W9-BVD-553

ENGLISH HISTORICAL DOCUMENTS

General Editor

DAVID C. DOUGLAS

M.A., D.Litt., F.B.A.

Emeritus Professor of History
in the University of Bristol

ENGLISH HISTORICAL DOCUMENTS

General Editor: David C. Douglas, M.A., D.LITT., F.B.A.

VOLUMES

I, *c.* 500–1042. Dorothy Whitelock, C.B.E., M.A., LITT.D., F.B.A.
II, 1042–1189. David C. Douglas, M.A., D.LITT., F.B.A., and G. W. Greenaway, M.A.
III, 1189–1327. Harry Rothwell, B.A., PH.D.
IV, 1327–1485. Alec R. Myers, M.A., PH.D., F.R.HIST.S., F.S.A.
V, 1485–1558. C. H. Williams, M.A.
*VI, 1558–1603. Douglas Price, M.A., B.LITT., F.S.A.
*VII, 1603–1660. Ivan Roots, M.A., F.R.HIST.S.
VIII, 1660–1714. Andrew Browning, M.A., D.LITT., F.B.A.
IX, American Colonial Documents to 1776. Merrill Jensen, M.A., PH.D.
X, 1714–1783. D. B. Horn, M.A., D.LITT., and Mary Ransome, M.A.
XI, 1783–1832. A. Aspinall, M.A., D.LITT., and E. Anthony Smith, M.A.
XII, Pt 1, 1833–1874. G. M. Young, M.A., D.LITT., and W. D. Handcock, M.A., B.LITT.
*XII, Pt 2, 1874–1914. W. D. Handcock, M.A., B.LITT.

* *in preparation*

GENERAL PREFACE

ENGLISH HISTORICAL DOCUMENTS is a work designed to meet a present need. Its purpose is to make generally accessible a wide selection of the fundamental sources of English history.

During the past half-century there has been an immense accumulation of historical material, but only a fraction of this has been made readily available to the majority of those who teach or who study history. The transcendent importance of the original authorities is recognised, but direct approach to them remains difficult, and even some of the basic texts (which are frequently quoted) are hard to consult. A gulf has thus opened between the work of the specialist scholar and those students, both at schools and universities, who best can profit by his labours. Historical studies tend too often today to consist of a commentary on documents which are not included in the available books; and, in the absence of any representative and accessible collection of the sources, the formation of opinion proceeds without that direct study of the evidence which alone can give validity to historical judgment.

The editors of these volumes consider that this situation calls for a remedy. They have striven to supply one by providing what they hope can be regarded as an authoritative work of primary reference.

An enterprise of this nature could be effective only if planned on a large scale. In scope and content, therefore, these volumes differ materially from the conventional "source-books" which usually contain only a restricted number of selected extracts. Here, within much wider limits, the editors have sought to produce a comprehensive *corpus* of evidence relating generally to the period with which they deal. Their aim, in each case, has been to present the material with scholarly accuracy, and without bias. Editorial comment has thus been directed, in the main, towards making the evidence intelligible, and not to drawing conclusions from it. Full account has been taken of modern textual criticism to compile a reliable collection of authentic testimony, but the reader has in general been left to pass his own judgment upon it, and to appraise for himself the value of current historical verdicts. Critical bibliographies have been added to assist further investigation.

The decision to display the texts, when necessary, in an English translation was thus dictated by the general purpose of the work. A translated text can, of course, never be a complete substitute for the original, but those who, today, can utilise a document in Anglo-Saxon, Latin or old French are few and are decreasing in number. This is doubtless to be regretted. But there seems no adequate reason why the majority of those interested in English history should be arbitrarily deprived of the opportunity to consult the basic sources of their study. In this work, therefore, there is nothing that cannot be used by those who can only read English.

The material to be included in each volume naturally varies according to the needs of each period as assessed by the editors. The years 1189–1327 have long been recognised as marking an age of cardinal importance in English history, and the complex developments which then occurred are reflected in the documents contained in this book. The narrative sources are fully represented, and a central position has been given to texts of constitutional, administrative and legal relevance. New translations have been supplied of many of the famous statutes of the period, including Magna Carta, and life in the manors and in the boroughs of England is likewise illustrated. Special attention has been paid to the Church. Ecclesiastical records have been selected to indicate the work of the secular hierarchy in the dioceses of England, and also the varied activities of the monasteries and of the friars. The development of canon law, and the operations of papal policy find expression in such texts as the canons of the Fourth Lateran Council. Here as elsewhere, as also in his comments and in the maps which illustrate them, the editor has been concerned to stress the community of ideas pervading western Christendom at this time, and to demonstrate how essential were the links between thirteenth-century England and the continent of Europe.

All concerned in this series are fully aware of the magnitude of the undertaking to which they have addressed themselves. They are conscious of the hazards of selecting from the inexhaustible store of historical material. They realise also the difficulties involved in editing so large a mass of very varied texts in accordance with the exigent demands of modern scholarship. They believe, however, that the essential prerequisite for the healthy development of English historical studies is wider acquaintance with the original authorities for English history. And they are content that their work should be judged by the degree to which they have promoted this object.

DAVID DOUGLAS

VOLUME III

ENGLISH HISTORICAL DOCUMENTS

1189–1327

DA26
E55
v.3

ENGLISH HISTORICAL DOCUMENTS

1189–1327

Edited by
HARRY ROTHWELL
B.A. PH.D
Emeritus Professor of History
in the University of Southampton

NEW YORK
OXFORD UNIVERSITY PRESS
1975

188443
JUL 1 0 1975

© 1975 Eyre & Spottiswoode (Publishers) Ltd
Printed in Great Britain
for Oxford University Press, New York
by Butler & Tanner Ltd
Frome and London

matri meae
in Christo
dormienti

ACKNOWLEDGEMENTS

EVERY document in this volume – even No. 38 – is, of course, translated into modern English. Where a translation is not my own, this is indicated in the editorial matter at the head of the document in question. Either the work there given as the source of the document will, in such cases, be found to be a translation into English or, if not, the source of the translation too is given. I am greatly indebted to the scholars, publishers and institutions concerned and am particularly indebted where copyright is still involved. Thus to the Keeper of the Public Records, Public Record Office, London, in respect of access to manuscript material and permission to translate and publish extracts in Nos 70, 72–3 and 78; and to the Controller of Her Majesty's Stationery Office for permission to reproduce (normally brief) passages from the Calendars and other publications of the public records by that office; to the Selden Society and the respective editors (chiefly Professor G. O. Sayles and Mr H. G. Richardson, separately or together) in respect of Nos 67, 108–10, 112–13, 115, 183, 191, 199, 204, 207 and 212–13; to the President of St John's College, Oxford, and the Council of the Royal Historical Society in respect of No. 239; to the Anglo-Norman Text Society and Basil Blackwell in respect of No. 233; to the Society for the Promotion of Christian Knowledge, and J. M. Wilson and C. J. Offer, respectively, in connection with Nos 144, 147, 155, 161, 166–7 and 189; to the Canterbury and York Society and C. Deedes in respect of No. 145; to Dr C. M. Fraser and the Surtees Society in respect of No. 159 and to the Society of Antiquaries of Newcastle-upon-Tyne and J. Conway Davies, R. K. Richardson, and R. J. Whitwell and Charles Johnson, respectively, in connection with Nos 128, 169 and 225; to the Lincoln Record Society in respect of No. 126; to the Wiltshire Archaeological and Natural History Society Records Branch, now the Wiltshire Records Society, and C. A. F. Meekings and M. T. Clanchy in respect of Nos 107 and 205–6; to the Chetham Society and G. H. Tupling in respect of Nos 110 (c) and 135; to the Bedfordshire Historical Record Society and R. F. Hunnisett and A. T. Gayton, respectively, in connection with Nos 110 (b) and 127; to the Bristol Record Society and N. D. Harding in respect of No. 176; to the Southampton Records Series (University of Southampton) in respect of No. 237; to W. O. Ault and the American Philosophical Society in respect of No. 212 (a); to the Jewish Historical Society of England in respect of No. 223; to the *Agricultural History Review* and *The Ancestor*, respectively, in connection with Nos 184 and 192; to the editors and Thomas Nelson and Sons Ltd and the Oxford University Press, respectively, for Nos 1, 9, 13, 17, 21, 86, 109 (b), 148, 150–3, 164 and 199 (a); also to Thomas Nelson and Sons Ltd and the editors for Nos 31, 56, 65, 142 and 172; to the Clarendon Press for Nos 162, 228 and 232; to the Oxford University Press for No. 137; to the Cambridge University Press for Nos 116, 160 and 229; to Butterworth and Co. Ltd for No. 25; to G. Bell and Sons Ltd for No. 101; to the University of Chicago Press for No. 238; to J. M. W. Bean and Manchester University Press for No. 35; to Blackfriars and Eyre and Spottiswoode Ltd for the greater part of No. 231; to Methuen and Co. Ltd for Nos 45, 111 (a) and 233 (d); and to H. G. Richardson and G. O. Sayles and Edinburgh University Press in respect of Nos 98 and 210 (a). I acknowledge with particular pleasure my debt, indeed that of all scholars, to C. E. Lugard not only for a translation but for the Latin text, privately printed, of "Trailbaston" proceedings in Derbyshire (No. 133).

If I have omitted acknowledgement of any other debt it is an oversight and a quite unintentional discourtesy, for which I offer my apologies.

As to the maps, I am obviously indebted to the *South Wales and the Border in the Fourteenth Century* and the *Historical Atlas of Wales* of Professor William Rees for the foundations of my maps of Wales on pp. 424 and 425 and I thank him and Faber and Faber Ltd, the publishers of the *Historical Atlas*. Historical maps of Ireland are rarer still and the map of Ireland *c.* 1300 (p. 470) even more obviously relies on that of Professor Otway-Ruthven in her *History of Medieval Ireland* (1968), which I am grateful for her permission to use. The map illustrating the Anglo-Scottish war (p. 471) draws on a number of sources and a variety of evidence, but more especially on the maps of Professor G. W. Barrow's *Feudal Britain* (1956) and *Robert Bruce* (1965). I am grateful to him too. On the map of England *c.* 1300 the basic detail as to roads is inevitably derived from the Gough map in the Bodleian Library and for the purpose I have, with the permission of Bodley's Librarian, used the splendid facsimile edition with introduction (Oxford, 1958). I am indebted to Mr W. Bromage for the professional skill with which he redrew my maps. With the resulting clarity, they are, I believe, a feature of this volume.

To my friend and one-time colleague, Professor G. J. Hand of University College, Dublin, I am more indebted than he is aware, but particularly for helpful discussion with him of some of the knottier passages of Nos 57 and 235. Professor C. R. Cheney and Dr Kathleen Edwards have each helped me with answers to questions I put to them. My greatest debt of all is, however, to the General Editor, Professor David Douglas, and to all concerned with the production of this volume, whether as publishers or printers, unnamed here, for their patience.

Finally to those who use the book. In a work of this size and range I cannot think I have never stumbled over a technicality and I promise my gratitude for rescue from any pits into which I may have fallen.

H. R.

CONTENTS

Part II. ROYAL GOVERNMENT

A. THE TESTING TIME 1189–1227

B. THE RULE OF HENRY III 1227–67

C. RECONSTRUCTION 1267–94

D. ENGLAND AT WAR 1294–1327

Part III. ROYAL GOVERNMENT IN ACTION

Part IV. THE CHURCH IN ENGLAND

A. THE WESTERN CHURCH

B. THE COMING OF THE FRIARS

C. THE UNIVERSITY MOVEMENT

D. THE BISHOP AND HIS DIOCESE

Part V. LAND AND PEOPLE

APPENDICES

ILLUSTRATIONS

CHART

MAPS

EDITOR'S NOTE

The original text of all documents printed in this volume is, unless otherwise stated, in Latin. The place of publication of any book, unless otherwise indicated, is London. The year begins on 1 January unless specially mentioned in a note.

ABBREVIATIONS

Ann. Monast.	*Annales Monastici*, ed. H. R. Luard, 5 vols (1864–9), in Rolls series
Bémont, *Chartes*	Ch. Bémont, *Chartes des libertés anglaises 1100–1305* (Paris, 1892)
Berry	*Statute Rolls of the Parliaments of Ireland*, vol. I (entitled *Statutes and Ordinances and Acts of the Parliament of Ireland, King John to Henry V*), ed. Henry F. Berry (Irish Record Office, 1907), *see* Mullins, p. 41
Cant. & York Soc.	Canterbury and York Society for the publication of Episcopal Records
Cal. Chart. Rolls	*Calendar of Charter Rolls*
Cal. Close Rolls	*Calendar of Close Rolls*
Cal. Pat. Rolls.	*Calendar of Patent Rolls*
Camden	Camden Society, *see* Mullins, p. 239 ff.
	Camden Series of the Royal Historical Society, *see* Mullins, p. 264
Chron. Maj.	*Matthaei Parisiensis, Chronica Majora*, ed. H. R. Luard, 7 vols (1872–83), in the Rolls series
E.H.D.	*English Historical Documents*
Foedera	Record Commission incomplete re-edition of Rymer, *Foedera* (*see* Mullins, p. 11), 3 vols in 6, folio (1816–30), vol. I, i and ii (1816)
Glanvill	*Tractatus de legibus* . . . ("The treatise on the laws and customs of England commonly called Glanvill"), ed. G. D. G. Hall (1965)
Hist. MSS Com.	Reports and calendars issued by the Royal Commission on Historical Manuscripts
K.R. Memor. Roll	Exchequer, King's Remembrancer's Memoranda Roll in the Public Record Office
L.T.R. Memor. Roll	Exchequer, Lord Treasurer's Remembrancer's Memoranda Roll in the Public Record Office
Q.R. Mem. (p. 503 below)	K.R. Memor. Roll
Linc. Rec. Soc.	Publications of the Lincoln Record Society
mr	*magister*, master
Mullins	E. L. C. Mullins, *Texts and calendars: an analytical guide to serial publications* (Roy. Hist. Soc. Guides, 1958)
P.R.O.	Public Record Office

Parl. Writs	*Parliamentary Writs and Writs of Military Summons of Edward I and Edward II*, ed. Sir Francis Palgrave, 2 vols in 4, Rec. Com. folio (1827–34)
Plucknett, *Legislation*	T. F. T. Plucknett, *Legislation of Edward I* (Oxford, 1949)
Rec. Com.	Publications of the Record Commissioners (*see* Mullins, p. 3)
Rock, *Church of our Fathers*	D. Rock, *The Church of our Fathers as seen in St Osmund's Rite for the Cathedral of Salisbury*, ed. G. W. Hart and W. H. Frere, 4 vols (1903–4)
Rolls series	Chronicles and Memorials of Great Britain and Ireland during the Middle Ages published under the direction of the Master of the Rolls
Rot. Parl.	*Rotuli Parliamentorum* (Rolls of Parliament), 6 vols, folio and index vol. (*see* Mullins, p. 12), vol. I (1767)
Rymer	Thomas Rymer, *Foedera, conventiones* (etc), *see* Mullins, pp. 11–12
s.a.	*sub. anno, annis* . . . Under the (chronicle) year(s) . . .
Stat. of the Realm	*Statutes of the Realm*, vol. I (Rec. Com., 1810), *see* Mullins, p. 4
Stubbs, *Sel. Charters*	*Select Charters and other illustrations of English Constitutional History . . . to the Reign of Edward I*, ed. William Stubbs, 9th edn by H. W. C. Davis (Oxford, 1913)

INTRODUCTION

(i) THE PERIOD

THE first of the reigns covered by this volume is that of Richard I. Bishop Stubbs wrote of it, "there is abundance of personal adventure and incident, and there is a certain quantity of legal and constitutional material which it is easier to interweave into a general disquisition on such subjects than to invest with a unity and plot of its own."

In a ten-year reign, one who gave so little of his time, and less of his mind, to the business of being king of England cannot be expected to have left much of a mark. But, king apart, it is not true that "there is no great national change, no very pronounced development"[1] in England in these ten years. Human societies do not go into a state of suspended animation except in fairy tales. Processes of great permanent import were at work in England between 1189 and 1199: what they require for their understanding is a larger perspective than the decade itself.

By 1189 the Normans had been settled for more than a century in this country. Already it was difficult to tell, among freemen at any rate, who was of English and who of Norman birth. And in their speech men were coming together. It would be rash to assume anything other than that English remained the language of the majority of men, but what is certain is that French was spreading downwards in society and outwards into the Church and into trade. The end will be a French "after the school of Stratford atte Bow", a long-lingering French in the law-courts, and an English enriched by Englishmen who were also French-speaking, a world language. All that contemporaries knew was that to speak only English was increasingly a mark of rusticity, while the possession of French was no evidence of ancestry.

The assimilation of the conquerors and their speech must be reckoned the greatest of the processes in train at this time. It was helped by another. In his ten-year reign Richard visited England only twice and spent not more than six months there all told. When he was not crusading he was defending his dominions in France, and he died defending them. Their loss, except for Gascony, soon after was decisive for those French families who preferred to stay with their English properties and so become ultimately (even in their own eyes) Englishmen.

The next reign is that of John, who is best known as the king who lost Normandy and from whom Magna Carta had to be wrested. He has had to wait until the twentieth century for even rough justice. We now reject the wild judgments of Wendover and Paris. We no longer equate the testimony of the other chroniclers, as J. R. Green and Stubbs did, with "the sober judgment of history", for we look at the records of the reign as well, and they give a different John.[2] They confirm, in so far as it is their

[1] This too is quoted from Stubbs.

[2] These records were accessible in Green's and Stubbs's day and some of them were in print: see the Introduction to Part II below. But neither made sufficient use even of those which were printed. Stubbs's famous

nature to do so, the man (but not the monster) of the chronicles: a cruel, violent, grasping man, treacherous himself, suspicious of others, genial if he chooses to be, superstitious, a womaniser. As king, however, whatever else he was, he is revealed as no fainéant, but a real king with ability in government and a liking for it, intervening personally more perhaps than by that date he need have done, particularly in the processes of justice, travelling his kingdom more than any ruler of this country before him – or since for that matter. But (if we try to balance the credit of the records with the debit of contemporary opinion – for, with all corrections made, there is no denying that the chronicles are almost solidly against him) he would seem to have lacked the highest qualities needed for the kingly office when rule was personal.

The more we know of him, the more we are reminded of his father. He seems to have had much the same merits and demerits, but in meaner measure – which, after all, without the rhetoric, the elaborate comparison with the whole family, is what Stubbs really meant.[1] Like his father he was competent in the arts of war, if not his brother's equal. "No medieval English king before or since his time dealt more successfully", we are taught, "with the Welsh, the Scots, or the Irish." But he failed in France where it mattered most. One may ask whether even Richard, had he lived, could have done any better in the end. Equally idly, one may recognise that the problem in France was not of John's making. He assumed responsibility for it in assuming the crown, and we know from *Glanvill*[2] that while part of a king's function was to be "continually impartial in dealing with his subjects", the other part was "to be always victorious in wars with his enemies". It was not in John to command success. His inadequacy is clearer still in domestic affairs. He showed great ability in administration and his interest in it is unmistakable, but when kings were allowed to rule as well as reign, the real test of kingship was political and Magna Carta is proof that he failed it. Though not all his policies were unjustifiable – his financial exactions, for example, in view of the changing character and ever increasing cost of warfare at that time – he failed to carry opinion, or enough of it, with him. That before representative parliaments this meant carrying the magnates of the country, or enough of them, with him is simply clearer proof of a personal failure. He lacked that trust in men which inspires trust, that blend of honesty and deviousness, the steadiness and the sure judgment of men and of situations, which mark the successful political leader in any age and which kings need when they lead.

Though it began with a minority and ended in civil war, the next reign seems placid by comparison. It was a long reign and an important period. One thinks of Bracton and of Grosseteste; of Salisbury cathedral and the vitality of the clergy who founded it and served it in the first generation; of the friars; of Oxford and Franciscan

characterisation of John in the introduction to his edition of Walter of Coventry's *Memoriale* (reprinted, *Historical Introductions to the Rolls Series*, ed. A. Hassall (1902), pp. 439 ff.), despite its mention of "abundant records", is based almost exclusively on chronicles.

[1] *Historical Introductions*, ed. Hassall, pp. 442 and 444: "John, then, as far as I can read his character from his acts, was a mean reproduction of all the vices and of the few pettinesses of his family" and "the faults which come out in this form in him are faults so ingrained in the Angevin family that they can scarcely be regarded, except in the particular manifestation, as distinctive of John".

[2] Glanvill's prologue (ed. Hall, p. 1). Cf. pp. 28, n. 1, and 890 below.

philosophy; Flanders and English wool; of the Basings and the Bukerels of London and of Nicholas of Ludlow. But King Henry III escapes one. If he had personality he failed to impose it in thirty years of personal rule. If he had a policy he failed to achieve it. He was not an incompetent: he ran the country, or was responsible for its running, from 1227 to 1258 without serious trouble. But he won no glory and he lost credit with his barons. He failed the tests his father failed. More fortunate than his father, he lived through his troubles. The achievement of this respectable but mediocre king was to confirm in a long reign, after two short and troubled ones, the strength of Henry II's machinery of government and hand it on, easily and unimpaired, to an abler son.

The reign of Edward I is universally regarded as one of the really great reigns of English history. Unlike his father's, which rightly or wrongly gives an impression of drift, there is vigour and a sense of purpose about it. But there is no such agreement about Edward himself. Taught at various times that he was "English to the core" and "the conscious creator of English greatness", opposition to whom, if it was not factious, was mistaken, for "he saw what was best for his age and people, he led the way and kept faith", we are also taught that "no more than Philip the Fair" had he "any conscious intention of taking the people into partnership with him or of promoting any sort of constitutional freedom", that his policy was "on the verge of collapse at the moment of [his] death". The picture of the great general who showed "masterly strategy" at Evesham, "dash" at Kenilworth, "masterly conduct of the great Welsh campaign", "genius" at Falkirk and in organisation took "important steps in the process which led to the English victories at Crécy, Poitiers, and Agincourt", is now contradicted: "he lacked . . . military ability. However good a tactician he may have been, he was a pitiable strategist . . . The art of war is a difficult art, which Edward failed to master".[1] The picture of the faithful husband and wise father, not above a bet with his washerwoman, is also questioned. Perhaps this shows nothing more than the futility of trying to elicit personality from formal records. But there is difference of opinion about the reign too, as part of the reaction from the glorification, adulation even in some cases, of Edward. There is a break, we are taught, at his accession. "Political history imposes the accession of Edward I as the beginning of an age." He broke "with the feudal past" and founded "a new regime upon the basis of prerogative". It was his "rule" to legislate by prerogative and "all the great business of state is coming to pass under prerogative". The idea of the continuity of his reign with that of his predecessor is abandoned. Now prerogative has its place in his reign, but not that place; and it has been rightly answered that "to call [his] policy anti-feudal is to cut him off from the air he breathed, from the medium in which he worked, from the political and legal assumptions of his whole life". Moreover, the sharpness of the contrast between Henry III's reign and Edward's, in legislative activity may turn out to have been illusory, once the records, legal and otherwise, of the father's reign have been properly explored.[2] As to Edward himself, we have no

[1] H. G. Richardson in *E.H.R.*, lxxx (1965), p. 555

[2] For work done and still to be done on the records of the years 1227–58, see the Select Bibliography to Part II below.

Joinville to tell us what he was like, but he was neither a saint like one of his uncles nor brilliant and versatile like another, the Emperor Frederick II: he was (the records do show this) a workaday monarch, possibly a great one, but neither more far-seeing nor more sinister than most other men of affairs outside the pages of a history book.

There is no doubt about the continuity between the reigns of Edward I and Edward II. Indeed, the son would have been less obviously inadequate if he had inherited fewer of his father's difficulties. Thus far Edward II deserves our sympathy, but no more. We need not believe all that was said about him at the time or has been written since: it is as clear as can be that, more than a failure as we have said John and Henry III were failures, he was a positive misfit as king, and the fairest yet severest verdict upon him is by the most sympathetic modern writer on him – "His real offence at the bar of history lies . . . not in his personal preferences but in his failure to subordinate them to his obligations as a king"[1] – a verdict with which one may reasonably suppose his father would have agreed. More important, however, than the monarch, to present thinking, is the reign. It is a lacuna, and therefore a crucial period, in the history of our representative institutions. It has been shown to be a time of administrative reform. Its political history has still to be elucidated. It cries out for workers.

(ii) THE COUNTRY AND THE PEOPLE

The slow operation of natural forces created these islands on the submerged shelf of Europe's Atlantic seaboard. It determined their resources. It still alters their coastline and decrees their dubious climate.

Much more rapidly but scarcely less mysteriously (so complex is man), human agencies have decided their population, their languages, their social, cultural and economic heritage, their political development – in short, their history.

We are not concerned with the whole of that history. But it is useful – as it is logical – for us to begin with the land.

It has been described as a palimpsest, though our leading landscape palaeographer, Dr W. G. Hoskins, likens it rather to a symphony or chamber music. Whatever the metaphor, man has left his mark. A straight line on the Ordnance Survey map, composed it may be of a stretch of road, a footpath, a hedge, a length of parish boundary, a piece of motorway, a farm-track and a woodland walk, even if interrupted by a river or an aerodrome, may be the line of an old road or the earlier route of an existing one. In appropriate country, parish boundaries between riverside settlements in two adjacent valleys, leading up to and ending at the watershed between, could indicate an earlier, possibly pastoral economy. A field-name or a place-name can be a clue. The O.S. 1/25,000, 2½ inches to one mile, carrying most of the detail of the 6″ scale but covering a larger area, is best for following up anything that may have been detected on the 1″ map. On the ground itself, where the evidence is, most of it still unmapped, at the right time of year for crop-markings to show, or early or late enough in the day for the shadows to be right, air photography can reveal what is

[1] Hilda Johnstone, *Edward of Carnarvon* (Manchester, 1946), p. 131

otherwise not visible. In built-up areas excavation is usually needed to expose the past. But field work with a map, a trained eye and a prepared mind normally suffices. The historian will naturally prepare himself with a knowledge of such local historical records as may have survived. Thus, from the hamlet where this is written, in what was one of the large manors (and correspondingly large parish) of the medieval bishops of Winchester, a path, now disused, still goes to the then parish church two miles away. Within a furlong is the massive earthen bank of the bishop's deer park, which appears and reappears in the woods – quite unpredictably until the puzzle was solved by an entry in the bishop's pipe roll for the year 1258. There were two parks, the Inner and the Outer, interlocking. Their banks are still not completely traced. This southern, wooded portion of the manor is, today, one of scattered farmsteads, identifiable in the custumal of the manor as thirteenth-century clearings. Its northern boundary on the chalk downs which fed the sheep whose wool was sold in 1315 to a London wool merchant, in 1316 to the Bardi of Florence, was the Roman road from Winchester to Old Salisbury.

So much of the landscape of the period 1189–1327, the period covered by this volume, is so obviously man-made – roads; buildings, ecclesiastical, monastic, military and civil, still used or ruined; works which today would be called public, Richard I's development of Portsmouth as a time-saving haven nearer the sea than Southampton, the bishop of Winchester's reservoir and canals to ensure the navigation of the R. Itchen above Southampton for the benefit of his annual fair of St Giles – that it is plain to see. The main effort required is to travel it, with a map ("England *c.* 1300", below) and perhaps in the company of the author of No. 230, though before setting out it will be well to know what and what not to expect. Travel will be by road, less frequently by river. It will be as safe as the king's peace can make it, but no more. It will, in any case, be slow. There was little improvement in transport between Roman and modern times. The roads will be the Roman ones where they are still usable, for they were well routed. But there are many others. As on the continent centuries of *défrichement, Innencolonisation*, so in Britain since the Romans clearance of ancient woodland had greatly increased the area of cultivation and settlement. Figures are hard to come by and harder still to interpret, which is what in this country makes Domesday Book so precious and at the same time so tantalising, but it is clear that the population too had increased, and particularly rapidly since Domesday, i.e. in the century just past. Yet for all the signs of life we shall see, the villages, single farmsteads, the new parish churches, little market towns, the countryside will seem bare and the roads empty compared with today. On no reckoning has England's population been put at a tenth of today's. London, far and away the biggest place in the country, may on a generous estimate have had a population of up to 50,000, Bristol under 20,000, York under 10,000, the rest under (most of them very much under) 5,000. One recalls Maitland's description of the "rusticity" of the county town of Cambridge. The ordinary local market town (*villa mercatoria*) was very often literally a vill, as rural except on market-days as the locality it served. The vast open fields of arable, without the hedges, coverts and cunningly-placed windbreaks of today, emphasised the bareness of even the most settled areas. Elsewhere the woodland will come closer, the stretches of heath and moor get longer and the signs of habitation fewer as we journey, particularly as we go north or west. One other thing we shall notice. Water will be more of a hindrance to us than either wood or mountains. There had been more land-clearance than drainage since Roman times and the seventeenth century and Vermuyden were still to come. Still, as in Roman times, the rivers flowing into the Wash and all the tributaries of the Humber at their confluence, all flow in their last stages through unreclaimed fens, which the great medieval road to the North, like its Roman predecessor, must still skirt. As the Disinherited after Evesham knew, Ely and Axholme were still islands. The North road on the other side of the Pennines, faced at the Mersey with a similar passage between mountain and marsh, takes the lower of the two Roman crossings of the river, the ford at Warrington (the other being at Stretford for Manchester). River-crossings generally are important, especially when because of undrained valleys there is difficulty too over the approaches.[1] Tide-water, of course, can be a further difficulty.[2]

The fastest way into England was, obviously, at the Narrows as in Roman times, and the Roman lighthouses at Boulogne and Dover (two at Dover) still stood.[3] From Dover the road was Roman, that known by now as Watling Street, through Canterbury and Rochester to London. No. 230 below mentions the castle at Dover. Matthew Paris, the St Albans chronicler, mentions it too. It was being converted between 1181 and 1256 at immense expense from a twelfth-century into the up-to-date thirteenth-century castle we know today. At Canterbury there was the shrine of St Thomas à Becket to be seen. At Rochester the Medway was crossed by a wooden bridge on nine stone piers eked out at either end it would seem across the wide wet valley by what would appear to have been the remains of a Roman causeway. The first glimpse of London would be St Paul's cathedral from the heights above Greenwich, then the river, Southwark and the bridge. This in 1189 was a wooden bridge, quite possibly Roman,[4] with beside it about a hundred feet upstream a new bridge of stone begun thirteen years before but not yet finished. From 1209 when it was completed the stone bridge was London bridge, until it was in its turn superseded and pulled down in 1831. It had no rival until the eighteenth century, and Westminster was reached either by river or across the bridge into the city, out by Ludgate, by the bridge over the Fleet, past the New Temple and the Bar,[5] along the ridge above the Thames[6] to the hamlet of Charing,[7] then south with the bend of the river to Westminster, the abbey and the palace.

The river, less embanked, was broader and shallower than now and had been broader and shallower still. London was where it was because there, near the tidal

[1] No. 182 below for one such case.

[2] Not merely for river-crossings, but also for coastal flats (cf. No. 183 below) and the complicated, interesting situations which can arise where there is a conflict between river-water and tides and a struggle of man with both. For the Channel ports, cf. Nos. 174, 175, and the references there given; for the Fen country, No. 183, and as background, N. Neilson, H. C. Darby, and H. E. Hallam in the Select Bibliography to Part V below; for the marshes of the Humber and the Vale of York, June A. Sheppard in the same bibliography.

[3] That at Boulogne until the middle of the seventeenth century; both stood at Dover until the eighteenth century and one of them (to a height of 13 metres) is still standing.

[4] Miss M. B. Honeybourne's conclusion (p. 39) in her important article, "The pre-Norman bridge of London", *Studies in London History presented to P. E. Jones*, ed. Hollaender and Kellaway (1969).

[5] see no. 180 below

[6] Now the Strand.

[7] cf. No. 230 (line 5) below

limit at that time, there was a hard foreshore for river traffic and trade and the bridge, Roman, Saxon or Norman, wooden or stone, was where it was because there was hard ground exactly opposite on the other, Surrey bank. Elsewhere, below the bridge and for miles above, on both banks, there was marsh or easily flooded meadow. As to the city itself, little remained in 1189 but the walls and the gates – not even the street plan – of Roman London. For a time after the end of Roman rule, though not necessarily immediately (Roman London may have been a very long time in dying), its population had not been enough to fill the walls: now they could no longer contain it. There were suburbs on all the main roads outside the gates. In a more disorderly country these might have been taken in by further walling, as happened twice at Cologne, for instance, in the twelfth century. Instead, their extent was marked by bars, as at Temple Bar, and the city's jurisdiction over them was recognised after 1222. By then, however, newer suburbs beyond the bars were appearing. This was particularly so beyond Temple Bar on the way to Westminster, though we may reasonably suppose that the church of St Martin-in-the-Fields was on the outskirts when it was founded in the early thirteenth century. The pressure showed itself inside the walls too. Empty spaces were filled, plots divided and subdivided. Men built higher and also outward, since letting an upper storey overhang the ground-floor shop gave more space for living quarters: though if a street or a lane or alley were built up on both sides it would obviously be at the expense of light and air and, in medieval conditions,[1] of health too, just as it would certainly increase the risk of fire. Ordinary building was done in timber, roofed (in the words of a London by-law[2]) "with straw and stubble and such like thack" and (the passage goes on) "so that when any house caught fire, the greater part of the city was burnt by fire". Stone was recognised as safer material for houses as well as bridges, but it was beyond most men's pockets, especially in London, where to the cost of quarrying and dressing had to be added the expense of getting it from a distance.[3] Aware of this and "in order that citizens might build willingly of stone",[4] the by-law emphasised chiefly the need for at least a stone wall between houses and provided for arrangements between neighbours of different means.[5] Later by-laws and the record of later fires show, however, that "stone walls never became common".[6] London continued to grow despite the disadvantages of urban life. It was "no mere regional market" in 1189.[7] Fitz Stephen, writing a few years before that, much as he idealises it, is clearly describing a prosperous city. Its river was full of shipping. Besides visiting aliens it had

[1] cf. No. 215 below and, for medieval London, the articles by E. L. Sabine mentioned in the Select Bibliography to Part V below.
[2] No. 214 below
[3] L. F. Salzman (*Building in England*, p. 119) estimated that carriage even a distance of twelve miles would about double the cost. London's sources of supply (ibid. pp. 128–30) were farther away than this. The economy of water carriage, cheaper in itself, could be largely cancelled out by unavoidable extra charges involved and by distance, should it be greater than by land.
[4] No 214 below
[5] ibid.: "if anyone wishes to build of stone . . . and his neighbour through poverty cannot, or perchance will not . . ."
[6] T. Baker, *Medieval London*, p. 246
[7] Sir Frank Stenton's phrase: *Norman London* (1934), p. 19. This pamphlet contains also a translation of Fitz Stephen's description of London, referred to in the next sentence.

strong resident colonies. It was the one place in England of a size and importance to bear comparison with the great European centres. Like them it developed communal ambitions.[1] By the end of the period covered by this volume it had grown still more and become even more cosmopolitan. But the native element, always great,[2] had been strongly reinforced from the provinces, so strongly from the East Midlands that Londoners' speech was permanently affected,[3] though most parts of England contributed in some measure to the influx. It is symptomatic that so many of the apprentices had a provincial English place-name as their surname, even if, as could be, they themselves were of the second or third and not the incoming generation. Symptomatic too that a growing proportion of the country's trade was handled in London and that the Londoners' share of it was increasing at the expense of that of aliens, but that at the same time new men were breaking into, had indeed broken into, the preserves commercially, politically and socially of the older merchant dynasties.[4]

London was destined to dominate the provinces, as Westminster was in government. England's medieval road system,[5] like the Roman, radiated from it, though as we shall see this was for continuing geographical rather than historical reasons – there is a good measure of identity but no necessary connection otherwise. The road to the north-east was out by Bishopsgate and the suburb to Ware, leaving Waltham Abbey and the Lea valley to the right. This was the Roman Ermine Street. Beyond Ware a road went off through Barkway, Cambridge, Newmarket and Bury St Edmunds to Norwich, keeping as long as possible to higher ground because of the fens. This brought East Anglia too into London's orbit. After Ware and Royston, Huntingdon, Wansford and Stamford, still as in Roman times the lowest practicable crossings of the great Fenland rivers. After Stamford Ermine Street had made for Lincoln, the Winteringham–Brough ferry over the Humber, and York, going east, that is, of the marshes at the confluence of the Humber's many tributaries. There was still a road at least as far as Lincoln in the Middle Ages, slightly lower at spring level to the west of Ermine Street, and a ferry over the Humber, and this kept Lincoln in touch with its enormous diocese and enlarged the market for the county's corn and wool. Traffic for York might still take this road if consignments were bulky and time not vital, after Lincoln to Torksey-on-Trent, then the rest of the way by water, down the Trent and up the Ouse. But it could be held up by storm and contrary winds at the junction of the Trent with the Humber and most traffic left Ermine Street earlier for Grantham to do the whole journey by road, crossing the Trent at Newark, then west of the great water-logged Humber basin via Tuxford, Blyth, Doncaster, Pontefract and Tadcaster to York.

The other road to the north was out by Newgate, via Barnet, St Albans and Dunstable. It went on via Coventry and Lichfield – with an offshoot to the port of Chester – west of the Pennines to Carlisle. It had a military and political importance

[1] Their outcome is traced in G. A. Williams, *Medieval London: from Commune to Capital.*
[2] For early twelfth-century London, Stenton, *Norman London*, p. 16.
[3] From a southern dialect to East Midland, neither a southern nor Northumbrian but a Mercian dialect destined to become the standard English.
[4] For analysis of London names, E. Ekwall's studies, particularly *Studies in the Population of Medieval London*: for analysis of the commercial evidence, Williams, op. cit. and the accompanying tables.
[5] see map, "England *c.* 1300"

of its own not only for campaigns in North Wales but also as the road to the earldoms of Chester and Lancaster, both of which were in this period within the control of the royal family and considered (merely hopefully in one case, as it proved) safer so. But for part of its way it served also as an alternative road to the north-east. Turning off at Stony Stratford to Northampton, then on through Leicester, Nottingham and Worksop to join the north-east road proper above Blyth but before Doncaster, this instead of hugging the fens of the lower reaches of the Ouse, Nene and Welland kept higher ground much nearer their sources on the Midland ridge between them and the waters of the Severn basin. So that quite apart from its advantages as a truly Midland route and the places it thereby linked, it was the better road to or from the north, well above fen and storm-driven tidal water and with easier river-crossings, in winter or bad weather. As his Eleanor Crosses show, after his wife's death near Lincoln in late November, the widowed Edward I sent her body home this way.

There were two roads to the west. They were not alternatives. One went as directly as possible to Gloucester and Hereford, and ultimately to St David's in farthest Wales. The other equally directly to Bristol. From Newgate, across the Holborn,[1] along "Holeburnestrete"[2] past the Old Temple[3] and the leper hospital of St Giles-in-the-Fields and on by what is now High Holborn, Oxford Street and Bayswater Road north of Hyde Park, the former kept in fact the line of the great Roman arterial road to Silchester, but at present-day Notting Hill instead of bearing south with it to Staines went straight on to Uxbridge, going directly from the lower to the upper Thames valley by High Wycombe over the Chilterns to Tetsworth; then from Oxford by Witney, Burford and Northleach over the Cotswolds to Gloucester. Gloucester, important in itself as the centre of a rich district, a manufacturing town and a river port,[4] was then as until quite recently the bridge town of the Severn, with none above it before Worcester, and so at once a gateway for all purposes for all South Wales as well as an outlet for the iron of the Forest of Dean, England's chief source of supply, and the high quality wool of the Welsh Marches. The main Bristol traffic probably left by Newgate too, for it was a better road than that along the Strand from Ludgate, though we must assume that this also was used. If so, it would probably be joined at Charing[5] by traffic from Westminster, increasingly the seat of royal government; then keeping to the higher ground by what is now Piccadilly and Knightsbridge, on through Kensington, it had joined the other Bristol traffic from Newgate by the time it reached Brentford. There, or soon after, as the Gloucester road had already done after Notting Hill, the Bristol road went straight on instead of to Staines – in this case to Colnbrook, Maidenhead and Reading, then up the Kennet valley to Newbury and Marlborough and so on to Chippenham and Bristol. Favoured by nature,[6] Bristol was a sea as well as a river port with a large and still growing[7]

[1] Now beneath Farringdon Street, crossed by Holborn Viaduct.

[2] The usual name for modern Holborn until the fourteenth century (Ekwall, *Street-Names of the City of London*, p. 193).

[3] For the move from Holborn to Thames-side, No. 129 below, editorial note.

[4] The Severn was navigable as far as Shrewsbury. For the river trade, No. 177 below.

[5] See above, p. 6

[6] Bristol's natural advantages are emphasised by E. M. Carus-Wilson at the beginning of her essay on "The overseas trade of Bristol in the fifteenth century", *Medieval Merchant Venturers* (1967).

[7] cf. No. 176 below and J. W. Sherborne, *The Port of Bristol in the Middle Ages*, p. 2

overseas trade, but, doubly favoured, was by no means dependent upon it. It had an Irish and a large coastal trade with South Wales as well, and was also a manufacturing and distributive centre: a western capital as truly as York was capital of the north, but larger and richer; surpassed in size and wealth, in fact, only by London.[1] The main road to the south-west went all the way to St Ives via Kingston and Cobham to Guildford, on to Farnham and Alton, by the notorious[2] Pass of Alton to Alresford and then to Winchester, which if it were early September would be full for the bishop's fair on St Giles's Hill,[3] from Winchester to Salisbury, after 1244 to New Salisbury, where the most remarkable body of clergy in England at that time was building[4] not only a new cathedral but also a new city in the valley below the hill-top castle, cathedral and city of Old Sarum. After that, Shaftesbury, Honiton, Exeter, Okehampton, Launceston, Bodmin and St Ives very much as today.

The principal cross-county roads too are shown on the map "England *c.* 1300". They bring out particularly clearly the importance of Oxford, Northampton, Coventry and Doncaster in the medieval road system. The clearest representation of the physical features which, we have suggested, governed the road system is the contoured map on the scale of 1/625,000 (about 10 miles to 1 inch) adopted by the Ordnance Survey as the foundation of its *Map of Monastic Britain* (South Sheet and North Sheet), 2nd edition, 1954–5. The bold way in which the Gloucester and Bristol roads from London drive straight to their destinations instead of getting out of the lower Thames basin to higher ground at Silchester before fanning out (as Roman westward traffic had done) is a reminder of how much clearance of the land there had been and how much reclamation of marsh and fen since Roman times.[5] "England *c.* 1300" does not attempt to show the network of minor roads which new settlements, rural markets, urban trades, the supply of raw materials for them and the provisioning of urban populations (as for instance at Winchester and Lincoln, Nos 228, 229 below), the getting of Cornish tin or iron of the Forest of Dean to market, the cartage to Clifton above York for shipment down the Ouse of Cistercian wool bought by Florentines (for the woolcrops of Fountains Abbey in 1276, No. 221 below), the visitation by a zealous bishop such as Swinfield of Hereford in 1290[6] of the parishes of his diocese, presuppose.

[1] cf. Nos 207, 227, and 13, below. Bristol castle was the administrative centre of the large establishment provided for the young Lord Edward by his father, Henry III, in 1254. On its extent, Powicke, *King Henry III and the Lord Edward*, p. 233. An edition of the accounts of the constables of Bristol castle by Dr Margaret Sharp is awaited.

[2] Notorious in the early thirteenth century (*Royal Letters . . . Henry III*, ed. Shirley, Rolls ser., I, p. 167, and Matthew Paris, *Chron. Majora*, ed. Luard, Rolls ser., V, pp. 55–60) and still notorious in the late fourteenth century, when Langland in *Piers Plowman* tells us that Poverty "could even walk through the Alton Pass without fear of robbery"; cf. No. 230 below, line 48.

[3] cf. Nos 216, 217 below

[4] cf. No. 162 below. By 1225 enough of the east end had been built for services to be held, after which the clergy and more and more of the civil population moved down from Old Sarum and the new town grew as well as the cathedral. The building of the Harnham bridge over the Avon in 1244 brought the road too down to the valley and along it, away from the old through the new Salisbury. The cathedral was advanced enough by 1258 to be consecrated and was completed eight years later. But not with the two-tiered tower or the spire which Constable painted and which we see. They are post-1327 and no part of the original plan.

[5] cf. pp. 5–6 above

[6] Or the other examples mentioned in J. R. H. Moorman, *Church Life in England in the Thirteenth Century*, ch. XIV with references. The chapter gives an account of Swinfield's journey in 1290, based on his Household Roll, in detail.

The map "English interests in France and the Low Countries" (p. 885 below) is best read in conjunction with the *Cambridge Medieval History*, VI (1929), map 58, to which it is the economic counterpart. The two bring together the geographical, feudal, political and economic aspects of the country's relationships with its nearest and most powerful European neighbour, the France of Philip Augustus and his successors. The loss of the Angevin empire, the antecedents of the Treaty of Paris of 1259, the value to the king of England of the cession to him by that treaty of rights in the "Three Bishoprics" area, the opposition on the French side to such cession, particularly by the count of Poitiers-Auvergne, who by marriage was also count of Toulouse, the importance of the rivers of the Gascon wine trade, the importance for economic as well as other reasons of north–south communications through the area, bastide-building, appeals or not to the authority of the French king's *parlement* at Paris, currency questions, the precise implications of the liege homage owed to the king of France: on all these matters a sharper light is thrown. On, too, relations with powers politically or economically within the orbit of France, whether in the Midi or in the Low Countries. Over the period covered by this volume one thinks particularly of Castile, Provence, Flanders and the Flemish market for English wool.

This is to remind oneself of Bristol and Southampton and the annual wine-fleet from Bordeaux in the autumn, of the Flemish hanse in London, of Jean Boinebroke of Douai, Riccardi and Frescobaldi, natives in the trade such as the Basinges of London, the Ludlows, father and son of Shropshire and the Duraunts[1] of Dunstable, and of those who in 1297 claimed that "the wool of England is worth nearly half what the whole land is worth a year".[2] England's has been described as a "colonial" economy in the larger economy of north-western Europe.[3] It is one aspect. Another is that even the whole body of those who lived by trade or manufacture, including those whose business was entirely in home markets as well as those who exported or imported, was small compared with the numbers who lived on the land or on its proceeds. Except, as we have seen, for London and one or two other places, the urban communities in which for the most part they congregated were islands, so to speak, in the ocean of rural society. Relatively they were few, but they were having an influence out of all proportion to their numbers.

Trade and manufacture were, of course, not new, but on a scale which now invited description as commerce and industry they presented both problems and new situations to an agrarian society in which the dominant elements were feudal and ecclesiastical. Here was something too big now to be ignored, but with a different ethos and ethics as well as a host of mundane problems. It could not be assimilated without changes in the old order – in church and state alike. The church proved the less reluctant to change. There was the physical problem of the cure of souls in overgrown communities. At Antwerp about the year 1100 a single priest laboured "in a community which had been transformed from a little fishing village into a town by

[1] Power, *Medieval English Wool Trade*, p. 113 (though the name is John Duraunt, not Thomas) and No. 171 below, s.a. 1275, 1277, 1280–1, 1283–4, 1292 (and see s.a. 1294 for a comment on Laurence, son of Nicholas of Ludlow).

[2] No. 69 below

[3] e.g. Professor Postan in *Cambridge Economic History*, II, p. 233

increase of its trade".[1] In the territorial dioceses of the Middle Ages a parish of a few hundred souls would appear to have been considered manageable. The urban problem was solved not by one minster or central church with a sufficient team of clergy but by division, keeping the country parish as model for size and organisation and creating as many parishes as required. This explains the many City of London churches. London had about a hundred parishes, Norwich over fifty, York and Lincoln about forty and a number of others between ten and twenty.[2] In addition, the church was inspired enough to break with the past and recruit as missioners and social workers the friars, who believed that service was as sure a way to Heaven as the withdrawal of a Carthusian and sought "their Grande Chartreuse in the wretched slums of over-crowded cities, their mountain-tops of contemplation in the haunts of plague and fever".[3] There was also a moral problem. The church devoted a great deal of attention to the ethics of buying and selling – whether, for instance, it is lawful to sell a thing for more than it is worth, whether a sale is unlawful through a fault in the thing sold, whether a seller is bound to state the defects of a thing sold, whether it is lawful to sell a thing at a higher price than was paid for it; or again, as to the borrowing or lending of money, whether it is a sin to take usury for money lent, whether it is lawful to ask any other kind of consideration for money lent, whether a man must restore profits made out of money got by usury, whether it is lawful to borrow money on terms of usury.[4] Its answers to these questions became too refined for practical purposes. Its teaching could not be and was not literally observed. It acquiesced in much, and indeed itself in its administration and through its members practised perforce much that it never accepted in principle. As the mechanism of the Champagne fairs shows,[5] credit was by now essential to the smooth working of business.[6] Secular authority on the other hand (in its various medieval manifestations) felt contempt rather than concern for traders and artisans. 'They stoop," wrote the aristocratic Otto of Freising, uncle of the emperor Frederick Barbarossa, of the overweening Lombard towns, bishop though he was too, "to confer the belt of knighthood and honourable rank on youths of lowly conditions or indiscriminately on artisans engaged in contemptible mechanical industries, whom other nations exclude like the pest from liberal and honourable occupations."[7] Townsmen might be allowed to purchase liberties of their lord, but if they dared to say they were wholly free of him and to appoint their own magistrates they threatened more than him: a "commune" was a revolutionary thing. The communal movement, which went so far in Italy with its civic traditions and in the Empire, had no such success in these islands. London was "the only city or borough . . . that ruled over a district without its own walls"[8] or even approached communal independence, though the movement was not without

[1] J. Westfall Thompson, *Econ and Soc. Hist. of the Middle Ages*, p. 645
[2] Figures from Moorman, *Church Life in England*, p. 5.
[3] The fine words of H. B. Workman, *Evolution of the Monastic Ideal*, p. 272.
[4] The articles of Aquinas's treatment of the subject in *Summa Theologiæ*, 2a2æ, Qu. 77 and 78.
[5] R. D. Face's article in *Econ. Hist. Rev.*, n.s. x (1957–8), pp. 427–38, and xii (1959–60), pp. 239–46.
[6] For a brief general survey, Henri Pirenne, *Econ. and Soc. Hist. of Medieval Europe* (1936), ch. IV, sect. 4 on "Credit and the traffic in money".
[7] In the translation of R. G. D. Laffan, *Select Documents of European History*, I, *800–1492* (1930), p. 77.
[8] C. G. Crump, *Legacy of the Middle Ages* (Oxford, 1926), p. 12

its repercussions.[1] In this country as on the continent, however, neither feudal nor ecclesiastical pride could resist opportunities, if they presented themselves; and just as in an earlier age lords had founded churches and monasteries with profit as well as piety or public spirit in mind,[2] so now they were ready to found towns or construct fulling mills on their land or exploit its natural resources of coal or ore or wood or peat, for example, if there was money to be made.[3]

Trade and industry and towns, it can be said, forced themselves on a social order which was neither organised so as to receive them easily nor (even in the church's case) eager to receive them. They succeeded because they made themselves necessary to it. Business acumen, craftsmen's skills, financial expertise, credit and, for long-distance trade, credit instruments, which had made it possible to enlarge the economy, were as necessary for running it. Church and state alike, at all levels, used them and, willy-nilly, were changed by them. Merchants' loans financed at all stages the conquest of Sicily from the Hohenstaufen at the instance of the papacy after the death of the emperor Frederick II; their organisation transmitted as a normal thing papal revenue from all parts of Christendom; Dunstable priory was business-like in managing its affairs,[4] and Simon Lovel did business with St Mary Clerkenwell to provide for his mother for the rest of her days.[5] Kings anticipated revenues by borrowings, financed their wars by them (what consequences, political and constitutional, could follow, the reigns of Edwards I to III in our history show). Among their subjects buying and selling, borrowing and even lending were increasingly practised outside merchant circles. Neither the feudal classes nor feudalism, which was not and never had been as static as theory would make it, were immune. Knights fees had become units of account reckoned in fractions, in England, long before the time of Edward I; knight service commutable and preferred that way. Knights who fought were "strenuous" (*milites strenui*) to distinguish them from those who lived on their estates and served their shires and were, in any case, too few in number for the duties they were expected to perform, so that men of sufficient substance might be compelled to become knights[6] – the Sir Roger de Coverleys of a later date. Feudal tenures were not yet the archaisms which antique a modern deed of conveyance, but were already obstacles for a clever lawyer to find his way over or round if the wishes or family needs of a large section of thirteenth-century feudal society itself required (as Plucknett, *Legislation of Edward I* has shown they did) a flexibility which the law of lord and vassal and fief did not permit. Transactions in land were in fact general from the king downwards, despite the law, and the money market was open to all people of sufficient substance to enter it. The most brilliant though difficult chapter of Plucknett's

[1] On their great importance for the future of the English borough, J. Tait, *The Medieval English Borough* (Manchester, 1936) ch. IX and especially p. 240.
[2] Ulrich Stutz's classic essay on proprietary monasteries and churches as investments, in English translation in G. Barraclough, *Studies in Mediaeval History: Mediaeval Germany 911–1250*, II (Oxford, 1938), pp. 35–70.
[3] "Six new towns of the bishops of Winchester 1200–55" (Part V below, Select Bibliography, s.v. Beresford); "An industrial revolution in the thirteenth century" (loc. cit., s.v. Carus-Wilson); and (for example) No. 185 below and "The making of the Broads" (Part V below, Select Bibliography, s.v. Lambert, J., and others) and for peat-cutting in the Somerset levels, loc. cit., s.v. Helm.
[4] see below, No. 171
[5] below, No. 154
[6] e.g. No. 51 below

Legislation of Edward I is the most illuminating demonstration of the extent to which the townsman, his money and his mentality had commercialised the old order in this country by the 1280s, when the statutes of Acton Burnell (No. 54 below) and of Merchants (No. 58) and the clause *Elegit*, the 18th clause, of Westminster II (No. 57) were worked out for the benefit of creditors – all creditors, not merely merchants native or foreign. Neither the common law nor existing statute law had kept pace with the changes. The problem was to provide effective remedies for a creditor against a defaulting debtor, especially one not amenable either to the pressure of the recognised good custom of merchants or to the special mercantile courts. Trade and industry had by the thirteenth century created a new sort of wealth, property in "movables" as well as landed property, bringing with it a new distribution of wealth, which neither church nor state could afford to ignore. This brought about a revolution in taxation too, the taxing of "movable" wealth, which with the different distribution meant also a new incidence of taxation. This in turn gave possessors of the new wealth political importance – so beginning yet another (if slow) revolution when, along with knights of the shire, burgesses of the cities and boroughs were called in to play, however humbly at first, a part in the counsels of the nation.

(iii) CHURCH AND PEOPLE

For most of us the phrase "the medieval church" is synonymous with monks, clergy, popes, crusades, church and state, Abelard, heresy, Inquisition – the textbook topics. Implicit, but neglected in the books because we know so little about him, is the lay foundation of the structure, the parishioner.

The church's concern, of course, was first and foremost with his soul. In the early days, having by the end of the fourth century triumphed with the help of the emperor Constantine in the Graeco-Roman world, it had gone on to convert the Germanic and Slav gentiles too. A vast, sustained effort directed from both Rome and Constantinople was in the end successful. Wulfilas, Boniface, Cyril and Methodius are simply the greatest of many in the European mission field in these centuries. (Incidentally, mention of St Boniface, who was by birth Winfrith of Crediton, should remind us of the great contribution of Anglo-Saxon England to this mission.) By 1189 only pockets of outright paganism were left in Europe.

The church had been active in consolidation too. In the now large territorial dioceses it had developed a parochial system and priesthood, for the cure of the newly-won souls. Its fatherly care was, however, a stern paternalism. The textbook image of an authoritarian, persecuting church is not untrue. It used authority to create a Christian society: governing men into goodness, not merely persuading them. It preserved the learning of the ancient world in the West, as everyone knows, but suppressed what it regarded as dangerous learning. Abelard, whom St Bernard considered "presumptuously prepared to give a reason for everything, even of those things which are above reason", was silenced. When the "Physics" and the "Metaphysics" of Aristotle were recovered they were at first prohibited. It protected the parishioner as well as the scholar and, possessor, as it believed, of a divinely-revealed truth, sure of its mission and sure of its message, it could only regard individual deviation, any individual claim (especially by the ordinary layman) to perceive truth as likely to be human error – dangerous alike to the individual and to the community. The penalty for heresy, tempered though it might be, was death. The responsibility for detecting and eradicating it was the bishop's in his diocese. Faced with mass heresy so that the diocesan machinery broke down, as in the Albigensian lands, the church declared a crusade; elsewhere it developed a central, papal inquisition to supplement the diocesan and, if interrogation failed, first allowed torture, then ordered it. This was not just unfortunate and unintended. The highest authority in the church was usually the slowest to act (indeed authority often lagged behind public opinion) but when it acted, it did so deliberately and on principle.[1]

We cannot understand, let alone do justice to such a church unless we appreciate the situation it had to deal with. The delayed, but when it came after three whole centuries, the swift and sweeping success of Christianity brought with it all the problems of position and of unprecedented numbers. The growth was in some ways too rapid. For the first time in its history Christianity now attracted time-servers. Its ranks were no longer purified by pagan persecution. Wealth came, and responsibility, and the thousand and one problems that come from sheer size and the consequent need of organisation. Its leaders were increasingly taken up with business, if they were not corrupted by it. Again, a distinction grew between clergy and laity when in the earliest ministry of the church an ordained Christian, with increased calls for his ministrations, found it increasingly difficult to follow a secular calling, had perforce to be paid for his ministry and, being paid, was in the end required to give up his secular livelihood. An ordained clergy had become also a professional clergy, visibly distinct from the laity. Finally, unprecedented numbers lowered the standards – especially after the wholesale conversion of barbarian peoples beyond the Roman frontiers.

This was the time of SS Anthony and Pachomius, of St Benedict of Nursia, of the monastic movement in Christianity. The spectacle of the secular church – the church in the world – was already too much for many Christians, particularly among the laity. Revulsion from what they considered an over-worldly church was for many one cause at least of their adopting the monastic life, and we know that, despite what happened later, the earliest Christian monasteries were communities of laymen.

The church entered the Middle Ages, therefore, with a twofold problem. On the one hand, some of the best of its laity were leaving it for the monastic life; on the other, an alarming and increasing proportion of the remainder professed Christianity, but for them conversion had not meant any deep change. This was especially true of the mass conversion of barbarians. The medieval church had to find room in its system for the monastic institution. It had also to tolerate for centuries – throughout and indeed beyond the Middle Ages – the barbarian and still half-pagan rites,

[1] At the height of the crisis, the Fourth Lateran Council restated its standard of orthodoxy, took the "momentous step" of making it obligatory on every Christian to show in confession to his parish priest at least once a year his fitness for church membership (A. Hamilton Thompson, *Cambridge Medieval History*, VI, pp. 690–1), strengthened the authority of the bishop for detecting heresy and commanded him to use it (No. 136 below, canons 1, 21, and 3).

superstitions and idolatries, of popular religion. As it presided over tribal marriage until it could make a sacrament of it, so it presided over the ordeals by fire, water, etc. of tribal justice until it felt able to denounce them as superstitious. "It is impossible to efface everything at once," Pope Gregory the Great had warned Augustine, his missionary-bishop in England. In this spirit pagan temples were continued as Christian shrines, heathen festivals turned into church-occasions, and men accustomed to sacrifice to devils allowed to "kill cattle to the praise of God". But medieval man walked in fear of much else besides the fear of the Lord. There were demons that could strike you by the wayside, the women that ride by night, spells, magic, the malevolent in many forms. There were the spirits of places, of trees, rivers and wells to be propitiated, fairies to be invoked, charms for one's crops or for sick cattle and sheep. The church tried in vain to prevent offerings and vows elsewhere than at church, and to stop mummings and dancings or recourse in time of trouble to charms and divinations. It was fighting a paganism that was not yet remote, and that was liable at any moment somewhere or other to get out of control. In this country King Canute in the eleventh century had forbidden in his laws every heathen practice: "it is heathen practice if one worships idols, namely if one worships heathen gods and the sun or the moon, fire or flood, walls or stones or any kind of forest trees, or if one practises witchcraft or encompasses death by any means, either by sacrifice or divination, or takes any part in such delusions".[1] Between 1161 and 1186, that is only a few years before the beginning of this volume, in the diocese of Exeter, Bartholomew, the bishop at that time, still found it necessary to condemn a long list of heathen practices.[2] A century later synodal statutes for the diocese of Winchester mention child-exposure "with or without salt"[3] – this is paralleled in France at the time and explained by the French Dominican, Etienne de Bourbon (d. *c.* 1261).[4] And under the year 1282, the Lanercost chronicler tells of the parish priest of Inverkeithing, named John, who in Easter week "revived the profane rites of Priapus, collecting young girls from the villages, and compelling them to dance in circles to Father Bacchus". We are told that "out of sheer wantonness, he led the dance . . . and singing and dancing himself like a mime, he viewed them all and stirred them to lust by filthy language" and that "those who held respectable matrimony in honour were scandalised by such a shameless performance, although they respected the parson because of the dignity of his rank". We learn, however, that later in the same year his parishioners turned upon him when he inflicted other indignities on them and he "fell the same night pierced by a knife".[5]

But the typical medieval parishioner was not only in many respects still half-pagan: he was also an illiterate peasant. This was, of course, a major difficulty in putting over Christ's teaching. Mass education is something very new in our civilisation. The church had to wrestle with the ignorance, not as today the sophistication, of the laity. It put its spiritual message over as best it could. We must not assume the sermon,

[1] *E.H.D.*, I, *c. 500–1042*, ed. D. Whitelock (1955), p. 420
[2] G. G. Coulton, *Life in the Middle Ages* (Cambridge, 1930), I, No. 14 (pp. 33–5)
[3] No. 145 below
[4] Coulton, op. cit. No. 54 (p. 93)
[5] *The Chronicle of Lanercost, 1272–1346*, trans. Sir Herbert Maxwell (Glasgow, 1913), pp. 29–30

which, when given, was normally in Latin to an appropriate audience and was as much above the capacity of the ordinary parish priest as it would have been above the heads of his congregation. He, for oral instruction, normally relied on his contacts with parishioners individually in the confessional, though the example and competition of the friars brought about a change. By the time this volume ends in 1327 he is to be found more often giving his parishioners a sermon, and giving it in English. For laity who could read, the church increasingly provided works of edification: vernacular renderings of the Lord's Prayer, paraphrases of the Creed, manuals for confession, tracts on the deadly sins, penitence, and so on. Innumerable friars devoted themselves to such work as well as to preaching. The greatest of the works for this purpose was the *Legends of the Saints* (the "Golden Legend") of a learned theologian whose learned theology is forgotten, but not this, the Dominican archbishop of Genoa, James de Voragine (d. *c.* 1298). From it and other sources a Nottingham Franciscan, Nicholas Bozon, was translating and versifying saints' lives at the end of the century. For those who could not read, such lives could be set to the church's music and sung to them. Similarly, there was the religious, semi-liturgical drama, of which a good example is the "Adam" play, scenes interspersed at intervals in the liturgy, telling the story of the Fall and the murder of Abel: all – clergy, choir, actors, stage Paradise with Forbidden Tree and serpent, Hell and its pandemonium – in the open air, at the church door and the open space in front of it where Adam and Eve cultivated ceremonial soil, Cain and Abel played their parts, and Hell's demons ran about among the onlookers, the church itself being off-stage for the occasion and serving as dressing room. Again, sculpture, such as the sequence of sixty Old Testament scenes in the chapter house at Salisbury, contributed. Paintings on the walls of Norman churches, and stained glass in the windows of Gothic, also served as "the bible of the illiterate".

There is no way of knowing precisely how much success the church had by these methods. We must not exaggerate "the Age of Faith": there is evidence of indifference too.[1] But many undoubtedly were receptive, showing that the ground was fertile. The simple gospel simply told offered the humble dignity, the oppressed, hope. It generated enthusiasm, sometimes embarrassing such as mob crusades, sometimes unwelcome such as that of the followers of Arnold of Brescia or those of Peter Waldo when they contrasted the existing church with the simplicity and poverty of early Christianity, sometimes plainly heretical, but always sincere. Even the heresy in many cases sprang from nothing more alien or sinister than a desire to live the Christ-like life more perfectly. A church today would be considered healthy which could arouse such fervour and at the same time find energy to reform and reorganise itself.

This the western church did in the eleventh, twelfth and thirteenth centuries. By the eleventh, a sufficiently influential minority in it had realised that it was more enmeshed in the affairs, the social order, the economic activities, and the legalities of the world than ever before. After the disintegration of the Roman empire of the west it had fallen under the control of the barbarian kingdoms, particularly the expanding

[1] cf. Powicke and Cheney, *Councils and Synods*, II, *1205–1313*, p. 1,020, on non-attendance at church as one evidence of indifference.

Frankish kingdom. It is realistic, for example, to use the term "the Frankish church". Clovis and his successors appointed its bishops. Missions to the still pagan Germans beyond the Rhine worked under their patronage. In his capitularies Charlemagne legislated for it as well as for his lay subjects, and the pope at Rome was subject to him. Lay control had also established itself in monasticism and at the parochial level, not so much as an abuse as, by Germanic law, a recognised founder's proprietary right. To better thinking such lay appointment to ecclesiastical office, however decently disguised, was a cause of evil in the church, whether evil itself or not. There was once again a spontaneous reaction to the spectacle of a worldly church, once again most easily finding monastic expression – Cluny leading the way. As a monastic movement it persisted and grew into the great monastic revival of the late eleventh and the twelfth centuries. But it was not solely monastic. Ordinary clergy as well as monks worked for reform and after a reforming emperor had reformed Rome itself, after the choice of pope was lifted out of local politics, and especially after Cardinal Hildebrand, a man dedicated to the cause, became Gregory VII, they had the papacy behind them. From then on the Roman church asserted its responsibility to no one except God, its supremacy over other churches, and the authority of its head, the pope, as successor of Peter and then as vicar of Christ, over all other authorities ecclesiastical and lay.

There was little in this that was new as a statement of principle but, as a programme for action in the eleventh century, to lay powers and to most churchmen it was revolutionary. It meant often challenging instead of cooperating with lay rulers. It meant for churchmen a drive against simony and married clergy, centralisation under the bishop of Rome, less lay control but more ecclesiastical discipline.

Lay rulers, except in special cases or special circumstances,[1] would not in fact have papal overlordship: they were equally unwilling to admit that a pope had any right as pope even to arbitrate in temporal matters.[2] Backed by "evil prelates" (the adjective is Hildebrand's), they forced a compromise over the election and investiture of bishops and abbots. Lay appointment at lower levels was so widespread and so entrenched that it had to be approached circumspectly. Popes in the end put their main effort into ensuring proper cure of souls despite it. The clergy proved more amenable. They were stubborn over celibacy, and all too human when it was enforced,[3] but they were ready to accept a high view of their office. Bishops over and above their ordinary duties took on others as agents of the pope, the universal ordinary. The parish clergy, little as there was in other ways to distinguish most of them from their parishioners, accepted the view, even though it meant stricter ecclesiastical control, that the fact of being in orders set them apart. The church claimed a special position and privileges for them as clerks and added to their powers as priests.[4] Gregory VII's successors had not abandoned reform. In waiting until they had a firmer foundation for it in the church itself – a papal authority grounded in law and practice as well as tradition – they had made it possible.

[1] e.g. No. 17 below

[2] e.g. No. 87 below

[3] C. R. Cheney, *From Becket to Langton*, pp. 14–15, 126–7 and 137–8 and, below, Nos 136 (canc 1 14) and 145. For clergy in the Canterbury diocese in 1292–4, No. 146.

[4] On this, Cheney, op. cit. pp. 104–5 and 156–7.

The achievement of the twelfth century is evident in the Canons of the Fourth Lateran Council of 1215 (No. 136), though reform did not wait for them. It is Cheney's conclusion in *From Becket to Langton* that "English church government was transformed between 1170 and 1213", that "the law of the decretals was being applied in England in the last decade of the twelfth century much as it was applied after 1215', that the Fourth Lateran Council "made no break and caused no change of direction".[1] It does not diminish Innocent III to say this: seen in line, he still towers. Nor are the Canons of the council a less valuable source because they did not initiate the policy they represent, for there is no better formulation of it. They open with a restatement of the Faith, as a standard for true believers, but quite clearly also for the better recognition of heresy and action against it. They continue, after an affirmation of the primacy of the Roman over other patriarchates and churches, with a thoroughgoing survey of that Roman church, its clergy, its organisation and its working, highlighting shortcomings and decreeing remedies. They conclude by fixing a date in 1217 for the talked-of crusade, with equally decisive instructions for mounting it, but their main concern is church reform.

Innocent III's church had the vitality to reform itself and, as we have seen from the English evidence, had in fact already begun to do so. It now, these canons show, had confidence too, and in Innocent it had a man who combined with the qualities which made him pope those which in other circumstances could have made him a great king, and who was a born leader. That he was also by nature an authoritarian, raised at an exceptionally early age to authority in a church which had itself lately become more authoritarian,[2] argued little difference between him and council on policy, and we should expect none.

It is not surprising that the church should have become more authoritarian. Magnificently as it had met most of the demands made upon it in the new conditions of the century just past, in religion itself it had – perhaps because it did not understand it – failed to satisfy the mass enthusiasm as it had satisfied the monastic urge, which it did understand. One reason for this failure, perhaps the basic one, was its lack of confidence as custodian of the truths of a revealed religion in spontaneity in its illiterate and in any case half-pagan laity – an ecclesiastical prejudice which Pope Innocent III shared. In 1201, even in recognising the Humiliati, a Lombard fraternity of devout lay men and women, he had laid it down that in their meetings brethren of approved faith and knowledge of religion licensed by the bishop of their diocese might "set forth words of exhortation to those assembled . . . admonishing them to live good lives and do works of piety: but so that they do not speak of the articles of the Faith and the sacraments of the Church."[3] A second reason was that mass enthusiasm had led to mass heresy, amounting in some dioceses to a loss of control. This was particularly the case in Albigensian areas in southern France, where every conventional method had failed and in the end a crusade – no less – had been declared. It did nothing to diminish alarm that the Albigensian problem, though serious, was a

[1] ibid., p. 176
[2] On the evidence as regards heresy, *Cambridge Medieval History*, VI, pp. 715–16. But the Canons of the Fourth Lateran Council as a whole veritably breathe authority.
[3] cited in Father Cuthbert, *Life of St Francis of Assisi* (1927), p. 335

special case; that much heresy, even there, was misguided, Christian in origin, avoidable given understanding; that much of this stirring manifesting itself in so many forms and in so many districts, excessive and ill-regulated though it might be, was not actually heretical. Besides heresy there was a strong anti-clerical feeling about, even among the faithful: the feeling which the emperor Frederick II would think still worth appealing to in 1227 when in a manifesto he reminded the lay world that "the primitive church was founded in poverty and simplicity".[1] Here was reason for less trust than ever in the laity.

Innocent was not the man to shirk the use of authority: he was prepared to be the mainspring of it indeed (as the Canons of the Lateran Council obviously expect). But the true measure of his greatness is that he also had use for the methods of the priest Dominic and even for those of the layman Francis, so like those of other gospellizers – sharing as he did the belief of the one in the power of the Word itself over men's souls and recognising when he met it in the other the power also of simple faith. He took over the church at the end of the twelfth century and in eighteen years made it ready for the thirteenth. Not underrating past failures and setbacks, planning for the future. We have his "grand design" in the canons of his council: a church reformed, for its critics to be silenced, for its teaching to be credible, its authority unquestionable; heresy eradicated – in addition to the present emergency action locally, a policy for the future for the church generally, for taking action early enough at diocesan level, in the ordinary course, to prevent it from ever again being a danger;[2] a church inflexible of purpose but not set in its ways.

This last point illustrates a neglected aspect of medieval thought, which we are too ready to think of as static but which did in fact allow for change. Passage of time may, for instance, make a law no longer appropriate.[3] There is emergency power in government, for necessity knows no law.[4] Generally, "in a world of change there can be nothing that is altogether and immutably stable"[5] and "it should not be judged reprehensible if men's decrees are varied at some time or other in accordance with changing circumstances".[6] This, of course, need not involve expediency as the word is normally used today. There is not, and was not in medieval thinking, necessarily any compromise with principle or sacrifice of purpose.[7] It need be no more than a readiness to "move with the times": as shown by the council by its refusal in 1215 to continue to countenance ordeals[8] and by Innocent himself in choosing to fight heresy,

[1] see R. G. D. Laffan, *Select Documents of European History 800–1492* (1930), p. 123

[2] This, it will be seen, involved (No. 136, canons 1 and 3) a restatement in the light of current heresies (as the emphasis shows) of the orthodox belief, and an official statement of policy for the future, this requiring not only full cooperation from lay authorities but also a strengthening of existing diocesan procedures.

[3] Augustine: "Temporal law, however just it be, can be justly changed with the passage of time", quoted by Aquinas, who takes up the whole question of law and change (*Summa Theol.*, 1a2æ, Qu. 97, extracts from which are given below, No. 231).

[4] On this generally, the present writer in *E.H.R.*, lx (1945), pp. 18–23, for the theory; for its practical importance in England and France in 1297, the rest of the article. cf. Aquinas extracts, No. 231 below.

[5] Aquinas, *Summa Theol.* 1a2æ, Qu. 97 (art. 1)

[6] From the opening sentence of the canons (50–2) of the 1215 council, dealing with marriage. For the full sentence see No. 136 below.

[7] On medieval thinking on this matter there is a valuable article by Ewart Lewis, "Natural law and expediency in medieval political theory", *Ethics*, l, No. 2 (January 1940), pp. 144–63.

[8] No. 136 (canon 18) below; cf. No. 25 also.

harness the enthusiasm his predecessors had let run wild, disarm anti-clericalism and overcome indifference or worse by new methods as well as the church's traditional ways. With him, in supplementing authority by a missionary effort, supplementing the establishment by recruiting auxiliaries, and giving the church hope through them of reaching out to those whom the parochial system was failing to reach, there was no change of purpose, simply greater flexibility in the choice of means.

It is remarkable because of its significance, though it should not surprise us, that the canons show little change in the church's general attitude towards the laity, even its dutiful laity. Canon 1, with its revised statement (there are accretions in the penultimate paragraph) of the belief required for church membership and eternal salvation, and canon 21, with a new compulsory annual test of fitness for membership, may have had chiefly heresy and laxity in mind. But there is nothing elsewhere which shows confidence in even the zealous layman. He had little or no place in church government, none if he was an ordinary layman.[1] Active participation by him in the worship and ministry of his parish had been reduced in the course of the twelfth century – English evidence of this is given by Professor Cheney, who comments, "It is not always realised what a revolution this constituted."[2] There is nothing in the canons of 1215 to reverse this: instead, the greater authority of the parish priest is confirmed.[3] The picture changes again in the fourteenth century[4] and it would be interesting to explore the reasons for this. But for the greater part of the period covered by this volume the layman's role is little more than passive. Layfolk were, essentially, sheep to be shepherded.

At the same time, the church's attitude was benevolent. It cared for them. It stood for social justice for them, as then understood. It had a place for them in the church, if they believed what it taught them to believe and if they submitted to its discipline. They too would be of the universal church of the faithful: "Not only virgins and the continent, but married people too, find favour with God by right faith and good works and deserve to attain to eternal blessedness."[5] And it could be indulgent. Its discipline allowed for human frailty.

The history of the development of the practice of public confession and penance in the early church into the sacrament of penance, and especially into its culmination in 1215 as compulsory private confession to a priest and imposition of the penance by him,[6] could be used as an illustration of the direction the church was taking generally. But its only relevance here is that penances both came to be graded in severity according to the gravity of the sin and quite early in their history could, because of their severity, be partially remitted in deserving cases, the rest of the penance being commuted for some act of piety, such as alms instead of fasting or, in the case of mortal sin and a wealthy penitent, perhaps the founding of a monastery.[7] Such commutation is, of course, the perfectly respectable origin of the indulgence, later so dubious and as Luther showed challengeable. It took on the character of commutation in reverse if,

[1] Cheney, *From Becket to Langton*, pp. 155–60 [2] ibid., pp. 156–7
[3] No. 136 below, canons 1 and 21
[4] Professor Cheney draws attention to this, op. cit. p. 160. [5] No. 136 below, canon 1
[6] ibid., canon 21. For this whole development, *Cambridge Medieval History*, VI, pp. 686–94.
[7] *C.M.H.*, VI, p. 693

for example, gifts for pious purposes were raised from the faithful by promising them remission for a stated time of the penances enjoined upon them by their priest.[1] Plenary indulgence, full remission, first promised so far as we know[2] in 1095 by Pope Urban II to crusaders, was also, strictly speaking, remission of penance but in practice (and practice preceded theory) not so clearly understood and not, even in official statements, so clearly defined. The concluding canon of the Lateran Council of 1215, announcing the benefit of plenary indulgence for the forthcoming crusade, speaks of "full pardon for their sins".[3] Thirteenth-century theologians (the age was not unaware of the danger in unregulated practice[4]) found a rationale for indulgences in a "treasury of merits" theory and this was officially adopted by the church in 1343. We do not need to trace the further development of indulgence practice.[5] The theory is enough. Essentially, it was that Christ gave his whole life, whereas one drop of his blood would have sufficed for the redemption of the human race, and many saints too contributed a superfluity of merit. This "treasury" of merits, so built up, administered in the first instance by the pope as head of the church but a partial power of administering might be conveyed by him to others, could be drawn on to make up the shortcomings of those who could not themselves furnish the full satisfaction required of them. Such was the theory. It appeared after, long after, the practice. Whether or not it was framed according to the practice[6] is not our concern, any more than whether or not it was, as Catholics before Luther claimed,[7] unbiblical. It is a striking enough demonstration of the medieval church's readiness to take medieval man as he was. "It is impossible to efface everything at once," Pope Gregory the Great had advised Augustine of Canterbury, his missionary-bishop in England.[8]

It cared for his material condition too and stood, we have said, for social justice for him, as then understood. This more sophisticated way of saying that it was faithful to Christ's teaching to succour those in distress will be seen to be entirely appropriate. It has also, for the historian, two immediate advantages. On the one hand it is a reminder of the immense change in Christianity in the twelve centuries after Christ, of its changed position in society and of the changes in society itself during that time. On the other hand, it links up with later developments. The history of the treatment of the poor in this country is, academically, a strand of Modern History. We distinguish the Later Poor Law from the Early Poor Law, and begin the early for all practical purposes with the legislation of the Tudors. Before that, except perhaps for a

[1] *C.M.H.*, VI, p. 694. cf. No. 155 below, a grant by the bishop of London of an indulgence of this partial sort in 1308.

[2] *C.M.H.*, VI, p. 694; the "record", however, is not official, still less an official text. Urban's sermon is known only from contemporary chroniclers.

[3] No. 136 below, canon 71. The Latin *peccatum* (sin) was itself ambiguous. It could also mean the penalty for sin (Harnack, *History of Dogma*, VI (New York, 1907), p. 260, n. 1).

[4] No. 136 below, canons 60 and 62; cf. *C.M.H.*, VI, pp. 695–6.

[5] for which, B. J. Kidd, *Documents of the Continental Reformation* (Oxford, 1911)

[6] Harnack, op. cit. VI, p. 260

[7] ibid., pp. 267–8

[8] A good deal of English evidence for the church's attitude towards its laity will be found by a careful reading of the texts given in Part IV (D) below, particularly in Nos 145–53. Attention should be drawn also to two articles by Rosalind Hill on public penance and excommunication respectively – for references see the Select Bibliography to Part IV below; and to another item in that bibliography, C. Drew, *Early Parochial Organisation in England . . . the Office of Churchwarden*. This deals with one aspect of the fourteenth-century revival of activity by parishioners (see above p. 21 and n. 4), but, concerned as it is with origins, is centred on the thirteenth-century evidence.

reference to the Black Death, the familiar quotation from More's *Utopia* about "husbandmen" being "thrust out of their own" by enclosures for sheep-farming, and the relief given by monasteries before the Dissolution, it is, or has been until recently, *terra incognita*. We propose to work backwards, from the known to the unknown.

The books stress the modernity of Sir Thomas More. I believe the medievalism of his outlook has been underestimated. As to *Utopia*, the "Utopian" book, Book II, was in fact written before Book I, and it describes a pagan state organised on communist lines and governed by reason. But its author was more than a student of Plato's *Republic*. Book I was obviously written as a preface (not the only preface to be written last) to make his meaning explicit. When he wrote it he was a leading English common lawyer and a future lord chancellor and his message was that "to find citizens ruled by good and wholesome laws, that is an exceeding rare and hard thing" and in England the criminal law, for theft for instance, was at once irrational ("unreasonable") and unjust ("passeth the limits of justice"), "For great and horrible punishments be appointed for thieves, whereas much rather provision should have been made that there were some means whereby they might get their living, so that no man should be driven to this extreme necessity, first to steal, and then to die."

The severity of the laws which More calls unjust is not in doubt. Their brutality by present-day standards, not for theft or any other offence, but merely for being a "rogue, vagabond, or sturdy beggar", is sufficiently illustrated by 39 Eliz. I, c. 4 of 1598, a companion Act of the Poor Relief Act of that year and milder than some of the century:

> . . . every person which is by this present Act declared to be a rogue, vagabond or sturdy beggar . . . taken begging, vagrant, wandering, or misordering themselves . . . shall . . . be stripped naked from the middle upwards and shall be openly whipped until his or her body be bloody, and shall be forthwith sent . . . the next straight way to the parish where he was born. . . .

Tudor legislation on the problem of the poor, with some later changes, "determined the main features of national policy in relation to the poor until the reforms which followed the Poor Law Commission of 1834".[1]

It is one of the "common errors in history" still to see new policies in these Tudor laws. The error has been aggravated by attributing them for too long to a particular cause – the dissolution of the monasteries and the consequent failure of monastic relief for the poor. Even J. R. Tanner, while rejecting the dissolution as anything more than a contributory factor, stresses the novelty of Tudor policies time and time again.[2]

Now of course it is not true that only monasteries looked after the needy in the Middle Ages. It is easily shown that medieval society itself felt concern for and accepted a responsibility for its poor. There was a medieval poor law and, in fact, it was not to the monasteries that the poor would look for relief in the first instance. Recent work in this country and America makes it clear that just as the sixteenth century

[1] J. R. Tanner, *Tudor Constitutional Documents* (Cambridge, 1922), p. 472. G. R. Elton's chapter on local government omits Tanner's pages 469–95 (*Tudor Constitution* (Cambridge, 1962), p. 455, n. 1).
[2] Tanner, op. cit. pp. 469–73

inherited the problem from the Middle Ages for the most part, so (for the most part) it persisted in medieval attitudes to poverty. The true novelty of Tudor legislation, our Early Poor Law, is that, in a situation in which the older agencies for relief were no longer adequate, the state, of its own secular authority, took over the responsibility. But what it took over was a medieval system of poor relief that had gone wrong. Tudor government can be charged with building on it without putting it right.

What then was the medieval system, before it "went wrong"? The first element was the family. Under the Christian obligation of charity, incumbent on all men, a man's first obligation was to his family – charity literally began at home. This was retained by the state as a legal obligation on parents or children able to do so to "relieve and maintain" "at their own charges".[1] A second element was organised charity: urban craft guilds or religious fraternities in the countryside who helped their members. Manorial custom, too, could provide for the poor. This was found on a group of Cambridgeshire manors and has since been found on Ramsey Abbey estates,[2] though it is too early to say how generally this was the practice. On the Cambridgeshire manors a tenant too old or infirm to perform his services and without family to do them for him had his holding given to another villein and he was allowed a cottage and garden (worked by the other) and the produce of six acres or so of the holding to live on. If he died, leaving a widow and children, his widow was allowed to hold without payment of heriot and hold until death or remarriage, when (by the local custom in this case) the youngest son succeeded. Above all, there was the church's provision for the poor, the only one that can properly be called systematic.

The provision, in one form or another, was as old as the church itself, older than the medieval organisation of the church, older than medieval society, and recent American scholarship has shown how busy theologians and canonists were in the late twelfth and thirteenth centuries working out a properly-grounded yet up-to-date theory of Christian charity. This, it seems, is how they went about it.[3] Gratian's *Decretum* (*c.* 1140), a concordance of earlier church law, opens with "The human race is ruled by two [principles], namely by natural law and by customs". Natural law he defines as something that is "common to all nations, so that it is held everywhere by instinct of nature, not by any legal enactment – as, for instance, the coming together of men and women, the succession and rearing of children, the common possession of all things [etc.]" Private property he finds room for by his distinction, already quoted, between the two [principles] that rule the human race. "Natural law differs from customs and enactments, for by natural law all things are common to all men. . . . By the laws of custom and legal enactment, this belongs to me, that to another." Commentators on the *Decretum* found a way of reconciling the natural instinct towards common possession with private property by glossing the word "common" –

[1] In the words of 39 Eliz. I, c. 3 (Tanner, op. cit. p. 491).

[2] F. M. Page, "The customary poor law of three Cambridgeshire manors", *Cambridge Historical Journal*, iii, No. 2 (1930), pp. 125–33; J. A. Raftis, *The Estates of Ramsey Abbey* (Toronto, 1957); *Tenure and Mobility*, (Toronto, 1964); and "Social Structures in five East Midland villages", *Econ. Hist. Rev*, 2nd ser., xviii (1965) pp. 83–100

[3] This and the two following paragraphs are based on Brian Tierney's exposition of the subject in *Medieval Poor Law: a sketch of canonical theory and its application in England* (University of California Press, Berkeley and Los Angeles, 1959).

"according to this law of nature all things are called common, that is they are to be shared in time of necessity". This sets limits to property rights by attaching to the possession of property an obligation of charity. It does not deny the right to private property, or the rightness of it; what it does deny is the right of a man in all circumstances to say "I can do what I like with my own", to keep in all circumstances more than suffices for his own needs. There was no obligation on a man to "deprive himself of his own necessities in order to help another in need. He could even retain superfluities, provided others were not in want. But in time of necessity any superfluous wealth of an individual was to be regarded as common property to be shared with those in need."

What constituted a superfluity of wealth and when almsgiving was a duty and when a voluntary (and therefore a meritorious) act interested these theologians and canonists very much. It became accepted doctrine that to give superfluities was an obligation and, "as the beggar received only what was properly his own", an act of justice, but to give of one's necessities was an act of mercy and of merit. But, medieval society not being democratic, a man's necessities were what his station required: his superfluous wealth was what was beyond that. This it was his duty to share with the poor. By the same token a poor man had a right to a share and in extreme need it was not theft if he took it. We are reminded of Jean Valjean in Victor Hugo's *Les Misérables*.

Such was the general theory of charity worked out by theologians and canonists, applicable to all property and to all owners. Church property, however, was not a simple case. Exemption was out of the question and was not sought. But after twelve centuries, with the endowment of churches, monasteries and hospitals, the accumulated pieties of the faithful, offerings and fees, and income from tithes, the church had enormous wealth. Moreover, the simplicity of the early church, when the bishop administered the revenues of his diocese and the responsibility for dispensing its charity was his, was no longer possible. He no longer received most of the wealth which accrued to the church in his diocese. For a variety of reasons, legal and feudal as well as the size of his responsibility in the large territorial diocese of medieval centuries, not only had he delegated many matters: there were others where his authority (as over religious houses) was supervisory rather than immediate, and others again where it had to be shared with lay interests. His *familia* had become an elaborate diocesan administration; cure of souls had devolved upon a parochial system and a parochial priesthood. Of ecclesiastical property in his diocese little was now vested in him and over its administration therefore, provided there was no scandal, he had little control. As Gratian's sources were too early even to be aware of this change, and as, in any case, the church was always reluctant to admit ownership of church property by the bishop or priest who administered it (hence the fictions of giving to God or the patron saint of a church or monastery), it was now difficult to pin down the responsibility for the church's charity. Canonists, with the help of a pronouncement by Pope Innocent IV, found a way of recognising the facts while preserving the principle:

> No prelate, but Christ, has possession and domination of the things of the church . . . that is to say the community of the faithful which is the body of Christ, the head. They are said to

belong to the poor as to sustenance [that is the poor were to be supported from them]. For the common welfare they are divided among the churches of divers places by authority of the supreme pontiff, and administration of them is conceded to bishops and other prelates.

So far so good. It did not solve every problem – how, for instance, to reconcile communal ownership with the idea of a beneficed clergy. But a practical solution was more important than a watertight theory and the theory did preserve the right of the poor. It also squared with the general theory. A cleric had a right to the necessities his status required. The right of the poor was to be relieved out of the superfluities of the benefice. Monastic wealth, of course, continued to be liable, and with the amount of wealth by now vested in parochial benefices it would have been unrealistic not to include them. As to theory, the only other thing that needs to be said is that the total charges on a benefice could vary so much between one benefice and another (even if the revenues were the same and even if, for instance, no provision had to be made for the endowment of a vicarage for a non-resident rector) that, wisely, there was no longer any attempt to require a specific proportion of the revenue to be given to the poor, and as local, e.g. English, evidence shows there could be great variation in practice.[1]

As to practice, it is likely, but we do not know, that the parochial form of ecclesistical charity was the main form. Yet, because it was closest to the needy and knew best their need, it is likely to have been the most efficient. It is certainly the medieval church's only systematic provision for the relief of want; and, as far as we yet know, it was the only systematic provision in existence in medieval society. The medieval poor law, it would seem, was the law of the ecclesiastical state.

Evidence of its application by the church in England has been assembled by Mr Tierney[2] and can be followed up in Powicke and Cheney, *Councils and Synods*.[3] Its parochial basis is implicit in a mandate of Pope Alexander IV in 1261 on the dislocations of parish life caused by the appropriation of benefices to episcopal, capitular, and especially monastic uses:

Mandate to the bishops of Worcester, Lincoln, Salisbury, Coventry, and Llandaff, on the reported cupidity of religious in getting churches appropriated to them, to the extinction in such churches of divine worship, the loss of episcopal rights, and the closing of the doors of promotion against poor and proficient clerks; the religious in some cases boasting that they have bought such churches. The pope, having received information from the above bishops . . . has ordered that examination should be made into the motive for such appropriations, whether they have been made under the pretext of poverty, and also what benefices have been annexed to episcopal and secular chapter uses, and whether vicarages with sufficient stipends have been instituted, and how many are served by monks themselves; plurality also is to be restrained, and the proportion of proceeds of the churches distant four or five miles from the monasteries to which they are appropriated is to be regulated, an eighth or tenth part being set aside for poor parishioners. The above bishops are to apply fitting remedies. . . .[4]

---

[1] See Tierney, op. cit. p. 78, and the evidence in ch. V.
[2] ibid. ch. V.
[3] See Select Bibliography to Part IV below, s.v. "Councils and Synods . . .".
[4] *Cal. Papal Registers: Papal Letters I*, ed. W. H. Bliss, p. 375

Such special problems apart, it is Mr Tierney's conclusion that the "ecclesiastical poor law worked tolerably well in thirteenth-century England".[1]

And yet, the following extract from a coroner's inquest in a thirteenth-century eyre roll creates doubt in one's mind:

> Richard of Rye that was ten years old begged for his livelihood through the countryside. He died from weakness and exhaustion, and the jury brought it in Misadventure.[2]

Perhaps it worked with no more anomalies than modern social institutions work, or no more than human institutions at any time.

If so, why did it no longer suffice in the sixteenth century? To answer this we must consider the causes of poverty. "There was no mass unemployment in the high Middle Ages such as we have seen in modern times."[3] The problem in the thirteenth century was distress arising from old age, sickness, death, the ordinary fluctuations of harvest etc. By the fifteenth century, because of the dislocation of, especially, rural society due to processes of economic change as well as calamity and evidenced in the decay of the manorial system, deserted villages, enclosures and the like as well as plagues, the problem of poverty and its relief contained the question, "Can a man who could work be numbered among the poor?" It was a problem of able-bodied and vagrant (because dislocated) poor. There was not a collapse of the medieval system of poor relief, or the secular state could not have taken over the working of it in the sixteenth century. What happened in the fourteenth and fifteenth centuries was that the state stepped in to add its authority. The failure of ecclesiastical authority in these centuries was its failure to do again what it had done so successfully in the thirteenth, rethink its theory of charity – in this case, face the intellectual problem presented by able-bodied poverty. Tudor governments took over the machinery, but did not rethink either.

(iv) GOVERNMENT

The period 1189 to 1327 is best known for its constitutional history, but it could be said that it was the fourteenth century, not the thirteenth, that was decisive for our constitutional development and that the real achievement of 1189–1327 was administrative and legal, monarchy but not limited monarchy, the common law not the constitution.

The truth in this will be seen if we let ourselves forget the words "constitution" and "crisis" for a moment and ask ourselves what, from the evidence there is, were the preoccupations of government in the long intervals between 1215, 1258–65, and 1297.

In the first place, it must be said, with being a king; which could mean also restoring authority after civil war, as in the case of Henry II, the regency for Henry III, and Edward I at the outset of their reigns, but at all times meant upholding the laws and customs of the realm (and if necessary making new law) to ensure justice and good

[1] Tierney, op cit. p. 109
[2] W. C. Bolland, *The Year Books* (Cambridge, 1921), p. 75
[3] Tierney, op. cit. p. 58

government for all men.[1] Feudal monarchy, as we are accustomed to describing monarchy in the middle centuries of the Middle Ages, is best seen (it could almost be defined) as an older monarchical principle of government surviving in a feudalised society. It meant in theory as well as practice very much less than autocracy. The "law of the land" and the "good customs" which it was such a king's function to uphold (and adapt if need be) were some of them older than kingship itself and certainly most of them were not of royal making. Maitland has described the rivals to the king's authority at the beginning of the twelfth century in justice alone, how limited his direct authority was, how long it was to be – even with the idea of the *king's* peace – before "every, [even] the slightest, wrongful application of physical force" was brought "within the cognisance of the royal court".[2] It is also true that in government generally at the beginning of the twelfth century the king was a remote figure whose authority was only occasionally felt directly by most men, and that even in 1327 church, township and manor were still the realities for most of them for most of their life for most of the year.[3] Nonetheless, feudal monarchy in England, thanks first to the Conqueror, then to Henry II, then to adjustment to the loss of Normandy, was stronger than many. At his death in 1189 Henry left a monarchy which stood the test of time and change – even violent change: on top of Richard I's neglect, a minority, wars, two civil wars, and deposition by 1327. It is presupposed in Magna Carta itself. It was not shaken by *feudal* rising in the minority of Henry III as that of France was in the minority of St Louis. It was not as undeveloped as that in Germany of the emperor Frederick II who as he moved about doing justice could only be in one place at once; did so by Swabian law if he was in Swabia, by Saxon if in Saxony, and so on, there being no common law; and kept no record of cases decided, so that a common law could not grow, before a timid decision of a diet at Mainz in 1235 for a judge to be appointed to act in his stead, and a notary to be appointed to make a record to serve as a precedent in like cases. We are inevitably reminded of the justices acting in the king's name, their eyres and their records, already at work in England. Governmentally, fortune and misfortunes had made England an advanced country, not a Sicily, but one of the more centralised states. That said, it should not be necessary to say that it was, of course, still a medieval state equipped for administration with nothing specifically royal, simply the personal household organisation that any of the king's subjects with estates great enough might have,[4] and like all other governments of the day still handicapped, as Charlemagne in his empire five centuries before had been, by poor communications. Space here simply would not allow any detailed account of how much remained to be done – and was done – by 1327 (still less of how it was done) to enthrone the monarchical principle at the expense of the feudal, to draw the older communal institutions of shire and hundred into a centralised royal system, and to

[1] A comparison of the proem to Justinian's Institutes, the prologues to "Glanvill" on the laws and customs of the realm of England and "Fleta", and of these with a careful reading of the material (crisis documents or not, in this case) given below in Part II and Nos 231–5 in Part VI will show that this is more than literary commonplace; that it is the commonplace of government and politics too, and not less significant because it is common to the king and his opponents alike.

[2] Lecture II of his, on the forms of action at common law (*Equity and the Forms of Action* (Cambridge, 1920)).

[3] This point is enlarged upon in the Introduction to Part III below.

[4] For this, see the Introduction to Part III below.

subordinate local custom to common law.[1] An index to the magnitude of it (there is no reason to suppose that the case is exceptional) may be the instance of the hundred of Amounderness in Lancashire where, we learn from a complaint in 1334, the hundred bailiff's work, most of it due to the increase in the volume of royal business, had increased fourfold in a century: "Under Henry III, Alan of Singleton," Miss Cam tells us, "was hereditary bailiff . . . and he did all the work himself, and at his own expense, and so did his son after him, but his grandson found the work grown so much that he appointed a whole-time subordinate to do the work for him, and the process went on till in 1334, Alan's great-great-great-grandson had let the office to a man who employed five others to help him in doing the work . . . In spite of their complaints, the men of Amounderness admitted that at least four were necessary."[2]

A second preoccupation of thirteenth-century government was with good government. We remarked earlier that Magna Carta presupposes monarchy, meaning that its begetters, in their meticulously detailed and undoctrinaire way of saying so by reciting grievances instead of principles, required the king to act within the law, as they themselves undertook to act within it[3] towards their men; and this, in the same meticulously detailed and undoctrinaire form, the king agreed to for himself and his heirs. Kingship, the institution, is not for them the issue. Their concern is that the king should govern rightly.

There is plenty of evidence that so it remained, whatever means they and their children might be driven to.[4] There is, however, at least as much evidence of royal concern for good government. A king would see it rather as a matter of administration and naturally be less critical than his subjects of royal policies. But he stood to gain from good administration and to lose by bad, and the problem in medieval conditions of controlling from a distance the conduct of local officials, which was not new when Henry II made a clean sweep of his sheriffs in 1170, could never be far from the minds of his successors. The promptings of self-interest would only be reinforced by the evidence of public discontent on the same subject. Miss Cam observed the change in the instructions given to the justices in eyre after 1215.[5] A mixture of motives no doubt, kingly duty, self-interest and political prudence in

[1] There is ample illustration, of course, in Parts II and III below, and much contemporary comment in Part I.

[2] H. M. Cam, *The Hundred and the Hundred Rolls* (1930), pp. 6–7. Indirectly a similar effect seemed to have been caused in London, where at least three-quarters of the civic officials in the early fourteenth century "simply did not exist in the reign of Henry III", we are told by G. A. Williams (*Medieval London* (1963), p. 89), who continues, "The demands of the monarchy governed London's life . . . and for much of the thirteenth century civic 'financial' policy must have been almost entirely a matter of fiscal relations with the Crown.'

[3] Below, No. 19 (article 48) and No. 20 (c. 60). *Mutatis mutandis* there is no difference between the barons' Articles and the royal grant, the Charter itself, on this.

[4] The petition put forward at the Oxford parliament in 1258 (*Annales Monastici*, ed. Luard, I, pp. 438–43; more conveniently in Stubbs, *Sel. Charters*, ed. H. W. C. Davis, pp. 373–8), described by the Burton annalist (*Ann. Monast.*, I, p. 438), who gives them, as "articles that need correction in the kingdom" (No. 5 below, p. 154). Articles 16–20 and 22–3 are notable. Then the opening provision of the "Provisions of Oxford" (No. 37 below); No. 39 below, the editorial note as well as the text; No. 40 below, the Provisions of Westminster, 1259. This is a closely-knit group for no more than the first two years of the next big crisis after 1215–25. Relevant texts for subsequent crises will be easily recognisable in the list of contents to this volume apart from the incidental information to be found at other times.

[5] *The Hundred and the Hundred Rolls*, p. 23, but the whole chapter should be read, indeed the whole book as a counterpoise to all the work done on central administration. Chapter I of the same author's *Studies in*

whatever proportions, explains it; but there is equally no doubt about the large measure of common ground between a king and his subjects on the question of official misconduct or, from the evidence of action in this volume alone, about royal concern over the problem. Edward I showed it within ten weeks of his return to this country in 1274,[1] within less in 1289,[2] less still in 1298[3] after his return from Flanders. Only when his prerogative is touched, his prises are involved, or officials of his curia (even "hors de leur place") are impugned, is there between him and his subjects head-on collision.

Good government, however, was more than either the king's own conduct or that of his officials. It was also a matter of keeping the peace between subjects themselves – or at least due process of law between them. The maintenance of order was a constant preoccupation and one which presented special problems in this period.

In the first place there was the problem of the law itself. The Fourth Lateran Council in 1215 forbade clergy to take any part in future in trials by ordeal,[4] thus officially recognising long-held[5] doubts about these as the judgment of God on the innocence or guilt of the accused. The lay power had already shown its doubts. Henry II had banished from the realm for life those with a thoroughly bad reputation even if by ordeal they were innocent.[6] No. 25 below reflects, however, the difficulties created by the Lateran decree. The problem was to find a substitute for the ordeal. The solution evolved was trial by jury as well as indictment by a jury.[7] The Statute of Westminster I (1275)[8] declared it "the common law of the land" that known felons and those manifestly of bad repute should be tried by jury. Significantly, though, the nearest it went to insisting upon jury trial was to authorise pressure to be put on them to agree to it – *prison forte et dure* which became *peine forte et dure* and in the end torture.[9] Public opinion, with all its doubts about ordeals, was slow to say that a man must accept men's judgment rather than God's. Secondly there was the problem of procedure, the prior problem of bringing a criminal to justice. Henry II had found that the old procedure of private accusation ("appeal of felony") was insufficient. Men were reluctant to face the risks to themselves in this and criminals were going scot-free. He had introduced collective accusation as an alternative, presentment or indictment (the distinction is technical) by a jury of the neighbourhood; but this in its

---

the Hundred Rolls (Vinogradoff, *Oxford Studies in Social and Legal History*, VI (Oxford, 1921)) surveys the growth in the Articles of the General Eyre from 1194 to 1341. No. 15 below may be compared with No. 45 below.

[1] No. 45 below.

[2] Below, Nos 61 and 234, and chroniclers in Part I

[3] No. 80 below

[4] below, No. 136, c. 18; and on the ordeals, Plucknett, *Concise History of the Common Law* (1948), pp. 111–14

[5] Plucknett, op. cit., pp. 114–16; and the same author's *Edward I and the Criminal Law* (Cambridge, 1960), pp. 68 ff.

[6] The Assizes of Clarendon and Northampton, Nos 24 and 25 in the preceding volume in this series, *E.H.D.*, II, *1042–1189*, ed. Douglas and Greenaway; cf. Plucknett, *Concise History*, p. 110; *Edward I and the Criminal Law*, p. 68; for textual questions, H. G. Richardson and G. O. Sayles, *The Governance of Mediaeval England* (Edinburgh, 1963), Appendix IV.

[7] On this evolution, Plucknett, *Concise History*, pp. 116–25. The irrationality of the solution compared with inquisitorial procedures found on the continent and with procedures already used in England on the civil side is emphasised in *Edward I and the Criminal Law*, pp. 70–6.

[8] below, No. 47, c. 12

[9] No. 109 below and, for the sixteenth century, *Concise History*, p. 122

turn was failing and an enormous amount of crime was again going unpunished.[1] The classic case is the attack on two merchants of Brabant in the Pass of Alton, near Winchester, in or shortly before 1249 and the conspiracy of silence in the neighbourhood when an attempt was made to identify the wrongdoers.[2] The failure is admitted in the preamble to the Statute of Winchester (1285)[3] and attributed to juries which "had rather suffer felonies done to strangers to go unpunished than indict wrongdoers the greater part of whom are people of the same district, or at least, if the doers are of another district, their receivers are of the neighbourhood" and this is put down to two things, first they have no fear of breaking their oath as jurymen and secondly there has been no penalty for concealment. Along with a tightening-up[4] of existing machinery, hue and cry, watch and ward, the Assize of Arms, and regulations for making the highways safer, a penalty is therefore now provided. The practice in the case of a homicide, of making the hundred where it happened responsible if it could not produce the killer, was extended to robberies: after a robbery the hundred in which it was committed must either produce those responsible or be itself held responsible, and that within forty days. It did not work. Proof is the "trailbaston" enquiry twenty years later, the commissioners, the articles of the enquiry, and proceedings thereon at Derby relating to a single wapentake of Derbyshire, the Peak District, in 1306.[5] We learn that men, if indicted, have "slipped away" (*se subtraxerint*) – swelling, no doubt, the number of footpads in the Pass of Alton and elsewhere or forming the gangs of thugs (*trailbastons*, "clubmen") we now hear of – or, better still, have avoided indictment by frightening into silence the juries who should have indicted them or suborning the very constables or bailiffs responsible for enforcing the statute of Winchester.[6] Authority given on 16 June 1306[7] to prevent escape by arresting on suspicion, despite Westminster II, c. 13 (which had been ordained to prevent another evil),[8] cannot have had great effect. The overriding impression remains, of a terrorised countryside and a near-breakdown of law and order.

(v) THE POLITICS OF GOVERNMENT

The heading of this section probably requires elucidation. We have spoken of constitutional history as a branch of political history, and see no harm done to the political by the present emphasis on social history if this is understood not in any narrow or superficial sense, but as covering the whole activity of man in society. "Political history could then be taken for what it is: the history of the frictions generated in

[1] F. W. Maitland speaks of "an enormous mass of crime" going "absolutely unpunished in the days of King John" (*Pleas of the Crown for the county of Gloucester, A.D. 1221*, p. xxiii).

[2] cf. Pollock and Maitland, *History of English Law* (2nd edn, Cambridge, 1923), II, 655. The story is told vividly by Matthew Paris (*Chron. Majora*, v. 56–60; in a translation in J. A. Giles, *Matthew Paris's English History*, vol. 2 (1853), pp. 294–8). Official record in the unpublished record of the Hampshire eyre in 1249: P.R.O., J.I. 1/776 and K.B. 26/223.

[3] below, No. 59

[4] Through constables in each hundred and liberty, who are to supervise the working of these institutions and the statute and report defects to justices, who shall in turn report to the king and he will provide remedies.

[5] below, Nos 93 (a) and (b) and 133

[6] Articles 7–9 of No. 93(b) are particularly revealing.

[7] below, No. 95

[8] No. 57 below

a society."[1] We have also said, of King John, that "when kings were allowed to rule as well as reign, the real test of kingship was political" and Magna Carta is proof that John failed it. Not that all his policies were unjustifiable, but "he failed to carry opinion, or enough of it, with him" and, before representative parliaments, this meant carrying the magnates, or enough of them, with him.[2]

In principle, there was a great deal of common ground between a medieval king and his subjects. The object of government was the common good. They could conceivably be in agreement too on what this for them would be. It was less likely (or there would be no political history) that they would always be agreed on whether a particular line of action would be for the common good. But over king and subjects alike there was the law. This Christian theory saw as – ultimately – the Law of God,[3] men of affairs as "the laws and customs of the land".[4] In either case it set standards and, in principle at least, made politics a matter not of personalities and expedients but of interpreting the law.

In principle, therefore, the area of conflict was much reduced and a further safeguard was the practice of consultation. It was a tradition that a king should take counsel with his magnates, and a prudent king did so. It prevented many a difference of opinion from becoming a straight trial of strength and was, moreover, in line with contemporary thinking,[5] though the king's freedom to seek counsel where he would, and reject it if he chose, became increasingly a political issue during the period.[6]

If it did come to a trial of strength, as it did from time to time, subjects might win, but their problem was how to bind a king. The pre-parliamentary limitations on monarchy were few. A ruler might promise, as he did and as he or she still does, in the coronation oath. He might amplify his oath in a charter, as Henry I did at his coronation. He might be forced, as John was, to issue a special charter during his reign, longer, detailed, specific, emphatic[7] that it was the outcome of consultation, even accepting a sanction – a right of resistance (call it feudal defiance or common distraint or what you will) to keep John to his promises. There was little left but deposition or tyrannicide or both.

Magna Carta and the Forest Charter which grew out of it ("the Charters") became a synonym for good government for ninety years. The problem was to enforce them. Oaths and charters were the most binding things men knew. But John sought and got the release from his undertakings which he had sworn not to seek, and his son and grandson got release from theirs. The sanction clause of Magna Carta 1215[8] was dropped from reissues, possibly because like other clauses which were dropped it may have been felt to have gone too far against royalty, but equally likely (and conveniently) because in 1216 it may have been considered not necessary in a charter issued in the name of a boy king who was in tutelage. Still, Magna Carta was a public act, in charter form because no better was known, partaking of law, and given the

[1] See below, in the Select Bibliography to Part II.
[2] See above, in section (i) of this Introduction
[3] as, for example, in No. 231 below
[4] e.g. Stubbs, *Select Charters*, 9th edn, p. 434
[5] As evidenced by Aquinas on law and government (No. 231 below) and the lawyer Bracton (Bk I, c. 1) on custom as law (Stubbs, op. cit. p. 412)
[6] See Introduction to Part III below, paragraphs "In No. 106(b) there is . . . had still to be", and the quotations and references there given.
[7] See below, No. 20, preamble: ". . . on the advice of . . ."
[8] See below, No. 20, c. 61

publicity of law from the outset. Adopted by the regency in Henry III's minority, protected by the church to the extent of excommunicating infringers of it other than the king himself, it became the basis of efforts to secure government acceptable to the governed for the rest of the century. The idea towards the middle of Henry III's reign of elective counsellors in attendance on the king among others of his own choosing, wherever it came from,[1] suggests some concern over royal policy. It was taken up again and acted on in a more stringent form in 1258[2] and was, of course, Simon de Montfort's idea of government in his year of power after the battle of Lewes.[3] In that same year regular publication of the Charters was ordered twice a year.[4] A move towards ecclesiastical, as well as royal, publication failed in 1279,[5] but it was allowed in 1297 in the fullest way and as a regular thing along with excommunication of offenders against the Charters.[6] Again, in 1297[7] it was granted that the Charters should be allowed in pleadings and judgments at common law; in 1300,[8] besides now being published four times a year, to avoid the delays of the common law or the difficulty when there was no remedy at common law elective county commissions elected by the county itself were to be appointed as royal justices with full powers to hear and determine summarily infringements of them; in 1301,[9] in case of conflict between them and statutes the statutes are to be amended or annulled.

Acceptable government was not in fact secured by charter. Edward I was an abler politician than his father and grandfather. But here we must distinguish. Edward was masterful but not reactionary. As Lord Edward he had concurred in the charters his father had granted and as king he never repudiated them, not even in 1297. On the contrary he refuted the very idea that he was opposed to them. Similarly, he never challenged the convention that he should govern with his people. No king before him had consulted his people more: nobody did more than he to establish the "parliamentary" occasion[10] as part of normal practice – even to adopting the novelty of shire and borough representation when it suited him. Far from retreating from this in 1297, he went beyond it: from the earls to the shires. Desperately late already for crossing to Flanders, he took emergency measures, but not without planning a propaganda campaign too, to win the country's support for them.[11]

Events enabled his subjects to impose their ideas. He had to accept an addition[12] – part revision, part supplement – to the charters his father had granted. This, which would have been a further limitation of royal power, he managed to undo[13] before he died. Like his father and grandfather before him, moreover, he got himself released from his undertakings by the pope.

[1] below, No. 34; and see the paragraph beginning "The genesis of No. 106 (b) . . ." in the Introduction to Part III below
[2] No. 37 below [3] Stubbs, *Select Charters*, 9th edn, p. 401 [4] ibid. pp. 405–6
[5] Faith Thompson, *The First Century of Magna Carta* (Minneapolis, 1925), pp. 96–7; together with Powicke and Cheney, *Councils & Synods*, II, *1205–1313* (Oxford, 1964), p. 851; and *Cal. Close Rolls, 1272–9*, p. 582
[6] below, No. 74 [7] loc. cit. [8] No. 85, c. 1, below [9] No. 89 below
[10] In the sense of an occasion when the king took counsel with a larger number of advisers than usual; cf. the Introduction to Part III below, the paragraph beginning "Discontent with royal government . . .".
[11] No. 70 below; and an article on "The Confirmation of the Charters, 1297", *English Historical Review*, lx (1945). [12] No. 74 below
[13] On this, the present writer's contribution to *Studies in Medieval History presented to F. M. Powicke*, ed. Hunt, Pantin and Southern (Oxford, 1948).

It is tempting to see in this failure to modernise the Charters and to bind the king by them the reason for a shift of emphasis in the new reign. But, however this may be, a shift there is. In the first place, Edward I had challenged his critics with his coronation oath.[1] In 1308 for Edward II a new clause was added to the coronation oath[2] and, apart from the specific reference to this clause in the interesting "baronial" logic of No. 98 below, his oath is referred to again and again.[3] Secondly, in the New Ordinances of 1311[4] the Charters[5] are still "in the pharmacopoeia" of good government but are "no longer the sovereign remedy". The emphasis is now on the need for good counsel – which steps are to be taken to see is in attendance on the king but which is chiefly to be found (and is to be sought) in parliament. When by 1322 Edward II is able to find the Ordinances of 1311 restrictive[6] (particularly, it would be, as to his choice of ministers) he is still not able to dispense with parliaments.[7] And again, when in 1341 the financial curbs of 1297 (No. 74 below) were revived and imposed on Edward III verbatim it was with the addition of the words "and that in parliament".

The partnership of parliament in royal government was the beginning of an event of world significance, the more as it was accompanied (as it happened, for we must not attribute credit for this) by the establishment of parliament permanently on a representative as well as a baronial basis. This too happened in the first quarter of the fourteenth century. H. G. Richardson's statistics in the first edition of the Royal Historical Society's *Handbook of British Chronology* (1939) may have been over-precise[8] but their revision in the second edition (1961)[9] does not affect the trend they indicated. It was exceptional for representatives to be summoned before 1300,

[1] At Lincoln in 1301 (No. 88 below).
[2] below, No. 97
[3] Nos 98, 100, and 103 below
[4] below, No. 100
[5] i.e. those of 1225 confirmed by Edward I
[6] The Statute of York (below, No. 103) "restricted . . . contrary to what ought to be, to the weakening of his royal lordship, and against the estate of the crown".
[7] ibid. "but things which . . . formerly"; cf. the Introduction to Part III below, the paragraph "Discontent . . . still to be".
[8] As Richardson's paragraph on the subject was not retained in the new edition, it is given here: "The position is, perhaps, most clearly expressed by stating that, out of all the parliaments between 1258 and 1300 . . . we have no evidence to show that representatives either of the shires or of the towns attended on more than nine occasions, namely:

Michaelmas 1258	Michaelmas 1275	November 1295
Hilary 1265	Michaelmas 1283	November 1296
Easter 1275	Easter 1290	Michaelmas 1297

The proportion is about one in nine. And although, as will be seen from the explanatory notes, there were a few occasions, other than session of parliament, when popular representatives were summoned, the inclusion of such gatherings even if it were legitimate, would not affect the result; for there were, during this period, many specially full meetings of the council to which the name of parliament is not properly applied and which equally find no place in our list.

After 1300, instead of setting down the parliaments which the commons attended, we find it easier to set down those parliaments for which there is no evidence that the commons were summoned, namely: Midsummer 1302, September 1305, Easter and Michaelmas 1308, July 1309, Candlemas 1310, Hilary 1320, and Michaelmas 1325. Out of thirty-four occasions between 1301 and 1325, the commons were invariably absent on no more than eight. And after 1325, the commons were invariably present." (*Handbook* (1939), pp. 339–40)
[9] *Handbook*, 2nd edn (1961), ed. Powicke and Fryde, pp. 492–544

between 1300 and 1325 it was exceptional for them not to be, thereafter they were normally present.

Over the centuries representation has transformed the partnership between parliament and ruler by now almost beyond recognition. Its early appearance should not in the least surprise us. In his *Making of the English Constitution*, A. B. White saw "something of the representative idea" as "present in almost any kind of government" and considered it "useless to seek the origin of so general a principle". Another American, G. H. Sabine, reminds us[1] of the Germanic folk and its idea of law as the law of the people, not given or made, but customary, which had survived the enormous change of the transition in the earlier Middle Ages from tribal to territorial law (from one's law being determined by one's kindred to one's law being determined by one's locality), and even survived also the revived study of Roman law in and after the eleventh century, so that it was commonplace still in the thirteenth[2] century that law was rather "found and declared" than made, that it was found and declared in the name of the people who lived it and that their approval and consent was necessary for the statement or modification of it. But he reminds us also that this idea was "very vague so far as concerned the procedure of government" and "implied no definite apparatus of representation". It is not that we cannot find the origin of the representative idea: the history of the practice is more important than the history of the theory.

And it should not surprise us after this that there are early instances of representative practice.[3] The important question is *why* the development after the twelfth century of "parliamentary" institutions to implement representation: to put a finer point upon it, why did even rulers (such as Edward I and Philip IV of France) take the initiative in developing (for their purposes) machinery of representation? The question involves social, economic and political, as well as constitutional history. The answer is, on the one hand, in the social history touched on above in the concluding paragraph of section (ii) and, on the other, in royal policies themselves. The part played by the wartime needs of England's three Edwards in the securing of English liberties is too often overlooked.

[1] *A History of Political Theory*, ch. XI
[2] cf. Nos. 231 and 232 (esp. pp. 909–10) below
[3] cf. C. H. McIlwain in *Cambr. Med. Hist.*, VII, ch. 23

GENERAL BIBLIOGRAPHY

This bibliography surveys briefly sources and modern work dealing generally with English history between 1189 and 1327. A very much fuller bibliography of source material and more specialised work on aspects of the period accompanies the Introduction to each Part of this volume.

A. MODERN WORKS

Since the appearance of *The Political History of England* (ed. W. Hunt and R. L. Poole in 12 vols) and *A History of England* (ed. Sir Charles Oman in 7 vols) much about the same time at the beginning of the century, so much record material has been available and used, in print or manuscript, that the volumes of G. B. Adams and T. F. Tout in the former and of H. W. C. Davis and K. H. Vickers in the latter, while still useful, need to be supplemented. The mid-century *Oxford History of England* (ed. G. N. Clark, 14 vols) is now standard. The volumes *From Domesday Book to Magna Carta* (A. L. Poole), *The Thirteenth Century* (Sir Maurice Powicke) and *The Fourteenth Century* (May McKisack) between them cover 1189 to 1327.

Recent brief surveys of a greater sweep chronologically than this period but which may serve as an introduction to it because of the quality of their authors are F. M. Powicke, *Medieval England 1066–1485* (Home University Library, reprinted 1942); Doris M. Stenton, *English Society in the Early Middle Ages, 1066–1307* (Penguin Books, 1951); Helen Cam, *England before Elizabeth* (2nd edn, 1960); and G. W. S. Barrow, *Feudal Britain: the Completion of the Medieval Kingdoms 1066–1314* (1956); though as an introduction the least useful will be the Powicke volume. It will probably be best read last of them as a commentary on the facts. Barrow is a textbook, but original and fresh. Stenton is excellent.

Powicke's *King Henry III and the Lord Edward* (Oxford, 1947; 2 vols paginated as one) is a masterly study in the grand manner, from which we all can learn. But like all Powicke's work, we get the more the more we bring to it: so not a beginner's book. Whether this quality makes his *The Thirteenth Century* in the Oxford History series a better textbook could be doubted, but it is indispensable. For insight, intellectual power and sheer brilliance of exposition F. W. Maitland's classic, Pollock and Maitland's *History of English law before the time of Edward I* (Cambridge, 2nd edn, 1898 and reprints, in 2 vols; now available in paperback), is not likely to be surpassed. But a work of great distinction and great influence on historical as well as legal-history studies is T. F. T. Plucknett, *Legislation of Edward I* (Oxford, 1949). Another kind of book of major importance is J. C. Holt, *Magna Carta* (Cambridge, 1965), an *historical* commentary superseding W. S. McKechnie's *Magna Carta* (Glasgow, 2nd edn, 1914), an over-legalistic commentary with which historians and their pupils have had to make do for so long as the only modern treatise. In a different field a work of equal impact, not because it needed to supply but because it has changed historical perspective, is C. R. Cheney, *From Becket to Langton: English Church Government 1170–1213* (Manchester, 1956). Here, inevitably, comes to mind the writing of David Knowles, especially *The Monastic Order in England* (Cambridge, 1940) and *The Religious Orders in England* (3 vols, Cambridge, 1948, 1955, 1959), on the spiritual and religious aspect of the medieval church, not only for its intrinsic quality but for its breadth, never failing to give us the larger background of Christianity in England: altogether, in insight, construction and presentation, an achievement surpassing even that of Powicke in his field.

Of reference books, bibliographies are indispensable. The standard bibliography, Charles

Gross, *The Sources and Literature of English History from the earliest times to about 1485* has long been out of print. A revision, recasting and expansion of it, taking its place, was announced in 1973 by the Oxford University Press: Edgar B. Graves, *A Bibliography of English History to 1485*, sponsored by the Royal Historical Society and by the American Historical Association and the Mediaeval Academy of America. The generous bibliographies in the volumes of the *Oxford History of England*, that of Powicke, for example, in *The Thirteenth Century*, will not, as personal selections of reading rather than formal bibliography, be entirely superseded. Not likely to be superseded are specialised bibliographies such as, for example, those of Kathleen Edwards, *The English Secular Cathedrals in the Middle Ages* (Manchester, revised edition, 1967); W. A. Hinnebusch, *The Early English Friars Preachers* (Rome, 1951); David Knowles in the books already mentioned on the monastic order and the religious orders; W. E. Lunt, "List of sources cited", *Financial Relations of the Papacy with England to 1327* (Cambridge, Mass., 1939) or, indeed, those in the economic field, in the *Cambridge Economic History* volumes.

The Royal Historical Society has published in 5 vols a bibliography of *Writings on British History 1901–1933* (volume II of which deals with the Middle Ages) and from 1934 annual volumes on the whole of the history since about 450. The annual volumes include the publications of societies, the *Writings . . . 1901–1933* did not. This, however, has been corrected by E. L. C. Mullins, *A Guide to the Historical and Archaeological Publications of Societies in England and Wales, 1901–1933* (1968), so that, with this, "every significant book and article issued on the subject during the twentieth century" is recorded. There are similar works by C. S. Terry and C. Matheson recording society publications for Scotland.

Other works of reference valuable for the period 1189–1327 include F. M. Powicke and E. B. Fryde, *Handbook of British Chronology* (2nd edn, 1961), not to be confused with C. R. Cheney, *Handbook of Dates for Students of English History* (1970). Both are indispensable. In the series of Royal Historical Society Guides and Handbooks are: N. R. Ker, *Medieval Libraries of Great Britain* (2nd edn, 1964), which is a list of surviving books which have been identified, with in each case their present location – the result of fascinating detective work; and (though this will be mentioned again as a bibliography of source material) E. L. C. Mullins, *Texts and Calendars* (1958), an "analytical guide to printed texts and calendars relating to English and Welsh history issued in general collections or in series by a public body or private society". Indispensable for the higher clergy of the church in England is the revision and expansion of John Le Neve's *Fasti Ecclesiae Anglicanae* now being published by the University of London Institute of Historical Research, for practical reasons in two series. That for the period 1300–1541 is now complete in 12 vols; the series for the period before 1300 is still in progress. Volume I, *St Paul's, London*, compiled by D. E. Greenway, has already appeared (1968).

For religious foundations: D. Knowles and R. Neville Hadcock, *Medieval Religious Houses: England and Wales* (the 2nd edn, 1971, is essential); D. E. Easson, *M.R.H.: Scotland* (1957); A. Gwynn and R. N. Hadcock, *M.R.H.: Ireland* (1970). There is a very informative "Short Catalogue" of *Medieval Cartularies of Great Britain* (1958), published and unpublished, by G. R. C. Davis.

Of a different kind, *Historic Towns*, I, edited by M. D. Lobel, with maps (Oxford, 1969), is the first volume for the British Isles in a series planned by the International Committee for Town History. In this volume, by working back from modern maps, the medieval lay-out of eight towns is recovered.

Periodicals: Among the more relevant are the national reviews – the *English Historical Review*, the *Scottish Historical Review* (Glasgow, 1903–28 and new series 1947–), the *Welsh History Review*, *Irish Historical Studies*; also the *Bulletin of the Institute of Historical Research*, *Speculum* (Medieval Academy of America), *Annales du Midi*, the *Journal of Ecclesiastical History*, *Economic*

History Review, *Agricultural History Review*, *Business History*, *History* (The Historical Association), the *Bulletin of the John Rylands Library, Manchester*.

B. SOURCE MATERIAL

It is told in the Introductions to Parts I and II below how government and learned societies took over in the nineteenth century the work of editing and publishing the source material for English history – chronicles and records. And we shall see that their achievement was immense, if uneven in quality. The work has continued in the twentieth century. There have been casualties among the societies, but also recruits – new societies, national, like the Canterbury and York Society and the British Society of Franciscan Studies, and active local societies like the Lincoln Record and Surrey Record Societies. Some idea of the present position (as its preface explains it is not an exhaustive list and it does not, of course, include publications after March 1957) may be gathered from Mullins's guide to texts and calendars of source material issued, the E. L. C. Mullins, *Texts and Calendars: an analytical Guide to serial publications* (1958) mentioned in section A. above. The English Historical Society, it will be seen, no longer exists. The Camden Society survives as a Camden series of the Royal Historical Society. The "Rolls" series (*Chronicles and Memorials . . .*), like the earlier Record Commissions an expensive undertaking even for governments, was brought to an end. Official publication is now in the hands of the Record Offices and various Royal Commissions. In the case of the Public Record Office at least, i.e. for England and Wales, the emphasis is on record publication, rightly of course as so much more remains to be done there than on chronicles; and, with the switch to publishing normally calendars of the records instead of the full texts, such progress has been made (for the scholar a matter of more importance than the price of the volumes published) that Exchequer as well as Chancery records are now beginning to be systematically calendared and published. This will, of course, greatly enhance the value of the Exchequer Pipe Rolls, the main burden of publishing which has been carried by a special Pipe Roll Society. If section A. of the Select Bibliography in Part III below is consulted, it will be seen that though more legal than financial records have been printed so far, the situation is not dissimilar for them: a special society again, the Selden Society, still bears the main burden, and systematic official publication has barely begun, whereas in this case, the society's policy is one of selective publication. Local societies who take some of the burden by publishing legal records from time to time, as many do, tend to publish extracts, to translate, to summarise, having regard to their locality, their membership, and economy. So theirs is not systematic record publication either. To say this is, of course, simply to emphasise the scholar's need of such work as urgently on the legal as the financial records, not to belittle local record societies. Their methods, which are usually those suited to their purposes and circumstances, are not the same as their standard of scholarship, which (as, for example and to mention no other, that of the Lincoln Record Society shows) can be of the highest.

The establishment of local record offices, usually though not necessarily on a county basis, to prevent further loss of the records and other source material for the local history of this country by keeping them for the future in official custody (and by accepting custody of earlier material which has survived destruction if offered) will surely be reckoned one of the great services of this century to historical scholarship. The emphasis in some local offices is on the current records, but the professional archivists themselves are usually no less interested in the earlier administration and other evidence of the past of the area they serve. They have won the confidence of owners of older material in very many instances and most offices have by now, by gift, on indefinite loan, or by special arrangement less formally in their care, a considerable amount of material interesting to historians. The Essex and the West Sussex Record Offices have been outstandingly successful in this.

The invaluable work the Selden Society continues to do has been mentioned. In 1960 it published also an essential guide to its publications to that date: A. K. R. Kiralfy and Gareth H. Jones (compilers), *General Guide to the Society's Publications* (1960), a very "detailed and indexed summary of the contents of the Introductions" to vols I–LXXIX. A similarly useful guide to the publications of the original Camden Society, the Camden series and other publications of the Royal Historical Society, including its *Transactions*, to 1968 is A. T. Milne, *A Centenary Guide to the Publications of the Royal Historical Society 1868–1968 and of the former Camden Society 1838–1897* (1968). It is, however, a detailed and indexed list, rather than summary of contents. On the Exchequer Memoranda Rolls: for such of them as have been printed and for plans for further publication, for microfilm and indexes of those as yet unpublished, the Introduction to *Calendar of Memoranda Rolls (Exchequer) preserved in the Public Record Office, Michaelmas 1326 to Michaelmas 1327* (H.M.S.O., 1968), which should in any case be read by those working on earlier rolls, published or unpublished, of the period for its usefulness to them too.

Part I

SELECT CHRONICLE AND NARRATIVE SOURCES FOR THE HISTORY OF ENGLAND, 1189–1327

INTRODUCTION

THE characteristic forms of medieval historical writing, annals, chronicles and histories, differ more in scale than in kind. They are dominated by a common chronological framework. A year's entry may be a single fact such as "This year died Frithwald, the abbot" (or nothing at all) or it may run to many thousands of words as with Matthew Paris (No. 4 below). But even Matthew, however much he distorts it, never abandons the chronological form.

Another feature is that annals, chronicles and histories conventionally begin at a date well in the past, the Creation, the Fall of Troy, the Foundation of Rome, the Birth of Christ. They may compromise – English chronicles can be found beginning with the coming of Hengist and Horsa, the Norman Conquest, even the reign of Stephen. But such foreshortenings were, on principle, to be regretted. History was part – the past part – of a divinely ordered plan of the ages, the revelation (to date) of God's Will. Matthew Paris, it must be admitted, lost sight of this pious purpose of historiography in devoting half his chronicle to the last twenty-five years, but at least he observed the convention in beginning at Creation.

A third feature of historical writing in the Middle Ages is that so much of it is compilation. The explanation could, in part, be that a chronicler seeing history as revelation and himself as a recorder adding the evidence of his own day, a continuator, would not be inclined to question the earlier record; but what is most certainly a part is that there was little else he could do but compile. For questioning the past, speculative reason alone was not enough and most of the tools of modern historical scholarship did not then exist. He was almost compelled to accept authority, to use, however disposed he might be to question, the past that was given him, and he is most valuable to us when he is writing what we now call contemporary history and valuable for an earlier time only when the source he himself has used is lost to us.

To read chronicles, then, one must find out what system of chronology they employ, in particular, when they begin their year; and to use them, one must be able to put a value on their testimony. The chronology is usually, in this volume, what one would expect of material of ecclesiastical origin, years of the Julian calendar counted from the year of Christ's birth, but the beginning of the year is not standard, as today. It is far more likely to be 25 December (Christmas), 25 March (the Annunciation) or, more awkwardly, a movable feast, Easter, than 1 January. The chronicler is exceptional who states his practice, but with the help of, for instance, E. A. Fry's *Almanacks* or its successor, C. R. Cheney's *Handbook of Dates*, and by a process of approximation from events of known date mentioned in the chronicle, it can be discovered. Evaluation, on the other hand, requires answers to many questions: authorship, date of composition, sources of information, methods of using it; when part is compilation, how much, source or sources, methods as compiler; where original, means of information then, if any documentary, methods of handling that; general accuracy, reliability, impartiality or lack of it.

The finest period of English historical writing was almost over by 1189,[1] but there was still no lack of quantity. Matthew Paris alone would take up this volume and more. Selection is difficult. To attempt to "cover" the period from one aspect, however important (say, the political history), is simply to compile an artificial chronicle of extracts too short to be useful, out of context, and denatured. Extracts of sufficient length from fewer sources can fail to be representative. I have chosen to illustrate the variety of material of the narrative sort which is available for this period, compromising on "coverage" (since compromise one must) by selecting, in the main, years rather than passages as extracts so that chronicles can be compared, and compared in units that are comparable.

SELECT BIBLIOGRAPHY OF CHRONICLE AND NARRATIVE MATERIAL

The subject, including the English contribution, is focussed in H. Rothwell, "The Middle Ages", a section of the article on Historiography in *Chambers's Encyclopaedia*. Essential reading is R. L. Poole, *Chronicles and Annals* (1926). It may be supplemented, for present purposes, by W. L. Jones's chapter on "Latin chronicles from the 11th to the 13th centuries" in the *Cambridge History of English Literature*, I (1908); T. F. Tout, *The Study of Medieval Chronicles* (Manchester, 1922); and V. H. Galbraith, *Historical Research in Medieval England* (1951). The subject of J. Taylor, *The "Universal Chronicle" of Ranulf Higden* (Oxford, 1966), a well-organised monograph, falls outside the limits of this volume, but it is a work of great range and should not be neglected. *The Use of Medieval Chronicles* (Hist. Assoc. Pamphlet, 1965) by the same writer is a helpful survey of thirteenth as well as fourteenth century English work; his *Medieval Historical Writing in Yorkshire* (York, 1961), and H. S. Offler's *Medieval Historians of Durham* (Durham, 1958) are useful for historical writing in northern England. The books referred to in the introduction to this section are E. A. Fry, *Almanacks for students of English History* (1915) and C. R. Cheney, *Handbook of Dates for students of English History* (1945). An excellent little guide on chronological matters generally, R. L. Poole, *Medieval Reckonings of Time* (Helps for Students of History, 1921), deserves to be reprinted.

Any chronicle had a limited circulation before the days of printing. Most, including even Paris's *Chronica Majora*, "the fullest and most detailed of all medieval chronicles"[2] (and, it could be added, one of the liveliest), were scarcely known outside the communities for which they were written. The occasional copy, or copy of a copy, for another house was their limit. The few multiplied on any scale by hand,[3] because they proved of interest to a growing lay public and there was a market for them, were also, for the same reason, among the first things printed.[4] The dissolution of the monasteries released the rest, but led only gradually to their printing. Among the pioneers in this was Matthew Parker, Elizabeth I's first archbishop of Canterbury. It was to him, for example – though this was not his only service – that Matthew Paris owed his appearance in print.[5] Seven chronicles, all important, were printed together in the *Rerum*

[1] A survey of medieval historiography and England's contribution (pre-Conquest and post-Conquest) to it is given in *Chambers's Encyclopaedia*, art. "Historiography" (medieval section).
[2] See Vaughan, *Matthew Paris*, pp. 153 ff.
[3] Increasingly by trade copyists.
[4] Thus the Brut Chronicle and Higden's Polychronicon, both of which achieved wide manuscript circulation, were printed by Caxton. Taylor, *The "Universal Chronicle" of Ranulf Higden*, p. 13.
[5] For this and later editions of Paris, Vaughan, op. cit. pp. 154–5.

Anglicarum Scriptores post Bedam (1596), the work of Henry Savile (1549–1622). Over thirty others saw print in the next hundred years: [Roger Twysden], *Historiae Anglicanae Scriptores X* (1652); [William Fulman], *Rerum Anglicarum Scriptores*, I (Oxford, 1684); and Thomas Gale's two volumes, of which the second appeared before the first, *Historiae Anglicanae Scriptores quinque* (Oxford, 1687) and *Historiae Britannicae . . . Scriptores XV* (Oxford, 1691); apart from the individual achievement of Henry Wharton (1664–95) in *Anglia Sacra*. All this was eclipsed in the next generation by Thomas Hearne (1678–1735), who single-handed in circumstances of almost unbelievable difficulty surpassed every predecessor not only in the number of chronicles he edited or re-edited but also in the quality of his editions. Hearne's scholarship, in its field, completes that of the seventeenth century or anticipates that of the nineteenth, as one chooses, but action by government and by learned societies was needed in the nineteenth century to match it. The Surtees Society, the Camden Society and the Caxton Society all sponsored editions of chronicles, but the most successful in this was the English Historical Society between 1838 and 1856. The most ambitious project and, no doubt because its editors were paid by the page, the bulkiest, as it proved, was the government-financed *Chronicles and Memorials of Great Britain and Ireland during the Middle Ages* (the "Rolls" series), which in fifty-four years (1857–1911) issued 99 separate works in 253 volumes – not all chronicles, but enough of them chronicles, edited or re-edited as considered necessary, to enable one to say that the dream of the pioneers is almost realised and that, in editions passable or better, not quite all but nearly all the main chronicle-sources for the study of English history in the Middle Ages are now in print.

The relevant chronicles for the period covered by this volume, grouped according to reigns, are:

RICHARD I

Of first importance are the *Gesta Regis Henrici secundi Benedicti Abbatis: The Chronicle of the Reigns of Henry II and Richard I, 1169–1192, known under the name of Benedict of Peterborough*, ed. W. Stubbs (Rolls ser., 2 vols, 1867), and *Chronica Magistri Rogeri de Houedene*, ed. W. Stubbs (Rolls ser., 4 vols, 1868–71). These were once believed to be by different authors, but are now considered to be the work of Hoveden (Howden) in both cases and indeed first and second versions of the same chronicle. (Lady) D. M. Stenton, "Roger of Hoveden and Benedict", *E.H.R.*, lxviii (1953), pp. 574–82. Cf. F. Barlow, "Roger of Howden", *E.H.R.*, lxv (1950), pp. 352–60. A translation of the second version, from which extracts from the years 1190–2 are taken (No. 2 below), is *The Annals of Roger de Hoveden*, trans. H. T. Riley (2 vols, 1853).

Other chronicles for Henry II's reign extend into Richard's. The "Imagines Historiarum" of Ralph de Diceto (also edited for the Rolls series by Stubbs, *Radulfi de Diceto . . . opera historica*, 2 vols, 1876: vol. 2 is the relevant volume) continues to 1202. William of Newburgh's "Historia" (*Chronicles of the reigns of Stephen, Henry II, and Richard I*, ed. R. Howlett, Rolls ser., 4 vols, 1884–9) goes down to 1198 (the rest, 1198–1298, is by hands elsewhere). The *Historical Works of Gervase of Canterbury*, ed. Stubbs (Rolls ser., 2 vols, 1879–80), which supersedes Twysden's text in *Scriptores X*, extends into John's reign. Ralph of Coggeshall's *Chronicon Anglicanum* (1066–1223), ed. J. Stevenson (Rolls ser., 1875), increases in authority as it leaves Henry II's reign.

Roger Howden accompanied Richard on crusade. The Latin and French accounts of the crusade, the "Itinerarium Peregrinorum et gesta regis Ricardi" (ed. Stubbs, *Chronicles and Memorials of the reign of Richard I*, vol. 1, 1864) and the *Estoire de la Guerre Sainte* by Ambroise (ed. G. Paris, Paris, 1897), are related: see J. G. Edwards in *Historical Essays in honour of James Tait*, ed. Edwards, Galbraith and Jacob (Manchester, 1933), pp. 59–77. Some account of it is given by Richard of Devizes, whose chronicle "Of the Time of King Richard I" has been re-edited with a translation by J. T. Appleby in the series "Nelson's Medieval Texts" (1963), extracts from which (No. 1 below), however, relate to events in England in the king's absence.

JOHN

Again chronicles continue from the previous reign. The *Chronica* of Roger of Hoveden continues to 1201; the "Imagines Historiarum" of Diceto, to 1202; Gervase of Canterbury's "Gesta Regum" (in vol. II of *Historical Works*, ed. Stubbs) covers the first ten years of John's reign; Coggeshall's *Chronicon* (1066–1223) is now at its best and, with the Barnwell annals preserved in the *Memoriale* of Walter of Coventry (ed. Stubbs, Rolls ser., 2 vols, 1872–3) is one of the main authorities for the reign.

With this reign the *Annales Monastici*, ed. H. R. Luard (Rolls ser., 5 vols, 1864–9), a collection of the annals of ten different houses, becomes important. The *Flores Historiarum* of the St Albans chronicler, Roger Wendover, an important source in the lack of Hoveden and Diceto after 1201–2, is better edited by H. O. Coxe, *Rogeri de Wendover chronica* (English Historical Society, 5 vols, 1841–4) than by H. G. Hewlett (Rolls ser., 3 vols, 1886–9), but neither edition is satisfactory. Wendover's influence on modern writing has been too great: his shortcomings, which must have been obvious if Hoveden and Diceto, for example, had given us their accounts of the years after 1201–2, have been exposed by V. H. Galbraith, *Roger Wendover and Matthew Paris* (Glasgow, 1944). R. Vaughan examines textually the relationship between Wendover and Paris in chap. II of his *Matthew Paris* (Cambridge, 1958). A brief but judicious statement on the value of the chronicle evidence as a whole for this reign is J. C. Holt, *King John* (1963), an Historical Association pamphlet.

HENRY III

St Albans writing, through Wendover and then Matthew Paris, dominates. For Matthew's revision of Wendover for his "Chronica Majora", the relationship of this to his other historical works, particularly to his own "Flores Historiarum", which circulated more widely and was therefore more influential before printing than his larger work – all matters of extreme complexity – Vaughan's *Matthew Paris* (as above) is essential. Galbraith's *Roger Wendover and Matthew Paris* (for which also see above) is as important for Paris as for Wendover. For the full bibliography of the subject, Vaughan, op. cit. pp. 267 ff. The editions of the *Chronica Majora* (ed. H. R. Luard, 7 vols, 1872–3), the *Historia Anglorum* (ed. F. Madden, 3 vols, 1866–9), and the *Flores Historiarum* of Paris (ed. Luard, 3 vols, 1890), all in the Rolls series, are standard. English translations (though from earlier editions) of both the *Chronica Majora* and Paris's *Flores* exist, the former by J. A. Giles under the title *Matthew Paris's English History* (3 vols, 1852–4 – from the year 1235 only), the latter by C. D. Yonge under the title *Matthew of Westminster's Flowers of History* (2 vols, 1853).

For the years 1216–19 the metrical life of the regent, William the Marshal, *Histoire de Guillaume le Maréchal*, ed. and translated into modern French prose by P. Meyer (3 vols, Paris, 1891–1901), "a private production for record, not light reading" (M. D. Legge, *Anglo-Norman Literature and its Background*, Oxford, 1963, p. 170) is indispensable. See No. 3 below.

Coggeshall's *Chronicon* continues into this reign (–1223). Canterbury and Dover annals are preserved in continuations of Gervase of Canterbury's "Gesta Regum" (see above, under John's reign). The annals collected in *Annales Monastici*, ed. Luard (see above, also under John) are indispensable for this reign. For other monastic annals, the need to examine their relations with each other ("they are not separate works of equal value") and for the importance of London chronicles for this reign, the reader is best referred to the appropriate section of Sir

Maurice Powicke's bibliography in *The Thirteenth Century, 1216–1307* (Oxford History of England). Few such annals, however local, domestic, otherworldly even, they may be, can have no interest at all for the modern student of history as this is now interpreted, but those with a concern for the larger world are just what he needs to protect himself from the dangers of looking at that world only from St Albans. Fortunately they reach their best as the crisis of the reign approaches; and when the *Chronica Majora* ceases in only the second year of it we can still follow it, and follow it with more than one pair of eyes. This is illustrated by Nos. 4–7 below. No. 4 gives in a translation based on that of J. A. Giles but thoroughly revised and greatly changed in the light of Luard's edition (see above) the full text of the *Chronica Majora* under the years 1258–9. No. 5 translates the Burton annals for those years. Their different character, their independence of the *Chronica Majora*, and their different contribution are obvious. Nos. 6 and 7 illustrate what can still be done after 1259.

One of the *fables convenues* of the period, not merely of this reign, was that the beginning of history in these islands was the conquest of them from the giants, the only previous inhabitants, by Brutus, a Trojan prince who in the great dispersion after the fall of Troy came here from Spain. Geoffrey of Monmouth's brilliant embroidery of the theme some fifty years before 1189 in his *History of the Kings of Britain*, through Gaimar, Wace and Layamon translated and versified first from the Latin to French then to English, became literature. It also affected the "serious" history which it itself claimed to be. With William of Newburgh's criticisms soon forgotten and Ranulf Higden's doubts not yet expressed,[1] it quickly led to a proliferation of "Brut" chronicles in Latin, French, Welsh[2] and English[3] beginning with or associated with the Brutus story though, of course, their value is as continuations bringing the story down to the writer's own day.

EDWARD I

(The reader can again be referred to the "Narrative sources" section of Powicke's bibliography in *The Thirteenth Century*.)

The student of the reign of Edward I is not really well-served with chronicles. The monastic annals so valuable for the last reign are the great stand-by for the early years. All but three of those in the *Annales Monastici*, those in vol. I, continue into Edward's reign.

The *Flores Historiarum* of Matthew Paris is continued into it too, but not at St Albans, and, in any case, it is difficult to use as printed. The "post-Paris" section presents problems relegated to a 100-page appendix in Luard's edition as well as problems of its own relationship to other chronicles, notably those contained in the Rolls series volume *Willelmi Rishanger . . . et quorundam anonymorum Chronica et Annales, 1259–1307*, ed. H. T. Riley (1865). The *Chronica* of Rishanger is in turn related to the *Annales sex regum* of Nicholas Trivet (ed. T. Hog, English Historical Society, 1845). An imposing body of chronicles must, in fact, be regarded as a group until their relationships can be clarified; Trivet and Rishanger, in particular, treated as one where they agree, and not independent authorities as they have been.

V. H. Galbraith, "The St Edmundsbury Chronicle, 1296–1301", *E.H.R.*, lviii (1943), pp. 51–78, strips away the confusions of previous editors of the Bury St Edmunds chronicle and prints the hitherto unedited and, as will be seen, invaluable portion. *The Chronicle of Bury St*

[1] See T. D. Kendrick, *British Antiquity* (1950), pp. 12–15.
[2] The origin of the "Brut y Tywysogion" is discussed by J. E. Lloyd in "The Welsh Chronicles", *Proc. of the British Academy*, vol. xiv (1928). For the best edition of this, a translation, and the *Annales Cambriae*, the other important chronicle of Welsh affairs for this period, see Powicke, *The Thirteenth Century*, p. 754.
[3] The metrical chronicles of Robert of Gloucester and, in the northern dialect, of Thomas of Castleford. The former in a Rolls series edition, the latter unpublished. Cf. *Brut or the Chronicles of England*, ed. F.W.D. Brie (Early English Text Soc., 1906–8).

Edmunds 1212–1301, ed A. Gransden (1964), gives the Latin text from 1212 with English translation.

The Norwich chronicle, the "Historia Anglicana" of Bartholomew Cotton from Hengist and Horsa to 1298 (ed. Luard, Rolls ser., 1859), indispensable for 1291–8, is mostly compilation before that, chiefly from St Albans and Bury St Edmunds sources.

Even the Guisborough chronicle (*The Chronicle of Walter of Guisborough, previously edited as the chronicle of Walter of Hemingford or Hemingburgh*, ed. H. Rothwell, 1957), like Cotton indispensable for its last years, is systematic compilation until the end of the twelfth century and a hotch-potch for a surprising amount of the thirteenth. It is only spasmodically of importance before the twelve-nineties for Edward's reign and then chiefly for his Welsh campaigns.

The student is not well-served for the second half of the reign either, for different reasons. In the first place, because, as we have seen, a number of the available chronicles cannot, until their relationships are clarified, be treated as independent authorities, the chronicle evidence at his disposal for the critical years of this reign, 1296–1301, years of major domestic crisis in time of war, is severely limited. Secondly, limited in effect to three chronicles, Bartholomew Cotton, Walter of Guisborough and the Bury chronicle, he quickly finds himself relying more and more on one. Cotton, quite the most valuable as far as it goes, stops quite suddenly in 1298. In the same year Guisborough shrinks, just as, when for lack of Cotton and also because the centre of government and of politics had shifted to the north, its evidence was all the more desirable. It is in these circumstances that the last years of the Bury chronicle become indispensable. Fortunately they are as valuable as they are brief, but the student of this reign would indeed be in difficulty if he had not also a wealth of documentary evidence.

Nos 8–10 below enable the three major chronicles to be compared for the first of the crisis years. No. 11 is offered by way of contrast, but also as a sample of a chronicle of value as well as interest, and not least among a number of its claims to attention is that it takes into its perspective the whole reign.

EDWARD II

(One cannot improve on the section on "Narrative sources" in the bibliography to M. McKisack, *The Fourteenth Century 1307–1399*, Oxford, 1959, though, as it is not arranged by reigns, items for 1307–27 have to be dug out.)

The Guisborough chronicle continues into this reign and though brief is valuable down to 1312, where it ends. St Albans annals attributed to Trokelowe and Blaneforde (ed. H. T. Riley, Rolls ser., 1866) cover most of the reign, as do (from Westminster) the *Flores Historiarum* (vol. III, ed. Luard, 1890), a valuable source. The London annals of St Paul's ("Annales Paulini") and the lay London "Annales Londonienses" (both in vol. I of *Chronicles of Edward I and Edward II*, ed. Stubbs, Rolls ser., 2 vols, 1882–3) are both important. Of the rest (for which see the McKisack bibliography) the Bridlington "Gesta Edwardi de Carnarvan" (in vol. II of *Chronicles of Edward I and Edward II*, as above) is important, particularly for its northern view, and the *Vita Edwardi secundi* to 1325 (ed. and translated by N. Denholm-Young, 1957), anonymous, once attributed to a monk of Malmesbury but believed by its latest editor to be a West Countryman indeed, but of Herefordshire, a royal official and a canon of St Paul's, mr John Walwayn, D.C.L., is both individual and well-informed and therefore indispensable. See No. 13 below. For the French "Brut" chronicles, mainly unprinted, for this reign the best introduction is J. Taylor, "The French Brut and the Reign of Edward II", *E.H.R.*, lxxii (1957), pp. 423–37. No. 12 below, the Lanercost chronicle for the years 1315–22, is included because it is not over-political, reminding us that, whatever historians may use them for, chronicles could still be seen as the story of the divinely ordered plan of the ages being gradually revealed to man, and that Divinity does not reveal its plan solely through politics.

FURTHER READING

Chaytor, H. J., *From Script to Print* (Cambridge, 1945)

Douglas, D. C., *English Scholars, 1660–1730* (2nd edn, 1951)

Ker, N. R., *Medieval Libraries of Great Britain: a List of Surviving Books* (2nd edn, 1964)

Knowles, M. D., "Great Historical Enterprises: IV, The Rolls Series", *Trans. Roy. Hist. Soc.*, 5th ser., vol. 11 (1961), pp. 137–59

Legge, M. D., *Anglo-Norman in the Cloisters* (Edinburgh, 1950)

McKisack, M., *Medieval History in the Tudor Age* (Oxford, 1971)

(and as examples of twentieth-century chronicle-scholarship at its finest:)

Galbraith, V. H., "The Chronicle of Henry Knighton", *Fritz Saxl, 1890–1948 . . . Memorial Essays*, ed. D. J. Gordon (Edinburgh, 1957), pp. 136–48

—— "An Autograph MS. of Ranulph Higden's Polychronicon", *Huntington Library Quarterly*, vol. xxiii, No. 1 (November 1959), pp. 1–18

1. Richard of Devizes, "Of the Time of King Richard I": selected passages from the years 1190–2

(*The Chronicle of Richard of Devizes of the Time of King Richard the First*, trans. J. T. Appleby (Nelson's Medieval Texts, 1963), pp. 9–13, 27–35, 39–43, 45–6, 48–53, 55, 59–64)

The following extracts from the chronicle of Richard of Devizes, a monk of St Swithun's at Winchester, illustrate the struggle for power that went on in England during Richard I's absence on crusade. Richard had left the government of the country ambiguously divided between the princely bishop of Durham, Hugh of Le Puiset, almost if not quite the most powerful man in the north of England, and a career official, a man of his own making in whom he seems to have had greater confidence, his chancellor bishop William Longchamp of Ely. The rivalry between these two ended in the fall of Longchamp but left his successors, notably Walter of Coutances, another career official, who had intervened on the authority of the absent king, with the problem of curbing the king's brother, John, whose conduct throughout had been devious and to some seemed disloyal.

Richard of Devizes is contemporary, independent and well-informed. Here he is, unusually for him, "judicious and restrained". For a full appreciation of the brilliance, originality and raciness of his comment upon his times his short chronicle must be read as a whole.

[Before setting out on his crusade, the king crossed over to his French possessions.]

In the year of our Lord 1190,

The king crossed over to Normandy, having delegated the care of the whole kingdom to the chancellor . . .

William, bishop of Ely and the king's chancellor, another Jacob by nature, although he did not wrestle with an angel, a remarkable person who made up for the shortness of his stature by his arrogance, counting on his lord's affection and presuming on his good will, expelled Hugh of Le Puiset from the exchequer, because all power always has been, still is, and always will be jealous of anyone sharing it. Scarcely leaving the bishop the bare sword with which the king's hand had girded him a knight, he took away from him the honour of the earldom, which he had held only a short time. And to make sure that the bishop of Durham did not suffer alone, he spared no one and was more savage than a wild beast to everyone. He even persecuted the bishop of Winchester. The custody of the castles and of the county was taken away from him, and he was not even allowed to enjoy his own patrimony. The kingdom was thrown into an uproar, and those who were offended accused the king of bad faith. An appeal by all against the tyrant was carried across the sea to the king, but the tyrant crossed the sea first and defended the whole series of his actions and exactions before the king with a few words. The king instructed him very fully in all the things he was to do, thus forestalling the complaints of the envious. He was back before his attackers had access to the king. Thus he returned to the English no less powerful and prosperous, so that "whatever he wanted to do he did" . . .

When the king returned from Gascony, where he had overcome the brigands by force of arms and demolished the fortifications they were occupying, those whom the chancellor had injured came to him. He made each one feel that he had been satisfied and sent them all back to the chancellor with whatever letters they wanted. . . . The bishop of Durham hastily proceeded to London, but, since he was not received by the barons of the exchequer, he quickly set out, as though he were expecting to stage a triumph, after the chancellor, who at that time had gone on a military sortie towards Lincoln. When he overtook him, he saluted him on the king's behalf, neither simply nor without a frown. He haughtily began straightway discussing the affairs of the country with him, as though nothing were allowed to be done without his consent. "He burst into bombast and words half a yard long" and, glorying greatly in a power he had not yet received and forgetting whom he was talking to, he discussed matters concerning which he should have kept silent. At the end of his speech, the club was brought forth that put a stop to idle words; the sacred letter of the king, greatly to be revered, was brought forth to be proclaimed. "The mountains are in labour; a ridiculous mouse will be born." It was ordered that complete silence be kept before the king's mandate. "All were still and kept attentive silence." The letter, which would have been more impressive if its contents had not already been known, was read in public. When the chancellor heard it, the cunning man, skilled in hiding his deceit, put off answering for a week and appointed Tickhill as the place for the conference. On the appointed day the bishop of Durham came to the castle and, ordering his attendants to wait outside the gates, went in alone to the chancellor. The one who had kept silent before was now the first to speak, and forced the deceived bishop to read with his own lips a letter that had been written after the first one and that was contrary to what he had hoped for. When the bishop was getting ready to answer, the chancellor said: "The other day, when you were speaking, it was my time to keep silent. Now, in order to make you realise that while you keep silent it is my turn to speak – for my lord the king is still living – you will not leave here till you have given hostages that you will surrender to me all the castles you hold, for I seize you, not as a bishop seizing another bishop, but as the chancellor seizing a castellan." The duped man had neither the firmness nor the means to resist. The hostages were handed over, and at the appointed time the castles were surrendered in order to redeem them. . . . All the others who had crossed over to complain against the chancellor got less than nothing for their pains . . .

In order that he might use either hand as his right hand and in order that Peter's sword might help Caesar's, William, that marvellous bishop of Ely, the king's chancellor and the chief justiciar of the realm, a man with three titles and three heads, received the office of legate to all England, Scotland, Wales and Ireland, obtained from the supreme pontiff at the instance of the king, who would not otherwise set out on the crusade, by Reginald, bishop of Bath. Blessed thus by fate with everything he wanted, he came and went through the kingdom like a flash of dazzling lightning . . .

King Richard exacted an oath from his two brothers, John the legitimate one and Geoffrey the bastard, that they would not enter England within three years of his pilgrimage, the three years to be computed from the day he set out from Tours. However, at his mother's request, he so far dispensed John as to allow him to come to England with the chancellor's permission and to stay there according to his judgment: at the chancellor's pleasure he might either remain in the realm or be exiled from it . . .

[The king left on crusade.]

In the year 1191,

. . . Walter,[1] archbishop of Rouen, was, as is common among the secular clergy, cowardly and timid. Having saluted Jerusalem from afar, unasked he laid aside his anger against Saladin. He gave the king, who was going to fight in his stead, everything he had brought with him for the expedition. He also laid aside the cross. Forgetting all shame, he gave as his excuse a devotion that even the most wretched of mothers would bear with distrust. He alleged (that is to say) that the shepherds of the church should preach rather than fight and that it was not fitting for a bishop to bear any other arms than those of the virtues. The king, however, to whom the sight of his money was more necessary than the presence of his person, approved his excuses, as if overcome by his exceedingly lively logic, and sent him back to England with his letters to William the chancellor, to be furnished with a certain number of men and horses from the exchequer for three years. The king added at the end of his letter, for the archbishop's honour and as a general directive, that the chancellor should use his counsel in the affairs of the kingdom . . .

The archbishop of Rouen came to England to the chancellor, by whom he was honourably received and entertained, even much better than the king had ordered. Others followed him with many orders, all of which had the conclusion that the chancellor was to be obeyed by all.

The king especially ordered his brother John, by each of the messengers, to support the chancellor, to help him against all men, and not to break the oath he had sworn to him.[2]

The king of England ordered the chancellor and the convent of Canterbury and the bishops of the province to take counsel together canonically concerning the see, because Baldwin's death[3] had deprived it of a head. Concerning the office of abbot of Westminster, however, now vacant, the chancellor alone was permitted to arrange matters at his pleasure.

John, the king's brother, who had kept his ears open, so that he knew for certain that his brother had turned his back on England, now went about the country, with a larger following. He did not prohibit or restrain his followers from calling him the king's heir.

And as the earth shudders at the absence of the sun, so the face of the realm was altered at the king's departure. Certain nobles became busy; castles were strengthened; towns were fortified, and moats were dug. The archbishop of Rouen, foreseeing the future no better than he who was praised as the father of error, knew how to please the chancellor greatly, but in such a way that he did not displease even his rivals.

Letters were secretly sent (or went) amongst the leaders of the clergy and the people, and the support of each one was solicited against the chancellor. The knights willingly but secretly consented to count John; the clergy, however, more cautious by nature, did not dare openly to swear to the words of either instructor. The chancellor pretended not to be aware of this, scorning to admit that anyone would presume to dare anything against him in any way. At last the lid was taken off the pot. It was

[1] Walter of Coutances, an Englishman despite his name and an experienced official of the previous reign.
[2] i.e. not to be in England in the king's absence without the chancellor's permission.
[3] The archbishop had died while on crusade with the king.

reported to him that Gerard of Camville, a factious man, prodigal of his allegiance, had done homage to count John, the king's brother, for Lincoln Castle, the custody of which was recognised to belong to the inheritance of Nicholaa, the wife of this same Gerard, but under the king. This act was believed to be an offence against the crown, and the chancellor went to punish the one who had committed it. He quickly collected an army and went to those places. First he made an attack on Wigmore, and then he forced Roger of Mortimer (who was charged) with having formed a conspiracy against the king (or the realm) with the Welsh, to surrender the castles and to abjure England for three years. As he went into exile, he was blamed by his accomplices for faintness of heart, for although he was supplied with many soldiers and had abundant castles and provisions, before a blow was struck he surrendered at the mere threats of a priest.

The reproach after the event was too late. Roger left the kingdom, and the chancellor ordered (or caused) Lincoln to be besieged. Gerard was with the count, and his wife, Nicholaa, whose heart was not that of a woman, defended the castle manfully. The chancellor was wholly occupied around Lincoln, when count John, having forced the custodians to surrender solely through fear, occupied Nottingham castle and that of Tickhill, both exceedingly strong. Moreover, he ordered the chancellor to lift the siege, or else he would avenge the injury to his man. It was not fitting [he said] to take their custodies away from law-worthy men of the realm, well-known and free and hand them over to foreigners and unknown men. The chancellor's argument that he had entrusted the king's castles to such men because they were left unprotected against passers-by and that any barbarian who might go by could take them with the same ease that he [John] had done was mere foolishness. He was no longer willing to bear in silence the desolation of his brother's possessions and his realm. The chancellor was greatly disturbed by these messages. He summoned the nobles and the chiefs of the army and said: "Don't believe anything I say, if this man is not seeking to conquer the kingdom for himself. He is too hasty in his presumption, for even if he were bound to share the crown with his brother in alternate years, Eteocles has not yet reigned for a full year." He spoke many words of grief in this fashion. Then his spirits rose again, for he was greater in courage than in body and he conceived things on a grand scale. He sent the archbishop of Rouen to the count to order him in a peremptory manner to give up the castles and to answer for his broken oath to his brother before the king's court. The archbishop, who knew how to keep more than one iron in the fire, praised the chancellor's firmness. Then he went to the count. After he had delivered the chancellor's demands, he put it in the count's ear that, whatever others might say, he should dare something big, "worthy of Gyaros and prison", if he wanted to be someone of importance. In public, however, he advised that the count and the chancellor should come to a conference and that they should put an end to their differences by committing them to arbitrators. The count, more than angry at the presumption of the chancellor's orders, became unrecognisable in all his body. Wrath cut furrows across his forehead; his burning eyes shot sparks; rage darkened the ruddy colour of his face. I know what he would have done to the chancellor if in that hour of fury he had fallen like an apple into the hands of the raging count. Indignation so swelled in his closed breast that it had either to burst or to vomit forth its venom somewhere. "This son of perdition," he said, "the worst of the worst, who first carried across to Englishmen from the foolishness of the French the preposterous custom of serving on bended knee, would not trouble me as you now see [me troubled], if I had not refused to pay any attention to this new knowledge offered me." He wanted to say stronger things, either true or false, but out of respect for the archbishop's presence he recollected himself and restrained his vehemence. "If I have spoken amiss, archbishop," he said, "I beg pardon." After these frivolous words they turned to serious matters. A discussion was held concerning the chancellor's orders, and each one agreed to the archbishop's advice to have a conference on a day of mediation. The day was fixed for 28 July; the place, outside Winchester. The chancellor agreed to abide by these provisions, and he raised the siege and returned to London. The count, however, distrusting his crafty designs, brought with him 4,000 Welshmen, so that if the chancellor attempted to seize him during the truce, these men, concealed near the conference-place, might quickly check his attempt. Furthermore, he ordered the summons and request to be made that all his men and everyone else who loved him should assemble, ready for war, and go with him at the appointed place and day to the conference, which he had agreed to but distrusted, with the lord of the whole land, so that he might at least escape alive if that man, more than a king and mightier in his own eyes, should do anything contrary to the decision of the tribunal or should not agree to the transaction. The chancellor, on the other hand, ordered a third of the knighthood of all England to come fully armed to Winchester on the appointed day. He took with him, too, the Welshmen from the king's levy, so that if there should be a struggle with the count, he would have equal forces "and spear threatening spear".

An agreement was reached at the conference, as it was proclaimed and published, which brought things to a better end than had been feared. The agreement made between the count and the chancellor was of this nature and made the following provisions:

First, three bishops were named, those of Winchester, London, and Bath, on whose trustworthiness each side relied. The bishops chose, on the chancellor's side, three earls, those of Warenne, Arundel, and Clare, and eight other nominees; and on the count's side, Stephen Ridel, the count's chancellor, William of Wenneval, Reginald of Wasseville, and eight other nominees. All these men swore, some while looking at the holy gospels and others while touching them, that they would provide a settlement of the complaints and differences between the count and the chancellor to the honour of each party and the peace of the realm, and that if any disagreement should arise between them thereafter, they would faithfully put an end to it. The count and the chancellor also swore to agree to whatever the jurors should provide. And these were the provisions:

The custody of Lincoln castle remained in good peace with Gerard of Camville, who was to be received into the chancellor's favour. The count surrendered the castles he had taken. When he received these castles, the chancellor turned them over to faithful liegemen of the king, to wit: to William of Wenneval, Nottingham castle, and to Reginald of Wasseville, the castle of Tickhill. Each of these men gave a hostage to the chancellor to ensure that he would keep these castles for the king in true peace and faith to the lord king, if he should return alive. If, however, the king should die before he returned, they would give the aforesaid castles back to the count, and the chancellor would return the hostages.

The constables of the castles belonging to the count's honours were to be changed by the chancellor, if the count should show a good reason for changing them. The chancellor would not try to disinherit the count if the king died, but he would, in so far as he was able, advance him to the crown.

This was solemnly done at Winchester, on 25 April[1]. . .

Geoffrey, the brother, but not on the mother's side, of king Richard and count John, who had been consecrated archbishop of York at Tours by the archbishop of Tours at the command of the supreme pontiff, several times sent letters to John, the king's brother and his own, begging that at least with his consent he might be permitted to return to England. When John consented, he made ready to return. The brothers' correspondence did not escape the notice of the chancellor. Taking precautions lest the quality of their innate perversity might increase through their being together, he gave orders to the guardians of the coast that wherever the archbishop, who had abjured England for the three years of the king's pilgrimage, might land within that period, he should not be permitted to proceed onward except with the consent of the jurors to whose arbitration the count and the chancellor had by oath agreed to submit everything that might be a subject of difference between them (or that might afterwards arise) . . .

Geoffrey, archbishop of York, presuming on the consent of count John his brother, got his ship ready and landed at Dover. As soon as he set foot to land he sought a church where he might pray. There is a priory of monks there of the profession of Canterbury, whose oratory he entered with his clerks to hear mass, while his servants were busy round the ships, which were being unloaded.

All his household furniture was already unloaded, when suddenly the constable of the castle reading more into the order of his lord the chancellor than he had commanded, had everything that was thought to be the archbishop's dragged into the town. Some soldiers, also, armed under their cloaks and girded with swords, came into the monastery to seize the prelate. When he saw them, aware of their intention, he took his cross in his hands. Speaking to them first and stretching out his hands to his followers, he said: "I am the archbishop. If you are seeking me, let these men go." The soldiers said: "Whether you are the archbishop or not is nothing to us. One thing we do know: that you are Geoffrey, the son of king Henry whom he begot in some bed or other, who, in the presence of the king, whose brother you make yourself out to be, abjured England for three years. If you have not come into the realm as a traitor to the realm, if you have brought letters releasing you from your oath, either speak or take the consequences." Then the archbishop said: "I am not a traitor, nor will I show you any letters." They laid hands on him there before the very altar. By violence they dragged him, unwilling and resisting, but not fighting back, out of the church. As

[1] inconsistent with 28 July above

soon as he was past the threshold he excommunicated by name those who had laid hands on him, who were present and hearing him and still holding him. He refused a horse offered him, so that he might ride with them to the castle, because it was the property of excommunicated men. Forgetful of all mercy, with their hands they dragged him, on foot and carrying his cross, through the mud of the streets into the castle. After all this, when they wanted in their kindness to act in a more humane manner to their captive, they brought him some better food, which they had prepared for themselves. He, however, made more determined by what he had already borne, spat out their food as that of idolators and would not eat anything except from his own provisions. The story went through the country more quickly than the wind. Those who had followed their lord from afar followed it, reporting and lamenting to everyone that the archbishop, the king's brother, had been thus driven, thus dragged, and thus kept in prison . . .

The archbishop had already been in custody three days, when the chancellor, as soon as the affair was reported to him, gave all his possessions back to him and set him free to go wheresoever he chose. Moreover, he wrote to count John and all the bishops, declaring on his oath that this man had suffered all these injuries without his knowledge. The excuse was of little avail, for what had formerly been sought and purchased with promises was [now seized upon and] retained more tenaciously than if by birdlime, since he, of his own initiative, had furnished his enemies with an accusation against him. Those who had presumed to such temerity and had laid hands on the archbishop were excommunicated individually from every church in the whole realm. The authors of the deed and those who had consented to it were excommunicated in general, so that the chancellor, who was hated by all, might be involved at least in a general curse . . .

Count John, sharpening his jaw-teeth against the chancellor, whom he did not love, laid a most grave complaint before each of the bishops and nobles of the realm concerning the agreement to a (sworn) peace that had been broken by the other party and concerning the seizure, shameful to himself, of his brother. The jurors were begged and adjured to stand by their sworn promise and to act quickly lest the situation become worse, so that the man who had broken faith and betrayed his oath might wipe out by a fitting satisfaction the wrong he had done.

The affair, which up till this time had been conducted in the clouds, now proceeded to certain action. The chancellor was summoned by the valid authority of all of his and the count's mediators to come to answer the count's accusation and to submit himself to the law, at Loddon bridge, on 5 October.

The count, with a large part of the nobles of the realm all favouring him, waited for the chancellor at the conference place for two days. On the third day he sent some of his followers ahead of him to London, while he still waited (at the conference place) to see if the man for whom he was waiting would dare or deign to come. The chancellor, fearing the count and distrusting the judges, delayed for two days to go to the conference place. On the third day (for "as each man's conscience is, so within the breast it conceives its hopes and fears as facts") between hope and fear, he started to go to the conference. Behold! Henry Biset, a man faithful to him, who had seen those of the count's household who had been sent ahead going by "at full gallop, spurring heavily", came to the chancellor and swore that the count had gone armed on the day before to seize London. Who on that day would not accept as gospel truth whatever he might say, unaware that he was lying? But he did not lie, for he thought that what he said was true. The chancellor, deceived, as any man would be, by this turn of affairs, had all the soldiers who were with him arm immediately, and, thinking that he was following directly after the count, he reached the city ahead of him. Because the count had not yet arrived, he asked the citizens to shut the gates to the count when he arrived, but they refused and called the chancellor a disturber of the land and a traitor.

The archbishop of York, however, with an eye to the future, had stayed there for several days to see the end of the affair, and assiduously stirred up everyone against the chancellor by complaints and prayers. The chancellor, realising for the first time that he had been betrayed, fled to the Tower, and the Londoners kept watch by land and by sea lest he escape. When the count learned of his flight, he pursued the chancellor with his forces. The count was received by the citizens, who came out to meet him with lanterns and torches, for he entered the city by night. Nothing was lacking in the salutations of the fawning populace save that parrot-cry, "Chere Basileos!". . .

On the next day the count and all the nobles of the realm met in St Paul's church. The accusation of the archbishop of York was heard first of all.

After it, anyone was admitted who had anything against the chancellor. The accusers of the absent man had a full and careful hearing, and especially that wordy Hugh, bishop of Coventry, but yesterday his most familiar friend. Since the worst plague is an enemy who was once a friend, he spoke the most severely and gravely of all against his intimate friend and did not cease till everyone said: "We will not have this man to reign over us."

Then the whole assembly without delay declared count John, the king's brother, supreme governor of the whole realm and ordered that all the castles should be turned over to whomever he wanted. Three only (of the least valuable ones), which were at a great distance from each other, they left to the chancellor, already chancellor only in name. The chief justiciar, who was supreme after the count, the itinerant justiciars, the keepers of the exchequer, and the constables of the castles: all were new men, newly appointed. Among others who received something at that time, the bishop of Winchester received all the custodies that the chancellor had taken away from him, and the lord bishop of Durham received the earldom of Northumberland.

On the same day a commune of the citizens of London was granted and instituted, to which all the nobles (of the realm) and even the bishops of that province were forced to swear. Now London first realised that the king was absent from the realm by this conspiracy granted to it, which neither king Richard himself nor his predecessor and father, Henry, would have allowed to be done for a million silver marks. How many evils indeed arise from the conspiracy may be gathered from its very definition, which is this: a commune is the tumult of the people, the terror of the realm, and the tepidity of the priesthood.

When that ill-starred day was drawing near to evening, four bishops and a like number of earls, sent to the chancellor on behalf of the assembly, explained to him to the letter all that had been done that day. He was filled with horror at the unexpected boldness of the presumptuous men. His spirit failed him. He fell to earth so wan that he emitted foam from his mouth. When cold water had been thrown in his face, he revived. Standing erect, he pierced the messengers with a savage look and said: "'The one safety of the vanquished is to expect no safety.' You have vanquished and fettered me when I was unaware. If the Lord God lets me see my lord the king with my two eyes, this day will bring woe to you, you may be sure. In so far as you can, you have already given the count whatever was the king's in the realm. Tell him that Priam is still alive. You who have forgotten your still living king and have chosen another to be your lord, you tell that lord of yours that everything will turn out differently from what he thinks. The castles I will not give up; the seal I will not resign." The messengers left him and reported what had happened to the count, who ordered the Tower to be more closely besieged.

The chancellor was sleepless for the greater part of the night, for the man who "does not turn his mind to study and to honest matters will be racked to sleeplessness by envy or by love". In the meantime his followers racked him more (or not less) than his conscience, begging him with tears, prostrate at his feet, to give way to necessity and not to try to swim against the current. He, harder than iron, was softened by the tearful counsel of those weeping around him. Fainting again and again from sorrow, at last he reluctantly consented that those things be done that he, helpless as he was, was being forced to do. He did not send but, rather, permitted one of his brothers and three men, not ignoble, with him, to announce to the count at that same hour of the night that the chancellor, no matter in what frame of mind, was ready to suffer and to do what had been provided. Let delay be removed, they urged, for "it was always harmful to put things off when they were ready". Let it be done on the next day, lest the wind so change that it might have to be put off for a year. They returned to the Tower, and before daybreak the count notified his party that these things would be done.

"Meanwhile the new-born Aurora left the ocean", and the count with all his party went out to a level place outside London to the east, immediately after sunrise.

The chancellor, too, went there, but not so early as his adversaries. The great men were in the centre; around them was a circle of citizens, and the rabble, estimated at 10,000 men, was looking on from the fringe. First the bishop of Coventry came up to the chancellor and repeated each of the accusations of the previous day, always adding something of his own. "It is," he said, "neither fitting nor endurable that the knavery of one such man should cause so many noble and honourable men to come together from such distant parts for nothing. And because it is better to suffer once than for ever, I will bring all these things to a close with a few words. It does not please us, because it does not suit us, that you should rule any longer in the realm. You will be content with your bishopric, with the three castles we have allowed you, and with the shadow of a great name. You will give dependable hostages that you will surrender all the rest of the castles and that you will not stir up troubles or excite tumults, and (afterwards) you may freely go wherever you will." Many people said many things about these matters, but no one opposed them. Only (the lord bishop) of Winchester, although he was more eloquent than most, kept silent all the time. At last the chancellor, when with difficulty he got permission to speak, said:

"Am I always to be only a listener, and shall I never answer? Before all else, let each and every one of you know that I do not consider myself guilty of anything that should make me fear the verdict of any of you. I declare that the archbishop of York was seized without my knowledge or consent, and if you will hear it I will prove it either in the civil or in the ecclesiastical courts. If I have done anything concerning the king's escheats and the women in his gift, Geoffrey son of Peter, William Briwere, and Hugh Bardolf, whom I had as advisers by the king's appointment, will give satisfaction for me, if they are allowed to speak.

"I am ready to give an account to the last farthing as to why and for what I have spent the king's money. Although in this matter I fear the king more than I do you, I shall not refuse to give hostages for surrendering the castles, for I must submit to force. I do not relinquish the title that you cannot take away and the reputation that I shall still have. Finally I say, so that you may all know, that I do not lay down any of the duties given me by the king. You, being many, have beset one man. You are stronger than I, and I, the king's chancellor and justiciar of the realm, judged contrary to all law, give way to stronger men because it is necessary."

The sun, sinking in the west, put an end to the allegations of the parties. (Two) brothers of the former chancellor and a certain third person, who had shared his secrets as his chamberlain, were received as hostages.

The keys of the Tower of London having been surrendered, the council was dissolved on 10 October.

The chancellor went to Dover, which was one of the three castles of which mention has been made, and the count turned over all the fortified places of the land, which had been surrendered to him, to whomever he pleased and most trusted . . .

Messengers were sent immediately, both by the condemned man and by those who had condemned him, to the king himself in the Promised Land, and they were adequately instructed either to accuse or to excuse.

The chancellor in name only, disturbed by the thought of his lost power and his present condition, tried in every way to get round the prohibition against his crossing the Channel, and in a variety of ways and more than once he made a laughing-stock of himself.

I shall not mention that he was caught and held both in a monk's habit and in woman's clothing, but it is well remembered what vast stores of goods and what enormous treasures the Flemings took from him when he landed at last in Flanders. When his crossing over became known, whatever revenues he possessed in England were confiscated. Then there was an ominous contest among the strong. The chancellor laid an interdict on the diocese that had been taken away from him, and he marked down his attackers and bound them by an anathema. Nor was the archbishop of Rouen inferior to him in courage, for in punishment of this presumptuous excommunication of the exchequer officials he ordered William Longchamp to be denounced throughout Normandy and to be held as excommunicate. He did not want to appear afraid of the curse laid upon those who entered upon the aforesaid diocese, nor did he deign to believe that the sentence of the fugitive prelate could ascend to the throne of his majesty. Therefore the face of the church of Ely was foul; all the Lord's work was silenced throughout the whole diocese; and the bodies of the dead lay unburied along every road. In Normandy, in retaliation, no one of the archbishop's party had any dealings with the chancellor. At his entry every function of the church was suspended; at his leaving all the bells were rung; and the altars where he had celebrated mass were thrown down . . .

The archbishop of Rouen, having been appointed chief justiciar of the realm and supreme in affairs by the count . . .

In 1192,

. . . That matron, worthy of being mentioned so many times, queen Eleanor, was visiting some cottages that were part of her dower, in the diocese of Ely.[1] There came before her from all the villages and hamlets, wherever she went, men with women and children, not all of the lowest orders, a people weeping and pitiful, with bare feet, unwashed clothes, and unkempt hair. They spoke by their tears, for their grief was so great that they could not speak. There was no need for an interpreter, for more than what they wanted to say could be read on the open page [of their faces]. Human bodies lay unburied here and there in the fields, because their bishop had deprived them of burial. When she learned the cause of such suffering, the queen took pity on the misery of the living because of their dead, for she was very merciful. Immediately dropping her own affairs and looking after the concerns of others, she went to London. She requested, indeed commanded, the archbishop of Rouen that the confiscated revenues of the bishop be repaid to the bishop and that the same bishop, in the name of the chancery, be proclaimed throughout the province of Rouen as freed from the excommunication that had been pronounced upon him. And who would be so savage or cruel that this woman could not bend him to her wishes? She forgot nothing and sent word over to Normandy to the bishop of Ely that his public office and private affairs in England had been restored to him as she had requested, and she forced him to revoke the sentence he had laid upon the officers of the exchequer. Thus through the queen's mediation the open enmity between the warring parties was laid to rest, but, unless she were to shatter the hearts of both parties, the habits of thought contracted through an old hatred could not be changed.

Count John sent messengers to Southampton and ordered that a ship be made ready for him immediately, so that he might go over, as it was thought, to the king of the French. His mother, however, fearing that the lightminded youth might be going to attempt something, by the counsels of the French, against his lord and brother, with an anxious mind tried in every way she could to prevent her son's proposed journey. Her maternal heart was moved and pained when she called to mind the condition of her older sons and the premature deaths of both of them because of their sins.

With all her strength she wanted to make sure that faith would be kept between her youngest sons, at least, so that their mother might die more happily than had their father, who had gone before them. All the great men of the realm were called together, therefore, first at Windsor, secondly at Oxford, thirdly at London, and fourthly

[1] The diocese lay under an interdict imposed by its bishop, the disgraced chancellor, William Longchamp.

at Winchester. Through her own tears and the prayers of the nobles she was with difficulty able to obtain a promise that he would not cross over for the time being. The count, when he was prevented from making his intended journey, did what he could. He secretly summoned the king's constables of Windsor and Wallingford and took possession of those castles. When he had received them he turned them over to men sworn to him, to keep for him.

At the order of the archbishop of Rouen, the pillars of the church and the scribes of the law gathered at London to discuss, as is so often the case, little or nothing concerning the affairs of the realm. All were one of mind: to summon count John to account for taking over the castles. But, because each one in turn did not believe that it was his affair, each one, fearing the count, wanted the question to be put by another's mouth rather than by his own.

Everyone aired his views, therefore, to this purpose and in this spirit. Only Aeacus was not there, who everyone agreed should be summoned. But even while, among the matters to be attended to, the former chancellor, as it happened, was being discussed, behold! Crispinus was once more present. Messengers of the chancellor, now legate once more, came before the assembly and saluted the queen, who was present, and all the others, whom they found, as it happened, all together, on behalf of their lord, who had landed safely at Dover the day before. He revealed that the purpose of his legation would be to carry out his orders to the very last clause. "All held their tongues for a long time; their mouths hung open" in great astonishment. At last the desire came to all of them humbly to summon as their ruler and lord that same man whom they had been going to judge as a perjurer and an offender against his lord. Many of the great men, therefore, of whom Echion was one, were urgently and often sent to the count, who was then resting at Wallingford and laughing at their assemblies. Humbly and with smooth faces they begged him to make haste "to attack the he-goat". "My lord," they said, " 'he wears a horn; beware!' "

The count, not greatly moved, allowed himself to be humbly begged for a long time. At last, satisfied with the honour paid to him, he came to London with the latest suppliants, whom he liked better than the others. He was sufficiently informed to be able to answer to every "wherefore?" if any questions should happen to be asked. The assembly stood up and made flattering speeches to the newcomer, not observing the order of age and rank. Whoever could first do so ran up first and tried to be seen before the others, wanting to please the prince, for "to have pleased princes is not the least praise for a man". The leaders sat down in council. There was no mention of the castles; the whole complaint and consultation was concerning the chancellor. If the count so advised, they were all ready to proscribe him. They were busy trying to persuade the count to that opinion in every way, "but the beast was to their right". When the count was begged to reply, he said briefly: "This chancellor does not in the least fear the threats or seek the friendship of any or all of you, if he can only have my favour alone. He is to give me seven hundred pounds of silver within the week if I will not meddle between you and him. You see that I need money. 'To the wise, enough has been said.' " He spoke and withdrew, having dropped the conclusion into the middle of his first proposition. The council quickly concluded the matter brought before it. It seemed wise to each one to coax the man with more than promises, and it pleased each one to give or lend money, but not his own, since the whole would in the end fall into the absent man's treasury. Five hundred pounds sterling were lent to the count from the exchequer by the exchequer officials, and letters against the chancellor were received according to their desire. There was no delay. The queen wrote; the clergy wrote; the people wrote; all with one voice urged the chancellor, for his own safety, to make the leap and cross the sea without delay, unless he wanted to listen to threats and live with armed guards.

The chancellor went pale at the harshness of their orders and turned as white "as one who steps on a snake with bare feet". In departing, however, he made this one manful reply: "Let all who are persecuting me know that they shall see whom they have been afflicting. I am not destitute of all comfort, as they think. Someone is always dinning in my well-rinsed ear with truthful writings. 'As long as I am a pilgrim,' he says, 'bear patiently whatever you are exposed to. To a strong man, every country is his fatherland. Have confidence in one who has been tried by experience; be of stout heart and preserve your spirit for better things. With me the welcome hour will come to you when it is not expected.

" 'Unlooked-for I shall come and triumph over my enemies, and once more my victory will make you a citizen in my kingdom, which has been forbidden to you and is now disobedient to me Perhaps some day it will indeed be a pleasure to remember this.' "

2. The Chronicle of mr Roger of Howden: selected passages from the years 1190–2

(*The Annals of Roger de Hoveden*, trans. H. T. Riley, II (1853), extracts from pp. 134–271)

Another account of the struggle for power in England during Richard I's absence on crusade, by a not less well-informed contemporary, and so interesting to compare. A modern account is that by William Stubbs in the Introduction to vol. III of his edition of Howden, *Chronica Rogeri de Houedene*, 4 vols (Rolls ser., 1868–71), or in his *Historical Introductions to the Rolls Series*, ed. A. Hassall (1902), pp. 209 ff.

[Before setting out on his crusade, the king crossed over to his French possessions.]

Immediately after the king had passed over, a dispute arose between the before-named bishops of Durham and Ely, which of them was to occupy the highest place; for the thing that pleased the one, displeased the other. So true it is that "All authority is impatient of a partner"; and, not to go further for an illustration, "The first walls were steeped in a brother's blood"[1]. . .

[In the year of grace 1190] . . . the king appointed William, bishop of Ely, his chancellor, chief justiciary of England; while he made Hugh, bishop of Durham, justiciary from the river Humber to the territory of the king of Scotland. He also compelled Geoffrey, archbishop elect of York, and John, earl of Mortaigne, his brothers, to make oath, touching the Holy Evangelists, that they would not enter England for the next three years, except with his permission. However, he immedi-

[1] "*fraterno primi maduerunt sanguine muri*"; alluding to the death of Remus at the hands of his brother Romulus, or of Celer, his lieutenant, on the walls of infant Rome.

ately released his brother John from the oath which he had made, and gave him permission to return to England, after swearing that he would faithfully serve him.

The king also sent to England William, bishop of Ely, his chancellor, to make the preparations necessary for him and his expedition; and, as he wished to exalt him above all other persons in his dominions, both clergy as well as laity, he sent envoys to pope Clement, and prevailed upon him to entrust to the before-named chancellor the legateship of the whole of England and Scotland . . .

In the meantime, the king's envoys, whom he had sent to Rome to obtain the legateship of England and Scotland for William, his chancellor, returned to him with letters of our lord the pope relative thereto. Accordingly, on the strength of his legateship, the said bishop of Ely, legate of the apostolic see, chancellor of our lord the king, and justiciary of all England, oppressed the clergy and the people, confounding right and wrong; nor was there a person in the kingdom who dared to offer resistance to his authority, even in word.

After Easter, the said chancellor of the king came to York with a great army, for the purpose of seizing those evil-doers who had destroyed the Jews of that city; and, on learning that this had been done by command of the sheriff and the keeper of the tower, he deprived them both of their offices; while he exacted of the citizens of the city a hundred hostages, as security for their good faith and keeping the peace of the king and the kingdom, and that they would take their trial in the court of our lord the king for the death of the Jews. After this, the said chancellor placed in charge of Osbert de Longchamp, his brother, the jurisdiction of the county of York, and ordered the castle, in the old castelry which William Rufus had erected there, to be fortified. The knights, also, of that county who would not come to make redress, he ordered to be arrested.

The said chancellor, by virtue of his legateship, next suspended the canons, vicars, and clerks of the church of St Peter at York, because they had refused to receive him in solemn procession; and laid the church itself under an interdict until the canons, vicars, and clerks of the church of St Peter should come and throw themselves at his feet; he also caused the bells of that church to be laid upon the ground.

In the meantime, Richard, king of England, gave to Hugh, bishop of Durham, leave to return to his country: who, on meeting the chancellor at the city of Ely,[1] presented to him the king's letters, in which the king had appointed him justiciary from the river Humber to the territories of the king of Scotland; on which the chancellor made answer, that he would with pleasure execute the king's commands, and took him with him as far as Suwelle,[2] where he seized him, and kept him in custody until he had surrendered to him the castle of Windsor and others which the king had delivered into his charge. In addition to this, the bishop of Durham delivered to the chancellor, Henry de Pudsey, his son, and Gilbert de la Ley, as pledges that he would keep faith to the king and his kingdom; on which, the bishop of Durham, being liberated from the custody of the chancellor, came to a vill of his, which bears the name of Hoveden.[3] While the bishop was staying at this place for some days, there came to Hoveden

[1] erroneously called "Blie" in the text
[2] Southwell
[3] Howden, in Yorkshire, the native place of our author

Osbert de Longchamp, brother of the chancellor, and William de Stuteville, with a considerable body of armed people, intending, by command of the chancellor, to seize the bishop; however, the bishop gave them security that he would not depart thence, except with the permission of the king or of the chancellor. Accordingly, the bishop of Durham sent messengers to the king of England, to inform him of everything that had happened to him through the chancellor . . .

While Richard, king of England, was staying at Marseilles, there came to him the messengers of Hugh, bishop of Durham; and, on hearing from him the injuries which the before-named chancellor had inflicted on him, the king ordered the earldom of Northumberland and the manor of Sedbergh to be delivered to the bishop of Durham . . .

In the same year, William, bishop of Ely, legate of the apostolic see, chancellor of our lord the king and justiciary of all England, oppressed the people entrusted to his charge with heavy exactions. For in the first place he despised all his fellows whom the king had associated with him in the government of his kingdom, and disregarded their advice. Indeed, he considered no one of his associates in the kingdom his equal, not even John, earl of Mortaigne, the king's brother. Accordingly, he laid claim to the castles, estates, abbeys, churches, and all the rights of the king as his own. On the authority also of his legateship, he came to take up his lodging at bishoprics, abbeys, and priories, and other houses of the religious orders, with such a vast array of men, horses, hounds, and hawks, that a house where he took up his abode for only a single night, was hardly able within the three following years to recover its former state. From the clerks and laity he also took away their churches, farms, lands, and other possessions, which he either divided among his nephews, clerks, and servants, or else, to the loss of the owners, retained possession of them himself, or squandered them away to supply his extraordinary expenses.

Did not this wretched man consider that he should one day have to die? Did he not think that the Lord would demand of each an account of his stewardship, or honourable conduct in his government? But well is it said as to such men as this: "Nothing is more unendurable than a man of low station when he is exalted on high. On every side he strikes, while on every side he fears; against all does he rage, that they may have an idea of his power; nor is there any beast more foul than the rage of a slave let loose against the backs of the free . . ."

[In the year of grace 1191] . . . a serious difference happened in England between the king's chancellor and John, earl of Mortaigne, the king's brother, and the other principal men of the kingdom; which increased to such a pitch that they all wrote to the king relative to the state of his kingdom, and the excesses that the said chancellor was guilty of toward the people of his kingdom. Accordingly, when the king heard of the excesses and annoyances that the chancellor was guilty of towards his people, he sent to England from Messina, Walter, archbishop of Rouen, and William Marshal, earl of Striguil, with commands to the chancellor that in all business of the kingdom he should have the said archbishop of Rouen, and William Marshal, Geoffrey FitzPeter, William Bruere, and Hugh Bardolph, as his associates and witnesses. On their arrival in England, these persons did not dare deliver their letters to the chancellor, fearing lest they should rather incur his hatred, than derive honour therefrom. For the chancellor set at nought all the king's commands, and would have no one an equal with himself, or any associate in the kingdom . . .

In the meantime, a serious dissension arose in England between the king's chancellor and John, earl of Mortaigne, the king's brother, relative to the castle of Lincoln, which the chancellor besieged, having expelled Gerard de Camville from the keepership and the office of sheriff of Lincoln; which former office the chancellor gave to William de Stuteville, and made him sheriff as well. But while the said chancellor was besieging the castle of Lincoln, the castle of Nottingham and the castle of Tickhill, which belonged to the king, were surrendered to earl John, who immediately sent word to the chancellor that, unless he quickly gave up the siege, he would visit him with a rod of iron.

Consequently, the chancellor, being alarmed at the commands of John, earl of Mortaigne, broke up the siege; and, through the mediation of many of the bishops, and other faithful servants of our lord the king, they appointed a day for an interview, at which an agreement was made between them on the following terms:

"Be it known to all men to whom this present writing shall come, that the dispute that has arisen between the earl of Mortaigne and our lord the chancellor has been, through the mediation of the archbishop of Rouen, and the bishops of Durham, London, Winchester, Bath, Rochester, and Coventry, and other faithful servants of our lord the king, set at rest; inasmuch as the earl of Mortaigne has restored to our lord the king, by the hands of the lord archbishop of Rouen, the castles of Tickhill and of Nottingham, to be given into the charge of William Marshal and of William de Wendenal; that is to say, the castle of Nottingham to William Marshal, and the castle of Tickhill to William de Wendenal; which said castles they shall, having made oath thereto, keep to the honour of and in fealty to our lord the king, until such time as he shall return; and when he shall return, then they shall do therewith according to his will and command. And if, which God forbid, it shall so happen that our lord the king shall depart this life during the pilgrimage, then the said persons shall, without detaining the same or any delay, deliver up the before-mentioned castles to the said earl. And if it shall so happen that, in the meantime, our lord the chancellor shall be guilty of any excesses against the said earl, and, on being requested to make amends for the same without delay, in conformity with the advice and opinion of the said lord archbishop of Rouen and others of the household of our lord the king and of his court, shall refuse so to do, then they shall restore and give up the said castles to the said earl. These other castles also, with the honours thereof granted to him by our lord the king, have been delivered into the charge of faithful servants of our lord the king; that is to say, the castle of Wallingford has been given up to the lord archbishop of Rouen, the castle of Bristol to the lord bishop of London, the castle of the Peak to the lord bishop of Coventry, the castle of Bolsover to Richard of the Peak, and, if the said Richard should decline it, the lord bishop of Coventry is to take it, the castle of Eye to Walter Fitz-Robert, the castle of Hereford to earl Roger Bigot, the castles of Exeter and of Launceston to Richard Revel; who have in like manner sworn that, as they owe fealty to our lord the king, they will faithfully keep the same for his service.

And, further, three castles, which belong to the crown of our lord the king, have been delivered in trust as follows: the castle of Windsor to the earl of Arundel, the castle of Winchester to Gilbert de Lacy, and the castle of Northampton to Simon de Pateshull, who have in like manner sworn that, as they owe fealty to our lord the king, they will faithfully keep the same for his service. It has been further agreed, that bishops, abbots, earls, barons, vavasours, and freeholders shall not, at the will of justices or deputies of our lord the king, be disseised of their lands and chattels, but shall be dealt with by judgment of the court of our lord the king, according to the lawful customs and assizes of the realm, or according to the command of our lord the king. And in like manner the lord John shall cause similar provisions to be made in his lands. And, if any person shall presume to do otherwise, at the prayer of the before-named earl, the same shall be rectified by the lord archbishop of Rouen, if he shall be in England, and by the justices of our lord the king, and by those who have thus sworn to keep the peace; and, in like manner, at their prayer, the said John shall cause due reparation to be made. All new castles built after the departure beyond sea of our lord the king on his pilgrimage, whether begun or whether finished, shall be razed, and no other new ones shall be fortified until the return of our lord the king, except in manors demesne of our lord the king, if need there shall be, or in case such shall be done in the service of some person named by the precept of our lord the king, conveyed hither by letter or by some trusty messenger. Gerard de Camville shall be reinstated in the office of sheriff of Lincoln, and on the same day a proper day shall be appointed for him to make his appearance in the court of our lord the king, there to abide his trial; and if in the judgment of the court of our lord the king proof can be given that he ought to lose that office as also the keepership of the castle of Lincoln, then he is to lose the same; but, if not, he is to keep it, unless in the meantime an agreement can be come to relative thereto on some other terms. And the lord John is not to support him against the decision of our lord the king, nor is he to harbour such outlaws, or enemies to our lord the king, as shall be named to him, nor allow them to be harboured on his lands. But if any person shall be accused of any offence committed against our lord the king, it shall be lawful for the earl to harbour him in his lands so long as he shall offer to make due redress in the court of our lord the king. To maintain and observe this treaty of peace in good faith and without evil intent, the said earl, and chancellor, and fourteen barons, on the two sides, have made oath at the hand of the said lord archbishop of Rouen; namely, on the part of the chancellor, the earl of Arundel, the earl of Salisbury, the earl Roger Bigot, the earl of Clare, Walter Fitz-Robert, William de Braose, and Roger Fitz-Rainfray; and, on the part of the earl, Stephen Ridel, his chancellor, William de Wenneual, Robert de Mara, Philip de Worcester, William de Kahannes, Gilbert Basset, and William de Montacute. And if within the time of the truce anything shall have been taken or intercepted on either side, it shall be lawfully returned and made good. And this treaty has been made, saving in all things the authority and commands of our lord the king; but so that if, before his return, our lord the king shall be unwilling that this treaty shall hold good, the before-named castles of Nottingham and Tickhill shall be restored to the lord John, whatever commands our lord the king may give relative thereto."

In the same year, a short time after the abovementioned treaty of peace made between the chancellor and the earl, Geoffrey, the archbishop elect of York was consecrated by William, archbishop of Tours, by command of Celestinus, the supreme pontiff; and, immediately after his consecration, being unmindful of the oath which he had made to the king, his brother, to the effect that he would not return to England till after the expiration of three years from the time that the king left England, he hastened to return to England. However, on his arrival at Witsand, in Flanders, for the purpose of crossing over to England, he was forbidden on the part of the chancellor to presume to return to England, contrary to the tenor of the oath which he had taken before the king; but the archbishop refused at his command to abandon his purpose; wherefore, the chancellor ordered him to be seized, if he should come into England.

Accordingly, the archbishop of York came over to England, and landed at Dover, in the month of September, while the servants of the chancellor were standing on the shore for the purpose of laying hands on him. Being, however, forewarned of this, before he left the ship he changed his clothes, and mounting a horse in whose speed he had confidence, fled to a monastery of monks in that town. It was about the sixth hour of the day, and the monks had begun mass, and the epistle was being read, in which they had just come to the passage where the holy apostle says, "He that troubleth you shall bear his judgment, whosoever he be",[1] and again, in the same epistle, "I would they were even cut off which trouble you",[2] when the archbishop of York entered the church, putting his trust in the Lord; and he received the same as a pleasing omen, referring it to the lasting quiet of his own holy office, and the approaching confusion of the chancellor.

Upon this, the servants of the chancellor whom he had sent to apprehend him, besieged the church on all sides, so that he could not come forth without falling into their hands; and one day, after the celebration of the mass, while the said archbishop clad in his sacerdotal habiliments, was still standing at the altar, these sinister satellites effected an entrance into the church, and laid violent hands upon him, and dragged him forth from the church. After dragging him out, or rather tearing him away therefrom, they vilely and ignominiously led him through the mud of the streets, and along the lanes, while the people stood shouting after them, "O cowards! Why do you take him in this manner? What harm has he done? He is an archbishop, the brother of a king, and the son of a king!"

However, not attending to the words of the people, they took him to Dover castle, and delivered him into the custody of Matthew de Clare, the constable thereof. When this was told to earl John, the brother of the said archbishop, he enquired of the chancellor if this had been done by his order, on which he admitted that it was, and did not deny it; whereupon the earl gave orders that the archbishop should be set at liberty, which was done accordingly.

On his arrival at London, he made complaint to earl John, and the bishops, and other nobles of the kingdom, respecting the injuries done to him and his people by the chancellor and his men; and the earl gave orders that the chancellor should take his trial in the king's court for the injury which he had done to his brother the archbishop of

[1] Gal. v. 10 [2] Gal. v. 12

York, and to Hugh, bishop of Durham. On the chancellor delaying to do this from day to day, the earl John, and the archbishop of Rouen, and the bishops and principal men of the kingdom, named a peremptory day for his appearance at Reading: on which day there came thither the earl of Mortaigne, and nearly all the bishops, earls, and barons of the kingdom; but though they waited there after the peremptory day, expecting the arrival of the chancellor, he declined to come, or even to send a message. Upon this, earl John, and the bishops who were with him, prepared to set out for London, that being there met by a more considerable number of persons, they might enjoy the benefit of the advice of the citizens of London, what to do as to their chancellor, who had created this confusion in the kingdom, and refused to take his trial.

On the chancellor hearing this, he left Windsor and hastened to London, and, while on the road, it so happened that his household and knights met the knights of earl John, on which a sharp engagement took place between them. In this affair one of the knights of earl John, by name Roger de Planis, lost his life; however, the earl prevailed, and the chancellor and his men taking to flight, he entered London, and took refuge with his people in the Tower of London. Earl John, and nearly all the bishops and earls of England, also entered London on the same day, namely, the third day after the octave of St Michael, and, on the following day, the said earl John, the king's brother, and the archbishop of Rouen, and all the bishops, and the earls, and barons, met the citizens of London in St Paul's churchyard, and there made accusation against the said chancellor of many offences, and especially the injuries he had done to the lord archbishop of York and the lord bishop of Durham.

The associates also of the said chancellor whom the king had associated with him in the government of the kingdom, accused him of many offences, saying that, despising their advice, he had transacted all the affairs of the kingdom according to impulse and his own will. The archbishop of Rouen also, and William Marshal, earl of Striguil, then for the first time produced before the people the sealed letters from our lord the king, in which the king had sent orders from Messina that they should be associated with him in the government of the kingdom, and that, without the advice of them and the other persons so appointed, he was not to act in the affairs of the king and the kingdom, and that if he should do anything to the detriment of the kingdom, or without the consent of the persons before-named, he should be deposed, and the archbishop of Rouen substituted in his place.

It seemed good therefore to John, the king's brother, and all the bishops, earls, and barons of the kingdom, and to the citizens of London, that the chancellor should be deposed, and they accordingly deposed him, and substituted in his place the archbishop of Rouen, who was willing to do nothing in the government of the kingdom except with the will and consent of the persons assigned to him as associates therein, and with the sanction of the barons of the exchequer. On the same day, also, the earl of Mortaigne, the archbishop of Rouen, and the other justiciaries of the king, granted to the citizens of London the privilege of their commonalty; and, during the same year, the earl of Mortaigne, the archbishop of Rouen, and the other justiciaries of the king, made oath that they would solemnly and inviolably observe the said privilege, so long as the same should please their lord the king. The citizens of London also made oath that they would faithfully serve their lord king Richard, and his heirs, and would, if he should die without issue, receive earl John, the brother of king Richard, as their king and lord. They also swore fealty to him against all men, saving always their fealty to king Richard, his brother. Upon this, the chancellor, being deposed, made oath that he would surrender all the castles throughout England, and immediately surrendered to him the Tower of London; and he delivered it to the archbishop of Rouen, as also Windsor, and some other castles, but not all of them.

On this occasion, Hugh de Nunant, the bishop of Coventry, wrote to the following effect:

The letter of Hugh, bishop of Coventry, on the deposition of William, bishop of Ely, the king's chancellor

"The things that are committed to writing are beyond doubt bequeathed to posterity, to the end that the page that is confirmed by the testimony of a few, may either advise for the safety, or redound to the benefit of, many: and may what is here set down be considered as an illustration of the truth of the same. For many things are committed to writing by way of caution, that the same may be done; and many, again, that they may not be done; that so the church of Christ may profit on either side, and may both seek what is to be coveted and shun what is to be avoided. For this reason it is our wish that the fall of the bishop of Ely should, by letters attesting the same, be brought to the notice of all; to the end that in this illustration humility may always find that by which to profit, and pride that which to hold in dread. For he was a great man among all the people of the west, and, as though gifted with a twofold right hand, wielded the power of the kingdom and the authority of the apostolic see, and was in possession of the king's seal over all lands, so as to be enabled to govern according to his own will, and of his own power to bring all things to completion; even in the same degree of estimation as both king and priest together was he held: nor was there any person to be found to dare to offer resistance to his will. For he said and the thing was done, he commanded and all means were discovered. In his hands were the royal treasures, the whole of the king's riches, and the entire exchequer, so much so that all property whatsoever that swam beneath our skies was no longer said to belong to the king, but to him. For there was neither that which is hunted for on land, fished for in the water, or flying in the air, which was not compelled to be at the service of his table, insomuch that he appeared to have shared the elements with the Lord; leaving the heaven of heavens alone to the Lord, and reserving the other three to advantage by the use or rather abuse and luxurious enjoyment thereof. All the sons of the nobles acted as his servants, with downcast looks, nor dared they to look upwards towards the heavens, unless it so happened that they were addressed by him; and if they attended to anything else, they were pricked with a goad, which their lord held in his hands, fully mindful of his grandfather of pious memory, who being of servile condition in the district of Beauvais, had for his occupation to guide the plough and whip up the oxen;[1] and who at length, to gain his liberty, fled to the Norman territory. The grandchildren and relatives of this man, even any females whatsoever who were akin to him, though

[1] This is said in a spirit of caustic malevolence.

sprung from a poor cabin, earls, and barons, and nobles of the kingdom, longed with the greatest avidity to unite with themselves in marriage; thinking it a matter for pride, under any title whatever, to acquire the favour of his intimate acquaintanceship; nor was there a churl who longed for a field, a citizen who longed for a farm, a knight who longed for an estate, a clerk who longed for a benefice, or a monk who longed for an abbey, who was not obliged to become subservient to his power and influence. And although all England, bending the knee, was ever at his service, still did he always aspire to the free mode of life of the Franks, and removed his knights and yeomen, and all his household, to Oxford; where, slighting the English nation on all occasions, attended by a troop of Franks and Flemings, he moved pompously along, bearing a sneer in his nostrils, a grin on his features, derision in his eyes, and superciliousness on his brow, by way of fit ornament for a priest. For his own aggrandisement and for the glorification of his name, he was in the habit of getting up verses that he had picked up by begging, and adulatory jingles, and enticed jesters and singers from the kingdom of France by his presents, that they might sing about him in the streets; and but lately it was everywhere said that there was not such a person in all the world. And really, if it had been the time of the Caesars, he would with Liberius[1] have had himself styled the living God. But when the king had given him certain earls as his associates, in order that at least the more weighty concerns of the realm might be managed by their counsels in common, he could not at all endure to have any partner therein, as he thought that the greater part of his glory would be thrown into the shade, if he should stand in need of the advice of any mortal being. Therefore he ruled alone, therefore he reigned alone, and from sea to sea was he dreaded as though a God; and were I to say still more, I should not be telling a falsehood, because God is long-suffering and merciful; while he, ruling every thing according to his own impulses, was neither able to observe justice when acting, nor to endure delay in waiting the proper time. Hence it arose that he set at nought all the letters and mandates of his lord; that he might not seem to have a superior, nor be supposed to be subject to any one, having always made every one act as the servant of his own will. Therefore, after England had for a considerable time suffered under so heavy a burden and a yoke so insupportable, at length, while groaning at his deeds, she cried aloud with all her might. Her cries went up to the Lord, and He, rising, looked down on her from on high, who by His own might treads under foot the necks of the proud and haughty, and exalts the humble by the might of His arm. The sun of justice, indeed, may shine upon the good and the bad, still the eyes of the overwise it dazzles, and by the brilliancy of its light brings forth fruit in the minds of the humble. For although this chancellor may perchance have read that it is denied us long to dwell on high,[2] and that 'He who stands must take care lest he fall',[3] and that 'He who exalteth himself shall be abased',[4] and that before a downfall the heart is elated; still, being forgetful of the lot of mankind, which never remains in the same condition, and of the volubility of the wheel that elevates the lowly man, and, when elevated, is wont to depress him, he was never willing to understand that he ought to act virtuously; but meditating iniquity in

[1] a misprint for Tiberius
[2] perhaps alluding to Is. xxvi. 5
[3] alluding to I Cor. x. 12
[4] St Luke xiv. 11, and xviii. 14

his bed, where he was sleeping with the ministers of wickedness, and with youths in his chamber, he added iniquity to iniquity, so as by his pride and his abuses, through the just retribution of God, to precipitate himself into the powerful hands of the Lord; so that now there was no longer any room for mercy for him, but solely for the exercise of power. Nor indeed was there an opportunity for taking compassion on him or sparing him. For it was he himself who dictated the sentence against himself, who goaded vengeance on, who aimed at crimes so great, that he thereby provoked the anger not only of men, but still more, of God. For although the Lord can do all things, still He is unable to condemn a man who is innocent, or to save one who is guilty, nor would He spare him if the guilty man should chance to be obstinate in his guilt. For against an obstinate mind and the forehead of a harlot may be brought the hardness of real adamant, so as to be worn away thereby; for nothing is there so strong but that it must give way before what is stronger. As, therefore, a man so powerful could not be overcome by man, the Father of mercies and the God of consolation came to the aid of the people who supplicated God, and supplanting the hand of mercy in his case, hurled him down from his power, and brought this accuser, or rather destroyer, to such a pitch of giddiness of mind, that he was unable to recover or arouse himself therefrom; but He so hardened his heart, blinded his mind, and infatuated his counsels, that he first besieged the archbishop of York in a church, then seized him, and after seizing him, violently tore him away; after tearing him away, strongly bound him; after strongly binding him, dragged him along; and after dragging him along, threw him into prison. And although there was a concourse of people who exclaimed, 'What has this righteous man and friend of God been guilty of, that he should be taken to prison? His innocent blood is condemned without a cause,' still, pity could not listen where pride reigned, and God was not heard where the tyrant held sway. For the said archbishop was coming from the country of Normandy with his pastoral staff and mitre, and ring, and superhumeral, which in later times has been styled the pall. And although he was the son of king Henry, of happy memory, and the brother of king Richard, who now reigns, and the brother of John, earl of Mortaigne, still, his royal blood could be of no service to him; and although he had been recently consecrated, the recent performance of that sacrament could not avail him. Consequently, it was in public the universal cry of the laity throughout the whole island, 'Perish he who hastens on the ruin of all things! That he may not crush all, let him be crushed. If he has done this in a green tree, what will he do in a dry one?'[1] And behold! Under the guidance of the Holy Spirit, all persons meet together from the north, and from the sea, and from all parts of the whole island, and flock in crowds, that the archbishop may be set at liberty. But the cords of his sins tightening apace around the chancellor, and his conscience strongly accusing him, clad in a coat of mail, he flies from before the faces of men, and hides himself, and shuts himself with his people in the Tower of London. As we entered the city at a late hour, many of his household in arms attacked us with drawn swords, and slew one of our knights, a noble man, and wounded a great number. However, in the morning a council was held by nearly all the nobles of the kingdom, in presence of the lord John, the king's brother, the archbishops of

[1] St Luke xxiii. 31

Rouen and York, and the bishops of Durham, London, Winchester, Bath, Rochester, Norwich, Lincoln, Hereford, St David's and Coventry; and in the presence of all the people of the city, and of the justiciaries of our lord the king, who approved thereof, we did, with the assent of all, agree that such a person should thenceforth no longer rule in the kingdom of England, by whom the church of England was reduced to a state of ignominy, and the people to want; for, to omit other matters, he and his revellers had so exhausted the whole kingdom, that they did not leave a man his belt, a woman her necklace, a nobleman his ring, or anything of value even to a Jew. He had likewise so utterly emptied the king's treasury, that in all the coffers and bags therein, nothing but the keys could be met with, after the lapse of these last two years. On the third day he positively promised, and gave his word by one of his followers, in the presence of all, that he would not leave the island until certain castles which he kept in his own hands, and had given into the charge of some foreigners, unknown and obscure persons, and which were than named, should have been fully surrendered by him and given into the charge of certain persons named; for the performance of which he gave his brothers and his chamberlain as hostages. He then hastened to Canterbury, that there, as became him, he might assume the cross of pilgrimage, and lay aside the cross of the legateship, which for a year and a half since the death of pope Clement, he had wielded to the prejudice of the church of Rome, and to the detriment of that of England. For all the churches of England had that cross put to their ransom; that is to say, had compelled them to submit to the extortion of fines; nor was there any one exempt from feeling the blows of that cross. And then, besides if by chance it happened that he entered the house of any bishop, you will be able to learn from him that his entertainment cost him the price of one or two hundred marks. After he had remained in the castle of Dover some days, unmindful of his profession and of the obligation of his promise which he had given, forgetful also of his brothers, whom, having given as hostages, he was disgracefully exposing to peril of death, he determined to set sail, and as he did not care to do this openly, he hit upon a new kind of stratagem, and pretending to be a woman, a sex which he always hated, changed the priest's robe into the harlot's dress. Oh shame! The man became a woman, the chancellor a chancelloress, the priest a harlot, the bishop a buffoon. Accordingly, although he was lame, he chose to hasten on foot from the heights of the castle down to the sea-shore, clothed in a woman's green gown of enormous length instead of the priest's gown of azure colour;[1] having on a cape of the same colour, with unsightly long sleeves, instead of a chasuble, a hood on his head instead of a mitre, some brown cloth in his left hand, as if for sale, instead of a maniple,[2] and the staff of the huckster in his right in place of his pastoral staff. Decked out in such guise the bishop came down to the sea-shore, and he who had been accustomed much more frequently to wear the knight's coat of mail, wondrous thing! became so effeminate in mind, as to make choice of a feminine dress.[3] Having seated himself on the shore upon a rock, a fisherman, who immediately took him for a common woman, came up to him; and, having come

[1] *hyacinthina* in the text
[2] The *manipulum*, *fanon*, or *sudarium*, was either a napkin or a short sleeve worn over the left wrist by the priesthood when officiating.
[3] *animum* is probably a mistake for *amictum*

nearly naked from the sea, perhaps wishing to be made warm, he ran up to this wretch, and embracing his neck with the left arm, with his right began pulling him about, upon which he almost immediately discovered[1] that he was a man. At this he was greatly surprised, and, starting back, in a fit of amazement, shouted out with a loud voice, 'Come all of you and see a wonder; I have found a woman who is a man!' Immediately on this, his servants and acquaintances who were standing at a distance came up, and with a gentle kind of violence pushed him back and ordered him to hold his tongue; upon which the fisherman held his peace and the clamour ceased, and this hermaphrodite sat waiting there. In the meantime a woman, who had come from the town, seeing the linen cloth, which he or rather she, was carrying as though on sale, came and began to ask what was the price, and for how much he would let her have an ell. He, however, made no answer, as he was utterly unacquainted with the English language; on which she pressed the more; and shortly after another woman came up, who urgently made the same enquiry, and pressed him very hard to let her know the price at which he would sell it. As he answered nothing at all, but rather laughed in his sleeve, they began to talk among themselves, and to enquire what could be the meaning of it. Then, suspecting some imposture, they laid hands upon the hood with which his face was covered, and pulling it backwards from his nose, beheld the swarthy features of a man, lately shaved, on which they began to be extremely astonished. Then rushing to the dry land,[2] they lifted their voices to the stars, crying out, 'Come, let us stone this monster, who is a disgrace to either sex.' Immediately a crowd of men and women were collected together, tearing the hood off his head, and ignominiously dragging him prostrate on the ground by his sleeves and cape along the sand and over the rocks, not without doing him considerable injury. In the meanwhile his servants made an attack two or three times on the multitude for the purpose of rescuing him, but were not able, as all the populace were inflicting vengeance upon him with insatiate eagerness, reviling him, inflicting blows and spitting upon him; and after much other disgraceful treatment, they dragged him through the whole of the town, and then, dragging him, or rather dragging him to pieces, they shut him up in a dark cellar with a guard over him, for a prison. Thus was he dragged who had dragged another, made captive who had been the captor, bound who had been the binder, incarcerated who had been the one to incarcerate, that so with the extent of the offence the extent of the punishment might seem to be commensurate. For he became an object of extreme disgrace to his neighbours, of dread to his acquaintances, and was made a laughing-stock for all the people. I only wish that he had polluted himself alone, the priest, and not the priestly office. May, then, the church of Rome make due provision that such great guiltiness may be punished in such a way that the offence of one may not contaminate all, and that the priestly authority may not be lessened thereby. And further, may the king of England take all precaution to

[1] This passage has been necessarily modified in the translation; it stands thus in the text: *Cucurrit ad moustrum et manu sinistra collum complectens, dextera partes inferiores rimatur. Cumque tunicam subito sublevasset, et nimis inverecunde ad partes verecundas manum extendisset audacter, femoralia sensit et virum in faemina certis indiciis agnovit.* The story is not told with all these circumstances by all the chroniclers, and no doubt the bishop of Coventry was wishful that it should lose nothing in his way of telling it. The first part of this extract is exceedingly improbable.

[2] *terram*, in contradistinction to the sea-shore

appoint such a person over his realm, that by him the royal dignity may be preserved, and his authority may suffer no diminution through him; but rather that the clergy and the people may have cause to congratulate themselves upon his government."

The letter of master Peter of Blois on behalf of William, bishop of Ely

"To his former lord and friend, Hugh, so called, bishop of Coventry and Chester, Peter of Blois, archdeacon of Bath, may he remember God with fear. The excesses of a traitorous faction this day reveal to what lengths malice may proceed, what envy may be guilty of. The bishop of Ely, one beloved by God and men, a man amiable, wise, generous, kind, and meek, bounteous and liberal to the highest degree, had by the dispensations of the Divine favour, and in accordance with the requirements of his own manners and merits, been honoured with the administration of the state, and had thus gained the supreme authority. With feelings of anger you beheld this, and forthwith he became the object of your envy. Accordingly, your envy conceived vexation and brought forth iniquity; whereas he, walking in the simplicity of his mind, received you into the hallowed precincts of his acquaintanceship, and with singleness of heart, and into the bonds of friendship and strict alliance. His entire spirit reposed upon you, and all your thoughts unto him were for evil. 'Woe,' says Ecclesiasticus, 'to a double heart and to wicked lips, and to the sinner that goeth two ways.'[1] The face of the hypocrite veiled the wickedness of the conscience within with a kind of pretence of friendship, and in secret you were inflicting upon an innocent man the injuries caused by a seditious and petulant tongue. Solomon says, 'Curse the whisperer and double-tongued: for such have destroyed many that were at peace.'[2] All his inward thoughts did he pour forth into your bosom: you he looked upon as a second self, and yet you, to find a pretence for causing his fall, thought fit to ply him with the adulation of a betrayer. Oh detestable treachery! Judas betrayed with a kiss, you with words; without, you made a show of the regard of an attentive friend, and your tongue was planning treachery. As you sat, you spoke against your brother, and in the way of the son of your mother did you lay a stumbling-block. 'Woe to that man by whom the offence cometh.'[3] This guilty conduct, indeed, has branded you with the lasting stain of bad opinion, and if by the bounty of nature you had received any commendable points, this fault has done away with them for ever. In like manner, Joab acted valiantly on many occasions, but his treachery to Amasa and Abner, blackened in him all the glories of his valorous deeds. Oh lips of detraction! Oh tongue of abuse and treachery! What, O Lord shall be applied to this treacherous tongue? Would that arrows might be applied thereto, that they might pierce it through and through, and that desolating coals of fire might consume it; would that thou, seraph, who with the live coal from heaven[4] didst purge the lips of the prophet, wouldst with the flames of hell, in purging his whole face and tongue, destroy the same, that so we might be able to sing and say, 'In cleansing him thou hast destroyed him.' Lips consecrated by the gospel, are never ceasing to babble forth their lying words to the winds. That is entirely devoted to vanity which was due and owing to truth. But the man of froward

[1] Ecclus ii. 12
[2] Ecclus xxvii. 31
[3] St Matt. xviii. 7
[4] alluding to Isaiah vi. 6, 7

tongue will not be guided on the earth; wherefore, 'let him that standeth take care lest he fall', for before ruin the heart is exalted. Do you exult, unhappy man, and make it your boast that you have supplanted an innocent man? But know beyond a doubt, that he has been thus laid low for both the downfall and the uprising of many, for the uprising of himself and of his people, and for the downfall of yourself and your accomplices. This punishment will fall upon your own head.[1] For every deceit suffers from its own recoil: from your treachery[2] nought but the fruit of sorrow will you gather; and you have commenced the web, that you may be wrapped in a double cloak. It is Isaiah who says, 'Ye who begin the web and put your trust in the darkness of Egypt, await the day of bitterness.'[3] You publicly make it your boast and vaunt that it was you who created this tumult, that it was you who deceived him when not on his guard, and that it was you induced the multitude to attack with arms an unarmed man, and an innocent man with insidiousness. Why boast of your malice, you, who are so powerful in your iniquity? Why vaunt of your malice, which in most countries, as your infamous character has become circulated, is in the mouths of all classes? But about you and persons like you it may justly be said, 'They rejoice when they have done evil, and they exult at things that bring the greatest disgrace'. Besides, it is the remark of a wise man, that he 'who rejoiceth at the ruin of another, shall be punished';[4] and Solomon says, 'Rejoice not when thine enemy falleth – lest the Lord see it, and He turn his wrath upon thee.'[5] Indeed, it was always the usual accomplishment, and one peculiar to your family, to sow the materials for dissension; and the pestilent branch has contracted its evil qualities from the root of the noxious tree. Oh evil generation! Oh provoking race! 'Oh generation of vipers, who hath taught you to flee from the wrath to come?'[6] Do you think that God will not behold this, and require an account thereof? It was for this same reason that the wicked man caused the anger of the Lord, 'For he said in his heart, he will not require the same.'[7] But, beyond a doubt, the Lord will require it; He will also require to know as to whose misfortunes you are now boasting; and at a future day, by the bounty of the Lord, he shall breathe again. For wisdom will not forsake the righteous man when sold, and in time shall he gain respect. It rather befitted the gravity of your rank to promote peace among the people, to allay sedition, and especially in England, which, receiving you poor enough, amplified you with mighty honours. Also, when speaking to those who were in the Babylonish captivity, he says, 'Seek the peace of the city, in which the Lord has caused you to be carried away captives, for in the peace thereof shall ye have peace.'[8] On another occasion I wrote to you, and with salutary warning entreated you to abstain from such courses. However, the harp of David never fully allayed the madness of Saul; and your hand has been extended to the commission of such deeds as these. Therefore, remember, man, if only man you are, remember, I say, your condition;

[1] *Faba haec recudetur in caput tuum*. It is not improbable that the archdeacon was a reader of Terence.
[2] He puns upon the resemblance between *dolo* and *dolore*.
[3] This may perhaps allude to Is. xix. 9.
[4] alluding probably to Ecclus viii. 7
[5] Prov. xxiv. 17. 18
[6] St Matt. iii. 7; St Luke iii. 7
[7] Ps. x. 13
[8] Jer. xxxix. 7

remember the shortness of this life; remember the strict and dreadful judge; remember the punishment so fearful, so terrible, so interminable, and so intolerable, which is reserved for you to everlasting, if you desist not from such a course of wickedness."

In eight days after this, John, earl of Mortaigne, gave orders that the chancellor should be liberated from prison, and should take his departure. Accordingly, he took his departure, and, crossing the sea, landed at Witsand, in Flanders. But while he was on his road, some nobles of that country, whom he had injured while in England, laid hands upon him, and kept him till he had made satisfaction to them. Proceeding thence, he arrived at Paris, and gave to Mauricius, the bishop, sixty marks of silver, upon condition that he should be received there with a procession, which was accordingly done. After this, he returned into Normandy; but, by the command of the archbishop of Rouen, he was considered there as an excommunicated person, and in every place to which he came, throughout the whole of the archbishopric of Rouen, an end was put to divine service as long as he was staying there.

On this, he sent messengers to pope Celestinus, and to his lord the king of England, informing them, how John, earl of Mortaigne, and his accomplices, had expelled him from the kingdom; and, complaining of the injuries done him, he demanded restitution of what had been taken from him, at the same time making offer, on his part, to obey the law, and further stating, that if his acts and expenditure should not prove satisfactory to his lord the king, he would in all things give satisfaction according to his demands. Upon this, the supreme pontiff was provoked to anger, and wrote, to the following effect, to all the archbishops and bishops of England:

The letter of pope Celestinus to the prelates of England, in behalf of William, bishop of Ely

"Celestinus the bishop, servant of the servants of God, to his venerable brethren the archbishops and bishops throughout the kingdom of England appointed, health, and the apostolic benediction. Whereas our dearly beloved son in Christ, Richard, the illustrious king of the English, having assumed the cross, and prepared himself for avenging the injuries done to the Redeemer, has therein, like a prudent man and one who seeks the Lord, considered that the cares of governing his kingdom ought to be postponed to the performance of his duty, and has left the same under the apostolic protection: it is, therefore, our wish and our duty, with the greatest zeal, to preserve the integrity and the rights of his realm, and the honour of himself, in the same degree that, trusting in our protection, he has exposed his person and his property to the greatest danger for the upholding of the holy religion, and is known, in obedience to the Creator, to have behaved himself in a praiseworthy manner, the Lord dealing with him and giving good tokens of success, and most zealously, as is manifest from his exploits. Therefore, inasmuch as we have heard that certain attempts have been made upon his kingdom itself, as well as against your venerable father, William, bishop of Ely, the legate of the apostolic see, to whom he has committed the government of his kingdom, both by John, earl of Mortaigne, and certain other persons, which in themselves contain some grounds of suspicion, and, if they are true, are known to redound in no slight degree to contempt of the apostolic see, we have deemed it our duty at this early period to meet such presumption, inasmuch as from delay very great injury might possibly accrue to the king before-named and the land of Jerusalem, and to ourselves and the Roman church. Wherefore, by these apostolic writings, we do command the whole of you, and in virtue of your obedience enjoin you, that if (as has been reported to us) the said earl or any one else has dared to lay violent hands on the bishop before-mentioned, or to seize him, or to extort from him any oath by means of violence or to keep him in confinement, or in any way to change the state of the kingdom from the position in which it was placed by his serene highness at his departure, in such case, all pretexts and excuses laid aside, you will meet together, and, with candles lighted and bells ringing, all appeals and excuses, and all respect for persons on your part utterly laid aside, publicly announce as under the ban of excommunication the said earl, and all his counsellors, advisers, accomplices, and abettors in the said acts of presumptuous daring. You are also to cause them, when thus excommunicated, to be strictly avoided by all, both in their own lands as also in others which they may have invaded, and you are entirely to forbid the celebration there of divine service, except penance and the baptism of children, all obstacle thereto by appeal being entirely removed; until such time as, the said legate having been released from confinement, as well as from the stringency of his oath, and the kingdom having been replaced in the same position in which it was left by the said king at his departure, envoys shall come to the apostolic see, with the testimony of letters from him and from yourselves as well, for the purpose of absolution. And know for certain that if, in the execution of this our precept, you shall be negligent or remiss, we have resolved, with the help of God, to inflict upon you no less a punishment than if the said injury had been done to our own person, or to one of our brethren. Given at the Lateran, on the fourth day before the nones of December, in the first year of our pontificate."

Upon the authority, therefore, of these letters of the supreme pontiff, the said bishop of Ely wrote to Hugh, bishop of Lincoln, to the following effect:

"William, by the grace of God, bishop of Ely, legate of the apostolic see, and chancellor of our lord the king, to his venerable brother and most dearly beloved friend, [Hugh], by the same grace, bishop of Lincoln, health, and sincere love and affection. The more full the confidence that we feel in your affection, the greater the constancy we have found in you, so much the more confidently do we entrust to your discreetness, and to that of the church of God, the interests of our lord the king, and our own, to be duly watched over; putting our trust in God as to you, that your brotherly love will, in your pontifical character, show all due regard to the apostolic precepts and our own. We do, therefore, in virtue of your obedience, enjoin, and, on the strength of the authority which has been conferred upon us, command you, that, for the purpose of performing the apostolical mandate issued to all the archbishops and bishops of England, as also to all other your brethren whatsoever, you will with all speed convene the same, to the end that the iniquity of the laity may no longer cast a slur on the church of God and its priesthood, and lest, through any tergiversation or dissimulation, their malice may be imputed as a crime to yourselves. But as to the order which our lord the pope has given with regard to the person of John, earl of Mortaigne, we have modified the same, deferring the occasion until the Lord's day when '*Esto mihi*'[1] is sung; to the end that, if in the meantime he shall think fit to repent, we may return thanks to God for the same, and in his behalf, in the sight of our lord the pope, and of our lord the king of England, the champion of Him who was crucified, pour forth our affectionate prayers, that he may be deemed deserving of pardon for his offence, and give him our strenuous aid and all efficacious attention, saving always our fealty to our lord the king, and the honour of our priestly office. But, on the lands of those excommunicated, you are to permit the celebration of no divine service, the baptism of children and penance excepted. The names of those who have been excommunicated by our lord the pope, and have been denounced as such by ourselves, of whose doings the evidence is so notorious that it cannot by any equivocation on their part be invalidated, are as follows: Walter, archbishop of Rouen, Godfrey, bishop of Winchester, Hugh, bishop of Coventry, William Marshal, Geoffrey Fitz-Peter, William Bruyere, Hugh Bardolph, Richard Malebisse and his brother Hugh, James and Simon Fitz-Simon, Simon de Avranches, Roger Fitz-Rainfray, Gilbert and Rainfrid his sons, Gerard Camville, earl of Salisbury, John Marshal, earl of Mellent, Gilbert Basset, Thomas Basset, Henry de Vere, Jocelyn Fitz-Rainfray, Stephen Riddel, chancellor of the earl of Mortaigne; whom, both as bishop and as his legate, we do denounce to you as excommunicated; as also master Benedict, who, contrary to the statutes of the king and the kingdom, and against our prohibition, has dared to employ the seal of our lord the king, together with John, archdeacon of Oxford. In addition to this, we do distinctly and in especial order you publicly to denounce, as excommunicated, Hugh, bishop of Coventry, whom we have solemnly excommunicated, not only because in word and deed he has disowned the bishop, and because he gave his bodily oath at the hand of Baldwin, archbishisop of Canterbury, of pious memory, as to not holding courts, but also because he has been manifestly a counsellor and adviser to the entire subversion of the realm of England, a disturber of the peace, and a public advocate against the royal dignity and interests: and to cause him to be strictly avoided by all, that in future a sheep so diseased may not be able to blemish and corrupt the flock of the Lord. But Hugh Bardolph, who took no part in our expulsion and confinement, we do except from the said sentence of excommunication, if, immediately upon being warned, he shall surrender the castles of Scarborough, and those throughout the whole of Yorkshire and Westmoreland which he holds in his hands, to William de Stuteville. You are also to forbid all persons in your diocese, under pain of excommunication, to do anything in obedience to those who conduct themselves in England as though they were justices, or in any way to obey a power founded on violence and usurpation. Farewell."

[1] Quinquagesima Sunday; when the introit begins, "*Esto mihi in Deum protectorem*", "Be thou, O God, a protector to me"

The said bishop of Ely also wrote to Hugh, bishop of Lincoln, to the following effect:

"William, by the grace of God, bishop of Ely, legate of the holy apostolic see, and chancellor of our lord the king, to his venerable brother and friend, by the same grace, bishop of Lincoln, greeting. By that authority which has been conferred upon us, we do command you, and in virtue of your obedience enjoin, that you seize and take into your own hands, and retain possession of, the archdeaconry and all the revenues of John, archdeacon of Oxford, until such time as you shall have received commands from the apostolic see, or from ourselves; inasmuch as with his uncle, the Pilate of Rouen, he is disturbing the peace and tranquillity of the kingdom of England, and is seeking to do whatever mischief he possibly can to our lord the king and to his realm, as being an enemy of the realm and to ourselves. For, by the authority of our lord the pope, we have placed him under the ban of excommunication. Farewell."

The said bishop of Ely also wrote to a similar effect to some others of the bishops of England; though not one of them performed the commands of either the apostolic see or of himself; as they did not consider him as legate, or as the king's chancellor. But the said archbishop of Rouen, and the other justices of England, deprived him of his bishopric, and collected his revenues for the behoof of the king, in return for the king's treasures which he had made away with.

After this, the said justices and all the bishops, earls, and barons of England joined in a letter, and wrote word to the king how his chancellor had laid waste the kingdom of England and his treasures, and how, by the common consent of the kingdom, he had been deposed. On the other hand, the chancellor wrote to the king, signifying how that his brother John had taken possession of his kingdom, and would place the crown on his own head, unless he should make haste and return with all speed . . .

[In the year of grace 1192] During Lent . . . the archbishop of York came to London by command of the king's justices; but when he came to Westminster with his cross, he was forbidden by the bishop of London and the other bishops of England thenceforth to presume to carry his cross in the province of Canterbury. On this, he contumaciously made answer that he would not lay it aside for them; but, listening to the advice of his own people, he hid it from before the face of the people, lest a tumult might arise among the clergy. The bishop of London, however, holding him as an excommunicated person, in consequence of this transgression, suspended the New Temple, at which place the said archbishop of York had taken up his abode, from the performance of divine service and from the ringing of bells, and in consequence, he was obliged to leave the city; but before he left, queen Eleanor, the archbishop of Rouen, himself, and all the nobles of the kingdom, met together and swore fealty and faithful service to Richard, king of England, and his heir, against all men.

During the same Lent, the bishop of Ely, the chancellor, returned to England, by command of the earl of Mortaigne, and remained some days in the castle at Dover, not daring to proceed any further. The earl of Mortaigne, however, in consideration of five hundred pounds of silver which the chancellor had promised him for the restoration of his office, tried in every way to induce the chief men of the kingdom to receive the chancellor in his former position; but they refused, and sent word to the chancellor, that if he did not make haste and leave the kingdom with all speed, they would take him prisoner. On hearing this, the chancellor, not daring to stay in England against the will of the chief men, crossed over at the Supper of our Lord . . .

3. The "History of William the Marshal" for the years 1216–19

(*Histoire de Guillaume le Maréchal*, ed. Paul Meyer, 3 vols (Paris, Société de l'histoire de France, 1891–1901), vol. 3, pp. 209–69 [French])

This long extract from the metrical life of the regent, William the Marshal, earl of Pembroke, written about 1226 on information given by his squire, John de Erley, is today our main authority for the years 1216–19. The editor, Paul Meyer, gives also a modern French prose rendering, somewhat shortened but omitting little of historical importance: it is this which is here translated.

I must pass rapidly over the war that broke out between the king and his barons, because there were too many circumstances that are not creditable to relate. Harm might come to me because of them. The barons having formed a league came to the king and demanded of him their liberties. He refused: then they made it known that if they did not obtain their liberties they would withdraw from his service and do him all the harm they could. They kept their word and betook themselves to London to act against him. But note well that the Marshal took no part whatever in this movement. He grieved for the excesses into which those on both sides had allowed themselves to be drawn, and had no share in the agreement concluded between the barons and the citizens of London. The barons, having collected at London, sent messengers to summon Louis, the son of the king of France, whom they intended to make king of England. This was folly. Before Louis arrived, the king besieged Rochester. He spent a great deal of money there before he gained possession of it. He went to Dover by sea. Why by sea rather than by land I need not say for that is not my concern. Then he called in some Flemings, knights and serjeants, who thought only of plunder and were less concerned with helping him in his war than with laying waste his land. In five weeks he had exhausted his treasure. That is what must happen: a man who spends without earning anything and associates with evil men, is soon broke. Eventually he took Rochester.

The Londoners brought in Louis, who for a long time was master of the country. He captured Farnham, Winchester, Porchester and Southampton. There the ribalds of France drank very many tuns [of wine]. They were boasting foolishly that England was theirs and that the English, having no right to the land, could only evacuate it. These boasts had no effect. Later I saw eaten by dogs a hundred of them whom the English slew between Winchester and Romsey. That was how they kept the land. In a number of places in England, people did the same or worse, witness Willikin of the Weald.

When the king had no more money, most of those who served him for wages went off with what they had earned. The Marshal however stayed with him in misfortune, serving him faithfully as his lord and his king. From this moment to his death, he never deserted him. And, besides, he invariably acted towards the king as a loyal subject whatever the king might do to him.

Meanwhile, as the war dragged on, the king lost much of his land. Finally he made his way towards Lindsey. On the way he was seized by the illness of which he died. He was forced to stop at Newark. With him were the bishop of Winchester, John of Monmouth, Walter Clifford, sire Rogier, John Marshal and a number of other men of high rank. All were deeply distressed.

Feeling his illness growing worse, king John summoned his faithful subjects and said to them, "My lords, I must die; I cannot hold out against this illness. For God's sake, beg the Marshal to pardon me all the wrongs I have done him, of which I fully repent. He has always served me faithfully; he has never acted against me, whatever I did or said to him. For God's sake, my lords, beg him to forgive me for it. And since I am more sure of his loyalty than that of any other, I ask you to entrust to him the guardianship of my son, who will never manage to hold the land, except with his help."

So spoke the king. Pitiless death pressed so hard upon him that soon he was reduced to helplessness. At least he died repentant. His body was carried to Worcester.

The Marshal was grieved when he heard of the death of the king. He left Gloucester to go ahead of the corpse that was being carried to Worcester. The bier was escorted by the legate Gualo, and by numerous clerks and knights. A splendid service was held, as was fitting for a king. Thus the prophecy of Merlin was fulfilled, that said that he [John] would lie between sovereigns. And this was the truth, for he lies between St Wulfstan and another saint's body.

When the king was buried, the great men made their way to Gloucester and summoned thither the earl of Chester and the adherents of the late king. When they came together in council, they resolved to send Thomas of Samford to Devizes to bring from there the king's son and all those that were with him. The Marshal made his way ahead of them and rejoined them outside Malmesbury on the plain. Ralph de St Sanson who was the young prince's governor was there, carrying him in his arms. The child, who was well bred, greeted the Marshal and said to him, "Sire, greetings. I entrust myself to God and to you. May God grant you look after us well." The Marshal replied, "Sire, upon my soul, I shall neglect nothing to serve you faithfully so long as I have strength to do so." All burst into tears, the Marshal like the rest. Then they set out again for Gloucester.

There they deliberated whether to await the earl of Chester or to proceed without him. Some were for waiting, others advised them to crown the king immediately, for no one knows what the future holds for him. This latter counsel won the day. Then someone asked who was to dub the king knight. "Who indeed," said someone, "if not he who amongst a thousand men would deserve the honour more than the rest? William Marshal, he who girded the sword upon the young king.[1] Not one of you rivals his greatness. It is he who ought to gird the sword upon this one and so he will have knighted two kings." All agreed to this. The child was dressed in royal robes made to his size: he was a fine little knight. The great men who were present

[1] i.e. Henry (1155–83), son of Henry II

carried him to the monastery. Rich gifts were distributed when he was anointed and crowned. The legate Gualo sang the mass and crowned him, assisted by the bishops who were assembled there.

When he was anointed and consecrated, and the service was over, the knights carried the child in their arms, particularly Philip de Aubeney and Richard de Ferrers. A number of others lent a hand, who were not much help. He was carried to his chamber, where he was dressed in other less heavy clothes. At this moment, just as the company was going to sit down at table, there came bad news. A messenger, more foolish than wise, told the Marshal, in front of everybody, that his castle of Goodrich had been besieged the previous day and that his constable was asking him for help. The Marshal immediately sent there knights, serjeants and crossbowmen. Many of those present considered that this event, on the very day of the coronation, was a bad omen.

The great men came to the Marshal and asked him to take upon himself the guardianship of the king. "I cannot," he replied. "I have no longer the strength needed for such a charge. I am too old. You must give this responsibility to another. Wait till the earl of Chester arrives." They left the matter at that for the night and each man went home.

The Marshal, on returning to the castle, called into counsel John Marshal, Ralf Musard, and John de Erley, and said to them: "Those men want me to undertake the guardianship of the king and the government of the realm. But it is a heavy responsibility and I want first to be guided by your opinions." John Marshal and Ralf Musard advised him to accept. "You will be in a position," said the latter, "to advance your dependents and others besides, and us who are here." John de Erley, on the other hand, dissuaded him from it, pointing out to him that it was a heavy burden for one weakened by age; that, moreover, as the king had little money, it would be to him, the Marshal, that people would turn, and that he would as a result suffer much trouble and vexation to put up with. "Let us wait for the coming of the earl [of Chester]," the Marshal answered; "we shall have better advice; let us go to bed. God grant us there counsel and peace."

The next day, after mass, the earl of Chester arrived. He greeted the king, who received his homage and that of the other barons. Many of those who came with the earl regarded it as unfitting that the others had not waited for him to arrive before crowning the king. But the earl silenced them by saying that they had done the right thing by proceeding without delay to the coronation. Then they all took counsel together and deliberated on the choice of the one to whom the guardianship of the king and the kingdom should be entrusted. The bishop of Winchester asked Alan Basset his opinion. "By my faith," he replied, "I see only the Marshal or the earl of Chester." "In truth, my lords," replied the Marshal, "I cannot accept so exalted a mission. I am too weak. I am over eighty. But you, earl of Chester, make it your charge, and as long as I live, I will give you all the help I can. There is nothing you can command me that I will not do, so long as God gives me the strength for it." "No indeed, Marshal," said the earl, "that may not be. You are so fine a knight, so upright, so respected, so loved and so wise that you are considered one of the finest knights in the world. I say this to you in all sincerity, it is you that ought to be chosen. I will serve you and will perform, as best I can, all the tasks you wish to command me."

Then the legate took the Marshal aside into another room with the earl of Chester, the bishop of Winchester and some of the great men, and they began to deliberate afresh. But they would never have managed to overcome the resistance of the Marshal had the legate not begged him to accept the regency for the remission and pardon of his sins. On this condition, he would grant him absolution from them before God. "In God's name," said the Marshal, "if at this price I am absolved of my sins, this office suits me, and I will take it, though it weigh heavily upon me."

The legate entrusted it to him, and the noble Marshal received at the same time the king and the regency. He performed it well so long as he lived, but we lost him too soon for the wellbeing of England.

When the Marshal had taken charge of the kingdom, he spoke thus, "My lords, behold this young and tender king. I could not undertake to lead him with me about the land. And I cannot stay in the same place, for I shall have to go to the marches of the kingdom to protect them. That is why I ask you to name an upright man to whom the young king shall be entrusted." "Do as you please, sire," said the legate, "you will know how to put him into good hands." Upon which the Marshal entrusted the child to the bishop of Winchester.

When it became known that the Marshal had charge of the king and the kingdom, there was universal rejoicing. "God protects us," people said, "for there is no one in England who would be capable of acquitting himself as well of this charge."

The Marshal called into counsel the three faithful friends whom he had consulted the previous day, and said to them, "Advise me, for by the faith I owe you I see myself embarking upon a sea without either bottom or shore. May God come to my aid. They have entrusted to me an almost hopeless governorship. The child has no money and I, I am a man of great age." Tears came into his eyes as he uttered these words, and the others wept too, out of pity. "Yes," said John de Erley, who had understood his way of thinking, "you have undertaken a task that must be carried through at all costs. But when we reach the end, I tell you that, even putting things at their worst, only great honour can come of it. Let us suppose that all your supporters go over to Louis, that they surrender to him all the castles, to the point that you can find no refuge anywhere in England, and that pursued by Louis you are obliged to quit the country and seek refuge in Ireland: that will still be a great honour. And as the worst possible outcome is so honourable, the most propitious will bring you both great honour and great joy. No man will ever have earned such glory on earth." "By God's sword," said the earl, "this advice is true and good; it goes so straight to my heart, that if all abandoned the king, do you know what I would do? I would carry him on my shoulders step by step, from island to island, from country to country and I would not fail him, not even if it meant begging my bread." "You cannot say more, and God will be with you," replied his friends. "Now," concluded the Marshal, "let us go to bed, and there may God grant counsel and help, He who comes to the help of those who wish to do good and act loyally."

The king and his court left Gloucester and made their way to Bristol. Savari de Mauléon was there and presented himself before the king and asked his permission to go back to his own land. At that time Louis was besieging Hertford. The defenders of the castle, without waiting for help, asked Louis for a twenty-day truce. He granted them it on condition that they gave up Berkhampstead and Hertford to him. He took possession of these two places. Shortly afterwards the justiciar and sir Fawkes with numerous barons joined the king at Bristol.

When the truce expired, those who were guarding Hertford agreed to another of twenty days without consulting the Marshal. That was wrong. They gave up two strong castles: Norwich and Orford, and so Louis found himself in possession of four castles. But he did not observe the truce as he had agreed to do. The French, proud as ever, did not allow him to. So he decided to go to France. When the Marshal saw that Louis was not observing the truce, he resolved not to observe it either.

The Marshal reassembled all the men who held loyally to this king's side, and made his way to Chertsey. Louis, on his part, made his way to Winchelsea, where he had not the chance to embark with his following because he found the road to the sea closed. The Marshal having consulted his allies had had the town of Rye occupied by Philip de Aubeney and a sufficient troop of knights and serjeants. Then he sent round to the seaward side a well-equipped fleet. Next he rode towards Louis and pressed him so hard that he no longer knew in which direction to turn, since he had the Marshal on one side, Philip de Aubeney, who was killing many of his men, on the other, and the fleet in front of him. Furthermore, Willikin of the Weald was harrying him and had many of Louis's men beheaded.

Thus hemmed in, Louis lost a good thousand of his men who died by the sword, unconfessed. The troop of ribalds who boasted of conquering England was almost destroyed there. And no bad thing. Two rich undertenants were captured there who had left Louis to return to their own land, one William of Pont de l'Arche and John, son of Hugh, and with them a number of other Englishmen who even now are hated for their conduct. Louis would have been captured had he not been helped by fortune, who is ill disposed to the heirs of England and robs them of their land. Hearken how strong fortune is and how she sustains those whose part she takes! Meanwhile sir Hugues Tacon, who was our enemy, arrived. He brought with him a large fleet to help Louis and forcing his way through took him back to France. But first of all we must tell you how he destroyed our fleet and how Louis came, with a host of knights, to Rye. The king's men who were occupying this town realised that they could not defend it, their opponents being over 3,000 in number, and they evacuated it. Louis continued his journey to Dover, where he embarked.

When the Marshal learnt that Louis had returned to his own country, he made his way to Shoreham and stayed there one night. The next day, as he was leaving the town, he met on the way the young Marshal and William of Salisbury, who loved one another like brothers. They all made their way together to Knap, which immediately surrendered.

The next day the young Marshal and the earl of Salisbury went to Winchester, where they laid siege to the castle, while the Marshal, the father, went with some of the great men to besiege Farnham. The young Marshal and the earl of Salisbury took up their abode at Hyde and besieged the city of Winchester. The first day they accomplished little, but on the second they made an assault. That same day the elder Marshal ordered them to rejoin him without delay. They set off, but at Alresford fell in with messengers who told them of the capture of the castle. At this news, the two counts retraced their steps in good order, advising their men to be on their guard for fear of being surprised by the besieged.

Meanwhile the garrison of the castles [of Winchester], seeing the host of the English depart, made a sortie, plundered the town and set fire to it, because the townsfolk had harboured their enemies. They could not, however, do all they wanted, because the host returned so suddenly that they were obliged to retreat into their castles. But the unfortunate thing was that the inhabitants of the suburb sided with the garrison – which cost them dear. The earl of Salisbury besieged and captured the smaller of the two castles. The young Marshal besieged the larger and for a week pressed it so hard that the defenders dared not rest nor lay aside their arms.

The earl of Salisbury taking one of the castles by force then hurried to the aid of the young Marshal, and the two made such efforts that the garrison was not long in losing heart. Meanwhile the elder Marshal arrived with so great an army that the countryside and the town were filled with it. The defenders of the castle realised that they could not resist for long.

When the elder Marshal arrived they took counsel and it was decided that the young Marshal and the earl of Salisbury should go to besiege Southampton. Winchester meanwhile surrendered and there was so much plunder, that the poor who cared to help themselves became rich on the possessions of their enemies. The two earls for their part wasted no time in taking the castle [of Southampton] and having installed a constable there, they returned to Winchester.

Then the Marshal sent sir Philip de Aubeney to take Rochester. That was quickly accomplished and Philip returned to Winchester. Shortly afterwards, the young Marshal came to his father and asked his permission to go and lay siege to Marlborough. This was granted him, the father remaining at Winchester. According to what is written it was on the first Friday after Easter that the young Marshal set siege to Marlborough and succeeded in taking it, though not without difficulty.

After an absence of seven weeks and five days Louis returned to England with a large and proud army. Before this happened, knowing nothing of his arrival, the holders of the castle surrendered, saving their lives. The Marshal was annoyed at the return of Louis. He had all the castles he had taken dismantled with the exception of Farnham. When those who had surrendered Marlborough learnt of the arrival of Louis they were ashamed of what they had done.

When Louis learnt that the castles of which he thought himself master had surrendered he was displeased. Having assembled a large number of carters, serjeants, crossbowmen and ribalds, he went by Farnham without stopping to lay siege to it, and came straight to Winchester. In a little while, he had restored the tower and the high walls with stone and mortar and had the breaches repaired. He left the count of Nevers on the spot, a cruel proud man, with a strong garrison. Subsequently he committed various excesses with which he has been reproached, but I do not want to talk about them.

On leaving Winchester, Louis divided his great army into two bodies. With one he went to besiege Dover, and he sent the other to Mountsorel, which the earls of Chester and of Ferrers held under siege. These men believing that Louis in person was descending upon them raised the siege and retired to Nottingham. The French having relieved Mountsorel made their way to Lincoln where they wanted to besiege the castle.

When the Marshal learnt that the siege of Mountsorel had been raised, he was greatly distressed by the news. He was no less annoyed to hear that the French had made their way to Lincoln and that Louis was not with them. He himself was at Northampton with the royalists the day before Pentecost. God inspired them to a marvellous enterprise from which they earned great profit and honour. Listen how that came about.

Hearken then; give ear! You shall hear how God counselled the noble man who had been chosen out of them all! "Hear ye, true and loyal knights!" said William the Marshal. "At a time when, to preserve our reputation, to defend ourselves, our wives, our children, our friends and our land, to win great honour, for the peace of the holy church which our enemies have broken, to be pardoned our sins, we support the burden of arms, beware that there is amongst you no coward! A portion of our enemies have gone to Lincoln to besiege our castle, but they are not all there, and Louis is elsewhere. His supporters have acted like fools in coming here. We should indeed be soft if we did not take vengeance upon those who have come from France to rob us of our heritage. They desire our destruction. For God's sake, let us make a great effort, for, if we are victorious, we shall have increased our glory and defended our freedom and that of our lineage. It is God's will that we should defend ourselves. Their host is divided; we shall overcome it more easily than if it were united. You all see that we must open the way with iron and steel. No more threats, but attack them. God is giving us the chance to revenge ourselves."

These words inflamed them and, full of fire, they set out. On the Wednesday of Whit-week, they rode as far as Newark where they spent the night. On the Thursday they rested. The Normans in the army sought out the young Marshal and said to him, "My lord, you were born in Normandy. You know that the Normans have the right of striking the first blows in battle; do not let the tradition die out." But the earl of Chester declared that if he did not command the front line, he would not take part in the action. The Marshal and his men, to avoid a quarrel, granted him what he asked, without prejudicing the Normans' right.

When this matter was settled, the legate gave them absolution and excommunicated the Frenchmen. Then he made his way to Nottingham. The host set out for Torksey where it spent the night. The next day, which was a Saturday, they armed themselves and arranged the battle order. The earl of Chester had the first line. Next came the Marshal with his sons. The noble earl of Salisbury had the third line and the bishop of Winchester the fourth. When the host had been counted, it was found to consist of only 406 knights and 317 crossbowmen. They were few in number, but their bearing was resolute. When they were in line, the Marshal harangued them in true orator's style. "The men who are seizing our lands and our goods are at your mercy there. They are ours, if heart and spirit do not fail us. If we die in this enterprise, God, who knows well how to distinguish the good, will place us in his paradise, and if we are victorious, we shall have won lasting glory for ourselves and for our families. Besides, you know the enemy are under sentence of excommunication; those of them that die will go straight to hell. It is God who has put them in our power. Let us attack! The time has come."

After having spoken in this way, the Marshal delegated the command of the crossbowmen to the noble bishop of Winchester, Peter, who knew what he was about, advising them to . . . and to marshal themselves in an extended line in order to kill the horses of the French as they charged. Next he ordered 200 serjeants to be prepared to kill their own horses to serve as barriers should they be needed. All those to whom the earl spoke in this way showed great delight; they were as gay as if it were only a question of a tournament.

At Lincoln the French numbered 611 knights with a thousand foot soldiers, not to mention the English who were on their side. Simon de Poissy, the count of Perche and the earl of Winchester sallied out from the city to reconnoitre the king's army. They returned having found out that it was in fine fettle. No one in any land had ever seen a force better equipped or better prepared for war.

In accordance with the report that was made to them, the French barricaded themselves within the town and said that the royalists were not in a state to challenge them there, in spite of the airs they gave themselves, and that they would have to beat a retreat. But, they added, the royalists would not go off peacefully without challenging them, particularly as their horses were exhausted with travelling night and day. On this last point the French were right, and yet the royal army made its way boldly against the town. The Marshal made them another speech saying that it was an initial success for them to see the French, usually in the forefront of a tourney, hiding themselves behind walls.

My lords, here I no longer know what to say, because my sources of information are not in agreement and I cannot follow each of them. I should lose the right way and deserve less credence. One must not introduce lies into true history. When the Marshal learnt that the French had retired into the town, he ordered John Marshal, his nephew, to go to the castle, to find out the state of the besieged. Sir John performed his mission well, and as he approached the castle, sir Geoffrey de Serland met him and showed him an entrance by which one could pass unchallenged. John turned back and as he went, some Frenchmen who were on the alert attacked him. He was not daunted, and set upon them so bravely that they fled. Having driven them off, he sought out his uncle and reported to him what he had done.

The bishop of Winchester went off to reconnoitre with a troop of crossbowmen. He told them to wait for him and penetrated into the castle with a single serjeant. At the entrance he met sir Geoffrey de Serland. He saw the walls and the houses knocked down by the trebuchets. People begged him to take shelter because of the mangonels and the trebuchets which were destroying everything in the vicinity, and he went into the tower, where he found the noble lady to whom the castle belonged and who was defending it as best she could. The lady was greatly delighted by the arrival of the bishop; who reassured her by the news he gave her. The bishop did not stop there long: he went out on foot by a postern into the town and as he was examining it, he noticed an old gate that had allowed communication between the castle and the town, but which had been walled up in former days. He had it knocked down to give entry to the host. The bishop rejoined his men who came to meet him singing as though they were already victorious. Laughingly the bishop said to them that they must save the bishop's house for him since he had been responsible for the entrance by which his men would get in. When Fawkes's men heard these words, they invaded the town but were repulsed in an ugly fashion by those inside.

The bishop said to the Marshal, "They have not found the undefended entrance I meant. There is an opening there that the enemy does not know about. Come, I'll take you to it." "By God's sword, here with my helm!" replied the Marshal. "Sir," answered the bishop, "we must not attack so precipitately, but let two men from each of our battle lines go to reconnoitre the area round the tower and we will be guided by their report."

The Marshal agreed to this and set out. The bishop of Winchester chose ten men, two from each line, with whom he went off to reconnoitre. On the way they met the serjeants who had given ground disgracefully and ill treated them. The Marshal cried to his companions, "Charge, they will soon be defeated. Shame on him who tarries longer." The bishop said to him, "Sir, wait for your men. It is safer to go all together; our enemies will fear us all the more." The Marshal did not want to hear him. Quicker than a falcon, he spurred his horse and all those who were with him grew reckless at the sight. A squire had to point out to him that he had not got his helm. He said to the young Marshal, "Wait for me while I get my helm."

When his helm was on, he looked the finest of them all and as light as a bird. He spurred on his horse. A hungry lion is not quicker to fall upon its prey than was the Marshal when rushed upon his enemies. He carved his way three lances deep into the throng, scattering his adversaries and forcing them to turn tail. The bishop followed him crying, "Now! God help the Marshal!" I forgot to tell you that when our men arrived the most skilful of those who were working the enemy's trebuchets was killed. It was the man who was firing upon the tower. When he saw our knights approaching, he thought they were men of his own side. He redoubled his efforts; he put a stone into the trebuchet, and as he grunted with the effort, they cut off his head.

The young Marshal made it very obvious that he did not wish to stay behind, for his banner was always to be seen in the front line. He had entered the city by the breach at the moment when the Marshal was having his helm laced on. Those in the town outnumbered the attackers, but he charged so energetically that soon many of them were unhorsed. Before the end of the struggle, the French had the worst of it. The elder Marshal and his son forced them to retreat. The former, accompanied by the earl of Salisbury (whom God pardon for his sins!) turned to the right, leaving a monastery on the left. Then they found a large group of very scared Frenchmen. One of them, Robert de Ropelai, broke his lance against the earl of Salisbury but the Marshal dealt him such a blow between the shoulders that he almost unseated him. Robert let himself slide from his horse and went off to hide. Continuing on their way, they found the count of Perche who, surrounded by his men, was defending himself in front of the monastery.

At that place many men were wounded, stunned or captured. A number of our men too were badly wounded because no one dreamt of giving himself up: all wanted to fight. The count of Perche performed many a feat. The Marshal saw that the French were drawing back their men from the top to the foot of the hill; he advanced upon the count and seized his horse by its bridle. But by this time he was already mortally wounded by a blow from a lance with which sir Reginald Crok had struck him through the eye-hole of his helm. In spite of this he took his sword in both hands and with it aimed three blows at the Marshal whose helm carried the marks of them. But immediately afterwards, he swayed and fell from his horse. When the Marshal saw him fall, he thought he had simply lost consciousness and ordered William de Montigny to take off his helm. When this was done, they saw that he was dead. It was grievous that he should die in this way.

When the French saw that in spite of their numbers, they could no longer hold out against the vigorous attacks of our men, they went off down a street to the left and made their way towards Wigford. There to their great satisfaction they found a party of their men, with whom they rallied to start the struggle afresh. But they would have done better, as some of them did, to keep as far away as possible. Looking towards the right they saw to their great displeasure the earl of Chester and his valiant band.

The French and the English who were on their side advanced in an orderly fashion up the slope. But before they got to the top they met our men who were emerging from between the church and the castle and who drove them back with a vigorous charge. At this moment, Alan Basset and his brother Thomas, followed by their men, fell upon them from behind. Seeing themselves thus surrounded, they were overcome with surprise and had no respite till they reached Wigford bridge. There they found themselves on soft ground and there was no need to go far to find feats of arms, for anyone who cared to join in had his hands full. This was not the time for challenges to combat delivered the night before; there were other things to do. Fighting was so fierce on both sides, that even the strongest were exhausted by it.

William Bloet, the standard bearer of the young Marshal, charged so impetuously that he fell with his horse over the bridge. But he soon picked himself up. The struggle did not last long on the side of the French, who shortly before had boasted of chasing the English out of England.

In this action Saer de Quincy, earl of Winchester, sir Robert FitzWalter, sir Robert de Quincy and a number of others were taken prisoner. The rest took flight down the street that leads to the hospital. The street proved difficult going for them as far as the gate. There they were unfortunate. A cow had wandered on to the drawbridge and blocked the passage. The fugitives killed it but nevertheless a number of knights were captured just as though someone had handed them over. When the gate was broken down Simon de Poissy and the constable of Arras were seen in flight. All who managed to escape were so terrified that every bush seemed to them full of marshals. They stopped nowhere. This was very evident at Holland bridge, which was broken; they slaughtered their horses to make a bridge over which they passed, so eager were they to cross.

When sir Richard of Samford saw that the French were in flight, he took his wife up in front of him to save her. A knight called out to him, "Leave her, you can't take her." Immediately he put her gently to the ground and turning on the knight he unseated him with a blow of his lance in the chest, then took up his wife again and saved her.

The good bishop of Winchester, Peter des Roches, who on this day directed our men so well, took many prisoners. He and his men made a considerable profit. But the one who earned most was the pious and loyal John Marshal. He captured seven barons with banners flying and many of the knights of their company.

As I told you before, the knights on the king's side were only 406 in number, whereas on the other side there were 611. And yet it was the latter who were defeated. Such is the fate of those that take up arms against God.

When the Marshal and his men had defeated their enemies and taken prisoner the most important of them, counsel was taken on the policy to pursue. Opinion was divided. Many thought it wise to go and besiege London; others said they would go to Dover to force Louis to raise the siege of that town. The Marshal, who had more experience, advised them to take away their prisoners and have them enter into engagements, and arranged a rendezvous with them for a certain day at Chertsey. He ordered the legate to attend this assembly, where they would consider what measures to take for the defence of the kingdom.

Louis was greatly distressed when he heard that his men had been utterly defeated at Lincoln, and that the count of Perche had perished there. Abandoning the siege of Dover, he made his way to London at full speed, fearing that that city would be taken by the royalists, by main force or by surprise, and he sent to France for help.

When king Philip learnt of the defeat of his men, he was heartbroken and asked if king John were dead. "Yes," he was told, "his son is already crowned and the Marshal has vowed to defend him." "Then we have nothing to gain in England. The land is lost for Louis and in a short time he and his supporters will be chased out of it, as the Marshal has taken the matter in hand."

So he spoke, then he prepared the despatch to England of a large number of troops that would have helped his son and facilitated the conquest of the kingdom, if they had been able to land. But God did not allow it. His [Louis's] wife ransacked France for assistance in men and money. She went at her task so energetically that if all those she assembled had come in arms to London, they would have conquered the whole kingdom.

The Marshal was in a quandary. The king was young and penniless. The majority of the great men had sided with Louis. As a last straw, the greatest barons of France were coming to conquer the land. These were sir Robert de Courtenay, sir Raoul de la Tournelle, Guillaume des Barres. There was also Eustace the Monk, who was never behindhand in wrongdoing. He had taken command of the fleet but that day was his feast day, for on the same day his head was cut off. There were many other men whom we cannot name, having learnt only the names of those who were taken prisoner.

The Marshal promptly made for the coast with such forces as he could assemble. He summoned the mariners of the Cinque Ports, and by dint of bribes and promises, he induced them to go and meet the French. The mariners trusted him and assembled at Sandwich. There they made all the preparations necessary for abasing the pride of the French.

The Marshal hurried to reach the shore with his men, for he had a strong desire to measure swords with the French, but he was not allowed to embark. People remonstrated with him, saying that he ought to remain on land, for, if by chance he was killed or captured, who then would defend the country?

The Marshal so exerted himself that he soon had 22 ships armed. He had promised the sailors to make good their possible losses with the ships they would capture. The mariners bound themselves to him by oath but they complained of the wrongs they had been made to suffer by king John, who had treated them like serfs. When they saw the large French fleet approaching they went to meet it as they had undertaken to do. But, having no leader they panicked, in utter bewilderment, abandoning their ships, with the sails still set, and taking refuge in their boats. The Marshal, nonetheless, succeeded by his encouragement in restoring their confidence, showing them that they were accompanied by good knights and serjeants and that he himself would readily have hazarded himself with them if his men had allowed him to do so. For if this fleet managed to land, it would be the end of England.

On the feast of St Bartholomew [24 August] the Marshal made his way to Sandwich at the head of a large army. He had the knights of his son, of Richard the son of king John, of the earl Warenne, of Philip de Aubeney and of a number of brave young men. They spent the night near Canterbury and, at an early hour, set out for Sandwich. The weather was clear, and one could see far out to sea. They saw the enemy fleet advancing, in close line as for a set battle. Ahead sailed the ship of Eustace the Monk, who was in command. But, that day, he died without confession. There were a good 300 ships in the fleet.

The Marshal lost no time. He embarked his men, and would himself have put to sea had he not been prevented. The justiciar of England, Hubert, embarked in a fine well-armed ship; Richard the son of king John did likewise. The previous evening the Marshal's serjeants had taken up their stations. The rest manned the ships as best they could. The Marshal kept with them, encouraging them to do well. "My lords, you ought to remember that God has granted us on land a first victory over the French. And now here they are returning to England to take the kingdom from us. But God can help the good at sea as well as upon land and this time too he will help his own. You have the advantage: you will prevail over the enemies of God."

They sailed straight for the rising tide. The French saw them come out of the harbour but despised them. They clewed up their sails saying, "It's only foot; there's not a knight amongst them. They are ours. A happy chance has sent them to us: they won't be able to resist us. They'll pay our expenses. We'll take them with us to London or else they'll fish for flounders in the sea." They spoke thus, remembering the mischance our men had recently suffered in similar circumstances. Besides, they saw that our men had few ships. Sir Hubert de Burgh's ship advanced ahead of the others as if to attack. But she passed by under full sail without giving battle. The French ribalds, full of bravado, yelled out, "*La hart! la hart!*". But finally they were cornered and drowned.

The great ship of Bayonne, which the king's treasure was in, was ahead of the others. It was in this ship that the great men named above were. There was also the châtelain of St Omer, and the count of Blois. Sir Richard, the son of king John, steered towards this ship to attack it. But he had little effect till he was rejoined by the cog carrying the serjeants. The "castle", being lightly loaded, was high above the water, whereas the Monk's ship was so low that the water was almost coming in. It was carrying the trebuchet and the valuable horses sent to Louis. Those who were in the cog had great pots full of lime that they threw down into the Monk's ship to blind those who manned her.

Renaut Paien of Guernsey, a valiant serjeant, leapt from the cog into the ship. In his fall he knocked over Guillaume des Barres and Robert de Courtenay and sent Raoul de la Tournelle spinning. He attacked this last so energetically that he ended by taking him prisoner. After Renaut, Thébaut and the others leapt in their turn. All on board the ship were captured. Eustace, to save his life, offered 10,000 marks, but in vain. He met his master. There was one Stephen of Winchelsea who reminded him of the miseries he had inflicted on him on land and at sea and gave him the choice of having his head cut off either on the trebuchet or on the side of the ship. Then they cut off his head. In the ship were 32 knights who would have suffered the same fate, had the English knights not prevented it. And they had a hard job to do so.

When this great ship had been captured, our men fought with such courage that the French retreated. Our fleet kept in close pursuit and routed them. When they captured a ship, they did not fail to kill all they found on board and threw them to the fishes, leaving only one or two, and occasionally three alive. They pursued the French in this way nearly to Calais. There was one who thought to draw to himself with a boathook a fine coverlet of scarlet, when it was only congealed blood. According to witnesses of the affair, we can say that a good four thousand men were killed, without counting those who leapt into the sea and were drowned. I was not there, and I take no responsibility for the figures. The world despises those who digress from their subject to record the false or the trivial.

After the battle, our men came back to land, bringing with them their spoil, which was very considerable. Sir Hubert had captured two ships. Some ships had won such spoils that the sailors were handing out money in bowlfuls. The Marshal ordered distribution to be made in a way that would satisfy all the sailors. Then he decided that with the part put aside they would found a hospital in honour of St Bartholomew, who on this day had given them victory. The sailors did what he ordered and founded the celebrated house where God's poor are lodged and entertained.

One ought to have seen, the next day, the sailors coming and going dressed in scarlet and silk, and outdoing one another in boasting: "My robe is worth two of it," said one. "Bah!" replied another, "mine is all cisemus fur, cote and surcoat, mantle and cape. There isn't a better between here and Aleppo." "And mine," said a third, "is all ermine edged with gold." And as they provoked each other in this wise, the others dragged provisions out of the ships, meat, wine, corn, and iron and steel utensils from which the whole country benefited.

When the Marshal had completed the division of the wealth found in the captured ships, the French prisoners were taken to Dover – 32 knights, all men of importance. They were entrusted to the justiciar.

Louis soon heard in London of the defeat of those who had come to his aid, and was greatly distressed. The same news soon spread through France. King Philip, fearing that his son had been captured or betrayed, assembled his counsellors and said to them, "My lords, did I not say that if the Marshal came into this, Louis and his enterprise would be ruined? Now, what do you advise me to do?" The opinion of the council was to order Louis to return at all costs. The order was sent to Louis secretly. He received it and appeared to take no notice of it.

The Marshal and his men, and the earl Warenne too, left Dover. Shortly after, Louis resolved, after taking counsel with his men, to seek an interview with the Marshal. The latter discussed the matter with the king's supporters. Certain amongst them, who had kept far from the sea at the critical moment, spoke loftily: "We have only to pretend to treat with Louis," said they, "let us go and besiege London." The sensible men who were present spoke more moderately, and counselled the Marshal to do all he could to rid the land of the French; and not to spare money in the process, for they would help him to their utmost. The Marshal followed this advice and consented to the interview Louis had asked for. All this was not done in a day; there were several meetings and agreement was not reached without difficulty. The French so acted that their English supporters were not allowed to take any part in the negotiations. Eventually it was decided that Louis should leave the country, that he would receive, in compensation, a great sum of money and that, above all, he would be absolved. They met, to conclude the agreement, on an island near Kingston, but the legate would not consent to grant Louis absolution except on condition that he should present himself barefooted, in woollen garments and without shirt. The French eventually got this concession: that he should present himself with his mantle over his woollen garments. When absolution was pronounced a day was fixed to conduct Louis to Dover. It had been agreed that the English who had sided with him should get back their lands except those who had sold or given them away for their ransom.

When Louis had gone, the Marshal took care to place keepers in the royal castles; but I have forgotten to tell you that when the truce was agreed, Louis had ordered his men, French, Scottish, Welsh and English, to respect it. All did in fact respect it, except Morgan of Caerleon, who made war against the Marshal, so that Llywelyn ordered him through William de Coleville to take steps to observe the peace. But Morgan did no such thing. He replied that as long as the Marshal held a foot of his land, he would not cease to fight him. He said this and did not go back on it, for it was during Louis's truce that sir Roland Bloet was killed, as well as Walter . . . and Robert de Colombiers and 7 other men of gentle birth. Morgan did not cease to harry the English after Louis's departure. But the following year, after Michaelmas, he suffered a considerable check, for the bailiff of the Marshal, sending for his men and his friends, besieged Caerleon and took it. The war went on for a long time after this and the countryside suffered from it. To end it, a "parliament" was convened at Worcester. The archbishops and bishops were summoned to it. The legate Gualo came, and so did Llywelyn of Wales, and a number of earls and barons whose names I do not know. In this council, Llywelyn asked the king, with the backing of the earl of Chester and the bishop of Winchester, to restore to Morgan, his cousin, the lands that the Marshal had taken from him by force and would not restore to him, in spite of the terms of the peace that everyone ought to get back the possessions he had before the war.

The Marshal took counsel with his men, quite prepared to give back the land if that were their advice. But, on the contrary, they showed him that he was entitled to keep it. The Marshal entrusted the defence of his cause to one of his friends who was an accomplished speaker. This man came to the king and spoke to him thus: "Hear, beloved king, what my lord wishes to say to you. My lord points out to you that Morgan's claim is ill-founded. When Louis ordered his supporters to observe the truce, Morgan refused to do so. He did not wish to be a party to it. The Marshal can prove that it was during this truce that Morgan killed several of his knights. He burnt down 22 churches, ravaged the land, so much so that he has for this deed incurred excommunication. There is no need to prove anything else."

The assembly decided in favour of the Marshal; the land and castle of Caerleon remained in his possession with all dependencies. Then the "parliament" broke up.

I do not want to try to relate all that was done in this "parliament" – it is not my subject – but I will tell you its date. It was held one year after the departure of Louis at Michaelmas. At Candlemas, the Marshal was attacked by the illness of which he died. He made his way on horseback, in spite of his illness, to the Tower of London. Doctors came from various parts of the country to visit him but they did not help him much. He remained bedridden until Lent, with the countess by his side. When he realised he was getting worse, he summoned his son and his men and spoke to them as he knew how to. He comforted them to the best of his ability, and, on advice, he made his will in good time. He called his son and Henry Fitz Gerold to his side and ordered them to have him carried without delay to Caversham to his manor there. He did not wish to stay any longer in an unhealthy town. It seemed to him that in his own house he would bear his illness better; and when the time came for him to die, he would prefer to die at home rather than elsewhere. Boats were prepared and he was comfortably settled in one of them. The countess took her place in another. They sailed slowly to Caversham. It was at this time that the legate Gualo was on his way to the Alps. He was replaced by Pandulf.

Then a council was held, which, because of the Marshal's illness, took place at Reading. The king, the legate, the justiciar were there and many other barons.

When they were all assembled the earl begged the king, the legate and the earls to come to him, for he wished to speak with them. They hastened to go at his call. After exchanging greetings they sat down around him. He addressed the king and said, "Dear gracious lord, when death struck your father, the legate Gualo made his way to Gloucester with the leading barons who stood by you, and there by the will of God, you were crowned. You were entrusted to my keeping. I have served you loyally, defending your land which, at that time, was difficult to defend. I would still serve you, were it God's will for me to be strong enough for it. But it no longer pleases him that I should remain in this world, as you all see. That is why it is right that your barons should choose someone to guard you, you and the kingdom, to the satisfaction of God and the world. May God grant you a master who will do you credit."

The bishop of Winchester stood up and said, "Listen! the kingdom was entrusted to you, Marshal, I grant: but it was to me that the king was given." "Never," replied the Marshal. "Lord bishop, these are unbecoming words, and such as you ought not to utter. You were a witness of what happened. It was not so long ago that you begged me, with tears in your eyes, you and the good earl of Chester, to take guardianship of the king and the kingdom at the same time. You forget this, it seems. The legate exerted his influence and pressed me so much that, to please you all, I accepted the king and the kingdom. It is true only that after receiving the king I gave him to you to keep because he was too young to travel."

Then the Marshal, who was in great pain, spoke to the legate and said, "Leave me; take the king with you and tomorrow, if you will, come back here. I will deliberate with my son and my men. I shall try to make the best choice, and may God guide me."

They took their leave and went off, taking the king with them. The next morning he summoned his son, the countess, sir John Marshal and those of his men whom he most trusted, and said to them, "My lords, I have thought over what we said yesterday about the choice of a guardian for the king. There is no country where the people are so divided in their opinions as in England. If I entrusted the king to some, the others would be jealous. That is why I have decided, if you agree, to entrust him to God and the pope, and particularly to the legate as their deputy. No one could reasonably blame me for this choice, for if, in the state we are in, the land is not protected by the pope I do not know who will protect it." All agreed with him.

At this moment the king entered, accompanied by the legate and other great men, all strung up with anxiety. The Marshal raised himself, and leaning on his elbow took the king by the hand and, in front of all, said to the legate, "Sir, I have reflected long on what we talked about yesterday. I wish here, in the presence of all, to entrust the king to God, to the pope and to you who represent him." Then, turning to the king, "Sir, I pray God, if ever I have done anything that has pleased him, to grant you grace to be a good man. And if it so happen that you must follow the example of any criminal ancestor, I pray God not to grant you a long life." "Amen," replied the king. Those present rose and took their leave.

The earl said to John Marshal: "Tell my son from me to go and hand over the king to the legate in the presence of the barons." He did not want anyone to be able to say that this act had been done by private agreement. The son went to take the king by the hand and presented him in front of all to the legate. The bishop of Winchester immediately stepped forward and took the king by the head. But the young Marshal said to him, "My lord bishop, leave off. Your efforts will be in vain.

I shall do as my father has commanded me." The legate became angry with the bishop and received the child as he had already done once. Then he [the young Marshal] went back to his father and mother, and related to them the presumptuous action of the bishop.

The next day, it was the Marshal's pleasure to summon his people to him. He said to the countess . . . "Lord, thanks be to God, whether I am about to live or to die, I can boast that I am now relieved of a heavy burden. It would be well for me to finish my will and care for my soul, for my body is in a parlous state. This is the moment for me to unburden myself of all earthly things and to think of the things of heaven." Then he turned his attention to his children and divided his lands among them as he intended. He said, "My lords, one of my sons, Anselm, has nothing from this division and yet he is truly dear to me. If he lives long enough to be dubbed knight, though he has no land, he will find, provided he deserves it, people to love him and to honour him greatly above other men. God grant him prowess and wisdom." "Ah, my lord," said John de Erley, "you must not do that. Give him at least money enough to pay for the shoeing of his horses." The Marshal without more ado, gave him 140 pounds worth of land for his support. Then he said, "Now I feel free. I am anxious only for my daughter Jeanne. If while I was alive I had married her well, my soul would be more at ease. I wish her to have 30 pounds worth of land and 200 marks in cash to help her to live until God takes care of her."

When he had distributed his belongings he said to John de Erley: "Go to your bailiwick. I am anxious about my men who are at Nether Gwent and also about your son who, with bad advice, could well risk his life in an expedition in which our men would suffer. Go without delay, my strength is failing. On your return, you will bring me two silken sheets that I have left with Stephen [d'Evreux]. But above all be quick back." John de Erley fulfilled his mission faithfully, travelling many hours a day. When he returned, the earl, whose illness was worse, asked him for news of his people. "They are well, God be praised," he replied, "and here are the silken sheets that I was to bring you." The earl took them and said to Henry Fitz Gerold, "Henry, look at these cloths." "Yes, sire, but they look a bit worn, if I see well." "Unfold them," replied the count, "we'll take a better look." And when the cloths were unfolded they looked very fine. The Marshal having summoned his son and his knights to his side, said to them, "My lords behold. I have had these cloths for 30 years. I brought them with me when I came back from crusade to serve the purpose for which I intend them, that is to say to be spread over me when I am laid in the ground." "Sir," said his son, "we do not know where you wish to rest." "My good son, I will tell you. When I was away on crusade, I then gave my body to the Temple for burial. Know that I shall give them Upleadon, my rich manor. I wish it so and I shall be buried in the Temple, for that was my vow."

He then said to John de Erley, "Take these cloths. When I am dead put them over me; you will cover the bier on which I am carried with them. If it snows or the weather is bad, you will buy grey burel, which you will put over the cloths to protect them from the weather; and when I am buried you will give the cloths to the brothers of the house to do with them what they please."

When he had thus spoken his son began to weep, tenderly. All the knights who were there wept too and the varlets and the serjeants and all his household. His son went out and having called the knights told them that they must watch over his father so that there should always be three knights by him. He himself would watch at night with John de Erley and Thomas Basset, the others would watch by day, three at a time in rotation. So long as the earl lived, his son did not fail a single night to watch over him.

The next day, the earl summoned his men and his almoner, brother Geoffrey, a Templar, and had his letters done. Then he summoned brother Aimery de St Maur, who was master of the Temple and a wise man, deeply religious. He then sent his will sealed with his seal and those of his wife and son to the archbishop, to the legate, who was then regent, and to the bishops of Winchester and Salisbury, asking them to be his executors and to affix their seals to his will. They did so gladly and excommunicated all those who wished to dispute it. Then they sent it back to him, wishing him to see it before he died.

Meanwhile brother Aimery de St Maur presented himself. The Marshal called back his wife and his men. "It is long," he said, "since I gave myself to the Temple. Now I am going there." Then he told his almoner Geoffrey to go and get his cloak from his wardrobe. He had had this cloak made a year before, but no one knew anything of it. The earl then said to the countess, "Fair one, you will kiss me, but it will be for the last time." She stepped forward and kissed him. Both wept, as did the brave men who were present. The earl at once had the cloak laid out in front of him. It was necessary to remove the countess and her daughters who were distraught and inconsolable.

Brother Aimery said, "Marshal, I am glad that you are returning to God. He has granted you in this world a great favour; that you should never alienate yourself from Him or from His company. He shows you this in life and in death. In the world, you have been honoured – no knight more – for courage, judgment and loyalty. When God has thus graced you, you can be sure that He will receive you at the last. You leave this world honourably. You were noble, and nobly you leave it. I shall go to London to do what you wish to have done."

Brother Aimery set off. As soon as he reached London he was taken ill and died. But in dying he asked to be buried before the minster cross, "beside the good knight, brother William Marshal, who acquired so great a name on earth for his prowess and who now wishes to acquire it in heaven. I have rejoiced greatly in his company in this world and I wish to lie beside him. May God grant us his company in the life above."

When he was dead the news was taken to Caversham, where it caused great grief. They kept it from the Marshal for fear of aggravating his condition. The knights of his entourage said, "It is indeed proof that God loves the earl: brother Aimery has gone to take his place in heaven near that which is reserved for the earl, just as he wished to rest on earth beside him."

What more shall I say? The earl's illness got worse, until he could no longer eat or drink. He grew steadily weaker, for nature was failing in him. He could no longer eat anything except mushrooms. His attendant moistened the bread so that he would eat it without being conscious of doing so. He remained in this state for 15 days before he died. One day as he lay on his bed, supported by Henry Fitz Gerold, with his knights about him, all greatly grieved by the pain they saw him suffering, sir Henry said to him, "Sire, you must think of your salvation. Death respects no one and clerks teach us that no one will be saved if he does not restore what he has taken." The Marshal replied to him, "Henry, listen to me. The clerks are too hard upon us. They shave us too close. I have taken 500 knights, whose arms, horses and equipment were forfeit to me. If for that I am denied the kingdom of God, there is nothing to be done, for I could not give them back. I can do no more for God than give myself up to him, repenting all my faults. Unless the clerks desire my utter damnation, they ought to refrain from hounding me further. Either their argument is false, or no one can be saved." "Sire," said John de Erley, "it is the truth. And I assure you, you have hardly a neighbour who in his last days could say as much."

The next day his daughters came to see him. They were very taken aback to see him so ill. They did not all come together each day, but that day came my lady Mahaut [Matilda], wife of le Bigod, the countess of Gloucester, lady Eve and lady Sibyl, all displaying great grief, and Jeanne, who more than once swooned – and that was very natural for she was still without a counsellor, but he to whom her father left her knew well how to counsel her.

The son of the Marshal was seated by his father. There also was a large company of knights. The Marshal called John de Erley and said to him, "I'm going to tell you something quite extraordinary." "Tell me, sir, provided it doesn't tire you." "I don't know why, but it is quite three years or more since I had such a desire to sing as I have had these last 3 days." "Sing, my lord, if you can," replied John. "Nature would pick up again in you and that would be a good thing, for your appetite would come back." "Be quiet," said the earl, "that would do me no good. People would take me for a madman." He did not want to sing and he could not. Henry Fitz Gerold advised him to summon his daughters. "They will sing you something, and that will comfort you." They were sent for and they came. "Sing first, Mahaut," said the earl. She did not want to, yet she did it to please her father, and sang a verse of a song in a sweet, simple voice. "Jeanne, it is your turn to sing." She sang a verse of a chorus, but did so timidly. "Don't look ashamed when you sing," the earl admonished. "You will never sing well that way." And he began to show her how to do it. When they had sung, he said to them, "My daughters, trust in Jesus Christ. I pray him to keep watch over you." When they had left, returning to their mother, he sent for his son and gave him instructions for the funeral, telling him to remain close to him when the cortege entered London and to distribute money generously to the poor. He enjoined him also to give food, clothes and shoes on that day to a hundred poor people.

When all that had been arranged, the abbot of Nutley appeared, on his way back from his chapter. He was welcome. He was a black canon of the order of Arrouaise. He observed the rule of his order strictly, holy man that he was, and took good care of his abbey. He came to the earl and having greeted him, said, "My lord, I have talked with our sovereign abbot and the brethren of our order. I told them in chapter of your illness, and asked them to let you share in the benefit of their prayers and to pray for you as long as the order shall last. The abbot told me he knew you to be a good man and one of great worth, and that he would willingly admit you as a participant in all the benefits of the order. Here are letters sealed with the abbot's seal testifying to this decision." "A thousand times thanks," replied the earl. "You have granted me a great boon, and you will be repaid for it, for, if you have thought of me, I have not forgotten you either. I have left 50 marks to your house. I have made a similar gift to each of the abbeys on my land overseas, and to each chapter I have left 10 marks; for I wish to have a share of their merit for ever." The abbot replied, with tears in his eyes, "My lord, you have given generously and God, I am certain, will return it with interest in the glory of paradise."

The next day his son and many of his household were beside him. John de Erley asked him what he wished to be done with the fur robes that were kept in the house. The earl did not hear clearly what John de Erley said. But the clerk Philip said in a loud voice, "Sire, there is there a number of fine robes of scarlet and ermine, quite new, and at least 80 cisemus furs. One could raise a lot of money with them to buy absolution for you." "Quiet, you wicked man," said the earl, "I have had more than enough of your advice; I wish to hear no more. It will soon be Pentecost; my knights have a right to their robes; it will be the last time I shall give them them, and here you're trying to cajole me." Then he said, "Come here, John de Erley. I command you to see to the distribution of the robes; and if there is not enough of them for everyone, have some got from London, for I do not want anyone to have cause of complaint because of me." Then he said to his son, "My good son, I beg you to take leave for me of all those who are not here and who have served me well. May they have God's thanks and mine."

The robes were distributed in such a way that each of the knights of his following had one. As for the clothes that were left over, they were given to the poor. Everyone spent the night there. The son of the Marshal and those who were with him did not go to bed. The next day they were replaced by others at the Marshal's side, but they hardly slept, so anxious and wretched were they.

The day I am talking about was the Monday before Ascension. The son knelt before his father and said, "Sire, for the love of Jesus Christ, eat something, it will do you good." "Well," he replied, "I will eat as much as I can." He sat up and a knight supported him. When the cloth was spread before him, he said to John de Erley, "Listen to me. Do you see what I see?" "Sire, I don't know." "By my head! I see two men in white, one on my right, the other on my left. Never have I seen men so beautiful anywhere." "My lord, these are the companions God has sent you to lead you on the right road." And the earl said: "Blessed be God, our Lord, who to the very last has granted me his grace!" Sir John did not ask the Marshal who the men were, for he thought to have plenty of time to do so later. But afterwards he regretted always not having asked.

All the evening, the illness continued to get worse. The young Marshal watched all night. The next day, the Tuesday before Ascension, he returned about midday with the knights. The earl had turned towards the wall and was resting peacefully.

Thinking that he slept, the young Marshal commanded silence. I do not know if the earl heard him, but he awoke and said, "Who is there?" John de Erley said, "It is I, John de Erley." "Is it you, John?" "Yes my lord." "I cannot get to sleep." "How could you get to sleep when you haven't eaten for more than 15 days?" The earl moved as though to turn, and at that moment the pangs of death seized him. He said, "John, open the doors and windows quickly; call the countess and the knights, for I am dying; I cannot tarry and I wish to take leave of them." John rose, did as he was asked and took the earl, who was fainting, in his arms. When he came round, the Marshal said, "John, did I faint?" "Yes my lord." "I have never seen you so upset. Why did you not take some of this rose water and bathe my face with it, so that I would have time to talk to these good men, for I shall not do so for long?" John quickly took the rose water, which was in a phial, and bathed his face for he was going pale with the anguish of death.

The young Marshal and the countess went closer, with all the knights, and the earl said to them, "I am dying, I commend you to God. I can no longer be with you, and cannot ward off death." His son came to sit beside John de Erley; he took his father in his arms and wept silently. A cross was placed before the Marshal; he adored it and prayed God to grant him a good end. The abbot of Nutley came in with a group of religious. But the earl, leaning against his son, said no more. While all gave way to grief, a serving man ran up to John de Erley, and touching his arm, told him that the abbot of Reading requested permission to enter. John did not hear him for his mind was far away, and he pushed the young man aside. But the earl had heard, he opened his eyes and signed to John to have the abbot brought in. "My lord," said the abbot, when he was introduced, "the legate, who was last night at Cirencester, greets you. He tells you through me that in the night he had a vision about you. He was so distressed by it that he told me to make haste here to tell you of it. The legate tells you that God has granted to St Peter and to all the popes after him the power to bind and loose all sinners. In virtue of this power, which has been delegated to him by the pope, he absolves you of all the sins you have committed since your birth and which you have confessed." The earl turned towards him, put his hands together and bowed his head.

From the outset of his illness the earl had confessed every week. The abbot of Reading, assisted by him of Nutley and other religious, pronounced absolution. When he was absolved, the Marshal joined his hands and adored the cross. Then God did with him according to his will as he does with all good men whom it pleases him to recall to himself. Let us pray God that he place him in the glory of paradise with his friends.

So died the Marshal. We believe that his soul is in the company of God, for he was good in life and in death. His body was interred with honour, as was fitting for such a man. Then before his body was carried out of the enclosure [the abbot of Reading] said mass in the rich chapel founded by the Marshal. During the mass, it was noticed that the countess could no longer hold herself upright, so worn out was she with grief and watching. She and her sons gave Reading abbey 100 shillings in rents to participate in the benefits of the house. This donation was given when the body was set down in the abbey. From there it was carried to Staines. There the cortege was joined by the earl Warenne and by earl William of Essex, famous for his liberality. The earl Robert de Ver came too, with the earl of Gloucester and many great barons, bishops and abbots, who all showed great grief when they saw the Marshal dead. At London was the archbishop with a bishop and many clergy. By order of the archbishop, vigil was kept over the body with great pomp with singing and rich lighting. The next day the body was buried, before the cross, beside brother Aimery de St Maur, as the earl had ordered.

When the masses were sung, the archbishop, assisted by the bishop and numerous religious, archdeacons and canons, performed the burial service in such a noble manner that all were satisfied with it and thanked God for the honours he had granted the Marshal in the course of his long life and in his death. Before the tomb the archbishop began to speak and said: "Behold what earthly life is worth. When one is dead one is no more than a bit of earth. You see what remains of the best knight that ever lived. There is what you will all come to. Each man dies when his day is come. We have here our mirror, you and I alike. Let everyone say his paternoster that God may admit to his glory this Christian and place him in the company of the faithful, as we believe he has deserved."

When the body had been laid in the ground, those who had been charged with the distribution of the alms took care that it was done equitably. It took place at Westminster, for in London there would not have been room enough, so numerous were the poor. All had a share in the distribution and it happened that when all were satisfied there was neither money nor bread left over. As for the robes, after the 100 poor people had each received theirs, 3 were left over.

The news of the Marshal's death spread quickly. It soon reached the king of France, who was then in Gâtinais with his court. The king said to the messenger: "Wait a while, before speaking, that Richard Marshal may have his meal with the others, for he will be greatly distressed."

When the cloths were removed, those who had served sat down to eat. Meanwhile king Philip took aside Guillaume des Barres, who was sitting near him, and said to him: "Did you hear what he said to me?" "What did he say, sire?" "That the Marshal who was so upright and so loyal, was buried." "Which Marshal?" "Him of England, Guillaume, who was worthy and wise." "Indeed, sire, it is a great pity, for, in our time there was not a better knight or a more valiant man in war." "What do you say?" "I say that never in my life have I seen a better man than that one. I cannot say more." "Indeed," replied the king, "that is great praise. And, in truth, the Marshal was the most loyal man I have ever known." Sir Jean de Rouvrai said in turn: "Sire, I say this was the wisest knight who lived in our time." "God! what a happy star is he born under of whom such witness is borne after his death! What encouragement for all upright men who hear of his life."

Here ends the history of the earl Marshal, which, wherever it is heard, ought to be listened to with love and with joy. It is fitting now to mention all those who have had a hand in this book, that it may be known, when you hear it read, who it was who furnished the material, who caused it to be written, who paid for it. First shall be named the good son of the Marshal, the earl William, renowned for his fine deeds. From a good tree comes good fruit. When he was advised to have the history of his father written, he did not rest until it was done. One sees this clearly now and will see it more clearly still. He who provided the material until the work was done (God be praised!) showed clearly that he loved his lord. It was John de Erley who put his heart, thought and money into it, and now you see the result. True love proves itself in all good deeds; indeed, this is not a lie, for John who commissioned and composed this book, has given ample proof of it. And may God who rewards all good men for their good deeds, grant the joys of paradise to those who have had a hand in this work!

When the children of the Marshal, the brothers and sisters, hear that the good Marshal, their brother William, has had executed in honour of their father, a work such as this, they will be touched to the bottom of their hearts. And may God grant them the joy of it! I know well that they will find pleasure in this book when they hear it read and see all the good that is said of their father.

Here ends the history of the earl. May God vouchsafe his soul a place in eternal glory among his angels!

4. The "Greater Chronicle" (Chronica Majora) of Matthew Paris of St Albans for the years 1258–9

(*Matthew Paris's English History*, trans. J. A. Giles, 3 vols (1852–4), III, pp. 256 ff, thoroughly revised in the light of H. R. Luard's edition (Rolls ser., 1872–3), V, pp. 661–748; the entries s.a. 1258 and 1259 are given in full)

How the king of England kept Christmas at London

In the year 1258 which was the forty-second year of the reign of king Henry the third, the said king spent Christmas at London, where, awaiting the arrival of the messengers he had sent to France, he celebrated that festival with great solemnity and splendour in company with many of the nobles. The said king was also present at the feast in honour of St Edward, in which solemnly . . .[1]

Of the arrival of the bishop of Ely and the abbot of St Edmunds

Also during this time, the bishop of Ely and the abbot of Bury St Edmunds arrived in England on their return from the court of Rome, where they had succeeded in obtaining from the pope a decree confirming them in their respective positions, despite the opposition and ill-will of the king and the archbishop of Canterbury. Thus daily did the king, on the worst of counsel, destroy his kingly dignity, and endeavour to injure the church in manifold ways.

Of the disturbances at Rome

At this time, and for some little time previously, serious disturbances were occurring in the city of Rome, in consequence of the proceedings of the senator M., a citizen of Brescia, who, deviating from the paths of justice, impoverished and oppressed the people of Rome in many ways, at the instigation of the nobles, and made it his only

[1] The rest of the sentence is erased.

business to please the said nobles, especially the Annibaldi. The people, then, by the advice of one Matthew of Belvoir, an Englishman and fellow-citizen of theirs, head of the bakers in the city, assembled together in crowds, and making a violent attack on the prison where their former senator, Brancaleone, was imprisoned, succeeded in breaking it open and releasing him: this done, they appointed him senator, and, according to the former custom of the city, swore fealty to him. Thus supported, Brancaleone drove his enemies from the city, and laying aside all reverence for the pope, caused two of the Annibaldi, who were relations of one of the cardinals, to be hanged on the gallows. And when the pope wished to excommunicate Brancaleone and his partisans, they declared that they had a privilege which prevented any pope from excommunicating them; therefore, they not only ridiculed him, but threatened to injure and persecute the pope and his cardinals to the death. This excited the fears of the pope for his own safety, and he said to his brethren, "When fury is in its course, yield to its torrent." And in order that worse evils might not ensue, he suddenly withdrew to Viterbo, intending a further removal to Assisi.

Of the death of William Heron, sheriff of Northumberland

At this same time died William Heron, sheriff of Northumberland, a most avaricious man, a hammer of cruelty to the poor, and a persecutor of the religious orders. From worldly avarice and thirst for wealth, he passed, as is believed, to the infernal regions, to experience the thirst of Tantalus.

About the Epiphany of our Lord, the deputation of nobles from the king of England appeared before the French king, who treated them with civility and honour, and answered them with kindness on the matter which had brought them there, namely, the demand for the restoration of Normandy and other rights on the continent. But his brothers, and some other nobles, flatly refused to accede to their demands; so that the messengers returned home without accomplishing their errand.

Of the accusation made against certain citizens of London

During this time the middling sort, the populace, and the plebs of the citizens of London made a serious complaint to the king that the rich appointed to collect the money for rebuilding the walls of the city, as the king had ordered for their honour, had fraudulently kept the greatest part of this money in their own purses, to the injury of the lower order of citizens; in fact, that they had done the same in all the taxes and talliages they had collected. Of this they were accused and proved guilty: however, their lives were spared after great difficulty, on the intercession of John Mansell; but they were obliged to pay a ransom for themselves.

Of the death of John of Avesnes

About the same time, died John of Avesnes, seneschal of the king of Almain, in whom reposed all the hopes of that king.

At this time, too, the Welsh, who now entirely despaired of making their peace with the king, and of obtaining mercy from him, seized on some borough towns on the confines of Wales, which belonged to Edward and to some other nobles, carried off all the stores with which they were provided, destroyed and burned all the rest, and cut off the heads of all the men found in the said towns, without mercy, and without allowing them to ransom themselves.

How the pope humbled himself to the senator Brancaleone

About the same time, like London, which was the scene of great excitement and disturbance, Rome was agitated by a serious schism amongst the citizens; for when the Roman nobles complained to the pope, and tried to get him to excommunicate the Roman people and Brancaleone their senator and all his partisans, the latter only laughed at them, and treated their threats with contempt, and thus, not only did they pay but little heed to the power to be enforced against them, but even vilified and treated it with contempt. The senator Brancaleone, thus lately elevated to that dignity and beloved by all the people, now boldly exerted his authority to punish all the malefactors of the city, and especially revenged himself on those who had brought about his imprisonment and consigned them to the gibbet; neither did he spare the friends or relations of the pope, nor was he corrupted by the entreaties, threats, or bribes of any. What was more, he issued a general edict, ordering all the people of the city, under penalty of disinheritance and perpetual exile, to provide themselves with arms, and to sally forth as one man on an expedition against Anagni, the pope's birthplace. The people of that place, on hearing of this order, especially the pope's relatives and friends, went to the pope, and gave vent to their grief, saying: "Your holiness, at least have pity on your friends and relations, and on the whole city of Anagni, which is your birthplace; for an edict has been issued by the senator Brancaleone and the Roman people for all to take arms and lay siege to our city. In their anger they will come as one man, will destroy the city, demolish the castles, raze the houses to the ground, seize on the property of the besieged, and slay them all without mercy." On hearing this address, the pope, although enraged, and though he hated the senator Brancaleone, willy nilly sent special messengers and asked him repeatedly and most humbly to curb his anger and spare Anagni, the city of his birth, lest he should become a lasting object of reproach to all mankind. The senator therefore took compassion, and acceded to the entreaties of the humbled pope, although he had great difficulty in restraining the people from destroying like wild animals all obstacles they met with. This matter gave the greatest joy to Manfred, who hated the pope, and had a heartfelt affection for the senator; for he was delighted at seeing him, who a little before was throwing out threats of thundering forth sentence of excommunication, now so humbled, that he was compelled to ask for peace. Prince Manfred, therefore, promised the senator Brancaleone that he would assist him in all things necessary. And thus was [his] friend Henry, king of the English, whom he was accustomed to give powerful support, forsaken; and all that incalculable sum of money, which he had laid out and sent thither for the sake of acquiring possession of the kingdom of Apulia, was insufficient to pay off the interest, which, silently creeping on, had enshackled the unwary and imprudent king. Moreover, the pope accused him of having deceived and tricked the church; and he fell into very ill repute with all nations in consequence.

Of the pope's anger against the king of England

During this time, the pope's anger blazed against the king of England, because, not keeping promises repeated so often, he volunteered, on pain of losing his kingdom, to amend his usual faults. At the pressing entreaties, therefore, of Lawrence bishop of Rochester, and many others, the pope, after fruitless admonitions, conceived the idea of thundering forth sentence of excommunication against the king, of laying the kingdom under an interdict, and of piling on severer and severer punishment. The king, in a confused state of mind, paid five thousand marks in cash to the pope to temper his anger and postpone this sentence for a time; and the pope yielded to his price and his prayers. Thus was England impoverished and stripped of its wealth on all sides, whilst hopes of acquiring possession of the kingdom of Apulia almost vanished into thin air, except for what little there was in the breast of the new king of Almain; and this was slight, for he had not yet attained to the imperial dignity.

Of the return of Rustand to England

At this time, too, mr Rustand, a clerk of the pope's, came to England; for what reason it was unknown, unless it was to visit and collect his revenues, for he had an abundance of wealth in England, acquired in a short time. On that account, when he had last gone to Rome he incurred strong indignation; but by the application of the usual remedy for that complaint, he escaped the threatened punishment.

Of the consecration of three bishops at Canterbury

On the Sunday of the Passion of our Lord Jesus Christ, three bishops were consecrated at Canterbury – namely, mr Simon of Walton, to the diocese of Norwich; mr Roger of Meuland, to that of Chester; and to that of Exeter mr Walter of Exeter (who was elected, confirmed, and consecrated within a fortnight) – with due solemnity by Boniface, archbishop of Canterbury.

Of the arrangement made as to provisions between the abbot and brethren of St Albans

In this same, year, too, as the convent of St Albans had frequently made strong complaint to their abbot, John the second, not without good reason, that they were not suitably and adequately provided with bread and beer for their own use, and for distribution amongst their guests, religious and secular, as the monastery was founded to provide sufficient support for them in the aforesaid things, the said abbot devoted his attention to provide a proper remedy for this want. The following arrangement was, in consequence, made between the abbot and convent; to wit, that the convent should from that time forth receive a certain and fixed allowance of bread and beer, sufficient to provide proper and decent refreshment for themselves and for guests, as is fully set forth in the said arrangement, sealed with the seals of both parties and confirmed by the king. In return for this arrangement and the kindness done to them, the convent, by way of thanks, discharged, by themselves and by means of the priors of the cells dependent on St Albans, certain debts to the amount of . . .[1] marks, due from the aforesaid abbot to certain merchants on the continent. But there still re-

[1] The number of marks is wanting in the text.

mained to be discharged some heavy debts owing by the said abbot. And in order that the particulars of this liberal and gratuitous act of kindness may be known to all who wish it, we have thought proper to insert in this book the king's charter in confirmation of the above arrangement.

The charter in confirmation of the foregoing

Henry, by the grace of God, king of England, lord of Ireland, duke of Normandy and Aquitaine, and count of Anjou; to the archbishops, bishops, abbots, priors, earls, barons, justices, sheriffs, reeves, ministers, bailiffs, and all his bailiffs and faithful, greeting. We have inspected a provision and arrangement made between John of Hertford, abbot of St Albans, and his conventual brethren of the same place, as follows:

John of Hertford, by the grace of God, abbot of St Albans, to all Christ's faithful, greeting in the Lord. It is fitting for us to afford a willing consent to the just requests of petitioners, and to carry their wishes into full effect, so long as they do not stray from the path of reason. Therefore we have thought fit to make it known to you all that [as] both we and the abbots of St Albans our predecessors, have been accustomed in times past commonly to provide victuals, to the extent of bread and beer, for our brethren of the said monastery, as well as for unexpected guests, from the proceeds of our barony, as well as from our churches in which we have pontifical rights, and from the other churches in which we have not pontifical rights, and also from our farms and from revenues pertaining to the said monastery, we, instigated by a twofold motive of charity and wishing to better and make more honourable the condition of the said convent as regards the said provisions so that the brethren may henceforth remain in peace and tranquillity in future, and also wishing to release the abbots our successors from supplying the said provisions for the support of the said convent, have determined, with the fear of God before our eyes and by the common wish, advice, and connivance of our brethren, to assign the undermentioned portions to the aforesaid convent: that is to say, the churches of Hartburn and Eglingham in the diocese of Durham, and the churches of Norton and Waldon, with forty shillings which the vicar of Waldon at the time shall pay annually: also the tithes, together with the hay, which we usually receive in the parish of Watford, with ten marks from the vicar of Watford for the time being: also the church of Houghton, with six marks annually from the vicar of Potsgrove; with two marks and a half from the church of Hertburn, in the diocese of Lincoln; and with six marks annually from the vicar of Appleton, in the diocese of York: also all offerings proceeding from the two festivals of St Albans: and also the manor of Kingsbury, with all its appurtenances and with five men in the vill of Westwick, together with the manure of the court of St Albans, to improve the condition of the said manor when they shall see fit. Be it known, too, that the corn and malt of the aforesaid convent should be ground at our mills within as well as beyond the court of St Albans, as free of expense as if it were our own corn, without any charge being made on the said convent for millstones, mills, repairing mill-ponds, or on any other grounds soever. And we will find for the said convent suitable houses needed for brewing and baking, and for making malt;

as also for storing up corn, and for stabling of their horses, together with all utensils necessary for all the above matters. As regards our manors where the aforesaid tithes are placed, we will find houses suitable for storing the corn and hay and for lodging their men and horses, and all utensils necessary for cooking their food, as well as wood for fuel in sufficient quantities, both within and without the court of St Albans, and timber for repairing the aforesaid houses as often as necessary. And we and all our successors will warrant, acquit, and defend at our own expense, to the said convent and against all men, the aforesaid portions, with all their appurtenances, easements, and liberties aforesaid; and we will bear, for ever, all ordinary and extraordinary burdens in the aforesaid churches and pensions, whenever such shall occur. And for the further security of this arrangement, we have pronounced sentence of excommunication against all who, whether at the instigation of the king or of the pope or of their own free will, shall invalidate, or cause to be invalidated, the aforesaid ordinance, unless it happens that such alteration shall take place by the common consent and wish as well of the abbot as of the whole convent, for the greater good and benefit of the convent and their church. We, furthermore, of our own free will and by the common consent of our aforesaid convent, pledge ourselves both to the king (who is our patron) and his heirs for the time being and to the pope and his successors, that if we or our successors shall at any time rashly venture (which God forbid!) to contravene the aforesaid ordinance, either wholly or in part, and without the common consent of the said convent, as above stated, he the said king and his heirs may by seizure of our barony, and the pope and his successors by ecclesiastical censure, lawfully compel and effectually coerce us to a strict observance of the aforesaid ordinance by all the means they deem expedient. And in order that all the things aforesaid may have full force for ever, we have affixed our seal, as well as the seal of our convent, to this writing. Given at St Albans, in our full chapter, on the Wednesday after the feast of St Matthew the Apostle, in the year of our Lord one thousand two hundred and fifty-seven.

And whereas, by the examination we have caused to be made, we have learned that the aforesaid proviso and ordinance will tend to relieve and be to the advantage of us and our heirs during the vacancies of the said abbey, we ratify, grant, and confirm the same for ourselves and our heirs, as the aforesaid writing between us testifies. In further proof whereof, it is our will, and we, in our own name and in that of our heirs, grant authority to the prior and conventual brethren of the same place, in case of the resignation or decease of the aforesaid abbot or of his successors as abbots of the aforesaid church of St Albans, to have and to hold free and peaceable possession for ever, both in times of vacancy of the said abbey and at other times, of all the aforesaid portions for the uses above stated, and to dispose of them at their pleasure, without any hindrance on our part or on the part of our heirs, or of any of our bailiffs or of our keepers [of the said abbey for the time being]. Nor will we allow the said ordinance to be altered in any way by any of our keepers of the said abbey or our other officers. As witness, Geoffrey de Lusignan and William de Valence, our brothers; Simon de Montfort, earl of Leicester; Richard of Clare, earl of Gloucester and Hertford; Roger Bigod, earl of Northumberland and marshal of England; Peter of Savoy;

Hugh Bigod; John Mansell, treasurer of York; Philip Lovel; Henry of Bath; Robert Waleran; William de Gray; Walter of Merton, Hubert [Pogeys,] and others present. Given under our hand at Westminster, this eighth day of March, in the forty-second year of our reign.

Who it was that brought about the aforesaid arrangement

These arrangements were brought to the wished-for effect by the aforesaid abbot, through the diligence and skill of William of Horton, the chamberlain, and John of Bulum, the abbot's bailiff, who were possessed with zeal in God's service and affection towards their brethren. William of Huntingdon was appointed, in the name of the convent, master of the guests, guardian of the aforesaid possessions, and initial proctor.

Of the return of Rustand from the court of Rome

About the middle of Lent, mr Rustand returned from the court of Rome, shorn of his former power; for he had been accused before the pope by his enemies, of thirsting after money in a greedy and unbecoming way, and, laying aside the fear of God, of having clutched hold of a great many rich revenues, thus getting above himself. In acquiring these he had, in order to obtain greater favour with the king, asserted that he was a native of Bordeaux, and had promised, as being consequently a natural subject of the king, to give him unceasing and effectual assistance at the court of Rome and elsewhere, in obtaining the sovereignty of Apulia, and in arranging other business of the king's. By such promises and soft speeches he imposed on the king's simplicity, and was enriched by the gifts of many revenues; but at length, at the instance of some of his enemies, he was summoned to return to Rome. There he was severely reproached by the pope for his conduct, and had great difficulty in regaining his favour as formerly; nonetheless, he was deprived of his former dignity and power, and disgraced.

Of the arrival of Herlot, the pope's nuncio, in England

Soon afterwards, that is to say, in the week before Easter, mr Arlot [Herlotus], a notary and confidential clerk of the lord pope, came to England; who, although he was not called a legate, wanted the pomp and splendour of one. For he came to London attended by twenty mounted followers; and the persons in close attendance on him lorded it in their finery of eight [*sic*] cloaks;[1] namely, five close and five sleeved, of the finest murrey. The king, as usual, greeted him with rapture on his arrival, for he was invested with the greatest powers and authority.

Of the arrival in England of some ships laden with wheat

At this same time, too, when an unheard-of famine occurred to such a degree that many simply pined away and died and a measure of corn was sold at London for nine shillings or more, about fifty large ships, sent by Richard, king of Almain, arrived there from overseas, having been laden with wheat, barley, rye and bread.

[1] *octo capis . . . superbivit redimita*

A proclamation was then made by royal authority, forbidding any of the citizens of London to buy any of that corn for storing up, with the view of selling it at a dearer price to those wanting it, as they made a general practice of doing. Indeed, the said citizens were notorious for having, in time of want, either treacherously sent away ships laden with provisions, or for having purchased their cargoes entirely, in order to sell them at pleasure to those requiring such articles of consumption. It was stated as a positive fact, that any three counties of England united had not produced so much corn as was brought by these vessels; but, owing to the scarcity of money, although it in some slight degree mitigated the effects of the famine, which was general throughout England, it did not entirely do away with them. For the king, to the injury of his own kingdom, which was despoiled of its wealth by him, exalted and enriched all strangers who chose to come there.

Of the remarkable nature of the season

In this same year, the mildness and moderate temperature of autumn lasted to the end of January, so that the surface of the water was not frozen anywhere at any time. But from that time, that is to say, from the Purification of the Blessed Virgin till the end of March, the north wind blew without intermission, a continued frost prevailed, accompanied by snow and such unendurable cold, that it bound up the face of the earth, afflicted the poor, suspended all cultivation, and killed the young of the cattle to such an extent that it seemed as if a general plague was raging amongst the sheep and lambs.

Of the prosperous condition of Richard, king of Almain

Richard, king of Almain, subdued his enemies, and enticed and attached them to his cause with such prudence, that the citizens of the noble cities of Italy offered him the right hand of friendship. The threats of his enemies, namely the French, Spanish, the people of Treves and the neighbouring countries, were also silenced, although they had designed injury to him.

Of the arrival of Thomas of Savoy in England

In the fortnight of Easter, Thomas, formerly count of Flanders, came to London, carried on a litter, being in ill health. He had been released from prison at Turin, for which liberation merchants of Asti were made to pay a large amount. For the French king had, at the pope's request, made many of these merchants prisoners, and compelled them to ransom themselves, until the aforesaid Thomas should be at liberty to return to England, where he would receive abundant presents.

Of the heavy fine imposed on the citizens of London

The citizens of London having been accused to the king of some irregularities, were punished in manifold ways, and compelled to ransom themselves; yet had great difficulty in regaining the king's favour. The chief amongst them, Ralph Hardel, who was mayor of the city, died of grief.

Of the expiration of the truce between the English and Welsh

At this time the truce between the English and Welsh expired. The king's adherents oppressed them so ruthlessly that they could not procure salt, corn, or any other necessaries. However, trusting to the king's attention being engaged by his quarrel with the nobles of Scotland, who were raising their heads against him, and with the bishop of Durham, who when summoned to appear at the king's court, impudently refused to attend there, nay contumaciously heaped injury upon injury, the Welsh increased their ravages, and foraged at large on the Welsh borders to provide for their wants.

How the knights of England were convoked against the Welsh

About the same time, the king summoned all the knights of England by royal warrant with horses and arms, for a general invasion of Wales to crush and ravage it to its utter ruin. The knights when summoned deplored being so often troubled by loss and useless expense to no purpose.

Of the parliament held at London at that time

After the Tuesday which is commonly called Hokeday, a parliament was held at London; for the king was weighed down with anxiety over many difficult matters; amongst others, that of the matter of the kingdom of Apulia, concerning which a formal envoy, mr Arlot, had been specially sent to get a definite and precise answer. The king, moreover, demanded an immense sum of money, for the payment of which the pope had bound himself to certain merchants on behalf of and at the urgent request of the king, who was entangled in heavy penalties, such as I think it dishonourable to mention. The amount required was so large a sum that it would alike astonish and horrify those who heard it; and the nobility of the kingdom grieved at being reduced to such ruin by the supine simplicity of one man. The king was moreover greatly vexed by the Welsh who boasted that they had so often injured and repulsed him and his whole army, and that they had often gained the best of the battle when opposed to the whole of the nobility of England. To add to his anger and vexation, he had heard that at the expiration of the truce, about the feast of St Elphege, they had taken to pillage, slaughter, and incendiarism, had invaded the parts of Pembroke and attacked the inhabitants, slaughtering great numbers of them with great ferocity and heaping abuse and ill-treatment on those they allowed to escape with their lives. Of these proceedings William himself[1] complained strongly to the king, to which the latter replied, "Expend, expend my well-beloved brother, some of the money of which you have such an abundance, to avenge our injuries." But William heaping threats on threats and adding insult to insult, declared that all these things occurred with the cunning consent and connivance of English traitors. And a little while afterwards to the disgrace of many nobles he particularised what he had before uttered in confusion and as a general remark. At this the earl of Gloucester and the earl of Leicester were much ashamed and angered. William intensifying his reproaches against the earl of Leicester, dared in the presence of the king and many nobles to

[1] William of Valence, lord of Pembroke

assert with abuse that the earl was an old traitor and had lied. To this the earl, flaming with anger and vexation, replied, "No, no, William, I am not the son of a traitor, nor a traitor myself; our fathers were not alike." And wishing to take vengeance there and then for such a great injury, he endeavoured to attack William, but was prevented by the king himself, who got between them, although with great difficulty; and thus the earl's anger was curbed for a time. It would be no easy matter to recount the injuries done in South Wales during the aforementioned struggle with the Welsh; suffice it to say, that those who were victorious wisely laid in a stock of wheat, salt, and other necessaries, of which they were formerly in need.

Of the assembling of the knights to proceed against the Welsh
On the morrow and the succeeding days, the king and the magnates held careful deliberation as to how they should crush such intolerable insolence on the part of the Welsh and check their frequent irruptions. There was therefore a general summons to the whole of the knighthood of England that all who were bound to render knight service to the king were to be ready and prepared at Chester on the Monday before the Nativity of St John the Baptist to follow the king with horses and arms into Wales. In consequence of this, manifold murmurs and complaints resounded amongst the people, because the king so often impoverished and harassed his nobles without honour or profit, and disturbed them by so often requiring scutage of them on the approach of harvest-time, especially when such an unheard-of famine had destroyed so many people. The king, however, paying little heed to the peril of the kingdom, and utterly destitute of money as he was, and although about to make war immediately, gave on the spot hastily and incautiously a thousand marks to Thomas of Savoy, formerly count of Flanders, who had lately arrived borne on a litter after a recent illness. He also gave two hundred pounds to a certain Poitevin, who generally waited at the royal table and carved his meat for him; and they, not heeding the imminent peril to which the kingdom was exposed, received everything with wide-open purses. Thomas, with his bags well filled, at once took leave of the queen (whose gifts he did not refuse any more than he did the king's), and went back over-seas for the purpose of destroying the city of Turin, without caring for the hostages detained there. The name of the aforesaid Poitevin was William de St Hermes, who would not take his departure just at present, but remained in expectation of still richer presents.

Of the consecration of R. de Chause as bishop of Carlisle
On the festival of St Tiburtius and his companions, mr Robert de Chause, a clerk of the queen's, was consecrated as bishop of Carlisle, by the bishops of Bath and Salisbury, at Bermondsey, in London.

Of the death of the archbishop of Armagh
And in the same week died, at London, the archbishop of Armagh, who had at one time been dean of St Paul's church, London.

Of the troubles of the archbishop of York

About the same time, too, the pope laid his heavy hand on the archbishop of York, whose position, as regards the world, was worsened, but bettered in the sight of God; for his patience increased in proportion to his manifold persecutions. Thus, in fulfilment of the prophecy of St Edmund the archbishop of Canterbury, he was prepared for martyrdom; in fact, we read that many have received the crown of martyrdom without shedding their blood. For besides many offences which had preceded this one, they now deprived him of the privilege of having the cross carried before him by his chief clerk, as was customary. However, he still refused to bow the knee to Baal, and to give the rich benefice of his church to unworthy, nay filthy foreigners like throwing pearls to swine.

How the bishop of Hereford was attacked by polypus

The bishop of Hereford, who had by his treachery injured the whole kingdom of England, was, by a visitation of the Lord, deservedly disfigured by a most foul disease, namely morphew.[1]

How Edward gave up his manors to W. of Valence

The king's eldest son, Edward, gave up his lands and rich manors, which he had received as a gift from his father, namely, those of Stanford, Grantham, and many others, as it were at farm or keepership, to William of Valence, who possessed abundance of money, in order that he, Edward, might thus obtain assistance in his need, and satisfy his avarice from the overflowing treasure of his uncle. This proceeding gave a sad presage of the future for both; for in the case of the young man it showed, that when he came to the full possession of the kingdom, he would waste and squander its wealth; and in the case of William, that he would be despoiled of his superfluous wealth.

Of the arrival of brother Mansuetus, a Minorite, on a mission from the pope

About the same time, there arrived in England, at the instance of the king, a certain brother of the Minorite order, named Mansuetus, who was sent by the pope, invested with great powers, and following in the footsteps of mr Arlot. His power, indeed, was such that, as it was stated, he absolved at will the partisans of the king, whoever they might be, when changing their vows, or when excommunicated, and even justified false-speakers and perjurers; in consequence of which, many assumed boldness in sinning; but among wise and prudent persons this only gave rise to contempt and derision, as the following narrative will fully show.

Of the reply given to the king in the parliament at London

At the aforesaid parliament, held at this time, the nobles strongly and steadfastly gave the king, who had urgently demanded an immense sum of money for the purpose of expediting his business in Apulia, and for prosecuting other matters of difficulty, a joint answer that they could not in any way, without irreparable ruin to themselves,

[1] a skin disease

so often drain themselves, and expend their small substance so often and so uselessly; that if he without consultation and improperly had obtained the kingdom of Apulia from the pope for his son Edmund, he must put it down to his own simplicity, and because he acted imprudently and without the advice of his nobles, alike rejecting all deliberation and prudence, which generally consider the results of actions beforehand, he must bring the matter to the best conclusion he could; that he ought really to have learned wisdom, and taken pattern by his brother Richard, king of Almain, who, when the said kingdom of Apulia was offered to him as a gift from the pope, and mr Albert was sent to announce it to him, refused it with contempt, especially as England was separated from Apulia by so many unknown kingdoms using various languages, by so many principalities, by so many cities well provided with soldiers and arms, by seas and mountains, and by an extent of country so toilsome to traverse. What earl Richard most feared, and with good reason, was the cavilling conduct of the Roman court, and the manifold treacheries of the Apulians, who destroyed their allies and relations by poison. However, not to appear insolent to the pope, who by reason of his office takes pre-eminence of all princes and prelates, and who had out of friendship selected him, the earl, for such a high dignity, he wrote back signifying that he would willingly acquiesce in his plan, if the pope would allow all the crusaders to assist him, which could well be arranged on account of the city of Nucera, in Apulia, which was inhabited by infidels, and would allow him half of the expenses to be incurred in that war, and would also give him possession of certain cities and castles which he, the pope, then had, together with good hostages, that he might on coming thither find a safe place of refuge and protection in them against rebels, if any should rise against him; and if, moreover, he would grant him the protection of valid documents in writing, sealed with the papal bull.

How the pope imposed upon the king of England

When the pope was informed of all these demands, he would not agree to them in any way. He therefore privately sent messengers who were well able to seduce the minds of their hearers by their cunning arguments, and imposed upon the supine and credulous simplicity of the king by offering him the kingdom of Apulia for his younger son Edmund, and promising him effective assistance and advice in bringing the matter to a conclusion. By this vague promise the king's heart was so elated and infatuated, that he lavished on the pope and his messengers whatever he had in his possession, and whatever he could obtain by any means, and confidently promised more. In consequence of this, the pope's messengers vied with one another, as it were, in coming to England to the king, for the purpose of carrying off his rich presents: for they smelled the sweet savour of his money from afar. First came the bishop of Bologna, who, in the pope's name, invested the said Edmund with the kingdom of Apulia, by means of a ring: then the archbishop of Messina, who went back not empty-handed: and he was followed in succession by John of Diva, mr Bernard, mr Sinitius, Rustand, Arlot, and many others too numerous to mention, every one of whom the king received with the greatest reverence and honour, to the injury and ruin of his whole kingdom. The nobles of England, therefore, being justly provoked at the silence of the timid prelates, endeavoured to regulate the king's proceedings, if they could by any means do so.

Of the death of the archbishop of Trier

About this same time died the archbishop of Trier, who had formed an alliance with the duke of Brabant, and was opposed to the king of Almain.

How the king was refused pecuniary aid

During this time, too, as the nobles of the kingdom as if with one voice had replied steadfastly and precisely to the king's urgent demand for pecuniary assistance that they neither would nor could any longer submit to such extortions, the king betook himself in anger to other cunning devices to extract a large sum from the church. He therefore addressed himself, in the first place, to the abbot of Westminster, and wheedled him over by deceitful promises to affix his seal and that of his convent to a deed in writing, whereby he became surety for the king to the amount of two thousand five hundred marks, in order that this pernicious example might give him the means of extorting as much from other monasteries.

How Simon Passelewe was sent on a mission to the various abbots, to extort money from them

The king then sent the said Simon in all haste with these letters to other monasteries in order that their abbots might take on them the same burden: and by this proceeding the king injured his good fame in no slight degree; for the act itself clearly showed how eagerly he longed to oppress the church without remedy. The crafty and lying Simon Passelewe, who was a clerk and counsellor of the king, in his desire to execute the king's orders, however improper, but not explain them, went with all haste to Waltham, and produced the king's letter entreating the abbot and brethren of Waltham to take on them a similar obligation to that which the abbot of Westminster had freely imposed on himself; namely, by a deed in writing, under his hand and the hands of the brethren, to become surety for the king for the payment of two thousand five hundred marks on the king's behalf. He also showed the letters patent on this matter of the abbot and conventual assembly of Westminster, bearing their seals; at sight of which the abbot of Waltham was in great alarm, and inquired of him if he had similar letters addressed to other convents. Simon replied, "Indeed I have; to St Albans, to Reading, and elsewhere." The abbot then took counsel with the brethren of the convent in chapter, and at length gave Simon to understand, in reply to his demand, that whatever might be done in this matter by the abbot and convent of Westminster (who of necessity showed favour to the king, and were bound to obey him in matters of difficulty, as being the restorer of their church), he would not on any account become security, or pledge himself in any way for the payment of so much money for the king: that no prelate was allowed according to what is written in the Decretals, in the chapter on obligations, to subject his church to such great peril and risk. To this speech Simon replied, "The king will give you what security you wish, in writing, for the certain payment of your money." But, rejoined the abbot, "We do not wish to have any occasion for disputing or engaging in a lawsuit with the king; for we have not the means of contending with him on equal grounds, and we cannot bring him to justice or distrain on him for payment, if he should be weak enough to listen to evil counsel." Then added Simon, "Pity, for God's sake, pity your lord and especial protector. For this chapel will be laid under interdict immediately, that is to say, within three or four days; and harsher measures will follow afterwards, unless you accede to his entreaties. As you well know, he is the most Christian and most pious of kings, and would not be obliged to desist from the observance of divine duties for an untold amount of pure gold."

How Simon Passelewe went to the abbot and convent of St Albans

As he could not succeed thus, or by any roundabout arguments and lies, he went away in anger, heaping threats upon threats, and took his way to St Albans, accompanied by a certain clerk of the king's, who was his companion, for the purpose of binding both abbot and convent of that place to accede to the king's wish by his deceitful speeches, or by some means or other, whether right or wrong. But the abbot of Waltham sent word privately and in all haste to the abbot of St Albans of all that had taken place; how Simon Passelewe, by deceitful and perverted arguments, endeavoured, at the king's urgent request, to bind the church of Waltham to the payment of two thousand five hundred marks for the king, and wished the abbot and brethren to become surety for him by a deed in writing. The aforesaid Simon (or more properly speaking "Sinon") reached St Albans before the hour of chapter, pretending to have come from London that day, and to have ridden nearly all night (although he had come direct from Waltham); and throwing himself into a seat, he leaned his head down on it and went to sleep. After this he went with all haste to the abbot, and said in a tone of sorrow, "My lord, I and my companion have been compelled by the greatest necessity to travel the distance between London and this place this last night"; and he produced the king's letter, which made mention of a different sum to what he had verbally stated, and he also openly exhibited the letter of the abbot and convent of Westminster, proving that they had promptly acceded to the king's request – for by this example he hoped to bend the abbot and convent of St Albans to the king's will. He also promised, in the king's name, that any deed in writing which we might choose should be prepared for securing the payment of the money, which he asked to be lent to him for a time, under a bond in writing; and the sum required, he stated, amounted to two thousand five hundred marks. And, if the abbot refused, he would incur the king's lasting anger; for his chapel was in danger of being suspended, which he would not on any account put up with. The abbot and convent, and indeed everyone who heard this message, were astounded at the tyranny and cunning of the king, especially as he had by his earnest entreaties obtained a writing of the abbot and brethren similar to that which he had obtained from the abbot and convent of Westminster. A council was therefore held in the chapter, and finally the reply was given decisively, that they could not in any way agree to the king's request, because it would be contrary to the pope's prohibition, contrary to right, and contrary to honour. Simon was also shown instruments in writing, and one in particular, addressed to Warin, formerly abbot of St Albans, and his successors, in which was contained a clause, forbidding them to lay their church under obligation in any way, under penalty of suspension, interdiction, and excommunication. The abbot and convent of St Albans chose, therefore, to incur the anger of an earthly king who made unjust demands, rather than by violating the pope's prohibition suffer the displeasure of the heavenly king and be bound by the chains of anathema. When Simon heard their reasons for refusal, he assumed a placid and kind look, and eagerly replied: "My well-beloved friends, do not disquiet yourselves at all about that; for our king has with him a certain most holy man, a brother of the Minorite order, named Mansuetus, who is sent by the pope as a protection, who has full power and is absolutely ready to absolve all who violate their oaths for the sake of assisting the king in this his most pressing necessity. But if you will not assist the king at this crisis, I shall at once return to London and tell him both that you lay aside all respect for the king and despise his protection and that you regard the kindness and power of the said brother with contempt." To this Simon received for answer: "It would not appear sensible to wish to be excommunicated and to be absolved at the same time; in the same way as we should not attend to the orders of a quack who might say, 'Fearlessly break your leg, or some other limb, and I will find you a good surgeon who will heal and reset the broken limb.' Besides, if we were to do this, we should sin in manifold ways: in the first place, we should knowingly lie: in the next, if we were to affix our seals, which are pledges of our faith, to such a document, they would cry out against us that we had acted iniquitously; but this we will not do on any account." Simon rejoined: "What does this mean? Am I to go away empty-handed? My lord the king will believe that I have awakened some quarrel between you and him, and thus all the blame will recoil on my head, although I am innocent. Why should my lord meet with such a repulse at your hands? You have nothing but what my lord the king or his ancestors have given you; therefore you are bound in justice to assist him in such a pressing emergency, since everything belongs to the prince." To these arguments the abbot and brethren replied: "It is true all belongs to the prince; but it is for protection, and not for destruction. This is what the king swore at his coronation and many times since; therefore we pay no attention to these cavilling arguments of yours." Simon, on hearing this, had recourse to another kind of deceit: "If," said he, "you will do nothing else for the king, at least do this: draw up a writing favourable to the king's demand, in accordance with his request and desire, seal the same, and keep it in your possession in your treasury, so that if at any time your hearts are softened and humbled, the king or his deputy may find it ready, and take it away when the proper time comes. Do this, that your contempt and effrontery may not be too apparent." To this also the abbot and brethren replied: "No, Simon, no; for you would then say, and could say, that we had consented, and had drawn up a written statement of our consent to his wishes, as is now the case with the letter of the abbot of Westminster which you are showing. And thus we should afford a pernicious example to others whom you are desirous of assailing and bending to your will, which we will never do." Thus the tempter went away in confusion, without accomplishing his object.

Of the deceits put in practice by the aforesaid Simon to impose upon certain abbots
I have inserted these particulars in full, that the reader of this may learn how dangerous domestic enemies are, and how much this degenerate Englishman, Simon, would have played the stepfather to the kingdom and the church. The aforesaid abbot and brethren, by writing in terms of moderation and friendship, and excusing themselves on just grounds, escaped the danger which threatened them. As for Simon, although he had declared with an oath that he would go at once to the king at London, not being ashamed at being charged with another lie, he altered his course and went full speed to Reading, to entrap the abbot and brethren of that place with his usual crafty devices; but they forewarned of his coming and informed of his proceedings, manfully resisted him to his face. Thus *iniquity, which was false to itself*, failed in its purpose. In what I have written above, I have stated the whole sum of money in full, because the king's written demand was to the effect that each of the four houses, namely, Westminster, St Albans, Reading and Waltham, should become security, each for the other, for the full amount; so that each house should be responsible for itself, and for each of the other three, to the amount of five hundred marks; that is, for two thousand marks, and five hundred marks for interest. And the king wanted to have this money with all haste, so that it would be necessary to borrow it from the merchants of Cahors.

How the Minorite brethren forced their way into the city of St Edmunds
About this same time, the Minorite friars, by virtue of authority from the pope, forced themselves into the city of St Edmunds, against the will and despite the opposition of the abbot and brethren of that place. They were introduced and established there by force, by the agency of laymen; namely the earl of Gloucester, who was a declared enemy of the said abbot and convent, and Gilbert of Preston. A few days previously, the abbot had come from the Roman court, where he had been taking precautions for the future against the violence of the said friars, and had forearmed himself with a papal letter; but immediately afterwards, the friars obtained another, directly to a contrary purport, by means of that additional clause, "Notwithstanding". On hearing of this proceeding, people could hardly express their astonishment that such holy men – men who had voluntarily chosen poverty for their lot – should thus, laying aside all fear of God, despising the anger of the reverend martyr and of men, and heedless of the protection of privileges, violently disturb the peaceful state of that noble church, which was well known to be of great dignity and antiquity. The abbot was not so much harassed by his toilsome journey across the Alps or by the incalculable debts in which he was involved, [as he was by this proceeding.] And under stress at the height of his difficulties, he chose essoins of bed-sickness in the plea of the earl of Gloucester.

The continuation of the parliament lately commenced
The altercation between the king and the magnates of the kingdom at the aforementioned parliament, continued until the Sunday after Ascension day, and complaints multiplied daily against the king, because he did not keep his promises, having

little regard for the keys of the church and for the tenor of his Great Charter so many times paid for. Also he exalted his uterine brothers in a most intolerable manner, contrary to the law of the kingdom as though they had been born in this country, and would not allow any writ to issue from the chancery against them. And although the impudence of all the said brothers of the king, and of the other Poitevins, was intolerable, yet William de Valence exceeded them all in insolence. The earl of Leicester, in particular, complained heartily of this, not only to the king but also to everybody, demanding that he be given justice at once. In addition, the king was reproached with advancing and enriching all aliens, and with despising and pillaging his own natural subjects, to the ruin of the whole kingdom. And he was so needy, whilst others possessed money in abundance, that he could not, for want of money, recover the rights of the kingdom, nay, that he could not even ward off the wrongs done by the Welsh, who were the very scum of mankind. In short, the king's aberrations require special consideration. The king, on reflection, acknowledged the truth of the accusations, although late, and humbled himself, declaring that he had been too often beguiled by evil counsel, and he promised and made solemn oath at the altar and shrine of St Edward, that he would fully and properly amend his old errors, and show favour and kindness to his natural subjects. But his frequent earlier transgressions rendered him entirely unworthy of belief, and as the nobles had not yet learned what knot to bind their Proteus with (for it was an arduous and difficult matter), the parliament was prorogued to the feast of St Barnabas, when it would be actively resumed at Oxford. In the meantime, the nobles of England, for instance, the earls of Gloucester, Leicester, and Hereford, the earl marshal, and other men of distinction, took precautions and provided for their safety by forming a confederation, and as they greatly feared the traps and snares of the aliens and had overmuch respect for the king's nets, they turned up with horses and arms and the protection of an ample escort.

Of the unseasonableness of the weather

In this year too the north wind blew incessantly for several months and when April, May, and the greater part of June had already passed, scarcely any of the small and rare plants were visible with few shoots; and, in consequence, but small hopes were entertained of the fruit crops. Owing to the shortage of food, a very large number of poor people died; and dead bodies were found everywhere, swollen and livid, lying by fives and sixes in pigsties, on dunghills, and in the muddy streets. Those who had houses did not dare, in their own state of need, to take in the dying, for fear of contagion. When a number of corpses were found, large and spacious pits were dug in the cemeteries, and a great many bodies were laid in them together.

Of the impressive mission to the French king

During the time which elapsed previous to the holding of the parliament at Oxford, important messengers, selected from the earls and barons of England, were sent to the French king, to obtain some consolation from him or at least to prevent any impediment from being thrown in the way to hinder them in their designs. For they were endeavouring, for their own benefit, and for that of neighbouring countries, to end and pacify the disturbance which had arisen in the kingdom of England in consequence of the long-continued supine simplicity of the king.

Of the founding of a religious house by John Mansell

During this same year, too, John Mansell, provost of Beverley, a clerk and a particular counsellor of the lord king, a wise, prudent, and wealthy man, founded near Romney, about two miles from the sea, a house of religious, that is to say, of Canons Regular, and endowed it at his own expense, and established canons therein. This he was induced to do by consideration that a king's favour is not hereditary, and that the prosperity of the world is not everlasting. He was influenced by the example of Peter Chaceport, who a short time previously had piously and happily founded a house of the same order so that in this way when he passed from the possession of temporal goods, he might not lose those which were eternal.

Of the death of Sewal, archbishop of York

About the feast of the Ascension the archbishop of York, in order to ascend with the Lord and, quitting the prison of this world, take flight to heaven, wearied by the many tribulations he had undergone while manfully fighting to the utmost of his power for his church against the tyranny of the court of Rome, and crowned with laurel for his merits, exchanged, it was truly believed, this earthly life for the kingdom of heaven. This archbishop Sewal followed step by step in the track of St Edmund (whose discourses he had listened to, and of whom he had been a fellow-scholar and disciple), and endeavoured to assimilate himself in his actions and to conform in his morals to that saint. I think I ought not to omit mentioning that St Edmund, when lecturing in theology at Oxford used to say to this dearest friend and special pupil of his, "Oh Sewal! Sewal! you will pass from this world a martyr; you will be assailed and slain by the sword, or at least by heavy and insuperable tribulations in the world. However, let Him be your comforter who inspired his psalmist to say, 'Many are the tribulations of the just; but from all of these the Lord will one day release them.' " It is an evident fact that many martyrs have passed from the world without their blood being shed, as for instance, St John the Evangelist, and many others.

Of the sayings and doings of the aforesaid archbishop on the near approach of death

This holy archbishop, too, when he sensed that death was undoubtedly approaching, and that he was about to pass from this world, raised himself up, and, with clasped hands and a tearful countenance turned towards heaven, gave utterance to the following prayer: "Oh Lord Jesus Christ, most just of judges, by thy infallible scrutiny thou knowest how in my innocence I have been harassed in manifold ways by the pope, whom thou has permitted to be established as ruler of thy church, because (as God knows, and as is no secret to the world) I refused to admit unknown and utterly unworthy persons to the ministry of the churches intrusted by thee to my care, unworthy as I am. However, lest by a contempt of the pope's sentence, unjust though it was, it should become a just one, I humbly beg to be absolved from the shackles of excommunication; but I accuse that pope before the supreme and incorruptible

Judge, and heaven and earth will be my witness as to how unjustly he has vexed, provoked, and slandered me manifold times." In the bitterness of his soul, therefore, he wrote to the pope (influenced by the example of Robert, bishop of Lincoln), expressing his inconsolable grief that the pope had harassed him in so many ways (because he refused, as above stated, to accept persons inexperienced and ignorant of the English language) at one time by suspending him, at another by excluding him from the church, at another by taking the cross from him, and at another by publicly excommunicating him throughout the kingdom (amazingly the agents of such excommunication performing their task unwillingly), and thus injuring his good name in divers ways, to his great temporal injury. He furthermore complained bitterly that, although he did so with patience, he could ill endure the violent attacks of certain clerks who impudently asserted they had papal authority for what they were doing, especially of mr Jordan, who was longing for the office of dean [of York]; he repeated, he bore all this with patience, that he might not be said to be ridiculing the disgrace of his father, like Ham, by revealing it, but to be anxious to hide and veil it like Shem, often recalling to memory the following brief precept: "In revealing the disgrace of thy father, thou art like Ham; like Shem in concealing it." In his letter, therefore, as the aforesaid Robert, bishop of Lincoln, had done, he humbly yet earnestly begged of the pope "to mitigate his usual tyranny, and to follow the example set by the humility of his predecessors. For the Lord said to Peter, 'Feed my sheep'; and not shear or flay them, nor disembowel, nor devour them." But the pope ridiculed his request, and treated it with contempt; and conceived the greatest indignation that they broke out into such great presumption as to trouble him, the pope, in any way whatever; and he refused to listen to the salutary warnings of either archbishop Sewal, or the said Robert, bishop of Lincoln.

Of the miracle of the water turned into wine

It happened one day, when the mortal disease under which he was suffering pressed heavily upon him, that he felt thirsty, and asked for some spring water; and on its being offered to him he devoutly blessed it, as he said it was of no benefit to his complaint. On tasting it, he found the flavour to be that of wine, not water, and reproached his attendant for having deceived him, saying, "Why have you deceived me with this drink? Where did you find this?" The servant replied, "At the spring, my lord, and I was not alone there"; then bringing forward two other attendants who stood by, he added, "Here are credible witnesses to the truth of what I say." The attendants then tasted the beverage, and declared it to be new wine. The archbishop, hearing what the man said, for fear his attendants should spread it abroad, drank all that was in the cup, and begged of his servants in mild terms (for he was a man of gentle speech) not to say anything about the matter. This took place just previous to his death.

Of the great famine which prevailed throughout the whole of England

About the feast of the Trinity in this year, a frightful and intolerable pestilence attacked the people, especially those of the lower orders, and spread death among them in a most lamentable degree. Not to mention others, I think it worthwhile to mention the following incident. In the city of London, where fifteen thousand of the poor had already perished of hunger, it happened that it was publicly proclaimed: "Go all you who are in want of it, and receive a portion of the bread of such and such a noble", and the crier specified the person and place from whom and where they were to receive alms . . .[1] and insolent, urging him with threats to give up his kingdom of Almain, and take his departure forthwith. To this demand the king [of Almain] replied at once undauntedly and cheerfully, "If he chooses to come and attack me, he will find me ready to meet him outside the boundaries of my kingdom, and to receive him at the sword's point." The king of Spain, provoked the more by this reply, combined his army with the forces of the king of Arragon and Navarre, and headed for Italy; but whilst he was absent, the Saracens of Spain tried to take Cordova; on hearing of which he retraced his steps to check their incursions. He did, however, send emissaries of distinction to the pope, claiming his right and calling upon the Roman court not to admit to the government of the empire any other than the most excellent king of Spain, who had extended the limits of Christendom more than all other Christian kings. In answer to this, the pope, on behalf of the king of Almain, replied: "Well-beloved sons, you know, and are bound to know, that the proper order of proceeding, and the usual and approved custom from times of old is for the kingdom of Almain to be considered as an earnest of the empire, a dignity to be previously held, and, as it were, a primitive possession of it. Let, therefore, your lord, the illustrious king of Spain, be duly elected king of Almain, at Aix-la-Chapelle, by the clergy and nobles of that country, with whom such election rests, as is the ancient custom; first strive prudently and powerfully to be consecrated and solemnly crowned king; after which we, as far as in our power lies, and with the fear of God before our eyes, will show ourselves favourable and agreeable to the advancement of your lord, the illustrious king of Spain, who is worthy of all honour." The messengers, therefore, weighing the pope's reply and the king's on the beam of reason, announced to their lord, the king of Spain, the strict rule of procedure and advised him that it would be wise and beneficial to protect his own kingdom, against which the Saracens were plotting. This result being made known to the Italian nobles, many of them gave the right hand of friendship to the king of Almain, and spontaneously gave him their allegiance. The king received them kindly, and paid a very large sum of money to release certain cities of Germany from debts, in which his predecessors had involved them; by which proceeding he would have gained immense favour with men of power amongst the Germans, if he had been as vigorous in warlike proceedings as he was prudent and circumspect in counsel.

Of the return of the abbot of Bury St Edmunds from the Roman court

About this same time, the abbot of St Edmund king and martyr, after a prolonged and expensive sojourn at the court of Rome, returned home involved in heavy debts. Moreover, the Friars Minor had, as before stated, built themselves a house, in spite of the opposition of the said abbot and his convent. He had, during his late visit to Rome,

[1] A folio is missing from the chronicle here.

obtained a privilege, whereby the said brethren were forbidden to attempt such a proceeding on any account; but they invalidated all that he had gained by means of the additional clause, "Nothwithstanding".

Of the parliament held at Oxford

As the feast of St Barnabas drew near, the magnates and nobles of the land hastened to the parliament which was to be held at Oxford, and gave orders to all those who owed them knight service, to come with them, ready to defend them against enemy attacks. Which they did, concealing their real reasons for so doing under the pretence that their coming in such a way was to show themselves ready to set out with their united forces against the king's enemies in Wales. The fact was they were in no slight fear that, in consequence of the disagreement of parties, civil war would break out between them and that the king and his Poitevin brothers would call in aliens to aid them against his native-born subjects. Forewarned, the magnates therefore took the precaution of securing the sea-ports. When parliament opened the proposal and unalterable intention of the magnates was adopted, most firmly demanding that the king should faithfully keep and observe the charter of the liberties of England, which his father, king John, had made and granted to the English and sworn to keep; and which he, king Henry the third, had many times granted, and sworn to keep, and infringers of which he had caused to be excommunicated by all the bishops of England in the presence of himself and the whole baronage, he himself being one of the excommunicators. They moreover demanded that a justiciar should be appointed to dispense justice to those suffering injury, with equal impartiality towards rich and poor. They also asked for other things touching the kingdom for the common good, the peace, and the honour of the king and kingdom alike. And they insisted that the king should frequently and regularly consult them, and conform to their counsel and necessary provisions; plighting faith on oath, and offering their right hands to one another that they would prosecute their design, at the risk of losing their money or their lands, or even the lives of them and theirs. All of which the king allowed and solemnly swore that he would follow their counsel; and his son Edward was bound down by the same oath. But John earl Warrenne and the uterine brothers of the king, William de Valence and the others, refused. Orders were, moreover, given for the ports of England to be strictly guarded, and for the gates of London to be carefully fastened at night with better bars; on which someone said, "Through the night the gates of London are shut, for fear the deceit of Frenchmen should break into the city."

After they had prolonged their stay there for some days deliberating what to do in such a difficult matter as reckoning the condition of the disturbed kingdom they met together at the house of the Friars Preachers. There they renewed afresh their alliance and oath, and confirmed their determination that neither for death nor life, or for tenements, or hate or love, would they allow themselves in any way to be turned from, or weakened in, their design of both purging of aliens the kingdom in which were begotten men of noble stock, their own begetters, and of restoring commendable laws. And if any man, whosoever he might be, should resist, he should be forced to join them even against his will. Although the king and his eldest son, Edward, had taken the oath, Edward began, as far as he could, to draw back from it, as did also John earl Warenne. Henry, the son of Richard the king of Almain, wavered and said that he would on no account take such an oath without the permission and advice of his father; whereupon he was told plainly that even his father, if he would not make common cause with the baronage, would not keep possession of one furlong of land in England. In addition, the aforesaid [Poitevin] brothers had sworn most definitely, by the death and wounds of Christ, that they would never, as long as they lived, give up the castles, rents, or wardships which their brother, the king, had delighted to give them, although Simon, the earl of Leicester, had freely given up to the king his castles of Kenilwithe and Odiham, which he had even repaired a few days previously. When they made this declaration, intensifying it by unrepeatable oaths, the earl of Leicester, addressing himself to William de Valence, who was blustering more than the others, replied: "Know for certain and make no mistake about it, you will either give up the castles which you hold of the king, or you will lose your head." And the other earls and barons said the same, adding their witness in a most determined manner. The Poitevins were, as a result, in great alarm, not knowing what to do; for if they betook themselves for concealment to any castle quite without provision and were besieged, they would perish of hunger; for even if the nobles did not do so, all the populace of the realm would besiege them, and destroy their castles utterly. They therefore suddenly and secretly took to flight, whilst dinner was being prepared; and that their design might not be found out, they pretended that they wished to sit down to dinner. As they fled, they frequently looked behind them, and made some of their retainers ascend high towers to watch if the barons followed in pursuit of them; nor did they spare their horses' flanks till they reached Winchester, where, in their fear, they placed themselves, as it were, under the protecting wings of the bishop elect of Winchester, on whom all their hopes depended; and moreover, they had hopes of finding a safe place of refuge in the castles belonging to him, the said bishop elect. The nobles in the mean time became more firmly leagued together, and appointed as their justiciar a native Englishman of noble birth, an illustrious knight and a man well skilled in the laws of the country, Hugh Bigod, brother of the earl marshal; and he discharged the office of justiciar with vigour and would not allow the law of the kingdom to falter on any account. When the magnates learnt for certain of the aforesaid flight of the Poitevins, they feared that getting near to the sea they might call aliens to their help, that is Poitevins and others from overseas. Seeing, therefore, danger in delay, they gave strict orders to their following and all their partisans, to take to arms, and to horse with all haste. And thus ended the parliament at Oxford, uncertainly and inconclusively.

Of the disagreement at Rome between the pope and the senator Brancaleone

At this time, too, Richard, king of Almain, prudently released certain cities of Germany from the heavy debts and pledges in which they had been involved by kings of Almain, his predecessors. The archbishop of Trier, also, who had been long ill, and was, in fact, believed to be dead many days before this, sent word to the said king, that unless the king of Spain came, as he had positively promised to do, to the aid of him, the archbishop, and the duke of Brabant, who were in league with the said king of Spain, they would both give their firm and faithful support and obedience to him, the said king of Almain. The inhabitants of many of the cities of Italy, moreover, gave the right hand of friendship to him, as they eagerly longed for his arrival and his promotion to the empire. In the mean time, Brancaleone, the senator of Rome, destroyed the towers of the Roman nobles, and imprisoned their owners. He also hanged and mutilated very many relatives and connections of the cardinals, and would not act in any way so as to conflict with the wishes of the people of Rome. This senator was in favour of Manfred, a prince who aspired to the empire, and consequently, both of them hated the king of Almain, and made plans to oppose him. For that very reason, the pope, who hated the senator and prince Manfred, showed favour to the aforesaid king of Almain.

How the abbot [of Ramsey] recovered the fair of St Ives

In this same year by the skilful management of the abbot Ralph, Ramsey abbey regained its full right to the fair of St Ives, which it had obtained by gift of king Edgar and confirmation by other kings of old; and its possession of which had also been strengthened by authentic writings of St Thomas, archbishop and martyr. The said abbot Ralph had, as was reported, paid five hundred marks of silver for the recovery of the right to the said fair, which had been lost, not by any fault of the said church, but by the cavillings of others, which it was evident to many were false and groundless.

Of the death of R., abbot of Westminster

On 18 July in this year, near Winchester, died Richard, abbot of Westminster, a man of handsome appearance, eloquent, and well versed in both kinds of law, canon and civil; he was also a most particular friend of the king's, in whose service he had willingly undergone great toil and incurred much expense, both on the continent and at home. This said Richard had, by his great prudence, for which he was much distinguished, increased the possessions of his abbey by twelve hides of land, and obtained a great many liberties for it; but as some vices usually go with virtues, he put his seal and that of his convent to a document of the king's, that other abbots named therein might the more willingly and more boldly apply theirs. This document was drawn up at that time to induce some of the superior abbots in England to pledge themselves for the king to overseas merchants for no small sum of money; on the promise, however, of giving security to the same abbots and their successors for the payment of the said money by the king, and of preserving their churches indemnified. But as no confidence was placed in this promise, his consent alone was to no purpose, for all the other abbots vigorously and unanimously opposed it, adding, by divine inspiration as it were, that if such an obligation were commenced by them, the consent of others would be inferred from their example. The body of the deceased Richard was taken to Westminster, and buried with honours in his conventual church there.

How Philip, the abbot elect of Westminster, died before his election was confirmed

Philip, the prior of the said monastery, was now elected abbot thereof; but when he heard of his election, he expressed great reluctance in giving his consent, through fear of that most oppressive decree of the pope, requiring a journey to Rome in person; as he was fat and heavy in body. For he preferred, and it would have been better for him to have done so, to remain at home in his former mode of life, rather than to expose himself to such danger for the sake of worldly dignity. Being, however, overcome by the exhortations of the brethren, and by his legitimate election by the whole community, he was pleased to accede to their wishes, on condition, however, that they would send others to the curia to get confirmation of his election. Some of the more eminent of the brethren, therefore, went, putting to the pope the most urgent reasons and excuses for the non-attendance of their abbot elect; and after much difficulty, owing to the opposition of the cardinals, they at length obtained the required favour by the payment of a large sum of money. On their way back with their difficult business settled, they heard that their abbot elect was dead and that another person had already been appointed as quickly as possible in his stead. In great grief, they quickly resumed their journey to the curia.

Of the election of G. de Kimeton as archbishop of York

At this same time, the canons of York assembled and elected their dean, that is mr Godfrey of Kimetone,[1] as their archbishop, who went in person to the court of Rome, and after much trouble and expense brought his business to a satisfactory termination, and as quickly as possible returned home safely.

Of the mortality caused by the famine amongst the people

About the same time, such great famine and mortality prevailed in the country, that a measure of wheat rose in price to fifteen shillings and more, at a time when the country itself was drained of money, and numberless dead bodies were lying about the streets. No one, indeed, could remember ever having before beheld such misery and such a famine, although there were many who had seen prices rise higher than they then were. And if corn had not been brought over for sale from the continent, the rich would scarcely have been able to escape death. Moreover, the dead lay about, swollen up and rotting, on dunghills, and in the dirt of the streets, and there was scarcely any one to bury them; nor did the citizens dare or wish to receive the dead into their houses, for fear of contagion. So great, too, was the scarcity of money that even if corn could have been sold for a small price per measure, scarcely any one could have been found with the means of buying it. But the Lord in his benign mercy supplied a speedy remedy, as above stated.

Of the departure of the king's brothers from England

In the octave of the Translation of St Benedict, namely, on 18 July, the aforesaid brothers of the king bade farewell to the English, and withdrew, accompanied by certain other Poitevins, that is to say William de St Hermes (who used to stand by

[1] mr Godfrey of Ludham

the king at his meals with a napkin, and to carve his food for him), and many others who had oppressed the whole kingdom and pillaged it of its wealth, especially of its coin. These Poitevins rested themselves first at Winchester, and afterwards at the house of the bishop elect of Winchester in London, that is at Southwark, and it was reported that many of the nobles of England were treacherously poisoned there and elsewhere; and the result proved such to be the fact. When they reached the coast, the nobles who had conducted them consigned them to the care of Neptune. On their arrival at Boulogne, they wrote to the French king for leave to travel peaceably through his country, or to take up their abode there for a time, in accordance with the old-established liberty and custom of France; and for permission for the bishop elect of Winchester to remain for a while at Paris as a scholar. But the king of France refused, being exasperated by a complaint made against these Poitevins by the queen of France to the effect that they had shamefully scandalised and defamed her sister, the queen of England, adding to his refusal that they had been "driven from England in disgrace, on account of their crimes". On hearing of this the earl of Leicester's son Henry suddenly crossed the Channel to attack them, either without the knowledge or against the will of his father, or it might have been with his connivance. On the way he met with many friends, who, out of respect and affection for his father, were ready and willing to avenge his injuries; for he had mentioned how William of Valence, relying on the favour of the king of England and the support of his other brothers who were present, had gone beyond all bounds with his blustering at the parliament at London, had publicly given the lie to his father, the earl, and called him an old traitor, to the great amazement of people on the continent, who wondered that men much less noble than he, although they were near relations of the king, should wish or dare to reproach or defame, by thought, word, or deed, a man so noble in disposition, of such noble birth, and one pre-eminent amongst all, both at home and on the continent. Indeed, it was not proper, and scarcely to be believed, that men connected with royalty should utter such dishonourable words. The friends of the earl, therefore, on learning the truth, prepared to join Henry in his attack on the Poitevins. The latter, finding how matters stood, secretly withdrew into Boulogne; but their pursuers kept watch over that place on all sides, by sea as well as land, and thus hemming them in, deprived them of all means of escape, and were thus at liberty to harass and annoy them as they deserved.

How the castellan of Dover intercepted a large sum of money

Richard de Gray, a brave and faithful man, who had been appointed castellan of Dover on behalf of the barons, looked carefully at everybody who crossed or wanted to cross over, strictly scrutinising everything; and he found a considerable treasure ready to be conveyed secretly to the said Poitevins, all of which was seized and kept in the castle. At the new Temple in London, also, a very large sum was seized, the amount of which excited great astonishment in those who heard of it, and which had been hidden there by the said Poitevins, although the Hospitallers made an attempt to deny it. This money was taken possession of, to be expended usefully, at the option of the king and the barons, for the benefit of the kingdom.

Of the desire of the Welsh to make amends to the king of England

About the same time, the Welsh, who had quarrelled and gained ill repute with the king of England, offered him honourable terms of peace, and declared themselves ready to clear themselves by judicial trial from all the charges made against them, as well of murder as of robbery.

How the Londoners acquiesced in the resolutions of the barons

On the feast of St Mary Magdalene special messengers, sent to London on behalf of the community at large of England, convoked all the citizens (who are styled barons) and in the hall which is called the Guildhall, the question was put to them, whether they would faithfully acquiesce in the decrees of the barons, and adhere firmly to their cause, vigorously oppose their adversaries and give them effective assistance. To this they all readily conceded and made them a charter on it sealed with the common seal of the city. They did not intend yet to make public however what had been resolved; for the illness of the earl of Gloucester, which he had contracted from a dose of poison, as is commonly reported, seriously alarmed all of them; but they had hopes he would recover from his illness, because gory matter emanated from numerous pustules which broke out on his body, and his hair, nails, and skin fell off, and his teeth dropped out. Thus shaven and purged, he was consigned to the care and medical treatment of mr John of St Giles, a friar of the order of Preachers, who had once cured bishop Robert of Lincoln of a similar disease.

How many nobles were poisoned in England

Many of the nobles of England, who had been poisoned at the same time, as is said, by the Poitevins, began now to pine away of themselves, and some of them departed this life, whilst others continued lingering betwixt life and death; some of them being laymen of rank and power, and others noblemen and men of learning. It was not as yet clear to the English that the Poitevins had given them the poisonous draughts, for they thought that this disease might proceed from some other calamity, and thus show itself openly. There were, moreover, some other evilly-disposed poisoners left behind, who were engaged in evil designs and plots against the magnates; in consequence of which these nobles entertained suspicions of their stewards, cooks, and butlers, lest they should be bribed to perpetrate similar crimes upon their lords.

Of the instability of Fulk, bishop of London

In all this difficult and important affair, and this new and most happy arrangement of the affairs of the kingdom, Fulk, bishop of London, was more lukewarm and remiss than was becoming or advantageous, and by thus acting, he injured his good name the more, because he was more exalted by birth than the rest. As the hopes of the barons rested on him, his weak conduct provoked their anger, as they relied on him to justify the king with the people.

Of the harsh speech of the king to the earl of Leicester

The fears and anxieties of the barons were increased by the coming on of the month of July, which, with its plague-bearing lion and furiously-raging dog, generally disturbs the repose of the air. What more alarmed them than all the rest was the fickleness and inscrutable duplicity of the king, which they discovered to be existing from a certain alarming conversation of his. For one day when he had left his palace at Westminster, and embarked in a vessel to take his dinner, and to enjoy an excursion on the Thames, the sky on the way became obscured and a thunderstorm came on, attended with lightning and heavy rain; and the king, who feared a storm of that kind more than others, gave orders to be put ashore at once, the vessel being, at the time, opposite to the noble palace of the bishop of Durham, where the earl of Leicester was then staying. When the earl knew of the king's arrival, he went joyfully and serenely to meet him, and, greeting him reverently, as was fitting, and by way of comforting him, said, "What is it you fear? The storm has now passed over." To which the king replied, not jestingly but seriously and with a severe look, "I fear thunder and lightning beyond measure; but, by God's head, I fear you more than all the thunder and lighting in the world." The earl mildly replied, "It is unjust and incredible, my lord, that you should fear me, your firm friend, who am always faithful to you and yours and the kingdom of England; rather ought you to fear your enemies, your destroyers, and false-speaking flatterers." Every one suspected that these astounding words broke forth from the king, because the earl of Leicester boldly and firmly persisted in carrying out the determination to compel the king and all opposed to their plans to adhere to them, and utterly banish his brothers, who were corrupting the whole kingdom.

Of the finding, on the death of Berard, of a chest filled with blank sheets sealed with the bull

Master Berard de Nympha, a native of the suburbs of Rome, died suddenly about this same time. He was a crafty and wealthy man, had been a clerk of Richard, earl of Cornwall, and had extorted money from the crusaders on various specious pretexts. Amongst his goods was found a coffer full of blank sheets sealed with the bull, which might be filled up at pleasure and applied to any misuse, such as fraudulently extorting money from the unsuspecting as if by authority of the pope.

Of the convocation of the prelates of England at Oxford

About the same time, all the prelates of England were convoked to assembly at Oxford, for the purpose of reforming the condition of the tottering English church, which, being driven about in manifold ways hither and thither, was in danger of falling altogether. To that place there came four bishops, specially deputed for this, namely, the bishops of Norwich and Chichester and two others whose names I do not recollect. These bishops convoked all the exempt abbots, and others of the other order, or their competent proctors, wanting to know if they would acquiesce in their decrees and unite with them in maintaining and defending them. But as some were absent on some excuse or other, and some hesitated to give their assent, they could give no positive reply just then; so they all went away, leaving the business unfinished. The things decreed are given in the Book of Additions.

Of the finding of poison

After the lapse of a short time, a report was circulated and complaints were made, that deadly poison had been administered to different people in England, and especially to the nobles, and that its effects were spreading in all directions in a lamentable way; and, as above stated, the outcome proved this to be the fact very soon. For in certain most secret places some jars, commonly called "costrells", were found which were filled with this poison and securely fastened. These fastenings having been opened, though with great difficulty, there was found in them, according to general report, a blue liquor, which was deadly poison and which being offered to some hungry dogs, they refused to taste it, but when it was mixed with their other food and offered to them, they partook of it and died at once. This was said to be a plot of foreigners to cause death of the English.

Of the cruelty of the bishop elect of Winchester towards a certain clerk

It happened, a little time ago, that John Fitz Geoffrey, justiciar of Ireland, a man of illustrious descent, rich and powerful, had given a church to one of his clerks. The bishop elect of Winchester, hearing of this, claimed the patronage of the same church, and in great anger ordered the said clerk to be ejected from it, and if he made any opposition, that he should be dragged from it in disgrace and by force, and thrust into any vile place. The agents of the said bishop elect accordingly ejected him from the church with great brutality, and, because he accused them, went so far as to kill him, and abused and wronged and beat and wounded some of his servants, driving them from their houses, and pillaging the church. Some of them they treated so inhumanly that they languished and died within a few days. This detestable deed was notified to the Roman pontiff by the barons, and when John [Fitz Geoffrey] heard of it, he was enraged, not surprisingly, and complained of it to the king. The king, however, as usual, made light of and excused the fault of the bishop elect, eagerly beseeching the complaining party not to accuse the bishop elect of or slander him with such grievous sin, or institute any proceedings against him. The said John, therefore, stayed proceedings and awaited a more convenient time for vengeance. Finding at this present time that the pride of the Poitevins was falling away, he renewed his complaint, accusing certain Poitevins, servants, that is, of the bishop elect of Winchester, of the above enormous crime, and the bishop elect himself of ordering it to be done.

Of the convalescence of the earl of Gloucester

The earl of Gloucester, who was staying at Sunning, a place not far from Reading, found himself now somewhat improved in health; though he did not dare, owing to the virulence of his disease, to exert himself, lest it should recur. For he was suffering no little grief both inwardly and outwardly; inwardly, for the death of his brother W[illiam], whose loss was one for the whole of England to deplore; outwardly, because, although convalescing, he was dreadfully disfigured, having lost his hair, as well as his complexion, whilst his teeth and nails were scabby and livid, and threatened to fall away from him like leaves.

How the senator Brancaleone destroyed the towers of the Romans

In this year, too, the Roman senator Brancaleone, finding that the insolence and pride of the Roman nobles could not be repressed in any other way than by throwing down their strongholds, which were, as it were, places of resort for thieves, caused about one hundred and forty of the towers of the said nobles to be destroyed and razed to the ground. Thus peace and tranquillity was completely established, the robbers whom they call Birri and the Roman malefactors being dispersed, both in Rome itself and in the neighbourhood.

Of the complaints instituted against the Poitevins

Instructions were sent by letter to many of those who had been so shamelessly injured by the aforesaid Poitevins, to make their complaints upon the matter and to show to the magnates of the realm proofs of the injuries done to them by the said brothers of the king; and they were assured that, if they showed their complaints to be well grounded and resolutely prosecuted them, every reparation would be made to them in accordance with the dictates of justice. But as harvest-time was near at hand, and as they thought of the inconveniences of such proceedings, and that perhaps at that moment their trouble would be to no purpose, they refused to sue until they saw a better opportunity.

How the Poitevins were permitted to pass freely through France

The aforesaid brothers of the king, being as it were closely besieged at Boulogne, as previously stated, sent once more to the king of France, humbly beseeching him not to abandon those who fled to his protecting bosom in their trouble, but rather, in accordance with the privilege of his kingdom (which is bound by it to receive and protect in peace all those who flee to it), to send them messengers of peace and guides for their journey and allow them to pass through his kingdom on their way into Poitou. This request of theirs was willingly complied with by that most pious king; and no one can doubt that to show mercy to the wretched, though they be not deserving of it, is the perfection of charity.

Of the increase of the famine, owing to the harvest being spoiled by the heavy rains

At this time, too, that is, at the end of July and the beginning of August, owing to the failure of this year's as well as the previous year's crops, such misery, want, and famine prevailed, that those who usually aided others were amongst the unfortunates who perished from want. What alarmed the lower orders more than the magnates, was the continued deluge of heavy rain, which threatened to drown the rich crops which God had given hopes of previously. To put it briefly, England would have failed in herself, had she not been restored to life by the arrival of some vessels, belonging to overseas brokers, which were laden with corn and bread brought from Germany and Holland for public sale; still, many who spent all their money, died of hunger and want. There might be seen persons of high rank, who formerly possessed abundance of all things, but whose wealth was entirely expended, now compelled to live on the charity of others, and to beg from door to door, overcome with shame, their faces pallid with hunger and want of rest, their nights being passed sleeplessly, in sorrow and lamentation. At the feast of the Assumption of the Blessed Virgin, when the barns are usually bursting with the annual crops of corn, scarcely even a single sheaf was ripe; and as the deluge increased daily, the hired labourers and their cattle caused a great expense daily, without being able to leave their houses, or to do any good in the fields. In consequence, a circumstance hitherto unknown, at the feast of All Saints, the corn was standing ready to be cut down, but useless and spoiled almost. In some places, indeed, although late, and the crop of little use, it was cut and carried, whilst in many others it was left altogether in the fields to be used as manure to enrich the soil. It should be known also, that in that year the land produced such an abundant crop, that, had it all been saved, it would have been sufficient for nearly two years' consumption.

Of the proclamation of a fast, and the procession in consequence, and for the preservation of the crops

As all human means of consolation failed, recourse was now had to the divine Comforter. It was therefore decreed, at the chapter of St Albans, that through the archdeacon a solemn and general fast should be proclaimed amongst the people, and in all the churches of the town the inhabitants should assemble in deep devotion on St Oswald's day, that is, 5 August, and should follow the brethren of the convent in procession, barefooted, to the church of St Mary de Pré[1] and there humbly beseech the Lord and His Mother that the Lord be moved by the intercession of his martyr [St Alban] and the attendant merits of the other saints to have pity on his people and deign to grant a due measure of propitious weather. On hearing this, the people of London reproached themselves for their tardiness and, influenced by this example, decreed that the same should be done with their religious orders, citizens and populace, that a general fast should be imposed on either sex, and that observing the due forms of contrition and repentance, they should go in turn in procession to the church and offer up devout prayers to the Lord that by giving them good weather, he would preserve the fruits of the earth, of which he had given hopes, and allow the people to gather them into their barns by checking the fall of rain. "For," they said, "we endure with more equanimity a failure unforeseen, than the withdrawal of a benefit after it has been promised." These things were done willingly and devoutly, as the result quickly showed. For within a short time, by the intercession of that most powerful advocate of ours [the Virgin Mary], and the blessed proto-martyr Alban and other saints, the bad weather, which had lasted so long, ceased, or came more seldom, and the price of corn diminished from that time until it was sold for half what it previously cost; for the devout prayers of the people and the subsequent change in the weather and temperature promised a speedy and abundant crop both of corn and fruit.

Of the death of H. Lexington, bishop of Lincoln

About this time, that is to say on 8 August, Henry of Lexington, bishop of Lincoln, died at Netlington, a manor of his near Lincoln, and his body was buried with all due respect in the cathedral church of Lincoln.

[1] Later a Benedictine nunnery, but at this date still a leper hospital dependent on St Albans Abbey.

Of the departure of Arlot, the pope's nuncio from England

As the feast of the Assumption of the glorious Virgin drew near, Arlot, the pope's nuncio, left England. He was a clerk, intimate counsellor and notary of the pope's, and had come to England armed with the greatest powers by the pope, but seeing the disturbed state of the kingdom, he wisely took his departure quietly, until a wind of peace and unity, more auspicious for him, should blow.

Of the interception of some money belonging to the bishop elect of Winchester

In the mean time the castellan[1] of Dover, who kept a careful watch over the coast and was an unfailing scrutiniser of travellers, found many laden with the much-desired coin, which they were taking out to the aliens; these he quickly relieved of their burdens, that they might travel more easily. And a thousand marks belonging to the bishop elect of Winchester, which he had deposited there, were found at that time; and these were given to four knights as pay and travelling expenses for going to Rome in the name of the king and the magnates to plead the cause of the baronage of England briefly and summarily without delay or dispute; and to announce to him the finding of some blank sheets sealed with the bull, in a chest belonging to mr Berard de Nympha, after his death, and show by these sealed blank sheets the many and manifold devices by which the Romans studied to defile the land; which blank forms sealed with the bull, the deputies took with them just as they were discovered.

Of the anxiety of the king of France to establish a lasting peace with the English

The most pious king of France is now earnestly and carefully considering how a lasting peace can be established between the two kingdoms, that is, of France and England; for, said he, "The utmost effort should be made to establish a firm and durable peace between my sons and those of the king of England, who are cousins and who, under God's favour, will become kings, in order that the two kingdoms may no longer gnaw each other at the instigation of the enemy of the human race, nor the inhabitants pillage and slay each other, and thus be thrust into hell." He therefore had a very large sum of money collected to enable him to carry through to the desired end this happy design, promising his French subjects that great advantages would accrue to them from this taxation, and begging them not to be annoyed at a short-lived burden, from which they could derive lasting benefit for the future.

Of the appointment of four knights in each county to examine into the grievances of the lower orders

A writ of the lord king was sent at this time to each county, to four knights appointed in each of these counties, who were to make faithful and strict inquiry into the nature and measure of the grievances which the lower orders suffered at the hands of their more powerful neighbours, to carefully inquire into each complaint and injury, by whomsoever committed, and on whomsoever inflicted, for many a long time past;

[1] *oppidanus*. The castellan referred to above, Richard de Grey.

and to bring with them before the barons the results of their enquiry, enclosed under their seals, at a time prescribed for them in the writ. Any one wishing to know the contents of these letters, can find them in the Book of Additions at the sign

Of the king's anger against Philip Lovel, on account of the injuries done to the forests

At the commencement of harvest-time in this year, the king made a strict examination into the state of his forests in the vicinity of Stony Stratford, and it was intimated to him that Philip Lovel, a clerk and intimate counsellor of his, and his treasurer, had done irreparable damage to the royal forests. The king, in fact, had, out of pure and royal generosity, kindly granted him up to a certain number of beasts of the chase for stocking his parks and for the use of his table; but he abused this favour, shamelessly exceeding the number given, so it was said, him by a tenfold. Much enraged at this, the king made an examination of the recesses of the forests, and on finding them devoid of animals, and being told, as above stated, that the said Philip was the cause of it, he seized him roughly by the arm, saying, "Philip, by God's head, I arrest thee as the basest of my subjects." Philip, thereupon, wishing to appease the king's anger, replied with moderation and frankly and humbly, "My lord king, whom I have served faithfully for some time in your exchequer, there are many foresters, especially in Whittlewood, tyrannising over their fellow-countrymen, whose own crimes render them unworthy of belief, as the abbot and convent of Beccles can prove. Do not, therefore, if it please you, so hastily listen to the tale-bearing of such accusers; for they endeavour to blacken the reputation of the king, in order that his enemies may have reason to say, 'The king finishes, like the devil, by confounding those who serve him, even those who serve him best in their offices.' " The king was still more roused by this speech, and consigned Philip there and then to the custody of the marshal, saying, with a loud and threatening voice, "If I have exalted you and some others, and as a favour, appointed you to high and profitable offices, you are so much the more strictly bound to serve me with fidelity, and you ought to be more severely punished for faults and offences." These were the same words he had made use of frequently to Robert Passelewe, when that person was kicking against his authority some years before. But Philip, who had conferred many benefits on a great many people, was not without friends, and on finding some persons of high rank as pledges for him until he could establish his innocence, he was set at liberty for a time, with the hope of finally being released entirely.

Of the committal of the sheriff of Northampton to prison

The sheriff of Northampton, following in the track of his predecessor, William de Lisle, the late sheriff, and stimulated by avarice, inflicted injuries on several innocent persons, and a complaint having been made of his proceedings to Hugh Bigod, the chief justiciar, he was found guilty of very many wrongdoings and when the feast of the blessed Mary's Nativity was near he was seized and committed to a hard and horrible prison, narrowly escaping the gallows.

Of the death of Roger of Whitchester

About this time died Roger of Whitchester, a clerk and intimate counsellor of the king, who relying on the office of judge used his utmost endeavours to give satisfaction to the king by carrying out his orders.

Of the death of William de Tarente of the Cistercian order

About this same time, also, died William de Tarente, a brother of the Cistercian order, a proctor and sort of steward of the queen's. This man strayed widely from the rule of St Benedict, and, instigated by an insatiable avarice, took on the selling or mortgaging of all the lands and manors for the queen, whereby he greatly increased her possessions, but by augmenting the losses and risks of others he damaged his reputation irreparably. And although religious, especially those of his own order, were reproached with the said William's fault, as it redounded and threw scandal on all of them, the queen shrewdly made excuses and palliated his fault, and thus allowed his errors to go on increasing for many years.

How messengers were sent to the pope on behalf of the community of England

Solemn messengers were sent to the pope on behalf of the kingdom and the community of all England, with orders to deliver their messages fully to the pope and return as quickly as possible, without waiting to listen to any arguments or discussions. One of these, Peter Branche, a most eloquent and extraordinarily skilled man, died at Paris, which spread alarm and grief to the rest; but they continued their journey, determined to persevere in carrying out the object of their mission. Any one who wishes to learn the object of their journey, and to see a copy of the document drawn up by the barons, will be able to find them in the Book of Additions at the sign.

Of the treachery perpetrated against the Welsh

On a certain occasion, whilst the English were holding a peaceful parley with the Welsh, they saw they were more numerous and stronger than the Welsh and one of the English knights said to Patrick, who was their chief, "My lord Patrick, you are a great baron of the king's, and our illustrious chief and protector. Look, the Lord God of Hosts, the avenger, has delivered our enemies into our hands; we are stronger and more numerous than the Welsh. Let us attack them unawares, and send them as prisoners to our lord the king, to whom that triumph will be most acceptable. But if you do not accede to my request, I will accuse you to the king of treason." When the English, that is the frontier people, whom we call Marchers heard this, they rushed suddenly on the Welsh, and by this treachery slew many of them. But after a while the battle turned against these treacherous Marchers, and great numbers of them fell slain in their turn, amongst them one baron, the aforesaid Patrick. The one who had counselled their act of treachery was a coward and escaped, slipping away from the field whilst the others were fighting fiercely. The leader of the Welsh in that bloody conflict was David, the youngest of three brothers, the three sons [*sic*] of the great Llewellyn, the prince of North Wales, whose innumerable triumphs would require special mention; but much has been said of him earlier in this book in the proper place. Another of the brothers, the middle one, whose name was also Llewellyn, was not present at this battle, but conducted himself bravely enough in the war against the English, following his father's example in every way, and striving not to be a degenerate. The remaining brother, the eldest of the three, was kept a close prisoner in prison and in chains.

Of the consecration of Godfrey as archbishop of York

Round about the anniversary of the Nativity aforesaid,[1] mr Godfrey of Kimeton was consecrated[2] at Rome as archbishop of York, having been found by the pope and all his examiners to be a fit and commendable person for that office; and when he had settled in praiseworthy fashion the affairs of his church, he returned in proper time to take the government of it.

Of the archbishop of Canterbury's wish to administer holy orders in the church of St Albans

The church of Lincoln being at this time vacant, the archbishop of Canterbury indicated to the abbot of St Albans that he proposed to come there and conduct ordinations (if it was agreeable to the abbot) in the conventual church there. On hearing this, the abbot was alarmed lest his church should be deprived of its liberties in any way by it, and after taking counsel, resolved to resist it. The archbishop, therefore, was told in reply, that he would not be received to do this on any account, as it was well known that the monastery of St Albans had been from times of old exempt, which ought not to be unknown to him, and because he at that time held the government of the church at Lincoln, which was vacant, and which, it was well known, was excluded altogether from the liberty of St Albans. On hearing this, the archbishop quietly gave way, considering that perseverance in this matter would be of no avail; and he therefore went through with his ordinations at Dunstable. Nevertheless, because he asked for hospitality at St Albans as a favour, he was received with kindness and respect both on the way and on the return journey, and provided excellent presents at table; with all which he was well satisfied, and thanked them, blessing both hospice and hosts, and leaving the church and all its possessions undisturbed and uninjured.

Of the election of R. of Gravesend as bishop of Lincoln

On the Monday before Michaelmas mr Richard of Gravesend, dean of the church of Lincoln, was elected bishop of Lincoln; he was by general consent a praiseworthy person, and one not likely to neglect the interests of any of those under him.

Of the dedication of the church of Salisbury

Also on the day after Michaelmas, the church of Salisbury was dedicated by Boniface, archbishop of Canterbury, in the presence of the king and a numerous body of the

[1] Nativity BVM, 8 September
[2] For Godfrey's election, see above, p. 126.

prelates, the bishop providing outstanding entertainment for all whom he could get together at the ceremony.

Of the deposition from office of Philip Lovel and many others

About the feast of St Luke the Evangelist in the same year, Philip Lovel, the king's treasurer, was deposed from his office by the judgment of the barons, for the offence above mentioned, and John de Crachal, archdeacon of Bedford, was appointed in his stead. Philip, who was not so much grieved at the deposition itself, as inconsolable at the manner of it, and the suddenness of his fall from such a high position, offered the king a large sum of money to obtain a re-establishment of his good name, and to be, or at least in appearance to be, a friend of the king. In like manner, by the advice of the barons, and especially of the chief justiciar, many others were dismissed from their offices in the exchequer along with Philip, and others substituted. Thomas of Wymondham, precentor of Lichfield, was appointed treasurer at the exchequer, where writs of the green wax are sealed.

How a check was put upon the rapacity of the sheriffs

The rapacity of the sheriffs was prudently and with good reason checked; for, mercenary beyond measure, they hitherto made a practice of extorting gifts from the inhabitants by any means, whether right or wrong, and fell over each other in increasing their farms. They rode about with large retinues, busy oppressing all the country people by their manifold exactions, and injuring them on frivolous and unreasonable grounds. It was therefore decreed, that if any one, from that time forth, should secretly or openly give presents to them, the sheriffs, or any of them, for the sake of obtaining justice, or of impeding the due course of justice, unless such presents should consist of a moderate supply of food and drink, both the briber and the bribed should be severely punished.

Of the deputation sent from England to the parliament held at Cambray

About the feast of St Leonard, the community of the barons, who were then assembled at London, decided to send special messengers to the great secret conference appointed to be held at Cambray between the kingdoms of France, England, and Germany, the king, by the advice of all his barons, remaining in England the while. Those chosen to be sent there for this purpose, on behalf of the king and the kingdom of England, were the bishops of Worcester and Lincoln; Roger Bigod, the earl marshal, and the earl of Leicester; who crossed over but could not bring matters to any result at all, as the French king purposely absented himself owing to the absence of the other king.

Of the consecration of R. of Gravesend as bishop of Lincoln

On the Sunday after All Saints' day, the bishop of Lincoln was consecrated at Cambridge, and immediately afterwards he crossed the Channel as above stated, on the king's business. Thus he abandoned the church of Lincoln, although he was made bishop of the same, and did not visit it for a long time afterwards.

How Joan, wife of William de Valence, demanded her dowry

About the same time, whilst the king was at London, Joan, the wife of William de Valence, came to him, and in the presence of Hugh Bigod, the chief justiciar, and the barons, urgently demanded that justice should be done her and she be allowed at least the dowry which belonged to her. After careful deliberation on the matter, a portion of the lands which had belonged to her before she was married to the aforesaid William was granted to her, that is to say, to the value of five hundred marks, which was out of her inheritance, although the lands concerned were valued at more than a thousand marks; for they feared that if more was allowed her, she would send the greater part of it to her husband, who was a public enemy of the kingdom; and they did not wish to take it all away from her, lest an innocent woman should be punished for another's fault.

How Manfred was crowned king of Apulia

At this same time, too, the Roman curia began to fall into low repute, inasmuch as the prelates and magnates of Apulia, contrary to the pope's wish, elected and had crowned as their king, the emperor Frederick's son Manfred; because not only Manfred himself but also the whole family was held in great contempt and detested by the pope and the whole curia. Moreover, the king of Apulia created archbishops and bishops without the pope's consent, nay even against his wish, and all of them were unanimous, despite the papal prohibition, in showing greater obedience and in paying more honour and respect to the said king than to the pope. The magnates, also, made no mention of Edmund, son of the king of England (to whom the pope had given the kingdom of Apulia, and who had been invested with the same by a ring delivered him by the bishop of Bologna), but had done homage and sworn allegiance to this same Manfred, and given him full seisin and possession of their cities and castles. In consequence of this, the king of England complained strongly, not without reason, of the pope, for having, in conjunction with his cardinals, so plausibly and improperly dragged away so much money from his kingdom for the sake of obtaining that kingdom of Apulia, but all to no purpose; yet he, the said king of England, had received with all honour the pope's messengers who were sent to England; for instance, brother John of Diva, mr [Bernard] of Siena, bishop of Bologna, the archbishop of Messina, and a great many others, who had come as proctors for the purpose of expediting the business of his son Edmund in the matter of the kingdom of Apulia, and whom he had allowed to extort rich procurations from the religious orders. In addition at this same time, the citizens of Florence razed to the ground a certain castle which cardinal Octavian had built, because it was an object of suspicion to them.

How the uncle of Brancaleone was appointed senator of Rome

The senator Brancaleone dying, the Roman citizens, not troubling to obtain the pope's consent (though he asserted that even if it was as a simple citizen, he ought to be called in for the election of a senator), unanimously elected as senator the uncle of the aforesaid Brancaleone, who was likewise detestable to the pope as a relation of

Brancaleone's. The head of Brancaleone placed in a precious vase, they over-superstitiously and grandly, as if it were a holy relic, set up on a marble column in memory of his valour and probity. And indeed he was a hammer and exterminator of the proud and powerful and of malefactors, a protector and defender of the poor, and a lover of and striver after truth and justice. Following his advice, which he had handed down to them as a sort of inheritance, they listened with obedience to the commands of the new senator, whom they had elected by the advice of the aforesaid Brancaleone, with the same readiness as they did to those of his predecessor. All these proceedings the pope considered to be indubitably insults to himself and to the court of Rome; for immediately after the death of aforesaid Brancaleone, he had sent solemn messengers to the Romans, forbidding them to elect anyone as senator without his assent; but they treated the pope's message with ridicule and contempt, and at once elected the uncle of Brancaleone and solemnly installed him as senator in his stead, as above stated.

Of the death of Philip, prior of Westminster, who was elected abbot of that place

At the end of October, Philip, prior of Westminster, who had been elected abbot of that church and was in daily expectation of the return of his messengers from the court of Rome, went the way of all flesh, to the great disquiet of the church and convent of Westminster; and being thus deprived of his wished-for earthly dignity, he was gathered to the heavenly host.

Of a violent thunderstorm

*In the following month, that is to say, on the first night of December, there was violent and horrible thunder and lightning, wind and pouring rain; interpreted by many as a sad and lamentable omen, which thunder in winter usually signifies.

Of the announcement of the deaths of several people made to the king at St Albans

*On the feast day of St Cecilia the Virgin,[1] which fell on a Friday, the king came to St Albans, staying for the three following days, and on St Catherine's day[2] he caused the [image of] the martyr to be carried in solemn procession round the cloister, the brethren of the convent being robed fittingly for a prince, and he himself with his attendants following in procession and devoutly and reverently making offerings. Whilst he was staying there, messengers arrived, announcing that Walter Comyn the most powerful earl in Scotland, had yielded to fate, having died from the effects of a fall from his horse, which, stumbling over some obstacle in the road, threw him and broke his legs. Another message, too, was brought to him, announcing that John Fitz Geoffrey had gone the way of all flesh near Guildford. For him the king, before his departure, caused a solemn mass to be performed. It was further announced to the king that Brancaleone, the Roman senator already mentioned, had been taken from

* These two paragraphs occur in this order, but, as the dates show and marks in the chronicle indicate, a strictly chronological order would require them to be reversed.

[1] Friday, 22 November 1258

[2] Monday, 25 November 1258

amongst us, to the great injury [of the city of Rome], and his uncle appointed in his stead.

Of the return of the archbishop of York, after being consecrated by the pope

When the king left St Albans, he went towards Ely and [Bury] St Edmunds. Just at that time, too, the archbishop of York arrived in England from beyond the Alps, where he had been consecrated by the pope. On reaching London he caused his cross to be carried publicly before him through the midst of the city; then he went to the king, and was received with due honour by him; after which he set off for the north of England, and was received in his archdiocese with great joy and exalted as pastor and father. A short time afterwards he appointed as dean of York mr Roger of Holderness, a clerk of St Albans, as a reward for his merits, and because he was himself a fellow countryman of St Albans, and in conferring his benefits studied to remunerate all according to their deserts.

Of the proscription and banishment of Guy de Rochfort

About this same time, Guy de Rochfort, a Poitevin by birth, to whom the king had two years before granted the castle of Colchester by charter, with the honour pertaining thereto, incurred the grave anger of the king and baronage, and was condemned to exile and to be deprived of all his property: for many and reiterated complaints were made against him, that he had outrageously oppressed and injured the people of the county, especially those subject to him; but the fact that he was a Poitevin gave more offence than any other faults.

Of the accusation brought against W. of Scotenny, who absconded

Walter of Scoteny, seneschal of the earl of Gloucester, withdrew from the earl's sight and concealed himself with unnamed friends in out-of-the-way places. For he was accused of having basely and treacherously administered poison to the earl his master and William the earl's brother, from the effects of which the latter died, and the life of the former was endangered. The accusation against him had more weight from the fact that the aforesaid William, before his death, had declared that the said Walter of Scoteny was guilty of the treachery; and one thing certain was that soon after making this statement he died suddenly. However, the aforesaid Walter oftentimes offered to clear himself publicly and in due form of the crime imputed to him.

Of the imprisonment of W. de Bussey

At this same time, William de Bussey, seneschal of William de Valence, and a most wicked man, was seized and committed to close custody in the Tower of London, for his base and iniquitous offences and crimes.

Of the departure of Joan, wife of W. de Valence

During Advent Joan, the wife of William de Valence crossed the Channel to share in her husband's exile, being incited to do so, either by love of him and a desire of being in his company, or by anger at the distribution of her lands, in which, although she was to receive four hundred marks, she seemed to have no part.

Of the dispute amongst the scholars of Oxford

At this time also, there arose a serious quarrel between the scholars of Oxford, who were of various nations, there being amongst them Scotchmen, Welshmen, and men from the north as well as the south of England; and the quarrel rose to such a pitch that (sad prognostic as it was) they displayed hostile banners, and the different parties attacked each other, with deaths and injuries on both sides.

How the Welsh desired to make peace with the king

In the same year, too, the Welsh notwithstanding their frequent victories over their opponents, prudently enough weighing future events in their minds and taking counsel amongst themselves, said, "We know that the kingdom of England is in a very disturbed state, but when peace is established – a result the nobles of the country are trying to bring about – we shall not be able to resist them, as they will all unite in falling upon us. Let us consider, above all, that Llewelyn's brother, the eldest son of our lord Griffith, who died in prison at London, is kept in chains, and if he is released he will be provoked to take vengeance; and that his other brothers, David and Rhodri, will also incline the same way, and we shall be divided and desolate. In this helpless state, if the English attack us, they will pound us down, will demand an account at our hands of the blood of their brethren, and will blot us out from the face of the earth, and crush us irreparably, like a clay pitcher." By common assent, therefore, they offered four thousand marks to the king, three hundred to Edward, and two hundred to the queen, on condition that all cause of dispute, offence, and discord, should be entirely forgiven on both sides, and that they should be allowed to enjoy their accustomed peace, tranquillity and liberty. The king, on hearing this proposition, trusting to evil counsel, replied with anger, "What means this? One good man is of more value than the amount they offer for the peace they ask." Thus the request made by the Welsh for peace remained unanswered; however, they waited quietly for peace, always declaring that, as had ever been their custom, they would defend themselves, would resist the attacks of their enemies, and sustain their own cause, like men, to the utmost of their power.

Of the general disposition of events during the whole year

This year throughout was very unlike all previous ones, bringing disease and death, stormy and very rainy; to such an extent that although in the summer a fair promise of abundant crops of corn and fruit was given, in the autumn the continual heavy rains spoiled the corn, fruit, and all kinds of pulse once more; and in Advent, in some parts of England as above stated, the barns were empty and the crops remained standing ready for cutting, but entirely spoiled: for as the grain germinated, the ear and the straw rotted together, and as men died from the want of corn, so the cattle died from want of fodder; and though England was drained empty of money on many pretexts, yet the people were obliged, at the instigation of hunger, to pay sixteen shillings for a measure of corn still moist and germinating. Consequently the poor pined away with hunger, and died. The dying staggered away into various by-ways to yield their last pitiable breath; and of these there was such a great number, that the gravediggers were overcome with weariness and threw a number of bodies in a heap into a single grave. The middling sort, short of food, sold their animals, reduced their households, and left their land uncultivated, whereby the hope of rising again from the abyss, which generally consoles the despairing, was entirely extinguished. And if corn had not been brought for sale from the continent, there is no doubt but that England would have perished in herself.

Of the vision of a certain holy woman

Quite genuine at this time, appears to have been the terrifying vision of a certain holy recluse at St Albans, which was, as the archdeacon of the place was reliably informed, plainly not a dream but a manifestation of the divine will and a fearful threat. For she saw a person of advanced age and venerable appearance, whose beard gave him a severe aspect, standing in her parlour; from which place he withdrew in anger, ascended a tower and, turning a stern and threatening look towards the town, thundered forth, "Woe, woe, to all dwellers upon earth," and repeating this several times he vanished.

The king at London at Christmas

Anno Domini 1259, which was the forty-third year of the reign of king Henry the third, the said king was at London at Christmas, where the nobles of the kingdom were deeply engaged in deliberating how, while abiding by their salutary design, they could comply with the wish of Richard, king of Almain, who ardently longed, as he told them, to come to England to visit his relatives and friends, his properties and his native land. For they suspected that on his coming he would vent his displeasure and revenge on the barons, reproaching them with pursuing with a deadly hatred his brother, king Henry the third, as they had done his father, king John; and of lately condemning his uterine brothers to exile, as though they had been found guilty of the greatest crimes, when they were innocent. They feared moreover that he would make these same brothers of his common enemies of the kingdom, either by bringing them back with him by stealth, or at some future time effecting a reconciliation, and then treacherously exhorting them to return to England to trample it underfoot once again, which would tend to the greater undoing of the inhabitants, and be a new and worse error. They likewise feared that he would oppose and impede their salutary design for the happiest arrangement of the affairs of the kingdom, and that he would re-establish the old order of things, and having deceived them all he would punish them one by one and in course of time disinherit them.

How the Jew was convicted of treason, and escaped punishment by being baptised

As the time drew near when our Lord was born in the flesh, one of his creatures was reborn in the spirit. Elias the Jew, of London, who was surnamed Bishop, fearing danger and damnation manifold, fled to the font for safety and protection; for, being purified by the wholesome process of baptism, in company with two others, he was snatched from the ranks of the devil, and saved from the punishment due for a most base crime formerly perpetrated by him. For report stated that it was in his house that the poisonous liquor was made which had brought danger or death to many of the nobles of England, and it was said that he willingly allowed the transaction to be carried on. But at that time he was a demon; but being now changed to a Christian, his works were altered in accordance with his condition.

How a large sum of money was sent abroad through the cunning of the wife of W. de Valence

As mentioned above, a rumour was spread through the kingdom, that the king's brothers, whom fame had aspersed, as above stated, had been enriched by a large sum of money, thanks to a woman's activity, and perhaps the instruction of the Poitevins, by Joan, wife of William de Valence, who as if following her husband out of love, left England with a large amount of money, to the incalculable danger and detriment of the kingdom. According to report, the aforesaid Joan, with womanly ingenuity, procured a large quantity of wool, among which as it was packed in sacks she hid a large sum of money. Then she had it loaded on very strong carts, as if it were only wool, and at a convenient opportunity sent to Poitou. Therefore, although it was stated by many that the money belonging to the aforesaid William was confiscated, wherever it was stored, it is evident from this that no reliance can be placed on such statements.

Of the death of Philip Lovel

Whilst the festivities of Christmas were being kept up, lest the joys of this world should come unalloyed to mortals, Philip Lovel, a particularly intimate counsellor of the king's, and one-time treasurer, died on St Thomas's day,[1] at his church of Hamestable, through grief, as was stated, and bitterness of spirit, at not having reconciled himself to the king, whom he had formerly served. The king demanded from him an immense sum for the offence committed by him according to report, in his forests. When informed of Philip's death, he ordered all the property that had belonged to him to be confiscated, until his demand was satisfied.

Of the election of H. de Wengham as bishop of Winchester

At this same time, too, the monks of Winchester, finding that the king would not accept any one whom they elected as bishop unless it was someone he particularly approved of,[2] especially since the banishment of his brother, elected as their bishop and pastor of their souls Henry of Wengham, the king's chancellor. He, however, considering it an uncertain matter, likely to cause litigation, would not unreservedly[3] consent to the election made of himself, although he had no doubt of finding the king in his favour. He declared that he was unfitted for such high office, and the cure of souls; neither was he instructed in theology and scriptures, or (as would be seemly) opposed to office.[4] In the end, however, he gave some sort of consent, and was willingly

[1] 29 December
[2] *sibi carissimum*
[3] *plene*
[4] *aut, ut decet, renitentem*

accepted by the king though on the following condition; namely, that his (the king's) brother Aymer, elected before him, should, if he could obtain from the pope the favour of consecration, have the precedence of all others in being instituted to the church of Winchester; but if not, he, Henry de Wengham, should, saving his brother's right to maintenance, be appointed in his stead.

How a deputation was sent to meet Richard, king of Almain

About the feast of St Hilary after holding a general council, at which careful discussion took place concerning the coming of king Richard of Almain to England, they sent a formal deputation to meet him, consisting of the bishop of Worcester, the said abbot of [Bury] St Edmunds, Peter of Savoy, and John Mansel, for him to inform them of the cause of his sudden and unexpected coming, and as to the length of his proposed stay in England. The earl of Leicester, Simon, to the astonishment of many people, was still away overseas, so that the council of the barons was in a great measure incomplete, and they had great fears of concealed plots. They were afraid that the king, although he wore a serene expression, would feel for his brothers in exile, and would have complained strongly to the aforesaid king of Almain, his brother, that "the English, after hounding their father king John to the death with their mortal hatred, were now in the same way pursuing his sons and relatives, as if the angry feeling was transmitted by inheritance;[1] and as the king of England so the king of Almain – they were suffering similar wrongs". The magnates of England therefore proposed to get an oath from the king of Almain, before he landed, that he would not in any way do injury to the kingdom of England, nor impede the common provision.[2] But of what benefit would this be? For he might perhaps say afterwards that he had been compelled to take the oath against his will. But as it is unknown to the generality of the people whether this would have come to pass, I do not venture to determine the matter in this book; but it is generally said that he took the oath, as mentioned above, and gave letters patent in accordance therewith.

How the king set out to meet his brother Richard

The king hastened to the sea coast, and was accompanied by a great body of the magnates, who, by way of caution, were well armed and mounted. For it was said that the said king Richard purposed to bring with him one or more of his brothers, whom by common consent they had banished, in order that, by thus annulling the decision in that matter, he might be able to restore them to their former position – which the barons would ill bear. The king had proclamation made by the crier of London, ordering the city to be cleared of sticks, blocks of wood, mud and filth, and decorated with hangings and, with everything that could offend the eyes of beholders removed, made resplendent with all sorts of novelties.

The reply of Richard, king of Almain, to the deputation from the community of England

To the formal deputation thus sent by the community of England, the king of Almain, who was waiting on the coast at the other side of the Channel, and collecting a strong

[1] *traduce* [2] specifically the Provisions of Oxford in another chronicler, Thomas Wykes

and numerous army, replied with a stern look and threatening tone, swearing by God's throat, "I will neither take the oath which you require, nor will I give you a date for the end of my stay in England." And he added, "I have not my peer in England; for I am the son of the late king, and the brother of the present one, and am also earl of Cornwall. If, therefore, the nobles of England wished to reform a deformed kingdom, they ought in the first place to have sent for me, and not have so hastily and presumptuously attempted such a difficult matter without my agreement or presence." When one of the deputation wished to reply to this speech, he was restrained by a word[1] from a colleague. The reply would have been: "We have often appointed you our leader in effecting a reform of the declining kingdom, but, driven by avarice, you have always sought to entrap us by your cunning and unexpected devices, when we were studying to improve the condition of the king as well as the kingdom and not anticipating such things; in consequence of which, the king, going back on wholesome intentions, has injured everyone he could thereafter." Lest such reproaches should cause strife the deputation, well enough aware of the excited state of the feelings of the king of Almain, straightway returned as quickly as they could; for a large number of people, equipped in various ways, were awaiting him. When this outcome of the mission was announced to the English nobles on this side of the Channel, they caused ships and galleys to be assembled from the Cinque Ports, as well as from very many other ports. And, armed in advance with arms and armour as a precaution, and the ardent desire of all of them being to attack the enemy, they boldly got ready to meet him. They were also encouraged by the fact that when Louis, the son of the king of France, was heretofore in England, a very few ships of the English, beyond everybody's expectation, attacked and destroyed a numerous and well-equipped French fleet. Furthermore, they assembled a large army of horse and foot soldiers on this side, so that, if the enemy should gain the advantage in a sea fight and come on (of which result they had, however, no fear), they could give them a lively reception at sword's point on the beach and make a stand against them on dry land. When the king of Almain, Richard, by means of diligent spies got a trustworthy account of these things, he yielded to the advice of common friends, calmed his angry feelings, and promised in writing that he would take with equanimity the oath which the barons of England in their zeal for the welfare of the state demanded.

Of the return of king Richard of Almain to England

King Richard of Almain, then, accompanied by his queen, set sail for England, and landed at Dover at St Julian's day.[2] He entered England with a chastened and reduced household, consisting of two counts from Almain who had only three knights with them; and the king himself with eight knights and his queen and his son Edmund. They, on coming ashore, were not allowed to enter the castle of Dover, nor even was the king of England, for the nobles of England were still afraid to allow any one who had not taken the oath to enter that castle, which is England's principal barrier. The king, however, met him when he landed, welcoming him very warmly. And

[1] *secreto moderamine*
[2] 27 January

entertained by the archbishop of Canterbury, they spent days feasting together with great pleasure in each other's company.

How R., king of Almain, swore to assist the magnates of England

On the morrow the magnates of England went into the chapter-house at Canterbury respectfully conducting the kings of England and Almain and ordered the text of the gospel to be placed on the pulpit. Richard, earl of Gloucester, then stood up in the presence of all, and in a loud though respectful voice called the earl of Cornwall to him, addressing him not as king of Almain, but by name, "Richard, earl of Cornwall", who, in obedience to the call, came forward respectfully and pronounced clearly and distinctly the oath imposed upon him, which was to the following effect:

The oath of Richard king of Almain

"Hear all of you, that I hereby swear upon the holy Gospels that I, Richard, earl of Cornwall, will faithfully and diligently join with you in reforming the kingdom of England, hitherto exceedingly deformed by evil counsellors. I will also give you powerful help in expelling all rebels and disturbers of the kingdom. And this oath I will inviolably observe, on pain of losing all the lands I hold in England." And when everyone said, "that is enough, he is sufficiently bound to keep faith with us," the aforesaid earl [of Gloucester] replied, "Because we have sometimes been immensely hurt in such cases, and because he who has once been scalded always dreads boiling water, I am not at all sure that we have done enough; which Almighty God forbid."

How the nobles of Almain took their departure on their king's arrival at London

On the day of St Mary's Purification[1] the two kings and their queens, accompanied by a great many nobles of England, reached the city of London, which in accordance with the orders above mentioned, had been properly cleared of filth, and richly decorated for the arrival of such great princes; and they were met, on their approach, by a large number of citizens, uttering shouts of welcome. The city indeed was so full of people that the pavements of the streets were entirely covered by the crowds assembled; and as Richard's uterine brothers were not in his train, as had been threatened and as was suspected (they having been left on the continent), they gave vent to their joy with still greater eagerness. But they wondered very much that the Germans should give him so much liberty and allow him to go to England in company with his queen and his son, the objects most dear to him; that they had not retained at least one of them, as a sort of hostage or at least because he had left them behind him their lord and prince might the more readily and quickly return to them. But in a short time his fame began to diminish, and his power as a king to be little or not at all feared amongst the English; and in consequence of this the German nobles, who had come to England in attendance on their king, considering that he was not treated in England with the favour and respect due to his kingly dignity, took their departure in indignation, and hastened home, saying to themselves, "If his fellow-countrymen do not respect him, how can we treat him with honour? We have what

[1] 2 February

we have chosen: money, rather than a man who will make money; a treasure amassed, rather than one who will amass it. But if he will give us all he has left of it, we will not trouble ourselves any more with his personal presence." For their object was, as they had in a great measure done, to drain him dry of the rest of his money.

Of the parliament held at London

On the octave of the Purification the nobles of England assembled in London, as they had previously arranged, and the earl of Leicester, whose prolonged absence had been a source of regret to all the people of England, who knew not what could have happened to him on the continent, came to this present council. In addition, a member of the French king's privy council, the dean of Bourges, was there. At this parliament much discussion took place concerning the business which was on the go between the two kings, of France and England that is, and what had been done and approved of with regard to it on the continent. The result of the discussion was, that within a short space of time, that is to say, on St Valentine's day, peace was arranged and made between them at London; provided that each party would, without dispute, observe what, as will be fully stated hereafter in its proper place, had been pre-arranged and determined between their special and solemn messengers.

Of the capture and imprisonment of W. Scotenny and William Bussey

At the end of February and beginning of March in this year, Walter Scotenny, the principal and most intimate adviser and seneschal of the earl of Gloucester, was taken prisoner at London, on suspicion of having administered poison to the said earl, and to his brother William, from the effects of which the earl had barely escaped with his life, and the said William had actually died. He had been before under the custody of sureties, but he was now taken to the Tower of London and placed in the closest confinement there. Likewise, William Bussey, the seneschal and principal adviser of the king's uterine brother William de Valence, was made prisoner; and it would require a special narrative, were a full statement of his crimes to be given. After having been up to this kept in the custody of his sureties, he was now taken up for judgment before the judges; and as he could not satisfactorily answer the charges made against him (for he was implicated in many crimes), he wanted to undo the fastenings of his coif, to show publicly that he had the tonsure of a clerk. He was not allowed to do so, however, but by order of the judges he was savagely and violently hurried away, to be tormented in a worse place of imprisonment. The warder who took him away seized him, not by the fastenings of his coif, but by his throat, and whilst dragging him to prison, said derisively, "If I do you injustice, who will do you justice?" These were the words which the aforesaid William generally employed to parties who frequently appeared before him to complain of injuries they had suffered, and to demand justice of him. He was accustomed, too, to say on many occasions, "The lord king's will is what my master William de Valence wills, but not *vice versa*." Thus he deigned to show respect neither to the king nor to any of the magnates, nor indeed to afford justice to any one of a lower order, asserting that his master had obtained a privilege from the king that no writ could be sued out against him in chancery, and that he need not answer to any injured party, whatever the offence might be, except at his own pleasure. Whilst this William, then, was being quickly taken off to prison, everybody derided and insulted him for his intolerable pride, his inexorable tyranny, and his plundering and wrongdoing. Although it would be tedious to enumerate these things, we think it worth while to mention one in this book, that the rest may be imagined.

A certain detestable action of W. de Bussey's

It happened that a certain young man was going along a lane in Trumpington, when a dog barked at him, and wishing to stop this, the young man carelessly threw a stone at the dog. The stone, glancing off to one side, accidentally killed a hen belonging to some poor woman, who happening to come out of her house, saw the occurrence, and raising a cry of complaint, brought many of the neighbours together round her. The young man humbly declared upon his oath, that it was an accident, and duly offered to pay the price of the hen, and twice that amount as a compensation for the offence committed; but the wicked woman refused all his offers, and insisted on a more profitable revenge. An insolent retainer of William de Valence, taking courage from the high rank of his master, seized the innocent young man, and placed him in prison in the most confining chains, where, in a few days, he died from his intolerable sufferings. The priest of the place having called the neighbours together, and become assured of the young man's innocence, buried the corpse in the cemetery, and performed the burial services over it as well as he could, after it had lain two or three days on a dunghill, where it had been thrown, and had become putrid. Three days afterwards, William Bussey happened to be passing, and hearing of what had been done, he ordered the body, which had been rotting for four days, to be dragged from the tomb and hung on a gibbet. All these cruelties, and other similar ones, were perpetrated without any judgment, but not without drawing down vengeance from the Lord. The wife of the dead man having made a complaint of this act of cruelty, is now bringing a suit against a dead man, and the most just Judge now requites this most iniquitous judge for his actions, by sentencing him to eternal perdition.

Of William Horton, who had been sent to Scotland by the king of England

In the same year about 1 March William de Horton, monk and chamberlain of the church of St Albans, returned from the remotest parts of Scotland, whither he had, long before, namely about the feast of St Catherine in the same year, undertaken the laborious journey by command of the lord king and by provision of his (the lord king's) counsellor, and also by the kindness of his abbot. For difficult and secret affairs had been intrusted to him by the king and queen and magnates of England to announce to the king and queen and magnates of Scotland; and when he got there, he found the king, queen, and magnates of the realm assembled for discussion,[1] as he wished. He then explained the cause of his journey and in the name of the king and queen and barons of England, presenting his credentials asked the king and queen of Scotland most urgently to come to England without fail, to hear and negotiate those

[1] *ad parlamentum*

matters which urgently required arduous and secret negotiation. Although they offered many objections, and threw many obstacles in the way, yet, after much dispute William, by urgently pressing his request, skilfully induced them to give their consent to what he wished. They therefore gave William their letters patent, sealed jointly with the king's seal and with the seals of all the magnates of Scotland, addressed to the king and the whole community of England, whereby they willingly promised to act according to their wish, provided that the king and magnates of England would give them security in the matter of the document in writing, faithfully promised to them previously. They moreover sent letters to the king and queen, and magnates of the land, commending the discretion, indefatigability, and diligence of the said William in the business intrusted to him; and immediately after his departure, they sent a special and solemn deputation into England, comprised of the earl of Buchan, mr William the chancellor, and the lord Alan, the usher, to treat more fully with the king of England and his council on the aforesaid matter. These persons on their arrival conferred with the aforesaid William, who had preceded them, but returned home without making public any information as to the success of the negotiations with the king and the community of the kingdom.

Of the death of Thomas, formerly count of Flanders

At this time also died Thomas, one-time count of Flanders,[1] who had extorted from the simple minded king and queen so many thousand marks, which were wasted like seed sown on the seashore, just as, to the injury and loss of the kingdom, many others were often distributed amongst and seized on by aliens. He had also, without any cause, annoyed and inflicted enormous injury on the church of St Albans, if only that he shamelessly sowed discord between it and the king. He was, according to report, poisoned on the continent, and departed from this life to reap the reward of his ways.

How a deputation was sent to the French king's conference

About 1 April, by order of the king of England, advised by the whole baronage, the earls of Clare and Leicester, John Mansel, Peter of Savoy, and Robert Walerand, went overseas to hold a great parley with the king of the French in France over a number of difficult matters concerning the kingdoms of France and England. They took with them a document from the king of England about the giving up of Normandy and also credentials authorising them to agree terms with the king of France and his council concerning the matters by this time long disputed between the two kings and their kingdoms, and, as had been arranged in advance, to confirm things previously agreed between their confidential and expert messengers, and render them unalterable. But as, owing to the dispersal of the said deputies, nothing has been made public about what was done in this matter, nothing certain about it can be committed to writing as yet.

[1] Thomas of Savoy, Queen Eleanor's uncle and count of Flanders in right of his wife, the countess Joan (d. 1244).

How the Friars Preachers live in Dunstable

At this same time, also, a house in Dunstable with the land belonging to it was given out of charity to the Friars Preachers and some of them secretly betook themselves to it immediately, to the great injury of the prior and convent of Dunstable, encouraged in this by the example of the Friars Minor, who had obtained a messuage[1] at [Bury] St Edmunds, maugre the abbot and convent of that place and to the no small injury of that house, and had built such costly dwellings there that all who beheld them were struck with amazement at the sudden expenditure of so much money by poor friars, persons who professed voluntary poverty. The said friars therefore, by a sudden and secret move, erected an altar, and without waiting for any kind of licence publicly performed divine service there. They were, in fact, emboldened by the facility with which they obtained whatever privileges they wished, and by the protection afforded them by cardinal Hugh, a friar of their order, which was by no means inconsiderable. Building day after day, to the great detriment of the house [of Dunstable], from properties roundabout which very many people confer upon them and from which the prior and convent ought to get rents, to extend quickly. And the bigger they grow in buildings the broader their acres, the more straitened the prior and convent are in their possessions and rights; because the rents they had received from messuages bestowed upon the friars are now lost to them, and the offerings which used to be given to them these newly-come friars, by their high-pressure preaching,[2] completely usurp.

Of the death of the countess of Boulogne

In the first week in Lent of this same year the countess of Boulogne, through whose tyranny so many thousand human beings were slain a few years back, died and went to reap the fruits of her ways.

How two new senators were created at Rome, who commenced hostilities against the one lately appointed

At this time, in consequence of the destruction of the towers of the city of Rome, the [Romans] assembled in a state of furious anger, and created for themselves two new senators, who collecting a large force, composed of the middling class of Romans, rose against the lately-appointed senator, that is, the uncle of Brancaleone, and besieged him in a certain castle at Rome, to take and hack him to pieces. He, however, trusting to the oath of fealty given him, and relying on the hostages which he had in keeping in his native city of Bologna, defended himself with vigour, to prove that he did not fall short of the noble spirit of his nephew and predecessor. Thus Rome was in a great measure worn away and consumed in itself internally.

Of the quarrels which arose in three universities

In this same Lent a very serious quarrel broke out at Oxford and Cambridge, in consequence of a person accused of a death and committed to gaol having been released by force by clerks, who had broken his prison open and carried him off to a

[1] *mansionem* [2] *praedicationibus suis urgentibus*

church for protection. The university of Paris too was not a little disturbed by the Preachers and the Minorites. So many orders, indeed, have sprung up, that the one supplants the other and people's alms are not enough to support them, as they used to be.

Of the disagreement between the earls of Gloucester and Leicester

At this time, also, whilst all were diligently employed, during the suspension of the parliament, in making beneficial statutes and ordinances, angry words passed between the earls of Gloucester and Leicester, in such sort that the earl of Leicester, enraged at the other earl's wavering in his adherence to their proposed plans, uttered words of this sort: "I do not care to live among or have dealings with people so fickle and deceitful. For these things we have promised and sworn that we are dealing with. And as for you, my lord earl of Gloucester, the higher your position is above us all, the more are you bound to these wholesome statutes"; with which he left England soon after. The earl of Hereford, and the other nobles and their compeers, when they heard this, intimated to the earl of Gloucester, that the earl of Leicester, who had gone away because of him, would be recalled as soon as possible, and, mollified and in nowise exasperated by such injuries, he would stand by his colleagues; also, that he, the earl of Gloucester, should faithfully honour things he had provided and sworn to and cease to oppose them and correct what needed correction in his own lands in accordance with them; otherwise they would unite to attack him as an enemy. This frightened the said earl, who sent his seneschal Hervey throughout his lands with orders to see that justice was done as decreed and promised and everything done without delay in accordance with his recent promise. Thus the tempest was mitigated for the most part; and although the earl of Leicester still remained overseas, yet, in consequence of this change for the better, they had greater confidence of a happy return on his part.

Of the impediments in the way of establishing peace between the kings of France and England

The peace arranged for between the kings of France and England by the mediation of the many and important solemn envoys named earlier received an unexpected check, just as it was thought to be on the point of being concluded. For the countess of Leicester would not on any account quitclaim[1] her portion of Normandy, which the king of England was, according to the terms of the agreement, to resign to the king of France. It was in consequence of this that the earl of Gloucester upbraided and hurled insulting words at the earl of Leicester. But with stinging words the earl of Leicester cut him short.[2] This nearly led to bloodshed; but they were restrained by mutual friends, in order that the French might not have cause to rejoice from the circumstance. And so, amidst the ridicule of the French, they (the envoys) came back empty-handed, their business unaccomplished.

Of the battle between the Templars and Hospitallers

During this time, too, the Templars, the brethren of St Lazarus and St Thomas of Acre,[3] the Hospitallers and their fellows in the province, as well as some others, the

[1] i.e. renounce her claim to [2] *verba retundebat* [3] Knights of St Thomas of Acre, an English order

Genoese and Pisans, for example, quarrelled among themselves in the Holy Land, and those whom the church was actuated to consider its legitimate defenders then showed themselves breakers of the peace, each other's undoing, and its bloodiest destroyers. For the Hospitallers, to a man, rose against the Templars, in consequence of some deadly feud between them, and, after very large losses of their own, utterly destroyed them, so that barely one of the Templars, but a great many of the Hospitallers, it is said, survived and never, it was said, had there been between Christians, especially between religious, such pitiable slaughter. As a result, all Templars remaining on this side, in a hastily assembled council, made it known with all speed, it was said, to all brethren of their order staying in the houses of the order wherever they might be that without delay and without any excuse, appointing the necessary keepers for each house, they were to come there all at the same time first to replenish to a slight extent their houses at Acre, emptied by the destruction of so many of their brethren there, then to wreak a fearful vengeance as on an enemy on the Hospitallers. From this there was in turn great fear that, if the Almighty did not mitigate things,[1] the peace and stability of Christendom would in a measure be destroyed through their unbearable fury.

How the pope obtained the imperial dignity for earl Richard, whilst the latter was in England
In the mean time, whilst the king of Almain was peaceably staying in England, the way was being prepared for him to receive the imperial dignity unopposed. The pope attended to this cunningly but quietly, not to show himself openly opposed to the king of Spain. The king of Almain, however, in order to amass more money, still remained quietly in England, as if in hiding. For the magnates of England were applying themselves vigorously to what they had provided[2] and begun to give effect to, caring little or nothing whether the aforesaid king stayed or went, giving instead their whole and united attention to destroying evil customs, injustices, and corrupt practices.

Of a severe pestilence, and the death of Fulk, bishop of London
About the same time when the sun was entering the sign of Cancer, an unexpected pestilence and mortality fell upon mankind; so that, to say nothing of the great numbers that died in other places, in Paris alone more than [ ][3] thousand human beings were consigned to the tomb. Oil, wine, and corn, moreover, were infected. And as the sword of death, which spares no one, strikes sometimes one and sometimes another and carries off rich and poor alike, so Fulk, bishop of London, died during that deadly pestilence. That prelate was a man of noble disposition and high breeding and had he not some little time before wavered in giving his support to their generally-agreed provisions, he would have been considered by the whole kingdom an anchor of stability and a buckler of defence; though as a pastor and eminent father of the church he was buried with due solemnity on St Urban's day in St Paul's church, London.

[1] *mitigationem immisceat* [2] *statutis*
[3] the number is omitted

Of the condemnation of W. de Scotenay
In the same week, Walter de Scotenay, formerly chief seneschal of the earl of Gloucester, who, as said earlier, was accused of poisoning, taken, and committed to close confinement in three counties, but especially at Winchester, submitted to trial.[1] But what is lamentable both to relate and to hear is that the very circumstance which gave him greater confidence of liberation, was the cause of his more quickly being rightly condemned. Asked by the judges how well they knew this in offering such a judgment,[2] they replied, "We never knew or heard that William de Valence, or any of his brethren, were indebted in any way to the said Walter; but we have learned well and truly that the said Walter lately received a very large amount of money from the aforesaid William, and we consider the better view is that this was paid to reward him for having administered the poison to his lord the earl, to William de Clare the brother, and to many others, as stated above, to satisfy the vengeance of the exiled rather than on account of any debt previously contracted or contrived between them; and we are more confirmed in this opinion by the fact that William de Clare, realising he was poisoned and approaching death, said publicly that all should know without a doubt that he had been consigned to the jaws of death by Walter de Scotenay." At this, he was convicted of this act of treachery, by judicial sentence at[3] Winchester, dragged [by a horse] and hanged horribly on the gallows.

It should be known that thus far wrote[4] the venerable man, brother Matthew Paris; and though the hand on the pen may vary, nevertheless, as the same method of composition is maintained throughout, the whole is ascribed to him. What has been added and continued from this point onwards may be ascribed to another brother, who presuming to approach the works of so great a predecessor, and unworthy to continue them, as he is unworthy to undo the latchet of his shoe, has not deserved to have even his name mentioned on the page.[5]

5. The Annals of Burton for the years 1258–9

(*Annales Monastici*, ed. H. R. Luard, I (Rolls series, 1864), pp. 409–91)

The annals of the Benedictine abbey of Burton upon Trent are particularly valuable for the undigested material thrown into them. The annals for the years 1258 and 1259 are given as an example of the compiler's method.

1258

[The pope's commission to his nuncio Arlot.]

The same mr Arlot sent similar letters to the archbishop and suffragans of the whole

[1] *se posuit discutiendum:* a loose untechnical equivalent of "*posuit se super patriam*" ("put himself on the country", i.e. a jury; cf. other chroniclers, *Ann. Monastici*, ed. Luard, I, p. 167; II, p. 98; IV, p. 120), which emphasises the quasi-judicial element in the jury (Pollock and Maitland, *History of English Law*, II, pp. 624–5) and which I have kept; "liberation" in the chronicler's next sentence would appear to be a characteristic medieval play upon words.
[2] *ita judicialiter proferendo;* cf. *History of English Law*, op. cit., II, pp. 624–5, and 625 nn. 1 and 2
[3] "Winton" in the MS. (R. Vaughan, *Matthew Paris* (Cambridge, 1958), Plate 1); and other chroniclers say "at Winchester". [4] *perscripsit.*
[5] This rubric closes the text of the *Chronica Majora.* As it is critical for the date of Paris's death and for the composition of the chronicle, I have adopted Professor Galbraith's translation of it in V. H. Galbraith, *Roger Wendover and Matthew Paris* (Glasgow, 1944), p. 12. The manuscript text is reproduced photographically in Vaughan, op. cit., Plate 1, with discussion of the critical points and further references on pp. 7–11.

kingdom. On account of which the lord archbishop of Canterbury, as in the previous year, summoned a convocation of his suffragans and prelates for a given date at Merton.

[The letter of summons.]

On the stated day therefore the suffragans of the lord Boniface archbishop of Canterbury and the prelates of the kingdom and the clergy assembled before him at Merton and the following articles were provided for the reform and improvement of the condition of the church in England.

[Articles provided at Merton.]

[An earlier statement by Grosseteste, bishop of Lincoln, of the church's grievances.]

Because of the many grievances and oppressions of this sort which contrary to the liberties of the church used daily and unabatingly to come to light among the clergy all over the kingdom, the clergy assembled in the presence of the archbishop at Merton and the aforesaid articles were decreed.

[A statement of the privileges of the clergy compiled by Robert de Marisco by order of Grosseteste.]

[Letter of pope intervening in dispute between the university and the Dominicans of Paris.]

[Letter of prior of the Dominicans on complaints against them.]

The lord pope granted that, where it has not been sought all brothers should be freed and absolved from the canonical portion[1] up to the present, and that they should be freed in their consciences, as previously, if it is not sought from them. If however it is sought, it is sufficient for them to stand their trial. This the pope granted on the fourth day before Ash Wednesday.

[Regulations for regent masters at Oxford who transgress the university statutes.]

Thus was peace restored between the Oxford masters.

A papal letter odious to God and man

A papal letter sent in A.D. 1253 about providing for a certain Roman in the church of Lincoln, to the archdeacon of Canterbury and mr Innocent, to whom the lord Robert, bishop of Lincoln replied as is contained above under that year.

[The papal letter follows.]

After this digression on things that arose in the kingdom of England previously but were not recorded and so have been inserted here among the happenings of this year, let us return to the events of this year in the kingdom.

While the lord king Henry was at Woodstock, the magnates of the whole kingdom were summoned to and met at Oxford with horses and greater and lesser arms together with the clergy, to provide for the reform and better ordering of the kingdom, and there under an oath of fealty were produced the following articles that need correction in the kingdom.

[The petition of the barons at Oxford.[2]]

[1] The reference is to apportionment of the burial fee when a lay person is given mendicant instead of ordinary parochial burial, a matter of dispute referred to in the preceding letter of the prior of the Dominicans.
[2] See, for summary, R. F. Treharne, *Baronial Plan of Reform*, pp. 70–1.

Letter from someone at the king's court about the Oxford parliament

Greeting. Know that in the Oxford parliament the lord Hugh le Bigod was made justiciar of England, and he swore that he would show justice to all complainants, and that he would not fail in this for the lord king or the queen or their sons, or for any living person, or for anything, neither for hatred nor love, for prayer or price, and that he would not receive anything from anyone, save food or drink which it is customary to bring to the tables of the rich. Afterwards all the castles of the lord king, which formerly were nearly all in the hands of aliens, were there committed to reliable English persons. And afterwards when the aforementioned articles had been set forth, there was discussion among the twenty-four sworn men of the fact that because of the king's poverty, if he or his kingdom were attacked by some neighbouring prince, he and the kingdom would be in great danger and perhaps the whole realm would be overwhelmed. Therefore it was provided that all the lands and all the tenements and castles alienated from the crown by him should be restored to him. This article his Poitevin brothers and some of their English supporters, namely Henry son of the king of Germany, and John de Warenne, gainsaid, and all, except the king of Germany's son, withdrew towards Winchester without asking leave. But he, when the barons demanded his oath that he would stand by their provisions, answered that he had land only at his father's will, and so he did not wish to do so without consulting him, and he ought not to take any oath, as he was not their equal. He was then given time in which to consult his father, namely forty days.

Afterwards all the barons, with horses and arms, went with the king to Winchester, ready to besiege the elect of Winchester's castle, Wolvesey, and afterwards his other castles, and the castles of W[illiam] de Valence, and to pursue them to ultimate destruction if they did not retreat from the wrong course they had undertaken against the community of the realm over the provisions of the barons. Afterwards John de Warenne made his peace with difficulty and took the oath as they wished. Then the king's brothers at Wolvesey sent messengers to the barons wishing to be reconciled, saying that they were ready to observe all their provisions. They were told in reply that as they had sworn at the start to provide with them for the reform and benefit of the lord king and the kingdom, and as they had withdrawn from Oxford like traitors to the lord king and the community, like perjurers contradicting their articles and provisions, they could not have any confidence whatever in them. They would therefore all have to leave the kingdom with all their following until such time as the kingdom was reformed; and afterwards the lord king on advice given him would send for them. And as the lord king offered to give security for them that they would in no way impede or trouble the barons or oppose their provisions, it was conceded and provided that they should choose and do one of two things, either leave the kingdom as already said, or that two of them, namely Guy and Geoffrey de Lusignan, should leave the country for ever and that the elect of Winchester and William de Valence, who had lands in England might stay in England under safe but honourable custody, that would be arranged by the barons, while the kingdom was being reformed. In the end they chose all to leave the kingdom, provided they might have the issues of their lands. That was by no means fully granted them, but that they might have what in the judgment of the barons was suitable provision for their maintenance from the issues of their lands and the rest should stay in the country kept for them and in course of time, if considered expedient, handed over to them – which it is not believed will happen. And when afterwards they asked to be allowed to take their treasure with them, they were allowed only 6,000 marks and the rest will remain in the country and from it will be met the claims of all complaining of them or their bailiffs, and what is left over will be kept for them. Later, when they had asked for and obtained safe conduct, they all withdrew with no more than the said 6,000 marks and on the first Sunday after the Translation of the blessed Thomas the Martyr they crossed over from Dover. And knights were sent to arrest and seal up their treasures in various religious houses.

Afterwards the lord Edward was with the greatest difficulty induced to subject himself to the regulation and provision of the barons. They also appointed to him four reliable counsellors, namely the lords John de Balliol, John de Gray, Stephen Longespée and Roger de Mouhaut. They will soon provide concerning the state of his household and that of the lord king. The lord king quite frequently asked them that none but Englishmen should remain with him, and so it will be. The barons have great and difficult matters to provide for, that cannot quickly or easily be settled and carried into effect. Also they with the lord king will soon in London provide many things concerning aliens, as well Romans as merchants, money-changers, and others. Also the barons definitely propose to strive for the deposition and deprivation of the elect of Winchester, and they have already reached an agreement with the monks of St Swithun's. The barons set to work furiously. Would that they may succeed![1]

Also in the same Oxford parliament were chosen twenty-four, namely twelve on the part of the lord king, and as many on the part of the community, to whose ordinances and provisions the lord king and the lord Edward his son subjected themselves, as is noted above, as regards the correction and reform of the state of themselves and of the whole realm of England. Many other things also there and elsewhere were hammered out that are contained below.

The provision made at Oxford

[A text of the Provisions of Oxford follows.[2]]

At the same time by the common counsel of the lord king and the community the following charters of the lord king were drawn up, written in Latin, French and English and sent to all shires throughout the kingdom of England, there to be read by the sheriffs and understood and for the future firmly observed intact by all.

[Proclamations (French) of 20 and 18 October 1258 (in that order).[3]]

[Commission, dated 28 July 1258, for enquiries into conduct of local officials.[4]]

In this year, messengers were sent on the part of the lord king and the community

[1] The above newsletter was, according to Treharne, *Baronial Plan of Reform*, p. 80, n. 1, written between 7 and 12 July 1258.

[2] See below, No. 37.

[3] See below, Nos. 39 and 38.

[4] cf. Treharne, *Baronial Plan of Reform*, p. 108, n. 9.

with letters to the supreme pontiff about the state of the kingdom and of the church, sealed with the seals of the magnates named in them and in these words:

[A text follows of the barons' manifesto of late July 1258 to the pope.[1]]

After the lord king and the barons of England had withdrawn from the Oxford parliament, very many of the magnates of England were at a repast in Winchester with the lord Edward; and among them a certain son of perdition caused poison to be served and tasted there. Some chose and consumed it and died groaning and moaning the same day – among them the abbot of Westminster and some others drew their last breath. Richard de Clare, earl of Gloucester, too, escaped half alive, his hair dropping out and his nails dropping off. His brother, William de Clare, had already succumbed to the said deadly draught.

The same year there was a parliament at Cambrai between the kings of France, England and Germany for the making of a peace between them and their heirs, to be put into writing and to last for ever, about Normandy and certain other lands of the lord king of England overseas, so that the better part should remain with the king of France not to be taken from him or his for ever.

Richard king of Germany came to England about Michaelmas and, being met by the barons at Canterbury, swore in their presence to keep together with the community of the realm faithfully the ordinances they had made and would make.

In the same year Sewall, lord archbishop of York, died. Mr Godfrey of Ludham, dean of York, is consecrated archbishop of that place. The lord Henry of Lexington, bishop of Lincoln, died. Richard of Gravelage, dean of Lincoln, succeeded him as bishop. John fitz Geoffrey died.

On the peace between the kings of the Romans, of the French and of England

[Oration expounding the baronial cause to pope and cardinals.[2]]

[Letter ("fabulous"[3]) of Richard of Cornwall to pope against Alfonso X of Castile.]

1259

[Letter of pope to Richard of Cornwall, 30 April 1259.[4]]

Fulk Basset, bishop of London, died.

Henry of Hengham [Wingham], the chancellor, was elected bishop of London.

On the feast of St Edward, king and confessor, which the lord king celebrated royally at Westminster a fortnight after Michaelmas, the community of the bachelery of England made known to lord Edward, the king's son, the earl of Gloucester and others sworn of the council at Oxford, that the king had done and fulfilled completely every single thing that the barons had provided and required him to do, but that the barons themselves had done nothing for the commonweal as they had promised, but only for their own advantage and at the king's expense everywhere; and that if

[1] Better preserved by the Tewkesbury annalist (*Ann. Monastici*, I, pp. 170–4); cf. Powicke, *Henry III and the Lord Edward*, p. 387, n. 3; and, for a partial translation, Bémont, *S. de Montfort* (ed. E. F. Jacob), pp. 162 ff.

[2] See Powicke, *Henry III and the Lord Edward*, pp. 387–8; and Treharne, *Baronial Plan of Reform*, pp. 104–5.

[3] N. Denholm-Young, *Richard of Cornwall* (Oxford, 1947), p. 96, n. 2.

[4] ibid., p. 100.

something was not done to better this, other measures would be taken to restore what had been agreed on. The lord Edward at once replied for himself that he had taken a certain oath at Oxford even against his will, but he was not on that account unprepared to stand readily by the said oath and to expose himself to death for the community of England and for the commonweal, as was sworn at Oxford. And he told the barons who were sworn of the council flatly that unless they fulfilled their said oath, he would stand by the community to the death and cause what had been promised to be carried out. In the end, reckoning it better to have what they had promised done by themselves rather than others, the barons caused the following provisions of theirs to be publicly proclaimed.

The provisions of the barons
[A text of the Provisions of Westminster, October 1259, in French.[1]]
Form of the inquisition to be made by the escheator of the lord king into the lands and tenements and other things contained in the same of archbishops, bishops, earls, barons, abbots and priors and other tenants-in-chief of the king after their death.
[The form of inquisition.]

Also the above provisions in Latin
[The Provisions of Westminster, October 1259, in Latin.[2]]

These articles are to be inquired into in houses of religious
[A list of 57 articles follows.]

Concerning the peace and concord between the kings of France and England
In this year peace and concord between the kings of France and England over Normandy and the other overseas lands of the kings of England was made at Paris and confirmed by writings drawn up and sealed by both sides, both kings being there with their advisers. In such wise that the king of France should retain Normandy and the two words, viz, duke of Normandy, be forever ignominiously deleted from the style and the seal of the king of England, wherein and whereon they had hitherto been accustomed to appear: so was fulfilled the writing of Merlin Silvester which says "By a miraculous change the sword shall be separated from the sceptre" i.e. the duchy of Normandy from the kingdom of England.
[Letter of pope to the magnates of England replying to one from them.[3]]

[1] cf. Treharne, *Baronial Plan of Reform*, pp. 165–9 and 390.
[2] An inferior text. cf. Treharne, loc. cit.
[3] Neither letter otherwise known. Printed from this source in Rymer, *Foedera*, I, i, 393, under date January 1260; cf. Powicke, *The Thirteenth Century*, p. 461 and n.

6. The "Chronicles of the Mayors and Sheriffs of London" for the years 1259–66 (Michaelmas 1259 to Michaelmas 1267)

(The translation is that of H. T. Riley, *Chronicles of Old London* [Chron. of Mayors and Sheriffs, and the French Chronicle of London] (London, 1863), pp. 44–101)

The "Chronicles of the Mayors and Sheriffs" is the main item in a miscellaneous ?London collection known as the Book of Ancient Laws. It was edited for the Camden Society by Thomas Stapleton, *De Antiquis Legibus Liber: Cronica Maiorum et Vicecomitum Londoniarum* (London, 1846). The entries cover the years 1188–1274 but only for the last twenty are they at all full. We give those for the years 1259–66. It is important, however, to remember that the year is the year of office of the sheriffs, the twelvemonth from Michaelmas to the Michaelmas of (in our reckoning) the following year. What we give is in fact the chronicle of 29 September 1259 to 29 September 1267. It follows that the first nine months of any year (in our reckoning) must be looked for in the chronicle entry for the previous year: the battle of Lewes, for example, which was fought on 14 May 1264 will be found s.a. 1263.

1259 Adam Bruning
Henry de Coventre } Sheriffs

This year, within the quinzaine of St Michael there was a very great wind, and a most dreadful tempest both by land and sea, so that numberless vessels, going forth from the port of Gernemue[1] to fish, were lost, together with their men.

In the same year, on the Friday before the feast of Simon and Jude [28 October], there was held a great and long parliament; and his lordship the king, being in the Great Hall at Westminster, where many earls and barons, and a countless multitude of people, had met, caused the Composition to be openly and distinctly read, that had been made by the barons (as noticed in the other book[2]) as to amending the usages and laws of the realm. The archbishop of Canterbury, and many other bishops, arrayed in pontificals, pronounced sentence of excommunication against all those who should make any attempt upon the said Composition. And then, his lordship the king took leave to cross over into France, for the purpose of making peace with the king of France; and delivered his kingdom into the safe keeping of the archbishop of Canterbury, the bishop of Worcester, [and] the lords Roger Bigot, Hugh Bigot, and Philip Basset.

In this year William Fitz-Richard was made mayor.

In the same year, on the day before the feast of St Leonard [6 November], his lordship the king came to the Cross of St Paul's, a countless multitude of the city being there assembled in folkmote, and took leave of the people to cross over, just as he had done before at Westminster; and promised them that he would preserve all their liberties unimpaired, and, for the amendment of the city, granted them certain new statutes which he commanded to be inviolably observed; to the effect, that in future it should not be necessary to have a pleader in any plea moved in the city, either in the Hustings or in any courts in the city, save only, in pleas pertaining to the crown, or else pleas of land or of distresses unjustly taken. But every one was to set forth his complaint with his own lips, and the other side in like manner, without hindrance, so that the court, in its prudence, being certified as to the truth of the matter,

[1] Yarmouth in Norfolk

[2] What this alludes to, it seems impossible to say. Perhaps "another leaf" is the meaning.

might render equal and righteous judgment unto the parties. Also, that if with any pleader there should be an agreement made for him to have part of the tenement for which he was pleading, in respect of his pay, and he should be convicted thereof, he should lose such share, and be suspended from his calling. The same too was to be done as to the others, who, upon being convicted of such an offence, were to lose their own portion, acquired, and be heavily punished as well.

On the same day, John Maunsel said, on behalf of his lordship the king, that he had been certified that Arnulf Fitz-Thedmar, of whom mention has been made above, had committed no offence, and had been unjustly indicted; wherefore he recalled him to his peace and favour, and commanded that he should be reinstated in his [former] position.

This year, upon the morrow of the feast of St Leonard [6 November] his lordship the king took his departure from London for the sea-coast; and on the Monday following, in the Hustings, the said Arnulf was replaced in seisin of his ward, from which he had before been deposed.

Afterwards, on the feast of St Brice [13 November], which at that time fell on a Friday, his lordship the king crossed over; having first recalled to his grace and favour Nicholas Fitz-Joce, John le Minur, and Matthew Bukerel, of whom mention has been made above. Ralph Hardel, Nicholas Bat, and John Tulesan, were dead.

This year, just before our Lord's Nativity, the seal of his lordship the king was changed,[1] he being still beyond sea; the superscription being to the following effect – "*Henricus Dei Gratia Rex Anglie, Dominus Hibernie et Dux Aquitannie*," – "Henry by the Grace of God King of England, Lord of Ireland, and Duke of Acquitaine."

At this time also, a lasting peace was made between him and the king of France, in form under-written; that is to say, he quitted claim unto the king of France as to all right and title which he had to Normandy, Poitou, and Anjou, retaining unto himself only Gascoigne and certain other parts of Acquitaine, for which he did homage to the king of France. At the same time, the king of England gave his daughter Beatrice in marriage to the son of the earl of Bretagne.

This year, on the morrow of St Valentine [14 February], which then fell on a Sunday, Henry de Wengham was consecrated bishop of London by Boniface archbishop of Canterbury, in the church of St Mary of Suwerk.[2]

In the same year, when it had been arranged by sir Edward, the king's son, and the earl of Gloucester, who were then at variance, that they should hold a general parliament at Westminster, three weeks after Easter day, and it was also proposed that they, and many other earls, and barons, and knights, should, with their horses and arms, take up their abode within the city; seeing that very great loss and peril might have accrued therefrom to the citizens and to the city, sir Richard, king of the Romans, came to Westminster in Easter week, and summoning the mayor and certain discreet men of the city in presence of himself and the chief justiciar, and sir Philip

[1] "As to this new seal of the king, the prophecy was then fulfilled which says 'By reason of a wondrous change, the sword shall be severed from the sceptre,' a thing that was then fulfilled. For upon his old seal the king held the sword and the sceptre; whereas, upon the new one, the sceptre without the sword." *Marginal note*

[2] St Mary Overy in Southwark

Basset, held conference with them as to avoiding this peril. Wherefore, it was then provided, that neither sir Edward, nor the said earl, nor any one else, as to whom any suspicion might be entertained, should be harboured within the walls of the city; which was accordingly done. It was also provided, that all persons of fifteen years and upwards, each to the best of his ability, should be well provided with arms; and that all the city gates should be closed at night and watched by armed men, and should not be opened in the daytime; with the exception of Bridge gate, Ludgate, and Alegate,[1] which also were to be well fortified with armed men. Also, that the king beforementioned, the justiciars aforesaid, and Philip, as well as those whom they might think proper to bring with them, and against whom no suspicion existed, might be harboured within the city, and, together with the citizens, protect the city if necessary.

Afterwards, on the second day before the feast of St Mark the Evangelist [25 April] his lordship the king, coming from the parts beyond sea, landed at Dover; and on the fifth day after the said feast, came to London and took up his abode in the hostel of the bishop of London, causing the earl of Gloucester, and many others, at his will, to be harboured within the city, the gates in the meantime being well fortified with armed men, by day and night. Sir Edward however and the earl of Leicester, and their followers, were lodged without the city, both at the Hospital of Jerusalem,[2] and in all the other houses which lay between the city and Westminster. The king of Almaine however took up his abode in his own house at Westminster, as it was not necessary for him to be in the city, while his lordship the king was making stay there. Afterwards, the king having made a stay in the city of fifteen days and more, returned from thence to Westminster on the 17th of the calends of June [16 May], and a day was named for holding another parliament, the quinzaine[3] of St John the Baptist [24 June].

After this, the king of Almaine took his departure from London for the sea-coast, on the feast of St Botolph [17 June], that is to say; and, on the third day after the said feast, put to sea at Dover.

In the said parliament, as varying and different opinions existed between his lordship the king and the barons of England, a day was named for holding a parliament, the feast of St Edward [5 January] namely.

1260 Richard Pikard
John de Norhamton } Sheriffs

This year, on the feast of the Translation of St Edward [13 October], John, son of the earl of Bretagne, who had married the daughter of his lordship the king, was made a knight, as also many other nobles, at Westminster, amid the greatest hilarity and rejoicing.

In the same year, on the Monday before the feast of Simon and Jude [28 October], sir Hugh le Despenser was made justiciar of England; and in the same year William Fitz-Richard was again made mayor.

Afterwards, on the morrow of Simon and Jude, the king of Almaine, returning

[1] Aldgate [2] in Clerkenwell [3] a fortnight after

from the parts beyond sea, came to London; and on the following day, the king of Scotland came, with his queen; who, upon her lord returning home, remained with her mother the queen of England, until the time of her delivery.

In this year, on the Monday after the feast of St Edmund the King [20 November], it was provided in full Hustings, that, because such pleas as were moved by many kinds of writs of his lordship the king, could not in one day, between morning and vespers,[1] or even complines,[2] be, all of them, brought to a conclusion; from that day forward, all pleas moved by writ of dower *unde nihil habet*,[3] and all pleas of customs and services, should be heard on the same day on which the common pleas are heard.

The same year, after the Purification of the Blessed Mary [2 February] the king came to London, and afterwards, on the Sunday before the feast of St Valentine [14 February], had the folkmote summoned at St Paul's Cross; whither he himself came, and the king of Almaine, the archbishop of Canterbury, John Maunsel, and many others. The king also commanded that all persons of the age of twelve years and upwards should make oath before their alderman, in every ward, that they would be faithful unto him, so long as he should live, and, after his death, to his heir; which was accordingly done. Then all the gates of the city were shut, night and day, by the king's command, the Bridge gate, and the gates of Ludgate and Alegate, excepted, which were open by day, and well fortified with armed men.

Be it remembered, that in an affray that took place this year, at the Fair of Norhamptone,[4] between the Londoners and the men of Norhamptone, certain persons of Norhamptone were wounded, and one of them afterwards died; but whether he died from the injury so inflicted or by a natural death, is not known. The bailiffs however of that town, who are always envious of the Londoners, seized four men of London, imputing the death to them, and, after imprisoning them, seized all their goods, as well as those of the other Londoners. Upon hearing this, the mayor and citizens, seeing that no Londoner is bound to plead without the walls of the city, except in pleas as to tenures without, obtained royal letters directing them to deliver up such persons to the mayor or to his messenger bearing such letters, that they might take their trial before the king, as they ought to do, according to the laws of the city; the said bailiffs, however, would not let them go, either for that writ or for another, which the mayor obtained on a second request. But, in contravention of the precepts of his lordship the king and of the liberties of London, they kept them still more closely and more cruelly confined; and so they remained there until after the Purification of the Blessed Mary [2 February]; at which time the king came to London and sojourned at the Tower.

On the morrow of his arrival, the mayor and citizens went to his lordship the king, and obtained from him a third writ for delivery of the prisoners aforesaid, as also, another writ, directed to the sheriff of the county of Norhamptone, to the effect that if the bailiffs should be unwilling to release them, he should enter their liberties and deliver them up to the bearer of the letters of his lordship the king, to take them before

[1] from about 3 or 4 in the afternoon to seven
[2] or second vespers, about 7 o'clock
[3] "Of which she has nothing" – meaning, the woman making claim.
[4] Northampton

his said lordship the king, there to do what, in accordance with the laws of the city, they ought to do. These letters being obtained, behold! news came that the aforesaid prisoners were at Cherringe[1] near Westminster, whither the mayor and bailiffs of Norehamptone had brought them. Upon hearing this, the mayor of London sent to them certain citizens, carrying the writ before-mentioned: which writ being read and understood, they still would not agree to deliver the prisoners to the said messengers. Upon this therefore, the mayor of London, waiting upon the king with a countless multitude of people, showed unto him, making grievous complaint, how that the said bailiffs, in despite of his royal majesty, and to the very great disgrace of his city of London, for all his third writ, would do nothing. The king, moved to anger, upon this sent Peter de Nevile, a certain marshal of his household, to Cherringe; who immediately brought the prisoners before the king, and they were delivered to the mayor.

The citizens however forthwith made plaint against the people of Norhamptone, of the trespass that had been committed against them, and their contempt of the writs of his lordship the king; to which the others made answer. As to this plaint and answer, the king named for them the next day as a day for hearing judgment; the giving and receiving of which judgment was however, by collusion, respited from day to day for more than five weeks; at the end of which, on the third day before the feast of the Annunciation of our Lady, the mayor and citizens came to the Tower, as also the bailiffs of Norhamptone, and appeared before the king in his chamber there; there being also present, the chief justiciar, Philip Basset, John Maunsel, Robert Walerand, and others of the council of his lordship the king. The citizens hereupon demanded their judgment that had been so respited, as between them and the people of Norhamtone, in reference to their plaint and the answer made thereto. The people of Norhamtone however said that they never made any answer to them, but only to his lordship the king, seeing that they were not bound to plead without the walls of their own borough; and made profert of a charter of his lordship the king to that effect, which had been made in the forty-first year of the king now reigning. The citizens however said that that charter ought not to avail them, seeing that they were not then in the enjoyment of many of the articles contained therein, and more especially, because they had made answer in all the fairs of England. For that they had made answer at the fairs of St Ives,[2] St Botolph's,[3] Lenne,[4] and Stanford;[5] and even here they had departed from their charter, by making answer to the plaint of the citizens. After this, the record of the justiciar's roll was read, in which was specified the answer that had been made by them unto his lordship the king as to contempt of his writs, the same being openly and distinctly enrolled. But as to the plaint of the citizens and the answer made by the burgesses thereto, little or nothing was entered therein. The citizens however declared that they had made plaint against them, to the effect that they had wrongfully detained their own freemen, in contravention of the franchises of London, after receiving the writs of his lordship the king, and did still detain the chattels of the persons before-named; and further, made plaint against

[1] This passage deserves remark, as confuting the assertion that has been erroneously made, that Charing owes its name to the cross erected there in memory of the *chère reine*, Eleanor, wife of Edward I.
[2] in Huntingdonshire
[3] Boston, in Lincolnshire.
[4] Lynn, in Norfolk
[5] Stamford, in Lincolnshire

them as to other trespasses, whereby they had been injured and had received damage to the value of ten pounds. To which the others made answer, that in part they acknowledged and in part denied the same, and as to the same they placed themselves upon the record of the bishops and barons, who were present on that day, and demanded judgment thereon. [The citizens] also demanded judgment as to the new charter of the burgesses, which ought to be of no validity [they said] as against the charters of the citizens, of which they made profert; namely, the charter of king Henry the second, of king Richard, of king John, and that of his lordship the king now reigning, and that they were then in enjoyment of all the liberties in the aforesaid charters contained.

At length, after much altercation had taken place between them, conference and counsel was held thereon by his barons before his lordship the king; and because the bishops and others who had been present on the day of the plea being heard, were not then present, judgment was respited until five weeks after Easter.

About the same time, during Lent, Philip de Boklaunde, a marshal of his lordship the king, who had always claimed that the citizens of London ought to make answer before the king's seneschal, whensoever any one of the king's household might make complaint against them, impleaded a certain merchant, in contravention of his liberties, who had been born in the parts beyond sea. This plea was brought into the city before the sheriffs of London and there determined.

In this year, the bishop elect of Winchester, who was consecrated at Rome, and of whom mention has been made above, died about the feast of our Lord's Nativity, while coming to England with letters from the pope; and, by assent of the barons, William de Valence, his brother, returned to England about Easter.

After this, when the five weeks after Easter had expired, judgment in the aforesaid matter between the Londoners and the men of Norhamtone, was again respited until the quinzaine after the feast of St John [24 June].

Be it remembered, that at the Easter aforesaid, his lordship the king, while at Winchester, made Philip Basset his chief justiciar, without the assent of the barons, who refused to admit him to such office; and so, for this reason and for other causes, there arose a dissension between his lordship the king and the said barons, and that too without any manifest reason for the same.

1261 Philip le Taillour
Richard de Walebrok } Sheriffs

In this year, just before the Translation of St Edward [13 October] the aforesaid dissension was allayed between his lordship the king and his barons, the king and his queen then sojourning at St Paul's,[1] and the king of Almaine at St Martin's le Grand; a reconciliation however, which did not last. On the contrary, the barons, after this, in some places removed the sheriffs of his lordship the king, and appointed others there, whom they styled "Wardens of the Counties"; and further, would not allow the justiciars to do their duty, who had been sent throughout the kingdon on eyre.

[1] Probably in the house of the bishop Henry de Wengham, who was in great favour with Henry III.

This year, Thomas Fitz-Thomas was made mayor.

In this year, at Lent, his lordship the king caused to be read at St Paul's Cross a certain bull of pope Urban,[1] who had been made pope the same year; which confirmed the bull of pope Alexander,[2] his predecessor, who had previously absolved the king and all the others of the oath which they had made in the parliament at Oxford, as before noticed in this record. The king also sent his writ throughout all the cities of England, commanding that no one should gainsay such absolution, and further, that if any one should in deed or word presume to do the contrary of such command, he should be taken, and not liberated without order of his lordship the king.

In this year, the king of Almaine took his departure from London, on the day before the feast of St Alban [22 June], and crossed over the third day after.

After this, on the Sunday next after the feast of Peter and Paul [29 June], his lordship the king took leave of the citizens of London, at St Paul's Cross, to pass over into France, and on the morrow departed from Westminster for the sea-coast, and the queen with him; there being at that time beyond sea sir Edward and sir Edmund, sons of his lordship the king. The king and queen soon afterwards crossed over.

About this time died Richard de Clare, earl of Gloucester, and Henry de Wingham, bishop of London.

After this, the king fell ill of a grievous sickness, about the feast of St Mary in the month of September;[3] by reason of which sickness, he remained in the parts beyond sea until after the feast of St Nicholas [6 December].

About the same time Richard Talebot, dean of St Paul's, was elected bishop of London; who, returning from the parts beyond sea, where he had been presented to his lordship the king, came over to England; but falling ill, he took to his bed and died, just before the feast of St Michael, and before consecration.

1262 Osbert de Suthfolch[4] } Sheriffs
Robert de Munpelers[5] }

This year, Thomas Fitz-Thomas was again made mayor of London.

In this year, just after the feast of St Martin [11 November] about the time of vespers, a certain Jew having wounded a Christian with an anelace,[6] in Colecherche street, many Christians, indeed a countless multitude of people, ran in pursuit of the Jew, and broke into many houses belonging to the Jews; not content with which, afterwards at nightfall they carried off all the goods of the said Jews, and would have broken into many more houses, and carried off the goods, had not the mayor and sheriffs repaired to the spot and driven away those offenders by force of arms. For which reason, inquisition was made on the morrow, and so from day to day, by the mayor and sheriffs in the Guildhall, twelve men from each of the wards of London, to whom no suspicion attached in reference to that felony, being sworn thereunto. And afterwards, all the aldermen made inquisition upon this matter, each in his own

[1] Urban IV, previously Patriarch of Jerusalem
[2] Alexander IV
[3] about 8 September, the Nativity of BVM
[4] Suffolk
[5] Montpellier
[6] a knife or dagger, worn in the girdle, at the side

wardmote; and those who were indicted or accused, were taken by the sheriffs and imprisoned, part of them in Neugate and part in Crepelgate.[1] But afterwards, those who were free of the city and who could find pledges, were liberated on surety.

In this year his lordship the king returned from France, and putting to sea, together with the queen, at Witsand, landed at Dover on the vigil of St Thomas the Apostle [21 December], and on the Wednesday before the Epiphany [6 January] arrived in London.

This year there was a great frost and thick ice, the frost beginning on the fifth day before the Nativity and lasting for three whole weeks; the Thames too was so frozen that at one time it was covered from shore to shore, so much so, that it had all the appearance of being able to be crossed over on foot and on horseback.

In the same year, on the seventh day of February, were burnt, by reason of a fire breaking out there, the Lesser Hall of his lordship the king at Westminster, the chamber, the chapel, the receiving-room,[2] and many other official buildings as well.

In this year, just before St Peter's Chair,[3] the mayor and citizens of London shewed unto sir Philip Basset, justiciar of England, and others of the council of his lordship the king, at Westminster, that the constable of the Tower, in contravention of their franchises, wished to arrest and seize vessels in the Thames before the Tower, and take prisage of corn and other things, before they had reached the wharf; further saying, that just then he had caused a vessel belonging to Thomas de Basinges, laden with wheat, to be stopped before the Tower, and was for taking one hundred quarters therefrom, at a price, by the quarter, two pence less than it would have sold for when brought ashore. To which the said constable made answer, that this he was quite at liberty to do, in behalf of his lordship the king; whereupon, the citizens replied, that attachments on the Thames pertain solely to the sheriffs of London, seeing that the whole water of Thames belongs to the city from shore to shore, as far as the Newe Weat; as had been repeatedly shown before the justiciars itinerant at the Tower, and as had been assented to at Bermundesheie, by twelve knights of Sureye, upon oath, before his lordship Hugh Bigot, justiciar of England, then itinerant there.

They said also, that his lordship the king takes no prisage of corn, before the vessel has reached the wharf, and that then he is to have the quarter of wheat at two pence less than it would sell for; and this, only for the support of his own household. Also, that neither the constable nor any other person is to have prisage of corn; but that, if he wishes to buy anything, he must buy it in the market of the city, like the citizens, and at the option of the vendor; and they entreated his lordship the king, that he would preserve their liberties; always claiming however, that there they neither would, nor ought to, undergo judgment or receive the same. Then, after conference had been held between the justiciars and others of the king's council, sir William de Wilton made answer to the citizens: "His lordship the king is wishful that your liberties be preserved, and it is our duty to be wishful that his rights be not lost; and because we are ignorant what are the rights which pertain unto the Tower, we will make in-

[1] in the stations probably for the armed watch, at the sides of, and perhaps over, the gate
[2] *Receptaculum*
[3] There were two festivals of this name; that instituted at Rome was on 28 January, and that at Antioch, 22 February.

quisition at the end of three weeks after Easter, of other persons who have been constables there, what kind of seisin his lordship the king has had there; but the city, in the meantime, may enjoy its own seisin wholly and in peace, saving however such claim on part of the constable, as upon the said day he shall be able reasonably to show." Whereupon, it was provided by the citizens and injunction was given to the sheriffs, that they should not allow the constable to make any attachment on the Thames, and should repel force by force, if necessary.

In this year, his lordship the king again gave his assent to the maintenance of the statutes of Oxford, and sent his writs, in which the said statutes were set forth in writing, throughout all the counties of England, enjoining that the same should be observed, as well as others which the earl marshal, the earl of Leicester, Philip Basset, and Hugh Bigot, were about to prepare: an ordinance which held good for no long time.

Afterwards, on Sunday in mid-Lent, many people of the city meeting at St Paul's Cross, the mayor did fealty to sir Edward as the king's heir;[1] and on the morrow all the aldermen did the same in the Guildhall, those who were absent through illness doing the same at home, before the mayor. On the Sunday following, all males of twelve years of age and upwards, made the same oath before their respective aldermen, each in his own wardmote.

In this year, before Pentecost, the barons who had given their assent to the observance of the ordinances and statutes made at Oxford, sent a certain letter to his lordship the king, under the seal of Roger de Clifford, requiring of him that he would maintain those statutes; and defied all those who should attempt to contravene the same, saving always, the persons of the king, the queen, and their children. Immediately after this, the said barons, with a great army, levied war against all their adversaries, and, in the first place, at Hereford seized the bishop of Hereford,[2] and all his canons who were aliens, carried off all their treasures, sold all that they could find upon their manors, and ravaged many of the manors with fire. And in the same way they did as to all the manors by which they passed, belonging to those, that is to say, who attempted to infringe the said statutes, ecclesiastics as well as others; in their churches also, they placed new rectors, and more especially in the churches that were held by aliens, doing no harm to any persons except their adversaries, but strictly maintaining the peace as towards them. Seizing however the castles belonging to his lordship the king and some others, they placed new constables in them; all of whom they made to swear fealty to his lordship the king, always carrying before themselves the king's standard. After this, about the feast of St John [24 June], they sent a letter to the citizens of London, under the seal of Simon de Montfort, earl of Leicester, desiring to be certified by them whether they would observe the said ordinances and statutes, made to the honour of God, in fealty to his lordship the king, and to the advantage of all the realm, or would in preference adhere to those who wished to infringe the same.

And be it known, that the prayer of the barons was to the following effect: "The

[1] *post vitam suam*
[2] Peter de Aigueblanche; who was obnoxious to them as being a native of Savoy

barons do humbly and duteously request of his lordship the king, that the ordinances and statutes made at Oxford, and confirmed by oath as well of his lordship the king as of the nobles, and after that, of all and singular of the realm of England, shall be strictly and inviolably observed. Provided however, that if anything in them, by award of good men thereunto elected, shall be found to the prejudice or injury of his lordship the king or of the realm, the same shall be wholly withdrawn therefrom; and that if anything shall be doubtful or shall need correction, the same shall be made clear or corrected; and that as to other points, those namely that are good and beneficial, security shall be provided that the same shall be for ever strictly observed. They do further request, that the realm shall in future be governed, under his lordship the king, by trusty and skilful natives of the same and not by others than such; the same as in all other kingdoms throughout the world is commonly done."

Upon receiving the message, the citizens showed the same to his lordship the king, who was then at the Tower, the king of Almaine, the queen, sir Edward, and Robert Walrand being the only other persons who were then present; and they further said, that all the community was willing to observe those statutes which were to the honour of God, in fealty to the king, and to the advantage of the realm; which statutes, by the king's command, had before been ratified by the said community by oath; and further, that it was their wish that no knights [or] serjeants, aliens by birth, should be allowed to sojourn in the city; for that it was through them[1] that all the dissensions had arisen between the king and his barons. After this, by the king's command, certain of the citizens were sent to Dover with the king's council, to treat for peace with the barons. On the occasion of which journey, answer was made to the barons, that all the community was willing to observe the said statutes, to the honour of God, in fealty to his lordship the king, and to the advantage of the realm, saving always the liberties of London: and thus was a league made between the barons and the citizens, with this reservation, "saving fealty to his lordship the king".

At this season, and indeed before, all aliens, both knights and serjeants, were dismissed from the city; who were afterwards placed by sir Edward in garrison at Wyndleshore. And at this time also the citizens kept watch and ward, riding by night throughout the city with horse and arms; though among them a countless multitude of persons on foot obtruded themselves; some evil-minded among whom, under pretext of searching for aliens, broke open many houses belonging to other persons, and carried off such goods as were there to be found. To restrain the evil designs of these persons, the watches on horseback were therefore put an end to, and watch was kept by the respective wards, each person keeping himself well armed within his own ward.

Afterwards, on the Sunday before the feast of St Margaret [20 July], the barons came to London, and on the morrow the king and queen withdrew from the Tower to Westminster. At this time, with the assent of his lordship the king, Hugh le Despencer was made by the barons justiciar of all England, and the Tower of London delivered into his charge.

Be it here remarked, that this mayor, during the time of his mayoralty, had so

[1] i.e. the aliens residing in the kingdom

pampered the city populace, that, styling themselves the "Commons of the City", they had obtained the first voice in the city. For the mayor, in doing all that he had to do, acted and determined through them, and would say to them, "Is it your will that so it shall be?" and then, if they answered, "Ya, ya," so it was done. And on the other hand, the aldermen or chief citizens were little or not at all consulted on such matter; but were in fact just as though they had not existed. Through this, that same populace became so elated and so inflated with pride, that during the commotions in the realm, of which mention has been previously made, they formed themselves into covins, and leagued themselves together by oath, by the hundred and by the thousand, under a sort of colour of keeping the peace, whereas they themselves were manifestly disturbers of the peace. For whereas the barons were only fighting against those who wished to break the aforesaid statutes, and seized the property of such, and that too by day, the others by night broke into the houses of the Cahorsins and of other persons in the city, who were not against the said statutes, and by main force carried off the property found in such houses, besides doing many other unlawful acts as well. As to the mayor, he censured these persons in but a lukewarm way.

Afterwards, these same persons, like so many justiciars itinerant, wished to remove all purprestures,[1] new and old, observing no order of trial; and endeavoured to throw open lanes, which, by writ of his lordship the king and with the sanction of the justiciars itinerant, the community assenting thereto, had been stopped up and rented to certain persons; so much so, in fact, that some of them they opened, without judgment given, and in like manner did they remove certain purprestures, and some of them after dinner;[2] and this they did, not only for the purpose of removing them, but for the opportunity of carrying off the timber and other things there to be found.

After this, on the morrow of St Margaret, a writ of his lordship the king was sent to the mayor and citizens, and was read in the Guildhall; it being set forth therein, that the dissensions which existed between the king and the barons had been allayed, and that the king commanded that his peace should be strictly observed, as well within the city as without; and that, when any one should be known to contravene the aforesaid statutes, he should be arrested by the bailiffs, and all his goods seized, and kept in safe custody until the king should have issued his precept to other effect thereupon. And further, that from that day forward all matters should be conducted and determined according to the law of the land.

At this season, the barons aforesaid, to conciliate still further the good will of the citizens, addressed them, and said that they would make provision, in case aught should be subtracted from their liberties; and even more, that such other matters, as, consistently with justice and honour, might tend to augment their liberties, if put in writing, they, the barons, would show unto the king and his council; and that the king would confirm the same with his seal, to be held by the said citizens and their heirs for ever. The mayor too had all the populace of the city summoned, telling them that the men of each craft must make such provisions as should be to their own advantage, and he himself would have the same proclaimed throughout the city, and

[1] alleged encroachments by building on, or enclosing, common ground, or land belonging to the Crown
[2] This passage appears to be incomplete.

strictly observed. Accordingly, after this, from day to day individuals of every craft of themselves made new statutes and provisions – or rather, what might be styled "abominations" – and that, solely for their own advantage, and to the intolerable loss of all merchants coming to London and visiting the fairs of England, and the exceeding injury of all persons in the realm. At this time too, nothing whatever was done, or treated of, for the common advantage of the city or for the increase of its liberties; though still, the aforesaid enactments and provisions[1] were not carried into effect.

After this, on the vigil of St James [25 July] the barons too departed from London for Windleshore, with the view of besieging the castle there: which castle however was surrendered by sir Edward, and peace made, on the day after the feast aforesaid, the king and barons still staying in the neighbourhood of Fuleham;[2] immediately after which, the aliens who were within the castle returned to their native land.

At this time also, many nobles and others, making complaint, set forth unto the king and his council, that they, among others, had been plundered, and that too unjustly, adding that they were not opposed to the said statutes of Oxford, and demanding justice: a matter however, which was postponed until the quinzaine of St Michael.

Afterwards, on the second day after the feast of St Matthew [21 September], which then fell on a Sunday, his lordship the king, the queen, and their sons, with many nobles of England, crossed over to be present at a conference with the king of France at Boulogne; where the pilgrimage of himself and of other crusaders to the Holy Land was treated of, as also the coronation of his son[3] as king; there being there present nearly all the dukes and nobles of France, Burgundy, Champagne, and Spain.

1263 Thomas de Ford, Gregory de Rokesle } Sheriffs

In this year,[4] on the day after the octaves of St Michael, his lordship the king, returning from Boulogne, arrived in England, and, on the Friday after, reached London.

Be it observed, that whereas for many years there had been a dispute between the abbot of Westminster and the citizens of London as to some liberties which the said abbot, by a certain charter obtained of his lordship the king, demanded in the county of Middlesex, at length, on the Tuesday after the octaves of St Michael in this year, the said dispute was determined by judgment given at the exchequer of his lordship the king, in presence of Gilbert de Preston, justiciar, by writ of the king thereunto specially deputed, and of the barons of the exchequer. For, by verdict upon oath of twelve knights of the county of Middlesex, it was decided that the sheriffs of London may enter all vills and tenements which the abbot holds in Middlesex, even unto the gate of his abbey, and there in every way make summons and distraint, the same as in the tenements of other freeholders of the county; and that the tenants of the abbot are bound to do suit at the county courts and at the hundred courts, and to do all

[1] those namely, made by the various trades with the city
[2] Fulham
[3] Philip III of France
[4] This passage shows that the years are computed throughout from the feast of St Michael, 29 September.

other services, as the freeholders of the county aforesaid are wont to do. Afterwards, in process of time the said abbot and his convent, by charter sealed with the common seal, remitted for ever unto the citizens all right of action which they had in Middlesex by reason of the before-named charter obtained of his lordship the king to the prejudice of the citizens: which however was not afterwards adhered to.

This year, in the parliament held after the quinzaine of St Michael, a dissension again arose between his lordship the king and the aforesaid earl of Leicester and his accomplices. For the king and sir Edward, and many nobles of the realm who adhered to them, desired that justice should be done to all those, upon whom depredations or trespasses had been unjustly committed; while the other party would not consent thereto. After this too, the king desired that those who were to be of his own household, should be chosen and put in office by himself.

At this season, sir Edward, under colour of paying a visit to his wife, entered the castle of Wyndeshor, and there continued to abide. The king also, on the morrow, departed in the morning from Westminster in the direction of the said castle, and entered it with such of his own people as he thought proper; many earls and barons following, who adhered to him, while the earl of Leicester and his accomplices were staying in London. Afterwards, however, the two parties submitted the dispute to the arbitration of the king of France.

This year, Thomas Fitz-Thomas was again elected mayor by the populace, the aldermen and principal men of the city being but little consulted thereon; and immediately after the election he was sworn, just as he had been the two preceding years; a thing that no other mayor had ever been, unless he had been first admitted by the king or his barons of the exchequer. On the morrow however he was presented to the aforesaid barons at Westminster; but was not admitted, the king forbidding it by his writ, he being for many reasons greatly moved to anger against the city.

After this, his lordship the king, who had before sent letters to the king of France, signifying that he would abide by his arbitration as to the dispute existing between himself and the barons, crossed over in the week of the Nativity, and sir Edward and others in his council, to hold a conference with the king of France. Peter de Montfort also, and certain others on part of the barons, whose letters patent the aforesaid king also had, to the effect that they would abide by his arbitration, crossed over.

Accordingly, the king before-mentioned, on the Wednesday before the Conversion of St Paul [25 January], made known his award, the tenor of which is as follows:

"We, the parties being convened at Amiens, his lordship the king of England in person, and some of the barons personally, and other by their proctors, appearing before us, after hearing the allegations and defences on either side, and fully understanding the reasons by the parties alleged, considering that, by the provisions, ordinances, statutes, and obligations, of Oxford, and by the results which therefrom have ensued, and by reason thereof, the royal right and honour have been greatly impaired, [and] that disturbance of the realm, oppression, and plunder of churches, and most grievous disasters to other persons of the said realm, ecclesiastical and secular, natives and aliens, have ensued; as also – a thing that was reasonably to be apprehended – to the end that evils still more grievous might not in future arise; after taking counsel of good and high personages, do, by our award and our ordinance, quash and annul the aforesaid provisions, ordinances, statutes, and obligations, by whatsoever name the same may be observed, and whatsoever through them, or by reason of them, has ensued; and this the more especially, as it appears that the supreme pontiff has by his letters pronounced the same quashed and annulled; we ordaining, that as well the said king as the barons, and such other persons as have agreed to this present compromise, and have in any way bound themselves to observe the aforesaid, shall wholly acquit and absolve themselves thereof. We do also add that, by force or virtue of the aforesaid provisions, or ordinances, or obligations, or of any power by the king granted thereon, no person shall make new statutes, or shall hold or observe those already made; nor ought any one, for non-observance of the aforesaid, to be held guilty of a capital crime or in any other way to be an enemy, or to undergo any punishment by reason thereof. We do also decide, that all letters made as to the aforesaid provisions, and by reason thereof, shall be null and void, and do further ordain that the same shall be restored by the barons unto the king of England, and duly returned. We do also say and ordain, that all castles which have been delivered for safe custody, or by reason of the aforesaid, and which are still withheld, shall, by the said barons unto the king be freely restored, by the said king to be held, in such manner as, before the time of the aforesaid provisions, he was wont to hold the same. We do also say and ordain, that it shall be lawful unto the same king, freely to appoint, depose, institute, and remove, the chief justiciar, chancellor, treasurer, minor justiciars, sheriffs, and all other ministers and officials of his realm and his household whomsoever, at his own free will, in such manner as, before the time aforesaid, he was wont. Also, we do revoke and quash the statute made, to the effect that the realm of England shall in future be governed by natives, as also that aliens shall depart therefrom, not to return, those only excepted whose stay the faithful subjects of the realm should in common allow. We do ordain by our award, that it shall be lawful for aliens to remain in security within the said realm, and that the said king shall be at liberty to call aliens to his counsel, such as he shall deem to him to be advantageous and trustworthy, in such manner as before the time aforesaid he might do. Also, we do say and do ordain, that the said king shall have full power and free rule within his realm and the appurtenances thereof; and that he shall be in the same position and with the same plenary power, in all things and by all things, that he was in before the time aforesaid. We further are unwilling, nor by this present ordinance do we intend, in any way to derogate from the royal privileges, charters, liberties, statutes, or praiseworthy customs, of the realm of England, which before the time aforesaid existed. We do also ordain, that the said king shall withhold and remit all rancour as towards the said barons, which against them he may entertain by reason of the premises, and the barons, also in like manner; and that no person shall in future, himself or by any other, in any way aggrieve or offend another by reason of the premises, which unto us by way of compromise have been referred."

After this, his lordship the king returned to England from the parts beyond sea.[1]

The barons however were not content with the award of the said king of France,

[1] "On the 15th of the calends of March" (15 February). *Marginal note*

but immediately levied war upon Roger de Mortimer in the marches of Wales; and levelled all his castles, pillaged his lands, and burnt his manors and vills; sir Edward also, on coming to his succour with a strong force, was nearly taken prisoner. At this time also, another parliament was held at Oxford between his lordship the king and the barons aforesaid. The Londoners however, and the barons of the Cinque Ports, and nearly all the middle class of people throughout the kingdom of England, who indeed had not joined in the reference to the king of France, wholly declined his award.

Wherefore, the Londoners appointed one of their number, Thomas de Piwelesdone by name, to be their constable, and as marshal, Stephen Buckerel, at whose summons, upon hearing the great bell of St Paul's, all the people of the city were to sally forth, and not otherwise; being prepared as well by night as by day, [and] well armed, to follow the standards of the said constable and marshal wheresoever they might think proper to lead them. After this, Hugh le Despenser, the justiciar, who then had charge of the Tower, with a countless multitude of Londoners, went forth from the city, following the standards of the aforesaid constable and marshal; none of them knowing whither they were going, or what they were to do. Being led however as far as Ystleworthe,[1] they there laid waste and ravaged with fire the manor of the king of Almaine, and plundered all the property there found, and broke down and burned his mills and fish-preserves, observing no truce, at the very time that the said parliament was in existence. And this was the beginning of woes, and the source of that deadly war, through which so many manors were committed to the flames, so many men, rich and poor, were plundered, and so many thousands of persons lost their lives.

The parliament however, being concluded without any agreement being arrived at, the earl of Leicester came to London, and many of the barons with him. Immediately upon this, his lordship the king and sir Edward, with a strong force, fought at Norhamptone, and took that place, and the castle there as well, as also Peter de Montfort, and Simon, son of the earl before-mentioned, and all the barons there found, together with all their harness; they also seized all the burgesses, the whole of whom the king caused to be kept in safe custody. At this time, the barons and Londoners entered into a league by written instrument and by oath, all in fact of twelve years of age and upwards; to the effect that they would stand together against all men, saving however their fealty to their lord the king.

Afterwards, in the week before Palm Sunday, the Jewish quarter in London was destroyed, and all the property of the Jews carried off; as many of them as were found, being stripped naked, despoiled, and afterwards murdered by night in sections, to the number, that is to say, of more than five hundred. And as for those who survived, they were saved by the justiciars and the mayor, having been sent to the Tower before the slaughter took place; and then too, the chest of chirographs[2] was sent to the Tower for safe custody. Then also, as well as before, much money belonging to the men of Italy and of Cahors, which had been deposited in the priories and abbeys about London for safe custody, was dragged forth and carried off to London. Afterwards, in the week before Easter, the barons and the Londoners attacked Rochester and took it, and laying siege to the castle there, took the bailey; but, on hearing news of the

[1] Isleworth in Middlesex [2] or *Starrs*

king's approach, they withdrew and returned to London in Easter week. After this, on the feast of St John Port Latin [6 May], the barons and Londoners went forth from the city to meet his said lordship the king, who was then in the neighbourhood of Liawes,[1] with a very great force. Making a halt there, the barons sent letters to his lordship the king and the king sent them letters of his in answer; and in like manner the king of Almaine and sir Edward – which letters see written on the reverse of this leaf. On the ninth day after that day, which fell on a Wednesday, very early in the morning, the contending parties met without the town of Liawes; and at the first onset, the greater part of the Londoners, horse and foot, as well as certain knights and barons, took to flight towards London. The [other] barons however, and those who remained, fought with the king's army until nightfall, and after a countless multitude on either side had been slain, the barons gained the victory, and took the town of Liawes. The king of Almaine also was taken, and many other earls and barons either surrendered themselves or were slain. In this conflict, apart from the kings and sir Edward, twenty-five barons, bearing banners, were either taken or slain; certain barons, however, of the king's army took to flight and escaped.

Be it remarked, that on the same night, between the king and the barons it was provided and ordained, that the provisions of Oxford should stand unshaken, and that if aught in them should need correction, the same should be duly corrected by four of the most noble men of England, bishops or persons of rank; and that if any dissension should arise between them, so much so that they could in no way come to an agreement thereon, they should then abide by the decision of the count of Anjou and the duke of Burgundy; if indeed the greater part of the barons should be willing to agree thereto. And that they would faithfully observe this provision, the two kings before-mentioned gave their eldest sons, as hostages and prisoners, unto the barons; and it was determined that a parliament should be held in London at the feast of Pentecost then next ensuing; an arrangement which was never carried into effect.

Afterwards, on the Tuesday before Ascension day, the peace between the king and the barons was proclaimed in London, and on the morrow the army of the barons came to London, and his lordship the king with his own people; as also the king of Almaine and many prisoners, who had been taken in the aforesaid battle; sir Edward and sir Henry of Almaine, who were hostages, as already stated, being kept in custody in Dover castle. The king of Almaine however, and many other prisoners, were put in the Tower of London. As to his lordship the king, he was lodged at St Paul's when many members of his household were removed from him; added to which, nothing was allowed to him or to the king of Almaine until they had delivered their hostages unto the barons.

Copy of the letters[2] which the barons sent to his lordship the king, before the battle before-mentioned, and of the letters which the said king, in return, sent to them; as also, of the letters which the king of Almaine sent to the barons in return:

"To their most excellent lord, Henry, by the grace of God, the illustrious king of

[1] Lewes, in Sussex

[2] See above, "written on the reverse of this leaf".

England, lord of Ireland, and duke of Acquitaine, the barons and other his faithful subjects, desiring to observe their oath and the fealty that is due unto God and to him, health and devoted service, with all reverence and honour. Whereas by many proofs it is evident, that certain persons about you have suggested unto your lordship many falsehoods as to ourselves, and that too, intending as great evils as they may, not only unto ourselves but also unto you and the whole of your realm; be it known unto your excellency, that it has been our wish, with the fealty which unto you we owe, to maintain the safety and security of your person with all our might; it being our purpose, to the utmost of our power, to aggrieve not only our own enemies, but also yours as well, and those of all your realm. Be pleased therefore, not to believe them as to the matters aforesaid; for we shall always be found to be faithful unto you. And we, the earl of Leicester and Gilbert de Clare, at the prayer of the others, for us and for them, here present, have hereto set our seals."

"Henry, by the grace of God, etc., to Simon de Montfort and Gilbert de Clare, and their accomplices. Whereas by the war and general commotion in our realm, which by you have lately been raised, as also by the conflagrations and other enormous acts of devastation, it is manifestly evident that you do not regard the fealty that from you is due unto us, nor do care in any way for the safety of our person; seeing too that you have outrageously aggrieved the nobles and other our faithful subjects, who with constancy do adhere unto their fealty to us, and do, to the utmost of your power, as by your letters you have signified unto us, purpose to aggrieve them; we, considering the grievance of them to be our own grievance, and the enemies of them to be our own enemies, the more especially as our said faithful subjects, in the observance of their fealty, do faithfully and manfully aid us against your unfaithfulness, do care nothing for your assurances or for your love, but, as being our enemies, do defy you. Witness myself at Lewes, this 12th day of May, in the forty-eighth year of our reign."

"Richard, by the grace of God, king of the Romans, ever august, and Edward, of the illustrious king of England the first-born, and all other the barons and nobles, who in the works of sincere fealty and devotion do testify their constant adherence unto the aforesaid king of England, to Simon de Montfort, Gilbert de Clare, and all and singular other the accomplices of their perfidy. From your letters which you have sent unto the illustrious king of England, our most dear lord, we have heard that we by you are defied; although this your verbal defiance has already been sufficiently proved unto us by fact of your hostility, in the destruction by fire of our property and the laying waste of our possessions. We therefore do wish you to know that you, as public enemies by enemies, are defied by all and singular of us; and that from this time forward we will, with all our mind and our strength, wheresoever we shall have the means of so doing, do our utmost to inflict injury alike upon your persons and your possessions. And further, whereas you do falsely impute unto us, that we do give neither faithful nor good counsel unto our said king, you do say that which is not the truth. And if you, sir Simon de Montfort, or Gilbert de Clare, do wish to assert that same in the court of the said king, we are ready to procure for you a safe-conduct to come unto the said court, and by another, your peer in nobility and in birth, to make proof of our innocence herein, and, as being a perfidious traitor, the falsehood of yourself. We all are content with the seals of the lords aforesaid, that is to say, of the king of the Romans, and sir Edward. Given at Lewes, this twelfth day of May."

After this, the king of Almaine was taken to the castle of Berkamstede.

Then the bishops and barons held a parliament, in which it was ordained, as is set forth in the letters of his lordship the king, which he himself made, and sealed with his seal; which letters begin as follows: "For the reformation of the present state of the realm, there shall be chosen three of the most discreet persons of the realm, etc."[1]

At the same time provision was made as to depredators, as well clerical as lay, how proceedings were to be taken against them. Also, as to clerks who have borne arms in war, or in the company of robbers. Also, as to clerks and laymen who have carried off ecclesiastical property in one diocese, and have benefices or domiciles in another; when they cannot be reached with citation where they have perpetrated their offences. Also, as to clerks and laymen who have made clerks captive.

[2]To the first, answer was made; if any one should think proper to act otherwise [than right], let due course of law be observed; but where rapine has been committed upon a church, either by clerk or layman, or at their moving, or where violence has been committed upon an ecclesiastical person by a person ecclesiastical or lay, or upon a layman by a clerk; because through fear of greater peril, injuries committed upon churches, as also those of a private nature, might, after many such wrongful deeds had been left unpunished, possibly be checked through the risk of such peril; I[3] do deem it in such cases to be agreeable and expedient, that the bishop shall in his diocese cause inquisition to be made thereon, as to who, from whom, what, how much, and from what place, has with violence stripped and despoiled the house; and further, that the names being specified, the persons shall be lawfully cited, and in the case of notorious and manifest acts, after monition has issued, condemnation shall follow. But in secret cases where there is denial, purgation is to be awarded. And because a multitude is implicated herein, it is expedient, I think, that there should be some little tending to severity.

To the second, answer was made; that clerks, bearing arms in actual conflict, if on the side of those who were supporting justice and repelling violence, shall for a time be suspended from office, and, after the period of such suspension shall have expired, may be restored to office; provided however they have struck or wounded no one in the said conflict. From this you may form a judgment what I think as to other like cases. But where such persons have leagued themselves with robbers or depredators, and have been partakers in robbing or depredation, especially of churches and ecclesiastics, they must incur the peril of their order, and may by strict right be

[1] For the whole of this document, see *Liber Custumarum*, ed. H. T. Riley, Rolls series (1860–2), pp. 663, 664.
[2] The whole of this passage is evidently corrupt and imperfect; and its meaning can only be guessed at.
[3] It is probably the legate who is speaking.

deprived of their benefices: against such persons, when accused, proceedings must be taken by way of inquisition, as already stated.

To the third, answer was made; that when misdoers betake themselves to other parts, so that citations cannot reach them there, an edict must be publicly put forth by the bishop, to the effect that the same bishop, at a certain time and place, will make inquisition as to such acts of rapine and such depredators; and notice must be given to all who are in any way interested, that they may be present at such inquisition, if they shall deem it expedient. And whoever shall be found guilty, shall by the bishop of the place in which he has committed the offence, be excommunicated, and execution of such sentence shall be demanded of the bishop in whose territory he has domicile or benefice. And if any person shall wish to bring such offender to trial, the bishop of the place in which the offence was committed, must cite the bishop in whose diocese he has benefice or domicile, who in such case must do for his peer whatever is necessary.

To the fourth, answer was made; that those who make clerks captive are by the canon rendered excommunicate, and after satisfaction has been made for the injuries committed, and the costs and damages, they must be sent for absolution to the apostolic see; and if they shall have extorted anything by way of ransom, the same shall be restored, simply or twofold, according to the award of the bishop. Also, in this case, procedure may be had by way of action, if there be any one who may wish to proceed by inquisition, in case the injured parties have shown a purpose to act through the influence of fear, or through slothfulness, or collusion. – This ordinance was not at that season carried into effect.

At this season, because news came that through the queen's contrivance, and that of Peter de Sauveie,[1] John earl of Warenne, Hugh Bigot, William de Valence, John Maunsell, and others, who were then in the parts beyond the sea, certain aliens intended to invade the kingdom of England by force of arms, a writ of his lordship the king was sent to the sheriffs of England, to the effect under-written:

"Henry, by the grace of God, king of England, lord of Ireland, and duke of Acquitaine, to the archbishops, bishops, abbots, priors, earls, barons, sheriffs, knights, freemen, and all the commons, of the county of Essex, greeting. Whereas we have heard for certain, that a great multitude of aliens, collecting ships from every quarter, are making preparations to enter our realm by force of arms, to the confusion and the everlasting disherison of us, and of all and singular persons in this realm, unless indeed we shall deem it proper to meet them with a strong hand, we do command you, in virtue of the fealty in which unto us you are bound, and do strictly enjoin, that manfully and strenuously you do forthwith equip with horses and with arms, all knights and freeholders who shall thereunto suffice; that so, you be with us at London, with all your array, on the Sunday next after the feast of St Peter's Chains [1 August], to proceed with us forthwith against such aliens, in defence by us and by you of all this realm. And you, the sheriff, taking with you the keeper of the peace of the same county, are to give notice unto the bishops, abbots, priors, barons, and all others who owe service unto us, and are strictly to enjoin on our behalf, by virtue of the fealty

[1] Savoy

and the homage in which unto us they are bound, and as they love themselves, their lands and tenements, that each one of them do come, not only with the military service which unto us is due, but with all the might and power that he may, or else send unto us upon that day such horses, and arms, and chosen foot-soldiers, as he shall be able; that so by their aid we may be enabled the more efficiently to meet this peril. And let no one, by reason of the shortness of this notice, and because that it does not contain a reasonable time of summons, excuse himself; seeing that urgent necessity does not allow of postponement to a future day; nor is it our intention or our wish, that even this shall be drawn into a precedent, to the prejudice of others. And further, from every vill, upon the same day, you are to summon eight, six, or four at the least, according to the size of such vill, of the best and most able foot-soldiers, well provided with befitting array, that is to say, with lances, bows and arrows, swords, arbalests, and axes, and have them provided therewith at the common expense for forty days. In the case also of cities, in like manner, castles, and boroughs, where there is a greater multitude of men, according to the extent and means of every such place, omit not, in manner aforesaid, to send as well foot as horse, in such numbers as, taking into consideration the nature of the business, you shall think proper to provide. Nor is any one to make allegation of the approaching time of harvest, or of his being occupied with his family affairs of any other kind, seeing that it is more safe and more advantageous, with security to the person, to be in goods in some small measure damnified, than, with total loss of land and of goods, by the impious hands of those who, thirsting for your blood, will spare neither sex nor age, if they can prevail, to be delivered up to the sufferings of a cruel death. This our mandate therefore you are to have published throughout your county in form aforesaid, and notice thereof given unto each, that, as they love our honour and that of our land and their own lives, and as they would avoid their own disherison and the everlasting disherison of their posterity, they hasten to make preparations as manfully and as efficiently as they may; that so, all excuses laid aside, at the very latest, on the Sunday next after the feast of St Peter's Chains [1 August] they appear at the place aforesaid. And you are to know, that if you shall find any persons to hold this mandate in contempt, or to be in reference thereto negligent and remiss, we shall heavily exact from their persons and their property for the same; in such manner as against those whose fault it will not be, if we and our realm are delivered over to confusion and to everlasting disherison. In testimony whereof, we have caused these our letters patent to be written. Witness myself, at St Paul's, London, this 7th day of July, in the forty-eighth year of our reign."

After this, in obedience to the precept of the before-stated writ, countless multitudes of horse and foot gathered together from all the counties of England; and, well provided with arms, set out for the sea-coast, to defend the realm against aliens; and in like manner, numberless ships of the Cinque Ports and other places put to sea with crews well-armed, for the purpose of resisting the said aliens with a strong hand.

Afterwards, about the feast of the Assumption of the Blessed Mary [15 August], his lordship the king and the barons set out for Dover, where there was a conference held between envoys sent by the king and the barons of England on the one hand, and the aliens whom the queen of England, John Maunsell, Peter de Sauveie, and their accomplices had induced, at a vast outlay, to make a descent upon England.

Afterwards, about the feast of the Exaltation of the Holy Cross [14 September], sir Hugh le Despenser, justiciar of England, Peter de Montfort, and other nobles, the bishop of London, the bishop of Worcester, and other bishops, crossed over for the purpose of arranging and confirming a treaty of peace.

At this time, the ecclesiastics throughout all England gave the tenth part of the issues of their churches.

1264 Edward Blund, Peter Fitz-Auger } Sheriffs { They were not sworn at the exchequer when presented

This year, on the second day before the feast of the Translation of St Edward the Confessor [13 October], the king returned to London from the sea-coast.

At this time, about the feast of Simon and Jude [28 October], it was provided that three bishops should be chosen, unto whom should be given by his lordship the king and the barons, full power of reasonably correcting all injuries done to the church in this kingdom between Easter in the year of our Lord 1263 and the said time; a thing that the barons conceded in good faith, and by their letters patent confirmed the same. And if any one should decline to be judged by the said bishops, he was to be excommunicated, and by the lay power compelled to make satisfaction; and it was then provided, that such bishops should collect all issues of benefices of aliens which had existed in contravention of the Provisions of Oxford, and should deposit the same in safety, until peace throughout the realm should be fully confirmed.

Be it remembered, that Thomas Fitz-Thomas, who in the preceding year had been elected mayor, though he had not been admitted, still remained in office throughout the whole year: but in that year no pleas of land were pleaded, save only pleas of intrusion, as also pleas on plaint made, which pertain to the assizes;[1] nor was any Hustings held. Hence it was, that no affidavits as to tenements were sworn from foreign courts, nor was any testament proved. The same Thomas also was again elected mayor on the feast of Simon and Jude, and on the morrow admitted by the king.

In this year, it was provided in the Hustings, on the morrow of All Souls [2 November], that all measures by which wine, ale, and other liquors, are sold, should be of the same dimensions, the mouth of the gallon being ordered to measure four inches across. On the same day, it was enacted and provided that no advocate should be an essoiner[2] in the Hustings, or in any other of the city courts.

In this year, about the Nativity, the barons of the March of Wales, who before had adhered to the king and had been with him at the battle of Liawes, and had afterwards fought at the head of a large army in the March aforesaid, committing depredations and many mischiefs, concluded peace at Gloucester, his lordship the king being there, as also the earls of Leicester and Gloucester, and many other nobles. Some of

[1] or, regulations as to the sale of victuals, and other commodities, within the city

[2] an agent or attorney, whose sole duty it was to proffer essoins for defendants, and support them before the court

these barons however abjured the realm of England for a year and a day, to proceed to Ireland in exile, and there to stay the whole of the said year, their lands, tenements, and castles, remaining in the hands of the earl of Leicester in the meantime. But after such year should have expired, and when the said barons should have returned to England, they were to abide by the award of their peers, and to be bound to be at the sea-coast ready to cross over, on the twentieth day after our Lord's Nativity; an arrangement which did not hold good.

This year, on the octaves of St Hilary [13 January], there came to London, by summons of his lordship the king, all the bishops, abbots, priors, earls, [and] barons, of the whole realm, as also the barons of the Cinque Ports, [and] four men of every city and borough, to hold a parliament; in which parliament, on St Valentine's day, it was made known in the Chapter House at Westminster, that his lordship the king had bound himself by his charter, on oath, that neither he nor sir Edward, would from thenceforth aggrieve, or cause to be aggrieved, the earls of Leicester or Gloucester, or the citizens of London, or any of those who had sided with them, on pretence of any thing done in the time of the past commotions in the realm; and he thereby expressly gave orders, that the charters of Liberties and of the Forest, which had been made in the ninth year of his reign, together with the other articles which had been enacted in the month of June in the forty-eighth year of his reign, should be inviolably observed.

Afterwards, on the day before the feast of St Gregory [12 March], sir Edward and Henry of Almaine, who had surrendered themselves as hostages at the battle of Liawes, until peace should be restored in England, were delivered up to his lordship the king, free and quit, before all the people in the Great Hall at Westminster; and at the same time there were read certain letters obligatory of his lordship the king and sir Edward, in which it is set forth how and under what penalties they, upon oath, had promised to maintain the peace and tranquility of the realm. And then, nine bishops, arrayed in pontificals, with lighted tapers, pronounced excommunicate all those who should presume to do aught against the charters of Liberties and the Forest, or against the statutes which had been enacted in the preceding year. There were also then read certain other letters of sir Edward, in which, upon oath, he promised to surrender three castles which he held in the march of Wales; the same to be given, by counsel of his lordship the king, into the custody of men of the realm, not suspected, by them to be held for three whole years.

He further promised, that he would give due care that the knights of the March of Wales should duly fulfil what they had undertaken, and that if they should not, he would prove their deadly enemy, and, by force of arms, to the utmost of his power would compel them to do the same. He further promised, that for three years from the Easter next ensuing he would remain in England, and would not depart therefrom, without leave of the council. He further promised, that he would not bring, or cause to bring, aliens into the realm of England; and that if any should come, and he by the council of his lordship the king should be warned thereof, he would, to the utmost of his power, resist the same. And faithfully to observe all these things he bound himself, upon peril of all the lands, tenements, honours, and dignities, which he then possessed or should possess, if he should contravene any one of the articles aforesaid, and the same should be manifestly proved. And for the more sure observance thereof, sir Henry of Almaine, of his own accord, offered himself as hostage for sir Edward aforesaid, to remain in custody of sir Henry de Montfort until St Peter's Chains [1 August]; and if, in the meantime, any army of aliens should prepare to come into England by force of arms, in such case the said Henry was to remain hostage in the same custody for sir Edward, until the feast of All Souls [2 November] then next ensuing; that so, in the meantime it might be ascertained how sir Edward should be inclined to conduct himself as towards the aliens aforesaid.[1]

On the same day it was made known, that whereas his lordship the king, before the battle of Liewes, had by counsel of his advisers defied the earls of Gloucester and Leicester, and those who adhered to them, it was now provided that all free men of the realm of England should do homage and fealty to him anew, saving however all articles in his letters obligatory, and in the letters of sir Edward, contained.

After this, on the 17th day of March, the mayor and aldermen of London in the church of St Paul did fealty[2] to his lordship the king, who was there present; and on the Sunday following, all persons in the city, of the age of twelve years and upwards, made the same oath, each before his own alderman, in his own ward.

Afterwards, between Easter and Pentecost there arose certain dissensions between the earl of Gloucester and the earl of Leicester, his lordship the king being then at Gloucester. For the earl of Gloucester said, that many of the articles which had been prepared at Oxford and at Liawes, had not been fully observed; and those articles were put in writing by the said earl. Whereupon, the aforesaid earls of Gloucester and Leicester, upon oath and by their letters obligatory, submitted to the arbitration of the bishop of Worcester, sir Hugh le Despenser, sir John Fitz-John, and sir William de Munchensy; which arrangement however was not carried into effect.

In this year, by assent and consent of certain nobles of England, namely the earl of Leicester and his sons, the men of the Cinque Ports roved about the sea in keels[3] and other vessels, plundering all those whom they found coming into England or leaving it; and they cruelly threw men overboard into the sea, sparing no one, whether English or aliens. Of all the plunder so acquired, the said earl of Leicester and his sons received a third part, it was said.

Afterwards, on the Thursday in the week of Pentecost, sir Edward departed from Hereford without leave, his lordship the king, the earl of Leicester, and many other earls and barons, then being there; and took his departure in the direction of Chester.

After this, sir Edward, accompanied by the earl of Gloucester and the barons of the March and others, as also the earl of Warenne and William de Valence, who had recently landed at Penbrok, took Gloucester and the castle there. At this time, his lordship the king, listening to evil counsel, gave and granted unto Leuwelin, prince of

[1] "It should be known, that all the aforesaid letters of his lordship the king and of his son, were quashed after the battle of Evesham, as set forth below in this book." *Marginal note*

[2] "Then, those who were present might see a thing wondrous and unheard of in this age; for this most wretched mayor, when taking the oath, dared to utter words so rash as these, saying unto his lordship the king in presence of the people; 'My lord, so long as unto us you will be a good lord and king, we will be faithful and duteous unto you.' " *Marginal note*

[3] a kind of merchant vessel

Wales, the greater part of the March, with the castles thereof, as also, lands and castles of orphans, who were under age and in guardianship: whereupon, Lewelin, as soon as ever he received seisin of any castle, at once levelled the same, to the very great loss and detriment of the realm of England. For the Welsh had never before entered into such a league with the English, nor ever will enter into any such, without fraud and estrangement through them thence ensuing. This gift his lordship the king made unto the said Lewelin, in order that he might give him aid against his son and his followers.

In the same year, upon the morrow of St Swithun [15 July], Simon de Montfort the Younger, with other barons and their adherents, took and plundered Winchester, and destroyed the Jewry there; because the citizens would not admit them into the city without his lordship the king being present. After which, they laid siege to the castle there; but, upon hearing rumours of the approach of sir Edward, although he did not come, through fear they withdrew.

Be it remembered, that at the same time that the before-mentioned dissension arose between the said earls of Gloucester and Leicester, it was provided and enacted among the Londoners, and confirmed by oath of every person of twelve years and upwards, that the peace of his lordship the king should be strictly observed within the city and without; and that if any person should contravene the same, and should be convicted thereof, he should immediately undergo capital punishment, notwithstanding any franchise that he might possess; and this was proclaimed throughout all the city, as also by letters patent of the commons of the city, published in the four adjoining counties, in all hundreds and vills within a distance from London of twenty-five miles: wherefore, certain persons who had followed the army of Simon de Montfort the Younger to London, and who had been convicted of the commission of robberies in Stebenhe and Hackenheie,[1] were hanged, about the feast of the apostles Peter and Paul [29 June].

After this, on the night after St Peter's Chains [1 August], sir Edward, the earl of Warenne, William de Valence, and their adherents, came with a strong armed force, to Kenelworthe, and there found all the army of Simon de Montfort the Younger buried in sleep. Upon this, sir Edward caused immediate proclamation to be made, that no one of his people should slay any of the army of the said Simon; but that they should be taken alive. Accordingly, there were captured there the earl of Oxford, William de Munchensy, Adam de Newmarket, Baldwin Wake, Hugh de Nevile, and many others, barons, knights, and serjeants, all of whom were carried prisoners to Gloucester, having lost their horses and arms, and all their harness. As to Simon before-named, he and certain others, taking to flight, threw themselves into the castle of Kenelworthe; while as many as were able, took to flight and escaped.

Be it observed, that his lordship the king, with the earl of Leicester and his adherents, had been staying at Hereford for many weeks, being unable to pass the Severn, as all the bridges had been broken down by sir Edward and the earl of Gloucester; the said Edward, and the earl and the barons of the march of Wales, with their army, preventing the king from crossing over with his troops. At last, while the said Edward was with his army at Kenelworthe, as already mentioned, his lordship the king, with his

[1] Stepney and Hackney

forces, crossed the Severn at Worcester on the morrow of St Peter's Chains, which day[1] then fell upon a Sunday. After this, on the Tuesday following, such Tuesday being the third day after the Chains, and the fourth of August, they arrived at Hevesham,[2] where sir Edward and the earl of Gloucester surprised them with all their army; and on the same day, the two parties engaging without the said town, the said Edward and the earl of Gloucester gained the victory, and the earl of Leicester and his eldest son, Henry, were slain; Hugh le Despenser also, and Peter de Montfort, and all the barons and knights who had adhered to them, were slain, a few only excepted, who however were badly wounded and made prisoners. It was said also, that many knights and men-at-arms on that side were slain, while on the other side but very few lost their lives.

The head of the earl of Leicester, it is said, was severed from his body, and his testicles cut off and hung on either side of his nose; and in such guise the head was sent to the wife of sir Roger de Mortimer, at Wiggemor castle. His hands and feet were also cut off, and sent to divers places to enemies of his, as a great mark of dishonour to the deceased; the trunk of his body however, and that only, was given for burial in the church of Evesham. On the same day and at the same hour that the battle took place, there was a very great tempest at London and elsewhere, accompanied with coruscations,[3] lightning, and thunder.

After this, when certain news was heard of the battle aforesaid, all the prisoners who had been taken at the battle of Liewes and put in the Tower of London and the castle of Windleshores, were set at liberty and released without ransom. In like manner, the king of Almaine was liberated from the castle of Kenelworthe, and all the other prisoners who had been taken by the said earl of Leicester and his accomplices during the aforesaid disturbances in the realm of England.

After this, about the feast of the Nativity of the Blessed Mary [8 September], his lordship the king held a parliament at Winchester, where Simon de Montfort the Younger, who had a safe-conduct from his lordship the king and sir Edward, appeared; but as he was not able at that season to make peace on his own terms, he withdrew and threw himself into the castle of Kenelworthe, whither he had summoned many knights and men-at-arms, who still adhered to him. In the said parliament, it was provided that all who were taken at Kenelworthe, as already noticed, as also those who were taken at the battle of Evesham, as well as the heirs of those who were slain there, should be disinherited, because, as it was said, they had in reality been against the king, although fighting together with him as following his standard. For it was resolved that he was not in full enjoyment of his power, after he had been taken at the battle of Liawes; but rather, under the rod and power of the earl of Leicester, who did whatever he pleased with the king's seal, and all things pertaining unto the realm of England. His lordship the king also then recalled all donations of lands, churches, [and] prebends, which between the day of his capture and the day aforesaid he had granted; and all letters, charters, and writings, which he and his son

[1] i.e. 2 August, the day after St Peter's Chains
[2] Evesham, in Worcestershire
[3] "*choruscationes*" here probably means something of the nature of the Aurora Borealis

had executed by compulsion throughout the whole time aforesaid, were recalled and made of no effect.

1265 Gregory de Rokesle } Sheriffs
Simon de Hadestok }

On the morrow of St Michael, as the custom is, the mayor and citizens proceeded to Westminster, to present them to the barons of the exchequer; but finding no one there, they returned home. And so, they were not admitted[1] sheriffs. Be it remembered, that at the close of the parliament before-mentioned, his lordship the king had summoned to Wyndleshores all the earls, barons, [and] knights, as many as he could, with horses and arms, intending to lay siege to the city of London, [and] calling the citizens his foes.

Then was all the city in great alarm. The fools and evil-minded persons, however, who had previously been adherents of the earl of Leicester against the king, proposed fortifying the city against him; while the discreet men of the city, who always maintained their fealty to his lordship the king – although some part of them, but by compulsion, had given their adherence to the said earl – would not assent thereto; but, though they sent many letters, through men of the religious orders, to his lordship the king, for the purpose of beseeching his favour, it was of no avail to them. At length, after holding counsel among themselves, the whole community gave its consent to throwing themselves on the mercy of his lordship the king, and made letters patent thereupon, sealed with the common seal; eight men being selected to carry and show the same unto his lordship the king, and to present such letters to him at Windleshores. Upon the road, they were met by sir Roger de Leiburne, who said that he, for the benefit and advantage of the city, had come to make arrangements for peace between his lordship the king and the citizens: upon hearing which, the men who had been so sent, returned home; and the said Roger took up his quarters in the Tower of London.

The next morning however, the said Roger went to the church called Berkinge cherche;[2] where the mayor and a countless multitude of the citizens had met; and then, summoning the mayor and more discreet men of the city, the said Roger said to them that if it was their wish to become reconciled with his lordship the king, they must wholly subject themselves unto the will of his lordship the king as to life and limb, and as to all things movable and immovable. The citizens accordingly gave assent thereto, and caused letters patent to be made, sealed with the common seal; which letters the said Roger took with him to his lordship the king at Windleshores.

Afterwards, on the Friday next after the feast of St Michael, the same Roger came to London, and on the morrow proceeded to the church before-mentioned; the mayor also and citizens met there, to whom the same Roger said, that it was the desire of his lordship the king, that all chains which had been placed across the streets,

[1] "They were not admitted, because his lordship the king had then taken the city into his own hands; because that the citizens had been adherents of the earl of Leicester in the disturbances of the realm; and he retained the same for nearly six years." *Marginal note*
[2] Allhallows Barking, near the Tower

should be removed, and that all the posts to which the said chains had been attached, should be rooted up, and carried, all of them, to the Tower; and so it was afterwards done.

It was also the wish of his lordship the king, that the mayor and principal men of the city should come to him at Windleshores, to confirm what was said in the letters aforesaid. The said Roger also brought letters patent of safe-conduct of his lordship the king, for the mayor and citizens, so that they might safely go to Windleshores, there to stay and thence to return, the same to last until the Monday then next ensuing, and throughout the whole of the Monday aforesaid. Wherefore, on the same day, the mayor, and about forty of the more substantial men of the city, set out and arrived at Stanes. On the morrow, which was a Sunday, after the citizens had awaited the arrival of the said Roger until the third hour,[1] he came, and then the mayor and citizens accompanied him to Windleshores; where he entered the castle, the citizens remaining without until evening. His lordship the king also then caused proclamation to be made, that no knight, serjeant, or other person, should presume to say or to do anything affronting to the citizens, seeing that they had been summoned to the peace of his lordship the king.

After this, there were sent on part of his lordship the king, the said Roger, and sir Robert Walraven and others, to inform the mayor and citizens that the king was not then advised in what form to make known his will unto them; but that they were to enter the castle, and on the morrow should learn the same. Upon this, they entered, and all of them were lodged in the tower[2] in safe custody, the letters of safe-conduct granted by the king availing them nought. They also remained there throughout the whole of that night and the whole of the following day; but at a later hour, were separated and sent into the bailey of the castle, and there lodged, all of them, the mayor excepted, Thomas de Piwelesdon, Michael Thovi, Stephen Bugerel, [and] John de Flete, whose bodies the king gave to sir Edward; and they remained in the tower.

After this, his lordship the king departed from Windleshores and came to London, calling the citizens his enemies, and giving away more than sixty houses belonging to citizens; they, with all their families, being expelled. In like manner also, he gave away all such goods belonging to the citizens as they possessed without the city, as at Lenne,[3] for example, Gernemue,[4] and other sea-ports. He also took all their foreign lands,[5] into his hands, and destroyed and wasted all goods there found. At this time, sir Hugh Fitz-Otes, constable of the Tower, was made warden of the city, and styled "Seneschal", appointing under him two bailiffs, John Addrien, namely, and Walter Hervi, who, in place of sheriffs, were to have charge of the city.

After this, the citizens aforesaid, who were in the bailey at Windleshores, were liberated by leave of his lordship the king and of his son, and returned home, all of them, to London, on the Thursday next after the feast of St Luke the Evangelist [18 October], with the exception of Richard Bonaventure, Simon de Hadestoke, William de Kent, Eadmund de Essex, and William de Gloucester, who remained.

[1] nine in the morning [2] or keep [3] Lynn, in Norfolk
[4] Yarmouth, in Norfolk
[5] i.e. lands without the liberties of the city

At this time, his lordship the king had hostages taken for keeping the peace, from more than sixty citizens, who accordingly were put in the Tower; and at the same time the king had the citizens spoken to, to the effect that they must make fine to him for their offence. Upon this, after holding conference, they made answer that the citizens had not equally offended; for that some of them had always maintained the peace of his lordship the king, and whom in those times he used to call his friends. Others again had been adherents of the earl of Leicester; but this, because compelled thereto. Many others again, evil-minded persons, had spontaneously sided with the said earl and his accomplices, committing depredations both within the city and without. Wherefore it seemed unto the citizens, that they ought not equally to be punished; and they accordingly entreated the king and his council, that each of them might individually be allowed to make fine in proportion to his offence, and that everyone might be punished according to his transgressions. And this was granted them, though it was not carried into effect.

After this, on the Tuesday next after the feast of St Nicholas [6 December], the king took his departure from Westminster for Norhamptone, and on the same day, John de la Linde, knight, and John Waleraven, clerk, were made seneschals, the Tower of London being delivered into their hands. On the same day, there came to Westminster upon summons more than twenty-four of the most substantial men of the city; all of whom made oath before the council of his lordship the king, that they would faithfully and safely keep the city in his behalf, sir Roger de Leiburne telling them that his lordship the king had delivered his city into their keeping, under the seneschals before-mentioned.

Be it remarked, that at the time when the city submitted itself unto the mercy of his lordship the king, many persons in the city who had spontaneously sided with the earl of Leicester, took to flight; having committed depredations and many mischiefs within the city and without, and, in the time of the aforesaid mayor, styling themselves the "Commons of the City", having had the first voice there, the principal men thereof being but little consulted in reference thereto.

Be it remarked, that in the week of our Lord's Nativity in the same year, in presence of sir Roger de Leiburne and Robert Walraven, sent by his lordship the king, who was then at Norhamptone, the citizens made fine to his lordship the king in the sum of 20,000 marks sterling, for all trespasses and excesses during the disturbances of the realm imputed to them; in consideration whereof, he granted unto them his charter, in form under-written:

Letters of his lordship the king, whereby he remitted his indignation unto the citizens.

"Henry, by the grace of God, king of England, etc. to all men, etc. greeting. Know ye, that in consideration of a fine of 20,000 marks, which our citizens of London have made unto us as their ransom, by reason of trespasses or excesses against us, and our queen, and Richard the illustrious king of Almaine, our brother, and Edward our eldest son, by them committed, or unto them imputed, we do, for ourselves and our heirs, so far as in us lies, wholly remit and pardon unto the said citizens and their heirs all such trespasses and excesses, in form as follows, that is to say; that they shall have all issues of rents arising from houses and tenements as well in the city aforesaid as in the suburbs thereof, from the time of our Lord's Nativity last past, upon the understanding that from henceforth they shall, from such rents, satisfy all persons whatsoever in such manner as shall be right; and shall have all goods and chattels of such misdoers within the same city, as, in the disturbances aforesaid, have been against us and Edward our eldest son, and who thereof have been, or shall be, indicted; save and except the goods and chattels of those whose bodies we have granted unto our said son, and except the houses, lands, tenements, and rents, of the same citizens, which are and ought to be our escheats, by reason of the trespasses aforesaid; and shall have all goods and chattels of citizens of the same city in the parts of Flanders arrested, save and except the chattels and goods of those who by lawful inquisition may be found or convicted to have been our enemies. And that all prisoners of the same city, except those whose bodies we have given unto our firstborn son aforesaid, shall from prison be delivered; save also such prisoners as have by the same citizens been indicted and taken, and shall be indicted and taken. And that the hostages of the citizens aforesaid, for the safe-keeping of the same city unto us delivered, save and except the hostages of the prisoners of our son aforesaid, and the hostages of those who have taken to flight, if any such there shall be, shall in like manner be set at liberty; and that from the goods of such citizens as have died in the city aforesaid, since the time that the said citizens have submitted themselves unto our will, a contribution shall be proportionally levied towards the said ransom, according to the means of the deceased, in the same manner as in regard to the means of the other citizens who are still living in the city aforesaid; and in like manner it shall be done as to the goods of all men of the same city who are there in our exchange.[1] We have also granted unto them, that all goods and chattels of the reputable men of the city aforesaid, which have been taken from each and every of them, from the time when the citizens aforesaid submitted themselves unto our will, without our warrant aforesaid – the goods of Richard de Walebrok excepted – shall unto them be wholly restored; and that the said citizens shall throughout all our territories and dominions, freely and without impediment on part of us or ours, as well by sea as by land, trade with their wares and merchandise, in such manner as they shall deem expedient, quit of all custom, toll, and passage;[2] and shall sojourn wheresoever they shall think proper, in the same our realm, for purposes of business, in such manner as in past times they have been wont to do, until such time as of our counsel it shall as to the state of the city aforesaid be more fully provided. And that no one of the said city, as to whom it may manifestly be proved that in the disturbances aforesaid he has been our enemy, or the enemy of our eldest son aforesaid, shall in future sojourn or be harboured in the city aforesaid. In testimony whereof, we have caused these our letters patent to be made. Witness myself, at Norhamptone, this tenth day of January, in the fiftieth year of our reign."

By reason of this ransom, then were set at liberty William de Gloucester, Richard Bonaventure, William de Kent, [and] Simon de Hadestoke; Eadmund de Essex having been previously released.

[1] at the Tower, and acting as moneyers at the Mint, or their assistants
[2] a toll levied for passing over ferries

After this, Simon de Montfort the Younger, while his lordship the king was at Norhamptone, threw himself upon his mercy, to abide by the award of the king of Almaine and the legate of his lordship the pope, then in England, and certain others, barons of England. Afterwards, having come to London and made a stay for some time in the court of sir Edward, not awaiting his award, he escaped stealthily without leave and by night, making for Winchester, where he joined the pirates of the Cinque Ports; who then, as before, were seizing all the merchants they could, whether coming to England or departing from England, and either slaying them or plundering their goods. Still however, these pirates did not dare to attack any foreign prince or knight, coming in armed guise to England, or leaving it. This Simon however afterwards crossed the seas.

The same year, in the week before Palm Sunday, sir Edward received into the favour of his lordship the king, his father, and of himself, all the men of the Cinque Ports, as well misdoers as others; and granted that they should have all their liberties, and possess all their lands and tenements. And in like manner it was granted unto knights, serjeants, and all others who had been their adherents in the disturbances aforesaid, that they should freely have and hold all the possessions and lands, which they had before held; also, all acts of depredation and homicide by land or by sea were forgiven, whatsoever the same might be, which they had committed upon men of the realm of England, Ireland, Scotland, Wales, and Gascoigne; those lands namely, which belong to the dignity of his lordship the king. And if any person of a land other than the lands above-mentioned, should wish to proceed against such persons for depredations committed against them, or for homicide committed against their kinsfolk, he was to come into the court of the Cinque Ports aforesaid, and there have justice awarded him. But for what reason or through what necessity all the concessions aforesaid were made unto them, I know not.

The bishops who, for their disobedience, were sent to Rome, must not be passed over in silence here. A year and a half before, when the queen of England, Peter de Sauweye,[1] the earl of Warenne, Hugh Bigot, and a countless multitude of knights and men-at-arms, together with a large fleet, were in Flanders and intending to cross over to England with a strong and armed force, against the earl of Leicester and his accomplices; the Roman legate, who is now pope,[2] then being in those parts, pronounced sentence of excommunication against the said earl and all who adhered to him in the disturbances of the realm of England before-noticed, and placed the city of London under ecclesiastical interdict, as well as all persons and places belonging to the said earl and his adherents; and this he enjoined upon certain bishops there, in order that they might publish his said sentence and the aforesaid interdict throughout all England. And because they failed to do so, Ottoboni,[3] who is now legate from Rome, summoned them before him at London, and addressed them, pronouncing them contumacious. Wherefore, after much altercation had passed between them for

[1] Savoy

[2] Guy le Gros or le Foulques; previously archbishop of Narbonne and cardinal bishop of Sabina. As he died in November 1268, the present passage tends to show that the latter part of this chronicle is by the hand of a writer previous to that date.

[3] Ottoboni di Fresco; cardinal of St Adrian, and pope (for about five weeks) as Adrian V, in 1276

the reason aforesaid, and because they had showed themselves so luke-warm during the said disturbances in the realm, in not chiding or rebuking those evildoers who were striving against his lordship the king, the week before Palm Sunday in this year he suspended Henry,[1] bishop of London, and Stephen,[2] bishop of Chichester, from duty and benefice, sending them to Rome, to be punished according to their deserts by his lordship the pope.

After this, on the Monday next after the quinzaine of Easter, for the same reason the same legate suspended John,[3] bishop of Winchester, from duty and benefice, naming a peremptory time for him to appear in presence of his lordship the pope, there to receive penance according to his deserts.

About the same time, the exchequer of his lordship the king was transferred from Westminster to St Paul's, so that the pleas in bank which used to be held at Westminster, were now held in the hall of the bishop of London; the exchequer[4] too being placed in the chamber of the said bishop.[5] The legate however was lodged in the Tower of London.

In the same year and at the same season, the persons who had been deprived of their possessions, as already mentioned, collected in bands, and fought by force of arms, in Norfolch, Suthfolch, and Holand,[6] as also in divers other places throughout England, plundering many persons; on which occasion, some of them entered Lincoln, certain persons of that city siding with them, and plundered many of the citizens there. The boroughs and vills also, through which some of them passed, made fine to them, in order that they might not be attacked. Those however who had entered Lincoln, on hearing news of the approach of sir Edward, withdrew.

At this time, about the feast of the apostles Philip and James [1 May], his lordship the king held a parliament at Norhamptone. To this parliament were sent formal messengers from the city of London, begging his lordship the king that he would be pleased to reinstate them in their former position, and that they might elect sheriffs from among themselves, who should be answerable to the king's exchequer for the ancient ferm. Whereupon, returning from the parliament, they came to London on the vigil of our Lord's Ascension, and brought letters of his lordship the king, both close and patent, the tenor of which is as follows:

Letters of his lordship the king as to leave to elect bailiffs.

"Henry, by the grace of God, king of England, lord of Ireland, and duke of Acquitaine, to his well-beloved and trusty, the barons[7] and citizens of London, greeting. Whereas we have granted unto you, that you may elect one of your fellow-citizens, a trusty and discreet person, who has heretofore constantly adhered unto his fealty to us and to Edward, our eldest son, the same to attend to the duties of sheriff of Middlesex and of warden of the city of London; such person by you to be presented at our exchequer, and there to take the oath of fealty, as the usage is, and to be

[1] Henry de Sandwich [2] Stephen de Barksteed [3] John Gervais
[4] the table so called, at which the officers of the Exchequer sat
[5] who was now in disgrace, and on his way to Rome
[6] Holland, or Hoyland, in Lincolnshire
[7] the aldermen and tenants *in capite* were so styled

answerable unto us at the exchequer aforesaid for the ferm thereof; for which ferm the sheriffs thereof respectively from of old have been wont there to be answerable; all which things we have granted unto you of our own free will; provided however that the said sheriff and warden shall with the liberties of the abbey of Westminster in no way interfere: – we do command you that of your fellow-citizens you elect such a person thereunto, and make known unto us his name. Witness myself, at Norhamptone, this first day of May, in the fiftieth year of our reign."

"Henry, by the grace of God etc., to all to whom these present letters shall come, greeting. Know ye, that we have granted unto our well-beloved barons and citizens of London, that they may elect one of their fellow-citizens, a trusty and discreet person, who has heretofore constantly adhered unto his fealty to us and to Edward, our eldest son, the same to attend to the duties of sheriff of Middlesex and of warden of the city of London; the name of such person to be made known unto us, that so he may be presented at our exchequer, and there take the oath of fealty, as the usage is, and be answerable unto us at our exchequer aforesaid for the ferm thereof; all which things we have granted unto them of our own free will. It is our will, however, that the said sheriff and warden shall with the liberties of the abbey of Westminster in no way interfere. In testimony whereof we have caused these letters patent to be made. Witness myself, at Norhamptone, this 30th day of April, in the fiftieth year of our reign."

Accordingly, on the morrow, being the day of our Lord's Ascension, which on this occasion fell upon the feast of St John Port Latin [6 May], the citizens met at the Guildhall, and William Fitz-Richard was elected by them and sworn, to attend to the office of sheriff of Middlesex and the wardenship of the city of London, in form in the aforesaid letters contained: and on the morrow was presented to the barons of the exchequer at St Paul's, and there admitted and sworn.

Be it remarked, that many of the common people, on the day that the aforesaid election took place, gainsayed the same, crying – "Nay, nay," and saying, "We will have no one for mayor, save only Thomas Fitz-Thomas, and we desire that he be released from prison, as well as his companions, who are at Windleshores." Such base exclamations did the fools of the vulgar classes give utterance to, on the previous Monday, in the same Guildhall. Wherefore his lordship the king, on hearing rumours to this effect, fearing an insurrection of the populace against the principal men of the city, who maintained their fealty towards him, sent to London sir Roger de Leiburne; who, on the Saturday next ensuing, came into the Guildhall with a great retinue of knights and serjeants, with arms beneath their clothes; whither a countless multitude of the city had already resorted, and that without summons. And the same sir Roger gave orders, on behalf of his lordship the king, that all who were suspected, should be seized and put in arrest, lest they might enter into some confederacy with the enemies of his lordship the king. Wherefore, on the same day there were taken more than twenty persons, no one of the populace making any opposition thereto.

Be it remarked, that those who adhered unto his lordship the king had frequent conflicts with their adversaries; for example, on one occasion in the county of Derby, where John de Eyvile, Baldwin Wake, and the earl of Ferrers (who two days before had withdrawn from his allegiance to the king, and had given in his adherence to them upon oath), with many others, had met together, with horses and arms, in the vill that is known as Cestrefeld.[1] Here sir Henry of Almaine, sir John de Baliol, and others who maintained their fealty to his lordship the king, surprised and attacked them, on the vigil of Pentecost, many of them being taken prisoner and many slain. The earl of Ferrers also was taken, and carried to the castle of Windleshores. As to John de Eyvile and Baldwyn Wake, they took to flight.

After this, on Friday in the week of Pentecost, sir Edward attacked Adam Gurdan and his accomplices in the wood of Aulton, where many were slain and captured, and lost their all. Afterwards, on the fourth day of June, Boneface, archbishop of Canterbury, came to London from the parts beyond sea, where he had been staying all the time of the aforesaid disturbances in the kingdom of England.

In the same year, after the feast of the Nativity of St John the Baptist [24 June], his lordship the king laid siege to the castle of Kenelworthe, having with him a countless army of earls, barons, knights, men-at-arms, and others who adhered to their fealty. The same year, on the second of the Ides of July [12 August], at night, the wife of sir Edward was delivered of her first-born son, at Windleshores; on hearing news of which, the citizens of London caused proclamation to be made in the city, that on the morrow the whole community should celebrate the same by doing no handicraft, for joyousness at the birth of the said child. Accordingly on that day, all selds[2] and shops being closed, all the men and women, clergy as well as lay, went on foot and horseback to Westminster, to give thanks unto God for the birth of the child, and to offer prayers for its safety. Also, throughout the streets of the city there was dancing and singing of carols for joy, as is the usual yearly custom upon the feast of St John the Baptist. The name that was given to the child was John.

Be it observed, that on the vigil of St Michael a writ of his lordship the king was read in the Guildhall before all the people; in which was set forth, that he had given orders that the charter of liberties which he had granted unto his barons of England, in the ninth year of his reign, should be read before all the people, and that all the articles therein contained should throughout the whole realm of England be strictly observed. Also, in the same manner, at this time a writ of his lordship the king, in like form, was sent to all the sheriffs of England.

Also, on the same day there were immediately read certain letters patent, setting forth that the king had delivered the city into the custody of William Fitz-Richard, who before had been elected by the citizens bailiff of the city; as also, the sheriffwick of Middlesex, he making payment, according to the ancient ferm, at the exchequer. But these letters were contrary to the aforesaid charter, by which the city is entitled to have all its franchises and free customs, and by virtue whereof the citizens ought to elect their own sheriffs and mayor. For which reason, the citizens sent to the court of his lordship the king envoys on their behalf; though the same William continued to be warden of the city and of Middlesex; as the citizens declined to elect any one,

[1] Chesterfield
[2] or warehouses

in contravention of the letters aforesaid, without leave of his lordship the king. Still however, they sent envoys to the court, as already mentioned.

[1266] At the feast of St Michael, in the year of our Lord 1266, William Fitz-Richard, warden of the city and of Middlesex, still continued in his bailiwick; but being removed on the feast of St Martin [11 November], by election of the citizens John Addrien and Luke de Batencurt were made bailiffs[1] of the city and of Middlesex.

In this year, about the feast of St Michael, there were chosen twelve men of the nobles of the realm, ecclesiastics as well as laymen, in whose arbitration and ordinance were placed such matters as touched the state of the realm, and of those more particularly who had been disherisoned; that so, whatever decision they might give thereon, the same should be strictly observed. Accordingly, their ordinance was published on the Sunday before the feast of All Saints [1 November] at Warewyc,[2] before his lordship the king and his council, and a countless multitude of earls, barons, and others, by the legate, after his sermon; who declared that no one of those who had been disherisoned should lose his lands; but that those who had most offended against his lordship the king, should be ransomed at the value of their lands for five years, and certain others at the value of theirs for two. As to those whose offences had not been so great, the sum was to be the value of their lands for half a year; such ransoms to be the property of those who then held such lands. It was also provided, that if any one could immediately make payment of his ransom, he was immediately to have back his lands; and if unable to do so, he was to have back his land in proportion to such part of his ransom as he was able to pay; the residue thereof remaining unto him who was then in possession of the land, until the periods before-mentioned, unless in the meantime he should make payment of the residue of his ransom. After the like form, it was granted unto those who were in the castle of Kenelworthe, if it should be their wish, with the exception of sir Henry de Hastinges, sir John de la Ware, and the person who had cut off the hand of an envoy of his lordship the king. Those however who had been disherisoned, but had been guilty of no offence, were to have their lands free, and their damages by award of court. It should also be noticed that, first of all, the legate declared that the charter which the king had granted unto the barons, and of which mention has been previously made, should in all its points be strictly observed, etc.; as is set forth in a certain writing made thereon, a copy of which was sent to every county in the kingdom of England, under seal of his lordship the king, there to be read.

After this, the messengers of the city returned from the court, bringing with them letters from his lordship the king, both close and patent, on the vigil, namely, of St Martin [11 November]; whereby it was granted unto them, that they should elect two bailiffs of their number to take charge of the city and the sheriffwick of Middlesex, upon payment of the ancient ferm. Wherefore, on the morrow there were elected unto that office in the Guildhall, before all the people,[3] John Addrien and Luke de Batencurt, who, being presented at the exchequer, were admitted and sworn.

[1] i.e. substitutes for sheriffs

[2] Warwick

[3] This is a repetition, in more circumstantial detail, of what has been already stated.

After this, on the feast of St Lucy the Virgin [13 December], the castle of Kenelworthe was surrendered to his lordship the king; upon the siege of which castle, his lordship the king had been engaged, with a great army, from the feast of the Nativity of John the Baptist [24 June] until that day; his enemies and those who had proved unfaithful, holding the said castle against him by force of arms.

In this year, before the feast of St Michael preceding, those who were called the "disherisoned"[1] threw themselves into the Isle of Ely, fortifying it with arms; and repeatedly sallied forth therefrom, laying waste and burning manors in divers places in Essex, Norfolch, and Suthfolch, as also in the county of Cantebrigscire:[2] they also took and plundered the city of Norewych, and compelled the vills and boroughs to pay ransom.

In this year, when the earl of Gloucester, who by command of his lordship the legate was coming to London, was at Windleshores, the citizens went to the said legate, to advise with him as to whether the earl ought to enter the city; who said, that he was certain that the earl was the king's friend, and that it would be a disgrace to deny him admission into the city. Afterwards, on the Friday next before Palm Sunday, the citizens sent certain of their fellow-citizens to the earl, who was approaching the city, to request him not to take up his quarters within the city, by reason of the great number of his troops; which request he acceded to, and, passing through the middle of the city, took up his quarters in Suwerk, with his people. But on the morrow, as the legate would not come to him on the other side of the bridge, by command of the legate he came into London, to hold a conference with him in the church of the Holy Trinity,[3] and so remained in the city with his people. From this it is clear that the earl had entrance into the city by counsel and assent of the legate; by whose counsel the citizens, by order of his lordship the king and of the queen, were required to abide. On the Monday following, John de Eyvile and his confederates, who were called the "disherisoned", came to Suwerk and took up their quarters there: the citizens understanding which, put the city in a state of defence, and for greater safety drew up the drawbridge, that they might not enter the city. For the citizens themselves had not the means of attacking them without the assistance of the earl; who declined to give them such assistance; as in fact it was through him, and at his instigation, that they had come so near the city, and had committed much mischief in divers places.

After this, soon after Easter, the earl took all the keys of the city gates, and delivered them to such of his own people as he thought proper, for the purpose of watching all entrance into, and exit from, the city; and always, in the meantime, they who had taken up their quarters in Suwerk, had free admission, day and night, by the bridge into the city. Upon this, many citizens departed from the city, through fear of his lordship the king; and their goods the earl ordered to be carried off.

Thereupon, the low people arose, calling themselves the "Commons of the City", as had been the case in the time of the earl of Leicester, and had the chief voice in the city; so that many persons of the city, and of the principal men even, were seized by them and put in the earl's keeping, because they had manifestly maintained their

[1] *exheredati* [2] Cambridgeshire [3] at Aldgate

fealty towards his lordship the king; their goods being either sequestrated by the earl or made away with. And then, by election of the said populace, Robert de Lintone and Roger Marshal were made bailiffs;[1] sir Richard de Culeworth being also made high bailiff of the city by the earl. Then all those who had been, as it were, outlawed from the city in the time of the earl of Leicester, for breach of the peace of his lordship the king, came into the city and were spontaneously admitted; and all those who had been imprisoned in Newgate for the cause aforesaid, were set at liberty.

Afterwards, on the Wednesday after the close of Easter, the legate issued a prohibition of bells being rung in the city, and of divine service being celebrated with song; but the same was to be performed in silence; the doors of the churches being closed, that so the enemies of the king, known as the "disherisoned", might not be present at the celebration of divine service. After this, at the end of three weeks after Easter, his lordship the king came with his army to Hamme, and took up his quarters there, in the abbey of the monks; and soon after, the legate left the Tower and took up his abode in the same abbey, where for some time he turned the cloister of the monks into a stable for his horses.

After this, from day to day his lordship the king and the earl held conference, through envoys, as to making peace; the earl however, always in the meantime, protecting the city and the entrance thereto with armed men, against the army of his lordship the king.

Be it remarked, that during these commotions, the earl did not allow those who had come with him to commit acts of depredation without the city; though still, the persons who had their quarters beyond the bridge, committed depredations and many acts of mischief in Sureye, Kent, and elsewhere. And even – alas for such wickedness! – they went so far as to repair to Westminster and there despoil the palace of his lordship the king, breaking the seats, windows, and doors, and carrying off whatever they could. And although the earl had daily caused proclamation to be made, that no act of depredation should be committed, still, many persons in the city were plundered; whereupon, the earl had judgment executed upon some of his own people. For, on one occasion, where four men-at-arms of sir William de Ferers had been concerned in an act of depredation where one of the citizens had been slain, he had them bound hand and foot and cast into the Thames, and there drowned. And such was the sentence executed during all this period upon those who were condemned.

Afterwards, in the week after the feast of the Holy Trinity, peace was made between his lordship the king and the earl through the king of Almaine and sir Henry his son, and Philip Basset, who had frequently intervened, as also through some other persons: so that the earl and his people withdrew thereupon from the city, and took up his quarters in Suwerk; and his lordship the king, on the Saturday before the feast of the Nativity of St John the Baptist [24 June], came to London with all his army, and took up his quarters there. And immediately thereupon, he had his peace proclaimed, and granted to the disherisoned a truce for eleven days from that day, that in the meantime they might treat for peace; and at the same time also, by precept

[1] substitutes for sheriffs

of his lordship the king, John Addrien and Luke de Batencurt were replaced in their bailiwick, and all the aldermen in their wards, in which the earl had previously placed new wardens [in their stead].

On the Monday following, about the sixth hour,[1] the legate laid a general interdict upon the city; which however was taken off about the third hour on the following day, upon two men making oath before commissioners of his lordship the legate at St Paul's, and swearing upon the souls of all the commons, that they would abide by the award of holy church. Also, at this time, the whole of the covered way which the earl had made between the city and the Tower, was entirely broken up, and the timber carried away. At this time also, on the vigil of St John the Baptist, sir Alan la Suche[2] was made constable of the Tower and warden of the city by his lordship the king, in presence of all the people, at St Paul's Cross.

On the Sunday after this, his lordship the king gave orders that on the morrow twenty men should come from each ward, in readiness to level the foss which the earl had had made, that so the place thereof might not be seen.

Be it remembered, that peace was made between his lordship the king and the earl of Gloucester in form underwritten, namely; his lordship the king remitted unto him and all of his household, fellowship, and friendship, and unto all the people of London, all anger, rancour, and indignation, and all ill-will, which he entertained towards them by reason of trespasses and other things by them committed by land or by water, since the said earl had last departed from Wales, and while he was making sojourn in the city. And his lordship the king was to hold them acquitted thereof as towards all persons, and not to permit any one of them to be molested or appealed by reason of the trespasses aforesaid; save only, that such merchants as had not intermeddled with the war were to have full right of action for recovery of chattels, only their own, without amercement on behalf of his lordship the king, according to the law of the land. Also, that grants of lands, houses, and rents, which had been made, as well by the king as by the earl, after the aforesaid departure of the earl from Wales, were to be wholly revoked. The said earl also bound himself by oath, that he would not wage war against his lordship the king, and made letters thereupon, and found sureties in a penalty of ten thousand marks. And this penalty was to hold good, until it should be known from his lordship the pope, whether the same should appear to him to be a sufficient penalty; and whatsoever his lordship the pope should ordain thereupon, the said earl was held bound to observe. And this ordinance was to be made before the feast of the Purification of the Blessed Mary [2 February] then next ensuing.

On this occasion his lordship the king, by his letters patent and under-written, agreed to forgo as against the Londoners all the ill-will which for the reasons aforesaid he had entertained towards them. At the same time, at the instance of the king, the citizens promised the king of Almaine one thousand marks for the damages which he had sustained at Istleworthe.

[1] twelve in the day
[2] more generally "Zouche"

Letters of his lordship the king, by way of forgiveness for the harbouring of the earl of Gloucester in the city.

[1]"Henry, by the grace of God, king of England, lord of Ireland, and duke of Acquitaine, to all those who this letter shall see or hear, greeting. Whereas by reason of the commotions that have of late existed in our territory, we have been moved to anger against the people of London, because of the sojourn of Gilbert de Clare, earl of Gloucester and of Hertford, in the city aforesaid, and for other things which have been done since the late departure of the earl from Wales for the city, and since his entry into the same; as also, for things which have been done by the earl and on part of others of his household, and of his fellowship, and of his friendship, and by those of London within the city and without, in divers counties and lands, as well by water as by land;[2] we have, by the counsel and by assent of our dear brother the king of Almaine, and of the earls, and barons, and commons, of our land, remitted and forgone, as against all those of London, all manner of wrath and of rancour, and of ill-will, and have granted and accorded, that unto them no harm or mischief we will do or will cause to be done, or will suffer to be done; and that they shall not be molested or impleaded for the matters aforesaid, save only by merchants who have not interfered in the war, the which shall have their action according to the law of the land, if they shall so wish;[3] but that nevertheless, as regards them, or as regards others against whom they shall have offended, all the people of London shall be quit, so far as we and our heirs are concerned, of all forfeits and amends; and that, upon suit by such merchants, no one impleaded shall suffer any harm or damage, such merchants being solely to receive their chattels. Besides this, we do will and do grant, that those of London, who are not in London upon the day on which this acquittance is made, shall go acquitted the same as the others; that so, if they do nothing against our peace, between now and then,[4] they may of the peace that is now so made, be fully assured. And we have also granted and accorded, that all lands in London which have been seized by reason of this commotion since the time aforesaid, shall be now restored unto them, and returned. And if there shall be any land that has been taken since the time aforesaid, by reason of the commotions aforesaid, the same shall forthwith be delivered. In witness of which thing, we, and our dear brother, sir Richard, by the grace of God, king of Almaine, have unto this writing set our seals. Done at Est Ratford,[5] the sixteenth day of June, in the fifty-first year of our reign."

Soon after this, his lordship the king received into his peace John de Eyvile, Nicholas de Segrave, William Marmeyun, and their confederates, who had taken up their quarters on the other side of the bridge. About the same time, while his lordship the king was staying at London, in a parliament held at Wyndleshores, there being present his lordship the king of Almaine, sir Henry his son, sir Philip Basset, and other nobles of the realm of England, a reconciliation was effected between sir Edward and the earl of Gloucester.

At the same time also, the Isle of Ely was surrendered to sir Edward, who received

[1] written in Anglo-Norman
[2] This is probably the meaning; though the passage seems to be imperfect.
[3] The original is here apparently in a corrupt state, and difficult to be understood.
[4] the time of their return
[5] East Retford, in Nottinghamshire

those whom he found there into the peace and favour of his lordship the king, his father, and caused all the covered ways and fortifications, around it and within it, as well by land as by water, to be levelled with the ground. In the same manner, all the fortifications, the barbican, and the covered way, which had been made around Suwerk, his lordship the king caused to be destroyed and levelled even, so that the place where they were is no longer to be seen.

After this, his lordship the king, departing from London, set out for Salopesbery[1] with many barons, and knights and others, foot and horse, to hold a conference at Salopesbery with Lewelin, the prince of Wales.

This year was more fruitful than any year in times past, in memory of persons then living, as well in reference to fields, abundance of corn, trees, and plenty of fruit, as well in woods and spinneys, as in gardens and vineyards.

Be it remarked, that on the Monday next before the feast of St Michael, when the commons had met in the Guildhall to elect the sheriffs according to their usages, there was sent a writ of his lordship the king to sir Alan la Zuche, warden of the city, and to the citizens, commanding that John Addrien and Luke de Batencurt should continue to be bailiffs[2] until his arrival in London; and accordingly, they continued to be bailiffs until the Easter next ensuing.

7. The Annals of Dunstable for the years 1260–4

Annales Monastici, ed. Luard, III (Rolls series, 1866), pp. 214–38)

Dunstable was two days out (St Albans, one day) on the medieval road from London to the north-west. For information on the movements between London, Kenilworth and Northampton at this time the chronicler was therefore well-placed, quite apart from the fact that his sympathies are obviously with the king's opponents.

1260

King Henry of England, the son of king John, stayed in France a long time after he had completed the peace with the king of France; nor did he make any move to return to England until the English bishops and magnates sent him a letter ordering him to hasten his return to England and if he did not do that he would not come back when he wanted to. Hearing this, the king came to himself and returned to England. But certain people by false rumours maliciously sowed discord between the father and his son Edward, declaring that the said Edward and his counsellors were taking steps to wage war on the lord king; on which account the lord king was exceedingly angry and brought with him to London many knights from overseas. Leaving them behind beyond the bridge in parts of Surrey, he himself entered the city of London and stayed there for some time with the gates of the city closed and locked and he set guards that no one might enter without his permission. The earl of Gloucester, though, and John Mansel and certain others of the king's council could go in and out at will. The king, however, forbade his son Edward, or anyone in his counsel, to come into his presence, saying, "Let not my son Edward appear before me because if I see him I shall not restrain myself from kissing him." In the end, moved by a

[1] Shrewsbury

[2] substitutes for sheriffs

father's love and prevailed upon by the entreaties of the magnates, he admitted him to the kiss of peace, and so did his mother, the queen, who (as was said) was the cause of all the malice. How magnificently the lord Edward did the honours while these things were taking place and how much expense he was at for all who cared to come the tongue can scarcely convey.

After this the lord king unloosed his anger on the earl Simon de Montfort through false accusers and proposed to condemn him on many counts. But he, sustained by God's help, so replied to all the charges either by written document or by spoken argument that they were stupefied and were able in no way to make head against him.

In the same year there died William Beauchamp the elder; and the lady Ida received her dower at her pleasure and immediately turning on[1] Simon Pattishull entered his manor at Crawley, threw down the houses, cut down trees and committed an enormous amount of other damage there.

In the same year died John, the vicar of Ashbourne, who throughout his time had paid fifty marks a year to the dean of Lincoln from the aforesaid church, and all the rest, viz, two hundred marks he spent there. The dean wished to keep the said church for his own use, but the king, saying that he himself had rights in the patronage of that church, presented to it the clerk Peter of Winchester. The dean and chapter, afraid for themselves, by way of settlement[2] offered the king 1,000 marks and to his clerk who had been presented property yielding a rent of 100 pounds.

The same year, about St Margaret's day, Lawrence, the abbot of Burton, died, and within a month there was put in his place John of Stafford, a monk of the same house.

The same year the elect of Winchester, Aymer, brother of the lord king, who was banished from England by the council of all England for homicide, was ordained priest by the lord pope on the vigil of the Trinity and next day consecrated bishop; and about Michaelmas he died at Paris.

The same year, about the Nativity of the Blessed Mary, there died John Crakhale, archdeacon of Bedford and at that time treasurer of the lord king. And the monks of Bardney presented to the church of Edlesborough mr David of St Frideswide, at that time archdeacon of Derby. He took possession of that church by proxy and held it for some time: but Walter of Rudham came on the scene with many armed men, ejected the others, took the church by force and held it in virtue of a provision that had been made for him. The abbot and monks of Ramsey presented to the church of Shillington mr Roger of Ravenigham at that time archdeacon of Huntingdon, he entered it boldly, took possession of it and held it in peace.

The same year the lord Edward with a large company of knights went overseas to take part in tournaments. He and all his men were badly used in many places, suffered many bodily injuries and lost completely the horses, arms and other things they had taken with them.

The same year after Christmas, the lord king entered the Tower of London and greatly strengthened it. He closed the gates of the city and ordered the magnates to

[1] *conversa ad* [2] *pro bono pacis*

come to parliament at the Tower; and they refused, announcing that, if it pleased him they would come to Westminster, where they were accustomed to hold parliament, and nowhere else. There was dissension between them over this.

The same year the king of Scotland came to London with his wife, the king of England's daughter, who was pregnant. And after spending some days there he asked leave and withdrew from the lord king, leaving his wife with her mother until she should give birth. And she bore a daughter at Windsor.

1261

The magnates appointed sheriffs and officials throughout almost the whole of England, against the authority and wishes of the king. And the sheriffs and bailiffs that the king had appointed they degraded and in no wise wished to obey them.

Meanwhile the earl of Gloucester apostasised as it were, withdrawing from the counsels of Simon de Montfort and the other magnates, with whom he had entered into a sworn confederacy to maintain the good laws of the land; leaving them completely, he sided with the king. Hearing this, Simon de Montfort left England, saying he would rather die landless than withdraw from the truth and be perjured.

1262

On the quinzaine of Easter the justices in eyre came to Bedford: viz, the lord Nicholas de Turri, Robert de Brus, William de Englefield, William Bonquer, Adam de Greynvile, knights; and they were in session there for over three weeks. [The chronicler then mentions four cases the priory was party to, before these justices.]

Also, the same year, during the quinzaine of St John the Baptist, the lord king Henry, son of king John, went overseas with the queen and his privy household, almost everybody on this side ignorant of the reason for his journey and beginning greatly to fear future evils from it.

Also, the same year, in the month of June, the lord Edward, son of king Henry, was badly beaten in a certain tournament overseas and gravely wounded.

Also, the same year, in the month of July, Henry of Wengham, bishop of London died; and Richard, earl of Gloucester.

The same year, about the feast of John the Baptist, we ran out of ale; and we received on loan from H. Chadde malt to the amount of £20; and besides that five tuns of wine for 10 marks; and from the previous Michaelmas, we bought 400 quarters of oats for sowing and for the horses, domestic and other. And besides, from the octave of the Purification, we gave bread to provender the horses, domestic and other, until the new grain was ready.

While the king was overseas there died over there Baldwin earl of Wight [*de Insula*], Ingram de Percy and others of the king's household to the number of sixty. The king was stricken almost to death with quartan fever; and then Richard de Clare, earl of Gloucester, died, by evildoing, at the table of Peter of Savoy, the queen's uncle; and W[illiam] Beauchamp likewise died.

At the same time pope Urban conferred the bishopric of Winchester on mr J[ohn] of Exeter; on whose advice the king came back to England to be cured by his native air.

And he, reaching the coast on the Wednesday before Christmas, crossed and landed at Dover. And from there he came to Canterbury, where he celebrated Christmas.

At the same time there died Ralph of Stodham and Richard of Dodington, canons.

At the same time, on the Saturday before the feast of St Nicholas, prior Geoffrey voluntarily resigned the office of prior into the hand of Richard, bishop of Lincoln, at Dunstable, and when the licence of the lord king to elect another prior had been sought and obtained by canons S[imon] of Etone and Henry of Neutone the whole house delegated the election to Reginald of Reading, Simon of Etone, William Britone, Thomas of Leistone, W. of Hannes, Henry of Neutone and Richard of Mentmore, who unanimously elected on behalf of the whole house the said Simon of Etone as prior on the Friday in the octave of the Epiphany [i.e. on Friday, 12 January 1263] and he got confirmation by the bishop and seisin of lands and possessions from the lord king before the following Friday [i.e. before Friday, 19 January 1263]. And he was installed as prior on the morrow of the next feast of SS Fabian and Sebastian [i.e. on Sunday, 21 January 1263], when the lord Peter de Aldham, archdeacon of Bedford, asked for the prior's palfrey, but did not get it.

At the same time, after St Lucy's day [13 December], the lord Roger of St Albans was admitted by the bishop of Chester to the guardianship of our church in accordance with the form of our presentation: viz, that he should answer to the bishop for the spiritualities and to us for the temporalities, his power to be revocable when the honour of the order or the need of our house required it.

The same year, about the Purification of the Blessed Mary [2 February], while the king was at Westminster ill, a flame from the chimney of his room set fire to it and the chapel of St Laurence, and the conflagration spread to the chamber of receipt and set fire to it.

The same year the abbot of Peterborough, the king's treasurer at that time, died at Launde, and Nicholas, the archdeacon of Ely, was made treasurer in his place.

At the same time the king caused his magnates to be called together at Westminster to do homage and fealty to his son Edward; which indeed many did, but Gilbert de Clare refused to do it.

It should be known that prior Simon found his house burdened with debt to the amount of 400 marks due in part on the day of his installation, and in addition all the wool of that year sold, payment received and the money spent except [ ]. Also we bought all our oats from that time until the following autumn.

The same year, about the feast of St Gregory, we had the lord king's writ to Laurence de Broc for the delivery of Dunstable gaol; and then a certain man was hanged for theft; and the others were delivered.

1263

Llywelyn got together a considerable army and invaded and burnt the March and took certain castles.

The same year about the Finding of the Cross [3 May] an agreement was reached with the lord Geoffrey de Barton, formerly our prior, about the provision to be made for him, at the command of the lord bishop of Lincoln.

The same year we acquired a certain part of the wood in Flitwick from Simon fitz Wirnart; and half of the pasture of Brademor from the daughter of Peter of Tingrith, paying her corn in exchange as is contained in the deed.

The same year about the feast of St Mark the Evangelist [25 April] Simon de Montfort came back to England; and, unknown to the king and his council, Richard, then king of Almain, the aforesaid Simon, the earl Warenne, Gilbert de Clare and many others of the barons gathered together for a parliament at Oxford; where it was provided that all contravening the "statutes" of Oxford should be reckoned mortal enemies, as had been provided by the king and the barons at Oxford on another occasion and confirmed by them in writing. And when the same earl Simon and the others told this to the lord king, the king did not give his assent to their provision. And then the earl collected an army beyond number; and with him in counsel and in deed were the earl Warenne, Henry the son of the king of Almain, Hugh the Despenser, Henry of Hastings, Roger Clifford, John FitzJohn, Roger Leyburn, Gilbert de Clare, John de Vaux, John Giffard, Hamo Lestrange, Nicholas of Segrave, Geoffrey de Lucy, and others without number. And they first attacked Peter, the bishop of Hereford, and took him and seized all his goods; doing the same with the manors of Geoffrey de Langley and his goods; inflicting no evil or loss on anyone at all save aliens; and on them because they gave counsel or aid contrary to the statutes of Oxford or because they were not willing to come to them when summoned; and they reckoned them all breakers of their oath and called them felons; and all their goods, wherever they were found, were plundered, besides the lands and churches of aliens, the enfeoffment with and institution to which they gave away. But this was contrary to right and could not stand.

At the same time, about the feast of the Blessed Augustine the apostle of the English, the king went with the queen to the Tower of London, the lord Edward staying at the hospital of Clerkenwell. As they were all short of money and there was no one in London who would give them a halfpennyworth of credit, the lord Edward, not wishing to be disgraced, went on the feast of the apostles Peter and Paul, along with Robert Walerand and many others to the New Temple when the gates were closed; and when at his request he was given the keys, he said he wished to see the jewels of his mother, the queen, and summoning the keeper, he by this deceit entered with his men the Temple treasury and there, breaking open with iron hammers that they had brought with them the chests of certain people, he took and had carried away a large sum of money to the amount of a thousand pounds. At this outrage the citizens of London rose against him and others of the king's council who were staying in the city; they went so far as to break into the house of John de Grey outside Ludgate and carry off thirty-two horses of his and whatever else they found there, John himself escaping with the greatest difficulty across the bed of the Fleet. They did the same with the houses and goods of Simon Passelewe.

At the same time John Mansel left the Tower of London by the Thames with the countess of Wight [*de Insula*] and other women from overseas and went by boat to Wissant. He caused the lord Henry, son of the king of Almain, who was crossing overseas there for certain matters, to be seized and detained by the lord Ingram de Fiennes. He was afterwards freed by the king of France and returned to England.

At the same time we redeemed from John of Elston and Walter Gode liveries in which we were bound to them.

The same year, on St Mildred's day, the queen left the Tower by the Thames on her way to Windsor by boat and came to London Bridge; when the Londoners assailed her and her men shamefully with foul and base words and even casting stones; so that freed with difficulty by the mayor of London and driven by necessity she went back to the Tower. The king would not let her enter, but she was conducted by the mayor of London safely to St Paul's and lodged in the house of the bishop.

Meanwhile the bishops of Lincoln, London and Chester, treating for the reestablishment of peace between the lord king at the Tower and the barons who were at Dover, learnt from the lord Simon, the earl, and the barons that they would in no wise agree to peace if the lord king and the queen would not first release the lord Henry, who had been taken prisoner while overseas, hand over to them Dover castle and all other castles, cleanse England completely of aliens, and – with good security given for this – cause the statutes of Oxford to be more fully observed: all which the lord king, in a difficult situation, granted. The earl, on hearing this, came with the barons from Dover to London, where he was received by the citizens with the utmost delight. Then he went to the Tower, greeted the king and enquired of him whether he had conceded the aforesaid articles and was willing to keep them. The king answered "Yes" and pledged himself to this by a charter, so that by the decision of certain people chosen for the purpose the statutes of Oxford should be added to or subtracted from as would be to the advantage of the king and the kingdom. Then it was ordered by letters of the lord king that Dover castle and the other castles be restored to the barons to keep. Windsor castle, though, which was in the custody of the lord Edward, was with the greatest difficulty restored to the lord king and the barons, on condition that all the aliens there might freely depart with their horses and arms after first swearing not to come back again without being sent for by the community. After this, to seek the assent of the community, all the bishops, the earls, barons, abbots and priors were summoned by letters of the lord king for the morrow of the Nativity of the Blessed Mary, and in St Paul's church, London, there was read in the presence of all the aforesaid and of the lord Edward and other magnates the previously mentioned charter of the lord king – to which all gave their assent, the lord Edward included.

Meanwhile the lord Edward, from whom Robert the earl Ferrers had taken three castles, and others who had been deprived of their goods had it in mind to rise against those who had dispossessed them; but on the advice of the magnates it was provided that the lord king, personally and by judges specially appointed by him for the purpose, should do full justice to those complaining of plunderers – as was contained in a certain form put into writing.

While these things were happening the lord king and the queen secretly arranged with the king of France for him to summon them, the lord Edward, the earl and certain others to appear before him at Boulogne on the next octave of Michaelmas for it to be more fully ascertained who was wronging whom. And there when the lord king and the queen and the lord Edward and the earl and many other nobles had appeared, the king and queen laid many serious complaints against the earl about wrongs, imprisonments, seizures of their castles, and depredations of churches done to him and his in his kingdom. The said Simon replied to all and singular of which things, in all respects to the satisfaction of the king of France, and then, by permission, returned with honour to England so that on the quinzaine of Michaelmas as said above, he might with the others chosen for the purpose, ordain concerning the statutes. On that day many Londoners came with arms, and Welshmen likewise. And as the lord Edward would not agree to the aforesaid things, he withdrew from the parliament towards Windsor with a numerous following, and the king with him. The earl however withdrew with his following to the Tower of London. And the earl Warenne and Hugh Bigod and others who were for the king were turned out of London and the gates of the city shut. And after a while the earl went to Kenilworth. The lord Edward meanwhile won over very many who were previously on the earl's side, by giving them manors of his, viz, the earl Warenne and Henry, the son of the king of Almain, Roger Clifford, Roger Leyburn, John de Vaux, Hamo Lestrange and others.

At the same time the king summoned a parliament to Reading; to which the earl did not come for fear he might be made captive. From there the king went towards Dover, having taken advice, with a large force, that the castle which was in the custody of Richard de Grey might be given back to him. He came to the gates, sought entry, but did not obtain it. On the news that the king was making for Dover, the earl left Kenilworth for London by way of Northampton, where he received the fealty of the burgesses, and thus came through Dunstable. And when Simon, the prior of Dunstable, had hastened to meet him and greetings had been exchanged, he sought the fraternity of the house, and the prior agreed and received him. And thus he came to London, wanting with his men to attack the king at Dover. And when the king could not get entry to the castle, he returned through the Weald, where certain citizens of London met him and promised him faithfully that if the earl came to London he would not be admitted.

Hearing this, the king and Edward were overjoyed, and convinced that they would capture the earl and his men, who were in Southwark, the king commanded the earl to surrender. He replied that this he would never do to perjurers and renegades. When the earl saw that he had far fewer men than the king, so that he could in no way resist, he wanted to enter the city, but the gates were shut and he could not. After careful consideration the earl armed himself and his men, and in the name of God had himself and the others marked back and front with the sign of the cross, and meanwhile confessing their sins, they all took the sacrament, ready to meet the onslaught of their enemies and to struggle with them for the sake of the truth. But when it was known in the city that the earl was shut out, the commonalty at once broke open the gates, and the earl entered with his men. When the other side heard this, they were thrown into extreme confusion.

While these things were being done, the king gave three of the earl's vills that were in the March to Roger Mortimer, who destroyed them and took and imprisoned the earl's bailiff until the earl ransomed him for 100 marks.

[The same year, canon W. of Waterford died at Michaelmas.[1]]

When these things were all over, the king and the earl, with the mediation of certain bishops, agreed to submit themselves to the arbitration of the king of France and to stand by his award on all disputed points arising out of the Provisions of Oxford. And when the earl was on his way to France from Kenilworth to hear the award of the said king his palfrey fell near Catesby and a bone in his leg was broken; because of that he returned to Kenilworth and sent certain wise clerks and laymen to hear on the barons' behalf the said king of France. The king of England went over in person, and the lord Edward. In mid-channel a great and terrible storm arose, so that the lord Edward out of fear made very many vows, and they reached Wissant with the greatest difficulty. The king of France at the instance of his wife and the queen of England, as is said, regardless of his honour and exceeding the authority given him and keeping in sight neither God nor truth, pronounced against the barons in the matter of the statutes and all other things even not pertaining to the statutes.

While these things were happening the earl, neither he nor the barons being willing to acquiesce in such an award, sent two of his sons, the knights Simon and Henry, with a very large force, to avenge their father, to the castles and vills of Roger Mortimer, which they laid waste and burnt.

Having done this, the said sons of the earl came to Gloucester and the town was forthwith surrendered to them, while the castle, with the wives of Roger Clifford, Roger Leyburn and others in it, was in the keeping of the earl of Hereford. To this the aforesaid sons of the earl laid siege, but when the greater part of the army had gone off to places in the neighbourhood for recreation, the lord Edward secretly passed through the army with his men and seeing the smallness of it he resolved to attack it on the morrow and made his intention known. The barons, afraid because they were few, sent for the earl Ferrers and others who were near, and they came with all haste. Henry and John FitzJohn and very many others of the more important of those who were not knights, choosing rather to die as knights than as squires, received the belt of knighthood in the field, ready for battle. Seeing therefore a large body arrive unexpectedly and being exceedingly afraid, the lord Edward went unarmed to the barons with Henry the son of the king of Almain and others and, in the presence of the bishop of Worcester, offered them peace and sought a truce until the morrow of St Gregory's day for him to get the said peace and the will of the barons in all things made perpetual by his father the lord king, by that day; the said Henry going surety and Edward offering himself as warranty. And so unfortunately was it agreed by the lord Henry, the earl's son, against the wishes of his fellows; for the advantageousness of the site, the time, and many other favourable circumstances disposed the said barons to capture or rout their adversaries. Securities, therefore, having been exchanged, the army of the barons withdrew towards Kenilworth, and the lord Edward contrary to the terms of peace took the burgesses of Gloucester, imprisoned them and deprived them of all their goods and then went back to Oxford, where the king was,

[1] an entry in the margin

sending William de Valence and others out in all directions to pillage the countryside and particularly their adversaries. Then because the lord Edward had been thus foolishly allowed to go, the earl was greatly disturbed and ashamed, and he bitterly rebuked his son Henry for it. Because the lord Edward had not kept to the day agreed on, the barons were greatly disturbed and they made for London with an innumerable multitude to take counsel with the Londoners, their allies, as to what should be done.

1264

The king meanwhile sent messengers throughout England summoning all his tenants to come to him at Oxford with horses and arms at mid-Lent. When he had taken counsel with them, he first (as it was said) had three bishops who were present and twenty-four priests excommunicate all who opposed the statutes of Oxford, who plundered sacred places, or who deprived religious or clerks of their goods. Afterwards on a Thursday he had his standards unfurled preceded by the dragon standard[1] and took the road from Oxford to Northampton, wishing to know who denied him entrance, especially since the barons had the custody of the town, the custody of the castle having been handed over to lord Roger of Walton by them. Now there were within the town the lord Simon de Montfort the younger, Peter of Montfort, Ralph Pirot, Hugh Gubiun, Osbert Giffard, Simon de Pateshull and many others. Those of the king's party who came on the Friday and sought entry did not obtain it. The king himself, however, when he approached the gate on Saturday with some of his men, was admitted with all ceremony. Others meanwhile approached the town walls surrounding the garden of the prior of St Andrew's, which the prior, it was said, had treacherously weakened in some way and indicated to the king and his men, and made a sharp assault with great violence. When the lord Simon (the younger) was told this, when a great part of the wall had already fallen, he resisted manfully, twice driving back the assailants with the help of the lord Ingram de Balliol and a certain squire. When he wanted to contain them yet a third time and could not, he charged with great impetuosity, bearing himself manfully right in their midst. And due to his horse falling he was honourably taken prisoner with his men. When the others saw this, some fled ignominiously to a church, some retreated into the castle. What more need be said? All were taken and held fast, and those who were on the side of the king pillaged the burgesses and everyone else to the last halfpennyworth.

Henry de Montfort captured the earl and countess of Warwick and many others. The lord Edward burnt all the manors of the barons round about and took Tutbury castle, and he was promised £200 not to burn the wapentake of Wirksworth, of which £10 was required of the prior of Dunstable in respect of Bradeburne.

The earl Simon, who was in London, made ready with his men to set out for Northampton. When he reached St Albans he was informed that the Jews of London had prepared a rebellion in the city, so he immediately returned and found they had Greek fire in their possession with which they were going to set fire to the city on the vigil of Palm Sunday. And false keys which they had made themselves for every gate

[1] his personal standard

of the city. And, it was said, they had underground passages to every gate. Because of this he had the Jews, from the least to the greatest, put to death, save certain elders of whom he wished to make further enquiries, and save those who were willing to receive baptism. Gilbert de Clare did the same to the Jews of Canterbury.

While this was happening the earl set out for the castle at Rochester, in which the earl Warenne and a certain other earl, Roger Leyburn, Reginald FitzPeter and many others were in hiding. These were ready to enter the city of London as soon as the Greek fire had been set to it and occupy and destroy it. When earl Simon reached Rochester, the burgesses broke down the bridge and also fortified their side of the bridge against an assault. But the earl skilfully set fire to the fortifications of the bridge and took the town by force of arms after four or five of the burgesses had been killed. When the earl laid siege to the castle, he took the outer bailey on the first day, and with the Londoners applied himself carefully and manfully to the business of taking the keep.

The king, who was at Nottingham, hastened to Rochester with his army to raise the siege. Meanwhile it was reported to earl Simon that unless he came quickly to London, the city would be handed over by certain seditious people to the lord Edward. At this the earl abandoned the siege and returned to London without delay and finding the news was true, he took hostages from the seditious for their future fidelity to the barons. When the king reached the neighbourhood of Rochester, the earl with his men, with the traitors in front of them, left London and followed the king and his son Edward, who were making for the coast. In this way came it to pass that at Lewes, where they were with their army, he, first through knights, secondly and thirdly through bishops, urged them to make peace.

While these things were happening, on St Fremund's day some thieves entered the fields near Sewell at the hour of vespers and in spite of the shepherds drove off the almoner's sheep in the direction of Leighton. When the news reached Dunstable, the priory servants went out with men of the town and caught two with sheep at Sewell, and on the morrow they were tried and hanged at Passecumbe.

On that day there came to Segenhoe twenty or more men mounted and armed and many on foot and they carried off whatever they could find in the house of the prior, Henry of Northwood, W. Beyvin [*sic*]. Followed by the hue and cry of the neighbourhood, seventeen with arms were taken the same day at Beadlow with all that they had carried off. Afterwards they were rashly set free by the prior of that place.

The same day, the 14th May, with the lord king of England and the lord Richard king of Almain and the lord Edward at Lewes with all their army and in no wise agreeing to a peace, the earl of Leicester with his men, mindful of God and justice and choosing to die for the truth rather than go against his sworn oath, going by the advice of the bishops and other men of religion, went fortified by faith towards the king and his men to fight the Lord's fight. After the battle had begun, the lord Henry of Hastings, Geoffrey de Lucy, Humphrey de Bohun the younger who was wounded, and all the Londoners turned tail and fled to London, leaving the earl and Gilbert de Clare and John FitzJohn and a few others with their men in the field. And although the lord king had four times the numbers and the strength the earl of Leicester had, the earl and those who were with him, by a miracle and with God's help, took captive the king of England and the king of Almain and Edward the son of the king[1] and Henry the son of the king of Almain,[1] Philip Basset, the earl of Hereford, Roger Leyburn[1] and very many other barons; and everyone[2] was found except John, the earl Warenne, Hugh Bigod, Roger Mortimer[1] and William de Valence, who fled to Pevensey. And except Roger Mortimer, John Balliol, Roger Clifford, Roger Leyburn, Hamo Lestrange and certain others, who were allowed to go, on leaving hostages for themselves and the lord king, viz, the lord Edward and the lord Henry son of the king of Almain, that they would come to parliament when summoned and stand trial by their peers.

The earl of Leicester and the earl of Gloucester and others who were with them left Lewes for Canterbury taking the king with them and sending the lord Edward and Henry son of the king of Almain to Dover to be kept in the castle as hostages. The barons fearing dissension around themselves sent them to Wallingford; the king of Almain who was confined to the Tower of London was subsequently sent to Wallingford.

The same year, round about the feast of St John the Baptist, when the barons heard that the queen of England, who was abroad, had in her distress and extreme grief at the result of the battle solicited the king of France, Peter of Savoy and other magnates overseas diligently, promising much and disbursing many things, and that she would bring to the coast an innumerable force to cross over and invade England to the confusion and utter destruction of the English, the king on their advice had his letters sent to all the shires of England commanding all the adjacent sea coasts of England to be guarded by an ample force of armed men against adversaries coming from foreign parts; and this was done in the autumn. Wherefore indeed had we at the sea four men with horses and arms, and six footmen. Besides this we gave a tenth of the total valuation of our churches, the vicars contributing nothing at all: so that altogether, besides the purchase of horses and arms, we paid out 30 marks. Meanwhile, with the foreigners on the other side of the sea and ours on this side facing each other, messengers were sent both ways to try and restore peace.

In the same year and at the same time through the queen of England and the king and queen of France a legate was procured from the apostolic see with great state to come to England with the power of both swords: with one to depose bishops who would not excommunicate the barons of England, and with the other to disinherit certain barons to the number of thirty. And besides, to utterly annul the statutes of Oxford and the peace entered into between the lord king and the said barons. And when he was at Boulogne, as was said, he cited by proclamation in consistory the bishops of London, Lincoln, Worcester, Chester, Salisbury, Chichester and the elect of Bath and certain other clerks of a lower order. They, hearing rumours of this citation and wanting to make every effort to cross over to the said legate but their crossing, or that of proxies for them, being obstructed by the barons, sent over to the legate after the permission of the barons had been obtained with the greatest difficulty

[1] These four names have been scored through.
[2] *omnes quot*

men properly accredited and instructed with lawful grounds of excuse to excuse them. And when before the said lord on behalf of their lords the bishops they put forward the legitimate grounds of excuse, he would not allow these and reviled them greatly. On account of this the said excusers with legitimate cause appealed in writing to the apostolic see or a general council on behalf of their lords and on behalf of the whole of the clergy of England. And the clergy of England as a body, on being called to Westminster on the Sunday after the feast of St Luke the Evangelist, approved of the appeal.

[We admitted as canons Robert of Pulloxhill and Edmund of Tril.[1]]

The same year, the aforesaid Roger Mortimer, Roger Clifford, Roger Leyburn and the others who withdrew from Lewes after giving hostages went to the March, took possession of Gloucester, Bridgenorth and Marlborough castles and very many others, and laid waste the surrounding countryside, wishing not to make peace but rather to infringe it. The lord king, however, hearing of their temerity, on the advice of the earls of Leicester and Gloucester and of other barons sent his letters of summons to every shire in England for all owing him military service to be at Northampton the fortnight after the feast of St Martin with horses and arms ready to set out with him for wherever he might think fit.

In the same year and at the same time Robert de Ferrers, earl of Derby, taking with him many knights, and footmen to the number of 20,000, set out for Chester. William la Zuche, David the brother of Llewelyn, James of Audley and many others, on encountering him did not dare to give battle, but fled. He, following them with his men, killed up to a hundred of them and took some prisoner; and none of his own men was wounded except one.

The same year, on the Sunday within the octave of St Martin, we received Ralph of Tingrith as a canon, and Ralph of Bray as a lay brother.

The same year, Roger Mortimer and the others for whom the lord Edward was given in custody were summoned to come to a parliament at Oxford, but were afraid for themselves and did not come. On hearing of this the lord king by common assent set out for the March with earl Simon and other barons to subdue the aforesaid rebels, to find all the bridges over the Severn completely destroyed by them. And when the lord king and the earl were ready to cross in whatever fashion with their men, the aforesaid rebels came to parley,[2] upon which Roger Mortimer, Roger Clifford, Roger Leyburn and certain other accomplices of theirs were sentenced to be exiled from England for a year and more. And then a parliament at London was decided on, at which by common counsel they might deliberate on the freeing of the lord Edward, the observing of statutes, the sending throughout England of justices to enquire into unjust robberies, and other things for the betterment of the kingdom.

The parliament was fixed for the octave of St Hilary and the lord king, Simon earl of Leicester, Gilbert earl of Gloucester, bishops and very many other magnates were there. And when they dealt with the freeing of the lord Edward, his liberation was effected on conditions laid down in the following form.

[The annalist here incorporates the text of the pacification and acceptance of the provisional government (*forma regiminis*) of June 1264 by the king and lord Edward in March 1265.[3]]

---

[1] an entry in the margin [2] *ad parliamentum* [3] Given in Stubbs, *Select Charters*, pp. 404–6

Meanwhile the earl of Gloucester got himself ready with a large band for a tournament at Dunstable against the earl of Leicester's son Henry on Shrove Tuesday; but in letters addressed to the prior of Dunstable the king forbade it.

8. The "English History" of Bartholomew Cotton of Norwich for the domestic crisis of November 1296 to 10 October 1297

(*Bartholomaei de Cotton . . . Historia Anglicana . . .*, ed. Luard (Rolls series, 1859), pp. 312–39)

In the same year the king of England ordered his parliament to meet at Bury St Edmunds on the morrow of the feast of All Souls and returned to England.

In the same year knights appointed to keep the sea (coast) assessed bishops, abbots and priors and other ecclesiastics, according to the value of their lands, for horses and arms, that is, for twenty pounds a year worth of land one horse fully equipped.

In the same year, many seamen, subjects of the king of France, sailed the sea with a great fleet and armament, inflicting many losses on merchants who were subjects of the king of England and wished to cross the sea with their merchandise; on which account the lord king forbade the crossing of the sea for the time being by a writ in these words . . .

[King to sheriff of Norfolk and Suffolk, 30 August 1296, Westminster, attested Philip of Willoughby as lieutenant of the treasurer.]

In the same year, earls, barons and knights, the archbishop and many bishops, abbots, priors, archdeacons, and clergy of the kingdom of England, met at the king's command, in the parliament of the lord king at Bury St Edmunds and there a twelfth of all goods was granted to the lord king by the laity, an eighth, however, by the inhabitants of cities, boroughs and manors of the lord king. But when the king put forward the promise, made to him the previous year by the archbishops and the rest of the bishops and abbots who were present at the same time, of a more generous subsidy than hitherto, the archbishop replied that he would consider these things with his clergy. The next day however, when the whole of the aforesaid clergy were gathered together in the chapter house of the monastery of Bury St Edmunds and he had told them of the king's request, the archbishop proposed to them four points for discussion: namely the promise already made to the king of a subsidy, as the king asserted; secondly the pope's statute newly published, which most firmly binds as well those who promise and give as those who receive and extort; thirdly the imminent danger to the whole realm of England from our enemies of the kingdom of France; fourthly the diminution of the clergy's goods owing to various previous contributions. The clergy divided into four parts to discuss these points. In the first part were the archbishop, those bishops who were present, and the proctors of the absent bishops. In the second part abbots exempt and not exempt, also priors and the rest of the religious. In the third all in positions of authority. In the fourth all the proctors of the body of the clergy. And when they had meditated and conferred diligently on these points for many days, without being able to find any sure way of making a contribution or levy which would not contravene the statute, the archbishop at length went to the king, and sought from him permission to postpone until the next feast of St Hilary their final answer on the matter. This being granted, the same archbishop not long afterwards caused to be summoned to appear at St Paul's, London, on the aforementioned day all his fellow bishops and suffragans, also abbots exempt and not exempt, priors, archdeacons and all in positions of authority in person, every chapter of a cathedral or collegiate church through one proctor, and the clergy of each diocese through two. For the letter of citation look above, where the other letters are written.

In the same year, a certain clerk, John de Yvone by name, came to the counties of Norfolk and Suffolk, had all the hundred bailiffs and certain others of the said counties summoned to his presence and instructed them on behalf of the lord king to take, according to every man's means, corn, barley and oats for the king's use; in which taking those most troubled and burdened were the religious and other ecclesiastical persons, though how much corn was provided, and how much barley and oats, you will find above in the letter directed to the sheriff about it.

In the same year, the lord William Rocelin, knight, and William de Crostweyt, clerk, were assigned by the lord king's writ to collect a twelfth and eighth, according to the form of their instructions, granted to the lord king by the laity. In the same year the lord pope sent word to two cardinals who were in France to publish the statute recently issued for the benefit of the church and its clergy, and sent to them sealed with the same bull, and they, publishing it in France, sent the said statute to the archbishop of Canterbury under their seals, firmly enjoining him, on behalf of the lord pope, to have the said statute published in England, and he at once demanded of his suffragans that they should do the same. The suffragans similarly instructed their archdeacons, and the archdeacons the deans, and so it scarcely got proper publication because of the negligence of the prelates. Look for the pope's statute above in the letter the cardinals sent to the archbishop.

The king remained for some time at Bury St Edmunds, then went to Ipswich, where he solemnly celebrated Christmas. There John, count of Holland and Zeeland, married Elizabeth the daughter of the king of England; and they took at will from the inhabitants of Norfolk and Suffolk almost everything that was laid out on that feast, paying little or nothing for it. Also many magnates and leading men of Holland and Zeeland came there, and, with a great company of leading men and magnates of England, conducted their lord, the aforesaid count, to his country, to receive the homage of his men. And in this company Margaret, wife of John, duke of Brabant, was escorted to her husband in Brabant. But while the king set out on a pilgrimage through Norfolk to Walsingham, his son the lord Edward and his [the lord Edward's] sister Elizabeth, countess of Holland, left their father and retired to Windsor to stay there for a time.

During that time, that is to say on the feast of St Hilary, the archbishop, very many of his suffragans, abbots, priors and the whole clergy of the kingdom met in accordance with the archbishop's summons, at St Paul's, London, to make their final reply to the king, as already mentioned, and the archbishop preached, and after that had all the clergy divided into four grades; that is, in the first grade were the bishops who were present and the proctors of absent bishops. In the second all the religious, both exempt and not exempt. In the third all in positions of authority. In the fourth all the proctors of the body of the clergy. And the archbishop enjoined them under pain of excommunication, to provide for some suitable middle course between the two dangers, namely, of the pope's bull, and the subversion of the whole kingdom, of which there was great danger; and each one was to say in the end, without any pretence or disguise, what he thought on the matter. There also were messengers of the lord king, namely the lords Hugh le Despenser, knight, and John of Berwick, clerk, bringing credentials from the king to the archbishop and all the clergy, of whom the lord John explained the dangers threatening the kingdom from foreigners if it were not defended strongly, which could not be done, he said, except with the help of the clergy. The archbishop however caused to be read in the presence of the king's messengers and all the clergy the recently-published statute of the lord pope against those seeking, receiving, promising or paying contributions of this kind, on hearing which the said lord Hugh said: "I on behalf of the lord king, the earls, barons, knights and other faithful subjects of the king say to you that you should provide from the goods of the church for such a subsidy for the defence of the land, lest the lord king, the earls and barons order and dispose of your ecclesiastical goods as they will." This said, the aforementioned messengers withdrew from the assembly of clerks. However, the clergy, divided up in the way mentioned, discussed the said matter for many days on end with great diligence and labour and with varied and arduous disputations, turning over carefully in their minds on the one hand the pope's statute and the penalty contained in it, and on the other the danger threatening the kingdom, and in the end each grade replied separately that it could not at present find a sure way of assisting by means of a contribution or levy. Finally the archbishop with the advice of the clergy, sent the lord bishops of Norwich, Hereford, Exeter, the abbots of Ramsey and Colchester and the archdeacon of Norfolk to the lord king, who was then in Norfolk at Castleacre, to give the answer with letters on his behalf and that of all the clergy, after first drawing up certain articles on behalf of the clergy, which were to be explained to the king by word of mouth. But when these articles were exceedingly well explained in the king's presence by the bishop of Hereford, all that the king said was: "As you do not hold to the homage and oath that you made to me for your baronies, neither am I bound to you in any way." When they heard this, the aforesaid messengers returned home. And the letter sent to the lord king and the articles conveyed to him by word of mouth, you will find above, where letters are given.

Now the king, before the arrival of the messengers of the clergy, knowing from his own messengers what the decision and reply of the clergy was, and greatly angered, on the Wednesday before the feast of the Purification of Blessed Mary ordained certain severe, and in England unheard-of, measures against the clergy, namely that no archbishop, bishop, archdeacon, or any one else of the clergy, should be heard in his court for any wrong done them or should sue out any writ, and that he would take into his own hand and seize all lay fees of archbishops, bishops, all religious and clerks whatsoever, whatever their status or condition, and if any of the laity met a religious or any of the clergy who had a better horse than his own, he should seize it for his own and take it away. And lo! in a wonderful way and as though by the vengeance of God, on the same day and hour when he had ordained these things, the army of the king of England in Gascony was attacked by the army of the king of France while taking victuals from one place to another, some being captured, some killed, some drowned, while the rest with the victuals escaped by flight. Those captured there were the lord John of St John, lord William de Mortimer, lord William de Sully, lord John of Ros, lord Adam of Hudleston, lord John de la Garde, lord Reginald de Noers, lord Thomas de Mose, lord William of Ponton, lord Henry of Schadewrche, lord Gerard de Leseyn, and lord William of Berningham; lord Philip de Mattesdon was killed, the lord Alan de Tuycham and his son and their squires were drowned.

In the same year, on the feast of the Purification of the Blessed Mary, while the king was at Walsingham, certain knights and other magnates for the count of Flanders, who had renounced his homage to the king of France on account of various wrongs which the latter had done him, came to the lord king there to make for the said count a treaty with the king of England. When the terms of the said treaty had been drawn up between them, certain knights for the king of England, on the soul of that king, and some from Flanders on the soul of the count of Flanders, swore on the milk of the Blessed Virgin Mary and on other relics there, that they would inviolably and faithfully keep the said treaty in every part of it and in respect of every single thing contained in it. While they remained there some days with the king for a holiday, the lord king treated them lavishly with his gifts, and at last, having sought and obtained the king's leave, they returned home with great joy.

In the same year the king decreed his parliament at Salisbury on the feast of St Mathias the Apostle, to which were called earls, knights and barons, but no archbishop, bishop, abbot or prior, or any clerk. Now while the king was at Ely on the way to the parliament, the edict went out which had previously been made against the clergy; for the king's writs were sent out from there on the twelfth of February to all the sheriffs of England, that they should take into the king's hand and hold all lay fees of archbishops, bishops, all religious and the whole of the clergy; so that none of the clergy, nor anyone on their behalf, should lay hands upon them, until they had word otherwise from the king. They carried out these orders to the full so that not only were all lay fees seized into the king's hands, but also nearly all fees annexed to churches. You will find a copy of the writ above among the other letters.

In the same year on St Scholastica the Virgin's day, the archbishop at Canterbury consecrated [John of Monmouth] to the bishopric of Llandaff. The archbishop preached after the mass, and after the sermon, having first announced the king's reply to the messengers of the clergy, he solemnly and publicly excommunicated all contravening in any way the pope's statute, while the bishops who were there for the consecration were still present.

In the same year, certain bishops, abbots and priors, and certain others of the clergy, notwithstanding the reply sent by the whole of the clergy in common, as has been said, about not contributing a subsidy for the lord king from the goods of the church lest they might infringe the statute, seeing their goods seized into the king's hands, redeemed them by means of money without consulting the archbishop.

In the same year, in the aforementioned parliament of the king at Salisbury, certain persons were appointed by the king himself, to go to each of the counties of England, and cause the bishops, abbots, priors, and all the clergy to be summoned to their presence at a certain place, and to say on the king's behalf, that they should redeem their lands from the king's hands before the next Easter, and should accept his protection under certain penalties. For this purpose, coming personally to the county of Norfolk, the lord Robert of Tattershall sent word to the sheriff of Norfolk to have it publicly proclaimed in every market town that he (Robert) would cause all bishops, abbots, priors and the whole of the clergy to be summoned before himself at Norwich on a certain day. When he carried out this order, many of the clergy came there, but few accepted the king's protection; many however, not surprisingly, did not bother to come at his order.

In the same year the lord Robert, archbishop of Canterbury, considering that the lord king Edward had caused all his lay fees to be seized, and those of the bishops, religious, and also those of all the clergy not only lay fees, but even many fees annexed to churches, and also that in many places officers of the king had entered the houses of religious and taken them into the hand of the lord king, and that they could not get hold of any of their goods, unless they were released by the said officers, caused to be summoned all the bishops, abbots, priors, chapters, archdeacons and clergy to appear at St Paul's London, in the middle of Lent, to discuss these recent events.

In the same year the sheriff of Kent had the doors of the prior and convent of Canterbury, of both cellar and kitchen, closed, with food standing on the hearth, so that the prior and convent of that place had nothing to eat or drink for several days from their own goods, except what their friends brought them out of charity or previous friendship.

In the same year when the lord Robert the archbishop set off to go to the king a number of armed men, on the instructions of the sheriff of the district, kept guard around him, lest he should turn aside somewhere out of their sight. And when he had reached Maidstone, the king's officers took his and very many of his clerks' horses, and held them; however he came as best he could to the king but could obtain no satisfaction concerning the release of his horses or holdings, or those of other ecclesiastics, from the king's hand; all the king did was to send word to the sheriff that from the goods found in the holdings of the clerks he should have the holdings that had been seized sown.

In the same year, a large number of men of religion and other clerks were made to come off or were thrown off their horses, and their horses taken away. For the king put all bishops, religious and other clerks outside his protection, nor was any clerk given a hearing for any kind of wrong done to him before any of the lord king's justices or officers whatsoever, so that the clerical order was reckoned the lowest, lower than the common people.

In the same year the lord king went to Plymouth in person in order to send money and corn to his army in Gascony, and he made a long stay in those parts.

In the same year, in the middle of Lent, the lord Robert, archbishop of Canterbury and his suffragans, the religious, and the clergy of the province of Canterbury, met in London and after various discussions over several days it seemed to the lord archbishop that because of the statute of the lord pope they could in no way contribute anything to the king without incurring excommunication; but to nearly all the other bishops, religious and clergy it seemed that they must make the king a contribution, saying that the necessity imposed upon them excused them from the excommunication carried in the statute, because otherwise they must perish of hunger and need or be dispersed. For, so it was said, the king made a statute at Salisbury, that if the ecclesiastics did not buy back his peace and protection before the following Easter, all holdings of the church, whether they were annexed to churches, or granted in any other manner whatever, would be forfeited with all the goods found in them, for ever. Also those who did not buy back peace and protection, would remain outside his peace and protection. The lord archbishop followed his conscience and would contribute nothing to the lord king; he conceded to all the others, however, that they might follow their own consciences without any punishment being imposed by him. And so nearly all, great as well as small, personally or through their friends or proctors, bought back for themselves the peace and protection of the lord king, giving a fifth part of their goods according to the taxation of the lords of Lincoln and Winchester, and so left London, with letters allowing them to get back their goods and holdings. But the holdings and goods of the archbishop, and of those who did not make peace, remained in the hand of the lord king. And after the following Easter he did with them what he wished.

In the year 1297 the lord king sent word to all the sheriffs of the kingdom of England to give notice to all in their bailiwicks, both tenants in chief of the lord king and those not tenants in chief, to be ready with horses and arms to go with the lord king in person for the defence of the kingdom, whenever he summoned them.

In the same year the king sent word to each of the sheriffs of the kingdom specially to ask and require all those who had twenty pounds a year worth of land and rents, or more, both within liberties and without, from whomsoever they held them, and also firmly to enjoin them, to be with the lord king at London on the Sunday next after the octaves of St John the Baptist, with horses and arms, that is to say each of them as befits his standing, ready to cross overseas with the lord king. And that each of them [the sheriffs] should notify the lord king of all the names of those who were thus called upon.

In the same year the lord king ordered the sheriffs to cause the archbishops, bishops, abbots, priors, and other ecclesiastical persons, and also widows and other women in their bailiwicks, who hold of the king in chief by military service or by serjeanty, or of wardships in the hand of the king, to be summoned to have at London on the Sunday next after the octaves of St John the Baptist all the service due to the lord king equipped and ready to cross the sea with the lord king. And immediately afterwards there issued another letter to the sheriffs under the king's privy seal, to have it proclaimed throughout their counties that archbishops, bishops, abbots, priors and the rest of the religious, and widows, owing service to the lord king, could make fine for it, if they wished.

In the same year there issued a certain letter to the sheriffs that all the goods and chattels of prelates, religious and whatsoever other clerks with benefices of the value of forty shillings or more in their bailiwicks, and movables which had been taken into the lord king's hand, who had not the lord king's protection at Easter, should be put up for sale, and that for the proceeds thereof they (the sheriffs) should answer at the exchequer. And they should nevertheless hold in the king's hands and keep safely the lands and holdings of the said clerks who at Easter had not protection or were not making fine for the same, until they should receive word otherwise from the lord king.

In the same year there issued another letter to the sheriffs, that immediately on seeing the letter they should inquire diligently the names and the number of the clerks in their counties with ecclesiastical benefices worth forty shillings, in rectories and vicarages or in any other way whatever, who had not the lord king's protection, and immediately take into the lord king's hand and put up for sale all their goods and chattels found outside sanctuary, and the same sheriffs should answer for the proceeds thereof at the lord king's exchequer.

In the same year on the Sunday next after the Nativity[1] of St John the Baptist, the archbishop of Canterbury, bishops, earls, barons, and those having twenty pounds a year worth of land met together at London, and the lord Roger Bigod, earl of Norfolk and marshal of England, the lord Humphrey, earl of Hereford and constable of England, with their confederates and followers, made objections on behalf of the commonalty of the kingdom, saying that neither they nor any others, who were bound to service, were bound to go with the king to Flanders in the army, and they put forward many other articles for the commonalty of the land, which were as follows – or so it was said; as will appear later, however, the king afterwards asserted the contrary.

[The chronicler here inserts one of the three surviving texts of the French version (*Monstraunces*) of the Articles of Grievance given as No. 69 below.]

They also put forward many other articles for the commonalty, which are not written here.

In the same year, after many and various altercations, the king granted to all who owed him service, and to all with twenty pounds a year worth of land that they were not bound to go with him to Flanders, except at wages and in return for payment by the lord king.

In the same year and in the same parliament, the lord king granted that the great charter of the liberties of England and the charter of the forest would be confirmed if the archbishop, bishops, and clergy would act generously towards him in return for the said confirmation, and the earls, barons and people would grant him an eighth.

In the same year the lord archbishop, deliberation being requested about the lord king's request, caused the bishops, abbots, priors and clergy, deans of cathedral churches and priors to be summoned to appear personally, cathedral chapters by a proctor, the clergy of each diocese by two proctors, at London on the feast of St Laurence with

[1] This should be not the Nativity, but the octaves of the Nativity. See above, p. 214.

continuation and prorogation day by day until the business was finished, to treat of difficult matters, namely of advantageously renewing the great charters of liberties and of the forest and of recovering from the lord king the rights and liberties of the English church, which had for so long been falling and were still continuing to fall into disuse, and of other difficulties touching the state of the clergy and the church.

In the same year, on St Laurence's day, the lord archbishop, bishops, and the others summoned by the lord archbishop, met at London and treated of the aforesaid things, and the opinion of all resolved on this, that they could contribute nothing to the king because of the statute of pope Boniface, and that they should signify this to the lord king, who was then at Winchelsea, by two bishops. In addition they should say to the lord king that he should not take it amiss that they had not dared to dissimulate further by not declaring excommunicate all those who contravened or infringed the statute of pope Boniface; and it was also provided in the same discussion, that each bishop, in his cathedral church if it could be done, otherwise in an appointed place of the same diocese, should on the first of September begin solemnly to denounce them, and on the next following feast days in the more important places of each diocese by the bishops personally. In other places, however, namely in the churches of those dioceses, in the presence of the clergy and people during the celebration of mass, the bells having been rung as a warning of all these things and the candles lit, and extinguished at the end of the denunciations, the excommunications should be solemnly published, and expounded for all to hear by officers of the bishops or subordinates suitable for the purpose. And all bishops hindered from beginning it in their cathedral churches on the day mentioned shall do it in the same churches as soon as they can, namely that all shall be denounced as excommunicate, who have consumed, taken away or interfered with the goods of the church and of ecclesiastical persons, that is to say of archbishops, bishops, abbots, priors, rectors or vicars of parish churches, or other ecclesiastics, from their houses, manors, granges, or other places of this kind belonging to churches and ecclesiastical persons, contrary to the wish and ready permission of the same or of the custodians of those goods, or have caused those things, or any of those things, to be done. Also those who have laid violent hands or have rashly caused or procured them to be laid on any cleric or religious lay brother. Also those who through the lay power have entered or occupied churches or their houses contrary to the ecclesiastical law, or detained any thus occupied, and those who have counselled or countenanced those things or any of them. Also those who without the authority of the apostolic see have imposed on, exacted or received from churches or ecclesiastics levies, tallages or other exactions payable to laymen in any quantity, portion or quota, or who have anywhere whatever arrested, seized or occupied the goods of ecclesiastical persons or church goods deposited in sacred buildings, or have received goods thus taken or seized, and those who knowingly have tacitly or explicitly given advice in or countenance to the aforesaid matters. Also it should be publicly forbidden in the aforesaid denunciations for anyone in future to do or procure the aforesaid things or any of them, on pain of excommunication – under which anyone disobeying would fall *ipso facto*. And lest the said general denunciations should remain fruitless, or should be of little use, malefactors of this kind, of whom mention has been made above and against whom a case has been made out in proper legal form by evidence of the fact or inquests diligently made about the matter at a convenient time, shall all be publicly declared by name with the aforesaid solemnity in the churches in whose parishes these things were done, and in churches neighbouring on the same, and also in other places which according to the circumstances seem suitable, to have incurred the sentence of major excommunication, and after this has been carried out, as against the aforementioned malefactors who presume to continue their wrongdoing, according to the nature of their excesses, the aforesaid denunciations shall continue with the same solemnity from day to day. In addition it shall be forbidden in all the aforesaid denunciations, under pain of the excommunication which contraveners incur *ipso facto*, for anyone to hinder, or cause to be hindered, the carrying out of any of the aforesaid, or for that reason to cause or procure loss or injury to be inflicted on anyone in person or things. In the said denunciations it shall also be publicly and expressly forbidden for any prelate or ecclesiastical person to do or attempt anything contrary to the pope's constitution lately published about granting anything in the least to laymen, by way of tallage or levy, under whatever manner, title or colour it may be sought lest they incur the penalties contained in that constitution.

In the same year and the same parliament, the aforesaid earls marshal and constable, withdrew without being reconciled to the king, and afterwards the lord king had the truth of the whole matter sent to the sheriffs, as he said, telling them to make known to the people not to believe anything against the king other than what truth dictated, in this form . . .

[The chronicler here inserts the royal proclamation of 12 August 1297, translated (from a superior text) as No. 71 below.]

In the same year, the lord archbishop, the bishops and clergy sent to the lord king the bishops of Exeter and Rochester to lay before him certain articles; and the first article was this, namely that the archbishop, bishops and clergy could not make him a subsidy from ecclesiastical goods, on account of the pope's constitution forbidding it. To this article, the king replied thus: "That being so, we are placed in a position of such necessity, that we shall have a contribution taken from the church goods by royal authority, however, it shall be done so moderately and so quietly that you will not be able to say that you have been excessively burdened or oppressed in this matter."

Another article was this, that the archbishop and the bishops and clergy would, if the king was agreeable, send messengers to the court of Rome to ask permission from the pope to grant the king some subsidy, to which the king did not consent on that occasion.

The third article was about publishing the sentence against those laying hold of things ecclesiastical, which the king forbade to be done and had letters forbidding it handed to all the bishops then present, under pain of forfeiture of all things which they could forfeit, and had similar prohibitions sent to the lord archbishop and the other absent bishops. He gave all these answers with a calm expression and quiet bearing, and, asking a blessing from each bishop there present, arranged his journey to the ships, and in a pleasant speech gave the said bishops leave to depart. These things took place on a Wednesday.

In the same year the lord archbishop, on the day appointed, namely the first of September, denounced as excommunicate all laying hold of things ecclesiastical, in the prescribed form, in his cathedral church at Canterbury. Some others pronounced the sentence; but they excepted the king and his sons provisionally. Some put off on account of the lord king's prohibition until they had the lord archbishop's advice, and afterwards made the denunciation, excepting however the king and his children; others did little or nothing in the matter.

In the same year, the lord Edward, the son of the illustrious king Edward of England, caused the archbishop, bishops, abbots, priors of cathedral churches, earls, barons, and very many other knights, to be summoned to appear on the morrow of Michaelmas at London, to treat with the said lord Edward the said king's son, and with the council of the lord king, of difficult and urgent matters concerning the whole realm of England and to advise upon them.

In the same year the lord Edward, the king of England, crossed over to Flanders about the feast of St [Bartholomew], to the help of the count of Flanders, who was allied to the said king of England, because the lord king of France entered Flanders with a great army against the said count of Flanders, to destroy and lay waste his lands and capture the count if possible.

In the same year, after the king had reached Flanders and was at Bruges, fearing an insurrection of the townspeople, he went from there, and the count of Flanders with him, to Ghent, and there made a long stay.

In the same year the Welsh, leaving the king of England's army, set fire to many vills in the count of Hainault's territory and invaded certain fairs in the said territory, and returned to the king of England's army with a very great deal of booty.

In the same year, the Scots rose against the king of England, having as leader of their army William Wallace who had previously been outlawed and was supported secretly by the magnates of Scotland. On a certain day the lord the earl Warenne, lieutenant of the king of England in Scotland, and the lord Hugh de Cressingham, treasurer of the said king, who were there with their followers and only a small army, because they had caused many to leave their army, being deceived by a promise of the magnates of Scotland that the Scots would make peace, came to Stirling, and since the army of the Scots was large, they nearly all hid themselves in the mountains. But when the English crossed the bridge of Stirling on the Wednesday next before the feast of the Exaltation of the Holy Cross, before the English were drawn up for battle, the Scots, with their lines of battle drawn up ready, fell upon the English and killed the lord Hugh de Cressingham, the treasurer of Scotland, and many others, both knights and squires, and some clerks. The earl Warenne, and others who could, fled, and afterwards reached Berwick; but when the English who lived there saw this, they all fled from the said town of Berwick, and left it quite unguarded.

In the same year, on the morrow of Michaelmas, the archbishop of Canterbury, bishops, prelates, clergy, earls, barons, many knights, proctors of counties and cities, assembled at London, and after much and varied discussion, the lord Edward the king's son and all of the king's council conceded that the charters of the liberties of the kingdom of England and of the forest should be granted and confirmed anew. Also that prises should not be taken, nor mises nor aids imposed, except with the consent of the archbishops, bishops, prelates, earls and barons, unless they were due by ancient custom. Also that, in future forty shillings should not be taken for a sack of wool, for fells or hides, as they were now taken because of the war, but half a mark only. If you wish to know more, see above. Also the said lord Edward the king's son on his own account, and all of the king's council, granted and faithfully promised to procure the king's remission of all rancour and all ill will, if he had any, towards Roger Bigod, the marshal of England, Humphrey Bohun, the constable of England, and John Ferrers and their accomplices, confederates or supporters, and to procure the lord king's letter under his great seal on all the aforesaid matters.

In the same year the lord kings of England and France made a truce between themselves and their allies on either side, that is the lord king of England made truce for the duchy of Aquitaine and for the county of Flanders and some other places with the agreement of the king of France, from kingdom to kingdom, from land to land, from people to people, by land and by sea to last only until the feast of the Lord's Epiphany next to come, in the case of the duchy of Aquitaine; and in the case of the other territories, until the octave of St Andrew the Apostle next to come, and while this truce lasted all merchants and anyone else whatever could safely go from kingdom to kingdom and return thence and stay and trade; and each king promised for his own part, in good faith, that if any injury were done meanwhile, he would cause it to be suitably compensated, and to this end Walter Beauchamp took the oath for the lord king of England on the soul of the lord king.

In the same year the lord king had all the wool in the kingdom of England taken, promising that he would pay for it as soon as he could, and this was largely the reason why the magnates, as has been written, rose against the king.

In the same year, because he had lately learnt both by letters sent swiftly from Scotland and by the earl Warenne's report telling the same tale, that an army of Scots, enormous in numbers, after occupying the whole of the kingdom of Scotland and slaughtering very many English, sparing neither age nor sex, had invaded the kingdom of England beyond doubt, the lord archbishop caused to be summoned all the bishops, abbots, priors, deans and clergy, to discuss with him how the wickednesses of the Scots could be resisted and the said dangers guarded against, and to discuss with him both what aid would be lawful and the manner of granting it.

In the same year the bishops, prelates and clergy attended on the feast of St Edmund, king and martyr, and a tenth of all the goods of archbishops, bishops, prelates and deans, according to the taxation last made, was granted to help those going in the army against the Scots, and a tenth of the goods of the clergy, according to the taxation of Norwich.

In the same year, at the same time and place, the lord Edward the king's son, earls, barons, and magnates were present, and the great charter of the liberties of England was read, and the charter of the Forest, and that the lord king remitted all rancour against the earls and barons, and all the other things which are written above in the

6th chronicle were sealed with the great seal of the lord king in Flanders by his will, consent, and deed, and precept, and there, namely at London, all were brought back signed with the great seal of the lord king, read and recited before all who were present, and the charters were handed over to the custody of the lord archbishop of Canterbury, and thus was a good state of peace reestablished between the lord king, his earls and magnates, and then they discussed the expedition against the Scots, and in all things God was blessed. Amen.

9. The Chronicle of Bury St Edmunds for the domestic crisis of November 1296 to 10 October 1297

(*The Chronicle of Bury St Edmunds 1212–1301*, ed. A. Gransden (1964), pp. 134–42. The translation is, with certain changes, that of Dr Gransden)

[1296]

. . . The king held his parliament at Bury St Edmunds on the morrow[1] of All Souls' day, especially to ask the clergy and the rest of the people for an aid to help his country. When he arrived he went to the house of Henry de Lynn, outside the limits of the monastery; he slept there as long as he remained in town. Many people were offended by this form of hospitality as unworthy of royalty and not usually offered to kings in former times. Lest the archbishop's presence, which was regarded with mistrust in respect of the bearing of his cross and his bestowal of benediction, should detract from the privileges and exemption of St Edmund's church, he granted letters patent formally drawn up before he entered the exempt limits of this church, making them binding for its perpetual protection both for himself and for his successors. Whoever should have hesitated to comply with the king's demand mentioned above or refused as much as he could, was publicly attacked by the king and dishonoured. After a brief consultation the laity granted the king a twelfth penny of all revenues, and the burgesses granted a seventh[2] penny. The archbishop held his council with the clergy at Bury St Edmunds. In it the new papal constitution was made public. It definitely forbids any ecclesiastical person to pay anything to the secular power in any manner or under any pretext whatever, however elaborate, without consulting the pope. This is the papal bull. "Boniface, etc. In perpetual memory of this affair past history teaches us that the laity are very hostile to the clergy. . . ." After a debate on this constitution they could find no way by which they could concede the king's wish without danger. So the archbishop, speaking for himself and the whole clergy, informed the king of this. When the king heard this he decided from that day to harass and molest the archbishop and other prelates and all the clergy of England: and arranged a later day for the clergy on the octave[3] of the feast of St Hilary, in London. Till then he declared peace between himself and the church. The king solemnly kept the feast of St Edmund[4] with the chief men of the realm and entertained the convent.

[1] 3 November
[2] An eighth, in fact, but probably a scribal error only (vij for viij).
[3] 20 January 1297 [4] 20 November 1296

The king of England's ambassadors crossed the sea to [attend] the parliament of the king of France. Rhys, son of Rhys, a powerful man backed by the strength of Wales and apparently a strongly entrenched enemy of the English, voluntarily submitted with his confederates to the king's peace on the feast of St Edmund at the hour when the king was attending high mass at Bury. He bowed his neck in dutiful subjection to the king. Because of this the king gave due thanks to the martyr, whose miraculous power is universal, and made offerings with humble devotion.

After the king had stayed at Bury St Edmunds for three weeks he set out for Clare. Before he left he dismantled and broke into small pieces the altar which he had erected by a special dispensation outside the boundaries of the monastery, lest as a result it should be prejudicial to the church. The king kept Christmas at Ipswich. The king of England's ambassadors left the French court after they had lost all hope of peace and returned to England.

[1297]

In the following year the Dominical letter was F.

Margaret, the king of England's daughter and duchess of Brabant, set sail for Brabant on St Sebastian's day.[1] Elizabeth, the king of England's daughter, was married to the count of Holland. It should be remembered that the king's eldest daughter, called Eleanor, married the count of Bar. His second daughter, Joan, married Gilbert, earl of Gloucester. The third, Margaret, was married to the duke of Brabant, as has been said. The fourth, Elizabeth, was married to the count of Holland. The fifth became a nun at Amesbury. The count of Flanders sent formal ambassadors with letters of alliance to the king of England concerning the treaty he had already discussed with him. Thus he calmed the strife at sea between the English and the men of Flanders; and those who before had been bitter enemies were made friends.

A general convocation of the clergy met in London on the octave[2] of the feast of St Hilary to discuss the peace of the holy English church and the king's threats and how to resist "voluntary" extortions.[3] As the assembly feared the eternal King more than him who was king for the time and the peril of their souls more than the hazards of worldly affairs, it was ordained by the common assent of everyone that the holy decree of the chief shepherd of the universal church ought to be maintained with passionate consistency inviolate and untouched. This was announced to the king by formal messengers, together with the punishments threatened in the papal decree. At this the king was angry and determined to treat holy church with unheard-of rigour, to the extent of depriving the lady and queen of the world, abandoned without a shadow of rightful protection and exposed to the fangs of wicked men and robbers, of all the protection and services of the law courts; indeed he seemed rather to spur on her enemies. Moreover according to some he published an edict that the censure of the courts of law should not extend to laymen attacking clerks and robbing them of horses worth more than 40*s*. On the day when the king issued this cruel sentence against the clergy, many of the nobles in his army in Gascony fell in battle against the French. Some were captured, among whom was John de St John, formerly

[1] 20 January [2] 20 January [3] *pressuris*

the king's seneschal in Gascony, and many others, for the enemy triumphed by weight of numbers after lying in ambush and attacking suddenly. Many of the clergy forgot their own salvation and were worldly-wise; they acted with the weakness of women, as for instance the king's clerks and courtiers who immediately tried to make peace with the king. They put the papal statute wholly on one side and granted the king a fifth part of all their revenues both spiritual and temporal. The king seized into his hands all the lay fees of the archbishops, bishops, the religious orders and the other clergy of every rank and condition who had not accepted protection, and all their property wherever it was to be found outside ecclesiastical boundaries. For which reason the aforesaid property which had been taken in this way was confiscated and suffered grave pillage. The king held his parliament, with the laity who alone had been summoned, at Salisbury on Ash Wednesday[1] to discuss the question of his military expedition against the king of France. There the king asked certain earls, that is the constable and marshal of England, to cross the Channel with him or at least go to Gascony. They did not consent to his request and explained firmly by way of excuses that they neither could nor would quit their own country when it was surrounded by so many enemies and leave it deserted. From that day the king bore their reply in mind without saying anything.

It must be remembered that on Ash Wednesday all the goods of the abbot and convent of Bury St Edmunds were confiscated and all their manors together with St Edmund's borough. The whole clergy met for the third time in London about the middle of Lent to discuss in detail the innumerable exactions, injuries and unjust losses daily inflicted on the church and clergy. When they had argued this way and that for eight days over the contributions requested, they still did not find any way of complying with the royal authority without peril. And this in the end was the reply they gave to the king's council. In this council[2] a certain friar of the preaching order publicly affirmed before everyone that the king's request was just and declared with shameless effrontery that he would defend its justice before the pope. The king named a day after which all the chattels found on the manors of those of the clergy who did not have protection should be adjudged forfeited, and they should have no service from laymen. The king would also distribute their property as he wished. And if at some time or other they were found without the protection of the council they were to be punished by imprisonment as public enemies.

The bishop of Salisbury died and was succeeded by master Simon de Gaunt, a canon of Salisbury.

In the year of the Lord 1297 the Dominical letter was F and Easter day was on 14 April.

It should be recorded that on the second night after Palm Sunday[3] before matins there was a terrible storm; thunder, lightning, fire[-balls] and hail came in turn with unheard-of violence. The hailstones were immense and astonishing to witness, for their size was as big as a man's thumb. After the night hymns there was an eclipse of the moon and then the storm started again, raging with renewed violence. On the

[1] 27 February 1297

[2] Here, of course, the ecclesiastical assembly is meant.

[3] Sunday, 7 April 1297

feast of the Translation of St Edmund[1] there was a big earthquake in many parts of Norfolk before sunrise. A certain monk of Walden named Simon, having drunk deep at the fount of ecclesiastical learning, incepted at the university of Cambridge and taught canon law.

The king summoned a parliament at Lincoln[2] on the octave of the feast of St John the Baptist. In it a dispute arose between him and some of the earls and barons of the realm because he had tried to lay an unbearable burden on both the clergy and the laity. For he had again asked the clergy for half of all their revenues, the laity for a sixth penny and the boroughs for a third penny. The earls and barons replied without the agreement of the archbishop of Canterbury and all the clergy that they would on no account submit to such a heavy and unbearable exaction, but rather they earnestly asked that the property of holy church and their own, which together had been unjustly seized by the royal officials, should be restored without delay, and that henceforth the clauses and terms contained in Magna Carta should be observed. The king did not agree to these just demands but artfully postponed the question. At last the king, moved by a kindlier spirit, came to himself; he freely restored to his peace and protection by royal letters all those who from the bosom of church had observed the papal statutes and not feared the transient tyranny of the king. The archbishop held a general council of the clergy in London on the Sunday[3] after the feast of St Laurence, especially to discuss making the grant which was repeatedly sought by the king, but against which the clergy always protested, alleging that it hurt their consciences. On the eve[4] of St Bartholomew's day the king put to sea from Winchelsea and three days later reached the Zwyn in Flanders. There the Portuguese burnt seventeen ships from Yarmouth and cruelly butchered the sailors. When the king heard this he pondered it in silence. On St Giles's day[5] a general sentence of excommunication was fulminated by each and every archbishop and bishop of England in their dioceses by papal authority against everyone who lately forced their way contrary to canon law into churches and ecclesiastical liberties and made a scrutiny of the sacred places, and against all those who had in any way countenanced them.

On the morrow of the feast of the Exaltation of the Holy Cross[6] the Scots rose against the English because they had been informed that the king of England had crossed the sea. In the clash Hugh de Cressingham, who had lately been made treasurer of Scotland, was captured and beheaded. The earls and barons held their parliament at Northampton on St Matthew's day[7] to discuss the quarrel which had arisen between the king and themselves. Edward, the king's son, held his parliament in London on Michaelmas day[8] to discuss a peace and agreement between his father, the king, and

[1] 9 June

[2] This should be London, not Lincoln, and the Sunday after the octave (i.e. not 1 July, but 7 July 1297). Also, as Cotton (pp. 214–15 above) knew, the writs of summons were for a muster, not a parliament, however political the occasion became.

[3] 11 August: the summons (to the New Temple, London) was however for the feast itself (10 August) and the following days.

[4] 23 August

[5] 1 September

[6] 15 September. The battle of Stirling Bridge took place on 11 September, the Wednesday before, not the day after the Exaltation of the Holy Cross.

[7] 21 September

[8] 29 September

the barons. These by the common consent of the king's council remaining in England, and of the archbishops, bishops, earls and barons, the great charter of England and certain additions which had been made to it were renewed and confirmed by the king's exchequer seal and the seals of all the chief men of the king's council. They sent the charter in great haste to the king, who was occupied across the seas. The king received it, and after talking the matter over with his magnates who were there with him, approved what had been done and gave it permanent force by applying his great seal. He returned the charter to the barons in England by formal messengers with a noteworthy promise.

10. The Chronicle of Walter of Guisborough for the domestic crisis of November 1296 to 10 October 1297

(*The Chronicle of Walter of Guisborough*, ed. H. Rothwell (Camden series, 1957), pp. 286–313)

The king of England put the clergy outside his protection

On the day after the feast of All Souls in the same year the king held his parliament at Bury St Edmunds, where at his request a twelfth penny was granted to him by the people, an eighth by the cities and boroughs. The clergy's reply was, however, that they could not give or grant him anything, nor could he receive anything, without each of them incurring the sentence of excommunication contained in the bull: which they did not think the king wanted and which they knew was not expedient for them. But this reply did not please the king. So they were adjourned to another parliament at London on the day after the feast of St Hilary, to give them time to consult and deliberate and so give him a better answer. When at length the day came, and the clergy were assembled there, the archbishop of Canterbury, mr Robert de Winchelsey, gave the decision to those who were sent on the king's behalf, replying in these words: "It is well enough known to you, my lords, nor can it be hidden, that under Almighty God we have also two lords on earth, to wit a spiritual and a temporal; the spiritual the lord pope, and the temporal, the king. And although we owe obedience to both, we owe a greater obedience to the spiritual than to the temporal. But so that we can please both, we grant and are willing to send at our expense our confidential messengers to the spiritual father the lord pope to get permission to grant something, or at least have an answer from him what we ought to do. For we believe our lord the king, like ourselves, both fears and wishes to avoid the sentence of excommunication contained in the bull." To this the king's messengers said: "Appoint, dearest lords, some of yourselves to tell to the king such things for you: we, knowing what he is like when his anger is aroused, are quite afraid to tell him." This done, the king's anger flared and, burning with rage, he put the archbishop of Canterbury himself and all the clergy of England outside his defence and protection, ordering, too, all the lands and endowments of the whole English church to be taken into his hand. And miraculously, as is believed, it happened that the very same day the king put the clergy outside his protection, his knights were confounded in Gascony and defeated by the French, as told below.[1] The king's justice in the Bench, too, sitting in judgment for the king, said publicly to all who were around, "You lords who are attorneys of archbishops, bishops, abbots and priors and all the rest of the clergy, tell your lords that henceforth in the court of the lord king no justice shall be given them in any matter whatsoever, even if the most atrocious wrong has been inflicted on them. Justice however shall be done to all complaining of them and wanting it." Wonderful to relate, common justice which is granted to the people is – I know not by what spirit – denied to the clergy! And mother church is enslaved and serves, who formerly used to rule over her sons. However, the elect of York, Henry of Newark, as well as the bishops of Durham, Ely and Salisbury and certain others, fearing the king's extreme anger and conjecturing that grave danger threatened, declared themselves willing to deposit a fifth of the ecclesiastical goods of that year in a religious house, for the protection of the English church and against an emergency, so as to escape in this way the king's anger and not incur the sentence contained in the bull. Whatever the clergy deposited, however, the state removed. By this arrangement, under pretence granting a fifth, they obtained the king's protection. The archbishop of Canterbury however, did not change his mind and would neither grant nor deposit anything. He chose rather to incur the king's anger than the sentence of excommunication. So all his goods and his gold and silver vessels were taken and all his horses; and the members of his household left him, and nothing remained from which the poor man of Christ could be supported. And it was ordered, on pain of the king's heavy forfeiture, that no one should give him hospitality in a monastery or outside. And the saying of the apostle: "Receive ye one another as Christ also received you" was made void. Thus cast out, he stayed in the house of a certain simple rector, with a single priest and one clerk, and he had nowhere in his whole archbishopric where he could lay his head. He was constantly active, however, for the Word of God, preaching publicly and everywhere declaring that all who granted anything either to the king or to a secular person contrary to the will of the lord pope had undoubtedly by the very act incurred the force of the condemnation (contained in the bull), and he was always readier for death than for concession. But friends of Oliver, bishop of Lincoln, unknown to him and, when he did know, without his agreement, arranged however, that the sheriff of Lincoln should levy a fifth of the bishop's goods and then restore to him his possessions and lands. All the monasteries too of the diocese and the whole province of Canterbury were taken into the king's hand and by his order keepers appointed, who were to serve the religious with only what was necessary, the rest to be turned over to the state. As a result abbots and priors, driven by necessity, went to the king's court and redeemed not their sins but their goods with a gift of a fourth. No justice was dispensed to the clergy at that time and clerks suffered many wrongs. The religious were also robbed of their horses on the king's highway and got no justice, until they redeemed themselves and got the king's protection.

Oppression of the land by prises

In the same year too, during Lent, the king ordered all who had wool and hides to

[1] above, in fact, not below

carry them to certain sea-ports before a certain day, on pain of losing the same and of imprisonment, and of the king's heavy penalty. When they had done this, the king's servants took all the sacks of wool over the number of five for the king's use, giving tallies, and for each sack not over the number of five, they extorted from their owners[1] forty shillings as maletote. Furthermore the king ordered that in preparation for his crossing to France, two thousand quarters of corn and the same amount of oats should be taken from each county by the sheriff and carried to the sea-ports. And so it was done, and men were tallaged at a certain number of quarters, even those who had no corn; also carcases of beef and pork were taken up to a certain number, and many were the oppressions inflicted on the people of the land.

The count of Flanders came to an agreement with the king

The same year, the count of Flanders, having been wronged by his lord, the king of France, when he had already expended much money on his behalf, seeing that he had laboured in vain although he had deserved much, repudiated his fealty to his king. And to be the more acceptable to the king of England, he expelled all Frenchmen from his land. And considering his land was, so to speak, exhausted because his citizens had not English wool and hides to work with, as they had been accustomed to have by way of trade, whereas there are many workmen there, and that the fishermen also of his land were impoverished because they had not free access to the sea, and finally, seeing that he could hold out no longer against the king of the English, he sent envoys to him, seeking and asking for conditions of peace and friendship. And the request pleased our king, and he praised and commended him for expelling the French from his land. And he made a firm peace with him and had it publicly proclaimed. And besides entering into a firm treaty, they became close friends as well.

The disagreement that arose between the king and his earls

On the feast of St Matthias the Apostle that year, calling together the leading men of the kingdom without the clergy, the king held his parliament at Salisbury, where he asked certain of the magnates to cross over to Gascony. And one after the other they began to excuse themselves. And the king was angry and threatened some of them, that either they went or he would give their lands to others who were willing to go. And many were offended at this and a split began to appear between them. The earl of Hereford and the earl marshal excused themselves, saying that their offices, which belonged to them by hereditary right, they would gladly perform by going with the king himself. And the request was repeated and the earl marshal asked to go, and he said, "With you I will gladly go, O king, in front of you in the first line of battle as belongs to me by hereditary right." And the king replied, "You will go without me too, with the others." But he, "I am not bound, neither is it my will, O king, to march without you." Enraged, the king burst out, so it is said, with these words, "By God, O earl, you will either go or hang." And he, "By the same oath, O king, I will neither go nor hang." And, without leave, he went away. And the council was dissolved for the day. Immediately, however, the two earls, Hereford and the

[1] *dominis*

marshal, joined by many magnates and more than thirty picked bannerets, grew into a multitude. They numbered one thousand five hundred men on armed horses ready for war and the king began to fear them. He did not show it, however. They went off to their own lands, where they would not allow the king's servants to take either wool or hides or anything whatever out of the ordinary or to exact anything from anyone against his will. Indeed they forbade them entry to their lands under penalty of head and members, and made ready to resist.

The archbishop of Canterbury is reconciled to the king and the king got leave to cross

In the year of the Lord 1297, the king, persisting in his plan ordered all who owed him service and all others who held twenty pounds worth of land from anyone within the kingdom of England to be at London on the feast of St Peter's Chains,[1] ready with horses and arms to cross with him without any delay or excuse whatever. And when many had come there, and seen that the king was persisting in the plan he had embarked on, some of the magnates said to him, "It is not advisable, king, nor is it a good thing thus to cross, unless by first reconciling your spiritual father the archbishop of Canterbury you yourself are found by your magnates reckoned in the bosom of mother church." At this he came to himself and seeing that this was just and consonant with reason, sent at once for the archbishop of Canterbury who was at hand and putting aside all rancour, took him and his back into his particular friendship as before and made it greater still. For, trusting in his goodness and firmness of character, he committed to him, in association with the lord Reginald de Gray, in the presence of all the people the care and custody of his son Edward and the whole land of England. He ordered too that everything should be restored to him to the very last farthing. And so by God's favour, he was restored with honour, who, not fearing death, for the honour of God resisted unto death. And all the magnates who were there did fealty to the king's son on the father's order, and he was acclaimed by all the people with their right hands raised the true heir, future lord and successor to the kingdom. The king, also, excused himself for the exactions and prises which he had taken from the people, saying that he could not continue what he had begun if their liberal hand did not come to his assistance, especially as he was acting as their protector and defender in a cause which was not his alone but indeed that of the whole people. And in taking leave, he asked the people to forgive him everything and pray for him. And some prayed publicly, but others cursed secretly. The aforesaid earls, Hereford and the marshal, withdrew themselves from the king and, as they would not obey his wishes, were dismissed from their offices. And the king gave their offices to certain others who would serve him. This they took badly, especially as the cause they were striving for was not only their own but also that of the whole community, and they said to mediators who were riding between them and the king, that not only they themselves but the whole community of the land was burdened beyond what they could bear with unjust exactions, tallages and prises, and especially that they were not treated in accordance with the liberties of the great charter; and when they saw that the king's mind was unalterable, not wishing to beat the air in uncertainty any longer,

[1] 1 August

they sent messengers to the king and asked him to order the articles written below to be amended for them and for the people, adding that if he would confirm the charter of liberties and correct the articles they were all prepared to follow him to life or death.

The articles which the earls asked for in the name of the community

[Here the chronicler incorporates one of three surviving texts of the French version (*Monstraunces*) of the Articles of Grievance given at No. 69 below.]

Concerning the king's reply

And while the king was on his way to Portsmouth[1] nearly ready to cross, the aforesaid earls sent messengers to him to find out what his will was on the aforesaid. In reply to them he said, "My full council is not here with me. For, as you know, part has stayed behind in London and part has gone ahead to Flanders, and without the full council I cannot reply to your questions. But go and say to those who have sent you, that if they will come with me it will please me much; but if they will not, I ask them at least not to do me or the kingdom any harm. I hope indeed, if the Lord favours me so far, to return to this land and to be received back into my kingdom." And with a light dismissal the messengers went away. And the king crossed to Flanders about the feast of St Bartholomew, and put in at the port of the Swyn. His doings we will not follow here, but later in their proper place. The said earls returned to London with certain barons who were in league with them and forbade the king's chancellor and the barons of the exchequer to demand or levy in any way whatever the eighth penny which the king had demanded from the people, or the fifth from the clergy, or any exaction. They also asked the Londoners, as friends and associates, to be willing to help them in demanding the liberties of the great charter and to be diligent in recovering their lost rights and protecting them when recovered. And so that they could not be accused later on of rapine or unlawful extortion, the said earls had it publicly proclaimed that none of their followers should take anything, however small, from anyone, without giving a just price, and this on penalty of losing the right hand, or even head if the guilt demanded it. And they went back to their lands, without inflicting harm or burden on anyone.

[Seven chapters dealing with events in Scotland, the English defeat at Stirling Bridge, and the resulting Scots invasion of England are here omitted.]

Our earls are reconciled by the king's son

While such things were being done by the treacherous nation of the Scots, the counsellors of our king who were with the king's son, seeing great danger threaten not only the king in his activities far away, but also the whole land of England, urged the king's son, who on account of the danger of sedition, was staying in London within the walls of the city, to invite the aforesaid earls, namely the marshal and Hereford, who, as has been said, had in part separated from his father, and appeal to them for peace and compromise. He therefore sent letters inviting them to come to his parlia-

[1] an error for Winchelsea

ment, because he was taking his father's place in England, which was to be held in London on the 10th of October. And they, embracing the invitation of their new ruler and future prince, came on that day, not indeed unarmed, nay with one thousand five hundred armed horse, and a large force of picked footmen. They would not for all that enter the gates of the city unless they were first allowed to place their guards at all the city gates beforehand, for fear they might be accidentally shut in like sheep in a sheepfold if they entered without arms. When this was granted, they entered, where at last after many consultations and various discussions, by the mediation of the venerable father the archbishop of Canterbury, namely mr Robert Winchelsey, of blessed memory, there were no other terms they would agree to save that the lord king himself would grant and confirm the great charter with certain articles added and the charter of the forest; and that he would not in future ask for or demand any aid or exaction from the clergy or people without the will and assent of the magnates; and that he would remit all rancour of spirit against them and all associated with them. And a writing of this kind was drawn up, conceived in these words.

Confirmation of the Great Charter

[Here the chronicler incorporates a text of the official French articles granted in his father's name by the lord Edward at London on 10 October 1297, which are given at No. 74 below; followed immediately, in Latin, by:]

And this same writing was sent to Flanders to the king for him to set his secret seal[1] to it. For the great seal had remained with the king's son. Sent also were transcripts of the great charter and of the charter of the Forest with the underwritten articles inserted at the end of the great charter for him to seal them likewise.

The articles inserted in the Great Charter

[Here the chronicler gives the mysterious Latin articles now known as *De Tallagio non concedendo* (No. 75 below), followed immediately by:]

Also Edward himself, the king's son, by his letters patent remitted to the said earls and all their followers all rancour of spirit and ill will, and promised in the same letters to use all means to induce his father to do the same. All the king's counsellors too who were there present, by a writing of theirs made specially on this subject, promised the same thing, and everyone was glad on that day. For there on behalf of the king were the archbishop of Canterbury and Henry, the elect of York, also the bishops of London, Ely, Bath and Coventry, also the earls of Cornwall, Warenne, Warwick and Oxford, also barons John Giffard, Henry Percy and Reginald de Grey, with many other clerks and laymen. These one and all swore on holy gospel, for greater security, to keep the aforesaid earls and all their followers unharmed and immune from attack by the king. It was agreed also that on the day after the feast of St Nicholas [6 December] the bishops should receive a definite reply about this from the king himself, under this additional condition, that if the king returned the aforesaid writings

[1] Almost certainly the seal better known as the privy seal (which was generally entitled *secretum* in its legend down to the reign of Henry VIII).

sealed, and ratified everything, then at the king's order the same earls would set out either to the king in Flanders or against his enemies in Scotland as desired. Messengers were therefore sent to the lord king, and his secretaries wrote to him that, if he meant to save and keep his honour, estate and kingdom, he should send back all the aforesaid things sealed. He, to be sure being in a difficult position, after hesitating for three days did in the end however, in order to keep the hearts of his people, agree to their wishes in the aforesaid matters and granted and confirmed them all in turn. Now for this confirmation of the aforesaid charters, with their aforesaid additions, the magnates of the land with the common people gave a ninth penny, the archbishop of Canterbury with his clergy a tenth, and the archbishop-elect of York with his clergy, who were nearer the danger, a fifth penny, as a subsidy for the king's war in Scotland. The king had previously received the wool also of religious and others of the people, with however a declaration that it would be allowed for in the fifth.

11. The Chronicle of Peter Langtoft of Bridlington for the years 1297 to 1307

(*Chronicle of Pierre de Langtoft*, ed. T. Wright, 2 vols (Rolls series, 1866–8), II, pp. 265–383 [French])

This verse chronicle in Yorkshire French by Peter Langtoft, an Augustinian canon of Bridlington in the time of Edward I, is an example of history in a vernacular and in "geste" form for an audience. It is also an authority of original value for the reign of Edward I, which historians could profitably have made more use of. It is contemporary, demonstrably well-informed on details in some respects, but above all precious for its contemporary perspectives – its "Arthurian" setting, its view of the reign from the later years reflecting the war-fever of those years, its complete view of the ten critical last years, like, yet so unlike, that of the Chronicle of Walter of Guisborough. Like it in being a "Northern" view, unlike it in being complete and in being royalist (though not uncritically royalist).

The translation is that of Langtoft's editor, T. Wright. Modern work on Langtoft has been done by M. Dominica Legge, *Anglo-Norman in the Cloisters* (Edinburgh, 1950), and *Medium Aevum*, iv (1935), pp. 20–4. A modern, critical edition of the text is needed.

Of the union of England and Scotland

Ah, God! how often Merlin said truth
In his prophecies, if you read them!
Now are the two waters united in one,
Which have been separated by great mountains;
And one realm made of two different kingdoms
Which used to be governed by two kings.
Now are the islanders all joined together,
And Albany reunited to the royalties
Of which king Edward is proclaimed lord.
Cornwall and Wales are in his power,
And Ireland the great at his will.
There is neither king nor prince of all the countries
Except king Edward, who has thus united them;
Arthur had never the fiefs so fully.
Henceforward there is nothing to do but provide his expedition

Against the king of France, to conquer his inheritances,
And then bear the cross where Jesus Christ was born.

His enemies,
Thank God!
Are chastised;
They are all defeated,
And taken like rats
In trap.
He has run about,
And combated
Quite enough,
With two kings
At one time,
And overthrown them.
Let the one on this side
Now go over there
With his barons.
John and Thomas
Will not leave him
Without aid.
Cuthbert comes to him
Who holds with him
In his battles.
In God I tell you,
Merlin of him
Has prophesied,
Three regions
Into his power
Shall be gained;
Let not be blemished
The prophecy
By sin!
Lord God almighty,
At St Edmund's at the parliament
Give him counsel;
And upon false Philip of France,
By thy virtue, to have vengeance
Grant him.

Of the parliament at St Edmunds

At the town of St Edmunds, on the day fixed,
Are come the bishops, with the company
Of the archdeacons and clergy, whom the king has asked
For aid and courtesy of the goods of holy church,

According to the promise they made formerly in the abbey
Of Westminster, for which the king trusts to it
In aid of his war, which is not finished.
Earls and barons and the knights,
For themselves and for the people, grant him in aid
The tenth penny, and for the mercantile class
The seventh among them for his treasury.
And the archbishop who holds the primacy
Of the see of Canterbury, studies an answer,
And by two bishops signifies to the king
The state of holy church, which is much impoverished.
The archbishop afterwards goes to the king, and says,
"Sire, for God there above, do not be angry,
I certify thee for all holy church,
Under God on earth there is no soul alive
Who has over holy church power and mastery
Except the pope of Rome, who holds the vicarate
Which St Peter the apostle had in his trust.
The pope is our head, he keeps and rules us;
He has made a statute which binds us strictly,
Upon privation of rent and prelacy,
That tenth, nor twentieth, nor moiety, nor part,
No one of us give to thee or to other,
Without his commandement as our authority.
Upon that he solemnly excommunicates and curses
All the sons of mother who by lordship
Put in subjection holy church, which God has freed."
"Sir clerk," says the king, "thou hast spoken folly.
Promise is debt due, if faith be not forgotten.
But let me see thee possessed of the bull,
As well as all the others, by the Son of Mary!
You will not be able to escape this aid."

The reply of the clergy on the demand for aid

"Sire," says the bishop, "very willingly
To thee, as to our lord, we are willing all to give aid
By leave of the pope, if thou wilt send
By one of thy clerks with our messenger,
Who shall be able to state thy condition and ours.
And according to the message which the pope shall send us back,
We will aid voluntarily according to our capabilities."
"Sir clerk," replies the king, "I have no need
Of thy sending to consult the pope.
But if thou desire to have respite in this case,

Cause when thou wilt thy clerks to assemble,
Talk with them of the promise, talk of it heartily;
After St Hillary's day come to Westminster,
To perform the promise without more talking of it."
"Sire," says the archbishop, "for God and St Richer,
Deign to give order here and there to thy people,
Who are thy ministers for the twelfth penny,
That they cause not to be molested us or our tenants,
Nor tax our temporal goods with the laity."
"Sir," says the king, "that need not be feared,
For they will do nor good nor evil to any one of thy power."
Nevertheless the king prays and requires him,
"Throughout thy diocese give orders to pray
For me and mine, and to thank God
Who has done largely for us hitherto."
The archbishop grants it, and does his duty.
A little before this time returned the treasurer,
Walter de Langton, who had passed the sea
With the cardinals to treat of peace.
The reply which he brings no man can know,
Except those of the council, who dare not reveal it.
Afterwards messengers came to announce
To the king, sir Edward, a form of conciliating
The strife of Gascony, and of reconciling
Him with king Philip without further hostilities,
Accordingly as the cardinals have caused to be arranged.
King Edward thereupon has sent back
Walter de Langton and Hugh le Despenser,
And John de Berwick, clerk, a prudent baron;
May God give them good guidance and bring them back successfully!

Of the respect yielded to the Scots

Of the barons of Scotland in this parliament
Was no account rendered, or judgment given.
The king is so courteous, of such charitable feelings,
And of so great compassion, I believe veritably
That his mercy will be the salvation
Of those who have fully deserved death,
And attainted of acts of felony.
Of the great generosity of heart which he has often shown
To the felons of Wales, all people talk.
When he had most work before him for his own advancement,
They have raised war upon him, and given him trouble,
Through which he was obliged to abandon his expeditions elsewhere.

Of the above aid sought from the clergy

After St Hillary's day, when the king thought
To hold a parliament in London as he had ordained,
News came to him by him who was then
Come from Cambrai, and announced to him
That the conference on peace was carried on without effect.
Wherefore king Edward remains and provides,
By land and by sea, that he be not betrayed;
And he sends some of his people to Westminster
To treat on the aid which the clergy would give him.
The lord of Canterbury held himself inflexible on that subject,
For himself and for his diocese he vowed to St Thomas
That no one of his church should be taxed in future,
Nor put in servage, as long as he lived,
Without command of the pope, who ought to be their governor.
The lord of Lincoln agreed to the same,
Bishop Oliver, who was not used to give way.
The king thereupon became angered against the clergy,
And ordered them to be judged out of his peace
But soon afterwards he repealed that act.
That caused the bishops who showed willingness
To give their lord aid, whereby to recover his right,
And protect holy church from shame and injury.
The elect of York, who desired peace,
Said that willingly, for as much as touched himself,
He would contribute the fifth penny for the defence of holy church.
No soul spoke of the wretched Scots;
They are remaining still in custody in the same position
As they were before; listen what caused that.

While the king and his counsellors
Were in debate with the clergy,
Count William of Flanders has sent messengers,
The lord of Blancmount, a prudent and bold knight,
And the lord of Kew, and the treasurer,
Receiver of Flanders, who will willingly
Make entire friends of the English and Flemings,
That in one land and the other, on all coasts,
The merchants may in good love and peace
Arrive with their wares, and sell for money.
And when king Edward shall raise his banners,
The count and his Flemings shall be his allies
Against king Philip and against the twelve peers,
Who wrongfully hold from him the land with the manors

Which king Arthur to the duke sir Beduer
Gave in Aquitaine, as to his butler;
Which king Edward and king Henry his father,
And all their ancestors, held hitherto.
The gentle count of Henault, with all the Henaulters,
The duke John of Brabant, and his Hollanders,
Have by the count of Flanders and his knights
Confirmed the alliance as his dear friends.

I have openly related to you the reason
Why king Edward, for the occupation
Of the affairs of Flanders, could not at St Edmund's,
Nor at Salisbury, treat of ransom,
Nor save or condemn earl or baron
Of the realm of Scotland, for death nor for burning.
Still they remain there under custody in prison.
I cannot conceal from you another cause;
Listen, and I will tell you the narration.

Of the capture of John de St John at Belgarde

Grievous news was then spread
In the king's household, of his knights
Who were in Aquitaine, and were to have stored
The castles with provisions and part with money.
At vespers on the Wednesday before the Purification
Of the holy mother of God, the glorious Mary,
They were passing through a narrow pass, led by their spy,
Who tells them for truth that in the company
Of the French at that time in the country were no more
Than five hundred men-at-arms, having lied by a thousand
and more.
Sir John de St John, who trusts in that,
Places himself in the van-guard, and displays his banner.
When the pass was passed, he found in ambush
Fifteen hundred men-at-arms, and battle formed
In four great squadrons; and the baron raises the cry upon them,
Discomfits the first, and engages the rest.
The earl of Lincoln, Henry de Lacy,
Returned by advice, the rear-guard agrees to it,
The provision is lost, and the money plundered.
Sir James de Beauchamp has abandoned the battle,
With many of our English of his cowardice,
In fleeing he is drowned, alas! the disgrace!
Sir John de St John, combating with the sword,

And eleven knights, are taken in the flight,
And eighteen gentlemen of their esquiery.
In the departure of Israel, Egypt was disgraced,
And Pharaoh drowned in his presumption;
Through sin perished Gomorrah and Sodom;
David in his youthful age delivered Goliath to death;
Lucius the emperor died through covetousness;
Joseph, son of Jacob, was sold through envy;
And king Arthur surprised through treachery,
And Modred slaughtered through his madness;
Cadwallader for poverty lost Britain,
By force the people of Germany drove him from it;
Afterwards Harold, son of Godwin, held it wrongfully,
Who in his first year lost the lordship;
William the Conqueror acquired it by the sword;
Llewellyn, formerly prince of the Welshery,
And David his brother, have lost their lordship;
He with the long shanks is seised of all.
King John de Baliol has lost by folly,
For himself and his heirs, the kingdom of Albany.
Alas! that no man corrects himself by the example of another!
Oh, rich king Edward! for God, have mercy;
Suffer not to perish the great nobility
Of those who are left to conquer Aquitaine.
Haste you thither, the people appeals to you;
Be reconciled with the church and with the clergy,
And Thomas of Kent, and John of Beverley,
And Cuthbert of Durham, will come to thee in aid.
For, if thou hast not aid of God in the struggle,
For all thou wilt do I would not give a garlic.
Upon him whom God loves least will fall the ruin.
In war and in battle God gave formerly
Honour and victory to the son of Matathias;
So he does to all who are most dear to him.
The Prince who died on the mount of Calvary
Loves king Edward and his barons.
I was obliged to relate the controversy,
Afterwards I will talk to you of the folly
Of the remnant of Scotland, accursed of the Lord.

Of the passage of the above-named king into Flanders

After the holy feast of the Ascension,
King Edward sent through his kingdom
To archbishop, bishop, to earl, and to baron,

And to all the others who have for maintenance
Twenty pounds of land in possession,
To come to his court and make redemption,
Or proceed with his body against the felonious French,
Who wrongfully hold from his land of Gascony.
The barons converse on it; some say no,
For to do new service without condition
Would be disinheritance by custom.
They consult with the lord of Canterbury;
Ask him for advice in the dispute,
And he offers himself as a champion for holy church,
And he goes to the parliament, bearing down upon them
like a lion.
The king then addresses them, and says in his speech,
"I am castle for you, and wall, and house,
And you the barbacan, and gate, and pavilion;
My land of Gascony is lost through treason,
I must recover it, or lose my process.
I have undertaken the expedition, I have finally made
the vow;
It is the duty of each of you by name to pass with me,
Of that not a soul has excuse by evasion."
"Sire," says the archbishop, "to thy perdition
Wilt thou undertake war without correction
Performing devoutly for the offence
That thou hast often done, by thy misbehaviour,
To God, and to holy church, and to the clergy?
Listen to thy trespass for thy salvation,
And make amends, and pray for pardon
To God and holy church, by satisfaction
For thee and for all the others of the nation.
Suspend the passage, upon the curse
Of him who suffered passion for us all."

After the archbishop, Roger, the earl Marshal,
Began to speak to king Edward;
He demanded respite, and time to consult about it;
He told him that the barons, nor any one of their power,
Nor of their homage, owe beyond sea
To pass, except at his cost by agreement.
The king took the speech angrily to heart,
Spoke haughtily, would not grant respite;
Commanded the earl to equip himself,
For, whether he would or not, he must go,

Or quit there the office of the marshalship.
Earl Roger replies that so lightly
He will not think of there resigning his office;
And out of the court he departs without further dealing there.
The king then sends for Geoffrey de Genevile
And presents to him the rod of the marshalship,
And thereupon orders his familiars to arm,
And intends on the morrow to arrest the barons.
The earl Marshal hears tell of it, makes himself ready,
With earls and barons, to restrain the king;
And thus, as battle was at the point of beginning,
Bishop Anthony arrives, and proceeds to show the king
What evil and what peril may fall upon him,
If he and his barons were to disagree.
Then bishop Anthony goes to beg of the barons
That they will deign to bend to their liege lord,
Inasmuch as he has now need of their aid.
The barons consult on it, and send back their reply
By petitions of diverss manner,
And that they will willingly come to St Albans,
To hold a conference with king Edward upon it,
If he will go down there with his council.
The king sire Edward cannot wait;
It was necessary he should visit his allies beyond sea.
He raises his sail without company of earl,
And goes suddenly to arrive in Flanders.
Never in time back was such a sovereign served
Thus by his people, when he was going to make war.
He is too cowardly who draws back
When he sees his lord going into danger.

How the aforesaid Edward arrived in Flanders

The earls remained, king Edward crossed the sea;
Now listen how he arrived in Flanders:
Of wines and meats his depot was
In the town of Bruges, where he lodged.
The Saviour of mankind, who knows and sees all things,
There saved him from great disaster.
The provost of the town aimed at depriving of his heritage
The earl his liege lord, who ruled Flanders;
To king Philip of France, who was at war with him,
He sends his letter privately by messengers;
Tells him at whatever hour he would approach Bruges,
All the commune would deliver the town up to him,

And that he would there take king Edward suddenly,
So that he would escape nowhere else.
King Philip of France at once agrees to it;
He marshalled his army towards the town of Bruges.
King Edward heard tell of it and talk of deceit,
Ordered to trumpet to arms, and made preparation for his departure
To the noble burgh of Ghent, where he expected to come
The king of the Germans, who had his money
To aid in the war so long as it lasted.
The king of the Germans sent word to him there,
That he was overtaken by war, through which he could not come.
Alas! that such a prince should belie his faith!
King Edward remains, and eats and drinks;
His Welsh issued forth often for plunder.
The warlike count of Bar rode out with them,
And invaded and plundered the territory of the king of France;
Robbed his markets and his fairs of their chattels,
Spared not to do evil everywhere;
And king Philip did as much to him.
The bishop of Durham continually laboured
To put an end to the war without strife and dispute.
King Philip knew the force of the English,
Insomuch as it was small, he held himself the more unguarded.
King Edward, I tell you, would have gained a great advantage,
If he had had his earls then and there.
Listen to the fault in which all the sin lay.

An example of the noble king sir Arthur

In ancient histories we find written
What kings and what kingdoms king Arthur conquered,
And how he shared largely his gain.
There was not a king under him who contradicted him,
Earl, duke, or baron, who ever failed him
In war or in battle, but each followed him.
The king sir Edward has given too little;
Whereby at his departure, when he put to sea
Against the king of France, the affront was shown him
That not one of his earls undertook the expedition.
The commonalty of Scotland hears the news,
Each on his own part rejoices over it.
The rabble of the lower people resumed war anew;
The earl and the baron suffered by dissimulation
That William Wallace made himself their chieftain

By false pretence, which none understood,
That he sought to raise himself up a great man of Scotland.
The Wallace immediately assaulted the castles
Through the land of Scotland, and took them from the English.
Hugh de Cressingham had done wrong a while before,
When he was so very sparing of sir Edward's money,
That much of the foot of the army deserted.
The earl John de Warenne, as soon as he learnt
That the peace was broken which the Scot promised,
He proceeds towards Stirling with the army which remains,
Where William Wallace discomfited the earl,
By his own folly, when he went to bed.
For while the earl was sleeping in the morning,
William Wallace laid siege to the head of the bridge;
Of spears and gavelokes none ever saw before
So thick an assemblage; the earl fled,
The English died there, the Scot pass there quit.

At this misfortune were slain
Courteous vavasors of noble kindred,
Robert de Somerville and his eldest son;
Knights and serjeants there took their leave,
Northerns and Southerns, who are not named here.
Hugh de Cressingham, not accustomed to the saddle,
From his steed in its course fell under foot,
His body was cut to picces by the ribalds of Scotland,
And his skin taken off in small thongs,
As an insult to the king, whose clerk he was called.
May Marmaduke de Thweng, may he be honoured of God!
Behaved like a lion in all the combats;
He did so much that day that his are the congratulations;
Earl nor baron was compared to him:
Combating with the sword he has recovered the ward
Of the castle of Stirling, and remained there.
Now afterwards the Scot has sent
Beyond sea into Flanders a ribald in disguise,
To spy sir Edward in towns and cities.
He returns and tells for perfect truth,
He saw where sir Edward was dead and buried.
The commonalty of Scotland rouses itself at this time,
And promises and vows to God in trinity
To destroy England without having pity;
To confound holy church and the clergy.
In Northumberland the madmen have begun

To burn and destroy both houses and corn.
People are sent into Flanders to king Edward,
Who have presented on the part of the Northerns their complaint
How they have lost their lands and their fees,
And how they will lose more, and all those of most account
Who are in England in towns and cities,
If they be not aided by him in time.
The king was tormented on all sides,
So that on the morrow he sent for his privy councillors;
They consulted on the matter, as you will hear.
Immediately after, the king is counselled,
That he must grant to clergy and to the barons
The petitions which were laid before him.
To the earls and barons who were not gone with him,
To the primates of England who hold the two sees,
And to all the other consecrated bishops,
To the abbots and priors and beneficed clergy,
To the earls and barons, the king before named
By letter and by mouth has earnestly prayed
For aid and succour and friendship
Against the Scots and their wickedness;
Faithfully he promises them they shall be well rewarded,
And shall have their demand at their will.
The lord of Canterbury is rejoiced by the promise;
He has given answer for himself and his province,
With reservation of the statute the pope has published,
He has there granted the tenth of the goods of holy church,
Wherewith to save and defend him in his dignities,
So that the money be raised by the clergy,
And by the same clergy delivered to the barons,
When they shall go into Scotland with their allies,
To save holy church throughout the kingdoms.
And the clergy of the North are charged with the fifth,
At the strict valuation as they were taxed
When they gave to king Edward the moiety.

Now after when the Scots knew
How his clergy were willing to aid king Edward,
How his barons talked among themselves,
As soon as they saw sealed by the king
The charter of liberties which they had formerly,
That they would all go willingly into Albany
Against the Scots to prevent their doing more evil,
The Scots were in fear of the coming of the barons.

They went to the castle of Stirling as men of peace,
Offered hostages to Marmaduke de Thwenge,
And promised and swore on their baptism,
If he would come out they would treat of peace with him,
And there they would submit to king Edward.
Marmaduke went out to those who solicited him,
Who without further delay took him and put him on horseback,
Took with him the young constable
Straight to Dumbarton, and put him in prison;
Their friends know not if they be dead or alive there.
The treason was done, for the Scots imagined,
If misfortune came upon them, they would by them have the better.
Now hear of the charter what people brought it
To the clergy and barons, who procured it.

While the clergy of the South were employed in contriving
That by the tenth granted they could have no harm,
Nor offend the pope, returns the treasurer
Of the king of England, who was beyond sea.
He began to address the clergy,
And to announce to the barons as follows:
"Friends, the king, your lord, seeks with gentle heart
Of his lordship to ease all England,
It is his will to you to confirm the charter of liberties,
And to amend the assize of the forest,
As king Henry his father formerly provided."
The charter was shown and read at Westminster
The lord of Canterbury will not delay thereupon,
He has caused it to be published throughout his parish.
Thereupon the earl Marshal Roger,
And the earl of Hereford, Humphrey the noble baron,
Go to York, to the minster of St Peter;
The high men of the land come to meet them,
Earl John of Surrey with all his power,
The warden of Gloucester, Ralph de Monthermer,
With Joan the countess, his lawful wife,
And all the others who carry banner
From Dover to Durham, they come willingly.
On the day of St Agnes they summon thither
The bishop of Carlisle, who comes to pronounce
In the pulpit of the minster the solemn sentence,
Between the two earls, with book and candle,
Against all those who cause the charter to be violated,
Or infringed, or any point of the whole to be destroyed.

Then they go towards Scotland to protect Northumberland,
They recover the lands which Wallace the thief
Had previously seized, and then he flies back.

Amidst these transactions, of the great dispute
Between king Edward and the king of France
A delay is taken until a certain day,
And the war appeased and put in sufferance,
Until the pope has made order
And provided the accord between the two kings.
By two marriages the peace is in negotiation;
King Edward shall have her of whom was talk,
And his son Edward, may God there above advance him!
Shall have Philip's daughter, who is only seven years of age.
Clerks and laymen, in whom the kings have trust,
Are gone to Rome, with letters of credit,
To explain to the pope how, and by what agreement,
Gascony was given up with the appurtenance.
The pope has understood by their explanation
What evil, and what damages, and how frequently grievance,
English and French have had by the quarrel,
He has made discussion of the great disagreement,
And has sent to the king part of his will.
May God by his power put there a good accord!

Anno Domini 1298

While pope Boniface waits
To provide the accord between the two kings,
The king sir Edward takes his way back
Right towards England, with sail and with wind.[1]
The earl of Menteith, who was his kinsman,
And the earl of Asketil, the Comyn likewise,
Son of him of Badenagh, and others to the number of thirty,
Whom king Edward without gold or silver
Let quit out of his prison,
Prayed devoutly to go on a pilgrimage.
When they have leave, hear how
They went treacherously to king Philip of France,
Prayed him for succour and advancement
Wherewith to recover Scotland with the appurtenance,
To hold of him for ever.
King Philip replies, "Fools, go away with you,
The pope by his letter sends and forbids me

[1] He landed at Sandwich on 14 March 1298.

To attack the land which belongs to king Edward,
So long as our truce remains upon judgment."
The false company finds itself without aid,
They go hastily to the port of the sea,
They find there the passage ready, promise largely,
Cause themselves to be embarked, do not hesitate for storm,
Arrive in Scotland without impediment.
The king sir Edward learns by hearsay
How the Scots have betrayed him often.
Then he goes to visit St Thomas of Kent
St John of Beverley, very devoutly,
St William of York, St Cuthbert likewise;
Then he goes towards the North to his liege people,
Causes them to assemble, and holds a parliament.
These speak, and provide, and are of one assent,
To go into Scotland and take vengeance,
And deprive the Scots of land and tenement.
Now hear what vengeance God Almighty
Took there by his power on the false people,
Who robbed holy church of its garment,
And renewed the war contrary to their oath.

On the day of the Magdalen, after Midsummer,
The wretched people of Scotland and Galloway,
As many as were bred and born in the Marches,
Each with spear in fist ready to do mischief,
Are come to Falkirk in a morning,
Arranged in order of battle against the English.
In their van guard back was placed against back,
And point of lance on point, in squadrons so serried,
Like castle in plain surrounded with wall.
The multitude was so very fierce,
And so eager to destroy the English,
They imagined not for truth that all the race
Through the whole length of the land from Perth to Pevensey
With king Edward, could have pierced through them.
King Edward sees them coming down the meadow,
He shouts to his barons, "Let us advance in God's name!"
Then earls and barons spur their steeds;
He who can run quickest goes into the battle.
The knights on the other side who were mounted,
When they see the banner of Edward the wise
With the three leopards displayed in the field,
Now fled and left without aid

All their footmen, have abandoned and lost them.
The army of the common soldiers was now severed
By the power of the English, who had no mercy;
Like flies died there a hundred thousand by sword blows;
The others fled, the place was cleared
Of all the race between prime and none,
And not one of the English was killed or left on the field,
Except brother Brian de Jai, a knight of worth,
Appointed high master of the Temple on this side the sea.
He pursued the Scots to a slough,
And following without succour there was slain.
The Welsh gave no assistance in the battle,
They voluntarily took their position on a mountain,
Until the battle there was terminated.

Anno Domini 1299

After the battle the king came back,
He gave the custody of the realm of Scotland
To his English barons, by whom he believed he should
Curb the Scot, that he would rebel no more.
When he came to London, the pope sent to command him.
That he should take to wife the sister of the king of France,
Whereby the war of Gascony should cease;
Not the lady Blanche, of whom people spoke first,
But the lady Margaret, in whose least finger
There is more goodness and beauty, whoever looks at her,
Than in the fair Idione whom Adamas loved.
The king receives the message courteously,
And from day to day provides for that.
On which affair when he was most occupied,
The earl Marshal approached to London,
Earl Humphrey de Bohun came there with great retinue,
He found there enough of earls and barons.
Earl Roger for the commons went to the king,
And in good love earnestly prayed him
That without further delay the perambulation should be made.
The king wishes to delay the perambulation,
Nevertheless he gave a very courteous reply,
Showed to earl Roger the pope's message,
And in good faith promised and swore
That, when he had espoused the damsel,
He would appoint people to execute the perambulation,
With whom no one of his kingdom would be dissatisfied.
So courteous was his saying which he then spoke to the earl,

So fair his word, and it sounded so well,
That count and baron that time believed it,
And each returned to his country.
The earl Humphrey de Bohun after this lay down ill;
Death takes him, alas! his son Humphrey by right
Claims the heritage of his father, and receives it.

Now after, king Philip of France
Has heard news that, by the alliance
Of his sister Margaret, the common ordinance
Of the court of Rome would cause to be appeased the quarrel
About the duchy of Aquitaine with the appurtenance.
King Philip consents to it like an obedient son,
And causes purveyance to be made for the damsel;
He sends her into England with people of knowledge.
She is arrived at Dover without any impediment,
Where people meet her with great ceremony;
They take her to Canterbury, where without delay
The espousals are made according to the same covenant
Of which the court of Rome drew up the terms.

The archbishop Robert de Winchelsea
Performed the ceremony of the espousals,
The Wednesday before the Nativity
Of the glorious virgin Mary, the mother of God.
In the winter following, the king ill advised
Went towards Scotland without aid of his barons;
When he came to the March, he has reviewed his army,
Sees it small, and poor, and disheartened.
The Scot on the other side sees him, has shown him his face,
Offers him battle; the king has not power there
To visit Scotland or support a battle.
As before he has left the March under a warden,
Without doing more this time he is returned to the south;
He has spent his money, and gained no more there.
His chance was very poor in the year of the Jubilee;
Know for certain that was caused by the perambulation,
Which was not performed as it was granted.

Of the parliament of the perambulation

At Easter following the king has summoned
Archbishops, bishops, earls, and barons,
Four knights of each of the counties,
To London to parliament for several causes.

At the beginning are named the persons
To make the perambulation round the country.
When that shall be completed through the kingdoms,
The commons have granted to the king in reward
The twentieth penny of their possessions.
Afterwards it was debated, agreed to by some,
To send to the pope to know his reply,
Why to king Edward he will not by his reasons
Judge back the possession of the land of the Gascons.

In the third article of that parliament,
King Edward asked for succour of his people
Wherewith to reassemble his army against the stinking Scot
After Midsummer, by common assent,
Their adjournment was at Carlisle;
Southerns and Northerns for their lordships
Who owe him service go thither well-willing,
The earl Marshal Roger feels himself discouraged,
Presents sir John de Segrave in his place,
To do the service in as much as belongs to him.
Queen Margaret, by command
Of her lord the king, proceeds towards the North;
She was advanced in pregnancy; by will of God Almighty,
At Brotherton on the Wharf she is safely delivered
Of a son, who is named Thomas in his baptism.
King Edward receives information of it, prepares quickly
To visit the lady, like a falcon before the wind.
After her purification made solemnly,
The king resumes his road towards Scotland;
The queen with her son waits at Cawood,
On the river Ouse, much at her ease.

Of the entrance of the king into Scotland

The king at Carlisle talks with his barons,
So that by some he is advised
To pass through Galloway and destroy the countries,
Sweep and clear pastures and meadows
Of the cattle to salt, where he found enough.
The country is warned, the people informed of it
Drive their cattle among the bogs,
Into the moors and marshes of such depth
A foreigner knows not where to hold his feet.
Then the weather changes, the showers come,
They descend from the mountains into the plains and valleys,

Overflow the rivers, cover the ditches,
King Edward knows not on what side to pass the fords,
Changes his roads, takes to the easiest.
A poor little castle, called Caerlaverok,
King Edward takes, no soul found in it,
Except ribalds who hold it, vanquished at the entrance.
Among these affairs, in form of friendship,
The king of France has asked king Edward
Peace for the Scots in the name of the Trinity.
In the year after following he has granted him the truce,
And king Edward is returned to London.

Idleness and fained delay, and long morning's sleep,
Delight in luxury, and surfeit in the evenings,
Trust in felons, compassion for enemies,
Self-will in act and counsel,
To retain conquest without giving distributions of gain,
Overthrew the Britons in old times.
We may take example of Arthur the wise;
He was always the first in all his expeditions
In morning and in evening, with great magnanimity;
Felons in company, and hostile people,
According to their desert, he condemned them all.
He was temperate in deed and in counsel;
A prince more courteous in conquering lands
Was never born among Christians.
Wherefore I tell you, listen to the reason,
If our king had performed the perambulations
Through England, as he had granted
And strengthened by writing, as is well witnessed,
And of the land of Scotland had shared and given
To his English barons, by just quantities,
The land over there would have been in his power,
And his men heritors of it for ever.
The end of this war you will hear afterwards.

Anno Domini 1300

At the Easter afterwards, the king caused to be assembled
At Lincoln on the Witham his entire parliament,
Of earls and barons, of prelates of the minster,
Who come willingly at the day appointed,
And to Edward first make their complaint

How he has not carried out the perambulation according
to his duty;
How the great charter, which cost much money,
He suffers not to be held nor the points acted upon;
How his ministers go to ravage the land
By seizures for forfeit,[1] without paying money;
And thereupon they complain of his treasurer,
Who through the land gives command for the wrongs,
And from day to day labours to overthrow
Old usages and the laws of the exchequer.
They pray him in love to dismiss this man,
And by common assent appoint another,
Who may be able to execute this office with safety.
King Edward replies with anger in his heart,
"I see that through pride you intend to insult me,
When you think to drive me to so low condition;
There is not one of you who has not full power,
Without assent of another, to arrange his household,
To appoint bailiffs and stewards under him,
Whom at his pleasure he will be able to judge.
Nor ought any one to push a lord lower than himself,
Nor will I suffer it as long as I am to reign.
But if my officers have caused injury to you,
When I know the truth I will cause the wrong to be amended
That you shall hear no more talk of such acts of violence.
The charter of liberties and of the perambulation
Will undo my crown, if I were to grant them;
Which you ought to join with me in supporting,
That it be not damaged by taking by force or by prayer.
Wherefore I grant you the right to examine
By twenty-six discreet men, who will give judgment,
If I can yield to your petitions,
And save the crown in dismembering it so much.
On another side, I say to you, I am without money,
Of which I must have aid of my land,
If I am to recommence the war of Scotland.
You know my reasons, now go and discuss them."
The clergy and the barons go now to the discussion;
The twenty-six discreet men, who go to consult,
They treat on the things, avoid erring,
Lest they might be afterwards accused of disloyalty;
They desire to discharge themselves of so great an oath,
And return answer to the king: "Sir, it is not the manner

[1] ? excessive prises

For a king or a prince to overthrow his covenant,
Nor put in question a thing sold dear;
It would be fairer in thee to advance thy people
By thy courtesy, than by putting questions to arbitration,
Or to the judgment of him who is not thy peer;
Repay that which thou owest, and we ought to love thee,
And serve and honour thee as a liege lord,
And aid thee in taking vengeance of thy enemies."
The king covertly sends them back an answer,
As he who has no desire to ease his people with what is his,
Nor they truly him by gift or by tax;
But they go in parties to dispute against
All his demands, without allowing any.
It was so hard to bear the altercations,
That the people were in doubt between peace and war;
But God interposed his counsel, who can aid when he will,
And he threw so much of his grace into it, that all agree,
After Michaelmas, to raise for the king's use
The fifteenth penny, in exchange for well confirming
The charter of liberties without abating anything,
And for fixing exact bounds for the perambulation
Through the kingdom, without sparing any one
And they agree to go to the war of Scotland.
Of the dispute about Gascony they wait messengers,
The earl of Lincoln, who was beyond sea,
The earl of Savoy, and Hugh le Despenser,
Sir John de Berwick, a very wise baron,
Who were then at Rome to argue with the pope,
That without more delay he would declare
To whom the right to Gascony ought to remain,
And by his decree pronounce peace.
Let us hear pope Boniface tell the case.
He sent for the messengers of France into his presence,
And likewise the English, began to preach them,
"They say in your two lands there are people of great knowledge,
Who ought by reason to support their kings,
Without giving so much trouble to us or our court;
Return to your lands, announce to your kings,
That they come to agreement of themselves, if not, by St Peter,
On St Andrew's day, at the approach of winter,
We will give the decree with judgment so solid,
That one and the other must need respect it."

The messengers return, without further report.
Let us return to the history; we must record
The end of the parliament, be willing to listen to it.

The king sir Edward, at that parliament,
Gave fully to his son Edward
The lordship of Wales, without reserve,
The county of Chester with its appurtenance,
And Pontivy and Montreuil, with the honour belonging.
The son is prince and earl, and takes the homages;
He prepares himself earnestly towards the war of Scotland
With thirty thousand Welshmen, besides other good men,
Earls and barons, knights at will,
And they come to Carlisle with pavilion and tent,
Talk and provide on which side and how
They shall be able to pass the sea of Scotland towards the west.
King Edward the father goes towards the east,
By way of Berwick-on-Tweed, where he waits a while
With his knights, and they are of one accord
To clear that march at the beginning
Of the false lineage of Scotland by whom they are often betrayed.
Amid these affairs, by command
Of pope Boniface, there arrives suddenly
The bishop of Spoleto, with new messages;
And from the king of France a man of convent,
The abbot of Compiegne, I know not nor for what purpose,
Nor for what message truly;
Wherefore we must remain quiet upon the history,
Until the news is made known openly,
That no one may say that this writing lies.

The king has received the letter of credit,
And by the messenger understood its substance;
He has put in abeyance his war against Scotland;
His son returns to Linlithgow without delay.
The king then proclaims his peace, the Scot is in balance;
As he did before, he remains in his tenancy.
The king returns to London, and holds there conference,
In which a truce is arranged on good assurance
Until St Andrew's day, confirmed by pledges.
That the pope did in holy hope
Within the time of peace to make accord

Between the two kings of England and France.
I have discovered to you the fact, now hear the mishap
Which is happened to France, and what honour
Is accrued to Flanders by stroke of sword and spear,
Over the fraud of France, the pomp, and the boasting;
Shortly to tell it, listen to the vengeance.

Count Guy of Flanders, against whom contention
The king of France had by sudden cause,
Was shamefully betrayed by Charles,
Who was bound by agreement the count
To bring and take back in safety
To the parliament of France among the barons.
The count, when he came, was taken like a thief,
And carried and put in prison like a felon.
King Philip of France, after the treason,
Causes Flanders to be seized to his subjection;
He places there wardens of his own in land and houses.
They make destruction of the goods of the rich men,
Violate their wives and daughters at will.
The townships consult upon it, the people around
Drive out the French without any remaining;
Some left there what they carried in their hats.
King Philip hears tell of it, provides an army of occupation
To destroy Flanders without redemption.
The army is fitted out, raises its banners;
The leader of it was the count of Artois by name.
He was the first who lost his escutcheon;
A ribald slew him without confession.
The count of Eu lost both head and heel,
And the count of Albermarle member and chin.
The lord Pierre de Flote, Godfrey de Brabazon,
The two lords de Nele, knights of renown,
Sir William de Fens, his kinsmen in fine,
The most renowned of France by election,
And bannerets without number, of whom I have no mention,
Died in the battle, falling on the sand.
The man of Henalt falls like a bird in a snare.
Of Norman, or Picard, or the Burgundian,
Or Viennese, or Basque, or Brabanter, or Breton,
Neither this time nor other, was there abundance.
In each occurrence since the dissension,
The defeat is fallen upon France;
As long as the world lasts in each kingdom

The shame is lasting, the fact in mockery
Of king Philip of France and of his nation.
May He who sustained Abacuc in prison,
And saved Daniel from the bite of the lion,
Save the Flemings and their action,
That they lose not their heritage by extortion.
Let us return to the history, let us resume the lesson,
To speak of the English without making mixture,
Except so far as the matter reasonably demands.

In truth, in the year a thousand, as we find written,
And three hundred and two, from the birth of Jesus Christ,
The earl of Carrick deserted the Scots,
He willingly surrendered himself to the people of king Edward.
The earl Humfrey de Bohun that year took to wife
The daughter of king Edward, Elizabeth is she called.
Amid these affairs counsel interfered
Between the two kings that war should not happen,
To continue the truce, so that peace should be preserved
Until after Easter; Philip thereupon requires
That king Edward would in love
A conduct through his land, without evil and without ill-feeling,
Grant to the Scots, for whom he sent
To come to him in France, and sir Edward assented;
And to avoid danger immediately afterwards provides
That John de Hastings, a knight of choice,
And Emery de la Brette, no little baron,
Should go into Gascony immediately without contradiction,
To wait the term of the aforesaid truce.
We English believe that negligence is accursed;
For when we have most pleasure in striking well,
Dishonour comes upon us and loss by delay.
I speak for the Scot who the other day attacked
Our English in Scotland by a sudden onset;
Sir John de Segrave took to flight,
His son and his brother, after rising from bed,
And sixteen knights undressed, [the Scot] took by surprise,
Serjeants as many as thirty, of whom all surrendered;
He there slew sir Thomas de Nevile, knight,
And Ralph the cofferer, who offered much money
To Simon Fresel that he should not die there.
Fresel looks at him, Fresel replies to him,
"Thou hast betrayed the king who made thee treasurer,
And me and many others, of whom not one is acquitted

Of the wages which thou owest by reckoning and by writing;
Now art thou found here without alb and without amice,
In hauberk of iron, which is not a habit
For clergy of holy church in which he chants and reads;
Thou shalt have judgment according to thy merit."
A ribald near at hand, who heard it all so well,
Now seized the wretched cofferer,
Cut off his hands, his head departed from him;
By such manner of war he took leave of arms.

Amidst these affairs, great quarrel
Between the king of France, lord of St Denis,
And Boniface the pope, arose through hastiness of temper.
The king laid to the charge of the pope heresy,
The sin of Sodom, usury, and simony,
Error and misbelief in idolatry,
Robbery of holy church, fraud, and heretical tenets,
Fatal for ever to soul as well as to life.
Of such misbelief Philip accuses the pope;
Crime more horrible, or greater disgrace,
Was never heard of the head of holy church.
Boniface takes counsel by wisdom and by clergy;
Causes to be assembled the masters in theology,
These talk and provide that the quarrel be appeased,
And that king Philip correct himself in that,
And make amends for his offence
To God and holy church; if not, the pope grants
That for the error France be punished
By common interdict and by crusade,
As land renegate, which sets God at defiance.
In time afterwards you will hear the end of this madness;
Let us return to the history, that it be not forgotten.

Anno Domini 1303

In the summer after, without more delaying,
The king sir Edward goes to lay Scotland waste;
By the advice of some, he first causes to be built of timber
Ships, boats, and barges, and crossed with hurdles,
In manner of a bridge, by chance there was no need of it,
The shore is passed without ship and mariner.
The Scot sees him come, turns his behind upon him,
Flying back towards moors and mountains like a thief.
The king causes his army to be divided in parts:
Some of the barons, with the earl of Ulster,

Go towards the west to despoil the land;
The king undertakes his expedition towards the east.
Hamlets and towns, granges and barns,
Both full and empty, he burns everywhere;
So does the prince, without sparing anything.
The king goes so far to the north pursuing the Scot,
Where never English king carried banner before.
The aliens of the isles hear talk of it,
Their earls go to hold counsel on it,
They submit to peace, and go to the king to swear
That they will be loyal to him by land and by sea.
The weather afterwards changes, and winter comes on;
The king goes to take rest at Dumfermlin.
The queen comes thither, the king causes her to be sent for.
The lord of Badenagh goes skulking about,
Fresel and Wallace go with him robbing.
Henceforth they have nothing to fry, or drink, or eat,
Nor power remaining wherewith to manage war;
They are come to the king to solicit his peace.
The king on the demand gives them a day,
Whereby I fear me much that courtesy of heart
Will make ſor us the new sauce worse than the first,
Trust in a felon may no man have.

Now listen how, in the year beforesaid,
To our pope was done great despite
By the Colonnas, of the lineage of Rome elected
Cardinals they were, I know not by what merit.
The pope deposed them and deprived them of the habit;
Destroyed their lands, threw down their castles,
Gave their dignities away, sent them into exile.
Their kindred was large, felt itself aggrieved,
They went without delay to the others in Sicily;
Philip king of France sent them aid.
They went to Anagni, where Boniface was born;
The entered the city, the citizen joined them.
The Colonnas in truth captured there the pope,
And then seized the whole of his treasure.
The pope was two days in confinement without meat;
He got out on the third day through aid which arrived;
Of all the great treasure which he amassed in his time,
He had no more left than Job when he sat on the dunghill.
The sum of money which Boniface lost,
Nor how much they returned him back,

Nor of fees of cost, it was never known;
But I have learnt for truth that he went away terrified
Thereupon towards Rome, where he lived three days,
He is dead there without fail, and lies at St Peter's.
We have a new bull, the name written Benedict,
Which repeals part of what Boniface provided.
The robber is absolved who before did so much wrong.
He is very foolish and mad who puts his trust in Rome.
For however much he may give to great and to little,
Rome mocks us by doing and undoing.
No more! we have sufficiently dwelt upon matters abroad.

Our subject compels us to return to the history,
To treating with the Scots for peace without molestation,
To William Wallace who lies in the forest.
At Dunfermlin, after the holy festival
Of Christmas, through friends he has made request to the king,
That he may submit to his honest peace,
Without surrendering into his hands body or head;
But that the king grant him, of his gift, not as a loan,
An honourable allowance of woods and cattle,
And by his writing the seisure and investment
For him and for his heirs in purchased land.
The king, angered at this demand, breaks into a rage,
Commends him to the devil, and all that grows on him,
Promises three hundred marks to the man who makes him headless.
Wallace makes ready to seek concealment by flight
Into moors and mountains, he lives by robbery.

Anno Domini 1304

Now hear the form which the king grants
Of peace to the Scots who are at his mercy,
And who were adjourned for their outrage,
To receive judgment, that no one find fault with it.
The king has granted them by his courtesy,
Land and domain and limb and life,
Except on all parts to his lordship
Ransom of each according to his folly.
Sir Simon Fresel, excepted in the party,
Is condemned to exile for his felony
Into a foreign kingdom, where he has no friend.
He shall make his dwelling there two years, the third, if he be alive,
He shall repair in peace to his lordship.
In Lent after this affair finished,

The king proceeds to St Andrews, proclaims his peace there.
The bishop of Glasgow comes there, with the clergy
Of the realm of Scotland, and each binds himself
To the king's peace, the king yields to that,
Excepted the amends to his lordship,
As they shall be ordered, without other escape,
By him and the communalty of his barony.

Of the taking of the castle of Stirling

The king after Easter takes his departure,
With his knighthood, to besiege Stirling.
When they are come there, they go and examine the place,
And cause to be raised there thirteen great engines.
Two knights had the castle in ward,
Sir William Olifard was the first,
I heard the other named sir William of Dipplyn,
And twenty gentlemen, besides pages and porter,
A Jacobin friar, a monk as counsellor,
And thirteen gentlewomen with their laundress;
No more persons they numbered there.
They had an engine, and brought it out to cast;
The rod broke, afterwards it was of no use.
The engines without are put to work,
And cause the stones to pass walls and towers;
They overthrow the battlements around,
And throw down to the ground the houses inside.
In the midst of these doings the king causes to be built of timber
A terrible engine, and to be called Ludgar;
And this at its stroke broke down the entire wall.
Three months and eight days, reckoning by days,
Lasted the storm; the endurance was hard
To wretches within, who had nothing to eat.
From no side came to them succour or power,
Wherefore they desire much to have the king's peace;
By intermessengers they often solicit him.
The king sends them word that he will not grant it so soon.
So long the conference for peace dragged out,
That I know not nor can I record the half of it;
But I have heard well that, in the sequel,
The castle was surrendered to the king at his will,
So that those within, knight, squire,
And all the others, without making conditions,
Put themselves in his pardon with piteousness of heart.
The castle is taken possession of; the king causes to be appointed

Wardens throughout the land to judge the people;
He will not dwell in a land so wasted,
Returns with victory back into England.

How Stirling was surrendered

In September following, Stirling is surrendered;
The king sir Edward has felt his labours.
He has taken his way towards Brustwick-on-Humber;
Takes there his sojourn a while for his health.
Sir John de Warenne, an earl well known,
Was then dead, and ready to put in his coffin.
The king, whom God preserve! in going towards the south
Through Lindsey, inquires from place to place,
While he was in his war in Scotland,
Who have broken his peace, who have held his peace;
In order that according to his will remedy might be provided
For him who was convicted of his peace broken.
People of good will have made reply to the king,
How throughout the land is made a great grievance
By common quarrellers, who are by oath
Bound together to a compact;
Those of that company are named Trailbastons,
In fairs and markets they offer themselves to make an engagement,
For three shillings or four, or for the worth,
To beat a freeman who never did injury
To Christian body, by any evidence.
If a man offends any one of the confederacy,
Or a merchant refuses to give him credit with his wares,
In his own house, without other dealing,
He should be well beaten, or to make it up
He shall give of his money, and take acquittance.
If there be not some stop put to this turbulence,
A war of the commons will arise by chance.
The king has heard the complaint and the talk;
Now hear how the vengeance is provided.

Anno Domini 1305

Through England people of great judgment
Are appointed judges upon the Trailbastons.
Some by trial are condemned to imprisonment,
Others gone to hang about on gallows;
Several are deprived of their property;
Who offended least are allowed to escape by fines.
If there were no chastisement of ribalds and rogues,

A man would not dare to live in house.
O how God is good in his righteous rewards!
Who so often has revenged us on felons.
We have heard news, among companions,
Of William Wallace, the master of thieves;
Sir John de Meneteith followed him at his heels,
Took him in hiding by the side of his concubine;
Carried him to London in shackles and bonds,
Where he was judged on the following conditions:
In the first place to the gallows he was drawn for treasons,
Hanged for robberies and slaughters;
And because he had annihilated by burnings,
Towns and churches and monasteries,
He is taken down from the gallows, his belly opened,
His heart and his bowels burnt to cinders,
And his head cut off for such treasons as follow:
Because he had by his assumptions of authority
Maintained the war, given protections,
Seized into his subjection the lordship
Of another's kingdom by his usurpations.
His body was cut into four parts;
Each one hangs by itself, in memory of his name,
In place of his banner these are his gonfanons.
To finish his history,
His head is at London,
Of the body is made partition
In four good towns,
Wherewith to honour the isles
Which are in Albany.
And thus may you hear
To teach a lad
To build in peace;
It falls in his eye,
Who hacks over high,
Take example of Wallace.

By the death of Wallace may one bear in mind
What reward belongs to traitor and to thief,
And what divers wages to divers trespasses.
Of earl Robert de Brus we must now relate,
In the Lent following how he invited
The lord of Badenagh to come and talk with him,
At Dumfries in the church of the Friars Minors;
Where earl Robert, leaning upon the altar,

Slew the Badenagh through felony of heart,
Because he would not agree with him
To raise war against king Edward,
And by dint of sword obtain the kingdom
For him, who then said he was the right king.
After the felony, without remaining long,
He caused to be re-erected a new seat at Scone,
And he took there the garland which the king used to wear,
In sign of lordship, at his coronation.
Now after he caused everywhere to be proclaimed
To voyd cities, boroughs, and towns of the English.
Two bishops were primates at the investment,
With the abbot of Scone, who afterwards paid it dear,
Earls and barons, knights and squires,
Were councillors of the kingdom of Scotland,
Sworn to aid the Bruce by land and by sea;
Their names you will hear afterwards in talking of the vengeance.
The Bruce goes as king to order his wars.
King Edward hears tell of it, sends thither sir Aymer,
Earl of Pembroke, to check the madman.
He causes him to be accompanied with English barons,
Who, thank God! have done their duty well over there.

Anno Domini 1306

After the festival of Easter in the year here named,
The king has proclaimed his feast of Whitsuntide
To be held at Westminster, with clergy and with barons,
Where, with great nobleness, to his eldest son,
Edward prince of Wales, he has given arms.
Three hundred knights of account in truth
Were dubbed at the cost of king Edward.
Several of the most noble were married on that occasion.
The earl of Warenne, with his newly received title,
Espoused the daughter of the count de Barre.
The earl of Arundel, in possession of his fees,
Took there the damsel whose father was named
William de Warenne, who had departed to God.
Sir Hugh son of Hugh, called Despenser,
Took there the maiden of noble kindred,
Whom Gilbert de Clare had begotten
On Joan the countess surnamed of Acres.
No soul wonders there was game and joy enough,
Where a feast was held with such ceremonies.
Never in Britain, since God was born,

Was there such nobleness in towns nor in cities,
Except Caerleon in ancient times,
When sir Arthur the king was crowned there.
The prince, whom God preserve! of whom we have spoken,
After the said feast has taken his leave
With joyous company, and gone towards the north,
To seek king Robin wherever he may be found.
King Edward, his father, afterwards made his progress
As far as Lanercost, where he is laid down ill,
Until God above has restored his strength.

Now after spring up the griefs
For abbots, for bishops, and for the clergy, for many of the laity,
Of the land of Scotland, for people often perjured.
Sir Aymer de Valence, with his cavalry,
Had taken his residence within St John's Town [Perth];
There were there the best of the barons of Scotland.
King Robin receives information of it, consults with his adherents,
Summons sir Aymer by his ambassadors
To give up to him the town, to deliver the traitors
Who had deserted him to their dishonour.
On the morning of the morrow, Robin in his wanderings,
His armour covered with surplices and skirts,
Offers battle, he will try his courage.
Sir Aymer de Valance sallies out of the walls;
Robin slew his steed at the first attack,
The earl is remounted, he has succour from his own people;
Robin turns his back upon him, flies elsewhere.
Then began the chace, and lasted so many hours,
Till Robert had neither castles nor towers,
Nor refuge in town or among receivers.
Fresel, I know not how, escaped from the battle;
He is taken, carried to London, drawn, and hanged on gallows,
His head was cut off, and without chaplet of flowers,
Raised up on the bridge, the body was burnt.
In him, through his falseness, perished much worth.

Now hear what disgrace is come upon the clergy
Of the land of Scotland, disturbed by the war.
The bishop of St Andrews has lost honour,
And the abbot of Scone, and the bishop of Glasgow,
Are sent in fetters on hackneys towards the south;
Each is held in a separate prison,
Until the pope has become better acquainted with the fact.

To clergy and laymen without number who have maintained the war,
Equally as to a robber is judgment rendered.
Christopher de Seaton, not unknown,
Is drawn and hanged on account of John of Badenagh;
And the earl of Asketil has received judgment
Similar to that of the Fresel, and in the same place,
By command of the king the drawing was omitted.
Alas! the noble blood which was thus spilt!
King Robin has drunk of the drink of dan Warin,
Who lost cities and towns by the shield,
Afterwards in the forest, mad and naked,
He fed with the cattle on the raw grass.
His book bears witness of it, which is read concerning him.

While king Robin is running about and committing violence,
Sir Arthur of Britany, a duke of high kindred,
Comes into England to seek his inheritance,
Richmondshire, with the rents and profit,
With wards and reliefs, forest and pannage,
To hold by homage of the king sir Edward.
To speak briefly, he had a light answer.
Duke Arthur returns with heavy spirit;
To sir John his brother, of younger age,
Is given the county, without new services,
To hold in fee by ancient usage
Of the king sir Edward and of his lineage.
The King of kings, through whom storm of sea becomes calmed,
Grant there arrive neither loss nor damage!

The duke is repassed the sea to Britany;
Who would discourse further of the mad king Robin,
He may make mention of sir Thomas de Bruce,
And of sir Alexander, of whom my heart doubts,
High dean of Glasgow and rich beneficiary;
By appointment of king Robin, to their trouble,
Whose friends they were, they went to spy,
In order to destroy the English without sparing any.
A sergeant of Galloway, I heard him named Macdowel,
On Ash Wednesday, as they were coming from the minster,
Took them by surprise, and caused them to be bound,
And to be sent to Carlisle to king Edward.
When the king was informed of it, he caused judges to be appointed,
And Thomas de Bruce to be hanged and drawn,
And sir Alexander to be sent to the gallows,

And after the hanging the two to be beheaded.
Pope Boniface caused to be determined,
In the sixth book which he had compiled,
What clerks in what case one ought to save,
And what clerks in what habit one ought to condemn,
As robbers and thieves, when attainted of felony.
Were it not for the statute made in such manner,
The clergy would be more daring to violate God's peace.

Anno Domini 1307

At the Easter following, at Carlisle with his people
The king sir Edward holds his parliament;
A cardinal from Rome comes there solemnly,
For that marriage of which was often speech,
Between the prince of Wales and the fair maiden
Daughter of the king of France, if one successfully
Could then make an arrangement of that treaty.
Of several things they treated likewise.
By clerks of holy church fairly enough
A statute was made, repelled without assent.
The earl and the baron reject it unjustly.
Of all the great counsel the end was
That king Edward, without delay,
Should cause to be sent to London people of wisdom,
To see and explain to king Philip how
The said marriage will be able profitably
To be confirmed, without further negotiation about it.
Now may God Almighty grant it be well!

King Robin still in moors and marshes
Wanders in his turbulence, sir John Wallace
Is taken in the plain pursued by the northerners,
And sent to London fettered on a hackney.
When he came to Westminster among the southerners,
According to his deserts he was judged by the laws.
His punishment was divided into three punishments;
He was let down from the gallows in shirt and breeches,
His head afterwards cut off and carried by the Londoners
On the bridge of London, and raised with shouts
Near the head of his brother William the wicked,
Who never had pity on an English Christian,
Knight and parson, citizen and burgher,
And canon and monk, and brothers of abbeys,
He put them all to the sword without having peace.

May everywhere be honoured the high true God,
By whose holy grace Edward our king
Has destroyed the thief and all his puny line.

Of the death of the illustrious king Edward

O Lord Almighty, whom the Christian adores,
Every earthly creature is thy work,
In making the world was formed the law,
That man, woman, and beast must die by nature.
Belinus and Brennius, Britons in their pride,
Took Rome by force, and put a truce upon it;
King Arthur afterwards, without wound and without blemish,
Conquered all France, and took possession as his own.
Gawain and Angusele, of his nourishing,
In wars and battles used to follow Arthur.
One must well, among kings who have reigned since that time,
Speak of king Edward and of his memory
As of the most renowned combatant on steed.
Since the time of Adam never was any time
That prince for nobility, or baron for splendour,
Or merchant for wealth, or clerk for learning,
By art or by genius could escape death.
Of chivalry, after king Arthur,
Was king Edward the flower of Christendom.
He was so handsome and great, so powerful in arms,
That of him may one speak as long as the world lasts.
For he had no equal as a knight in armour
For vigour and valour, neither present nor future.
We have of him news dolorous and hard;
Death has taken him, alas! henceforth who will do justice
Upon John of Badenagh, except him who has the care,
Edward the son of Edward, king of the tenure
Which is held by vow to destroy king Robin.

Of the day and death of king Edward aforesaid Anno Domini 1307

In the year just named as we have heard,
The seventh day of July, for truth we certify you,
That our king Edward, whose soul may God bless!

At Burgh-upon-the-Sands, on his way to Albany,
In true faith has ended his life.
Now after his death was made public,
The body is transported by barons and by clergy
To Waltham near London, his own abbey,
Four months entire served with solemn service.
It lay embalmed on the bier, without sparing of
wealth
Distributing to the poor who pray for that soul.
Thirty-four years, eight months, and five days, I tell
you,
He reigned over England by established law,
By reason and right he maintained the monarchy;
Of vigour and worth, and full of understanding,
He had no equal in ruling a lordship.
Beside his kindred now is the body buried,
At Westminster, in tomb of marble well polished.
May the Prince who for us was punished under
Pilate
Receive king Edward into his mercy;
Give remission to his soul of the sins committed in
his life,
Take him to his company there into regal mansion,
Where there is no service except joy and melody.

12. The Chronicle of Lanercost for the years A.D. 1315–23

(*Chronicon de Lanercost*, ed. Joseph Stevenson, 2 vols (Edinburgh, for the Maitland and Bannatyne Clubs, 1839); the 1315–23 portion trans. Sir Herbert Maxwell, *The Chronicle of Lanercost 1272–1346* (Glasgow, 1913), pp. 212–46)

Basically a Franciscan chronicle adapted, abbreviated and interpolated at the Augustinian priory of Lanercost: a masterly examination of these questions of authorship is by A. G. Little, "The authorship of the Lanercost chronicle", *E.H.R.*, xxxi (1916), pp. 269–79 and xxxii (1917), pp. 48–9, reprinted in *Franciscan Papers, Lists and Documents* (Manchester, 1943), pp. 42–54.

The extract translated by Maxwell gives not only vivid illustrations of the insecurity of the north but also a northern, as distinct from the southern English attitude to the Scots war.

[1315] At this time also the Scots again wasted Northumberland; but from the aforesaid Nativity of our Lord until the Nativity of St John the Baptist [24 June 1315] the county of Cumberland alone paid 600 marks in tribute to the king of Scots.

The Scots, therefore, unduly elated, as much by their victory in the field[1] as by the devastation of the March of England and the receipt of very large sums of money, were not satisfied with their own frontiers, but fitted out ships and sailed to Ireland in the month of May, to reduce that country to subjection if they could. Their commanders were my lord Edward Bruce, the king's brother, and his kinsman my lord Thomas Randolf, earl of Moray, both enterprising and valiant knights, having a very

[1] at Bannockburn, the year before

strong force with them. Landing in Ireland, and receiving some slight aid from the Irish, they captured from the king of England's dominion much land and many towns, and so prevailed as to have my lord Edward made king by the Irish. Let us leave him reigning there for the present, just as many kinglets reign there, till we shall describe elsewhere how he came to be beheaded, and let us return to Scotland.

The Scots, then, seeing that affairs were going everywhere in their favour, invaded the bishopric of Durham about the feast of the apostles Peter and Paul [29 June], and plundered the town of Hartlepool, whence the people took to the sea in ships; but they did not burn it. On their return they carried away very much booty from the bishopric.

Also, a little later in the same year, on the feast of St Mary Magdalene [22 July], the king of Scotland, having mustered all his forces, came to Carlisle, invested the city and besieged it for ten days, trampling down all the crops, wasting the suburbs and all within the bounds, burning the whole of that district, and driving in a very great store of cattle for his army from Allerdale, Copland, and Westmorland. On every day of the siege they assaulted one of the three gates of the city, sometimes all three at once; but never without loss, because there were discharged upon them from the walls such dense volleys of darts and arrows, likewise stones, that they asked one another whether stones bred and multiplied within the walls. Now on the fifth day of the siege they set up a machine for casting stones next the church of Holy Trinity, where their king stationed himself, and they cast great stones continually against the Caldew gate[1] and against the wall, but they did little or no injury to those within, except that they killed one man. But there were seven or eight similar machines within the city, besides other engines of war, which are called springalds, for discharging long darts, and staves with sockets for casting stones, which caused great fear and damage to those outside. Meanwhile, however, the Scots set up a certain great berefrai like a kind of tower, which was considerably higher than the city walls. On perceiving this, the carpenters of the city erected upon a tower of the wall against which that engine must come if it had ever reached the wall, a wooden tower loftier than the other; but neither that engine nor any other ever did reach the wall, because, when it was being drawn on wheels over the wet and swampy ground, having stuck there through its own weight, it could neither be taken any further nor do any harm.

Moreover the Scots had made many long ladders, which they brought with them for scaling the wall in different places simultaneously; also a sow[2] for mining the town wall, had they been able; but neither sow nor ladders availed them aught. Also they made great numbers of fascines of corn and herbage to fill the moat outside the wall on the east side, so as they might pass over dry-shod. Also they made long bridges of logs running upon wheels, such as being strongly and swiftly drawn with ropes might reach across the width of the moat. But during all the time the Scots were on the ground neither fascines sufficed to fill the moat, nor those wooden bridges to cross the ditch, but sank to the depths by their own weight.

[1] on the west of the town

[2] A siege engine which was constructed to contain men, who, when the sow was wheeled up to the wall, should proceed to sap the foundation under shelter.

Howbeit on the ninth day of the siege, when all the engines were ready, they delivered a general assault upon all the city gates and upon the whole circuit of the wall, attacking manfully, while the citizens defended themselves just as manfully, and they did the same next day. The Scots also resorted to the same kind of stratagem whereby they had taken Edinburgh castle; for they employed the greater part of their army in delivering an assault upon the eastern side of the city, against the place of the Minorite friars, in order to draw thither the people who were inside. But Sir James of Douglas, a bold and cautious knight, stationed himself, with some others of the army who were most daring and nimble, on the west side opposite the place of the canons and preaching friars, where no attack was expected because of the height [of the wall] and the difficulty of access. There they set up long ladders which they climbed and the bowmen, whereof they had a great number, shot their arrows thickly to prevent anyone showing his head above the wall. But, blessed be God! they met with such resistance there as threw them to the ground with their ladders, so that there and elsewhere round the wall some were killed, others taken prisoners and others wounded; yet throughout the whole siege no Englishman was killed, save one man only who was struck by an arrow (and except the man above mentioned), and few were wounded.

Wherefore on the eleventh day, to wit, the feast of St Peter ad Vincula [1 August], whether because they had heard that the English were approaching to relieve the besieged or whether they despaired of success, the Scots marched off in confusion to their own country, leaving behind them all their engines of war aforesaid. Some Englishmen pursuing them captured John de Moray, who in the aforesaid battle near Stirling[1] had for his share twenty-three English knights, besides esquires and others of meaner rank, and had taken very heavy ransom for them. Also they captured with the aforesaid John, Sir Robert Bardolf, a man specially ill-disposed to the English, and brought them both to Carlisle castle; but they were ransomed later for no small sum of money.

[1316] In the octave of the Epiphany[2] the king of Scotland came stealthily to Berwick one bright moonlit night with a strong force, and delivered an assault by land and sea in boats, intending to enter the town by stealth on the waterside between Brighouse and the castle, where the wall was not yet built, but they were manfully repulsed by the guards and by those who answered to the alarm, and a certain Scottish knight, sir J. de Landels, was killed, and sir James of Douglas escaped with difficulty in a small boat. And thus the whole army was put to confusion.

About the same time, on the morrow of the Conception of the Blessed Mary,[3] my lord Henry de Burgh, prior of Lanercost, died, and was succeeded by sir Robert de Meburne.

About the feast of the Nativity of St John the Baptist[4] the Scots invaded England, burning as before and laying waste all things to the best of their power; and so they went as far as Richmond. But the nobles of that district, who took refuge in Richmond castle and defended the same, compounded with them for a large sum of money so that they might not burn that town, nor yet the district, more than they

[1] Bannockburn [2] 14 January 1316. It was full moon. [3] 9 December [4] 24 June

had already done. Having received this money, the Scots marched away some sixty miles to the west, laying waste everything as far as Furness, and burnt that district whither they had not come before, taking away with them nearly all the goods of that district, with men and women as prisoners. Especially were they delighted with the abundance of iron which they found there, because Scotland is not rich in iron.

Now in that year there was such a mortality of men in England and Scotland through famine and pestilence as had not been heard of in our time. In some of the northern parts of England the quarter of wheat sold for forty shillings.

After the Scots had returned to their own country, their king Robert provided himself with a great force and sailed to Ireland, in order to conquer that country, or a large part thereof, for his brother Edward. He freely traversed nearly all that part of it which was within the king of England's dominion, but he did not take walled towns or castles.

About the same time died master William de Grenefeld, archbishop of York, to whom succeeded my lord William de Meltoun; who, albeit he was one of the king's courtiers, yet led a religious and honourable life. Also in the same year there died my lord Richard de Kellow, bishop of Durham, to whom succeeded my lord Louis de Belmont, a Frenchman of noble birth, but lame on both feet, nevertheless liberal and agreeable. He was appointed by the pope, as was reported, because of a deceitful suggestion, whereby the pope was led to believe that he [Louis] himself would hold the march of England against the Scots.

After the feast of St Michael [29 September], the earl of Lancaster with his adherents marched towards Scotland as far as Newcastle in compliance with the king's behest; but the king declined to follow him as they had agreed upon together, wherefore the earl marched back again at once; for neither of them put any trust in the other.

In the month of October in that year, in the night after the day of St Remigius [1 October], and rather more than an hour after midnight, there was a total eclipse of the moon, and the whole moon was hidden for the space of one hour.

About the same time a certain knight of Northumberland, to wit, sir Gilbert de Middleton, seized and robbed two cardinals, who had landed in England not long before, because they came in the company of the aforesaid Louis de Belmont in order to consecrate him bishop of Durham, as had been commanded by the pope.

Also at the same time a certain knight of Richmond county, to wit sir John de Cleasby, having gathered together a number of malefactors and rogues, rose and devastated the district, plundering, robbing and wasting, at his own and his people's pleasure, just as Sir Gilbert was doing in Northumberland with his accomplices and rogues. But, by God's ordinance, both of them were soon taken. Sir John was put to his penance, because he refused to speak when brought before the justiciaries, and he soon afterwards died in prison. Sir Gilbert, after [suffering] other punishments, was cut into four quarters, which were sent to different places in England.

[1317] About Pentecost [22 May] the king of Scotland returned to his own land from Ireland. In the same year before noon on the sixth day of September there was an eclipse of the sun.

After the feast of St Michael [29 September] the pope sent a bull to England wherein he advised a truce between England and Scotland to last for two years after the receipt of the said bull. Now the English received the said bull with satisfaction, both on account of the dissension between the king and the earl of Lancaster and because of excessive molestation by the Scots arising out of the said dissension, and they hung the bull according to the pope's command in the cathedral churches and other important places. But the Scots refused to accept it, and paid it no manner of respect, and therefore came deplorably under the sentence of excommunication delivered by the pope and contained in the said bull.

In the middle of the said truce pope Clement the fifth died, and pope John the twenty-second was elected.[1]

[1318] On the second day of the month of April, in mid-Lent, about midnight on Saturday, the Scots treacherously took the town of Berwick through means of a certain Englishman, Peter of Spalding, living in the town, who, being bribed by a great sum of money received from them and by the promise of land, allowed them to scale the wall and to enter by that part of the wall where he himself was stationed as guard and sentry. After they had entered and obtained full possession of the town, they expelled all the English, almost naked and despoiled of all their property; howbeit, in their entrance they killed few or none, except those who resisted them.

Also the castles of Wark and Harbottle, to which they had already laid siege, were surrendered to them in that season of Lent, because relief did not reach them on the appointed day. Also they took the castle of Mitford by guile, and subdued nearly the whole of Northumberland as far as the town of Newcastle, except those castles which have not been mentioned above. Howbeit the castle of the town of Berwick defended itself manfully against the town, but at length capitulated through want of victual.

About the same time there arrived in England for the first time the seventh book of Decretals, and the statute of pope Boniface VIII was renewed – *Super cathedram et caetera* – dealing with the relations between prelates of the churches and the orders of Preachers and Minorites, and the statute of pope Benedict XI was revoked, because it seemed to be too much in favour of the friars. Also there came the decree of pope John XXII, under a bull and with the addition of severe penalty, that no cleric should have more than one church; whereas before that time a single rector or parson of a church could accept and hold as many churches as different patrons might be willing to confer upon him, notwithstanding that each such church depended upon his ministrations alone. During the whole of that time these two cardinals remained in England.

In the month of May the Scottish army invaded England further than usual, burning the town of Northallerton and Boroughbridge and sundry other towns on their march, pressing forward as far as the town of Ripon, which town they despoiled of all the goods they could find; and from those who entered the mother church

[1] Clement V died 14 April 1314 and the Holy See was vacant 27 months. John XXII was elected in 1316

and defended it against the Scottish army they exacted one thousand marks instead of burning the town itself.

After they had lain there three days, they went off to Knaresborough, destroying that town with fire, and, searching the woods in that district whither the people had fled for refuge with their cattle, they took away the cattle. And so forth to the town of Skipton in Craven, which they plundered first and then burnt, returning through the middle of that district to Scotland, burning in all directions and driving off a countless quantity of cattle. They made men and women captives, making the poor folks drive the cattle, carrying them off to Scotland without any opposition.

In the same year, about the Nativity of the blessed John the Baptist [24 June], there arrived in Oxford a certain unknown and ignoble individual, who, establishing himself in the king's manor (where the Carmelite friars now dwell), made claim to the kingdom of England, alleging that he was the true heir of the realm as the son of the illustrious king Edward who had long been dead. He declared that my lord Edward, who at that time possessed the kingdom, was not of the blood royal, nor had any right to the realm, which he offered to prove by combat with him or with any one else in his place. When this was reported the whole community became excited and greatly wondered, certain foolish persons yielding adherence to this fellow, all the more readily because the said lord Edward resembled the elder lord Edward in none of his virtues. For it was commonly reported that he [Edward II] had devoted himself privately from his youth to the arts of rowing and driving chariots, digging pits and roofing houses; also that he wrought as a craftsman with his boon companions by night, and at other mechanical arts, besides other vanities and frivolities wherein it doth not become a king's son to busy himself.[1] So when the said report reached the king, who was then at Northampton, he commanded that this man should be brought before him. When he came, the king addressed him derisively, "Welcome, my brother!" but he answered, "Thou art no brother of mine, but falsely thou claimest the kingdom for thyself. Thou hast not a drop of blood from the illustrious Edward, and that I am prepared to prove against thee, or against any one else in thy room."

When he heard these rough words, the king commanded that he should be imprisoned as guilty of lese-majesty, and took counsel with his advisers what should be done with him. After a few days, when the council had been held and a very large number of the people had been assembled, he was brought before the king's steward sitting in judgment, who asked the said man before the people what was his name. He answered that he was called John of Powderham. Whereupon the steward straightway pronounced sentence upon him, saying, "John of Powderham, whereas, either by the most wicked counsel of some other, or out of the iniquity and device of thine own heart, thou hast dared falsely and presumptuously to usurp and claim for thyself the right of inheritance of the realm of England, and whereas thou hast no right in that realm, but art an ignoble and unknown man, I pronounce upon thee as doom that thou be first drawn at the heels of horses, and secondly be hanged on the gallows, and thirdly be burnt."

[1] When John XXII became pope he addressed a long letter to Edward II rebuking him for his fondness for light and boyish pursuits, and reminding him that, now he was king, he should put away childish things.

When this sentence had been pronounced and horses had been brought up to draw him, he, seeing none of the succour at hand which had been promised to him, and perceiving that he had been deceived, besought a hearing for the love of God the lord of Heaven. Having obtained a hearing he began to relate how a certain evil spirit[1] had appeared to him in dreams on various occasions before that time, and had promised him carnal pleasures and many other things that he desired; and always those things which that spirit promised him came to pass shortly afterwards. On one occasion as he was going to walk abroad alone in the fields, a certain man met him, who, after some little familiar conversation, asked him, "Wouldst thou become rich?" When he replied in the affirmative, the other enquired further whether he would like to be king of England. And when he, greatly wondering, replied that he would like to reign if that were by any means possible, the other said to him, "I, who now appear to thee in the likeness of a man, am that spirit which hath often before this appeared to thee in dreams"; and then he added, "Hast thou ever found me untruthful? Have I not fulfilled in act all that I promised thee in words?" He answering said, "I have found no falsehood in thee, but all that thou hast promised thou hast faithfully fulfilled." Then said the other, "Nor shalt thou find me faithless now. Do homage unto me and I will cause thee to reign. And if the king, or any one else in his name, will offer to fight thee for the realm, I will assist thee and cause thee to conquer."

Whereupon he made homage to him, who said, "Go to Oxford taking with thee a dog, a cock and a tom-cat; enter the king's manor, and there publicly claim thy right to the realm of England, and I will cause the hearts of the people to turn to thee, forasmuch as king Edward is by no means deeply beloved by the people."

And when he [John] had related these things – "Thus did that evil spirit beguile me, and behold! I die a shameful death." After this confession had been listened to, he was immediately drawn to the gallows, hanged there and afterwards burnt. Wherefore let everybody beware of the devil's falsehood and his cunning, nor pay any heed to the dreams which he may dream, according to the precept of Jeremy the prophet, as is said in the Book of Wisdom, "Dreams excite the unwary, and as one who catcheth at a shadow and pursueth the wind, so is he who taketh heed to the deceptive visions of a dream."

In the same year, about the feast of the Nativity of the Blessed Virgin [8 September], the cardinals, who then were still in England, wrote to all the prelates of England that in every solemn mass on ordinary days as well as festivals, they should thrice denounce Robert de Brus, with all his counsellors and adherents, as excommunicate; and, by the pope's authority, they proclaimed him infamous and bereft of all honour, and placed all his lands and the lands of all his adherents under ecclesiastical interdict, and disqualified the offspring of all his adherents to the second generation from holding any ecclesiastical office or benefice. Also against all prelates of Scotland and all religious men, whether exempt or not exempt from episcopal jurisdiction, who should adhere to the said Robert or show him favour they promulgated sentence of excommunication and interdict, with other most grievous penalties. Howbeit the

[1] *Spiritus Domini*, in Stevenson's edition, probably a misreading for *spiritus demonis*.

Scots, stubbornly pertinacious, cared nothing for any excommunication, nor would they pay the slightest attention to the interdict. It is not to be wondered at therefore, that afterwards the weighty vengeance of God in the appearance of a true heir of the realm, visited so rebellious a people, whose head (I will not call him king, but usurper) showed such contempt for the keys of holy mother church.

Let us now hear what happened to his brother Edward in Ireland. Within fifteen days after the feast of St Michael,[1] he came to the town of Dundalk with his Irish adherents and a great army of Scots which had newly arrived in Ireland to enable him to invade and lay waste that land and [to harass] the king of England's people to the best of their power. But by God's help, nearly all these were killed by a few of the commonalty, excepting only those who saved themselves by flight; for they were in three columns at such a distance from each other that the first was done with before the second came up, and then the second before the third, with which Edward was marching, could render any aid. Thus the third column was routed, just as the two preceding ones had been. Edward fell at the same time and was beheaded after death; his body being divided into four quarters, which quarters were sent to the four chief towns of Ireland.

[1319] About the feast of the Nativity of St John the Baptist the Christians were defeated by the Saracens in Spain.[2] Also in the same year a permanent agreement, as was thought, having been come to between the king and the earl of Lancaster, they entered Scotland together, with a large army, about the feast of the Assumption of the Glorious Virgin, and set themselves to attack the town of Berwick, and almost scaled the wall in the first assault delivered with great fury, which when those within the wall perceived, many of them fled to the castle; but later, when the English slackened their attack, the inhabitants regained courage and defended themselves with spirit, manning the walls better than before and burning the sow[3] which had been brought up to the wall to mine it.

Meanwhile my lord Thomas Randolf, earl of Moray and sir James of Douglas, not daring to encounter the king of England and the earl [of Lancaster], invaded England with an army, burning the country and taking captives and booty of cattle, and so pressed as far as Boroughbridge. When the citizens of York heard of this, without knowledge of the country people and led by my lord archbishop William de Meltoun and my lord the bishop of Ely, with a great number of priests and clerics, among whom were sundry religious men, both beneficed and mendicant, they attacked the Scots one day after dinner near the town of Mytton, about twelve miles north of York; but, as men unskilled in war, they marched all scattered through the fields and in no kind of array. When the Scots beheld men rushing to fight against them, they formed up according to their custom in a single schiltrom, and then uttered together a tremendous shout to terrify the English, who straightway began to take to their heels at the sound. Then the Scots, breaking up their schiltrom wherein they were massed, mounted their horses and pursued the English, killing both clergy and laymen, so that about

[1] that is, 14 October, the date of the battle of Dundalk

[2] at Granada, on 24 June

[3] see above, p. 266, n. 2

four thousand were slain, among whom fell the mayor of the town, and about one thousand, it was said, were drowned in the water of Swale. Had not night come on, hardly a single Englishman would have escaped. Also many were taken alive, carried off to Scotland and ransomed at a heavy price.[1]

When the king of England, occupied in the siege of Berwick, heard of such transactions in his own country, he wished to send part of his forces to attack the Scots still remaining in England, and to maintain the siege with the rest of his people; but by advice of his nobles, who objected either to divide their forces or to fight the Scots, he raised the siege and marched his army into England, expecting to encounter the Scots. But they got wind of this and entered Scotland with their captives and booty of cattle by way of Stanemoor, Gilsland and those western parts. Then the king disbanded his army, allowing every one to return home, without any good business done.

But the excommunicate Scots, not satisfied with the aforesaid misdeeds, invaded England with an army commanded by the aforesaid two leaders, to wit, Thomas Randolf and James of Douglas, about the feast of All Saints [1 November], when the crop had been stored in barns, and burnt the whole of Gilsland, both the corn upon which the people depended for sustenance during that year and the houses wherein they had been able to take refuge; also, they carried off with them both men and cattle. And so, marching as far as Borough under Stanemoor, they laid all waste, and then returned through Westmorland, doing there as they had done in Gilsland, or worse. Then, after ten or twelve days, they fared through part of Cumberland, which they burnt on their march, and returned to Scotland with a very large spoil of men and cattle.[2]

Howbeit, before the Nativity of our Lord, the wise men of both nations met, and by common consent arranged a truce between the kingdoms, to last for two years, and that truce was proclaimed in the march on the octave of the Nativity of our Lord [1 January 1320].

[1320] At the same time the plague and the murrain of cattle which had lasted through the two preceding years in the southern districts, broke out in the northern districts among oxen and cows, which, after a short sickness, generally died; and few animals of that kind were left, so that men had to plough that year with horses. Howbeit, men used to eat cattle dying in the aforesaid manner, and, by God's ordinance, suffered no ill consequences. At the same time sea fishes were found dead on the shores in great multitude, whereof neither man nor other animal nor bird did eat. Also in the southern parts of England the birds fought most fiercely among themselves and were found dead in great numbers; and all these three [phenomena] seem to have happened either in vengeance upon sinners or as omens of future events.

About the feast of St Michael [29 September] a mandate came from the pope for

[1] This affair was called "the Chapter of Mytton" because of the number of clergy engaged.

[2] These incessant raids provide very monotonous reading; but nothing short of constant repetition could give any adequate notion of the horror and cruelty of this kind of warfare, or of the utterly defenceless condition into which the lamentable rule of Edward II allowed the northern counties to fall.

the denunciation of Robert de Brus as excommunicate with all who held intercourse with him. This, however, was no addition to the sentence pronounced before; and he [Robert] paying no attention thereto, remained as obstinate as ever.

[1321] All lepers who could be found in nearly all parts across the sea as far as Rome, were burnt; for they had been secretly hired at a great price by the pagans to poison the waters of the Christians and thereby to cause their death.

In summer of the same year Humfrey de Bohun, earl of Hereford, sir John de Mowbray, sir Roger de Clifford, with many other barons, knights, esquires and a great force of other horse and foot, entered the March of Wales, and speedily took and occupied without opposition the various castles of sir Hugh Despenser the younger, who was, as it were, the king of England's right eye, and after the death of Piers de Gavestoun, his chief counsellor against the earls and barons. These castles they despoiled of treasure and all other goods, and put keepers therein of their own followers; also they seized the king's castles in those parts, and although they removed the king's arms and standard from the same, they declared that they were doing all these things, not against the crown, but for the crown and law of the realm of England. But all these things were done by advice and command of the earl of Lancaster. These earls and barons were specially animated against the said sir Hugh because he had married one of the three sisters among whom the noble earldom of Gloucester had been divided, and because, being a most avaricious man, he had contrived by different means and tricks that he alone should possess the lands and revenues, and for that reason had devised grave charges against those who had married the other two sisters, so that he might obtain the whole earldom for himself.

The aforesaid [knights], then, holding the castles in this manner and prevailing more and more against the king from day to day, in the following autumn they, as it were, compelled the king to hold a parliament in London and to yield to their will in all things. In this parliament sir Hugh Despenser the younger was banished for ever, with his father and son, and all their property was confiscated.

[1322] Now after the Epiphany [6 January], when the truce between the kingdoms lapsed, the Scottish army invaded England and marched into the bishopric of Durham, and the earl of Moray remained at Darlington. But James of Douglas and the steward of Scotland went forward plundering the country in all directions, one of them raiding towards Hartlepool and the district of Cleveland, the other towards Richmond. The people of Richmond county, neither having nor hoping to have any defender now as formerly, bought off the invaders with a great sum of money. This time the Scots remained in England a fortnight and more; and when the northern knights came to the earl of Lancaster at Pontefract, where he usually dwelt, ready to fight against the Scots if he would assist them, he feigned excuse; and no wonder! seeing that he cared not to take up arms in the cause of a king who was ready to attack him.

Howbeit, as time went on, the king, through the efforts of some of his adherents, drew to his party by large gifts and promises the citizens of London and other southerners, earls as well as barons and knights. And he granted leave for the said two exiles to return,[1] received them to his peace, and caused this to be publicly proclaimed in London.

When this report was received, the party of the earl of Lancaster besieged the king's castle of Tykhill with a large army; and thus war was declared and begun in England, and the enmity between the king and the earl was made manifest.

When, therefore, the whole strength of the king's party south of Trent was assembled at Burton-upon-Trent, some 60,000 fighting men, in the second week of Lent, about the feast of the Forty Martyr Saints [10 March], the earl of Lancaster and the earl of Hereford (who had married the king's sister) attacked them with barons, knights and other cavalry, and with foot archers; but the earl's forces were soon thrown into confusion and retired before the king's army, taking their way towards Pontefract, where the earl usually dwelt. The king followed him with his army at a leisurely pace, but there was no slaughter to speak of on either side; and although the earl would have awaited the king there and given him battle, yet on the advice of his people he retired with his army into the northern district.

Now when that valiant and famous knight sir Andrew de Harcla, sheriff of Carlisle, heard of their approach, believing that they intended to go to Scotland to ally themselves with the Scots against the king of England, acting under the king's commission and authority, he summoned, under very heavy penalties, the knights, esquires and other able men of the two counties, to wit, Cumberland and Westmorland, all who were able to bear arms, to assemble for the king's aid against the oft-mentioned earl. But when the said sir Andrew, on his march towards the king with that somewhat scanty following, had spent the night at Ripon, he learnt from a certain spy that the earl and his army were going to arrive on the morrow at the town of Boroughbridge, which is only some four miles distant from the town of Ripon. Pressing forward, therefore, at night, he got a start of the earl, occupying the bridge of Boroughbridge before him, and, sending his horses and those of his men to the rear, he posted all his knights and some pikemen on foot at the northern end of the bridge, and other pikemen he stationed in schiltrom, after the Scottish fashion, opposite the ford or passage of the water, to oppose the cavalry wherein the enemy put his trust. Also he directed his archers to keep up a hot and constant discharge upon the enemy as he approached. On Tuesday, then, after the third Sunday in Lent, being the seventeenth of the kalends of April,[2] the aforesaid earls arrived in force, and perceiving that sir Andrew had anticipated them by occupying the north end of the bridge, they arranged that the earl of Hereford and sir Roger de Clifford (a man of great strength who had married his daughter) should advance with their company and seize the bridge from the pikemen stationed there, while the earl of Lancaster with the rest of the cavalry should attack the ford and seize the water and the ford from the pikemen, putting them to flight and killing all who resisted; but matters took a different turn. For when the earl of Hereford (with his standard-bearer leading the advance, to wit, sir Ralf de Applinsdene) and sir Roger de Clifford and some other knights, had entered upon the bridge before the others as bold as lions, charging fiercely upon the enemy, pikes were thrust at the earl from all sides; he fell immediately and was killed with his

[1] the Despensers [2] 16 March 1322

standard-bearer and the knights aforesaid, to wit, sir W. de Sule and sir Roger de Berefield; but Sir Roger de Clifford, though grievously wounded with pikes and arrows, and driven back, escaped with difficulty along with the others.

The earl [of Lancaster's] cavalry, when they endeavoured to cross the water, could not enter it by reason of the number and density of arrows which the archers discharged upon them and their horses. This affair being thus quickly settled, the earl of Lancaster and his people retired from the water, nor did they dare to approach it again, and so their whole array was thrown into disorder. Wherefore the earl sent messengers to sir Andrew, requesting an armistice until the morning, when he would either give him battle or surrender to him. Andrew agreed to the earl's proposal; nevertheless he kept his people at the bridge and the river all that day and throughout the night, so as to be ready for battle at any moment.

But during that night the earl of Hereford's men deserted and fled, because their lord had been killed, also many of the earl of Lancaster's men and those of my lord de Clifford and others deserted from them. When morning came, therefore, the earl of Lancaster, my lord de Clifford, my lord de Mowbray and all who had remained with them, surrendered to sir Andrew, who himself took them to York as captives, where they were confined in the castle to await there the pleasure of my lord the king.

The king, then, greatly delighted by the capture of these persons, sent for the earl to come to Pontefract, where he remained still in the castle of the same earl; and there, in revenge for the death of Piers de Gaveston (whom the earl had caused to be beheaded), and at the instance of the earl's rivals (especially of sir Hugh Despenser the younger), without holding a parliament or taking the advice of the majority, caused sentence to be pronounced that he should be drawn, hanged and beheaded. But, forasmuch as he was the queen's uncle and son of the king's uncle, the first two penalties were commuted, so that he was neither drawn nor hanged, only beheaded in like manner as this same earl Thomas had caused Piers de Gaveston to be beheaded. Howbeit, other adequate cause was brought forward and alleged, to wit, that he had borne arms against the king of England in his own realm; but those who best knew the king's mind declared that the earl never would have been summarily beheaded without the advice of parliament, nor so badly treated, had not that other cause prevailed, but that he would have been imprisoned for life or sent into exile.

This man, then, said to be of most eminent birth and noblest of Christians, as well as the wealthiest earl in the world, inasmuch as he owned five earldoms, to wit, Lancaster, Lincoln, Salisbury, Leycester and Ferrers, was taken on the morrow of St Benedict Abbot [22 March] in Lent and beheaded like any thief or vilest rascal upon a certain hillock outside the town, where now, because of the miracles which it is said God works in his honour, there is a great concourse of pilgrims, and a chapel has been built. In the aforesaid town sir Garin de l'Isle, a king's baron, also was drawn and hanged, and three knights with him. But the aforesaid sir Andrew [de Harcla] was made earl of Carlisle for his good service and courage.

Besides the decollation of the most noble earl of Lancaster at Pontefract, and the slaying of the earl of Hereford and two knights at Boroughbridge, eight English barons, belonging to the party and policy of the earl and his friends, were afterwards drawn and hanged, as I have been informed, and one other died in his bed, it is believed through grief. Four others were taken and immediately released; ten others were imprisoned and released later. Also fifteen knights were drawn and hanged; one died in his bed, and five escaped and fled to France; five were taken and released at once, and sixty-two were taken and imprisoned, but were released later. O the excessive cruelty of the king and his friends!

In addition to all these aforesaid, the following barons were taken with the earl at Boroughbridge and in the neighbourhood: sir Hugh de Audley, who owned a third part of the earldom of Gloucester, sir John Giffard, sir Bartholomew de Badlesmere, sir Henry de Tyes, sir John de Euer, sir William Touchet, sir Robert de Holand, sir Thomas Maudent. Now sir John de Mowbray and sir Roger de Clifford, were drawn and hanged with sir Jocelyn de Dayvile, a knight notorious for his misdeeds; but sir Bartholomew de Badlesmere was taken near Canterbury, and was there drawn, hanged and beheaded, sir Henry Tyes was drawn and hanged in London, each of them in his own district for their greater disgrace, except the aforesaid sir Hugh de Audley and others. Also there were imprisoned at York about sixty-seven knights, but most of these afterwards obtained the king's pardon.

After this the king held his parliament at York and there Hugh Despenser the elder, sometime exiled from England, was made earl of Winchester.

About this time the question was raised and discussed in various consistories and before the pope, whether it was heresy to say that Christ owned no private property nor even anything in common; the preaching friars held that it was [heresy] and the Minorite friars that it was not, chiefly on the strength of that decretal in Sextus – *Exiit qui seminat*. Of the cardinals and other seculars, some held one opinion, others another.

The king mustered an army in order to approach Scotland about the feast of St Peter ad Vincula [1 August]; hearing of which Robert de Brus invaded England with an army by way of Carlisle in the octave before the Nativity of St John the Baptist [17 June], and burnt the bishop's manor at Rose,[1] and Allerdale, and plundered the monastery of Holm Cultran, notwithstanding that his father's body was buried there; and thence proceeded to waste and plunder Copeland, and so on beyond the sands of Duddon to Furness. But the abbot of Furness went to meet him, and paid ransom for the district of Furness that it should not be again burnt or plundered, and took him to Furness abbey. This notwithstanding, the Scots set fire to various places and lifted spoil. Also they went further beyond the sands of Leven to Cartmel, and burnt the lands round the priory of the black canons,[2] taking away cattle and spoil: and so they crossed the sands of Kent[3] as far as the town of Lancaster, which they burnt, except the priory of the black monks and the house of the preaching friars. The earl of Moray and sir James of Douglas joined them there with another strong force, and so they marched forward together some twenty miles to the south, burning everything and taking away prisoners and cattle as far as the town of Preston in Amoundness, which also they burnt, except the house of the Minorite friars. Some of the Scots even went beyond that town fifteen miles to the south, being then some eighty miles within

[1] about seven miles from Carlisle
[2] Austin canons
[3] the river Kent, between Westmorland and Lancashire whence Kendal takes its name, i.e. Kent dale

England; and then all returned with many prisoners and cattle and much booty; so that on the vigil of St Margaret Virgin [12 July] they came to Carlisle, and lay there in their tents around the town for five days, trampling and destroying as much of the crops as they could by themselves and their beasts. They re-entered Scotland on the vigil of St James the Apostle [24 July], so that they spent three weeks and three days in England on that occasion.

The king of England came to Newcastle about the feast of St Peter ad Vincula [1 August], and shortly afterwards invaded Scotland with his earls, barons, knights and a very great army; but the Scots retired before him in their usual way, nor dared to give him battle. Thus the English were compelled to evacuate Scottish ground before the Nativity of the Glorious Virgin [8 September], owing as much to want of provender as to pestilence in the army; for famine killed as many soldiers as did dysentery.

After the retreat of the king of England the king of Scotland collected all his forces, both on this side of the Scottish sea[1] and beyond it, and from the Isles and from Bute and Arran,[2] and on the day after the feast of St Michael [30 September] he invaded England by the Solway and lay for five days at Beaumond, about three miles from Carlisle, and during that time sent the greater part of his force to lay waste the country all around; after which he marched into England to Blackmoor[3] (whither he had never gone before nor laid waste those parts, because of their difficulty of access), having learned for a certainty from his scouts that the king of England was there. The king, however, hearing of his approach, wrote to the new earl of Carlisle,[4] commanding him to muster all the northern forces, horse and foot, of his county and Lancaster, that were fit for war, and to come to his aid against the Scots. This he [Carlisle] did, having taken command of the county of Lancaster, so that he had 30,000 men ready for battle; and whereas the Scots were in the eastern district, he brought his forces by the western district so as to reach the king. But the Scots burnt the villages and manors in Blackmoor, and laid waste all that they could, taking men away as prisoners, together with much booty and cattle.

Now my lord John of Brittany, earl of Richmond, having been detached with his division by the king to reconnoitre the army of the Scots from a certain height between Biland abbey and Rievaulx abbey, and being suddenly attacked and surprised by them, attempted by making his people hurl stones to repel their assault by a certain narrow and steep pass in the hill; but the Scots forced their way fiercely and courageously against them; many English escaped by flight and many were made prisoners, including the aforesaid earl. Justly, indeed, did he incur that punishment, seeing that it was he himself who had prevented peace being made between the realms.

When this became known to the king of England, who was then in Rievaulx abbey, he, being ever chicken-hearted and luckless in war and having [already] fled in fear from them in Scotland, now took to flight in England, leaving behind him in the monastery in his haste his silver plate and much treasure. Then the Scots,

[1] the Firths of Forth and Clyde
[2] *De Brandanis:* the Atlantic was known as *Brendanicum mare*
[3] *Blakehoumor*, Blackmoor in the North Riding, the old name of the moorland south of Cleveland
[4] Sir Andrew de Harcla

arriving immediately after, seized it all and plundered the monastery, and then marched on to the Wolds, taking the earl [of Richmond] with them, laying waste that country nearly as far as the town of Beverley, which was held to ransom to escape being burnt by them in like manner as they had destroyed other towns.

Now when the aforesaid earl of Carlisle heard that the king was at York, he directed his march thither in order to attack the Scots with him and drive them out of the kingdom; but when he found the king all in confusion and no army mustered, he disbanded his own forces, allowing every man to return home. The Scots on that occasion did not go beyond Beverley, but returned laden with spoil and with many prisoners and much booty; and on the day of the commemoration of All Souls [1 November] they entered Scotland, after remaining in England one month and three days.

[1323] Wherefore, when the said earl of Carlisle perceived that the king of England neither knew how to rule his realm nor was able to defend it against the Scots, who year by year laid it more and more waste, he feared lest at last he [the king] should lose the entire kingdom; so he chose the less of two evils, and considered how much better it would be for the community of each realm if each king should possess his own kingdom freely and peacefully without any homage, instead of so many homicides and arsons, captivities, plunderings and raidings taking place every year. Therefore on 3 January [1323] the said earl of Carlisle went secretly to Robert the Bruce at Lochmaben and, after holding long conference and protracted discussion with him, at length, to his own perdition, came to agreement with him in the following bond. The earl firmly pledged himself, his heirs and their adherents to advise and assist with all their might in maintaining the said Robert as king of Scotland, his heirs and successors, in the aforesaid independence, and to oppose with all their force all those who would not join in nor even consent to the said treaty, as hinderers of the public and common welfare. And the said Robert, king of Scotland, pledged himself upon honour to assist and protect with all his might the said earl and all his heirs and their adherents according to the aforesaid compact, which he was willing should be confirmed by six persons [from] each [kingdom] to be nominated by aforesaid king and earl. And if the king of England should give his assent to the said treaty within a year, then the king of Scots should cause a monastery to be built in Scotland, the rental whereof should be five hundred marks, for the perpetual commemoration of and prayer for the souls of those slain in the war between England and Scotland, and should pay to the king of England within ten years 80,000 marks of silver, and that the king of England should have the heir male of the king of Scotland in order to marry to him any lady of his blood.

On behalf of the king of Scotland my lord Thomas Randolf, earl of Moray, swore to the faithful fulfilment of all these conditions without fraud, and the said earl of Carlisle in his own person, touching the sacred gospels; and written indentures having been made out, their seals were set thereto mutually.

Now the earl of Carlisle made the aforesaid convention and treaty with the Scots without the knowledge and consent of the king of England and of the kingdom in parliament; nor was he more than a single individual, none of whose business it was to transact such affairs. But the said earl, returning soon after from Scotland, caused all the chief men in his earldom to be summoned to Carlisle, both regulars and laymen, and there, more from fear than from any liking, they made him their oath that they would help him faithfully to fulfil all the things aforesaid. But after all these things had been made known for certain to the king and kingdom of England, the poor folk, middle class and farmers in the northern parts were not a little delighted that the king of Scotland should freely possess his own kingdom on such terms that they themselves might live in peace. But the king and his council were exceedingly put out (and no wonder!) because he whom the king had made an earl so lately had allied himself to the Scots, an excommunicated enemy, to the prejudice of the realm and crown, and would compel the lieges of the king of England to rebel with him against the king; wherefore they [the king and council] publicly proclaimed him as a traitor. So the king sent word to sir Antony de Lucy that he should endeavour to take him [Harcla] by craft; and if he should succeed in doing so by any means, the king would reward him and all who helped and assisted him. Therefore sir Antony, taking advantage of a time when the esquires[1] of the aforesaid earl and his other people had been scattered hither and thither on various affairs, entered Carlisle castle on the morrow after St Matthew the Apostle's day [25 February], as if to consult with him as usual upon some household matters. With him went three powerful and bold knights, to wit, sir Hugh de Lowther, sir Richard de Denton, and sir Hugh de Moriceby, with four men-at-arms of good mettle, and some others with arms concealed under their clothing. When they had entered the castle, they were careful to leave armed men behind them in all the outer and inner parts thereof to guard the same; but sir Antony, with the aforesaid three knights, entered the great hall where the earl sat dictating letters to be sent to different places, and spoke as follows to the earl: "My lord earl, thou must either surrender immediately or defend thyself." He, perceiving so many armed knights coming in upon him on a sudden, and being himself unarmed, surrendered to sir Antony.

Meanwhile the sound arose of the earl's household crying – "Treason! treason!" and when the porter at the inner gate tried to shut it against the knights who had entered, sir Richard de Denton killed him with his own hand. Nobody else was killed when the earl was arrested, for all the earl's men who were in the castle surrendered and the castle was given up to the aforesaid sir Antony. But one of the earl's household ran off to the pele of Highhead and informed master Michael, the earl's cousin (an ecclesiastic) of all that had been done at Carlisle. Michael went off in haste to Scotland, and with him sir William Blount, a knight of Scotland, and sundry others who had been particular friends of the earl. Then a messenger was sent to the king at York, to announce to him the earl's arrest and all that had taken place, that he might send word to sir Antony how he wished the oft-mentioned earl to be dealt with.

Meanwhile, to wit, on the morning after his arrest, the earl made confession to the parish priest about his whole life, and afterwards, before dinner on the same day, to a

[1] *armigeri*

preaching friar, and later to a Minorite friar, and on the following day to the warden of the Minorite friars – each and all of these about the whole of his life, and afterwards repeatedly to the aforesaid Minorite; all of whom justified him and acquitted him of intention and taint of treason. Whence it may be that, albeit he merited death according to the laws of kingdoms, his aforesaid good intention may yet have saved him in the sight of God.

On the feast of St Cedda Bishop [2 March] (that is, on the sixth day after the earl's arrest), there arrived in Carlisle from the king a number of men-at-arms, with whom was the justiciary sir Galfrid de Scrope, who on the next day, to wit, 3 March, sat in judgment in the castle, and pronounced sentence upon the earl as if from the mouth and in the words of the king, condemning him first to be degraded and stripped of the dignity of earldom by being deprived of the sword given him by the king, and in like manner of knightly rank by striking off from his heels the gilded spurs, and thereafter to be drawn by horses from the castle through the town to the gallows of Harraby and there to be hanged and afterwards beheaded; to be disembowelled and his entrails burnt; his head to be taken and suspended on the Tower of London; his body to be divided into four parts, one part to be suspended on the tower of Carlisle, another at Newcastle-on-Tyne, a third at Bristol and the fourth at Dover.[1]

When this sentence was pronounced the earl made answer: "Ye have divided my carcase according to your pleasure, and I commend my soul to God." And so, with most steadfast countenance and bold spirit, as it seemed to the bystanders, he went to suffer all these pains, and, while being drawn through the town, he gazed upon the heavens, with hands clasped and held aloft and likewise his eyes directed on high. Then under the gallows, whole in body, strong and fiery in spirit and powerful in speech, he explained to all men the purpose he had in making the aforesaid convention with the Scots, and so yielded himself to undergo the aforesaid punishment.[2]

The king made ample recognition to sir Antony and the others who arrested the earl, to wit – sir Antony de Lucy [received] the manor of Cockermouth, sir Richard de Denton the village of Thursby close to Carlisle, sir Hugh de Moriceby of part of the village of Culgaythe, being the part belonging to the aforesaid earl Andrew, sir Hugh de Lowther [ ], Richard de Salkeld the village of Great Corby.

Before Christmas came the bull of my lord pope John XXII, *Cum inter nonnullos*, wherein he pronounced it to be erroneous and heretical to affirm obstinately that our Lord Jesus Christ and his apostles possessed no private property even in common, since this is expressly contrary to scripture; and likewise that consequently it is heretical to affirm obstinately that the Lord Jesus Christ and his apostles had no legal right to those things which holy scripture testifies that they possessed, but only actual use of them, and that they had not the right to sell or give away those things, or of themselves acquiring other things, which aforesaid things holy scripture testifies to their

[1] It appears from the Parliamentary Writs (ii. 3,971) that the destination of the earl's quarters was to Carlisle, Newcastle, York and Shrewsbury.

[2] It is not difficult to discern in this most tragic fate of a gallant knight the influence upon the king of men who were jealous of Harcla's rapid rise. Harcla had been appointed by the king to treat with King Robert: he agreed to little more than what the king two months later was obliged to concede at Newcastle in fixing a truce for thirteen years. The terms of Harcla's indenture with King Robert are given in Bain's *Cal. Doc. Scot.* iii. 148.

having done, because such use of them would have been illegal. Friar Michael, minister general, appealed against this finding of the pope, wherefore the pope had him arrested, as is explained below, in the year 1328.

13. The "Life of Edward the Second" of the so-called Monk of Malmesbury: selected passages from the years 1315–16 and 1322

(*Vita Edwardi Secundi*, ed. and trans. N. Denholm-Young (1957), pp. 59, 61, 64, 69–74, 121–6)

An educated and informed contemporary's view of the personalities and events of his time.

[1315] . . . at the Purification of the Blessed Mary the earls and all the barons met at London, to treat of the state of the king and the realm, and of fighting the Scots. . . . In this parliament, because merchants going about the country selling victuals charged excessively, the earls and barons, looking to the welfare of the state, appointed a remedy for this malady; they ordained a fixed price for oxen, pigs and sheep, for fowls, chickens, and pigeons, and for other common foods. It was also provided and granted that the Gascons should carry their wines to English ports, and there sell it by the barrel according to the price assigned in parliament, and that Englishmen should not in future cross the sea as forestallers seeking wine. . . .

. . . the Irish are woodland people and dwell in the mountains and forests of their country; they do not cultivate the land, but live on their flocks and the milk thereof; and if from time to time they need bread, they come down to the English towns on the coast, selling livestock and buying corn. . . .

. . . the hand of God appears to be raised against us. For in the past year there was such plentiful rain that men could scarcely harvest the corn or bring it safely to the barn. In the present year worse has happened. For the floods of rain have rotted almost all the seed, so that the prophecy of Isaiah might seem now to be fulfilled; for he says that "ten acres of vineyard shall yield one little measure and thirty bushels of seed shall yield three bushels"; and in many places the hay lay so long under water that it could neither be mown nor gathered. Sheep generally died and other animals were killed by a sudden plague. It is greatly to be feared that if the Lord finds us incorrigible after these visitations, he will destroy at once both man and beasts; and I firmly believe that unless the English church had interceded for us, we should have perished long ago. . . .

[1316] . . . The lord king had summoned the barons to Lincoln. . . . The regulations formerly made about food were completely abolished. Those who travelled about the country were indeed suffering much hardship. For as a result of that statute little or nothing was exposed for sale in the markets, whereas formerly there had been an abundant market in goods, though they seemed dear to travellers. But it is better to buy dear than to find in case of need that there is nothing to be had. For although scarcity of corn raises the price, subsequent plenty will improve the situation.

After the feast of Easter the dearth of corn was much increased. Such a scarcity has not been seen in our time in England, nor heard of for a hundred years. For the measure of wheat was sold in London and the neighbouring places for forty pence, and in other less thickly populated parts of the country thirty pence was a common price. Indeed during this time of scarcity a great famine appeared, and after the famine came a severe pestilence, of which many thousands died in different places. I have even heard it said by some, that in Northumbria dogs and horses and other unclean things were eaten. . . . Spare, O Lord, spare thy people! . . . Yet those who are wise in astrology say that these storms in the heavens have happened naturally; for Saturn, cold and heedless, brings rough weather that is useless to the seed; in the ascendant now for three years he has completed his course, and mild Jupiter duly succeeds him. Under Jupiter these floods of rain will cease, the valleys will grow rich in corn, and the fields be filled with abundance. For the Lord shall give that which is good and our land shall yield her increase, etc.

A long time ago discontent arose in the town of Bristol, over the customs on the harbour and the market, over privileges and other matters in which fourteen of the greater townsmen were understood to have a prerogative. The "community" opposed them, maintaining that all the burgesses were of one rank and therefore equal in liberties and privileges. Over such matters they had frequent disputes among themselves, until they asked the king's court to provide judges to take cognisance of the case and duly terminate it. Now the said fourteen had so arranged matters that strangers should be on the panel, and these men were believed to have been won over and to lean wholly to the side of the said fourteen. The community alleged that it would be contrary to the liberties of the town for domestic issues to be subject to the judgment of strangers; but the justices regarded such allegations as frivolous, and would not allow them their liberties or privileges in this. The leaders of the commons[1] seeing that their exceptions were rejected, that their rights were destroyed rather by favour than by reason, were much distressed as they left the hall where judgments are customarily given, and spoke to the people saying, "Judges have come favourable to our opponents, and to our prejudice admit strangers, whence our rights will be lost for ever." At these words the senseless crowd turned to rioting, and the whole populace trembled from fear of the disorder. Returning once more they entered the hall with a large following and there turned their right to wrong. For with fists and sticks they began to attack the crowd opposed to them, and in that day nearly twenty men lost their lives for nothing. A very natural fear seized noble and commoner alike, so that many leapt out of the top-storey windows into the street, and seriously injured their legs or thighs as they fell to the ground. The judges, too, were afraid, humbly seeking to leave peacefully, but the mayor of the town, with difficulty repressing the frenzy of the populace, got them away safely.

About eighty men were indicted for this, and after a searching enquiry before the royal justices at Gloucester, were condemned, and the county ordered to produce them. As they neither came nor obeyed they were ordered to be exiled. They found good protection within the town and held out there; they will not obey the king's command unless they are forced to.

The said fourteen, who were opposing the commons, left their houses and rents

[1] *communitatis*

and departed from the town, judging it useless to linger with their opponents during such a storm. This rebellion of the commons of Bristol lasted for two years and more [1313–16] though they were many times summoned by the king to make their peace. For the king thought it better to exact a moderate penalty from the lawbreakers if they should be willing to comply, than by taking full vengeance to destroy a good town. But they persisted still in their rebellion, always disregarding the king's command and order. They did not come when they were summoned; they did not obey when bidden, pleading that the whole process against them was unjust, because it was entirely contrary to their privileges and liberties.

Unwilling any longer to put up with their wickedness the king summoned the knights and more important men of the county of Gloucester to London, and enjoined them by virtue of an oath there taken to expound openly the case of Bristol and who had suffered wrong. And they all said that the commons of Bristol had embraced the wrong cause and that the eighty men were the authors of this wrongdoing. So the king sent to Bristol Aylmer, earl of Pembroke, who called together the leaders of the commons and spoke to them on the king's behalf: "The lord king," he said, "on hearing your cause has found you guilty, and he warns and commands you to obey the law. Hand over the homicides and the guilty, and you and your town shall remain in peace. I promise that if you do this, the lord king will be easy with you and you will find mercy." The commons replied: "We were not the authors of this wrong; we have not failed the lord king in anything. Certain men strove to take away our rights, and we, as was proper, strove to defend them. Therefore if the lord king will remit his penalties, if he will grant us life and limb and rents and property, we will obey him as lord and do whatever he wishes; otherwise we shall continue as we have begun, and defend our liberties and privileges to the death."

The king hearing of their stubbornness, and thinking that this was a bad example, ordered the town to be besieged, and not left until the besieged had been taken. Siege was laid to the town forthwith, fortifications and siegeworks made. Maurice de Berkeley guarded the approach by sea. John de Charlton, the king's chamberlain, was present, Roger Mortimer, John de Wylington, and very many other barons and knights, and Bartholomew de Baddlesmere was in charge of the whole business. There were also in the castle which lies over against the town, men assaulting it with mangonels and other engines. For some days the besieged strove to defend the town, hoping that those outside would not stay long, both because the earl of Gloucester had long ago besieged the town, but had at length departed without taking it, and also because they knew that the king was going to Scotland, and needed the help of his magnates. This vain hope deceived them: the besiegers will not depart until the town is taken. For a mangonel of the castle, vigorously handled, beat down the walls and buildings. When the townsmen saw this they were troubled and stricken with fear, and fearing that the whole town [would be destroyed they agreed upon] surrender, and the leading captives were sent to prison. The whole multitude could not be punished, but when there are many lawbreakers an example is needed. The Bristollians now know that they have made a bad mistake, and that their rebellion has achieved nothing. If they had formerly accepted the condition of peace offered, almost all the commons and their goods would have remained safe, but because they have followed bad advice they are all at the king's mercy. The advice indeed was useless since the advantage of individual citizens turned to the common loss. They ought, indeed, to have remembered the tragic fate of the besieged at Bedford, and of those who held the castle of Kenilworth against the king; the former were captured and almost all hanged; the latter were cast into prison or exiled. . . .

[1322] . . . The barons could still have come to peace, seeking the king's pardon and mercy, but . . . puffed-up by the earl of Lancaster's protection they killed those who opposed them, plundered those who offered no resistance, sparing no one, and to their greater guilt attacked the king's own castle at Tickhill, and to take it put forth their best efforts, though in vain.

The lord king was certainly very much enraged at this and set out for Coventry, where he awaited the arrival of his army for some days. Thence he led his army to the great river called Trent. There is there a great bridge which offers a passage to those who wish to cross. The king sent forward to the bridge a strong phalanx of cavalry and infantry, wishing to know if there would be any opposition to his crossing. But the earl of Lancaster had arrived with all his retinue at the town of Burton on the other side.

When it was known that the king proposed to cross the river, the earl sent horse and foot to defend the bridge. But when the two sides had fought together for three or more days, and returned to the same battle on the morrow, the king found a ford higher up, where he himself crossed with the remainder of his army. When the barons heard, and now saw for themselves that the king had crossed the river, they left the bridge, took horse, and fled. But why does the earl of Lancaster, so often accustomed to resist the king, now take to flight, particularly as he had with him the earl of Hereford, and the flower of English chivalry? The king's forces were indeed now great and powerful. For he had about 300,000 men all told.

The earl had ordered Robert Holland, whom he had put in charge of his treasure, to bring an army of his best men, and had arranged a day for his coming; but on the appointed day Robert did not come, but as an apostate in his lord's cause deserted to the lord king; hence the earl's followers seeing that not enough help was present left the bridge, took horse, and fled.

The king pursued the fugitives to Tutbury castle, which belonged to the earl of Lancaster, and he found the gates open, because after the earl's flight no one dared to offer resistance. The warden of Kenilworth castle, too, on hearing of the earl's flight, at once surrendered the castle to the sheriff. . . . Thus the earl of Lancaster and the earl of Hereford, with all their adherents, were put to flight and came to Pomfret. After a short delay there it was decided to press on towards Scotland. They hoped to find a refuge in Scotland, because Robert Bruce, as was said, had promised help against the king.

When they reached Boroughbridge, that there at any rate they might rest for a night, who should be there but Andrew Harclay, that active soldier, already aware of the earl's flight. He had fully informed himself of the earl's order of march and his plans, and had arrived with some four thousand men, whom he had led with all speed to that place. The earls were settling into their lodgings in the town, when they heard that Andrew and his followers had come to destroy them utterly, so they left the town to meet their opponents in two columns. The earl of Hereford crossed by the bridge with his men-at-arms, but none of them was mounted. For the bridge was narrow, and offered no path for horsemen in battle array. The earl of Lancaster with his knights made their way to the ford of the river. But Andrew Harclay, like a prudent knight, had shrewdly stationed a force of men-at-arms opposite each crossing. The earl of Hereford forthwith attacked the enemy, but at length fell badly wounded in the fighting and died. Three or four knights were killed with the earl in that conflict. Roger de Clifford and very many others returned to the town badly wounded. Others, trying to cross the ford, were lamentably cut up by a shower of arrows; but after the death of the earl of Hereford their zeal for battle cooled off, and they at once retreated. But the earl of Lancaster made a truce with Andrew Harclay to keep the peace until the morrow; and when this was done each returned to his lodging. On that same night the sheriff of York came with a large force to attack the king's enemies; relying on his help Andrew Harclay entered the town very early, and taking the earl of Lancaster and almost all the other knights and esquires scatheless, led them off to York and imprisoned them. Some left their horses and putting off their armour looked round for ancient worn-out garments, and took to the road as beggars. But their caution was of no avail, for not a single well-known man among them all escaped.

O calamity! To see men lately dressed in purple and fine linen now attired in rags, bound and imprisoned in chains! A marvellous thing and one indeed brought about by God's will and aid, that so scanty a company should in a moment overcome so many knights. For the earl's side were more than seven times as numerous as their adversaries. There were captured with the earl of Lancaster and the other barons more than a hundred valiant knights. The number of esquires no less valiant was, I believe, much greater. Why therefore should they not have stood and fought manfully for their safety? Indeed the criminal is always fearful and so less effective in action. They saw that the whole countryside was up-in-arms in front of them, and thus their advance was blocked. They knew that the king's army threatened them from the rear, and therefore their retreat was not secure. Thus as men having no plan nor even time to deliberate, they fell into the hands of their enemies, etc.

On the fourth or fifth day after the capture of the earl of Lancaster, the king coming to Pomfret ordered him to be brought up without delay. He was at once brought up by the king's command, and for that night he was shut up in a certain new tower. It is said that the earl had recently built that tower, and determined that when the king was captured he should be imprisoned in it for life, and so to have made the prince a lion after the manner of the Lombards. This was the common story, but I have not heard evidence of its truth.

On the morrow the earl was led into the hall before the justices assigned for the purpose, and charged one by one with his crimes, and to each charge a special penalty was attached, namely, that first he should be drawn, then hanged, and finally decapitated. But out of reverence for his royal blood the penalty of drawing was remitted, as also that of hanging, and one punishment was decreed for all three. The earl, however, wishing to speak in mitigation of his crimes, immediately tried to make some points; but the judges refused to hear him, because the words of the condemned can neither harm nor be of any profit. Then the earl said: "This is a powerful court, and great in authority, where no answer is heard nor any excuse admitted." Here was a sight indeed! To see the earl of Lancaster, lately the terror of the whole country, receiving judgment in his own castle and home. Then the earl was led forth from the castle, and mounted on some worthless mule was led to the place of execution. Then the earl stretched forth his head as if in prayer, and the executioner cut off his head with two or three strokes.

14. The Pipewell Chronicle on the deposition of Edward II, 1327

(Maud Clarke, *Medieval Representation and Consent* (1936), pp. 123–4 and 193–5, for text and a translation which has been followed as far as possible [French])

And on the feast of St Hilary in the year of our Lord 1326[1] there came to the great hall at Westminster the archbishops, bishops, earls and barons, abbots and priors and all the others from cities and boroughs alike together with the whole community[2] of the land. There, by the common assent of all it was solemnly declared by the archbishop of Canterbury how the good king Edward when he died had left his son the lands of England, Ireland, Wales, Gascony and Scotland quite at peace and how the son had as good as lost the lands of Gascony and Scotland through bad counsel and bad custody, and how likewise through bad counsel he had caused to be slain a great part of the noble blood of the land, to the dishonour and loss of himself, his realm and the whole people, and had done many other astonishing things. Therefore it was agreed by absolutely all the aforesaid that he ought no longer to reign but that his eldest son, the duke of Guyenne, should reign and wear the crown in his stead. For when the bishops of Hereford and London who had been sent to him on behalf of the community of the land to Kenilworth to request him to come[?][3] to the parliament bore witness that he remained as cruel and malevolent as before, it was accordingly ordained and agreed that such[?] great folk as bishops, abbots, priors, earls, barons, knights, justices and others should go to him and renounce entirely[?] their homage to him and on behalf of the whole land; and so it was done. It was further ordained that our lady the queen, for the great anxiety and anguish she had suffered as well this side as overseas, should stay queen all her life. And that our lord the king who now is should take to wife the daughter of the count of Hainault.

On the feast of SS Fabian and Sebastian [20 January] in the aforesaid year . . . there came to Kenilworth the undermentioned, namely, the bishops of London, Winchester and Hereford, the abbots of Glastonbury and Dover, the earl Warenne and the earl of Lancaster, the barons sir Hugh de Courtenay, sir Richard de Grey, the justices

[1] 13 January 1327 in modern reckoning
[2] *communalte*, here and elsewhere
[3] The manuscript is in places barely legible. Doubtful readings (and so translations) are indicated by a query.

sir Geoffrey le Scrope and John de Bourser[?], two[?] barons of the [Cinque] Ports, four burgesses of London and four knights on behalf of the community of the land. And they recited to our lord the king the aforementioned shortcomings as they had been charged to do. He, before them all, quite freely admitted that he had governed them and the land badly and with tears and on his knees he cried them mercy for this and asked them to pardon him and to ask in full parliament for them [parliament] to pardon his trespasses against them. He also granted and ordained that sir Edward his eldest son should be king in his place and wear the crown the Sunday, the eve that is of the Purification [1 February] and that every kind of homage and service should in no wise be done to him – be to him[?]. And on this there came sir William Trussel of Petling and knelt before our lord the king and cried him mercy, begging him to pardon him his trespasses against him and he pardoned him and gave him the sign of peace in front of them all.

Part II
ROYAL GOVERNMENT

INTRODUCTION

THE generation which founded the Surtees, Camden, Caxton and English Historical societies and secured government finance for the publication of chronicles showed no less concern for the records of over six centuries of royal government surviving in over fifty different places. The Public Record Office Act of 1838 provided for their concentration under the charge of the Master of the Rolls. The present Public Record Office on the "Rolls" estate in Chancery Lane (meant to be sufficient to house "all . . . documents whatsoever of a public nature belonging to Her Majesty", but which, if ever it was, has long since ceased to be so) was begun in 1851 and occupied from 1856, the year before the Master of the Rolls, who had been active in promoting it, was given the direction of the Chronicles and Memorials (the "Rolls" series) project too.

Those who sought by establishing a single record office to provide "a better custody" for the archives of the English monarchy knew their value. Because of the continuity of English history since the Norman Conquest no other country in Europe had such series of records beginning so early and surviving with so few gaps. The nation had already spent a great deal of money on putting some of them, on selected topics, into print. Thomas Rymer's *Foedera*, the *Rolls of Parliament* (commissioned in 1767), *Domesday Book* (1783) and at vast expense (no less than £260,000 at those days' prices) the vast volumes of the six record commissions between 1800 and 1837. This last enterprise was wound up, but the Public Record Office Act of 1838 provided, subject of course to parliament's financial provision, for the continued printing and sale of "Records, Calendars, Catalogues and Indexes of the said Records", and the first of these, a *Calendar of State Papers Domestic 1547–80*, continuing in different form the work of the by now absorbed State Paper Office, appeared in 1856. The continuous preparation and surprisingly regular publication thereafter of other calendars, since 1886 of medieval as well as later records, must be reckoned one of the greatest of the services of the unified record office to scholarship.

There could be access, it seems, to the records even in the Middle Ages.[1] The Act of 1838 respected this tradition and provided for the admission of such members of the public "as ought to be admitted" and, at discretion, without payment of the traditional fees. This was defined in 1851 as meaning that persons using the records for literary as distinct from legal purposes would not be charged. But these privileges were not quickly claimed. Macaulay sought access. Stubbs apparently did not. Student's tickets were not introduced until 1908. It was never difficult to get a seat in the Search Rooms until after the First World War: never impossible until after the Second. English history, for the medieval period at least, continued to be written from the chronicles plus the earlier printed collections of record evidence (notably the Record Commissions' volumes) and such of the new Public Record Office *Calendars* as had yet appeared and these for the medieval period were indeed few

[1] *Guide to the Public Records, Pt I: Introductory* (H.M.S.O., 1949), pp. 47–8

before 1890. Thus William Stubbs, *Constitutional History of England down to 1485*, in the eighteen-seventies, which superseded Hallam's and "gave a new direction to the study of medieval English history" but which he never had time to revise after he became a bishop in 1884, adopts for the reign of Edward I the perspectives of the Guisborough chronicle.[1] Today, exactly a hundred years after the appearance of Stubbs's first volume, it is the chronicles which are neglected. English history is being rewritten from the documents and with over fifty million documents (any of which "may be only a sheet of modern paper" but could be "some hundreds of yards of fifteenth-century parchment") in the Public Record Office alone, it must continue to be so for a very long time to come.[2] The danger is that, in general, the document-trained scholar of today is likely to be less proficient in the use of chronicles than Stubbs was in using documents – if only because the professionalism of the twentieth-century historian has raised standards in the techniques of chronicle criticism as in everything else except literary presentation.

Documents are usually more precise and therefore better evidence on matters of fact than are chronicles. They can be misleading, sometimes deliberately so, especially if they give reasons, as in preambles to statutes, but this is not usually the case. Their obvious fault is at first sight their recommendation: that they were not written for the historian, either to guide or misguide him, in the normal case, but to enable some official at the time to do his job, so that historical evidence has to be extracted from them and this can be a highly technical proceeding. Their real shortcoming lies in what (by their nature) they cannot give: the unofficial contemporary view which chronicles, despite their prejudices, their at best incomplete knowledge and the fact that for different reasons they are not ready-made evidence either, can give and do.

SELECT BIBLIOGRAPHY

The first requisite with a document is to establish its authenticity, though this logical priority rarely in practice precedes and its conclusion usually comes after other processes to be mentioned. Thus, at the period we are concerned with, a document is unlikely to be written in English and, to save both time and materials, it will be written in a sort of shorthand: one must be able to read it. Then its dating must be right for what it professes to be or do. A complication is that, early in this period, a date may not be given and so have to be inferred; and an incongruous member of a body of witnesses to an undated charter, for example, should alert one to the possibility of forgery. But there can be forgery without any such give-away. Also, in the Middle Ages there could be quite respectable, innocent reasons for forgery. It did not necessarily carry a stigma. Again, there is the forgery which is not a complete forgery.[3] This, obviously, need not be rejected outright, but like all half-truths it is more difficult to detect.

Then its wording and other things about it must be right. There is a science of Diplomatic or Diplomatics which deals with these things. A wrong choice of writ, a mistake in a writ, even a *stultiloquium* (a blunder in the choice, use or order of words in court in an oral pleading) could

[1] cf. the bibliography to Part I above, under "Edward I", and the present writer in *Studies in Medieval History presented to Frederick Maurice Powicke*, ed. Hunt, Pantin and Southern (Oxford, 1948), pp. 319–32.
[2] *Guide . . . Pt I: Introductory*, p. 19
[3] No. 193 below

be fatal to one's case. Offices developed particular forms of document for particular purposes, and formularies of them in advance for economy of effort.[1] They developed too for the benefit of recipients – for the age had its own problems of authentication – particular ways of folding and sealing, and even more sophisticated methods such as a set of rhythms in the latinity of a document, which, read aloud, as most reading was done, would betray a false quantity – a watermark of language as it were.[2] When form is as important as this, one must know such things.

The reader will observe at this stage that many of the documents in this volume are printed, directly or indirectly, not from the originals but from office copies entered either in registers or on rolls. This probably means that some of the recognised tests of authenticity cannot be applied. There is no fold or seal to an enrolment, for example, and common form in wording (especially legal common form) is very often replaced by an "etc.". Calendars, of Patent or Close Rolls for instance, suppress even more, of course. But official enrolment is itself evidence of authenticity, if the enrolment has remained in official custody.

The language difficulty can be overrated. With the increasing amount of source material becoming available in translation, a student can now go farther before he meets it, and when he does it need not be insuperable. The trained linguist has an advantage, as one would expect. But the classical scholar has much to learn and to unlearn in dealing with medieval Latin, which was a living language and not decadent except by comparison with Ciceronian Latin, from which it was not in any case descended. The modern linguist is in not much better case, unless he has specialised in the early history of his language. The essential is a minimum of Latin grammar, which anyone can acquire, together with a quite small list of the basic Latin words. Both these things can be got from a schoolbook. After which an ordinary Latin dictionary, supplemented, for new words and new forms in medieval Latin, by the *Revised Medieval Latin Word-List*, ed. R. E. Latham (1965). A direct approach to medieval Latin for complete beginners is *Latin for Local History*, by Eileen A. Gooder (1961), again supplemented, of course, by Latham's *Word-List*. Ultimately indispensable will be Karl Strecker, *Introduction to Medieval Latin*, trans. and rev. by R. B. Palmer (Berlin, 1957), and H. P. V. Nunn, *An Introduction to Ecclesiastical Latin*, 3rd edn (London, 1951). There is no short cut to Anglo-Norman. Given some knowledge of modern French, an excellent introduction to the vocabulary is Kenneth Urwin, *A Short Old French Dictionary for Students*. Both J. Vising, *Anglo-Norman Language and Literature* (1923) and F. W. Maitland, "Of the Anglo-French Language in the Early Year Books" in the Introduction (pp. xxxiii–lxxxviii) to his edition of the *Year Books of 1 & 2 Edward II, 1307–9*, Selden Soc., vol. 17 (1903), are useful at every stage. There is no short cut to "Middle" English either, but documentary material in English in the period covered by this volume is so exceptional that in practice there is little problem for the historian.

Handwriting and abbreviations: the sections by E. A. Lowe and V. H. Galbraith in *The Legacy of the Middle Ages*, ed. C. G. Crump and E. F. Jacob (Oxford, 1926) and *Medieval England*, ed. A. L. Poole, I (Oxford, 1958) respectively for a general introduction; C. Johnson and H. Jenkinson, *English Court Hand* (Oxford, 1915) for the cursive script of the English royal administration; and C. T. Martin, *The Record Interpreter*, 2nd edn (1910), a guide to the abbreviations and (as the title implies) much else, by an Assistant-Keeper of the Public Records.

Dating: R. L. Poole, *Medieval Reckonings of Time* (London, 1921) as a general introduction. As a vade-mecum, in the useful almanac form of an earlier work, Fry's *Almanacks* (1915), C. R. Cheney, *Handbook of Dates for Students of English History* (1945) is indispensable: as valuable for the other information it contains (the select bibliography deserves special mention) as for

[1] An extreme instance is in No. 215.
[2] known as the *cursus*

the almanacs. The *Handbook of British Chronology*, ed. Sir F. Maurice Powicke and E. B. Fryde, 2nd edn (1961), is no substitute for Cheney's *Handbook* but a reference book, giving in the form of lists a vast amount of supplementary information.

Proper form etc.: reference may be made to the section on "Diplomatic, etc." in the Select Bibliography of Cheney's *Handbook of Dates* – for English documents the works of Madox, Hall, Maxwell-Lyte, Stenton, and Galbraith there mentioned, supplemented by L. C. Hector, *Palaeography and Forgery*, St Anthony's Hall Publications No. 15 (York, 1959) and H. G. Richardson, "The Forgery of Fines, 1272–1376", *E.H.R.*, xxv (1920), pp. 405–18. cf. Helen M. Cam in *Speculum*, vol. 32 (1957), pp. 433–4. For the *cursus*, R. L. Poole, *Lectures on the History of the Papal Chancery* (Cambridge, 1915), ch. 4, and Karl Strecker, *Introduction to Medieval Latin*, trans. and rev. by R. B. Palmer (Berlin, 1957), pp. 86–90.

In the Introduction to this part a brief account was given of the assembling of the royal records in the nineteenth century and of the measures taken since then to make them available for study. It is essential to know also the working of the machinery of government which produced them. This will be further considered in the Introduction to Part III. Meanwhile V. H. Galbraith, *An Introduction to the Use of the Public Records* (Oxford University Press, 1934) is essential reading, supplemented by the official *Guide to the Contents of the Public Record Office* (H.M.S.O., 2 vols, 1963), though for records prior to 1509 only volume I of this is necessary.

The difference between chronicle and record evidence needed to be emphasised. But the object of Part II is to illustrate some of the problems facing the kings of England in this period and the policies they pursued in trying to solve them. Political and constitutional texts inevitably loom large and from the plan of the volume they fall naturally into this part of it. They are far from dominating it, as will be seen; yet a word at this stage on the place envisaged for them in that plan may save words later. The emphasis in both the teaching and the writing of history has shifted in this century from the political and constitutional, the backbone of university degree courses only fifty years ago, to social aspects of the subject. This harms nothing except vested interests and can only enrich the older sorts of history, provided that, having moved away from "drums and trumpets", we do not move into fashion and follies – to social history, in any narrow or superficial sense. Social history should include, for example, economic history, the getting as well as the spending; the whole activity indeed of men in society. Political history could then be taken for what it is: the history of the frictions generated in a society. And constitutional history as the history of such of those frictions as relate to the government of men, the question of who exercises authority, the institutions through which it is exercised. Political history thus understood is not narrow. It is more than power-politics, who is "in" and who is "out". The tracing of frictions back to their causes (surely part of the historian's task) makes it as wide and as varied as society itself. Part II is not planned to be self-sufficient. Those who consider it central will not find the other parts wholly irrelevant.

The achievement of Henry II, could he but have known it in the humiliation of his last days, was to have succeeded to a kingdom shaken to its foundations by civil war, yet leave it strong enough to survive the test in quick succession after him of an absentee king, civil war again, and a minority, the trilogy of calamities to which kingdoms are prone. Not that Richard was being untrue to his office in defending the Cross and defending his inheritance, or indeed in being absent except in being outrageously so. The circumstance was provided for in the practice of his father, particularly in his last years, of using his justiciar not only as chief minister under him but also as his deputy with complete authority in his absences. The fact remains that Richard was absent for nine and a half of his ten years as king and England was governed for him; and the evidence we have supports a conclusion that it was governed normally and well.

What is lacking in sufficient quantity is direct evidence of the kind we have increasingly from 1199 onwards: the official records of their actions kept by royal officials. To what extent such records were kept before 1199 is not clear. Contrast V. H. Galbraith, *Studies in the Public Records* (1948), pp. 65–6 and 74, and H. G. Richardson and G. O. Sayles, *The Governance of Medieval England from the Conquest to Magna Carta* (Edinburgh, 1963), pp. 170–1. The ordinance of 7 June 1199 (Rymer's *Foedera*, I, i (1816), p. 75) does not itself order records to be kept. On the other hand, there is force in the contention (Galbraith, op. cit. p. 69) that "a far less elaborate record" than we find from 1199 "would have served equally well" the financial purposes of the Exchequer, and, with reference to Richardson and Sayles (op. cit. p. 171, n. 3, "Arguments not based on the records leave us unmoved"), their own argument is not based on the records at the critical point, being no more than an inference from the ordinance of 7 June 1199, and a questionable one at that. Whatever the answer to this, it is clear that if enrolment began in Chancery before 1199, the rolls have not survived. The contrast between the record evidence available for Richard's reign and for John's is very obvious in the formal bibliography by Powicke in *Cambridge Medieval History*, VI (1929), section I(A), pp. 881–3. The more up-to-date statement in A. L. Poole, *Domesday Book to Magna Carta* (Oxford History of England), Bibliography, sect. 2 and 4, shows little change in the interval in the balance of chronicle and record evidence for Richard's reign and little fresh work since 1929 directly on the reign. The truth here would seem to be that research like Blitzkrieg is a probe for soft spots; and that, rather than hold up advance, Richard's reign has been bypassed, to be reduced from any promising angles there may be later. There have been break-throughs, through the financial and legal records. The *Curia Regis* rolls have been published by the Public Record Office (for details, E. L. C. Mullins, *Texts and Calendars*, Royal Hist. Soc., 1958, p. 22), with an introduction to them by their editor separately published by the Selden Society, *Introduction to the Curia Regis Rolls, 1199–1230 A.D.*, ed. C. T. Flower (1944). cf. C. Johnson, "Notes on Thirteenth-Century Judicial Procedure", *E.H.R.*, lxii (1947), pp. 508–21. D. M. Stenton has edited *The Earliest Lincolnshire Assize Rolls, 1202–9* (Lincoln Rec. Soc., 1926) and *The Earliest Northamptonshire Assize Rolls, 1202 and 1203* (Northamptonshire Rec. Soc., 1930). Other legal records are mentioned in Poole's bibliography. For details of the Exchequer *Pipe Rolls* and other records published by the Pipe Roll Society see Mullins, *Texts and Calendars*, pp. 232–8. Valuable light is thrown on Richard's reign by the above, but it is mostly indirect light and it is significant that in recent writing scholars have preferred to give this reign of ten years a larger setting. This is true even of a work which is of the utmost relevance, the monograph of F. J. West, *The Justiciarship in England, 1066–1232* (Cambridge, 1966). For a brief but discerning review of this book see F. Barlow in *History*, lii (1967), pp. 184–5.

In John's reign the king is on stage and there is high drama. Also, the scholar can now expect record evidence to set alongside that of the chronicles. The reign continues to stimulate fine work. It is surprising how much of the older work (Powicke's bibliograph of 1929, *Cambridge Med. Hist.*, VI, pp. 884 ff.) has held its ground. Much of the publication mentioned above for the indirect light it throws on Richard's reign is direct evidence for John's. General works taking this evidence into account are: A. L. Poole, *Domesday Book to Magna Carta* (Oxford History of England); Doris M. Stenton, *English Society in the Early Middle Ages (1066–1307)* (1951), brief and as it says a social history, descriptive not narrative, but masterly; after Kate Norgate's *John Lackland* (1902), Sidney Painter's *The Reign of King John* (Baltimore, 1949) and W. L. Warren, *King John* (1961) and the brief, but balanced assessment of the character of John by J. C. Holt, *King John* (Hist. Assoc. Pamphlet, 1963). Further source-material made available includes, besides W. Farrer's *Honors and Knight's Fees*, 3 vols (London and Manchester, 1923–5), his *Early Yorkshire Charters*, vols I–III (Edinburgh, 1914–16), followed by vols IV–X, ed. by

C. T. Clay (Yorkshire Archaeological Society, Record ser., extra series, 1935–55); C. T. Clay's *Three Yorkshire Assize Rolls for the reigns of King John and King Henry III* (Yorkshire Arch. Soc., Record ser., 1911); and *The Letters of Pope Innocent III concerning England and Wales*, ed. C. R. and Mary G. Cheney (Oxford, 1967). J. C. Holt, *The Northerners: a Study in the Reign of King John* (Oxford, 1961) is important, as is D. M. Stenton, *English Justice between the Norman Conquest and the Great Charter* (1965), which includes an earlier lecture on "King John and the Courts of Justice". H. G. Richardson and G. O. Sayles, *The Governance of Medieval England from the Conquest to Magna Carta* (Edinburgh, 1963) is constructive as well as critical of accepted views. Important articles of C. R. Cheney and others are listed in Warren's *King John* (pp. 324–7). On war and finance, F. M. Powicke, *The Loss of Normandy* (Manchester, 1913, 2nd edn, rev., 1961), ch. 8. Quite the most important recent publication on the reign is J. C. Holt, *Magna Carta* (Cambridge, 1965).

The best account of the minority of Henry III, since Kate Norgate's book of that title (1912), is in the opening chapters of F. M. Powicke, *King Henry III and the Lord Edward*, 2 vols (Oxford, 1947), or more briefly in the same author's *The Thirteenth Century, 1216–1307* (Oxford, 1953), ch. 1. The important articles of G. J. Turner in *Trans. Royal Hist. Soc.*, new ser., xviii (1904). pp. 245–95, and 3rd ser., i (1907), pp. 205–62, are not superseded. For William the Marshal, S. Painter, *William Marshal* (Baltimore, 1933). As one would expect, financial and legal questions were important. Mabel H. Mills, "Experiments in Exchequer Procedure", *Trans. Royal Hist. Soc.*, 4th ser., viii (1925), pp. 151–70 and S. K. Mitchell, *Studies in Taxation under John and Henry III* (1914) and *Taxation in Medieval England* (New Haven, 1951). The earliest surviving wardrobe account comes from this period and has been printed in T. F. Tout, *Chapters in Medieval Administrative History*, I (Manchester, 1920). On the annual Memoranda and Pipe rolls, the bibliography in Powicke, *Thirteenth Century, 1216–1307* (section 2, sub-section "Exchequer"). As to legal records, the editing of Curia Regis rolls and rolls of Justices in Eyre was continued by C. T. Flower and D. M. Stenton respectively; for details, Mullins, *Texts and Calendars* (as above), pp. 22–3, 283 and 282–3 respectively. The ultimate importance of the minority, however, is the decision of those who ruled for the boy-king to adopt Magna Carta. But it took them three revisions (1216, 1217 and 1225), five drafts (Nos 22, 23, 24, 26 and 27 below) and ten years to work out an acceptable text of it. If we ask why, all we can do is learn what we can of the situation they faced and infer what we can from their drafting (which is why we give the drafts in order and in full). Powicke's second chapter (*King Henry III and the Lord Edward*, pp. 42–83) is probably as near the truth as it is possible to get, but it leaves no doubt that the decade after John was as important for the future of this country as the decade before him.

Henry III took over in 1227 the government of a country as near normal, thanks to men of real statesmanship during his minority, as any king could expect and led it into civil war. That he lived on until 1272 is probably the least important thing we know about him. The task of reconstruction facing his successor dated from 1267. Reign and reality do not correspond in Edward I's case either. The contrast between the earlier and the later years of his reign is plain enough. The years 1290–1 are usually taken as marking the turn, but 1294 would seem to account better for what follows. After 1267, Welsh and other distractions apart, there seems to have been no diversion of the main effort of English government from home affairs until 1294, when – with lasting domestic consequences – England went to war. There is no comparable change after that in the rest of the period. 1307 changed the monarch but not the situation, except perhaps in the person of Edward II to aggravate it.

Down to 1307 there is no substitute for the general bibliography in Powicke's Oxford History volume, *The Thirteenth Century, 1216–1307*. The following notes are merely meant to supplement the relevant sections of it on the subject of royal government.

The fullest and best account of Henry III's reign is now Sir Maurice Powicke's own, F. M. Powicke, *King Henry III and the Lord Edward*, 2 vols (Oxford, 1947), though his later and briefer textbook statement in *The Thirteenth Century* (Oxford, 1953) should also be read, for it is much more than a summary of the other. In addition to their recognition of the "social" foundations of "political" history, a further merit of these writings is the emphasis they give to the years before 1258. As with John's reign compared with Richard I's, more attention has been paid to the crisis years – which are dramatic and where the issues are explicit. It is too often not appreciated that Henry III was nineteen when he took full responsibility in 1227 and fifty in 1258: that he ruled for thirty years before the Provisions of Oxford and the Barons' Wars. Those years cannot be unimportant.

The rapid publication, in full or in calendar, from the opening years of this century of chancery records of the reign, the Charter, Patent and Close Rolls, the Liberate Rolls, Chancery Warrants and Inquisitions Post Mortem, most of them before the First World War, the rest before the Second,[1] freed the student from dependence on chronicles. Between the wars Mabel H. Mills's work on exchequer records elucidated in a number of important studies the thirteenth-century working of that institution, so laying a foundation for further work on a critical period of royal finance: the long and valuable Introduction to her edition of *The Pipe Roll for 1295, Surrey Membrane, Pipe Roll 140*, Surrey Rec. Soc. Publication No. 21 (1924); "Experiments in Exchequer Procedure", *Trans. Royal Hist. Soc.*, 4th ser., viii (1925), pp. 151–70; "The Reforms at the Exchequer 1232–42", *T.R.H.S.*, 4th ser., x (1927), pp. 111–34; "Adventus Vicecomitum, 1258–72" and "1272–1307", *E.H.R.*, xxxvi (1921), pp. 481–96 and xxxviii (1923), pp. 331–54 respectively. T. F. Tout pioneered the study of English administrative history with *Chapters in the Administrative History of Medieval England: the Wardrobe, the Chamber and the small seals*, 6 vols (Manchester, 1920–33). The legal history had already been brilliantly pioneered by F. W. Maitland with *Bracton's Note Book*, 3 vols (1887) and Pollock and Maitland, *The History of English Law before the time of Edward I*, 2 vols (2nd edn, Cambridge, 1898). The Selden Society, which he did more than anyone else to establish, has continued his work – notably for this reign with *Select Cases of Procedure without Writ under Henry III*, ed. H. G. Richardson and G. O. Sayles (1941), *Brevia Placitata*, ed. G. J. Turner and T. F. T. Plucknett (1951) and *Casus Placitorum*, ed. W. H. Dunham, jr (1952).[2] It was a critical time in legal as well as financial development and studies such as these, of cases and of treatises other than Bracton's on case law, are needed.[3] Helen M. Cam, *The Hundred and the Hundred Rolls* (1930) is still the best account of local government. But the system there described was not universal. Nor was it static. The county (shire) court and the sheriff alike find themselves threatened, the one by royal justice, the other by new and equally royal officials. For further reading on these things, see Powicke, *Thirteenth Century*, Bibliography, sections 1 (Legal) and 6, esp. pp. 729–30 (local courts) and 749–50 (local government).

It is surprising how much authoritative work on the crisis years too was done in these inter-war years. R. F. Treharne, *The Baronial Plan of Reform, 1258–63* (Manchester, 1932); E. F. Jacob, *Studies in the Period of Baronial Reform and Rebellion, 1258–67* (Oxford, 1925); a new edition, in English, Ch. Bémont, *Simon de Montfort* (Oxford, 1930), of the original French work of 1884 (but without the latter's valuable appendices of documents); and other work mentioned in the Powicke bibliography (sect. 5).

Since then the Wiltshire eyre roll for 1249 in an English version, splendidly edited, has appeared: *Crown Pleas of the Wiltshire Eyre, 1249*, ed. C. A. F. Meekings (Devizes, 1961) and

[1] see the General Bibliography above [2] see General Bibliography (Selden Soc. Publications) above
[3] as Maitland, whose own work rested chiefly on Bracton, was well aware. cf. T. F. T. Plucknett, *Early English Legal Literature* (Cambridge, 1958), pp. 104–5

Civil Pleas of the Wiltshire Eyre, 1249, ed. M. T. Clanchy (Devizes, 1971); on the origin and the office of the coroner, R. V. Hunnisett in *Trans. Royal Hist. Soc.*, 5th ser., viii (1958), *The Medieval Coroner* (Cambridge, 1961) and *Bedfordshire Coroners' Rolls* (Bedfordshire Hist. Rec. Soc. Publication No. 41, Streatley, 1961). On the Mise of Amiens of January 1264, with R. F. Treharne on the subject in *Studies in Medieval History presented to F. M. Powicke*, ed. Hunt, Pantin and Southern (Oxford, 1948), pp. 223–39 read P. Walne, "The Barons' Argument at Amiens, January 1264", *E.H.R.*, lxix (1954), pp. 418–25, and lxxiii (1958), pp. 453–9.

Powicke's writing sums up and is also the culmination of modern scholarship on Henry III's reign. With a sympathetic study in the Epilogue of *King Henry III and the Lord Edward*, the shift of emphasis to Edward in the *Thirteenth Century* and the essay on "King Edward in Fact and Fiction" in *Fritz Saxl 1890–1948*, ed. D. J. Gordon (London, 1957), pp. 120–35, he was moving into the son's reign. His account of it in the *Thirteenth Century* (nine of the fourteen chapters) is in fact the only adequate modern statement. E. L. G. Stones, *Edward I* (1968), intended for a different public is scholarly, and excellent, but too slight. L. F. Salzman, *Edward I* (1908), equally scholarly, of course, is more interested in the king as a person than in his problems as king.

The period 1267–94 is pre-eminently one of resettlement and reconstruction and, to supplement the common law at a time of increasing social complexity, of massive and detailed legislation. T. F. T. Plucknett, *Legislation of Edward I* (Oxford, 1949) is essential reading. See also *A Concise History of the Common Law*, by the same writer, 4th (1948) or later edition, for background; Powicke, *The Thirteenth Century* (1953), ch. viii; Richardson and Sayles, "The Early Statutes", *Law Quarterly Review*, vol. 50 (1934), pp. 201–23 and 540–71, and *Select Cases of Procedure without Writ under Henry III* (Selden Soc., 1941); G. O. Sayles, *Select Cases in the Court of King's Bench*, 3 vols (Selden Soc., 1936–9) and Introduction to vol. III. Plucknett, *Edward I and Criminal Law* (Cambridge, 1960) lacks the immediacy of *Legislation of Edward I*. D. W. Sutherland, *Quo Warranto Proceedings in the Reign of Edward I, 1278–1294* (Oxford, 1963) provides the analysis of the "abundant material for studying the course of decisions between 1278 and 1290" which Plucknett (*Legislation of Edward I*, pp. 45–6) called for.

Powicke's *Thirteenth Century*, ch. ix and Bibliography, sect. 8, affords the best introduction to Anglo-Welsh relations in this period. Subsequent work shows the same interest in differences in law and social organisation: J. G. Edwards, "Historical Study of the Welsh lawbooks", *Trans. Royal Hist. Soc.*, 5th ser., xii (1962), pp. 141–55 and "The Royal Household and the Welsh lawbooks", op. cit., xiii (1963), pp. 163–76; R. R. Davies, "The Twilight of Welsh Law, 1284–1536", *History*, li (1966), pp. 143–64 and "The Survival of the Bloodfeud in Medieval Wales", op. cit., liv (1969), pp. 338–57. On the Welsh March, to which the Statute of Wales of 1284 did not apply, A. J. Otway-Ruthven's valuable paper, "The Constitutional Position of the Great Lordships of South Wales", *Trans. Royal Hist. Soc.*, 5th ser., viii (1958), pp. 1–20.

On relations with the king of France over the duchy of Aquitaine as reconstituted by the treaty of Paris of 1259 the best modern account in English[1] is also in Powicke's *Thirteenth Century* – chapter vii. cf. M. C. L. Salt, "Embassies to France, 1272–1307", *E.H.R.*, xliv (1929), pp. 263–78, and, for Edward I's itinerary in Gascony in 1286–9, *Bull. Inst. Hist. Research*, xxv (1952), pp. 160–203. Since then the most important relevant publication has been the *Treaty Rolls preserved in the Public Record Office*, I (1234–1325), ed. P. Chaplais (H.M.S.O., 1955).

C. Johnson, *The "De Moneta" of Nicholas Oresme and English Mint Documents* (1956) sketches

[1] The study of Mr J. P. Trabut-Cussac, on which Powicke's chapter is chiefly based, has since been published, but, of course, in French – *L'Administration anglaise en Gascogne sous Henri III et Edouard Ier de 1254 à 1307* (Paris, 1972).

the history of English coinage in the period and gives documents. H. G. Richardson, *The English Jewry under Angevin Kings* (1960) ranges far more widely than its title, ending in fact with a valuable discussion of the expulsion in 1290.

For a valuable survey of work done in 1937–67 on medieval Irish history, A. J. Otway-Ruthven in *Irish Historical Studies*, xv, No. 60 (September 1967), pp. 359–65. Since then, A. J. Otway-Ruthven, *A History of Medieval Ireland* (1968); J. F. Lydon, *The Lordship of Ireland in the Middle Ages* (Dublin, 1972) and G. J. Hand, *English Law in Ireland 1290–1324* (Cambridge, 1967) and "English Law in Ireland 1172–1351", *Northern Ireland Legal Quarterly*, vol. 23, No. 4 (Winter 1972), pp. 393–420, have appeared. Relevant articles are: G. J. Hand in *Proc. Royal Irish Acad.*, vol. 62, sect. C, No. 2, pp. 9–20, A. J. Otway-Ruthven, "Royal Service in Ireland", *Journ. Royal Soc. Antiqu. Ireland*, vol. 98, pt 1 (1968), pp. 37–46; and R. Frame in *The Irish Jurist*, ii, n.s., pt 2 (1967), pp. 308–26, on procedure without writ, scutage, and keepers of the peace respectively in Ireland.

On medieval Scotland three notable works have appeared since Powicke's *Thirteenth Century* (ch. xii and bibliography sect. 7): W. C. Dickinson, *Scotland from the earliest times to 1603* (Edinburgh, 1961); G. W. S. Barrow, *Robert Bruce and the community of the realm of Scotland* (1965); and E. L. G. Stones, *Anglo-Scottish Relations 1174–1328* (1965), a source-book, which is to be followed by a modern edition of the material for Edward I's adjudication in the Scottish succession question and the resulting reign of John Balliol. See also R. Nicholson, "The Franco-Scottish and Franco-Norwegian Treaties of 1295", *Scottish Historical Review*, xxxviii (1959), pp. 114–32.

From 1294 England was more or less continuously at war or on a war footing. Powicke's synthesis to 1307 has been carried forward to 1327 by M. McKisack, *The Fourteenth Century* (1959), the next volume in the Oxford History of England. Neither has been modified except in detail by work done since. More spade-work is needed before there can be a fresh synthesis and in the last twenty years the main effort has been editorial and critical. For work done on the chronicle evidence see the Bibliography to Part I above. The Selden Society followed G. O. Sayles's three volumes of *Select Cases in the Court of King's Bench under Edward I* with a fourth by the same editor for Edward II's reign (1957). Of the new Public Record Office series, *Treaty Rolls*, I (1234–1325), ed. P. Chaplais appeared in 1955, but neither *Diplomatic Documents* nor *Calendar of Liberate Rolls* is yet available for these years. The chancery's Gascon rolls down to 1307 were printed long ago: *Rôles Gascons*, ed. Francisque-Michel and C. Bémont, 3 vols in 4 (Paris, 1885–1906). They are now available down to 1317: *Gascon Rolls . . . 1307–1317*, ed. Y. Renouard (H.M.S.O., 1962). Of exchequer records the Memoranda Rolls are by the later thirteenth century more important than the Pipe Rolls but they have not yet had such systematic treatment. They are the next most obvious and most direct line of enquiry into the reigns of Edwards I–III. They are described by J. Conway Davies in his *Studies presented to Sir Hilary Jenkinson* (1957), pp. 97–154. Their interpretation has been facilitated by the publication of them for 1326–7 with an introduction: *Calendar of Memoranda Rolls (Exchequer) preserved in the Public Record Office, Michaelmas 1326 to Michaelmas 1327* (H.M.S.O., 1968–9). Their relationship to the final record of the exchequer, the Pipe Roll, will be seen by comparison with Mabel H. Mill's edition and interpretation of the Pipe Roll record for the county of Surrey in 1295: *The Pipe Roll for 1295, Surrey Membrane, Pipe Roll 140*, Surrey Rec. Soc. Publication No. 21 (1924). C. A. F. Meekings's important article on "The Pipe Roll Order of 12 February 1270" in *Studies presented to Sir Hilary Jenkinson*, ed. J. C. Davies (1957), pp. 222–53 explains the problem of auditing such county accounts due to growth in the amount of royal government. An important event was the publication of another Wardrobe book, *The Book of Prests of the King's Wardrobe for 1294–5: presented to John Goronwy Edwards*, ed. E. B. Fryde

(Oxford, 1962). E. M. Carus-Wilson and O. Coleman, *England's Export Trade 1275–1547* (Oxford, 1963) tabulates the Enrolled Customs Accounts.

There has been no further progress in the debate on the origin and nature of the English parliament. J. G. Edwards assessed the importance of judicial business in parliaments at this time: "Justice in Early English Parliaments", *Bull. Inst. Hist. Research*, xxvii (1954), pp. 35–53. H. G. Richardson and G. O. Sayles reaffirmed their original positions of 1928–1946 in the *Law Quarterly Review* for 1961 in articles reprinted as *Parliaments and Great Councils in Medieval England* (1961). E. Miller, *The Origins of Parliament* (1960), an Historical Association pamphlet, remains an excellent summary of the debate.

In political as well as parliamentary history the reign of Edward II is a dark but critical time. A new attack on the politics of it is being made by means of monographs: J. R. Maddicott, *Thomas of Lancaster 1307–22* (1970) and J. R. S. Phillips, *Aymer de Valence, Earl of Pembroke 1307–1324*. At the very outset of the reign is the problem of the Coronation Oath of Edward II, 1308 (No. 97 below). The scholarship lavished on this short text has so far thrown more light on the coronation ceremony as a whole than on the oath, and more on other occasions than on 1308. It has, in other words, abundantly justified itself (particularly in the work of Mr H. G. Richardson as summed up in *Traditio*, vol. 16 (1960), pp. 111–202), without accounting for the novelty of Edward II's oath, the addition of a fourth clause, or helping to interpret it. But Professor McKisack is surely right when she says that "the most plausible explanation" of the addition is that it was "intended to cover [I would say safeguard] any changes in law and custom which might arise during the reign as a result of enactments promulgated by the king with the consent of the community" and in saying that it is likely to have been "prompted by memories of Edward I's violations" of enactments of his reign (*The Fourteenth Century 1307–1399* (Oxford, 1959), pp. 5–6). Few who were present when Edward II was crowned can have been unaware of the struggle and defeat of the previous decade or of Clement V's bull barely two years before (cf. H. Rothwell in *Studies in Medieval History presented to Frederick Maurice Powicke*, ed. Hunt, Pantin and Southern (Oxford, 1948), pp. 319–32, and Ch. Bémont's *Chartes des libertés anglaises* (Paris, 1892), No. XVII) and one of their first concerns after the coronation was to rescue the Articles upon the Charters of 1300 from the previous reign (No. 85 below) and, in a parliament fully representative of the "community", exact substantially, in the Articles of Stamford of 1309 (Rolls of Parliament, *Rotuli Parliamentorum* (6 vols, 1767 – and Index (Rec. Com., 1832), I, 443–5), a virtual reissue of them. The king is being bound (as far as a king can be bound) by the commonplace of "*Quod omnes tangit ab omnibus approbetur*". Not only when it is convenient, as it was for Edward I when he made the maxim famous in 1295, but also when it is irksome. This is the emphasis, the only novelty, and the limit of the revolutionary in the coronation oath of Edward II. There is no attempt at a definition of the way in which approbation is to be sought or given, or in which a king, having had it, may test whether he still has it. We may not anticipate parliament, least of all a parliament of any particular composition. The authors may or may not have had such things in mind at the coronation, but they are not in the oath. Nor, if we did not know what happened afterwards, would we venture to read them into it.

A description of the coronation in 1308 is printed by H. G. Richardson in *Bulletin of the Institute of Historical Research*, xvi (1938–9), pp. 8–10.

The oath, in the original French, is preserved (unusually) in a special schedule to the Close Roll of the year, whence printed in *Parliamentary Writs*, ii, part 2, App. pp. 10–11; in Rymer, *Foedera* (Rec. Com.), II, i, 36; and most recently in Chrimes and Brown, *Sel. Docs. of Engl. Constit. Hist.* (1961), pp. 4–5 with verification from the Close Roll.

It is also preserved, unofficially, in two Winchester texts, a cartulary of St Swithun's (whence printed in A. W. Goodman, *Chartulary of Winchester Cathedral* (Winchester, 1927), pp. 175–6) and the Custumal of St Swithun's in the cathedral library, f. 180v (edited by K. A. Hanna in her unpublished University of London M.A. dissertation (1954), pp. 646–7). The bishop of Winchester, Henry Woodlock, deputised for the archbishop of Canterbury, Winchelsey, at the coronation.

The text printed in *Statutes of the Realm*, I (1810), p. 168, is of Canterbury (Christ Church) provenance, "Cant. Chapter Libr., MS. K.11". Brit. Mus. Cotton Vitellius C. xii, fos 231–1b, printed by H. G. Richardson, *Bull. Inst. Hist. Research*, xvi (1938–9), p. 9, is also from Canterbury (St Augustine's).

A Latin text from the Coronation Roll is printed in Rymer, *Foedera* (Rec. Com.), II, i, 33, but the oath was taken in French.

Discussion of the oath, revived by B. Wilkinson, "The Coronation Oath of Edward II", *Historical Essays in honour of James Tait*, ed. J. G. Edwards, V. H. Galbraith and E. F. Jacob (Manchester, 1933), pp. 405–16, continued first of all with a series of articles by H. G. Richardson and G. O. Sayles in the *Bulletin of the Institute of Historical Research* on "Early Coronation Records", vols xiii (1935–6), pp. 129–45; xiv (1936–7), pp. 1–9 and 145–8; xv (1937–8), pp. 94–9; and xvi (1938–9), pp. 1–11, then by P. L. Ward, "The Coronation Ceremony in Medieval England", *Speculum*, xiv (1939), pp. 160–78; H. G. Richardson, "The English Coronation Oath", *Transactions of the Royal Historical Society*, 4th ser., xxiii (1941), pp. 129–58; B. Wilkinson, "The Coronation Oath of Edward II and the Statute of York", *Speculum*, xix (1944), pp. 445–69; H. G. Richardson, "The Annales Paulini", *Speculum*, xxiii (1948), pp. 630–40 and "The English Coronation Oath", *Speculum*, xxiv (1949), pp. 44–75; Robert S. Hoyt, "The Coronation Oath of 1308: the background of 'Les leys et les custumes' ", *Traditio*, xi (1955), pp. 235–57 and "The Coronation Oath of 1308", *English Historical Review*, lxxi (1956), pp. 353–83; and H. G. Richardson, "The Coronation in Medieval England: the Evolution of the Office and the Oath", *Traditio*, xvi (1960), pp. 111–202.

Since T. F. Tout's *The Place of the Reign of Edward II in English History* (Manchester, 1914, revised edn, 1936) and J. Conway Davies's *The Baronial Opposition to Edward II: its character and policy* (Cambridge, 1918) until lately, most contributions to the political history of this reign appeared in article form. Kathleen Edwards, "The Political Importance of the English Bishops during the Reign of Edward II", *English Historical Review*, lix (1944), pp. 311–47; J. G. Edwards, "The Negotiating of the Treaty of Leake, 1318", *Essays in History presented to R. Lane Poole* (ed. H. W. C. Davis (Oxford, 1927)), pp. 360–78 and, on the chronology of the negotiations, B. Wilkinson, "The Negotiations preceding the 'Treaty' of Leake, August 1318", *Studies in Medieval History presented to F. M. Powicke* (ed. Hunt, Pantin and Southern (Oxford, 1948)), pp. 333–53; W. J. Smith, "The 'Revolt' of William de Somertone", *E.H.R.*, lxix (1954), pp. 76–83 suggests local Lancastrian action in 1319–20; though book rather than article, G. H. Tupling, *South Lancs. in the Reign of Edward II* (1949) must be mentioned here as an important edition of a roll of Proceedings *coram rege* showing the disturbed state of the north in 1323; E. L. G. Stones, "Sir Geoffrey le Scrope (*c.* 1285–1340), Chief Justice of the King's Bench", *E.H.R.*, lxix (1954), pp. 1–17, shows continuity in at least one career through the "revolution" of 1326.

Books on the reign include, of course, on the young Edward, Hilda Johnstone, *Edward of Carnarvon, 1284–1307* (Manchester, 1946) and quite recently, Harold F. Hutchison, *Edward II the Pliant King* (1971). On Edward's fall, Maud V. Clarke, "Committees of Estates and the deposition of Edward II", *Historical Essays in honour of James Tait*, ed. J. G. Edwards, V. H. Galbraith and E. F. Jacob (Manchester, 1933), pp. 27–45; May McKisack, "London and the Succession to the Crown during the Middle Ages", *Studies in Medieval History presented to F. M. Powicke*, ed. Hunt, Pantin and Southern (Oxford, 1948), pp. 76–89. G. W. S. Barrow, *Robert Bruce* (1965) is of major importance for Edward's wars. In this connection Jean Scammell, "Robert I and the North of England", *E.H.R.*, lxxiv (1958), pp. 385–403 and E. L. G. Stones, *Anglo-Scottish Relations 1174–1328* (1965). For relations with Ireland, A. J. Otway-Ruthven, *A History of Medieval Ireland*, and G. J. Hand, *English Law in Ireland 1290–1324* (Cambridge, 1967). On finance, W. E. Lunt, *Financial Relations of the Papacy with England to 1327* (Cambridge, Mass., 1939) and J. F. Willard, *Parliamentary Taxes on Personal Property 1290–1334* (Cambridge, Mass., 1934).

Among source material for the reign an important recent publication is *Records of the Trial of Walter Langeton, bishop of Coventry and Lichfield, 1307–12*, ed. Alice Beardwood (Camden, 4th ser., vol. 6 (1969)).

The Selden Society has made excellent progress with printing legal material for the reign. With Year Books in particular: volumes 27, 29, 31, 33, 34, 36, 37, 38, 39, 41, 42, 43, 45 52, 54, 61, 63, 65, 70 all relate to Edward II's reign. Similarly, G. O. Sayles has extended for the Society his editing of *Select Cases in the Court of King's Bench* to cover the reign of Edward II as well as that of Edward I.

A. THE TESTING TIME 1189–1227

15. Form of proceeding in pleas of the crown, 1194

(Preserved by the chronicler, mr Roger of Howden, cf. No. 2 above, s.a. 1194; reprinted in W. Stubbs, *Select Charters . . . of English Constitutional History* with division into clauses. It is translated from this conveniently articulated text (9th edn, ed. H. W. C. Davis, Oxford, 1913, pp. 251–7) for the present volume)

Form of proceeding in pleas of the crown of the king

In the first place, four knights are to be chosen from out of the whole county, who, upon their oaths, are to choose two lawful knights from each hundred or wapentake, and these two are to choose upon their oath ten knights from each hundred or wapentake, or free and lawful men if there are not enough knights, in order that these twelve together may answer to all the articles from every hundred or wapentake.

The articles of pleas of the crown of the king

[1] Of pleas of the crown new and old and all not yet concluded before the justices of the lord king.

[2] Also of all recognitions and all pleas which have been summoned before the justices by writ of the king or of the chief justice, or which have been sent before them from the chief court of the king.

[3] Also of escheats, what they are, and what they were after the king set out for the land of Jerusalem; and what were at that time in the king's hands, and whether they are now in his hands or not; and of all escheats of the lord king, if they have been taken out of his hands, how, and by whom, and into whose hands they have come, and by what right, and if any one has had the issues thereof, and what these are, and what were they worth, and what are they worth now; and if there is any escheat which belongs to the lord king which is not in his hands.

[4] Also of churches which are in the gift of the lord king.

[5] Also of wardships of children, which belong to the lord king.

[6] Also of marriages of maidens or widows, which belong to the lord king.

[7] Also of malefactors, and those who harbour them and those who abet them.

[8] Also of forgers.

[9] Also of killers of Jews, who they are; and of the pledges of Jews who are killed, and the chattels, lands, debts and charters, and who has them, and who owes them what, and what pledges they had, and who holds, and what they are worth, and who has the issues thereof, and what these are; and all the pledges and debts of Jews who are killed are to be taken into the hands of the king; and those who were present at the killing and have not made fine with the lord king or with his justices are to be taken and not liberated except by the lord king or his justices.

[10] Also of all aids given for the ransom of the lord king, who promised how much, and how much he has paid and how much is in arrears.

[11] Also of the adherents of earl John, who have made fine with the lord king and who not.

[12] Also of the chattels of earl John or of his adherents, which have not been converted to the use of the lord king; and how much the sheriffs or their bailiffs have received, and who has given anything contrary to the ancient customs of the kingdom.
[13] Also of all the lands of earl John, of demesnes and wardships, and escheats, and of his gifts and why they were given, and all earl John's gifts are to be taken into the hands of the lord king except those which were confirmed by the king.
[14] Also of the debts and fines due to the earl John and for what reason; and all are to be exacted for the use of the lord king.
[15] Also of deceased usurers and their chattels.
[16] Also of wines sold contrary to the assize, and of false measures as well for wine as for other things.
[17] Also of crusaders who died before setting out for Jerusalem, and who has their chattels, and what these are and how much.
[18] Also of grand assizes, which are of 100*s* worth a year of land and less.
[19] Also of defaults.
[20] Further, in every county three knights and one clerk are to be elected as keepers of the pleas of the crown.
[21] And no sheriff is to be a justice where he is sheriff, or in a county he has held since the first coronation of the lord king.
[22] Furthermore, all cities, boroughs and demesnes of the lord king are to be tallaged.
[23] The justices named, together with the bailiffs of William of St Mary Church and of Geoffrey fitzPeter, William de Chimelli, William Brewer and Hugh Bardolf and of the sheriffs of the places concerned, shall cause the knights named in the roll in a county to appear at a time and place which they shall signify to them and have them swear in their presence that they will use all their lawful endeavours to stock the wardships and escheats of the lord king and to value them to the lord king's advantage, and they shall not through hatred, favour or goodwill of anyone omit to do so. And the aforesaid knights who are named shall on their oath elect twelve lawful knights, or free and lawful men if knights have not been found for the purpose, in the different parts of each county in the eyre of the aforesaid justices, as they see fit, who shall in like manner swear to do what they lawfully can and afford counsel and aid to stock and value and strengthen wardships and escheats in those parts to the king's advantage, as aforesaid. And the said jurors shall on their oath select from the free men of the escheats and wardships as many men of the right kind as they find they require to execute the aforesaid business of the lord king as well as it can be done to the lord king's advantage. And be it known that the said wardships and escheats shall be stocked from the issues forthcoming from them until Michaelmas and also from the issues at that time. And if they are not sufficient, what is short shall be supplied from the toll of the lord king, yet so that they who hold these wardships and escheats at farm shall answer from Michaelmas onwards for them and for what is stocked as well. And the lord king for those who hold them at farm will guarantee those wardships and escheats from year to year until the end of their term, so that even if the lord king gives any of them to anybody a farmer shall still hold his farm

until the end of the year by paying the farm which the king got for it to him to whom the king has given it. The judicial authority attaching to an escheat he gave shall remain with the lord king, unless the lord king has given it expressly. The farmer, when he gives up his farm, shall have his stock and everything of his which he has put into the farm over and above the king's stock, freely and in full. They shall also have letters patent of the lord archbishop thereon, containing the tenor of the lord king's charter made about this.

Most diligent enquiry shall also be made what is the fixed rent for every single manor in the demesne and what all other things that are fixed in the said manors are worth, and how many carucates there are and how much they are worth each, not estimating them at the price of 20 shillings only, but according to whether the land is good or bad the price shall increase or decrease. Those who take up farms shall stock their farms, as already said, according to the above-mentioned price from the issues of the escheats and wardships.

Enquiry shall be made too with how many oxen and livestock the carucates ought each to be stocked, and how many and how much stock the manors can each support. And the answers shall immediately be set down plainly and distinctly in writing. The price of an ox shall be 4 shillings, and cows the same, and draft-animals the same; and of a curly-fleeced sheep 10*d*; and of a sheep with coarser wool 6*d*; and of a sow 12*d*, and of a boar 12*d*; and when farmers give up their farms they shall be answerable at the aforesaid prices or in animals payable instead at the option of the farmers. And when all the aforesaid have been stocked and valued, everything is to be clearly and distinctly recorded and taken to the exchequer. Exempted from this assize are bishoprics and abbeys and the lands of barons who are nearly of age.

Enquiry shall also be made upon the oaths of the aforesaid about all wardships and escheats which are not in the king's hands; and let them be taken into the lord king's hands and dealt with like other escheats and wardships.

[24] *Articles about the Jews*

A written record is to be made of all Jews' debts and pledges, lands, houses, rents and possessions. And a Jew who conceals any of these things shall forfeit to the lord king his body and what he has concealed, and all his possessions and all his chattels, and no Jew shall ever be allowed to recover what he has concealed.

Also, let six or seven places be appointed at which they shall make their loans, and two lawful Christians and two lawful Jews and two lawful scribes shall be appointed, and before them and a clerk of William of St Mary Church and of William de Chimilli loans are to be made, and charters of loans shall be made in the manner of a chirograph. One part shall remain with the Jew, sealed with the seal of him to whom the money is given, and the other part shall remain in the common chest, whereon there shall be three locks, of which the two Christians shall have one key, and the two Jews one, and a clerk of William of St Mary Church and of mr William de Chimilli shall have the third; and moreover three seals, and those who have the keys shall apply the seals. The clerks of the aforesaid William and William are to have a roll of transcripts of all the charters, and as charters are altered, so shall the roll be altered. Three pence shall be paid for each charter, half by the Jew and half by him for whom the money is intended; of which the two scribes shall have two pence and the keeper of the roll the third. And in future no loan shall be made, no payment made to Jews, no alteration of charters made, except in the presence of the aforesaid, or of the greater part of them if all cannot be present. And the aforesaid two Christians are to have a Receipt Roll of the Jews of payments made to them in future, and the two Jews are to have one, and the keeper of the roll one.

Also every Jew shall swear on his scroll[1] that he will have all his debts, pledges, rents, and all his property and possessions recorded, and that, as aforesaid, he will not conceal anything; and that if he is able to learn that anyone has concealed anything, he will secretly disclose the fact to the justices sent to them; and that forgers of charters and clippers of coins, when he knows them, he will expose and point out; and the like with regard to the charters they forged.

[25] Furthermore, the enquiry which was to be held into things taken and protection-money demanded by all bailiffs of the lord king, as well justices as sheriffs and constables and foresters and their servants, since the first coronation of the lord king Richard, and why those things were taken, and by whom; and into all the chattels, gifts and promises made on the occasion of the possession taken of the lands of earl John and his adherents,[2] and who received them, and what, and how much, was postponed by command of Hubert, archbishop of Canterbury, at that time the king's chief justice.[3]

16. Franco-Welsh treaty of alliance, 1212

(This important letter would appear to have been written in July or early August 1212. It is today J.655,14 in the Archives Nationales in Paris. The translation is of the best printed text: that of R. F. Treharne, in *Bulletin of the Board of Celtic Studies*, vol. 18, Pt 1 (November 1958), pp. 74–5)

To his most excellent lord, Philip, by God's grace the illustrious king of the French, Llywelyn prince of North Wales his faithful subject greeting and devoted and due service of fealty and reverence. How am I to repay the excellence of your nobility for the singular honour and priceless gift with which you the king of the French, nay foremost of kings on earth, anticipated me, not so much munificently as magnificently, in sending me, your knight, your letter sealed with the seal of gold in testimony of the treaty between the kingdom of the French and the principality of North Wales – which letter I will have kept in the aumbreys of the church as if it were a sacred relic, to be a perpetual memorial and an inviolable witness that I and my heirs, adhering inseparably to you and your heirs, will be friends to your friends and enemies to your enemies and I confidently ask and request that the very same be observed in all respects by your royal dignity in royal fashion towards me and my friends. That it may be inviolably observed, by the testimony of my seal, having summoned the council of my chief men and having obtained the

[1] *rotulum* [2] cf. articles 12–14 above
[3] Hubert Walter, archbishop 1193–1205, was chief justice 1194–8

common assent of all the princes of Wales, all of whom I have bound to you in the friendship of this treaty, I promise that I will be faithful to you for ever and just as I faithfully promise I will most faithfully fulfil my promise. Furthermore, from the time I received your highness's letter, I have made neither truce nor peace, nor even parley, with the English, but, by God's grace, I and all the princes of Wales unanimously leagued together have manfully resisted our – and your – enemies, and with God's help we have by force of arms recovered from the yoke of their tyranny a large part of the land and the strongly defended castles which they by fraud and deceit had occupied and having recovered them we hold them strongly in the might of the Lord. Hence we, all the princes of Wales, ask and request that you make no truce or peace with the English without us, knowing that we will not for any terms or price bind ourselves to them by any peace or treaty unless we know in advance we have your approval.

17. John's surrender of his kingdoms of England and Ireland to the pope, May and October 1213

(*Selected Letters of Pope Innocent III concerning England (1198–1216)*, ed. C. R. Cheney and W. H. Semple (London, 1953), No. 67)

King John accepted Pope Innocent III's terms for raising the interdict in May 1213 and on 15 May, in the presence of the nuncio, Pandulf, surrendered his kingdoms of England and Ireland to the pope to receive them back as fiefs of the Roman see. The surrender was repeated in the presence of a legate on 3 October 1213 in terms which are recited in the pope's acceptance of it in the following privilege of 21 April 1214.

For what became of the legal relationship thus established, see Powicke, *Henry III and the Lord Edward* (1947), pp. 347–8 and the further reading there given.

INNOCENT, BISHOP, SERVANT OF THE SERVANTS OF GOD, TO HIS WELL-BELOVED SON IN CHRIST, JOHN ILLUSTRIOUS KING OF THE ENGLISH, AND TO HIS LEGITIMATE FREE-BORN HEIRS FOR EVER

The King of kings and Lord of lords, Jesus Christ, a priest for ever after the order of Melchisedech, has so established in the church His kingdom and His priesthood that the one is a kingdom of priests and the other a royal priesthood, as is testified by Moses in the Law and by Peter in his Epistle; and over all He has set one whom He has appointed as His vicar on earth, so that, as every knee is bowed to Jesus, of things in heaven, and things in earth, and things under the earth, so all men should obey His vicar and strive that there may be one fold and one shepherd. All secular kings for the sake of God so venerate this vicar, that unless they seek to serve him devotedly they doubt if they are reigning properly. To this, dearly beloved son, you have paid wise attention; and by the merciful inspiration of Him in whose hand are the hearts of kings which He turns whithersoever He wills, you have decided to submit in a temporal sense yourself and your kingdom to him to whom you knew them to be spiritually subject, so that kingdom and priesthood, like body and soul, for the great good and profit of each, might be united in the single person of Christ's vicar. He has deigned to work this wonder, who being alpha and omega has caused the end to fulfil the beginning and the beginning to anticipate the end, so that those provinces which from of old have had the holy Roman church as their proper teacher in spiritual matters should now in temporal things also have her as their peculiar sovereign. You, whom God has chosen as a suitable minister to effect this, by a devout and spontaneous act of will and on the general advice of your barons have offered and yielded, in the form of an annual payment of a thousand marks, yourself and your kingdoms of England and Ireland, with all their rights and appurtenances, to God and to SS Peter and Paul His apostles and to the holy Roman church and to us and our successors, to be our right and our property – as is stated in your official letter attested by a golden seal, the literal tenor of which is as follows:

"John, by the grace of God king of England, lord of Ireland, duke of Normandy and Aquitaine, count of Anjou, to all the faithful of Christ who may see this charter, greeting in the Lord.

"By this charter attested by our golden seal we wish it to be known to you all that, having in many things offended God and holy church our mother and being therefore in the utmost need of divine mercy and possessing nothing but ourselves and our kingdoms that we can worthily offer as due amends to God and the church, we desire to humble ourselves for the sake of Him who for us humbled Himself even unto death; and inspired by the grace of the Holy Spirit – not induced by force nor compelled by fear, but of our own good and spontaneous will and on the general advice of our barons – we offer and freely yield to God, and to SS Peter and Paul His apostles, and to the holy Roman church our mother, and to our lord pope Innocent III and his catholic successors, the whole kingdom of England and the whole kingdom of Ireland with all their rights and appurtenances for the remission of our sins and the sins of our whole family, both the living and the dead. And now, receiving back these kingdoms from God and the Roman church and holding them as feudatory vassal, in the presence of our venerable father, lord Nicholas, bishop of Tusculum, legate of the apostolic see, and of Pandulf, subdeacon and member of household to our lord the pope, we have pledged and sworn our fealty henceforth to our lord aforesaid, pope Innocent, and to his catholic successors, and to the Roman church, in the terms hereinunder stated; and we have publicly paid liege homage for the said kingdoms to God, and to the holy apostles Peter and Paul, and to the Roman church, and to our lord aforesaid, pope Innocent III, at the hands of the said legate who accepts our homage in place and instead of our said lord, the pope; and we bind in perpetuity our successors and legitimate heirs that without question they must similarly render fealty and acknowledge homage to the supreme pontiff holding office at the time and to the Roman church. As a token of this our perpetual offering and concession we will and decree that out of the proper and special revenues of our said kingdoms, in lieu of all service and payment which we should render for them, the Roman church is to receive annually, without prejudice to the payment of Peter's pence, one thousand marks sterling – five hundred at the feast of St Michael and five hundred at Easter – that is, seven hundred for the kingdom of England and three hundred for the kingdom of Ireland, subject to the maintenance for us and our heirs of our jurisdiction, privileges, and regalities. Desiring all these terms, exactly as stated, to be forever ratified and valid, we bind ourselves and our successors not to contravene them; and if we or any of our successors shall presume to contravene them, then, no matter who he be, unless on due warning he come to his senses, let him lose the title to the kingdom, and let this document of our offer and concession remain ever valid.

"I, John, by grace of God king of England and lord of Ireland, will from this hour henceforward be faithful to God and St Peter and the Roman church and my lord pope Innocent III and his catholic successors. I will not take part in deed, word, agreement, or plan whereby they should lose life or limb or be treacherously taken prisoners; any injury to them, if aware of it, I will prevent and will check if I can; and otherwise, I will notify them as soon as possible, or inform a person whom I can trust without fail to tell them; any counsel they have entrusted to me either personally or by envoys or by letter I will keep secret, nor will I wittingly divulge it to anyone to their disadvantage. I will help in maintaining and defending, to the utmost of my power, against all men, the patrimony of St Peter, and particularly the kingdom of England and the kingdom of Ireland. So help me God and the holy gospels of God whereon I swear.

"To prevent any questioning of these terms at any time in the future, and for the greater surety of our offer and concession, we have caused this charter to be made and to be sealed with our golden seal; and as tribute for this the first year we pay a thousand marks sterling to the Roman church by the hand of the said legate.

"Witnessed by his lordship Stephen archbishop of Canterbury, and by their lordships William bishop of London, Peter bishop of Winchester, Eustace bishop of Ely, and Hugh bishop of Lincoln, and by our chancellor, Walter de Gray, our brother William earl of Salisbury, Ranulf earl of Chester, William Marshal earl of Pembroke, William earl of Ferrers, Saer earl of Winchester, Robert de Ros, William Briwerre, Peter FitzHerbert, Matthew FitzHerbert, and Brian de Lisle our steward.

"By the hand of master Richard Marsh archdeacon of Richmond and Northumberland, at St Paul's London, the third of October A.D. 1213, in the fifteenth year of our reign."

This offer and concession so piously and wisely made we regard as acceptable and valid, and we take under the protection of St Peter and of ourselves your person and the persons of your heirs together with the said kingdoms and their appurtenances and all other goods which are now reasonably held or may in future be so held: to you and to your heirs, according to the terms set out above and by the general advice of our brethren, we grant the said kingdoms in fief and confirm them by this privilege, on condition that any of your heirs on receiving the crown will publicly acknowledge this as a fief held of the supreme pontiff and of the Roman church, and will take an oath of fealty to them. Let no man, therefore, have power to infringe this document of our concession and confirmation, or presume to oppose it. If any man dare to do so, let him know that he will incur the anger of Almighty God and of SS Peter and Paul, His apostles. AMEN, amen, AMEN.

(Rota) I, Innocent, bishop of the catholic church, have signed. Farewell.

✠ I, John, bishop of Sabina, have signed.

✠ I, Hugh, bishop of Ostia and Velletri, have signed.

✠ I, Benedict, bishop of Porto and S. Rufina, have signed.
✠ I, Cinthius, cardinal priest of the title of S. Lorenzo in Lucina, have signed.
✠ I, Cencius, cardinal priest of SS Giovanni e Paolo of the title of Pammachius, have signed.
✠ I, Peter, cardinal priest of the title of S. Marcello, have signed.
✠ I, Leo, cardinal priest of the title of Santa Croce in Gerusalemme, have signed.
✠ I, Peter, cardinal priest of Santa Pudenziana of the title of the pastor, have signed.
✠ I, Guala, cardinal priest of S. Martino of the title of Equitius, have signed.
✠ I, John, cardinal priest of the title of Santa Prassede, have signed.
✠ I, Guy, cardinal deacon of S. Nicola in Carcere Tulliano, have signed.
✠ I, Octavian, cardinal deacon of Santi Sergio e Bacco, have signed.
✠ I, John, cardinal deacon of Santi Cosma e Damiano, have signed.
✠ I, Angelus, cardinal deacon of S. Adriano, have signed.

Rome, St Peter's, by the hand of master Raynaldus, acolyte and chaplain to the lord pope Innocent III, the 21st of April, indiction 2, A.D. 1214, in the 17th year of the pontificate of the lord Innocent.

18. The "Unknown" Charter of Liberties, before 15 June 1215

(Paris, Archives Nationales: Archives du Royaume J. 655, as printed in J. C. Holt, *Magna Carta* (Cambridge, 1965), App. II, more particularly pp. 302–3)

The problem presented by this text and the discussion it has given rise to are summarised in Holt, loc. cit.

[1] King John concedes that he will not take a man without judgment, nor accept anything for doing justice and will not do injustice.
[2] And if my baron or my man should happen to die and his heir is of age, I ought to give him his land at a just relief without taking more.
[3] And if it be that the heir is under age, I ought to put the land in charge of four knights from among the more lawful men of the fief, and they with my official ought to render to me the revenues of the land without sale of woods and without letting men be redeemed and without destruction of park and preserve; and then when the heir comes of age I will let him have the land without payment.
[4] If a woman is heir to the land, I ought to give her in marriage on the advice of her relatives so that she is not disparaged; and if I give her once in marriage I cannot give her again, but she can marry as she pleases, though not to my enemies.
[5] If my baron or man should happen to die, I grant that his money[1] be divided as he himself willed; and if he dies unexpectedly through arms or unforeseen illness, his wife or children or relatives and close friends shall divide it for the good of his soul.
[6] And his wife shall not leave the house within forty days and until she has had her proper dower, and she shall have her marriage portion.
[7] In addition, I grant to my men that they should not serve in the army outside

[1] *pecunia*

England save in Normandy and Brittany, and this properly, because if anyone owes me the service of ten knights it shall be alleviated by the counsel of my barons.
[8] And if a scutage takes place in the land one mark of silver will be taken on the knight's fee, and if the burden of an army occurs more may be taken by the counsel of the barons of the kingdom.
[9] Further, I grant that all the forests which my father and my brother and I have made forest I disafforest.
[10] Furthermore, I grant that knights who have their own wood in my ancient forests are to have the wood from now on for their rights of herbage and for burning; and they are to have their forester[1] and I one only to protect my beasts.
[11] And if any of my men dies in debt to the Jews, the debt shall not bear interest as long as his heir is under age.
[12] And I grant that a man is not to lose life or limb for a beast.

19. The articles of the barons, 15 June 1215

(Brit. Mus. Add. MS. 4838 – the original. Now best read in print in J. C. Holt, *Magna Carta* (Cambridge, 1965), App. III, but also conveniently in W. Stubbs, *Select Charters*, 9th edn, pp. 285–91)

This document "the preliminary draft terms not yet put into charter form . . . the true original [of Magna Carta] which must have been seen and handled by both parties [at Runnymede]", has been called "the most momentous single document in our history" and its survival, "a miracle" (V. H. Galbraith, *Studies in the Public Records*, p. 124).

These are the articles which the barons ask for and the lord king grants
[1] After the death of their predecessors, heirs who are of full age shall have their inheritance on payment of the old relief, which is to be stated in the charter.
[2] Heirs who are under age and are wards shall have their inheritance when they come of age without paying relief and without making fine.
[3] The guardian of the land of an heir shall take reasonable revenues, customary dues and services without destruction and waste of his men and goods, and if the guardian of the land causes destruction and waste, he shall lose the wardship; and the guardian shall keep in repair the houses, parks, preserves, ponds, mills and other things pertaining to the land out of the revenue from it; and that heirs shall be so married that they are not disparaged and on the advice of those nearest in blood to them.
[4] That a widow shall not pay anything to have her dower or marriage portion after the death of her husband, but shall remain in his house for forty days after his death, and within that term the dower shall be assigned to her; the marriage portion and her inheritance she shall have forthwith.
[5] King or bailiff shall not seize any land for debt while the chattels of the debtor suffice; nor shall those who have gone surety for the debtor be distrained while the principal debtor is himself able to pay; if however the principal debtor fails to pay, the sureties shall, if they wish, have the lands of the debtor until that debt is fully paid, unless the principal debtor can show that he has discharged his obligation in the matter to the sureties.

[1] a private forester, i.e. woodward

[6] The king shall not grant any baron the right to take an aid from his free men, except for ransoming his person, for making his eldest son a knight and for once marrying his eldest daughter, and this he shall do by a reasonable aid.

[7] That no one shall do greater service for a knight's fee than is due from it.

[8] That common pleas shall not follow the court of the lord king, but shall be assigned in some fixed place; and that recognitions be held in the counties to which they relate,[1] in this manner – that the king shall send two justices four times a year, who with four knights of the same county chosen by the county shall hold assizes of *novel disseisin*, *mort d'ancestor* and *darrein presentment*, nor shall anyone be summoned on account of this save the jurors and the two parties.

[9] That a free man shall be amerced for a trivial offence in accordance with the degree of the offence, and for a grave offence in accordance with its gravity, yet saving his way of living;[2] a villein also shall be amerced in the same way, saving his means of livelihood;[3] and a merchant in the same way, saving his stock-in-trade;[4] by the oath of good men of the neighbourhood.

[10] That a clerk shall be amerced in respect of his lay fief after the manner of the others aforesaid and not according to his ecclesiastical benefice.

[11] That no vill shall be amerced for the purpose of making bridges at river banks save where they used to be legally and of old.

[12] That the measure for wine, corn and widths of cloths and other things be improved; and so with weights.

[13] That assizes of *novel disseisin* and of *mort d'ancestor* be shortened; and similarly with other assizes.

[14] That no sheriff shall concern himself with pleas pertaining to the crown without coroners; and that counties and hundreds be at the old rents without any additional payment, except the king's demesne manors.

[15] If anyone holding of the king dies, it shall be lawful for the sheriff or other bailiff of the king to seize and make a list of his chattels under the supervision of law-worthy men, provided that none of the chattels shall be removed until it is more fully known whether he owes any manifest[5] debt to the lord king and then the debt to the king is paid in full; the residue however shall be left to the executors for carrying out the will of the deceased. And if nothing is owing to the king, all the chattels shall accrue to the deceased.

[16] If any free man dies without leaving a will, his goods shall be distributed by his nearest kinsfolk and friends and under the supervision of the church.

[17] That widows shall not be forced to marry, so long as they wish to live without a husband, provided that they give security not to marry without the consent of the king, if they hold of the king, or of the lords of whom they hold.

[18] That no constable or other bailiff shall take corn or other chattels unless he pays on the spot in cash for them, unless he can delay payment by arrangement with the seller.

[19] That no constable shall be able to compel any knight to give money instead of

[1] *in eisdem comitatibus* [2] *contenementum* [3] *waynagium*
[4] *marcandisa* [5] *liquidum*

castle-guard if he is willing to do the guard himself or through another good man, if for some good reason he cannot do it himself; and if the king leads him on military service, let him be excused guard in proportion to the time.

[20] That no sheriff or king's bailiff or anyone else shall take the horses or carts of any free man for transport work save with his agreement.

[21] That neither the king nor his bailiff shall take another man's timber for castles or other works of his, except with the agreement of him whose timber it is.

[22] That the king shall not hold for more than a year and a day the land of those convicted of felony, but then it shall be handed over to the lord of the fief.

[23] That all fish-weirs be henceforth cleared completely from the Thames and Medway and throughout all England.

[24] That the writ called *Praecipe* be not in future issued to anyone in respect of any holding whereby a free man may lose his court.

[25] If any one has been disseised of or kept out of his lands, franchises and his right by the king without a judgment, let it be immediately restored to him; and if a dispute arises over this, then let it be decided by the judgment of the twenty-five barons; and that those who were disseised by the father or the brother of the king get justice without delay by the judgment of their peers in the king's court; and let the archbishop and bishops by a certain date give their decision, which shall be final,[1] whether the king should have the respite allowed to other crusaders.

[26] That nothing be given for the writ of inquisition of life or limbs, but that instead it be freely granted without charge and not refused.

[27] If anyone holds of the king by fee-farm, by socage, or by burgage, and of another by knight service, the lord king shall not, by reason of the burgage or socage, have the wardship of the knights of the fief of the other, nor ought he to have custody of the burgage, socage or fee-farm; and that a free men shall not lose his knight service[2] by reason of petty serjeanties, such as those who hold any holding by rendering knives or arrows or the like for it.

[28] That no bailiff be able to put anyone to trial[3] upon his own bare word without reliable witnesses.

[29] That the body of a free man be not arrested or imprisoned or disseised or outlawed or exiled or in any way victimised, nor shall the king attack or send anyone to attack him with force, except by the judgment of his social equals or[4] by the law of the land.

[30] That right be not sold or delayed or forbidden to be done.

[31] That merchants be able to go and come safely for buying or selling by the ancient and right customs, free from all evil tolls.

[32] That no scutage or aid be imposed in the kingdom unless by common counsel of the kingdom, except for ransoming the king's person, for making his eldest son a knight, and for once marrying his eldest daughter; and for this a reasonable aid shall be levied. Be it done in like manner concerning tallages and aids from the city of

[1] *appellatione remota*
[2] *militia*
[3] *lex* (here a technical term for a trial, such as compurgation, ordeal or combat)
[4] *vel*

London and from other cities which have liberties in respect thereof, and that the city of London have in full its ancient liberties and free customs as well by water as by land.

[33] That it be lawful for any one, without prejudicing the allegiance due to the lord king, to leave the kingdom and return, save, in the public interest, for a short period in time of war.

[34] If anyone who has borrowed from the Jews any sum, great or small, dies before it is repaid, the debt shall not bear interest as long as the heir is under age, of whomsoever he holds; and if the debt falls into the hand of the king, the king shall not take anything except the principal which is mentioned in the bond.

[35] If anyone dies indebted to the Jews, his wife shall have her dower; and if children are left, they shall be provided with necessaries befitting the holding; and the debt shall be paid out of the residue, reserving, however, service due to lords of the land; other debts shall be dealt with in like manner; and that the guardian of the land shall restore to the heir when he comes of full age his land stocked, according to what he can reasonably bear from the revenues of the land, with ploughs and the means of husbandry.

[36] If anyone who holds of some escheat such as the honour of Wallingford, Nottingham, Boulogne, and Lancaster or[1] of other escheats which are in the king's hands and are baronies, dies, his heir shall give no other relief or do no other service to the king than he would have done to the baron; and that the king hold it in the same manner in which the baron held it.

[37] That fines made for dowers, marriage portions, inheritances and amercements unjustly and against the law of the land be entirely remitted, or else let them be settled by the judgment of the twenty-five barons, or by the judgment of the majority of the same, along with the archbishop and such others as he may wish to associate with himself, provided that if any one or more of the twenty-five are in a like suit they be removed and others put in their place by the rest of the twenty-five.

[38] That hostages and charters given to the king as security be returned.

[39] That those who were outside the forest need not come before justices of the forest upon a general summons, unless they are impleaded or are sureties; and that wicked customs connected with forests and with foresters and warrens and sheriffs and river-banks be amended by twelve knights of every county who are to be chosen by good men of the same county.

[40] That the king remove completely from office[2] the relations and all the following of Gerard d'Athée so that they have no office in future, namely Engeland, Andrew, Peter and Guy de Chanceaux, Guy de Cigogné, Matthew de Martigny and his brothers and his nephew Geoffrey and Philip Marc.

[41] And that the king remove foreign knights, mercenaries, cross-bowmen, routiers and serjeants, who come with horses and arms to the detriment of the kingdom.

[42] That the king make justices, constables, sheriffs and bailiffs of such as know the law of the land and mean to observe it well.

[1] *et*
[2] *de balliva*

[43] That barons who have founded abbeys, for which they have royal charters[1] or ancient tenure, have the custody of them during vacancies.

[44] If the king has disseised or kept out Welshmen from lands or liberties or from other things in England or in Wales they shall be immediately restored to them without a lawsuit;[2] and if they were disseised or kept out of their holdings in England by the king's father or brother without the judgment of their peers, the king shall without delay do justice to them in the way that he does justice to the English, for their holdings in England according to the law of England, and for holdings in Wales according to the law of Wales, and for holdings in the March according to the law of the March; Welshmen shall do the same to the king and his men.[3]

[45] That the king give back the son of Llywelyn and, besides, all the hostages from Wales and the charters that were handed over to him as security for peace [46] That the king act towards the king of the Scots concerning the return of hostages and concerning his franchises and his right in the same manner in which he acts towards the barons of England	unless, in the judgment of the archbishop and of such others as he may wish to associate with himself, it ought to be otherwise by the charters which the king has.

[47] And let all forests that have been made forest by the king in his time be disafforested, and so be it done with river-banks that have been made preserves[4] by the king himself.

[48] All these customs and liberties which the king has granted to be observed in the kingdom as far as it pertains to him towards his men, all of the kingdom, clerks as well as laymen, shall observe as far as it pertains to them towards their men.

[A space in the manuscript between [48] and [49].]

[49] This is the form of security for the observance of the peace and liberties between the king and the kingdom. The barons shall choose any twenty-five barons of the kingdom they wish, who must with all their might observe, hold and cause to be observed, the peace and liberties which the lord king has granted and confirmed to them by his charter; so that if the king or the justiciar or the king's bailiffs or any one of his servants offends in any way against any one or transgresses any of the articles of the peace or the security and the offence be notified to four of the aforesaid twenty-five barons, those four barons shall come to the lord king, or to his justiciar if the king is out of the kingdom, and, laying the transgression before him, shall petition him to have that transgression corrected without delay; and if the king or his justiciar does not correct it, if the king is out of the kingdom, within a reasonable time to be determined in the charter, the aforesaid four shall refer that case to the rest of the twenty-five barons and those twenty-five together with the community of the whole land shall distrain and distress the king in every way they can, namely, by seizing castles, lands, possessions, and in such other ways as they can, saving the

[1] *cartas regum*
[2] *sine placito*
[3] *suis*
[4] literally, "are 'in defence'"

person of the lord king and the persons of the queen and his children, until, in their opinion, amends have been made; and when amends have been made they shall obey the lord king as before. And anyone in the land who wishes shall take an oath to obey the orders of the said twenty-five barons for the execution of the aforesaid matters, and with them to distress the king as much as he can, and the king shall publicly and freely give anyone leave to take the oath who wishes to take it and he shall never prohibit anyone from taking it. Indeed, all those in the land who are unwilling of their own accord and of themselves to take an oath to the twenty-five barons to help them to distrain and distress the king, the king shall make them take the oath as aforesaid at his command. Also, if any of the said twenty-five barons dies or leaves the country or is in any other way prevented from carrying out the things aforesaid, the rest of the twenty-five shall choose as they think fit another one in his place, and he shall take the oath like the rest. In all matters the execution of which is committed to these twenty-five barons, if it should happen that these twenty-five are present yet disagree among themselves about anything, or if some of those summoned will not or cannot be present, that shall be held, as fixed and established which the majority of them ordained or commanded, exactly as if all the twenty-five had consented to it; and the said twenty-five shall swear that they will faithfully observe all the things aforesaid and will do all they can to get them observed. Furthermore, the king shall give them security by charters of the archbishop and bishops and master Pandulf that he will procure nothing from the lord pope whereby any of the things here agreed[1] might be revoked or diminished, and if he does procure any such thing, let it be reckoned void and null and let him never use it.

20. Magna Carta, 1215

(There is no "original" of the Charter of Liberties of 1215. Four copies sent out from the royal chancery shortly after the meeting at Runnymede on 19 June survive: two are in the British Museum, one at Lincoln Cathedral, and one at Salisbury Cathedral. Each consists of a single sheet of parchment measuring approximately 15 × 20 in. The punctuation, division into paragraphs, and numeration of them in the translation which follows are in accordance with the practice of modern editors. The Latin text has been printed many times, most conveniently in Stubbs, *Select Charters* (9th edn, ed. H. W. C. Davis, pp. 292–302), most recently by J. C. Holt, *Magna Carta* (Cambridge, 1965), App. IV)

Professor Holt's book just mentioned is quite indispensable, superseding for the historian that of W. S. McKechnie, *Magna Carta*, 2nd edn (Glasgow, 1914).

John, by the grace of God, king of England, lord of Ireland, duke of Normandy and Aquitaine, and count of Anjou, to the archbishops, bishops, abbots, earls, barons, justiciars, foresters, sheriffs, stewards, servants, and to all his bailiffs and faithful subjects, greeting. Know that we, out of reverence for God and for the salvation of our soul and those of all our ancestors and heirs, for the honour of God and the exaltation of holy church, and for the reform of our realm, on the advice of our venerable fathers, Stephen, archbishop of Canterbury, primate of all England and cardinal of the holy Roman church, Henry archbishop of Dublin, William of London, Peter of Winchester, Jocelyn of Bath and Glastonbury, Hugh of Lincoln, Walter of

[1] *istarum conventionum*

Worcester, William of Coventry and Benedict of Rochester, bishops, of master Pandulf, subdeacon and member of the household of the lord pope, of brother Aymeric, master of the order of Knights Templar in England, and of the noble men William Marshal earl of Pembroke, William earl of Salisbury, William earl of Warenne, William earl of Arundel, Alan of Galloway constable of Scotland, Warin fitz Gerold, Peter fitz Herbert, Hubert de Burgh seneschal of Poitou, Hugh de Neville, Matthew fitz Herbert, Thomas Basset, Alan Basset, Philip de Aubeney, Robert of Ropsley, John Marshal, John fitz Hugh, and others, our faithful subjects:

[1] In the first place have granted to God, and by this our present charter confirmed for us and our heirs for ever that the English church shall be free, and shall have its rights undiminished and its liberties unimpaired; and it is our will that it be thus observed; which is evident from the fact that, before the quarrel between us and our barons began, we willingly and spontaneously granted and by our charter confirmed the freedom of elections which is reckoned most important and very essential to the English church, and obtained confirmation of it from the lord pope Innocent III; the which we will observe and we wish our heirs to observe it in good faith for ever. We have also granted to all free men of our kingdom, for ourselves and our heirs for ever, all the liberties written below, to be had and held by them and their heirs of us and our heirs.

[2] If any of our earls or barons or others holding of us in chief by knight service dies, and at his death his heir be of full age and owe relief he shall have his inheritance on payment of the old relief, namely the heir or heirs of an earl £100 for a whole earl's barony, the heir or heirs of a baron £100 for a whole barony, the heir or heirs of a knight 100*s*, at most, for a whole knight's fee; and he who owes less shall give less according to the ancient usage of fiefs.

[3] If, however, the heir of any such be under age and a ward, he shall have his inheritance when he comes of age without paying relief and without making fine.

[4] The guardian of the land of such an heir who is under age shall take from the land of the heir no more than reasonable revenues, reasonable customary dues and reasonable services, and that without destruction and waste of men or goods; and if we commit the wardship of the land of any such to a sheriff, or to any other who is answerable to us for its revenues, and he destroys or wastes what he has wardship of, we will take compensation from him and the land shall be committed to two lawful and discreet men of that fief, who shall be answerable for the revenues to us or to him to whom we have assigned them; and if we give or sell to anyone the wardship of any such land and he causes destruction or waste therein, he shall lose that wardship, and it shall be transferred to two lawful and discreet men of that fief, who shall similarly be answerable to us as is aforesaid.

[5] Moreover, so long as he has the wardship of the land, the guardian shall keep in repair the houses, parks, preserves, ponds, mills and other things pertaining to the land out of the revenues from it; and he shall restore to the heir when he comes of age his land fully[1] stocked with ploughs and the means of husbandry[2] according to what the season of husbandry requires and the revenues of the land can reasonably bear.

[1] *totam*

[2] *waynagiis*, cf. c.20 below

[6] Heirs shall be married without disparagement, yet so that before the marriage is contracted those nearest in blood to the heir shall have notice.

[7] A widow shall have her marriage portion and inheritance forthwith and without difficulty after the death of her husband; nor shall she pay anything to have her dower or her marriage portion or the inheritance which she and her husband held on the day of her husband's death; and she may remain in her husband's house for forty days after his death, within which time her dower shall be assigned to her.

[8] No widow shall be forced to marry so long as she wishes to live without a husband, provided that she gives security not to marry without our consent if she holds of us, or without the consent of her lord of whom she holds, if she holds of another.

[9] Neither we nor our bailiffs will seize for any debt any land or rent, so long as the chattels of the debtor are sufficient to repay the debt; nor will those who have gone surety for the debtor be distrained so long as the principal debtor is himself able to pay the debt; and if the principal debtor fails to pay the debt, having nothing wherewith to pay it, then shall the sureties answer for the debt; and they shall, if they wish, have the lands and rents of the debtor until they are reimbursed for the debt which they have paid for him, unless the principal debtor can show that he has discharged his obligation in the matter to the said sureties.

[10] If anyone who has borrowed from the Jews any sum, great or small, dies before it is repaid, the debt shall not bear interest as long as the heir is under age, of whomsoever he holds; and if the debt falls into our hands, we will not take anything except the principal mentioned in the bond.

[11] And if anyone dies indebted to the Jews, his wife shall have her dower and pay nothing of that debt; and if the dead man leaves children who are under age, they shall be provided with necessaries befitting the holding of the deceased; and the debt shall be paid out of the residue, reserving, however, service due to lords of the land; debts owing to others than Jews shall be dealt with in like manner.

[12] No scutage or aid shall be imposed in our kingdom unless by common counsel of our kingdom, except for ransoming our person, for making our eldest son a knight, and for once marrying our eldest daughter; and for these only a reasonable aid shall be levied. Be it done in like manner concerning aids from the city of London.

[13] And the city of London shall have all its ancient liberties and free customs as well by land as by water. Furthermore, we will and grant that all other cities, boroughs, towns, and ports shall have all their liberties and free customs.

[14] And to obtain the common counsel of the kingdom about the assessing of an aid (except in the three cases aforesaid) or of a scutage, we will cause to be summoned the archbishops, bishops, abbots, earls and greater barons, individually by our letters – and, in addition, we will cause to be summoned generally through our sheriffs and bailiffs all those holding of us in chief – for a fixed date, namely, after the expiry of at least forty days, and to a fixed place; and in all letters of such summons we will specify the reason for the summons. And when the summons has thus been made, the business shall proceed on the day appointed, according to the counsel of those present, though not all have come who were summoned.

[15] We will not in future grant any one the right to take an aid from his free men, except for ransoming his person, for making his eldest son a knight and for once marrying his eldest daughter, and for these only a reasonable aid shall be levied.
[16] No one shall be compelled to do greater service for a knight's fee or for any other free holding than is due from it.
[17] Common pleas shall not follow our court, but shall be held in some fixed place.
[18] Recognitions of *novel disseisin*, of *mort d'ancester*, and of *darrein presentment*, shall not be held elsewhere than in the counties to which they relate,[1] and in this manner – we, or, if we should be out of the realm, our chief justiciar, will send two justices through each county four times a year, who, with four knights of each county chosen by the county, shall hold the said assizes in the county and on the day and in the place of meeting of the county court.
[19] And if the said assizes cannot all be held on the day of the county court, there shall stay behind as many of the knights and freeholders who were present at the county court on that day as are necessary for the sufficient making of judgments, according to the amount of business to be done.
[20] A free man shall not be amerced for a trivial offence except in accordance with the degree of the offence, and for a grave offence he shall be amerced in accordance with its gravity, yet saving his way of living;[2] and a merchant in the same way, saving his stock-in-trade;[3] and a villein shall be amerced in the same way, saving his means of livelihood[4] – if they have fallen into our mercy: and none of the aforesaid amercements shall be imposed except by the oath of good men of the neighbourhood.
[21] Earls and barons shall not be amerced except by their peers, and only in accordance with the degree of the offence.
[22] No clerk shall be amerced in respect of his lay holding except after the manner of the others aforesaid and not according to the amount of his ecclesiastical benefice.
[23] No vill or individual[5] shall be compelled to make bridges at river banks, except those who from of old are legally bound to do so.
[24] No sheriff, constable, coroners, or others of our bailiffs, shall hold pleas of our crown.
[25] All counties, hundreds, wapentakes and trithings[6] shall be at the old rents without any additional payment, except our demesne manors.
[26] If anyone holding a lay fief of us dies and our sheriff or bailiff shows our letters patent of summons for a debt that the deceased owed us, it shall be lawful for our sheriff or bailiff to attach and make a list of chattels of the deceased found upon the lay fief to the value of that debt under the supervision of law-worthy men, provided that none of the chattels shall be removed until the debt which is manifest[7] has been paid to us in full; and the residue shall be left to the executors for carrying out the will of the deceased. And if nothing is owing to us from him, all the chattels shall accrue to the deceased, saving to his wife and children their reasonable shares.
[27] If any free man dies without leaving a will, his chattels shall be distributed by

[1] *in suis comitatibus*
[2] *contenementum*
[3] *mercandisa*
[4] *waynagium*
[5] *homo*
[6] i.e. ridings
[7] *clarum*

his nearest kinsfolk and friends under the supervision of the church, saving to every one the debts which the deceased owed him.

[28] No constable or other bailiff of ours shall take anyone's corn or other chattels unless he pays on the spot in cash for them or can delay payment by arrangement with the seller.

[29] No constable shall compel any knight to give money instead of castle-guard if he is willing to do the guard himself or through another good man, if for some good reason he cannot do it himself; and if we lead or send him on military service, he shall be excused guard in proportion to the time that because of us he has been on service.

[30] No sheriff, or bailiff of ours, or anyone else shall take the horses or carts of any free man for transport work save with the agreement of that freeman.

[31] Neither we nor our bailiffs will take, for castles or other works of ours, timber which is not ours, except with the agreement of him whose timber it is.

[32] We will not hold for more than a year and a day the lands of those convicted of felony, and then the lands shall be handed over to the lords of the fiefs.

[33] Henceforth all fish-weirs shall be cleared completely from the Thames and the Medway and throughout all England, except along the sea coast.

[34] The writ called *Praecipe* shall not in future be issued to anyone in respect of any holding whereby a free man may lose his court.

[35] Let there be one measure for wine throughout our kingdom, and one measure for ale, and one measure for corn, namely "the London quarter"; and one width for cloths whether dyed, russet or halberget, namely two ells within the selvedges. Let it be the same with weights as with measures.

[36] Nothing shall be given or taken in future for the writ of inquisition of life or limbs: instead it shall be granted free of charge and not refused.

[37] If anyone holds of us by fee-farm, by socage, or by burgage, and holds land of another by knight service, we will not, by reason of that fee-farm, socage, or burgage, have the wardship of his heir or of land of his that is of the fief of the other; nor will we have custody of the fee-farm, socage, or burgage, unless such fee-farm owes knight service. We will not have custody of anyone's heir or land which he holds of another by knight service by reason of any petty serjeanty which he holds of us by the service of rendering to us knives or arrows or the like.

[38] No bailiff shall in future put anyone to trial[1] upon his own bare word, without reliable witnesses produced for this purpose.

[39] No free man shall be arrested or imprisoned or disseised or outlawed or exiled or in any way victimised, neither will we attack him or send anyone to attack him, except by the lawful judgment of his peers or[2] by the law of the land.

[40] To no one will we sell, to no one will we refuse or delay right or justice.

[41] All merchants shall be able to go out of and come into England safely and securely and stay and travel throughout England, as well by land as by water, for buying and selling by the ancient and right customs free from all evil tolls, except in time of war

[1] *lex* (here a technical term for a trial, such as compurgation, ordeal or combat)
[2] *vel*

and if they are of the land that is at war with us. And if such are found in our land at the beginning of a war, they shall be attached, without injury to their persons or goods, until we, or our chief justiciar, know how merchants of our land are treated who were found in the land at war with us when war broke out;[1] and if ours are safe there, the others shall be safe in our land.

[42] It shall be lawful in future for anyone, without prejudicing the allegiance due to us, to leave our kingdom and return safely and securely by land and water, save, in the public interest, for a short period in time of war – except for those imprisoned or outlawed in accordance with the law of the kingdom and natives of a land that is at war with us and merchants (who shall be treated as aforesaid).

[43] If anyone who holds of some escheat such as the honour of Wallingford, Nottingham, Boulogne, Lancaster, or of other escheats which are in our hands and are baronies dies, his heir shall give no other relief and do no other service to us than he would have done to the baron if that barony had been in the baron's hands; and we will hold it in the same manner in which the baron held it.

[44] Men who live outside the forest need not henceforth come before our justices of the forest upon a general summons, unless they are impleaded or are sureties for any person or persons who are attached for forest offences.

[45] We will not make justices, constables, sheriffs or bailiffs save of such as know the law of the kingdom and mean to observe it well.

[46] All barons who have founded abbeys for which they have charters of the kings of England or ancient tenure shall have the custody of them during vacancies, as they ought to have.

[47] All forests that have been made forest in our time shall be immediately disafforested; and so be it done with river-banks that have been made preserves[2] by us in our time.

[48] All evil customs connected with forests and warrens, foresters and warreners, sheriffs and their officials, river-banks and their wardens shall immediately be inquired into in each county by twelve sworn knights of the same county who are to be chosen by good men of the same county, and within forty days of the completion of the inquiry shall be utterly abolished by them so as never to be restored, provided that we, or our justiciar if we are not in England, know of it first.

[49] We will immediately return all hostages and charters given to us by Englishmen, as security for peace or faithful service.

[50] We will remove completely from office[3] the relations of Gerard de Athée so that in future they shall have no office in England, namely Engelard de Cigogné, Peter and Guy and Andrew de Chanceaux, Guy de Cigogné, Geoffrey de Martigny and his brothers, Philip Marc and his brothers and his nephew Geoffrey, and all their following.

[51] As soon as peace is restored, we will remove from the kingdom all foreign knights, cross-bowmen, serjeants, and mercenaries, who have come with horses and arms to the detriment of the kingdom.

[1] *tunc*
[2] literally, "put 'in defence'"
[3] *de balliis*

[52] If anyone has been disseised of or kept out of his lands, castles, franchises or his right by us without the legal judgment of his peers, we will immediately restore them to him: and if a dispute arises over this, then let it be decided by the judgment of the twenty-five barons who are mentioned below in the clause for securing the peace:[1] for all the things, however, which anyone has been disseised or kept out of without the lawful judgment of his peers by king Henry, our father, or by king Richard, our brother, which we have in our hand or are held by others, to whom we are bound to warrant them, we will have the usual period of respite of crusaders, excepting those things about which a plea was started or an inquest made by our command before we took the cross; when however we return from our pilgrimage, or if by any chance we do not go on it, we will at once do full justice therein.

[53] We will have the same respite, and in the same manner, in the doing of justice in the matter of the disafforesting or retaining of the forests which Henry our father or Richard our brother afforested,[2] and in the matter of the wardship of lands which are of the fief of another, wardships of which sort we have hitherto had by reason of a fief which anyone held of us by knight service,[3] and in the matter of abbeys founded on the fief of another, not on a fief of our own, in which the lord of the fief claims he has a right;[4] and when we have returned, or if we do not set out on our pilgrimage, we will at once do full justice to those who complain of these things.

[54] No one shall be arrested or imprisoned upon the appeal of a woman for the death of anyone except her husband.

[55] All fines made with us unjustly and against the law of the land, and all amercements imposed unjustly and against the law of the land, shall be entirely remitted, or else let them be settled by the judgment of the twenty-five barons who are mentioned below in the clause for securing the peace,[5] or by the judgment of the majority of the same, along with the aforesaid Stephen, archbishop of Canterbury, if he can be present, and such others as he may wish to associate with himself for this purpose, and if he cannot be present the business shall nevertheless proceed without him, provided that if any one or more of the aforesaid twenty-five barons are in a like suit, they shall be removed from the judgment of the case in question, and others chosen, sworn and put in their place by the rest of the same twenty-five for this case only.

[56] If we have disseised or kept out Welshmen from lands or liberties or other things without the legal judgment of their peers in England or in Wales, they shall be immediately restored to them; and if a dispute arises over this, then let it be decided in the March by the judgment of their peers – for holdings in England according to the law of England, for holdings in Wales according to the law of Wales, and for holdings in the March according to the law of the March. Welshmen shall do the same to us and ours.

[57] For all the things, however, which any Welshman was disseised of or kept out of without the lawful judgment of his peers by king Henry, our father, or king Richard, our brother, which we have in our hand or which are held by others, to whom we are bound to warrant them, we will have the usual period of respite of

[1] c. 61
[2] cf. c. 47
[3] cf. c. 37
[4] cf. c. 46
[5] c. 61

crusaders, excepting those things about which a plea was started or an inquest made by our command before we took the cross; when however we return, or if by any chance we do not set out on our pilgrimage, we will at once do full justice to them in accordance with the laws of the Welsh and the foresaid regions.[1]

[58] We will give back at once the son of Llywelyn and all the hostages from Wales and the charters that were handed over to us as security for peace.

[59] We will act toward Alexander, king of the Scots, concerning the return of his sisters and hostages and concerning his franchises and his right in the same manner in which we act towards our other barons of England, unless it ought to be otherwise by the charters which we have from William his father, formerly king of the Scots, and this shall be determined by the judgment of his peers in our court.

[60] All these aforesaid customs and liberties which we have granted to be observed in our kingdom as far as it pertains to us towards our men, all of our kingdom, clerks as well as laymen, shall observe as far as it pertains to them towards their men.

[61] Since, moreover, for God and the betterment of our kingdom and for the better allaying of the discord that has arisen between us and our barons we have granted all these things aforesaid, wishing them to enjoy the use of them unimpaired and unshaken for ever, we give and grant them the under-written security, namely, that the barons shall choose any twenty-five barons of the kingdom they wish, who must with all their might observe, hold and cause to be observed, the peace and liberties which we have granted and confirmed to them by this present charters of ours, so that if we, or our justiciar, or our bailiffs or any one of our servants offend in any way against anyone or transgress any of the articles of the peace or the security and the offence be notified to four of the aforesaid twenty-five barons, those four barons shall come to us, or to our justiciar if we are out of the kingdom, and, laying the transgression before us, shall petition us to have that transgression corrected without delay. And if we do not correct the transgression, or if we are out of the kingdom, if our justiciar does not correct it, within forty days, reckoning from the time it was brought to our notice or to that of our justiciar if we were out of the kingdom, the aforesaid four barons shall refer that case to the rest of the twenty-five barons and those twenty-five barons together with the community of the whole land shall distrain and distress us in every way they can, namely, by seizing castles, lands, possessions, and in such other ways as they can, saving our person and the persons of our queen and our children, until, in their opinion, amends have been made; and when amends have been made, they shall obey us as they did before. And let anyone in the land who wishes take an oath to obey the orders of the said twenty-five barons for the execution of all the aforesaid matters, and with them to distress us as much as he can, and we publicly and freely give anyone leave to take the oath who wishes to take it and we will never prohibit anyone from taking it. Indeed, all those in the land who are unwilling of themselves and of their own accord to take an oath to the twenty-five barons to help them to distrain and distress us, we will make them take the oath as aforesaid at our command. And if any of the twenty-five barons dies or leaves the country or is in any other way prevented from carrying out the things

[1] Clauses 56–7 do for dispossessed Welshmen what clause 52 does for dispossessed Englishmen.

aforesaid, the rest of the aforesaid twenty-five barons shall choose as they think fit another one in his place, and he shall take the oath like the rest. In all matters the execution of which is committed to these twenty-five barons, if it should happen that these twenty-five are present yet disagree among themselves about anything, or if some of those summoned will not or cannot be present, that shall be held as fixed and established which the majority of those present ordained or commanded, exactly as if all the twenty-five had consented to it; and the said twenty-five shall swear that they will faithfully observe all the things aforesaid and will do all they can to get them observed. And we will procure nothing from anyone, either personally or through anyone else, whereby any of these concessions and liberties might be revoked or diminished; and if any such thing is procured, let it be void and null, and we will never use it either personally or through another.

[62] And we have fully remitted and pardoned to everyone all the ill-will, indignation and rancour that have arisen between us and our men, clergy and laity, from the time of the quarrel. Furthermore, we have fully remitted to all, clergy and laity, and as far as pertains to us have completely forgiven, all trespasses occasioned by the same quarrel between Easter in the sixteenth year of our reign and the restoration of peace. And, besides, we have caused to be made for them letters testimonial patent of the lord Stephen archbishop of Canterbury, of the lord Henry archbishop of Dublin and of the aforementioned bishops and of master Pandulf about this security and the aforementioned concessions.

[63] Wherefore we wish and firmly enjoin that the English church shall be free, and that the men in our kingdom shall have and hold all the aforesaid liberties, rights and concessions well and peacefully, freely and quietly, fully and completely, for themselves and their heirs from us and our heirs, in all matters and in all places for ever, as is aforesaid. An oath, moreover, has been taken, as well on our part as on the part of the barons, that all these things aforesaid shall be observed in good faith and without evil disposition. Witness the above-mentioned and many others. Given by our hand in the meadow which is called Runnymede between Windsor and Staines on the fifteenth day of June, in the seventeenth year of our reign.

21. Pope Innocent III declares Magna Carta null and void, 24 August 1215

(Trans. C. R. Cheney and W. H. Semple, *Selected Letters of Pope Innocent III concerning England (1198–1216)* (London, 1953), No. 82)

Despite the concluding sentence of the Articles of the Barons (No. 19 above) and King John's *personal* undertaking – ecclesiastical security on this point, the barons' demand, was not obtained (Magna Carta, c. 61, No. 20 above) – Pope Innocent III did annul Magna Carta.

INNOCENT, BISHOP, SERVANT OF THE SERVANTS OF GOD, TO ALL THE FAITHFUL OF CHRIST WHO WILL SEE THIS DOCUMENT, GREETING AND APOSTOLIC BENEDICTION.

Although our well-beloved son in Christ, John illustrious king of the English, grievously offended God and the church – in consequence of which we excommunicated him and put his kingdom under ecclesiastical interdict – yet, by the merciful inspiration of Him who desireth not the death of a sinner but rather that he should turn from his wickedness and live, the king at length returned to his senses, and humbly made to God and the church such complete amends that he not only paid compensation for losses and restored property wrongfully seized, but also conferred full liberty on the English church: and further, on the relaxation of the two sentences, he yielded his kingdom of England and of Ireland to St Peter and the Roman church, and received it from us again as fief under an annual payment of one thousand marks, having sworn an oath of fealty to us, as is clearly stated in his privilege furnished with a golden seal; and desiring still further to please Almighty God, he reverently assumed the badge of the life-giving Cross, intending to go to the relief of the Holy Land – a project for which he was splendidly preparing. But the enemy of the human race, who always hates good impulses, by his cunning wiles stirred up against him the barons of England so that, with a wicked inconsistency, the men who supported him when injuring the church rebelled against him when he turned from his sin and made amends to the church. A matter of dispute had arisen between them: several days had been fixed for the parties to discuss a settlement: meanwhile, formal envoys had been sent to us: with them we conferred diligently, and after full deliberation we sent letters by them to the archbishop and the English bishops, charging and commanding them to devote earnest attention and effective effort to restoring a genuine and full agreement between the two sides; by apostolic authority they were to denounce as void any leagues and conspiracies which might have been formed after the outbreak of trouble between the kingdom and the priesthood: they were to prohibit, under sentence of excommunication, any attempt to form such leagues in future: and they were prudently to admonish the magnates and nobles of England, and strongly to enjoin on them, to strive to conciliate the king by manifest proofs of loyalty and submission; and then, if they should decide to make a demand of him, to implore it respectfully and not arrogantly, maintaining his royal honour and rendering the customary services which they and their predecessors paid to him and his predecessors (since the king ought not to lose these services without a judicial decision), that in this way they might the more easily gain their object. For we in our letters, and equally through the archbishop and bishops, have asked and advised the king, enjoining it on him as he hopes to have his sins remitted, to treat these magnates and nobles kindly and to hear their just petitions graciously, so that they too might recognise with gladness how by divine grace he had had a change of heart, and that thereby they and their heirs should serve him and his heirs readily and loyally; and we also asked him to grant them full safeconduct for the outward and homeward journey and the time between, so that if they could not arrive at agreement the dispute might be decided in his court by their peers according to the laws and customs of the kingdom. But before the envoys bearing this wise and just mandate had reached England, the barons threw over their oath of fealty; and though, even if the king had wrongfully oppressed them they should not have proceeded against him by constituting themselves both judges and executors of the judgment in their own suit, yet, openly conspiring as vassals against their lord and as knights against their king, they leagued themselves with his acknowledged enemies as well as with others, and dared to make war on him, occupying and devastating his territory and even seizing the city of London, the capital of the kingdom, which had been treacherously surrendered to them. Meantime the aforesaid envoys returned to England and the king offered, in accordance with the terms of our mandate, to grant the barons full justice. This they altogether rejected and began to stretch forth their hands to deeds still worse. So the king, appealing to our tribunal, offered to grant them justice before us to whom the decision of this suit belonged by reason of our lordship: but this they utterly rejected. Then he offered that four discreet men chosen by him and four more chosen by themselves should, together with us, end the dispute, and he promised that, first in his reforms, he would repeal all abuses introduced into England in his reign: but this also they contemptuously refused. Finally, the king declared to them that, since the lordship of the kingdom belonged to the Roman church, he neither could nor should, without our special mandate, make any change in it to our prejudice: and so he again appealed to our tribunal, placing under apostolic protection both himself and his kingdom with all his honour and rights. But making no progress by any method, he asked the archbishop and the bishops to execute our mandate, to defend the rights of the Roman church, and to protect himself in accordance with the form of the privilege granted to crusaders. When the archbishop and bishops would not take any action, seeing himself bereft of almost all counsel and help, he did not dare to refuse what the barons had dared to demand. And so by such violence and fear as might affect the most courageous of men he was forced to accept an agreement which is not only shameful and demeaning but also illegal and unjust, thereby lessening unduly and impairing his royal rights and dignity.

But because the Lord has said to us by the prophet Jeremiah, "I have set thee over the nations and over the kingdoms, to root out, and to destroy, to build and to plant," and also by Isaiah, "Loose the bands of wickedness, undo the heavy burdens," we refuse to ignore such shameless presumption, for thereby the apostolic see would be dishonoured, the king's rights injured, the English nation shamed, and the whole plan for a crusade seriously endangered; and as this danger would be imminent if concessions, thus extorted from a great prince who has taken the Cross, were not cancelled by our authority, even though he himself should prefer them to be upheld, on behalf of Almighty God, Father, Son, and Holy Spirit, and by the authority of SS Peter and Paul His apostles, and by our own authority, acting on the general advice of our brethren, we utterly reject and condemn this settlement, and under threat of excommunication we order that the king should not dare to observe it and that the barons and their associates should not require it to be observed: the charter, with all undertakings and guarantees whether confirming it or resulting from it, we declare to be null, and void of all validity for ever. Wherefore, let no man deem it lawful to infringe this document of our annulment and prohibition, or presume to oppose it. If anyone should presume to do so, let him know that he will incur the anger of Almighty God and of SS Peter and Paul His apostles.

Anagni, the 24th of August, in the eighteenth year of our pontificate.

22. Magna Carta, 1216

(*Statutes of the Realm*, I (1810), Charters, pp. 14-16)

That the changes made in reissuing the charter shall be clear, the text is given in full with the differences shown—alterations and additions by italics,[1] omissions by footnotes. Only a few verbal or stylistic changes affecting neither the sense nor the translation have been ignored.

Henry, by the grace of God king of England, lord of Ireland, duke of Normandy and Aquitaine, and count of Anjou, to the archbishops, bishops, abbots, earls, barons, justiciars, foresters, sheriffs, stewards, servants, bailiffs and to all his faithful subjects, greeting. Know that we, out of reverence for God and for the salvation of our soul and those of all our ancestors and *successors*, for the honour of God and the exaltation of holy church, and for the reform of our realm, on the advice of our venerable fathers, *the lord Gualo, cardinal priest of St Martin, legate of the apostolic see, Peter of Winchester, R. of St Asaph, J. of Bath and Glastonbury, S. of Exeter, R. of Chichester, W. of Coventry, B. of Rochester, H. of Llandaff, — of St David's, — of Bangor and S. of Worcester, bishops,* and of the noble men *William Marshal earl of Pembroke, Ranulf earl of Chester, William de Ferrers earl of Derby, William count of Aumale, Hubert de Burgh our justiciar, Savari de Mauléon, William Brewer the father, William Brewer the son, Robert de Courtenay, Fawkes de Breauté, Reynold de Vautort, Walter de Lacy, Hugh de Mortimer, John of Monmouth, Walter de Beauchamp, Walter de Clifford, Roger de Clifford, Robert de Mortimer, William de Cantilupe, Matthew fitz Herbert, John Marshal, Alan Basset, Philip de Aubeney, John Lestrange* and others, our faithful subjects:

[1] In the first place have granted to God, and by this our present charter confirmed for us and our heirs for ever, that the English church shall be free, and shall have its rights undiminished and its liberties unimpaired.[2] We have also granted to all free men of our kingdom, for ourselves and our heirs for ever, all the liberties written below, to be had and held by them and their heirs of us and our heirs. [1215, c. 1]

[2] If any of our earls or barons or others holding of us in chief by knight service dies, and at his death his heir be of full age and owe relief he shall have his inheritance on payment of the old relief, namely the heir or heirs of an earl £100 for a whole earl's barony, the heir or heirs of a baron £100 for a whole barony, the heir or heirs of a knight 100*s*, at most, for a whole knight's fee; and he who owes less shall give less according to the ancient usage of fiefs. [1215, c. 2]

[3] If, however, the heir of any such be under age, *his lord shall not have wardship of him, nor of his land, before he has received his homage; and after being a ward such an heir* shall have his inheritance when he comes of age, *that is of twenty-one years*, without paying relief and without making fine, *so, however, that if he is made a knight while still under age, the land nevertheless shall remain in his lord's wardship for the full term.* [1215, c. 3]

[4] The guardian of the land of such an heir who is under age shall take from the land of the heir no more than reasonable revenues, reasonable customary dues and reasonable services, and that without destruction and waste of men or goods; and if we commit the wardship of the land of any such to a sheriff, or to any other who is

[1] Thus, Latin terms (regularly printed in italics) here revert to roman. See also Nos 23, 26 and 27 below.
[2] The rest of the sentence of M.C. 1215 ("and it is our will . . . good faith for ever") is omitted.

answerable to us for the revenues *of that land*, and he destroys or wastes what he has wardship of, we will take compensation from him and the land shall be committed to two lawful and discreet men of that fief, who shall be answerable for the revenues to us or to him to whom we have assigned them; and if we give or sell to anyone the wardship of any such land and he causes destruction or waste therein, he shall lose that wardship and it shall be transferred to two lawful and discreet men of that fief, who shall similarly be answerable to us as is aforesaid. [1215, c. 4]

[5] Moreover, so long as he has the wardship of the land, the guardian shall keep in repair the houses, parks, preserves, ponds, mills and other things pertaining to the land out of the revenues from it; and he shall restore to the heir when he comes of age his land fully stocked with ploughs and *all other things in at least the measure he received. All these things shall be observed in the case of wardships of vacant archbishoprics, bishoprics, abbeys, priories, churches and dignities except that wardships of this kind may not be sold.* [1215, c. 5]

[6] Heirs shall be married without disparagement.[1] [1215, c. 6]

[7] A widow shall have her marriage portion and inheritance forthwith and without *any* difficulty after the death of her husband; nor shall she pay anything to have her dower or her marriage portion or the inheritance which she and her husband held on the day of her husband's death; and she may remain in her husband's house for forty days after his death, within which time her dower shall be assigned to her, *unless it has already been assigned to her or unless the house is a castle; and if she leaves the castle, a suitable house shall be immediately provided for her in which she can stay honourably until her dower is assigned to her in accordance with what is aforesaid.* [1215, c. 7]

[8] No widow shall be forced to marry so long as she wishes to live without a husband, provided that she gives security not to marry without our consent if she holds of us, or without the consent of her lord[2] if she holds of another. [1215, c. 8]

[9] *We or our bailiffs will not* seize for any debt any land or rent, so long as the *available* chattels of the debtor are sufficient to repay the debt *and the debtor himself is prepared to have it paid therefrom;* nor will those who have gone surety for the debtor be distrained so long as the principal debtor is himself able to pay the debt; and if the principal debtor fails to pay the debt, having nothing wherewith to pay it *or is able but unwilling to pay*, then shall the sureties answer for the debt; and they shall, if they wish, have the lands and rents of the debtor until they are reimbursed for the debt which they have paid for him, unless the principal debtor can show that he has discharged his obligation in the matter to the said sureties. [1215, c. 9][3]

[10] The city of London shall have all its ancient liberties and free customs.[4] Furthermore, we will and grant that all other cities, boroughs, towns, *the barons of the Cinque Ports*, and *all* ports shall have all their liberties and free customs. [1215, c. 13][5]

[11] No one shall be compelled to do greater service for a knight's fee or for any other free holding than is due from it. [1215, c. 16]

[1] The rest of 1215, c. 6, is omitted.
[2] Here the "of whom she holds" of 1215, c. 8, is omitted.
[3] Here articles 10–12 of M.C. 1215 are omitted.
[4] In M.C. 1215 this sentence begins with "And" and ends with "as well by land as by water".
[5] Here articles 14–15 of M.C. 1215 are omitted.

[12] Common pleas shall not follow our court, but shall be held in some fixed place. [1215, c. 17]

[13] Recognitions of novel disseisin, of mort d'ancestor, and of darrein presentment, shall not be held elsewhere than in the counties to which they relate, and in this manner – we, or, if we should be out of the realm, our chief justiciar, will send two justices through each county four times a year, who, with four knights of each county chosen by the county, shall hold the said assizes in the county and on the day and in the place of meeting of the county court. [1215, c. 18]

[14] And if the said assizes cannot all be held on the day of the county court, there shall stay behind as many of the knights and freeholders who were present at the county court on that day as are necessary for the sufficient making of judgments, according to the amount of business to be done. [1215, c. 19]

[15] A free man shall not be amerced for a trivial offence except in accordance with the degree of the offence, and for a grave offence[1] in accordance with its gravity, yet saving his way of living; and a merchant in the same way, saving his stock-in-trade; and a villein shall be amerced in the same way, saving his means of livelihood; if *he has* fallen into our mercy: and none of the aforesaid amercements shall be imposed except by the oath of good *and law-worthy* men of the neighbourhood. [1215, c. 20]

[16] Earls and barons shall not be amerced except by their peers, and only in accordance with the degree of the offence. [1215, c. 21]

[17] No clerk shall be amerced[2] except after the fashion of the aforesaid and not according to the amount of his ecclesiastical benefice. [1215, c. 22]

[18] No vill or individual shall be compelled to make bridges at river banks, except *one* who from of old *is* legally bound to do so. [1215, c. 23]

[19] No sheriff, constable, coroners, or others of our bailiffs shall hold pleas of our crown. [1215, c. 24][3]

[20] If anyone holding a lay fief of us dies and our sheriff or bailiff shows our letters patent of summons for a debt that the deceased owed us, it shall be lawful for our sheriff or bailiff to attach and make a list of chattels of the deceased found upon the lay fief to the value of that debt under the supervision of law-worthy men, provided that none of the chattels shall be removed until the debt which is manifest has been paid to us in full; and the residue shall be left to the executors for carrying out the will of the deceased. And if nothing is owing to us from him, all the chattels shall accrue to the deceased, saving to his wife and *his* children their reasonable shares. [1215, c. 26][4]

[21] No constable *or his bailiff* shall take the corn or other chattels of anyone *who is not of the vill where the castle is situated* unless he pays on the spot in cash for them or can delay payment by arrangement with the seller; *if the seller is of the vill, he shall be bound to pay within three weeks.* [1215, c. 28]

[22] No constable shall compel any knight to give money instead of castle-guard if he is willing to do *it* himself or through another good man, if for some good reason

[1] Here the "he shall be amerced" of M.C. 1215, c. 20, is omitted.
[2] Here the "in respect of his lay holding" of 1215, c. 22, is omitted.
[3] Here article 25 of M.C. 1215 is omitted.
[4] Here article 27 of M.C. 1215 is omitted.

he cannot do it himself; and if we lead or send him on military service, he shall be excused guard in proportion to the time that because of us he has been on service. [1215, c. 29]

[23] No sheriff, or bailiff of ours, or *other person* shall take *anyone's* horses or carts for transport work unless *he pays for them at the old-established rates, namely at ten pence a day for a cart with two horses and fourteen pence a day for a cart with three horses.* [1215, c.30]

[24] Neither we nor our bailiffs will take, for castles or other works of ours, timber which is not ours, except with the agreement of him whose timber it is. [1215, c. 31]

[25] We will not hold for more than a year and a day the lands of those convicted of felony, and then the lands shall be handed over to the lords of the fiefs. [1215, c. 32]

[26] Henceforth all fish-weirs shall be cleared completely from the Thames and the Medway and throughout all England, except along the sea coast. [1215, c. 33]

[27] The writ called Praecipe shall not in future be issued to anyone in respect of any holding whereby a free man may lose his court. [1215, c. 34]

[28] Let there be one measure for wine throughout our kingdom, and one measure for ale, and one measure for corn, namely "the London quarter"; and one width for cloths whether dyed, russet or halberget, namely two ells within the selvedges. Let it be the same with weights as with measures. [1215, c. 35]

[29] Nothing shall be given[1] in future for the writ of inquisition of life or limbs: instead, it shall be granted free of charge and not refused. [1215, c. 36]

[30] If anyone holds of us by fee-farm, by socage, or by burgage, and holds land of another by knight service, we will not, by reason of that fee-farm, socage, or burgage, have the wardship of his heir or of land of his that is of the fief of the other; nor will we have custody of the fee-farm, socage, or burgage, unless such fee-farm owes knight service. We will not have custody of anyone's heir or land which he holds of another by knight service by reason of any petty serjeanty which he holds of us by the service of rendering to us knives or arrows or the like. [1215, c. 37]

[31] No bailiff shall in future put anyone to trial upon his own bare word without reliable witnesses produced for this purpose. [1215, c. 38]

[32] No free man shall be arrested or imprisoned or disseised or outlawed or exiled or victimised in any *other* way, neither will we attack him or send anyone to attack him, except by the lawful judgment of his peers or by the law of the land. [1215, c. 39]

[33] To no one will we sell, to no one will we refuse or delay right or justice. [1215, c. 40]

[34] All merchants, *unless they have been publicly prohibited beforehand*, shall be able to go out of and come into England safely and securely and stay and travel throughout England, as well by land as by water, for buying and selling by the ancient and right customs free from all evil tolls, except in time of war and if they are of the land that is at war with us. And if such are found in our land at the beginning of a war, they shall be attached, without injury to their persons or goods, until we, or our chief justiciar, know how merchants of our land are treated who were found in the land at war with us when war broke out; and if ours are safe there, the others shall be safe in our land. [1215, c. 41][2]

[1] Here the "or taken" of M.C. 1215, c. 36, is omitted.

[2] Here article 42 of M.C. 1215 is omitted.

[35] If anyone who holds of some escheat such as the honour of Wallingford, Nottingham, Boulogne, Lancaster, or of other escheats which are in our hands and are baronies dies, his heir shall give no other relief and do no other service to us than he would have done to the baron if that *land* had been in the baron's hands; and we will hold it in the same manner in which the barons held it. [1215, c. 43]

[36] Men who live outside the forest need not henceforth come before our justices of the forest upon a general summons, unless they are impleaded or are sureties for any person or persons who are attached for forest offences. [1215, c. 44][1]

[37] All barons who have founded abbeys for which they have charters of the kings of England or ancient tenure shall have the custody of them during vacancies, as they ought to have *and as it is made clear above*.[2] [1215, c. 46]

[38] All forests that were made forest in the time *of king John, our father*, shall be immediately disafforested; and so be it done with river-banks that were made preserves by *the same J. in his* time. [1215, c. 47][3]

[39] No one shall be arrested or imprisoned upon the appeal of a woman for the death of anyone except her husband. [1215, c. 54][4]

[40] *And* if *king J. our father* disseised or kept out Welshmen from lands or liberties or other things without the legal judgment of their peers in England or in Wales, they shall be immediately restored to them; and if a dispute arises over this, then let it be decided in the March by the judgment of their peers – for holdings in England according to the law of England, for holdings in Wales according to the law of Wales, and for holdings in the March according to the law of the March. Welshmen shall do the same to us and ours. [1215, c. 56][5]

[41] All these aforesaid customs and liberties which we have granted to be observed in our kingdom as far as it pertains to us towards our men, all of our kingdom, clerks as well as laymen, shall observe as far as it pertains to them towards their men. [1215, c. 60][6]

[42] *However, because there were certain articles contained in the former charter which seemed important yet doubtful, namely On the assessing of scutage and aids,*[7] *On debts of Jews and others,*[8] *On freedom to leave and return to our kingdom,*[9] *On forests and foresters, warrens and warreners,*[10] *On the customs of counties,*[11] *and On river-banks and their wardens,*[12] *the abovementioned prelates and magnates have agreed to these being deferred until we have fuller counsel, when we will, most fully in these as well as other matters that have to be amended, do what is for the common good*[13] *and the peace and estate*[14] *of ourselves and our kingdom. Because we have not yet a seal, we have had the present charter sealed with the seals of our*

[1] Here article 45 of M.C. 1215 is omitted.
[2] c. 5 above.
[3] Here articles 48–53 of M.C. 1215 are omitted.
[4] Here article 55 of M.C. 1215 is omitted.
[5] Here articles 57–59 of M.C. 1215 are omitted.
[6] All the rest of M.C. 1215 (i.e. articles 61–63) is omitted and the following new article (42) substituted.
[7] M.C. 1215, articles 12, 14 and 15.
[8] M.C. 1215, articles 10, 11 and 27.
[9] M.C. 1215, article 42.
[10] M.C. 1215, article 48.
[11] M.C. 1215, articles 25 and 45.
[12] M.C. 1215, article 48.
[13] *ad communem omnium utilitatem*
[14] *statum*

venerable father, the lord Gualo cardinal priest of St Martin, legate of the apostolic see, and William Marshal earl of Pembroke, ruler of us and of our kingdom.[1] *Witness all the aforementioned and many others. Given by the hands of the aforesaid lord, the legate, and William Marshal earl of Pembroke at Bristol on the twelfth day of November in the first year of our reign.*

23. Magna Carta, 1217

(*Statutes of the Realm*, I (1810), Charters, pp. 17-19)

The further changes made in the charter in this reissue compared with that of 1216 are shown in the same way that the differences of 1216 from 1215 were shown in No. 22 above.

It will be noticed that, unlike the Forest Charter (No. 24 below), this 1217 reissue of Magna Carta is not dated: from c. 20 of it (and the footnote thereto) it is clear, however, that it was drafted after the decision had been taken to make a separate charter for forest questions.

Henry, by the grace of God king of England, lord of Ireland, duke of Normandy, Aquitaine, and count of Anjou, to the archbishops, bishops, abbots, *priors*, earls, barons,[2] sheriffs, stewards, servants and to all his bailiffs and faithful subjects *who shall look at the present charter*, greeting. Know that out of reverence for God and for the salvation of our soul and *the souls* of[3] our ancestors and successors, for[4] the exaltation of holy church and the reform of our realm, *we have granted and by this present charter confirmed for us and our heirs for ever*, on the advice of our venerable *father, the lord Gualo, cardinal priest of St Martin and legate of the apostolic see, of the lord Walter archbishop of York, William bishop of London and the other bishops of England* and of[5] *William Marshal earl of Pembroke, ruler of us and of our kingdom, and our other faithful earls and barons of England, these liberties written below to be held in our kingdom of England for ever.*

[1] In the first place *we* have granted to God, and by this our present charter confirmed for us and our heirs for ever, that the English church shall be free and shall have its rights undiminished and its liberties unimpaired. We have also granted to all free men of our kingdom, for ourselves and our heirs for ever, all the liberties written below, to be[6] held by them and their heirs of us and our heirs. [1216, c. 1]

[2] If any of our earls or barons or others holding of us in chief by knight service dies, and at his death his heir be of full age and owe relief he shall have his inheritance on payment of the old relief, namely the heir or heirs of an earl £100 for a whole earl's barony, the heir or heirs of a baron £100 for a whole barony, the heir or heirs of a knight 100*s*, at most, for a whole knight's fee; and he who owes less shall give less according to the ancient usage of fiefs. [1216, c. 2]

[3] If, however, the heir of any such be under age, his lord shall not have wardship of him, nor of his land, before he has received his homage; and after being a ward such an heir shall have his inheritance when he comes of age, that is of twenty-one years, without paying relief and without making fine, so, however, that if he is

[1] *rectoris nostri et regni nostri*
[2] Here the "justiciars, foresters" of M.C. 1216 is omitted.
[3] Here the "all" of 1216 is omitted.
[4] Here "the honour of God and" of 1216 is omitted.
[5] Here "the noble men" of 1216 is omitted.
[6] Here the "had and" of 1216 is omitted.

made a knight while[1] still under age, the land nevertheless shall remain in the wardship of his *lords* for the full term. [1216, c. 3]

[4] The guardian of the land of such an heir who is under age shall take from the land of the heir no more than reasonable revenues, reasonable customary dues and reasonable services, and that without destruction and waste of men or goods; and if we commit the wardship of the land of any such to a sheriff, or to any other who is answerable to us for the revenues of that land, and he destroys or wastes what he has wardship of, we will take compensation from him and the land shall be committed to two lawful and discreet men of that fief, who shall be answerable for the revenues to us or to him to whom we have assigned them; and if we give or sell to anyone the wardship of any such land and he causes destruction or waste therein, he shall lose that wardship and it shall be transferred to two lawful and discreet men of that fief, who shall similarly be answerable to us as is aforesaid. [1216, c. 4]

[5] Moreover, so long as he has the wardship of the land, the guardian shall keep in repair the houses, parks, preserves, ponds, mills and other things pertaining to the land out of the revenues from it; and he shall restore to the heir when he comes of age his land fully stocked with ploughs and all other things in at least the measure he received. All these things shall be observed in the case of wardships of vacant archbishoprics, bishoprics, abbeys, priories, churches and dignities *that pertain to us* except that wardships of this kind may not be sold. [1216, c. 5]

[6] Heirs shall be married without disparagement. [1216, c. 6]

[7] A widow shall have her marriage portion and inheritance forthwith and without any difficulty after the death of her husband, nor shall she pay anything to have her dower or her marriage portion or the inheritance which she and her husband held on the day of her husband's death; and she may remain in the *chief* house of her husband for forty days after his death, within which time her dower shall be assigned to her, unless it has already been assigned to her or unless the house is a castle; and if she leaves the castle, a suitable house shall be immediately provided for her in which she can stay honourably until her dower is assigned to her in accordance with what is aforesaid, *and she shall have meanwhile her reasonable estover of common.*[2] *There shall be assigned to her for her dower a third of all her husband's land which was his in his lifetime, unless a smaller share was given her at the church door.*[3] [1216, c. 7]

[8] No widow shall be forced to marry so long as she wishes to live without a husband, provided that she gives security not to marry without our consent if she holds of us, or without the consent of her lord if she holds of another. [1216, c. 8]

[9] We or our bailiffs will not seize for any debt any land or rent, so long as the available chattels of the debtor are sufficient to repay the debt and the debtor himself is prepared to have it paid therefrom; nor will those who have gone surety for the debtor be distrained so long as the principal debtor is himself able to pay the debt; and if the principal debtor fails to pay the debt, having nothing wherewith to pay it or is able but unwilling to pay, then shall the sureties answer for the debt; and they

[1] "while" is wanting, but its omission would appear to be no more than accidental and M.C. 1225 restores it.

[2] i.e. reasonable allowances from the estate of things necessary to maintain her pending provision out of it of the dower

[3] The amount of dower was usually arranged at the church door at the time of the marriage.

shall, if they wish, have the lands and rents of the debtor until they are reimbursed for the debt which they have paid for him, unless the principal debtor can show that he has discharged his obligation in the matter to the said sureties. [1216, c. 9]

[10] The city of London shall have all its ancient liberties and free customs. Furthermore, we will and grant that all other cities, boroughs, towns, the barons of the Cinque Ports, and all ports shall have all their liberties and free customs. [1216, c. 10]

[11] No one shall be compelled to do greater service for a knight's fee or for any other free holding than is due from it. [1216, c. 11]

[12] Common pleas shall not follow our court, but shall be held in some fixed place. [1216, c. 12]

[13] Recognitions of novel disseisin, of mort d'ancestor[1] shall not be held elsewhere than in the counties to which they relate, and in this manner – we, or, if we should be out of the realm, our chief justiciar, will *send justices through each county once a year, who with knights of the counties shall hold the said assizes in the counties.* [1216, cc. 13–14]

[14] *And those which cannot on that visit be determined in the county to which they relate by the said justices sent to hold the said assizes shall be determined by them elsewhere on their circuit, and those which cannot be determined by them because of difficulty over certain articles shall be referred to our justices of the bench and determined there.* [1216, cc. 13–14]

[15] *Assizes of darrein presentment shall always be held before the justices of the bench and determined there.* [1216, cc. 13–14]

[16] A free man shall not be amerced for a trivial offence except in accordance with the degree of the offence and for a grave offence in accordance with its gravity, yet saving his way of living; and a merchant in the same way, saving his stock-in-trade; and a villein *other than one of our own* shall be amerced in the same way, saving his means of livelihood; if he has fallen into our mercy: and none of the aforesaid amercements shall be imposed except by the *oaths* of good and law-worthy men of the neighbourhood. [1216, c. 15]

[17] Earls and barons shall not be amerced except by their peers, and only in accordance with the degree of the offence. [1216, c. 16]

[18] No *ecclesiastical person* shall be amerced *according to the amount of his ecclesiastical benefice but in accordance with his lay holding and in accordance with the degree of the offence.* [1216, c. 17]

[19] No vill or individual shall be compelled to make bridges at river banks, except one who from of old is legally bound to do so. [1216, c. 18]

[20] *No river bank shall henceforth be made a preserve, except those which were* preserves *in the time of king Henry, our grandfather, in the same places and for the same periods as they used to be in his day.* [1216, c. 38][2]

[21] No sheriff, constable, coroners, or others of our bailiffs shall hold pleas of our crown. [1216, c. 19]

[22] If anyone holding a lay fief of us dies and our sheriff or bailiff shows our letters patent of summons for a debt that the deceased owed us, it shall be lawful for our

[1] Here the "and of darrein presentment" of 1216 is omitted; the resulting rough edge is smoothed in M.C. 1225 by the insertion of "and" *before* "of mort d'ancestor".

[2] The residue of 1216, c. 38, after the forest part had been transferred to the separate Charter of the Forest: it is now promoted to bring it and article 19 of M.C. 1217 together.

sheriff or bailiff to attach and make a list of chattels of the deceased found upon the lay fief to the value of that debt under the supervision of law-worthy men, provided that none of the chattels shall be removed until the debt which is manifest has been paid to us in full; and the residue shall be left to the executors for carrying out the will of the deceased. And if nothing is owing to us from him, all the chattels shall accrue to the deceased, saving to his wife[1] their reasonable shares. [1216, c. 20]

[23] No constable or his bailiff shall take the corn or other chattels of anyone who is not of the vill where the castle is situated unless he pays on the spot in cash for them or can delay payment by arrangement with the seller; if the seller is of *that* vill *he shall pay* within *forty days*. [1216, c. 21]

[24] No constable shall compel any knight to give money instead of castle-guard if he is willing to do it himself or through another good man, if for some good reason he cannot do it himself; and if we lead or send him on military service, he shall be excused guard in respect *of the fief for which he did service in the army* in proportion to the time that because of us he has been on service. [1216, c. 22]

[25] No sheriff, or bailiff of ours, or other person shall take anyone's horses or carts for transport work unless he pays for them at the old-established rates, namely at ten pence a day for a cart with two horses and fourteen pence a day for a cart with three horses. [1216, c. 23]

[26] *No demesne cart of any ecclesiastical person or knight or of any lady shall be taken by the aforesaid bailiffs.*

[27] Neither we nor our bailiffs *nor others* will take, for castles or other works of ours, timber which is not ours, except with the agreement of him whose timber it is. [1216, c. 24]

[28] We will not hold for more than a year and a day the lands of those convicted of felony, and then the lands shall be handed over to the lords of the fiefs. [1216, c. 25]

[29] Henceforth all fish-weirs shall be cleared completely from the Thames and the Medway and throughout all England, except along the sea coast. [1216, c. 26]

[30] The writ called Praecipe shall not in future be issued to anyone in respect of any holding whereby a free man may lose his court. [1216, c. 27]

[31] Let there be one measure for wine throughout our kingdom, and one measure for ale, and one measure for corn, namely "the London quarter"; and one width for cloths whether dyed, russet or halberget, namely two ells within the selvedges. Let it be the same with weights as with measures. [1216, c. 28]

[32] Nothing shall be given in future for the writ of inquisition *by him who seeks an inquisition* of life or limbs: instead, it shall be granted free of charge and not refused. [1216, c. 29]

[33] If anyone holds of us by fee-farm, by socage, or by burgage, and holds land of another by knight service, we will not, by reason of that fee-farm, socage or burgage, have the wardship of his heir or of land of his that is of the fief of the other; nor will we have custody of the fee-farm, socage, or burgage, unless such fee-farm owes knight service. We will not have custody of anyone's heir or land which he holds of

[1] Here the "and his children" of 1216 is omitted, but quite obviously from the plural ("their reasonable shares") unintentionally, and M.C. 1225 restores it.

another by knight service by reason of any petty serjeanty which he holds of us by the service of rendering[1] knives or arrows or the like. [1216, c. 30]

[34] No bailiff shall in future put anyone to *manifest* trial *or to oath* upon his own bare word without reliable witnesses produced for this purpose. [1216, c. 31]

[35] No free man shall be arrested or imprisoned or disseised *of his freehold, liberties or free customs,* or outlawed or exiled or victimised in any other way, neither will we attack him or send anyone to attack him, except by the lawful judgment of his peers or by the law of the land. [1216, c. 32]

[36] To no one will we sell, to no one will we refuse or delay right or justice. [1216, c. 33]

[37] All merchants, unless they have been publicly prohibited beforehand, shall be able to go out of and come into England safely and securely[2] and stay and travel throughout England, as well by land as by water, for buying and selling by the ancient and right customs free from all evil tolls, except in time of war and if they are of the land that is at war with us. And if such are found in our land at the beginning of a war, they shall be attached without injury to their persons or goods, until we, or our chief justiciar, know how merchants of our land are treated who were found in the land at war with us when war broke out; and if ours are safe there, the others shall be safe in our land. [1216, c. 34]

[38] If anyone who holds of some escheat such as the honour of Wallingford, Boulogne, Nottingham, Lancaster, or of other escheats which are in our hands and are baronies dies, his heir shall give no other relief and do no other service to us than he would have done to the baron if that[3] had been in the baron's hands; and we will hold it in the same manner in which the baron held it. *Nor will we by reason of such a barony or escheat have any escheat or wardship of any men of ours unless he who held the barony or escheat held in chief of us elsewhere.* [1216, c. 35][4]

[39] *No free man shall henceforth give or sell to anyone more of his land than will leave enough for the full service due from the fief to be rendered to the lord of the fief.*

[40] All *patrons of* abbeys *who* have *charters of advowson* of the kings of England or ancient *tenure or possession* shall have the custody of them during vacancies, as they ought to have and as is made clear above.[5] [1216, c. 37][6]

[41] No one shall be arrested or imprisoned upon the appeal of a woman for the death of anyone except her husband. [1216, c. 39][7]

[1] Here the "to us" of 1216 is omitted (but restored in 1225).
[2] Here in the text as printed in *Stat. Realm,* "conduct" is given (*salvum et securum conductum exire*). There is no warrant for it in the 1215, 1216 or the 1225 issues and it is scarcely explicable save as an interpolation. It should be added that *conductum* is given in the text which was confirmed by inspeximus in 1297 and 1300 (*Stat. Realm,* I, p. 33 (Charters), p. 114, and p. 38 (Charters)).
[3] Here the "land" of 1216 is omitted.
[4] Here article 36 of M.C. 1216 (on the forest) is omitted, being transferred to the separate charter on forest matters (Charter of the Forest, 1217, c. 2, No. 24 below) and replaced as article 39 here by a new article on alienation.
[5] article 5 above.
[6] Here article 38 of 1216 is omitted and divided, the forest part being taken into the new Charter of the Forest (No. 24 below), and the residue about river banks becoming an article in its own right as c. 20 above.
[7] Here article 40 of 1216 is omitted, but before continuing with article 41 of 1216 three new articles are introduced, presumably so as to have them too covered by article 41 (which becomes c. 45 below). Of the new articles (cc. 42–44 below) two, 42 and 44, in fact reintroduce matters deferred by 1216, c. 42, for further consideration. Article 43 is entirely new.

[42] *No county shall in future be held more often than once a month and where a greater interval has been customary let it be greater. Nor shall any sheriff or his bailiff make his tourn through the hundred save twice a year (and then only in the due and accustomed place), that is to say, once after Easter and again after Michaelmas. And view of frankpledge shall be held then at the Michaelmas term without interference,*[1] *that is to say, so that each has his liberties which he had and was accustomed to have in the time of king Henry our grandfather or which he has since acquired. View of frankpledge shall be held in this manner, namely, that our peace be kept, that a tithing be kept full as it used to be, and that the sheriff shall not look for opportunities for exactions,*[2] *but be satisfied with what a sheriff used to get from holding his view in the time of king Henry our grandfather.*

[43] *It shall not in future be lawful for anyone to give land of his to any religious house in such a way that he gets it back again as a tenant of that house. Nor shall it be lawful for any religious house to receive anyone's land to hand it back to him as a tenant. And if in future anyone does give land of his in this way to any religious house and he is convicted of it, his gift shall be utterly quashed and the land shall be forfeit to the lord of the fief concerned.*

[44] *Scutage shall be taken in future as it used to be taken in the time of king Henry our grandfather.*

[45] All these aforesaid customs and liberties which we have granted to be observed in our kingdom as far as it pertains to us towards our men, all of our kingdom, clerks as well as laymen, shall observe as far as it pertains to them towards their men. [1216, c. 41][3]

[46] *Saving*[4] *to archbishops, bishops, abbots, priors, Templars, Hospitallers, earls, barons and all other persons, ecclesiastical and secular, the liberties and free customs they had previously.*

[47] *We have also with the common counsel of our whole realm decreed that all adulterine castles, that is to say, those built or rebuilt since the beginning of the war between the lord John our father and his barons of England, shall be destroyed immediately.* Because we have not yet a seal, we have had *this* [charter] sealed with the seals of *the aforesaid lord legate and the earl W. Marshal, ruler of us and of our kingdom.*

24. The Charter of the Forest, 1217

(*Statutes of the Realm*, I (Rec. Com., 1810), Charters, pp. 20-1)

Henry by the grace of God, king of England, lord of Ireland, duke of Normandy, Aquitaine, and count of Anjou, to the archbishops, bishops, abbots, priors, earls, barons, justices, foresters, sheriffs, stewards, servants, and to all his bailiffs and faithful subjects, greeting. Know that out of reverence for God and for the salvation of our soul and the souls of our ancestors and successors, for the exaltation of holy church and the reform of our realm, we have granted and by this present charter confirmed for us and our heirs for ever, on the advice of our venerable father, the lord Gualo, cardinal priest of St Martin and legate of the apostolic see, of

[1] *sine occasione*
[2] *non querat occasiones*
[3] All the rest of M.C. 1216 (art. 42, including the final protocol) is omitted and the following (articles 46–47) substituted.
[4] In the Latin this article is not a sentence but an ablative absolute. Both the construction and the context are changed in the 1225 reissue (No. 26 below, article 37).

the lord Walter archbishop of York, William bishop of London and the other bishops of England and of William Marshal earl of Pembroke, ruler of us and of our kingdom, and our other faithful earls and barons of England, these liberties written below to be held in our kingdom of England for ever.

[1] In the first place, all the forests which king Henry our grandfather made forest shall be viewed by good and law-worthy men, and if he made forest any wood that was not his demesne to the injury of him whose wood it was, it shall be disafforested. And if he made his own wood forest, it shall remain forest, saving common of pasture and other things in that forest to those who were accustomed to have them previously.

[2] Men who live outside the forest need not henceforth come before our justices of the forest upon a general summons, unless they are impleaded or are sureties for any person or persons who are attached for forest offences.

[3] All woods made forest by king Richard our uncle, or by king John our father, up to the time of our first coronation shall be immediately disafforested unless it be our demesne wood.

[4] Archbishops, bishops, abbots, priors, earls, barons, knights and freeholders who have woods within forests shall have them as they had them at the time of the first coronation of the aforesaid king Henry our grandfather, so that they shall be quit forever[1] in respect of all purprestures, wastes and assarts made in those woods between that time and the beginning of the second year of our coronation. And those who in future make waste, purpresture or assart in them without licence from us shall answer for wastes, purprestures[2] and assarts.

[5] Our regarders shall go through the forests making the regard as it used to be made at the time of the first coronation of the aforesaid king Henry our grandfather, and not otherwise.

[6] The inquest or view of the expeditating of dogs in the forest shall henceforth be made when the regard ought to be made, namely every third year, and then made by the view and testimony of law-worthy men and not otherwise. And he whose dog is then found not expeditated shall give as amercement three shillings, and in future no ox shall be seized for failure to expeditate. The manner, moreover, of expeditating by the assize shall generally be that three claws of the forefoot are to be cut off, but not the ball. Nor shall dogs henceforth be expeditated except in places where it was customary to expeditate them at the time of the first coronation of king Henry our grandfather.

[7] No forester or beadle shall henceforth make scotale or levy sheaves of corn, or oats or other grain or lambs or piglets or make any other levy. And by the view and oath of twelve regarders when they make the regard as many foresters are to be set to keep the forests as shall seem to them reasonably sufficient for keeping them.

[8] No swanimote shall henceforth be held in our kingdom except three times a year, namely a fortnight before the feast of St Michael, when the agisters meet to agist our demesne woods, and about the feast of St Martin, when our agisters ought to receive

[1] i.e. of payments at the Exchequer

[2] *purprestures:* required by the context, an accidental omission, supplied from the Forest Charter of 1225

our pannage-dues; and at these two swanimotes foresters, verderers and agisters shall appear but no one else shall be compelled to do so; and the third swanimote shall be held a fortnight before the feast of St John the Baptist for the fawning of our beasts, and for holding this swanimote foresters and verderers shall come but no others shall be compelled to do so. And in addition every forty days throughout the year the verderers and foresters shall meet to view attachments of the forest both of the vert and of the venison on the presentment of those foresters and with the attached present. The aforesaid swanimotes however shall only be held in counties in which they were wont to be held.

[9] Every free man shall agist his wood in the forest as he wishes and have his pannage. We grant also that every free man can conduct his pigs through our demesne wood freely and without impediment to agist them in his own woods or anywhere else he wishes. And if the pigs of any free man shall spend one night in our forest he shall not on that account be so prosecuted that he loses anything of his own.

[10] No one shall henceforth lose life or limb because of our venison, but if anyone has been arrested and convicted of taking venison he shall be fined heavily if he has the means; and if he has not the means, he shall lie in our prison for a year and a day; and if after a year and a day he can find pledges he may leave prison; but if not, he shall abjure the realm of England.

[11] Any archbishop, bishop, earl or baron whatever who passes through our forest shall be allowed to take one or two beasts under the supervision of the forester, if he is to hand; but if not, let him have the horn blown, lest he seem to be doing it furtively.

[12] Every free man may henceforth without being prosecuted make in his wood or in land he has in the forest a mill, a preserve, a pond, a marl-pit, a ditch, or arable outside the covert in arable land, on condition that it does not harm any neighbour.

[13] Every free man shall have the eyries of hawks, sparrowhawks, falcons, eagles and herons in his woods, and likewise honey found in his woods.

[14] No forester henceforth who is not a forester-in-fee rendering us a farm for his bailiwick may exact any chiminage[1] in his bailiwick; but a forester-in-fee rendering us a farm for his bailiwick may exact chiminage, namely for a cart for half a year 2*d* and for the other half year 2*d*, and for a horse with a load for half a year ½*d* and for the other half year ½*d*, and only from those who come from outside his bailiwick as merchants with his permission into his bailiwick to buy wood, timber, bark or charcoal and take them elsewhere to sell where they wish; and from no other cart or load shall any chiminage be exacted, and chiminage shall only be exacted in places where it used to be exacted of old and ought to have been exacted. Those, on the other hand, who carry wood, bark, or charcoal on their backs for sale, although they get their living by it, shall not in future pay chiminage. In respect of the woods of others no chiminage shall be given to our foresters beyond [that given] in respect of our own[2] woods.[3]

[1] A toll levied on transport in the forest.
[2] literally, demesne
[3] An obscure Latin sentence, not found in the 1225 or later reissues of the Forest Charter. This would seem to be its meaning.

[15] All who from the time of king Henry our grandfather up to our first coronation have been outlawed for a forest offence only shall be released from their outlawry without legal proceedings and shall find reliable pledges that they will not do wrong to us in the future in respect of our forest.

[16] No castellan or other person may hold forest pleas either of the vert or the venison but each forester-in-fee shall attach forest pleas of both the vert and the venison and present them to the verderers of the districts[1] and when they have been enrolled and closed under the seals of the verderers they shall be presented to the head forester when he arrives in those parts to hold forest pleas and be determined before him.

[17] These liberties concerning the forests we have granted to everybody, saving to archbishops, bishops, abbots, priors, earls, barons, knights, and other persons, ecclesiastical and secular, Templars and Hospitallers, the liberties and free customs, in forests and outside, in warrens and other things, which they had previously. All these aforesaid customs and liberties which we have granted to be observed in our kingdom as far as it pertains to us towards our men, all of our kingdom, clerks as well as laymen, shall observe as far as it pertains to them towards their men. Because we have not yet a seal we have had the present charter sealed with the seals of our venerable father the lord Gualo cardinal priest of St Martin, legate of the apostolic see, and William Marshal earl of Pembroke, ruler of us and of our kingdom. Witness the aforenamed and many others. Given by the hands of the aforesaid lord, the legate, and of William Marshal at St Paul's, London, on the sixth day of November in the second year of our reign.

25. Temporary instructions to justices in eyre because of prohibition of ordeal, 1219

(*Foedera*, I, i (Rec. Com., 1816), p. 154. The translation is that of T. F. T. Plucknett, *Concise History of the Common Law*, 4th edn, rev. (1948), p. 115, with omissions supplied)

The king to his beloved and faithful . . . justices itinerant in the counties of . . . and . . ., greeting. Because it was in doubt and not definitely settled before the beginning of your eyre with what trial those are to be judged who are accused of robbery, murder, arson, and similar crimes since the trial by fire and water has been prohibited by the Roman church, it has been provided by our council that, at present, in this eyre of yours, it shall be done thus with those accused of excesses of this kind: to wit, that those who are accused of the aforesaid greater crimes and of whom suspicion is held that they are guilty of that whereof they are accused, of whom also, in case they were permitted to abjure the realm, there would still be suspicion that afterwards they would do evil, they shall be kept in our prison and safely guarded, yet so that they do not incur danger of life or limb on our account.

But those who are accused of medium crimes and to whom would be assigned the ordeal by fire or water if it had not been prohibited, and of whom if they should

[1] *provinciarum*

abjure the realm there would be no suspicion of their doing evil afterwards, they may abjure our realm.

But those who are accused of lesser crimes and of whom there would be no suspicion of evil, let them find safe and sure pledges of fidelity and of keeping our peace and then they may be released in our land.

As our council has provided nothing more certain in this matter at present, we therefore leave to your discretion the observance of this aforesaid order in this eyre of yours, in order that you, who are better able to know the people, the nature of the offence and the truth of things, may in this way proceed to this effect in accordance with your own discretion and consciences.

In witness of which, etc.

Witness the lord P. Winton, at Westminster, 26 January 1219.

By the same and H. de Burgh, the justiciar.

26. Magna Carta, 1225

(*Statutes of the Realm*, I (1810), Charters, pp. 22–5)

The further changes made in this reissue of the Charter compared with that of 1217 are shown in the same way as the differences between previous reissues (cf. Nos 22 and 23 above).

The modern editorial division of the text into clauses is again preserved, not because it is in this case the best possible, but because it is by now conventional and therefore necessary for ease of reference.

Henry by the grace of God, king of England, lord of Ireland, duke of Normandy, Aquitaine, and count of Anjou, to the archbishops, bishops, abbots, priors, earls, barons, sheriffs, stewards, servants and to all his bailiffs and faithful subjects who shall look at the present charter, greeting. Know that we, out of reverence for God and for the salvation of our soul and the souls of our ancestors and successors, for the exaltation of holy church and the reform of our realm, have *of our own spontaneous goodwill given and granted to the archbishops, bishops, abbots, priors, earls, barons and all of our realm* these liberties written below to be held in our kingdom of England for ever.

[1] In the first place we have granted to God, and by this our present charter confirmed for us and our heirs for ever, that the English church shall be free and shall have *all* its rights undiminished and its liberties unimpaired. We have also granted to all free men of our kingdom, for ourselves and our heirs for ever, all the liberties written below to be *had and*[1] held by them and their heirs of us and our heirs *for ever*. [1217, c. 1]

[2] If any of our earls or barons or others holding of us in chief by knight service dies, and at his death his heir be of full age and owe relief he shall have his inheritance on payment of the old relief, namely the heir or heirs of an earl £100 for a whole earl's barony, the heir or heirs of a baron £100 for a whole barony, the heir or heirs of a knight 100*s*, at most, for a whole knight's fee; and he who owes less shall give less according to the ancient usage of fiefs. [1217, c. 2]

[3] If, however, the heir of any such be under age, his lord shall not have wardship of

[1] Here the "had and" omitted in 1217 is restored.

him, nor of his land, before he has received his homage; and after being a ward such an heir shall have his inheritance when he comes of age, that is of twenty-one years, without paying relief and without making fine, so, however, that if he is made a knight *while*[1] still under age, the land nevertheless shall remain in the wardship of his lords for the full term. [1217, c. 3]

[4] The guardian of the land of such an heir who is under age shall take from the land of the heir no more than reasonable revenues, reasonable customary dues and reasonable services, and that without destruction and waste of men or goods; and if we commit the wardship of the land of any such to a sheriff, or to any other who is answerable to us for the revenues of that land, and he destroys or wastes what he has wardship of, we will take compensation from him and the land shall be committed to two lawful and discreet men of that fief, who shall be answerable for the revenues to us or to him to whom we have assigned them; and if we give or sell to anyone the wardship of any such land and he causes destruction or waste therein, he shall lose that wardship and it shall be transferred to two lawful and discreet men of that fief, who shall similarly be answerable to us as is aforesaid. [1217, c. 4]

[5] Moreover, so long as he has the wardship of the land, the guardian shall keep in repair the houses, parks, preserves, ponds, mills and other things pertaining to the land out of the revenues from it; and he shall restore to the heir when he comes of age his land fully stocked with ploughs and all other things in at least the measure he received. All these things shall be observed in the case of wardships of vacant archbishoprics, bishoprics, abbeys, priories, churches and dignities that pertain to us except that wardships of this kind may not be sold. [1217, c. 5]

[6] Heirs shall be married without disparagement. [1217, c. 6]

[7] A widow shall have her marriage portion and inheritance forthwith and without any difficulty after the death of her husband, nor shall she pay anything to have her dower or her marriage portion or the inheritance which she and her husband held on the day of her husband's death; and she may remain in the chief house of her husband for forty days after his death, within which time her dower shall be assigned to her, unless it has already been assigned to her or unless the house is a castle; and if she leaves the castle, a suitable house shall be immediately provided for her in which she can stay honourably until her dower is assigned to her in accordance with what is aforesaid, and she shall have meanwhile her reasonable estover of common. There shall be assigned to her for her dower a third of all her husband's land which was his in his lifetime, unless a smaller share was given her at the church door. No widow shall be forced to marry so long as she wishes to live without a husband, provided that she gives security not to marry without our consent if she holds of us, or without the consent of her lord if she holds of another. [1217, cc. 7–8]

[8] We or our bailiffs will not seize for any debt any land or rent, so long as the available chattels of the debtor are sufficient to repay the debt and the debtor himself is prepared to have it paid therefrom; nor will those who have gone surety for the debtor be distrained so long as the principal debtor is himself able to pay the debt; and if the principal debtor fails to pay the debt, having nothing wherewith to

[1] Here the "while" omitted in 1217 is restored.

pay it or is able but unwilling to pay, then shall the sureties answer for the debt; and they shall, if they wish, have the lands and rents of the debtor until they are reimbursed for the debt which they have paid for him, unless the principal debtor can show that he has discharged his obligation in the matter to the said sureties. [1217, c. 9]

[9] The city of London shall have all its ancient liberties and free customs. Furthermore, we will and grant that all other cities, boroughs, towns, the barons of the Cinque Ports, and all ports shall have all their liberties and free customs. [1217, c. 10]

[10] No one shall be compelled to do greater service for a knight's fee or for any other free holding than is due from it. [1217, c. 11]

[11] Common pleas shall not follow our court, but shall be held in some fixed place. [1217, c. 12]

[12] Recognitions of novel disseisin *and*[1] of mort d'ancestor shall not be held elsewhere than in the counties to which they relate, and in this manner – we, or, if we should be out of the realm, our chief justiciar, will send justices through each county once a year, who with knights of the counties shall hold the said assizes in the counties, and those which cannot on that visit be determined in the county to which they relate by the said justices sent to hold the said assizes shall be determined by them elsewhere on their circuit, and those which cannot be determined by them because of difficulty over certain articles shall be referred to our justices of the bench and determined there. [1217, cc. 13–14]

[13] Assizes of darrein presentment shall always be held before the justices of the bench and determined there. [1217, c. 15]

[14] A free man shall not be amerced for a trivial offence except in accordance with the degree of the offence and for a grave offence in accordance with its gravity, yet saving his way of living; and a merchant in the same way, saving his stock-in-trade; and a villein other than one of our own shall be amerced in the same way, saving his means of livelihood; if he has fallen into our mercy: and none of the aforesaid amercements shall be imposed except by the *oath* of good and law-worthy men of the neighbourhood. Earls and barons shall not be amerced except by their peers, and only in accordance with the degree of the offence. No ecclesiastical person shall be amerced according to the amount of his ecclesiastical benefice but in accordance with his lay holding and in accordance with the degree of the offence. [1217, cc. 16–18]

[15] No vill or individual shall be compelled to make bridges at river banks, except one who from of old is legally bound to do so. [1217, c. 19]

[16] No river bank shall henceforth be made a preserve, except those which were preserves in the time of king Henry, our grandfather, in the same places and for the same periods as they used to be in his day. [1217, c. 20]

[17] No sheriff, constable, coroners, or others of our bailiffs shall hold pleas of our crown. [1217, c. 21]

[18] If anyone holding a lay fief of us dies and our sheriff or bailiff shows our letters patent of summons for a debt that the deceased owed us, it shall be lawful for our sheriff or bailiff to attach and make a list of chattels of the deceased found upon the

[1] The rough edge smoothed. See 1217, c. 13, p. 334, n. 1 above.

lay fief to the value of that debt under the supervision of law-worthy men, provided that none of the chattels shall be removed until the debt which is manifest has been paid to us in full; and the residue shall be left to the executors for carrying out the will of the deceased. And if nothing is owing to us from him, all the chattels shall accrue to the deceased, saving to his wife *and his children*[1] their reasonable shares. [1217, c. 22]

[19] No constable or his bailiff shall take the corn or other chattels of anyone who is not of the vill where the castle is situated unless he pays on the spot in cash for them or can delay payment by arrangement with the seller; if the seller is of that vill he shall pay within forty days. [1217, c. 23]

[20] No constable shall compel any knight to give money instead of castle-guard he is willing to do it himself or through another good man, if for some good reason he cannot do it himself; and if we lead or send him on military service, he shall be excused guard in respect of the fief for which he did service in the army in proportion to the time that because of us he has been on service. [1217, c. 24]

[21] No sheriff, or bailiff of ours, or other person shall take anyone's horses or carts for transport work unless he pays for them at the old-established rates, namely at ten pence a day for a cart with two horses and fourteen pence a day for a cart with three horses. No demesne cart of any ecclesiastical person or knight or of any lady shall be taken by the aforesaid bailiffs. Neither we nor our bailiffs nor others will take, for castles or other works of ours, timber which is not ours, except with the agreement of him whose timber it is. [1217, cc. 25–27]

[22] We will not hold for more than a year and a day the lands of those convicted of felony, and then the lands shall be handed over to the lords of the fiefs. [1217, c. 28]

[23] Henceforth all fish-weirs shall be cleared completely from the Thames and the Medway and throughout all England, except along the sea coast. [1217, c. 29]

[24] The writ called Praecipe shall not in future be issued to anyone in respect of any holding whereby a free man may lose his court. [1217, c. 30]

[25] Let there be one measure for wine throughout our kingdom, and one measure for ale, and one measure for corn, namely "the London quarter"; and one width for cloths whether dyed, russet or halberget, namely two ells within the selvedges. Let it be the same with weights as with measures. [1217, c. 31]

[26] Nothing shall be given in future for the writ of inquisition by him who seeks an inquisition of life or limbs: instead, it shall be granted free of charge and not refused. [1217, c. 32]

[27] If anyone holds of us by fee-farm, by socage, or by burgage, and holds land of another by knight service, we will not, by reason of that fee-farm, socage or burgage, have the wardship of his heir or of land of his that is of the fief of the other; nor will we have custody of the fee-farm, socage, or burgage, unless such fee-farm owes knight service. We will not have custody of anyone's heir or land which he holds of another by knight service by reason of any petty serjeanty which he holds of us by the service of rendering *to us*[2] knives or arrows or the like. [1217, c. 33]

[1] Here the "and his children" omitted in 1217 is restored.

[2] Here the "to us" omitted in 1217 is restored.

[28] No bailiff shall in future put anyone to manifest trial or to oath upon his own bare word without reliable witnesses produced for this purpose. [1217, c. 34]

[29] No free man shall *in future* be arrested or imprisoned or disseised of his freehold, liberties or free customs, or outlawed or exiled or victimised in any other way, neither will we attack him or send anyone to attack him, except by the lawful judgment of his peers or by the law of the land. To no one will we sell, to no one will we refuse or delay right or justice. [1217, cc. 35–36]

[30] All merchants, unless they have been publicly prohibited beforehand, shall be able to go out of and come into England safely and securely and stay and travel throughout England, as well by land as by water, for buying and selling by the ancient and right customs free from all evil tolls, except in time of war and if they are of the land that is at war with us. And if such are found in our land at the beginning of a war, they shall be attached without injury to their persons or goods, until we, or our chief justiciar, know how merchants of our land are treated who were found in the land at war with us when war broke out; and if ours are safe there, the others shall be safe in our land. [1217, c. 37]

[31] If anyone who holds of some escheat such as the honour of Wallingford, Boulogne, Nottingham, Lancaster, or of other escheats which are in our hands and are baronies dies, his heir shall give no other relief and do no other service to us than he would have done to the baron if that[1] had been in the baron's hands; and we will hold it in the same manner in which the baron held it. Nor will we by reason of such a barony or escheat have any escheat or wardship of any men of ours unless he who held the barony or escheat held in chief of us elsewhere. [1217, c. 38]

[32] No free man shall henceforth give or sell to anyone more of his land than will leave enough for the full service due from the fief to be rendered to the lord of the fief. [1217, c. 39]

[33] All patrons of abbeys who have charters of advowson of the kings of England or ancient tenure or possession shall have the custody of them during vacancies, as they ought to have and as is made clear above. [1217, c. 40]

[34] No one shall be arrested or imprisoned upon the appeal of a woman for the death of anyone except her husband. [1217, c. 41]

[35] No county shall in future be held more often than once a month and where a greater interval has been customary let it be greater. Nor shall any sheriff or[2] bailiff make his tourn through the hundred save twice a year (and then only in the due and accustomed place), that is to say, once after Easter and again after Michaelmas. And view of frankpledge shall be held then at the Michaelmas term without interference, that is to say, so that each has his liberties which he had and was accustomed to have in the time of king Henry our grandfather or which he has since acquired. View of frankpledge shall be held in this manner, namely, that our peace be kept, that a tithing be kept full as it used to be, and that the sheriff shall not look for opportunities

[1] For "that" 1225 gives "*ipsa*" instead of the "*illa*" of 1217, but (curiously, in view of the other omissions by 1217 which are restored) 1225 restores neither the "land" of 1216 (c. 35) nor the "barony" of 1215 (c. 43).
[2] Here the "his" of M.C. 1217, c. 42, is omitted.

for exactions but be satisfied with what a sheriff used to get from holding his view in the time of king Henry our grandfather. [1217, c. 42]

[36] It shall not in future be lawful for anyone to give land of his to any religious house in such a way that he gets it back again as a tenant of that house. Nor shall it be lawful for any religious house to receive anyone's land to hand it back to him as a tenant. And if in future anyone does give land of his in this way to any religious house and he is convicted of it, his gift shall be utterly quashed and the land shall be forfeit to the lord of the fief concerned. [1217, c. 43]

[37] Scutage shall be taken in future as it used to be taken in the time of king Henry our grandfather. *And let there be saved*[1] to archbishops, bishops, abbots, priors, Templars, Hospitallers, earls, barons and all other persons, ecclesiastical and secular, the liberties and free customs they had previously. All these aforesaid customs and liberties which we have granted to be observed in our kingdom as far as it pertains to us towards our men, all of our kingdom, clerks as well as laymen, shall observe as far as it pertains to them towards their men. *In return for this grant and gift of these liberties and of the other liberties contained in our charter on the liberties of the forest, the archbishops, bishops, abbots, priors, earls, barons, knights, freeholders and all of our realm have given us a fifteenth part of all their movables. We have also granted to them for us and our heirs that neither we nor our heirs will procure anything whereby the liberties contained in this charter shall be infringed or weakened; and if anything contrary to this is procured from anyone, it shall avail nothing and be held for nought. These being witness: the lord S. archbishop of Canterbury, E. of London, J. of Bath, P. of Winchester, H. of Lincoln, R. of Salisbury, B. of Rochester, W. of Worcester, J. of Ely, H. of Hereford, R. of Chichester and W. of Exeter, bishops; the abbot of St Albans, the abbot of Bury St Edmunds, the abbot of Battle, the abbot of St Augustine's, Canterbury, the abbot of Evesham, the abbot of Westminster, the abbot of Peterborough, the abbot of Reading, the abbot of Abingdon, the abbot of Malmesbury, the abbot of Winchcombe, the abbot of Hyde, the abbot of Chertsey, the abbot of Sherborne, the abbot of Cerne, the abbot of Abbotsbury, the abbot of Milton, the abbot of Selby, the abbot of Whitby, the abbot of Cirencester, H. de Burgh the justiciar, R. earl of Chester and Lincoln, W. earl of Salisbury, W. earl of Warenne, G. de Clare earl of Gloucester and Hertford, W. de Ferrers earl of Derby, W. de Mandeville earl of Essex, H. le Bigod earl of Norfolk, W. count of Aumale, H. earl of Hereford, John the constable of Chester, Robert de Ros, Robert fitz Walter, Robert de Vipont, William Brewer, Richard de Munfichet, Peter fitz Herbert, Matthew fitz Herbert, William de Aubeney, Robert Grelley, Reginald de Braose, John of Monmouth, John fitz Alan, Hugh de Mortimer, Walter de Beauchamp, William of St John, Peter de Maulay, Brian de Lisle, Thomas of Moulton, Richard de Argentein, Geoffrey de Neville, William Mauduit, John de Balun. Given at Westminster on the eleventh day of February in the ninth year of our reign.*[2]

[1] cf. 1217, c. 46, n. 4, above

[2] Article 37 gives article 44 of 1217, articles 46 and 45 (in that order), omits 47 and, instead, concludes the charter with "In return . . . year of our reign". This writes into the charter the fact that the fifteenth was a *quid pro quo*, restores the dropped provision of 1215 (article 61) that any attempt to annul the charter shall itself be null, and substitutes for 1217's rather perfunctory ending a full final protocol in proper charter form.

27. Charter of the Forest, 1225

(*Statutes of the Realm*, I (1810), Charters, pp. 26–7)

The differences between this and the Forest Charter of 1217 (No. 24 above) are shown in the same way that the changes made in reissuing Magna Carta are shown: see the editorial note to No. 22 above.

Henry by the grace of God, king of England, lord of Ireland, duke of Normandy, Aquitaine, and count of Anjou, to the archbishops, bishops, abbots, priors, earls, barons, justices, foresters, sheriffs, stewards, servants and to all his bailiffs and faithful subjects *who shall look at the present charter*, greeting. Know that we, out of reverence for God and for the salvation of our soul and the souls of our ancestors and successors, for the exaltation of holy church and the reform of our realm, have *of our own spontaneous goodwill given and granted to the archbishops, bishops, earls, barons and all of our realm* these liberties written below to be held in our kingdom of England for ever.

[1] In the first place, all the forests which king Henry our grandfather made forest shall be viewed by good and law-worthy men, and if he made forest any wood that was not his demesne to the injury of him whose wood it was, it shall be disafforested. And if he made his own wood forest, it shall remain forest, saving common of pasture and other things in that forest to those who were accustomed to have them previously. [For. Ch. 1217, c. 1]

[2] Men who live outside the forest need not henceforth come before our justices of the forest upon a general summons, unless they are impleaded or are sureties for any person or persons who are attached for forest offences. [For. Ch. 1217, c. 2]

[3] All woods made forest by king Richard our uncle, or by king John our father, up to the time of our first coronation shall be immediately disafforested unless it be our demesne wood. [For. Ch. 1217, c. 3]

[4] Archbishops, bishops, abbots, priors, earls, barons, knights and freeholders who have woods within forests shall have them as they had them at the time of the first coronation of[1] king Henry our grandfather, so that they shall be quit forever in respect of all purprestures, wastes and assarts made in those woods between that time and the beginning of the second year of our coronation. And those who in future make waste, purpresture or assart in them without licence from us shall answer for wastes, purprestures and assarts. [For. Ch. 1217, c. 4]

[5] Our regarders shall go through the forests making the regard as it used to be made at the time of the first coronation of[2] king Henry our grandfather, and not otherwise. [For. Ch. 1217, c. 5]

[6] The inquest or view of the expeditating of dogs in the forest shall henceforth be made when the regard ought to be made, namely every third year, and then made by the view and testimony of law-worthy men and not otherwise. And he whose dog is then found not expeditated shall give as amercement three shillings, and in future no ox shall be seized for failure to expeditate. The manner, moreover, of expeditating by the assize shall generally be that three claws of the forefoot are to be cut off, but

[1] Here the "the aforesaid" of For. Ch. 1217 is omitted.
[2] Here the "the aforesaid" of For. Ch. 1217 is omitted.

not the ball. Nor shall dogs henceforth be expeditated except in places where it was customary to expeditate them at the time of the first coronation of *the aforesaid* king Henry our grandfather. [For. Ch. 1217, c. 6]

[7] No forester or beadle shall henceforth make *scotales* or levy sheaves of corn, or oats or other grain or lambs or piglets or make any other levy. And by the view and oath of twelve regarders when they make the regard as many foresters are to be set to keep the forests as shall seem to them reasonably sufficient for keeping them. [For. Ch. 1217, c. 7]

[8] No swanimote shall henceforth be held in our kingdom except three times a year, namely a fortnight before the feast of St Michael, when *our* agisters meet to agist our demesne woods, and about the feast of St Martin, when our agisters ought to receive our pannage-dues; and at these two swanimotes foresters, verderers and agisters shall appear but *no others* shall be compelled to do so; and the third swanimote shall be held a fortnight before the feast of St John the Baptist for the fawning of our beasts, and for holding this swanimote foresters and verderers shall come but *others* shall *not* be compelled to do so. And in addition every forty days throughout the year the *foresters and verderers* shall meet to view[1] attachments of the forest both of the vert and of the venison on the presentment of those foresters and with the attached present. The aforesaid swanimotes however shall only be held in counties in which they were wont to be held. [For. Ch. 1217, c. 8]

[9] Every free man shall agist his wood *which he has* in the forest as he wishes and have his pannage. We grant also that every free man can conduct his pigs through our demesne wood freely and without impediment to agist them in his own woods or anywhere else he wishes. And if the pigs of any free man shall spend one night in our forest he shall not on that account be so prosecuted that he loses anything of his own. [For. Ch. 1217, c. 9]

[10] No one shall henceforth lose life or limb because of our venison, but if anyone has been arrested and convicted of taking venison he shall be fined heavily if he has the means; *but* if he has not the means, he shall lie in our prison for a year and a day; and if after a year and a day he can find pledges he may leave prison; but if not, he shall abjure the realm of England. [For. Ch. 1217, c. 10]

[11] Any archbishop, bishop, earl or baron whatever who passes through our forest *on his way to us at our command* shall be allowed to take one or two beasts under the supervision of the forester, if he is to hand; but if not, let him have the horn blown, lest he seem to be doing it furtively. *They shall be allowed to do the same as is aforesaid on their return journey*. [For. Ch. 1217, c. 11]

[12] Every free man may henceforth without being prosecuted make in his wood or in land he has in the forest a mill, a preserve, a pond, a marl-pit, a ditch, or arable outside the covert in arable land, on condition that it does not harm any neighbour. [For. Ch. 1217, c. 12]

[13] Every free man shall have the eyries of hawks, sparrowhawks, falcons, eagles and herons in his woods, and likewise honey found in his woods. [For. Ch. 1217, c. 13]

1 "*ad videndum*" (1217); here "*ad faciendum*"

[14] No forester henceforth who is not a forester-in-fee rendering us a farm for his bailiwick may exact any chiminage in his bailiwick; but a forester-in-fee rendering us a farm for his bailiwick may exact chiminage, namely for a cart for half a year *2d* and for the other half year *2d*, and for a horse with a load for half a year ½*d* and for the other half year ½*d*, and only from those who come from outside his bailiwick as merchants with his permission into his bailiwick to buy wood, timber, bark or charcoal and take them elsewhere to sell where they wish; and from no other cart or *any*[1] *load shall chiminage* be exacted, and chiminage shall only be exacted in places where it used to be exacted of old and ought to have been exacted. Those, on the other hand, who carry wood, bark, or charcoal on their backs for sale, although they get their living by it, shall not in future pay chiminage.[2] [For. Ch. 1217, c. 14]

[15] All who from the time of king Henry our grandfather up to our first coronation have been outlawed for a forest offence only shall be released from their outlawry without legal proceedings and shall find reliable pledges that they will not do wrong to us in the future in respect of our forest. [For. Ch. 1217, c. 15]

[16] No castellan[3] may hold forest pleas either of the vert or of the venison but each forester-in-fee shall attach forest pleas of both the vert and the venison and present them to the verderers of the districts and when they have been enrolled and closed under the seals of the verderers they shall be presented to *our* head forester when he arrives in those parts to hold forest pleas and be determined before him. [For. Ch. 1217, c. 16]

[17] These liberties concerning the forests we have granted to everybody, saving to archbishops, bishops, abbots, priors, earls, barons, knights, and other persons, ecclesiastical and secular, Templars and Hospitallers, the liberties and free customs in forests and outside, in warrens and other things, which they had previously. All these aforesaid customs and liberties which we have granted to be observed in our kingdom as far as it pertains to us towards our men, all of our kingdom[4] shall observe as far as it pertains to them towards their men. *In return for this grant and gift of these liberties and of the other liberties contained in our greater charter on other liberties, the archbishops, bishops, abbots, priors, earls, barons, knights, freeholders and all of our realm have given us a fifteenth part of all their movables. We have also granted to them for us and our heirs that neither we nor our heirs will procure anything whereby the liberties contained in this charter shall be infringed or weakened; and if anything contrary to this is procured from anyone, it shall avail nothing and be held for nought. These being witness* [the list of witnesses is the same as in M.C. 1225 (No. 26 above)]. *Given at Westminster on the eleventh day of February in the ninth year of our reign.* [For. Ch. 1217, c. 17]

[1] Here "*aliquo*", agreeing with "*summagio*". This is suspiciously like a slip for *aliquod* (agreeing with *chiminagium* as in 1217), but it is confirmed by the inspeximuses of 1297 (*Stat. Realm*, I, p. 121) and 1300 (ibid. Charters, p. 43) as the reading of 1225.

[2] Here the obscure final sentence ("In respect . . . our woods") of 1217, c. 14, is omitted.

[3] Here the "or other person" of 1217 is omitted.

[4] Here the "clerks as well as laymen" of 1217 is omitted.

B. THE RULE OF HENRY III 1227-67

28. Statute concerning the Jews, 1233

This statute of 4 April 1233 is known only from an early manuscript collection of documents, not from any official record. But there is no reason to doubt its authenticity. See H. G. Richardson in *Law Quarterly Review*, vol. 54 (1938), pp. 393-4, and *English Jewry under the Angevin Kings* (1960), pp. 293-4, where it is printed.

In the seventeenth year of the reign of king Henry son of John on the fourth day of April on the morrow of Easter, it was ordained by the same king at Canterbury that no loan may be contracted with Jews by tally, but by chirograph, whose other part the Jew shall have, with the seal[1] of the Christian contracting the loan appended, and the other part let the Christian contracting the loan have. The third part, however, that is called the foot, let that be placed in the chest to be safely kept by the chirographers, Christian and Jew, and a chirograph whose foot shall not have been found in the chest, as stated, shall not be valid.

No Jew may lend anything by penalty,[2] but let him take interest at twopence per pound per week[3] and no more, so that nothing is put to hazard save the sum first loaned.

No Jew may remain in our kingdom unless he is such that he can be of service to the king and find good pledges for his loyalty. Other Jews, who have nothing with which they can be of service to the king, shall leave the kingdom before Michaelmas of the seventeenth year of the aforesaid king's reign [Michaelmas 1233]. If they stay longer let them be cast into prison and not released without the king's special mandate.

No Jew may make an advance henceforth on church plate or on cloths that are bloodstained or sodden or holed[4] as if by violence.

29. Hundred Courts: Magna Carta clarified, 1234

(*Close Rolls . . . Henry III, 1231-4*, pp. 588-9)

This official guidance on correct practice was prompted by the uncertainties described by J. C. Holt, *Magna Carta* (1965), pp. 279-84. Holt (p. 284, n.) has some pertinent criticism of the importance Sir Maurice Powicke (*King Henry III and the Lord Edward*, I, p. 148) would attach to it: a similar public-spiritedness (whether one should attribute it to the barons or not) is, however, shown in the royal proclamation of 20 October 1258 (No. 39 below).

For how far this ruling of 1234 was observed and for the subject generally: Helen M. Cam, *The Hundred and the Hundred Rolls*, in particular p. 168.

The king to the sheriff of Lincolnshire, greeting. Because we have heard that since we granted to all our realm the liberties contained in our charters which we then made while we were under age you and your bailiffs and also the bailiffs of others who have hundreds in your county do not understand how hundreds and wapentakes ought to be held in your county, we have lately caused the same charter to be read in the presence of our lord of Canterbury and of the greater and sounder part of all the bishops, earls and barons of the whole of our realm in order that in their presence

[1] *signo* [2] *per penam*
[3] amounting to $43\frac{1}{3}\%$ per annum
[4] MS. *confunctos*. Mr Richardson has confirmed this in correspondence with me as the reading of the manuscript. I have regarded this as a corruption of *conpunctos* and so translated it.

and through them this clause contained in our charter of liberties might be explained, namely, that no sheriff or bailiff may make his tourn through the hundreds more than twice a year and only in the due and accustomed place, that is once after Easter and again after Michaelmas[. And view of frankpledge shall then be held at the Michaelmas term] without molestation, so, that is,[1] that everyone has his liberties which he had and was wont to have in the time of king Henry our grandfather or which he afterwards acquired. Concerning which it was by many there said and testified that in the time of king Henry our grandfather both the hundreds and wapentakes and the courts of magnates of England used to be held fortnightly. And much though it would please us to provide for the common easement of the whole realm and the sparing of the poor, yet because those two tourns do not fully suffice for the preservation of the peace of our kingdom and for the redress of wrongs done to rich and poor, which matters pertain to hundred courts, by the common counsel of the aforesaid lord of Canterbury and of all the aforesaid bishops, earls and barons and the others it is provided that hundreds and wapentakes and also courts of magnates are to be held between the aforesaid two tourns every three weeks, where formerly they used to be held fortnightly; so, however, that to those hundreds and wapentakes and courts no general summons as to the aforesaid tourns is to be made, but only plaintiffs and their adversaries and those who owe suit through whom the pleas will be held and judgments given shall come to those hundreds, wapentakes and courts – unless it be that at those hundreds and wapentakes inquiry ought to be made about pleas of the crown, such as a man's death, treasure trove and this sort of thing, for inquiry into which there shall come, with the aforesaid suitors, the four nearest townships, that is, all from those vills who are necessary for the holding of those inquests. And therefore we command you to have the aforesaid hundreds, wapentakes and courts, both our own and those of others, held henceforth in accordance with what is aforesaid every three weeks, except the aforesaid two tourns, which are to be held in the future as they were wont to be held in the past. Witness the king at Westminster, 11 October.

30. The so-called Statute of Merton, 1236

(*Statutes of the Realm*, I, pp. 1–4)

It was provided in the court of the lord king on Wednesday the day after the feast of St Vincent[2] in the 20th year of the reign of king Henry the son of king John at Merton in the presence of the archbishop of Canterbury and his suffragan bishops and of the greater part of the earls and barons of England who were there for the coronation of the lord king and queen Eleanor, for which they had all been summoned, after discussion of the common good of the realm upon the underwritten articles it

[1] From a comparison of Magna Carta (1217 or 1225), which is, of course, what is being recited, it seems likely (and I have assumed) that there has been an accidental omission of *Et visus . . . sancti Michaelis* after *sancti Michaelis*; and here too it makes better sense to restore *scilicet* rather than *saltem*.
[2] i.e. Wednesday, 23 January 1236

was thus provided and granted both by the aforesaid archbishop, bishops, earls and barons and by the king himself and others:

[1] Concerning widows who after their husbands' deaths are expelled from their dowers and cannot get their dowers or their quarantine without sueing for them,[1] namely, that whoever withholds from them their dowers or their quarantine out of the lands of which their husbands died seised and those widows afterwards recover by sueing, those who are convicted of [such] wrongful deforcement are to pay those same widows their damages, that is to say the full value of the dower which is theirs from the time of their husbands' deaths to the day when they recovered seisin of it by judgment of court. And the deforcers are nonetheless to be in the king's mercy.

[2] Also all widows can from now on bequeath the corn from their land, as well from their dower-lands as from their other lands and tenements, saving the services due to the lords for their dower-lands and their other tenements.

[3] Also if any is disseised of his freehold and recovers his seisin by assize of *novel disseisin* before the justices in eyre, or on the confession of those who did the disseisin, and is put in possession by the sheriff, if those same disseisors subsequently after the eyre of the justices again disseise him and are convicted of it they are to be at once arrested and detained in the king's prison until on payment of fine or in some other way they are discharged by the lord king . . . The same is to be done in the case of those who recover seisin by assize of *mort d'ancestor*, and in the case of all lands and tenements recovered by juries in the king's court, if they are subsequently disseised by the original disseisors from whom they have recovered in any way by jury.

[4] Also because many magnates of England who have enfeoffed their knights and freeholders with small tenements in their large manors have complained that they could not profit from what remained of the manors, such as wastes, woods and pastures, although those feoffees have sufficient pasture as belongs to their tenements, it is thus provided and granted that whenever such feoffees bring an assize of *novel disseisin* for their common pasture and it is acknowledged before the justices that they have as much pasture as suffices for their tenements and that they have free access and egress from their tenements to their pasture, then they are to be content with it and they of whom they have complained may go quit for having profited from the lands, wastes, woods and pasture. If, however, they say that they have not sufficient pasture or sufficient access and egress as belongs to their tenements, then the truth is to be enquired into by the assize. And if it is found by the assize that their access or egress is by the same deforcers in some respect impeded or that they have not sufficient pasture and sufficient access and egress as aforesaid, then they are to recover their seisin by view of the jurors, so that by their discretion and oath the plaintiffs may have sufficient access and egress in the way aforesaid. And the disseisors are to be in the lord king's mercy and pay damages as they were wont to be paid before this provision. If, however, it is recognised by the assize that the plaintiffs have sufficient pasture with free and sufficient access and egress as said before then the others may lawfully make their profit from the remainder and go quit from that assize.

[1] *sine placito*

[5] Likewise it is provided and by the lord king granted that in future interest[1] is not to run against anyone under age from the time when his ancestor, whose heir he is, died until his coming-of-age; so nevertheless that on this account payment of the principal together with the interest [for the time] before the death of his ancestor, whose heir he is, is not to be stayed.

[6] Concerning heirs forcibly abducted or withheld by parents[2] or others it is thus provided: that every layman whatsoever convicted of so [withholding, abducting or][3] giving in marriage a child is to pay the loser the value of the marriage and for the offence is to be physically arrested and imprisoned until he has compensated the loser for the marriage, if the child is married, and furthermore satisfied the lord king for the trespass; and this is to be done in the case of an heir under fourteen years of age. In the case, though, of an heir aged fourteen years or more, up to full age, if he marries without his lord's permission in order to deprive him of his marriage, when the lord offers him a reasonable marriage where he will not be disparaged, then his lord shall hold his land beyond the coming-of-age, that is twenty-one years, long enough for him to receive therefrom twice the value of the marriage on the estimate of lawful men or according to what was earlier offered him without fraud and malice for the marriage and according to what can be proved in the court of the lord king. Concerning lords who have married those whom they have in ward to villeins or others such as burgesses whereby they are disparaged, if such an heir is under fourteen and of such an age that he cannot consent, then if the relatives complain, the lord shall lose the wardship until the heir comes of age, and all the profit that he would have received from it shall be converted to the profit of him who is under age as the relatives arrange and provide, in return for the shame inflicted upon him. But if he is fourteen or over, so that he can consent, and has consented, to such a marriage no penalty shall follow.

[7] If any heir of any age whatever will not marry for the benefit of his lord he is not to be compelled to do so, but when he comes of age he shall give and satisfy his lord with as much as he could have got from anybody for the marriage; and this whether he wishes to marry himself or not, for the marriage of him who is under age belongs of clear right to the lord of the fee.

[8] Concerning statement of descent in a writ of right from an ancestor from the time of king Henry the Elder, the year and the day, it is provided that henceforth no mention be made of so long a time, but from the time of king Henry our grandfather, and this provision shall take effect at Whitsuntide in the twenty-first year and not before: writs sued out before that are to proceed. Writs of *mort d'ancestor*, *neifty*, and of entry shall not go beyond the last return of the lord king John to England. Writs of *novel disseisin* shall not go beyond the first crossing of the lord king who now is to Brittany and this provision shall take effect from the time aforesaid, and writs sued out before that are to proceed.

[9] To[4] the king's writ about bastardy whether anyone born before matrimony can

[1] literally "usuries" [2] i.e. relatives

[3] On the textual difficulty, see T. F. T. Plucknett, *Statutes and their Interpretation in the Fourteenth Century*, pp. 13–14.

[4] cf. Powicke and Cheney, *Councils and Synods*, II (Oxford, 1964), pp. 198–9

inherit just as he can who is born after, all the bishops answered that they would not and could not reply to this because this was contrary to the general principle of the church: and all the bishops asked the magnates to agree that those born before matrimony were legitimate like those born after matrimony as regards hereditary succession, because the church reckons them as legitimate; and all the earls and barons answered with one voice that they were not willing to change the laws of England that were used and approved.

[10] It is provided and granted that every free man who owes suit to the county, tithing, hundred and wapentake or to the court of his lord can freely appoint an attorney to do those suits for him.

[11] Concerning malefactors in parks and preserves, it is not yet settled, for the magnates asked for their own prison for those whom they caught in their parks and preserves; but the king opposed it, and therefore it is put off.

31. Treaty between the kings of England and Scotland, 1237

(W. C. Dickinson, G. Donaldson and I. A. Milne, *A Source Book of Scottish History*, I (1952), pp. 82–3)

(a) *Treaty of York, 1237*

It was agreed

That the said Alexander king of Scotland remitted and quit-claimed for himself and his heirs to the said Henry king of England and his heirs in perpetuity the said counties of Northumberland, Cumberland and Westmoreland [*and fifteen thousand marks of silver which king John, father of Henry, received from William, former king of Scotland, father of Alexander, for certain agreements entered upon between the said kings which were not observed by king John, as Alexander king of Scotland says*] and all agreements made between king John and king William about marriages between Henry king of England or Richard his brother and Margaret or Isabella sisters of the said Alexander king of Scotland . . .

For this remission and quitclaim the said Henry king of England gave and granted to the said Alexander king of Scotland two hundred librates of land within the said counties of Northumberland and Cumberland if the said two hundred librates of land can be found in these counties outside towns where castles are situated, and if any is lacking, it shall be made up in suitable places nearest the said counties of Northumberland and Cumberland; to be had, held and retained in demesne by the said Alexander king of Scotland and his heirs the kings of Scotland of the said Henry king of England and his heirs; rendering from it annually one red falcon to the king of England and his heirs at Carlisle through the hands of the constable of the castle of Carlisle whoever he may be on the feast of the Assumption of the Blessed Mary for all services, customs and other demands which might be exacted for the same lands . . .

And the said king of Scotland shall do his homage from these lands to the said Henry king of England and shall swear fealty to him. [*Foedera*, I, i, 233]

(b)

As a firm peace has been entered upon between the king and the king of Scotland, so that the king is not now in fear of his castles as before, it is not necessary that there should be as great expense at the royal castles at Bamborough and Newcastle-on-Tyne as there used to be; and Hugh de Bolebec is commanded to spend as little as he can on the maintenance of the aforesaid castles. . . . [*Cal. Close Rolls, 1234–7*, p. 498]

32. The king is refused an aid, 1242

(Matthew Paris, *Chronica Majora*, ed. Luard, Rolls series, IV, pp. 185–7; whence more conveniently in Stubbs, *Select Charters*, 9th edn, pp. 360–2. Translation based on that of J. A. Giles, *Matthew Paris's English History*, I (Bohn's Antiquarian Library, 1852), pp. 400–2)

Preserved only by the chronicler Matthew Paris and given after his own account of the negotiation, as a record of it. At a discount to the extent that it is not demonstrably official, it is nonetheless "the first detailed account" of the deliberations in a parliament and "an early and very important instance of an aid being absolutely refused" (Stubbs) and, whatever its origin, valuable because (as Paris says it was meant to do) it preserves the prelates' and magnates' reasons for refusing.

Whereas the lord archbishop of York, all the bishops of England, abbots, priors, either in person or by their proctors, and also the earls, and almost all the barons of England have assembled at the command of the lord king at Westminster on the Tuesday before the Purification of the Blessed Mary in the year of our Lord one thousand two hundred and forty two, the twenty-sixth year of the reign of king Henry, to hear the king's will and the business for which he has summoned them, and whereas the said lord king, sending to them the said lord archbishop of York, the noble lord the earl Richard and Walter of York, provost of Beverley, concerning his will and his affairs, those, that is to say, expounded to them by those eminent messengers, asked all the magnates of his kingdom to give him counsel and aid to obtain possession of his inheritance and his rights overseas which belong to his kingdom of England: the said bishops, abbots, priors, earls and barons, after lengthy discussion among themselves, in the end advised the king through the aforesaid nobles first to await the expiration of the truce made between him and the king of France. And if by chance the said king of France should have made any attacks contrary to the terms of the truce, then the said king of England should send illustrious messengers to him to request, warn, and induce him to observe the truce entered into and to make amends for attacks, if any had been made by him or his. And if the king of France should refuse to do so, they would in this connection willingly give their utmost consideration to giving him an aid. All unanimously agreed on this answer. At the same time, since he had been their ruler they had many times, at his request, given him aid, namely, a thirteenth of their movable property, and afterwards a fifteenth and a sixteenth and a fortieth, carucage, hidage, and several scutages; and lastly one grand scutage, for the marriage of his sister, the empress. Scarcely, however, had four years or so elapsed from that time, when he again asked them for aid, and, at length, by dint of great entreaties, he obtained a thirtieth, which they granted him on the condition that neither that exaction nor the others before it should in the future be made a precedent of. And regarding that he gave them his charter. Furthermore, he then granted them that all the liberties contained in Magna Carta should thenceforward be fully observed throughout the whole of his kingdom, and on this he made a certain small charter of his for them which they still have, in which these things are contained. Besides this, the lord king granted to them, of his own free will and by the advice of all his barons, that the whole of the money from the said thirtieth should be safely deposited in his castles under the custody of four magnates of England, namely, the earl Warenne and others, by whose view and advice the money should be expended for the benefit of the said king and kingdom as necessary. And because the barons do not know, and have not heard, that any of the said money has been expended by the view or the advice of any one of the said four magnates, they firmly believe and are well aware that the lord king has the whole of that money intact still, and from it he can provide himself now with a great deal of aid. Further, they well know that since that time he has had so many escheats (the archbishopric of Canterbury, and several of the richer bishoprics of England, and the lands of deceased earls and barons and of knights who held of him) that from those escheats alone, if they were well kept, he ought to have a large sum of money. Furthermore, from the time of their giving the said thirtieth, itinerant justices have been continually going on eyre through all parts of England, alike for pleas of the forest and all other pleas, so that all the counties, hundreds, cities, boroughs, and nearly all the vills of England are heavily amerced; wherefore, from that eyre alone the king has, or ought to have, a very large sum of money, if it were paid, and properly collected. They therefore say with truth that all in the kingdom are so oppressed and impoverished by these amercements and by the other aids given before that they have little or no goods left. And because the king had never, after the granting of the thirtieth, abided by his charter of liberties, nay had since then oppressed them more than usual, and by the other charter had granted to them that such exactions should not be made a precedent of, they told the king flatly that for the present they would not give him an aid. But, inasmuch as he was their lord, he could behave in such a manner towards them until the end of the said truce that they would then give the matter as favourable consideration as they could.

When the said nobles who were his messengers had conveyed this reply to the king, they returned to the barons and said that they had to the best of their ability given the king a sufficient answer, but he wanted to know from them what they would do if the king of France should break the truce before it ended. Also, on behalf of the king, they promised that, if he had done injury to any of the magnates of England, he would make amends for it as adjudged by Peter of Savoy and others of his council. To which things the magnates replied that, if the king of France should break the truce and be unwilling to make amends for the attacks, they would then give the matter the consideration they had previously said they would give at the expiration of the truce, provided they were assured of the truth of the French king's having done so. As to the fact that, on behalf of the king, the messengers promised amends for injuries inflicted on them, they said they were unwilling at present to wrangle with[1] the king.

[1] *placitare*

At the time of the grant of the thirtieth, W[illiam] of Raleigh had promised them as well and faithfully on the king's behalf as they were now doing, and how the king kept his promises he may see for himself.

Afterwards the king tried many of them privately one by one; what they individually granted the community[1] does not know.

33. Form for keeping the peace, 1242

(*Close Rolls 1237–42*, pp. 482–5)

Stubbs's misdating of this (*Select Charters*, 9th edn, pp. 362–5) is corrected by Helen Cam, *Hundred and the Hundred Rolls*, p. 189. Stubbs took it from *Foedera*, I, i (1816), p. 281, which took it from Matthew Paris. The correct date is established and a better text afforded by the official record in the Close Roll for 26 Hen. III.

For Henry II's assize of arms (1181), see *E.H.D.*, II, No. 27. Now, it will be observed, villeins are definitely brought into the system. Edward I's Statute of Winchester is No. 59 below. A survey of these developments at hundred level is Cam, op. cit., pp. 188–94.

The king to the sheriff of Worcester, greeting. Know that for our peace to be firmly maintained, it has been provided by our council[2] that watches be kept in each city and borough and in all other vills of your county from the day of the Lord's Ascension to Michaelmas, that is to say, in each city by six men at each gate, equipped with arms, and in each borough by twelve men and in each whole vill[3] by six men, or at least four, according to the number of the inhabitants, likewise equipped with arms, and let them keep watch continually all night from sunset to sunrise; so that, if any stranger pass by them let them arrest him until morning and then, if he is of good character, he shall be set free, but, if suspect, he shall be handed over to the sheriff, who shall receive him without any difficulty or delay and keep him safely. If however such passing strangers will not suffer themselves to be arrested, then the said watchmen shall raise the hue on all sides against them and pursue them, with the whole vill and the neighbouring vills, with hue and cry from vill to vill until they are taken and then they shall be handed over to the sheriff as is aforesaid: it being provided that for such arrest or taking into custody of strangers no one shall have legal proceedings taken against him by the sheriff or his bailiffs. And let each city, borough and vill be warned to perform the aforesaid watches and pursuits so diligently that we have not to punish severely their shortcoming. It is provided also that the sheriffs shall each along with two knights appointed specially for this purpose go round their shires from hundred to hundred and cities and boroughs and have convened before them in each hundred, city and borough the citizens, burgesses, freeholders, villeins and others, from the age of 15 to the age of 60 years, and have them all assessed and sworn to arms according to the amount of their lands and[4] chattels, that is to say, for fifteen pounds worth[5] of land a hauberk and a helmet of iron, a sword, a knife and a horse; for ten pounds worth of land, a haubergeon, a helmet of iron, a sword and a knife; for a hundred shillings worth of land, a doublet, a helmet of iron, a sword, a lance and a

[1] *universitas*
[2] The king himself was in France at this time.
[3] *villa integra*
[4] On the disjunctive use of *et*, cf. *Dialogus de Scaccario*, ed. C. Johnson (Medieval Classics), p. 71.
[5] i.e. an estate in land worth this much a year, not its capital value

knife; for forty shillings worth of land and over up to a hundred shillings worth, a sword, a bow, arrows and a knife. And those who have less than forty shillings worth of land shall be sworn to have scythes, gisarmes, knives and other small weapons. For sixty marks worth of chattels, a hauberk, a helmet, a sword, a knife and a horse; for forty marks worth of chattels, a haubergeon, a helmet, a sword and a knife; for twenty marks worth of chattels, a doublet, a helmet, a sword and a knife; for ten marks worth of chattels, a sword, a knife, a bow and arrows; for forty shillings worth of chattels and over up to ten marks worth of chattels, scythes, knives, gisarmes and other small weapons. Also all others who can do so, shall have bows and arrows outside the forest; those within the forest, however, bows and bolts. And in each city and borough all those sworn to arms shall obey the mayors of the cities and the reeves and bailiffs of the boroughs, where there are not mayors. In each of the other vills, however, let there be appointed one constable or two according to the number of the inhabitants and the provision of the aforesaid. In each hundred let there be appointed a chief constable on whose orders all in his hundred who are sworn to arms shall assemble and obey him in doing what concerns the keeping of our peace. The chief constables of all the hundreds shall obey the sheriff and the aforementioned two knights in coming at their order and doing at their command what concerns the keeping of our peace. The sheriffs shall each have it proclaimed in the cities and boroughs and at all the markets of their bailiwicks that none assemble for tourneying or jousting or any other knightly adventure whatsoever; also that no one shall come armed unless they are specially deputed to preserve our peace. And if any are found thus appearing armed contrary to this our provision, let them be arrested and handed over to the sheriffs; and, if they will not allow themselves to be arrested, then the constables of every hundred and vill and others whosoever they are shall raise the hue on all sides against them and with the neighbouring vills pursue them from vill to vill until they are taken and handed over to the sheriffs as is aforesaid. As often as it happens that the hue is raised against disturbers of any kind of our peace, robbers, and malefactors in parks and preserves, let the hue be raised immediately and the offenders[1] pursued until they are taken and handed over to the sheriffs as already said about the others. And all sheriffs and their bailiffs, constables, those sworn to arms, citizens, burgesses, freeholders, villeins and others shall make such pursuit of the aforesaid malefactors that they do not escape and if through any shortcoming of theirs they do escape, those whose fault it is shall be so punished by our council that their punishment shall strike fear into others and remove the disposition to offend. Suspects arrested while it is still day by anyone whatsoever shall be received by the sheriffs without delay and difficulty and kept safely until they are delivered by the law of the land. And therefore we order you, as you cherish your body and all that you have, to carry out, along with our well-beloved and faithful William Corbet and Peter de Wyk',[2] whom we have associated with you in this, all the aforesaid with all diligence in the way prescribed, lest for any shortcoming of yours and of our aforesaid faithful we be

[1] *ipsos*

[2] The two knights associated with the sheriff of Worcestershire. The names differ, of course, in the writ sent to other sheriffs.

obliged to proceed against you and them. You should cause all liberties of your bailiwick to make return of these letters without delay in order that they execute all the aforesaid in the prescribed fashion. And if they do not do this, you shall, notwithstanding the aforesaid liberties, have it done without delay. Witness W. archbishop of York, at Westminster, the 20th day of May.

34. The so-called "Paper Constitution" preserved by Matthew Paris, 1238–44

(*Matthaei Parisiensis: Chronica Majora*, ed. H. R. Luard, Rolls series, IV, pp. 366–8)

This text, which Matthew Paris alone has preserved, is given by him under the year 1244, but N. Denholm-Young (*E.H.R.*, lviii (1943), pp. 401–23) argued for a date as early as February 1238 and has adhered to this (*Richard of Cornwall* (Oxford, 1947), p. 36, and p. 55, n. 2). The argument, however, is not completely convincing and both B. Wilkinson (*Constitutional History of England*, I (1948), ch. III) and C. R. Cheney (*E.H.R.*, xlv (1950), pp. 213–21) give reasons for retaining 1244 as the date, despite the difficulties of Matthew Paris's text.

Sir Maurice Powicke saw other possibilities between these extremes (*King Henry III and the Lord Edward* (Oxford, 1947), pp. 291, n. 2, and 300, n. 2), but would not commit himself to a precise date (ibid., p. vi; and *The Thirteenth Century*, Oxford History of England (1953), p. 77, and Additional Note on p. 79).

Precision, while it would be very satisfying, is not in this case essential. There is no evidence that this text was ever put into effect (which is why Stubbs, *Constit. Hist.*, II, 4th edn, repr., p. 64, wondered "whether or no it were more than a paper constitution"). Its importance is that it reflects somebody's (or some group's) attitude to the politics of these years. In the history of baronial action it cannot be placed chronologically, but it fits easily into the history of baronial thinking, and shows its direction.

These things the magnates provided with the king's consent to be inviolably observed thereafter

With respect to the liberties purchased, granted, and confirmed by the lord king's charter on another occasion, that they be observed in future. For the greater security whereof let a new charter be made, which shall make particular mention of these things. And those who knowingly and purposely venture either to assail the liberties granted by the lord king or to hinder their observance shall be solemnly excommunicated by all prelates; and the status of those who have suffered any infringement of their liberties since the last grant shall be restored. And because, without either regard for the oath taken or fear of the sentence the saintly Edmund pronounced, what was promised on that occasion has not so far been kept and lest there should be a danger of this sort of thing happening in the future, and so the last state become worse than the first, four men of rank and power shall be chosen by common consent from the most discreet persons of the whole realm to be of the king's council and sworn to handle faithfully the affairs of the king and of the kingdom and do justice to all without respect of persons. These shall follow the king, and if not all, at least two of them shall always be available[1] to hear each one's complaints and be able to help quickly those suffering an injustice. The lord king's treasure shall be managed under their supervision and authority[2] and money granted by them all[3] specially and for the benefit of the lord king and the kingdom shall be expended as they think best. And they shall be conservators of liberties. And as they are elected by the assent of all, so none of them shall be removable without general consent. Should one of them be taken from our midst,[4] another, by the assent and choice of the [other] three, shall be

[1] *presentes*
[2] *per visum et testimonium eorum*
[3] *ab universis*
[4] i.e. by death

put in his place within two months. And the whole body shall not meet again without them, but when necessary and at their instance. Writs sued out that are contrary to the law[1] and custom of the realm shall be utterly revoked. Remember too the sentence to be pronounced on those who oppose. Also the bond of a mutual oath. Also the eyre of the justices. Justiciar and chancellor[2] shall be chosen by all. And as they ought to be frequently with the lord king, they can be numbered among the conservators.[3] And if for any reason the king takes the seal away from the chancellor, whatever is sealed in the interval shall be treated as null and void. Then the seal shall be given back to the chancellor. No justiciar or chancellor shall be appointed in place of another, save with the assent of all in solemn assembly. Two justices in the bench. Two barons in the exchequer. At least one justice of the Jews. This time they shall be appointed by general choice; so that, just as they will handle the affairs of all, so everyone shall concur in their election. But afterwards, when it is necessary for someone else to be appointed in place of any of them, the appointment shall be by provision by the four councillors aforesaid. Those thus far suspect and not needed are to be removed from the lord king's side.

35. Royal ordinance on alienations by tenants-in-chief, 15 July 1256

(*Law Quarterly Review*, vol. 12 (1896), pp. 299–301. Translation based on that of J. M. W. Bean, *The Decline of English Feudalism 1215–1540* (Manchester, 1968), p. 67)

The king to the sheriff of York greeting. Because it is manifestly to our most grievous loss and unendurable damage to our crown and royal dignity that any one enters the baronies and fees which are held of us in chief in our kingdom and power at the will of those who hold those baronies and fees of us through which we lose wardships and escheats and our barons and others who hold those baronies and fees of us are so weakened that they are unable to perform sufficiently the services due to us therefrom, whence our crown is seriously damaged; which matter we are unwilling to suffer any longer: OF OUR COUNSEL WE HAVE PROVIDED that no one henceforth may enter a barony or any fee which may be held of us in chief by purchase or by any other means without our assent and special licence. And on that account we strictly enjoin you in the fealty by which you hold to us and as you value your person and all your possessions that you do not permit any one henceforth to enter a barony or any fee which may be held of us in chief in your bailiwick by purchase or by any other means without our assent and special licence. And if any one should enter a barony or any fee which is held of us in chief in your bailiwick against this our provision, then you are to seize the land which he has entered by that means into our hand and keep it safely in your custody until we shall have ordered otherwise with regard to it. And in executing this our mandate you are so to behave that because of any fault or negligence of yours we do not sustain loss in this regard or

[1] Mr Denholm-Young's emendation of *regem* to *legem* has been adopted.
[2] To translate *Justitiarius et cancellarius* with either the definite or the indefinite article would be to beg the question of the date of this text.
[3] *esse de numero conservatorum*

damage to our crown or royal dignity on account of which we may have to act[1] severely towards you and your possessions. The king being witness at Bristol the fifteenth day of July.

Word sent in like terms to all the sheriffs of England. Witness as above.

36. The sworn confederation of seven barons, 12 April 1258

(Bémont, *Simon de Montfort* (Paris, 1884), App. 30 [French])

The move of this powerful group after the king's revelation of his financial predicament and his failure at Rome to gain time led directly to his submission and the "Provisions of Oxford". Matthew Paris of St Albans shows a knowledge of the confederacy, but the terms of it have been preserved only in a modern copy in the archives of the Montfort family and now in the Bibliothèque Nationale.

We, Richard of Clare, earl of Gloucester and Hertford; Roger Bigod, earl marshal and earl of Norfolk; Simon de Montfort, earl of Leicester; Peter of Savoy; Hugh Bigod; John fitz Geoffrey; and Peter of Montfort make known to all people that we have sworn on the holy gospels, and are held together by this oath, and we promise in good faith that each one of us and all of us together will help each other, both ourselves and those belonging to us, against all people, doing right and taking nothing that we cannot take without doing wrong,[2] saving faith to our lord the king of England and to the crown.

In witness of which thing we have made these letters sealed with our seals . . .

And this was done at London, on the Friday after the fortnight after Easter, in the year of our Lord twelve hundred and fifty-eight.

37. The so-called Provisions of Oxford, 1258

(*Annales Monastici*, I, 446–53 [Latin and French])

By "Provisions of Oxford" we should understand a programme of reform, not a document. The texts given below are not in proper documentary form and most of them are not officially recorded. They come to us via a chronicler (the annalist of Burton-on-Trent, see above, No. 5), a manuscript collection (Brit. Mus. MS. Cotton Tiberius B. IV), and modern transcripts of an abstract which is itself modern (analysed by H. G. Richardson and G. O. Sayles in "The Provisions of Oxford: a Forgotten Document and some Comments", *Bull. J. Rylands Library*, vol. 17 (1933), pp. 291–321). As Richardson and Sayles show, there is no question of restoring from these a single original text and their suggestions for a better order even of the Provisions cannot be more than conjectural. In the circumstances, Burton, the best of the texts as well as the best-known, has been chosen for translation.

The provision made at Oxford

It was provided that from each county there are to be chosen four discreet and law-worthy knights, who on every day when the county is held are to meet to hear all complaints of any trespasses and injuries whatsoever inflicted upon any persons whatsoever by sheriffs, bailiffs, or whatsoever others, and to make the attachments arising out of the said complaints pending the first coming of the chief justiciar to those parts. In such wise that they take sufficient sureties from the plaintiff that he will

[1] *carere* emended to *capere*

[2] *et prenant kanke nous porrons senz mesfeire* has been emended (in the light of the oath of the community in the Provisions of Oxford, No. 37 below)

proceed with the suit and likewise from him who is complained of that he will appear and submit to the law before the said justiciar at his first coming. And the aforesaid four knights are to have all the aforesaid complaints with their attachments enrolled in proper order and sequence, namely arranged according to hundred and each hundred separately. So that the aforesaid justiciar on his first coming can hear and determine the aforesaid complaints one by one from each hundred. And they are to let the sheriff know that they are summoning before the said justiciar at his next coming for days and places which he will make known to them, all his hundredors and bailiffs. So that every hundredor shall produce all plaintiffs and defendants of his bailiwick in the order in which the said justiciar shall think fit to take the pleas of that hundred; and enough men of such a sort – as well knights as other free and law-worthy men – from his bailiwick that the truth of the matter may be the better found, in such a way that all are not troubled at one and the same time, but as many appear as can have their cases heard and determined in one day.

Also it was provided that no regard is to be had for any knight of the aforesaid counties because of exemption by a charter of the lord king from being put on juries or assizes, nor is he to be quit in respect of this provision made in this wise for the common benefit of the whole kingdom.

Those chosen from the lord king's side

The lord bishop of London. The lord bishop elect of Winchester. The lord H[enry], son of the king of Germany. The lord J[ohn], earl Warenne. The lord Guy de Lusignan. The lord W[illiam] de Valence. The lord J[ohn], earl of Warwick. The lord John Mansel. Brother J[ohn] of Darlington. The abbot of Westminster. The lord H[enry] of Hengham.[1]

Those chosen from the side of the earls and barons

The lord bishop of Worcester. The lord Simon, earl of Leicester. The lord Richard, earl of Gloucester. The lord Humphrey, earl of Hereford. The lord Roger the marshal. The lord Roger of Mortimer. The lord J[ohn] fitz Geoffrey. The lord Hugh Bigod. The lord Richard de Grey. The lord W[illiam] Bardolf. The lord P[eter] of Montfort. The lord Hugh the Dispenser.

And if it should happen that of necessity any one of those cannot be present, the rest of them are to choose whom they will for the other one needed in place of the absentee to proceed with the business.

This the community of England swore at Oxford

We, so and so, make known to all people that we have sworn on the holy gospels, and are held together by this oath, and promise in good faith, that each one of us and all of us together will help each other, both ourselves and those belonging to us, against all people, doing right and taking nothing that we cannot take without doing wrong, saving faith to the king and the crown. And we promise upon the same oath that none of us will ever take anything of land or movables whereby this oath can be

[1] Wingham

disturbed or in any way impaired. And if any one acts contrary to this, we will hold him as a mortal enemy.

This is the oath of the twenty-four

Each one swore on the holy gospels that he for the glory of God and in loyalty to the king and for the benefit of the kingdom will ordain and treat with the aforesaid sworn persons upon the reform and improvement of the condition of the kingdom. And that he will not fail for gift or for promise, for love or for hatred, for fear of any one, for gain or for loss, loyally to act according to the tenour of the letter that the king has given on this and his son likewise.

This the chief justiciar of England swore

He swears that he will well and loyally according to his power do what belongs to the justiciar's office of dispensing justice to all men for the profit of the king and the kingdom, in accordance with the provision made and to be made by the twenty-four, and by the king's council and the magnates of the land, who will swear to help and support him in these things.

This the chancellor of England swore

That he will not seal any writ except a writ of course without the order of the king and of the councillors who are present. Nor will he seal a gift of a great wardship or of a large sum of money or of escheats without the assent of the full council or of the greater part of it. And that he will not seal anything that is contrary to what has been and will be ordained by the twenty-four or by the greater part of them. And that he will not take any reward otherwise than is agreed for others. And he will be given a companion in the way that the council will provide.

This is the oath that the keepers of the castles took

That they will keep the king's castles loyally and in good faith for the use of the king and his heirs. And that they will give them up to the king or his heirs and to no other and [do it] through his council and in no other way, that is to say, through men of standing in the land elected to his council or through the greater part of them. And this form above[1] written is to last full twelve years. And thenceforward they shall not be prevented by this establishment and this oath from being able to give them up freely to the king or his heirs.

These are those who are sworn of the king's council

The archbishop of Canterbury, the bishop of Worcester, the earl of Leicester, the earl of Gloucester, the Earl Marshal, Peter of Savoy, the count of Aumale, the earl of Warwick, the earl of Hereford, John Mansel, John fitz Geoffrey, Peter of Montfort, Richard de Grey, Roger of Mortimer, James of Audley.

The king's twelve have chosen from the twelve of the community: the earl Roger the marshal, Hugh Bigod.

[1] "above" is supplied from the patent roll (*C.P.R., 1247–58*, p. 637), an official record of the terms of this oath

And the party for the community has chosen from the twelve who are of the king's side: the earl of Warwick, John Mansel.

And these four have power to choose the council of the king, and when they have chosen, they shall show them to the twenty-four and what the greater part of these agree on shall hold good.

These are the twelve who are chosen by the barons to treat in three parliaments a year with the king's council for all the community of the land about the common business

The bishop of London, the earl of Winchester, the earl of Hereford, Philip Basset, John de Balliol, John de Verdun, John de Grey, Roger de Sumery, Roger de Mohaut, Hugh the Dispenser, Thomas de Gresley, Giles d'Argentein.

These are the twenty-four who are appointed by the community to treat of an aid for the king

The bishop of Worcester, the bishop of London, the bishop of Salisbury, the earl of Leicester, the earl of Gloucester, the Earl Marshal, Peter of Savoy, the earl of Hereford, the count of Aumale, the earl of Winchester, the earl of Oxford, John fitz Geoffrey, John de Grey, John de Balliol, Roger of Mortimer, Roger de Mohaut, Roger de Sumery, Peter of Montfort, Thomas de Gresley, Fulk of Kerdiston, Giles d'Argentein, John Kyriel, Philip Basset, Giles of Erdinton.

And if any of these cannot be there, or will not, those who are there are to have the power of choosing another in his place.

Of the condition of holy church

It is to be remembered that the condition of holy church is to be amended by the twenty-four chosen to reform the condition of the kingdom of England, when they see place and time, in accordance with the power they have in that regard by the letter of the king of England.

Of the chief justiciar

Furthermore that a justiciar be appointed, one or two, and what power he is to have, and that he is not to be for more than a year. So that at the end of the year he answer before the king and his council for his time and before the one who is to succeed him.

Of the treasurer, and of the exchequer

Likewise of the treasurer. Except that he is to render account at the end of the year. And other good men are to be put at the exchequer in accordance with the ordinance of the aforesaid twenty-four. And there all the issues of the land are to come and no part of them elsewhere. And what is seen to need amendment is to be amended.

Of the chancellor

Likewise of the chancellor. So that at the end of the year he answer for his time. And that he seal not out of course by the will of the king alone; but do it through the councillors who are with the king.

Of the power of the justiciar and of the bailiffs

The chief justiciar has power to amend the wrongs committed by all other justices and by bailiffs, and earls and barons and all other men, in accordance with the law and right of the land. And writs are to be pleaded according to the law of the land, and in proper places. And that the justiciar take nothing unless it be a present of bread and wine and such things, that is to say food and drink, as one has been accustomed to bring to the tables of men of quality for the day. And this same thing is to be understood of all the councillors of the king and of all his bailiffs. And that no bailiff because of a plea or of his office take any reward by his own hand or through another person in any way. And if he is convicted, that he be condemned to make fine, and he who gives also. And so it is necessary for the king to give to his justiciar and to his people who serve him, so that they have no need to take anything from anyone else.

Of sheriffs

Sheriffs are to be provided, loyal people and good men and landholders; so that in each county a vavassour of the same county be sheriff, to treat the people of the county well, loyally and justly. And that he take no reward, and that he is not to be sheriff for more than a year at a time. And that in the year he render his accounts at the exchequer and answer for his term. And that the king grant him of his own according to his estimate of how he can keep the county rightly. And that he take no reward, neither he nor his bailiffs. And if they are convicted, they are to be condemned to make fine.

It is to be remembered that such amendment is to be applied to the Jewry and to the wardens of the Jewry that the oath relating thereto may be kept.

Of escheators

Good escheators are to be appointed. And that they take nothing of the goods of the dead from such lands as ought to be in the king's hand. But that the executors have free administration of the goods as soon as they have satisfied the king if they owe him a debt. And this in accordance with the form of the charter of liberty. And that enquiry be made into wrongs done by escheators in the past, and that amendment be made of such and such. Neither tallage nor other thing is to be taken save as it ought to be according to the charter of liberty.

The charter of liberty is to be kept firmly.

Of the exchange of London

It is to be remembered about amending the exchange of London and about the city of London and all the other cities of the king that have gone to shame and destruction through tallages and other oppressions.

Of the household of the king and of the queen

It is to be remembered to amend the households of the king and queen.

Of the parliaments, when they shall be held in the year and how

It is to be remembered that the twenty-four have ordained that there are to be three parliaments a year. The first on the octave of Michaelmas. The second, the morrow of Candlemas. The third, the first day of June, that is to say, three weeks before St John's day.[1] To these three parliaments shall come the chosen councillors of the king, even if they are not summoned, to view the state of the kingdom and to treat of the common business of the kingdom and of the king likewise. And at other times they are to meet[2] when there is need, on a summons of the king.

And it is to be remembered that the community is to choose twelve good men who shall come to the parliaments and at other times, when there is need, when the king or his council shall summon them to treat of the common[3] business of the king and of the kingdom. And that the community are to hold as established what these twelve shall do. And this is to be done to spare the community expense.

Fifteen are to be named by these four, that is to say by the earl Marshal, the earl of Warwick, Hugh Bigod and John Mansel, who have been chosen by the twenty-four to name the aforesaid fifteen who are to be of the king's council. And they are to be confirmed by the aforesaid twenty-four or by the greater part of them. And they are to have authority to advise the king in good faith on the government of the kingdom and on all things pertaining to the king or the kingdom. And [authority] to amend and redress all the things they see need to be redressed and amended. And [authority] over the chief justiciar, and over all other people. And if they cannot all be present, what the majority does shall be firm and established.

These are the names of the principal castles of the king, and of those who have charge of them

Robert de Neville	Bamburgh Newcastle-upon-Tyne
Gilbert de Gant	Scarborough
William Bardolf	Nottingham
Ralph Basset of Sapcote	Northampton
Hugh Bigod	Tower of London
Richard de Grey	Dover
Nicholas de Moels	Rochester and Canterbury
	Winchester
Roger de Samford	Porchester
Stephen Longespee	Corfe
Matthew de Bezil	Gloucester
Henry de Tracy	Exeter
Richard de Rochele	Haldesham
John de Grey	Hereford
Robert Walerand	Salisbury

[1] i.e. beginning 6 October, 3 February and 3 June annually

[2] I have preferred here the reading of the "Coke Roll" abstract (*asemblerent*) to that (*ensement*) of the Burton Annals (*Ann. Monast.*, I, 452).

[3] Though "*comunes*" is wanting here in the Burton Annals text, "common business" is the phrase used elsewhere in that text (ibid. p. 452) and the "Coke Roll" actually gives *comunes* here.

Hugh the Dispenser	Horston
Peter of Montfort	Bridgwater[1]
The earl of Warwick	Devizes
John son of Bernard	Oxford

38. Proclamation of 18 October 1258

The following proclaims to the people in the shires the king's adherence to the new order and requires of them too the oath to observe it. The councillors named as participating in the act are members of the Council of Fifteen. Issued in all three languages, Latin, French and English (Burton annals, No. 5 above), the proclamation is here offered in the English version and in the original English as well as a fairly literal modern version. The use of English, after a century of eclipse of the vernacular as an official language, is interesting, as well as, of course, evidence of the exceptional nature of the occasion. Comparison of the two forms will enable the difference between the speech of the thirteenth and the twentieth-century Englishman to be seen.

The English version (a mixture of Southern and Midland forms probably characteristic of the London English of the time) is printed from that given in B. Dickins and R. M. Wilson, *Early Middle English Texts* (Cambridge, 1952), pp. 8–9. The French version is printed in Rymer, *Foedera*, I, i (Rec. Com., 1816), pp. 377–8. The modern English version is by H. Rothwell, first printed here.

MIDDLE ENGLISH

Henri, þurȝ Godes fultume King on Engleneloande, Lhoauerd on Yrloande, Duk on Normandi, on Aquitaine, and Eorl on Aniow, send igretinge to alle hise holde, ilærde and ileawede, on Huntendoneschire. Þæt witen ȝe wel alle þæt we willen and vnnen þæt, þæt vre rædesmen alle, oþer þe moare dæl of heom, þæt beoþ ichosen þurȝ us and þurȝ þæt loandes folk on vre kuneriche, habbeþ idon and shullen don in þe worþnesse of Gode and on vre treowþe, for þe freme of þe loande þurȝ þe besiȝte of þan toforeniseide redesmen, beo stedefæst and ilestinde in alle þinge a buten ænde. And we hoaten alle vre treowe in þe treowþe þæt heo vs oȝen, þæt hoe stedefæstliche healden and swerien to healden and to werien þo isetnesses þæt beon imakede and beon to makien, þurȝ þan toforeniseide rædesmen, oþer þurȝ þe moare dæl of heom, alswo alse hit is biforen iseid; and þæt æhc oþer helpe þæt for to done bi þan ilche oþe aȝenes alle men riȝt for to done and to foangen. And noan ne nime of loande ne of eȝte wherþurȝ þis besiȝte muȝe beon ilet oþer iwersed on onie wise. And ȝif oni oþer onie cumen her onȝenes, we willen and hoaten þæt alle vre treowe heom healden deadliche ifoan. And for þæt we willen þæt þis beo stedefæst and lestinde, we senden ȝew þis writ open, iseined wiþ vre seel, to halden amanges ȝew ine hord. Witnesse vsseluen æt Lundene þane eȝtetenþe day on þe monþe of Octobre, in þe two and fowertiȝþe ȝeare of vre cruninge. And þis wes idon ætforen vre isworene redesmen, Boneface Archebischop on Kanterburi, Walter of Cantelow, Bischop on Wirechestre, Simon of Muntfort, Eorl on Leirchestre, Richard of Clare, Eorl on Glowchestre and on Hurtford, Roger Bigod, Eorl on Northfolke and Marescal on Engleneloande, Perres of Sauueye, Willelm of Fort, Eorl on Aubermarle, Iohan of Plesseiz, Eorl on Warewik, Iohan Geffrees sune, Perres of Muntfort, Richard of Grey, Roger of Mortemer, Iames of Aldithele, and ætforen oþre inoȝe.

[1] error for Bridgnorth

And al on þo ilche worden is isend into æurihce oþre shcire ouer al þære kuneriche on Engleneloande, and ek in-tel Irelonde.

Henry, through God's help king of England, lord of Ireland, duke of Normandy, of Aquitaine, and earl [i.e. count] of Anjou, sends greetings to all his faithful subjects, clergy and laity, of Huntingdonshire. That know ye all well that we will and grant that that which all our councillors, or the greater part of them, that were chosen by us and by the community[1] of our kingdom, have done and shall do for the glory of God and in loyalty to us, for the benefit of the country in the judgment of the aforesaid councillors, be firm and lasting in all things always without end. And we command all our loyal subjects by the loyalty that they owe us, that they firmly hold and swear to hold and to defend the establishments made and to be made by the aforesaid councillors, or by the greater part of them even as it is said earlier; and that each should help the other to do that by the same oath against all men to do right and to receive it. And let no one take of land or of goods whereby this judgment[2] may be hindered or prejudiced in any way. And if any man or any men oppose,[3] we will and command that all our loyal subjects hold them deadly foes. And because we will that this should be firm and lasting, we send you this writ open, sealed with our seal, to keep amongst you in the archives.[4] Bear witness ourselves at London the eighteenth day of the month of October, in the two and fortieth year of our reign. And this was done before our sworn councillors, Boniface archbishop of Canterbury, Walter of Cantelupe, bishop of Worcester, Simon de Montfort, earl of Leicester, Richard of Clare, earl of Gloucester and of Hertford, Roger Bigod, earl of Norfolk and Marshal of England, Peter of Savoy, William de Forz, count of Aumale, John of Plessis, earl of Warwick, John fitz Geoffrey, Peter of Montfort, Richard de Grey, Roger of Mortimer, James of Audley, and before many others.

And all in the very same words is sent to every other shire over all the kingdom of England, and also into Ireland.

39. Proclamation of 20 October 1258

This was meant to reassure public opinion on the problem of the conduct of the king's local officials and, according to the Dunstable annalist (No. 7, above) was to be proclaimed several times a year. Is it significant that Dunstable appears to consider this, but not that dated 18 October, memorable and that the official enrolment (*Cal. Pat. Rolls 1247–58*, pp. 655–6) and the Burton annalist (No. 5, above) alike violate chronology by giving this of the 20th before that of the 18th?

This, like that of 18 October 1258, was written (by an Exchequer clerk, Robert of Fulham, see Treharne, *Baronial Plan of Reform*, p. 120, n. 1) in French and English as well as Latin and sent to all shires. The translation is of the official enrolment (French) of the Rutlandshire writ (printed in *Royal Letters*, ed. Shirley, II, pp. 130–2) and is from *Cal. Pat. Rolls 1247–58*, pp. 655–6.

Proclamation by the king to all the people of the county of Rotelande. Whereas the king desires that swift justice be done throughout the realm for poor as well as rich, he commands that the wrongs which have been done in his time in the said

[1] literally "the people of the country"; in the French version *le commun*
[2] "provision" (*purveaunce*) in the French version
[3] literally "come here against"; in the French version, *viegnent encountre ceste chose*
[4] *en tresor* in the French version

county, whoever has done them, be shown to four knights whom the king has attorned for this, if they have not before been shown to them, and the king will amend them as speedily as he can. But if he cannot do this thing as speedily as he would wish and as there is need, both for himself and them, they ought not to marvel, as the thing has so long gone ill to the damage of the king and them, that it cannot be amended so soon; but by the first amendments which will be made in the first counties where the king shall send his justices and other good men to do this, they can have certain hope that it will be done to them in like manner as soon as can be. And know that the king has made each of his sheriffs swear this oath, that he will serve the king loyally and will keep to the best of his power what is written above, that is, that he will do right commonly to all people according to the power which he has of his office, and will not fail for love or hatred, nor for fear of any nor for any covetousness, to do speedy justice well and quickly for the poor as for the rich, and will take nothing from anyone either himself or by another, or by any manner of art or devise by occasion of his bailiwick, except only food and drink which it is customary to bring to the tables for one day at most, and that he will only have five horses in the place where he lodges with anyone by occasion of his bailiwick, and that he will lodge with no one who has less than 40*l* yearly of land, nor in any house of religion which has less than the value of 100 marks yearly in land or rents, and only once a year or twice at most, and this only by their will, and that he shall not draw this into a custom, and if it is agreed that he lodge there, he shall not take any present or other thing worth more than 12*d*. And of serjeants he shall not have more than is necessary to guard his bailiwick, and he shall take such serjeants as he can be answerable for with certainty for their good faith, and such that the country shall not be too much aggrieved by their eating and drinking, and all, so long as they are in the exercise of their office[1] from no man, clerk or lay, free or villein, house of religion or township[2] shall demand or take lamb, sheaf or corn, wool or any manner of movable or money or money's worth, as many have been accustomed to do heretofore. This to do the sheriff shall make them swear, when he commits the bailiwick to them. And he shall not let to farm counties, hundreds, wapentakes or other bailiwick of the realm, to anyone. And sheriffs and all other manner of bailiffs may be sure that if anyone is indicted[3] of any other kind of prise than is written above, by reason of his bailiwick, he shall abide judgment,[4] and also the giver with the taker, for the king has provided by the counsel of his magnates that always for the future full and swift justice shall be done to all without any manner of hire. And for this the king forbids all persons male and female that they offer, permit or give anything to any of his bailiffs on pain of abiding judgment, for when the sheriff comes at the end of the year on his account, he will be allowed his proper expenses, that he has made in keeping the king's bailiwick both for himself and for the hire of his serjeants. And for this the king gives of his own, because he does not wish that they have occasion to take anything of another. And he wills that none of his bailiffs whom he places in his

[1] *en baillie*
[2] *vilee*
[3] *ateint*
[4] *reint*

land, whether sheriff or other, remain in his bailiwick more than a year, and therefore, the king gives it to be known, that if harshness or wrong be done to them, by the aforesaid bailiffs, they shall fear[1] them less and more securely[2] expose their wrongs.

40. The Provisions of Westminster, October 1259

(*Ann. Monastici*, ed. Luard, I, pp. 471–9 [French])

For the circumstances of the Provisions, Powicke, *King Henry III and the Lord Edward*, pp. 399–406. The provisions were written in French, but some of them were translated into Latin and have come down to us in Latin as well as French. On the texts and their relationships, R. F. Treharne, *Baronial Plan of Reform 1258–1263*, pp. 164–9. The French text preserved in the annals of Burton on Trent (*Ann. Monastici*, I, pp. 471–9) is the best single text available in that it gives both the "legal" and the "administrative" provisions, the best available French text of the former and the only complete text of the latter.

The provisions of the barons

On suits of court to lords it is thus provided: That from now on no one is to be distrained to do suits to the court of his lord if it is not specifically contained in his charter that he ought to hold his land in return for rendering a certain service and doing suit to the court of his lord, unless he or his ancestors have done it from before the first crossing of the king to Brittany that is to say twenty-nine [and a half] years [past]. If anyone distrains his tenant contrary to this provision let quick justice be done about it in the king's court as is subsequently provided.

If it happens that an inheritance is divided between several parceners (like an inheritance that arises as from one heir), the other parceners shall help (the eldest of the parceners) with the cost of doing the suit reasonably. And if tenants are enfeoffed[3] with the same inheritance the lord may no longer demand more than one suit as is aforesaid.

If any lords distrain their tenants contrary to this provision, then at the complaint of the tenant let them be attached to come to the king's court at an early date to answer them; on which day they shall have one excuse for non-appearance if they are in the realm and the beasts in this connection are to be released immediately to the plaintiff and so remain until the action between them is terminated.

And [if] these who have levied the distress do not appear on the date that was given them by way of essoin, or on the first date if they were not essoined, then shall the sheriff of the district be ordered to cause them to appear on another date and if then they do not appear the sheriff shall be ordered to distrain them by all that they possess in his bailiwick, and that he be answerable to the king for the issue therefrom, and that he produce them in person in court on another day. And then on that day if they do not appear the plaintiff shall go away without day[4] and the beasts shall stay released, so that the lords henceforth shall not be able to distrain them on that account until they have deraignment[5] by an action in the king's court, saving to the lords their rights in respect of the suits whenever they dare to institute legal proceedings about

[1] *dotez* [2] *seurement*
[3] i.e. if the fee has heen subdivided by alienations, as distinct from succession
[4] i.e. free from liability
[5] i.e. until their title thereto is established

them. And the lords are to come to the court of the king to answer. And the plaintiffs can have their plaints; then by judgment of the court they shall recover the damages they have had by reason of this distress.

On the other hand let [lords[1]] distrain [for[1]] their suit by the same speedy justice tenants who withhold from their lords suits which they owe and which they have done since the aforesaid term, and recover their damages just as their tenants do from them. As to suits which were withheld before the aforesaid term the common law shall run as usual.

Furthermore it is provided that archbishop, bishop, abbot or prior, earl or baron or any of religion, or women likewise, need not come to sheriff's tourns unless they have something special to do. But tourns are to be held in the way they were held in the time of the predecessors of our lord the king who now is. And if any have lands in several hundreds they are not to be distrained or to attend tourns except where they live. And they are to be held in accordance with the charter of liberties and as they were held in the time of king Richard and king John.

It is similarly provided that neither in the eyre of justices nor in county court nor in the court of a baron or a freeman, nor in a liberty or elsewhere is one in future to take fines in return for *beaupleader* or on condition that people are not molested.

Furthermore it is provided that in a plea of dower that is before the bench one should give four days in the year at least, namely one day each term. And if one can give more, one should give more.

Likewise in essoins of *darrein presentment* and of *quare impedit* of churches that are vacant one should give a day every fortnight or every three weeks according to whether the district is a long way off or near. And if anyone who is impleaded by *quare impedit* does not come on the first day and does not have himself essoined, on another day if he does not come let him there be distrained by all his lands and his chattels by the great distress, as said above.

Concerning charters that one has obtained to be quit of assizes and juries it is so provided that if justices see that justice cannot be done without the oath of those who have the charters, as in the grand assize or in a perambulation or where they are witnesses, by name either in charters in writing, in attaints or in other case which cannot be decided without the oath of knights, in such cases one should make them swear saving to them elsewhere their liberties.

No one except the king is in future to levy a distress outside his own fee or on the king's highway where everybody can come and go.

In addition, if it happens that the lord after his tenant's death takes his lands into his hand because the heir is under age and then when the heir comes of age will not surrender his land without being sued, that the heir get back his land into his hand by writ of *mort d'ancestor* together with the damages he has sustained on account of the detention after his full age. And likewise if the heir is of age when his ancestor dies and is in[2] as the heir apparent who is regarded and accepted [as such], that the chief lord may not evict him, or take anything or remove anything, except take a simple

[1] a conjectural emendation of a corrupt passage
[2] The meaning and the legal importance of being "in" is clearer in the Latin.

seisin only. And if the chief lord keeps him out, so that he is allowed to obtain a writ of *mort d'ancestor* or of cosinage, he may recover his land and his damages as by writ of *novel disseisin*.

On wardship of socage it is so provided that if land which is held in socage is held in wardship by his kinsmen because of the heir who is under age, the guardian cannot do waste, sale or any destruction of the land that is in his wardship, but shall safely keep it for the benefit of the heir so that when he comes of age the guardian shall answer to him loyally for the issues and the profits of the thing, saving to him his reasonable outlay. Nor can he sell or give the marriage except to the advantage of the minor.

In addition it is provided that escheators, those appointed to hold inquests, justices assigned to take assizes and justices assigned to hear and determine pleas of trespass, or any other bailiff, have no power to amerce for failure to obey a common summons, except the chief justice and the justices in eyre for all pleas.

It is likewise provided that no man of religion can buy any land without the agreement of the lord, namely that lord who is the nearest except for the mesne [lord].[1]

It is likewise provided on essoins that no one henceforth is to be distrained to take an oath in warranty of the essoin either in county court or elsewhere.

Henceforth no one except the king is to hold in his court a plea concerning false judgment given in the court of his tenant; because such a plea belongs to the king and to his crown.

It is provided that if any one is distrained and his beasts are kept against gage and surety, the sheriff when complaint has been made can freely release the beasts in accordance with the law of the land, if they were taken outside a liberty, without contradiction and without hindrance from him who took them. And if they are within a liberty and the bailiff will not release them [the sheriff shall release them] for default on the part of the bailiff of the liberty.

It is provided that no magnate can from now on distrain his tenants to answer for their freehold nor for any thing that appertains to their freehold without the king's writ, nor shall he cause his free tenants to take an oath against their will, inasmuch as no one can do it without the king specially ordering it.

It is provided that no bailiff who ought to render account is to take himself off away from his lord. And if he will not render his account and has no land or tenement whereby he can be distrained he is to be attached in person, so that the sheriff in whose bailiwick he is found shall make him come to render account if he is in arrears.

It is provided that no farmers during the period of their farm shall do sale or exile of woods, houses, men or other thing belonging to the tenement which they have at farm, unless they have special permission in writing to make this sale. And if they do it and are convicted, they shall render the damages for it.

Itinerant justices from now on shall not amerce townships in their eyre because not every man who has attained the age of twelve years has come to inquests held before the coroners for the death of a man or for other thing pertaining to the crown,

[1] *plus precein sanz le main*

provided that sufficient people come from those vills to enable the inquests to be properly held.

No coroner or sheriff or other bailiff from now on shall amerce townships because they do not come to inquests. But when they find a default, let it be put in the coroners' roll and presented before the justices in eyre who have power to amerce townships and no one else [has].

In the eyre of the justices murder[1] is not henceforth to be adjudged in respect of men who have died by misadventure, but only in respect of those killed by felony.

No justice or sheriff or other bailiff is from now on to amerce townships for hue and cry raised and not followed up if it is not raised for a reasonable cause, such as for the death of a man, robbery, wounding or other similar case which pertains specially to the crown.

Furthermore if any one is vouched to warranty in a plea of land in the eyre of the justices he is not from now on to be amerced for not being present,[2] inasmuch as no free man ought to be amerced for default except on the first day of the coming of the justices. But if he who is vouched to warranty is then within the same county, then it is for the sheriff to cause him to come on the third day or the fourth according to whether he is far away or near, as is the practice in the eyre of the justices. And if he is living in another county, then he shall have a reasonable summons of fifteen days in accordance with the common law.[3]

Furthermore, that justices are to be provided to go through the land. And there is to be one of the twelve or of others of the community to see that justice is done to plaintiffs[4] and to all others. And so they are to see that the order is sent to the counties that establishments made for the benefit of the realm, those that are made and those that will be, are to be kept.

Likewise that the provisions that have been made since the beginning of these establishments are to be upheld[5] and maintained.

Furthermore the rolls of these establishments are to be read and affirmed. And the charters of liberties and of the forest are to be kept and maintained.

It is likewise provided that no one is to come to attend parliament with horses or with arms, or armed, unless he is specially ordered by the king or by his council or by writ for the common business of the land.

Where itinerant justices were lately on circuit, good men and sage are to be appointed to hear and inquire into all complaints that could have been terminated without writ during the last seven years; similarly that if any one has not made plaint before the seven years and has not had justice he is to recover to get it. And they are to have power to inquire concerning the sheriffs and their bailiffs, how they have behaved towards their district since the establishments.

They are to enquire also concerning the bailiffs of the rich men of the land and concerning the rich men themselves.

[1] *murdre*, i.e. *murdrum*
[2] i.e. when called upon to warrant
[3] The foregoing are what historians call, for their convenience, the "legislative" provisions. Those following are what they call the "administrative" provisions.
[4] *pleinanz* – plaintiffs by plaint (*querela*) rather than by writ
[5] *levez*

Itinerant justices are to have the same power as sheriffs in their eyre; in addition they are to have their own power throughout their eyre.[1] And there are to be provided from the less important people[2] of the council two or three who are to be constantly in attendance on the king between parliaments. And they are to be changed at each parliament and others appointed. And their action is to be viewed at each parliament. And if there is anything in it to be amended, it is to be amended by those of the council. And if any important business arises between parliaments that cannot be settled by the aforesaid two or three, or that cannot well be delayed until the next parliament, all those of the council are to be summoned by writ to settle this business. And there is to be put in the writ the occasion of the summons, if this is not secret. And if any of the others of the council, or of the aforesaid two or three, come to court at the king's summons or on his own business, they are to be present at the king's council as long as the business lasts both as to[3] their own business and as to[3] the king's business for which they are summoned.

It is to be remembered that two good men are to be provided to sell the wardships that are now of right in the king's hand.

Furthermore that two good men are to be provided to ordain equally with the council of the exchequer concerning sheriffs and counties.

Furthermore people are to be provided to go with the king to France. And who shall stay in the land with the justiciar.

And that an answer is to be given to the envoys from Wales.

And it is to be provided how the writs of the provisions and of the establishments shall issue from the chancery without delay.

And likewise about the envoys who shall go to Rome.

For selling the wardships the justiciar, the treasurer, mr Thomas of Wymondham, sir Roger of Thirkleby [and] sir Henry of Bath are to be appointed immediately. And that these same are to ordain and provide on what items the queen ought to get gold.

It is provided that these same are to come to the exchequer and view the sums of all kinds of tallages that have been imposed since this king's accession. And that they are to estimate how much each one can raise.

And these same are to provide how one ought to proceed in pleas about customs and about services.

Likewise they are to provide how one ought to proceed in escheats and in wardships.

It is to be provided which people ought to go[4] to correct trespasses and wrongs done, which can be determined without writ.

The justiciar is to provide this with the others. And which are to be at the bench with the justices, and which at the exchequer.

[1] *ensement en lur poer demeine par lur eire*. I have adopted E. F. Jacobs's interpretation of this obscure clause (*Studies in the Period of Baronial Reform and Rebellion 1258–1267*, p. 90), the more readily as *en* may be a misprint, misreading or corruption of some form of the verb *avoir* (*eu* or *eient*?).

[2] *mesne gent*

[3] *ove*

[4] i.e. go on circuit, cf. the provision (p. 373 above) in which the decision to send such people had already been taken.

It is provided that four knights are to be appointed in each county to observe the wrongs which sheriffs do: that, if it happens that they do wrongs, these four are to admonish the sheriffs to have them corrected. And if they will not correct them, let them enter the wrongs done on a roll and show them to the chief justice at the end of the year when he asks for them; or earlier, if he asks for them, if so be that the plaintiffs to whom the wrongs were done are willing to prosecute. And that these aforesaid four knights are not to have any authority to interfere with the performance by the sheriffs of their office.

If a clerk is accused of the death of a man, of robbery, or larceny, or other crime that concerns the crown, and then is by command of the king delivered on bail to twelve good men that they have him before the justices or released by pledges without[1] command of the king [and] if the aforesaid twelve or the pledges have his person before the justices on the first day, they are not in future to be amerced, even though the clerk will not answer or stand his trial in the king's court, inasmuch as they were not pledged or going surety for anything other than to produce the clerk's person in court.

The justiciar,[2] the treasurer, sir Henry of Bath, sir Roger of Thirkleby and the barons of the exchequer are to provide this year instantly which good men, upright and sage, are to be sheriffs this year. And they are to be vavasours in the shire they are sheriff of.[3] On the other hand, next year at the last county court before Michaelmas there are to be chosen in full county court four good men, upright and who will be advantageous to the king and to the shire in this office. And they are to be at the exchequer at Michaelmas. And the barons[4] are to pick out the most sufficient in their estimation.

Furthermore good men are to be chosen by the justiciar[2] and the treasurer to provide during this Advent and the festival-days,[5] against the next parliament,[6] what is to be amended at the great exchequer and at the exchequer of the Jews. And by these same reasonable sustenance is to be provided for those who are at either exchequer.

It is provided that sir Thomas de Gresley, justice of the forest, is to take Nicholas of Ramsey and three knights from each county and they are to enquire into the condition of the forests, of vert and venison, and of sales and destructions, and by whom they are done. And they are to enquire about malpractices in connection with forest pleas and by whom they were established and from what time; and when he has done this he is to make it known to the king and to his council.

It is to be done the same way with the forests beyond Trent; that the chief justice[7]

[1] Burton (*Ann. Monastici*, I, p. 478) has *par*, but "without" (*sans, sine*) is the reading of the St Albans French version (Jacobs, *Baronial Reform and Rebellion*, p. 376) and the Latin version (*Ann. Monastici*, I, 484).

[2] *la haute justice*

[3] *de memes les cuntez*

[4] i.e. the Exchequer barons

[5] *en cest Advent e en ces jurs de festes*

[6] Advent began (in 1259) on 30 November, with the great cycle of church festivals stretching over to Twelfth Night, and (by the Provisions of Oxford) the next parliament was due on 2 February (Candlemas) 1260.

[7] *la haute justice*: Gresley was chief justice of the forests south of Trent. Here *la haute justice* is probably not the justiciar (Treharne, *Baronial Plan of Reform*, p. 182); but "chief justice" = the chief forest justice (north of Trent).

provide four knights and enquire about all the forests beyond Trent in the way aforesaid.

The archbishop, the bishop of Worcester, the earl marshal, the earl of Warwick are to be with the justiciar to deal with the important business of the kingdom as long as the king is out of England. And all those of the council and of the community's twelve[1] who stay in England are to be summoned if need be. Sir Philip Basset and sir Roger Mortimer are to be constantly with the justiciar.

It is provided that the justiciar is to provide that the castellans are to have reasonable sustenance for keeping the king's castles and maintaining them.

It is provided to put two good men from the community or from the community's twelve or from others with the justices at the bench. And that they are to see that justice is done. And in the same way two good men from the community or from the community's twelve or from others are to be put at the exchequer.

These are the provisions and the establishments made at Westminster at the Michaelmas parliament by the king and his council and the twelve chosen by the common counsel before the community of England which then were at Westminster in the forty-third year of the reign of Henry the son of king John.

41. The Treaty of Paris, 1259

(Printed in *Layettes du Trésor des Chartes*, ed. Teulet (A.), Laborde (J.), etc., 5 vols (Paris, 1863–1909), III, No. 4554 [French])

The final form of 13 October 1259, in the king of England's version. An earlier form, agreed as early as May 1258, had required similar renunciations to the king's from his brother, Richard of Cornwall, and his sister Eleanor, the wife of Simon de Montfort. Both made difficulties, the former until February 1259, the latter to the end. The form of October 1259 does not require their renunciations: Louis IX had helped his brother-in-law – and peace – by no longer insisting upon them as part of the treaty itself.

He would not, however, it should be noted, make peace without them as parallel transactions. Only on 4 December 1259, the very day the outstanding Montfort renunciation was received, but not before, would he complete the peace by receiving the homage and fealty of Henry III for Aquitaine and so give the treaty its force.

Henry, by God's grace king of England, lord of Ireland and duke of Aquitaine. We make known to all and to all who are to come that we by God's will have made and ratified peace with our dear cousin, the noble king Louis of France in this manner: namely that he give us and our heirs and our successors all the right that he has and holds in these three bishoprics and in the cities, namely, of Limoges, Cahors and Périgueux, in fief and domain, saving the homage of his brothers if they hold anything there for which they are his man, and saving the things that he cannot alienate owing to letters granted by him or his ancestors, which things he must take steps to acquire in good faith from those who hold these things so that we may have them within a year next All Saints day or give us a suitable exchange, in the opinion of men of standing nominated by either side the most suitable for the interests of both parties.—The aforesaid king of France shall also give us in money each year the value of the land of the Agenais according to the assessment to be made of it on the proper value of the land by men of standing nominated by either side, and payment

[1] cf. p. 364 above

shall be made at Paris at the Temple each year, half on the *quinzaine* of the Ascension and the other half on the *quinzaine* of All Saints. And should it happen that this land escheats from the countess Joan of Poitiers to the king of France or his heirs, he or his heirs shall be bound to surrender it to us or our heirs and when the land has been surrendered they shall be relieved of the payment. And if it comes to others than the king of France or his heirs, they shall give us the fief of the Agenais with the aforesaid payment. And if it comes in domain to us, the king of France shall not be bound to render this payment. And if it is decided by the court of the king of France that, to have the land of the Agenais, we ought to put down or hand over some money as security, the king of France shall return this money or we shall hold and have the payment until we have had what we have put down for this security.—Again, it shall be enquired in good faith and without impediment, at our request, by men of standing of either side chosen for the purpose, whether the land that the count of Poitiers holds in Quercy on behalf of his wife was given or granted by the king of England with the land of the Agenais as marriage portion or as security, either wholly or in part, to his sister, who was the mother of the last count Raymond of Toulouse. And if it is found that it had so been and this land escheats to him or to his heirs on the death of the countess of Poitiers, he shall give it to us or to our heirs, and if it escheats to another and it be found by this inquest however that it had been given or granted in the way said above, after the death of the countess of Poitiers, he shall give the fief to us and to our heirs, saving the homage of his brothers, if they hold anything there, while they live.—Again, after the death of the count of Poitiers, the king of France or his heirs, kings of France, shall give to us and to our heirs the land that the count of Poitiers holds then[1] in Saintonge beyond the R. Charente in fief and in domain that are beyond the Charente, if it escheats to him or to his heirs. And if it does not escheat to him, he shall take steps in good fashion to acquire it, by exchange or otherwise, so that we or our heirs shall have it, or he shall give us, in the opinion of men of standing who shall be nominated by either side, a suitable exchange. And for what he shall give us and our heirs in fief and in domain, we and our heirs will do him and his heirs, kings of France, liege homage, and also for Bordeaux, for Bayonne and for Gascony, and for all the land that we hold beyond the English Channel in fief and in domain, and for the islands, if there are any, that we hold that are of the kingdom of France, and we will hold of him as a peer of France and as duke of Aquitaine. And for all these things aforesaid we will do him our appropriate services until it be found what services are due for these things and then we shall be bound to do them just as they have been found. About homage for the county of Bigorre, for Armagnac and for Fezensac let what is right be done about them. And the king of France absolves us if we or our ancestor[2] ever wronged him by holding his fief without doing him homage and without doing his service, and all arrears.—Again, the king of France shall give us what, in the opinion of men of standing who shall be nominated by either side, 500 knights ought to cost to maintain reasonably for two years and shall be bound to pay this money at Paris at the Temple in six payments over the period of two years, namely the first payment, that is to say a sixth, on the *quinzaine* of next

[1] *ores*

[2] i.e. his father, king John

Candlemas, another payment on the *quinzaine* of the Ascension following and another on the *quinzaine* of All Saints and likewise with the remaining payments in the following year. And for this the king of France shall give the Temple or the Hospital or both of them together as surety. And we ought not to spend this money except in the service of God or of the church, or for the benefit of the kingdom of England, and this by view of men of standing of the land chosen by the king of England and by the magnates[1] of the land.—And in making this peace we and our two sons have renounced and do renounce completely all claim upon the king of France and his ancestors and his heirs and successors, and his brothers and their heirs and successors, for us and our heirs and successors if we or our ancestors have or ever had any right in things which the king of France holds or ever held, or his ancestors or his brothers held or hold, namely in the duchy and the whole land of Normandy, in the county and the whole land of Anjou, of Touraine and of Maine, and in the county and the whole land of Poitiers, or elsewhere in any part of the kingdom of France or in the islands, if the king of France or his brothers, or others from them, hold anything of them, and all arrears. —And likewise we have renounced and do renounce, we and our two sons, all claim upon all those who hold anything, by gift, exchange, sale, purchase, elevation or other similar way, from the king of France or from his ancestors or his brothers in the duchy and the whole land of Normandy, in the county and the whole land of Anjou, of Touraine and of Maine, and in the county and the whole land of Poitiers, or elsewhere in any part of the kingdom of France or in the islands aforesaid, saving to us and our heirs our right in the lands for which we ought by this peace, as set out above, to do liege homage to the king of France, and saving that we can ask for our right if we believe we have it in the Agenais, and have it there if the court of the king of France decides it, and likewise in respect of Quercy.[2] —And we have pardoned and renounced all claim upon one another and we pardon and renounce all animosity over disputes and wars, all arrears, and all issues which have been had or which could have been had in all the aforesaid things, and all losses and all expenses incurred on either side in war or in other ways. —And so that this peace may be kept firmly and stably, without any infringement, forever, the king of France has had an oath sworn on his soul by his proxies specially appointed for this and his two sons have sworn to keep these things as long as it concerns each of them, and they have bound themselves and their heirs to keep it by their letters pendant.[3] And that we will keep these things we are bound to give the king of France such surety from the knights of the aforesaid lands that he gives us and from the towns as he will require of us. —And the form of the surety for us from the men and towns shall be this: they shall swear that they will give neither counsel nor support nor aid whereby we or our heir may contravene the peace, and if it should happen, which God forbid, that we or our heir should contravene it and be unwilling to make amends on being requested to do so by the king of France or his heir, the king of France, those who have gone surety shall, within three months of being required by him to do so, be bound to help the

[1] *hauz homes*

[2] The requirement at this point in the earlier form of the treaty of similar renunciations by the king's brother and sister has been dropped. But see editorial note.

[3] i.e. letters with their seals appended

king of France and his heirs against us and our heirs until this thing is sufficiently amended in the opinion of the court of the king of France. And this surety shall be renewed every ten years at the request of the king of France or of his heirs, the kings of France. —And we promise in good faith for ourselves and for our heirs and successors, to the aforesaid king of France and his heirs and successors, loyally and firmly to keep this peace and this composition established between us and the aforesaid king of France and every one of the things aforesaid just as they are contained above, and we promise that we will not contravene them in any way either personally or through another, and that we have not and will not do anything whereby any or all of the aforesaid things, in whole or part, might be less firm. And so that this peace may be kept firmly and stably, without any infringement, forever, we have bound ourselves and our heirs to this and have had an oath sworn on our soul in our presence by our proxies to keep this peace, just as it is set out and written above, in good faith as long as it concerns us, and not to contravene it either personally or through another. —And in witness of all these things we have made for the king of France these letters pendant, sealed with our seal.[1] —And by our special commandment our sons Edward and Edmund have in our presence sworn to keep and hold firmly this peace and all the things which are contained above and not to contravene them either personally or through others. —This was given at London, the Monday before the feast of St Luke the Evangelist in the year of our Lord's Incarnation one thousand two hundred and fifty nine, in the month of October.

42. Commissions under the ordinance of Winchester, September 1265

(*Cal. Pat. Rolls 1258–66*, p. 490)

The ordinance was made on 17 September, the commissions themselves on 21 September.

Appointment in pursuance of the ordinance lately made by the counsel of the magnates at Winchester, of William Bagod and Robert de Grendon, with the sheriff of the counties of Warwick and Leicester, to take into the king's hands the lands of rebels in those counties, and extend them and to send the extent thereof to the king by the feast of St Edward [13 October] to Westminster. They are further to appoint two discreet persons in every hundred to enquire of and collect the rents of this instant Michaelmas term, and let these have the sum thereof in the several places and towns;[2] and they are to certify the king of the said sum and the names of the collectors. And if any persons happen to have received the said rents, they are to distrain them to make full restitution. Also if the said lands have been restored to any other than the king after Thursday next after the feast of the Exaltation of the Holy Cross [Thursday, 17 September 1265], they are to be revoked into the king's hands.

[The enrolment then gives the names of the knights appointed for other counties.

Some of the returns, in the required form, survive. Those for the Buckinghamshire hundreds of Ixhill, Ashendon, Waddesdon and Mursley, as calendared in *Cal. Inqu. Miscell.*, i, Nos 631 and 633, chosen for their relevance to No. 209 (b) below, will serve as illustration:]

[1] in green wax, appended to the vellum by cords of plaited red and green silk
[2] *villis*

Hundreds of Hikeshulle, Essestone and Wottestone

The manor of Crendon was held by sir S. de Monte Forti by reason of the dower of Eleanor his wife. It is worth 4*l* 5*s* a year with the rent of Chatendone. The rents due last Michaelmas came to 10*l* 9*s* 3*d* and were taken by Hugh Cheval, steward of Sir G. de Clare, earl of Gloucester and Hertford. Sir S. de Monte Forti was killed at Evesham because he was against the king and sir Edward.

Half the manor of Dorton was held by William de Bermingham and is worth 8*l* a year. Rents last Michaelmas amounted to 10*s* 4*d* and were paid to lady Isabel de Bermingham through Alexander reeve of the manor. The said William was killed at Evesham because he was against the king.

The hundred of Wottestone did not appear before the jury because it is of the honour of Walingeford.

Endorsed: Collectors' names – Hundred of Essendon, Robert son of Robert of Ovinge; Robert Justin, of the same. Hundred of Yckeshull, John le Mazun of Crendon; Adam son of Peter of the same.

Hundred of Muresle

John son of John had the manor of Waddon in demesne. He was with sir Simon de Monte Forti and was captured at Evesham. The manor is worth 21*l* ½*d* a year. Sir John de Gray is in seisin and his men took the Michaelmas rent of 4*l* 11*s* 5*d*.

John Passelewe held Drayton in demesne. He was captured on the side of Simon de Monte Forti at Evesham. The manor, with part of Muresle, is worth 16*l* 2*s* a year. The earl of Gloucester is in seisin and his bailiffs took the Michaelmas rent of 65*s* 11*d*.

William de Bermingham held the manor of Hoggeston in demesne. He was killed at Evesham on the side of sir Simon de Monte Forti. The manor is worth 10*l* a year. Sir Roger de Clifford is in seisin and his bailiffs received the Michaelmas rent of 26*s* 3*d*.

Robert son of Neal held the manor of Salden in demesne with part of Muresley. He was on the side of sir Simon de Monte Forti, and was killed at Evesham. The manor is worth, with the aforesaid part of Muresleye, 20*l* a year. Sir John de Grey is in seisin and his bailiffs received the Michaelmas rent of 30*s* 10*d* and a half a pound of pepper.

Endorsed: Names of collectors – Robert son of Alexander de Drayton, Walter le Sergaunt of Oggeston.

43. The Dictum of Kenilworth, 31 October 1266

(*Statutes of the Realm*, I (1810), pp. 12–17; more accessibly in Stubbs, *Select Charters*, 9th edn, ed. H. W. C. Davis, pp. 407–11)

The more important of the forty-one clauses into which the final form of the Dictum or Award of Kenilworth is conventionally divided.

In the name of the holy and indivisible Trinity, Amen. To the honour and glory of almighty God, the Father, the Son and the Holy Ghost, of the glorious and pre-eminent mother of God, the Virgin Mary, and of all the blessed, by whose merits and intercessions we are guided on earth; of the holy, catholic and apostolic Roman church, which is the mother and instructress of all the faithful; of our most holy father and lord, Clement, supreme pontiff of that universal church; to the honour and well-being, prosperity and peace of the most Christian prince, the lord Henry, illustrious king of England, and of the whole realm and of the English church, we, W. bishop of Exeter, W. bishop of Bath and Wells, N. bishop of Worcester and R. bishop of St David's, Gilbert de Clare earl of Gloucester and Hertford and Humphrey de Bohan earl of Hereford, P[hilip] Basset, John Balliol, Robert Walerand, Alan la Zouche, Roger de Somery and Warin of Bassingbourne, having from the aforesaid lord king and from the other barons, councillors[1] of the kingdom, and the leading men of England, by the terms of letters declaratory supported by the seals of the aforesaid king and the others, full power of providing for the state of the country, particularly with regard to the fact of the disinherited, have indeed with the help of the divine grace provided what according to the paths of righteousness and equity we consider accords with God's will and the peace of the realm, in this matter not listening to the representations of anyone but keeping God alone in mind; acting therefore above all as if in the sight of God Almighty and most fittingly mentioning in order head before members:

[1] We declare and provide that the most serene prince the lord Henry illustrious king of England shall have, fully obtain, and freely exercise his lordship, authority and royal power without impediment or contradiction from anybody whatsoever whereby contrary to the approved rights and laws and the long-established customs of the realm the royal dignity might be offended against; and that all and singular of high and low estate of the men of the realm shall be completely obedient and humbly submissive to the lord king and his lawful mandates and precepts. And all and singular shall seek justice through writs in the court of the lord king and answer in judicial proceedings there as used to be done up to the time of this disturbance.

[2] We also ask the lord king and with respect advise his piety to appoint such men to do justice and give judgment as do not seek things for themselves but things which are of God and of justice and will rightly settle the affairs of subjects in accordance with the laws and praiseworthy customs of the realm and thereby cause the seat of the royal majesty to be strengthened as regards justice.

[3] We likewise ask and advise the same lord king to keep and observe fully ecclesiastical liberties [and] the charters of liberties and the forest, which he is expressly and by his own oath bound to observe and keep.

[4] Let the lord king also see to it that concessions which he has made up to now of his own accord and not under compulsion are observed, and other things needful which were devised by his men by his good pleasure, let him establish them to last. And the English church too, let it be fully restored to the liberties and customs which it had and should have had before the time of this disturbance, and be allowed to use them freely.

[5] We declare and provide that the aforesaid lord king shall be in every way forgiving and forbearing to all and singular who, from the beginning of the present disturbance of the realm (and because of it) up to the present, have done any injury or offence to

[1] *consiliariis*

him or the royal crown and have come to his peace within forty days after the proclamation of this provision of ours, to the extent that he shall not in any way or for any reason or excuse take any revenge on those offenders for such past injuries or offences, or punish them in life, limb, by prison, in their estate[1] or fortune,[2] or mulct them,[3] apart from the things contained below[4] in our present provision.

[6] We also declare and provide that all places,[5] rights, incorporeal rights,[6] and other things pertaining to the royal crown shall be restored to that crown and the lord king by those who retain the occupation of them, unless they show they possess them by reasonable warrant from the lord king or from his ancestors.

[7] We also declare and provide that all writings, bonds and instruments which the aforesaid lord king or the lord Edward, his first-born, or other faithful subjects have made or put out up to now in connection with the provisions of Oxford or with the disturbance in the kingdom at the instance of the late Simon de Montfort, earl of Leicester, and his associates shall be utterly annulled and quashed and be treated as utterly quashed and annulled. Also things prejudicial and injurious done by the said Simon and his associates and contracts over immovable property made by them while it was in their power shall be annulled and treated as null.

[8] Humbly asking both the lord legate and the lord king that he, the lord legate, should absolutely forbid on pain of ecclesiastical punishment Simon earl of Leicester to be regarded by anyone as a saint or a just man, since he died excommunicate as holy church holds. And the vain and fatuous marvels told of him by some, ever to be uttered by any lips. And that the lord king be pleased strictly to forbid these same things on pain of bodily punishment.

[11] About London we recommend and urge and request the aforesaid lord king to provide with his council for reforming the state of the city as regards lands, rents, houses[7] and liberties, and that such provision be made quickly.

[12] On the matter and estate of the disinherited, among the other things we have ordained and decreed, wishing to walk in accordance with God's will and on the path of equity, we have thought right to so provide, with the assent of the venerable father O[ttobuono], cardinal deacon of St Adrian and legate of the apostolic see, and of the noble Henry of Almain, who have like power,[8] that the course to be followed is not disinheritance, but redemption; namely, that those who began the war and have continued it until now, those who violently and maliciously held Northampton against the king, those who attacked and defeated the king at Lewes, those taken prisoner at Kenilworth who had been at the sack of Winchester, or had been against the king elsewhere, and whom the king has not pardoned, those who fought at Evesham against the king, those who were at Chesterfield in battle against the king, those who freely and voluntarily and not under compulsion sent their men[9] against

[1] "exile" (waste of their estate)
[2] *pecunia*
[3] *vel vindictam* (i.e. by an arbitrary fine as distinct from the legal penalties mentioned)
[4] referring, of course, to the tariff of redemptions in c. 12
[5] *loca* [6] *res*
[7] *dominium*
[8] they were joint umpires in differences of opinion among the twelve responsible for the Dictum
[9] *servitia*

the king or his son, and the bailiffs and servants of the earl of Leicester who plundered their neighbours and instigated slaughter, arson and other evils – all these shall pay five times what their land is worth a year. And if they pay the redemption they shall have back their lands, provided that if the land has to be sold no one shall have it except the man who holds it of the lord king's gift if he is willing to give as much as anyone buying in the ordinary way and at the same terms. Similarly, if it has to be granted at farm no one shall have a better right than he who holds it of the lord king's gift, if he is willing to give as much as anyone else is willing to give for it at farm and have it at the same terms. He who pays at one time for the whole of the land shall have the whole, for a half shall have half, for a third shall have a third, straightway. Though if by the end of the term appointed the one who is redeeming has not paid in full, half of the land remaining shall remain to those on whom the lands were bestowed by the lord king; it shall however be open to one who is redeeming to sell the whole or a part of the land (in accordance with the method of selling noted above) within the term, and similarly to let it to farm.

[14] Also the earl of Ferrers[1] shall be punished by seven times what his land is worth a year, and knights and men-at-arms who plundered along with the chief plunderers in the battles and depredations, if they have no lands but have goods, shall pay half of their goods as their redemption and find sufficient surety that they will keep the peace of the king and the realm from now on. Those who have nothing shall come and swear on God's holy gospel and find sufficient surety that they will keep the peace of the king and the kingdom from now on, and shall submit to suitable satisfaction and penance in accordance with the judgment of the church, except those who have been banished, to whom the king alone can be lenient.

[17] All from the castle shall be comprised in the peace and its terms in the ordinary way, except Henry of Hastings[2] and the mutilators of the lord king's messenger, and they shall be punished by seven times [what their land is worth a year] or submit to the lord king's mercy.

[20] If there is anyone of whom it is feared that he wishes to make war or provoke it, the lord legate and the lord king shall provide themselves with the security they think expedient, by banishments out of the kingdom for a time or otherwise as they think expedient; provided however that, if it happens that he is prevented from paying his redemption, he shall not on this account be disinherited.

[21][3] If anyone is not content with this provision he may submit to judgment in the court of the lord king before Hilarytide,[4] or, if he is out of the kingdom he may have stay of proceedings for being overseas in accordance with the law and custom of the land, provided however that he keeps the peace, otherwise he shall not be comprised in the terms of the peace.

[22] Because the king is indebted to many who helped him and faithfully stood by him, for whom he has not provided as regards lands, and certain people have more

[1] an alternative style of the earls of Derby in this period
[2] the commander of the defending garrison
[3] The reader is reminded that clause divisions and enumeration are editorial devices and conveniences. Clauses [20] and [21] go together (cf. Powicke, *King Henry III and the Lord Edward*, p. 556, n. 2).
[4] i.e. before 13 January 1267

than they ought to have, the lord king shall see to it that he rewards them abundantly from the proceeds of the redemptions, lest it be the cause of a new war.

[23] The lord legate, the lord king and the lord Henry of Almain shall also see to it that they choose twelve to give effect[1] diligently and faithfully to these things, and the lord king and his heirs shall cause them to be observed and maintained. They shall ascertain what things have been ordained by the above-mentioned chosen twelve and do them, in accordance with the terms of the ordinances now made; otherwise they shall make reasonable and truthful valuations in accordance with what the twelve executors shall provide.

[26] Laymen who were openly active in the affairs of the lord earl and his associates, winning over men by lies, by falsities inciting to the side of the earl and his associates and disparaging the side of the lord king and his son, shall be punished by twice as much as their land is worth a year.

[27] Those compelled or induced by fear to come to battle, who did not attack or do any evil, helpless people forced or frightened into sending their men[2] against the king or his son, and those compelled or induced by fear to plunder and along with the chief plunderers commit depredations, but who withdrew from them when they conveniently could and went back home and lived in peace: these shall be redeemed by what their land is worth for one year.

* * * *

Given and made public in the castle at Kenilworth on the day before the kalends of November [31 October] in the year of grace 1266, but of the reign of the lord Henry king of England the fifty-first year.

C. RECONSTRUCTION 1267–94

44. The Statute of Marlborough, 18 November 1267

(*Statutes of the Realm*, I (Rec. Com., 1810), pp. 19–25)

Provisions made at Marlborough in the presence of the lord king Henry, R[*ichard*] *king of Almain, and the lord Edward, the first-born son of king Henry, and of the lord Ottobuono then legate in England*[3]

In the year of grace 1267, the fifty-second of the reign of king Henry son of king John, on the octave of Martinmas,[4] the lord king gave thought to the betterment of his realm of England and, as the exercise of kingly office requires, the better administration of justice, and in a gathering of the more discerning men, of high and low estate, of the realm it was provided, settled and unanimously ordained that, as the

[1] for clarification see Powicke, *King Henry III and the Lord Edward*, p. 552, n. 2
[2] *servitia*
[3] The heading given to the statute in the Red Book of the Exchequer
[4] i.e. on 18 November 1267

realm of England, oppressed of late by many tribulations and unprofitable dissensions, needs amendment of its laws and legal rules so that the peace and tranquillity of its people may be preserved and for this it was right and necessary for a wholesome remedy to be applied by the king and his faithful subjects, the underwritten provisions, ordinances and statutes shall be firmly and inviolably observed by all inhabitants of the realm, as well of high as of low estate, for ever.

[1] Whereas during the disturbance which lately arose within the realm, and since then, many magnates and others have disdained to receive justice from the lord king and his court, as they ought and were wont to do in the time of the lord king's predecessors and in his time too, but instead have themselves taken grave revenges and levied grave distresses on their neighbours and others until they received amends[1] of their own fixing,[2] and, furthermore, as some of them do not let themselves be brought to justice by the lord king's officers and do not suffer the distresses which they have levied of their own authority and at their own fixing to be released by them, it is provided and unanimously granted that men of high and low estate alike shall obtain justice and submit to justice in the court of the lord king, and no one in future take revenges or levy distresses at his own pleasure without a decision of the lord king's court, should it happen loss or injury is done to him for which he wishes to have amends from his neighbour, high or low.

Further to the above-mentioned article it is provided and granted that if anyone in future takes such revenge at his own pleasure without a decision of the lord king's court and is convicted thereof, he shall be punished by a fine[3] proportioned to the gravity of the offence. Similarly, if without a decision of the lord king's court he levies a distress on his neighbour whereby the latter suffers loss he shall be punished in the same way and this according to the gravity of the offence, and full and sufficient amends shall nonetheless be made to those who have suffered the loss by such distraint.

[2] Moreover, no one, of high estate or low, shall distrain anybody to come to his court who is not of his fee or over whom he has no jurisdiction by reason of a hundred or bailiwick which is his; nor shall he levy distresses outside his fee or the place where he has bailiwick or jurisdiction. And he who acts contrary to this statute shall be punished in the same way and that according to the gravity of the offence.

[3] If anyone, of high or low estate, will not let distresses he has levied be released by the lord king's officers in accordance with the law and custom of the realm, or even if he will not suffer executions of judgments of the lord king's court to be carried out or even will not suffer summonses and attachments to be made in accordance with the law and custom of the realm, he shall be punished in the way aforesaid as one not letting himself be brought to justice, and this according to the gravity of the offence.[4]

Though if anyone, of high or low estate, levies distresses on his tenant for services or customs which he alleges are due to him, or for something else whereby it pertains to the lord of the fee to levy distresses, and it is afterwards found that his tenant does not owe him them, the lord shall not on that account be punished by fine as in the

[1] *redemptiones* (on a possible significance of this, cf. Powicke, *King Henry III and the Lord Edward*, p. 548)
[2] *ad voluntatem suam*
[3] *redemptio* (cf. n. 1, above)
[4] The Latin text of this clause is, up to this point, more than usually doubtful: but the meaning is certain.

aforementioned cases if he lets the distresses be released in accordance with the law and custom of the realm, but shall be amerced as has been usually done up to now and the tenant shall recover his damages in full against him.

[4] No one henceforth shall cause distresses which he has levied to be driven out of the county in which they were. And if neighbour does this to neighbour of his own authority and without a judgment he shall be punished by fine as above, as for an infringement of the peace. If a lord presumes to do this to his tenant, however, he shall be punished by a heavy amercement.

Distresses, moreover, shall be reasonable and not unduly severe and if any one levies unreasonable and undue distresses he shall be heavily amerced for the excess of those distresses.

[5] The great charter shall be kept in every one of its articles, as well in those pertaining to the king as those pertaining to others, and when there is need this shall be entrusted to the justices in their eyres and the sheriffs in their counties, and writs against infringers shall be granted freely[1] [for action] *coram rege* or in the [common] bench or before the justices in eyre when they reach those parts. [The charter, moreover, of the forest shall be kept in every one of its articles everywhere and infringers when convicted thereof shall be punished by the lord king himself.[2]]

[6] Concerning those who are accustomed to enfeoff their eldest sons and heirs with their inheritance when they are under age in order that by this the lords of the fees shall lose their wardships, it is unanimously provided and granted that by reason of such a feoffment no chief lord shall lose his wardship.

As to those, moreover, who, wanting to let their lands for a term of years in order that the lords of the fees shall lose their wardships, contrive false feoffments having in them that they have been satisfied in respect of the whole of the service involved in them up to some term or other and that after that term such feoffees shall be bound to pay a certain sum greatly exceeding the value of the lands, so that in this way their land will after that term revert to them because no one will care to hold it at such a price,[3] it is provided and granted that no chief lord shall lose his wardship by fraud of this sort: yet it shall not be lawful for them [lords cheated by such frauds] to disseise such feoffees without judgment, but instead they shall get a writ to have such wardship given back to them and from the witnesses contained in the deeds of such feoffments together with other free and law-worthy men of the neighbourhood and from the value of the tenement and the size of the sum payable after the aforesaid term it shall be decided whether such feoffments were made in good faith or fraudulently to deprive the chief lords of their wardships. If, however, the chief lords by judgment of the court recover their wardship in such cases, such feoffees shall nevertheless have their action saved to them to recover their term or their fee when the heir comes of age.

[1] *gratis* (whether in the sense of "readily" or of "without charge" is not clear)

[2] This sentence is not given by some manuscripts and could be an interpolation. The Forest Charter was as usual mentioned along with Magna Carta in the Dictum of Kenilworth, however, and is not likely to have been ignored here, so soon after.

[3] This device and the tentative nature, as well as the inadequacy of the remedy here given is explained by T. F. T. Plucknett, *Legislation of Edward I*, pp. 79–80.

But if any chief lords have impleaded any feoffees maliciously, inventing a case of such a kind when the feoffments were made lawfully and in good faith, then their damages and their expenditure occasioned by that plea shall be awarded to the feoffees, and those who brought the action shall be grievously punished by amercement.

[7] In the common plea of wardships, if the deforciants do not appear at the grand distress, then the said writ shall be repeated two or three times at the terms when it can be done during the following half-year, so that each time the writ shall be read in full county unless the deforciant is found previously, and it shall there be publicly proclaimed that he should appear on a day prescribed for him. But if he withdraws so that he does not appear to answer within the said half-year and the sheriff is unable to find him so as to be able to produce him before the justices to answer according to the law and custom of the realm, then as a rebel and one not letting himself be brought to justice he shall lose seisin of such wardship, saving to him his action at another time if perchance he has a right to it. But in cases where wardships belong to the guardians of heirs under age and wardships which fall to those heirs as belonging to their inheritance are claimed from those guardians, such heirs under age shall not lose by the negligence or rebellion of their guardian, as in the case above-mentioned, but the law shall run in the way it did before.

[8] They who are taken and imprisoned for repeated disseisin shall not be delivered without the king's special command and this by making fine with the lord king for their trespass of this kind. And if it is found that the sheriff has delivered them otherwise he shall be heavily amerced on account of this, and those delivered by the sheriff without the king's command shall be punished for their trespass nonetheless.

[9] Regarding doing suit to the courts of magnates and other lords of courts, the observance henceforth shall be thus, namely, that no one who is enfeoffed by charter shall be distrained in future to do such suit to his lord's court unless he is specifically bound by the terms of his charter to do that suit, except those whose ancestors used to or who have themselves been used to do such suit before the lord king's first crossing to Brittany, from the time of which crossing thirty-nine and a half years[1] have elapsed at the time these constitutions were decreed. And likewise no one enfeoffed without charter[2] from the time of the Conquest or by other ancient enfeoffment shall be distrained in future to do such suit unless he and his ancestors used to do it before the above-mentioned crossing of the lord king. Those, however, who are enfeoffed by charter in return for a certain service, for example, free service of so many shillings to be paid annually in lieu of all service, shall not be bound to do suit or anything else beyond the terms of their enfeoffment. And if any inheritance from which one suit only is due descends to a number of heirs as coparceners of that inheritance he who has the "esnecy"[3] of the inheritance shall do the one suit for himself and his coparceners and his other coparceners for their shares shall contribute to the doing of that

[1] An error: 1230 is the year in question. This clause of the Statute of Marlborough incorporates the Provisions of Westminster (1259) on the subject, which with 29½ years (*Stat. of the Realm*, I, p. 8) is correctly calculated. From xxix to xxxix could be no more than a scribal error.

[2] Charters, though becoming commoner, were not yet essential to an enfeoffment, which was an oral and ceremonial act. Increasingly popular as a written attestation of the act, they were not yet necessary and were not, in law, insuperable evidence of enfeoffment. See Plucknett, *Legislation of Edward I*, pp. 66 and 51–2.

[3] i.e. the rights of the eldest-born in the inheritance

suit. Similarly if several have been enfeoffed[1] of an inheritance from which one suit only is due, the lord of that fee shall have only the one suit from it, and shall not be able to exact more from the inheritance than the one suit, as used to be done before. And if those who are enfeoffed have not a warrantor or a mean lord to acquit them of it, then all the enfeoffed shall contribute their share towards the doing of the suit.

But if it happens that lords of courts distrain their tenants for such suits contrary to this provision, then on complaint of those tenants they shall be attached to appear in the lord king's court at an early date to answer thereto and have but a single essoin if they are in the realm, and the beasts or other distresses levied in this connection shall be released to the plaintiff immediately and stay released until the plea thereon between them is determined. And if lords of courts who levied such distresses do not appear on the day for which they were attached or keep the day given them by essoin, then word shall be sent to the sheriff to cause them to come for another day, and if on that day they do not appear the sheriff shall be ordered to distrain them by all they have in his bailiwick, so that he, the sheriff, shall be responsible to the lord king for the issues and for producing their persons on a definite, prearranged day to the end that, if they do not appear on that day either, the plaintiff may go away with the business adjourned indefinitely[2] and the beasts or other distresses shall stay released until those lords recover the suit by award of the lord king's court: and such distraints shall cease meanwhile, saving to lords of courts their right to sue for those suits by process of law, when they wish to plead thereon. And when lords of courts appear to answer those who complain of this sort of distress and are convicted of it, then by judgment of the court the plaintiff shall recover from them the damages they have sustained by reason of the aforesaid distress.

In similar fashion, if after this constitution tenants withdraw from their lords suits which they ought to do and which from before the time of the aforesaid crossing until now they have been accustomed to do, lords of courts shall obtain justice concerning the suits, together with their damages, by the same procedure and with the same dispatch[3] in prearranging days and awarding distresses that tenants recover their damages. And this, namely this matter of recovering damages, is to be understood as relating to withdrawings of suit from themselves and not of withdrawings from their predecessors. Lords of courts shall not, for all that, be able to recover from their tenants seisin of such suits by default, as that has not been the custom hitherto. As regards suits withdrawn before the time aforesaid, the common law shall apply as it used to apply before.

[10] On sheriffs' tourns, it is provided that archbishops, bishops, abbots, priors, earls, barons shall not be bound to attend, nor any men of religion or women, unless their presence is especially required, but the tourn shall be held as it used to be in the days of the lord king's predecessors. And if they have tenements in various hundreds, they are not bound to attend such tourns save in the bailiwicks they ordinarily live in. And tourns shall be held in accordance with the terms of the king's great charter and as they used to be held in the days of king Richard and king John.

[1] i.e. by division and sub-infeudation
[2] *eat sine die*
[3] *per eandem justitiam et celeritatem*

[11] It is provided also that neither in the eyre of justices nor in county court, hundred court, or court baron shall fines be taken in future for *beaupleader* or on condition that they be not troubled. And be it known that fines certain or payments commuted to a yearly rent between the time the king first crossed into Brittany and now are not abolished by this constitution.

[12] In the plea of dower which is called *unde nihil habet* at least four days shall be given in the year in future, and more if it can conveniently be done, in order that six days or at least five a year may be managed.

In the assize of *darrein presentment* and in the plea *quare impedit* in connection with vacant churches, day shall be given every fortnight or every three weeks according as the place is near or far. And in the plea of *quare impedit* if the defendant neither appears nor sends an essoin on the first day for which he was summoned, then he shall be attached for another day, and if on that day he does not appear or send an essoin he shall be distrained by the aforesaid grand distress. And if then he does not appear, word shall be sent because of his default to the bishop [concerned] that the claim of the defendant shall not that time hinder the plaintiff, saving to the defendant his right another time when he wishes to sue therefor.

The same law as to the making of attachments in all writs where attachments lie shall henceforth be firmly observed in the making of distresses. So, however, that the second attachment shall be by better pledges and afterwards the last distress.

[13] And be it known that after anyone has put himself on any inquest which has arisen or can arise in writs of this sort, he shall have but one essoin or one default, so namely, that if he does not appear on the day given him by his essoin or makes a second default, then by his default the inquest shall be taken and in accordance with the inquest the court shall proceed to judgment. If however the inquest is taken in the county before the coroners or the king's justices for return on a certain day and the defendant[1] does not appear on that day, then because of his default another day shall be assigned to him at the justices' discretion and word sent to the sheriff to cause him to appear on that day to hear, if he wishes, his judgment in accordance with the inquest; and if on that day he does not appear the court shall proceed to judgment because of his default. Let it be done in the same way if he does not appear on the day given him by his essoin.

[14] Concerning charters of exemption and liberty that those who acquire them shall not be put on assizes, juries, or recognitions, it is provided that if their oath is so necessary that without it justice cannot be done, for example in the grand assize and in perambulations and when in charters or deeds of covenant they are named as witnesses, or in attaints or other like cases, they shall be compelled to serve,[2] saving to them their aforesaid liberty and exemption at other times.

[15] Save only for the lord king and his officers, it shall be lawful henceforth for no one for whatever cause to levy distresses outside his fee or on the king's highway or a public way.

[16] If any heir after the death of his ancestor is under age and his lord has the wardship

[1] *pars rea*
[2] *jurare*

of his lands and will not give them back to the said heir when he comes of age without being sued,[1] the heir shall recover his land by reason of the death of his ancestor[2] together with the damages he has sustained by the detention from the time when he came of age. Now if an heir is of full age on the death of his ancestor, is the heir apparent, and is acknowledged as heir and is found in the inheritance, his chief lord shall not eject him nor take or remove anything there, but shall take only simple seisin thereof as a recognition of his lordship. And if the chief lord maliciously withholds seisin so that it is necessary for the heir to sue by an action of *mort d'ancestor* or cosinage, then he shall recover his damages as in the action of *novel disseisin*.

As regards inheritances which are held in chief of the lord king, however, the observance shall be this: that the lord king shall have the first[3] seisin thereof as he previously used to; nor shall the heir or anyone else enter forcibly into the inheritance before receiving it from the hands of the lord king in the way inheritances of this sort used to be received from his or his ancestors' hands. And this shall be understood of lands and fees which used to be in the king's hands by reason of knight-service or serjeanty or right of patronage.

[17] It is provided also that if land held in socage is in the wardship of kinsmen of an heir because the heir is under age, those guardians shall have no power to do waste or sale or any destruction in the inheritance, but shall keep it safely for the use of the said heir; so that when he comes of age they shall answer to him by proper accounting for the issues of the said inheritance, saving to those guardians their reasonable costs. Neither can the said guardians sell or give the marriage of the said heir except for the benefit of the said heir. But next of kin[4] who have had this sort of wardship ever since the time when writs of impleading were not granted may keep such wardships for the benefit of the heir as before stated without committing waste, exile[5] or destruction.

[18] No escheator, anyone empowered to hold enquiries,[6] or justice assigned to take any assizes or to hear and determine any plaints shall henceforth have power to amerce anyone for defaulting on the common summons, save the chief justice or justices in eyre in their circuits.

[19][7] Concerning essoins it is provided that in county court, hundred court, court baron or other courts, no one shall be bound to swear to warrant his essoin.

[20][8] Henceforth no one except the lord king shall hold a plea in his court about a false judgment given in the court of his tenants; because such pleas pertain especially to the crown and dignity of the lord king.

[21] It is provided also that if anyone's beasts are taken and unjustly detained, the sheriff upon complaint made to him thereof can release them without hindrance or contradiction from him who took the said beasts if they were taken outside liberties. And if such beasts are taken within liberties and the bailiffs of the liberties will not release them, then because of the default of those bailiffs the sheriff shall have them released.

[1] *sine placito*
[2] i.e. by writ of *mort d'ancestor*
[3] i.e. *primer seisin* (but "*liberam seisinam*", *Stat. of the Realm*, I, p. 24)
[4] *parentes propinquiores*
[5] see below, p. 391, n. 2
[6] *inquisitor*
[7] wrongly numbered 20 in margin of *Stat. Realm*, I, p. 24
[8] wrongly numbered 19 in margin of *Stat. Realm*, I, p. 24

[22] No one henceforth can distrain his free tenants to answer for their freehold nor for any matters touching their freehold, nor shall he put his freeholders to the oath against their will; inasmuch as no one can do this without a precept of the lord king.[1]

[23] It is provided also that if bailiffs who are bound to render account to their lords take themselves off and have no lands or tenements by which they can be distrained, then they shall be attached by their bodies so that the sheriffs in whose bailiwicks they are found can make them appear to render their account.

Also farmers during the term of their farms shall not commit waste, sale or exile[2] in respect of houses, woods, men, or anything belonging to the tenements they have at farm, unless they have a special concession in writing or mention in the deed of covenant that they can. And if they do this and are convicted of it they shall restore damages in full and be heavily amerced.

[24] Also, justices in eyre shall not henceforth amerce townships in their eyre because not every one twelve years old appeared before the sheriff and coroners for the holding of inquests into robberies and arsons or other things pertaining to the crown, provided that sufficient come from those vills to enable juries for such inquests to be made up in full, except inquests concerning a man's death, when all who are twelve ought to appear unless they have reasonable cause of absence.

[25] Murdrum[3] shall not henceforth be adjudged before justices when [death by] misadventure only has been adjudged, but shall be imposed[4] in cases of death by felony and not otherwise.

[26] It is moreover provided that no one vouched to warranty before justices in eyre in a plea of land or tenement shall henceforth be amerced because he is not present when he is vouched to warranty, except on the first day of the coming of the justices; instead, if he is within the shire the sheriff shall then be commanded to have him appear within the third day, or the fourth, according to the distance of the places, as used to be done in the eyre of the justices. And if he lives outside the shire then he shall have a reasonable summons of at least a fortnight according to the discretion of the justices and the common law.

[27] If any clerk is arrested for any crime or charge pertaining to the crown and afterwards by the king's command delivered on bail or replevied on condition that they to whom he was delivered on bail have him before the justices, they to whom he was delivered on bail or his other pledges shall not henceforth be amerced if they have his body before the justices, even if he will not or cannot answer before them because of benefit of clergy.

[28] It is also provided that if any acts of plundering and pillaging are committed against abbots or other prelates of the church and they started legal proceedings over

[1] i.e. without a royal writ. On the absence of novelty in this and the significance of its reaffirmation now, see Plucknett, *Legislation of Edward I*, pp. 25–8.

[2] In this context exile is to be understood (in the words of *Fleta*, using Bracton) as "Waste and destruction are practically identical terms and may be applied equally as concerns houses, woods and gardens, but exile is the term to be applied when bondsmen are enfranchised and ejected from their holdings unjustly" (*Fleta*, II, ed. Richardson and Sayles (1955) (Selden Soc., vol. 72), p. 25).

[3] A judgment imposed on a hundred or other district involving payment of a common fine, not the killing (clandestine or otherwise) itself. A brief, clear statement of the matter is C. A. F. Meekings, *Crown Pleas of the Wiltshire Eyre, 1249* (Devizes, 1961), pp. 61–5.

[4] literally "take place" (*locum habeat*)

such depredations but were forestalled by death before they obtained justice therein, their successors shall have the right to take proceedings to reclaim from the hands of such transgressors the goods of their church recently removed by such violence before the death of their predecessors. The successors shall have like right of action, moreover, over those things recently removed from their house and church by such violence before the death of their predecessors, even if their said predecessors had not started legal proceedings while they were living.

And if any intrude themselves into the lands or tenements of such religious (of which their prelates died seised as by right of their church) during a vacancy, their successors shall have a writ[1] to recover their seisin, and their damages shall be awarded to them, as has customarily been done in *novel disseisin*.

[29] It is provided also that if the alienations for which a writ of entry used to be given are made through so many degrees that that writ cannot be had in the form previously used, the plaintiff shall have a writ for recovering seisin without mention of the degrees, into whosesoever hands the thing shall have come through such alienations, by original writs to be provided for the purpose by the king's council.

45. The inquests of 1274–5: the commission and the articles of 11 October 1274

(*Foedera*, I, ii, 517–18, trans. H. M. Cam, *The Hundred and the Hundred Rolls* (1930), pp. 39–40 and Appendix I)

The Commission

The king to his beloved and faithful . . . and . . ., greeting. Know that we have assigned you to inquire by the oaths of good and lawful men of the counties of . . ., . . ., and . . . by whom the truth may be fully ascertained concerning certain rights, liberties, and other matters affecting us and our estate and the estate of the community of the said counties, and moreover concerning the deeds and the behaviour of all sheriffs and bailiffs in the said counties, as is more fully contained in the articles on the subject which we have sent to you. We command you therefore to hold these inquests, according to the contents of the said articles, at fixed days and places which you shall appoint for the purpose. And these inquests, distinctly and openly made, you shall send to us without delay under your seal and under the seals of those by whom inquest was made. We have also commanded our sheriffs of the said counties to bring before you, at the fixed days and places which you shall signify to them, such and so many good and lawful men of their bailiwick that by them the truth of the above-mentioned matters may be well ascertained.

The Articles

1. How many and what demesne manors the king has in his hand in every county, that is, both of the ancient demesnes of the crown, and of escheats and purchases.
2. What manors, moreover, used to be in the hands of the kings who were the king's predecessors, and who hold them, by what warrant and since when, and by whom and how they were alienated.

[1] *litteras*

3. Also concerning the lord king's fees and tenants; who hold them now from him in chief, how many fees each of them holds; what fees used to be held in chief of the king and now are held through a mesne lord, and by what mesne, and from what time they have been alienated, how and by whom.
4. Also concerning the lands of tenants of the ancient demesne of the crown, whether free sokemen or serfs: whether held by deputies or by the tenants themselves, and by what deputies or tenants, and by whom they have been alienated, how and from what time.
5. Likewise inquiry shall be made concerning the farms of hundreds, wapentakes, ridings, cities and boroughs and of all other rents whatsoever and from what time.
6. Also how many hundreds, wapentakes and ridings are now in the lord king's hand and how many and which are in the hands of others, from what time and by what warrant, and how much a year every hundred is worth.
7. Concerning ancient suits, customs, services and other things withdrawn from the lord king and from his ancestors; who withdrew them, and from what time; and who have appropriated to themselves such suits, customs, services and other things belonging of established custom to the lord king, from what time, and by what warrant.
8. Also, what other persons claim from the king to have return or estreats of writs, who hold pleas of *vee de naam*, who claim to have wreck of sea, and by what warrant, and other royal liberties such as gallows, the assizes of bread and ale and other things which belong to the crown; and from what time.
9. Also concerning those who have liberties granted to them by kings of England and have made use of them otherwise than they should have done; how, from what time and in what way.
10. Again concerning liberties which obstruct common justice and overturn the king's power, and by whom they were granted and since when.
11. Who, moreover, have recently appropriated to themselves free chases or warrens without warrant, and likewise who have had such chases and warrens from old time by the king's grant and have gone beyond their bounds and landmarks, and since when.
12. What persons also, whether lords or their seneschals or bailiffs of any kind or even the lord king's officials, have not upheld the execution of the lord king's commands or have even scorned to carry them out, or have hindered the doing of them in any way, since the time when the constitutions were made at Marlborough in the fifty-second year of the reign of the lord king Henry, father of the king that now is.
13. Again concerning all encroachments whatsoever upon the king or upon the royal dignity: by whom they have been made, how and from what time.
14. Concerning knights' fees, of whomsoever held, and lands or holdings given or sold to monks or to other persons to the king's prejudice, by whom and from what time.
15. Concerning sheriffs who take gifts to consent to the concealment of felonies committed in their bailiwicks, or who neglect to attach such felons for favour to anyone, both within liberties and without. In like manner, concerning the clerks and

other bailiffs of the sheriffs, concerning coroners and all their clerks and bailiffs: who have acted thus in the time of the lord king Henry since the battle of Evesham, and who in the time of the present lord king.

16. Concerning sheriffs and all manner of bailiffs who take gifts to remove recognitors from assizes and juries, and at what time.

17. Again, concerning sheriffs and all other manner of bailiffs who have amerced for default men summoned to make inquests by the lord king's command, when a sufficient number of persons had responded to the summons to make the inquest; how much and from whom they have taken on this pretext, and since when.

18. Again, concerning sheriffs who have handed over to extortionate bailiffs, oppressing the people beyond measure, hundreds, wapentakes or ridings at high farms, so that they may thus raise their own farms; who those bailiffs were, on whom they have inflicted such losses, and at what time.

19. Again, whereas sheriffs ought not to hold their tourn more than twice a year, who has held his tourn more often, and from what time.

20. Again, when fines for redisseisins or for encroachments by land or sea, for concealment of treasure and such like matters belong to the lord king and sheriffs ought to attach them, what persons have taken such fines, and from whom and how much.

21. Again who have by the power of their office troubled any maliciously and thus have extorted lands, rents or any other contributions, and from what time.

22. Who have received the command of the lord king to pay his debts, and have received part of the money from the creditors for paying the rest to them, and yet have had the whole sum allowed them in the exchequer or elsewhere, and from what time.

23. Who have received monies owed to the king, or a part of them, and have not given the debtors quittance, both in the time of the lord king Henry and in the time of the lord king who now is.

24. Again, who have summoned any to be knighted, and have taken bribes from them to have respite; how much and from what time. And if any magnates or others have distrained any to take up arms without the king's command, and from what time.

25. Again, if sheriffs or any bailiffs of any liberty whatsoever have not made summons in due manner, according to the form of the lord king's writ, or in any other way have fraudulently or inadequately executed the king's commands for prayer, for bribe or for favour, and from what time.

26. Again, concerning those who have approvers in prison and have made them appeal honest and innocent persons for the sake of gain, and have sometimes hindered them from appealing guilty persons, and from what time.

27. Again, who have had felons in prison and have allowed them, for money, to get away and escape from prison free and unpunished; and who have extorted money for letting men out of prison on bail; when they have been bailed, and from what time.

28. Again, who have received any gifts or bribes for exercising or for not exercising or executing their offices, or have executed them or exceeded the bounds of the king's commands otherwise than belonged to their office, and from what date.

All these inquiries shall be made not only concerning sheriffs, coroners and their clerks, but also concerning the lords and bailiffs of all liberties whatsoever.

29. Again, what sheriffs or keepers of any of the lord king's castles or manors, or also what surveyors of such works wherever carried out by the king's command, have accounted for larger sums than they have rightly spent on them and have thereupon procured false allowances to be made to them. And likewise, who have retained or removed for their own use stone, timber or other things bought or provided for such works, and what and how much loss the lord king has thus suffered, and from what time.

30. Concerning escheators and subescheators occupying lands for the lord king who do waste and destruction in woods, parks, fishponds or warrens within the wardships committed to them by the lord king; how much, and in whose lands, and how and when.

31. Again concerning the same: if by occasion of such occupation they have unjustly taken the goods of the deceased or of the heirs into the lord king's hand till redeemed by them, and what and how much they have taken by way of such redemption, and what of it they have kept for themselves and at what time.

32. Again, concerning the same who have taken gifts from any for exercising or not exercising their office: how much, from whom, and at what time.

33. Again, concerning the same who have made inadequate valuations of any person's lands in favour of himself or of some other person to whom the custody of those lands ought to be given, sold or granted, thus deceiving the lord king; where, and how, and if they have received anything for doing this, and how much and when.

34. Again, concerning the same who for prayer, for bribe or for favour have agreed or advised that the lord king's wardships should be sold at a lesser price than they should be, by their true value, or marriages of the heirs of tenants-in-chief, or marriages of widow ladies, married without the lord king's leave; what they have taken for this, how much, when, and since what time.

35. Again, concerning the same who have procured or permitted jurors of inquests into the age of heirs to declare that the heirs were of full age when they were not, whereby the lord king has lost the marriage and wardship of such heirs.

36. Again, concerning the same who have reserved for their own use wardships or marriages at a trifling price or by concealment from the lord king; what loss the lord king has thereby suffered, and since when.

37. Again what sort of lands they have occupied, and for how long they have kept them in the hands of the lord king.

38. Again, concerning lands taken into the lord king's hands which ought not to have been taken, and afterwards restored, with their takings, by the lord king's command; whether they have restored the takings at the lord king's command or no.

39. Again, concerning those persons who, during the dispute between the lord king and the countess of Flanders, against the prohibition and veto of the late king or the present king, have conveyed or caused to be conveyed wool over seas; how much and at what port.

40.[1] Concerning the collectors of the twentieth penny, or common amercements and tallages imposed in towns and boroughs for the lord king's profit.
41. Who have levied payments for the breakdown of bridges or causeways contrary to the custom of the realm.
42. Concerning sheriffs, lords' seneschals or any manner of bailiffs who have extorted payment from men because of verdicts given before the justices.
43. Again; concerning magnates and their bailiffs who have taken distresses outside their fees, and have imposed and taken ransoms for such distresses; what they have taken, how much, from whom, and from what time.
44. Who have made rescues from the lord king's bailiffs and thus hindered them when taking distresses.
45. Concerning monks and others who have appropriated to themselves advowsons of churches which were wont and ought to be in the lord king's advowson, and from what time.
46. Concerning cities and boroughs and demesnes of the lord king that have been let to farm.
47. Concerning ancient tolls; who have increased them.
48. Concerning murages and pontages that have been granted.
49. Concerning weights and measures.
50. Concerning ecclesiastical judges.
51. Concerning forgers and clippers of coin.

46. Summons of knights and burgesses to Edward I's first parliament at London on 25 April –, 1275 (Woodstock, 26 December 1274)

(Stubbs, *Select Charters*, 9th edn, ed. H. W. C. Davis (Oxford, 1913), pp. 441–2)

Edward, by the grace of God king of England, lord of Ireland and duke of Aquitaine, to the sheriff of Middlesex, greeting. As for certain reasons we have postponed to the morrow of the Sunday after Easter next [i.e. to 22 April 1275] our general parliament which we proposed to hold with the prelates and other magnates of our realm at London a fortnight after the Purification of the Blessed Mary next [on 16 February 1275], we order you to cause four of the knights of your county with knowledge of the law[2] and also six or four citizens, burgesses or other good men from each city, borough and market town[3] of your bailliwick to come there on the aforesaid morrow of the Sunday after Easter to consider at the same time as[4] the magnates of our realm the affairs of that realm. You shall also have our letters addressed to various persons in your bailliwick handed to or sent to them on our behalf without delay. And this you shall in no wise omit, and you shall give us full information about the execution of this our command at the date aforesaid. Witness myself at Woodstock, on 26 December in the third year of our reign.

[1] Articles 40 onwards are extra articles, asked in some but not all counties (for details cf. Cam, *Hundred and Hundred Rolls*, pp. 254–6).
[2] *discretioribus in lege*
[3] *villis mercatoriis*, alternatively "towns of merchants"
[4] *una cum* – which does not in classical Latin necessarily imply a meeting with (the magnates)

47. Statute of Westminster I (3 Edw. I), 1275

(*Statutes of the Realm*, I (Rec. Com., 1810), pp. 26–39 [French])

These are the establishments of king Edward, son of king Henry, made at Westminster at his first parliament general after his coronation after the Close of Easter in the 3rd year of his reign, by his council and by the assent of archbishops, bishops, abbots, priors, earls, barons and the community of the land thereto summoned. Because our lord the king greatly wills and desires to set to rights the state of his kingdom in the things in which there is need of amendment, and this for the common profit of holy church and the kingdom; and because the state of holy church has been ill-managed and the prelates and religious of the land burdened in many ways and the people otherwise treated, and the peace less kept, than ought to be, and the laws abused and malefactors less punished than they ought to be and for that people are less afraid to do wrong, THE KING HAS ordained and established the things underwritten, which he intends to be profitable and suitable for the whole kingdom. [c. 1] First the king wills and commands that the peace of holy church and of the land be well kept and maintained in all points, and that common justice be done to all, as well to the poor as to the rich, without regard for anyone. Because abbeys and houses of religion have been overburdened and badly affected by the coming of the great and of others who had means enough to entertain themselves and the religious have as a result been so reduced and impoverished that they could not support themselves or the burden of their accustomed charity, it is for this reason provided that no one come to eat, lodge or lie in a house of religion of anyone's patronage other than their own at the cost of the house, if he is not specially invited or requested beforehand by the ruler of the house, and that no one henceforth come to lie in a house of religion at his own cost against the will of the house. And by these statutes the king does not intend that the grace of hospitality should be withheld from the needy or that patrons of houses should be able by their coming to overburden and ruin. It is likewise provided that no one, great or small, on the strength of relationship, special friendship or other connection or on any other pretext, shall course in another's park, or fish in another's pond or stay on another's manor, or in the house of a prelate, man of religion or any other against the will and leave of the lord or his bailiff, whether at the cost of the lord thereof or at his own. And if he comes, willy nilly the lord or his bailiff, he shall cause no lock, door, window or any sort of fastening to be opened or broken by himself or anyone else, and shall take no sort of provisions or anything else, by making a show of purchasing or otherwise. And that no one cause the corn to be threshed or the corn or any sort of provisions or other goods taken of any prelate, man of religion, parson or any other, clerk or lay, by making a show of purchasing or otherwise, against the will or leave of the owner or the custodian, be it within a market town or without. And that no one take horses, oxen, wagons, carts, ships or boats for transport without the goodwill or the leave of the owner, and if he does it with his consent, then he shall immediately pay according to the covenant made between them. And they who contravene the aforesaid statutes and are convicted of this shall be committed to the king's prison and after that shall make fine according to the quantity and the kind of the trespass, as the king or his court shall think fit. And be it known that if those against whom the trespass is committed wish to sue, the damage they have suffered shall be awarded and restored to them twofold, and they that have committed the trespass shall be punished in the aforementioned way; and if no one wishes to sue, the king shall have the suit as in respect of a thing committed against his orders and against his peace. And the king will have enquiry made year by year, as he thinks fit, what people have committed such trespass, and those who are indicted in such inquests shall be attached and distrained by the great distress to come on a certain day within the space of a month into the king's court where it pleases him; and if they do not come on that day, let them be distrained again by the same distress to come on a certain day within six weeks; and if they then do not come they shall be judged as convicted and render double damages, at the king's suit, to those who have suffered the damage, and shall be severely punished according to the nature of the trespass. And the king forbids and commands that no one shall henceforth hurt, damage or oppress any man of religion, person of holy church or anyone else because they have denied lodging or food to anybody or because someone complains in the king's court of feeling aggrieved in any of the things aforesaid, and if anyone does so and is convicted of it, he shall incur the aforesaid penalty. And it is provided that the aforesaid points shall bind as well our counsellors, justices of the forest and our other justices as other people. And so that the aforesaid points shall be maintained and kept, the king forbids, on pain of his grievous forfeiture, any prelate, abbot, man of religion, or bailiff or anyone of them or of anyone else to receive any man contrary to the aforesaid way of doing. And that no one send men, horses or dogs to stay at a house or manor of a man of religion or any other man, and that no one receive them; and he who does, shall, because it is contrary to the prohibition and command of the king, be severely punished. It is further provided that sheriffs shall not lodge in any place with more than five or six horses, or burden people of religion or others by often coming or lying at their houses or their manors.

[c. 2] It is likewise provided that when a clerk is taken on an accusation of felony and is claimed by the ordinary, he is to be handed over to him in accordance with the privilege of holy church, on such peril as pertains thereto, according to the customs used before now; and the king admonishes the prelates and enjoins them on the faith they owe him and for the common profit and the peace of the land that those who are indicted of such accusation by solemn inquest of men of standing made in the king's court they shall in no wise release without due purgation, so that the king will have no need to apply any other remedy thereto.

[c. 3] It is likewise provided that nothing from now on shall be demanded or taken or levied for the escape of a thief or a felon, until it is adjudged by justices in eyre; and he who does otherwise shall pay back what he has received to him or them who have paid it and the like amount to the king.

[c. 4] On wreck of the sea it is agreed that when a man, a dog or a cat escapes alive from a ship, neither the ship nor the boat nor anything that was in them shall be adjudged wreck, but the things shall be saved and kept, by view of the sheriff, the coroner or the king's bailiffs, in the hands of the people of the vill where the goods are found, so that if anyone sue for these goods within a year and a day and can prove that they are his or his lord's, or were lost when in his keeping, they shall be restored to him without delay; and if not, they shall remain the property of the king and be appraised by the sheriff and the coroner and given to the township to answer before the justices for wreck belonging to the king. And where wreck belongs to someone other than the king, he shall have it in like manner. And he who acts otherwise and is attainted of it, shall be sentenced to prison and make fine at the will of the king, and shall render damages also. And if a bailiff does it and is disavowed by the lord, and the lord has appropriated nothing for himself, the bailiff shall answer if he has the means, and if he has not the means the lord shall hand over the person of the bailiff to the king.

[c. 5] Because elections ought to be free the king forbids on pain of his heavy penalty any man, great or otherwise, to interfere by force of arms or by malicious conduct with the making of a free election.

[c. 6] And that no city, borough or vill, nor any man, is to be amerced without reasonable cause and in accordance with the degree of the offence, that is in the case of a freeman saving his way of living, a merchant, his stock-in-trade, a villein, saving his means of livelihood, and this by their peers.

[c. 7] On prises taken by constables or castellans from people other than those of the vills where the castles are situated, it is provided that no constable or castellan shall from now on take any sort of prise from any man other than a man from the vill where his castle is situated, and it is to be paid for or an agreement made within forty days, unless it is an ancient prise due to the king or the castle or the lord of the castle.

[c. 8] And that nothing is to be taken for *beaupleader*, as was formerly forbidden in the time of king Henry, father of the present king.

[c. 9] And because the peace of the land has been weakly kept until now for lack of good pursuit being made of felons in due manner, and especially because of liberties where felons are received, it is provided that all shall ordinarily be ready and apparalled, at the command and summons of the sheriffs or at the cry of the countryside, to pursue and arrest felons when need arises, as well within liberties as without; and the king will act severely towards those who do not do this and are convicted of it. And if default is found in the lord of a liberty, the king will take over the liberty; and if the default is in the bailiff he shall have one year's imprisonment and then be heavily fined, and if he has not the means he is to have two years' imprisonment. And if a sheriff or other bailiff, within liberties or without, for reward or on request or because of any sort of relationship, conceal or consent to or procure concealment of felonies committed in their bailiwicks, or pretend to arrest or to attach wrongdoers when in reality they could, or otherwise pretend to perform their office as any sort of favour to the wrongdoers, and are convicted of it, they shall have one year's imprisonment and then be heavily fined, and if they have no means they shall have four years' imprisonment.

[c. 10] Because of late unimportant and inexperienced people are commonly chosen for the office of coroner and there is need for substantial, lawful and experienced men to take up this office, it is provided that in every county men that are sufficient shall be chosen to be coroners from the most lawful and experienced knights who shall best know, watch over and be able to attend to this office and who will attach and present pleas of the crown according to law, and the sheriffs shall have counter-rolls with the coroners as well of appeals as of inquests, attachments and other things belonging to the office, and that no coroner shall demand or take anything from any one for doing his office on pain of the king's grievous forfeiture.

[c. 11] And because many accused of homicide, and guilty of the same, are by favourable inquests taken by sheriffs and by the king's writ called *odio et atia* replevied until the eyre of the justices itinerant, it is provided that these inquests shall from now on be taken by men of standing chosen by oath, of whom two at least shall be knights who are not connected with the prisoners by any relationship and are not otherwise suspect.

[c. 12] It is likewise provided that known felons and those who are manifestly of bad repute and will not put themselves upon inquests for felonies that men accuse them of at the king's suit before justices, shall be remanded to a prison strong and hard[1] as men who refuse to submit to the common law of the land. But this is not to be understood as applying to prisoners who are taken upon slight suspicion.

[c. 13] And the king forbids anyone to rape, or take by force a damsel under age,[2] either with her consent or without it, or a married woman or a damsel of age or any other woman against her will; and if anyone does so the king will, at the suit of him who will sue within forty days, do common justice therein; and if no one begins his suit within forty days the king will sue in the matter; and those whom he finds guilty shall have two years' imprisonment and then shall make fine at the will of the king, and if they have not the means from which to be fined at the king's pleasure they are to be punished by longer imprisonment, according to what the offence demands.

[c. 14] Because it has been the practice in some counties to outlaw people appealed of commandment, force, aid and receipt during the period that one is in the process of outlawing him who is appealed of the deed, it is provided and granted by the king that no one is to be outlawed because of appeal of commandment, force, aid or receipt until the one appealed of the deed is convicted, so that there may be one uniform law for this throughout the land; but he who appeals shall not because of this omit to make his appeal of them at the next county as well as of those appealed of the deed, but the exigent shall wait in their case until those appealed of the deed have been attainted by outlawry or otherwise.

[c. 15] Because sheriffs and others have arrested and kept in prison people accused of felonies and have many times released on bail people who were not replevisable[3] and have kept in prison those who were replevisable, for the sake of making a profit out of the one lot and of harassing the other; and because up to now it has not been determined with certainty who were replevisable and who not (except those who were arrested for homicide or at the command of the king or of his justices or for

[1] *prison forte et dure*

[2] cf. No. 115 below

[3] i.e. releasable on bail

forest offences), it is provided and commanded by the king that prisoners previously outlawed, those who have abjured the land, approvers, all who are taken with the mainour,[1] those who have broken the king's prison, common and notorious thieves, those appealed by approvers as long as the approver is alive (if they are not of good repute), those arrested for arson feloniously done or for counterfeiting money or forging the king's seal, persons excommunicate arrested at the request of the bishop, those arrested for manifest crime and those arrested for treason touching the king himself are to be in no wise replevisable by the common-law writ or without writ. But those indicted for larceny by inquests of sheriffs and bailiffs taken in the course of their office, either on slight suspicion or for petty larceny amounting to not more than twelve pence in value (provided that he has not been accused of larceny before, or accused of the harbouring of felons or inciting, supporting or helping) as also those accused of some other offence for which one ought not to lose life or limb, and a man appealed by an approver after the death of the approver if he is not a common thief, shall henceforth be released by sufficient surety (for which the sheriff shall be answerable) and this without any payment. And if sheriffs or others release on bail anyone who is not replevisable, if he be sheriff, constable or other bailiff of fee who has the keeping of the prisoners, and is convicted of this, let him lose the fee and the bailiwick for ever. And if an undersheriff, constable, or bailiff of him who has this fee for keeping the prisoners has done this without his lord's wish, let him or any other bailiff who is not of fee be imprisoned for three years and make fine at the king's pleasure. And if any one detains prisoners who are replevisable after the prisoner has offered sufficient surety he shall be liable to heavy amercement by the king. And if he exacts payment for releasing him he shall restore double the amount to the prisoner and also be liable to heavy amercement by the king.

[c. 16] In view of the fact that some people seize and cause to be seized the beasts of another and drive them out of the county in which they were seized, it is provided that no one shall do it and if anyone does he is to make heavy fine in accordance with the provisions of the statutes of Marlborough made in the time of king Henry, father of the king who now is. And those are to be treated in the same way who seize beasts and levy distress in the fee of another and they are to be more heavily punished if the nature of the offence requires it.

[c. 17] It is likewise provided that, if any from now on seize the beasts of another and has them driven to a castle or a fort and keeps them there within the enclosure of the castle or the fort against gage and pledge after they have been solemnly demanded by the sheriff or other bailiff of the king at the suit of the plaintiff, the sheriff or the bailiff taking with him the posse of his county or his bailiwick is to go and try to get release of the beasts from him who seized them or from his lord or from any other men whatever of his lord who may be found where the beasts were driven, and if release of the beasts is then forcibly prevented or if no man is found who will answer for the lord of him who seized the beasts and release them, then after the lord of him who seized the beasts has been warned by the sheriff or bailiff if he is in the district or near enough to be properly warned by him who seized the beasts or by another of

[1] i.e. with the stolen property

his men if he was not in the district when the seizure was made to cause the beasts to be released, if he does not straightway have them released the king for the despite and for the trespass will have the castle or fort razed beyond rebuilding and all the loss that the plaintiff has suffered in respect of his beasts or because of hindrance to his husbandry or in any other way since the first demand for the beasts was made by the sheriff or bailiff shall be restored to him twofold by him who seized the beasts if he has sufficient means and if he has not, then by the lord – whenever and however release is made after the sheriff or bailiff has come to effect the release, that is to say that where the sheriff ought to make return of the king's writ to the bailiff of the lord of the castle or fort or to another to whom the return of the king's writ in this matter belongs, if after receiving it the bailiff of this liberty does not make the release the sheriff is without delay to discharge his office as aforesaid and with the aforesaid penalty. And release is to be made in the same way by attachment of plaint made without writ and with the same penalty. And this is to be understood everywhere where the king's writ runs. And if it is in the marches of Wales or elsewhere where the king's writ does not run, the king, who is their sovereign lord, will do right therein to those who wish to complain.

[c. 18] Because the common fine and amercement of the whole county in justices' eyres for false judgment or for other offence is badly assessed by sheriffs and barrators in the counties so that the total amount is increased many times and the portions are assessed otherwise than they ought to be to the damage of the people and are often paid to the sheriffs and barrators who do not acquit the payers, it is provided, and the king's will, that from now on in justices' eyres this amount shall be assessed before them before their departure by the oath of knights and other good men on all those who ought to contribute to it, and the justices shall cause the portions to be put down in their estreats, which they will deliver to the exchequer, and not the total amount.

[c. 19] As regards sheriffs, and others who answer personally at the exchequer, who have received debts due to king Henry, the father of the present king, or the debts of the king himself up to now and have not given the debtors quittance at the exchequer, it is provided that the king shall send good men through every county to hear all those who wish to complain of this and to determine the business so that those who can show that they have paid shall be forever quit, whether the sheriffs or others are dead or alive, by a certain form that is to be given to them; and those [sheriffs and others] who have acted so [i.e. not acquitted the debtor][1] shall, if they are alive, be severely punished, and if they are dead their heirs shall answer and be charged with the debt. And the king commands that sheriffs and the others aforesaid shall henceforth lawfully acquit debtors at the next accounting after they have received payment of the debt and then the debt shall be allowed at the exchequer so that it shall not in future appear in the summons. And if a sheriff does otherwise and is found guilty of it, he shall pay the plaintiff treble the amount he has received and make fine at the king's pleasure; and let each sheriff take good care to have a receiver such as he is prepared to answer for, because the king will proceed against sheriffs and their heirs for the full amount. And if anyone else who answers personally at the exchequer does other-

[1] The French here is elucidated by the Latin of *Fleta* (ed. Richardson and Sayles, II, p. 136).

wise let him pay the plaintiff threefold and make fine in like manner. And that sheriffs make tallies for all those who pay them their debt to the king, and that they cause the summons of the exchequer to be shown to all debtors who care to ask to see it without denying anyone and without anything being given; and the king will take severe measures against him who does not do so.

[c. 20] It is provided concerning wrongdoers in parks and preserves that if anyone is convicted thereof at the suit of the plaintiff there shall be awarded appropriate and heavy damages according to the nature of the offence and three years imprisonment, from which he shall be ransomed, at the king's will, if he has the wherewithal to make fine, and then he shall find good security that he will not misbehave in future. And if he has not wherewith to make fine he shall after the three years imprisonment find the same security. And if he cannot find the security he shall abjure the realm. And if anyone accused of wrongdoing takes to flight and has neither land nor tenement by which he can be distrained, he is to be called county by county as soon as the king has discovered this by lawful inquest and if no one is forthcoming, let him be outlawed. And it is provided that if no one has sued within a year and a day of the wrong being done, the king shall have the suit, and those whom he finds guilty of it by lawful inquest shall be punished in the same way in all respects as is said above. And if any such malefactor is convicted of having taken domesticated animals or anything else in parks by way of robbery while coming, staying, or returning he is to be dealt with at common law as one convicted of open robbery and larceny, as well at the suit of the king as of another.

[c. 21] As regards lands of heirs under age who are in the wardship of their lord, it is provided that the guardians shall keep and maintain them without causing destruction of anything; and that with regard to wardships of this kind it be done in all respects as is contained in the great charter of liberties of king Henry, father of the present king, and be it so done from now on; and archbishoprics, bishoprics, abbeys, churches and dignities are to be kept in the same way in times of vacancy.

[c. 22] Concerning heirs under age married without the agreement of their guardians before the age of fourteen years, be it done according to what is contained in the provision of Merton. And of those who are married without the agreement of their guardians after they have reached fourteen years, the guardian is to have twice the value of the marriage according to the tenor of the same provision. In addition, those who have withheld the marriage are to render the full value of the marriage to the guardian for the offence; and the king is nonetheless to receive satisfaction in accordance with this same provision from him who has withheld it.[1]

Concerning female heirs who attained the age of fourteen and the lord to whom their marriage belongs will not marry them but out of desire to retain the land wishes to keep them unmarried, it is provided that the lord can not on the pretext of the marriage have or hold the land of these female heirs more than two years beyond the term of the aforesaid fourteen years. And if the lord does not marry them within these two years, then they shall have an action to recover their inheritance freely, without giving anything for the wardship or for the marriage. And if they, of malice

[1] See No. 30, cap. 6, for the whole of this first paragraph.

or by evil counsel, refuse to be married by their chief lord where they would not be disparaged, then the lord may hold the land and the inheritance until the age when a male attains his majority, namely the age of twenty-one and beyond that until he has received the value of the marriage.

[c. 23] It is likewise provided that no stranger who is of this kingdom is to be distrained in a city, borough, vill, fair or market for what he is neither debtor nor pledge for, and he who does this is to be severely punished and the distress is to be released without delay by the bailiffs of the place or by the other, the king's, bailiffs if need be.

[c. 24] It is likewise provided that no escheator, sheriff or other bailiff of the king is to disseise any man of his freehold or of anything touching his freehold on the strength of his office without special warrant or instruction or definite authority appertaining to his office, and if any does this, it is to be at the discretion of the disseised whether the king *ex officio* has the wrong amended on his complaint[1] or whether he sues at common law by writ of *novel disseisin.* And he who is convicted of this shall pay double damages to the plaintiff himself and shall be liable to heavy amercement by the king.

[c. 25] No royal official shall maintain, personally or through another, pleas, suits or business in the king's court concerning lands, tenements or any other thing, in consideration of receiving part thereof, or other advantage by agreement made between them,[2] and he who does is to be punished at the king's pleasure.

[c. 26] And that no sheriff or other royal official is to accept a consideration for discharging his office, but is to be paid by what he receives from the king, and he who does shall give back twice as much and be punished at the king's pleasure.

[c. 27] And that no clerk of a justice, escheator or of one conducting an inquiry is to accept anything for delivering chapiters,[3] except only clerks of justices in eyre and that two shillings from every wapentake, hundred or vill which answers by twelve or by six according to what used to be done. And he who does otherwise shall give back three times what he has taken and shall be suspended from his master's service for one year.

[c. 28] And that no clerk of the king or of his justices shall henceforth accept presentation to any church, about which there is an action or dispute in the king's court, without the special permission of the king; and the king forbids this on pain of dismissal from his service. And that no clerk of a justice or a sheriff shall maintain parties to quarrels or business in the king's court, or commit any fraud for the purpose of delaying or obstructing common justice; and if any does, he shall be punished with the penalty just mentioned or with a heavier one if the offence requires it.

[c. 29] It is likewise provided that if any serjeant-pleader or other commit any sort of deceit or collusion in the king's court or be a party to deceiving the court in order to delude the court or a party and is convicted of this, then he shall be imprisoned for a year and a day and be heard in court no more after that pleading for anybody. And if

[1] i.e. proceed by *querela* (complaint) without writ
[2] i.e. between him and a party to the case
[3] supplying copies of, or extracts from, documents

it be someone other than a pleader, he shall in like manner be imprisoned for a year and a day at least. And if the offence calls for a greater penalty, let him be at the king's pleasure.

[c. 30] Because many people complain that serjeant-criers at fee and other marshals of the justices in eyre unlawfully take money from those who recover seisin of land or who win their suits, from fines levied, from jurors, townships, prisoners and from others attached upon pleas of the crown, otherwise than they ought to do in many ways, and because there are more of them than ought to be, whereby people are badly oppressed, the king forbids such things to be done henceforth; and if any serjeant at fee does it his office is to be taken into the king's hands, and if justices' marshals do it they are to be severely punished at the king's pleasure, and both are to give back to all plaintiffs threefold what they took.

[c. 31] With regard to those who take excessive tolls contrary to the common usage of the realm in a market town, it is provided that if anyone does it in a town belonging to the king himself which is let at fee farm the king will take the franchise of the market into his own hands. And if it is someone else's town and this is done by the lord of the town, the king will act in the same way. And if it is done by a bailiff without orders from his lord, the bailiff shall give back to the plaintiff as much for the excessive prise as he would have taken from him if he had avoided paying his toll and in addition be imprisoned for forty days. With regard to citizens and burgesses to whom the king or his father has granted murage to enclose their town and who take such murage otherwise than it was granted to them and are convicted of this, it is provided that they shall lose this favour forever and be liable to heavy amercement by the king.

[c. 32] As to those who take victuals or anything else for the king's use on credit either for the provisioning of a castle or for another reason, and when they have received payment therefor at the exchequer, in the wardrobe or elsewhere, withhold it from the creditors, to their great loss and the king's discredit, it is provided, in the case of those who have lands and tenements, that it be immediately levied from their lands and their chattels and paid to the creditors together with the damages they have sustained and they are to make fine for their trespass; and if they have no lands or tenements, they are to be in prison at the king's pleasure. As regards those who accept part of the king's debts or accept other rewards from the king's creditors for getting them payment of these same debts, it is provided that they are to give back double what they received and be heavily punished at the king's pleasure. As to those who take more horses or carts for doing the king's carrying than are needed and accept a reward for releasing horses or carts, it is provided that if anyone belonging to the court does it, he shall be severely punished by the marshals, and if it be done out of court by someone of the court or by someone else who is convicted of it, he shall give back threefold and be in the king's prison for forty days.

[c. 33] It is provided that no sheriff shall allow a barrator to maintain suits in the county court, or stewards of magnates or anyone else, if he is not appointed attorney of his lord to perform suit, nor to render judgments of the county court or pronounce judgments if he is not specially prayed and requested to do this by all the suitors and attornies of the suitors who are there that day; and if any does the king will proceed severely against both the sheriff and him.

[c. 34] Because many have often invented and told lying tales, as a result of which there has often been discord or the intention of discord between the king and his people, or some magnates of his kingdom, it is forbidden, because of the damage that has been and that could still be, for anyone henceforward to be so bold as to utter or repeat false news or fabrications whence any discord, or intention of discord, or slander could arise between the king and his people or the magnates of his kingdom; and he who does is to be taken and kept in prison until he has declared in court who started the talk.

[c. 35] With regard to magnates and their bailiffs and others (except the king's officers to whom special authority has been given to do this) who on somebody's complaint or on their own authority attach others with their chattels who are passing through their dominion to answer before them concerning contracts, covenants and trespasses made outside their power and jurisdiction, whereas they (the attached) hold nothing either of them or within the liberty where their authority is, to the prejudice of the king and the crown and the damage of the people, it is provided that from now on no one is to do it; and if anyone does he shall pay him who is attached double the amount of his damages and be liable to heavy amercement by the king.

[c. 36] Because reasonable[1] aid for making sons knights or for marrying daughters has never yet been defined,[2] nor when it ought to be taken, nor at what time, whereby some levied excessive aid sooner than seemed necessary, at which the people felt aggrieved, it is provided that from now on for a whole knight's fee only 20*s* is to be paid, and for 20 librates of land held in socage 20*s* and for more, more and for less, less according to the assessment. And that no one can levy such aid for making his son a knight until his son is fifteen years old, or for marrying his daughter until she is seven years old, and there shall be mention made of this in the king's writ drawn up for the purpose when he wishes to claim it. And if it happens that the father, after he has levied such an aid from his tenants, dies before he has married his daughter, the father's executors are to be bound to the daughter for as much as the father received by way of aid and if the father's goods do not suffice, the heir is to be bound to the daughter for it.

[c. 37] It is likewise provided and agreed that if any man is attainted by recognition of assize of *novel disseisin* of disseisin committed in the time of the present king with robbery of any kind of goods or movables, the judgment is to be that the plaintiff shall recover his seisin and his damages as well in respect of the goods and movables aforesaid as in respect of the rest, and the disseisor shall make fine whether he is present or not, provided that if he is present he is first to be sentenced to prison. And the same is to be done in the case of disseisin by force and arms, although robbery is not committed.

[c. 38] Because some people in the land have less fear than they ought of swearing a false oath, whereby many people are disinherited and lose their right, it is provided

[1] Required by M.C. (1215), cc. 12 and 15 (No. 20 above), but not defined.
[2] *mise en certein*

that from now on the king will *ex officio* grant attaints on inquests in pleas of land or franchise [or anything] concerning a free tenement when it seems to him that there is need.

[c. 39] And because a long time has passed since the writs named below were limited, it is provided that in reckoning descent on a writ of right no one is to be given a hearing to claim seisin by an ancestor of his farther back than the time of king Richard, uncle of king Henry, the father of the present king; and that the writ of *novel disseisin* and that of purpartie which is called *nuper obiit* are to have the limitation "since the first crossing of king Henry, father of our lord the king who now is, to Gascony", and the writs of *mort d'ancestor*, *cosinage*, *ael* and entry, and the writ of *neifty* are to have the limitation "from the coronation of king Henry", and not before. Except that all writs purchased at once or purchased between now and a year after St John's day are to be pleaded from the time they used previously to be pleaded from.

[c. 40] And because many people are hindered from obtaining their right by false vouching to warranty, it is provided that in possessory writs (especially such as writs of *mort d'ancestor*, *cosinage*, *ael*, *nuper obiit*, intrusion and other like writs, whereby lands or tenements are claimed which ought to descend, revert, remain or escheat by the death of an ancestor or of another), if the tenant vouches to warranty and the demandant counterpleads it and is willing to aver, by the assize or by the country or otherwise as the king's court shall award, that the tenant, or his ancestor whose heir he is, was the first to enter after the death of him from whose seisin he (the demandant) claims, the demandant's averment is to be received if the tenant will abide thereupon; if he will not, he is to be driven to make another answer if he has not his warrantor present willing to warrant him voluntarily and enter immediately upon the defence, saving to the demandant his exceptions against him (if he wishes to vouch further) as he had before against the first tenant. Again, in all kinds of writs of entry which mention degrees it is provided that no one henceforth shall vouch out of the line. In other writs of entry where no mention is made of degrees (which writs are not to be maintained save where the aforesaid writs in the degrees cannot lie nor rightfully have place) and in writ of right, it is provided that, if the tenant vouches to warranty and the demandant wishes to counterplead it and is ready to aver by the country that neither he who is vouched nor his ancestors ever had seisin of the land or the tenement demanded whether in fee or in service by the hand of the tenant or of his ancestors since the time of him upon whose seisin the demandant bases his claim until the time when the writ was purchased and the plea moved so that he could not aver that the tenant or his ancestor was his feoffee, the demandant's averment is to be received if the tenant will abide thereupon; if he will not, the tenant is to be driven to make another answer if he has not his warrantor present willing to warrant him voluntarily and enter immediately upon the defence, saving to the demandant his exceptions against him as he had before against the first tenant. And the aforesaid exception is to have place in writ of *mort d'ancestor* and the other writs before named, as well as in writs that concern right. And if the tenant has perchance a charter of warranty from another man besides so that he is not obliged in any of the aforesaid cases to warrant voluntarily, his recovery is saved to him by a writ of warranty of charter from the king's chancery when he wishes to purchase it, but the plea is not to be held up because of this.

[c. 41] Concerning the oath of champions it is provided – because it seldom happens that a demandant's champion is not perjured, in that he swears that he or his father saw the seisin of his lord or of his lord's ancestry and that his father enjoined him to have it vindicated – that the demandant's champion is not henceforth to be compelled to swear this; but the oath is to be kept in all its other points.

[c. 42] Because in writs of assizes and of attaints and of juries *utrum*, the jurors are often harassed by tenants' excuses for non-appearance, it is provided that from the time that he [a tenant] has once appeared in court he cannot after that make excuse, but, if he will, is to appoint an attorney to sue for him; if he will not, the assize or the jury is to be taken because of his default.

[c. 43] Because demandants are oftentimes hindered from obtaining their right because there are many parcener-tenants, of whom one cannot answer without the other, or because there are many tenants jointly enfeoffed where none knows his several and these tenants often fourch by essoin, so that each of them has an excuse for non-appearance, it is provided that from now on these tenants are not to have essoin except on one day and no more than one sole tenant, so that in future they can fourch only with one essoin.

[c. 44] Because many people have themselves falsely essoined on the ground of being overseas when they were in England on the day of the summons, it is provided that from now on this essoin is not to be allowed at all if the demandant challenges it and is ready to aver that he was in England on the day the summons was made and for three weeks after, but is to be adjourned in this way: that, if the demandant on such and such a day prosecutes the averment by the country or as the king's court shall award and it is found that the tenant was within the four seas[1] the day he was summoned and for three weeks after so that he could have reasonable notice of the summons, the essoin is to be turned into a default – and this, be it understood, only before justices.

[c. 45] With regard to delays in all kinds of writs connected with attachments, it is provided that if the tenant or the defendant defaults after the attachment has been proved, the grand distress is to be awarded immediately and if the sheriff does not make sufficient return on the day he is to be heavily amerced. And if he returns that he has made execution in due fashion and delivered the issues to the sureties, the sheriff is then to be ordered to have the issues brought before the justices on another day; and if he who is attached comes to remedy his defaults, he is to have the issues, and if he does not come the king is to have them. And the justices of the king's pleas shall have them delivered into the wardrobe, the justices of the bench at Westminster shall have them delivered into the exchequer; and the justices in eyre to the sheriff of the shire where the pleadings are,[2] both of that shire and of other shires, and he is to be charged with this in the summons by the roll of the justices.

[c. 46] It is likewise provided, and ordered by the king, that justices of the king's bench and justices of the bench at Westminster are from now on to plead to the end

[1] i.e. the four seas bounding Great Britain, i.e. in Great Britain [2] *ou il pleident*

pleas started on one day before broaching or beginning the following day's pleas, except that essoins are to be entered, judged and allowed. And no one because of this is to presume not to come on the day which has been given him.

[c. 47] It is likewise provided that if any one from now on purchases a writ of *novel disseisin* and if he whom the writ proceeds against as principal disseisor dies before the assize is passed, the plaintiff is to have his writ of entry founded *sur disseisin* against the heir or against the heirs of the disseisor, of whatever age they are; in the same way let the heir or the heirs of the disseised have their writ of entry against the disseisors, of whatever age they are, if perchance the disseised dies before he has made his purchase of the writ; so that because of the nonage of the heirs of either of the parties the writ shall not be abated or the plea delayed, but as much as can be done without offending the law it shall be speeded up to make lively suit after the disseisin. In like manner this article is to be observed with regard to prelates, religious, and others to whom lands or tenements may come in any way after the death of another person. And if the parties in pleading proceed to an inquest and it passes against an heir who is under age, and especially against the heir of the disseised, in that case he shall have an attaint as an act of royal grace.

[c. 48] If a guardian who is the immediate lord enfeoff any man with land which is of the inheritance of a child who is under age and in his wardship, to the disinheritance of the heir, it is provided that the heir is to have his recovery immediately by writ of *novel disseisin* against his guardian and against the tenant; and the seisin is to be handed over by the justices, if it is recovered, to the next friend to whom the inheritance cannot descend to improve for the child's benefit and to answer to the heir for the issues when he comes of age; and the guardian is to lose for life wardship of the thing recovered and all the rest of the inheritance that he holds in the heir's name. And if a guardian other than the immediate lord does it, he is to lose the wardship of the whole and is to be liable to severe punishment from the king. And if the child is moved away or disturbed by the guardian or by the feoffee or by another with the result that he cannot sue for his assize, one of his next friends who is willing to do so may sue on his behalf and shall be admitted.

[c. 49] In a writ of dower in which the woman has nothing[1] the writ is not henceforth to be abated by the exception of the tenant that she has received her dower from another man before her writ was purchased, unless he can show that she had received part of the dower from himself and in the same vill before her writ was purchased.

[c. 50] And because the king does these things in honour of God and of holy church and for the common good and the relief of those who are oppressed, he does not wish them to turn at another time to his prejudice or that of the crown, but that the rights that belong to him should be saved to him in all points.

[c. 51] And because it would be very much a Christian act[2] to do right to all and at all times, it would be useful for assizes of *novel disseisin*, *mort d'ancestor* and *darrein presentment*, with the assent of the prelates, to be taken in Advent, on Septuagesima and in Lent as indeed is done with inquests; and the king asks this of the bishops.

[1] known as the writ of dower *unde nihil habet*

[2] *graunt Charite serroit*

Here ends the statute of the lord king Edward made at Westminster on the morrow of the Close of Easter in the third year of his reign, after his coronation.

48. Grant of custom on exported wool, woolfells and hides, (not later than 10 May) 1275

(*Parliamentary Writs*, I (1827), p. 1 (No. 2) [French])

Granted to Edward I in the first "general" parliament of his reign. Known first as the "new custom" but later as the "ancient custom" of 1275, to distinguish it first of all from the "maltote" of 1294–7 and then from the newer "new custom" of 1303. Sometimes also as the "great custom of 1275". The terminology is untangled by N. S. B. Gras in ch. II of his *The Early English Customs System* (Harvard Univ. Press, 1918), the standard work.

For the new custom granted by all the magnates of the realm and at the request of the communities of merchants[1] of all England, it is provided that in every county in the largest town where there is a port there shall be chosen two of the most upright and most influential men to have the custody of one piece of a seal and one man, who shall be appointed by the king, shall have another piece, and they shall be sworn to honestly receive and answer for the king's money, namely ½ mark on each sack of wool, ½ mark on each 300 woolfells (which make one sack) and 1 mark on each last of hides going out of the realm, as well in Ireland and Wales as in England, within liberties and without. In addition, in every port ships can put to sea from, there shall be two men of standing sworn not to suffer wool, woolfells or hides to go out without a letter patent with the seal which is at the chief port in the same county. And if there is anyone who goes out of the realm with them otherwise he shall lose all the chattels he has and his person shall be at the king's pleasure. And because this matter cannot be done immediately it is provided that the king shall send his letters to every sheriff throughout the realm and have it proclaimed and forbidden throughout the shires for anyone to cause wool, woolfells or hides to be taken out of the land before the feast of Trinity this year[2] on pain of forfeiture of his person and of all his chattels, and then by letters patent with seals as aforesaid, and not otherwise on pain of the aforesaid forfeitures. And the king has granted of his grace that all the lords through whose ports wool or hides go out shall each have the forfeitures happening in his own port, saving to the king ½ mark on each sack of wool and of woolfells and 1 mark on each last of hides.[3]

[On 25 May a text of the above was sent to the Justiciary of Ireland, Geoffrey de Genvill, together with instructions "to induce the archbishops, bishops, abbots, priors, earls, barons, commons and merchants of Ireland to grant to the king a custom of wool, woolfells and hides after the form of the grant made in England, and to admit Luke of Lucca and his fellows, merchants of Lucca, and Bonasius Bonalvity and his fellows, merchants of Florence, whom the king has deputed to collect the said custom, and to be intendant to them therein" (*Cal. Fine Rolls*, I (1272–1307), p. 60).

Luke of Lucca and his fellows had already been appointed on 21 May collectors of this custom for the ports of England and Wales (ibid., pp. 45–6). cf. Powicke, *The Thirteenth Century 1216–1307* (Oxford History of England), pp. 629, 631–2, 642.]

---

[1] *la priere des comunes de marchanz*

[2] 9 June 1275

[3] The writ printed by Stubbs, *Select Charters*, 9th edn, ed. H. W. C. Davis, pp. 443–4, is one of a number issued by such lords pursuant to this last sentence of the present document. cf. *Parl. Writs*, I (1827), p. 2 (No.7).

49. The Statute of the Jewry, 1275

(*Statutes of the Realm* (1810), I, pp. 221–3 [French])

Issued at Westminster in the Michaelmas parliament of 1275 (Richardson and Sayles, "The Early Statutes", *L.Q.R.* vol. 50 (1934), p. 220; and Roth, *History of the Jews in England*, p. 70). A far-reaching, but not necessarily benevolent or practicable "attempt to emancipate the Jews economically". On the difficulties to which it gave rise, see Roth, op. cit. ch. 4. The petition of the Jews in response to this statute is given as No. 50 below.

Because the king has seen that many evils and instances of the disinheriting of good men of his land have happened as a result of the usuries which the Jews have made in the past, and that many sins have followed thereupon, the king though he and his ancestors have always received great benefit from the Jewish people in the past, has nevertheless for the honour of God and the common benefit of the people ordained and established that from now on no Jew shall lend anything at usury, either on land or rent or any thing else, and that usuries shall not continue beyond the feast of St Edward last. Agreements made before that shall be kept, save that the usuries shall cease. All those who owe debts to Jews on pledges of movables are to clear them between now and Easter; if not the pledges shall be forfeited. And if any Jew shall lend at usury contrary to what the king has established the king will not concern himself either personally or through his officials to get him recovery of his loan, but will punish him at his discretion for the offence and will do justice to the Christian that he may recover his pledge.

And so that distresses for debts due to Jews shall not henceforth be so grievous, a half of the lands and chattels of Christians is to be kept for their sustenance, and no distress for a debt owing to a Jew is to be made upon the heir of the debtor named in the Jew's deed or other person holding the land that was the debtor's before the debt is proved and acknowledged in court.

And if a sheriff or other bailiff has by the king's command to give a Jew, or a number of Jews, for a debt due to them seisin of chattels or land to the value of the debt, the chattels are to be valued by the oaths of good men and be delivered to the Jew or Jews or to their agent to the amount of the debt, and if the chattels do not suffice, the lands shall be extended by the same oath before seisin is given to the Jew or Jews, to each one according to what is due to him, so that it may be known for certain that the debt is paid and the Christian may have his land again, saving always to the Christian half of his land and chattels for his sustenance as aforesaid, and the chief dwelling.

And if any movables be found hereafter in the seisin of a Jew and any one wishes to sue him, the Jew shall have his warranty if he is entitled to it, and if not, let him answer: so that in future he is not in this matter to be otherwise privileged than a Christian.

And that all Jews shall dwell in the king's own cities and boroughs, where the chirograph chests of the Jews are wont to be: and that each Jew after he is seven years old shall wear a distinguishing mark on his outer garment, that is to say in the form of two Tables joined, of yellow felt of the length of six inches and of the breadth of three inches. And that each one after he is twelve years old shall yearly at Easter pay to the king, whose serf he is, a tax of three pence, and this be understood to hold as well for a woman as for a man.

And that no Jew have power to enfeoff another, Jew or Christian, with houses, rents or tenements that he now has, or to alienate them in any other manner, or to acquit any Christian of his debt without special permission of the king, until the king shall have otherwise ordained thereon.

And as it is the will and sufferance of holy church that they may live and be preserved, the king takes them into his protection and grants them his peace; and wills that they may be safely preserved and defended by his sheriffs and his other bailiffs and faithful; and commands that none shall do them harm or damage or wrong in their bodies or in their goods movable or immovable and that they shall neither plead nor be impleaded in any court, nor be challenged or troubled in any court, save in the court of the king, whose bondmen they are. And that none shall owe obedience or service or rent save to the king or to his bailiffs in his name, unless it be for their dwellings which they now hold by paying rent, saving the right of holy church.

And the king grants them that they may live by lawful trade and by their labour and that they may have intercourse with Christians in order to carry on lawful trade by selling and buying. But that no Christian for this cause or any other shall dwell[1] among them. And the king wills that they shall not by reason of their trading be put to scot and lot or tallaged with those of the cities and boroughs where they live because they are liable for tallage to the king as his serfs and to no one other than the king.

Moreover the king grants them that they may buy houses and curtilages in the cities and boroughs where they live, so that they hold them in chief of the king, saving to the lords of the fee their services due and accustomed. And they may take and buy farms or land for the term of ten years or less, without taking homages or fealties or such sort of obedience from Christians, and without having advowsons of churches, that they may be able to gain their living in the world if they have not the means of trading or cannot labour. And this power of taking lands at farm shall be open to them only for fifteen years from this time forward.

50. Petition of the "commonalty" of the Jews, shortly after 1275

(A request for the interpretation and amendment of the Statute of the Jewry of 1275 (No. 49 above). P.R.O., Ancient Petitions, No. 2655, printed in G. O. Sayles, *Select Cases in the Court of King's Bench*, III (1939), p. cxiv [French])

To our lord the king and to his council the commonalty of the Jews ask the favour of their assent and discretion on the things written below.

Because the new statutes will that the Jews should have seisin of half only of lands and rents pledged to them, leaving the other half of the lands and rents and the chief messuage for the sustenance of the Christian who is the debtor of the Jew, this is their enquiry: if the debtor of the Jew dies without heir of his body and without wife and the lands and rents fall to a rich man or to someone who has enough of his own to

[1] *ne seit cochaunt ne levaunt*

live on without these lands and rents that are pledged to the Jew, in such circumstances shall the Jew have possession of the whole of the pledged property until the debt is paid, or not?

Besides this, our question is about a Christian who has borrowed money from Jews which is the king's money and this Christian has no lands, rents or chattels save a large house which he occupies worth 100*s* or 10 marks a year and if it were sold would fetch 100 marks or £100, what seisin will the Jew have of his pledge for the recovery of the debt seeing that this Christian has nothing save this house.

Further, the commonalty of the Jews beseech our lord the king that the poor Jews, who have nothing whereby to live or trade, may have leave to sell their houses and their rents to other Jews richer than themselves: it would be worth as much to our lord the king for the one lot of Jews to have the rents and houses as the other, and he could not lose by it. [[1]That if they have not leave to sell their houses they will have to demolish them and sell the stone and timber to various people.]

Furthermore, the commonalty of the Jews demonstrate that they would be compelled if they were to trade at all to buy dearer than a Christian and to sell dearer, for Christian merchants sell their merchandise on credit and if the Jew sold on credit he would never be paid a single penny. And Christian merchants can carry their merchandise far and near but if the Jew carried his beyond the . . .[2] he would be . . .[2] and robbed. And they beseech our lord the king and his council that . . .[2] such counsel in the Jewry that they can live in his time with his . . .[2] as in the time of his ancestors since the Conquest.[3]

51. Distraint of knighthood, 1278

(*Parliamentary Writs*, I (1827), p. 214; more conveniently in Stubbs, *Select Charters*, 9th edn, pp. 448–9)

Like writs were sent to all the sheriffs. For the returns of the sheriffs of Northumberland and Surrey and Sussex, see *Parl. Writs*, I, pp. 214–18. See also No. 111(b) below.

The king to the sheriff of Gloucestershire, greeting. We order and firmly enjoin you to distrain without delay all those of your bailiwick who have lands worth twenty pounds a year, or one whole knight's fee worth twenty pounds a year, and hold of us in chief and ought to be knights but are not, to receive from us before Christmas or on that feast the arms of a knight; to distrain also without delay all those of your bailiwick who have lands worth twenty pounds a year, or one whole knight's fee worth twenty pounds a year, whoever they hold of, and ought to be knights but are not, to receive such arms on that feast or before: so that you receive from them good and sufficient security for doing this[4] and cause the names of all of them to be entered under the supervision of two law-worthy knights of the aforesaid county on a certain roll and sent to us under your seal and the seals of the two knights without delay. And we wish you to know that we shall make careful enquiry into your conduct in carrying out this order of ours and have a suitable remedy provided for it forthwith. Witness the king at Westminster, the 26th day of June.

Like letters to all the sheriffs of England.

[1] Perhaps a later addition. [2] writing defaced [3] *pus le conquest de la terre* [4] *inde*

52. Statute of Gloucester, 7 August 1278

(*Statutes of the Realm*, I, pp. 45–50 [French])

The year of grace 1278 and the 6th of the reign of king Edward, son of king Henry, at Gloucester, in the month of August, the king himself providing for the betterment of his kingdom and for more fully doing justice, as the well-being of the kingly office requires, there having been called in the more discreet people of his kingdom as well of the greater as of the lesser sort: IT IS ESTABLISHED and by agreement ordained that, as the same kingdom in many divers cases as well of liberties as of other things in which aforetime the law was found wanting and to avoid the very grievous injuries and the innumerable disinheritances which such default of law caused to the people of the kingdom needs a number of supplementations to the law and new provisions, the underwritten statutes, ordinances and provisions shall be steadfastly observed by all the people of the kingdom from now on.

As prelates, earls, barons and others of the kingdom claim to have various liberties, for the examination and judgment of which the king gave these same prelates, earls, barons and others a date, it is provided and by agreement granted that the aforesaid prelates, earls, barons and others shall have the use of such liberties, provided that nothing accrues to them by usurpation or occupation and that they occupy nothing at the expense of the king, until the king's next coming through the county or the next coming of itinerant justices for common pleas into the same county or until the king orders otherwise, saving the king's right when he wishes to take proceedings thereon, as is contained in the king's writ. And writs shall be issued about this to sheriffs, bailiffs and others for each claimant, and the form of the writ shall be varied according to the sort of liberty each man claims to have.

And sheriffs shall have it publicly proclaimed throughout their bailiwicks, that is in cities, boroughs, market towns and elsewhere, that all those who claim to have any liberties by charters of the king's predecessors, kings of England, or in another way, shall be before the king or before the justices in eyre at a certain day and place to show what sort of liberties they claim to have and by what warrant. And the same sheriffs shall be there then personally with their bailiffs and officers to certify the king upon the aforesaid liberties and other things concerning these liberties. And this proclamation [about being] before the king shall contain three weeks' notice. And in the same way the sheriffs shall have proclamation made in the eyre of the justices, and in the same way they shall be there personally with their bailiffs and officers to certify the justices upon such liberties and upon other things concerning these liberties. And this proclamation shall contain forty days' notice, as the common summons [of the eyre] does; so that if the party that claims to have the liberty is before the king he shall not be put in default before the justices in eyre; because the king of his special grace has granted that he will keep the party from harm in respect of this adjournment. And if this party is impleaded over such liberties before two of the aforesaid justices, the same justices before whom they are impleaded shall keep the party from harm before other justices; and the king before himself, provided that he knows from the justices that the party is impleaded before them, as is aforesaid.

And if they who claim to have such liberties do not come on the day aforesaid, then the liberties shall be taken into the king's hand by the sheriff of the place as distress, so that they shall not use such liberties until they come to receive justice. And when they come in consequence of this distress their liberties shall be replevied, if they ask for them: once these are replevied they shall answer immediately in the way aforesaid. And if peradventure the parties except that they ought not to answer concerning this without an original writ, then, if it can be known that they have by their own act usurped or occupied any liberties at the expense of the king or of his predecessors, they shall be told to answer immediately without a writ, and then they shall receive such judgment as the king's court shall award. And if they say further that their ancestor or ancestors died seised of the same liberties, they shall be heard and the truth immediately enquired into and according to this the justices shall proceed in the business. And if it be found that their ancestor did die seised of them, then the king shall have an original writ from his chancery in the form made for the purpose: "The king to the sheriff, greeting. Summon by good summoners so and so to be before us at such and such a place on our next coming to the county, or, before our justices at the first assizes when they come into these parts, to show by what warrant he holds his view of frankpledge in his manor of N. in the same county, and let the sheriff have there the summoners and this writ"; or thus, "by what warrant he holds the hundred of B. in the aforesaid county"; or thus, "by what warrant he claims to be quit of toll for himself or his men throughout our kingdom, by continuance after the death of so and so late his predecessor. And have there the summoners and this writ". And the forms of the writs shall be changed according to the sort of liberty and according to the case and at the discretion of the chancellor and of the justices.[1] And if the parties come on the day, let them answer, and let replication be made and judgment given. And if they do not come and do not essoin themselves before the king and the king stays longer in the county, the sheriff shall be commanded to cause them to come on the fourth day – on which day, if they come not and the king stays longer in the county, let things be done as they are in the eyre of the justices. And if the king leaves the county, the parties shall be adjourned to an early date, and shall have reasonable delays at the discretion of the justices as in personal actions. And the justices in eyre shall act in this matter in their eyres according to the aforesaid ordinance and as such pleas ought to be conducted in the eyre.

Concerning complaints made and to be made about the king's bailiffs or others' bailiffs, it shall be done according to the ordinance made earlier on the subject and according to the inquests into it earlier. And the justices in eyre shall act in this matter as the king has enjoined them, and according to the articles that the king has issued to them.

[c. 1] As up to now damages have not been awarded in assizes of *novel disseisin* except against the disseisors only, it is provided that if the disseisors alienate the tenements and have nothing from which damages can be levied, those into whose hands the

[1] "And the forms . . . justices": this sentence is not given in the statute roll text (printed in *Stat. Realm*, I, pp. 45–50) or in certain others. It is not strictly necessary, but relevant, and it is given by the French text in "Reg. A" (i.e. P.R.O., Liber A, E.36/274, f. 276).

tenements come shall be charged with the damages in such a way that each shall be responsible for his time. It is likewise provided that the disseised shall recover damages in a writ of entry upon *novel disseisin* against him who is found to be tenant after the disseisor. It is likewise provided that where up to now damages have not been awarded in a plea of *mort d'ancestor*, except in a case where the tenement was recovered against the chief lord, from now on damages shall be awarded in all cases where a man recovers by an assize of *mort d'ancestor*, as said before in the assize of *novel disseisin*. In the same way shall one recover damages in writs of *cosinage*, *aiel*[1] and *besael*.[2] And whereas up to now damages have been calculated only on the value of the issues of the land, the demandant from now on shall recover against the tenant the costs of purchasing his writ as well as the aforesaid damages; and all this shall apply in all cases where one recovers damages.[3] And everyone shall in future be bound in like manner to render damages where recovery is obtained against him for his intrusion or his own act.

[c. 2] If a child under age is kept out of his inheritance after the death of his[4] cousin, grandfather or great-grandfather so that he has to buy a writ and his adversary comes into court and in answering alleges feoffment or says something else whereby the judges award an inquest, whereas the inquest was deferred until he came of age now let it take place as if he were of age.

[c. 3] It is likewise established that if a man alienates a tenement that he holds by the law of England, his son shall not be barred by the deed of his father, from whom no inheritance descended to him, from demanding and recovering his mother's seisin by a writ of *mort d'ancestor*, even though his father's charter states that he and his heirs are bound to warranty. And if an inheritance has descended to him from his father, then he shall be excluded from the value of the inheritance that has descended to him. And if an inheritance descends to him from the same father at a later date, then shall the tenant recover from him his mother's seisin by a judicial writ that shall issue out of the rolls of the justices before whom the plea was pleaded, to resummon his warrantor, as has been done in other cases where the warrantor comes into court and says that nothing descended to him from him by whose deed he is vouched. In the same way the son's issue [shall recover] by writ of *ael*, *cosin* and *besael*. Likewise, in the same way the heir of the wife, after the death of his father and mother shall not be barred from an action by his father's charter, if he demands the inheritance or marriage of his mother by a writ of entry that his father alienated in the time of his mother, of which no fine is levied in the king's court.

[c.4] Likewise if a man lets[5] his land at fee-farm or for finding estovers in food or clothing amounting to a quarter of the true value of the land and he who holds the land thus charged lets it lie unused, so that no distress can be found there, for two or three years without having the farm for it rendered or without doing what is contained in the deed of the lease,[5] it is established that after two years have passed the

[1] grandfather [2] great-grandfather

[3] "And whereas . . . damages": this sentence is not found in all manuscripts. Its text is uncertain, in any case.

[4] On absence of "father", see T. F. T. Plucknett, *Statutes and their Interpretation* (Cambridge, 1922), pp. 15–16 and 107–8.

[5] Not at this date to be understood as a lease for a term of years, but a subinfeudation (Plucknett, *Legislation of Edward I*, p. 90, n. 4)

lessor shall have an action to demand the land in demesne by a writ which he shall have out of the chancery. And if he from whom the land is demanded comes before judgment and renders the arrears and the damages and finds such security as the court considers sufficient for rendering thereafter what is contained in the deed, he shall retain the land. And if he waits until it is recovered by judgment, he shall be foreclosed for ever.

[c. 5] Likewise it is provided that one shall henceforth have a writ of waste out of the chancery made on this against the man who holds by the law of England or otherwise for term of life or for term of years, or a woman in dower; and he who is convicted of waste shall lose what he has wasted and in addition compensate with three times the amount the waste is assessed at. And in respect of waste done during wardship let there be done as is contained in the great charter. And where it is contained in the great charter that he who has committed waste during wardship shall lose the wardship it is agreed that he shall render damages to the heir for the waste, if it be that the wardship lost before the coming-of-age of the heir of the same wardship does not cover the value of the damages.

[c. 6] It is likewise provided that if a man dies and has several heirs, of whom one is a son or daughter, a brother or sister, a nephew or niece and the others are in a more remote degree, the heirs shall henceforth have recovery by a writ of chancery of *mort d'ancestor*.

[c. 7] Likewise if a woman sells or gives in fee or for term of life the tenement that she holds in dower, it is established that the heir or other person to whom the land ought to revert after the woman's death, shall at once have recovery to demand the land by a writ of entry made therefor in the chancery.

[c. 8] It is likewise provided that sheriffs shall hold pleas of trespass in counties as they used to be pleaded. And that no one from now on shall have a writ of trespass before justices unless he declares on oath that the goods taken away were worth at least forty shillings. And if he complains of battery, he shall declare on oath that his complaint is true. For wounds and mayhems one shall have a writ as one used to have it. And it is granted that defendants may make attornies in such pleas where there is not appeal, so that if they are convicted of the trespass in their absence it shall be required of the sheriff that they be taken and have the penalty that they would have had if they had been present when judgment was given. And if the plaintiffs henceforth in such trespass cause themselves to be essoined after the first appearance, let there be an adjournment until the coming of the justices, and the defendants meanwhile shall be in peace in such pleas and in other pleas where attachments and distresses lie. And if the defendant causes himself to be essoined of the king's service and does not carry his warrant at the day given him by his essoiner, let him render damages to the plaintiff for his journey of twenty shillings, or more at the discretion of the justices, and nevertheless grievously in the king's mercy.

[c. 9] The king commands that no writ of chancery shall be granted on account of the death of a man to enquire whether a man killed another by misadventure or in defending himself or otherwise by felony, but if he[1] is in prison and before justices in

[1] *tel* (*Stat. Realm*, I, p. 48, where, however, the text is obscure)

eyre or justices assigned to deliver gaol let him put himself upon the country for good and ill and should it be found by the country that he did it defending himself or by misadventure, then on receipt of the justices' record the king shall give him grace, if he pleases.

[1]It is likewise provided that no accusation shall be discontinued as lightly as has been the case in the past, but, if the accuser states the deed, the year, the day, the time and the place[2] where the deed was done, the accusation shall stand: and henceforth the accusation shall not be discontinued for default of fresh suit, provided that someone sues within a year and a day after the deed.

[c. 10] As it is contained in the statute of the present king[3] that two parceners, or two joint-tenants, may not fourch by essoin after they have once appeared in court, it is provided that the same be kept and observed where a man and his wife are impleaded in the king's court.

[c. 11] It is likewise provided that if a man in the city of London grants his tenement for a term of years and he to whom the freehold belongs causes himself by collusion to be impleaded and makes default after default, or comes into court and offers to surrender it to cause the termor to lose his term and the tenant has his plaint, then in order that the termor can recover by a writ of covenant the mayor and bailiffs can enquire by good men of the neighbourhood in the presence of the termor and the demandant whether the demandant sued in virtue of the right he had or by collusion or by fraud to make the termor lose his term; and if it is found by the inquest that the demandant brought the action in virtue of the good right he had, judgment shall be given at once; and if it is found that he sued by fraud to deprive the termor of his term, execution of judgment for the demandant shall be suspended until the term has expired. Let the same be done on grounds of equity in such a case before the justices, if the termor makes his challenge before the judgment.

[c. 12] It is likewise provided that if a man impleaded for a tenement in the same city vouches an outsider to warranty, he shall come to the chancery and have a writ to summon his warrantor for a certain day before the justices of the bench and another writ to the mayor and bailiffs of London that they shall stay proceedings in the plea that is before them by writ until the plea of warranty is determined before the justices of the bench, and when the plea at the bench is determined, the warrantor shall be told to go into the city and answer to the chief plea; and the demandant on sueing for it shall have a writ of the justices of the bench to the mayor and bailiffs that they shall proceed in the plea. And if the demandant recovers, the tenant shall come to the justices of the bench and have a writ to the mayor and bailiffs that if the tenant has alienated his land they shall have the land extended and return the extent to the bench by a certain day; and afterwards word shall be sent to the sheriff of the district where the warrantor was summoned to cause him to have its equivalent in value from the land of the warrantor.

[c. 13] It is likewise provided that from the time the plea is moved in the city of

[1] This paragraph is not given by all MSS.
[2] *le temps le Roy & la ville* (*Stat. Realm*, I, p. 49, where however the text is obscure)
[3] The reference is to Stat. Westm. I (1275), c. 43 (No. 47 above)

London by writ the tenant shall not have power to commit waste or stripping[1] of the tenement that is in dispute while the plea is pending. And at the suit of the demandant the mayor and bailiffs shall have it guarded. And the same ordinance and statute shall be kept in other cities and boroughs and elsewhere throughout the kingdom.

[c. 14] The king of his grace grants to the citizens of London that, whereas up to now those who were disseised of freehold in the same city could not recover their damages before the coming of the justices to the Tower, such disseisees shall henceforth have their damages by recognisance of the assize by which they recover their tenement; and the disseisors shall be amerced before two barons of the exchequer, who shall come once a year to the city to do this. And the treasurer and barons shall be ordered to do this each year through two of them, after their rising at Candlemas, and the amercements shall be levied by summons of the exchequer, and paid into the exchequer for the king's use.

[c. 15] It is likewise provided that the mayor and bailiffs, before the coming of these barons, shall enquire about wines sold contrary to the assize, and shall present it before them at their coming, and they shall be amerced then, whereas they used to wait for the coming of the justices.

Given at Gloucester on the Sunday next after the feast of St Peter at the Gules of August in the year aforesaid [Sunday, 7 August 1278].

53. Statute of Mortmain ("*de viris religiosis*"), November 1279

(*Councils and Synods II (1205–1313)*, ed. Powicke and Cheney (Oxford, 1964), pp. 864–5)

The king to his justices of the bench, greeting. As it was once[2] provided that men of religion should not enter anyone's fees without the licence and will of the chief lords from whom those fees are immediately held, and men of religion have, notwithstanding, from then until now entered both their own fees and those of others, appropriating them to themselves, buying them, sometimes receiving them from others as a gift, whereby the services which are due from such fees and which were provided from the beginning for the defence of the realm are unjustifiably withdrawn and chief lords in respect of them lose their escheats, We wishing for the benefit of the realm a suitable remedy to be provided for this have, on the advice of the prelates, earls and others faithful subjects of our realm who are of our council, provided, established and ordained that no religious or any other person whatever shall presume on pain of forfeiting them to buy, sell, receive from anyone under colour of gift or term of years or any other title whatsoever, or by any other means, art or artifice appropriate to himself lands or tenements, whereby such lands and tenements come in any way into mortmain. We have provided also that if any religious or any other presumes by any means, art or artifice to contravene the

[1] *estrepement*
[2] apparently a reference to the Provisions of Westminster (1259), c. 14: at any rate it follows its wording

present statute it shall be lawful for us and the other immediate chief lords of the fee so alienated to enter it within a year from the time of such alienation and hold it in fee and heritably. And if the immediate chief lord is negligent and does not wish to enter such fee within the year, then it shall be lawful for the lord immediately above[1] to enter the fee within the following half year and hold it as aforesaid; and so each mediate lord shall do if the nearer lord is negligent in entering such fee as is aforesaid. And if all such chief lords of such a fee who are of full age and within the four seas and not in[2] prison are negligent or remiss in this regard for the space of one year, we immediately the year from the time when such purchases, gifts or acquisition in other ways[3] happen to be made is over shall take possession of such lands and tenements and enfeoff others with them for certain services to be rendered to us for them for the defence of our realm, saving to the chief lords of those fees the wards, escheats and other things pertaining to them and the due and accustomed services therefrom. And therefore we command you to have the aforesaid statute read before you and henceforth firmly kept and observed. Witness the king at Westminster, 14 November.

54. Statute of Acton Burnell, 1283

(*Statutes of the Realm*, I (Rec. Com., 1810), pp. 53–4 [French])

The object of this statute was to enable a creditor to get prompt repayment without having to go to law for it. The legal problem and the relationship of this to Edward I's other experiments in commercial legislation, the "Elegit" clause of the second statute of Westminster, 1285 (No. 57 below, c. 18) and the Statute of Merchants, 1285 (No. 58 below), are explained by T. F. T. Plucknett in a chapter of his *Legislation of Edward I* (Oxford, 1949). For the historical background, Sir Maurice Powicke, *The Thirteenth Century*, pp. 619–26.

As merchants who in the past have lent their substance to various people are impoverished because there was no speedy law provided by which they could readily recover their debts on the day fixed for payment, and for that reason many merchants are put off from coming to this land with their merchandise to the detriment of merchants and of the whole kingdom, THE KING by himself and by his council has ordained and established that a merchant who wishes to be sure of his debt shall cause his debtor to come before the mayor of London, or York or Bristol, and before the mayor and before a clerk whom the king shall depute for the purpose, acknowledge the debt and the day of payment; and the recognisance shall be enrolled by the hand of the aforesaid clerk which will be known. And in addition the aforesaid clerk shall make with his own hand the bond, to which shall be affixed the seal of the debtor, with the seal of the king that is provided for this, which seal shall remain in the safe keeping of the mayor and the aforesaid clerk; and if the debtor does not pay on the day fixed for him, the creditor shall come to the mayor and the clerk with his bond, and if it is found by the roll and by the bond that the debt was acknowledged and that the day fixed is past, the mayor by view of lawful men shall immediately cause the goods of the debtor to be sold to the amount of the debt, such as chattels and devisable burgages totalling the amount of the debt, and the money to be paid

[1] *proximo capitali domino mediato feodi illius* [2] *extra*
[3] *aut alias appropriationes*

without delay to the creditors. And if the mayor finds no buyer let him have the goods on a reasonable valuation handed over to the creditor up to the amount of the debt in allowance of his debt. And to the sale and to the delivery of devisable burgages the aforesaid king's seal shall be affixed in perpetual witness. And if the debtor has no goods within the jurisdiction of the mayor from which the debt can be levied, but has elsewhere in the kingdom, then shall the mayor send to the chancellor under the aforesaid seal the recognisance made before him and the aforesaid clerk, and the chancellor shall send a writ to the sheriff in whose bailiwick the debtor has goods and the sheriff shall cause the creditor to be satisfied in the same prescribed way that the mayor would do it if the debtor's movables were in his jurisdiction. But let those who value the goods for delivery to the creditor take care to set a reasonable and fair price, for if they price them too high in favour of the debtor and to the loss of the creditor the thing so priced is to be delivered to those that have priced it, at the price they have put on it, and they themselves shall be responsible to the creditor forthwith for what is due to him. And if the debtor wishes to say that his movables have been sold, or delivered, for less than they are worth, he shall have no remedy for this, because the mayor or the sheriff have honestly sold the movables to the one that offered most, for he could blame himself that he could have sold his movables before the day of the prosecution and raised the money himself but had not been willing to do so. And if the debtor has not goods from which the whole debt can be levied, then he shall be arrested wherever he is found and kept in prison until he has paid, or his friends for him. And if he has nothing of his own on which he can be supported in prison, the creditor shall find him bread and water so that he shall not die of want; the cost of which the debtor shall repay with the debt before he comes out of prison. And if the creditor is a merchant from abroad, he shall stay at the expense of the debtor, all the time that he sues to levy his debt until the day that the movables of the debtor are sold, or are delivered to him. And if the creditor is not satisfied with the debtor alone as security, for which reason sureties are found for him, or mainpernors, the mainpernors or the sureties shall come before the mayor and the aforementioned clerk and bind themselves in writing and by recognisance, as aforesaid in the case of the debtor. In the same way, if the debt is not paid on the day fixed, let execution be done on the sureties or mainpernors as aforesaid in the case of the debtor, so nevertheless that as long as the debt can be levied in full on the movables of the debtor the mainpernors or the sureties shall suffer no loss. But in default of the debtor's movables, the creditor shall recover from the mainpernors or from the sureties in the way that is stated earlier in the case of the debtor. And to meet the costs of the aforesaid clerk, the king shall take a penny for every pound. The king wills that this ordinance and establishment be held from now on, throughout his kingdom of England, between any people whatsoever who wish of their own accord to make such a recognisance, except Jews, to whom this establishment does not apply.[1] And by this establishment a writ of debt shall not be abated. And the chancellor, the barons of the exchequer, the justices of both benches and justices itinerant shall not be prevented from taking recognisances of debts from those who wish to do

[1] There were other arrangements for Jews.

it before them. But the execution of recognisances before them shall not be done in the aforementioned way but in accordance with law and usage and the way previously used. Given at Acton Burnell on the twelfth of October in the eleventh year of our reign.

55. Statute of Wales, 19 March 1284, Rhuddlan

(*Statutes of the Realm*, I, pp. 55–68)

Edward by the grace of God king of England, lord of Ireland and duke of Aquitaine to all his faithful of his land of Snowdon and of all his other lands in Wales greeting in the Lord. Divine providence, which is unerring in its dispositions, among other gifts of its dispensation with which it has deigned to honour us and our kingdom of England has now of its grace wholly and entirely converted the land of Wales previously subject to us by feudal right with its inhabitants into a dominion of our ownership, every obstacle being overcome, and has annexed and united it to the crown of the said kingdom as a constituent part of it. So we, wishing with God's blessing our said land of Snowdon and our other lands in those parts, like others subject to our rule, to be governed to the honour and praise of God and holy church and from love of justice with due guidance, and the dwellers or inhabitants of those lands who have submitted themselves completely to our will and whom we have in like manner received into our will to be managed by fixed laws and customs in tranquillity and in our peace, have caused to be rehearsed before us and the leading men of our realm the laws and customs of those parts used hitherto: which being diligently heard and fully understood, we have on the advice of the aforesaid leading men abolished some of them, allowed some and corrected some, and some others also we have decreed are to be ordained and added thereto; and these we wish to be in future kept and observed in perpetuity in our lands in those parts in the form written below.

[II] We have provided and in our wisdom ordained that the justice of Snowdon shall have the keeping and administration of our royal peace in Snowdon and our adjacent lands of Wales, and do justice to anyone whatsoever in accordance with royal original writs and with the underwritten laws and customs. We will also and ordain that there shall be sheriffs, coroners and commote-bailiffs in Snowdon and our lands of those parts; a sheriff of Anglesey, under whom shall be the whole land of Anglesey with its cantreds, metes and bounds; a sheriff of Carnarvon, under whom shall be the cantred of Arvan, the cantred of Arthlencoyth, the commote of Creuthin, the cantred of Lleyn and the commote of Yorionith; a sheriff of Merioneth, under whom shall be the cantred of Merioneth, the commote of Ardudwy, the commote of Penllyn and the commote of Edeyrnion with their metes and bounds. A sheriff of Flint, under whom shall be the cantred of Englefield, the land of Maelor Saesneg, the land of Hope and all the land attached to our castle and town of Rhuddlan, as far as the town of Chester, shall in future under us be subordinate to our justice of Chester and answer for the issues of that commote at our exchequer of Chester. There shall be coroners in those shires, to be chosen by a writ of the king, the tenor whereof will be found among the original writs of the chancery.[1] There shall also be commote-bailiffs, who shall faithfully perform and execute their offices and diligently conduct them as ordered by the justices and sheriffs. A sheriff of Carmarthen with its cantreds, commotes and ancient metes and bounds. A sheriff of Cardigan and Llampeter with its cantreds, commotes and metes and bounds. There are to be coroners in these shires and commote-bailiffs as before.

[III] The sheriff ought to execute his office in this manner, namely . . . And it should be known that a shire-court ought to be held in this way. . . .

[IV] The sheriff shall make his tourn twice a year in each of his commotes. . . . And the sheriff by the oath of twelve of the more discerning and law-worthy freeholders, or more at his discretion, shall make careful enquiry on the underwritten articles touching the crown of the lord king. . . .

[V] It is provided that in every commote in Wales there shall be at least one coroner, who, by the writ of the lord king in the form contained in the following roll among the other royal writs,[2] shall be chosen in the full shire-court. . . . And his office shall be. . . .

[VI] The forms of royal original writs to be pleaded in Wales

The writ of *novel disseisin* for a freehold. . . .

Novel disseisin for common of pasture . . . or for (nuisance). . . .

Writs of *mort d'ancestor*. . . .

[Then follow the necessary administrative writs for summoning and taking the above assizes.]

A general writ (precipe for disseisin, modelled on the *Praecipe quod reddat* for land, the form[3] for which is given) . . .

Writ of dower in Wales. . . .

Writ of debt. . . .

Writ of covenant. . . .

Writ of attorney. . . .

Writ for choosing a coroner. . . .

[VII] Of pleas, some have to be decided by assize, some by jury. To be decided by assize:

[Pleas of land moved by the writs of *novel disseisin* and *mort d'ancestor* and their variations listed in [VI]. Procedure on these possessory writs.]

[VIII–XI] To be decided by inquest or by jury:

[Pleas concerning title to land to be decided by jury "because pleas concerning land in those parts are not to be decided by battle nor by the Grand Assize".]

[Pleas concerning movables (for which the writ of debt in [VI] is provided). Procedure on the writ of debt.]

[1] cf. c. VI below
[2] c. VI below (the last of the writs there set forth)
[3] cf. Glanvill, I, 6 (ed. G. D. G. Hall, p. 5). Its general utility is indicated by the way Glanvill introduces the *Praecipe quod reddat* for land: "When anyone complains to the lord king or his justices concerning his fee or free tenement, and the case is such that it ought to be, or the lord king is willing that it should be, tried in the king's court, then the complainant shall have the following writ. . . ."

WALES
c. 1200
Leading Marcher families
MARSHAL
The Kingdoms of independent Wales
GWYNEDD
EARLDOM of CHESTER
Chester
MADOC
POWYS
GWENWYNWYN
Severn
Shrewsbury
MORTIMER
Wigmore
Radnor
BRAOSE
BRAOSE
Builth
Hereford
Cardigan
DEHEUBARTH
English Crown Lands
Brecon
BRAOSE
ABERGAVENNY
BRAOSE
PEMBROKE
Carmarthen
MARSHAL
To BRAOSE 1203
Usk
MARSHAL
Earl of GLOUCESTER's HEIRESS
GOWER
Strigoil
GLAMORGAN
Miles
0
50
0
Km
80
W.Bromage del.

CONQUERED WALES c. 1300
English Crown Lands
English Marcher families
LINCOLN
Welsh Marcher family
GRUFFUDD
POWYS: Over two generations the rulers of S. Powys had intermarried with Marcher neighbours. In any case they disliked subordination to Gwynedd. In the war of 1282-3 Gruffudd ap Gwenwynwyn sided with the English. His reward was to retain his lordship in all the rearrangements of 1284, surrendering his rights as a native Welsh ruler and becoming, like his neighbours, a Marcher baron.
ANGLESEY
Beaumaris
Conway
Denbigh
FLINT
Chester
EARLDOM of CHESTER
LINCOLN
Ruthin
Carnarvon
CARNARVONSHIRE
GREY
BROMFIELD & YALE
WARENNE
FLT
Criccieth
MERIONETHSHIRE
MORTIMER
Chirk
Harlech
SUCCESSORS OF GRUFFUDD AP GWENWYNWYN
SHROPSHIRE
Shrewsbury
Bere
POWYS
Severn
Montgomery
MORTIMER
MORTIMER
Richard's Castle
Radnor
Wigmore
CARDIGANSHIRE
BOHUN
Huntington
Builth
TONY
HEREFORDSHIRE
Cardigan
CARMARTHENSHIRE
Hay
Hereford
Brecon
HASTINGS BOHUN
Haverfordwest
Carmarthen
BOHUN
MORTIMER
Abergavenny
HASTINGS
VALENCE
BRAOSE
Pembroke
Usk
BIGOD
Strigoil
CLARE
GOWER
GLAMORGAN
Miles
0
50
0
Km
80
W.Bromage del.

425

[Pleas moved by the writ of covenant (which can be used for either movables or immovables). Procedure on the writ of covenant.]

[Pleas of personal trespass in which damages of over 40*s* are claimed. No writ is mentioned and none is given in [VI], although the writ of trespass existed by that time in England. The procedure to be employed.]

[XII] And because women have not hitherto had dower in Wales, the king grants that they shall have it. A woman's dower is of two kinds. One is the assignment of a third part of the whole of the land which was her husband's in his lifetime, for which is used the writ *de rationabile dote* mentioned elsewhere in its place with the other writs for Wales.[1] The procedure on this writ is this. . . . The other dower is when a son endows his wife with his father's consent: the form of the writ for this will be found with the others,[2] and the procedure with this writ is this. . . .

[XIII] Because the custom is otherwise in Wales than in England with regard to succession to an inheritance inasmuch as the inheritance is partible among the heirs male and has been partible from a time whereof the memory of man is not to the contrary, the lord king does not wish that custom to be abrogated but inheritances to remain partible among like heirs as used to be, and the partition of the inheritance shall be made as it used to be made; with this exception, that bastards shall not in future inherit and also shall not in future have purparties with the lawful heirs or without them. And if perchance from now on any inheritance for lack of heir male descends to females as lawful heirs of their ancestor last seised thereof, we will of our special grace that those law-worthy females shall have their purparties thereof assigned to them in our court, although this is contrary to Welsh custom used up to now.

[XIV] And because the Welsh have petitioned us to grant them that concerning their immovable property, for instance having to do with lands and tenements, the truth may be inquired into by good and law-worthy men of the neighbourhood chosen with the agreement of the parties; and concerning movables, having to do for instance with contracts, debts, the giving of surety, covenants, trespasses, chattels and all other movables of this sort, that they can use the Welsh law they have been accustomed to use – which was this, that if anyone complain about another concerning contracts or things done, in such a place that the plaintiff's case[3] can be proved by those who saw and heard, when by witnesses such as these, whose testimony cannot be refuted, the plaintiff has proved his case he should recover the thing sought and the opposite party be condemned; and in other things which cannot be proved by those who saw and heard, the defendant should be put to his purgation, sometimes with many [compurgators] sometimes with few, according to the nature and the gravity of the thing or the deed; and in the case of theft when the thing stolen is found in the hand, [the thief] cannot purge himself but shall be regarded as convicted – we for the general peace and quiet of our aforesaid people of our land of Wales grant them the aforesaid things, on this condition however that those things

[1] i.e. c. VI above
[2] the variant provided for in c. VI above
[3] *intentio querentis*

shall have no place in cases of theft, larceny, arson, murder, manslaughter or manifest and notorious robbery and shall not apply to them at all, in which things we will the laws of England to be used as is expressly stated above.

And for that reason we command you to observe strictly the aforementioned in all things from now on, on condition however that we can as often as and whensoever and wheresoever we like clarify, interpret, add to or take away from the aforesaid statutes and every part of them at our pleasure and as seems to us expedient for our security and that of our aforesaid land.

In witness of which thing our seal has been affixed to these presents. Given at Rhuddlan on Sunday in mid-Lent, in the twelfth year of our reign.

56. Provision for succession to the Scottish kingship, 1284

(*Acts of the Parliaments of Scotland*, i, 424, in translation of Dickinson, Donaldson and Milne, *A Source Book of Scottish History*, I (1952), pp. 33–4)

To all Christ's faithful to whom this writ shall come, Alexander Comyn, earl of Buchan, constable and justiciar of Scotland, Patrick earl of Dunbar, Malise earl of Strathearn, Malcolm earl of Lennox, Robert de Bruce, earl of Carrick, Donald earl of Mar, Gilbert earl of Angus, Walter earl of Menteith, William earl of Ross, William earl of Sutherland, Magnus earl of Orkney, Duncan earl of Fife, John earl of Athole, Robert de Bruce, father, James, steward of Scotland, John de Balliol, John Comyn, William de Soulis, then justiciar of Lothian, Ingerram de Gynis, William de Moray, son of Walter de Moray, knights, Alexander de Balliol, Reginald le Chen, father, William de Sancto Claro, Richard Syward, William de Brechin, Nicholas de Hay, Henry de Graham, Ingerram de Balliol, Alan son of the earl, Reginald le Chen, son, J. [ ] de Lindesey, Patrick de Graham, [tus] de Maxwell, Simon Fraser, Alexander de Argyle, Angus son of Donald and Alan son of Roderick, barons of the realm of Scotland, greeting in the Lord.

Know ye that, since it has pleased the Most High that our lord Alexander eldest son of [king] Alexander has gone the way of all flesh with no legitimate offspring surviving directly from the body of the said king, we bind ourselves and our heirs completely by this document to our lord king and the heirs descended from his body directly or indirectly who by right ought to be admitted to the succession and in the faith and fealty by which we are bound to them we firmly and faithfully promise that if our said lord king happens to end his last day in this life leaving no legitimate son or sons, daughter or daughters of his body or of the body of the said Alexander his son, we each and all of us will accept the illustrious girl Margaret, daughter of our lord king's daughter Margaret, of good memory, late queen of Norway, begotten of the lord Eric, illustrious king of Norway, and legitimate offspring descended from her, as our lady and right heir of our said lord king of Scotland, of the whole realm of Scotland, of the Isle of Man and of all other islands belonging to the said kingdom of Scotland, and also of Tyndale and Penrith with all other rights and liberties belonging or of right belonging to the said lord king of Scotland . . . and against all men . . . we shall maintain, sustain and defend [her] with all our strength and power.

57. Statute of Westminster II (13 Edw. I), Easter 1285

(*Statutes of the Realm*, I (Rec. Com., 1810), pp. 71–95; and H. F. Berry, *Statute Rolls of the Parliament of Ireland* (Irish Rec. Office series of early statutes), I (1907), pp. 104–76)

I am indebted to my friend, Professor G. J. Hand, dean of the faculty of law of University College, Dublin, for xerox copies of the pages of Berry, a rare volume now, for actual collaboration on a number of clauses as well as for advice generally: though, of course, I alone am responsible for any errors.

Whereas not long ago the lord king, a fortnight after the feast of St John the Baptist in the sixth year of his reign, summoned to Gloucester the prelates, earls and barons, and his council, because many of his kingdom were suffering disinheritance, for in many cases where a remedy ought to have been applied none had been provided by his predecessors or himself, and issued certain statutes, very necessary and useful for his people, through which his people, English and Irish, subject to his rule, have obtained, in their tribulations, swifter justice than before; and yet certain cases, in which the law was inadequate, remained undetermined, and also some things remained to be enacted in order to restrain the oppression of the people; the lord king, in his parliament held at Westminster after Easter in the thirteenth year of his reign, to supplement the aforesaid statutes issued at Gloucester, caused many oppressions of the people and defects of the law to be recited, and issued statutes, as shall appear in the following.

[c. 1] First,[1] concerning tenements which are often given upon condition, that is, when someone gives his land to some man and his wife and the heirs begotten of the same man and woman with the added condition expressed that, if the man and woman should die without heir begotten of them, the land so given should revert to the donor or his heir; also in the case when someone gives a tenement in frank marriage, which gift has a condition attached, though it is not expressed in the deed of gift, which is, that if the man and woman should die without heir begotten of them, the tenement so given should revert to the donor or his heir; also in the case when someone gives a tenement to somebody and to the heirs issuing of his body: it seemed, and still seems, hard to such donors and heirs of donors that their wish expressed in their gifts has not heretofore been observed and still is not observed. For in all these cases, after offspring begotten and issuing from those to whom the tenement was thus conditionally given, these feoffees have hitherto had power to alienate the tenement so given and to disinherit their own issue contrary to the wish of the donors and the form expressed in the gift. And further, when on the failure of the issue of such feoffees the tenement so given ought to have reverted to the donor or his heirs by the form expressed in the deed of such a gift, notwithstanding the issue, if any there were, had died, they [the donors] have heretofore been barred from the reversion of the tenements by the deed and feoffment of those to whom the tenements were thus given upon condition, which was manifestly against the form of their gift. WHEREFORE the lord king, perceiving that it is necessary and useful to provide a remedy in the aforesaid cases, has enacted that the wish of the donor, according to the form manifestly expressed in his deed of gift, is henceforth to be observed, in such wise that those to whom the tenement was thus given upon condition shall not have the power of alienating the

[1] This clause is the famous *De donis conditionalibus*, often cited as if it were a separate statute.

tenement so given and thereby preventing it from[1] remaining after their death to their issue, or to the donor or his heir if issue fail either because there was no issue at all or because if there was issue it has failed by death, the heir of such issue failing. Neither shall, henceforth, the second husband of such[2] woman have anything by the curtesy[3] after the death of his wife in a tenement so given upon condition, or the issue of the woman and second husband have hereditary succession, but instead immediately after the death of the man and woman to whom the tenement was so given, it shall revert after their death either to their issue or to the donor or his heir as is aforesaid. And because in a new case a new remedy must be provided, the following writ is to be made as required: Command A. to render to B. justly etc. such and such a manor with appurtenances which C. gave to such and such a man and such and such a woman and the heirs of the bodies of that man and woman

or which C. gave to such and such a man in frank marriage with such and such a woman and which after the death of the aforesaid man and woman ought, by the form of the aforesaid gift, as he says, to descend to the aforesaid B., the son of the aforesaid man and woman

or which C. gave to so and so and the heirs of his body and which after the death of the same so and so ought by the form etc. to descend to the aforesaid B., the son of the aforesaid so and so.

The writ whereby the donor has his recovery when issue fails is in common use in the chancery. And it is to be understood that this statute applies to the alienation of a tenement contrary to the form of a gift made after this, and does not extend to gifts made before it. And if a fine[4] is levied hereafter on such a tenement, it is not to be legally binding, and the heirs or they to whom the reversion belongs will not be bound to lay their claim even if they are of full age, within England, and not in prison.

[c. 2] Because lords of fees who distrain their tenants for services due to them are frequently aggrieved in that their tenants replevy their distress with or without a writ, and then when the lords come by attachment on the complaint of their tenants to the county court, or to some other court having power to hold pleas of *vee de naam*, and avow the distraint as reasonable and lawful, the tenants disavow holding or claiming to hold anything of him who took the distress and avowed it, so that he who distrained is in mercy and his tenants go quit and no punishment can be inflicted on them[5] for such disavowal by record of the county or of other courts which do not have record, it is provided and enacted that henceforth as lords cannot obtain justice in county court or in such courts against tenants of theirs of this kind, as soon as they are attached at the suit of their tenants a writ shall be granted to them to bring the action before the justices, before whom and nowhere else can justice be done to such

[1] *quominus*

[2] Obviously means the wife in the joint estates already mentioned. Plucknett's inference from "such" (*Legislation of Edward I*, (1949), p. 132) seems questionable.

[3] A second husband normally had this right. Plucknett, *Legislation of Edward I* (1949), p. 118, n. 1, and the authorities there referred to.

[4] i.e. a final concord – for which see Pollock and Maitland, *History of English Law*, II, pp. 94–105; and for the bar which this sentence says shall not apply to heirs in tail, op. cit. p. 101.

[5] This is explained by Plucknett, *Legislation of Edward I*, pp. 61–2.

lords. And in the writ is to be inserted the clause "Because so and so distrained in his fee for services and customs due to him". Nor by this statute is the ordinary usage of the law, which has not allowed any plea to be brought before the justices at the petition of the defendant, infringed; for though at first sight the tenant seems to be the one who is bringing the action and the lord the defendant, yet having regard to the fact that the lord is distraining and suing for services and customs due to him which are in arrears, he will appear to be rather the bringer of the action or plaintiff than the defendant. And that the justices may be certain on how recent a seisin lords can avow reasonable distraint upon their tenants, it is agreed that henceforth reasonable distraint can be avowed on a seisin of their ancestors or predecessors from the time from which the writ of *novel disseisin* runs. And because it sometimes happens that the tenant, after he has replevied his beasts, sells or eloigns them so that their return to the distraining lord, if that is adjudged, cannot be effected, it is provided that sheriffs or bailiffs are not henceforth to receive from the plaintiffs merely pledges to prosecute the suit but also to return the beasts, if judgment is given for their return, before handing the beasts over. And if anyone accepts pledges in any other form, he is to answer for the value of the beasts and the distraining lord is to have his recovery by a writ, "that he render to him such and such a number of beasts or chattels to that amount", and if the bailiff has not the means to make restitution, his superior is to make it. And because it sometimes happens that the party so distrained, after the return of the beasts to the distrainor has been adjudged and the beasts accordingly returned, replevies them again and when he sees the distrainor appearing in court ready to answer him, makes default; on which account return of the beasts to the distrainor will again be adjudged and thus the beasts will be replevied a second time, a third time, and so on indefinitely and in this case the judgments of the king's court will have no effect, and because no remedy has yet been provided for this, the following procedure is ordained in this case: that as soon as return of the beasts to the distrainor has been adjudged, the sheriff is to be ordered by a judicial writ to have the beasts returned to the distrainor; in which writ it is to be stated that the sheriff shall not hand them over without a further judicial writ in which mention is made of the judgment given by the justices, and this cannot be done except by writ issuing from the rolls of the justices before whom the action was brought. When therefore the distrained party comes to the justices and asks for his beasts to be again replevied, let this judicial writ be made for him: that the sheriff, exacting surety to prosecute and also to return the beasts or chattels or their value if judgment for return is given, is to hand over to him the beasts or chattels previously returned and let him who distrained be attached to appear on a certain day before the justices before whom the plea is to be brought in the presence of the parties. And if he who has made the replevin makes default again or if for any other reason return of the distress, by now twice replevied, is adjudged, that distress is to remain forever irrepleviable. But if a fresh distraint is made for a fresh reason, the above-mentioned procedure is to be observed with regard to the new distress.

[c. 3] In cases where the husband lost by default a tenement which was the right of his wife, it was hard that the wife after the death of her husband had no recovery other than by a writ of Right: wherefore the lord king has ordained that a woman after the death of her husband may have recovery by a writ of Entry *cui ipsa in vita sua contradicere non potuit,*[1] which shall be pleaded in the following[2] way, namely, if the tenant excepts to the woman's claim on the ground that he had entry by judgment, and it be found that it was upon default (which the tenant must needs disclose if it be demanded of him), he must then further show his right according to the form of the writ which he first sued out against the husband and wife. And if he can prove that he has right in the tenement claimed, the woman shall take nothing by her writ; and if he cannot prove it, the woman shall recover the tenement claimed; this being observed that if a husband absent himself and refuse to defend his wife's right or wish to surrender it against his wife's will, if the wife come before judgment ready to answer the demandant and to defend her right, she is to be admitted. Likewise if a tenant in dower, by the law of England, or otherwise for term of life, or by gift wherein reversion is reserved, make default or wish to surrender, the heirs and those to whom the reversion belongs are, if they come before judgment, to be admitted to answer. And if judgment has been given upon default or surrender, then the heirs and those to whom the reversion belongs after the death of such tenants shall have recovery by a writ of Entry in which the same process shall be observed as is said above in the case of the husband losing by default his wife's tenement. Thus in the cases aforesaid two actions concur, one between the demandant and tenant, and the other between the tenant showing his right and the demandant.

[c. 4] In the case where a husband impleaded concerning a tenement surrenders the tenement demanded to his adversary, clearly after the husband's death the justices award the wife her dower if she claims it by writ; but in the case where the husband loses the tenement demanded by default and the wife after the death of her husband claims dower, it is found that by some justices dower is adjudged to her notwithstanding the default which her husband committed, while other justices are of the contrary opinion and adjudge the contrary. To do away henceforth with such uncertainty, it is ordained for certain that a woman claiming her dower shall in both cases be heard. And if it is excepted against her that her husband lost by judgment the tenement whereof the dower is demanded, for which reason she ought not to have dower, and it is asked by what judgment and it be found that it was by default (which the tenant must needs disclose), it then behoves the tenant to answer further and show that he had and has right in the aforesaid tenement according to the form of the writ which he first sued out against the husband. And if he can show that the woman's husband had not right in the tenement, nor anyone other than he the holder, then let him go quit and the wife recover nothing of her dower; and if he cannot show this, the wife shall recover her dower.

And so in these cases and in certain others following, that is to say, when the wife being endowed loses her dower by default, and tenants in marriage, by the law of England, or for term of life or in fee tail, a number of actions concur; for such tenants, when they have to claim their tenements lost by default and the point is reached that

[1] "whom during his life could not gainsay" or, more briefly, *cui in vita* "whom in life"
[2] To "*predicta*" I have preferred the reading "*subscripta*", for which there is MS. authority.

the tenant is compelled to show his right, they cannot make answer without those to whom the reversion of right belongs and are therefore allowed to vouch to warranty as if they were tenants, if they have a warranty. And when the warrantor has warranted, the plea shall proceed between him who is seised and the warrantor according to the tenor of the writ that the tenant first sued out and by which he recovered by default; and so from a number of actions in the end one judgment is arrived at, which is, that such demandants shall recover what they are claiming or that the tenants shall go quit. And if the action of such a tenant, who is compelled to show his right, is brought by a writ of Right, although the Grand Assize or battle cannot be joined by the usual words they can however be joined by words suitable, for since the tenants, in that they are showing their right which belongs to them by the writ they first sued out, are thus in the position of plaintiff, the warrantor may well defend the right of the tenant, who as said is held to be in the position of demandant, and offer to defend the seisin of his ancestor by the body of his freeman or put himself on the Grand Assize and ask for a recognition to be made to determine whether he has the greater right in the disputed tenement, or the aforesaid so-and-so; or the Grand Assize may be joined in another way, thus "So-and-so, the warrantor, defends the right etc. and acknowledges the seisin of his ancestor and puts himself on the Grand Assize and asks for a recognition to be made whether he has the greater right in the tenement aforesaid as in that whereof he enfeoffed such a man or that which such a man released and quitclaimed etc., or the aforesaid so-and-so has".

As it sometimes happens that a woman not having right to demand dower obtains while the heir is under age a writ of dower against the guardian and the guardian assigns the woman dower by favour or makes default or by collusion defends the plea so faintly[1] that the dower is adjudged to the woman to the heir's prejudice: it is provided that when he comes of age the heir shall have against such woman the action of demanding the seisin of his ancestor which he would have against any other deforciant; yet so that there be saved to the woman her exception against the demandant of showing that she has right to her dower and if she can show it she may go quit and retain her dower and the heir be in mercy and be amerced heavily at the direction of the justices, and if not the heir may recover his demand.

In like manner let the woman be protected if the heir or any other implead her for her dower if she lose her dower by default, in which case her default shall not be so prejudicial to her that she cannot recover her dower if she has right, and she may have this writ, "Command A. to render justly etc. to so-and-so, who was the wife of so-and-so, so much land with appurtenances in such-and-such vill, which she claims as her reasonable dower, or as part of her reasonable dower, and which the aforesaid so-and-so is withholding from her by force".[2] And to this writ let the tenant have his exception showing that she has no right in the dower, and if he can prove it let him go quit; otherwise the woman shall recover the tenement which before she had in dower.

And whereas in times gone by anyone who had lost his land by default had no

[1] *ficte*

[2] the statutory (as distinct from common-law) writ *Quod ei deforciat*, on which, see T. F. T. Plucknett, *Legislation of Edward I*, p. 124; and Fitzherbert, *New natura brevium* (London, 1666), pp. 17 and 377

other recovery than by a writ of Right, which was not appropriate for those who could not claim absolute right (such as tenants for term of life, in frank marriage, or in fee-tail, in which cases a reversion is reserved) it is provided that henceforth their default shall not be so prejudicial to them that they cannot have recovery of their estate, if they have right, by another writ[1] than by writ of Right. For land in frank marriage lost by default, let such a writ be made: "Command A. to render to B. justly etc. such-and-such manor with appurtenances, which he claims is his right and his marriage and which the aforesaid A. is unjustly withholding from him". Likewise, for a tenement held for term of life lost by default let there be made the writ "Command so-and-so to render to so-and-so justly etc. the manor etc. which he claims to hold for the term of his life and which so-and-so is unjustly etc." Similarly [for the tenant in fee-tail with the variant[2]] "which he claims to hold to himself and the heirs of his body and which so-and-so is unjustly etc."

[c. 5] Whereas concerning advowsons of churches there are only three original writs, that is to say the writ of Right and two of possession, namely, *darrein presentment* and *quare impedit*, and hitherto it has been used in the realm that when anyone having no right to present presented to any church and the one so presented was admitted, he who is the true patron could recover his advowson by no other writ than by a writ of Right, which had to be determined by judicial combat or by the Grand Assize and by this heirs under age, by the fraud and negligence of their guardians, heirs too, whether of full age or under age, by the negligence or fraud of tenants by the law of England or of women tenants in dower or otherwise for term of life or for years or in fee-tail, were often disinherited of their advowsons or at least, which was better for them, were compelled to resort to a writ of Right (and in that case hitherto were utterly disinherited): it is provided that such presentations shall not be so prejudicial to such rightful heirs, or to those to whom such advowsons ought to revert after the death of any persons, that they cannot, as often soever as anyone having no right presents during such wardships or during tenancies in dower or by the law of England or otherwise for term of life or of years or in fee-tail, have[3] at the next vacancy after the heir has come of age or when after the death of tenants of the sort aforesaid[4] the advowson reverts to the heir of full age, like action and exception by a possessory writ of advowson to that which the last ancestor of such heir would, being of full age, have had at the last vacancy in his time arising before his death or before demise[5] was made for term [of life or of years[6]] or in fee-tail as aforesaid. The same shall be observed of presentations made to churches belonging to the inheritance of wives while they were under the power of their husbands: they shall be helped by this statute by the aforesaid remedy. Men of religion, bishops, archdeacons, rectors of churches and other ecclesiastical persons shall be helped, too, by that same statute if anyone having

[1] the following variants of the writ *Quod ei deforciat*
[2] This is the significance of "*vel*" in *Statutes of the Realm*, I, p. 75; and "*similiter*" in H. F. Berry, *Statutes . . . of Ireland* (Dublin, 1907), p. 116.
[3] *habeat* (*Stat. Realm*, I, p. 76; and Berry, *Statutes . . . of Ireland*, I, p. 118, alike) emended to *habeant*
[4] literally, "after the death of those holding in the aforesaid manner"
[5] demise made: i.e. before a tenancy was created. On the technical difficulty of finding a special verb for the act of creating these tenancies, see Pollock and Maitland, *History of English Law*, II, p. 114.
[6] supplied, because evident from the context that both term of life and term of years are to be understood

no right to present presents to churches belonging to their houses, prelacy, dignity or parsonage during a vacancy in such prelacies, dignities or parsonages.

This statute shall not, however, be so largely understood that persons for whose remedy it was ordained may have their aforesaid recovery by asserting that guardians, tenants in dower, by the law of England, or otherwise for term of life or years, or husbands, have defended faintly the plea begun by them or against them, because judgments given in the king's court are not annulled by this statute, instead a judgment shall stand valid until it is annulled by the king's court as erroneous if error is found. Nor shall an assize of *darrein presentment* or an inquest by writ of *quare impedit*, if completed, be annulled by attaint or certification, which may be freely granted. And henceforth one form of pleading shall be observed among justices in writs of *darrein presentment* and *quare impedit* in this respect: if the defending party excepts the plenarty of the church by reason of his own presentation, the action shall not be stayed because of that plenarty provided the writ is obtained within six months although the presentation cannot be recovered within the six months. And whereas sometimes an agreement is made between several claimants to the advowson of a church and recorded[1] before justices in the roll or in a fine, in the form that one party shall present the first time and at the next vacancy another, at the third a third, and so on for as many as there are, but when one has presented and obtained the presentation due to him by the terms of the agreement, at the next vacancy he to whom the following presentation belongs is hindered by any party to the agreement or someone for him, it is provided that henceforth the one so hindered shall have no need to acquire a writ of *quare impedit*, but have recourse to the roll or to the fine, and if the aforesaid agreement or concord is found on the roll or in a fine word shall be sent to the sheriff to notify the hinderer to be ready at an early date within the next fortnight or three weeks, as the place is near or far, to show if he can say why so-and-so should not have his presentation. And if he does not come, or perhaps comes but cannot say why the one who is thus hindered should not – because of something done after the enrolling of or the making of a chirograph of the agreement – have his presentation, the latter shall recover his presentation with his damages. And where it happens that after the death of the ancestor who presented to a church the advowson of it has been assigned in the dower of any woman or is held by the law of England and those holding in dower or by the law of England have presented and, after the death of such tenants by the law of England or in dower, the true heir is hindered in presenting when the church falls vacant, it is provided that henceforth it shall be for him who is hindered to choose whether he wishes to sue by the writ of *quare impedit* or of *darrein presentment*. This is to apply also in the case of advowsons demised for term of life, or years, or in fee-tail. And henceforth damages shall be awarded in writs of *darrein presentment* and *quare impedit*, namely, if six months go by because of hindrance by anybody with the result that the bishop collates to the church and the true patron loses his presentation on that occasion, damages shall be awarded equivalent to two years value of the church; and if six months[2] have not elapsed but the right to present is established[3]

[1] *inrotulata*
[2] *si tempus*
[3] *disrationetur* (deraigned)

within that time, then damages equivalent to half a year's value of the church shall be awarded. And if the hinderer has not the means to pay the damages in the case where the bishop collates by lapse of time, he shall be punished by imprisonment for two years; and if the right to the advowson is established within the six months, the hinderer shall be punished by imprisonment for half a year. And henceforth writs are to be granted for chapels, prebends, vicarages, hospitals, abbeys, priories and other houses whose advowson is someone else's which before used not to be granted. And when by a writ of *Indicavit* the rector of any church is hindered in demanding tithes in a neighbouring parish, the patron of the rector so hindered shall have the writ[1] for claiming the advowson of the tithes demanded and when he has proved his right the plea shall proceed afterwards in the ecclesiastical court in accordance with what has been decided in the court of the king. When an advowson descends to parceners, although one presents twice and encroaches upon the coheir, he that was negligent shall not on this account be wholly excluded, but at another time, when it happens, he shall have his turn to present.

[c. 6] When anyone demands a tenement from another and the one sued vouches to warranty and the warrantor denies the warranty and the plea is held up a long time between the tenant and the warrantor, when it is at last proved incontestably that he who was vouched to warranty is bound to warrant, there was by the law and custom hitherto used no other punishment inflicted on the vouchee who refused to warrant save that he should warrant and be amerced because he did not warrant before, a thing which was hard on the demandant, who by collusion between the tenant and the warrantor often suffered great delays: on which account the lord the king has ordained that, just as the tenant should lose the tenement demanded if he vouched to warranty and the warrantor is able to rid himself of the warranty, the warrantor shall lose in the same way[2] if he denies the warranty and it is proved incontestably that he is bound to warrant. And if an inquest is pending between the tenant and the warrantor and the demandant asks for a writ to summon the jury, it shall be granted to him.

[c. 7] The writ for Measuring dower shall henceforth be granted to a guardian; but the heir shall not be barred by the guardian's suit from measuring the dower as it ought to be measured by the law of the land when he comes of age if the guardian takes proceedings against the woman tenant in dower faintly[3] and collusively. And as well in this writ as in the writ for Measuring pasture there shall in future be a speedier procedure than before, so that, when it comes to the great distress, days shall be given within which two counties may be held at which public proclamation shall be made that the defendant shall come on the day contained in the writ to answer the plaintiff: on which day, if he comes, the plea between them shall proceed, and if he does not come and proclamation in the manner aforesaid is witnessed to by the sheriff, let them because of the default proceed to the measuring.

[c. 8] Since, by a plea instituted upon a writ of Admeasurement of pasture, pasture is measured sometimes before the justices, sometimes in the county before the sheriff,

[1] i.e. the writ of Right of advowson of tithes
[2] i.e. lose the tenement to the demandant
[3] *ficte*

and it often happens that after such measuring he who overloaded the pasture before again puts more cattle on it than is appropriate for him to have and up to now no remedy has been provided: it is ordained that for the second overloading remedy shall be provided for the plaintiff in this manner – If the pasture was measured before the justices, the plaintiff shall have a judicial writ that the sheriff shall, in the presence of the parties if they have been forewarned and wish to be present, inquire into the second overloading and if the finding is that it in fact occurred,[1] this shall be returned to the justices under the sheriff's seal and the seals of the jurors; and the justices shall award the plaintiff damages and put in the estreats the value of the animals which after the measurement was made the overloader put in the pasture beyond what he ought to have done, and deliver the estreats to the barons of the exchequer for them to be answerable to the lord king for the animals.[2] If the pasture was measured in the county, then, at the request of the plaintiff, a writ shall issue out of chancery for the sheriff to inquire into such overloading, and for the cattle put in the pasture beyond the due number, or for their value, he shall be answerable to the lord king at the exchequer. And lest sheriffs defraud the lord king in this respect, it is agreed that all such writs of Overloading a second time[3] that issue out of chancery shall be enrolled and at the end of the year a transcript sent to the exchequer under the seal of the chancery for the treasurer and barons of the exchequer to see how the sheriffs answer for the issues of such writs. In the same way writs of redisseisin shall be enrolled and sent to the exchequer at the end of the year.

[c. 9] When chief lords distrain on their fee for services and customs due to them and there is a mesne who ought to acquit the tenant (since it lies not in the mouth of the tenant after he has replevied the first distress to deny the demand of the chief lord who maintains in the court of the lord king that the distraint is lawfully levied upon his tenant, that is upon the mesne tenant) many have hitherto been oppressed by such distraints, inasmuch as the mesne tenant, although he had the means by which to be distrained, made great delays before coming to court to answer his tenants on a writ of mesne, inasmuch also as it was hard when the mesne tenant had nothing, when also, if the tenant was ready to render to the chief lord the services and customs demanded, the chief lord refused to accept the services and customs due to him at the hands of any other than his nearest tenant and so such tenants in demesne lost the profit of their lands sometimes for a time, sometimes for the rest of their days, and up to now no remedy has been provided for this. There is for the future a remedy for this ordained and provided in this form. As soon as such a tenant in demesne with a mesne tenant between him and the chief lord is distrained he shall at once get himself a writ of mesne. And if the mesne tenant has land in the county but absents himself until the great distress, such day shall be given to the plaintiff in his writ of great distress that two counties can be held before it and the sheriff shall be ordered to distrain the mesne by the great distress as contained in the writ. And nevertheless the sheriff shall have it solemnly proclaimed in two full counties that such mesne shall come on the day contained in the writ to answer his tenant. If he comes on that

[1] *si inventa fuerit*
[2] *inde*
[3] *De secunda superoneratione*

day, the plea shall proceed between them in the usual way; if he does not come, the mesne shall lose his tenant's service, the tenant from then on not being responsible to him for anything, but, leaving out the mesne tenant, being responsible to the chief lord for the same services that previously the said mesne[1] had to perform. Nor shall the chief lord have power to distrain, so long as the said tenant offers him the services due and accustomed. And if the chief lord exacts more than the mesne ought to render to him, the tenant shall in that case have the exception the mesne would have. If however the mesne tenant has nothing within the king's jurisdiction, the tenant may obtain his writ of mesne to the sheriff of the county in which he is distrained all the same; and, if the sheriff sends word that the mesne tenant has nothing he can be summoned by, let him, notwithstanding, sue out a writ of attachment. And if the sheriff returns that he has nothing he can be attached by, let him, nevertheless, sue out a writ of great distress and let proclamation be made in the way aforesaid. If however the mesne tenant has no land in the county in which the distress is taken but has land in another county, then an original writ shall issue to the sheriff of the county in which the distress is taken to summon him, and when it has been testified by that sheriff that the mesne has nothing in his county, a judicial writ to summon him shall issue to the sheriff of the county in which it is testified that he has a tenement and let suit be made in that county and proceed as far as the great distress and proclamation as prescribed above in the case of a mesne who has land in the county in which the distress is levied, and let suit be made nevertheless in the county in which he has nothing, as prescribed above about a mesne with nothing, and proceed as far as the great distress and proclamation; and so after proclamation in both counties the mesne shall be adjudged deprived of his fee and service. As it sometimes happens that the tenant in demesne is enfeoffed to hold by less service than the mesne tenant had to do to the chief lord, when after such proclamation the tenant has been turned over to the chief lord, to the exclusion of the mesne tenant, the tenant shall be bound to answer to the chief lord for the services and customs which previously the mesne had to render to him. And after the mesne tenant has come into court and admitted, or it is adjudged, that he ought to acquit him, if after such admission or judgment there is complaint that the mesne is not acquitting the tenant, then a judicial writ shall issue that the sheriff distrain the mesne to acquit the tenant and to appear before the justices on a certain day to show why he did not acquit him sooner. And when because of the distress he does appear, the plaintiff shall be heard, and if the plaintiff can prove that he has not acquitted him he shall compensate for damages and the tenant shall by judgment of the court be quit of the mesne and be turned over to the chief lord. And if on this first distress he does not appear, let a writ issue for another distress and let proclamation be made. And after it has been testified, the court shall proceed to judgment as said above. And it is to be understood that by this statute tenants, if they are impleaded concerning their tenements, are not precluded from producing in court the warranty of their mesnes and the heirs of these as they did before. Nor are tenants precluded either from being able to institute proceedings

[1] *predicto medio: Statutes of the Realm*, I, p. 79, and Berry, *Statutes . . . of Ireland*, I, p. 128, alike; but I have here adopted T. F. T. Plucknett's emendation in *Legislation of Edward I*, p. 93

against their mesnes as used to be the custom, if they see that their action is more likely to be successful by the old custom than by this statute. And it is to be understood that by this statute no remedy is provided for any mesne tenant whatsoever but solely for the case where there is one mesne only between the lord who is distraining and the tenant, where that mesne is of full age, and where the tenant can turn himself over to the chief lord without prejudice to anyone other than the mesne, which is said for the benefit of women holding in dower, tenants by the law of England or otherwise for term of life or in fee-tail, for whom for certain reasons remedy is not yet provided, but, God permitting, shall be at another time.

[c. 10] When in the eyre it is proclaimed that all who wish to deliver writs should deliver them within a certain time, after which no writ will be received, many relying on this, when they have waited until that time and no writ has been served upon them, withdraw by licence of the justices and after their departure their adversaries perceiving their absence deliver their writs late[1] and these are accepted by the sheriff sometimes as a favour to them, sometimes in return for a gift, and they who thought they had left safely lose their tenements. To remedy such fraud hereafter, the lord king has ordained that justices in their eyres shall fix a period of a fortnight or a month, the shorter or the longer period according to the size of the county, within which, it shall be publicly proclaimed, all who wish to deliver writs shall deliver them and at the end of it the sheriff shall inform the senior[2] justices of the eyre of how many writs he has, and which; and that after that no writ shall be accepted and if it is accepted the proceedings begun by it shall be deemed invalid, except that a writ abated can be revalidated at any time during the whole circuit,[3] also writs of dower concerning men who die after the summons of the eyre, assizes of *darrein presentment* and *quare impedit* concerning churches falling vacant after the aforesaid summons may be accepted any time before the departure of the justices. Writs too of *novel disseisin*, at whatever time the disseisin was done, may be accepted.

In eyres the lord king as an act of special grace grants that those who have tenements in different counties in which the justices go on eyre, or are afraid of being impleaded concerning certain tenements in counties in which the justices go on eyre, and are impleaded concerning other tenements in counties in which the justices are not going on eyre before the justices at Westminster or in the king's bench or before justices assigned to take assizes or in any county before the sheriff or in any court baron, can appoint a general attorney to sue for them in the eyre in all pleas moved or to be moved for them or against them during the eyre, which attorney or attornies shall have authority in pleas moved in the eyre until a plea is finished or his principal removes him. Not that by this they are to be excused[4] from being on juries or assizes before the same justices.

[c. 11] On serjeants, bailiffs, chamberlains and all manner of receivers who are obliged

[1] *in cera* ("with seal unbroken") *Statutes of the Realm*, I, p. 80, and Berry, *Statutes . . . of Ireland*, I, p. 130, alike; but almost certainly a corruption of *in cero* (*sero*) ("at a late hour").

[2] *capitalem*

[3] *durante toto itinere releuari*

[4] *nec per hoc excusentur:* the proper punctuation is uncertain, but I have taken the antecedent of "they" to be the principals not the attornies and this is the sense in which the author of *Fleta* (II, ed. Richardson and Sayles, Selden Soc., vol. 72 (1953), p. 104) took it.

to render account, it is with one consent ordained and established that when the master of such servants appoints auditors of their accounts and it happens that they are in arrears on their account, they shall be arrested and on the testimony of the auditors of the account sent and delivered to the nearest gaol of the lord king in those parts and be received by the sheriff or the keeper of the gaol and committed to prison in irons and in good custody and remain in that prison living at their own expense until they have rendered full satisfaction to their masters for the arrears. If however anyone thus delivered to gaol complains that the auditors of the account have burdened him unjustly by debiting him with receipts which he did not receive or by not allowing expenses or reasonable disbursements, and finds friends willing to undertake to bring him,[1] let him be handed over to them. And the sheriff in whose power he has been shall instruct[2] the master to be before the barons of the exchequer on some appointed day with the rolls and tallies by which he[3] rendered account, and in the presence of the barons, or auditors whom it is their will to appoint, the account is to be gone through again and justice done between the parties so that, if he is in arrears, he be committed to the Fleet gaol as said above; and if he should flee and not be willing to render account voluntarily, he is to be distrained as is contained elsewhere in other statutes to come before the justices to render account if he has anything he can be distrained by. And if he comes to court, auditors of account shall be appointed before whom, if he is in arrears and if he cannot pay the arrears immediately, he shall be committed to gaol for custody in the manner aforesaid; and if he should flee and it is testified by the sheriff that he is not to be found, he is to be exacted[4] from county to county[5] until he is outlawed and such a prisoner[6] shall not be repleviable.[7] And the sheriff or keeper of the gaol, whether it is in a liberty or not, shall take care not to let him out of prison on the common writ called Replevin[8] or by other means without the assent of his master; and if he does and is found guilty of this, he shall be answerable to the master for the damage done to him by such servant as established by a jury and may have his recovery by a writ of debt. And if the keeper of the gaol has not the means by which he can be distrained[9] or with which to pay, his superior who entrusted the keeping of the gaol to him shall be answerable by the same writ.

[c. 12] As many, wishing out of malice to injure others, cause false accusations of homicide and other felonies to be made by accusers who have nothing with which to satisfy the king for the false accusation or pay damages to those accused, it is ordained that when anyone so accused has in due manner acquitted himself in the king's court of the felony attributed to him, the justices before whom such accusation has been heard and determined shall, at the suit of either the person accused or the king,

[1] common form: before a court (in this case before the barons of the exchequer) being understood.
[2] *scire faciat*
[3] i.e. the servant
[4] i.e. solemnly called on to appear
[5] Not county by county, but meetings of the county court. If he failed to appear after four successive meetings, he would be outlawed at the fifth.
[6] The assumption is that the threat of outlawry will cause him to appear. By the thirteenth century outlawry had (in Maitland's words) "lost its exterminating character and had become an engine for compelling the contumacious to abide the judgment of the courts" (Pollock and Maitland, *History of English Law*, II, p.449).
[7] i.e. cannot be released even if men can be found who are willing to go surety for his appearance in court.
[8] *replegiari* [9] *justicietur*

punish the accuser with imprisonment for a year and such accusers shall nonetheless make good to the accused their damages as decided by the justices, having regard to the imprisonment or arrest the accused sustained by reason of such accusations and to the ill-fame they incurred by imprisonment or otherwise, and shall nonetheless as regards the lord king be obliged to make grievous fine.[1] And if perchance such accusers have not the wherewithal to make good the said damages, enquiry, if the accused desires it, shall be made on the oath of good and law-worthy men at whose instigation such malicious accusation was framed. And if it is found by that inquest that someone was the instigator out of malice, he shall, by a judicial writ at the suit of the one accused, be distrained to appear before the justices; and if he is lawfully convicted of such malicious abetment he shall be punished by imprisonment and be bound to make restitution of damages as said above concerning the accuser. And in future no essoin shall lie for[2] the accuser in an accusation of homicide, in whatever court the accusation is to be determined.

[c. 13] As sheriffs, pretending that certain persons have been indicted before them in their tourns of thefts and other evil deeds, often arrest men who are not guilty and not lawfully indicted, and imprison them and extort money from them when they were not lawfully indicted by twelve jurors, it is ordained that sheriffs, in their tourns and elsewhere when they have to make enquiries about wrongdoers by the lord king's precept or in virtue of their office, shall make their enquiries about such wrongdoers by at the least twelve law-worthy men, who shall put their seals to those inquests, and shall arrest and imprison those whom through such inquests they find are guilty, as used aforetimes to be done. And if they imprison any other than those indicted by such inquests, such imprisoned shall have their action by writ of imprisonment against the sheriffs as they would have against any other person whatsoever who imprisoned them without warrant; and what has been said of sheriffs shall apply to any bailiff of a liberty.

[c. 14] As for waste committed in anybody's inheritance by guardians, tenants in dower, by the law of England, or otherwise for term of life, a writ of prohibition of waste used to be granted, by which writ many were misled, thinking that those who committed the waste needed only to answer for waste committed after the prohibition was directed to them, the lord king, to remove for the future this error, has ordained that for waste committed in any way whatever to the harm of anyone there shall in future be granted not a writ of prohibition of waste but a writ of summons so that he who is complained of shall answer for waste committed at any time, and if after the summons he does not appear let him be attached, and after attachment be distrained, and if after distraint he does not appear the sheriff shall be commanded to go personally to the place where the waste has occurred, taking with him twelve etc., and enquire into the waste and return the inquest and after the inquest has been returned the court shall proceed to judgment, in accordance with what is contained in the statute published earlier at Westminster.[3]

[1] *versus dominum regem gravius redimantur*
[2] i.e. be allowed to
[3] actually the Statute of Gloucester (1278), c. 5; not Westminster I; cf. Plucknett, *Statutes and their Interpretation*, ch. VIII, on this and other examples of contemporary ignorance

[c. 15] In every case in which minors under age can plead, it is granted that if such minors are eloigned[1] so that they cannot sue personally, their next friends shall be admitted to sue for them.

[c. 16] In the case where an inheritance descends to a minor from the side of his father, who held of one lord, and from the side of his mother, who held of another lord, there has been doubt hitherto to which of the two lords the marriage of the minor should belong. It is agreed that henceforth that lord shall have the marriage by whom the ancestor[2] was first enfeoffed, with no regard to the sex[3] or to the size of the tenement, but only to the more ancient feoffment by knight service.

[c. 17] In the eyre of the justices an essoin of bed-sickness[4] shall not henceforth be allowed for a tenement in the same county unless he who is causing himself to be essoined is genuinely sick; for if the demandant excepts that the tenant is not ill or in such a state that he could not appear before the justices, his challenge shall be permitted and if this on investigation is proved beyond doubt, the essoin shall be converted into a default. And henceforth this essoin shall not lie[5] in a writ of right between two people claiming by one descent.

[c. 18] When a debt has been recovered[6] or acknowledged[7] in the king's court, or damages awarded, it shall henceforth be for him who is suing for such debt or damages to choose whether to sue out a writ that the sheriff cause to be made[8] out of the lands and chattels or have the sheriff deliver to him all the chattels (except cattle and beasts of the plough) of the debtor and half his land until, on a reasonable valuation and extent,[9] the debt has been levied. And if he is ejected from the tenement he shall have recovery by writ of *novel disseisin*, and afterwards, if need be, by a writ of redisseisin.

[c. 19] When after the death of anyone who dies intestate and is bound to any persons for debt his goods come to the ordinary to be disposed of, the ordinary shall henceforth be bound to answer for the debts (to the extent that the deceased's goods suffice) in the same way that the executors would be bound to answer if he had made a will.

[c. 20] As justices in a plea of *mort d'ancestor*[10] have been accustomed to permit the

[1] i.e. forcibly kept away

[2] The text is obscure here, but there can be no doubt that "*maritagium antecessor*" in Berry, *Statutes ... of Ireland*, I, p. 138, is an accidental omission of "*de quo*", while Maitland's rendering of "*de qui auncestres*" (*Year Books of Edward II, vol. I, 1 and 2 Edward II, A.D. 1307–9*, Seld Soc. vol. 17, p. 60; cf. Plucknett, *Statutes and their Interpretation*, p. 73, n. 1) would seem to be a slip, especially in view of his rendering of the Latin in his footnote 2 on p. 60. The natural rendering of "ancestor" in the context is the ancestor (the dead ancestor, the immediate predecessor) of the minor.

[3] i.e. irrespective of the mode of descent, whether by father or mother

[4] *de malo lecti* [5] i.e. not be admissible

[6] i.e. at common law by the writ of debt

[7] i.e. a recognisance entered into; cf. Plucknett, *Legislation of Edward I*, p. 148

[8] The difficulty over the reference here to lands as well as chattels (Plucknett, *Concise History of the Common Law*, 4th edn, rev. and enlarged (1948), p. 370, n. 1) is most naturally overcome by assuming that if the debtor's chattels did not suffice, the writ *fieri facias* would be followed by a *levari facias* on the issues, as they accrued, of his lands (see Plucknett, *Legislation of Edward I* (Oxford, 1949), p. 149).

[9] of, presumably, the chattels and the accruing issues of the land, respectively

[10] By *mort d'ancestor* the remedy for disseisin was available only to "next heirs" of the deceased who were sons, daughters, brothers, sisters, nephews or nieces of his. To afford remedy to next heirs not so closely related *mort d'ancestor* was not itself enlarged, but supplemented by new actions, *aiel*, *besaiel* and *cosinage*, separate but "of the same nature". cf. Pollock and Maitland, *History of English Law*, II, pp. 56–7; and Maitland, *Equity, also Forms of Action* (Cambridge, 1920), pp. 323–5.

tenant to answer that the plaintiff is not the next heir of the ancestor on account of whose death he claims the tenement and to inquire into this by assize, it is agreed that in writs of *cosinage*,[1] *aiel*,[2] and *besaiel*,[3] which are of the same nature, that same answer shall be permitted and inquired into and in accordance with the inquest let the court proceed to judgment.

[c. 21] As in a statute made at Gloucester it is contained that if any demise to another a tenement at a rent of a quarter or more of the value of the tenement, he who demised it, or his heir, shall after cesser of payment for two years have an action for claiming in demesne the tenement so demised,[4] in like manner it is agreed that if anyone withholds from his lord the due or customary service over a period of two years the lord shall have an action for claiming the tenement in demesne by the following writ: "Order A. that lawfully etc. he render to B. such and such tenement, which C.[5] has held of him by such and such service and which ought to revert to the aforesaid B. because the aforesaid A. has for two years stopped doing that service, as he says." And not only in this case but also in the case mentioned in the aforesaid statute of Gloucester let writs of entry be made out for an heir claiming against the heir of the tenant, and against those to whom such a tenement may have been alienated.

[c. 22] When two or more hold wood, turbary, fishery or other such things in common without any of them knowing his severalty and any of them commits waste against the wish of another, an action may be brought by writ of Waste and the defendant when he comes to judgment shall have the choice either of taking his share in a particular place on the authority of the sheriff and by the view, oath and allotment of men of the neighbourhood chosen and sworn for the purpose or of agreeing not to take anything in future in such wood, turbary or other things except in accordance with what his coparceners are willing to take. And if he chooses to take his share in a particular place, let there be allotted to him in his share the place wasted at its value before he wasted it. The writ in this case: "As A. and B. hold the wood jointly, B. committed waste etc."

[c. 23] Executors shall henceforth have the writ of account and the same action and process by that writ as the deceased had and would have if he were alive.

[c. 24] In cases in which a writ is granted in chancery for an act done by somebody,[6] plaintiffs shall not henceforth depart from the court of the king[7] without remedy because the tenement has changed hands[8] and for that case no special writ is provided in the chancery's register (as for instance about a house, a wall, a market a writ is granted against him who set it up, yet if house, wall, and such like be conveyed to another person the writ is refused). Instead from now on when a writ is granted in

[1] consanguinity

[2] grandfather

[3] great-grandfather

[4] The foregoing is not Stat. Gloucester (1278), cap. 4 (No. 52 above) verbatim, and is not identical even substantially.

[5] Thus Berry, *Statutes . . . of Ireland*, I, p. 140, and *Statutes of the Realm*, I, p. 83, alike (which would seem to provide for the case of devolution, or alienation, on the tenant's side). The simple, direct case between A and B is provided in *Statutes of the Realm*, I, p. 83, n. 2, and *Fleta*, Bk II, ch. 45 (ed. Richardson and Sayles, II (Seld. Soc., vol. 72 for 1953), p. 151), both of which read "A" here, instead of "C."

[6] *de facto alicuius*

[7] *curia regis*

[8] literally, "is transferred from one to another"

one case, in a like case requiring like remedy it shall be made as before: "A. has complained to us that B. unjustly etc. has set up a house, wall, market and other things which are to the nuisance etc." If such things set up to the nuisance are transferred to another person, it shall henceforth be made thus: "A. has complained to us that B. and C. have set up etc." In the same way, just as the parson of a church can recover common of pasture by a writ of *novel disseisin*, so from now on shall his successor recover against the disseisor or his heir by the writ *Quod permittat* although this kind of writ has not been granted from chancery before. Likewise, just as a writ is granted as to whether[1] a tenement is the frankalmoin of some church or the lay fee of so-and-so, so from now on shall a writ be made whether it is the frankalmoin of one[2] or of another church in the case where the frankalmoin of one church is transferred into the possession of another church. And whensoever in future it happens in the chancery that a writ is found in one case, but in a similar case involving the same law and requiring similar remedy, it is not,[3] the clerks of the chancery shall agree in framing a writ, or shall adjourn the plaintiffs to the next parliament and[4] shall write down the matters[5] on which they cannot agree and refer them to the next parliament and a writ shall be framed by the joint opinion[6] of the learned in the law, that it may not happen hereafter that the court[7] long fails those who seek justice.

[c. 25] Because there is not any writ in the chancery whereby plaintiffs have so speedy a remedy as by a writ of *novel disseisin*, the lord king, desiring speedy justice to be done and delays in pleas to be done away with or reduced, grants that the writ of *novel disseisin* shall have a place in more cases than it has had before and grants that for estovers of wood, the profit to be taken from gathering nuts, acorns and other fruits in a wood,[8] a corrody, the delivery of corn or other victuals or necessaries due to be received annually at a certain place, the takings of toll, tronage, passage,[9] pontage and such like in certain places, the keeping of parks, woods, forests, chaces, warrens, gates, and other bailiwicks and offices in fee an assize of *novel disseisin* shall lie; and in all the aforesaid cases the writ shall be made out in the customary way with the words "of his freehold". And as it formerly lay and had a place in common of pasture, so shall it in future have a place in common of turbary, fishery and similar common rights which anyone has appendant to a freehold or by special deed for at least term of life without a freehold. In the case too when anyone holding a tenement for term of years or in wardship alienates it in fee and by that alienation transfers the freehold to the feoffee, remedy shall be by a writ of *novel disseisin* and both the feoffor and the feoffee shall be considered disseisors, so that while either of them is alive the writ shall be in place. And if by the death of the parties remedy by that writ shall cease, remedy shall be given by a writ of Entry. And although mention is made above of

[1] the assize *Utrum*
[2] *talis*
[3] I have followed early printed texts and Plucknett, *Concise History of the Common Law*, 4th edn, rev. (1948), p. 28, in supplying the negative which is obviously necessary.
[4] Thus *Statutes of the Realm*, I, p. 84, but Plucknett, loc. cit., prefers "or." Berry, *Statutes . . . of Ireland*, I, p. 142, gives neither "and" nor "or".
[5] *casus*
[6] *consensu*
[7] the *curia regis* mentioned at the beginning of cap. 24
[8] known later as "profits a prendre"; cf. *Novae Narrationes* (Seld. Soc., vol. 80 for 1963), p. lxxxiii
[9] a transport due

some cases in which the writ of *novel disseisin* had no place before, let no one for this reason think that that writ is not now competent where it was competent before. And though some have doubted whether there can be remedy by the aforesaid writ in the case where one pastures on the several[1] of another, let it be taken as certain that in that case there is a good and sure remedy by the aforesaid writ. And let those named as the disseisors take care henceforth not to put forward false exceptions to delay the taking of the assize, saying that an assize about the same tenement has passed between the same parties elsewhere,[2] or saying untruthfully that a writ of a higher nature is pending between the same parties about the same tenement, and on these and like matters vouching[3] rolls or record to warranty so that by that vouching they may be able to take away the crops and get the rents and other profits, to the great detriment of the plaintiff: because, although he who falsely advanced such untrue exceptions did not before bear any other penalty save only that on proof of his falsehood the court proceeded to take the assize, the lord king, to whom such false exceptions are hateful, has ordained that if anyone named as a disseisor puts forward personally the exception at the day given to him and fails in the warranty he has vouched he is, without[4] the recognition of the assize, to be adjudged a disseisor and shall make good the damages, those already ascertained and those to be ascertained later, twofold, and shall nonetheless be punished by being imprisoned for one year for his falsehood. And if the exception is put forward by an agent, the taking of the assize and the judgment on the restitution of the tenement and damages shall not be delayed on this account, so however that if the absent master of the bailiff appears later before the justices who took the assize and offers to prove by record or rolls that an assize about the same tenement between the same parties passed elsewhere,[5] or that the plaintiff withdrew from his suit in a like writ elsewhere, or that a plea by a writ of a higher nature is pending, a writ calling for the record of this to be brought[6] is to be made out for him, and when he has it and the justices see that the record so sent for for him[7] would have availed before the judgment for the plaintiff to be barred by it from his action, the justices shall straightway cause the party who before recovered to be warned to appear on a certain day for the defendant to recover his seisin and the damages, if any, he paid by the first judgment together with the damages he became liable for after the giving of the first judgment, which shall be restored to him, as is said above, twofold. And he who recovered before shall nonetheless be punished by imprisonment at the discretion of the justices. In the same way, if the defendant against whom the assize passed in his absence shows charters or quitclaims on the making of which the jurors were not examined, nor could be examined, because no mention was made of them in pleading, and probably could be ignorant of their making, the justice on seeing those writings shall cause the party who recovered to be warned to appear on a certain day and cause the jurors of the same assize to come. And if he

[1] on a several right as distinct from common of pasture, see Pollock and Maitland, *History of English Law*, I, p. 621

[2] *alias*

[3] *vocent*

[4] i.e. without waiting for

[5] *alias*

[6] a writ of *venire facias*

[7] an alternative reading is *eis*, "for them" (the justices) but the sense of the sentence is clear either way

verifies those writings by the verdict of the jurors, or it may be by an enrolment, he who requested the assize in contravention of his own deed shall be punished by the penalty aforesaid. And the sheriff shall not henceforth take an ox from the disseisee but from the disseisor only. And if there are several disseisors named in one writ he shall nevertheless be content with one ox, and shall exact an ox priced at only[1] five shillings and fourpence, or its value.

[c. 26] In writs of Redisseisin double damages shall henceforth be awarded and the redisseisors shall not hereafter be repleviable by the common writ. And just as in the statute of Merton[2] that writ was provided for those who were disseised after they had recovered by assize of *novel disseisin, mort d'ancestor* or other juries, that writ shall henceforth be further available[3] for those who have recovered by default, restoration or otherwise, without a recognition of assizes or juries.

[c. 27] After anyone has put himself on[4] an inquest an essoin shall be allowed him at the next day, but at other days following, the taking of the inquest shall not be delayed by essoin, whether or not he had an essoin before. And an essoin shall not be allowed after a day given at the prayer of the parties in a case in which the parties agree to appear without essoin.

[c. 28] Whereas by the statute of Gloucester[5] it is provided that after tenants have once appeared an essoin shall not be allowed them in writs of assizes, in like manner it shall henceforth be observed in the case of demandants.

[c. 29] A writ of Trespass to hear and determine shall not henceforth be granted before any justices except justices of either bench and justices in eyre, unless it be for a heinous trespass where it is necessary to apply a speedy remedy and the lord king considers it should be granted as an act of special grace. Nor, again, shall a writ to hear and determine appeals[6] before justices assigned be granted henceforth, unless in a special case and for a definite reason the lord king orders it. But to prevent such appealed or indicted persons being kept in prison a long time, they shall have a writ *de odis et atia* as stated in Magna Carta[7] and other statutes.

[c. 30] Henceforth two sworn justices[8] shall be assigned, before whom and not others assizes of *novel disseisin, mort d'ancestor*, and Attaint shall be taken, and they shall associate with them one or two of the more discreet knights of the county into which they shall come and shall take the aforesaid assizes and Attaints at most three times a year, namely once between the quindene of St John the Baptist and the Gules of August [8 July to 1 August] and again between the feast of the Exaltation of the Holy Cross and the octave of Michaelmas [14 September to 6 October] and the third time between Epiphany and the Purification of the blessed Mary [6 January to 2 February], and in every county at every taking of assizes they shall before their departure fix

[1] i.e. not more than
[2] No. 30 above, cap. 3
[3] *ulterius . . . habeat . . . locum*
[4] submitted the issue to the verdict of an inquest
[5] Another instance of contemporary ignorance of the statutes among lawyers: cf. Plucknett, *Statutes and their Interpretation*, p. 104. The correct reference is Westminster I (1275), c. 42 (No. 47 above).
[6] "accusations", of course, not the modern sense
[7] M.C. 1215 (No. 20 above), cap. 36; cf. Pollock and Maitland, *History of English Law*, II. p. 589, n. 1.
[8] i.e. two of the judges of the King's Bench or Common Pleas (Holdsworth, *Hist. of Engl. Law*, I (3rd edn, 1922), p. 278).

the day of their return, so that every one of the county may know of their coming, and they shall adjourn assizes from date to date[1] if on one day the taking of them is delayed by vouching to warranty, by essoin or by default of jurors. And if they see that it would be advantageous for any reason for an assize of *mort d'ancestor* which is postponed owing to an essoin or vouching to warranty to be adjourned into the bench, it shall be lawful for them to do this. And then they shall send the record with the original writ to the justices of the bench. And when the action reaches the taking of the assize, it, together with the original writ, shall be remitted by the justices of the bench to the previous justices for the assize to be taken before them. But henceforth the justices of the bench shall appoint at least four days a year for such assizes.

To save labour and expense inquisitions in connection with trespasses pleaded before justices of either bench shall be arranged[2] to be taken before the said justices assigned, unless the trespass is so heinous that it requires considerable examination. It shall also be arranged to take before them inquisitions of other pleas pleaded in either bench in which the examination is easy, as when entry or somebody's seisin is contradicted, or in the case of one article having to be inquired into: but inquisitions arising out of massive pleas and involving many articles, which require considerable examination, shall be taken before the justices of the benches unless both parties ask for the inquisition to be taken before some of them[3] when they come to those parts, which henceforth shall not be done save by two justices or by one along with some knight of the county upon whom the parties agree, and inquisitions of this sort shall not be arranged to be taken before any unless a definite day and place in the county is settled on with the parties present and day and place inserted in a judicial writ in these words, "We command you to cause twelve etc. to appear before the justices at Westminster on the octave of Michaelmas unless so-and-so and so-and-so come to those parts on such-and-such day and place." And when such inquisitions have been taken they shall be returned in the benches and there shall judgment be given and they shall be enrolled. And if any inquisitions are taken otherwise than in the aforesaid manner they shall be deemed invalid, except that it shall be arranged to take an assize of *darrein presentment* and inquisitions of *quare impedit* in their own county before one justice of the bench and one knight at a definite day and place decreed in the bench with or without the defendant's consent, and there judgment shall be given immediately. All justices of the bench and in eyres shall have clerks henceforth to enrol all pleas pleaded before them as they have been used from of old to have them.

It is also ordained that justices assigned to take assizes shall not compel the jurors to say categorically[4] whether it is disseisin or not, provided they are willing to speak the truth as to the facts[5] and to seek the help of the justices, but if they volunteer[6] that it is, or is not, disseisin, their statement shall be admitted at their own risk. And justices shall not henceforth put in assizes or juries any jurors other than those who were summoned for the purpose in the first instance.

[1] *de termino in terminum*. In their ordinary modern usage neither "from term to term" nor "from time to time" will do as a translation of this.

[2] *atterminentur*

[3] *aliquibus de societate*

[4] *precise*

[5] *veritatem facti*

[6] *si sponte velint*

[c. 31] When anyone who is impleaded before any of the justices puts forward an exception, praying the justices to allow it, and they will not allow it, if he who alleges the exception writes it down and requires a justice to affix his seal in witness, the justice shall affix his seal. And if one justice will not, another of them shall. And should the lord king, on complaint of the justices' action, have the record brought before him and should the exception not be found on the roll and the complainer[1] shows the exception written out with the seal of a justice affixed, the justice shall be commanded to appear on a certain day to acknowledge his seal or deny it. And if the justice cannot deny his seal, the court shall proceed to judgment having regard to the exception and the question whether it should be admitted or be quashed.[2]

[c. 32] Forasmuch as, when men of religion and other ecclesiastical persons implead anyone and the party impleaded defaults (on which account he should lose the tenement), justices have hitherto feared that if the impleaded party defaults collusively, in order that the demandant (when because of the statute[3] he cannot get seisin of the tenement by right of gift or alienation of another kind[4]) may get it because of the default, the statute would in this way be circumvented, it is ordained by the lord king and granted that in this case after the default inquiry shall be made by the country whether the demandant has a right to what he claims or not. And if it is found that the said demandant has a right, the court shall proceed to judgment for the demandant and he shall recover his seisin; but if he has not a right, the tenement shall accrue to the immediate lord of the fee if he claims it within a year from the time of the taking of the inquest. And if he does not claim it within the year, it shall accrue to the lord immediately above if he claims within half a year after that year; and so each lord in turn after the immediate lord shall have half a year within which to claim, until in the end it is the king to whom in default of other lords the tenement accrues. And each of the chief lords of the fees shall be allowed to challenge jurors of the inquest, and likewise he who wishes to challenge on behalf of the king. And after the judgment is clear the land shall remain in the king's hands until it[5] is deraigned[6] by some chief lord and the sheriff shall be charged to answer for it at the exchequer.

[c. 33] Because many tenants erect crosses in their tenements, or permit them to be erected, to the prejudice of their lords in order that the tenants can protect themselves by the privileges of the Templars and the Hospitallers against the chief lords of the fees, it is ordained that such tenements shall be forfeited to the chief lords or to the king in the same way as is provided elsewhere for tenements alienated in mortmain.

[c. 34] It is provided that henceforth if a man rapes a married woman, a maiden, or other woman, without her consent before or afterwards, he shall have judgment of life and limb; and likewise where a man rapes a woman – married woman, maiden, or other woman – by force even though she consents afterwards, he shall have the judgment beforestated if he is convicted at the king's suit, and there the king shall have his suit.[7]

[1] *querens*
[2] *secundum illam exceptionem prout admittenda esset vel cassanda*
[3] the Statute of Mortmain, 1279 (No. 53 above). On collusion in mortmain, see T. F. T. Plucknett, *Legislation of Edward I*, pp. 94–100, esp. p. 99.
[4] *alterius alienacionis*
[5] *tenementum*
[6] i.e. until a title is established to it
[7] This paragraph is in French.

As to women taken away with the husband's goods, the king shall have the suit for the goods thus carried off. And if a wife willingly leaves her husband and goes away and stays with her adulterer she shall be barred forever of action to claim her dower which she ought to have of her husband's tenements, if she is convicted thereof; unless her husband willingly and without the coercion of the church takes her back[1] and allows her to live with him, in which case action shall be restored to her.

He who takes a nun away from her house, although she consents, shall be punished by three years imprisonment and shall make adequate satisfaction to the house from which she was abducted and shall nonetheless make fine at the king's pleasure.

[c. 35] On children, male or female, seized and taken away, whose marriage belongs to someone: if he who seized them has no right to the marriage he shall, even if he subsequently restores the child unmarried or recompenses for the marriage, be nevertheless punished for the offence by imprisonment for two years. And if he does not restore, or marries the heir after marriageable age is reached and cannot recompense for the marriage, he shall abjure the realm or have imprisonment for life. And for this the complainant shall have the following writ: "If A. gives you security etc. put B. under gage etc. to be before our justices on such-and-such a day to show why he has ravished[2] and taken away a certain heir found in such-and-such place, who is under age and whose marriage belongs to him,[3] against the will of the said A. and against the peace etc." And if the heir is in the same county, then this clause shall be added: "And you shall diligently enquire where that heir is in your bailiwick and wherever he is found take and safely and securely keep him so as to have him before our aforesaid justices at the aforesaid term to be given back to whichever of the aforesaid A. or B. he ought to be given."[4] And there shall be legal action[5] against the party complained of until under distress he appears, if he has anything he can be distrained by, or, if he cannot be brought to justice he shall be exacted[6] and outlawed for contumacy. If perchance such an heir be conducted and transferred into another county, then a writ to the sheriff of that county shall be made in this form: "A. has complained to us that B. has lately seized a certain heir under age and in his wardship in such-and-such place in the county of so-and-so and abducted him from that county to such-and-such place in your county against the will of A. and against our peace. And therefore we command you wherever you can find him in your bailiwick to take the aforesaid heir and keep him safely and securely so as to have him before our justices at such-and-such day and place, which day the said A. has against the aforesaid B. to be given back to him to whom he ought rightly to be given."[7] And if the heir dies before he can be found or before he is restored to the plaintiff, the plea shall proceed between them nevertheless until it is determined to whom he ought to have been restored if he had survived, and he who unlawfully seized such an heir shall not be excused from or get any lightening of the punishment aforesaid after the death of the heir whose possessor in bad faith he was while he lived. And if the plaintiff dies before the plea is determined, if his right derived from his own fee, the action shall

[1] *eam reconciliet*
[2] in its original sense of "seized"
[3] i.e. to A.
[4] the writ of Ravishment of Ward.
[5] *fiat secta*
[6] On exaction procedure, see footnotes to cap. 11 above.
[7] a variant of Ravishment of Ward

be resummoned at the suit of the plaintiff's heir and the plea shall proceed in due order; if however the right was his[1] by another title, such as by title of gift, sale, or other sort of title, then the action shall be resummoned at the suit of the executors of the plaintiff and the plea proceed as aforesaid. In the same way if the defendant dies before the plea is determined or the heir restored, the plea shall proceed by resummons between the plaintiff, or his heir or executors, and the executors of the defendant, or his heir if the executors have not means enough to compensate for the value of the marriage in accordance with what is contained in other statutes, but not as regards the penalty of imprisonment – with which penalty no one should be punished for the offence of another. In the same way when a plea is pending between parties for the custody of land or of an heir or of both by the common writ which begins, "Command so-and-so that he render etc.,"[2] resummons shall be made between the heirs and the executors of the plaintiff, and likewise the heirs or executors of the defendant, if death overtakes either party before the plea is determined. And when the stage is reached of the grand distress a term shall be given within which at least three counties may be held, in each of which public proclamation shall be made that the deforciant shall appear in the bench to answer the plaintiff at the day contained in the writ. And if he does not appear on that day and it is certified once, a second time, and a third time, that proclamation has been made the court shall pass judgment for the plaintiff, saving the right of the defendant if afterwards he wishes to plead in the matter. The same shall be done in a writ of trespass, when anyone complains that he has been ejected from wardships of this sort.

[c. 36] Because lords of courts and others who hold courts, and stewards, when they wish to harass those subject to them and have no lawful means of doing so, procure others to bring complaints against them and to give gage and offer pledges, or to sue out writs and force them, at the suit of such plaintiffs, to attend county, hundred, and court[3] until they have made fine with them at their will, it is ordained that this shall not be done henceforth. And if anyone is attached upon such false complaints, let him replevy the distress there taken from him and have the action brought before the justices; before whom, if, after the one so distrained has formulated his complaint, the sheriff or other bailiff or lord avows that the distress was lawful because of the sort of complaints made before them and it is replied that such complaints were made against them maliciously at the instance or by procurement of the sheriff or other bailiffs or lords, that replication shall be admitted; and if they are convicted of this they shall make fine where the king is concerned and nevertheless pay triple damages to those so injured.

[c. 37] Because, too, bailiffs, whose office it is to take distresses, wishing to oppress those under their authority so as to extort money from them, send strangers to levy the distresses with the intention of being able to harass those under them on the ground that those distrained in this way (not knowing the persons) will not let such distresses be levied upon them:[4] it is ordained that no distress shall be levied save by bailiffs

[1] *competat ei*
[2] the writ *Praecipe quod reddat*
[3] seignorial, presumably, as distinct from communal courts
[4] *Fleta* (ed. Richardson and Sayles, II, Seld. Soc., vol. 72, p. 165) makes the point clearer by inserting at this point the gloss "and so a malicious action may be framed against them in order thus to extort money".

who are sworn and known. And those who distrain, if they do otherwise and are convicted of it, shall, if injured parties sue out a writ of trespass, pay damages to the injured parties and where the king is concerned be heavily punished.

[c. 38] Because, also, sheriffs, hundred-bailiffs, and bailiffs of liberties have been accustomed to oppress those subject to them by putting on assizes and juries men who are ailing, decrepit, permanently or temporarily incapacitated, and even men not living in the district at the time of the summons, as well as by summoning an inordinate number of jurors in order to extort money from some of them for letting them go in peace, so that assizes and juries are often made up of poor men, the rich because of their bribes staying at home: it is ordained that henceforth there shall be summoned not more than twenty-four in one assize, and old men (that is, over seventy years old), the chronically sick, those ill at the time of the summons, and those who do not live in the district, shall not be put in juries or in petty[1] assizes. Nor shall any be put in assizes or juries, even if these are to be taken in their own county, who hold tenements worth less than twenty shillings a year. And if such assizes and juries are to be taken outside the county, no one shall be put in them who has a tenement worth less than forty shillings a year, except those who are witnesses in charters or other writings, whose presence is taken for granted provided they are able to travel. Nor ought this statute to be extended to Grand Assizes, in which it is sometimes necessary because of the shortage of knights to put knights not resident in the district, provided they have tenements in the county. And if sheriffs or their under-sheriffs, or bailiffs of liberties, contravene in any article of this statute and are convicted of it, they shall pay damages to the injured parties and shall nonetheless be in the king's mercy. And justices assigned to take assizes shall, when they come into the county, have power to hear the plaints of all who have complaints in connection with the articles contained in this statute and to administer justice in the form aforesaid.

[c. 39] Because justices, whose duty it is to do justice to everyone who pleads before them, are very often hindered from being able to discharge their office in proper fashion because sheriffs do not return original and judicial writs and also because they return a false answer to the king's writs, the lord king has provided and ordained that those who fear wrongdoing on the part of a sheriff are to deliver their writs, original and judicial, in full county or in the rere-county at which the king's money is collected and a bill[2] is to be received from the sheriff, if he is present, or the under-sheriff, giving the names of the parties and of the tenements contained in the writ. And at the request of him who delivered the writ the seal of the sheriff or the under-sheriff is to be affixed in testimony and mention made of the day of the delivery of the writ. And if sheriffs or under-sheriffs will not affix their seals to a bill of this kind, the testimony of the knights and other trustworthy people present who affix their seals to the bill is to be accepted. And if a sheriff does not return writs delivered to him and complaint thereof reaches the justices let order be given by a judicial writ to the justices assigned to take assizes to enquire of those who were present when the writ was delivered to the sheriff if they were aware of its delivery and the inquest is to be returned. And if

[1] the petty or possessory assizes, as distinct from the Grand Assize
[2] i.e. an acknowledgement of receipt of the writ

it is found by the inquest that the writ was delivered to him, damages shall be awarded to the demandant or plaintiff, having regard to the gravity and the nature of the action and to the danger that could have befallen him because of the delay he suffered. And in this way let remedy be given when a sheriff replies that a writ reached him so late that he could not carry out the king's command.

Pleas are very often delayed too because a sheriff replies that he has sent instructions to the bailiffs of some liberty or other who have done nothing thereon, and he names liberties which have never had the return of writs; on which account the lord king has ordained that the treasurer of the exchequer shall provide a roll of all liberties having return of writs in any counties whatsoever. And if the sheriff replies that he has made return to the bailiffs of some other liberty than is contained in the aforesaid roll he is to be punished forthwith as a disinheritor of the lord king and of his crown. And if perchance he replies that he has made return to the bailiffs of some liberty which indeed has return, the sheriff shall be ordered not to omit[1] to execute the lord king's command by reason of the aforesaid liberty and to make it known to the bailiffs to whom he made the return that they are on the day mentioned in the writ to answer why they did not execute the lord king's command. And if they come on the day and clear themselves on the ground that a return was not made to them, the sheriff shall forthwith be condemned to restore damages to the lord of that liberty and likewise to the party injured by the delay. And if the bailiffs do not come on the day or come but do not clear themselves in the way aforesaid the sheriff is to be ordered in every judicial writ as long as the plea lasts not to omit by reason of the liberty etc. Sheriffs also very often give a false answer to the article about issues etc.,[2] sometimes reporting untruthfully that there are no issues, sometimes that they are small when they could return a bigger sum, sometimes not mentioning issues; wherefore it is ordained and agreed that if the plaintiff asks to hear the sheriff's reply, his request is to be granted. And if he offers to prove that the sheriff could have answered for greater issues, a judicial writ to the justices assigned to take assizes is to be made for him ordering them to enquire, in the presence of the sheriff if he wishes to be there, what were the issues and how much they were for which the sheriff could have answered from the day when the writ was received until the day contained in the writ. And when the inquest has been returned, if he did not previously answer for the full amount, he is to be charged with the deficit by estreats delivered into the exchequer, and be nonetheless heavily amerced for the concealment. And let the sheriff know that rents, corn in the grange, and all movables except harness, clothes, and household necessaries are included under the heading of issues. And the lord king has commanded that for such false answers sheriffs shall be punished the first time, and a second time if need be, by the justices. But if they offend a third time no one other than the king is to handle the matter. Very often, too, they give a false answer in reporting that they could not carry out the king's command because of the resistance of the armed force of some magnate, of which answer let sheriffs beware in future, for an answer of this kind redounds greatly to the lord king's dishonour; and as soon as his bailiffs aver

[1] on the clause "*non omittas*", see T. F. T. Plucknett, *Legislation of Edward I*, pp. 31 ff.
[2] *quod de exitibus etc.*

that they have encountered such resistance, a sheriff shall immediately put everything aside and, taking with him the posse of his county, go in person to carry out the command. And if he finds that his bailiffs have lied he shall so punish them by imprisonment that by their punishment others will be deterred. And if he finds they are telling the truth, let him punish those resisting them by imprisonment, from which they are not to be released without the lord king's special order. And if perchance the sheriff encounters resistance when he comes, let him inform the court of the names of the resisters and of those aiding, assenting, instructing or supporting them, and they are to be attached by a judicial writ to appear in person in court, and if they are convicted of such resistance, they are to be punished at the king's pleasure. Nor is any officer of the lord king to concern himself with inflicting such punishment, as the lord king specially reserves this matter to himself because resisters of this kind are deemed to be disturbers of his peace and of his realm.

[c. 40] When anyone alienates his wife's right, it is agreed that the suit of the woman or her heir shall not henceforth be delayed after the husband's death by the minority of the heir who ought to warrant; instead,[1] the buyer, who ought not to have been ignorant that he was buying another's right, shall wait to have his warranty until his warrantor comes of age.

[c. 41] The lord king has ordained that if abbots, priors, wardens of hospitals and of other religious houses founded by him or by his progenitors alienate henceforth tenements given to those houses by him or by his progenitors, those tenements shall be taken into the hands of the lord king and held at his will and the buyer lose his recovery both of the tenements and of the money he paid. If, on the other hand, the houses were founded by earls, barons or others, he by whom or by whose ancestors a tenement so alienated was given shall, for tenements so alienated, have a writ to recover the tenement in demesne in this form, "Command the abbot of so-and-so to render to B. justly etc. such-and-such tenement which was given by the aforesaid B. or his ancestors in frankalmoin to that house and which ought to revert to the said B. because of the alienation the said abbot has made of the said tenement contrary to the form of the said gift as he says." Likewise for a tenement given for maintaining a chantry, or lights in some church or chapel or to provide other alms, if, given on such condition, it is alienated. But if a tenement so given for a chantry, for lights, for feeding the poor or other good deed is perhaps not alienated but such alms withheld over a period of two years, an action shall lie for the donor or his heir to claim in demesne the tenement so given, as is ordained in the statute of Gloucester for tenements demised at a service or rent[2] of a quarter or more of the value of the tenement.

[c. 42] Concerning the lord king's marshals at fee, chamberlains, doorkeepers in the eyres of the justices and serjeant-vergers before the justices at Westminster who have the office in fee, who exact more by reason of their fee than they used to exact, as many complain on the authority of those who have seen and known the ways[3] of the court for a long time, the lord king has had enquiry made what standing[4] the

[1] *set*

[2] *dimissis ad faciendum vel reddendum*. Rather than Stat. Gloucester, 1278, cap. 4 (No. 52 above), cf. cap. 21 above of the present statute; cf. also T. F. T. Plucknett, *Legislation of Edward I*, pp. 88–93

[3] *statum*

[4] *quem statum*

aforesaid officers at fee used to have in times past. And as a result of the enquiries he has ordained and commanded that a marshal at fee who as an innovation[1] exacts a palfrey from earls and barons and others holding by a part of a barony when they have done homage and another palfrey, notwithstanding, when they are knighted, and as an innovation exacts a palfrey from some from whom he ought not to have one,[2] shall be content with one palfrey from every earl and baron holding a whole barony or the value of it in money which of old he used to receive by custom, so that if he takes the palfrey or its value in money in the way said when he does homage. he shall take nothing when he is knighted, and if it should be that he takes nothing at the homage, he shall take it at the knighting. As to abbots and priors holding a whole barony, when they have done homage or fealty for their baronies, he shall take a palfrey or its value in money, as aforesaid. The same to be done in the case of archbishops and bishops. From those, on the other hand, who hold a part of a barony, whether they are religious or seculars, he shall take proportionately to the part they hold of the barony. From religious who hold in frankalmoin and not by barony or part of a barony, a marshal shall henceforth exact nothing. And the lord king has granted that a marshal of his at fee shall not be precluded by this statute from demanding more if hereafter he can show that he has a right to demand more. The lord king's chamberlains shall in future receive from archbishops, bishops, abbots, priors and other ecclesiastics, earls and barons, who hold a whole barony a reasonable fine[3] when they do homage or fealty for the barony. And they shall accept a reasonable fine proportionate to what they hold, if they hold part of a barony. Other abbots, priors, religious and seculars, however, who do not hold by barony or part of a barony shall not be bound to make fine as is said of those who hold by barony or part of a barony, but instead a chamberlain shall be content with the outer garment – or with its value in money, which is said more for the benefit of the religious than for seculars because it is more seemly for religious to make fine for their outer garment than to be uncovered.

[c. 43] It shall be prohibited henceforth for Hospitallers and Templars to implead anyone in future before the conservators of their privileges on any matter cognizance of which belongs to the king's court, and if they do they shall after restoring damages to the injured party be severely punished as regards[4] the lord king. The lord king prohibits too the conservators of those same privileges from in future granting citations at the instance of Hospitallers or Templars or other privileged persons before it is expressly stated on what matter the citation ought to be made. And if such conservators see that the citation is requested over some matter cognizance of which belongs to the king's court, they shall neither make the citation nor treat it as valid. And if they do otherwise they shall be answerable to the injured party for damages and be nonetheless severely punished as regards the lord king. And because such privileged persons procure subpriors, precentors, sacrists and men of religion as conservators because they have nothing from which they can satisfy the injured

[1] *de novo*
[2] the words "ordained that the said marshal" (*ordinauit quod predictus marescallus*) given here I have rejected as an interpolation
[3] i.e. a fee
[4] *versus*

parties or the lord king and are readier to offend the lord king's dignity than are their superiors, on whom a penalty can be inflicted through their temporalities, let the superiors of such obedientiaries take care in future not to allow them to assume to themselves jurisdiction to the prejudice of the lord king and his crown. And if they do, the superiors shall be answerable for what they do, as if it were their own doing.[1]

[c. 44] With regard to doorkeepers in the eyres and vergers before the justices of the bench, it is ordained that for every assize and jury which they keep they shall take fourpence only, for chirographs nothing. From those who recover their claims by default, surrender, or in any other way by judgment without an assize and jury, from those who leave without a day through the default of the plaintiff or demandant, they shall take nothing. And if anyone recovers his claim against more than one person by the one writ and by verdict of an assize or jury, they shall be content with fourpence only. They shall similarly be content with fourpence only if several named in the one writ recover by verdict of an assize or jury. From those who do homage in the bench they shall be content with the outer garment. For Grand Assizes, attaints, juries and trial by battle they shall take twelve pence only. From those called before justices to prosecute or defend their plea they shall take[2] nothing for going in or out. At the pleas of the crown only twelvepence shall be taken from each jury of twelve; from each prisoner released only fourpence taken; from each person whose peace is proclaimed only twelvepence taken. From finders,[3] from neighbours and from others who are attached, from townships, from the four men and the reeve,[4] from tithingmen, nothing shall be taken. As regards chirographers and the making of chirographs, it is ordained that they are to be content with four shillings. As for clerks writing original and judicial writs, it is ordained that for a writ they are to be content with a penny. And the lord king enjoins every one of his justices on the fealty and oath by which they are bound to him that if such officials contravene in any way this statute and complaint reaches them, they are to inflict on them moderate punishment, and if they offend a second time, they shall inflict on them a greater punishment, with which they shall be punished as they deserve. And if they offend a third time, and are convicted of this, they shall, if they are officers at fee, lose their fee; if [they are] other than this, they shall be dismissed from the king's court and not return without the special order or grace of the king himself.

[c. 45] Because on matters[5] which are recorded before the chancellor of the lord king and justices of his who have record, and which are enrolled on their rolls, proceedings on a plea ought not to be by way of summons, attachment, essoin, view of land, and other necessary formalities of a court, as has been the customary practice with contracts and covenants made out of court, the practice in future shall be that those things which are found enrolled before those who have record, or are contained in fines, whether they are contracts, covenants, bonds, acknowledgements of services or

[1] *ac si de proprio facto suo convicti essent*

[2] "take" (*capiant*) is the reading of printed copies of the statutes (*Statutes of the Realm*, I, p. 93, n. 2) and I have preferred it because it gives a sentence which is in conformity with its context: "*dent*", the manuscript reading (*Stat. Realm*, I, p. 93; and Berry, *Statutes . . . of Ireland*, p. 170), would require "*De hiis . . . nichil dent*" to be translated, "As to those . . . plea, they shall give nothing."

[3] i.e. of corpses

[4] i.e. of a township

[5] *hiis*

customs, or whatever else is enrolled which the lord king's court can give authority to without breach of law and custom, shall henceforth have such force that it shall not hereafter be necessary to plead concerning them. Instead, when the plaintiff comes to the lord king's court he shall, if the recognition or fine is recent, that is to say drawn up in writing within the year, have forthwith a writ of execution of the recognition made.[1] And if perchance the recognition was made or the fine levied longer ago than that, the sheriff shall be commanded to inform the party complained of that he is to appear on a certain day to show if he knows any reason why such things as are enrolled or are contained in the fine ought not to be put into execution. And if he does not come on that day, or comes perhaps but cannot give any reason why execution should not take place, the sheriff shall be commanded to have what is enrolled or is contained in the fine carried out. The same instructions shall be given to the ordinary if the case concerns him,[2] subject however to what has been said above[3] about a mesne tenant who is bound by recognisance or a judgment to acquit [the tenant] being observed.

[c. 46] Whereas in a statute published at Merton[4] it was granted that lords of wastes, woods and pastures could approve[5] those wastes, woods and pastures, notwithstanding the opposition of their tenants, provided that those tenants have pasture adequate to their tenements and free access and egress to it, yet because no mention was made of relations between neighbour and neighbour many lords of wastes, woods and pastures have been hindered up to now by the opposition of neighbours with pasture enough and because "foreign"[6] tenants have no greater right of commoning in the waste or pasture of any lord than the lord's own tenants, it is henceforth ordained that the statute provided at Merton between lord and tenants shall in the future have effect between lords of wastes, woods and pastures and neighbours, so that such lords of wastes, woods or pastures can, saving sufficient pasture for their men and neighbours, approve the residue. And this shall be observed in the case of those who claim pasture as appurtenant to their tenements. But if anyone claims common by special feoffment or grant for a certain number of beasts or in any way other than he ought to have of common right, since covenant qualifies[7] the law he shall have the recovery he is entitled to by the form of the grant made to him. No one[8] shall be harassed henceforth by assize of *novel disseisin* for common of pasture because of a windmill, a sheepfold, a vaccary, the necessary enlargement of a court or curtilage. And as it sometimes happens that someone with a right to approve raises a bank of hedge and others[9], at night or some other time when they believe their action will not be noticed, level the bank or the hedge to the ground, and it cannot be ascertained by verdict of assize or jury who levelled it, nor will men of the neighbouring vills indict those

[1] An abbreviation of common form, which in the writ of execution would continue "made in the court at ..." and recite the parties and other details of the recognition.

[2] *in suo casu*

[3] in c. 9

[4] No. 30 above, c. 4

[5] i.e. "improve", literally "profit themselves from" (*appruiare se possint de*)

[6] *forinseci*

[7] *convencio legi deroget*. For other expressions of this, see *Year Books 5 Edw. II, 1311* (Seld. Soc., vol. 63 for 1944), pp. 31 and 33, and p. 31, n. 1; 179; 193. But as the verb is *derogare*, not *vincere*, and in view of the Classical distinction between *derogare* and *abrogare*, I have preferred "qualifies" to "overrides".

[8] i.e. no lord

[9] *aliqui*

guilty of such deed, let the vills immediately adjoining[1] be distrained to restore[2] the bank or hedge at their own expense and to pay damages. And when anyone without right of commoning usurps commons while heirs are under age or a married woman is under the power of living husbands or while the pasture is in the hands of tenants in dower, by the law of England, or otherwise for term of life or years or in fee-tail, and has used the pasture for a long time, many are of the opinion that pastures of this sort ought to be said to be appurtenant to the free tenement and that the possessor of such ought to have action by a writ of *novel disseisin* if he is deforced of such pasture; but from now on it must be held that those acquiring entry of it in the period within which the writ of *mort d'ancestor* runs shall not have recovery of it by writ of *novel disseisin* if they are deforced, if they had not common before.[3]

[c. 47] It is provided also that the waters of the Humber, Ouse, Trent, Don, Aire, Derwent, Wharfe, Nidd, Ure, Swale, Tees and all other waters in which salmon are caught shall be put in defence as regards the taking of salmon from the Nativity of the Blessed Mary [8 September] to St Martin's day [11 November]; and likewise that young salmon shall not be caught or destroyed by nets or by other engines at millponds from the middle of April to the Nativity of St John the Baptist [24 June]. And in the parts where such rivers are, let there be appointed conservators of this statute who, sworn to this, shall view frequently and enquire as to offenders. For the first offence they are to be punished by the burning of nets and engines. If they offend again, they shall be punished by imprisonment for a quarter of a year. If again they offend, they shall be punished by imprisonment for a whole year. And as the offence increases, so shall the penalty inflicted increase.

[c. 48] As to view of land, it is ordained and established that, in future, view shall not be granted except in cases where a view is necessary. Thus if someone loses a tenement by default, then[4] moves another writ to demand the same tenement, or[5] when someone by a dilatory exception abates a writ after the view of the land (on account, for instance, of non-tenure or misnomer of the vill or such like), if he moves another writ: in this case and in the previous one view shall not henceforth be granted, provided he had it in the earlier writs. In writs of Dower when dower is demanded of a tenement which the woman's husband alienated to a tenant or the tenant's ancestor, view nevertheless shall not henceforth be granted to the tenant, since the tenant ought not to be ignorant of what it was[6] the woman's husband alienated to him or his ancestor although the husband did not die seised. In also a writ of Entry abated because the demandant misnamed the entry, if the demandant moves another writ of[7] entry, the tenant if he had view in the first writ shall not have it in the second. In all writs too by which tenements are demanded by reason of a demise which the demandant or his ancestor made to the tenant (but not to his ancestor), as something he demised to him while he was under age, not in his right mind, in prison, and the

[1] *propinque villate circumadiacentes* [2] *levare*

[3] i.e. before 1216. cf. T. F. T. Plucknett, *Legislation of Edward I*, p. 86; and Stat. Westminster I, 1275 (No. 47 above), cap. 39

[4] *et ille qui amisit* [5] *et in casu*

[6] *quale tenementum*

[7] *Statutes of the Realm*, I, p. 95, interpolates "*aliquo*" at this point; Berry, *Statutes . . . of Ireland*, I, p. 176, "*alio*"

like, view henceforth shall not lie; but if the demise was made to the ancestor of the tenant, view shall lie henceforth as it did before.

[c. 49] [The chancellor,[1] the treasurer, a justice, or anyone of the king's council; a clerk of the chancery, of the exchequer, of a justice or other minister; or anyone of the king's household, clerk or lay, cannot accept a church or the advowson of a church, land, tenement or fee, by gift or by purchase, or at farm, or by champerty, or in any other way, so long as the thing is in plea before us or before any of our ministers; nor may any monetary reward be taken in connection with it. And he who does this, whether by himself or through another, or commits any fraud with regard to it, shall be punished at the king's pleasure, as well he who gains by it as he who does it.]

[c. 50] All the aforesaid statutes shall come into effect next Michaelmas: consequently for any offences against any of them committed before that feast the punishment prescribed in them for offenders shall not be inflicted. Where statutes provided to afford remedies where the law is deficient are concerned, however, suitors shall have the writs provided in their case, in order that they may no longer come to court and depart without a hope of remedy, but these shall not be pleaded until after the aforesaid Michaelmas.

58. Statute of Merchants (13 Edw. I), Easter 1285

(*Statutes of the Realm*, I (Rec. Com., 1810), pp. 98–100 [French])

A drastic revision of the Statute of Acton Burnell of two years before (No. 54 above), amounting to a change of policy: Plucknett, *Legislation of Edward I*, ch. VI. This is essential reading.

As merchants who in the past have lent their substance to various people are impoverished because there was no speedy law provided by which they could readily recover their debts on the day fixed for payment, and for that reason many merchants are put off from coming to this land with their merchandise to the detriment of merchants and of the whole kingdom, the king by himself and by his council at his parliament, which he held at Acton Burnell, after Michaelmas in the eleventh year of his reign, made and ordained an establishment on this as a remedy for merchants, which ordinance and establishment the king commanded should be held and firmly kept throughout his kingdom and by it merchants have had remedy and have recovered their debts with less hurt and trouble than they used to have before. But because merchants then complained to the king that sheriffs misinterpreted his statute and sometimes by malice and by misinterpretation delayed the execution of the statute to the great detriment of the merchants, THE KING at his parliament at West-

[1] This clause, in French not Latin, and uncertainly placed (in some manuscripts after, not before, the concluding c. 50), is not found in all manuscripts (see *Statutes of the Realm*, I, p. 95 and fn.). It is not given, either in Latin or in French, in the text sent to Ireland in 1285 as preserved in the Red Book of the Exchequer in Ireland and printed in Berry, *Statutes . . . of Ireland*, I, p. 176. It was, however, known not long afterwards to the author of Fleta, who gives a Latin rendering of it (*Fleta*, II, ed. Richardson and Sayles, Seld. Soc., vol. 72, pp. 138–9). Whether properly part of Stat. Westminster II, or not, it should be compared with Stat. Westminster I, 1275, c. 28 (No. 47 above).

minster after Easter in the 13th year of his reign had the aforesaid statute made at Acton Burnell read out, and to elucidate certain articles of his aforementioned statute has ordained and established that a merchant who wishes to be sure of his debt shall cause his debtor to come before the mayor of [[1]] or other chief warden of the town, or of other good town that the king shall appoint, and he before the mayor or chief warden or other man of standing chosen and sworn for the purpose when the mayor or chief warden cannot attend to it and before one of the clerks whom the king shall appoint for the purpose when neither of them can attend to it shall acknowledge the debt and the day of repayment, and the recognisance shall be enrolled by the hand of one of the aforesaid clerks whose hand will be known, and the roll shall be made in duplicate, one of which shall remain with the mayor or chief warden and the other with the clerk who is first named for the purpose. And in addition one of the aforesaid clerks shall make with his own hand the bond, to which shall be affixed the seal of the debtor, together with the seal of the king that is provided for this, which seal shall be in two pieces, of which the larger piece shall remain in the custody of the mayor or chief warden, and the other in the hand of the aforesaid clerk. And if the debtor does not pay on the day fixed for him, the merchant shall come to the mayor and the clerk with his bond, and if it is found by the roll or by the bond that the debt was acknowledged and if the day fixed is past, the mayor or chief warden shall arrest the debtor, if he is a layman, whenever he is found in his jurisdiction and hand him over to the town's prison, if there is a prison, to remain there at his own expense until he has paid the debt. And it is commanded that the keeper of the town's prison retain him in custody after he is handed over by the mayor or the warden; and if he will not receive him, the keeper of the prison shall immediately be responsible for the debt, if he has the means: and if he has not the means, he who gave him charge of the prison shall be responsible. And if the debtor cannot be found within the jurisdiction of the mayor or chief warden, then shall the mayor or chief warden send to the chancellor under the aforesaid seal of the king the recognisance made of the debt, and the chancellor shall send a writ to the sheriff in whose bailiwick the debtor is found to arrest him, if he is a layman, and keep him in a safe prison until he has paid the debt. And during a quarter[2] of a year after his arrest, he shall have his chattels and his lands handed over to him so that he can by his own efforts raise the money and pay the debt. And it is quite lawful[3] for him, during the quarter, to sell land and tenements to pay off his debts, and his sale shall be valid and effective. And if he does not give satisfaction within the quarter, let there be delivered to the merchant all the goods of the debtor, and all his lands at a reasonable valuation to be held until [from the proceeds] the debt is completely cleared off; and nevertheless he shall remain in prison as has been said, and the merchant shall find him bread and water. And the merchant or his assign shall have such seisin in the tenements delivered to him that he can take out a writ of *novel disseisin* if he is ejected, and redisseisin as well, to hold to him and his

[1] the name varies in the manuscripts

[2] i.e. during the first quarter, as in fact *Fleta* (ed. Richardson and Sayles), I, p. 213 makes clear, "*durante primo quarterio*".

[3] A valuable concession to the creditor. At common law the debtor could not have made a valid deed while he was in prison.

assigns as of freehold until the debt is paid. After the debt is levied and paid the debtor shall be set free with his land. And in the writ that the chancellor sends let mention be made that the sheriff shall certify the justices of the one bench or of the other of the manner in which he has executed the king's command for a certain day: on which day the merchant, if he has not had satisfaction for his debt, shall sue before the justices; and if the sheriff does not return the writ, or returns that the writ came too late, or that he has passed it on to the bailiffs of a liberty, the justices shall act in accordance with what is contained in the last statute of Westminster.[1] And if perchance the sheriff reports that the debtor has not been found, or that he is a clerk, the merchant shall have a writ to all the sheriffs where he has land to deliver to him all the debtor's chattels and tenements by a reasonable extent to hold to him and his assigns in the way aforementioned, and nevertheless he shall have a writ to what sheriff he will to arrest the debtor if he is a layman, and hold him in the aforementioned way. And the keeper of the prison shall take heed that he must be responsible for the person of the debtor or for the debt. And after the lands of the debtor are delivered to the merchant it will be quite lawful for the debtor to sell his land, provided that the merchant does not lose by his improvements. And there shall always be saved to the merchant damages and all necessary and reasonable costs in works, suits, delays and expenses. And if the debtor finds pledges who accept for themselves the liabilities of[2] principal debtors, the pledges shall after the day is past be dealt with in all things as is decreed for the principal debtor, as to arrest, delivery of lands and other things. And when the lands of the debtor are delivered to the merchant he shall have seisin of all the lands that were in the debtor's hand on the day that the recognisance was made, whoever's hand they have afterwards come into either by enfeoffment or in any other way. And after the debt has been paid lands alienated from the debtor by enfeoffment shall revert as before to the feoffee, just as the other lands to the debtor. And if the debtor or pledge dies the merchant shall have [remedy] not by arresting the heir, but by his lands as aforesaid, if he is of age, or when he comes of age. And a seal is to be provided for use at fairs. And this seal shall be sent to each fair under the king's seal by a sworn clerk. And there shall be chosen by the keeper of the fair and the community of the merchants two upright merchants of the city of London who shall take the oath, and the seal shall be opened before them and one piece shall be given to the aforesaid merchants and the other shall remain with the clerk. And before them, or one of the merchants if both cannot be there, the recognisances shall be made as is said earlier. And before any recognisance is enrolled the penalty of the statute shall be read publicly before the debtor, so that he cannot at another time say that the punishment he was given was not the one to which he had made himself liable. And to provide for the keep of the aforesaid clerk the king shall take a penny for every pound in every town where the seal is, except at a fair, where he shall take three halfpence for the pound. The king wills that this ordinance and establishment be observed from now on throughout his whole realm of England and of Ireland, between any people whoever they are who wish of their own accord to make

[1] (13 Edw. I) Westminster II (1285), c. 39 (No. 57 above)
[2] *se conoissent estre*

such a recognisance, except Jews, to whom this establishment does not apply. And by this establishment a writ of debt shall not be abated. And the chancellor, the barons of the exchequer, the justices of both benches and itinerant justices shall not be prevented from taking recognisances of debts from those who wish to make them before them. But the execution of recognisances made before them shall not be done in the aforementioned way, but in accordance with law and usage and the way provided elsewhere in another statute.

59. Statute of Winchester (13 Edw. I), Michaelmas 1285

(Stubbs, *Select Charters*, 9th edn, pp. 464-6 [French])

Because from day to day robberies, homicides and arsons are more often committed than they used to be, and felonies cannot be attainted by the oath of jurors, who had rather suffer felonies done to strangers to go unpunished than indict wrongdoers the greater part of whom are people of the same district, or at least, if the doers are of another district, their receivers are of the neighbourhood; and this they do because an oath is not now feared by the jurors, and for the district where the felonies were committed, with regard to restitution of losses, no penalty has hitherto been provided for their concealment and neglect; OUR LORD THE KING to reduce the power of felons establishes a penalty in such case, so that for fear of the penalty more than for fear of the oath, they shall henceforth not spare anyone nor conceal any felony, and commands that proclamation be solemnly made in all shire-courts, hundred-courts, markets, fairs and all other places where people assemble in considerable numbers – so that no one can excuse himself on the grounds of ignorance – that each district be henceforth so kept that immediately robberies and felonies are committed vigorous pursuit shall be made from vill to vill and from district to district.

[II] Likewise inquests shall be made, if need be, in vills by him who is lord of the vill, and then in hundreds and in liberties and in shires, and sometimes in two, three, or four shires in cases where felonies are committed on the borders of shires, so that malefactors can be attainted. And if the district does not answer concerning such manner of malefactors, the penalty shall be that each district, that is to say the people living in the district, shall answer for robberies committed and for the losses, so that the whole hundred in which the robbery is committed, together with the liberties within the boundaries of that hundred, shall answer for the robbery committed. And if the robbery is committed on the boundary of two hundreds, both the hundreds shall answer together with the liberties; and the district shall have no longer than forty days after the commission of the robbery and felony within which it will behove them to give satisfaction for the robbery and the misdeed or to produce the malefactors.

[III] And because he does not wish people to be suddenly impoverished by this penalty, which would seem hard to some people, the king grants that it shall not be immediately incurred, but shall be respited until next Easter and meanwhile the king will see how the district behaves and such robberies and felonies cease. After which time all may be sure that the aforesaid penalty will run generally, that is to say that each district, that is to say the people living in the district, shall answer for robberies and felonies committed in their district.

[IV] And the more to assure peace, the king has commanded that in the large vills that are enclosed the gates be shut from sunset to sunrise, and that no man lodge in a suburb or a detached part of the vill save by day, nor yet by day if the host be not willing to answer for him; and the bailiffs of vills shall make enquiry each week, or at the least each fortnight, into people lodging in suburbs and in detached parts of vills, and if they find any one receiving or otherwise harbouring people who are suspect of being against the peace the bailiffs shall do justice therein. And henceforth it is commanded that watches be kept as they were accustomed to be formerly, that is to say[1] from Ascension day to Michaelmas, in each city by six men at each gate, in each borough by twelve men, in each vill in the open country by six men or four according to the number of the inhabitants, and they shall keep watch continually all night from sunset to sunrise. And if any stranger pass by them, let him be arrested until morning: and if nothing suspicious is found he may go free, but if anything suspicious is found let him be handed over to the sheriff forthwith and he shall receive him without making difficulty and keep him safely until he is delivered in due manner. And if they will not suffer themselves to be arrested, let hue and cry be raised against them and those who keep watch shall follow them with the whole vill together with the neighbouring vills with hue and cry from vill to vill until they are taken and handed over to the sheriff as is aforesaid; and for the arrest of such strangers no one shall have legal proceedings taken against him.

[V] It is likewise commanded that the highways from market towns to other market towns be widened where there are woods or hedges or ditches, so that there may be no ditch, underwood or bushes where one could hide with evil intent within two hundred feet of the road on one side or the other, provided that this statute extends not to oaks or to large trees so long as it is clear underneath. And if by the default of a lord, who will not fill up a ditch or level underwood or bushes in the manner aforesaid, robberies are committed, the lord shall be answerable: and if murder is committed, the lord shall be condemned to make fine at the king's pleasure. And if the lord is unable to cut down the underwood, the district shall help him to do it. And the king is willing for the roads in his demesne lands and woods, within forest and without, to be widened as aforesaid. And if perchance there is a park near the highway, it will behove the lord of the park to reduce his park until there is a verge two hundred foot wide at the side of the highway as aforesaid, or to make a wall, ditch or hedge that malefactors cannot get over or get back over to do evil.

[VI] It is likewise commanded that every man have in his house arms for keeping the peace in accordance with the ancient assize; namely that every man between fifteen years and sixty be assessed and sworn to arms according to the amount of his lands

[1] The rest of this clause is in fact a recital of the provisions as to watch-keeping of the Form for keeping the peace, 1242 (No. 33 above).

and[1] of his chattels; that is to say, for fifteen pounds[2] of land, and[1] forty marks worth of chattels, a hauberk, a helmet of iron, a sword, a knife and a horse; for ten pounds worth of land and[1] twenty marks worth of chattels, a haubergeon,[3] a helmet, a sword and a knife; for a hundred shillings worth of land, a doublet,[4] a helmet of iron, a sword and a knife; for forty shillings worth of land and over, up to a hundred shillings worth, a sword, a bow, arrows and a knife; and he who has less than forty shillings worth of land shall be sworn to have scythes, gisarmes,[5] knives and other small weapons; he who has less than twenty marks in chattels, swords, knives and other small weapons. And all others who can do so shall have bows and arrows outside the forests and within them bows and bolts. And that the view of arms be made twice a year. And in each hundred and liberty let two constables be chosen to make the view of arms and the aforesaid constables shall, when the justices assigned to this come to the district, present before them the defaults they have found in arms, in watch-keeping and in highways; and present also people who harbour strangers in upland vills for whom they are not willing to answer. And the justices assigned shall present again to the king in each parliament and the king will provide a remedy therefor. And from henceforth let sheriffs and bailiffs, whether bailiffs of liberties or not, whether of greater or less authority, who have a bailiwick or forester's office, in fee or otherwise, take good care to follow the cry with the district, and, according to their degree, keep horses and arms to do this with; and if there is any who does not do it, let the defaults be presented by the constables to the justices assigned, and then afterwards by them to the king as aforesaid. And the king commands and forbids, for the honour of holy church, a fair or market to be held henceforth in a churchyard. Given at Winchester on the eighth day of October in the thirteenth year of the king's reign.

60. The writ "*Circumspecte agatis*", June–July 1286

(Powicke and Cheney (eds), *Councils and Synods II* (*1205–1313*), pp. 974–5)

The statute about the lord king's prohibition begins.

Edward by God's grace king of England etc. to Richard de Boyland and his fellow justices greeting. Act circumspectly in the matter of the lord bishop of Norwich and his clergy, not punishing them if they have held a plea concerning those things which are purely spiritual, that is concerning corrections which prelates impose for mortal sin, namely for fornications, adulteries and such like, for which sometimes corporal punishment is inflicted, sometimes a money penalty, especially if he who is convicted of such is a free man; also, if a prelate punishes for an unenclosed cemetery,

[1] On the disjunctive use of "*et*", cf. *Dialogus de Scaccario*, ed. C. Johnson (Medieval Classics), p. 71. It is clear from the Assize of Arms, 1181 (Stubbs, *Select Charters*, pp. 183–4), the Form for keeping the peace, 1242 (No. 33 above) and the Latin version in *Fleta* (ed. Richardson and Sayles, II, Selden Soc., vol. 72. p. 63) that the amounts for land and chattels are here alternatives.

[2] land, that is to say, worth that much a year, not its capital value

[3] a hauberk is a long coat of mail; a haubergeon, a sleeveless coat or jacket of mail

[4] a sword-proof or spear-proof coat

[5] pointed weapons resembling halberds

a church without roof or not properly provided with ornaments, in which cases no penalty can be inflicted other than a money penalty; also, if a rector claims a mortuary in places where mortuaries have customarily been given; also, if a rector claims from his parishioners oblations, [or] due and accustomed tithes, or a rector brings an action against a rector about tithes lesser or greater, provided a quarter of a church's value[1] is not claimed; also, if a prelate claims from a rector a pension due to him as advocate of a church: all such claims are to be made in a church court. With regard to laying violent hands on clerks and in a cause of defamation it was granted on another occasion that a plea concerning these things should be held in court Christian, provided money is not claimed but the action is for correction of the sin; also with regard to breach of faith, provided the action is for correction of the sin. In all the aforesaid cases and the like the ecclesiastical judge has cognisance, notwithstanding a writ of prohibition, even if it is delivered. Given at Paris, in the fourteenth year of our reign.

61. Enquiry into offences by royal officials during the king's absence, 1286–9, 13 October 1289

(*Cal. Close Rolls Edward I, 1288–96*, p. 55)

Edward I left England for Gascony on 13 May 1286 and was away until 12 August 1289 – more than three years. On his return he heard so much of misconduct by his officials in his absence that he appointed a carefully-chosen and exceptionally strong commission to hear complaints and by this letter of 13 October to all shires invited anyone with a grievance to bring it before these commissioners at Westminster. The proceedings have survived and have been analysed and a selection from them printed by T. F. Tout and Hilda Johnstone in *State Trials of the Reign of Edward the First 1289–1293* (London, 1906). The attention they attracted at the time is reflected in the chroniclers and in No. 234 below.

To the sheriff of Nottingham. Notification that the king has appointed J. bishop of Winchester, R. bishop of Bath and Wells, Henry de Lacy, earl of Lincoln, John de Sancto Johanne, William le Latimer, mr William de Luda, keeper of the wardrobe, and William de Marchia to hear any grievances and wrongs that have been committed during the king's absence from his realm by his ministers upon any persons of the realm, in order that they, after hearing the complaints and the answers of the ministers concerning them, may relate and explain them to the king in his next parliament to be duly corrected. The king therefore orders the sheriff to cause all and singular of his county who feel themselves to have been aggrieved during the king's absence by his ministers and who wish to complain of the same to be distinctly and openly warned throughout the sheriff's bailiwick to come to Westminster on the morrow of Martinmas next before the king's subjects aforesaid to show and prosecute their grievances. The sheriff is charged to execute this order as he loves himself and his goods, so that he may not be found remiss or negligent and so incur punishment as a contemner of the king's orders.

The like to all the sheriffs of England.

[1] *quarta pars alicuius ecclesie*

62. The Statute of Consultation, April–July 1290

(Powicke and Cheney (eds), *Councils and Synods II (1205–1313)*, pp. 1090–1)

As ecclesiastical judges because of the lord king's prohibition often refrain from proceeding with causes moved before them in cases where remedy cannot be given to complainants to the court of the lord king by a writ from his chancery, on which account those plaintiffs are to their grave loss dispossessed of their right and remedy in both the king's and the church's court (as the lord king has understood from the grievous complaint of certain people), the lord king wills and commands that, when because of a royal prohibition delivered to them ecclesiastical judges do refrain in the aforesaid cases, the chancellor or chief justice of the lord king at the time concerned, after seeing at the plaintiff's instance his libel[1] of the cause, shall, if they see that in his case remedy cannot be given to the plaintiff by a writ from the chancery but that it is for a church court to determine the cause, write to the judges before whom the cause was first moved to proceed with it notwithstanding the royal prohibition delivered to them earlier about it etc.

63. "Quo Warranto" (18 Edw. I), 1290

(A. *Statutes of the Realm*, I (Rec. Com., 1810), p. 107, and from there reprinted, more conveniently, in D. W. Sutherland, *Quo Warranto Proceedings in the Reign of Edward I, 1278–94* (Oxford, 1963), pp. 203–4;
B(1). *Ann. Monastici* (Rolls series), III, p. 361; and Sutherland, op. cit., p. 205, collated;
B(2). *Statutes of the Realm*, I, p. 107)

One of the important decisions in parliament in 1290 concerned the enquiry *quo warranto* which had been on the go from the beginning of the reign. What it was we do not know. Three texts have come down to us, A, B(1) and B(2) below. A is the "Parliament roll" record. B(1) and B(2) are Latin and French versions respectively of the so-called "summary" of A. A forthcoming article by the present writer will examine their relationships.

A.

Forasmuch as writs of *quo waranto* and also the giving of judgments on pleas of those writs have suffered long delay because justices in giving those judgments have not up to now been told the will of the lord king, that same lord king at his parliament after Easter at Westminster in the eighteenth year of his reign, of his special grace and also on account of the affection he has for the prelates, earls, barons and others of his kingdom, has granted that all of his kingdom whoever they are, as well religious as others, who can prove by good inquest of the neighbourhood or other[2] way that they and their ancestors or predecessors have used any whatsoever of the liberties about which they have been impleaded by the aforesaid writs before the time of king Richard his kinsman or during all his time and until now[3] may continue[4] and[5] provided they have not misused those liberties that the parties shall be

[1] In ecclesiastical procedure a statement in writing of the plaintiff's case.
[2] the word "sufficient" (*sufficienti*) is interlineated at this point in the parliament roll
[3] "without interruption" ditto
[4] "may continue": i.e. *continuarunt* emended to *continuent*
[5] "and": an interlineation in the parliament roll, but probably an original reading restored – though not necessarily to its original position. It could originally have been quite as well (perhaps better) after, rather than before the parenthetical "provided they have not misused those liberties".

further adjourned[1] to a date fixed to give them reasonable time to go to the lord king with the justices' record under the justices' seal[2] and get back and the lord king will confirm their estate by his letters.[3] And those who cannot prove seisin of their ancestors or predecessors in the aforesaid way shall be dealt with and judged according to the common law; and those who have royal charters shall be judged according to those charters.[4] Furthermore the lord king has of his special grace granted that all judgments which have been given in pleas of *quo waranto* by his justices at Westminster since the aforesaid Easter and given for him, the lord king, if the parties who have lost will come again to the lord king they shall have by the lord king's grace remedy of the sort granted above. The same lord king granted also, to save the people of his kingdom outlay and expense, that pleas of *quo waranto* shall henceforth be pleaded and determined in the eyres of the justices and that pleas[5] still pending[6] shall be readjourned[7] until the coming of the justices of those parts, etc.[8]

B(1)

Concerning the writ which is called *quo waranto* the lord king established on the third day of Pentecost that all who say they have had undisturbed possession of liberties before the times of king Richard and since without interruption and can show this by good inquest may enjoy the things thus possessed; which possession moreover, if it is claimed effectively,[9] he will confirm by a title.[10] And those who have old charters shall be judged according to the form and tenor of them. And those who have lost since last Easter by the aforesaid writ in the form previously used in a plea of the aforesaid writ shall have restitution of their losses and may plead again in accordance with the tenor of the present constitution.

B(2)

Concerning this writ which is called *quo waranto* our lord the king established on the day of Pentecost in the eighteenth year of his reign that all those who claim to have undisturbed possession of liberties before the time of king Richard[11] without interruption and can show this by good inquest may well enjoy[12] this possession; and if this possession is claimed rightly[13] our lord the king will confirm it by a title.[14] And those who have old charters of liberties[15] shall be judged according to the tenor and

[1] the phrase "before the same justices" is interlineated at this point in the parliament roll
[2] *recordo justiciariorum sub sigillo suo signato* in the parliament roll, "*sub*" being an interlineation and "*signato*" being scored out.
[3] In the foregoing punctuation has been omitted where to give it would prejudge the meaning. Elsewhere the punctuation is that of the *Statutes of the Realm* (I, p. 107) printed text.
[4] at this point "and their full content" (*et earundem plenitudinem*) is interlineated in the parliament roll
[5] "of *quo waranto*" is interlineated at this point in the parliament roll
[6] "before him" (*coram ipso*) is interlineated in the parliament roll at this point
[7] "in their respective shires" written at this point in the parliament roll, then scored out
[8] The parliament roll continues (but in a different hand) with "and that in the meantime after being adjourned in this way they shall be stayed without day".
[9] *cum effectu* [10] *titulo*
[11] and since: occurs at this point in the Latin version and seems required here also to make sense. Probably accidentally omitted from this particular manuscript of the French version.
[12] *bien se joient de*
[13] *par raison* [14] *par title*
[15] The manuscript here adds "the charters" as subject of the verb, but this must be an interpolation.

form of these same charters. And those who have lost their liberties[1] since last Easter and by the aforesaid writ in the form previously used in a plea of the aforesaid writ shall have restitution of their lost liberties and may plead again in accordance with the nature of the present constitution.

64. Statute of "Quia emptores" (18 Edw. I) (Stat. Westm. III), 8 July 1290

(*Statutes of the Realm*, I (1810), p. 106)

Also cited as the Statute of Westminster III, and this has contemporary warrant (*Walter of Guisborough*, ed. H. Rothwell, p. 226), but best known today by its opening words.

[c. 1] Because purchasers of lands and tenements belonging to the fees of magnates and others have often in times past entered into their fees to the prejudice of those magnates and others, in that their free tenants have sold their lands and tenements to the purchasers to be held in fee by them and their heirs of their feoffors and not of the chief lords of the fees, whereby the same chief lords have very often lost escheats, marriages and wardships of lands and tenements belonging to their fees, a thing which seemed to those magnates and other lords exceedingly hard and hard to bear and tantamount in this case to manifest disinheritance, THE LORD KING in his parliament at Westminster after Easter in the eighteenth year of his reign, namely on the quindene of St John the Baptist, at the instance of the magnates of his kingdom, granted, provided and enacted that henceforth it is to be lawful for each free man to sell at will his land or tenement or part thereof, so, however, that the feoffee shall hold that land or tenement of the same chief lord and by the same services and customs his feoffor previously held them by. And if he sells some part of those lands or tenements of his to anyone, the feoffee shall hold it immediately of the chief lord and be charged at once with as much service for that portion as pertains or ought to pertain to the same lord in accordance with the amount of land or tenement sold; and so in this case, that part of the service which is exactable by the feoffor shall fall to the chief lord, since the feoffee ought to be intendant and answerable to the same chief lord, according to the amount of land or tenement sold, for that portion of the service so due. And it is to be understood that by the aforesaid sales or purchases of lands or tenements, or any part of them, those lands or tenements can in no way, in part or wholly, come into mortmain, by art or artifice, contrary to the form of the statute ordained on this some time ago[2] etc. And it is to be understood that the present statute is applicable only to lands sold to be held in fee simply[3] and that it applies to the future; and it will begin to take effect at the next feast of St Andrew etc.

[1] "their liberties": possibly an interpolation

[2] 1279, the statute *De viris religiosis* (Mortmain), No. 53 above

[3] i.e. granted unconditionally. The technical term "fee simple" did not establish itself immediately, cf. A. W. B. Simpson, *An Introduction to the History of the Land Law* (Oxford, 1961), p. 53.

65. Treaty of Birgham, 18 July 1290

(*Documents Illustrative of the History of Scotland*, ed. J. Stevenson, 2 vols (Edinburgh, 1870), I, No. cviii [French]. The more important clauses as translated by Dickinson, Donaldson and Milne, *A Source Book of Scottish History*, I (1952), pp. 107–9)

A marriage treaty between England and Scotland. Confirmed at Northampton on 28 August. But invalidated by the death of Margaret, the "Maid of Norway" in September 1290.

. . . We, having due consideration to the peace and tranquillity of both kingdoms, and that mutual affection should continue between their peoples for all time, have granted in the name and on behalf of our lord king [Edward I] and his heirs that the rights, laws, liberties and customs of the kingdom of Scotland in all things and in all ways shall be wholly and inviolably preserved for all time throughout the whole of that kingdom and its marches. Saving always the right of our lord king, and of any other whomsoever, which has pertained to him, or to any other, on the marches, or elsewhere, over these things in question before the time of the present agreement, or which in any just way ought to pertain to him in the future.

We expressly will and grant in the name of our lord king and his heirs, and in our name, that, failing heirs to the aforesaid Edward and Margaret, or either of them, in the event that the aforesaid kingdom [of Scotland] ought of right to return to the nearest heirs, it shall return and be restored to them, wholly, freely, absolutely and without any subjection – if perchance in any way that kingdom shall happen to come into the hands of our lord king or his heirs – and in such a way that, by reason of these presents, nothing shall accrue to our lord king, or his heirs, or any other, and, in a like way, nothing shall be lost . . .

We promise in the name and on behalf of our lord king and his heirs that the kingdom of Scotland shall remain separate and divided from the kingdom of England, by its right boundaries and marches, as have hitherto in the past been observed, and that it shall be free in itself and without subjection; saving always the right of our lord king, and of any other whomsoever, which has pertained to him, or to any other, on the marches or elsewhere . . . before the time of the present agreement, or which in any just way ought to pertain to him in the future . . .

We expressly grant, for our lord king and his heirs, that the chapters of cathedral, collegiate, and conventual churches which hold their own elections shall not be compelled to pass outwith the kingdom of Scotland to seek leave to elect, or to present the persons elected, or to swear fealty or oath to the king of Scotland. And that no one holding in chief of the aforesaid king of Scotland shall be compelled to pass outwith the kingdom to do homage or fealty, or to pay the relief for his lands . . .

No one of the kingdom of Scotland shall be held to answer outwith that kingdom for any agreement entered into, or for any crime committed, in that kingdom, or in any other cause, contrary to the laws and customs of that kingdom; as has hitherto been reasonably observed . . .

No parliament shall be held outwith the kingdom and marches of Scotland on matters touching that kingdom or its marches or the position of those who inhabit that kingdom. Neither shall any tallages, aids, hostings, or maletots be exacted from the aforesaid kingdom, or placed upon the people of the same kingdom, except to meet the expenses of the common affairs of the kingdom and in those cases where the kings of Scotland were wont to demand the same . . .

We protest that all the clauses in this treaty are to be so understood that by this treaty the rights of neither kingdom are in any wise to be increased or decreased; nor are the rights of either of the kings, but each king is to have his own estate freely.

66. The "Fifteenth" of 1290 requested from Wales and Ireland also, *c.* 20 January and 26 October 1291

In 1290 an English parliament granted Edward I a tax of a fifteenth of movable property. In 1291 he requested his subjects in Wales and Ireland also to contribute. This was not Ireland's first experience of English taxation, but it was for newly-conquered Wales.

For the response to these requests, see J. F. Willard, *Parliamentary Taxes on Personal Property 1290–1334*, pp. 26–8.

(a)

(*Cal. Pat. Rolls 1281–92*, p. 419)

1291, *c.* 20 January
Request to the earls, barons, knights, free men and the whole commonalty of Wales to grant, in such manner as Richard de Massy and Master Adam de Bodindon whom the king is sending to them shall more fully request, a fifteenth like the rest of the realm, in order to pay the debts which the king incurred during his absence abroad in effecting the liberation of Charles, king of Sicily, his kinsman, whereby the state of the Holy Land and of the church was improved and peace secured; and to reply by the said messengers as to what they will do for the king.

(b)

(ibid. p. 448)

1291, 26 October, Abergavenny
Request, directed to all the king's subjects in Ireland, to graciously grant him a fifteenth for the relief of the manifold debts with which he is oppressed, in like manner as J. archbishop of Dublin, W. de Valencia, earl of Pembroke, G. de Clare, earl of Gloucester and Hertford, and Roger le Bygod, earl of Norfolk, marshal of England and many other barons and magnates having lands in Ireland have done, and as master Thomas Cantok, king's clerk, chancellor of Ireland, shall more fully declare. Each one is to inform the king by letters what he has done or will do in this respect; and the king promises that such grant shall not be to their prejudice or be drawn into a precedent.

D. ENGLAND AT WAR 1294–1327

67. "Quo Warranto" proceedings indefinitely postponed, November 1294

(*Select Cases in the Court of King's Bench under Edward I*, ed. G. O. Sayles (Selden Soc.), III, p. 28)

The lord king in his Michaelmas parliament at the close of the twenty-second year of the reign of the present king and the beginning of the twenty-third granted in consideration of his people's favour[1] and on account of the present Gascon war that all his writs, as well of *quo warranto* as of pleas of land, should remain for the present without day until he or his heirs wished to speak about them.

68. The "Evil toll" (Maltote) of 1294–7

(*Cal. of Fine Rolls I, 1272–1307*, p. 347)

The maltote, it will be seen, was much less for Ireland, but for England at the rate of 3 marks for ordinary wool (there was still a higher rate for dressed wool) it meant a sixfold increase on the custom of 1275 on wool (No. 48, above).

In force in England from at least 29 July 1294 until 23 November 1297.

A detailed account for almost the whole period has survived for the port of Newcastle-upon-Tyne, and an extract from it is given as No. 128 below.

Notable is the description of the maltote as a subsidy granted to the king by the merchants of England and granted for a limited period only. By 1297 at least, in the French version of the "Articles of Grievance" (the Latin calls it *vectigal lanarum*) and in the "Confirmatio Cartarum" of 10 October, it had acquired the name of the "maltote" (pp. 472 and 486 below).

1294, 28 October, Westminster

Order to the treasurer and barons of the exchequer of Dublin to cause a mark to be taken on each sack of wool or woolfells and each last of hides, whereon ½ mark used to be taken for custom, during the war which the king intends to wage for the recovery of Gascony against the French, appointing two men to collect the same in each town of Ireland where the same used to be collected, the king wishing to do grace to the merchants of Ireland; though the merchants of England have granted to the king as a subsidy 5 marks on each sack of dressed wool[2] taken beyond seas for two or three years if the war last so long, and 3 marks on each sack of other wool or woolfells and 5 marks on each last of hides.

69. Articles of Grievance (*Monstraunces*), 1297

(Translated from a collation of Sir Goronwy Edwards's edition of the French text (*E.H.R.*, lviii (1943), pp. 170–1) with an improved "Hemingburgh" text (*Chronicle of Walter of Guisborough*, ed. H. Rothwell, Camden ser., LXXXIX (1957), pp. 292–3 [French])

This petition has been preserved by chroniclers – notably by Guisborough and Cotton in French and by Trivet, "Rishanger" and derivatives in Latin. It is almost certain that the Latin text is no more than a translation of the French.

These are the representations that archbishops, bishops, abbots, priors, earls and barons and all the community of the land make to our lord the king, and they humbly pray him as their lord that he be willing to redress and amend these things

[1] He had been granted a tenth in this parliament.

[2] *lana fracta*

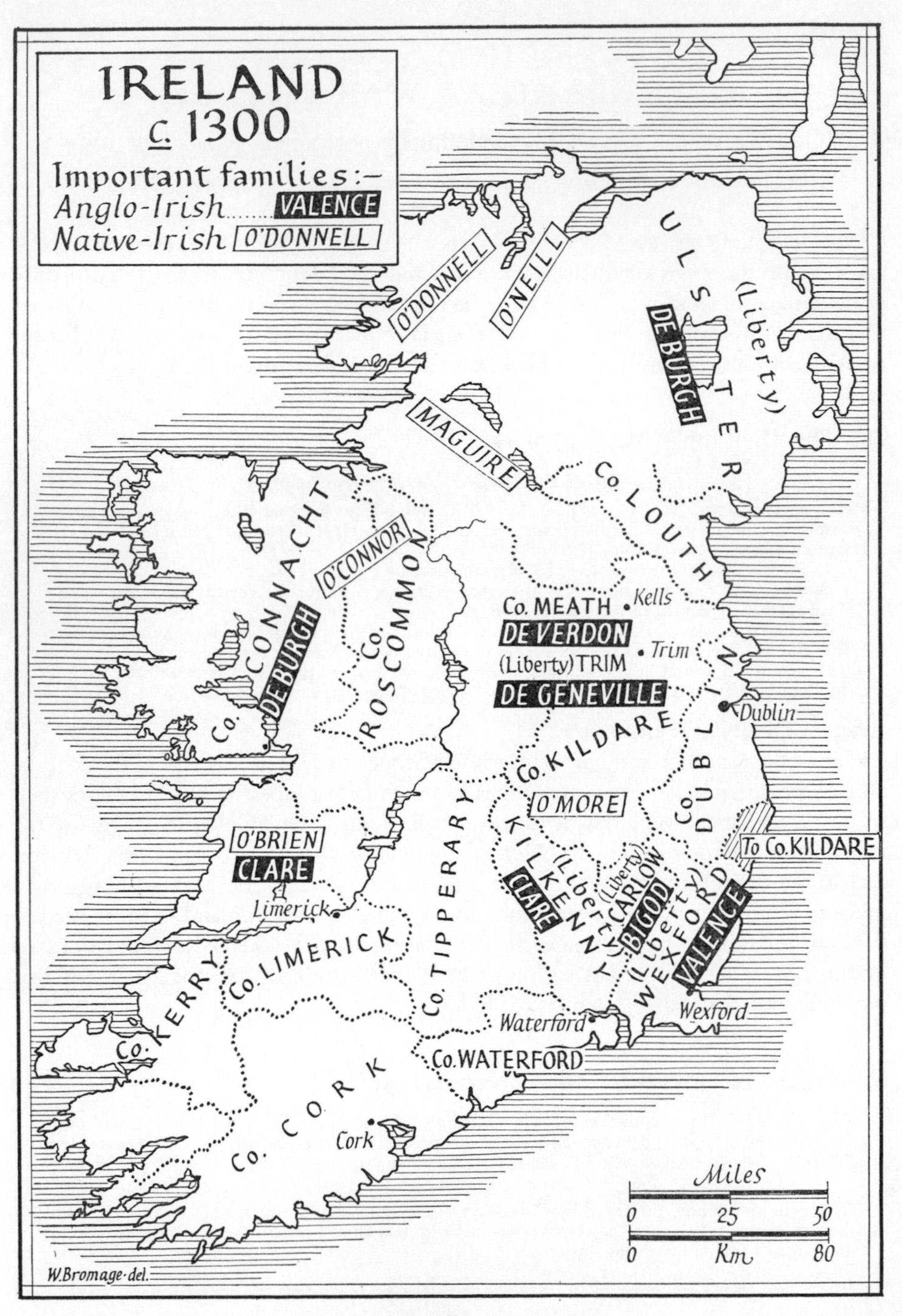
IRELAND
c. 1300
Important families:–
Anglo-Irish .... VALENCE
Native-Irish O'DONNELL
O'DONNELL
O'NEILL
ULSTER
(Liberty)
DE BURGH
MAGUIRE
Co. LOUTH
CONNACHT
O'CONNOR
Co. ROSCOMMON
Co. CONNACHT
DE BURGH
Co. MEATH
Kells
DE VERDON
Trim
(Liberty) TRIM
DE GENEVILLE
Dublin
Co. KILDARE
Co. DUBLIN
O'MORE
To Co. KILDARE
O'BRIEN
CLARE
Limerick
TIPPERARY
KILKENNY
(Liberty)
CLARE
(Liberty) CARLOW
BIGOD
(Liberty) WEXFORD
VALENCE
Co. LIMERICK
Co. KERRY
Co. TIPPERARY
Waterford
Wexford
Co. WATERFORD
Co. CORK
Cork
Miles
0
25
50
0
Km
80
W. Bromage del.

SCOTLAND and the NORTH of ENGLAND
to illustrate the Anglo-Scottish War
ORKNEY ISLANDS
SHETLAND IS.
Note: The Hebrides & Man acquired from Norway in 1266. The Orkneys & Shetland still Norwegian in 1327 – remained so until the late 15TH cent.
OUTER HEBRIDES
North Minch
HEBRIDES
INNER
Banff
BUCHAN
COMYN
Elgin
Spey
Inverness
BADENOCH
COMYN
Kildrummy
Aberdeen
Dee
THE MOUNTH
Pass
Loch Ericht
Pass
Brechin
Montrose
Dundee
Arbroath
Perth
St Andrews
Anglo-Scottish frontier
Ways through the Lowlands
Most used ways
Some important families
COMYN
Stirling
BANNOCKBURN
Firth of Forth
Dunbar
Falkirk
Edinburgh
Berwick on Tweed
Glasgow
Clyde
Lanark
Biggar
Lauder
Coldstream
Tweed
Irvine
Roxburgh
Forest of Selkirk
Jedburgh
Ayr
Crawford
Alnwick
Firth of Clyde
Nithsdale
COMYN
BRUS
Annandale
Redesdale
CARRICK
BRUS
N. Tyne
Dumfries
Fenland
Newcastle on Tyne
GALLOWAY
BALLIOL
S. Tyne
Hexham
ANTRIM
Caerlaverock
Carlisle
Penrith
Durham
Miles
0
50
0
Km
80
MAN
York
W. Bromage del.

for his own honour and for the preservation of the people. First, it seems to all the community of the land that the warning that was given them by the writ of our lord the king was not sufficient, because there was no definite place specified where they should go, for on the place depends the provision to be made and they could have known whether they ought to do him service or not. Because it is commonly said that our lord the king wishes to cross over into Flanders, it seems to all the community of the land that there they are not bound to do any service because neither they nor their predecessors or ancestors ever did service in this land. And even though it were that they ought to do service there as elsewhere, they would not have the power to do it because they have been so reduced by the various tallages and various prises, that is of corn, oats, malt, wools, hides, oxen, cows, salted flesh, without payment of the money with which they would have to support and maintain themselves. They say, besides, that they cannot pay an aid on account of the poverty they are in due to the aforesaid tallages and prises, because they scarcely have wherewith to support themselves and there are many of them that have no means of support and cannot till their lands. Besides, all the community of the land feel themselves greatly aggrieved that they are not treated according to the laws and customs of the land by which their ancestors used to be treated, nor have they their liberties which they used to have, but are arbitrarily put out, on which account they feel themselves greatly aggrieved. Besides, clerks and laymen feel themselves greatly aggrieved in that they used to be treated according to the clauses of the great charter, whose clauses are all neglected to the great loss of the people: on which account they pray our lord the king that he be willing for these things to be put right for his own honour and for the preservation of the people. Besides, the community of the land feel themselves greatly aggrieved about the assize of the forest which is not kept as it used to be in the past, nor the charter of the forest either, but attachments are made at will outside the assize otherwise than used to be done. Besides, all the community of the land feel themselves greatly aggrieved by the maletote on wools which is very burdensome – on each sack of whole wool 40*s* and of broken wool on each sack 5 marks – because the wool of England is worth nearly half what the whole land is worth a year, and the maltote paid at such a rate amounts in the year to a fifth of what the whole land is worth. Because the community of the land desire honour and safety for our lord the king, as they should, it does not seem to them that it would be for his good to cross over into Flanders without being more assured for himself and his followers about the Flemings and also about the land of Scotland which is beginning to rise against him whilst he is now in the land, and they well believe that they [the Scots] would do it in a worse way if they were sure that he had crossed the sea, and not only they but other lands that are not yet properly settled.

70. The Eighth and Fifth and Prise of Wool of 30 July 1297, and subsidiary documents

(*Parliamentary Writs*, I, pp. 54–5 (No. 9) and 394–5 (No. 36); subsidiary documents from P.R.O. Exchequer, K.R. Memor. Roll, No. 70, m. 118 [French and Latin])

The form of the taxation of the eighth and fifth granted to the king

It is ordained by the king and his council that the gift which is now granted to the king by the laity of the realm is to be taxed and levied in the following way: namely, first, that in each county two knights, or a knight and a serjeant, the most trustworthy that can be found and who do not belong to the county to which they are appointed and have no land in that county shall be the taxors and collectors; and that in the counties to which they are appointed these taxors and collectors shall cause to be chosen faithfully and with good examination from each vill of the county four or two lawful men (or less or more according to the size of the vills) who are of the more trustworthy and who are capable of answering at a future date for what they do, and equal to assessing everybody of the vill they belong to. And that these people so chosen from the vills shall be sworn honestly to examine and tax all the goods that everyone in the vills where they tax has in field, house or elsewhere on the day of the Nativity of our Lady next to come [8 September 1297] and value them at a good and proper[1] price, and honestly enrol all the items and the totals of those same goods thus priced and examined without sparing anyone or committing fraud by any sort of excuse of relationship, favour, or friendship. And the two above-mentioned chief examiners and taxors, after receiving the said oath of the said men of the vills, shall go from hundred to hundred and from vill to vill as thoroughly as they can to see and enquire whether everyone's goods have been well and lawfully examined, taxed and priced according to what by right and reason they ought to be by the aforesaid men of the vills. And they shall enquire whether anybody of the vills has removed any of his goods so that it would not be examined and taxed with his other goods on the above-named day. And if it is found that anyone has removed any goods, these goods shall be taxed to the same extent as the others. And if they find that these men of the vills[2] or any of them have concealed anything or in return for a gift or as a favour have taxed it for less than what it is worth, they shall increase and make up the amount at their discretion in the most appropriate way they can for the king's use. And they shall inform the treasurer and barons of the exchequer of the names of those who have thus infringed their oath. And the taxation of these men of the vills' own goods shall be done by other lawful persons of their neighbourhood who have no connection with them, to be assigned and well and properly sworn to this by the knights, the chief taxors. And the taxation of the goods of the chief taxors and collectors shall be reserved for the treasurer and barons of the exchequer. And as soon as the taxation of the goods is completed in the above-mentioned way, the chief taxors and collectors shall have the eighth and fifth levied and collected in the way laid down for them by the king. And this taxation shall be made of the goods of clerks as well as laymen, goods, that is, which are not appurtenant to their churches.

[1] *bon et leal*

[2] i.e. the men chosen and responsible for taxing their fellows in each vill

And there shall likewise be taxed in this taxation the goods of the villeins of archbishops, bishops, religious, and all other clerks, whoever they are. And be it known that in this taxation there shall be exempted the military equipment,[1] the mounts,[2] jewels and clothes of knights, gentle men,[3] and their wives, also their vessels of gold, silver and brass. And all cities and boroughs, small and large, of the realm, whosoever they are and by whatever tenure or liberty,[4] and all the king's demesnes shall be taxed at the rate of a fifth. And in cities, boroughs and market towns[5] there shall be exempted in this taxation one garment for the man, one other for the wife, one bed for them both, one ring, one buckle of gold or silver, and one girdle of silk which are in daily use, and also one cup of silver or of mazer-wood they drink from. The goods of lepers, where they are ruled by a master who is a leper, shall not be taxed or valued, and if they are lepers ruled by a healthy master their goods are to be taxed like those of other people. And no one's goods shall be taxed if they do not amount to 5 shillings. And the taxors shall have two rolls made straightway of the taxation that is made of goods, in which rolls shall be contained the name of everybody who is taxed and the amount they will be charged an eight or a fifth of. And one roll shall always correspond to the other.[6] And of these two rolls, when the taxation is completed and well and truly entered in the form stated above, one roll shall remain with the taxors and the other be sent at once under their seals to the treasurer and barons of the exchequer. And taxors and clerks shall take nothing for delivering chapiters,[7] making tallies, or for anything else pertaining to the said business. And the chief taxors shall accept the king's money by count as it is current in the realm, and not by weight. And let there be sent into each county some good and upright person who is an official of the king to survey, observe, enquire, and examine if need be: that the said taxation has been made and levied well and honestly in the way stated above, and that the people are not wrongly burdened or harmed in any way by sheriffs or other officials of the king other than by paying the grant of the aforesaid gift. And the chief taxors and collectors are each to have the rolls of the fifteenth[8] of the county they are appointed to and also a transcript of the form of this ordinance and a transcript of the oath which they must take. And for this gift thus made to the king on this occasion, our lord the king has confirmed the great charter and the forest charter for himself and for his heirs.

[The names of the taxors and collectors of this eighth and fifth in the various counties were announced to the counties in letters dated 30 July 1297 and are given, along with the oath they were to take, in *Parl. Writs*, I, pp. 53–5, or in calendar form in *Cal. Pat. Rolls 1292–1301*, pp. 297–9.]

The form of the ordinance made by the king and his council concerning the buying of wool in various counties for the king's use by various merchants appointed for the purpose and the collecting and sending of it overseas to the bishop of Chester and John of Berwick

Because it is in every way fitting that our lord the king, for the safety of himself, of all his allies, and of his whole realm, should loyally keep the agreements he has made

[1] literally "armour", but in a wider sense than today's
[2] *mounteure*
[3] *gentiz hommes*
[4] *fraunchise*
[5] *villes marchaundes* (alternatively "towns of merchants")
[6] *E lun roule siwe toutz jours lautre en escripture.*
[7] supplying copies of, or extracts from, documents
[8] the fifteenth of 1290

with his allies abroad and these agreements are such that he must cross over soon with a large force, and as soon as he has crossed over it is agreed he should pay the king of Almain without delay on his arrival over there 30,000 marks, and the duke of Brabant 25,500 marks, and it is fitting that he should have what he needs for his crossing, namely (to help his good people who cross, pay wages to the horsemen[1] and the foot,[2] and for sailors and other expenses of his household) 20,000 marks over and above everything that will come to the exchequer from the issues of the realm between now and the crossing, the sum total of the above-mentioned things is that the king, of absolute necessity, must have with him, as well as the other money which will come to the exchequer between now and the said crossing, 75,500 marks. And our lord the king and his council have thought and spoken of this and deliberated how and in what way and from what things the said sum can be raised with the least burden to the people and the least harm to them, and it is their opinion that the king cannot get the said sum quickly in any better way than by buying an equivalent amount of the wool of clerks and laymen in the following manner: namely, that there be selected the best and most reliable merchants of England who understand the buying of wool and that those merchants be appointed to various counties to buy the wool of archbishops, bishops, abbots, priors and all other clerks and other important people of the same realm to the number of 8,000 sacks at such price and such weight as other merchants buy identical wool in the same district as that in which the wool is thus bought. And if the said people reply to the king's merchants and his other people appointed for the purpose that they do not wish to sell their wool, let the king's merchants and his other people answer that it is incumbent on them to do so in view of a task as great as that the king has now to perform for himself and for the common profit of all the realm, but that their wool will be taken and paid for in such a way that they will be protected against loss. And the king's merchants shall cause each seller to get a suitable letter from the king for as much money as is agreed on between the seller and them, and they shall meanwhile give a letter of their own or a tally to those they buy from until the said royal letters are received from the chancery. And it is the king's wish that the clerks and laymen from whom wool is bought for his use in this way be paid quickly from the gift which has now been granted to him by the clergy and the laity in return for confirming the great charter and the forest charter. And that for each of them there be allowed for in reckoning the wool the amount he should pay of the aforesaid gift, and what more remains due to him is to be paid in money from the same gift as is said above. And the king wills that no poor man's wool be bought for his use in this manner. And these same merchants who buy the said wool shall cause it to go, with the help of the sheriffs, to the ports nearest to the counties where they are as is more fully enjoined in the letters patent which the said king's merchants have. And they shall also cause the wool to cross over in the quickest way they can, safely and well-escorted. And some of these same merchants or other experienced and trusty persons who are selected for this purpose and who

[1] *gentz darmes*: a generic term covering the knights as well as serjeants-at-arms. cf. J. E. Morris, *Welsh Wars of Edward I*, pp. 49–54.
[2] *gentz de pie*

know the job of middleman shall cross over with the wool, well-informed by all the buyers about the price, the weight, and the buying of the wool he or they[1] cross with, in such a way that they can deliver them at the other end[2] as the bishop of Chester and John of Berwick will fully instruct them when they get there – but they shall not discharge[3] before having their advice and knowing what they want to be done. And the sheriffs of counties where wool is bought shall bear the cost of carriage and other necessary things as far as the ports. And then the collectors of the customs shall ordain on them and clear the crossing[4] and quickly cause the said wool to cross over day by day as it comes to them in the way aforesaid. And that the collectors of the customs be well aware of the number of sacks they have received and allowed to cross.

[The merchants appointed to the various counties along with the sheriff of the county concerned to buy, collect, and ship the wool are named in letters again dated 30 July 1297: *Parl. Writs*, I, pp. 395–6, or in calendar form in *Cal. Pat. Rolls 1292–1301*, pp. 297–9.

The amounts to be taken were: from Yorks. 1,500 sacks, Lincs. 1,500, Notts. and Derbys. 1,000, Northants and Rutland 600, Cambs. and Hunts. 200, Beds. and Bucks, 350, Oxon and Berks. 600, Norfolk and Suffolk 400, Warwicks. and Leics. 400, Essex and Herts. 300, Som. and Dorset 300, Glos. and Worcs. 800, and Surrey 50 – a total of 8,000 sacks.]

[Exchequer records then take up the story (K.R. Memor. Roll, No. 70, m. 118)]

Afterwards the lord king sent his writ to the barons[5] in these words

Edward by the grace etc. We write to you firmly enjoining that you cause the writs and the ordinance concerning the aid from the laity to be sent out as soon as you possibly can after they are ready. And entrust them to such persons as know how to speak the people fair and how to manage the business well and wisely. And send us word back by your letters and by the bearer of this what you do about these things. Given under our privy seal at Sevenoaks on the fourth day of August in the twenty-fifth year of our reign [4 August 1297, Sevenoaks].

Because of this order clerks and others have been appointed in the underwritten counties to receive the oath of the above-appointed taxors in the counties where they are and to instruct them how they ought to speak to the people by a certain form, drawn up on this by the barons and John of Droxford, keeper of the king's wardrobe, set out below

[First, however, the appointments (dated 8 August 1297). These are to the more distant counties, arranged for the purpose in eight groups. Taxors in other counties, it is noted, took their oath and received these instructions at the exchequer itself, the usual practice. Then:]

The tenor of the aforesaid form for instructing the taxor is

Those who receive the oath of the taxors shall instruct them to tell the people of the counties to which they are appointed in the most civil[6] and the most courteous way they know or can that our lord the king is aware that his people are very burdened by the many aids they have often and freely granted and given him to defend his realm and his aforementioned people from his enemies, for which he cannot thank them enough,[7] though they are bound to this and regard themselves as bound to do a

[1] *il passera ou passerount*
[2] *par de la*
[3] i.e. unload cargo
[4] *aquitent le passage*
[5] the barons of the exchequer, of course
[6] *la plus beale*; cf. "speak (the people) fair" (*beau parler*) in the exchequer writ of 4 August, Sevenoaks, above
[7] literally "for which he thanks them as much as he can"

thing which can turn out a relief and a lasting benefit to them and their heirs; and instruct them to say that he has agreed at the request of the archbishops, bishops, abbots, priors, earls and barons to confirm the great charter and the forest charter in all their points and for this grant the said archbishops, bishops, abbots and priors have granted the king aid from the clergy in return, and the said earls and barons in return for the granting and confirming of the said charters and for the great task the king has at this very moment of defending and preserving himself, his people and his allies have granted the king, for themselves and for the people, an eighth and fifth in accordance with the form ordained thereupon. And [instruct them] to tell the people that this thing they should do loyally and with good will, as the king is committing his person and all that he has, both all his own money and whatever he gets from his realm, to preserve them and his realm. And it seems to our lord the king that he could not do more for them than endanger his person and his life for them as for those he truly cares for and wishes to do his utmost to protect and maintain in honour for as long as his own body can bear it or is equal to it: which they will naturally be good enough to take into consideration and do their duty to their lord of their own free will, as good men and loyal should and are bound to do for their liege lord in so great and so grave a matter, and withal pray for him that God of His grace grant him to acquit himself so well and with such result[1] in his expedition[2] that it may be to the honour of God, of himself and of the whole of his realm.

71. Royal proclamation, 12 August 1297, Udimore

Translated from the French text printed in Bémont, *Chartes* (Paris, 1892), No. XI, via Rymer, from the royal record. A text, somewhat inferior, is preserved by the chronicler, Bartholomew Cotton, pp. 330–4. Another in the archives of the Dean and Chapter of Canterbury is analysed in *Hist. MSS Comm. 8th Report*, Appendix, p. 347.

Bémont prints from Rymer a Latin title, "About the Constable of England and the Marshal abdicating their offices and about excusing the king for exactions made in the kingdom for the needs of divers wars".

Because the king desires always the peace and quiet and welfare of all the people of his realm and in particular desires that, after the journey he now proposes to make for the honour of God and to recover his rightful heritage of which he has been most deceitfully defrauded by the king of France and for the honour and common profit of his realm, all reasons for the said peace and quiet being in any way disturbed may be completely removed, but some persons might say and give the people to understand things that are not true, whereby the same people might be moved to behave towards their liege lord otherwise than they ought, as about the withdrawal of the earl of Hereford and the earl marshal from him lately or about other matters, THE KING, on this and on the condition of himself and of the kingdom and how the affairs of the kingdom have been going for some time, makes known and wishes all to know the truth thereof, which is as follows.

Recently, when a large part of the men-at-arms of England, some by request,

[1] *si bien faire e ouerir*
[2] "*voiage*" was not then restricted to a sea-journey

others at the king's summons, came to London, the king, wishing to provide for the deliverance of these same people and relieve their expenses and their discomforts, sent word to the said earls, as constable and marshal of England, to come to him on a certain day to arrange the deliverance of the said people; on which day the earl of Hereford and sir John de Segrave, who excused the earl marshal on account of illness, came to the king and in their presence and with their assent it was arranged that they should have it proclaimed throughout the city of London that all those who had come there on a summons or by request should be the next day at St Paul's before the said constable and marshal for it to be known and put on record how and with how much each of them was willing to serve or help the king on this journey abroad; and the king said to them that, in accordance with the said arrangement which was given to them in writing, they should cause the said proclamation to be made. And they, on receiving the said command and the said writing, went away; then the same night the said earls sent to the king by sir John[1] Esturmy knt a letter written in these terms:

"Because, dear lord, you sent word to the marshal by the constable, in writing, that he should have it proclaimed throughout the town of London that all those who have come at your summons or by request should be next day before them at St Paul's at the hour of prime, and that they should have enrolled how many horses from everybody and then let you know this, your constable and your marshal pray you to agree to order someone else of your household to do this thing. And because, lord, you well know that they have come here at your request and not on a summons, if they did this they would be entering on their office to do service, wherefore they pray you to agree to give the order to someone else."

And the king, having received the said letter and taken counsel on it, because it seemed to him that they had written somewhat inadvisedly and he did not wish them to be taken by surprise because of it, sent to them sir Geoffrey de Geneville, sir Thomas de Berkeley, sir John Tregoz, the constable of the Tower, the keeper of London, sir Roger Brabazon and sir William de Bereford to advise them better on this and to provide in such a way that they would not do anything that could turn out to be to the detriment of the king or of their own condition; and if they would not be otherwise advised, that then they should be asked if they acknowledged the said letter and the words contained in it as theirs – which things they acknowledged absolutely. And when this acknowledgement was reported to the king, he having taken counsel on it, put in place of the earl of Hereford, the constable, sir Thomas de Berkeley and in place of the earl marshal sir Geoffrey de Geneville, because the said earls had asked that the king should give the order to others, as is contained in the said letter. On this the earls withdrew from the king and his court. And soon after this the archbishop of Canterbury and several bishops of England came to the king and asked him for permission to speak with the said earls, and the king granted them it; whereupon the said archbishop and the other prelates asked the said earls to let them know where it would please them to come to talk with them; and the earls sent word back to them by letter that they would be at Waltham on Friday the day after the feast of St James.[2] On which day the said archbishop and bishops came to Waltham; and the

[1] "Robert" in Cotton, and in the Canterbury copy

[2] i.e. Friday, 26 July 1297

said earls did not come, but sent there sir Robert Fitz Roger and sir John de Segrave, knights, who said on behalf of the earls that for certain reasons they could not come then. And then, at the request of the said prelates and the said knights who came to the king at St Albans the Sunday next following,[1] the king granted safe conduct to the said earls and gave his letters to that effect to the said knights allowing in them a sufficient length of time within which the said earls could safely and on safe conduct come to the king and stay and return; and with these letters the said knights left the king at this time; but never since have the earls come or sent to the king, nor are they yet coming or sending, that the king knows.

Now it may be that some persons have given the people to understand that the earls showed the king certain articles for the common profit of the people and of the realm, and that the king must have refused and denied them absolutely: of which the king knows nothing, for they neither showed him anything nor caused anything to be shown to him, nor does he know why they withdrew, but expected every day that they would come to him.

Among which articles there is mention, according to what is said, of some burdens that the king has laid on his kingdom, which he is well aware of, such as the aids that he has oftentimes asked of his people, which he has had to do because of the wars that have been waged against him in Gascony, Wales, Scotland and elsewhere, from which he could not defend either himself or his kingdom without help from his good people; wherefore it grieves him greatly that he has so burdened and so exhausted them, and he asks them to be willing to consider him excused for it as one who has laid out the things not on buying lands or tenements or castles or towns, but on defending himself and them and all the realm. And if God grants him ever to return from the journey that he is now making he wishes very much that all should know that he has the will and great desire to amend it suitably to the will of God and the satisfaction of his people as far as he ought. And if it happens that he does not return, he proposes to ordain that his heir shall do as much as he himself would do if he came back about what he causes to be amended, for he well knows that no one is as bound to the kingdom or to love the good people of his land as he is. In addition, as they have undertaken to cross over to help the count of Flanders who is his ally and particularly to put such an end as God wills to the matter of himself and his kingdom (for much better to put an end to the matter as soon as one can than to have it drag on thus long), the great lords who were with him lately at London, because they well saw that he was not able (nor is it possible) to go on with or maintain so great a thing from his own resources and that the journey is so urgent owing to the great peril which the king's friends over there are in and, through them, if they lose, the kingdom could fall into great peril afterwards, which God forbid, and to get the confirmation of the great charter of the liberties of England and of the charter of the forest, which confirmation the king has duly granted them, have granted him a common gift such as he is very much in need of at the present moment. Wherefore he begs all men of property[2] and all the people of his realm, who have never failed him, not to let this gift annoy them, both since they well see that he is sparing neither

[1] Sunday, 28 July 1297

[2] *bones gentz*

his person nor his possessions to relieve them and himself of the great privations they have suffered and are still suffering with great distress every day, and since they know also that the need is greater than ever it was at any time. And because through this journey there will come, please God, a good and very long-lasting peace, on that account each one ought to consider himself less aggrieved by this gift, by which too they can be the soonest delivered from the hardships and the labours they have and have had before this time.

And if any should cause it to be understood in the land that the king has refused articles or anything else injuriously to the common profit of the realm in order to treat his people with contempt and to ruin them, or that he has acted otherwise towards the earls than in the way described, he begs that he should not be believed, for this is the right account and the whole truth of how things have gone up to now. And let every one consider how great discord there has been in the past in this realm through these words bandied between the lord and his people and the harm that has resulted from them. And if now these things are believed to be otherwise than they are, it could happen that a dispute would arise out of it, which would be more dangerous and more serious than any ever was in this land. And all those are excommunicated who disturb the peace of this realm in any way whatever, and all those, of whatever condition or estate they are, who give or secure aid or favour, in the form of money, horses, arms or otherwise, secretly or openly, for those disturbing the peace: from which sentence of excommunication no one can be absolved without special order of the pope, save at the point of death, as appears from a bill that the king has of the time of pope Clement,[1] which a great many of the prelates and other great lords of this land have well understood. Wherefor there is need for everyone to preserve himself from it. And the king, because for the honour of God and of himself and of them and of the realm and for the sake of a very long-lasting peace and in order to put his realm into good shape he has undertaken to make this journey and because he has great faith that the good prayers of his good people can help him much and avail to bring this matter to a good conclusion, begs all the good people of his realm to be willing to pray, and have prayers said, carefully for him and for those who go with him.

In witness, etc. Given at Udimore, the 12th day of August.

(*Like letters have been sent to all the sheriffs of England*)

72. The clergy to be taxed "by royal authority" (B. Cotton), 20 August 1297, Winchelsea

(*Parl. Writs*, I, p. 396, from Chancery record, and Exchequer L.T.R. Memor. Roll No. 68, m. 58*d*–59. Translated from a collation of the two [French])

The king to his barons of the exchequer, greeting. We send you under our seal the form of a certain ordinance made by us and our council on the levying for our use of a third or fifth part of the goods of prelates, clerks, and any ecclesiastical persons of our realm whatsoever in aid of our approaching expedition, with orders

[1] Clement IV (1266–8)

to appoint without delay certain persons on whose good character and industry you can rely by letters under the seal of our exchequer to tax and levy the said third or fifth part in accordance with the form of the aforesaid ordinance, which we wish to be issued to those whom you so appoint for public showing by them in the counties to which they are appointed. Witness myself at Winchelsea on the twentieth day of August in the twenty-fifth year [20 August 1297, Winchelsea] – *The tenor of the aforesaid form is:* As the king by the ordinance of God has received the government of the realm, by which he is bound to defend that same realm and all his subjects clerk and lay, and has felt and perceived the great dangers, evils and losses which have day after day befallen him and his people, to the subversion of the said realm and evident undoing of holy church, through the great power of the king of France and of his allies who have exerted themselves with all their might, and still do, to destroy him and his realm, he has made an alliance with the count of Flanders and other great lords by whose aid he intends with God's help to defend his realm, drive back his enemies and recover his right. Hence, so as not to lose his allies or his friends whom the king of France is doing his utmost to destroy (or their help especially in this business which is so important, and with their loss, if it happened, which God forfend, he could not expect to recover his right) and because his realm and all holy church and the people of this same realm would be in evident danger of both devastation and utter destruction, he has undertaken to cross the sea to places on the other side, not only to help his allies and his friends but also to recover his right and obviate the said dangers and repel his enemies and secure his own realm from the harm that could happen to it if his friends were in peril, and as these enemies he will with the help of God, his allies, and his friends be better and more certainly able to repel far off than near by[1] and this enterprise cannot be undertaken with honour and profit or to the salvation of himself and his realm without aid from the clergy and the laity alike[2] of his realm, he has for the aforesaid common good and defence ordained that as clerks ought not to defend themselves by force of arms the third part of the present year's temporalities of prelates and clerks and all persons of holy church, religious and other, is to be levied to undertake and maintain the said necessary enterprise: in such a way that nothing be levied because of this on tithes small or great, oblations, obventions, mortuaries[3] or on income assigned to lights or church-ornaments or on other purely spiritual revenues, and nothing be levied upon clerks whose benefices are not worth more than 5 marks in all, at the last assessment. And it is the king's intention that clerks' goods on their lay fiefs which are not appurtenant to churches shall not incur this taxation but be taxed in the taxation of the laity. It is also the king's intention that those who wish to give the fifth part of all their goods, temporal and spiritual, appertaining to their benefices may be taxed at the rate of a fifth. And as to this prise which the king will take, it is his intention to well satisfy as soon as he can those from whom he has taken, as he ought to, in such fashion that they will have occasion to consider themselves paid for it.

[1] *de loynz qe de pres*
[2] *sans commune ayde des clerks e de lays*
[3] For the tithes and these other, more casual sources of clerical income, J. R. H. Moorman, *Church Life in England in the Thirteenth Century*, chaps IX and X.

73. The appearance of Bohun and Bigod and supporters at the exchequer on 22 August 1297

([Hubert Hall], *Trans. Royal Hist. Soc.*, new series, III (1886), pp. 282–91, from the Exchequer L.T.R. Memor. Roll, with a translation. The present translation is based on this with essential corrections [French])

The treasurer's deputy and the barons of the exchequer despatched to our lord the king certain letters under the seal of the said exchequer in these words

Sire, this same Thursday next before the feast of St Bartholomew [Thursday, 22 August 1297] at the hour of tierce, there came to your exchequer, at the bar, the earl marshal, the earl of Hereford, my lord sir Robert le FitzRoger, sir Aleyn la Zouche, sir John de Segrave, sir Henry de Tyeys, sir John Lovel and many others, bannerets and batchelors. And the earl of Hereford said that he was charged to speak on behalf of the earl marshal and the others who were there and on behalf of all the commonalty of the realm, as well clerks as laymen, who felt themselves (they and the said commonalty) aggrieved by two things: in the one respect by certain grievances, the articles whereof they had had shown to you as their liege lord, and in the other by what they heard had been done by us of the exchequer without your knowledge as regards the levying of the eighth and the taking of wool; and said that in the writs issued for levying the eighth it is contained that the earls, barons, knights and the commonalty of the realm have granted the eighth as they and their ancestors have done in the past, whereas the said eighth never was granted by them or by the said commonalty; and said further that nothing sooner puts men in bondage than to redeem their own and to be tallaged at will, and that if the eighth were so levied it would lead to the disinheritance of them and of their heirs; and he said openly, and all the others after him, that such a tallage and prise of wool were quite insufferable and they would in no wise suffer them; and they prayed us to have these things redressed; and thereupon they departed without waiting for any answer. Wherefore, sire, be good enough, if you please, to let us have your will in this matter. Sire, our Lord give you prosperous life and long with increase of honours. Written at Westminster, the Thursday aforesaid at the hour of noon.

This letter was despatched to the lord king by Robert Dyvelyn, usher of the exchequer, at the aforesaid hour of noon.

Afterwards the lord king wrote his will to the same by his letters in these words

Edward by the grace of God king of England etc. To our treasurer's deputy and the barons of the exchequer, greeting. We have heard how the two earls came to the exchequer with their companions and the things also which you told us they said to you. And as to what they said, that they would in no wise suffer the eighth to be levied nor the prise of wool to be taken, we will that you leave nothing at all undone for going ahead with the taxing and levying of the aforesaid eighth in the form which is ordained for it. But because they said that the levy would lead to the prejudice and disinheritance of them and their heirs, we emphatically wish you to make it known to all, and it must be proclaimed throughout the counties in taxing the eighth, that if there be any who fears such prejudice or such disinheritance the king will gladly relieve him by his letters patent, in such manner that the taxing or levying of this eighth cannot lead to the prejudice or bondage of anyone, or be drawn into a custom in time to come, provided that the king may get help from it now for his great enterprise which is so urgent for his salvation and their own and that of the whole realm and for alleviating for him and for them the misfortunes with which they have now been burdened for a long time. And on this we will that our chancellor of England make out for them such letters with the seal which he will be keeping as long as we are away,[1] and you also with the seal of the exchequer, for those who wish to acquire them, as between you you consider good and sufficient. And we have sent orders to the aforesaid chancellor about this by our letters.[2] And as to the prise of wool, we will that the ordinance which has been made about it shall stand, and that it be said by all, as well by you as by those who have to do with it, that the king is not minded to take anything or have anything for nothing, but only by buying it, giving satisfaction therefor to everyone, and that otherwise-minded we never yet were, nor has the matter been set going in any other way. When you have to ask advice another time concerning this business, or any other which is urgent, you will cause it to be known to our son and his council which he has with him and they shall, after consultation between you, give such counsel as they deem good. Given under our privy seal, Winchelsea, the 23rd day of August in the twenty-fifth year of our reign [23 August 1297, Winchelsea].

Edward by the grace of God, etc. To the deputy of our treasurer and to the barons of the exchequer, greeting. We send you enclosed in these letters the transcript of our letters which we are sending to Edward our son and his council to make proclamation in our name throughout the counties of England as more plainly is contained in the transcript aforesaid. And we command you, when you come to where our son is, to be intendant in the matter and advise him and his council, so that, by consultation between you all, that which it seems to you is best done about it is done. Given under our privy seal, at sea off Dover, the 24th day of August in the twenty-fifth year of our reign [24 August 1297, at sea off Dover].

The tenor of the transcript aforesaid is as follows
Edward by the grace of God, etc. To Edward, our dear son our viceroy in England, and to his council, greeting. We command you now as we commanded you through our chancellor, forasmuch as the two earls and their abettors have chanced to disturb the levying of the eighth and the prise of wool as well, to have it proclaimed and solemnly stated throughout the counties of England and particularly in the presence of the said earls and to the earls themselves that they and all those who are in our allegiance and wish to be so shall suffer the aforesaid levy and prise to be made, seeing that these things are ordained for a need that is so great and so urgent and for the salvation of us and all our realm. And have it also prohibited for anyone to cause hindrance thereto or disturb anything that is ordained for the support of us who are

[1] *la outre*
[2] The text of this order, preserved in a transcript, is given below as the last item of this record.

their liege lord and of those who go with us. And have them know that you are ready as regards the levying of the said eighth to make out letters with the seal of the chancery which is to be used as long as we are away, and with that of the exchequer also, for all those who wish to acquire them, to the effect that this levy shall not lead to the prejudice or disinheritance of anyone or be again sought or asked for by us or by our heirs as any sort of bondage. And as to the prise of wool, let there be proclamation and prohibition in like manner. For we will give satisfaction therefor to all those from whom it has been taken, in such wise that they will have occasion to consider themselves properly paid. And it seems to us that we ought to be as free to buy wool in our country as anyone else. This proclamation [and] this prohibition we wish to be made speedily and generally throughout the counties, cities, boroughs and market-towns of England. And that all be charged with the homage and fealty they owe us and made responsible for all the wrong they may do us. And, as they have no desire to be accused of disinheriting us or of destroying us and those who go with us and the realm alike, that no one defeat or by word oppose, personally or through another, the aforesaid proclamation and prohibition. Still, we leave the making of this proclamation to your discretion, for it to be done if in your view it is the right thing to do. And because divers news could reach us[1] which we would not know what to make of, we command you to keep us frequently and fully informed of the facts of these matters and of all others which in your view could benefit us. Given under our privy seal, at sea off Dover, the 24th day of August in the twenty-fifth year of our reign [24 August 1297, at sea off Dover].

Edward son of the king of England, viceroy of the same king in England, to the treasurer's deputy and the barons of the exchequer, greeting. We send you, by William of Blyborough our clerk, enclosed in this letter the transcript of a letter which came from our lord, our father, to the chancellor and which he showed to us and our council: as to which and also as to having search made for the seal and as regards other matters concerning the custody of the town and the Tower and the making of proclamation in the city that none take victuals without payment, give credence to our aforementioned clerk and do on these things what he will tell you. Given at Robertsbridge, the morrow of St Bartholomew's day in the twenty-fifth year of the reign of our lord, the king, our father [25 August 1297].

The tenor of the transcript is as follows

Edward etc. to our chancellor, greeting. We command you that with the advice of those of the exchequer you have such letters made as again seem to you sufficient, to the effect that[2] the eighth which we are having taxed throughout the realm cannot lead to the prejudice or disinheritance of those of our realm or their heirs, or ever be drawn into a custom in time to come: which letters we wish to be sealed with the

[1] "... for it to be done ... reach us" (*si qele se face sil vous semble qe bon seit. E purcoe qe diverses noueles nous porount venir*) is omitted from the text as printed in *Tr. Roy. Hist. Soc.*, n.s. III (1886), p. 290. It is here supplied from the K.R. Memoranda Roll record.

[2] *coment*

seal of the chancery which is to be used as long as we are away. Given under our privy seal at Winchelsea the 24th day of August in the twenty-fifth year of our reign [24 August 1297, Winchelsea].

74–77. The Confirmation of the Charters, 1297

The outcome of the debates, "many and various" a contemporary tells us they were,[1] in the parliament of Michaelmas 1297 was agreement on 10 October to confirm Magna Carta and the Forest Charter once again – which was done by "inspeximus" of the 1225 texts of them by the regent on the king's behalf, recorded in letters patent dated 12 October[2] – and agreement on certain additional articles, conceded by the regent in his father's name in letters patent of 10 October and again on 5 November by the king himself at Ghent, the only (no doubt intended) difference being that the letters patent could then be sealed with the great seal itself instead of a seal of absence.[3]

With these officially recorded texts I give the so-called "*De Tallagio non concedendo*", which is known only from unofficial sources but which is obviously related in some way. The probability is that it is a statement of the opposition's demands, drawn up before or ("as a basis for discussion"[4]) in this parliament; though the possibility cannot be ruled out that it might be after it, a product rather of 1298, 1299 or 1300, but hardly later than the so-called Confirmation of the Charters of 1301 (No. 89 below, which is in reality, however important, very much a postscript to these other documents).

74. The additional articles (*Confirmatio Cartarum*), 10 October and 5 November 1297

(W. Stubbs, *Select Charters*, 9th edn, ed. H. W. C. Davis, pp. 490–1 [French])

[1] Edward, by the grace of God king of England, lord of Ireland and duke of Aquitaine, to all those who see or hear these present letters, greeting. Know that we, to the honour of God and of holy church and for the benefit of our whole realm, have granted for us and our heirs that the great charter of liberties and the forest charter which were made by common assent of all the realm in the time of king Henry, our father, be kept in all their points without any impediment to their working. And we will that these same charters be sent under our seal to our justices (to those of the forest as well as to the others), to all sheriffs of counties, and to all our other officials, and to all our cities throughout the land, together with our writs, in which it shall be contained that they cause the aforesaid charters to be published and have it declared to the people that we have granted they be kept in all their points; and to our justices, sheriffs, mayors and other officials, who have to administer under us and for us the law of the land, to have these same charters allowed in all their points in pleadings before them and in judgments – the great charter of liberties, that is, as common law and the forest charter in accordance with the assize of the forest – for the betterment of our people.

[2] And we will that if any judgments are given henceforth contrary to the points of the aforesaid charters by justices or by other officials of ours who hold pleas before them contrary to the points of the charters, they shall be undone and held for nought.

[3] And we will that these same charters be sent under our seal to cathedral churches throughout our realm and remain there, and be read before the people twice a year.

[1] Bartholomew Cotton of Norwich (No. 8 above)

[2] Nos 76 and 77 below

[3] I have given the king's own document (No. 74). The documents of 10 October are given together, semi-officially, in Archbishop Winchelsey's ecclesiastical register (*Registrum Robert Winchelsey*, ed. R. Graham (Cant. & York Soc.), pp. 201 ff.)

[4] Sir Maurice Powicke, *The Thirteenth Century*, p. 682

[4] And that archbishops and bishops pronounce sentences of greater excommunication against all those who contravene the aforesaid charters (whether of their own doing or by assisting or advising) or infringe or contravene any point of them. And that these sentences be pronounced and published twice a year by the aforesaid prelates. And if the same prelates, the bishops, or any of them are negligent over making the abovesaid denunciation, let them be reprimanded by the archbishops of Canterbury and York for the time being, as is proper, and be compelled to make this same denunciation in the form aforesaid.

[5] And because some people of our realm fear that the aids and contributions[1] they have furnished us with of their own granting and their goodwill before now for our wars and other needs in whatever way they were done could lead to bondage for them and their heirs because another time they might be found enrolled, and likewise the prises which have been taken throughout the realm by our officials in our name, we have granted for us and our heirs that henceforth we will not make a precedent of[2] such aids, mises or prises for anything that may have been done or that could be found out from a roll or in any other way.

[6] And we have likewise granted for us and our heirs to the archbishops, bishops, abbots, priors and other folk of holy church, and to the earls and barons and all the community of the land that for no need will we take such manner of aids, mises or prises from our realm henceforth except with the common assent of all the realm and for the common profit of the same realm, saving the ancient aids and prises due and accustomed.

[7] And because by far the greater part of the community of the realm feel themselves greatly burdened by the maltote on wool, namely 40 shillings on each sack of wool, and have entreated us to be good enough to relieve them, we at their request have completely relieved them and have granted that we will not take this or any other in future without their common assent and their goodwill, saving for us and our heirs the custom on wool, skins and leathers granted earlier by the community of the aforesaid realm. In witness of which things we have had these our letters patent made. Given at Ghent, the fifth day of November in the twenty-fifth year of our reign [5 November 1297, Ghent].

75. "De Tallagio non concedendo"

(*Engl. Hist. Review*, vol. 60 (1945), pp. 303–5)

[1] No tallage or aid shall be imposed or levied by us or our heirs in future in our realm without the will and common assent of the archbishops, bishops and other prelates, earls, barons, knights, burgesses and other free men of our realm.

[2] No official of ours or of our heirs shall take the corn, wool, leather, or any other goods of anyone whatsoever without the will and assent of him such goods belong to.

[3] Nothing shall be taken in future, by name of or by occasion of a maltote, on a sack of wool.

[1] *mises* [2] literally "draw into a custom". It was a medieval saying that "twice makes a custom".

[4] We also will and grant for ourselves and our heirs that all clerks and laymen of our realm shall have all their laws, liberties and free customs as freely and fully as they have enjoyed them at any time.[1] And if statutes have been issued by us or our ancestors, or customs introduced, contrary to them or to any article whatsoever contained in the present charter, we will and grant that such customs and statutes shall be null and void forever.

[5] We have, furthermore, pardoned Humphrey de Bohun, earl of Hereford and Essex, constable of England, Roger Bigod, earl of Norfolk, marshal of England, and other earls, barons, knights, serjeants-at-arms, John de Ferrers, and all others who belong to their circle, have joined with them or are of their way of thinking,[2] also all holders of twenty librates of land[3] in our realm, whether of us in chief or of any other person whatsoever, who were summoned for a certain, specified day to cross to Flanders with us but did not come, the rancour which was ours[4] and the ill-will which because of these things we felt towards them, and also the trespasses, if any, they have committed against us and ours up to the making of the present charter.

[6] And for greater assurance of this we will and grant for ourselves and our heirs that all the archbishops and bishops of England shall twice a year for all time to come, having the present charter and having recited it, excommunicate publicly in their cathedral churches, and have excommunicated or (if already excommunicated) denounced in every parish church of their dioceses, all who knowingly act, or instigate action, contrary to the tenor, force and effectiveness of the present charter in any article in any way. In witness of which thing our seal is appended to the present charter together with the seals of the archbishops, bishops, earls, barons and others who have voluntarily sworn that they will observe the tenor of the present charter, as far as in them is, in every single one of its articles and for its observance will faithfully afford their counsel and assistance for ever.

76. "Inspeximus" of Magna Carta 1225 by letters patent, 12 October 1297, Westminster

(*Statutes of the Realm*, I (1810), pp. 33–6 (Charters))

Edward by the grace of God king of England, lord of Ireland and duke of Aquitaine to all to whom the present letters come, greeting. We have inspected the great charter of the lord H. formerly king of England, our father, about the liberties of England, in these words:

> [Here follows "Henry by the grace of God . . . ninth year of our reign", being M.C. 1225 word for word as at No. 26 above except for a few verbal differences, interesting as suggesting access to a 1217 text also or to a somewhat purer 1225 text than that printed by *Stat. Realm*, I, pp. 22–5 (Charters) but (with one exception) affecting neither the sense nor the translation. The exception is a deliberate change to 100 marks instead of 100 pounds as the relief for a barony in clause 2.]

We ratifying and approving the aforesaid gifts and concessions, concede and confirm them for ourselves and our heirs and by the tenor of these presents renew them, willing and granting for us and our heirs that the aforesaid charter be observed firmly

[1] *sicut eas aliquo tempore melius et plenius habere consueverunt*
[2] *de eorum societate, confoederatione et concordia existentibus*
[3] i.e. land worth twenty pounds a year
[4] *rancorem nostram*

and inviolably in every single one of its articles for ever, although some articles in that same charter hitherto have perhaps not been observed. In witness of which we have caused these our letters patent to be made. Witness Edward our son, at Westminster, on the twelfth day of October in the twenty-fifth year of our reign.

77. "Inspeximus" of Charter of the Forest 1225 by letters patent, 12 October 1297, Westminster

(*Statutes of the Realm*, I (1810), pp. 120–2)

Edward by the grace of God king of England, lord of Ireland and duke of Aquitaine to all to whom the present letters come, greeting. We have inspected the charter of the lord H. formerly king of England, our father, about the forest, in these words:

[Here follows "Henry by the grace of God . . . ninth year of our reign", being For. Ch. 1225 word for word as at No. 27 above except for a few verbal differences of no importance or interest other than suggesting that (as with the inspeximus of Magna Carta – see No. 76 above) the draftsmen of 12 October 1297 either had access to a 1217 text as well as the 1225 text or had a somewhat purer 1225 text of the Forest Charter than that printed by *Stat. Realm*, I, pp. 26–7 (Charters).]

We ratifying and approving the aforesaid gifts and concessions, concede and confirm them for ourselves and our heirs and by the tenor of these presents renew them, willing and granting for us and our heirs that the aforesaid charter be observed firmly and inviolably in every single one of its articles for ever, although some articles in that same charter hitherto have perhaps not been observed. In witness of which we have caused these our letters patent to be made. Witness Edward our son, at Westminster, on the twelfth day of October in the twenty-fifth year of our reign.

78. The "Evil toll" (Maltote) of 1294–7 abolished, 23 November 1297

(P.R.O., L.T.R. Memor. Roll No. 69, m. 27)

Exchequer writs of the same date, and Chancery writs of 24 November, to all sheriffs ordered proclamation to be made of the abolition (P.R.O., L.T.R. Memor. Roll No. 69, m. 27 *r* and *d*, and *Cal. Close Rolls 1296–1302*, p. 187).

A writ of 26 November ordered its abolition in Ireland too (*Cal. Close Rolls 1296–1302*, p. 198).

The king to the keepers of the New Custom at Newcastle upon Tyne greeting. As we at the instance of the community of our realm have remitted the custom of 40*s* lately[1] granted to us in aid of our war against the king of France to be levied for two or three years, if that war should last so long, on each sack of wool leaving our realm, and have granted that we will not take that custom or any other at all[2] without the will and common assent of that community, saving however to us and our heirs the custom on wool, woolfells and leather granted to us earlier[3] by the community of the said realm,[4] WE ORDER you to receive the custom of ½ mark on each sack of wool and of woolfells and similarly the custom of 1 mark on each last of

[1] in 1294 (No. 68 above)
[2] *minime*
[3] in 1275 (No. 48 above)
[4] So far, of course, a recollection of the agreement of 10 October and 5 November 1297 on this subject (No. 74 above).

hides leaving the said realm as was wont previously to be done and to supersede entirely the taking of the said 40s on a sack of wool and of fells and of 5 marks on a last of hides. Witness W. bishop of Coventry and Lichfield, our treasurer, at Westminster, 23 November 1297. By the council.

§ It was likewise written to the keepers of that custom at Kingston upon Hull, Boston, Yarmouth, Ipswich, London, Southampton and Bristol. Witness as above.

79. Provision on sheriffs and their clerks, 14 February 1298

(*Statutes of the Realm*, I (Rec. Com., 1810), p. 213)

Because the punishment for every offence ought in justice to be inflicted on the offender and many sheriffs in the kingdom are wholly lay persons with no knowledge of returns of writs which hitherto are returned to the king's court and some, though they are lettered, still have so much faith in what their clerks do that they do not pretend to concern themselves in any way with supervising and also examining the writs directed to them, and in the past it was always the practice both in the exchequer and elsewhere in the king's court that for undue execution of writs the sheriffs to whom they were directed should be amerced and not their clerks who composed and made the false, feigned and frivolous replies to those writs, by which it is presumed and known to be true that those clerks have assumed a greater boldness in offending, THE VENERABLE FATHERS, brother William of Hotham, archbishop of Dublin, W. of Louth, bishop of Ely, R. of Gravesend, bishop of London, W. of Langton, bishop of Coventry and Lichfield, the king's treasurer, and John of Langton, the chancellor of England, John of Cobham and his fellows, barons of the aforesaid exchequer, also the justices of both benches and many others of the king's council, assembled at the same exchequer at Westminster on Friday, the feast of St Valentine, in the 26th year of the reign of king Edward, deliberating on the remedy to be applied in the aforesaid case so that in future sheriffs' clerks giving false answers to the king's writs may not suppose that their wickednesses of this kind will go unpunished as they have done hitherto and sheriffs may not be punished in that case for the deeds of their clerks and may not let them happen[1] as they have frequently done in the past, HAVE AGREED AND PROVIDED that both the clerks and the sheriffs themselves shall be answerable and be punished before the treasurer and barons of the exchequer and elsewhere in the king's court before any of his justices for a false return; on condition that if the defect in the return is found to be the fault of a clerk of the sheriff and not the sheriff's, that clerk shall make amends to the injured party for the damage which that party can lawfully show he has suffered from the defect in the aforesaid return and shall nevertheless as regards the king be punished at the discretion of the justices before whom he has been convicted, regard being had to the measure of the offence, and in that case sheriffs are to be quit, provided however that their clerks have sufficient means to make amends as stated—if not, in their default, the sheriffs under whom those clerks hold office are to answer and make amends.

[1] *et permittant*

§ And it is to be remembered that this provision has to be observed in respect of sheriffs and their clerks in London and Middlesex from the day of its being made because they are forewarned of it etc. And as regards the rest of the sheriffs of the kingdom and their clerks the said provision shall take effect from the morrow of the close of next Easter onwards because then the sheriffs are to be warned at their proffer. § Afterwards on the morrow of the Close of Easter in the 26th year of the king's reign the aforesaid provision was expounded in the exchequer to every sheriff of England and it was then agreed by the king's council that sheriff's clerks giving false answers to summonses of the exchequer on the accounts of the sheriffs shall be punished, if convicted of this, in the way it is provided above they are to be punished for falsely executing writs.

80. Ordinance for an enquiry into maladministration of prises by royal officials since the outbreak of the war with France in 1294 (30 March to 4 April 1298)

(J. F. Baldwin, *The King's Council* (Oxford, 1913), p. 465, corrected by the enrolment on the patent roll printed by W. S. Thomson, *A Lincolnshire Assize Roll for 1298* (Linc. Rec. Soc.), vol. 36 (1944), p. 136. The Parl. Proc., file ii, text printed by Baldwin is either corrupt or badly transcribed. [French])

As the king before his crossing to Flanders had the will and desire to have the grievances inflicted on his people in his name redressed and amended and on this sent his letters to all the counties of England, in order to put this thing into effect it is ordained by him and his council that four be appointed in each county, namely two knights (of whom one shall be sent by him, the other taken from the county), a clerk and a religious, who shall be responsible, upright and very prudent, to enquire concerning all manner of grievances, as of things removed from holy church, of prises of wools, woolfells, hides, corn, beasts, flesh, fish and all other kinds of things throughout the kingdom from clerks and from laymen since the beginning of the war between the king of France and him, whether this was for the custody of the sea or for any other purpose. And these same shall ask by whom and for whom and of what and in what amount and to what value and how and in what way these prises and grievances were inflicted on the people. And those appointed shall have full authority to enquire, hear and determine, both *ex officio* and at the suit of someone with a complaint to make. And when the truth of these things has been ascertained, whether it was with or without a warrant that these things were taken, what has been taken without warrant is to be returned to those who have suffered the damage if the wrongdoers have the means, and besides this they, the wrongdoers, are to be punished for the trespass. And if they have not the means, those to whom the warrants and commissions have come, such as sheriffs, clerks assigned, bailiffs and other officials of this kind, are to answer for their subordinates who have made such prises. And that the king is to be informed of what is found to have been taken by warrant and he will so act in the matter that those whose goods have been taken will consider themselves reasonably paid.

81. Statute "of fines levied" (*de finibus levatis*), 1299

(*Statutes of the Realm*, I (1810), pp. 126–30, from the Statute Roll)

Edward by the grace of God king of England, lord of Ireland and duke of Aquitaine, to the sheriff of Lancaster, greeting. As not long ago at Westminster before our crossing to Flanders we, having regard to the gracious services, payments and outgoings which the people of our realm had made and borne in various ways for us in peace as well as in war, had no small wish and desire to compensate them[1] as far as we could at that time and we granted to them[2] of our own free will for ourselves and our heirs that the great charter of liberties should be observed in all its points, and likewise the charter of the forest kept, saving, however, our oath, the right of our crown and our interests and those of other men too; which things we caused to be announced on our behalf and in our presence on that occasion by the venerable father R. archbishop of Canterbury, and then at Udimore on our way to Flanders we sent word under our seal ordering that same concession to be observed and kept throughout the whole of our kingdom in every county.[3] And because ever since that time we have in manifold ways been preoccupied with and distracted by the straits and stresses of wars in various far-away countries, for which reason we have not been able to know the state of our realm, we, holding to our first intention, have these days so far as our leisure allows deliberated on our aforesaid grant and, for the honour of God and holy mother church and the benefit of the whole of the people of our realm, will that the aforesaid great charter of liberties be observed in all its points, and the charter of the forest too in[4] the underwritten articles, which are:

[The Forest Charter of 1225 is given, in the text which had been used for the inspeximus of 12 October 1297 (No. 77 above), but only clauses 6–16 of it. The omission of clause 17, as well as clauses 1–5, is noteworthy. The ratifying clause of the inspeximus of 12 October 1297, confirming the charter in every single one of its articles ("We ratifying . . . hitherto have perhaps not been observed"), is ignored.]

And we will that the abovesaid articles be firmly and inviolably observed and held, willing nonetheless that there be a perambulation, always saving our oath, the right of our crown and our interests and claims and those of all other men,[5] which perambulation indeed we wish to take place, as said above, as soon as can be after the business we have to transact with messengers who are about to come from the court of Rome, which is so important that it concerns not only us and our realm but the whole of Christendom and to conduct it properly we need absolutely our entire council.

And besides our grant of the aforementioned, made as described above, we have carefully considered and meditated on certain defects in the law, the manifold grievances and the oppressions inflicted in many other ways on the aforesaid people in the past, and on those which occurred to us we wish at the present time, for the relief and benefit of that people, to render the law certain and apply remedy in this way. [1] Because fines levied in our court ought to put and do put an end to lawsuits and

[1] *populum ipsum* [2] *eidem populo* [3] cf. No. 71 above. [4] *secundum*

[5] At this point in the statute roll text printed by *Stat. Realm* is an interlineation "provided that that perambulation be reported to us before any effect is given to it or anything else is done about it". It is neither given in the text nor interlined in the exemplification received by London (now Brit. Mus. Cotton Charters VII, 11).

are for that reason called fines, especially as after the duel[1] and the Grand Assize they have in their case the last and final place and that for all time; and now for some time past, both in the time of the lord king H. our father of illustrious memory and in our own, parties to those fines and the heirs of those parties were, contrary to the laws and customs of the realm used of old, permitted, for the purpose of voiding and annulling such fines, to allege that before the fine was levied, at the time it was levied, and since, they, the demandants or plaintiffs, or their ancestors, were always seised of the tenements contained in the fines or of some parcel thereof, and so such fines, rightly levied, were often, by jurors of the country falsely suborned and maliciously procured, unjustly voided and annulled: we wishing to remedy the aforementioned have established in our parliament at Westminster that the said exceptions or answers, or inquests of the country on such exceptions or answers, contrary to such recognisances and fines shall by no means be permitted henceforth. And we will that this statute shall apply to fines levied previously as well as in future. And justices shall see that notes and fines levied in court in future are publicly and solemnly read and that pleas entirely cease meanwhile; and this shall be done on two days in the week at the justices' discretion.

[2] We have also ordained with our council that sheriffs shall not henceforth be charged with the levying of any issues, nor levy any, before they pass out of the exchequer, whither they are to be delivered by estreats of the justices; and that in these estreats every single individual shall be charged with issues forfeited as well as with amercements. And if perchance any sheriff answers for the issues of any juror or surety or mainpernor whom he appointed and returned into our court but who at the time of the return is not able to pay the issues or amercements, the sheriff shall be charged with them and answer at our exchequer. And sheriffs shall see to it, on pain of heavy forfeiture, that they make tallies henceforth for everyone for any moneys whatsoever received on our orders by them and their subordinates; and that they do not return anywhere names of mainpernors, jurors or others unless those mainpernors, jurors or others are legally and manifestly forewarned of this in accordance with our writs on the subject addressed to the sheriffs. Nor shall they return any names of freemen as sureties unless these have manifestly agreed to be sureties. And on this we have ordained that once every year one baron and one clerk shall be sent from our said exchequer to every single county of England to register the names of all who have that year paid debts exacted from them by the green wax; and the same baron and clerk shall inspect and register the tallies and hear and determine complaints against sheriffs and bailiffs who contravene the foregoing and offenders are to be severely punished.

[3] Because, contrary to the form of our recently published statute on those who are irrepleviable and who not,[2] sheriffs and others in times past have let out by replevin notorious and manifest thieves and people arrested and imprisoned for homicide and other felonies, who are not repleviable, whereby irrepleviable malefactors thus replevied procure and suborn, by themselves or through friends of theirs, jurors of

[1] *duellum*, i.e. trial by battle
[2] i.e. those who are repleviable. The statute referred to is (despite "recently", *nuper*) Westminster I (1275), c. 15

the country to secure falsely their deliverance before the coming of the justices in eyre or of others assigned to deliver them, and threaten others, whereby, both for fear of the sheriff and the others who let them out by such replevin and fear of the thieves or felons so delivered, homicides and thefts are suppressed before the justices assigned to deliver the gaols and, being so concealed, go quite unpunished: we for the benefit of our realm and the better keeping of our peace have decreed and ordained that justices assigned to take assizes, in every county where they do take the assizes as ordered, shall, immediately after the assizes are taken in those counties, stay on if both are laymen, but if one of them is a clerk then associated with the lay justice one of the more judicious knights of the county, and deliver by our writ the gaols in those counties, as well within liberties as without, of every prisoner in accordance with the form of gaol delivery hitherto used in those counties. And the same justices shall then enquire which sheriffs and others have let out by replevin any irrepleviable prisoners or have offended in any thing against the form of the aforesaid statute recently published at Westminster, and those whom they find guilty thereof they shall punish and chastise in all things according to the form of the aforesaid statute. [4] Also, as we have decreed that no one shall be put anywhere outside the shire on any inquests, recognitions and juries who has land worth less than 100 shillings a year,[1] because of which both they and those with more land are impoverished by frequent summonses both to the exchequer and before the justices of either bench: we, observing the intolerable burden of expense borne by our people, have, not only for the relief of such jurors but also to provide speedy justice for parties pleading in our court, decreed and ordained that henceforth inquests and recognitions determinable before the justices of either bench shall be taken during vacation before any of the justices before whom the plea was conducted, there being associated with him one knight of the county where such inquests occur, unless it is an inquest that requires a great deal of examination: and in taking such inquests henceforth let that rather be done which the justices consider should be done for the benefit of our realm, notwithstanding the statute on the taking of inquests recently published at Westminster, in which it is contained that if any inquests are taken otherwise than as prescribed in that statute they shall be treated as completely null.[2]

And therefore we command and firmly enjoin you to cause to be read and published immediately and without any delay in cities, boroughs, market towns and other customary places throughout your bailiwick where it seems most expedient to you all the above-mentioned articles as the ones we have granted and wish to be held and firmly observed in the aforesaid form in full and unaltered; and not to be dilatory in having every single one of the things above-written made known to all. Witness the king at Westminster on the second day of April.

The like statute, as far as "And therefore we command" etc. was sent to the underwritten, namely:

The treasurer and barons of the exchequer.

[1] The statute "Of persons to be put on juries and assizes" of 1293 (*Stat. Realm*, I, p. 113), following Stat. Westm. II (1285), c. 38 (ibid. p. 89).

[2] The reference seems to be to Stat. Westm. II (1285), c. 30.

Roger Brabazon and his fellows, justices assigned to hear and determine the king's pleas.

John Mettingham and his fellows, [justices of the king's bench,[1]] with this clause, "And therefore we command you to cause the aforesaid charter to be read before you in the aforesaid bench and cause, as far as they concern you and parties pleading before you, every single one of the aforesaid articles, as the ones we have granted and wish to be held, to be observed in full and unaltered. Witness the king at Westminster on the second day of April."

82. Statute of Stepney on bad money, 15 May 1299

(*Statutes of the Realm*, I (Rec. Com., 1810), pp. 131–3 [French])

Edward by God's grace king of England, lord of Ireland and duke of Aquitaine to the sheriff of Somerset and Dorset, greeting. Because our kingdom and the other lands of our lordship are full of various bad moneys, known by the names of pollards and crockards, and by other names, which are brought and left in the said kingdom and elsewhere in our power by various people from abroad and there spent in various ways to the great harm of us and of our people, we by the common assent of the prelates, earls and barons of the same kingdom have on this ordained and established a remedy according to the articles which follow:

First, that no one from now on shall bring such moneys into our said kingdom or elsewhere in our power on pain of forfeiture of life and goods and whatever else he can forfeit, yet so that all people of whatever land or country they are can safely bring to our exchange all sorts of money of good silver, of whatever foreign coin or of whatever value they are, without their being forfeited.

[To enforce this, watch is to be kept "in all places on the sea coast, at ports and elsewhere where there is any arrival" from abroad and wardens appointed at each port.]

It is further ordained that from now on no one of our kingdom or of our power may sell or dispose of wools, leather or skins, or lead or tin, except in return for good and lawful sterlings or plate of silver assayed and marked at our great exchange, or in exchange for good and lawful and sufficient merchandise. And if any one does otherwise and is convicted of it by the said wardens or other officers of ours, the things thus sold or disposed of are to be forfeit to us.

It is ordained in addition that no good money of silver, of our coin or of another's, or any silver in plate or other form, may leave or be taken out of our realm or out of our power in distant parts without special leave from us, on pain of the aforesaid penalty.

[The same wardens are to enforce this as well as the other points and are to be on oath to spare no man, on pain of forfeiture of their lives and all they possess.

There are to be tables for changing money – for travellers' necessary expenses – at Dover and other places through which traffic will be directed. Money may be changed only at these tables, and those to keep the table at Dover are named. cf. *Calendar of Patent Rolls 1292–1301*, p. 417.]

---

1 An interlineation in the Statute Roll, but as regards Mettingham, cf. Sayles, *Sel. Cases in . . . King's Bench: Edw. I*, I, p. xli, n. 2.

We send you therefore firm orders to have all the aforesaid articles and points proclaimed and published immediately you have seen these letters in cities and boroughs, market towns, ports and all other places throughout your bailiwick where in your view it should be done; and to have wardens appointed and sworn both to keep this our ordinance and to have it kept in the way aforesaid, on pain of the penalties contained in this same document. Given at Stepney on the fifteenth day of May in the twenty-seventh year of our reign.

Like letters sent to all the sheriffs of England and to the others underwritten, viz,

To Robert de Burghasshe, warden of the Cinque Ports
To the keeper of Berwick
To Reginald de Grey, justiciar of Chester
To John Wogan, justiciar of Ireland
To Walter de Pederton, justice of North Wales
To John de Havering, justice of West Wales
To Otto of Granson, keeper of the isles of Guernsey and Jersey, or his lieutenant

[Like letters to all the king's faithful bailiffs and officials, with instructions to proclaim them and to keep them and have them kept, and to the treasurer and barons of the exchequer likewise.]

83. "Inspeximus" of Magna Carta 1225 by charter, 28 March 1300, Westminster

(*Stat. of the Realm*, I (1810), pp. 38–41 (Charters), from the Charter Roll of 28 Edw. I)

The king to the archbishops etc., greeting.[1]

[Here follows "We have inspected . . . hitherto have perhaps not been observed", being No. 76, above, word for word, with only the formal changes involved in an inspeximus by charter as distinct from letters patent as in 1297, viz, the formal charter opening and, at the end, instead of "In witness of which . . . twenty-fifth year of our reign", the following:–]

These being witness: the venerable fathers, R. archbishop of Canterbury, primate of all England, A. bishop of Durham, R. of London, R. of Ely, T. of Exeter, W. of Coventry and Lichfield, S. of Salisbury, J. of Rochester, J. of Norwich, and J. of Llandaff, bishops; J. bishop-elect of Lincoln; John de Warenne earl of Surrey, Thomas earl of Lancaster, Roger le Bygod earl of Norfolk and marshal of England, Henry de Lacy earl of Lincoln, Ralph de Monthermer earl of Gloucester and Hertford, Humphrey de Bohun earl of Hereford and Essex, Guy de Beauchamp earl of Warwick, Richard fitz Alan earl of Arundel, Reginald de Grey, John de Hastings, Henry de Percy, Hugh le Despenser, Hugh de Veer, Robert de Tateshale, Hugh Bardolf, Hugh de Courtenay, John de Segrave, Henry de Grey, William de Ros of Helmsley, Alan la Zousche, Robert de Tony, Robert de Mohaut, William de Braose,

[1] The enrolment abbreviation of a charter opening, "The king" standing for the name and style of the monarch, while "to the archbishop etc." is enough to show that it is a charter which is being enrolled. cp. the rather fuller abbreviation in No. 84 below.

Thomas de Furnivall, John Engaigne, Peter Corbet, William of Leyburn, William le Latimer, Walter de Beauchamp steward of our household, Walter de Huntercumbe and others. Given by our hand at Westminster, on the 28th day of March in the 28th year etc.

84. "Inspeximus" of Charter of the Forest 1225 by charter, 28 March 1300, Westminster

(*Statutes of the Realm*, I (1810), pp. 42–4 (Charters), from the Charter Roll of 28 Edw. I)

The king to the archbishops etc., justices, foresters, sheriffs, stewards and all his bailiffs and faithful subjects who shall look at the present charter, greeting.[1]

[Here follows "We have inspected . . . hitherto have perhaps not been observed", being No. 77, above, word for word, with only the formal changes involved in an inspeximus by charter as distinct from letters patent as in 1297, viz, the formal charter opening and, at the end, instead of "In witness of which . . . twenty-fifth year of our reign", the following:–]

These being witness:

[The list is identical with that in the inspeximus of Magna Carta (No. 83 above) except for the omission of "J. of Norwich" (probably accidentally and possibly at the enrolment stage, not before) from the list of bishops.]

Given by our hand at Westminster, on the 28th day of March in the 28th year etc.

85. Articles upon the charters, Lenten parliament, Westminster, March 1300

(*Statutes of the Realm* (1810), I, pp. 136–41; Bémont, *Chartes des libertés anglaises 1100–1305* (Paris, 1892), No. XV [French])

Because the points of the great charter of liberties and the charter of the forest, which king Henry, father of the present king, granted to his people for the benefit of his kingdom, have not been held or kept hitherto because up to now no penalty has been established for offenders against the points of the aforesaid charters, our lord the king has granted, renewed and confirmed them afresh; and at the request of the prelates, earls and barons in his Lenten parliament at Westminster in the 28th year of his reign, has ordained and established a definite form and penalty for all those in any way contravening the points of the aforesaid charters or any point of them, in the following form.

[1] Namely that from now on the great charter of liberties of England granted to all the community of England and the charter of the forest in like manner granted be held, kept and maintained in each article and each point as fully as the king has granted, renewed and by his charter confirmed it; and that these charters be given to each sheriff of England under the king's seal to be read four times a year before the people in full county court: that is at the next county after Michaelmas, the next county after Christmas, the next county after Easter and at the next county after the feast of St John; and firmly to maintain these two charters in every point and in every article of them, where there was up to now no remedy at common law, let there

[1] See footnote on p. 495 above.

be chosen in each county by the community of that county three men of standing,[1] knights or other upright,[2] wise and prudent men, to be sworn as justices and assigned by letters patent of the king under his great seal to hear and determine, without other writ than their common warrant, the complaints that shall be made of all those who contravene or offend in any of the said points of the aforesaid charters in the counties to which they are assigned, as well within liberties as outside them, as well of the king's officers in their private capacities[3] as of others; and determine summarily the complaints heard day by day without allowing the delays that are allowed at common law; and that these same knights have power to punish all those convicted of offending against any point of the aforesaid charters, where as has been said there was previously no remedy at common law, by imprisonment or by fine or by amercement, according to what the offence demands. And by this neither the king nor any of those who were at the making of this ordinance intends that the aforesaid knights should hold any plea in virtue of the power that has been given them in a case where before now a remedy was provided at common law by writ, or that prejudice be done thereby to the common law or to the aforesaid charters in any of their points. And the king wills that if all three are not present or cannot every time attend to the performance of their office in the aforesaid form, that two of the three do it. And it is ordained that the sheriffs and the bailiffs of the king attend to the commands of the aforesaid justices in so far as they concern their office; and, besides these things granted on the points of the aforesaid charters, the king, of his special grace, in alleviation of the burdens that his people have had during the wars that have been and to amend their condition and in order that they may be readier in his service and more willingly helpful when they have the wherewithal to do it, has granted some articles which it is his intention shall hold as great a place in the estimation of his people and be of as great a benefit, or more, as the points afore granted.

[2] In the first place, because it is a great grievance in this kingdom and an incalculable harm that the king and his officers of his following, as well aliens as denizens, make their prises wherever they are as they move about the kingdom, taking people's goods, clerks' as well as laymen's, without payment or for much less than their value, it is ordained that from now on no one take prises in the kingdom except the king's takers and his purveyors for the king's household; and that these king's takers and purveyors for his household take nothing except for the same household; and that they pay for the prises of food and drink and other small necessaries for the household that they take in the districts or come to an agreement with those from whom the things are taken; and that all such king's takers, purveyors or buyers from now on have with them their warrant under the great seal or the privy seal[4] of the king, reciting their authority and the things that they are to make prise or purveyance of, which warrant they shall show to those from whom they take the prise before they take anything from them. And that these king's takers, purveyors or buyers take no more than is necessary for the king and his household and his children's households, and that they take nothing for those that are at wages or for any one else, and that they account fully in the household and in the wardrobe for all their prises, without

[1] *prodes hommes* [2] *loiaux* [3] *hors de leur places* [4] *le petit seal*

giving or delivering elsewhere anything taken for the king. And if any taker of the king's household makes prises or deliveries with the warrant that he has in any other way than is said above, on complaint made to the steward and to the treasurer of the king's household let the truth be enquired into; and if he be convicted of this let satisfaction be given at once to the plaintiff and let him be removed from the king's service forever and stay in prison as long as it is the king's pleasure; and if any one makes a prise without warrant and takes it away against the will of the owner of the goods, let him be immediately arrested by the vill where the prise is made and taken to the nearest gaol; and if he is convicted of this, let him be dealt with as a thief, if the amount of the goods demands it. And as for making prises in fairs and in good towns[1] and ports for the great wardrobe of the king, let the takers have their common warrant by the great seal, and for the things they are to take let them have the authority of the seal of the keeper of the wardrobe, and of the number, quantity and value of the things thus taken by them let there be made an indenture between the takers and the keepers of fairs, mayor or chief bailiffs of towns[2] and ports, by the view of the merchants to whom the goods thus taken belong; and let him not be allowed to take anything beyond what he puts in the indenture; and let this indenture be carried into the wardrobe under the seal of the keeper, mayor or chief bailiff aforesaid, and remain there until the account of the keeper of the king's wardrobe; and if it be found that any one has taken otherwise than he ought to have done, let him be punished at the account by the keeper of the king's wardrobe according to his deserts; and if any one take such prises without warrant, and is convicted of this, let him be dealt with like those who take prises for the king's household without warrant, as is said above. And it is not the intention of the king or his council that, by this statute, anything should lessen the king's right to the ancient prises due and accustomed, as of wine and other goods, but that it be preserved for him fully in all points.

[3] Concerning the estate of the steward and the marshals and the pleas that they ought to hold and in what manner, it is ordained that henceforth they hold no plea concerning freehold or debt or covenant or contract of people generally[3] but only of offences of the household and other offences committed within the verge, and of contracts and covenants that someone of the king's household has made with another of the same household and in the same household, not elsewhere; and hold no plea of trespass that is not set in motion by them before the king leaves the verge where the offence was committed and shall hold pleas quickly day by day so that they are heard and determined before the king goes beyond the bounds of the verge where the offence was committed; and if, perchance, they cannot be determined within the bounds of this verge, let these pleas cease before the steward and the plaintiffs be at common law; nor shall the steward henceforth take cognisance of debts or anything else, except of people of the aforementioned household; nor shall they hold any other plea by obligation[4] made at the distress of the steward and the marshals; and, if the steward or the marshals do anything contrary to this ordinance, what they do shall be held for nought. And because up to now many of the felonies committed

[1] *bones villes* [2] *villes* [3] *de gentz du pueple*
[4] a deed under seal acknowledging debt

within the verge have gone unpunished because the coroners of the districts have not concerned themselves to inquire into such manner of felonies within the verge, but [instead] the coroner of the king's household, who moves about, so that issue has not been made in proper manner, nor the felons put in exigent or outlawed, nor anything of this presented in the eyre, which has been to the great loss of the king and the less good keeping of his peace, it is ordained that henceforth, in case of homicide, in which it is the coroner's duty to view and hold inquest into the matter, the coroner of the district is to be informed and he together with the coroner of the household is to perform the office appertaining thereto and record it on the roll. And what cannot be determined before the steward because the felons cannot be attached there or for other reason, let it remain at common law, so that the exigents, outlawries and presentments in the eyre be made in this connection by the coroner of the district, as with other felonies committed outside the verge; but let not attachments cease because of this to be made with unabated vigour upon the felonies committed.

[4] In addition let no common plea be held henceforth at the exchequer contrary to the form of the great charter.

[5] In addition the king wills that the chancery and the justices of his bench follow him so that he may always have by him some men experienced in the law who will know how to dispose properly and as needed of matters that come to the court.

[6] Let no writ henceforth issue under the privy seal[1] that concerns the common law.

[7] Let not the constable of Dover castle henceforth hold at the gate of the castle any outside plea of the county that does not concern the keeping of the castle; the said constable shall not distrain the men of the Cinque Ports to plead in any other place or any other manner than they ought according to the form of the royal charters they have of their ancient liberties affirmed by the great charter.

[8] The king has granted to his people that they may if they wish have the choosing of their sheriffs in each county where the shrievalty is not of fee.

[9] The king wills and commands that no sheriff or bailiff put on inquests or on juries more people or other people or in any way other than is ordained by statute, and that they put on such inquests and juries the nearest, the most suitable and the least suspect; and he who does otherwise and is convicted of it, shall pay the plaintiff double his damages, and be grievously in the king's mercy.

[10] In respect of conspirators, false informers and evil suborners of twelves, inquests, assizes and juries, the king has ordained a remedy for plaintiffs by writ of chancery; and nevertheless wills that his justices of both benches and justices assigned to take assizes, when they come into a district to perform their office in this matter, make their inquests on every man's complaint without writ and without delay, and dispense justice to those with complaints.

[11] Again, because the king had previously ordained by statute[2] that none of his officers should take any plea by champerty[3] and by this statute people other than

[1] *le petit seal*

[2] the Statute of Westminster I (1275) c. 25 or, less likely, Westminster II (1285), c. 49. See Nos 47 and 57 above. Doubt attaches to c. 49 as part of Stat. Westm. II, but it may be compared with this enactment of 1300.

[3] i.e. on condition of receiving a share of the crop or other gain from the matter under litigation

officers were not up to now bound by this, the king wills that no officer or any other person, in order to have part of the thing that is in plea, shall undertake matters that are in plea, or that anyone on such an agreement shall surrender his right to another; and if anyone does it and is convicted of it, there shall be lost and forfeited to the king from the goods or the lands of him who undertakes the equivalent in value of what his gain by this undertaking amounts to. And to give effect to this let him who wishes to prosecute for the king be received before the justices before whom the plea has been, and by them let the award be made; but in this case it is not to be understood that a man cannot have help from pleaders and people learned in the law[1] by paying for it, or from his relatives and his neighbours.

[12] Again, the king wills that distresses for debts due to him be not made on beasts of the plough while anything else can be found to make them on, in accordance with what is ordained elsewhere by statute[2] with the penalty etc. And he does not wish too burdensome a distress to be taken for debts due to him, nor for it to be carried too far away; and if the debtor can find sufficient and suitable security until a day before the sheriff's day within which steps can be taken to obtain a remedy thereof or come to an agreement about the demand, let the distress be released meanwhile; and let him who does otherwise be severely punished.

[13] And because the king has granted those of the counties the choosing of the sheriff, he wills that they choose a sheriff such as will not burden them or put any officer in authority in return for payment or a gift, and such as will not lodge too often in one place or with the poor or with religious.

[14] Again, that bailiwicks and hundreds of the king or of other great lords of the land be not let at farm for too great a sum, whereby the people might be burdened or charged with contributing to such farms.

[15] In summonses and in attachments in a plea concerning land, let the summons and the attachment contain henceforth the term of at least 15 days, in accordance with the common law, if it is not in an attachment connected with holding assizes before the king or pleas before justices in eyre during the eyre.

[16] Let those be dealt with who make false returns to the king's writ, whereby justice is delayed, as is ordained in the second statute of Westminster, with the penalty.[3]

[17] And because many more evildoers are in the land than ever there were, and innumerable robberies, arsons and homicides are committed, and the peace is less well kept, because the statute which the king caused to be made but lately at Winchester has not been kept, the king wills that this statute be sent again into each county and read and published four times a year, like the two great charters, and firmly kept in every point, on pain of the penalties that are therein laid down; and let the three knights be charged to keep and maintain this statute who are assigned in the counties to correct infringements of the great charters; and for this let them have warrant.[4]

[18] In respect of wastes and acts of destruction committed in wardships of houses,

[1] *sages gentz*
[2] perhaps a reference to "Districtiones de Scaccario", c. 13 (*Statutes of the Realm* (Rec. Com.), I, p. 197)
[3] Stat. Westm. II, 13 Edw. I (1285), c. 39 (No. 57 above)
[4] the reference is to c. [1] above and, of course, to Stat. Winch., 13 Edw. I (1285) (No. 59 above)

parks, woods and preserves and all other things that escheat into the king's hand by escheator and sub-escheator, the king wills that he who has suffered the damage shall have a writ of waste in chancery against the escheator for what he has done or the sub-escheator for what he has done, if he has anything from which he can answer for it; and if he has nothing from which he can answer for it, then let his superior answer by such penalty as to damages as was last ordained by the statute on those who commit waste in wardships.[1]

[19] Again, when the escheator or the sheriff seizes in to the king's hand lands of another when he has no right to seize them and then, when the want of right has been established, the issues meanwhile have in the past been retained and not restored when the king has surrendered the lands, the king wills that from now on when lands have been thus seized and then surrendered because he has no right to seize or to hold them, the issues shall be fully restored to him to whom the land remains and who has suffered the damage.

[20] It is ordained that no goldsmith of England or elsewhere in the lordship of the king from now on work or make any manner of plate or jewels or any other thing of gold or of silver that is not of good and of true alloy, that is, gold of a definite assay and silver of the alloy of sterling or of a better alloy, according to the wishes of him who owns the things that are being wrought. And that no one work worse silver than money, and that no kind of plate of silver leave the hands of the workmen until it is assayed by the wardens of the craft and that it be signed with a leopard's head; that no one work worse gold than the assay of Paris, and that the wardens of the craft go from shop to shop among the workmen, testing that the gold is the same as the aforesaid assay, and if they find any worse than the assay, that the work be forfeit to the king. That no one make crossed[2] rings or crossed chains, that no one mount a stone in gold if it is not natural; that cutters of rings and of seals give everyone back his weight of silver and of gold, to the extent that they can honestly save it; and jewels of gold that they have in hand of old work they should make haste with as soon as they can; and if they buy this same work hereafter, they should buy it to take to pieces and not to resell it. And in all the good towns of England where there are goldsmiths, let them get themselves the same statutes that those of London have got, and let one from each town come for all to London to find out their fixed assay: and if any goldsmith be convicted of doing otherwise than is ordained above, let him be punished by imprisonment and by fine at the will of the king.

In all the aforesaid things, and each of them, the king wills and intends, he and his council and all those who were at this ordaining, that the right and the lordship of his crown be saved for him absolutely.

[1] a reference, apparently, to Stat. Gloucester (1278), c. 5 (No. 52 above)
[2] i.e. of more than one metal

86. The recoinage of 29 March 1300

(Red Book of the Exchequer, fo. 259, whence printed and translated by Ch. Johnson, *The De Moneta of Nicholas of Oresme and English Mint Documents* (1956), pp. 62–5 [French])

Be it remembered that the 29th day of March of the 28th year of the reign of king Edward it was ordained by the king and his council at Westminster to set up exchange and workers of money in the undermentioned places in the realm of England; namely, at the Tower of London, thirty furnaces; at Canterbury, eight furnaces as there have been before; at Kingston-upon-Hull, four furnaces; at Newcastle-upon-Tyne, two furnaces; at Bristol, four furnaces; at Exeter, two furnaces. And be it known that John Porcher, master of the mint of England, himself dwelling in London to coin the money, must set in each of the other places named a man in his stead to coin the money, and must find everything necessary for a master, for which he himself will answer at the same rate to the pound as in London. And Roger de Frowyke, changer, dwelling in London, must find a changer at Canterbury and another at Bristol, for whom he will answer, and must take for himself and a clerk, from the time when the pollards and other bad counterfeit moneys are put down till the main press is over, forty marks per annum. And for the changer of Canterbury, from the time of his appointment, twenty pounds a year; and for the changer of Bristol, from the time of his appointment, twenty pounds a year; so long as they shall remain in the said places. And Taldo Janiani and Coppo Cottenni and their companions, merchants of the company of the Frescobaldi of Florence, shall have the exchanges of Kingston-upon-Hull, Newcastle-upon-Tyne and Exeter and shall find changers and pence in the said exchanges to maintain them and all other things which pertain to the changers; provided that they render account to John de Sandale, warden of the king's exchanges; which John must set clerks in his stead in the said places to control and charge the said merchants and they shall answer to the said John for the issues and John shall answer for them to the king.[1] And Lapyn Roger, assayer, dwelling at London to make the assays of the control boxes and all other assays pertaining to the mint, must take from the time that the bad money is put down till the main press is over, forty marks a year. And if it happen that the said Lapyn be sent out of London elsewhere than to Canterbury to make assays, he must have his reasonable expenses for it from the king. And John de Sandale, warden of the king's exchanges aforesaid, must take for himself and his clerk dwelling in London, the same fee that his predecessors in that office have taken, and besides that ten marks a year for another clerk whom he will have to keep at the London mint as long as the press lasts. And for the clerks whom he shall find at Canterbury, Kingston-upon-Hull, Newcastle-upon-Tyne, Bristol and Exeter, who shall also be the keepers of the dies in those places, twenty marks a year each. And the keeper of the dies at London must also have as other keepers before him have had. And the ushers of the doors at London and at Canterbury must take each of them threepence a day. And whenever the said John de Sandale goes out of London on the king's business to visit the other places, he must take for his expenses three shillings every day.

[1] In the original draft the merchants were to answer directly to the king. The amendment was made by the council of 11 April 1300.

And furthermore, on the same day, it was ordained that Alexander Norman of Lucca must be master of the king's mint at Dublin in Ireland, and must take with him, at the king's cost, three furnaces, and must take of every pound of money that he shall make sixpence for all costs, on condition that he must find the engraver of the dies at his own cost and all other things pertaining to the master, as John Porcher does in England. And he must make money of like weight and alloy as has been made aforetime. And he has to answer well and lawfully to the king for all things which shall be delivered to him to keep and to work. The said Alexander has found the following security to the said Taldo and his companions, who must be answerable for everything, to wit:[1]

Taldo Janiani and Coppo Cottenni and their companions aforesaid shall have the exchange there and shall find a changer and pence and the other things which pertain to an exchange at Dublin out of the issues of the said exchange, and answer for the said issues to the king; so that the treasurer of the exchequer at Dublin shall assign them a clerk to control them and charge them with the aforesaid issues. And because the voyage between Ireland and England is perilous, and the box must be carried to England to be assayed, it is ordained that they make two boxes, so that if one were lost it might be replaced by the other. As to the wages, mises and expenses of the aforesaid merchants, they shall be taxed by the judgment of the treasurer and barons of the exchequer of England. And it is further ordained that these merchants of the Frescobaldi may change and buy silver, pollards, crockards and all manner of white money counterfeiting sterling throughout the realm of England, provided that they bring such silver and the plate as results from such counterfeit money to the king's exchanges to be coined.[2]

It was afterwards ordained by the council that there should be a mint at Chester, and that John de Sandale shall appoint a clerk there for himself, Roger de Frowyke a changer and John Porcher a master of the mint, for whom they shall be willing to answer in the form prescribed.

[1] The particulars of the security appear to be omitted.

[2] Q.R. Mem. adds: "In witness of all the above Walter by the grace of God, bishop of Chester, treasurer of our lord the king, of the one part, and John de Sandale, warden of the king's exchanges, of the other, to this indenture have mutually set their seals. Written at St Albans, 11 April, 28 Edward I."

87. A confidential state paper: papal diplomacy, 1300

(*E.H.R.*, xvii (1902), pp. 518–27 [French])

A report of private conversations of the king of England's envoys with Pope Boniface VIII at Sculcula near Anagni on 21, 22 and 24 August 1300. The matter under discussion was Gascony. The pope blames the king of England for giving it up in the first place in 1294, then for not getting it out of the hands of the French by agreeing to it being put into his hands as arbitrator. To the answer that the king of England had obeyed the pope in everything else, but the pope had not in his award of 1298 pronounced on the king of England's right to Gascony and had still to do so, Boniface replies that he had not done so because his English leanings make him suspect to the French, that in any case it would be useless for him to do so – he could be effective only with the plenitude of papal power behind him and what was needed was to let him arbitrate as pope and not, as at present, as Benedict Gaetano, a private person. This was, of course, precisely what the two kings had agreed from the start not to do, and Boniface's self-interest as arbitrator is clearly seen.

The first day the bishop of Winchester and the other envoys had audience of the pope, and when they had conveyed to him the king's greetings, the pope enquired very particularly after him. And then he said in the presence of six cardinals who were there at the time, "We have a great affection for the king of England, for we have tried him and found him loyal. And he will assuredly find us his peer and his friend, and we will not fail him now. God fail us, should we fail him."

The next day the said bishop put before the pope, who was quite alone with the said envoys, what the king of England had instructed them to do. And the pope answered in this way, "The king of England we listen to readily and more readily grant what he asks, and we readily receive [and] readily listen to his envoys, because we have a special affection for him and have had for a long time; and his father (God bless his soul) we greatly loved. They did us great honour. And we recall when we were in England with the lord Ottobon and were besieged in the Tower of London by the earl of Gloucester, this king, then a young man, came to deliver us from this siege and he did us many a service,[1] and his father did too. And it was then we gave this king our particular affection, and formed the opinion from his appearance that with him it was bound to happen that he would be the finest prince in the world, and we believe without a doubt that we did not err in this judgment, for we firmly believe that there is not now living a better prince. True enough, he has some faults, for no man is faultless, but comparing his shortcomings with his advantages, he is of all the princes of the world the best, and this we would say out boldly before all the world. And since then too, he has greatly honoured us at every stage of our career, both as notary and afterwards as cardinal, then later still as pope. Now the position is that he handed over his land of Gascony to the king of France. Most certainly he acted foolishly; and this one (he said about brother William of Gainsborough)[2] acted still more foolishly, for in virtue of the general authority he had he renounced both the fiefs and the homage to the king of France. The envoys of the king of France, namely the duke of Burgundy, the count of St Pol and the others, once relied greatly on this renunciation and used to say 'Sir, what more is needed? The king of England has

[1] *et nous fist multz dovurs:* "dovurs" could however be a corruption of *donurs* (*d'onurs*), in which case the meaning would be "and greatly honoured us".

[2] William of Gainsborough was most likely present when this was said. He is named on 15 April 1300 as a member of the embassy along with the bishop of Winchester and four others (*Foedera*, I, ii, p. 920). He (with Hugh of Manchester) had in fact carried Edward I's renunciation in 1294 (M. C. L. Salt, in *E.H.R.*, xliv (1929), p. 271).

by this renounced' and would not give up about it until we said one day to the bishop of Carcassonne, now dead, 'Tell me, you have studied law; in virtue of a general authority can renunciation be made of fiefs and homage?' and he replied 'No, sir, it requires special authority.' 'Certainly [I said] what you say is true, that in such a case there is needed not only special, but very special authority'; and they did not dare to speak of this in our presence ever after. In another thing has the king of England made a mistake, in that he has not kept to our award. On one occasion when the envoys of both kings were here, we worried a good deal and more than you, lord bishop of Winchester, who were one of them, know, how we, as was our inclination, [could] more discreetly ordain for the benefit of the king of England in the matter of this land of Gascony; and we thought of the great covetousness of the French and saw no better way of doing for the benefit of the king of England than that this land of Gascony be placed in our hands: for there is extreme covetousness in the French. What they once hold they never want to let go, and because of this he who has business with the French ought to take great care, for he who has business with the French has business with the devil. On another occasion when the said envoys of France were here, we rebuked them severely for their covetousness and said to them 'Your covetousness is something to wonder at, for what you once get hold of, whether rightly or wrongly, you never want to let go. And ought it not to more than suffice you that you have taken Normandy, which is a very great thing, from the king of England? It seems that your intention is to expel the king of England from whatever he has this side the sea.'[1] At which Pierre Flote answered with a smile, 'Certainly, sir, what you say is true.' And we said to him 'We verily believe that this would not be to the honour or the advantage of the king of France, rather we firmly believe that it would be more honourable and advantageous for the king of France that the king of England should have the very little land he claims this side the said sea, that he be not expelled from all the said land, for thus it would follow that the king and the kingdom of England would forever be hostile to the king of France.' They agreed with me on this, especially the laymen, that is the duke and the count, for them we found tractable and reasonable enough in public on everything that would benefit the king of England, and more so privately; but P. Flote and the other clerks were too hard and said 'Oh, the king of France will not let go his lands for anything.' 'We will tell you another thing (the pope had said[2] to the French). The Gascons would not wish at all to be under the sovereignty of the king of France without the mesne lordship of the king of England. It could well be, perchance, that some through some singular disposition might wish it, but I am speaking to you of the people generally. For such is the way of subjects: they wish to have several lords, so that they cannot be greatly oppressed by one.' On this they all agreed with me. And out of the regard we had to their covetousness, we provided that the land of Gascony should be placed in our hands and this the king of England has not done. True enough, we have heard that he was willing for it to be placed in our hands and that the king of France would never place what he held of it in our hands. The king is very prudent, but sometimes he wants his

[1] The English Channel went by the name of *la mer d'Engleterre* in the Middle Ages.
[2] The verb has to be supplied. The editors supply [*dit*], but a pluperfect seems preferable.

own way. He has gone ahead in good faith and with our confidence. We know him well, and we see him now as clearly in the mind's[1] eye as if we saw him here present before us. And in this the king of England has made a mistake, for he ought to have kept to our award and ought in no way to have departed from the terms of the award; and there could be a shorter way of ordaining about this land if it were in our hands. Now, lord bishop of Winchester, you say that we have pronounced peace between the kings, and that the king of England has obeyed us over his own marriage and his son's betrothal and the ladies' dowers, and that it still remains to pronounce on the land of Gascony, which is in the hands of the king of France. We can say with St Paul 'I have planted and Apollos has watered and God has given the increase.'[2] I have planted peace in bringing about and pronouncing peace, and I have watered and moistened it with the dews of marriage and betrothal. And because of this I expected for certain that God would send the increase and that the kings, because they were akin,[3] would come to an amicable arrangement over this land. Now that this has not been done, then, as St John said, the pope wears a two-edged sword,[4] that is, temporal authority and spiritual authority. For God gave the pope a double sword and double power, one by way of arbitration and the other by authority as pope: which power and authority we have not renounced in this business, and we do not intend to renounce it but will use it in its place if we see fit. And we marvel greatly that the king of England has not been willing to be advised by us or by the envoys he sent in the past. Either the envoys have been false in that they have not told him the truth or if they have told him they have not told it wisely. We well remember when we were a cardinal we advised the envoys who came on his behalf to this court in connection with this business that he should complain to this court about the king of France because the king of France was wrongly holding and detaining his land of Gascony and then we could have advised him who was pope at that time; and then again when we were pope we spoke privately to one who came to us on his behalf and recommended him to tell the king that he should make the aforesaid complaint, and if he had made it we can say to you with assurance that the business would now be in a different state. But as we saw that he did not wish to do it, that peace-talks had begun, and that the business was taking another course, we did not wish to hinder the peace. The truth is, and see that you keep it secret, that we carried on negotiations with the envoys of both kings once when they were here for an arrangement to be made over this land, and we found so great a covetousness in the French that an arrangement could then not be made for the French were asking for all the land of Gascony, we tell you, for they were asking for the best part, that is, Bordeaux and this land of the Agenais and another fortress as well, and there the matter rested at that time. Now we are in this state, and we believe that because of their covetousness it will be necessary for us to use main force.[5] (And then he quoted the Psalter) 'I am

[1] literally "in the eyes of the heart", the heart, not the head, of course, being to the medieval way of thinking the seat of all the faculties, intellectual as well as physical
[2] I Cor. iii. 6
[3] MS. [*freres?*]
[4] Rev. i. 14
[5] *mettre la mayn au fort*

a worm and no man' for nothing is softer than the touch of the worm and nothing touches more sharply than it.[1] You should know very well that we mean to use main force, but for certain reasons we have delayed doing some things that we would otherwise have done. We wish you to know that we very greatly desire to show the king of England by deeds the love we have for him, and please God that before we die he may perceive and recognise by the outcome the great feeling of love and goodwill we bear towards him."

Afterwards he said that at present he could not well reply to what the bishop of Winchester had asked, because the envoys of the king of France had not come who should come first of all more simply and then afterwards more solemnly and the same who had come before on the same matter, and because of the serious illness he had had also, which had left him very weak.

The archdeacon of Richmond said to him, "Sir, concerning what you say that the land of Gascony has not been placed in your hands, know, sir, that about this the king of England did what the bishop of Vicenza told him."

And the pope replied to him, "The bishop said well and you say ill."

On the remaining day the bishop of Winchester said to the pope, who was all alone with the envoys of the king of England, "Sir, the king of England instructed us that when we had given you our message and had heard your reply, we should inform him of all that had been done with regard to this business. And because, sir, you have said many kind and gracious things, which you have ordered to be and which indeed should be kept very secret, and which it could be dangerous to send him by letter if the letter was opened or lost in any way: because of this, sir, we have arranged, if it please your holiness, that one of us shall go to the king to tell him all these things and, if it please you, that you be good enough to write to him – that would please him."

Then the pope asked who this one was and from where and if each of them had authority individually or all together jointly. And when he had heard the reply to this and the letter of attorney had been read out before him he replied in this fashion. "The letter of attorney is good enough as regards proceeding by way of arbitration, but we have thought a great deal about this business and we do not think that it can be settled by way of arbitration, for the French would ask for unreasonable things as well as the whole or the greater part of the land as they have done formerly, and you would not be willing to grant it, nor would we ourselves wish . . . if the king of England wished it; and if we pronounce, the French will not abide by our pronouncement, nor can they be compelled by this method, except by applying the penalty and they will make light of this penalty. For this reason we consider that it will be necessary for us to use papal authority and our plenitude of power against them, and then it would be necessary to have power of attorney to complain of the king of France and of the sin that he commits by retaining his[2] land wrongfully; and that this thing should not be forgotten or left undone, for if he said that we ought not to meddle with fiefs, it would be answered that we could by reason of the sin

[1] the reference is to Ps. xxii. 6; the play is on *verme* as worm and as serpent
[2] i.e. the king of England's land

involved etc.[1] As regards the way of arbitration, the letter of attorney is sufficient, and although it could be challenged somewhat for not giving authority to cede or renounce anything, if it came to wanting to negotiate on that, nevertheless it is quite sufficient, because of the general nature of what is there,[2] for doing all other things, though they require special instructions." Then the pope said that he felt well-satisfied with this arrangement to send one of them to the king on account of the danger from letters that the bishop had mentioned; and he said to him who was to go, "Take care to be a faithful reporter and faithfully report to him what you have heard and will hear said. We have a great affection for the king of England and yet we have shown him no sign of affection. But we have refrained from showing him it for good reasons and for his own good. For the French are full of great suspicion and if they had seen that we had been partial to the king of England in any way the king of France would not have been brought round to accepting our arbitration. Because of this we have accorded the king of France many favours and the king of England we have accorded none. For another reason also have we refrained from showing him favour; for he made a great mistake and greatly angered us by going to Flanders, where neither he nor any of his ancestors ever had rights, and made alliance with the Germans and the Burgundians to wage war on the kingdom of France. If he had gone to Gascony, which is his land, to defend it or to recover it, that would have been another thing. [3]The position now is that he needs our favour and our help and he intends to petition us, as we have already heard by some means; and verily has he great need of our favour and our help with regard to the body and with regard to the soul, for he is in a bad way and in mortal sin, and not in one only but in many sins. He has caused churches to be robbed and has taken and wasted and squandered the goods of churches and of churchmen, and in this case he cannot have help except through us and through the church of Rome. He has sinned in other ways, for it is impossible in war for many killings and other sins not to be committed, but for these sins he can well have help perchance from other priests. Equally he has need with regard to the body, for he has in various ways greatly wasted and squandered his treasure: that we well know. And verily will we help him in these two ways, both spiritually with regard to the soul and temporally as regards the body, but this temporal help will not please this bishop."

After this he who was to come here said, "Sir, about what you said the other day that the king of England had not kept to your pronouncement, in that the land of Gascony was not placed in your hands, know sir, in the king of England's defence, that he has been and is willing to and is proposing to abide by your pronouncement and carry out your wishes. And to this end, sir, he sent his solemn envoys to the bishop of Vicenza and gave them full authority to place what he held in Gascony in your hands; and these envoys showed their power of attorney to the said bishop, and made an offer to him to place unreservedly in his hands what he held and to go with the bishop day after day continuously and stay until everything had been handed

[1] *par resoun du pecche* (i.e. *ratione peccati*)
[2] *pur la generale qe y est*
[3] In the margin opposite this paragraph, "Confessor, take heed".

over to him in your name. And the bishop would never move, because the king of France was in no way willing to place in your hands what he held; wherefor the king of England and his envoys did not see that they could do any more in this case."

And the pope replied, "Because of this the king of England ought to have remained firm and fixed without proceeding to make any alliance with the king of France."

The other then said to him, "Sir, besides what is contained in your pronouncement about the penalty imposed on the party through whom they might fail to make the alliances, you sent a letter to the king of England which contained among other things this clause: that you would require him to proceed without delay to make the alliances of marriage [and] betrothal which you had ordained for the better strengthening and keeping of the peace, for it was your firm belief that everything that the dissension of war had damaged the rapprochement following the alliances would mend and restore. In addition, the bishop of Vicenza came to him and asked him repeatedly in your name to proceed without any delay to make the alliances. So that, partly because of your letter, partly because of the request the bishop made in your name, the king of England did make the alliances."

The pope was silent for a while and then he said, "It is not good to trouble the king just now and don't trouble him over this, for what is done is done and let it be."

Then the bishop of Winchester said, "Sir, if you please, are you thinking of prolonging the truce, which is a short one?"

And he replied that Yes it would be a good thing, and then he said, "Now the king of France has not kept the truces we have ordained and we greatly wonder with what conscience he has asked for an aid to advance on Flanders: furthermore we are astonished that the prelates have granted him it, and most certainly we regard the king and the prelates of France as excommunicated. We spoke of it to the bishop of Soissons, who came to us the other day for the king of France, and said to him openly that the king and prelates were excommunicated, and he asked us for absolution, and we denied him it."

Endorsed: . . . by letters of credence from pope Boniface . . . concerning dangerous customs and reasons why it was necessary for him to use apostolic authority against the French and for the proctors to have full power to bring an action against the king of France on the ground of sin.

Also that a report be made on things aforesaid concerning the safety of the soul at this sign "Take heed, confessor".

88. Bills presented in the parliament at Lincoln, 1301

(Printed in *Parliamentary Writs*, I, pp. 104–5 (Nos 44–5), from a register preserved in the archives of the archbishop of Canterbury [French])

The king's bill is given in the register the date 20 January. The bill of his subjects in reply cannot be later than 14 February. It was presented on behalf of the whole community by a mere knight, Henry of Keighley, a knight of the shire for Lancashire in that parliament. Keighley had been involved in the political crisis at every stage since 1297 (Powicke, *The Thirteenth Century*, p. 704, and the further references there given). For his action on this occasion he was five years later imprisoned in the Tower – though more on principle than from vindictiveness, for we learn that it was not he but Robert Winchelsey, the archbishop of Canterbury, whom the king held chiefly responsible (see No. 94 below). Significantly, it is the archives at Canterbury that have preserved these texts.

Bill delivered to the prelates and leading men on behalf of the lord king in his parliament at Lincoln on the octave of St Hilary in the year of the Lord 1300 and the 29th year of the reign of king E[dward] [20 January 1301]

As to making the perambulation the king wills that it be shown to the good people who have come to this parliament. And when they have examined and well understood how and in what way and by what means of information, of recollection and of rights[1] it is done in all points and as a whole together with the evidence that the king means to have for it, if they are willing to say about it on their homage and the faith they owe him and the crown that it is done and carried out for the king, the crown and the people well and honestly and with sufficient consideration and reliable information, and that he can confirm it without infringing his oath and without disinheriting the crown and that they dare to advise him to do so, the king is quite willing that it should stand. And if there is anything to amend or to change, let it be put right without delay by any way suitable that can be ordained with their counsel on pain of the same charges. And if this way does not please, then let some middle way be provided how the thing can be done in good fashion with regard to the estate of the crown, as with regard to that by which it will be diminished, so that the king's oath may be saved and theirs in respect of the crown.

Bill of the prelates and leading men of the kingdom delivered to the lord king on behalf of the whole community in the parliament at Lincoln in the above-mentioned year

To our lord the king the people of the community of his land make it known that in respect of the two ways indicated to them by him they fail to appreciate why they should be challenged in any way and they do not dare to take it upon themselves to reply to the form to which these two ways are restricted[2] for perils that might ensue.

But the said community considers that, if it please our lord the king, the two charters of liberty and of the forest should from now on be fully kept in all their points.

It pleases the lord king expressly

And statutes contrary to the said charters should be voided and annulled.

It pleases expressly[3]

[1] *moevementz daprises de remembrances e de raisons*

[2] *contienent*

[3] Letters patent making this concession known issued from Lincoln under date 14 February 1301 – this is the so-called Confirmation of the Charters, 1301 and its sole purpose. See No. 89 below.

And that the authority of the justices assigned in the counties to keep the charters should be put beyond doubt with the counsel of the prelates, earls and barons.

It pleases silently

And the perambulation that is already done and completed by view of good men according to the form of the said charter of the forest should stand and become effective without delay by disafforestment in accordance with the bounds made manifest by the perambulators and that the community should be immediately put in possession thereof.

It pleases expressly

And the misdeeds and transgressions committed by the king's officers contrary to the tenor of the said charters, and prises wrongfully taken without agreement or payment contrary to the form of the statute of our lord the king made, at Westminster in Lent last[1] should cease from now on.

It pleases expressly

And what is done wrong by any officer should be amended in accordance with what the offence calls for by auditors assigned for the purpose who are not suspect to the prelates, earls and barons of the land, as he himself has done before now and that this should be put into effect immediately.

The lord king is willing to provide another remedy for this but not by such auditors.

And that sheriffs from now on should be answerable for issues as they used to be in his father's time, which issues have been and still are a cause of great impoverishment of the people; and that sheriffs should not be more heavily charged.

It pleases the lord king that a suitable remedy be provided for this by common counsel as quickly as it conveniently can be.

And that where the perambulation is not yet carried out or completed it should be done between now and next Michaelmas.

It pleases expressly

The people of the kingdom, so that all the above-mentioned things be done and be securely established and accomplished, grant him the fifteenth in place of the twentieth previously granted, provided that all the above-mentioned things are done between now and next Michaelmas, otherwise nothing shall be levied.

It pleases expressly

And that he should be good enough to have regard to the ninth given but lately for having these same things.[2]

It pleases expressly

[1] The reference is to Articles upon the Charters, 1300 (No. 85 above).

[2] This would seem to be a request that the fifteenth should be levied on the same basis as the ninth granted in return for the confirmation of the charters in the Michaelmas parliament of 1297. At all events, the form used for the collection of that ninth was used for the collection of the fifteenth of 1301.

And that this thing should be levied within a year after next Michaelmas in such a way that four knights shall be chosen from each county by the common assent of the counties to tax, collect and pay the aforesaid fifteenth to our lord the king.

It pleases expressly

And for these above-mentioned things the prelates of holy church cannot and dare not assent to a contribution being made from their goods or from the goods of the clergy contrary to the pope's prohibition.

It did not please the king but the community of leading men approved.

89. The so-called Confirmation of the Charters of 1301 (14 February 1301, Lincoln)

(*Statutes of the Realm* (Rec. Com.), I (1810), Charters, p. 44)

Edward by the grace of God king of England, lord of Ireland and duke of Aquitaine, to all to whom the present letters come, greeting. Know that as we have granted and confirmed and renewed by our own charter[1] the great charter of the lord Henry formerly king of England, our father, on the liberties of England along with the charter of the forest, and have ordered those charters to be kept and firmly observed in every one of their articles, we will and grant for us and our heirs that if any statutes are contrary to the said charters or to any article contained in those same charters, they shall be emended by the common counsel of our realm in due fashion, or even annulled. In witness of which thing we have had made these our letters patent. Witness myself at Lincoln the fourteenth day of February in the twenty-ninth year of our reign [14 February 1301, Lincoln].

90. Grant to Merchant Vintners of the Duchy of Aquitaine in return for custom on wine, 13 August 1302

(*Red Book of the Exchequer*, ed. H. Hall, Rolls series (1896), III, pp. 1060–4)

This is a custom on wine only.

On the liberties granted to the merchant vintners of the duchy of Aquitaine in return for paying the king and his heirs 2s on each tun of wine brought by them within the realm of England or the king's power.

The king to the archbishops etc., greeting. With regard to the well-being of the merchants of our aforesaid duchy [of Aquitaine] we are specially concerned how under our dominion the privilege of tranquillity and of full security may be provided for the same merchants in times to come in order that their willingness to serve us and our realm may be more abundantly increased, and assenting favourably to their petitions and ordaining in the form which follows for the fuller assurance of their

[1] "*per cartam nostram*": a clear reference to the confirmation of the Charters by charter in 1300. cf. Nos 83 and 84 above.

condition, we have decided for ourselves and our heirs forever to grant to the same merchants the things underwritten.

In the first place, namely, that all merchant vintners of the aforesaid duchy safely and securely under our defence and protection may come into our said realm of England and everywhere within our power with wines and any other merchandise whatsoever, and that within the same realm and our power in cities, boroughs and market-towns they may trade in large quantities as well with denizens or inhabitants of the realm as with aliens, strangers or friends,[1] and that their merchandise which they bring perchance into the same realm and our power or buy or otherwise acquire within the said realm and our power they may convey or have conveyed whither they will as well within the realm and our power as without and do what they want with it on paying the customs they owe, except only wines, which may in no wise be taken out of the same realm or our power without our approval. Item, that the said merchant vinters of the said duchy may lodge at their will in the cities and towns aforesaid, and tarry with their goods with the consent of those to whom the inns or houses belong. Item, that every contract entered into by the same vintners with any persons whatsoever, wheresoever they belong, touching all manner of merchandise, shall be firm and stable, so that neither of the merchants may disown that contract or withdraw from the same, after earnest-money has been given and received between the contractors. And if perchance dispute arises over such a contract, proof shall be made thereof according to the uses and customs of the fairs and vills where the said contract happens to have been made and entered into. Item, we remit and quit to the said merchants of the said duchy that ancient prise of two tuns of wine which we used to take from every ship laden with wines touching within our realm or power, one, to wit, from before the mast, and the other from behind it, promising further and granting to the same merchants for ourselves and our heirs for ever that we will in no wise hereafter make or suffer to be made the aforesaid prise, or any other, of wines or other their wares by us or another or others for any necessity or circumstance against the will of those merchants without immediate payment of the price at which the said merchants sell their wines and other wares to others, or satisfaction otherwise, so that they reckon themselves content and that no valuation or estimation be put upon their wines or other wares by us or our servants. Item, that on each tun of wine gauged, as the seller of the wine shall be bound to supply that which it lacks from the gauge, so he shall be satisfied by the buyer of that which is over the gauge according to the price at which the tun of wine shall be sold. Item, that as soon as ships with new wines touch within our realm and power, the old wines, wheresoever they be found in towns or other places to which the said ships shall come, shall be viewed and proved if they be sound and also uncorrupt, and of those who view the said wines one half shall be merchant vintners of the duchy aforesaid, and the other half good men of the town where this is done, and they shall be sworn to do the premises faithfully and without fraud, and they shall do justice as usual with corrupt wines. Item, whereas it was of old time accustomed and used that the buyer and seller should pay 1*d* for each tun for gauge, each of them, to wit, ½*d*, let it be so done in future and

[1] *privatis*

observed as a custom. Item, we will that all bailiffs and officials of fairs, cities, boroughs and market-towns, do speedy justice from day to day without delay according to the law merchant to the vintners aforesaid who complain before them of wrongs, molestations done to them or debts or any other pleas; and if by chance fault be found in any of the aforesaid bailiffs or officials whereby the same vintners or any of them sustain the inconveniences of delay, even though the vintner recover his losses against the principal party, nevertheless the bailiff or other official shall be punished by us as his offence demands, and we have granted that punishment as a favour to the aforesaid merchant vintners to speed up justice for them. Item, that in all kinds of pleas, saving the case of a crime for which the penalty of death should be inflicted, where a merchant vintner of the duchy aforesaid has been impleaded or has impleaded another, of whatsoever condition he is who is impleaded, stranger or friend, in fairs, cities or boroughs where there is a sufficient number of merchant vintners of the aforesaid duchy and inquest ought to be made, one half of the inquest shall be of such merchant vintners of the duchy aforesaid, and the other half of other good and law-worthy men of the place where the plea happens to be, and if it happens that a sufficient number of merchant vintners of the aforesaid duchy is not to be found, there shall be put on the inquest those who shall be found suitable there and the rest shall be of other good and suitable men of the places where the plea is. Item, that no other exaction or charge of prest shall be in any wise put upon the wines of the said merchants. Item, we have deemed fit to ordain – and we will for us and our heirs for ever that ordinance to be firmly observed – that for any liberty soever which we or our heirs shall grant hereafter, the aforesaid merchant vintners shall not lose the above-written liberties or any of them, willing that those liberties extend only to the said merchant vintners of our aforesaid duchy. And in return for the abovesaid liberties and free customs the aforesaid merchant vintners have granted to us that on each tun of wine which they bring or cause to be brought into our realm or power, and on which they are bound to pay freight to the sailors, they will pay to us and our heirs by name of custom 2*s*, beyond the ancient customs due and paid in money to us or to others, within forty days after the same wines are put ashore from the ships. And we will that the aforesaid merchant vintners, in respect of wines whereon they shall have paid to us the aforesaid custom of 2*s* in one place of our realm or elsewhere within our power, shall be entirely free and quit of payment of the aforesaid custom of 2*s* in all other places of our said realm and power; provided that for other merchandise whatsoever which they shall happen to employ within our realm and power they be bound to pay to us the same customs which the rest of the merchants shall pay to us for such merchandise. These being witnesses: – the venerable father, W. bishop of Coventry and Lichfield, John de Warenna, earl of Surrey, Roger le Bygod, earl of Norfolk and marshal of England, John of Britanny, Hugh le Despenser, William de Brewosa, Walter Beauchamp, steward of our household, Roger le Brabazon, John de Merk and others. Given by the king's hand at Westminster on 13 August.

91. Grant to foreign merchants in return for new custom (*Carta Mercatoria*), 1 February 1303

(N. S. B. Gras, *The Early English Customs System* (Cambridge, Mass., 1918), pp. 259–64)

In return for a new custom from them over and above the now "ancient" custom of 1275 (No. 48 above), the king granted foreign merchants these liberties. The new custom was on all important commodities of the foreign trade of the country, imports and exports alike, and was not, like the old, on the big export commodities, wool, woolfells and hides, only. Later in the year (No. 92 below) he tried but failed to get native merchants to accept this charter at the price.

The king to the archbishops etc. greeting. With regard to the well-being of all merchants of the underwritten kingdoms, land and provinces, to wit, Almain, France, Spain, Portugal, Navarre, Lombardy, Tuscany, Provence, Catalonia, our duchy of Aquitaine, Toulouse, Quercy, Flanders, Brabant, and all other foreign lands and places, by whatsoever name they be known, coming to our realm of England and having dealings[1] there, we are particularly concerned how within our dominion the benefit[2] of tranquillity and complete security may be provided for those merchants in days to come, so that they may be readier to serve us and our realm, and, inclining to their petitions and ordaining in the form which follows for the fuller safeguarding of their condition, we have decided to grant to the said merchants for ourselves and our heirs for ever the things underwritten. First, to wit, that all merchants of the said realms and lands with their wares whatsoever they are may come safely and securely under our defence and protection into our said realm of England and everywhere else within our power free and quit of murage, pontage and pavage, and that within our same realm and power they may trade, in large quantities[3] only, in cities, boroughs and market-towns with both denizens or inhabitants of our same aforesaid realm and power and aliens (strangers or connexions[4]) though the wares which are commonly called mercery and spices may be sold in small quantities as has usually been done in the past; and that all the aforesaid merchants can take their wares which they happen to bring to our aforesaid realm and power or to buy or otherwise acquire within our same realm and power, or have them taken, whither they will as well within our aforesaid realm and power as without (except to the lands of manifest and notorious enemies of our realm) on paying the customs they owe – wines only excepted, which it shall not be lawful for them in any wise to take out of our same realm or power without our will and special licence after they have been brought into our same realm or power.

Furthermore, that the aforesaid merchants may lodge at their will in the cities, boroughs and towns aforesaid, and tarry with their goods, at the pleasure of those to whom the inns or houses belong.

Furthermore, that every contract entered into by those merchants with any persons whatsoever, wherever they come from, touching any sort of merchandise shall be firm and stable, so that neither of the merchants can withdraw from or go back on that contract after God's penny has been given and received between the principal

[1] *conversantium*

[2] *immunitas*

[3] For the reason given by Gras, *Early English Customs System* (Cambridge, Mass., 1918), I have preferred this to "wholesale".

[4] *privatis*

contracting persons. And if perchance dispute arises over such a contract, let proof of or enquiry into the matter be made in accordance with the usages and customs of the fairs and towns where the said contract happens to have been made and entered into.

Furthermore, we promise and grant to the aforesaid merchants for ourselves and our heirs for ever that we will in no wise make or suffer to be made henceforth any prise, or arrest or delay because of prise, of their wares, merchandise or other goods by us or another or others for any necessity or circumstance against the will of those merchants, save upon immediate payment of the price at which the merchants can sell such wares to others, or satisfaction to them otherwise, so that they reckon themselves content, and that no valuation or estimation be put by us or our officials on their wares, merchandise or goods.

Furthermore, we will that all bailiffs and officials of fairs, cities, boroughs and market-towns afford to the aforesaid merchants who complain before them speedy justice from day to day without delay in accordance with the Law Merchant touching every single thing which can be determined by that law. And if by chance any of the aforesaid bailiffs or officials be found wanting in this, whereby those merchants or any of them suffer or suffers the inconveniences of delay, even if the merchant recovers in the main his losses against the (other) party, the bailiff or other official shall be punished nonetheless as regards us as the offence demands, and that punishment we grant as a favour to the aforesaid merchants to speed up justice for them.

Furthermore, that in pleas of every kind, save the case of a crime for which the penalty of death should be inflicted, where a merchant has been impleaded or has impleaded another, of whatsoever condition he is who is impleaded, stranger or a connexion, in fairs, cities, or boroughs where there is a sufficient number of merchants of the aforesaid lands, and enquiry ought to be made, one half of the inquest shall be drawn from those merchants, and the other half from other good and law-worthy men of the place where the plea happens to be, and if a sufficient number is not found from merchants of the said lands, let those found suitable there be put on the inquest and the remainder found from other good and suitable men of the place[1] where the plea is.

Furthermore, we will, ordain and decree that in each market-town and fair of our aforesaid realm and elsewhere within our power our weight be set in a fixed place, and before weighing the scales shall in the presence of buyer and seller be seen to be empty and the arms shall be level, and then the weigher shall weigh level, and when he has brought the balance level, forthwith move his hands away so that it remain level; and that throughout our realm and power there be one weight and one measure, and these shall be marked with the mark of our standard; and that each man may have scales of a quarter and less, where that is not against the lord of the place or a liberty granted by us or our ancestors, or against the hitherto-observed custom of towns or fairs.

Furthermore, we will and grant that a certain faithful and discreet man resident in London be assigned as justice for the said merchants before whom they may specially

[1] *locis*

plead and recover their debts speedily, if the sheriffs and mayors do not entirely afford them speedy justice from day to day, and that a commission granted to the aforesaid merchants in addition to the present charter be made thereon, to wit, on the things which are to be tried between merchants and merchants in accordance with the law merchant.

Furthermore, we ordain and decree – and we will for us and our heirs for ever that that ordinance and decree be firmly observed – that for each liberty which we or our heirs shall grant hereafter, the aforesaid merchants shall not lose the above-written[1] liberties or any of them.

In return for obtaining the above-mentioned liberties and free customs and the relaxation for them of our prises, the oft-mentioned merchants, every one of them, for themselves and for all others from their parts, have with one heart and mind granted to us that on each tun of wine which they bring into or have brought into our realm or power, and for which they are obliged to pay freight to the mariners, they will pay to us and our heirs by way of custom 2*s*, over and above the ancient customs due and accustomed to be paid in money to us or others, within forty days after the said wines are put ashore from the ships; also, on each sack of wool which the said merchants or others in their name buy and take or cause to be bought and taken out of our realm, they will pay 40*d* of increment over and above the ancient custom of half a mark paid before; and for a last of hides to be carried out of our realm and power half a mark above that which by ancient custom was previously paid and likewise on 300 woolfells for them to be taken out of our realm and power 40*d* over and above the fixed amount which was previously given by ancient custom; also, 2*s* on each scarlet[2] and each cloth dyed in grain;[3] also, 18*d* on each cloth wherein a part of grain is intermixed; also, 12*d* on each other cloth without grain;[4] also, 12*d* on each quintal of wax. And as some of the aforesaid merchants handle other wares, for instance avoirdupois and other fine goods, such as cloths of Tars',[5] silk, cendals, hair and divers other wares and horses also and other animals, corn and other things and merchandise of many kinds which cannot easily be given a fixed custom, those merchants have agreed to give us and our heirs on each pound of silver of the valuation or worth of things and merchandise of this kind, by whatsoever name they are known, 3*d* in the pound at the entry of those things and merchandise into our aforesaid realm and power within twenty days after such things and merchandise have been brought into our realm and power and there unladen or sold, and likewise 3*d* on each pound of silver at the export of any such things and merchandise bought in our realm and power aforesaid, over and above the ancient customs given to us or others previously. And as to the worth and valuation of things and merchandise of this kind, on which 3*d* on each pound of silver, as already said, are to be paid, credence shall be given to them by the letters which they are able to show from their owners or partners,[6] and if they have no letters, the matter shall be settled by the oaths of the

[1] *subscriptas*, but error for *suprascriptas*
[2] at this date a cloth, and the dearest of cloths, not a colour
[3] grain: a red dye and the dearest of all dyes
[4] i.e. not dyed in grain
[5] *pannis Tarsen*[*sibus*]
[6] *dominis aut sociis suis*

merchants themselves, if they are present, or of their servants in the merchants' absence. Moreover, it shall be lawful for the members of the fellowship of merchants aforesaid to sell wools within our aforesaid realm and power to their fellow-members, and likewise to buy from the same, without payment of custom – so, however, that the said wools do not get into such hands that we are defrauded of the custom due to us.

And furthermore, be it known that after the oft-mentioned merchants have duly paid once in one place within our realm and power the custom above granted to us for their wares and have their warrant therefor, they shall be free and quit by virtue of that warrant in all other places within our aforesaid realm and power of payment of such custom for the same goods or wares, whether such merchandise remain within our realm and power or be carried outside, except for wines, which shall, as is aforesaid, in no wise be taken out of our aforesaid realm and power without our will and licence.

It is our will, and for us and our heirs we grant, that no exaction, prise or prest[1] or any other burden be in any wise imposed on the persons, the merchandise or the goods of the aforesaid merchants against the form set out and granted above.

These being witnesses: the venerable fathers Robert, archbishop of Canterbury, primate of all England, Walter, bishop of Coventry and Lichfield; Henry de Lacy, earl of Lincoln, Humphrey de Bohun, earl of Hereford and Essex and constable of England, Aymer de Valence, Geoffrey de Geynvill', Hugh le Despenser, Walter Beauchamp, steward of our household, Robert de Bures and others. Given by our hand at Windsor on 1 February.

92. Failure of negotiation with native merchants, May to June 1303

(*Parliamentary Writs*, I, pp. 134–5, and more conveniently in Stubbs, *Select Charters*, pp. 496–7)

Edward by God's grace etc. to the mayor and sheriffs of London, greeting. Because we have been informed that divers merchants of our kingdom, to be able to be exempt from our prises and use and enjoy various liberties granted by us to merchants stranger and alien, are willing to pay us certain new levies and customs on their goods and wares which the said merchants stranger and alien pay us on their goods and wares within our kingdom and power, WE wishing to talk and treat with the merchants of our said kingdom on the aforesaid, order you to have two or three citizens come from our said city to our exchequer at York, to be there on the morrow of next St John the Baptist [Tuesday, 25 June], with full authority from the community of our said city to do and accept what with the counsel and assent of ourselves and them and the merchants of our said kingdom is then ordained in the aforesaid. And have this writ there then. Witness myself at Newcastle-on-Tyne, the eighth day of May in the 31st year of our reign [Wednesday, 8 May 1303].

[Forty-one other places sent representatives. They and their representatives are named in *Parl. Writs*, I, p. 135.]

---

[1] an advance of money

Who all appeared on 25 June before the lord king's council at York by summons of the aforesaid writ, and they said with unanimous agreement and will, both for themselves and for the communities of the said cities and boroughs, that they in no way consent to the increase of the maltote, or to the customs contained in the aforesaid writ, granted by merchants alien and stranger to the lord king, save only the customs due and accustomed of old.

93. The Trailbaston inquiry, 1304–5

(a) *Commission to enquire in cos. Lincoln, Nottingham and Derby, 23 November, Burstwick*

(*Parliamentary Writs*, I, 407 (No. 58), with similar commissions for Yorkshire and Norfolk and Suffolk on 9 January (Lincoln) and Lancashire on 12 March (Westminster) 1305)

The king to his beloved and faithful Edmund de Eyncourt, William Cressy and Thomas de Burnham greeting. Because many malefactors and disturbers of our peace commit homicides, depredations, arsons and very many other injuries by night and by day and wander and roam in woods, parks and divers other places, as well within liberties as without, in the counties of Lincoln, Nottingham and Derby and are there received, to the very great danger of both men passing through those parts and those dwelling in them and to the contempt of us and the manifest breach of our peace as we have heard, and by their incursion worse things than before can easily happen if a remedy is not quickly contrived for it, WE WISHING to oppose their wickedness in this regard and to provide against such injuries and dangers have assigned you to enquire, by the oath as well of knights as other upright and law-worthy men from the said counties within liberties and without through whom the truth can be better known, who these malefactors are and who are knowingly their receivers and who are in league with them; and also to enquire about those who in return for gifts from them have made and make pacts with malefactors and disturbers of our peace and have hired and hire them to strike, wound, ill-treat and kill many of our kingdom in fairs, markets and other places in the said counties out of enmity, envy and malice and also because they were put on assizes, juries, recognisances and inquests made concerning felonies and spoke the truth, so that by the hiring of such malefactors the jurors of those assizes, juries, recognisances and inquests, for fear of the said malefactors and their threats, quite frequently have not dared and do not dare at all to speak the truth or to indict the said malefactors; and also to enquire from them who have given and give such gifts and how much and to whom, and who have received and receive such gifts and from whom and what sort and in what way, and who keep, feed and maintain such malefactors in their malice in the aforesaid counties; and for you and our sheriffs of the aforesaid counties to arrest these malefactors and hand them over to our prison to be kept safely and securely in it by our sheriffs of the aforesaid counties so that they may in no way be delivered from that prison without our special order. And therefore we command you that on certain days and at certain places, which you or two of you shall arrange for the purpose, you shall hold those inquests and shall, taking with you if necessary a sufficient posse of the aforesaid counties, arrest the said malefactors who have thus been indicted of such things before you and hand them over to our prison in the way aforesaid, and also that you shall cause all the goods and chattels of those malefactors who have slipped away and taken to flight after being solemnly indicted of some felonies before you to be taken into our hand by the sheriffs of the aforesaid counties and safely kept for our use until we order otherwise in the matter. And we have sent word to our sheriffs of the aforesaid counties that on certain etc.[1] which you or two of you will let them know they shall cause to come before you or two of you such and such a number and such sort of men, as well knights as other upright and law-worthy men of those counties, within liberties and without, as through them the truth of the matter in the aforesaid things can the better be known and enquired into, and that all those who happen through those inquests to be found guilty of these things and whom you or two of you accordingly hand over to them they shall receive from you, and those whose names you let them know they shall, taking with them a sufficient posse of those counties, cause to be arrested without delay and kept safely and securely in our prison in the way aforesaid, and that all the goods and chattels of the aforesaid malefactors who have slipped away and taken to flight they shall as will be enjoined upon them by you cause to be taken into our hand without delay and kept safely for our use as is said above; and to the communities of the said counties that they together with the aforesaid sheriffs shall obey, assist and be intendant to you or two of you in the things aforesaid as often as need be and as you on our behalf shall enjoin them. In witness etc. Witness the king, at Burstwick 23 November [1304]. By the king himself and the council.

(b) *The Articles of Enquiry* [? *January 1305, Lincoln*]

(Ed. and trans. from a collation of *Chronicle of Walter of Guisborough*, ed. H. Rothwell (London, 1957), pp. 361–2, and the later, inferior text printed by F. M. Nichols in *Archaeologia*, xl (1866), pp. 102–4. cf. B. H. Putnam, *Proceedings before the Justices of the Peace, Edward III to Richard III* (1938), pp. 11, 13 and 15 [French])

The later (Nichols) text, of Edward II's time, carries the title "The Articles of Lincoln that are called Traylebastoun" and, as Nichols, op. cit. p. 95, observes, Lincoln, late December 1304 or early 1305 is quite a likely place and date.

1. Be it remembered concerning those who by force and wrong have entered contrary to the peace of our lord the king upon the lands of others and, when they cannot maintain their wrong and their force against those who withstand them by law, give and put the wrongful lands and tenements into the hands of great lords to continue by force and power their original wrong.

2. Concerning those who have prevented the jurors on assizes by menaces from daring to speak the truth, for if they said anything contrary to their wishes they would cause them to be beaten and so ill-treated that they would lose their lives or be maimed for ever after; so that for fear of harm the truth cannot be known before the ministers of our lord the king.

3. Concerning those who commit batteries in the country and who are ready and prepared to be in a band to do such thing as one is willing to hire them for or negotiate for a greater or lesser battery, that is for one of 2*s* or 3*s* or of half a mark or of 10*s* or of a mark or of 20*s*; and their abettors and who have maintained such a thing.

[1] i.e. days and at certain places

4. Concerning those who covet the lands of their poor neighbours, who are not willing to sell or lease at their wish, and cause them to be beaten and ill-treated without letting them be at peace until their wish is fulfilled.
5. Concerning those who have robbed and deprived worthy men of the country of their goods and heavily oppressed them and when they complain among their neighbours they are immediately ordered by the robbers to say no more about it and that if they do they will lose their lives as well as their goods.
6. Concerning those who reside in the country and are ready to be hired both to take seisin of churches and to enter lands and tenements to hold them by force and arms contrary to God and right and set an example of evildoing to others of the country: it would be a service to God and a creditable thing to punish and reprove their malice and their receivers and their abettors.
7. Concerning those who hinder the constables of vills, bailiffs or other ministers of our lord the king from performing their office as they have been charged by our lord the king to do to keep the peace of his land.
8. Concerning those who are constables of vills or bailiffs of our lord the king and have their warrant to attach felons and disturbers of his peace but take gifts or through friendships or for other reason let the felons go or have them warned in advance, so that the king's commands can in no wise be carried out.
9. Concerning those bailiffs who, when coroners or other ministers of the king should hold inquest in the country into homicides, murders or other trespasses committed against the peace, cause to appear before them poor people who know nothing of the matter and who do not dare to speak the truth and seek help and advice from people of the better sort who know better the truth; and if the coroner or other minister of the king finds among those present there some through whom the truth can be sufficiently ascertained and commands them in the name of the king to go to the book,[1] they in contempt of the crown and the dignity of the king are not willing to take the oath or obey them in any point, and thus felons and other malefactors remain unpunished.
10. Concerning those people who, when our lord the king commands his bailiffs to levy the green wax or other debts by order of the exchequer or of his justices and the demand comes on them, cause the bailiffs to be beaten and ill-treated so that they cannot and dare not levy the said debt.
11. Concerning those who commit homicides and murders by day and by night secretly or openly, who they are and with whose abetment they do it, and who maintains them.
12. Concerning those who commit arsons by day and by night secretly or openly, who they are and who maintains them after the commission of the felony.
13. Concerning those who go by night with force and arms against the peace and commit batteries and break the doors and windows of reputable people and commit other misdeeds against the peace when honest people should be having their rest, and what people maintain them in doing such things and receive them after the commission of the felony.

[1] "go to the book", i.e. to be sworn in as coroner's jurymen

14. Concerning those who in a market town or other village strike with the glove and push with the shoulders to pick a quarrel and then wish to threaten those they have pushed or struck in life and limb until they have paid or made fine with them at their will either in money or chattels or wine, so that the beaters get the compensation and the beaten nothing.

94. Henry of Keighley to be committed to the Tower, 5 June 1306

(Printed in Stubbs, *Constit. Hist.*, II, p. 158, n. 1 [French])

The bill referred to is in No. 88 above.

Edward by God's grace etc. to the honourable father in God Walter by the same grace bishop of Chester, our treasurer, greeting. We send to you by the bearers of these letters sir Henry of Keighley, who has been before us, and we have ascertained on his own admission that he is the one who brought us the bill on behalf of the archbishop of Canterbury and the others who pressed us outrageously at the Lincoln parliament and whom we have had so much search made for, and we order you to have the said Henry put in safe custody in the Tower of London, to remain there until we have reason to know that he is repentant for what he has done in the matter, and until we have ordained otherwise on this. And know that we wish the said Henry to be kept courteously and safely in the said Tower, without irons, but this courtesy and this confinement to be so arranged that it can be understood to proceed from your grace and not from ours. Given under our privy seal at Finedon the 5th day of June.

95. The problem of public order: to all sheriffs, 16 June 1306

(*Calendar of Close Rolls 1302–7*, pp. 396–7)

1306, 16 June, Westminster

To the sheriff of Kent. Order to cause the statute of Winchester to be read out in his county [court] and in cities, boroughs, hundreds, market towns, and other places in his bailiwick where he shall see fit, and to cause it to be observed in all its articles, as the king considers that the statute will be very useful for keeping his peace, especially when he is setting out for Scotland to repress the rebellion of Robert de Brus, and it is notorious that malefactors and felons and innumerable other persons of whom there is manifest suspicion of larceny and felony, both in the sheriff's bailiwick and elsewhere in the realm, wander about committing homicides and other enormities by day and night, secretly and openly, against the king's peace, and are harboured, maintained and are allowed to make open stay, which malefactors, harbourers, maintainers and their accomplices the sheriff may take and arrest if he will apply care, as he ought, to the keeping of the peace, which he is specially bound to preserve in the sheriff's bailiwick, since the posse of the county in certain such necessities is subject to his summons and distraint.

Moreover, as it is not unknown to the king what is known to all, to wit how divers traitors and felons do not permit themselves to be justiced before the justices appointed to hear and determine felonies and trespasses in divers counties of the realm, but transfer themselves, when they are placed in exigent, to other counties and lurk and dwell in them, so that open suspicion of felony or evil may be held and is held by their coming from other districts[1] and by their various journeys in the night,[2] and sometimes through their wanton manner of life;[3] and although it is contained in the statute of Westminster[4] that no one shall be taken or imprisoned unless he have been previously indicted by the oath of twelve jurymen, and unless their indictment have been afterwards testified by their seals, the king nevertheless wills and orders that all such persons who are suspected of felony or larceny found within the sheriff's bailiwick, both within liberties and without, shall be arrested without delay, although they are not thus indicted, and that the sheriff shall cause them to be kept safely in prison until they be delivered thence according to law. The sheriff is enjoined to cause the premises to be put into execution in such manner as he loves himself and as he would be free and immune from harbouring and consenting to the said malefactors and so that the king may not have to punish him[5] as guilty of the said evil deeds, and he is enjoined to apply such diligence against such suspected malefactors and manifest felons both by himself and by the posse of the county that it cannot and may not be imputed to him after the present order that such intolerable deeds are committed in his bailiwick hereafter through his negligence and consent. The king wills that the sheriff shall enjoin all bailiffs of his county to apply the same diligence for the conservation of the peace in their custodies and shall so conduct themselves in this behalf that they may not incur the penalty contained in the said statute and shall not be imprisoned at the king's will and be grievously ransomed thence. If they do not do so, the sheriff shall enter their liberties as often as necessary in their default, and shall cause the premises to be done and observed in all things in the form aforesaid. He shall arrest those whom he shall find contemning this order or remiss or negligent in executing it, or entirely unwilling to execute it, and shall certify the justices appointed to hear and determine felonies and trespasses in that county of their names immediately after their arrest, in order that they may come before the justices to answer for their contempt.

The like to all the sheriffs of England.

96. Keepers of the peace, coinage, and cost of living, 24 December 1307

(*Parliamentary Writs*, II, Pt 2, App., pp. 8–9)

The king to his beloved and faithful Richard de Windsore, William de Brok and the sheriff of Middlesex, greeting. As for certain difficult matters touching us and our kingdom we are with God's help soon to go overseas, and for that reason we the more earnestly desire our peace to be firmly maintained and observed inviolate, particularly while we are out of the kingdom, we appoint you keepers of our peace in the aforesaid county: strictly enjoining and ordering you not to leave the said county during our absence, but stay there in person, going from place to place throughout the said county, as well within liberties as without, as often as is necessary for

[1] *per eorum extraneos adventus* [2] *variosque incessus et nocturnos* [3] *voluptuosas expensas*
Westm. II (1285) c. 13 (No. 57 above) [5] *ad te . . . capere*

firmly keeping our peace there. So namely that you have it publicly proclaimed in every single city, borough, market town,[1] hundred, wapentake and other places where you think it expedient to do so, that our peace and the statute of Winchester in every one of its articles and likewise the things contained in the writs and mandates of the lord Edward of distinguished memory, formerly king of England, our father, lately sent to each of the sheriffs of the kingdom of England on the subject be firmly and inviolably observed, and should it chance that any fresh danger of a disturbance of our peace emerges anywhere in the aforesaid county (which God forbid) or any opponents or rebels who scorn to obey this our command are found, then taking with you if necessary the posse of the said county you shall prudently and strongly resist such danger and shall arrest such contrariants and rebels by their bodies and keep them safely and securely until you have other orders thereon from us. We also wish and firmly enjoin you to make it publicly, distinctly and openly known from us in each of the aforesaid places to all and singular that we, truly mindful that our coinage is of the same weight and the same value in all respects now as the coinage of our said father was, and that it has our name on it, have no wish to alter or change it. Nor do we wish it in future to be depreciated; or any goods for sale, either, or any merchandise whatsoever, to be sold or bought in future above their true value dearer than they used to be sold in the time of our said father, especially as the said money is reckoned to be worth as much in our time as our father's money was worth. And in order that these things may be firmly and inviolably observed in every single city, borough and market town of the said county, we by the tenor of these presents authorise you to select and appoint in our name two citizens from every city, two burgesses from every borough, and from every market town in the county two upright and law-worthy men to take oath before you to cause every single one of the things aforesaid to be strictly and firmly observed in the said cities, boroughs and (market) towns. Furthermore we will that if you find any acting contrary to or rebellious towards this our ordinance, or even any forestallers who buy or pay a deposit on others' goods in order in this way to sell them themselves at an undue and higher price later, you shall have them attached by their bodies and kept safely until we order otherwise thereon. And therefore we command and firmly enjoin you to see to it that you do and carry out every one of the aforementioned things in the manner stated with all the diligence you can, so behaving in these things that because of your diligence, circumspection and industry the things aforementioned be firmly kept in every one of their articles in the aforesaid county. In witness of which etc. Witness the king at Westminster, 24 December etc. [1307].

[Like letters of appointment for all other counties. The names of those appointed, along with the sheriff, for the individual counties may be read in *Parl. Writs*, II, Pt 2, App., pp. 8–9; or *Cal. Pat. Rolls 1307–13*, pp. 29–31.]

[1] *villa mercatoria*

97. The coronation oath of Edward II, 1308

(*Foedera*, II, i, p. 36, from a schedule attached to the Close Roll; more accessibly in Chrimes and Brown, *Sel. Docs. of Engl. Constit. Hist.* (1961), pp. 4–5 [French])

Sire, are you willing to grant and preserve and by your oath confirm to the people of England the laws and customs granted to them by former[1] kings of England, your righteous and godly predecessors, and particularly the laws, customs and liberties granted to the clergy and the people by the glorious king St Edward, your predecessor[?]
Response: I grant and promise them.

Sire, will you for God and holy church and for the clergy and for the people keep peace and accord in God, to the best of your ability, intact?
Response: I will.

Sire, will you in all your judgments have impartial and proper justice and discretion done in compassion and truth to the best of your ability?
Response: I will.

Sire, do you agree to maintain and preserve the laws and rightful customs which the community of your realm shall have chosen and will you defend and enforce them to the honour of God to the best of your ability?
Response: I agree and promise.

98. Articles against Gavaston presented by the earl of Lincoln to the king, March to April 1308

(Ed. and trans. H. G. Richardson and G. O. Sayles. *The Governance of Medieval England from the Conquest to Magna Carta* (Edinburgh, 1963), App. VII [French])

The first undertaking and the ordinance presented by the earl of Lincoln to the king
Homage and the oath of allegiance are more in respect of the crown than in respect of the king's person and are more closely related to the crown than to the king's person; and this is evident because, before the right to the crown has descended to the person, no allegiance is due to him. And, therefore, if it should befall that the king is not guided by reason, then, in order that the dignity of the crown may be preserved the lieges are bound by the oath made to the crown to reinstate the king in the dignity of the crown or else they would not have kept their oath. The next question is how the king should be reinstated, whether by an action at law or by constraint. It is not, however, possible by recourse to the law to obtain redress, because there would be no other judges than the royal judges, in which case, if the

[1] "former" (*aunciens*) appears in the French text on the schedule attached to the Close Roll, but may be the result of interpolation. It is not given by either of the texts preserved at Winchester cathedral priory, whose bishop crowned Edward, or by the French text preserved at St Augustine's, Canterbury (printed by H. G. Richardson, in *Bull. Instit. Histor. Research*, xvi, p. 9, from Cotton, Vitellius C. xii). The Latin version on the Coronation Roll, on the other hand, giving *antiquis*, makes no mention of "predecessors" or "predecessor".

king's will was not accordant with right reason, the only result would be that error would be maintained and confirmed. Hence, in order that the oath may be saved, when the king will not right a wrong and remove that which is hurtful to the people at large and prejudicial to the crown, and is so adjudged by the people, it behoves that the evil must be removed by constraint, for the king is bound by his oath to govern his people, and his lieges are bound to govern with him and in support of him.

As regards the person who is talked about, the people ought to judge him as one not to be suffered because he disinherits the crown and, as far as he is able, impoverishes it. By his counsel he withdraws the king from the counsel of his realm and puts discord between the king and his people, and he draws to himself the allegiance of men by as stringent an oath as does the king, thereby making himself the peer of the king and so enfeebling the crown, for by means of the property of the crown he has gathered to himself and put under his control the power of the crown, so that by his evil deeds it lies solely with him to determine whether the crown should be destroyed and he himself made sovereign of the realm, in treason towards his liege lord and the crown, contrary to his fealty.

Since the lord king has undertaken to maintain him against all men on every point, entirely without regard to right reason, as behoves the king, he cannot be judged or attainted by an action brought according to law, and therefore, seeing that he is a robber of the people and a traitor to his liege lord and his realm, the people rate him as a man attainted and judged, and pray the king that, since he is bound by his coronation oath to keep the laws that the people shall choose, he will accept and execute the award of the people.

99. Commissions to enquire touching all prises, 18 December 1309

(*Cal. Pat. Rolls 1307–13*, pp. 248–51)

1309, 18 December, Westminster

Commission to Henry de Cobeham the younger, John de Northwode and Roger de Tokton to enquire touching all prises taken in the county of Kent for the king's use, and for the use of other persons, contrary to the statute made in the parliament at Stamford; as well as the names of such persons who received gifts from persons wishing to be spared from prisage, and who unduly burdened others. They are to hear and reduce to writing the complaints of persons who are aggrieved; and to attach all offenders, who are to appear before the king and council. The names of such persons who are not to be found in the county are also to be returned before the king and council, as well as a full report of the entire proceedings of the justices.

Mandate to the coroners for the county of Kent to make proclamation that all aggrieved persons are to appear before the above-named justices to prefer their complaints.

The like appointments of the undermentioned, viz,

[for all counties separately and for London separately from Middlesex.]

100. The New Ordinances, 1311

(*Statutes of the Realm*, I (Rec. Com., 1810), pp. 157–67 [French])

The new ordinances made at London in the 5th year of the reign of our lord king Edward son of king Edward.

Edward by the grace of God king of England, lord of Ireland and duke of Aquitaine to all those to whom these letters come, greeting. KNOW THAT as on 16 March in the 3rd year of our reign to the honour of God and for the good of ourselves and of our realm we granted of our own free will by our letters patent to the prelates, earls and barons of our said realm that they could choose certain persons from the prelates, earls and barons whom they saw fit to call to them, and also granted by the same letters to those who should be chosen, whoever they might be, by the said prelates, earls and barons, full power of ordering the state of our household and of our aforementioned realm in such a way that their ordinances should be made to the honour of God and the honour and profit of holy church and the honour of ourselves and our profit and the profit of our people in accordance with right and reason and the oath we took at our coronation, as is more fully contained in our said letters; and the honourable father in God Robert by God's grace archbishop of Canterbury, primate of all England, the bishops, earls and barons chosen for this purpose by virtue of our said letters have ordained on the aforesaid things as follows.

Because through evil and deceptive counsel our lord the king and all his subjects[1] are dishonoured in all lands and in addition the crown is in many respects reduced and dismembered, and his lands of Gascony, Ireland and Scotland on the point of being lost if God does not give an improvement, and his kingdom of England on the point of rebelling because of oppressions, prises and molestations and these things being known and shown, our lord the king of his own free will granted to the prelates, earls and barons and other good people of his realm that certain persons should be chosen to order and establish the state of his household and of his realm as appears more fully from the commission of our lord the king made on the matter: Wherefor we Robert by the grace of God archbishop of Canterbury, primate of all England, the bishops, earls and barons, chosen by virtue of the said commission, ordain to the honour of God and of holy church and to the honour of the king and of his realm as follows.

[1] In the first place we ordain that the ordinances previously made by us and shown to the king be held and kept, which are written next below.[2] In the first place it is ordained that holy church have all its liberties to the extent that she ought to have.

[2] Again, it is ordained that the king's peace be firmly kept throughout the realm so that every one can safely go, come and abide in safety according to the law and usage of the realm.

[3] Again, it is ordained, to pay off the king's debts and restore his estate and the more honourably maintain it, that no gift of land or rent or liberty or escheat or wardship or marriage or bailiwick be made to any of the said ordainers during their power

[1] *les soens*

[2] The original ordinances are now recited as the first six of the "new" ordinances.

under the said ordinance nor to anyone else without the counsel and assent of the said ordainers or of the greater part of them or six of them at the least, but let all things from which profit could come be put to good use for the profit of the king until his estate is sufficiently restored and something else is ordained on this matter to the king's honour and profit.[1]

[4] Again, it is ordained that the customs of the kingdom be kept and received by people of the kingdom itself and not by aliens, and that the issues and the profits of the same customs together with all other issues and profits issuing from the kingdom from any things whatsoever shall come entirely to the king's exchequer and by the treasurer and chamberlains be paid out to maintain the household of the king and otherwise for his profit so that the king can live of his own without taking prises other than the ancient due and accustomed ones and that all others shall cease.

[5] Again, it is ordained that all alien merchants who have received the profits of the customs of the kingdom or of other things belonging to the king since the death of king Edward, the father of our lord the king that now is, be arrested with all their goods wherever they are found within the power of the king of England until they have rendered reasonable account of all that they have received of the issues of the kingdom within the time aforesaid before the treasurer and the barons of the exchequer and others joined to them by the said ordainers.

[6] Again, it is ordained that the great charter be kept in all its points in such a way that if there is in the said charter any point that is obscure or doubtful, let it be made clear by the said ordainers and others whom it is their will to call to them for this purpose, when they see an opportunity during their power.[2]

[7] And then again, because[3] the crown is so reduced and dismembered by divers gifts, we ordain that all gifts, made to the king's detriment and the diminution of the crown since we were given our commission, of castles, towns, lands and tenements and bailiwicks, wardships and marriages, escheats and releases, whatever they are, as well in Gascony, Ireland, Wales and Scotland as in England, be revoked, and we do revoke them completely so that they be not given back to the same people without common assent in parliament. And that if such manner of gifts or releases be made hereafter contrary to the aforementioned way of doing – without the assent of his baronage and that in parliament – until his debts are paid off and his estate is sufficiently restored, they shall be considered as null and let the taker be punished in parliament by the award of the baronage.

[8] Because it was formerly ordained[4] that the customs of the kingdom should be received and kept by people of the kingdom, and not by aliens and that the issues and the profits of the same customs together with all the other issues and profits issuing from the kingdom whatever they were should come entirely to the king's exchequer and be received and paid out by the treasurer and chamberlains to maintain the household of the king and otherwise for his profit so that the king can live of his own without taking prises other than the ancient, due and rightful ones, which

[1] cf. c.7 below

[2] They had not in fact found time and the matter is dealt with again in c. 38 below (when, it will be noticed, the opportunity is taken to include the Forest Charter as well).

[3] The further ordinance envisaged in c. 3 above.

[4] c. 4 above

things are not done; wherefore we ordain that the said customs together with all the issues of the kingdom as aforesaid shall be received and kept by people of the kingdom, and paid into the exchequer in the way aforementioned.

[9] Because the king ought not to undertake the act of war against anyone, or go out of his kingdom without the common assent of his baronage for the many perils that could happen to him and his kingdom, we ordain that hereafter the king shall not go out of his kingdom or undertake against anyone the act of war without the common assent of his baronage, and that in parliament, and if he does otherwise and for such undertaking has his feudal service summoned, the summons shall be as null. And if it happens that the king undertakes the act of war against anyone or goes out of the land with the assent of his baronage and needs to appoint a guardian in his kingdom, then he shall appoint him with the common assent of his baronage, and that in parliament.

[10] And because it is to be feared that the people of the land will rise on account of the prises and divers oppressions inflicted before this time, particularly because it was formerly ordained that our lord the king should live of his own without taking prises other than the ancient, due and accustomed ones and that all others should cease,[1] and nevertheless prises are taken every day contrary to this ordinance as before, we ordain that all prises shall cease from now on saving to the king and to others to whom they are due of right the ancient, rightful and due prises. And if any prises are taken contrary to the aforesaid ordinance whoever by or whatever his condition, that is, if any one appearing to purvey for the king's use or anyone else's takes corn, wares, merchandise or other kinds of goods against the will of those to whom they belong and does not immediately render the money to the true value, if he cannot have respite for it with the good will of the seller, in accordance with what is contained in the great charter about prises taken by constables of castles and their bailiffs, and leaving out of account as an exception the aforesaid due prises, notwithstanding the commission he has, let the pursuit by hue and cry be raised against him and let him be taken to the nearest gaol of the king and let the common law be applied to him as a robber or a thief, if he is convicted of that.

[11] Likewise new customs have been levied and old ones increased as upon wools, cloths, wines, merchandise sold by weight and other things, as a result of which merchants come more rarely and bring less goods into the land and foreign merchants stay for a longer time than they used to, by which staying things are made that much dearer than they used to be, to the detriment of the king and his people: We ordain that customs and maltotes of every kind levied since the coronation of king Edward son of king Henry shall be entirely removed and completely abolished forever, notwithstanding the charter that the said king Edward granted to alien merchants, because this was granted contrary to the great charter and contrary to the liberty of the city of London and without the assent of the baronage, and if anyone, whatever his condition, takes or levies anything beyond the ancient, due and rightful customs or creates any disturbance whereby merchants cannot do as they wish with their goods and is convicted of this, there shall be awarded to the plaintiffs their damages,

[1] in c. 4 above, but incidentally only. Here the problem of prises is treated for its own sake.

having regard to the purchase,[1] to the suit, to the costs and process[2] they have had, and to the violation of the great charter, and the offender shall be imprisoned according to the measure of the offence and according to the discretion of the justices and be no more in the king's service, saving nevertheless to the king the customs of wool, skins and leather, that is for each sack of wool ½ mark and for 300 wool fells ½ mark and for a last of leather 1 mark, if he ought to have it; and henceforth foreign merchants shall come, stay and go in accordance with the ancient customs and in accordance with what they used to do.

[12] To the honour of God and of holy church and against those who by malice purchase prohibitions and attachments against ordinaries of holy church in causes of corrections of sin and other causes purely spiritual that in no way pertain to the lay court, we ordain that by the justices who convict for such malices and who amerce the malicious plaintiffs there shall be judgment of damages to the ordinaries wrongfully molested, or if the said plaintiffs have nothing to pay with, judgment of imprisonment for a period in accordance with the wrong maliciously inflicted, saving the estate of the king and of his crown and the right of others.

[13] And because the king has been badly guided and counselled by evil counsellors, as is said above, we ordain that all the evil counsellors be ejected and dismissed altogether, so that neither they nor others like them shall be near him any more, or retained in the king's service, and that other suitable people be put in their place, and in the same way be it done with the attendants and the servants and others who are in the king's household who are not suitable.

[14] And because many evils have happened owing to such counsellors and such officers, we ordain that the king choose the chancellor, the chief justices of both benches, the treasurer, chancellor and chief baron of the exchequer, the steward of his household, the keeper of the wardrobe and the controller and his clerk suitable for keeping his privy seal, a chief keeper of his forests this side Trent and another for beyond Trent and also an escheator for this side Trent and another for the other side, and the chief clerk of the king in the common bench, with the counsel and the assent of his baronage, and that in parliament; and if it happens by any chance that any of the said officers must be appointed before there is a parliament, then let the king appoint thereto with the good counsel that he has near him until the parliament. And thus let it be done from now on with such officers when there is need.

[15] Likewise we ordain that the chief keepers of ports and of castles on the coast be appointed and chosen in the way aforesaid, and that these keepers be of the land themselves.

[16] And because the lands of Gascony, Ireland and Scotland are in danger of being lost for want of officers, we ordain that good and sufficient officers to keep guard in the said lands be appointed in the way contained in the article next but one above.

[17] In addition, we ordain that sheriffs be appointed henceforth by the chancellor, treasurer and the others of the council that are present, and if the chancellor is not present let them be appointed by the treasurer and barons of the exchequer and by the

[1] i.e. what they paid for their writ

[2] possibly a corruption for "losses"

justices of the bench, and that there be appointed and chosen such as are suitable and sufficient, and who have lands and tenements from which they could answer to the king and the people for their actions, and that none but such be appointed, and that they have their commission under the great seal.

[18] Because it is commonly said, and many representations have been made as well, that divers oppressions, such as false disinheritances, indictments and imprisonments and on top of this grievous exactions and many other kinds of burdens that keepers, bailiffs and officers of forests and others have inflicted in professing to perform their bailiwicks and their offices, of which burdens the people who are so heavily burdened do not dare openly to complain or to make their complaints in the king's court as long as they are in their bailiwicks and offices, we ordain that of all keepers bailiffs and officers of forests who before the time of the present king used to be removable at the king's pleasure as well as of those whose bailiwicks and offices have been already voluntarily granted for life, such grant notwithstanding, like the others, their bailiwicks or officers be seized into the king's hand; and that good and upright people be appointed justices to inquire into the aforesaid grievances and to hear and determine all the grievances and complaints of all those who are willing to prosecute for the king or for themselves against the said keepers, bailiffs and officers of the forests or others, according to the law and the custom of the kingdom, and as far as the law allows it the complaints shall be determined between now and next Easter, or before if it can properly be done according to law. And if the said keepers, bailiffs and officers are found guilty of inflicting the aforesaid burdens, then let them be removed for ever, and if not guilty, let them have back their bailiwicks and offices.

[19] And because many people have been disinherited, fined and ruined by the chief keepers of the forests this side and beyond Trent and by the other officers contrary to the form of the charter of the forest and contrary to the declaration that king Edward son of king Henry made in the following form, namely:

> We will and grant for ourselves and for our heirs concerning trespasses of the vert and of the venison committed in our forests, that the foresters in whose bailiwicks such trespasses shall have been committed present the same trespasses at the next swanimotes before the foresters, verderers, regarders, agisters and other officers of the same forests, and by such presentments before the foresters, verderers, regarders, agisters and other officers aforesaid, on the oath as well of knights as of other men of standing,[1] honest and not suspected, of the parts neighbouring on and closest to where such trespasses will be presented, so shall the truth be better and more fully enquired into and, the truth being so enquired into, such presentments shall be solemnly confirmed by the common accord and assent of all the aforesaid officers and sealed with their seals: and henceforth if any indictment is made in any other way, it shall be held for nought;

and because the chief keepers of the forests have not kept to the said form up to now, We ordain that from now on no one be taken or imprisoned for vert or for venison unless he is caught in the act[2] or has been indicted in the way aforementioned, and

[1] *prodeshoms*
[2] literally, "found with the mainour" i.e., in the case of theft, with the stolen goods on him

then the chief keeper of the forest shall let him go on bail until the forest eyre without taking anything for letting him go free and, if the said keeper will not do it, he shall have the writ in the chancery which formerly was ordained for such indicted persons to be at mainprise[1] until the eyre; and if the said keeper after receiving the said writ does not cause the said indicted persons to be let go on bail without delay and without taking anything [for letting him go], then the plaintiff shall have a writ in the chancery to the sheriff to attach the keeper before the king on a certain day to answer why he has not replevied[2] him who has been thus taken; and the sheriff, calling the verderers, shall cause him who has been taken to be delivered by good mainprise in the presence of the verderers and cause the names of the mainpernors to be delivered to the same verderers to answer in eyre before the justices. And if the chief keeper is convicted of this, the plaintiffs shall be awarded treble damages and the said keeper imprisoned and fined at the king's pleasure and not be henceforth in the king's service. And henceforth they shall be written to as chief keepers of the forest, since they ought not to be justices or have record except in eyre. And because it is said that the chief keepers of the forests have contrary to the form abovementioned taken and levied fines, amercements and ransoms, we ordain that the aforesaid keepers and the other chief keepers render their accounts of the aforesaid prises before the treasurer and barons of the exchequer between now and next Christmas.

[20] Because it is known, and by examination by the prelates, earls and barons, knights and other good people of the kingdom found, that Piers Gavaston has acted badly towards and has badly advised our lord the king and has incited him to do wrong in divers and deceptive ways; in taking possession of for himself all the king's treasure and sending it out of the kingdom; in drawing to himself royal power and royal dignity, as in making alliances on oath with people to live and die with him against all men, and this by the treasure he acquires from day to day; in lording it over the estate of the king and of the crown, to the ruin of the king and of the people; and especially in estranging the heart of the king from his lieges; in despising their counsels, not allowing good officers to carry out the law of the land; in removing good officers, appointing those of his own gang, as well aliens as others, who at his will and command offend against right and the law of the land; in taking the king's lands, tenements and bailiwicks to himself and his heirs; and has caused the king to give lands and tenements of his crown to divers people to the great loss and diminution of the estate of the king and of his crown, and this as well since the ordinance that the king granted to the ordainers to act for the profit of himself and his people as before against the ordinance of the ordainers; and in maintaining robbers and murderers and getting for them the king's charter of his peace, in emboldening wrongdoers to do worse, and in taking the king into a land where there is war without the common assent of his baronage to the danger of his person and the ruin of the kingdom, and in causing blank charters under the great seal of the king to be sealed to the deceit and disinheritance of the king and of his crown, and against his homage; and feloniously, falsely and traitorously has done the aforesaid things to the great dishonour and loss of the king and disinheriting of the crown and to the ruin of his people in many ways:

[1] i.e. on bail [2] i.e. released on bail

And in addition to this we having regard to what was done by the most noble king, the father of the present king, by whose adjudgment the aforesaid Piers abjured the realm of England and whose will it was that our lord the king, his son, should abjure forever his company, and that since by the common assent of all the realm and of the king and of the same prelates, earls and barons it was heretofore adjudged that he should leave the said realm, and he did leave it, and that his return was never by common assent, but only by the assent of some individuals who agreed to it on condition of his behaving well after his return: and now his bad conduct is established beyond doubt, for which conduct and for the great wickednesses aforementioned and for the many others that could befall our lord the king and his people, and in order to foster good understanding between the king and his people and avoid many kinds of discords and dangers, We ordain, by virtue of the commission our lord the king granted us, that Piers Gavaston as the evident enemy of the king and of his people be completely exiled as well from the kingdom of England, Scotland, Ireland and Wales as from the whole lordship of our lord the king overseas as well as on this side, forever without ever returning; and that he leave the kingdom of England and all the aforesaid lands and absolutely all the lordship of our lord the king between now and the feast of All Saints next to come; and we assign to him as port in the way aforesaid Dover and nowhere else for crossing and leaving. And if the said Piers stays in the kingdom of England or anywhere else in the lordship of our lord the king beyond the said day that has been given him for leaving and crossing as is aforesaid, then let there be done with him as would be done with the enemy of the king and of the kingdom and of his people. And let all those who from now on contravene this ordinance with regard to the said exile or the penalty that follows, be dealt with accordingly, if they are convicted of it.

[21] Also we ordain that Amerigo[1] and those of the company of Frescobaldi come to the accounting in the way that was ordained and published, notwithstanding the account they say they have rendered, within the fortnight after next Michaelmas and in the meantime let there be arrested all the persons and all the goods of members of the company of Frescobaldi that can be found in the power of the king of England, and that all the lands of the said Amerigo be seized into the hand of the king wheresoever they are in the said power of the king. And if the said Amerigo does not come within the day assigned, because the aforesaid ordinance has been infringed by him and by his non-appearance he renders himself culpable and suspect we ordain that he be banished from the power of the king and from now on be deemed an enemy and it be done with him as would be done with an enemy of the king and of the kingdom, if he be found anywhere in the power of the king as well overseas as on this side.

[22] Also because sir Henry de Beaumont has received from our lord the king to the loss and dishonour of the king, since the time of the ordinance of the ordainers to which the king agreed, the kingdom of Man and other lands, rents, liberties and bailiwicks and has caused lands and tenements liberties and bailiwicks to be given to others contrary to this ordinance, and because he has badly advised the king contrary to his oath, We ordain that he be removed from the king's counsel for ever and that

[1] Emery

he come no more near the king anywhere – unless it be at the common summons of parliament or in war if the king wishes to have him – save by common assent of the archbishop, bishops, earls and barons and that in full parliament; and all the other lands that he holds within the kingdom of England be taken into the hand of the king of England and held until the king has received from the issues of these lands the value of all the yield that the said sir Henry has had from the lands received contrary to the said ordinance, and if the said sir Henry in any point contravenes these ordinances let him be disinherited forever of all the lands that he has in England of the king's gift.

[23] Because it is found by examination by the prelates, earls and barons that the lady de Vescy has caused the king to give to sir Henry de Beaumont, her brother, and to others, lands, liberties and bailiwicks to the loss and dishonour of the king and the evident disinheritance of the crown and also caused to be sent out letters under the targe[1] against the law and the intention of the king, We ordain that she go to her house – and that within the fortnight after next Michaelmas – without ever returning to the court to stay there, and that for all these aforesaid things and because it is understood that Bamburgh castle belongs to the crown, we also ordain that this castle be retaken from her into the hand of the king and that it be no more given to her or to another except at the king's pleasure.

[24] And because the people feel greatly burdened by divers debts being demanded of them for the king's use by summons of the exchequer, which debts are paid and the people concerned have divers acquittances for them, some by tallies and writs and others by divers liberties that were granted to them by royal deeds that are allowable, We ordain that henceforth on the account of each sheriff and of other officers of the king who are required to render account at the exchequer such kinds of tallies, writs and liberties as are allowable on the account be allowed if the said acquittances are shown to the court, so that they continue no longer to be demanded for lack of allowance. And if the treasurer and the barons of the exchequer do not do this in the way aforesaid, the plaintiffs shall have their recovery by petitions in parliament.

[25] As common merchants and many others of the people are admitted to plead at the exchequer pleas of debt and of trespass, because they are sponsored by the officers of the said court[2] more readily than they ought to be, whereby the accounts and other things touching the king are the more delayed and in addition to this many of the people are burdened, We ordain that from now on pleas be not held in the said court[2] of the exchequer, except pleas touching the king and officers of his who are answerable in the exchequer *ex officio*, and the officers of the same court[2] and their attendants and servants that for the most part stay with them in the places where the exchequer stays. And if anyone is admitted to plead in the said exchequer by being sponsored by the said court[2] contrary to the aforesaid way of doing, let those whom the action is brought against have their recovery in parliament.

[26] Likewise, because the people feel much aggrieved that stewards and marshals hold many pleas that do not belong to their office and also because they will not receive attorneys for defendants as well as for plaintiffs, We ordain that from now on

[1] i.e. the privy seal [2] *place*

they receive attorneys for defendants as well as for plaintiffs; and that they do not hold pleas concerning freehold or debt or covenant or contract, or any common plea of people generally, but only of offences of the household and other offences committed within the verge and of contracts and covenants that someone of the king's household has made with another of the same household and in the same household, not elsewhere; and that they hold no plea of trespass that is not set in motion by them before the king leaves the verge where the offence was committed, and shall hold pleas quickly day by day so that they are heard and determined before the king goes beyond the bounds of the verge where the offence was committed; and if, perchance they cannot be determined within the bounds of this verge let such pleas cease before the steward and the plaintiffs go on with them by action at common law. Nor shall the steward henceforth take cognisance of debts or of other things, except of people of the aforementioned household and against people of the aforementioned household, nor shall they hold any other plea by obligation made at the distress of the steward and the marshals, and that no one of the household or any who follow the household be put on an inquest before them, except where both the plaintiff and the defendant are of the said household and the inquest is into things that were done in the same household; and if the steward and marshals do anything against this ordinance, what they do shall be held for nought. And that those who feel aggrieved against the said ordinance shall have a writ in the chancery pleadable in the king's bench and recover their damages against those who hold the plea and have drawn them into the plea, at the discretion of the justices having regard to their purchase,[1] costs, grievances and losses according to the measure of the offence, and they shall be no more in the king's service.

[27] And because up to now many of the felonies committed within the verge have gone unpunished because the coroners of the district have not concerned themselves to inquire into such manner of felonies within the verge, but [instead] the coroner of the king's household, so that issue has not been made in proper manner, nor the felons put in exigent or outlawed, nor anything of this felony presented in the eyre, which is to the great loss of the king and the less good keeping of his peace, We ordain that from now on in case of homicide, in which it is the coroner's duty to view corpses and hold inquest into the matter, the coroners of the districts or of the liberties where the dead persons are found are to be informed that together with the coroner of the household he is to perform the office appertaining thereto and record it on his roll; and what cannot be determined before the steward because the felons cannot be attached or found or for other reason, let the process remain at common law, so that the exigents, outlawries and presentments made in this connection be shown in the eyre by the coroner of the district, as with other felonies committed outside the verge; but let not attachments cease because of this to be made with unabated vigour upon the felonies committed if they can be found.

[28] As the people feel much aggrieved that men are emboldened to kill and rob people because the king by evil counsel so lightly gives them his peace contrary to the form of law, we ordain that no felon or fugitive be henceforth sheltered or protected

[1] i.e. what they paid for their writ

for any sort of felony by the king's charter of his peace being granted to him or in any other way unless in a case where the king can grant favour in accordance with his oath, and that by process of law and the custom of the realm, and if any charter is granted or made in any other way in future for anyone, it shall avail nothing and be held for nought; and that no evident evildoer against the crown and the peace of the land be aided or maintained by anyone.

[29] As many people are impeded in their claims in the king's court because the party alleges that the claimants ought not to be answered without the king, and also many people are aggrieved by the king's officers contrary to right, remedy for which grievances cannot be obtained without a common parliament, We ordain that the king hold a parliament once a year, or twice if need be, and that in a convenient place, and that in the same parliaments pleas that are held up in the way mentioned, and pleas in which the justices are of different opinions shall be recorded and determined; and in like manner shall bills that are delivered in parliament be determined so far as law and reason require it.

[30] Because every time a change of coinage is made in the kingdom the whole people suffers greatly in many ways, we ordain that, when there is need and the king wishes to make a change, he shall do it by the common counsel of his baronage and that in parliament.

[31] Likewise we ordain that all the statutes that have been made in amendment of the law and for the profit of the people by the ancestors of our lord the king be kept and maintained so far as they ought to be by law and reason, provided that they are not contrary to the great charter or to the charter of the forest, or contrary to the ordinances made by us, and if any statute be made contrary to the aforesaid form it shall be held for nought and utterly undone.

[32] Because the law of the land and common right have often been impeded by letters issued under the king's privy seal, to the great harm of the people, we ordain that from now on the law of the land and common right be not impeded or interfered with by letters of the said seal, and if anything is done contrary to right or the law of the land in any of the offices of the court of our lord the king or elsewhere by such letters issued under the privy seal, it shall avail nothing and be held for nought.

[33] Because many of the people besides known merchants feel greatly burdened and financially oppressed by the statute of merchants made at Acton Burnell, we ordain that henceforth this statute shall not hold except between merchants and merchants and in respect of business dealings between them, and that the recognisance be made as is contained in the said statute and by the testimony of four worthy and upright men who are known and that their names be entered in the recognisance to witness the deed; and that to no one shall other lands be delivered to hold in the name of freehold by virtue of the said statute except burgages of merchants and their movable chattels, and that, be it understood, between merchants and merchants, known merchants. In addition, we ordain that the king's seals that are assigned to witness the said recognisances be given to the richest and wisest men of the undermentioned towns, chosen for their custody by the commonalty of the same towns, namely, at Newcastle upon Tyne, at York and Nottingham for the counties beyond Trent and

the merchants there visiting and resident; at Exeter, Bristol and Southampton for merchants visiting and resident in the parts of the south and the west; at Lincoln and Northampton for merchants visiting and resident there; at London and at Canterbury for merchants visiting and resident in these parts; at Shrewsbury for merchants visiting and resident in these parts; at Norwich for merchants visiting and resident in these parts. And recognisances made elsewhere than in the said towns shall have no standing from now on.

[34] Because many prisoners become approvers to prolong their lives and by divers oppressions and punishments that sheriffs and gaolers in whose custody they are do to them and instruct them to bring an accusation against the richest of the district and people of good reputation, whom they [then] cause to be attached and put into vile and hard imprisonment and exact heavy ransom from them – from which tolls and exactions no advantage accrues to the king, We ordain that from now on those of good reputation who are accused by approvers (who by right should have no voice) shall not be put into prison, provided that they can find good mainpernors[1] that they will be at the next gaol delivery to submit to the law, and to clear themselves of the accusation according to the usage of the realm, without taking anything from them for being mainperned. And that whenever gaol delivery is delayed by the absence of the justices or other cause, they shall be left free on the said mainprise or on another sufficient one until the coming of the said justices, in the way aforesaid. Likewise we ordain that they who become approvers be not heard accusing any one for a longer time than the three days next after the time they became approvers.

[35] Likewise because many people holding land are accused through malice of divers felonies in counties where they have not lands or tenements and by malicious legal process are outlawed, to the loss of their lives and the disinheritance of them and their heirs, we ordain that from now on no one outlawed by such malicious process in a county where he has not land or tenement shall be put to death or disinherited, provided that they who are outlawed by such process surrender themselves to the king's prison and can clear themselves by the counties in which they were outlawed of the felonies and other trespasses for which they were outlawed and their lands shall be restored to them when they are acquitted if they are in the king's hand; and if someone other than the king holds the said tenements let them have their recovery by writ of entry formed upon the said case, and they at whose suit they were thus outlawed shall be taken and shall abjure the realm, and if they are not found let them be put in exigent and outlawed.

Because many people, by the false witness of sheriffs testifying that they have not been found and have not lands or tenements by which they can be distrained in their bailiwicks, although they have lands and tenements in other counties of the kingdom, are thereby put in exigent in counties where they have not lands or tenements and perchance outlawed in peril of their lives, in disinheritance of them and their heirs if they are outlawed for felonies, wherefore we ordain that people outlawed in such a way shall neither be put to death nor disinherited of their lands provided that they surrender themselves to the king's prison and can show themselves by the counties

[1] sureties

in which they were thus outlawed not guilty of the felonies or the trespasses laid to their charge, and they shall have recovery of their lands and their damages in the way aforesaid.

[36] Likewise because many are the more emboldened to kill and rob people because accusations pursued in the court of our lord the king are discontinued for reasons that are too slight and the accusers taken and imprisoned and fined at the king's pleasure, and those accused at the king's suit more lightly acquitted than they would be if the accusations were not discontinued, We ordain that from now on accusations of felonies be not discontinued from the time that the accusers make mention in their accusations of the day, the time and the place and what weapon he was killed with or the sort of goods he was robbed of; and if the accused can clear themselves of the said felonies they shall have their recovery from the abettors and the accusers in accordance with what is contained in the statute ordained on abettors of false accusations if the accused are not indicted of the said felonies by solemn inquest.

[37] Because many are impeded in their suits in the king's court by protections granted to people who pretend to go on the king's service and do so only to impede the plaintiff's suit as well in plea of land as in plea of debt and of trespass, to restrain such malice we ordain that if the tenant in a plea of land uses the protection of our lord the king after putting in an appearance and the demandant is able to aver that the tenant was not in the king's service the day the parol demurred[1] *sine die* because of the protection, the absence of the tenant shall be turned into a default; and if the tenant uses his protection before putting in an appearance it is quite lawful for the demandant, if it is to his advantage to do so, to take a writ in the chancery upon the tenant to aver that he was not in the king's service the day that his suit was impeded by the protection and, if the tenant is convicted of this, there shall be awarded to the demandant his damages at the discretion of the justices, having regard to his purchase,[2] costs, mises and losses, and the tenant shall be adjudged to prison for the deceit done to the king and to the court to stay a year and a day, and be fined at the king's pleasure; and if the said deceit be proved in a plea of debt or of trespass the defendant shall be punished, as well in respect of the plaintiff as in respect of the king, in the above-mentioned way.

[38] Likewise we ordain that the great charter of liberties and the charter of the forest that king Henry, son of king John, made be held in all their points, and that the points that are doubtful in the said charters of liberties be clarified in the next parliament after this by the advice of the baronage and of the justices and of other wise men of the law, and this thing shall be done because we have not been able to do it during our time.[3]

[39] Likewise we ordain that the chancellor, treasurer, chief justices of the one bench and of the other, the chancellor of the exchequer, the treasurer of the wardrobe, the steward of the king's household, all the justices, the sheriffs, escheators, constables, holders of inquests into anything whatever, and all other bailiffs and officers of the king shall be sworn, every time they receive their bailiwicks and offices, to keep and

[1] i.e. the action was adjourned
[2] i.e. what he paid for his writ
[3] as had been hoped (for Magna Carta at least) in the original ordinances. See c.6 above

hold all the ordinances made by the prelates, earls and barons chosen and assigned for this, and each one of them, without contravening any point of them.

[40] Likewise we ordain that in each parliament there be assigned one bishop, two earls and two barons to hear and determine all the complaints of those who wish to complain of the king's officers, whoever they are, who have contravened the above-mentioned ordinances; and if the said bishop, earls and barons cannot all attend or are prevented from hearing and determining the said complaints, then let three or two of them do so, and those that are found to have contravened the said ordinances shall be punished in respect of the king and in respect of the plaintiffs by the discretion of said persons assigned.

[41] Likewise we ordain that the aforementioned ordinances shall be maintained and kept in all their points, and that our lord the king shall have them put under his great seal and sent into every county of England to be made public, held and firmly kept, as well within liberties as without, and in the same way let order be given to the keeper of the Cinque Ports to have them made public, held and kept throughout his bailiwick in the aforesaid manner.

The which ordinances shown to us and published the Monday before last Michaelmas we agree to, accept and affirm; and we will and grant for us and for our heirs that all the said ordinances and each of them made according to the form of our letters aforesaid shall be published throughout our kingdom and henceforth firmly kept and held. In witness of which things we have caused these our letters patent to be made. Given at London the 5th day of October in the 5th year of our reign.

101. Arguments for the establishment of home staple towns, 24 April 1319

(*E.H.R.*, xxix (1914), pp. 94–7. A revised version of the translation printed in Bland, Brown and Tawney, *English Economic History: Select Documents*, pp. 180–1 [French])

A document emanating from a conference of merchants held at Westminster, though not, apparently, its unanimous recommendation. Those named in the endorsement are not all who had been summoned to the conference and they do not by any means represent all the wool-growing areas. Nor was the policy of home staples adopted until the ordinance of Kenilworth in 1326 (No. 104 below).

As to date, *E.H.R.*, xxix (1914), pp. 94–5; as to attendance, T. F. Tout, *The Place of the Reign of Edward I in English History*, 2nd edn, rev. (Manchester, 1936), pp. 228–9.

London. Whereas our lord the king by his writ has signified to us that in particular in his parliament last holden at York debate was raised touching the establishment of certain places within his realm whereat sales and purchases of wools should be made and not elsewhere, which business (whether it would be to the profit of our said lord and of the people of his realm, also the particular places most suitable for this) through certain disturbances remained undetermined, and signified also that divers moneys counterfeiting the coin of our said lord are brought by foreign people into his realm to the subversion of his money and to the prejudice of our said lord; whereon our lord the king wishes to have our advice and counsel: WE would inform him that in full treaty and discussion with divers merchants, citizens and burgesses of the realm, we have agreed if it please our lord the king, that there be two places established for the said sales and purchases, namely, one this side Trent and another one beyond it, which places should fulfil the conditions below-written, that is to say, the places should be strong, well situated and secure for the repair of foreign merchants and the safety of their persons and their goods, and there should be ready access for all manner of merchandise, an exchange good, easy and prompt, and a good and convenient haven in the same places; and that the law and usages and franchises which merchants repairing to the staple in these times have had and used they may be able to use and enjoy henceforth at the places where they shall be, without being drawn into another law or another custom; and that the foreigners who shall come to the said places go not further in the realm nor send privily or openly by any manner of people to make any purchase of wools elsewhere than at the places established; and by this the towns of our said lord which are now decayed and impoverished will be restored and enriched. If it be established in the form aforesaid, it will be of great profit to our lord the king and to all his realm: principally by the security of the persons and goods of merchants and other people of the realm, whom in these times death, robberies and other damages without number have in large measure befallen; and also by the increase of the profit of the change of our lord through the plate and bullion which shall be brought there; and also by the drawing of all manner of merchants and their merchandise that shall come there; moreover, owing to the great treasure of the goods of England that is and remains in the power of aliens, tort, trespass, robberies and homicide cannot be readily brought to justice or rightly punished in our parts on this side the sea out of fear for the persons and goods which they, the aliens, have in their power, whereby they are enriched and emboldened to maintain the king's mortal enemies and help them with men, arms, and victuals; and by the ordinance aforesaid the merchants and the people of our said lord, from whom he can take when need be, will be enriched, and the enemies of the king impoverished, and all alien merchants under his control; and innumerable other profits which we cannot fully describe. With regard to money, if it please our lord, let nothing be suffered to be brought from parts beyond the sea except gold, plate and bullion, and to do away with the counterfeit money current among the good, wheresoever it be found, let it be pierced and sent to the change.

[*Endorsed*] With which advice these counties of the realm are in agreement. [Here follow the names of London, Stamford and, it would seem, Shrewsbury, and the fourteen counties of Middlesex, Essex, Hertford, Bucks., Beds., Oxford, Berks., Gloucester, Hereford, Worcester, Shropshire, Staffs., Chester,[1] and Warwick.]

[1] It is unusual for Chester, a county palatine, to be thus listed with ordinary shires.

102. Letter of the Scottish barons to Pope John XXII ("Declaration of Arbroath"), 6 April 1320

(Lord (T. M.) Cooper of Culross, *Selected Papers 1922–1954* (Edinburgh, 1957), pp. 333–342)

To the most holy father in Christ and lord, the lord John, by divine providence supreme pontiff of the holy Roman and universal church, his humble and devoted sons Duncan earl of Fife, Thomas Randolph earl of Moray lord of Man and of Annandale, Patrick of Dunbar earl of March, Malise earl of Strathearn, Malcolm earl of Lennox, William earl of Ross, Magnus earl of Caithness and Orkney, William earl of Sutherland, Walter the stewart of Scotland, William de Soules butler of Scotland, James lord of Douglas, Roger Moubray, David lord of Brechin, David Graham, Ingram de Umfraville, John Menteith guardian of the earldom of Menteith, Alexander Fraser, Gilbert Hay constable of Scotland, Robert Keith marshal of Scotland, Henry Sinclair, John Graham, David Lindsay, William Oliphant, Patrick Graham, John Fenton, William Abernethy, David Wemyss, William Muschet, Fergus of Ardrossan, Eustace Maxwell, William Ramsay, William Mowat, Alan Murray, Donald Campbell, John Cameron, Reginald Cheyne, Alexander Seton, Andrew Leslie, Alexander Straiton and the other barons and freeholders and the whole community of the realm of Scotland all manner of filial reverence with devout kisses of the blessed feet.[1]

Most holy father and lord, we know and gather from the deeds and writings of the ancients that among other nations of renown our nation (of the Scots, that is) has been distinguished by many tributes to its fame. Crossing from Greater Scythia by the Tyrrhenian Sea and through the Pillars of Hercules, and residing in Spain for a long period of time among the most savage of peoples, by none of them anywhere however barbarous could it be subjugated. From there, twelve hundred years after the people of Israel crossed from the land of Egypt, it came and after expelling the Britons and completely destroying the Picts got for itself by many a victory and endless exertion, although it was repeatedly assailed by Norwegians, Danes and English, the places of abode in the west it has now, and, as the histories of the ancients bear witness, it has held them all the time free of any servitude. Within their realm one hundred and thirteen kings of their own royal stock have reigned, the line unbroken by a single foreigner.[2] Their nobility and worth, even if not evident from other things, shine out all the same clearly enough from the fact that the King of kings and Lord, Jesus Christ, after his passion and resurrection, called them, settled at the very ends of the earth, almost the first to his most holy faith, and would not have them confirmed in that faith by anyone save the first-called of his apostles (though second or third in rank) namely the gentle Andrew, blessed Peter's brother, whom he willed to be over them ever more as their patron.

The most holy fathers your predecessors, weighing these things carefully in their

[1] The courtesy of *Baiser la mule du Pape*.

[2] Here, as I cannot better it, I have borrowed Professor Duncan's happy rendering of *nullo alienigena interveniente* (A. A. M. Duncan, *The Nation of the Scots and the Declaration of Arbroath (1320)*, Histor. Assoc. Pamphlet (London, 1970), p. 35).

minds, fortified this kingdom and people, as the particular property of the blessed Peter's brother, with many favours and privileges. Under their protection our people accordingly lived free and undisturbed until the eminent prince, Edward king of the English, the father of the present king, in the guise of friend and ally but in unfriendly[1] fashion, molested our kingdom when it was headless and the people conscious of no evil or guile and at that time unused to wars or attacks. The wrongs – the slaughter, violence, pillage, arsons, prelates imprisoned, monasteries burnt down, their inmates robbed and slain, other enormities too – which he perpetrated on this people, sparing neither age nor sex, religion nor order, no one could describe or fully comprehend without having experienced them.

From which innumerable evils, with the help of Him who after wounding cures and heals,[2] we have been delivered by our most strenuous leader, king and lord, the lord Robert, who that he might free his people and his heritage from the hands of foes, like another Maccabeus or Joshua, cheerfully endured toil, weariness, hunger and peril. Divine providence, rightful succession according to our laws and customs, which we will maintain to the death, and the due consent and assent of us all have made him our leader and king. To him as the man through whom salvation has been wrought in our people,[3] we are bound both by right and as what he deserves for preserving our freedom, and to him we will in all things adhere. But were he to desist from what he has undertaken and be willing to subject us or our kingdom to the king of the English or the English we would strive to expel him forthwith as our enemy and as a subverter of right, his own and ours, and make someone else our king who is equal to the task of defending us. For, as long as a hundred men are left, we will never submit in the slightest to the dominion of the English.[4] It is not for glory, riches or honours we fight, but only for liberty, which no good man loses but with his life.

Hence it is, reverend father and lord, that we most earnestly pray and on bended knees and from our hearts entreat your holiness to recollect in all sincerity and piety that with Him whose vicegerent on earth you are there is not weight and weight[5] and no distinction of Jew and Greek, Scot or English; to look with a fatherly eye on the tribulations and distress brought on us and on the church of God by the English; and to think it fitting to admonish and exhort the king of the English (who should rest content with what he has, since England once used to be enough to satisfy seven or more kings) to leave us Scots in peace in our poor Scotland where we live at the limits of human habitation and covet nothing but our own. Whatsoever we can do to preserve our peace where he is concerned, with due consideration for our position, that we are indeed willing to do.

[1] The word play between friend and unfriendly (*amicus* and *inimicabiliter*) is further proof that *inimicabiliter* and not *innumerabiliter* (cf. Lord Cooper of Culross, *Selected Papers 1922–1954* (Edinburgh, 1957), p. 336) is the correct Latin reading.

[2] cf. Deut. xxxii. 39, and Job v. 18

[3] cf. I Sam. xi. 13.

[4] *dominio.* As the reference is, in any case, to the English, not the king of the English, I have preferred "dominion" to "lordship".

[5] Prov. xx. 10, *pondus et pondus.* Divers weights and divers measures, both of them are alike abomination to the Lord.

To do this, holy father, is your concern, for you see the savagery of the heathen (through the fault of the Christians) rage against the Christians and the bounds of Christendom contract every day. How much it will detract from your memory if (which God forbid) the church suffers eclipse or setback while you are pope you will see for yourself. Stir up therefore the princes of Christendom who, alleging a non-cause as a cause, pretend they cannot go to the help of the Holy Land because of wars with their neighbours – the real reason being that they reckon it more profitable and easier to vanquish smaller neighbours. How joyfully we and the said lord our king would go there, if the king of the English would leave us in peace, He from whom nought is hidden knows full well, and we declare and testify it to the vicar of Christ and to all Christendom. If your holiness, too ready to believe what the English say, will not take us at our word or stop favouring them at the cost of our undoing, the loss of life, the perdition of souls, and all the other evils which will follow, which they inflict on us and we on them, will, we believe, be attributed by the Most High to you.

Inasmuch as we are and shall be in duty bound ready, as obedient sons, to do your pleasure in all things as His vicar, and to Him as king and judge supreme we entrust our cause, casting our cares on Him and firmly expecting that He will endow us with fortitude and bring our enemies to nought, may the Most High keep your holiness in health for the benefit of his holy church for a long time.[1] Given at the monastery of Arbroath in Scotland on the sixth day of April in the year of grace one thousand three hundred and twenty and the fifteenth year of the reign of our aforesaid king.

103. Statute of York, repealing the Ordinances of 1311 (1322)

(*Statutes of the Realm*, I (1810), pp. 189–90 [French])

As our lord the king Edward, son of king Edward, on 16 March in the 3rd year of his reign, to the honour of God and for the good of himself and his realm, granted to the prelates, earls and barons of his realm that they could choose certain persons from the prelates, earls and barons and other loyal people[2] whom they saw fit to call to them to order and establish the state of the household of our said lord the king and of his realm in accordance with right and reason and in such a way that their ordinances should be made to the honour of God and the honour and profit of holy church and to the honour of the said king and his profit and the profit of his people in accordance with right and reason and the oath that our said lord the king took at his coronation, and the archbishop of Canterbury, primate of all England, the bishops, earls and barons chosen for this purpose made certain ordinances that begin thus, "Edward by the grace of God king of England, lord of Ireland and duke of Aquitaine, to all those to whom these letters come, greeting. Know that as on 16 March in the

[1] "Inasmuch as . . . long time": I have followed the guidance of the manuscript facsimile in Professor Duncan's pamphlet (Histor. Assoc., 1970), not the printed texts, in translating this.

[2] The letters patent of 16 March 1310 did in fact authorise the prelates, earls and barons to choose also certain other fit persons as well as members of their own ranks (*et des autres les queux il lour semblera suffisauntz dapeller a eux*; *Foedera*, II, i, p. 105), though in the end they did not do so.

3rd year of our reign, to the honour of God" etc. and finish thus, "Given at London on the 5th day of October in the 5th year of our reign",[1] which ordinances our said lord the king, at his parliament at York three weeks after Easter[2] in the 15th year of his reign, caused to be gone over and examined by the prelates, earls and barons (among whom were the greater part of the said ordainers who were then alive) and by the commonalty of the realm assembled there by his command;[3] and because by this examination it was found in the said parliament that by the things thus ordained the royal power of our said lord the king was restricted in a number of things, contrary to what ought to be, to the weakening of his royal lordship, and against the estate of the crown, and also because in time past, by such ordinances and provisions made by subjects concerning the royal power of the ancestors of our lord the king, troubles and wars have happened in the realm whereby the land has been in peril, IT IS AGREED AND ESTABLISHED at the said parliament by our lord the king and by the said prelates, earls and barons and the whole commonalty of the realm at this parliament assembled that all the things ordained by the said ordainers and contained in the said ordinances shall for the future from now on cease and forever lose repute,[4] force, virtue and effect, the statutes and establishments duly made by our lord the king and his ancestors remaining in force; and that after this any manner of ordinances or provisions made at any time by subjects of our lord the king or of his heirs by whatsoever authority or commission concerning the royal power of our lord the king or of his heirs or against the estate of our said lord the king or of his heirs or against the estate of the crown shall be null and of no sort of validity or force, but things which are to be established for the estate of our lord the king and of his heirs and for the estate of the realm and of the people shall be treated, agreed and established in parliaments by our lord the king and by the assent of the prelates, earls and barons and the commonalty of the realm as has been accustomed formerly.

104. Ordinance of Kenilworth, 1 May 1326

(Patent Roll, 19 Edward II, Part II, m. 8, in the translation of Bland, Brown and Tawney, *English Economic History: Select Documents*, pp. 181–4 [French])

Edward, etc., to the mayor of our city of London, greeting. We command you, straitly enjoining, that the things below written, ordained by us and our council for the common profit and relief of the people of all our realm and power, you cause to be proclaimed and published and straitly kept and observed in our city aforesaid and everywhere in your bailiwick.

First, that the staple of the merchants and the merchandise of England, Ireland and Wales, namely, of wools, hides, woolfells and tin, be holden in the same lands and nowhere else, and that too in the places below written, that is to say, at Newcastle

[1] This is, of course, No. 100 above.
[2] i.e. 2 May 1322, the date for which parliament was summoned
[3] It was the fullest sort of parliament, including, besides the magnates ecclesiastical and lay, representatives of the shires and boroughs and of the lower clergy, and "for the first time" (Tout, *Place of Edward II*, 2nd edn, p. 136) representatives of the commons of Wales.
[4] literally "lose name"

upon Tyne, York, Lincoln, Norwich, London, Winchester, Exeter, and Bristol, for England, Dublin, Drogheda and Cork, for Ireland, Shrewsbury, Carmarthen and Cardiff, for Wales. And for the tin of Cornwall, at Lostwithiel and Truro. And for the tin of Devonshire, at Ashburton, and not elsewhere in England, Ireland or Wales.

And that all alien people there and not elsewhere in England, Ireland or Wales, may freely buy and seek wools, hides and fells and other merchandise, and tin in Ashburton, Lostwithiel and Truro, and not elsewhere, and when they have bought their merchandise at the said places and in the form abovesaid and paid their customs, and have thereon letters sealed with the seal of the cocket,[1] they may carry the said wools, hides, fells, tin and other merchandise into what land soever they will, if it be not into a land that is at war or enmity with us or our realm. And that the merchant strangers be warned hereof.

And that no alien by himself or another privily or openly may buy elsewhere wools or other merchandise abovesaid except at the said places, upon forfeiture of the wools or other merchandise abovesaid which he shall have so bought.

And that the merchants of England, Ireland and Wales, who wish to carry wools, hides, fells or tin out of the staples to be sold elsewhere, may not carry them from the staples out of our power until they have remained fifteen days at any of our staples to sell them, and then they may go with the said merchandise whither they will, without making or holding a staple anywhere out of the said lands or within the said lands elsewhere than at the places abovesaid.

And that all the people of England, Ireland and Wales, may sell and buy wools and all other merchandise anywhere that they will in the said lands, so that the sale be not made to aliens except at the staple. And that wools, hides, fells and tin be nowhere carried out of the said lands by aliens or denizens except from the staples aforesaid.

And that the merchants of our power make not among themselves any conspiracy or compact to lessen the price of wools or other merchandise abovesaid, or to delay merchant strangers in the purchase or sale of their merchandise, and that those who shall do so and can be attainted hereof be heavily punished according to the ordinance of us and of our good council. And that every man be admitted on our behalf who will sue to attaint and punish such, and that such suit be made before our chief justices or others whom we will assign hereto and not elsewhere. And that the merchants and the people of Gascony and of the duchy of Aquitaine, who now are or for the time shall be of the fealty and obedience of us or of our son and heir, be holden as denizens and not as aliens in all these affairs.

And that all merchants, native and strangers, be subject to the law merchant in all things that touch trafficking at the places of the staples.

And that no man or woman of a borough or city, nor the commons of the people outside a borough or city in England, Ireland or Wales, after Christmas next coming, use cloth of their own buying that shall be bought after the said feast of Christmas, unless it be cloth made in England, Ireland or Wales, upon heavy forfeiture and punishment, as we by our good council will ordain hereon. And be it known that by the commons in this case shall be understood all people except the king and queen,

[1] the seal used by the customers (customs officers)

earls and barons, knights and ladies and their children born in wedlock, archbishops and bishops and other persons and people of holy church, and seculars, who can spend yearly from their rents 40*l* sterling, and this so long as it please us by our good council further to extend this ordinance and prohibition.

And that every man and woman of England, Ireland and Wales, may make cloths as long and as short as they shall please.

And that people may have the greater will to work upon the making of cloth in England, Ireland and Wales, we will that all people know that we shall grant suitable franchises to fullers, weavers, dyers and other clothworkers who live mainly by this craft, when such franchises be asked of us.

And that it be granted to the wool-merchants that they have a mayor of the staples aforesaid.

And that all merchant strangers may have the greater will to come into our power and may the more safely stay and return, we take them, their persons and goods, into our protection. And we forbid, upon heavy forfeiture, that anyone do them wrong or injury in person or goods, while they be coming, staying or returning, so that if anyone do them injury contrary to this protection and prohibition, those of the town to which the evildoers shall belong shall be bound to answer for the damages or for the persons of the evildoers, and that the mayor or bailiffs of the town where the shipping is take surety for which they will answer at their peril from the sailors of the same shipping every time that they shall go out of the havens, that they will not do evil or misbehave towards any man contrary to these articles.

In witness whereof we have caused these our letters to be signed with our seal. Given at Kenilworth, 1 May.

[The like sent to the mayors and bailiffs of the other staple towns (those mentioned in the second paragraph), to all the sheriffs of England, and to John Darci justice of Ireland and Edmund earl of Arundel justice of Wales, as well as to Ralph Basset warden of the castle of Dover and of the Cinque Ports and to the bailiffs of Sandwich.]

105. Export of materials for cloth-manufacture prohibited, 1 June 1326

(*Cal. Close Rolls 1323–7*, p. 565)

Within weeks of the Ordinance of Kenilworth of 1 May 1326 (No. 104 above), the king was informed of efforts to defeat his attempt in that ordinance at encouraging native cloth-manufacture. His counter-measure of 21 May, printed in Bland, Brown and Tawney, *English Economic History: Select Documents*, p. 186, was followed as promised by this general order under the great seal on 1 June 1326.

1326, 1 June, Saltwood

To the sheriff of Northumberland. Order to cause proclamation to be made prohibiting any merchant, native or alien, or other person whatsoever from carrying or sending out of the realm the thistles commonly called "tasles", fuller's earth, madder, woad, burs,[1] or other things necessary for the making of cloth, under pain of grievous forfeiture, or from buying and pulling up the herbs and roots of such thistles, or from

[1] corrected in the light of T. F. Tout, *Place of Edward II in English History* (2nd edn, Manchester, 1936), pp. 238–9

causing the same to be done, in order to send them to parts beyond sea, and to arrest and imprison until further orders any found doing the contrary, together with the thistles, etc., certifying the king from time to time of the names of those thus arrested, and of the value of the goods, as it is ordained by the king and his council, for the advantage and easement of the people of his realm, and of his lands of Ireland and Wales, that the staple of wool, hides, and wool-fells shall be held in certain places within the realm and the said lands, and not elsewhere, and that none of the realm and lands, certain persons excepted, shall use after Christmas next cloth of their own purchase made after the said feast out of the realm and lands, and the king now understands that many men of Flanders, Brabant and other foreign lands, endeavouring to hinder the making of cloth in the realm and lands, have bought all the thistles called "tasles" that could be found within the realm and lands, without which cloth cannot be made, and have bought fuller's earth, madder, woad, burs,[1] and other things necessary for the making of cloth, after the aforesaid ordinance, and have taken and sent them to parts beyond sea, and do daily take and send them, and, what is worse, have bought the herb and roots of the thistles, and have caused them to be pulled up by the roots in order to send them to parts beyond sea. By K.

The like to all the sheriffs of England.

[1] see above, p. 546, n.

Part III

ROYAL GOVERNMENT IN ACTION

INTRODUCTION

THE title given to this part of the volume possibly requires explanation. "The Machinery of State" would not do. Neither would "Machinery of Government" or "Government in Action". For one thing, men did not then speak of "The State", abstractly; but of the state of something, the state of the Church or the state of the realm, as an American president today in his annual Message to Congress on the state of the nation. For another thing, we must make it clear that it is royal government we are thinking of. England in the Middle Ages was a "much-governed" land, but the king was not the only governor. By 1189 he was ceasing to be the remote and occasional authority he had been at the beginning of the twelfth century, but even in 1327, rapidly as his authority had grown and was growing, church, township and manor were still the realities for most men for most of their life for most of the year.

So "Royal Government in Action" and the purpose is to look at the means the king had of imposing his policies. The first observation is by modern standards the primitiveness of the administrative machine at his disposal. There was no specifically royal machinery. For governing his realm he had nothing more than he had for managing his personal affairs, nothing of a higher order than any subject of his with great estates might have, a court (*curia*) – the king's court (*curia regis*) to distinguish it from other men's.

What is known of the *Curia Regis* in the twelfth century is summarised in chapters II and III of S. B. Chrimes, *Introduction to the Administrative History of Mediaeval England* (3rd edn, 1966). The essence of it was the king's household staff, responsible to him for the day-to-day management of his kingship as well as his domestic affairs, and indeed for any action needed on occasions when he "wore his crown" and deliberated with his magnates as well as his officials. We have an account of it written *c.* 1136, the "Establishment of the Royal Household" (*Constitutio Domus Regis*) in C. Johnson's edition of the *Dialogus de Scaccario*, pp. 129–35. It is also given in *English Historical Documents*, II in this series, No. 30.

This royal executive was still a unity in 1189. It was still simple and flexible enough to be responsive to changing needs and to be able to carry the extra burdens placed on it by Henry II without structural change. Even the Exchequer, formal – as from the *Dialogus*, written some ten or a dozen years before, we see it was – and leaving behind the bulk of its organisation when it travelled, was not an independent institution. Instead, organised already even for financial purposes as something more than a twice-yearly occasion of the *Curia* for audit, it had had channelled into it the new judicial business arising from Henry II's development of royal justice and had become "an office of general administration" for the *Curia*, by 1189 its chief office. The Exchequer ultimately went completely "out of court" in the physical sense as did other parts of the administration (there is a demand in 1215, granted in Magna Carta, for common pleas to be heard "in some fixed place" and "not follow the court of the lord king", Nos 19 (c. 8) and 20 (c. 17) above). But however partitioned, of physical necessity, the *Curia* became, it remained "the centre of administrative action". "No matter whether custom or expediency, convenience or routine, determines that some action shall normally be taken within a particular organisation within the *Curia*, in the Exchequer, the Chancery, or Chamber, or elsewhere, it is all action within the *Curia Regis*, and all is the application of the king's will and power." One's first observation was the primitiveness of the administrative machine at the king's disposal. The second must be (trite though it is in general terms) the essentially personal nature of royal government; for when royal government is challenged, as it repeatedly and increasingly is in the history of this country, it is important to bear in mind a third observation, that "In so far as the king has competence, the *Curia Regis* has competence, *and every part of it has equal competence,*[1] at least in theory."

Ninety years later, in 1279, though the ordinance of that year does not make possible a complete comparison, there is no essential change (No. 118 below). There has been growth, great growth. There has been change. But it is still personal government, working through the household with the counsel of the leading men of a now somewhat larger official circle and of a few intimate advisers with or without official position, such as the chancellor Robert Burnell, the ex-official Antony Bek and Sir Otho de Grandison later, and later still Piers Gavaston. It was still flexible, as the importance of the wardrobe in administration in and after 1279 shows, and of it and the great wardrobe in wartime. And, as a letter to the chancellor, Burnell, in 1281 (No. 106 (c) below) shows, it was small and intimate enough in operation to permit dominance (under the king himself) of an outstanding personality. The case of Robert Burnell is interesting and revealing. No other office succeeded to the pre-eminence of the Angevin justiciar. But that of the chancellor came near to it in the time of Burnell. As custodian of the great seal the main channel of the royal will when this had to be indicated in writing, equally a channel of access to that will, for he normally went with the king in his progresses, above all as loyal as he was able, and completely trusted by Edward I, he exercised until his death in 1292 a wider authority in administration (as the above-mentioned letter implies) and a greater influence in council than he had as chancellor – rather was the office dignified. It was a personal position and after him personality and wartime needs brought not the new chancellor, but the treasurer, Walter Langton, to the front.

No. 106 illustrates, besides the personal authority it was still possible for a minister to have irrespective of his position, the development, later than that of the Exchequer but in the same direction, of the chancellor's office – clerks of the chancery, chancery records, and "the great bench in the great hall at Westminster" where by 1310 "the king's chancellors were wont" to sit with their clerks, when of course they were not with the king elsewhere.

The records of the chancery were by this time voluminous, cf. p. 295 above, pp. 556 and 560 below for enrolment (of out-letters) quite apart from the files (in-letters), but the course of the chancery, the processes involved in issuing documents under the great seal, cannot begin to be traced before the reign of Edward I. The enquiry should start with Galbraith's chapter on the "secretariat" in *Use of the Public Records* and

[1] These italics are mine. The quotations are from Chrimes, *Introduction*, p. 45.

be pursued in Maxwell-Lyte, *Historical Notes*, where it will be seen that already warrants and other seals can be involved.

In No. 106 (b) there is mention of a council: "... the counsel (*conseyl*) of our magnates of our council (*conseyl*)". But this was in the year 1260 and that was an abnormal time and it was an abnormal body (cf. Nos 5 and 37 above). It would be unwise to read a hard institutional distinction into two uses of the one word *conseyl* or, for that matter (medieval orthography being what it was) into the difference between an "s" and a "c" (*consilium, concilium*) in the equivalent Latin. Administrative history, no less than constitutional history, is the history of persons.[1] It would be safer to think of normal conditions – of the king and his *curia* and advising as one of the functions of that *curia*, whether in the day-to-day sense of household officials and such others as the king chose to consult or in the larger, more formal sense of the occasions in the year when the king took counsel also with the great of the land. The king was drawing on a larger circle for advice as government (and so the *curia*) grew and grew more complex. The farther he went outside his immediate household circle into the expanding *curia*, and still more if he went outside the official circle altogether, the greater the need, probably, for a convenient name for these advisers as a body. We find *conseyl* (*consilium* or *concilium* in the Latin) in this second sense and, as often as not, (the king's) "advisers" or "body of advisers", or "counsel", would be an adequate translation, but if we wish to speak of an "advisory body", or more daringly still of a "council", it must not be understood in any institutional sense. These men are essentially a collection of individuals for a particular purpose. Their function is to advise. As such they have no executive power, whatever some of them, the officials among them, may have in another capacity. They are not "a court of record", obliged to keep records, so they keep none, and make none unless to further the immediate business of helping the king to a decision and, with him or for him, transmitting it for action on it in the *curia*. Their work is evidenced, if at all, by a note, a minute "endorsed on a bill or written on a scrap of parchment", occasional memoranda. They are too informal, too near king and *curia*, to need a seal of their own.

The genesis of No. 106 (b) and other abnormalities such as Nos. 34, 37–8, 40, 98 (p. 526) and 100 (esp. preamble and cc. 13–14) is political. In principle it was for the king to choose his advisers, but there was also a tradition, which was also political wisdom, that he should take counsel with his subjects, or at least their leaders. His magnates ecclesiastical and lay saw themselves as his natural advisers. Aquinas (No. 231 (b) below) in the *Summa Theologiae* 1a2æ, observing on "the right ordering of rulers" that "all should take some share in government; this makes for peace among the people, and commends itself to all, and they uphold it", wrote "the best system in any state or kingdom is one in which one man, as specially qualified, rules over all, and under him are others governing as having special endowments, yet all have a share inasmuch as those are elected from all, and also are elected by all" (Qu. 105) and again, in another way in another context (Qu. 95), a "type of regime blended of the others, and this is the best, and provides law as Isidore understood it, namely that 'which men of birth together with the common people have sanctioned' ". There

[1] "History, even constitutional history, is the history of persons" (Powicke, *King Henry III*, p. 342).

were already men in England thinking on these lines: before the "Provisions of Oxford" (No. 37) and before Edward I used the flourish about "what touches all" being "approved by all" when it served his own purposes to do so in 1295.[1] No. 34 above (however Matthew Paris came by it) fits easily into the history of baronial thinking as traced in an admirable chapter IV by Chrimes, *Introduction to Administrative History*, particularly pp. 120 ff. on "The Beginnings of Political Repercussions", in a prematurely parliamentary framework by Stubbs in *Const. Hist.*, II, ch. XIV, sections 174–5, and profoundly by Powicke in *King Henry III*, ch. 8. It would have provided for "four men of rank and power . . . chosen by common consent . . . to be of the king's council (*de consilio domini regis*)". Chosen "from the most discreet persons of the whole realm" and "elected by the assent of all", none of them would have been "removable without general consent". Persons, however, who were suspect and could be dispensed with were "to be removed from the lord king's side". Justiciar and chancellor were *ex officio* not removable ("they ought to be frequently with the lord king"), so their appointment should rest with all ("Justiciar and chancellor shall be chosen by all"). Intellectually the "Provisions of Oxford" and the Ordinances of 1311 are contained in this.

Discontent with royal government prompted demands for a larger voice in advising the king, amounting at times to a claim to control his choice of other advisers; in extreme cases to share his executive power. Our preoccupation with political and parliamentary history has obscured the course of political and administrative history. The word "parliament" apparently established itself in England in this connection (its primary sense of "parley" or "talks", without any suggestion in it of formality or regularity, would be a recommendation) as one way of referring to these occasions when the king took counsel with a larger number of advisers than usual. By 1327 parliaments were accepted as part of normal practice. This had come about by a shift of emphasis without institutional change. The "Provisions of Oxford" had been a bold experiment, Simon de Montfort's invocation in the fifteen months between Lewes and Evesham of a wider community even bolder. His defeat restored the royal power, but Edward I, for administrative convenience certainly but whether from political prudence too we do not know, took over parliament – and the novelty of shire and borough representation as well when it suited him – and made it so much a part of his system of government that his son, Edward II, at the height of his power in 1322 could not dispense with it (No. 103 above). Parliament had "arrived", though limitation of the monarchy by parliament and the shift within parliament from Lords to Commons had still to be.

The evidence we have shows, not surprisingly, little difference between business in parliament and the business of council. The memoranda of the Easter parliament in 1279, "the earliest surviving record of its kind", are printed in *Trans. Royal Hist. Soc.*, 4th ser., x (1928), pp. 48–53 and in *Rot. Parl. . . . hactenus inediti*, ed. Richardson and Sayles (1935), pp. 1–7 and described by Powicke (*The Thirteenth Century*, pp. 346 ff.). Much parliamentary business was judicial (which is not to say with Richard-

[1] For how much a commonplace this was cf. Stubbs, *Const. Hist.*, II (1906), p. 133, n. 4.

son and Sayles that "the essence of [parliaments] is the dispensing of justice"[1]), so much so that a means of dealing with most of the petitions that gave rise to it had to be developed[2] to lighten the burden and not impede other business. This is illustrated by No. 134 below, a classification of the petitions presented at the Michaelmas parliament of 1318 and, incidentally, a unique example.

To a medievalist J. E. Neale's *The Elizabethan House of Commons* (1949) is tantalising reading, for the light it is possible to shed on county elections almost three (but not six) hundred years before the ballot box. We have scanty knowledge of the election of medieval representatives to parliament. No. 135 below is one early piece of evidence – of the proper conduct of such an election, of misconduct, and the possibility in the circumstances (more it is not) of management.

Nos 111–13 below illustrate some of the routine and humdrum of the work of a sheriff, the king's "chief regular officials in the county for almost every variety of public business". He had, as later, an office with a permanent staff. It verges on the incredible that of the vast amount of record occasioned in every county over the centuries of his ascendancy so little apparently survives. No body of local government archive for a normal county, as distinct for example from co. Chester,[3] has come to light for the period covered by this volume. The earliest relates to the paired counties of Bedford and Buckingham and the years 1329–34. It is described by Hilary Jenkinson and Mabel H. Mills in *English Historical Review*, xliii (1928). Two of the three rolls in question can be studied in print in *Rolls from the Office of the Sheriff of Beds. and Bucks. 1332–4*, edited by G. H. Fowler for the Architectural and Archaeological Society for the County of Buckingham. This at least can be said: the system they reflect was not new in 1332. Some of the questions to which they give rise for the preceding period are discussed by T. F. T. Plucknett and G. H. Woodbine in the *Harvard Law Review*, xlii and xliii, for 1928 and 1929 and G. Lapsley in the *Law Quarterly Review*, li, for 1935.

SELECT BIBLIOGRAPHY

T. F. Tout, a pupil of Stubbs, paid the highest tribute in his power when he declared F. W. Maitland "the only great master of English mediaeval lore whom we may venture to put on the same plane as the author of the *Constitutional History of England*". He himself is now generally thought of as in their company. His *Chapters in the Administrative History of Mediaeval England* in six volumes (Manchester, 1920–33) as assuredly laid the foundations of the modern study of this central period of medieval English history as did Stubbs's work and Maitland's *History of English Law*. It showed the relevance and pioneered the method of a new line of enquiry, and put administrative history into the mainstream of historical scholarship.

The *Chapters* is, however, rough-hewn research and not a beginner's book. The student will be well advised to start with S. B. Chrimes's *Introduction to the Administrative History of Mediaeval England* (Oxford, 1952, now in its 3rd edn, 1966), which besides its helpfulness in showing the relevance of administrative to political and constitutional history takes account of work done since Tout. He will also turn again to Galbraith's *Introduction to the Use of the Public Records*, whose special distinction is that it never loses sight of the administrative system which produced the records.

---

[1] *Parliaments and Great Councils* (1961), p. 30.
[2] See *Rot. Parl. . . . hactenus inediti*, pp. vii–xiii and cf. Powicke, *Thirteenth Century*, pp. 348–9.
[3] For which see G. O. Sayles in *Sel. Cases in . . . K. B.: Edward I*, vol. 3 (Seld. Soc., 1939), p. xcvi, n. 1.

A. ORIGINAL SOURCES

Rotuli Chartarum in turri Londinensi asservati 1199–1216, ed. T. D. Hardy (Rec. Com., 1837)
Rotuli Litterarum Clausarum . . ., ed. T. D. Hardy (Rec. Com.), I, *1204–24* (1833); II, *1224–7* (1844)
Rotuli Litterarum Patentium . . . 1201–16, ed. T. D. Hardy (Rec. Com., 1835)

For other publications of the Record Commissioners prior to the Public Record Office *Calendars* of records, see the list in E. L. C. Mullins, *Texts and Calendars* (Royal Historical Society, 1958), pp. 1–15.

Calendar of Charter Rolls, I, *Henry III 1226–57* (1903)
——, II, *Henry III to Edward I 1257–1300* (1906)
——, III, *Edward I to Edward II 1300–26* (1908)
Calendar of Close Rolls, Henry III, I, *1227–31* (1902)
——, II, *1231–4* (1905)
——, III, *1234–7* (1909)
——, IV, *1237–42* (1911)
——, V, *1242–7* (1916)
——, VI, *1247–51* (1922)
——, VII, *1251–3* (1928)
——, VIII, *1253–4* (1930)
——, IX, *1254–6* (1931)
——, X, *1256–9* (1932)
——, XI, *1259–61* (1934)
——, XII, *1261–4* (1936)
——, XIII, *1264–8* (1937)
——, XIV, *1268–72* (1938)
Calendar of Close Rolls, Edward I, I, *1272–9* (1900)
——, II, *1279–88* (1902)
——, III, *1288–96* (1904)
——, IV, *1296–1302* (1906)
——, V, *1302–7* (1908)
Calendar of Close Rolls, Edward II, I, *1307–13* (1892)
——, II, *1313–18* (1893)
——, III, *1318–23* (1895)
——, IV, *1323–7* (1898)
Calendar of Fine Rolls, I, *Edward I 1272–1307* (1911)
——, II, *Edward II 1307–19* (1912)
——, III, *1319–27* (1913)
Calendar of Inquisitions Post Mortem and other analogous Documents, I, *Henry III* (1904)
——, II, *1–19 Edward I* (1906)
——, III, *20–8 Edward I* (1912)
——, IV, *29–35 Edward I* (1913)
——, V, *1–9 Edward II* (1908)
——, VI, *10–20 Edward II* (1910)
Calendar of Liberate Rolls, I, *Henry III 1226–40* (1917)
——, II, *1240–5* (1931)
——, III, *1245–51* (1937)
——, IV, *1251–60* (1959)
——, V, *1260–7* (1961)
——, VI, *1267–72* (1964)
Calendar of Miscellaneous Inquisitions, I, *Henry III and Edward I* (1916)
——, II, *Edward II to 22 Edward III* (1916)
Calendar of Patent Rolls, Henry III, I, *1216–25* (1901)
——, II, *1225–32* (1903)
——, III, *1232–47* (1906)
——, IV, *1247–58* (1908)
——, V, *1258–66* (1910)
——, VI, *1266–72* (1913)
Calendar of Patent Rolls, Edward I, I, *1272–81* (1901)
——, II, *1281–92* (1893)
——, III, *1292–1301* (1895)
——, IV, *1301–7* (1898)
Calendar of Patent Rolls, Edward II, I, *1307–13* (1894)
——, II, *1313–17* (1898)
——, III, *1317–21* (1903)
——, IV, *1321–4* (1904)
——, V, *1324–7* (1904)

Calendar of Chancery Rolls, Various: (i) *Supplementary Close Rolls* (ii) *Welsh Rolls* (iii) *Scutage Rolls 1277–1326* (1912)
Calendar of Chancery Warrants, I, *Privy Seals 1244–1326* (1927)
Treaty Rolls preserved in the Public Record Office, I, *1234–1325*, ed. P. Chaplais (1956)

Diplomatic Documents [*Chancery and Exchequer*] *preserved in the Public Record Office*, I, *1101–1272*, ed. P. Chaplais (1964)

Liber Quotidianus Contrarotulatoris Garderobae anno [*28 Edw. I*] (Society of Antiquaries, 1787)
Book of Prests of the King's Wardrobe for 1294–5 [P.R.O. Miscellaneous Books of the Treasury of Receipt, E.36/202], ed. E. B. Fryde (Oxford, 1962)
Book of Fees, I, *1198–1242* (1921)
——, II, *1242–93* (1923)
——, III, *Index* (1931)
Feudal Aids 1284–1431, I, *Bedford – Devon* (1899)
——, II, *Dorset – Huntingdon* (1901)
——, III, *Kent – Norfolk* (1904)
——, IV, *Northampton – Somerset* (1906)
——, V, *Stafford – Worcester* (1909)
——, VI, *York and additions* (1921)
Calendar of Memoranda Rolls (Exchequer) Michaelmas 1326 to Michaelmas 1327 (1968)
See also Pipe Roll Society publications in Mullins, *Texts and Calendars*, pp. 232 ff.
Great Rolls of the Pipe. See publications of the Pipe Roll Society, in Mullins, op. cit. pp. 232 ff.

Curia Regis Rolls preserved in the Public Record Office, 14 vols (1923–61), I–VII "of the reigns of Richard and John" and VIII–XIV "of the reign of Henry III" to 17 Hen. III. For editions of other legal records, see Selden Society publications in Mullins, op. cit. pp. 276 ff.

Ancient Deeds: Descriptive Catalogue, 6 vols (1890–1915)

The position over Scottish, Welsh and Irish records for the period is (for different reasons) difficult. See F. Maurice Powicke, *The Thirteenth Century* (Oxford, 1953), pp. 750–6. The publication of Gascon Rolls, *Rôles Gascons*, ed. F. Michel and Ch. Bémont, *Documents inédits sur l'histoire de France*, 4 vols (Paris 1885–1906), has been resumed by *Gascon Rolls preserved in the Public Record Office 1307–17*, ed. Y. Renouard (1962).

B. SECONDARY AUTHORITIES

COURT AND CHANCERY

Chaplais, P., "The Chancery of Guyenne 1289–1453", *Studies presented to Sir Hilary Jenkinson*, ed. J. C. Davies (1957), pp. 61–96
——, *English Royal Documents: King John to Henry VI, 1199–1461* (Oxford, 1971)
——, "Privy Seal Drafts, Rolls and Registers (Edw. I to Edw. II)", *English Historical Review*, lxxiii (1958), pp. 270–3
Chrimes, S. B., *An Introduction to the Administrative History of Mediaeval England* (Oxford, 1952), 3rd edn (1966)
Cuttino, G. P., *English Diplomatic Administration 1259–1339*, 2nd edn (1971)
Dibben, L. B., "Secretaries in the thirteenth and fourteenth centuries", *E.H.R.*, xxv (1910) pp. 430–44
Facsimiles of English Royal Writs to A.D. 1100 presented to V. H. Galbraith, ed. T. A. M. Bishop and P. Chaplais (Oxford, 1957)
Galbraith, V. H., *An Introduction to the Use of the Public Records* (1934)
——, *Studies in the Public Records* (1948)
Hill, Mary C., *The King's Messengers 1199–1377: a contribution to the History of the Royal Household* (1961)
List of Documents relating to the Household and Wardrobe, John to Edward I, Public Record Office Handbook No. 7 (1964)
Maxwell-Lyte, Sir H. C., *Historical Notes on the Use of the Great Seal of England* (1926)
Stamp, A. E., "Some Notes on the Court and Chancery of Henry III", *Historical Essays in honour of James Tait*, ed. Edwards, J. G. (etc.) (Manchester, 1933)
Van Caenegem, R. C., *Royal Writs in England from the Conquest to Glanvill*, Selden Society 77 (1959)
West, F. J., *The Justiciarship in England 1066–1232* (Cambridge, 1966)

JUDICIAL

Flower, C. T., *Introduction to the Curia Regis Rolls A.D. 1199–1230* (1944)
Hurnard, Naomi D., *The King's Pardon for Homicide before A.D. 1307* (Oxford, 1969)
Pugh, R. B., *Imprisonment in Medieval England* (Cambridge, 1968)

FINANCIAL

Brown, R. A., " 'The Treasury' of the later Twelfth Century", *Studies presented to Sir Hilary Jenkinson*, ed. J. C. Davies (1957), pp. 35–49
Davies, J. C., "The Memoranda Rolls of the Exchequer to 1307", *Studies presented to Sir Hilary Jenkinson*, ed. J. C. Davies (1957), pp. 97–154
Deighton, H. S., "Clerical Taxation by Consent 1279–1301", *E.H.R.*, lxviii (1953), pp. 161–92
Dialogus de Scaccario, trans. C. Johnson, Medieval Classics series (1950)
Ehrlich, L., "Exchequer and Wardrobe in 1270", *E.H.R.*, xxxvi (1921), pp. 553–4
Gras, N. S. B., *The Early English Customs System* (Cambridge, Mass., 1918)
Harriss, G. L., "Parliamentary Taxation and the Origins of Appropriation of Supply in England 1207–1340", *Recueils de la Société Jean Bodin pour l'Histoire Comparative des Institutions*, XXIV, pp. 165–79
Jenkinson, (Sir) Hilary, "An original Exchequer Account of 1304 with private Tallies attached", *Proceedings of the Society of Antiquaries*, 2nd ser., xxvi
——, "Exchequer Tallies", *Archaeologia*, lxii (1911), pp. 367–80, and "A note supplementary . . .", *Proceedings of the Society of Antiquaries*, 2nd ser., xxv
——, "Financial Records of the Reign of King John", *Magna Carta Commemoration Essays*, ed. H. E. Malden (Royal Hist. Soc., 1917), pp. 244–300
——, "Medieval Tallies, Public and Private", *Archaeologia*, lxiv (1925), pp. 289–351

Johnson, C., "The Exchequer Chamber under Edward II", *E.H.R.*, xxi (1906), pp. 726–7
——, "The system of Account in the Wardrobe of Edward I", *Trans. Royal Hist. Soc.*, 4th ser., vi (1923), pp. 52–72
Meekings, C. A. F., "The Pipe Roll Order of 12 February 1270", *Studies presented to Sir Hilary Jenkinson*, ed. J. C. Davies (1957), pp. 222–53
Willard, J. F., *Parliamentary Taxes on Personal Property 1290 to 1334: a study in Mediaeval English Financia Administration* (Cambridge, Mass., 1934)

COUNCIL AND PARLIAMENT

Baldwin, J. F., *The King's Council in England during the Middle Ages* (Oxford, 1913)
Edwards, J. G., *The Commons in Medieval English Parliaments* (1958)
——, "Justice in Early English Parliaments", *Bull. Inst. Hist. Research*, xxvii (1954), pp. 33–53
Jolliffe, J. E. A., "Some Factors in the Beginnings of Parliament", *Trans. Royal Hist. Soc.*, xxii (1940), pp. 101–39
Kingsford, C. L., "Sir Otho de Grandison", *Trans. Royal Hist. Soc.*, 3rd ser., iii (1909), pp. 125–95
Parliaments and related Assemblies to 1832 (a list with indispensable introduction. Supersedes earlier lists), in *Handbook of British Chronology*, ed. Sir F. Maurice Powicke and E. B. Fryde, 2nd edn (1961), pp. 492–544
Powicke, F. M., *King Henry III and the Lord Edward* (Oxford, 1947), ch. 8 ("King Henry and his Council")
——, Sir F. Maurice, *The Thirteenth Century 1216–1307* (Oxford, 1953)
Richardson, H. G., "The Origins of Parliament", *Trans. Royal Hist. Soc.*, 4th ser., xi (1928), pp. 137–49
——, and Sayles, G. O., "The King's Ministers in Parliament 1272–1377", *E.H.R.*, xlvi (1931), pp. 529–50
——, *Parliaments and Great Councils in Medieval England* (1961) (a reprint of articles in *Law Quarterly Review* for 1961)
Treharne, R. F., "The Nature of Parliament in the Reign of Henry III", *E.H.R.*, lxxiv (1959), pp. 590-610

LOCAL ADMINISTRATION

Cam, Helen M., *The Hundred and the Hundred Rolls* (1930)
Mills, Mabel H., "The Medieval Shire House (*Domus Vicecomitis*)", *Studies presented to Sir Hilary Jenkinson*, ed. J. C. Davies (1957), pp. 254–71
Morris, W. A., *The Medieval English Sheriff to 1300* (Manchester 1927)
Thomson, W. S., *A Lincolnshire Assize Roll for 1298 . . . with an Introduction on Royal Local Government in Lincolnshire during the War of 1294–8* (Lincoln Record Soc. vol. 36, 1944)

MISCELLANEOUS

Colvin, H. M. (ed.), *The History of the King's Works*, 2 vols (1963)
Handbook of British Chronology, ed. Sir F. Maurice Powicke and E. B. Fryde, 2nd edn (1961)

106. The Great Seal

(a) *Clerks of the chancery, 1244*

(*Close Rolls of . . . Henry III*, vol. 5, p. 275)

Mandate [10 December 1244] to the bailiffs of Windsor to send to Westminster for the approaching feast of Christmas, as instructed by William de Rading', two boatloads of firewood for the king's use and a boatload as well for the use of the clerks of the chancery. And when the king knows the cost he will have it paid to them. Witness as above.

(b) *Council and the great seal, 1260*

(Patent Roll, 44 Hen. III, pt 1, m. 2, printed in H. C. Maxwell-Lyte, *Historical Notes on the . . . Great Seal* (1926), pp. 180–1 [French and Latin])

Henry by the grace of God king of England etc. to all those who shall see these letters, greeting in our Lord. Know all of you that we received on the day of St Edward in the forty-fourth year from our coronation [13 October 1260] at our feast which we held then at Westminster, Henry the son of the king of Almain, our nephew, as the attorney of Simon de Muntfort, earl of Leicester, to serve for him at the aforesaid feast as pertains to the service of the stewardship. And in witness of this thing we have made to the abovesaid Simon these our letters patent by the counsel of our magnates [*hauz homes*] of our council. And this thing was done in the year and on the day aforesaid. [French]

This letter was read and approved before the lord king in his wardrobe, there being present Edward the king's son, Henry son of the king of Almain, the earl of Gloucester, the earl of Oxford, H[ugh] le Bygot the justiciar, J[ohn] Mansel and R[obert] Walerand, and others, and sealed by their order. [Latin]

(c) *To the chancellor, Robert Burnell, 1281*

(*Select Cases in the Court of King's Bench under Edward I*, I (1936), pp. cxlii–iii, trans. Sir Maurice Powicke, *The Thirteenth Century* (Oxford, 1953), p. 335)

To the reverend father in Christ and their most dear lord, the lord Robert by God's grace bishop of Bath and Wells, chancellor of the lord king, his devoted S[olomon] of Rochester and his fellows, justices on eyre in the county of Devon, greeting with all reverence and honour. Since we fully intend to finish the present eyre in Devon before Easter [13 April] we beg you to tell us as quickly as you can into what shire we should adjourn after Easter and to what date, and whether we must all come to parliament. Please note that, if we must all come, the shire of Cornwall cannot be summoned before the week or fortnight after Trinity [8 June] for the time between Easter week and the parliament is short and it is a long journey from London to Cornwall, and, as you know, parliament involves much delay. If you were willing to prorogue the eyre until after Michaelmas, you would do much service both to the whole shire and to us, for corn has failed there this year and if we go there in the summer we shall bring back meagre cheeks. Please let us know your good pleasure by the bearer. May your reverend lordship ever prosper.

(d) *Records of the chancery, 1289–92*

(*Cal. Close Rolls 1288–96*, p. 56; and ibid. pp. 245–6)

Enrolment [Close Roll 17 Edw. I, 1289] of grant by Godfrey, bishop of Worcester, to the king of his land in Wastull in the manor of Alveth', co. Worcester, which the bishop acquired from William de Wasthull, and all the land in Cokton, co. Warwick, which the bishop acquired from Roger de Spineto. Witnesses: sir John de Bello Campo, sir John de Cantilupo, sir John de Langel[eye], sir William le Poer, sir Robert de Bracy, sir Roger Corbet, sir Henry de Ribbesford, knights.

Memorandum, that this charter remains in a box in the chest in which the rolls of chancery are kept at the New Temple, London.

Memorandum, that Master William de Marchia, the king's treasurer, in the nineteenth year of the reign [1290–1], the king then being in Scotland and having with him Robert bishop of Bath and Wells, his chancellor, and the chancery with him, broke by the king's order a chest of rolls of the chancery at the New Temple, London, and examined [*quesivit*] the rolls and all other memoranda in the same, and extracted from it rolls and sent them to the king; and afterwards, upon the arrival of the king and chancellor at London at the feast of St Andrew, in the 20th year of the reign [1291–2], the said treasurer delivered by the hands of Hugh de Notingham, clerk, to John de Langeton new keys for the chest aforesaid, together with two rolls, to wit the patent roll 39 Henry III and the charter roll 22 Henry III, which the treasurer had previously taken out.

(e) *Westminster Hall, 1310*

(*Cal. Close Rolls 1307–13*, p. 326)

Memorandum, that, on Monday before the feast of the Translation of St Thomas the Martyr [Monday, 6 July 1310, 3 Edw. II], Adam de Osgoteby, keeper of the rolls of chancery, delivered the king's great seal, which had been in his custody under the seals of Robert de Bardelby and master John Fraunceis, to the king in the little chapel near the painted chamber, Westminster; who delivered it to Walter, bishop of Worcester, who received it from the king and took oath of office and re-delivered the seal to the said Adam, receiving it from him on the morrow "in the great hall at Westminster at the great bench where the king's chancellors were wont to sit" and opened it and sealed writs with it.

107. The Wiltshire Eyre of 1249: Downton Hundred and Township

(Civil pleas: *Civil Pleas of the Wiltshire Eyre, 1249*, ed. M. T. Clanchy (Devizes, 1971), pp. 32; 36 (No. 24); 57 (No. 118); 59 (No. 126) and 99 (No. 296). Crown pleas: *Crown Pleas of the Wiltshire Eyre, 1249*, ed. C. A. F. Meekings (Devizes, 1961), pp. 152 and 183–7 (Nos 163–74))

Pleas of juries and assizes at Wilton in the county of Wiltshire of the eyre of Henry of Bath and his fellow justices itinerant in the 33rd year of the reign of king Henry son of king John . . . Ralph Cole claimed in the county [court] against Robert Cole ½ virgate of land in Downton [Dudington'] as his right, whereof one Robert father of the aforesaid Ralph was seised in his demesne as of fee and right in the time of the present king by taking profits therefrom to the value etc., and from that Robert the right to that land descended to this Ralph who now lays claim as son and heir, and that such is his right he offers [to prove]. Consequently Robert came to the same county [court] and denied the right of that Robert [Ralph's father] and everything. He put himself on the king's grand assize and claimed that there be a recognition of which of them has the greater right in that land. The county [court] adjudged that a grand assize lay between them. Consequently 4 knights were summoned to be here to elect 12 to make a recognition of the grand assize. Ralph now comes and says that the grand assize between them should not proceed, because he says that they are brothers [born] of one father, so that this Robert is his elder brother and was begotten outside lawful wedlock. Ralph says that the land which he claims against Robert should descend to him by right of inheritance from Robert their father. The county [court] cannot deny this. So to *judgment on the county* [court]. Ralph is told that he may narrate anew against Robert if he wishes. Ralph now comes and narrates against Robert as above.

Robert comes and denies Ralph's right. He readily acknowledges that the aforesaid Robert Cole, father of Ralph and Robert, was seised of that land in his demesne as of fee and that Ralph is his son and heir. But he says that Robert enfeoffed him of that land by his charter, which he proffers and which attests this, so that if anyone else sued him for it, Ralph would have to warrant that land to him.

Ralph comes and readily acknowledges the charter. But he says that the charter should not injure him, because Robert his father died seised of that land in his demesne, so that Robert his brother never had any seisin thereof by that charter during the life of the aforesaid Robert his father. Thereon he puts himself on the country and Robert likewise. So let there be a jury.

The jurors say that Robert Cole did not die seised of that land. They say on the contrary that he enfeoffed Robert his son a long time before his death and that he put him in seisin and made a charter to him thereof. So it is adjudged that Robert is without day and Ralph is in *mercy*.

. . . Gillian who was wife of William Golde claims against Robert the cook $\frac{1}{3}$ of $\frac{1}{3}$ of 1 virgate of land in Downton [Dudington'] as her dower.

Robert came elsewhere and called Nicholas of Haversham[1] to warranty, who now comes and warrants him. Nicholas calls Matthew of Bimberton' to warranty, who comes and warrants him. Matthew knows nothing to say against her having her dower. So it is adjudged that Gillian recovers her seisin against him and Matthew is in *mercy*. Matthew is to make an exchange with Nicholas to the value [of Gillian's claim], because he has none of the land of William Golde, Gillian's former husband, wherefrom she can receive the value of her claim.

. . . Assize of *mort d'ancestor* to declare whether Aline of Downton [Dunton'], mother of Maud daughter of Aline and of Agatha her sister, was seised of 1 messuage

[1] See the next case but one.

in Dunton', which Nicholas of Wyli holds. He comes and they are agreed. Maud and Agatha give ½ mark for licence to agree. The agreement is as follows: Nicholas acknowledges the messuage to be Agatha's and Maud's right, and he has rendered it to them for 20*s*, which they will render him on the octave [6 June] of Trinity by surety of Laurence Aynel'. If they do not do so, they grant that the sheriff may do so from [their] lands.

. . . Walter[1] Goolde claims against Robert the cook ⅓ of 1 virgate of land in Downton [Dudinton'] as his right, into which Robert has no entry except by Nicholas of Haveresham, who unjustly and without judgment disseised William Goolde, Walter's father whose heir he is, after the first [crossing into Brittany, 1 May 1230].

Robert comes and calls Nicholas to warranty, who is present and warrants him. He readily maintains that he did not disseise William, Walter's father, of that land. For he says that William demised that land to one Matthew of Bymerton', who was seised thereof for many years, and later he enfeoffed Nicholas of that land. Walter cannot deny this. So it is adjudged that Robert is without day and Walter is in *mercy*. He is poor.

Pleas of the crown in the county of Wiltshire of the eyre of Henry of Bath and his fellows in the 33rd year of the reign of king Henry son of John
Englishry is presented in this county by three, namely by two on the father's side and one on the mother's side . . .

. . . *The hundred of Downton [Dunton'] comes by twelve*
John Lode was found drowned in the river Avon [Avene] near Stanleg' [? Standlynch]. The first finder, William the miller, does not come because he has died. William le Whyte of Chileton' [? Charlton, in Standlynch] was suspected of the death and imprisoned in Salisbury castle. Afterwards he was committed to bail by the king's writ. Nicholas of Haversham has not produced those to whom he committed the said William nor is he able to name them. So to judgment [on Nicholas]. William le Whyte comes and denies the death and for good [etc.]. The jurors say he is not guilty, so he is acquitted. The twelve jurors presented this matter falsely, so they are in *mercy*.

Later[2] it is testified that William was committed to the underwritten, namely to Walter the miller, William Govare, Walter Palmere, Gilbert de Aqua, Ralph Mody, Ralph Cok, John Foppinch, Gilbert Grant, Geoffrey Bren, Bernard Kanc and Andrew Fogel.

Roger Pygburd was found killed in his bed in Eblesburn'. Susan his wife first found him. She does not come and she was attached by Auger the tithingman of Falerston' with his tithing. So it is in *mercy*. Susan was attached for Roger's death and was committed to the tithings of Bishopstone, Croucheston and Netton and she escaped

[1] See the claim of Gillian, widow of William Golde, the case but one before this.
[2] This postea was added later.

from the custody of these tithings and fled to Bishopstone church, confessed to having killed Roger and *abjured* the realm. She had no chattels. Walter Scut, accused of the said death, does not come. The jurors say he is guilty, so let him be *exacted* and *outlawed*. He was in the tithing of Eblesburn', so it is in *mercy*. His chattels: *7s 6d* whereon [etc.].

Roger de Fonte came to the sheep pen of the bishop of Winchester, and there he trussed up a sheep and tried to carry it away by stealth. Walter the bishop's shepherd, seeing this, chased him to try to take the sheep from him. Roger struck Walter with a staff and Walter retaliated, striking Roger, so that he died at once. Walter comes and fully admits that he struck him, not to kill him but to defend himself from him and to save his lord's sheep, and on this he puts himself on the country.

The jurors say that Roger was a thief and went there to steal the sheep. Walter seeing him chased him and raised the hue and Roger, fearing the hue, ran upon Walter and struck him. Walter, in defence, struck Roger so that he killed him but not by felony, rather in self defence. So Walter is acquitted.

Joan, wife of Roger de Fonte, fled after her husband's death, put herself in Downton [Dunton'] church, admitted herself to be a thief and *abjured* the realm. Her chattels: *5s* whereon [etc.].

William Plance, the son of Robert of Boteham,[1] came to the house of the aforesaid Robert his father in the town of Buteham[1] and carried away two tunics worth 5 shillings and two cloaks [*pallia*] worth 3 shillings and pawned them in the Jewry. Robert comes and makes suit against him. William comes and fully admits that he pawned the tunics and cloaks in the Jewry at Wilton, but he emphatically denies [the larceny, saying] that he did not carry away the tunics and cloaks by stealth but compelled by necessity, since his father Robert would neither keep him nor permit him to enter into service with anyone. He puts himself on the country that he did no felony in the said deed.

The jurors say that William, driven by necessity and great want, pawned the said clothes as has been said by witlessness [*per simplicitatem*] and not by felony. They say that Robert suggested to William that he should appeal Andrew his brother and Robert's son and Maud his [Robert's] wife, as having been with him in stealing the clothes. He did this by fraud, desiring that William, Andrew his son and Maud his wife might be hanged. They say emphatically that William did no felony, so that he is acquitted. And that most wicked father, namely Robert, *let him be taken into custody*.

Hubert the shepherd and Ralph the cook and certain others found nine pennies, namely baselinges, in a moor that is called Monemora. It is testified by the jurors that nothing more was found but the steward of the bishop of Winchester claimed the said *9d* because it was found in the bishop's liberty. Therefore *a discussion* about this.

[1] Bodenham. Robert of Bodenham, a prosperous villein on the manor of Downton, a manor of the bishop of Winchester (*Crown Pleas of the Wiltshire Eyre, 1249*, ed. Meekings, p. 265).

Godfrey the hayward of Britford [is] accused of the death of Walter de Bereford by Agnes, Walter's wife, who appealed him. Godfrey comes. He was committed in bail to Ralph Sabode, John le Sankere, Walter atte Wythye, John le Blund, Walter in la Herne, Hugh Bruning, William atte Pyle, Gilbert Crume, Geoffrey Calveleye, William Hering, William Tylye and Richard Blund, who are all of Britford. Because they did not have him before the justices on the first day, all are in *mercy*. Geoffrey denies the said death and for good [etc.] The jurors say he is guilty. So to judgment. (*Hanged*).

Lucy, wife of Gilbert Morin, comes and appeals Adam le Traitur, in that Adam, on the vigil of St Barnabas the Apostle in the 28th year [10 June 1244] came in Bodenham [Botham] field and there, in robbery, took from her three piglings and gave her a wound in the head an inch long. That he did this wickedly and in felony she offers to prove as the court shall award.

Adam comes and denies the robbery and whatsoever is against the king's peace. He says that in truth he found the pigs in the field in his corn and that he tried to impound them. Lucy came, carrying a staff in her hand and obstructed the impounding. As Lucy tried to strike him on the head he caught the staff in his hand and Lucy, dragging away the staff towards herself, struck herself on the head. On this he puts himself on the country.

The jurors say that Adam did nothing to her in felony nor in robbery nor anything else against the peace etc. So Adam is acquitted, and *let her be taken into custody* for a false appeal.

Concerning defaults etc., they say that Walter de Ambdely, John de Bremlescote, Elias Tolose and William of Bereford did not come on the first day. So all are in *mercy*.

Concerning prises etc., they say that Laurence Aynel received, for the death of John Lude,[1] 8*s* from Andrew Fughel, 8*s*. 4*d* from William Dal, 7*s* 4*d* from Simon the smith, 16*d* from Ralph Pynnel, 12*d* from Walter le Fryssere [and] 12*d* from John Pys; and from Walter Tyrel,[2] for stealing a calf, half a mark. Laurence is present and cannot deny this, so *let him be taken into custody*.

Afterwards he makes a fine of 40*s* by pledges.

Afterwards[3] it is testified by sir Paulin Peyvere that the king had all the aforesaid moneys. So [Laurence is] acquitted thereon.

Margery Pytte comes and appeals William Fucher of the death of her daughter Maud, and she appeals him in that, as Maud was in Downton field, William came wickedly and in felony and against the king's peace and beat Maud and out of malice

[1] Probably the John Lode found drowned (above, in the first of these Downton pleas of the crown). Laurence Aynel or Aygnel was the bailiff of Downton and was accused of official misconduct, not killing.

[2] Possibly the William Torel of the next case but one.

[3] The first postea seems to have been written at the same time as the record; this one seems to have been written afterwards.

maltreated her, so that Maud was ill for six weeks and then died from the beating. That he did this wickedly etc., she offers etc.

William comes and denies the said death and whatsoever is against the king's peace, and for good [etc.].

The jurors say that William found Maud in the field of his lord, the bishop of Winchester, gleaning without permission and because she did this without permission he took his gage and struck her with a little stick. But they say emphatically that she did not die from this. They say that Maud afterwards was in good health and cheerful [*yllaris*] for a long time, whence they say that William is not guilty of the said death. So he is acquitted and *let* Margery *be taken into custody* for her false appeal.

Alard Fughel, accused of the death of Margery his stepsister, Brice the Devonian and Thomas Tripput, accused of the theft of a cow, William Torel,[1] accused of stealing a calf, and Roger Curefegel', accused of larceny, come except for William and Roger and for good [etc.]. The jurors say they are not guilty, so they are acquitted. And they say that a certain Peter de Forda indicted them out of hatred and malice. Peter is present and cannot deny this, so *let him be taken into custody*. They say also that William is guilty, so *let him be exacted and outlawed*. He was in the tithing of Robert le Man in the parson's tithing of Downton, so it is in *mercy*. He had no chattels. They say that Roger is not guilty, so he is acquitted and may return if, etc.

The township of Downton comes by twelve
Edith of Downton appealed Walter Chapun of rape and does not come because she has died. Walter does not come and he was attached by William le Teler of Downton and Anketyl Chapun of the same. So they are in *mercy*. The jurors concealed this matter, so they are all in *mercy*.

108. A prison, *c.* 1269

(*Select Pleas of the Forest*, ed. G. J. Turner (Selden Soc., vol. 13, 1901), p. 50)
From a forest eyre roll for the county of Rutland.

The same Peter [de Neville, chief forester] imprisoned Peter the son of Constantine of Liddington for two days and two nights at Allexton, and bound him with iron chains on suspicion of having taken a certain rabbit in Eastwood; and the same Peter the son of Constantine gave two pence to the men of the aforesaid Peter de Neville who had charge of him to permit him to sit upon a certain bench in the gaol of the same Peter, which is full of water at the bottom.[2]

[1] The same offence and perhaps the same person as Walter Tyrel in the case before last.
[2] Allexton, although in Leicestershire, not Rutlandshire, is near the R. Eye, the county boundary.

109. "Peine forte et dure", 1306 and 1322

"*Peine forte et dure*" (as it came to be known) – the torturing (as it came to be) of men who refused trial by jury – was not a necessary result of loss of faith in the ordeal. The difficulty of the courts in finding a substitute for the ordeal could have been resolved either by outright adoption of trial by jury (its use was being already greatly extended even before the abandonment of the ordeal) or by the development of an inquisitorial procedure (in which neither ordeal nor jury but the judge gave judgment). Both these alternatives were, in fact, experimented with and thought about. Quite certainly considered was the idea of enforcing acceptance of trial by jury. But authority was in the end reluctant to go so far: the statute of Westminster I in 1275 went far enough to declare that trial by jury was the common law of the land (No. 47[1]) but it would not say that men no longer had a right to refuse it. For this the general opinion was evidently not yet ready: so, instead, the statute legalised force to compel men not to refuse. The intention and the expected consequences of refusal are clear from official and unofficial evidence alike. Passage (a) below is the Exchequer's record of a decision of the king's council in the exchequer on 25 July 1306 and (b) is an extract under the year 1322 from a chronicle.

Why anyone should still refuse a jury is capable of a rational explanation. A "notorious felon" (in the phrase of the statute) could expect, if he pleaded, to be convicted and hanged, his lands would escheat to his lord and his goods and chattels would be forfeited to the crown: if he died under *peine forte et dure* he died untried and unconvicted and his possessions were saved for his heirs.

(a)

(*Select Cases in . . . King's Bench, Edward I*, ed. G. O. Sayles, II, p. clv)

Staff'

Memorandum that Henry Spigurnel, one of the justices assigned to deliver the king's gaols in several counties, now here before the king's council on the twenty-fifth day of July [1306] records that as he and his fellows etc. at the delivery of the king's gaol at Stafford, half a year and more ago now, found in the gaol a certain prisoner indicted for various felonies against the peace etc., and he refusing to clear himself of them before them by jury[2] in accordance with the law and custom of the realm, they condemned him, as is customary, to the *peine forte et dure* and handed him over for custody etc. to John de Dene, sheriff of the aforesaid county, and he, the justice, lately coming again to deliver the said gaol, they found the aforesaid prisoner alive: for which reason they manifestly have a dark suspicion of the sheriff etc., to wit, that he personally or by his men served food and drink to the prisoner otherwise than he ought to have done to the prejudice of the king's crown etc. as it has not hitherto been seen in a like case that anyone could exist for so long etc. on a diet as severe as that which the *peine forte et dure* requires in a case of this kind. On which account it is agreed by the said king's council that a royal writ attested by the aforesaid justice be made for attaching the aforesaid sheriff to be before the king on the octave of Michaelmas to answer the lord king on the aforesaid matters. And on this a royal writ of the exchequer is to be delivered to the usher for transmission to the coroners of the aforesaid county.

(b)

(*Life of Edward the Second by the so-called Monk of Malmesbury*, ed. and trans. N. Denholm-Young (1957), p. 128)

The customary punishment, indeed, for those mute of malice is carried out thus throughout the realm. The prisoner shall sit on the cold, bare floor, dressed only in the thinnest of shirts, and pressed with as great a weight of iron as his wretched body

[1] cap 12
[2] *per patriam*

can bear. His food shall be a little rotten bread, and his drink cloudy and stinking water. The day on which he eats he shall not drink, and the day on which he has drunk he shall not taste bread. Only superhuman strength survives this punishment beyond the fifth or sixth day.

110. Sanctuary and Abjuration of the realm, and outlawry

(a) *Fleta on sanctuary and abjuration*

(*Fleta*, II, ed. and trans. H. G. Richardson and G. O. Sayles (Selden Soc., vol. 72, 1955), pp. 76–7, being Fleta, Bk I, ch. 29)

There are some felons who, when they are liable to arrest, flee to a church or some other sacred place, whence they must not be drawn or thrust forth, lest laymen who draw them forth incur sentence of excommunication or clergy who thrust them forth incur the taint of irregularity by their rash act. For it has been enacted that the English church shall have its rights and franchises unimpaired and also that the peace of the church and the land shall be preserved inviolate and that equal justice shall be dispensed to all men alike. It is behoveful therefore that such felons should be left in peace in the church and that the coroners should straightway come to them, nor is there any other alternative than that they either come out of the dedicated place to stand their trial, should any man wish to proceed against them, or else that they acknowledge the misdeed, on account of which they seek the protection of the church. And it has been granted and enacted that such fugitives shall not stay in the church for more than forty days, and should they do so, food shall thereafter be denied them, so that they shall go forth voluntarily and seek what formerly they have refused with scorn, and in this event they are denied the privilege of abjuration. And he who supplies food to them after forty days shall be treated as the king's enemy and a reckless breaker of the peace and deservedly shall be so esteemed. Should a man, however, beg leave to go forth within the forty days the coroners shall come, and before them he must confess his misdeed and ask that, on account of his felony, he may be allowed to abjure the realm. And when he has acknowledged his misdeed, he shall swear as follows:

Hear this, ye coroners and other men, that I, so and so, for such and such a deed that I have wickedly committed, will go forth from the realm of England, and hither will I not return again without leave of the king and his heirs. So help me God etc.

And when his port or passage has been chosen, there shall be allowed to him certain days' journeys, more or less, according as the strength or weakness of his body shall require, and those shall be notified to him in writing or he may swear (and it is better so) that he will not make stay in any place for two nights together and that he will not stray from the direct road until he depart the realm. And then it shall be forbidden him to leave the king's highway until he shall have found passage. And ungirt and unshod, with head uncovered, in tunic alone, as though he were to be hanged on the gallows, he shall set out, with a cross clasped in his hands. And when he come to the sea, if he find no passage, he must plunge in up to the neck and, having raised the hue, he must remain on the shore until he find passage. And if he stray in the least from the roadway, by night or day, or if he return without leave, he may be beheaded, with impunity, unless he be arrested, in which event he must be committed to gaol. And likewise, if, after the forty days, [a fugitive] can be arrested outside the church, deservedly there is denied him any further privilege of abjuration.

There are, however, certain timid men who seek the protection of the church, although they have not committed a felony. In this event they will be well advised to acknowledge that they have slain someone whom they will be able to produce afterwards alive and well, so that they may be in a position to sue for the king's grace should they require it, and therefore diligent examination is necessary in abjurations and voluntary acknowledgments of felonies, lest they be actuated by fear or despair of life.

Those who commit sacrilege should not be protected by the church, but they must be judged and degraded by the clergy. And the same is to be said of apostate clerks, who, upon conviction, shall be straightway degraded by the clergy and then burnt by the lay power.

(b) *A case of sanctuary and abjuration*

(*Bedfordshire Coroners' Rolls*, ed. R. F. Hunnisett (Beds. Hist. Rec. Soc.), XLI (Streatley, 1961), No. 237)

Manshead Hundred. On 20 April [1276] John son of William of Westfields of Windridge, Hertfordshire, a hayward in Houghton Regis in the liberty of Eaton Bray, was arrested on suspicion of theft, imprisoned by Houghton Regis, escaped from the prison of that township and fled to Houghton Regis church. On 27 April he abjured the realm according to the custom of the kingdom before P. le Loreng, coroner, Houghton Regis, Totternhoe, Tilsworth and Chalgrave, and the king's bailiff, and was assigned the port of Dover, because he confessed before the coroner and townships that he was a thief, having robbed sir William of Gorhambury at Westwick, Hertfordshire, and he refused to surrender to the king's peace. On the same day he set forth on his journey, was followed by Houghton Regis after fleeing from the highway and was beheaded in the hue and the suit of the whole township.

Inquiry was made by the said townships concerning John's chattels. They said that he had sold 4 sheep to Matthew son of Stephen of Thorn of the parish of Houghton Regis for 4*s* 1*d*, which sale John recognised and warranted; he said that he had bought these sheep, but did not have his warranty nor was he known; the sheep were therefore delivered to Houghton Regis at the said price. Matthew found pledges, Richard son of William and John Alwynne of Thorn. [John] also had 2 sheets and a carpet worth 2*s*., a horn, a bow with 2 arrows, and a belt with a knife worth 6½*d*, which were delivered to Houghton Regis. They said that he had chattels at Dunstable, and the coroners of that liberty were ordered to inquire concerning them.

[At the eyre Houghton Regis was made answerable for John's escape. His chattels, worth 6*s* 7½*d*, were forfeited and the said 4 townships with Battlesden were amerced for appraising them falsely. It was also ordered that inquiry be made concerning his chattels in Dunstable. (J.1.1/10, m. 37)]

(c) *A returned outlaw*

(*South Lancashire in the Reign of Edward II, as illustrated by the Pleas at Wigan recorded in Coram Rege Roll No. 254*, ed. G. H. Tupling (Chetham Soc., Manchester, 1949), pp. 25–6)

William le Kyng of Rothelan [Rhuddlan] and Robert de Haldeleghes, having been taken for the death of John son of John de Clayton who was killed at Meluere [Mellor] on Saturday in Easter week in the sixteenth year of the present king's reign [2 April 1323], whereof they were indicted before the king now come. Both of them, being asked separately how they wish to clear themselves of the aforesaid felony, say that they are clerks and cannot answer thereon without their ordinaries. Thereupon comes Robert de Cliderhou, rector of the church of Wygan, acting as deputy for [Roger] the bishop of Coventry and Lichfield etc., and craves them as clerks etc. And in order that it may be known in what capacity they ought to be handed over to the ordinary, let the truth thereof be investigated by the country etc. The jurors say upon their oath that at another time before Robert de Lathum and Henry de Hambury, the present lord king's justices appointed to hear and determine a certain felony of the death of Henry de Biri, knight, the aforesaid John son of John was indicted of force and aid at the death of the aforesaid Henry de Bury; and that when proceedings were taken against the same John before the aforesaid justices, he was put in exigent to be outlawed, because he did not come before the justices to answer the charge, and afterwards he was outlawed. For this reason the same John son of John left the country for a long time, for almost six years. Later he returned to the country and came to Meluere where the aforesaid William le Kyng happened to meet the same John. And because the same John had been previously outlawed in the county court, and also because he had aided and abetted the death of a certain William de Farington, uncle of the aforesaid William le Kyng, the latter asked him to make amends and surrender himself to the lord king's peace; but the aforesaid John immediately raised his staff intending to strike the aforesaid William with it; and when the aforesaid William took up a certain crossbow and drew it with intent to shoot him, the aforesaid John dropped his staff and drew out a certain misericord[1] in order to kill the same William Kyng with it if he could, and the aforesaid William took out his knife. Thus they fought together and each of them struck the other, with the result that the aforesaid John was there killed by the aforesaid William le Kyng. And the aforesaid Robert de Haldeleghes was there in force and aid at the aforesaid death. On being asked whether the aforesaid William le Kyng and Robert could have taken the aforesaid John alive or not, the jurors say that they could not. The rolls of the coroner of the aforesaid county were thereupon examined and it was found therein that the aforesaid John son of John was outlawed, as is aforesaid; and [because] it is not in accordance with right that anyone of the king's realm etc. should suffer judgment for the death of anyone who has been outlawed and placed outside the law and has not been restored to the law, nor is willing to surrender himself to the lord king's peace, it is decided that the aforesaid William le Kyng and Robert de Haldeleghes may go quit thereof. [Margin: twice]

[1] dagger

111. A sheriff's office, 1278

(a)

(Helen M. Cam, *The Hundred and the Hundred Rolls*, pp. 65–6)

In 1273 Henry Malemeyns was ordered to deliver to his successor as sheriff of Kent, William de Hevre, "the county with the rolls and writs, the castle with the armour and victuals, and the hundred with its appurtenances" (*Cal. Pat. Rolls 1272–81*, p. 7). G. O. Sayles has discovered earlier references to such transfers (*Select Cases . . . King's Bench under Edward I*, III, p. xcvi, n. 1), and Helen Cam, direct evidence in an indenture between an outgoing and an incoming sheriff.

Be it remembered that on the Wednesday next before the feast of All Saints in the sixth year of king Edward's reign [Wednesday, 26 October 1278] Giles of Berkeley handed over to sir Roger of Burghull the county of Hereford and the castle with its appurtenances.

Also the statutes under the seal of the lord king and the letters patent as to the keeping of the new statutes. Also five writs to be returned on the morrow of Martinmas [specifying the names of the litigants], six writs to be returned on the octave of Martinmas, four writs to be returned on the quinzaine of Martinmas, one writ of *novel disseisin* and some writs of *mort d'ancestor*.

Also two prisoners; Osbert of Lugwardine who is appealed of homicide and has been arrested under the king's writ, and Lucy Baldwin who was convicted in the hundred court of Irchenfield of complicity in the death of Roger Oleyn and Wervella his wife.

Also the distresses taken for the summons of the exchequer, namely three beasts of Walter of Bastwick, taken for an amercement . . . and for having a writ; four beasts of Adam of Wygmore . . . for a Jew's debt; five pieces of Bruel, one of Brimenmow, and one of Russel; and one horse of Richard Manwood's, taken for tallage.

Also the rolls of the county and of the hundred of Irchenfield, with writs touching them.

[This does not suggest an office as big or as busy as that of the sheriff of Bedfordshire half a century later, which over seventeen months handled very nearly 2,000 writs (Cam, op. cit. p. 74, and G. H. Fowler, *Rolls from the Office of the Sheriff of Beds and Bucks 1332–1334* (Aylesbury, 1929)), but it is the same kind of office and a thirteenth-century sheriff already had clerical assistance: "And because the aforesaid business [a case in the King's Bench] cannot be determined without Henry Buckerell, clerk of the sheriff of Devon, who is appointed for the return of writs in the aforesaid county . . ." (Sayles, *Select Cases . . . King's Bench under Edward I*, II, p. 17).]

(b)

(*Parliamentary Writs*, I (1827), pp. 214–15)

The return for Northumberland (dated 22 September 1278) to the king's writ of 26 June 1278, for distraint of knighthood (see No. 51 above). The return for Surrey and Sussex (*Parl. Writs*, I, pp. 216–218) is made without distinguishing tenants in chief from the rest, and with six, instead of four, mainpernors per person.

The names of those distrained to assume the arms of a knight in the county of Northumberland in the sixth year of the reign of king Edward by writ of the lord king.

Of those who hold of the lord king in chief and have 20 pounds worth of land

Robert de Somervill his mainpernors	Walter de Witton, clerk Bartholomew de Wyndegatis Roger son of Andrew de Witton William de Camera	
Thomas de Dyveleston his mainpernors	Robert de Hydewyn Robert Wautlyn William de Slavely and William de Tyndall	
Robert de Glantedon his mainpernors	John de Esselinton John de Brempton William de Rodum John son of John de Edlingham	
Nicholas de Graham his mainpernors	Simon de Hedreslawe Walter his son William de Heddon Ralph son of Cecily of the same Robert son of Warin William Clerk of Belford	
Robert Taillebois his mainpernors	Thomas Scot de Warton Richard de Chartenay Patrick de Tossan John son of Michael	
Richard de Chartenay his mainpernors	Thomas Scot de Warton Robert Tailboys Patrick de Tossan Thomas de Heppehale	This Richard does not hold of the king but of Robert Tailboys
Walter Surteys his mainpernors	John Scot de Newcastle Peter de Faudon Ralph de Essingdon' John de Benewell	
pauper John de Eslington his mainpernors	Robert de Glantedon William de Glantedon John de Brempton Benedict de Glantedon	

Of the others who do not hold of the lord king in chief and have 20 pounds worth of land

Robert de Maners his mainpernors	John son of Tyock' de Ethale William Scot of the same Gilbert de Crukum—+ Adam Futur' of the same

Stephen de . . . his mainpernors	William Beupund de Beirmor William son of Isabella of the same Thomas son of Patrick Hugh son of Robert of the same
William de Ros his mainpernors	John de Oggil Robert de Pennebyr' William de Espell' and William de Stingelawe de Sindrum—+
Adam de Selby his mainpernors	Nicholas de Backeworth Hugh de Bacwrth Robert Tenement de Storton Thomas Gentil of the same Thomas son of John of the same William son of Clerk of the same
Maurice de Euurth his mainpernors	William de Yerdehill Thomas Baret de Ewrth Simon de Euurth Robert son of Thefania of the same
James de Houburne his mainpernors	Philip de Houburne Hugh son of Richard of the same William son of Henry of the same Hugh Modi of the same
. . .	Thomas de Dichend Richard de Dichend his brothers William de Dichend Richard le Forest of the same
. . .	Ralph de Olecestr' Odoullus his brother Robert son of William de Olecestr' Roger son of Adam of the same
Thomas de Rock' his mainpernors	John del Schele Ivo Rokard de Rock' John son of Ralph of the same Thomas Cissor' of the same
Thomas de Karleolo his mainpernors	William son of le Keu de Swarland Roger Uthorn Walter de Wyte Roger de Stanteby
Richard de Horsely his mainpernors	Simon de Plescetis Thomas de Cleuhill Ralph de Essingdon Walter de Hereford

Walter de Edlingham his mainpernors	Gilbert son of John Waldeif John son of John de Edlingham Adam Cl'us of the same Henry Tebaud of the same
John de Hilburn' his mainpernors	Richard de Crancestr' Peter de Emildon Robert de Fauldon Robert de Embirton
. . .	Richard de Wetwang Alexander de Broxefeld Michael de Rock John de Kertingdon
Roger Maudut his mainpernors	William de Bokingfeld William Blunvill William de Horsley Richard son of Sibyl de Eschete
Roger de Coygners his mainpernors	Robert de Botland John de Oggill Gilbert de Walington William Faudon
John de Belshowe his mainpernors	Walter Scot de Waltedon Robert his brother Richard de Denum John de Cokeman
Ralph de Essingdon his mainpernors	Roger de Woderington Peter de Faudon Gilbert de Walington John de Quinteley
Roger de Woderington his mainpernors	Peter de Faudon Ralph de Essingdon William de Echewick Robert Wautlyn
Simon de Pleseys his mainpernors	Philip de Keirwik Walter de Hereford Ralph de Essingden Roger de Woderington
Peter de Faudon his mainpernors	Roger de Woderington Ralph de Essingden William de Echwike Adam de Kynton

John de Ferlington his mainpernors	John de Apilton Adam de Donigton William Blundel William son of John de Brinklawe
Adam Baret his mainpernors	Richard de Sancto Petro de Berewik Richard de Killingworth William de Echewik Roger Baret de Borndon
Robert de Menevill his mainpernors	Ralph Bover de Milleburn John Bover his brother Robert son of John de Milleburne John son of Robert of the same
Thomas de Blencanshop his mainpernors	William de Ros Roger Baret de Throckelawe Richard de Doucestre Richard de Sancto Petro
William de Swineborne his mainpernors	Nicholas de Swineburne his brother William de Routhclyve Robert de Chilbeches William de Tindall
. . .	William son of Laurence Walter Beufrere Alan son of Alan de Swineburne Robert son of Alice of the same
. . .	William de Swynburne Nicholas de Swyneburne William de Routheclyue William son of Laurence
. . .	William de Swethorp Richard de Swethorp John Cole Ralph Plassage de Swinborne
. . .	Richard de Bocland junior William de Essindon Richard Freinde de Gunwarton Nicholas son of Ralph of the same
. . .	Robert de Walis William de Swyneburne Richard de Rucostr' William de Ruthclyue

Philip de Craudon his mainpernors	Nicholas de Schiringham Richard Tysun German de Hothton Peter de Haulton

This enrolment was made in the full county of Northumberland on Thursday the morrow of St Matthew the Apostle in the 6th year of the reign of king Edward [Thursday, 22 September 1278]. In witness of which William de Middelton' and Walter de Camhow, knights, set their seals to the present roll along with the seal of the sheriff.

112. The sheriff's gaol

(a)

(*Cal. Close Rolls 1307–13*, p. 167)

Sheriffs were responsible for guarding those suspected of felony. As early as 1166 they had been instructed in all counties where there was not a gaol to have one built. This scheme for county gaols was, however, slow of realisation, especially where, as here in the case of Warwickshire and Leicester, a sheriff had charge of two counties. cf. R. B. Pugh, *Imprisonment in Medieval England* (Cambridge, 1968), ch. 4. This is in strong contrast to the increasing pressure, especially in the later part of our period, on such prison accommodation as was available (cf. Pugh, op. cit. pp. 30-6). A sheriff's reluctance to accept custody of a suspect (cf. No. 59, c. 4, above "without making difficulty") is conceivable; even his lapses from official rectitude ought to be regarded in the light of his difficulties (see H. M. Cam, *Hundred and the Hundred Rolls*, pp. 67–74).

1309, 2 August, Westminster

To the sheriff of Leicester. Order to cause all prisoners hereafter made in co. Leicester to be led to the prison of Leicester, and not to send them to the prison of Warwick, the late king having ordained[1] for the easement of the men of the county of Leicester, with the consent of Thomas, earl of Lancaster, that a prison should be made in Leicester for prisoners from the same county, and the present king having ordered that the said prison, which was not then completed, should be finished as quickly as possible, so that no prisoner should be taken out of that county to Warwick, the said prison of Leicester being now well and securely made.

(b) *A problem*

(*The Mirror of Justices* (Selden Soc., VII), p. 33)

Whatever credit one may give to his views, the author of the *Mirror* is here drawing attention (as he undoubtedly meant to) to a problem of his time: how to ensure the keep of people in prison. The general principle was that they should keep themselves. But there was no single, regular, reliable machinery for ensuring even this in practice. Here is what the author of the *Mirror* proposes.

It is all he proposes. The problem of those who cannot keep themselves and die in prison he does not mention.[2]

All persons indicted before the coroners, accessories as well as principals, are to be taken on the order of the coroners by the sheriffs, and the principals are to be kept, and the accessories delivered to mainpernors. And in their presence, and in that of

[1] in the Lincoln parliament of 1301 (see *Cal. Close Rolls 1296–1302*, p. 428, and *Cal. Pat. Rolls 1301–7*, p. 477). The lapse of time will be noted.

[2] though those sin mortally who let them (*Mirror*, op. cit. p. 24)

the sheriffs, their movables and immovables are to be taken into the hands of the king; and by lawful extent and division these lands and movables are to be delivered to the townships, so that they may find therefrom for keep of prisoners and for their necessary retinue a reasonable sustenance, and may answer for the remainder thereof to the king, saving every right to the principals if they be acquitted, and to the accessories when mainprised.

(c) *An administrative accident*

(*Cal. Pat. Rolls 1292–1301*, p. 161)

1295, 8 June

Commission to William de Ormesby and Roger de Burton to deliver York gaol of all prisoners, as it appears that when the king, by reason of the disturbance by the Welsh, superseded the holding of further pleas by the justices in eyre in the county of York until further order, many persons indicted on that eyre were by judgment of the justices put in exigent, and upon the rumour thereof surrendered to York gaol, where a great multitude died of hunger and the residue in custody there remain in danger of death.

113. A sheriff's difficulties, 1307

(Printed and trans. by G. O. Sayles, *Select Cases in . . . King's Bench, Edward I*, III, pp. 194–6 [French])

A bill put forward before the lord king's council at Northampton on behalf of William of Chellaston, sheriff of Nottingham and Derby, in these words:

Derbyshire

Because it was testified before the sheriff of Nottingham and Derby by sundry people and by his bailiffs that sir Thomas Folejambe was accustomed to make rescue and offer resistance to the king's ministers and bailiffs who wished to distrain him for debts and other things due to the king, the aforesaid sheriff on Thursday[1] after the feast of the Assumption of our Lady in the first year of the reign of our lord the king Edward, son of king Edward, took with him his clerks, Giles de la Forth, our lord king's bailiff of the Peak, John the gaoler, the king's bailiff at fee, and others and came to Tideswell to make distraint upon the aforesaid Thomas for the debts he owes the king, in accordance with what was enjoined upon him by the king who is dead and as the present king has enjoined upon him by writ of his privy seal. Because he did not find as regards the aforesaid Thomas any distress save sheep, he went looking for another distress from prime until nones, and for lack of other distress he then caused his sheep which he found to be taken. And while he was elsewhere, there came people, who are still unknown, and rescued the said sheep and drove them away no one knew where. And the sheriff, when he heard this, caused the hue and cry to be raised from the place where the said sheep were rescued up to the vill and through the vill of Tideswell, as the vill would be able to testify, but the people of the vill would not come

[1] 17 August 1307

at the hue and cry as they ought to do. The sheriff was then told that the forenamed sir Thomas had other sheep in a sheepfold outside the vill. The sheriff went there and found some of sir Thomas's sheep, and his[1] men went into the sheepfold and would not allow the sheriff to have the sheep as a distress but held the sheepfold against him and against the king's peace by force and arms. Wherefore the sheriff ordered them through the constables of the peace of the said vill of Tideswell to come to him as to the king's sheriff like men of peace, and they would not do it. Wherefore the sheriff, in order to assemble more people to witness his action and to fulfil the king's command and preserve his estate and his peace, raised the hue and cry by horn again from the said sheepfold up to the vill of Tideswell and through the same vill, and still scarcely anyone wanted to come at the hue and cry. And whilst the sheriff was doing this, sir Thomas came to the said sheepfold and harshly abused those of the sheriff's men whom he found and others whom he found waiting at the said sheepfold so that the sheep and the men in the sheepfold should not be removed without being attached in due manner. Thereupon the sheriff came and asked sir Thomas whether he avowed the outrage that was done. And sir Thomas demanded of the sheriff by what warrant he had done this, and the sheriff showed him the present king's writ under his privy seal. And sir Thomas, [? biting his nails[2]] on his palfrey, read the writ and looked at the seal and said that he knew it well, and further said, "A fig for that! Produce another warrant." And the sheriff said that this and another warrant he had were sufficient for him, and he further asked whether he would hand over the distress and whether he avowed the outrage that his men had done. And sir Thomas said that he certainly avowed it and that he would have no distress there. And the sheriff said, "For the avowal and because you refuse to allow any distress, sir Thomas, I attach you on behalf of the king as a man who is against the king's peace," and he put his wand, which he as bailiff had in his hand, on his shoulder. And sir Thomas refused to be attached. Wherefore the sheriff caused the hue and cry by horn and mouth to be raised a third time, and in this way the day was continued from nones until the evening, when sir Thomas, on the advice of some people after he had been advised a long time, surrendered himself to the sheriff, and his three men who were in the sheepfold and his sheep who were kept in the same sheepfold, whereupon the sheriff asked him whether he had any other distress to hand over instead of his sheep so that his sheep could be delivered to him. And sir Thomas said that he had no other distress.

114. "Not guilty", 1266

(*Cal. Pat. Rolls 1258–66*, pp. 668, 677, 633)

1266

Commission to Gilbert de Preston to enquire by jury of Kent touching a complaint by Scoland, parson of the church of Stanes [Stone, co. Kent], that, whereas since disturbers of the peace lately came to Stanes and killed Andrew, vicar of Stanes there, certain enemies of the said Scoland, through hatred, charge him with taking part in the said killing that so they may defraud him of his right to the said church.

[1] i.e. sir Thomas's men

[2] *ungelant*

1266
Notification that the king has learned by inquisition made by Gilbert de Preston that, whereas Thomas, parson of the church of Fredesbyry [Frindsbury, co. Kent], and Abel his brother, parson of the church of Esse [Ash, co. Kent], and many others were at dinner with Scoland, parson of the church of Stanes, at Stanes, it happened that William the clerk, who carried the holy water of Stanes, was passing in the high way of the town, and there came two grooms who were with the said Thomas and Abel and assaulted the said William, who for fear fled to the house of Andrew, vicar of the church of Stanes, complaining of the assault of the said grooms, and the said vicar, hearing this, went out of his house with a falchion[1] drawn and struck one of the grooms on the right side of the head and almost cut off the thumb of the other groom. And when it came to the ears of Thomas and Abel that their men were thus wounded, they forthwith went out of the house of the said Scoland and went to the vicar's house, entered the house, and assaulted him, and the said Thomas took a pickaxe[2] from the hands of a groom who was with the vicar, and struck the vicar on the head as far as the brain, so that he died of the blow. And when the noise of this deed came to the ears of Scoland, he wondered much where Thomas and Abel were and went out of his house and found neighbours standing before the door of the vicar and asked what was the matter, and when they told him, he was much grieved and began to weep, and so returned home; and that the said deed was not perpetrated by the procurement of the said Scoland or by his assent.

1266, 28 August
Pardon to Scoland, parson of the church of Stanes, for the death of Andrew, sometime vicar of the said church; as it appears by inquisition made by Gilbert de Preston that he is not guilty thereof.

115. A crime unpunished, 1288

(Trans. G. O. Sayles, *Select Cases . . . King's Bench . . . Edward I*, I, pp. 176–7)

When crimes came to court normally by presentment, indictment or "appeal" (accusation), it was a question under what conditions the king could take action in criminal proceedings. The matter is discussed by G. O. Sayles in *Select Cases in the Court of King's Bench under Edward I*, III, pp. l–liii. The question was complicated by the impact of the growing body of statutes on the common law and the following case illustrates both the question and the complication: a man appealing *coram rege* against conviction in the eyre for rape and getting off scot-free on the ground that the offence was committed in 1284 before the king had suit in such a case. The astuteness of this appeal is seen if the statutes Westminster I (1275), c. 13 (No. 47 above) and Westminster II (1285), c. 34 (No. 57 above), are compared, but it succeeded. cf. Pollock and Maitland, *Hist. of Engl. Law*, II, pp. 490–1, and nn.

Word was sent to Solomon of Rochester and his fellows that, because the lord the king for some definite reasons wanted to be certified about the record of a certain presentment made before the same justices, lately on eyre in the county of Sussex, for which the same justices put Walter Bek in exigent, they should search

[1] *falcione*
[2] *hachiam a pik*

their rolls and without delay send for the aforesaid record and process to the king clearly and openly under their seal. And the justices sent their record in these words:

The jurors of the hundred of Rotherbridge present that Walter Bek, knight, about the quinzaine of St John the Baptist in the twelfth year, before a statutory penalty was enacted,[1] met Emma, daughter of Robert le Brid, aged ten years, between the vill of Petworth and Rotherbridge and threw her on the ground and lay upon her and forcibly raped her against her will. And he is now called and does not come. Therefore the sheriff is ordered to take him and safely etc. Afterwards at the end of the eyre the sheriff testifies that the aforesaid Walter is not to be found in his bailiwick etc., but has taken himself off. And the jurors, asked if they suspect the aforesaid Walter of the aforesaid deed, say that they do. Therefore let him be exacted and outlawed. He had no chattels nor was he in a tithing because a free man etc.

Afterwards the aforesaid Walter came here on this day and freely surrendered to the king's peace and prison. And asked why he caused the aforesaid record to come here, he says that it seems to him that the aforesaid justices in their eyre aforesaid did not rightly proceed to judgment in adjudging him to be put in exigent for that act, an act which must have been done before the statute when the lord king was not wont at that time to have suit in a case of that kind, as appears in the record, wherefore he prays remedy of that process. And after the aforesaid record and process had been read and understood by the lord king's council, because it seemed to the lord king's council that no one was wont to be put in exigent for a deed of this kind before the statute, especially as the lord king had no suit in a case of that kind, it is awarded that judgment was not rightly reached in adjudging him to be put in exigent, as aforesaid, and that it be altogether annulled and considered void etc. And Walter is to go thereof without day etc.

116. A model judgment, 1302

(*Rot. Parl.*, I, 140, trans. Pollock and Maitland, *History of English Law*, II, pp. 395–6)

William and Margaret Paynel sued for her dower as widow, by an earlier marriage, of John de Camoys. It was not contested that Margaret had deserted her husband for William, and had married the latter after John's death in 1298. Had petitioned in the "Articuli super Cartas" parliament of 1300, but adjourned to next parliament; this was the Lincoln parliament of 1301, but it too adjourned them. The parliament of 1302 delivered judgment (it is from the record of the 1302 parliament that we learn about 1300 and 1301). The case fell under the Statute of Westminster II (1285), c. 34 (No. 57 above). It was dismissed. The judgment (Pollock and Maitland, op. cit. II, pp. 394–6; D. M. Stenton, *English Woman in History*, pp. 48–9) is a model of its kind for the "measured dignity with which the judges set aside the plaintiff's claim" (D. M. Stenton, p. 49). Maitland calls it "the most elaborately reasoned judgment of the king's court that has come down to us from Edward I's day" (Pollock and Maitland, op. cit. II, p. 395).

Besides Stat. Westm. II (1285), c. 34, the paragraph on "Divorce and the temporal law" in Pollock and Maitland, op. cit. II, pp. 394–5 is essential background reading.

Whereas William and Margaret can not deny that Margaret in the lifetime of her husband John went off and abode with William, altogether relinquishing her husband John, as plainly appears because she never in the lifetime of her said husband raised any objection, and raises none now, either in her own person or by

[1] Stat. Westm. II (1285), c. 34

another in any manner whatsoever, but by way of making plain her original and spontaneous intention and continuing the affection which in her husband's lifetime she conceived for the said William, she has since John's death allowed herself to be married to the said William; And whereas William and Margaret say and show nothing to prove that the said John in his lifetime ever received her back as reconciled; And whereas it appears by the said writing which they have produced that the said Margaret was granted to the said William by the demise of the said John to remain with William for ever; And whereas it is not needful for the king's court to betake itself to an inquest by the country about such matters as the parties can not deny and which manifestly appear to the court, or about such matters as the parties have urged or admitted in pleading; And whereas it is more probable and to be more readily presumed in the king's court and in every other that, if a man's wife in the lifetime of her husband, of her own free will without objection or refusal, abides with another man, she is lying in adultery rather than in any due or lawful fashion, and this more especially when there follows so clear a declaration of her original intent as this, namely, that when her husband is dead she marries that other man: – Therefore it seems to the court that in the face of so many and such manifest evidences, presumptions and proofs, and the admissions of William and Margaret, there is no need to proceed to an inquest by the country in the form offered by them, and that for the reasons aforesaid Margaret by the form of the said statute ought not to be admitted or heard to demand her dower: And therefore it is considered that William and Margaret do take nothing by their petition but be in mercy for their false claim.

117. The *Dictum* of Kenilworth in the courts, 1276

(*Cal. Close Rolls 1272–9*, p. 333)

To master Roger de Seyton and his fellows, justices in eyre at the Tower of London. Order to cause to be observed in their eyre the following provisions made by the late king, the present king, and his council and others who had agreed[1] with the late king at Marleberge: that if appeal or complaint of robbery and breach of the peace or homicide should be made before justices in eyre or of other offences in the time of the war against any who were against the late king or against others, or if presentments of such offences should be made as are wont to be made at the *capitula* of the crown, no one should lose life or limb or incur the penalty of perpetual imprisonment on these grounds, but that justice should be done in another manner concerning damages or things lost or carried off and trespasses according to the discretion of the late king's justices, and moreover that the contents of the *Dictum* of Kenilleworth should be diligently observed, and that the justices should have in all their eyres a transcript of the *Dictum*, so that the said king's justices should do nothing concerning those things that had been determined or ought to be determined by other justices of the said king, without special order from the said king if he should enjoin anything upon them. They are to know that the war began on April 4, in the 48th year of the

[1] *convenerant*

late king's reign [4 April 1264], when the same king went with his army from Oxford to Northampton with banners displayed, and that it lasted continuously until September 16, in the 49th year [16 September 1265], when at Winchester, after the battle of Evesham, he caused his peace to be confirmed and proclaimed in the presence of the barons who had come thither. It was provided that no one should lose life or limb for robberies or homicides or other things done under the guise of war by those who were against the late king from 4 June, in the 47th year of his reign [4 June 1263], when they first, going through the land with banners displayed, committed robberies, homicides, and imprisonments on persons ecclesiastical and secular, until the said time when the said king went with his army from Oxford to Northampton. Concerning other things that were not done under guise of war during that time, [it was decided that] that time should be regarded as a time of peace. From the time aforesaid when he caused his peace to be strengthened and confirmed at Winchester, the law should run as in time of peace it was wont to run; provided that for those who were at Axeholm or at Kenill[eworth], or in the Isle of Ely, or at Cestrefeld or afterwards at Southwark[1] there should be observed fully their peace as they ought to have it, whether by the *Dictum* of Kenil[leworth] or by their privileges of the peace granted to them. Concerning those who were with the earl of Gloucester in the last disturbance, the peace made between the late king and the earl shall be observed, so that from the time when the earl went from Wales to London until the day when he went from the city aforesaid, justices should not proceed against him or against those who were in his peace, and this provision is to be understood of him only. Concerning depredations made on both sides during the time aforesaid, there should be observed what is contained in the peace made between the late king and the said earl.

118. The Household Ordinance of 13 November 1279

(Tout, *Chapters in Mediaeval Administrative History*, II, pp. 158–63 [French])

"The first royal ordinance concerning the government of the household that is now extant since the *Constitutio Domus Regis* of the late Norman period" (Tout), but not a systematic survey or a complete picture. It does not, for instance, bring in the king's chamber. It lists the chief officers (not including the chamberlain) and ordains on particular questions of organisation and working. Thus, besides detailed instructions upon accounting, the great wardrobe is (a matter of historical interest considering the enormous expansion of the great wardrobe in the war-years at the end of the century) most definitely subordinated to the wardrobe, and the running of the queen's household is geared to the running of the king's.

A modern description, based upon this ordinance, is Tout, op. cit., II, pp. 27–59: this may be supplemented by S. B. Chrimes, *Introduction to the Administrative History of Mediaeval England* (Oxford, 1952), pp. 129–53.

The ordinance of the king's household, made by the command [of the king] at Westminster on St Brice's day in the seventh year of king Edward's reign, concerning the stewards and the other officers in his household.

Stewards

Sir Hugh Fitzotho remains steward[2] and receives from the king neither fee nor wages nor hay nor oats, for the king has provided for him in land under wardship worth 50 pounds a year.

[1] Suwerk

[2] He had been steward under Henry III.

Sir Robert Fitzjohn, the other steward, receives yearly 10 marks as fee and 8 marks for robes, and wardships worth 25 pounds a year by gift of the present king.

Marshals

Sir Richard du Bois receives yearly 10 marks as fee and 8 marks for robes.
Sir Elys de Hauuile

Submarshals

Thomas de Maydenhach Reymund Ernald	submarshals of the hall; each of whom receives $7\frac{1}{2}d$ a day and 3 marks [a year] for robes

Ushers

Baldwin le Flemmieng Brian de Foxcote	ushers of the hall; and each receives $7\frac{1}{2}d$ a day and 3 marks [a year] for robes

Assessors

Thomas de Bikenore Henry le Lumbard	each of whom receives $7\frac{1}{2}d$ a day and 3 marks [a year] for robes

Pantlers

mr Robert le Normant Robert de Salisbury mr William le pestur	each of whom receives $7\frac{1}{2}d$ a day and $3\frac{1}{2}$ marks for robes

Butlers

Matthew of Colommiers Druet	nothing

Buyers

John Maupas, who receives $7\frac{1}{2}d$ a day and $3\frac{1}{2}$ marks for robes
Robert Poterel, who receives $4\frac{1}{2}d$ a day and $3\frac{1}{2}$ marks for robes

Cooks of the king's kitchen

mr Thomas, who receives $7\frac{1}{2}d$ a day and $3\frac{1}{2}$ marks for robes
William de Werewelle, [cook] of the dinner, new man[1]

Cooks of the kitchen of the household

mr Brice, who receives $7\frac{1}{2}d$ a day and $3\frac{1}{2}$ marks for robes
John Sauuare, who receives $7\frac{1}{2}d$ a day, new man[1]

Naperer

John le naper, who receives $4\frac{1}{2}d$ a day, and receives 3 marks for robes

Porter

Alexander le porter, who receives $7\frac{1}{2}d$ a day and 3[2] marks for robes

Of the kitchen

Walter le poleter Henry lesqueler	each of whom receives $4\frac{1}{2}d$ a day and $3\frac{1}{2}$ marks for robes

Thomas le Herbeiur, who should receive nothing, except 3 marks for robes

[1] *nouel home:* perhaps newcomer, perhaps occasionally engaged and not at regular wages. Despite Tout, op. cit. p. 159, n. 1, the line in each case in the MS. after *nouel home* probably means that these two men were *not* in receipt of the regular wages and allowances shown for their companions.

[2] possibly $3\frac{1}{2}$

Assessor before the king

William Fitzwarin, who receives 7½*d* a day and 3 marks for robes

Salser

mr Ralph le Sauser, who receives 7½*d* a day and 3½ marks for robes

Ushers of the king's chamber

John le Husser
Henry de Greneford
James de Stafford
William de Feltoun
Adenet le Taillur[1]
} each of whom receives 7½*d* a day and 3 marks for robes

Clerks of the offices

Richard de la Linde, clerk of the pantry and the buttery
Sir Ralph de Watervile, clerk of the kitchen
} each of whom receives 7½*d* a day and 4½[2] marks for robes

John de Maidenstan, clerk of the marshalcy, who receives hay and oats for 2 horses and 4½ marks for robes

Nicole Fermbaud, sub-clerk of the marshalcy, who receives hay and oats for 1 horse and 3 marks for robes

John de Gillingham, keeper of the carts, who receives hay and oats for 2 horses and 3 marks for robes

And the king's wardrobe

mr Thomas Bek, treasurer
Thomas Gunneys, controller
} who receives nothing except 8 marks for robes

A clerk under the treasurer,[3] who receives nothing from the king

mr William of Louth, who receives nothing except 8 marks for robes

Sir Stephen [of St George]
William of Blyborough
} each of whom receives 7½*d* a day and 3 marks for robes

Clerks of the wardrobe

mr Simon the surgeon, who receives 12*d* a day and 8 marks for robes

mr William de Seint-Pere, physician, who receives 7½*d* a day

John de Rede, usher of the wardrobe, who receives 4½*d* a day and 3½ marks for robes

Jakemin le Chaundeler, who receives 7½*d* a day and 3 marks for robes

Clerks of the king's chapel

Sir John le Chapelein, who receives nothing but 8 marks for robes

Sir Nicole le Chapelein
mr Nicole de Araz
} each of whom receives 7½*d* a day and 6 marks for robes

Sir Richard de Salisbury, who receives nothing but 6 marks for robes

Robert the clerk of the chapel, who receives 4½*d* a day and 3½ marks for robes

1 Adinctus, the king's tailor
2 possibly, but less likely, 3½
3 probably the origin of the officer, later known as the cofferer (Tout, *Chapters*, II, pp. 29 and 39)

[*On the dorse of the document*]

It is ordained and commanded that the stewards, or one, if both cannot, together with the treasurer[1] or with the controller, if the treasurer cannot, and one of the marshals of the hall, and the clerks and sergeants of the offices be each night at the account of the household; and there let there be examined the servings of the hall by the testimony of the ushers of the hall. And by the number of the servings let there be examined the issues from the pantry, from the buttery and from the kitchen. And if there is excess, let it be amended and the sergeants charged.[2] In the margin of the household roll let there be written each night the wine dispensed during the day, so that by the testimony of this roll, which is of record in the household, we can audit the account of the tuns of wine two or three times a year. In addition, there let there be examined the wages of the sergeants, yeomen[3] and serving-men, as is customary. And if there is any overpayment[4] presented at the account and the wrong is not so bad that it ought to be shown to the king, let it be amended there and then at the discretion of the stewards and the treasurer by deduction from their wages or in any other way they think fit, so that the lord is not bothered with things that can be put right by them.

The treasurer, having called to him one of the stewards, shall audit once or twice each year the account of the chamberlain of wines so that he may clearly know how many pieces[5] come from each port and from each individual[6] ship, and the names of the persons from whom the wines have been taken, all in detail, and how many by purchase and how many by prise. And this account shall be so audited and examined by the treasurer and one of the stewards that the treasurer can present it in summary fashion in his own account when he renders his own account on the feast of St Edmund, king.

Let the treasurer do the same with the account of the great wardrobe, having likewise called to him both one of the stewards and one of the king's council if there are any, and it shall be so audited and examined that the treasurer can render it in summary fashion each year in his own account. And be it known that the treasurer shall henceforth cause to be bought by a certain man at three fairs a year everything for the great wardrobe, and this man shall be keeper of the great wardrobe and shall go to the fairs to make the purchases. And he shall be made to take oath to the king specially for this work. And the usher of the wardrobe shall be controller for this man and go with him to the fairs and view purchases and testify to liveries at the account. And while the usher is thus absent, the treasurer shall put in his place someone with the ability and knowledge to be responsible for his work. And the aforesaid keeper shall neither buy nor issue anything to anybody without the treasurer's special order, and this in the controller's presence; and if he does, nothing shall be allowed him. And if the king orders him by word of mouth to make a livery, he shall report it straightway to the treasurer and get from him his warrant and so provide that the controller knows of it.

The usher of the wardrobe ought to have the wax and the wick, both for making-

[1] i.e. the above-mentioned treasurer of the wardrobe (also, but less often, known as keeper of the wardrobe) not the treasurer of the exchequer

[2] *respris*

[3] *esquiers*

[4] *trespas*

[5] *peces*, i.e., in this case, casks

[6] *chescun I nef*

up and for keeping in store,[1] weighed each day and weigh out the livery[2] each night and weigh again the next day what remains,[3] so that by the weight he can know the amounts used each night, and the total sum at the end of the year. And this same usher when he has received the candles, made by weight, he shall put them in safe-keeping, or[4] in his own keeping, and deliver to the chandler the amount needed for each night. And the chandler shall have nothing in his keeping except the amount for the night, as the usher delivers it.

And because it is fitting that the household of the queen[5] should be conducted according to the ordinance of the king's household, it is ordained that madame's steward, or his sergeant[6] who serves her household, be each night at the account of the king's household, together with the pantler, the butler, the master cook, and the marshal of her chamber. And let these be sworn in respect of the account and to safely keep and courteously dispense for the honour and the profit[7] of the lord [king] and of madame [the queen] and to honestly save or give back what remains. And if there are any of madame's people who offend by wasting her things, or in any other way, let them be summoned to the account and be charged[8] and be punished like the king's people at the discretion of those conducting[9] the account together with madame's steward, unless the offence is so notable that they ought to show it to the king or the queen.

It is furthermore ordained that the marshals, or one of them, go the round of the household each month of the year and clear it of ribalds and wantons and of the horses of those who do not receive[10] hay or oats or wages, or more often if they see the need. And they shall do it too for madame's household. And the marshals of the hall and the ushers shall also take care that the hall is well cleared of strangers and ribalds that ought not to eat. And that the hall is well served for everybody.[11] And that no knight has more than one squire[12] eating in the hall.

The evening livery of wine and candles shall be made entirely by the king's men, as well to madame's household as elsewhere. And let the treasurer and the stewards see to it that no outside livery is made to anyone except where it ought to be, whether of bread or wine or of candles; and each night let them check the liveries as well of madame's household as of other places and of the king's household.

[*continued on a second membrane*]

Further, it is ordained that no one sleep[13] in the wardrobe except the treasurer, sir Thomas Gunneys, mr William of Louth, the treasurer's clerk, mr Simon the surgeon, Orlandino[14] when he comes to the court, William of Blyborough, sir Stephen of St George, John de Rede who is chief usher of the wardrobe, and a footman[15] subordinate to him, and no one else.

[1] *au fere e au reteiner*
[2] i.e. of candles
[3] i.e. the candle ends
[4] *en*, but probably corruption of *ou*
[5] *madame*
[6] *ou cedlui suuens*
[7] *pui*
[8] *repris*
[9] *souereins de*
[10] i.e. not entitled to receive
[11] *ben seruie e comunaument*
[12] *esquier*
[13] literally, "lie"
[14] Orlandino di Poggio, of Lucca, at this time the king's chief banker and loosely attached to the wardrobe. He is the only layman and the only outsider allowed this privilege. The others, apart from the footman, are the six wardrobe officers and two of the four wardrobe clerks listed above.
[15] *vadlet a pe*

And it is ordained that no clerk who has a benefice from the king shall henceforth receive wages from the king. And it is ordained that no one shall eat in the wardrobe except the sub-usher, and the treasurer's chamberlain, and all the other chamberlains [shall eat] in the hall, if they are not lodged far from the court.

As to the king's transport, it is provided that for the king's wardrobe there shall be three long carts.

For the pantry one long cart, and a short one to carry the household flour and the mills of the saucery.

For the buttery one long cart and a short one.

For the kitchen one long cart and two short ones.

For sergeants-at-arms 20 have been picked: namely, John Ertaud, Michael de St Eadmund, Robert de Clopton, William de Hertford, Gerard de Broil, John le Conuers, Robert de Vilers, Nicole Ertaud, Guyot de Valery, William le Engleys, Thomas de Irpegrave, Guarsoun, Gailard de Morlans, Peres de Byly, Eble de la reine, William le Mareschal, Puche, Arnald de Clarac, and Carbonel. And each shall receive 3½ marks a year for robes.

And be it known that each time the steward orders the sergeants to keep three horses, they shall keep them and receive 12*d* a day. And when the steward shall order them to dispense with the third, they shall dispense with it and receive only 8*d* a day.

In addition it is ordered that each yeoman[1] receive 40*s* a year for robes, and each yeoman by calling[2] one mark. And each serving-man[3] who receives 2*d* a day for his wages shall receive 10*s* for robes. And each serving-man who receives 3 halfpennies a day and all the others who ought to receive robes shall receive half a mark.

[*Endorsement*] Ordinances of the king's household.

119. Licences for alienation in mortmain, May 1280

(*Cal. Pat. Rolls 1272–81*, pp. 372, 373)

In little over six months after the making of the Statute of Mortmain (No. 53 above) the king was, as these writs show, assuming a prerogative right in the matter and licensing alienations in mortmain. The matter is legally complex (on this, T. F. T. Plucknett, *Legislation of Edward I* (Oxford, 1949), pp. 94–102) and politically obscure. J. M. W. Bean, *The Decline of English Feudalism 1215–1540* (Manchester, 1968), has a chapter on alienation generally: on alienation in mortmain he is over-speculative on the politics behind Edward's moves, but advances the subject by exploring (as Plucknett, op. cit. p. 102 advised) the administrative records.

26 May, Westminster

Licence, notwithstanding the recent statute in mortmain, for the warden of the chapel of St Catherine, Wamberge, founded by Emelina, sometime countess of Ulster, in her lifetime, who assigned rents and possessions to it for the maintenance of five chaplains, and who left in her will a great part of her goods to buy rents and possessions to the value of 10*l* yearly in order to keep up hospitality, lights, ornaments, and other things pertaining to the praise of God there – to buy lands and possessions to that amount accordingly, on condition that neither the king nor the lord of the fees lose anything in this behalf.

[1] *esquier*
[2] *vadlet de mester*
[3] *garzon*

27 May, Westminster
Licence for the alienation in mortmain by Peter de Lenche and Margery his wife to the abbot and convent of Westminster of certain land of the inheritance of Margery which they hold of the fee of the abbot.

120. The escheatries, 1232–3, 1304

(a)
(*Cal. Close Rolls 1231–4*, pp. 129–31)

1232, 8 February, Westminster
The king to his beloved and faithful Fulk Baynard. Know that we have appointed you, along with our beloved and faithful Roger son of Osbert, to keep our escheats and wardships in the county of Norfolk and to answer for them to us at our exchequer. And we have commanded our sheriff of Norfolk and Suffolk to have you and the aforesaid Roger put in full seisin of our escheats and wardships as they fall in in the said county of Norfolk, as is aforesaid, and to receive from you and Roger in his full county the oath that you will keep faithfully the said escheats and wardships and answer to us for them. And therefore we command you to attend faithfully to this and to take the oath on these things to us, as is aforesaid, so that we may have to consider your faithfulness deserving of praise. Witness myself at Westminster, 8 February.

Roger son of Osbert is written to in the same way.

The king to the sheriff of Norfolk and Suffolk, greeting. Know that we have appointed our beloved and faithful Fulk Baynard and Roger son of Osbert to keep our escheats and wardships of co. Norfolk, and William de Ambel' and Hugh Talemasch' those of co. Suffolk, and answer for them to us at our exchequer. And therefore we order you to have them put in full seisin of the aforesaid escheats and wardships as they fall in, as is aforesaid, at the same time making them swear in your next full county after the receipt of these letters that (as we direct them in our letters which we send for you to deliver to them) they will keep faithfully our said escheats and wardships and answer to us at our exchequer. Witness as immediately above.

[Like letters to the sheriffs of other counties, the names of the appointed being given in each case.]

(b)
(*Cal. Pat. Rolls 1225–32*, p. 491)

1232, 16 July
On the custody of escheats. – The king has granted to P. de Rivaux etc. the custody for life of all escheats and wardships belonging to the king when they fall in in England, to answer for them at the king's exchequer. And word has been sent to the sheriff of Dorset and Somerset and Jordan de Clinton and John de Reigny, William Cusin and

Simon de Maneston to be intendant and answerable unto the said Peter for all wardships and escheats belonging to the king which have fallen in and are in their hands and those which fall in in future, as is aforesaid. Witness the king, at Lambeth, 16 July, 16 Hen. III.

The sheriff of Devon and Randolf de Albemarle and Warin son of Joel are written to in the same terms.

(c)

(*Cal. Pat. Rolls 1232–47*, p. 7)

1233, 13 January, Woodstock

Mandate to all sheriffs throughout England, whenever any wards or escheats fall in in their bailiwicks, to allow those who have the custody of the king's wards and escheats to have free administration thereof, not laying hands on them, or permitting hands to be laid on them by their men, in making seisin thereof; until further order.

(d)

(*Cal. Pat. Rolls 1301–7*, p. 275)

1304, 13 February, Dunfermline

The like [Commission of oyer and terminer] to Hervey de Staunton, Roger de Suthcote, John de Foxle and Roger de Bella Fago, on complaint by Adam de Kereseye, sub-escheator in the county of Berks, that Walter le Pouere [and ten others named] entered his houses at Bayworth while he was in Scotland and under the king's protection, broke his chests there and carried away charters, bonds, acquittances, tallies, rolls and muniments touching the office of the escheatry found there and at Sunnyngwell, co. Berks.

By p.s.

121. Wardships and marriages

(a)

(*Cal. Pat. Rolls 1247–58*, p. 481)

Like escheats, one of the incidents of feudal lordship which provided the king in particular with an unpredictable but regular source of revenue, applied in this case to paying an official.

1256, 12 June, Westminster

Whereas the king when in Gascony gave on 28 March, 38 Henry III [1254], by letters patent under the seal which he used in Gascony, to Robert Walround the wardship and marriage of the first girl that should fall in, whose inheritance should be worth 200*l* a year, with the wardship of her land, or the marriage of a lady whose land should be worth 200*l* a year, and the said Robert has not been thus provided for yet and has, with the king's will, granted the same to Alan de Plugenet, his nephew; the king grants to the said Alan that he will provide for him accordingly, when opportunity occur, and if the said Alan die before he be so provided for, the said Robert shall not be frustrated of the effect of the first grant made to him.

(b)

(*Cal. Pat. Rolls 1258–66*, pp. 36, 205, and 212)

1259, 2 August, Westminster

Grant to Ingram de Percy, Peter de Chauvent and Imbert de Muntferaunt of the wardship of the lands late of William de Fortibus with all the eschcats belonging thereto, in lieu of their fees at the exchequer. Grant also to the said Ingram, Peter and Imbert and Laurence son of Nicholas de Sancto Mauro of the marriage of the four daughters and heirs of the said William, to wit, to Ingram, the marriage of the eldest, to Peter, the marriage of one of the remaining three as he shall choose, to Imbert the marriage of one of the remaining two as he shall choose, and to Laurence, the marriage of the remaining one; saving to the daughter whose marriage is granted to Laurence for his service her purparty, when she come of age, of all the lands which fall to her and her co-parceners: so also that if they will not take these daughters as wives, Maud de Kyme, their mother, shall have preference over others if she shall wish to buy the said marriages, provided always that she give as much for them as others would.

By K.

1262, 10 March, Windsor

Whereas the king granted to Ingram de Percy and Peter de Chauvent the marriage of Joan and Cecily, daughters and the two heirs of William de Fortibus, on condition that if they were unwilling to take them as wives, Maud de Kyma, their mother, should be before all others if she wished to buy their marriages; the king grants to the said Maud that this condition shall be fully observed to her.

1262, 10 May, Westminster

Whereas the king lately granted to Imbert de Muntferrent the wardship of a third part of the inheritance of William de Fortibus with the wardship and marriage of one of the daughters and heirs of the said William, so that if he did not wish to take her to wife, Maud de Kyma her mother should have the preference over others if she wished to buy the marriage of that daughter, provided that she paid as much as another would give; the king grants that Imbert may assign the said wardship to whom he will, and with regard to the marriage of the said daughter, if he will not take her to wife and the said Maud will not buy her marriage from him or his assignee, then the assignee may, by taking the girl to wife or selling her marriage to another, do what seems best to him, but without disparagement of the said girl.

[Joan, the eldest of the four daughters, married her guardian, Ingram – presumably after 10 March 1262. But he was dead by February 1263 at the latest (ibid. p. 247) and she married again (C. Moor, *Knights of Edward I*, vol. 2, p. 80). The other three heiresses married otherwise it would seem.]

(c)

(*Cal. Close Rolls 1302–7*, pp. 486–7)

1307, 8 February, Lanercost
The king to Walter de Gloucestria, escheator beyond Trent. John de Suthewell, king's clerk, has besought the king by petition before him and his council to cause him to be provided with some wardship pertaining to the king in place of promotion, as he has long served the king faithfully in the chancery: the king orders the escheator to cause a wardship to be provided from the next wardships coming to the king's hands of the value of £10 yearly or thereabouts for the use of his said clerk, and to certify Walter, bishop of Coventry and Lichfield, the treasurer, as quickly as possible of the said wardship and of the age of the heir, in order that the wardship may be delivered to the said clerk by the treasurer's advice and ordinance.

By pet. of C.

122. A tallage, 1260

(*Cal. Pat. Rolls 1258–66*, pp. 75–6)

Appointment of William de Swyneford and William de Hecham to assess the king's tallage in the cities, boroughs and demesnes of the king in the counties of Norfolk, Suffolk, Cambridge and Huntingdon, by poll or in common, as they think best; with mandate to all the tenants to be intendent to them.

[Like letters making similar appointments for other groups of counties]

Writ of aid for them directed to the sheriffs of the respective counties.

[Appointment in the same form of H. le Bygod, the justiciar, to assess the tallage in the city of London and in Middlesex]

Mandate to Hamo Hauteyn, one of the above assessors, to make the assessment of the king's cities, boroughs and demesnes [he was one of the two assessors appointed for the Lincoln, Nottingham, Derby, Leicester and Warwick group of counties], as well those which S. de Monteforti, earl of Leicester, has in tenancy as others, by the gules of August [1 August]. And if any citizens, burgesses or tenants make fine with him in gross for the present tallage, as the king understands that in such cases the rich are often spared and the poor aggrieved, he is to provide that the tallage be assessed before his departure, so that this may not happen. He is to deliver extracts of the whole tallage to the sheriffs of the said counties for them to levy the same, so that a moiety be paid at the exchequer at All Saints and the other moiety at the quinzaine of Easter. And he is to be diligent herein – in no wise omitting to be with the king at the gules of August to certify what he has done and the king will satisfy him of his expenses.

In like form it is written to all the above knights.

123. Borrowing

(*Cal. Pat. Rolls 1247–58*, p. 629)

The note in the margin of the patent roll records for office purposes that the sum actually borrowed was £500, the acknowledgement providing for a concealed interest of £50 besides the forfeit of jewels, if repayment was not prompt to the day.

1258, 7 May, Westminster

Acknowledgement of the receipt of a loan of 550*l* from Paul Albertini, Erminius Erminii and Byncincn' Consilii, citizens and merchants of Siena, reckoning 13*s* 4*d* to the mark; with promise to pay the same within the octaves of Christmas at the New Temple, London. For the payment of which sum with the interest and damages the king binds himself and his heirs and goods and especially certain jewels of gold and silver sealed with the seal of J. Maunsel, treasurer of York, and Edward de Westmonasterio, and if it be not paid on that day, the king wills that the said merchants may dispose of the said jewels at their will.

[Note in the margin:] These 500*l* were borrowed for the expenses of William Bonquer and the other envoys to the court of Rome, whereof the said William received 250 marks at London, of which he ought to keep 100 marks to his own use, and pay 100 marks to Roger de Lentino and John de Monte Fusculo, knights of Apulia, and he ought to receive 500 marks in the court of Rome, to the use of the king's envoys going to the said court by ordinance of P. de Sabaudia, and others, who are at Paris on behalf of the king. And 50*l* are given for usury.

124. Royal prises (*ad opus regis*)

(*Cal. Pat. Rolls 1232–47*, p. 238)

1240, 16 November, Westminster

Mandate to the bailiffs and goodmen of Winchester to make known to all merchants coming to their city the provision of the king and council that all the king's prises from merchants shall be paid at four terms of the year, to wit, the prises due in the fair of Northampton in the fair of St Ives, [the prises due in the latter] in the fair of Boston, the prises due in the latter in the fair of Winchester, and those due in the latter in the fair of Northampton.

125. Payment for prises, 1256

(*Cal. Pat. Rolls 1247–58*, p. 483)

1256, June

Mandate to the abbot of Peterborough and Roger de Turkeby as the king has no ready money to pay for purchases which he has ordered to be made at Boston fair by the hands of Roger de Ros and Hugh de Turri, unless it be from the fines and amercements of the eyres of the said abbot and Roger in the northern counties, the amount of which he does not know, to command the sheriffs to cause the clearer of such fines and amercements to be levied to the amount of 700 marks. The king has commanded the said sheriffs to cause all money, which they levy by their command, to be carried to Boston and delivered to the said Roger and Hugh in the fair. And they are to provide for the king with all speed as they would save him from loss and perpetual scandal; and for the expedition of the business the king is sending them his clerk Richard de Sireburne.

Mandate to the sheriff of Northumberland accordingly. And when the king knows by letters of the said Roger and Hugh, keepers of the king's wardrobe, how much the sheriff has delivered to them, he will let the sheriff have a writ of *allocate*.

The like to the sheriffs of Cumberland, Westmoreland and Lancaster.

November 24, Winchester. *And because the said sheriffs did not deliver the whole of the money to the said R. and H. they are commanded to levy the residue without delay, and have it at the next fair of Stamford to deliver to the said R. and H. for them to make the king's purchases. And the king will cause it to be allowed to them.*

126. A wartime prise: Lincolnshire 1296–7

(*A Lincolnshire Assize Roll for 1298*, ed. W. S. Thomson (Lincoln Rec. Soc., vol. 36, 1944), App. IV, with translation pp. lxi–lxvi)

A prise of corn *ad opus regis* ordered on 29 November 1296: Lincolnshire to supply 500 quarters of barley, 1,000 qrs. of oats, 1,500 qrs. of wheat, and 500 qrs. of beans and peas, to be collected within a month of Easter 1297 (Thomson, op. cit. p. 181).

Cereals for the use of the lord king taken in the county of Lincoln by Richard of Hetherington, clerk, and Ralph Paynel, sheriff of that county, in the 25th year of the reign of king Edward: and expenses incurred with respect to the aforesaid cereals by the said sheriff, by view of the said Richard, about the feast of St John the Baptist [24 June 1297].

Sum of the whole receipt of cereals there taken: 2,741 quarters and half a bushel, as appears by the items below:

Of corn, 1,231 quarters 1 bushel 1 peck; and of beans and peas, 356 qrs. 1 bush.; of barley, 202 qrs. 1 bush. 1 peck; and of oats, 951 qrs. and half a bushel: of which were received as follows:

At Lincoln 780½ qrs. 1 bush., i.e.
of corn, 314½ qrs. 1 peck
of beans and peas, 65 qrs. 1 bush.
of barley 133½ qrs. 1 peck
of oats, 267 qrs. 1½ bush.

At Boston 1,275½ qrs. 1 bush., i.e.
of corn, 493½ qrs. ½ bush.
of beans and peas 232 qrs. 1 bush.
of barley 43 qrs.
of oats, 505½ qrs. 1 bush.

At Wainfleet 248 qrs. 1 bush., i.e.

of corn, 131 qrs. ½ bush.
of beans and peas, 5½ qrs. ½ bush.
of barley, nil
of oats, 111½ qrs.

At Grimsby 436 qrs. 1½ bush., i.e.
of corn, 292 qrs.
of beans and peas, 53 qrs. ½ bush.
of barley, 24½ qrs. 1½ bush.
of oats, 66 qrs. 1½ bush.

Sum of the whole of the corn milled in the aforesaid county: 239 qrs., of which were milled as follows:

At Lincoln 135 qrs., of which [there is]
of sifted flour, 123 qrs. 1½ bush.
of bran, 59½ qrs.

At Boston 62 qrs., of which [there is]
of sifted flour, 62 qrs.[1]
of bran, 22 qrs. 1½ bush.

At Grimsby 42 qrs., of which [there is]
of sifted flour, 42 qrs.[1]
of bran, 14 qrs.,

according to the report of the bakers selected and sworn for this.

Sum of the whole of the sifted flour: 227 qrs. 1½ bush. And the sum of the whole of the bran: 95½ qrs. 1½ bush., for the cost of which the aforesaid sheriff is answerable by a certain chirograph sewn to this.

Sum of flesh taken in the aforesaid county:
16 carcases of beef
43½ sides of bacon

Expenses incurred in respect of the aforesaid corn:

For milling 135 qrs. of corn at Lincoln: 33*s* 9*d*, viz, per quarter 3*d*. Item for milling 62 qrs. of corn at Boston: 15*s* 6*d*, viz, per qr. 3*d*. Item for milling 42 qrs. of corn at Grimsby: 10*s* 6*d*, viz, per qr. 3*d*.

Total 59*s* 9*d*

For bolting [sifting] flour obtained from corn milled at Lincoln, viz, 135 qrs.: 5*s* 7½*d*, viz, per qr. ½*d*. Item for bolting flour obtained from corn milled at Boston, viz, 62 qrs.: 2*s* 7*d*, viz, per qr. ½*d*. Item for bolting flour obtained from corn milled at Grimsby, viz, 42 qrs.: 1*s* 9*d*, viz, per qr. ½*d*.

Total 9*s* 11½*d*

For 40 ells of canvas bought at Lincoln for making a place for bolting the flour, after the manner of a granary: 11*s* 8*d*, of price per ell 3½*d*. Item for 20 ells of canvas bought at Boston for the same: 5*s* 10*d*, of price per ell 3½*d*. For 20 ells of coarse pieces bought at Grimsby for the same: 3*s* 4*d*, of price per ell 2*d*.

Total 20*s* 10*d*

[1] These figures are as in MS.

For carriage of 135 qrs. of corn milled at Lincoln, from the granary to the mill and from the mill to the place of bolting: 3*s*. Item for carriage of corn milled at Boston to the mill and from the mill: 2*s* 6*d*. Item for carriage of corn milled at Grimsby to the mill and from the mill: 1*s* 2*d*.

Total 6*s* 8*d*

For 37 ells of coarse pieces bought for making sacks for bearing and carrying corn received at Lincoln, of which were made 10 sacks: 4*s* 7½*d*, of price per ell 1½*d*. Item for 16 ells of coarse pieces bought for portage and conveyance of corn received at Wainfleet, of which were made four sacks, 2*s*, of price per ell 1½*d*. Item for nine used sacks bought for carriage of corn overseas and for portage and conveyance of corn received at Boston and at Grimsby: 15*s*, of price per sack 3*d*. Item for 111 used sacks bought for the same: 27*s* 9*d*, of price per sack 3*d*.

Total 49*s* 4½*d*

For 13 casks bought at Lincoln for containing the flour bolted there: 19*s* 6*d*, of price per cask 1*s* 6*d*. Item for 22 barrels bought there for the same: 18*s* 4*d*, of price per barrel 10*d*. Item for the wages of two men repairing, cleaning and refitting the said casks and barrels for 12 days: 8*s*, viz, to each of them per day 4*d*. Item for hoops and nails bought for the same: 7*s* 6*d*. Item for five Rhenish tuns bought at Boston for containing the flour bolted there: 12*s* 6*d*, of price per ton 2*s* 6*d*. Item for five casks bought there for the same: 8*s* 4*d*, of price per cask 1*s* 8*d*. Item for the wages of one man repairing, cleaning and refitting the said tuns and casks for eight days: 2*s* 8*d*, viz, per day 4*d*. Item for hoops and nails bought for the same: 2*s* 2*d*. Item for eight casks bought at Grimsby for containing the flour bolted there: 13*s* 4*d*, of price per cask 1*s* 8*d*. Item for hoops and nails bought for the same, 1*s* 3½*d*.

Total £4 13*s* 6½*d*

For the hire of 12 porters at Lincoln carrying corn from the granary to boats for three days: 9*s*, viz, to each of them per day 3*d*. Item for the hire of four porters there for one day for the same: 12*d*, viz, to each of them per day 3*d*. Item for the hire of a ferryman to convey 13 casks and 22 barrels on to the boats there: 6*s* 11*d*, viz, 3*d* per cask and 2*d* per barrel. Item for the hire of 16 porters at Boston for 12 days for carrying corn received there and for corn coming from Lincoln, to the great ships: 48*s*, viz, to each of them per day 3*d*. Item for hire of a ferryman to convey 10 tuns and casks filled there, and 13 casks and 22 barrels coming from Lincoln, into the great ships at Boston: 9*s* 5*d*, viz, 3*d* for each cask and 2*d* for each barrel. Item for the hire of six porters at Wainfleet for four days: 6*s*, viz, to each of them per day 3*d*. Item for the hire of eight porters at Grimsby for four days: 8*s*, viz, to each of them per day 3*d*. Item for the hire of a ferryman to convey eight casks filled there into the great ships: 2*s*, viz, 3*d* for each cask.

Total £4 10*s* 4*d*

For carriage of 179½ qrs. 1 peck of corn from Lincoln to Boston by water: 22*s* 5½*d*, viz, for each quarter 1½*d*. Item for carriage of 65 qrs. 1 bush. of beans and peas there: 8*s* 1¾*d*, viz, per qr. 1½*d*. Item for carriage of 133½ qrs. 1 peck of barley: 11*s* 1½*d*, viz, per qr. 1*d*. Item for carriage of 267 qrs. 1½ bush. of oats there: 16*s* 8½*d*, viz, per qr. ¾*d*. Item for the hire of dunnage for the boats carrying the said corn: 2*s* 10*d*. Item for carriage of the aforesaid 35 casks and barrels, which contained 123 qrs. 1½ bush. of flour, from Lincoln to Boston: 15*s* 5*d*, viz, 1½*d*. per qr.

Total 76*s* 8*d*

For the hire of five small boats carrying 540 qrs. of corn from Boston to Wainfleet to bigger ships: 15*s*, viz, for each boat 3*s*. And for the hire of one small boat by itself for the same: 2*s* 3*d*. Item for the hire of dunnage for the same small boats: 2*s* 6*d*. Item for the hire of one small boat carrying 32 qrs. 7 strikes of corn from the final remainder at Wainfleet to Boston, and for dunnage for the same: 8*s* 6*d*.

Total 38*s* 3*d*

For the hire of two men receiving and measuring corn at Lincoln at the granary, and from the granary to the boats, for 16 days: 8*s*, viz, to each of them 3*d* per day. For the expenses of one clerk living there for the same time, over the receipt and delivery of the aforesaid corn: 5*s* 4*d*, viz, 4*d* per day. Item for the hire of four men receiving and measuring corn at Boston for 14 days: 14*s*, viz, to each of them 3*d* per day. Item for the expenses of one clerk living there for the same time, over the receipt and delivery of the said corn: 7*s*, viz, 6*d* per day. Item for the hire of two men receiving and measuring corn at Wainfleet for 10 days: 5*s*, viz, to each of them 3*d* per day. Item for the expenses of one clerk living there for the same time, over the receipt and delivery of the said corn: 5*s*, viz, 6*d* per day. Item for the hire of two men receiving and measuring corn at Grimsby for eight days: 4*s*, viz, to each of them 3*d* per day. Item for the expenses of one clerk living there for the same time, over the receipt and delivery of the said corn: 4*s*, viz, 6*d* per day.

Total 52*s* 4*d*

For loading the ship of John de Nasingges which is called "Petre de Sancto Botulpho" bound for Flanders which holds 266½ qrs. of corn: 76*s* 6*d*. And for hire of dunnage of the same: 8*s*.

For loading the ship of Stephen of Stanham which is called "Katerine de Sancto Botulpho", which holds 152½ qrs. of beans and peas, transporting them to the parts of Flanders: 67*s* 6*d*. And for hire of dunnage of the same: 8*s* 6*d*.

For loading the ship of William de la Bothe which is called "Jonette de Sancto Botulpho" bound for Flanders, which holds 11 tuns of flour containing 54 qrs. and 73½ qrs. of beans and peas, and 145 qrs. of oats, 13½ carcases of beef, 33½ sides of bacon: 67*s* 6*d*. And for dunnage of the same: 7*s*. And for making a certain rope: 12*d*.

For loading the ship of Alexander Pyg' of Wintringham which is called "Godyer de Sancto Botulpho" bound for Flanders, which holds 34 casks of flour containing 131 qrs. 1½ bush. of flour; and 469 qrs. of oats; and 111 qrs. of barley: 75*s*. And for dunnage of the same: 9*s* 2½*d*. And for one pilot hired to take the ship out of port: 3*s*.

For loading the ship of Laurence son of Hugh and Walter son of Alan which is called "Belle de Weynflet" bound for Flanders, which holds 100 qrs. of corn and 120 qrs. of oats: 30*s*. And for dunnage of the same: ½ a mark.

For loading the ship of Laurence son of Hugh which is called "Blythe of Weynflet" bound for Flanders, which holds 110 qrs. ½ bush. of corn and 92 qrs. of oats: 56*s* 3*d*. And for dunnage of the same: ½ a mark.

For loading the ship of Alan of Wrangle and Peter son of Haco which is called "Godyer de Weynflet" bound for Flanders, which holds 135 qrs. of corn and 59 qrs. of beans and peas: 48*s* 9*d*. And for dunnage of the same: ½ a mark.

For loading the ship of Simon of Wrangle and Thomas of Swyne, which is called "Faucon de Weynflet" bound for Flanders, which holds 80 qrs. of corn and 60 qrs. of barley: 25*s*. And for dunnage of the same: 6*s*.

For loading the ship of Robert son of Alan of Grainthorpe which is called "Blythe de Grymmesby" bound for Flanders, which holds 81 qrs. of corn and 51½ qrs. and ½ bush. of beans and peas, and 5 qrs. 1 bush. of oats, 2½ qrs. of barley, eight casks containing 42 qrs. of flour: 38*s* 6*d*. And for dunnage of the same: ½ mark.

For loading another ship of Peter Duraunt which is called "Blythe de Grymmesby" bound for Flanders, which holds 160 qrs. of corn, 22 qrs. 3 bush. of barley, 61 qrs. of oats, 2½ carcases of beef and 10 sides of bacon: 60*s*. And for dunnage of the same: ½ mark.

For loading the ship of John Herny which is called "Gerlaund de Brummouth", of Boston, bound for Anuers [Antwerp] in Brabant, which holds 69 qrs. 1 bush. of corn, 20½ qrs. of beans and peas, 11 qrs. of barley and 75 qrs. of oats: £4. And for dunnage for the same: 7*s*.

	£	*s*	*d*
Total for loading the 11 ships aforesaid ..	31	5	0
Total of dunnage for the same		79	0½
And for a certain pilot and one rope ..		4	0

Sum total: £59 15*s* 9*d*, particulars of which are sent in.

This schedule was made in two parts, of which one part remains in the custody of the said Richard of Hetherington, clerk, for the use of the lord king; and the other part in the custody of the said Ralph the sheriff. But there ought to be withdrawn thence 3*s* for dunnage of the ship of John Herny, for that he did not receive above 4*s* where he ought to have received 7*s* for the said dunnage.

[Attached to the above schedule is the following, written on a portion of a membrane about eight inches wide and six long, not serrated on either side:]

Sale of bran extracted from the corn taken and milled in the county of Lincoln for the king's use by Richard of Hetherington, clerk of the lord king, and R. Paynel, sheriff of the said county, in the 25th year of the reign of king Edward:

The said Ralph the sheriff is answerable concerning 79*s* 4*d* for the sale of 59½ qrs. of bran extracted from corn milled at Lincoln, according to the report of the bakers of the city of Lincoln selected and sworn for this; of price per quarter, 16*d*. Item,

Ralph the sheriff is answerable concerning 18*s* 7*d* for the sale of 22 qrs. 1½ bush. of bran extracted from corn milled at Boston, of price per quarter 10*d*. The same Ralph the sheriff is answerable concerning 9*s* 4*d* for the sale of 14 qrs. of bran extracted from corn milled at Grimsby, as appears in the other chirograph to which this chirograph is sewn; of price per qr. 8*d*.

Total 107*s* 3*d*

Sale of canvas there made:

The said Ralph the sheriff is answerable concerning 6*s* 8*d*, for the sale of 40 ells of canvas previously bought for making a place for bolting flour at Lincoln; price per ell: 2*d*.

Total 6*s* 8*d*

Sum total 113*s* 11*d*

And memorandum, that from 20 ells of canvas bought at Boston for a place for bolting corn there, were made six sacks. And from 20 ells of coarse pieces bought for the same at Grimsby, as appears in the other chirograph to which this chirograph is sewn, were made five sacks. And 10 sacks were made at Lincoln for portage and carriage of corn from 37 ells of coarse pieces which were bought as appears in the other chirograph. And four sacks which were made from 16 ells of coarse pieces at Wainfleet for portage and carriage of corn there. And 171 sacks, bought as appears in the other chirograph, were sent overseas to Flanders with the ships transporting corn thereto, in accordance with the ordinance and writ of the lord king regarding this, directed to the said Richard and the sheriff.[1]

127. A tax on personal property ("movables"): local assessment roll of the Ninth of 1297 for Shillington (Flitt Hundred, Beds.)

(*The Taxation of 1297: a Translation of the Local Rolls of Assessment for Barford, Biggleswade and Flitt Hundreds, and for Bedford, Dunstable, Leighton Buzzard and Luton*, ed. A. T. Gayton (Bedfordshire Hist. Rec. Soc., Streatley nr Luton, Beds., 1959), pp. 58–9)

Taxation of the ninth granted to the lord king of the vill of Shillington

Richard de la Bere: 2 affers, 6*s*; 4 bullocks, 20*s*; 6 qr. wheat, 20*s*; 5 qr. drage, 2*s* 6*d*. Total 58*s* 6*d*. Ninth 6*s* 6*d*.

Robert de Barton: 1 affer, 3*s*; 1 bullock, 5*s*; 1 cow, 5*s*; 2 qr. wheat, 6*s* 8*d*; 2 qr. drage, 5*s*. Total 24*s* 8*d*. Ninth 2*s* 9*d*.

Elena de Chubbell: 1 affer, 2*s*; 1 cow, 5*s*; 1 qr. 2 b. wheat, 4*s* 2*d*; 1 qr. drage, 2*s* 6*d*. Total 13*s* 8*d*. Ninth 18¼*d*.

John de Brademere: 1 affer, 18*d*; 1 cow, 5*s*; 1 qr. wheat, 3*s* 4*d*; 1 qr. drage, 2*s* 6*d*. Total 12*s* 4*d*. Ninth 16½*d*.

Matilda de Wodemanend: 1 affer, 3*s*; 1 bullock, 5*s*; 1 cow, 5*s*; 1 young bullock, 18*d*; 1½ qr. wheat, 5*s*; 1 qr. drage, 2*s* 6*d*; 1 qr. beans, 3*s*. Total 25*s*. Ninth 2*s* 9½*d*.

[1] On the dorse a note that this chirograph with schedule was received by W. bishop of Coventry and Lichfield, the treasurer, from Richard of Hetherington, clerk, at the exchequer at York on 7 July 1298.

Thomas Worthynge: 1 affer, 2*s*; 1 cow, 5*s*; 1 young bullock, 2*s*; 1 qr. 2 b. wheat, 4*s* 2*d*; 1½ qr. drage, 3*s* 9*d*. Total 16*s* 11*d*. Ninth 22½*d*.

William Faber: 1 affer, 3*s*; 1 cow, 5*s*; ½ qr. wheat, 20*d*; 1 qr. drage, 2*s* 6*d*. Total 12*s* 2*d*. Ninth 16¼*d*.

William de Bradefen: 1 affer, 3*s*; 1 bullock, 5*s*; 1 young bullock, 2*s*. Total 10*s*. Ninth 13½*d*.

Henry le Parker: 1 affer, 4*s*; 1 bullock, 5*s*; 1 cow, 5*s*; 1 young bullock, 2*s*; 6 b. wheat, 2*s* 6*d*; 1½ qr. drage, 3*s* 9*d*. Total 22*s* 3*d*. Ninth 2*s* 5¾*d*.

William Lamberte: 1 affer, 3*s*; 1 bullock, 5*s*; 1 heifer, 4*s*; 1 pig, 2*s*; 1 qr. wheat 3*s* 4*d*; 1 qr. oats, 18*d*; ½ qr. peas, 15*d*. Total 20*s* 1*d*. Ninth 2*s* 3*d*.

Reginald de Hanescomp: 1 affer, 3*s*; 1 bullock, 5*s*; 1 cow, 5*s*; 1 pig, 2*s*; 1 qr. wheat, 3*s* 4*d*; 1½ qr. drage, 3*s* 9*d*; ½ qr. peas, 15*d*. Total 23*s* 4*d*. Ninth 2*s* 7*d*.

Adam Richard: 1 affer, 18*d*; 1 cow, 5*s*; 1 young bullock, 2*s* 6*d*; ½ qr. wheat, 20*d*; 1 qr. oats, 18*d*; ½ qr. peas, 15*d*. Total 13*s* 4*d*. Ninth 17¾*d*.

Nicholas Godmar: in all chattels,[1] 9*s*. Total 9*s*. Ninth 12*d*.

John le Carpenter: 1 affer, 3*s*; 1 bullock, 5*s*; 1 cow, 5*s*; 1 qr. wheat, 3*s* 4*d*; 1½ qr. drage, 3*s* 9*d*. Total 21*s* 4*d*. Ninth 2*s* 6*d*.

Robert Aylmar: in all goods,[2] 9*s*. Total 9*s*. Ninth 12*d*.

Thomas West: in all goods, 9*s*. Total 9*s*. Ninth 12*d*.

Alexander le Carecter: 1 affer, 3*s*; 1 cow, 5*s*; 1 heifer, 3*s*; 1 pig, 18*d*; 1 qr. wheat, 3*s* 4*d*; 1½ qr. oats, 2*s* 3*d*. Total 18*s* 10*d*. Ninth 2*s* 1¼*d*.

Robert le Carecter: in all goods, 9*s*. Total 9*s*. Ninth 12*d*.

Simon atte Welle: 1 affer, 3*s*; 1 cow, 5*s*; 6 sheep, 6*s*; 1½ qr. *berecorn*, 3*s*; 1 qr. oats, 18*d*. Total 20*s*. Ninth 2*s* 2¾*d*.

John atte Hulle: 1 affer, 18*d*; 1 cow, 5*s*; 8 sheep, 8*s*; ½ qr. wheat, 20*d*; 1 qr. oats, 18*d*. Total 17*s* 8*d*. Ninth 2*s*.

John Stefene: in all goods, 9*s*. Total 9*s*. Ninth 12*d*.

William Hereberd: in all goods, 9*s*. Total 9*s*. Ninth 12*d*.

Andrew atte Hull: 1 affer, 2*s*; 1 cow, 5*s*; ½ qr. wheat, 20*d*; 1 qr. *bericorn*, 3*s*. Total 11*s* 8*d*. Ninth 15½*d*.

Thomas le Rede: 1 affer, 18*d*; 1 cow, 5*s*; 3 sheep 3*s*; 1½ qr. *bericorn*, 4*s* 6*d*; 1 qr. oats, 18*d*. Total 15*s* 6*d*. Ninth 20¾*d*.

Editha vidua: 1 affer, 2*s*; 1 cow, 5*s*; 1 qr. wheat, 3*s* 4*d*; 1 qr. drage, 2*s* 6*d*; 1 qr. oats, 18*d*. Total 14*s* 4*d*. Ninth 19¼*d*.

John son of Hugh: 1 affer, 2*s*; 1 cow, 5*s*; 1 qr. *bericorn*, 3*s*; 1 qr. oats, 18*d*. Total 11*s* 6*d*. Ninth 15½*d*.

William Barefot: in all goods, 9*s*. Total 9*s*. Ninth 12*d*.

John Lewyne: 1 affer, 3*s*; 1 cow, 5*s*; 1 qr. wheat, 3*s* 4*d*; 1½ qr. drage, 3*s* 9*d*. Total 15*s* 1*d*. Ninth 20¼*d*.

John son of Edith: 1 affer, 18*d*; 1 cow, 5*s*; 4 sheep, 4*s*; 1 qr. wheat, 3*s* 4*d*; 1 qr. oats, 18*d*. Total 15*s* 4*d*. Ninth 20½*d*.

John atte Grene: 1 affer, 2*s*; 1 cow, 5*s*; 1 qr. wheat, 3*s* 4*d*; 1½ qr. oats, 2*s* 3*d*. Total 12*s* 7*d*. Ninth 17*d*.

[1] *in omnibus catallis ad valenciam*

[2] *in omnibus bonis ad valenciam*

Henry atte Netherhend: 1 affer, 4*s*; 1 bullock, 5*s*; 1 cow, 5*s*; 20 sheep, 20*s*; 1 pig, 2*s*; 1 qr. 2 b. wheat, 4*s* 2*d*; 1½ qr. drage, 3*s* 9*d*. Total 43*s* 11*d*. Ninth 4*s* 11*d*.

William atte Neth[er]end: 1 affer, 18*d*; 1 cow, 5*s*; 1 qr. *bericorn*, 3*s*; 1½ qr. oats, 2*s* 3*d*. Total 11*s* 9*d*. Ninth 15¾*d*.

Roger Wyttefelawe: 1 affer, 18*d*; 1 bullock, 4*s*; 1 cow, 5*s*; 1 qr. wheat, 3*s* 4*d*; 1½ qr. drage, 3*s* 9*d*. Total 17*s* 7*d*. Ninth 2*s* [*sic*].

Sum of the whole vill: 62*s* 11[½]*d*. [Approved]

128. Proceeds of the "evil custom" (Maltote) of 1294–7 in the port of Newcastle-upon-Tyne from 29 September 1296 to its abolition on 23 November 1297

From a detailed account for one port for almost the whole period of the maltote. The complete account is printed (in translation) in *Archaeologia Aeliana*, 4th ser., xxxii (1954), pp. 275–98.

The extract given is typical except that four ships in the 25th year carried wool for the king too. These items of cargo, which we mark with an asterisk, were indicated by *Lana Regis* (The King's Wool) in the margin of the manuscript. At first they were ignored for customs purposes, but at audit – for book-keeping reasons, no doubt – they were reckoned in (the totals in the manuscript being adjusted accordingly) and allowance made to the collectors of customs.

The 25th year (1296–7)[1]

The ship of William Cronan of Newcastle, called *The Wellfare*, which left the port of Newcastle, licensed, 11 October with the goods of the merchants, etc.:

Hermann Molle of Lubeck had in the same ship in ten sarplers, ten sacks by weight, whereon the custom £20. Of the same for tronage and the *Coket* 7*d*.

Totals:	Wool, 10 sacks	£20 0*s* 0*d*
	Tronage and the *Coket*	7*d*

Sum total £20 0*s* 7*d* Certified.

The ship of Walter, the son of Richard of Saltcott, called *The Cateline*, which left, etc., 1 November with the goods, etc.:

Nickolas of Elrekerr had in the same ship in seven sarplers and one bag, seven sacks eight stones of wool, whereon the custom £14 12*s* 4*d*.

The same had in the same two and a half lasts of hides, whereon the custom £8 6*s* 8*d*. The same had in the same one hundred wool-fells whereon the custom 13*s* 4*d*.

Peter le Graper and Peter Sampson had in the same ship two and a half lasts of hides, whereon the custom £8 6*s* 8*d*.

The same Peter and Peter had in the same two hundred wool-fells, whereon the custom 26*s* 8*d*. Of the same for tronage and the *Coket* 9½*d*, whereof for tronage 3½*d*.

Totals:	Wool, 7 sacks 8 stones	£14 12*s* 4*d*
	Hides, 5 lasts	£16 13*s* 4*d*
	Wool-fells, 300	40*s* 0*d*
	Tronage and the *Coket*	9½*d*

Sum total £33 6*s* 5½*d*

[1] The accounting year is the exchequer year not the regnal year. The "25th year" begins on 30 September, not 20 November, 1296.

The ship of Richard Gerard of Dunwich, called *St John*, which left, etc., 6 April with the goods, etc.:

The same Richard had in the same ship four dickers of hides, whereon the custom 13*s* 4*d*.

Lupus Bouretat of the Society of the White Friscobaldi had in the same ship in forty-seven sarplers, forty-seven sacks of wool, whereon the custom £94.

The same had in the same one and a half lasts six dickers six hides, whereon the custom £6 2*s*. Of the same for tronage and the *Coket* 2*s* 3½*d*, whereof tronage 23½*d*.

Totals:		
	Wool, 47 sacks	£94 0*s* 0*d*
	Hides, 2 lasts 6 hides	£6 15*s* 4*d*
	Tronage and the *Coket*	2*s* 3½*d*

Sum total £100 17*s* 7½*d* Certified.

The ship of Robert of Runeham of Yarmouth, called *The Palmer*, which left, etc., 8 April, etc.

Robert Pope of Yarmouth had in the same ship in one sarpler, one sack and one stone of wool, whereon the custom 41*s* 6½*d*.

The same had in the same eleven dickers 6 hides, whereon the custom 38*s* 4*d*. Of the same for tronage and the *Coket* 2½*d*.

Totals:		
	Wool, 1 sack 1 stone	41*s* 6½*d*
	Hides, 11 dickers 6 hides	38*s* 4*d*
	Tronage and the *Coket*	2½*d*

Sum total £4 0*s* 1*d* Certified.

The ship of William, the son of Peter of Flissing, called *Paradis*, which left, etc., 12 April with the goods, etc.:

The same William had in the same ten stones of wool in three bags, whereon the custom 15*s* 5*d*. The same had in the same fourteen wool-fells, whereon the custom 22¾*d*. Of the same for the *Coket* 2*d*. Total 17*s* 5¾*d*. Certified.

The ship of Walter Scot of Newcastle, which left the same 12 April, etc.:

Adam of Durham had in the same two dickers of hides, whereon the custom 6*s* 8*d*. Of the same for the *Coket* 2*d*.

Total 6*s* 10*d* Certified.

The ship of John, abbot of Blakeney, called *Joyland*, which left etc., 16 April, etc.:

Gilbert of Blakeney had in the same two and a half lasts four dickers three hides, whereon the custom £9 0*s* 12*d*. Of the same for the *Coket* 2*d*. Total £9 0*s* 14*d*. Certified.

The ship of John Prest, called *Backebrad*, which left, etc., 20 April with the goods, etc.:

Peter Sampson had in the same ship in ten sarplers, ten sacks of wool, whereon the custom £20. The same had in the same one last one dicker of hides, whereon the custom 70*s*.

Walter of Cowgate had in the same in four sarplers, four sacks of wool, whereon the custom £8. Richard of Emeldon had in the same in five sarplers, five sacks of wool, whereon the custom, £10. The same had in the same three lasts of hides, whereon the custom £10. The same had in the same a hundred and fifty wool-fells, whereon the custom 20*s*.

Cecilia, the widow of Alexander le Furbeor, had in the same in two sarplers, two sacks of wool, whereon the custom £4. The same had, etc., one last of hides 66*s*. 8*d*.

William of Pouncy had in the same one last of hides, whereon the custom 66*s*. 8*d*.

Guy of Barnard Castle had in the same in four sarplers, four sacks four stones of wool, whereon the custom £8 6*s* 2*d*. The same had in the same one last of hides, whereon the custom 66*s* 8*d*.

John le Especer of Durham had in the same in four sarplers, four sacks of wool, whereon the custom £8.

John Prest of Arnemuth had in the same in one bag, four stones of wool, whereon the custom 6*s* 2*d*.

Of the same for tronage and the *Coket* 2*s* 6½*d*, whereof for tronage 14½*d*.

Totals:	Wool, 29 sacks 8 stones	£58	12*s*	4*d*
	Hides, 10 lasts 1 dicker	£33	10*s*	0*d*
	Wool-fells, 150		20*s*	0*d*
	Tronage and the *Coket*		2*s*	6½*d*

Sum total £93 4*s* 10½*d* Certified.

The ship of John, the son of Mathew del Swyne, called *The Rose*, which left, etc., 23 April with the goods, etc.:

The same John had in the same in one bag, six stones of wool, whereon the custom 9*s* 3*d*. And the same had in the same three dickers of hides, whereon the custom 10*s*.

Roger Peyteuin of Newcastle had in the same one last of hides, whereon the custom 66*s* 8*d*. Robert of Norton of the same had in the same one last of hides, whereon the custom 66*s* 8*d*. John Lubald of the same had in the same in two sarplers, two sacks of wool, whereon the custom £4. The same had in the same fifteen dickers of hides, whereon the custom 50*s*. William le Porter of the same had in the same one last of hides, whereon the custom 66*s* 8*d*.

Roger of Burneton had in the same in one sarpler, one sack of wool, whereon the custom 40*s*. The same had in the same half a last of hides, whereon the custom 33*s* 4*d*. Matilda la Barber had in the same in two sarplers, two sacks of wool, whereon the custom £4. The same etc., in the same half a last of hides, 33*s* 4*d*.

Of the same for tronage and the *Coket* 18½*d*, whereof for tronage 2½*d*.

Totals:	Wool, 5 sacks 6 stones	£10	9*s*	3*d*
	Hides, 4½ lasts 8 dickers	£16	6*s*	8*d*
	Tronage and the *Coket*			18½*d*

Sum total £26 17*s* 5½*d* Certified.

The ship of William Fichet of Dunwich, called *St John*, which left, etc., 23 April with the goods, etc.:

Adam of Iribi had in the same in three sarplers and one bag, three sacks ten stones of wool, whereon the custom £6 15*s* 5*d*. The same had in the same two lasts one dicker of hides, whereon the custom £6 16*s* 8*d*. John of Blakedenn had in the same five dickers of hides, whereon the custom 16*s*. 8*d*.

Agnes, the widow of Sampson le Cotiler had in the same in three sarplers, three sacks two stones of wool, whereon the custom £6 3*s* 1*d*. The same had in the same one last of hides, whereon the custom 66*s* 8*d*. The same had in the same sixty wool-fells, whereon the custom 8*s* 1½*d*.

Thomas of Tyndal had in the same in five sarplers, five sacks of wool, whereon the custom £10. The same in the same half a last of hides, whereon the custom 33*s*. 4*d*.

Peter Sampson and Peter le Graper had in the same in ten sarplers, ten sacks of wool, whereon the custom £20. The same in the same one last one dicker 70*s*.

William of Pountney had in the same half a last one dicker of hides, whereon the custom 36*s* 8*d*.

Cecilia, the widow of Alexander le Furbeor, had in the same in two sarplers, two sacks of wool, whereof the custom £4. The same in the same half a last of hides, whereon, etc. 33*s*. 4*d*.

Elias, the servant of Alexander le Furbeor, the same half a last of hides, whereon the custom 33*s* 4*d*.

Walter le Orfeure had in the same in three sarplers, three sacks of wool, whereon the custom £6. The same in the same three dickers seven hides, whereof the custom 12*s*. 4*d*.

Of the same for tronage and the *Coket* 2*s*. 7*d*, whereof for tronage 13*d*.

Totals:	Wool, 26 sacks 12 stones	£52 18*s* 6*d*
	Hides, 6½ lasts 1 dicker 7 hides	£21 19*s* 0*d*
	Wool-fells, 60	8*s* 1½*d*
	Tronage and the *Coket*	2*s* 7*d*

Sum total £75 8*s* 2½*d* Certified.

The ship of Gau, the son of Hugh of Caumfre, called *The Blithe*, which left, etc., 23 April, etc.

Nicholas of Elrekerr had in the same in four sarplers, four sacks, whereon the custom £8. The same had in the same six hundred and sixty wool-fells, whereon the custom £4 8*s* 1½*d*. The same had in the same one and a half lasts of hides, whereon the custom 100*s*.

Walter of Cowgate had in the same in two sarplers, two sacks of wool, whereon the custom £4. The same had in the same one and a half lasts of hides, whereon the custom 100*s*. The same had in the same four hundred wool-fells, whereon the custom 53*s* 4*d*.

Cecilia, the widow of Alexander le Furbeor, had in the same fifteen dickers of hides, whereon the custom 50*s*. Agnes, the widow of Sampson le Cotiler had in the same in two sarplers, two sacks of wool, whereon the custom £4. Elias, the servant of Alexander le Furbeor, had in the same eleven dickers of hides, whereon the custom 36*s* 8*d*. The same had in the same one hundred wool-fells in one bag, whereon the custom 13*s* 4*d*. Of the same for tronage and the *Coket* 14*d*.

Totals:	Wool, 8 sacks	£8 0*s* 0*d*
	Hides, 4 lasts 6 dickers	£14 6*s* 8*d*
	Wool-fells, 1160	£7 14*s* 9½*d*
	Tronage and the *Coket*	14*d*

Sum total £38 2*s* 7½*d* Certified.

The ship of John of Yarmouth, called *The Wellfare*, which left, etc., 14 May, etc.:

Henry of Dunkirk had in the same two and a half dickers of tanned hides, whereon the custom 8*s*. 4*d*. Of the same for the *Coket* 2*d*. Total 8*s*. 6*d* Certified.

The ship of Richard of Paris, called *The Nicholas*, which left, etc., 14 May, etc.:

The same Richard had in the same one hundred wool-fells, whereon the custom 13*s* 4*d*. Of the same for the *Coket* 2*d*. Total 13*s* 6*d* Certified.

The ship of Gilbert Makerell which left, etc., 30 May with goods of the lord king and of the other merchants who follow:

*The lord king had in the same ship in seventy sarplers, seventy sacks, £140. The same had in the same three lasts nine dickers three hides, whereon the custom £11 11*s*.

John Sywater del Dam had in the same three dickers of hides, whereon the custom 13*s*. Of the same for the *Coket* 3*s* 1*d*.

Total £152 7*s* 3*d* Certified.

The ship of Adam Mouton of Great Yarmouth which left, etc. 30 May with goods of the lord king and of the other merchants, etc.:

*The lord king had in the same in sixty four sarplers, sixty four sacks of wool £128. And four lasts of hides, whereon the custom £13 6*s* 8*d*.

Villan Iscoldi of the Society of Black Circles had in the same in fifteen sarplers, of wool of Karram, fourteen sacks eleven stones of wool, whereon the custom £28 16*s* 11½*d*.

Elias of Crikelawe had in the same in one sarpler, one sack three stones of wool, whereon the custom 44*s* 7½*d*. Of the same for tronage and the *Coket* 3*s* 9½*d*.

Totals:	Wool, 89 sacks 14 stones	£159 0*s* 18½*d*
	Hides, 4 lasts	£13 6*s* 8*d*
	Tronage and the *Coket*	11½*d*

Sum total £172 12*s* 0½*d* Certified.

The ship of William, son of Alard of Cortekyn, which left, etc., 30 May with goods of the lord king and of the other merchants, etc.:

*The lord king had in the same in seventy sarplers, seventy sacks of wool, £140. And three lasts and six hides, whereon the custom £10 2*s*.

Ingelram of Cologne had in the same in two sarplers and one bag, two and a half sacks one stone of wool, whereon the custom 101*s* 6½*d*.

William Bayard had in the same three tanned hides, whereon the custom 12*d*. Of the same for tronage and the *Coket* 3*s*. 6*d*.

Totals:				
	Wool, 72½ sacks 1 stone	£145	0*s*	18½*d*
	Hides, 3 lasts 9 hides	£10	3*s*	0*d*
	Tronage and the *Coket*		3*s*	6*d*

Sum total £155 8*s* 0½*d* Certified.

The ship of William Ermeboud of Berflet, called *Wellfare*, which left, etc., 30 May with the goods of the merchants who follow, etc.:

Villan Iscoldi, merchant of the Society of Black Circles, had in the same in fifteen sarplers, fourteen sacks eleven stones of wool, whereof the custom £28 16*s* 11½*d*.

Isabel de Vesci had in the same in forty-one sarplers, forty-two and a half sacks two stones of wool, whereon the custom £85 3*s* 1*d*.

Of the same for tronage and the *Coket* 2*s* 8*d*, whereof for tronage 2*s* 4*d*.

Totals:				
	Wool, 57 sacks	£114	0*s*	0½*d*
	Tronage and the *Coket*		2*s*	8*d*

Sum total £114 2*s* 8½*d* Certified.

The ship of Peter of the Mill, called *Crusebergh*, which left etc., 2 June with the goods of the merchants, etc.:

The same Peter had in the same in one sarpler, one sack two stones of wool, whereon the custom 43*s* 1*d*.

John of Wolp had in the same in one sarpler, one sack one stone of wool, whereon the custom 41*s* 6½*d*.

Clays, the son of Walter, and Tankard, the son of Laurence, had in the same in eight bags, twenty-five stones of wool, whereon the custom 38*s* 5½*d*.

Clays, the son of Walter, had in the same five hides, whereon the custom 16*d*. Of the same for tronage and the *Coket* 11*d*.

Totals:				
	Wool, 3 sacks 2 stones	£6	3*s*	1*d*
	Hides, 5 hides			20*d*
	Tronage and the *Coket*			11*d*

Sum total £6 5*s* 4*d* Certified.

The ship of Arnald of Cortekyn, called *The Clostre*, which left, etc., 23 June, etc.:

The same had in the same in one sarpler, one sack of wool, whereon the custom 40*s*. William of Cortekin had in the same three and a half stones of wool, whereon, etc., 5*s* 4¾*d*. For tronage and the *Coket* 4½*d*.

Totals:			
	Wool, 1 sack 3½ stones	45*s*	4¾*d*
	Tronage and the *Coket*		4½*d*

Sum total 45*s* 9¼*d* Certified.

The ship of James of Fenying, called *Faireweder*, which left, etc., 6 June with the goods, etc.:

*The lord king had in the same in eighty-three sarplers, eighty-two sacks six stones of wool, whereon the custom £164 3*s* 1*d*. And two lasts six and a half dickers of hides from the county of Cumberland, whereon the custom £7 15*s*.

John del Dam had in the same in six sarplers, six sacks of wool by weight, whereon the custom £12.

Laurence of Fenying, Eustace of Kaleys, William, son of Henry, and John le Katter had in the same seven stones of wool, two dickers and two hides, whereon, etc., 18*s* 1½*d*.

Gocelin of Bruges had in the same in five sarplers and one bag, five sacks one and a half stone of wool, whereon the custom £10 2*s* 3¾*d*.

The same had in the same three and a half dickers of hides, whereon the custom 11*s* 11*d*. And the same had in the same three hundred and thirty wool-fells, whereon the custom 44*s* 0¾*d*.

Of the same for tronage and the *Coket* 5*s*.

Totals:	Wool, 93 sacks 10½ stones	£186 16*s* 2*d*
	Hides, 2½ lasts 2 dickers 2 hides	£8 14*s* 0*d*
	Wool-fells, 330	44*s* 0¾*d*
	Tronage and the *Coket*	5*s* 0*d*

Sum total £196 5*s* 4¾*d* Certified.

The ship of Peter Loef, called *Sauueterre*, which left 4 August, etc.:

The same Peter had in the same in one sarpler, one sack of wool, whereon the custom 40*s*.

Boidin Babard, Hanekin Mase, Peter, the son of Boidin, and Henry the son of Mabill, had in the same in four bags thirteen stones of wool, whereon the custom 20*s*. Of the same for tronage and the *Coket* 10½*d*, whereof for tronage ½*d*.

Totals:	Wool, 1½ sacks	60*s* 0*d*
	Tronage and the *Coket*	10½*d*

Sum total 60*s* 10½*d* Certified.

The ship of John de Camera, called *Gronewold*, which left 4 August with the goods of the merchants who follow:

Richard of Emelden had in the same in one sarpler, one sack of wool, whereon the custom 40*s*.

The same had in the same fifty wool-fells, whereon the custom 6*s* 8*d*.

Nicholas Coleuil had in the same in one bag, sixteen stones of wool, whereon the custom 24*s* 7½*d*.

Nicholas of Ellrekerr had in the same in five sarplers, five sacks of wool, whereon the custom £10.

The same had in the same one hundred wool-fells, whereon the custom 13*s* 4*d*.

Peter le Graper had in the same in six sarplers, six sacks of wool, whereon the custom £12.

Of the same for tronage and the *Coket* 14*d*, whereof for tronage 6*d*.

Totals:	Wool, 12½ sacks 3 stones	£25 4*s* 7½*d*

Wool-fells, 150	20*s* 0*d*
Tronage and the *Coket*	14*d*

Sum total £26 5*s* 9½*d* Certified.

The ship of William de Cruce, called *Bayard*, which left 16 September:

Richard of Emeldon had in the same in three sarplers, three sacks of wool, whereon the custom £6.

Nicholas of Elrekerr had in the same in ten sarplers, ten sacks of wool, whereon the custom £20.

John of St Omer had in the same in four sarplers, four sacks of wool, whereon the custom £8.

Walter Goldsmith had in the same in five sarplers, four sacks of wool, whereon the custom £8.

Simon of Brabant, Godfrey Edeler and John Perceval had in the same in six sarplers, six sacks of wool, whereon the custom £12. The same had in the same 3½ lasts 4 hides, whereon the custom £11 14*s* 8*d*. Of the same for tronage and the *Coket* 2*s* 3½*d*, whereof for tronage 13½*d*.

Totals:	Wool, 27 sacks	£54	0*s*	0*d*
	Hides, 3½ lasts 4 hides	£11	14*s*	7*d*
	Tronage and the *Coket*		2*s*	3½*d*

Sum total £65 16*s* 11½*d*

Sum total for the 25th year: £703 5*s* 11½*d* 19*s* 3½*d*.

Total of the 25th year:

Wool, 551½ sacks, 5 stones	£1,103	7*s*	8½*d*	£1,297 15*s* 9*d* Certified.
Hides, 53 lasts 4 dickers 9 hides	£177	9*s*	8*d*	
Wool-fells, 2,264	£15	2*s*	0*d*	
Tronage and the *Coket*		36*s*	4½*d*	

Of which:

Of the wool of the lord king 286 sacks 2 stones, whereon the custom	£572	3*s*	1*d*
Of the hides of the lord king 12 lasts 16 dickers 4 hides, whereon the custom	£42	14*s*	8*d*
For tronage and the *Coket* of the same wool		12*s*	6½*d*
Total	£615	10*s*	3½*d*
And this is the total whereof the Customers ought to answer	£683	19*s*	3½*d*

Certified.

The 26th year (1297–8)

The ship of William Deuener, called *Annota*, which left the port of Newcastle, licensed, 4 October, with the goods of the merchants, etc.:

Villan Iscoldi of the Society of Black Circles of Florence had in the same in twenty-five sarplers, twenty-four sacks of wool, whereon the custom £48. Of the same for tronage and the *Coket* 14*d*, whereof tronage 12*d*.

Totals:	Wool, 24 sacks	£48 0*s* 0*d*
	Tronage and the *Coket*	14*d*

Sum total £48 0*s* 14*d* Certified.

The ship of Thomas de Burgo, called *The Carite*, which left 16 October:

Richard Sparwe had in the same ship in eight sarplers, eight sacks of wool, whereon the custom £16.

Richard de Emeldon had in the same in five sarplers, five sacks of wool, whereon the custom £10.

The same had in the same one and a half lasts of hides, whereon the custom 100*s*.

The same in the same fifty wool-fells, whereon the custom 6*s* 8*d*.

Robert of Garton had in the same in four sarplers, four sacks of wool, whereon the custom £8.

Richard of Hoga had in the same in three sarplers, three sacks of wool, whereon the custom £6.

Hugh Hangard had in the same in seven sarplers, seven sacks of wool, whereon the custom £14.

The same had in the same six dickers four hides, whereon the custom 21*s* 4*d*.

John Thorald had in the same in two sarplers, two sacks of wool, whereon the custom £4.

The same in the same five dickers four hides, whereon the custom 18*s*.

The same had in the same one hundred wool-fells, whereon the custom 13*s* 4*d*.

Adam Lockesmyth had in the same in one sarpler, one sack of wool, whereon the custom 40*s*.

Simon of Brabant had in the same in nineteen sarplers, nineteen sacks of wool, whereon the custom £38.

Peter le Graper had in the same in three sarplers and one bag, three and a half sacks of wool, whereon the custom £7.

Elias of Crikelawe had in the same in one sarpler, one sack of wool, whereon the custom 40*s*.

Of the same for tronage and the *Coket* 3*s* 10½*d*, whereof for tronage 2*s* 2½*d*.

Totals:	Wool, 54½ sacks	£109 0*s* 0*d*
	Hides, 2 lasts 1 dicker 8 hides	£6 19*s* 4*d*
	Wool-fells, 150	20*s* 0*d*
	Tronage and the *Coket*	3*s* 10½*d*

Sum total £117 3*s* 2½*d*

Sum total for the 26th year to this time £165 4*s* 4½*d*. Certified.

Totals:	Wool of the two ships, 78½ sacks	£157 0*s* 0*d*
	Hides, 2 lasts 1 dicker 8 hides	£6 19*s* 4*d*
	Wool-fells, 150	20*s* 0*d*
	Tronage and the *Coket*	5*s* 0*d*

Sum total £165 4*s* 4*d* Certified.

From this 16 October to 4 January nothing in receipts, because here the receipts of the *New Custom* ceased.

Foreign receipts
25th year (1296–7). 4 May (1297), received 20*s* for eighty wool-fells in the ship of Thomas Fayreweder of Yarmouth, found and forefeited because without licence, etc., and sold by the hand of Symon of Tyndale in parts overseas. The same day, received 3*s* for four hides sold and found in the same ship and forfeited because without licence, etc.
Total 23*s* Certified.

129. The New Temple

In France, where the royal administration was not so developed as in England, the king kept his treasure at the Paris house of the Order of the Temple until 1295 and relied on it to manage his finances. The king of England, with royal institutions and staff, had no need to depend on the Order, but he regularly made great use of it. The following passages illustrate the use he made of it as a safe deposit and his use of its banking services. They have to be from the royal records as, except for one of the year 1185, the London Temple's own records are not known to exist. They could well have been destroyed at the dissolution of the Order. The "New" Temple because the Order had moved in 1185 from Holborn to Thames-side near the Fleet: the present round church dates from that time.

(a)

(*Cal. Pat. Rolls 1232–47*, p. 457)

Mandate to bro. Robert de Sickelingehal [the treasurer of the New Temple] to permit Peter Chaceporc [keeper of the royal wardrobe] to have access to the king's treasure deposited with him, to dispose of by view and testimony of the said Robert according to the injunctions of the king in letters which the said Peter will show him, notwithstanding that in his last retirement the king ordered that no one should have access thereto save in his own presence. [1245]

(b)

(*Cal. Close Rolls 1272–9*, p. 264)

To bro. Joseph de Chauncy, the measurer. Whereas the king has assigned the arrears of the tenth in England lately granted to him and of the tallage lately assessed upon the Jews to complete the works of the Tower of London, which arrears cannot be levied with the speed that is expedient, and the king wills that the works aforesaid shall not be in any way delayed, the king orders the treasurer to pay to Giles de Audenard, keeper of the works aforesaid, 1,000 marks out of the sum of money that the treasurer has in deposit at the New Temple, London, in the king's name. When the treasurer shall have paid this sum, the king will cause him to have his writ of *liberate* or of quittance. [1276]

(c)

(*Cal. Pat. Rolls 1258–66*, pp. 3, 4, 15, and 33)

Given here to illustrate use of the Templars as bankers, but the circumstances are that provision is being made for the wife of one of Henry III's Lusignan half-brothers during his absence abroad. He had chosen to go with his brothers rather than accept the baronial conditions. See the account of the Burton annalist s.a. 1258 (No. 5 above) and the Lusignan pedigree (Appendix II, B)

Grant, by ordinance of the magnates of the council, to Joan wife of William de Valencia, the king's brother, of 400*l* a year for her maintenance, to be taken at the New Temple, London, out of the money arising from the issues of the lands of the said William so long as he shall stay without the realm and his bailiffs have not free administration of the said lands; so that she shall have 200*l* this Michaelmas term, 42 Henry III, and 200*l* next Easter and so thenceforward. [6 November 1258]

Mandate to the preceptor and treasurer of the New Temple, London, to pay out of the first money which they receive of the issues of the lands of William de Valencia the above mentioned 400*l* a year to Joan the wife of the said William as aforesaid. [12 November 1258]

Appointment, during pleasure, of Robert de Creppinges with John de Mairy, steward of William de Valencia the king's brother, to keep the lands of the said William, to collect and receive the issues and deliver them under their seals at the New Temple, London, to remain there in deposit until further order. Further, all sheriffs and their ministers who by order of the king have had the keeping thereof before are to render account to the said John and Robert and to hand over to them what they have received so that all may be deposited together, and they are not to intermeddle herein hereafter; with mandate to the tenants to be intendant to the said John and Robert. [9 March 1259]

Grant, with the assent of the magnates of the council and of the bailiffs of William de Walens', the king's brother, to the king's nephew Henry son of the king of Almain of a loan of 200 marks from the issues of the lands of the said William in Northumberland, which sum he is to repay at the New Temple, London, on the quinzaine of Easter to be placed in deposit with the rest of the money of the said William; with mandate to the sheriff, on view of these letters, to deliver them to him and keep his receipt and the king will cause the same to be allowed to him. [July 1259]

(d)

(*Cat. Pat. Rolls 1292–1301*, p. 419)

Promise to Coppus Josep, Taldus Janiani and their fellows, merchants of Florence of the society of the Friskebaldi, dwelling in London, to recoup them for any loss they may incur in connection with a loan of 2,000 pollard marks and other money now current in England, which the king appointed them to receive from bro. Hugh of the order of Knights Templars, visitor of the order in England, to be repaid in one year after Michaelmas next at the treasury of the Knights Templars in Paris at the rate of 4 pence of Tours for every penny of the said money.

By K., on the information of J. de Drokenesford.

[25 May 1299]

130. Siege-engines for reduction of Stirling Castle, 3 January 1304

(J. Bain, *Cal. of Documents relating to Scotland*, IV, No. 1797)

A detail of the preparations for the campaign of 1304 against the Scots. The engines fresh from Brechin probably needed repair, "Segrave" was new (Bain, *Cal, Docs. Scotland*, IV, pp. 455–6). Old and new alike were ready by 6 April. They were intended to help in the reduction of Stirling Castle (ibid. II, Nos 1500 and 1498–9). By 1 August their work was done (ibid. II, No. 1599). For a vivid description of siege-engines in action, see the Lanercost chronicler's account s.a. 1315 of the Scots' siege of Carlisle (No. 12 above).

Memorandum of delivery by Thomas de Cotynge to Richard de Bremesgrave at Berwick-on-Tweed, of certain staves, hawsers, cords, lead and round stones for these engines, viz, the two made at Brechin, "Segrave", "Vernay", "Robynet", "Forster", and one from Aberdeen. Done at Berwick on 3 January 32 Edw. I.

131. The siege of Carlisle, 1315

(J. Bain, *Cal. of Documents relating to Scotland*, III, Nos 369, 621, 524 and 464)

The Lanercost Chronicle (No. 12 above) s.a. 1315 describes the siege of Carlisle by the Scots following their victory at Bannockburn the year before. The English resistance, particularly to the siege-engines of the attackers, can be both illustrated and checked by documentary evidence:

(a) "Intelligence" from Carlisle, 12 July 1315
(b) Reply to petition from the citizens of Carlisle for compensation, 12 December 1318
(c) Petition for compensation from the Prior of Carlisle [n.d.]
(d) Petition from John de Morpeth for compensation [n.d.]

(a) *To the king, from Carlisle, 12 July*

The writer tells him that they might have harassed the Scots oftener on the March of Carlisle if it had been strengthened by the men-at-arms and others appointed to come to Carlisle at the writer's late departure from him at York, as he has otherwise assured him. The present news is that the whole force of the Scots will enter England at this March [of Carlisle] this Tuesday, 14 July, and will make an "assaie" at the city, for which they have prepared ladders and other engines, as he knows by certain spies, and as Duugol Makdowelle the K's bachelor, the bearer, will tell him by word of mouth. That if they do not besiege Carlisle they intend to approach the K., wherever he may be. Whichever road they take, he hopes it will be the means of restoring the royal power, which may God ever increase and maintain.

(b) *1318, 12 December, York*

The K. considering a representation by the citizens of Carlisle, that on 5 March 1314–15, he committed to them their city, mills, fishings, etc., for three years from Easter thereafter, and Robert de Brus with his army besieged them from Monday next before the feast of St Margaret Virgin [14 July] 1315, till Sunday next after the feast of St Peter *ad vincula* [3 August] following, destroying all their growing crops and other goods; and that all the city gates were closed with a wall of stone and lime from the said Sunday till the Purification following, on account of the attacks of the enemy, whereby they could neither go in nor out, save only by a postern, and this but rarely in case of ambushes, and thus they got little good of the said mills, fishings, etc.; commands the barons, in reckoning with them, to have consideration of these losses, etc., in their discretion.

(c) *Petitions to the K. and council by the prior of Carlisle*
As sir Andrew de Harcla sheriff of Cumberland made a "fosse" through the prior's ground under the wall of Carlisle to strengthen the town, and he dare not level it for the sheriff, he prays remedy lest his church lose the ground.

As the said sheriff, on the approach of the enemy, set fire to and burned all the priory houses outside the walls . . . which could not be replaced for 100*l*, he prays remedy.

(d)

John of Morpeth shews the K. and council that he had houses within the walls of Carlisle worth 5 marks a year, and during the 12 days siege, when the Scots attacked it night and day with "berfrays" and other engines, sir Andrew de Harcla, sir Robert de Swyneburn, and the "Commune", knocked them down, and used the timber for "berfrays" and "bretages" to defend the town. He prays compensation.

132. Commissions of array

(*Cal. Pat. Rolls 1324–7*, pp. 27 and 96–7)

1324, 7 September, Petworth. Commission to Thomas le Botiller and William Walsh of Wolvestrop to select 300 foot archers in the forest of Dene, Berkeleyhirnes and elsewhere in the county of Gloucester, and the said William to be their leader to Portesmuth, by Monday after St Matthew to go thence at the king's wages against the king of France, in the duchy of Aquitaine, in the place of William Tracy and Robert Scliman, lately appointed for this, who cannot attend to the business.

1325, 26 February, Westminster. Appointment of Giles de Beauchamp and Alan de Cherleton to inspect the levies of north and south Wales and the Marches who are severally to muster at Shrewsbury on mid-Lent Sunday, and at Hereford on the Tuesday following, and to array and march them to Portsmouth with their sheriffs, sub-sheriffs, constables, and leaders, so that they shall neither do nor receive any harm. [French] By K.

Memorandum, from North Wales are to come 200 footmen with two constables armed, and their sheriffs, and the sub-sheriffs of the counties of Caernarvan, Anglese, and Merionith will lead them with four of the best of each of the said counties, so as to be at Balaa on Friday before mid-Lent, and there they shall receive wages from the chamberlain for two days as far as Shrewsbury, and thence order shall be made for their wages as far as Portsmouth for seven days.

There will come to Shrewsbury by mid-Lent Sunday the following levies from the following lands:

Mohautesdale	1 man at arms,		10 footmen	
Dynebegh	1	,,	60	,,
Dyffrencloyt	1	,,	30	,,

Bromfeld and Yal	1 man at arms,	50 footmen
The land of the earl of Arundel	1 ,,	50 ,,
La Pole	1 ,,	80 ,,
The county of Flint	1 ,,	50 ,,

Let order be taken for their wages to Portsmouth for seven days.

From Southgales there will come 200 footmen; two constables armed. Rees ap Griffith, sir Roger Pychard, will lead them with 6 men of the counties of Kardigan, Kermerdyn and the stewardship, and the chamberlain of Suthgales will find them wages as far as Portesmuth.

There will come to Hereford on Tuesday after mid-Lent the following levies from the following lands:

Breghenok	1 man at arms,	60 footmen
Buelt	1 ,,	20 ,,
Elvayl	1 ,,	20 ,,
Melnith	1 ,,	60 ,,
Radenore	1 ,,	40 ,,
Wenthrunion	0 ,,	10 ,,
Bergeveny	1 ,,	40 ,,

Let order be taken for their wages to Portsmouth, where they are ordered to be by Sunday after mid-Lent, for the chamberlain has a warrant for it. [French]

133. Trailbaston proceedings at Derby, 4 July 1306

(Text and translation in Cecil Edward Lugard, *Trailbaston: Derbyshire*, 3 vols (privately printed in an edition limited to 20 copies, Ashover, Derbyshire, 1934–5), vol. 2, pp. 1, 58–9, 60, 73–6 for extracts from Assize Roll No. 158; vol. 1, pp. 1, 14–23, 23–6 and vii for extracts from Assize Roll No. 159. The translation here given is that of Lugard with minimum change.)

Before Peter de Maulay and his fellows under commission of 6 April 1305 (see *Parl. Writs*, I, 408 (No. 61), and No. 93 above). Illustrated by the presentments and informal complaints (i.e. without writ) from one hundred or wapentake, that of the Peak District.

Assize Roll No. 158

Pleas and Complaints . . . at Derby, before Peter de Malo Lacu and his associates, justices of the lord the king assigned to hear and try [*sic*] divers felonies, on the Monday next after the octave of the Nativity of St John the Baptist . . . in the 34th year . . . of the reign of the lord king Edward son of king Henry. . .

[m. 5*d*] . . . PEK

It is presented by 12 of the Pek, that William, son of Brun of Little Hokelowe, beat Richard, son of Randolf de F . . . lowe and afterwards took from the same Richard 2*s* against the peace etc.

And William, son of Brun, attached at the king's suit, came and cannot deny the aforesaid trespass upon him presented. On that account let him be committed to gaol.

Afterwards the same William made fine by half a mark by the pledge of Clement de la Ford and Philip . . . leye, and they mainprised him, that he would be of good behaviour.

[m. 6] Still concerning complaints at Derby. MAULAY

PEK

It was presented by the jurors that Adam de Laddesehawebothme beat Richard Cue, against the peace etc. And the aforesaid Adam came and cannot deny the aforesaid trespass. On that account, let him be committed to gaol.

Afterwards he made fine by 40*d* by the pledge of John Folejaumbe and William, son of John del Hagh.

And likewise it was presented that William Haly is a common malefactor and a disturber of the king's peace, and that he beat William Curry, Robert de Smalley, and Roger Balymon, against the peace etc.

And William Haly came, and cannot deny this. On that account let him be committed to gaol. Afterwards he made fine by 100*s*, by the pledge of Hugh de Bukstones, Robert Woderoue, Henry de Hamilton, and Richard le Folejaumbe.

And likewise it was presented, that William Balgey, the elder, is a common conspirator and maliciously impoverished the king's men, especially Robert Ferebraz, whom he caused to be maliciously indicted for hunting, and took from William Palke half a mark, so that he should not be indicted for hunting. And he came and cannot deny this. On that account let him be committed to gaol.

Afterwards he made fine by 20 marks, by the pledge of Robert le Heyr, John de Bradewell, Ellis de Hope and John, son of Tele . . .

[m. 9*d*] . . . PEK

It is presented by 12 of the Pek, that William le Harper (by order of Richard de Vernun) beat Adam Sale of Aldeport, clerk, within the time limited to the justices.[1]

And Ranulf de Snytterton, junior, beat Henry de Northwood (and that Ralph, son of Richard de Baggeley, beat Robert Fox, chaplain, of Aldeport by order of Richard de Vernun) and Thomas le Convers, together with Thomas Hally, made an assault on William le Spenser of Tediswell, and Richard Danyell, senior, so that the said William and Richard fled to the house of William the vintner of Chapel de Freyt and there they dwelt throughout the whole night on account of their beating and the fear of death, until sir Richard Danyel came from his manor at Tediswell and brought help with him and rescued the said William and Richard.

And William de Stafford beat Matthew de Cokedonclif and the said William gave to the said Matthew ten shillings to have his peace.

And William de Lafford proceeded towards Ekynton on the king's business, and came into a certain place in the forest of the lord the king which is called Bedingdale, and in that place met with William son of John del Hawe, the attorney of sir Hugh le Despenser in the aforesaid forest, and there each insulted the other with quarrelsome

[1] The Ordinance of Trailbaston (25 September 1305) reached back to offences committed since 24 June 1297.

words, and afterwards they struck each other with swords and bows, and the aforesaid William de Lafford received the greater damage.

And William Hally and Robert Balgy, junior, and Robert Lillecok and Robert Gage of Tediswell and Henry le Haywart of the same are common bullies and disturbers of the king's peace.

And Thomas de Berleye ordered Hugh le Coroun and Hugh Ropstreit to beat William Holnet of Lytton, and he was beaten by order of the said Thomas within the time limited to the justices and against the peace etc.

And the aforesaid William le Harper, and Richard de Vernun and the others, attached at the king's suit, come. And for the observance of the king's peace, being asked how they wish to clear themselves, say that they are in no wise guilty. And concerning this, they place themselves on the country. On that account, let a jury be impanelled.

The jurors say upon their oath, as to William le Harper, that he is guilty of the aforesaid trespass made on Adam Sale, and by the order of Richard Vernun. On that account let him be committed to gaol.

And William de Stafford is not able to deny the trespass informed upon him. He made fine by one mark, by the pledge of William de la Ford and William del Haye.

And Thomas de Berleye, on his own behalf and for Hugh le Coroun and Hugh Ropstreit, made fine by one mark, by the pledge of William de la Ford and William de Stafford.

And Robert Lillecok made fine by 5*s*, by the pledge of Richard Danyel, knight.

And Robert Gage made fine by half a mark, by the pledge of Richard Danyel.

And Henry le Haywart made fine by half a mark, by the pledge of Richard Danyel, knight.

And Ranulf de Snytterton is not able to deny the trespass informed upon him. On that account let him be committed to gaol. Afterwards he made fine by one mark, by the pledge of Thomas de Berleye and Richard de Buckstanes etc.

Afterwards Richard Vernun came and made fine on his own behalf and for William le Harper by twenty marks, and for Ralph son of Richard de Bagleye he made fine by ten marks by the pledge of Henry de Brayllesford, Richard de Curzoun, Philip de Strell', John Bozoun, Richard Foljaumbe of Wormehull, Ralph Coterel, Richard Foljaumbe of Birchelis, Henry de Gratton, Peter de Roland, Thomas de Berlegh, John Foljambe and Robert de Wardelowe.

And the same pledges mainprised the aforesaid Richard de Vernun, William and Richard, that they would be of good behaviour in the future.

And afterwards Thomas Hally and Thomas le Convers are not able to deny the aforesaid trespass informed upon them. On that account let them be committed to gaol. Afterwards Thomas Hally made fine by 20*s* by the pledge of John, son of Tele, Robert Pek, John de Bradwell and William de Hagh.

And Thomas le Convers made fine by 100*s* by the pledge of William Willowe, Roger le Rus, William de la Ford and William de Bukstones.

And Robert Balgy, junior, is not able to deny the aforesaid trespass informed upon him. On that account let him be committed to gaol. Afterwards he made fine by 10 marks, by the pledge of Robert de Pek, William le Brewester, Roger le Ragged and John Martyn, junior.

And all the aforesaid mainpernors mainprised the aforesaid malefactors, that they would be of good behaviour according to the form etc. [for this cause provided] . . .

Assize Roll No. 159

Pleas of the crown at Derby, before P. de Malo Lacu and his associates, justices of the lord the king appointed for the purpose of hearing and determining divers felonies and trespasses in the county of Derby, on the Monday next after the octave of the Nativity of St John the Baptist . . . in the 34th year . . . of the reign of king Edward son of king Henry . . .

[m. 3] The Peak hundred comes by 12 jurors. MAULAY

The jurors present that Adam Warn of Glossop, on the Sunday next before the feast of All Saints [1 November] in the 31st year of the reign of the present king [1303] killed William del Helde in the vill of Chauelsworthe and that immediately after the deed he fled. And the sheriff was instructed to capture him if etc. And the sheriff testifies that he was not found. On that account let him be exacted and outlawed. His chattels 11*s* 3*d* whereon let Peter Picot the sheriff answer since . . . etc.

The jurors present that William de Chisseworth burgled the house of Alan de Arnicroft on the Wednesday next after the feast of the Apostles Simon and Jude [28 October] in the 31st year etc. [1303], and that the same William afterwards in fleeing because of the same burglary was beheaded at Arnicroft. His chattels 20*d* whereon let the same sheriff answer.

The jurors present also that Richard son of Matilda de Shakelcros on the Sunday in the feast of Pentecost, in the 30th year of the reign of the present king [1302], killed Hugh le Auyn of Whitehawe and immediately after the deed fled. And the sheriff was instructed to capture him if etc. And the sheriff testifies that he was not found. On that account let him be exacted and outlawed. His chattels 6*s* whereon let the same sheriff answer since etc. Afterwards the aforesaid Richard came and produced a charter of the lord the king, which testifies that the said king for the good service which the same Richard son of Matilda did the same lord the king in the parts of Scotland he had pardoned him the liability to prosecution for breach of the peace which pertained to him for the death of the aforesaid Hugh le Auyn of Whitehawe whereof he is indicted, with all trespasses whatsoever and also the outlawry if any etc. Provided that he stands trial in that court etc. if anyone etc.[1] And it is solemnly proclaimed if any etc. and no one came etc. On that account firm peace is granted to him according to the tenor of the charter. Date of the charter at Dunfermelyn in the 31st year of the reign of that king [1303]. And as regards him nothing is to be done about the outlawry.

Item they present that Adam son of Ellote de Buggesworth on the Wednesday next before the feast of St Andrew the Apostle [30 November] in the 31st year of the

[1] This pardon was enrolled on the Patent Roll under 10 November 1303, Dunfermline, and as warranted by privy seal. See *Cal. Pat. Rolls 1301–7*, p. 167.

reign of the present king [1302] killed Henry de Kendale in the aforesaid vill of Buggesworth and immediately after the deed fled. And the sheriff was instructed to capture him if etc. And the sheriff testifies that he was not found. On that account let him be exacted and outlawed. His chattels 18*d* whereon let the aforesaid sheriff answer since etc. And it was presented that the aforesaid Henry Sutor of Verd [or Berd] had knowingly received the aforesaid Adam after the aforesaid felony. On that account the sheriff was instructed to capture him if etc. And the sheriff testifies that he was not found etc. nor has anything etc. And because the aforesaid Adam of whose reception the same Henry is indicted is not yet convicted, for that reason the matter of the same Henry must wait until the aforesaid Adam is convicted etc.

It is presented that William son of Richard de Calwe on the Saturday next after the feast of the Ascension of the Lord in the 30th year of the reign of the present king [1302] killed William le Archer in the vill of Overton. And that Richard de Berdhawe, Philip Balgi of Hope, and Richard Abus of the same, on the Sunday in the feast of Pentecost in the 29th year etc. [1301], killed William de Chelaston in Eydale in the king's forest and that William son of the aforesaid Richard de Calwe and the others immediately after the committing of the aforesaid felonies fled. And the sheriff was instructed to capture them if etc. And the sheriff testifies that they were not found. On that account let them be exacted and outlawed. Chattels of the aforesaid Richard Abus of Hope 13*s* 2*d* whereon the same sheriff shall answer since etc. Afterwards it was testified that the same Richard Abus had died. On that account nothing concerning him to be done. And the others had no chattels.

[Philip Balgi was pardoned for the death of William de Chelaston by letters patent of 9 April 1302, "by reason of his service in Scotland" (*Cal. Pat. Rolls 1301–7*, p. 28).]

It was presented that Thomas de Lyndesey of Aldeporte, Richard Mathias and Nicholas, sons of the same Thomas, on the Monday next after the feast of the Epiphany of the Lord in the 28th year etc. [1300] killed Robert Keys of Aldeporte in the same vill of Aldeporte and immediately after the deed fled. And the sheriff was instructed to capture them if etc. And the sheriff testifies that they were not found. On that account let them be exacted and outlawed. Their chattels £8 10*s* whereon the same sheriff shall answer since etc.

It is presented that Walter Kay of Elton on the feast of the Ascension of the Lord in the 32nd year of the reign of the present king [1304] killed Henry son of Gene de Begheleye in the vill of Gratton. And that Hugh the smith (Faber) of Baucquell on the Monday next before Palm Sunday in the 29th year etc [1301] killed Roger Keys of Aldeporte in the vill of Baucquell. And that Matilda daughter of Robert le Bager of Yolegreve on the Thursday next after the feast of St John the Baptist [24 June] in the 31st year etc. [1303] freely and feloniously burnt the house of William le White of Yolegreve in the vill of Yolegreve. And that John son of Simon son of Nalle of Tadington on the vigil of the Circumcision of the Lord in the 34th year etc. [i.e. on 31 December 1305] killed Richard son of Herbert Hervy of Presteclove in the same vill of Presteclove at night. And that Robert son of Simon de Asscheford on the feast of the Assumption of the Blessed Virgin Mary [15 August] in the 27th year etc.

[1299] killed Thomas le Jager of Little Longsden in the vill of Asscheford. And that William son of Alan de Cley of Teddeswell on the Monday next after the feast of St Katherine the Virgin [25 November] in the 27th year etc. [1298] killed Ralph son of Juliana de Slack in the moor of Teddeswell. And that William son of Richard at the mill of Hauersegge on the feast of the Exaltation of the Holy Cross [14 September] in the 29th year etc. [1301] killed Philip del Hill of Hauersegge in the moor of Basselowe. And that Richard de Ryley son of Ralph le Streger of Hassop on Palm Sunday in the year aforesaid killed Eustace de Eyum in the same vill of Eyum in the evening. And that Richard Cut of Hertington on the Monday next after the feast of the Purification of the Blessed Virgin Mary [2 February] in the 28th year etc. [1300] killed Stephen le Wassher of Cheylmardon in the mill of Cheylmardon and that the aforesaid Walter Kay and all the others aforenamed immediately after committing the felonies aforesaid fled.

And the sheriff was instructed to capture them if etc.

And the sheriff testifies that they were not found etc.

On that account let the same Walter Kay, Hugh, John son of Simon son of Nalle, Robert son of Simon, William son of Alan, William son of Richard, Richard de Ryley and Richard Cut be exacted and outlawed. And let the aforesaid Matilda be exacted and waived. The chattels of the aforesaid Walter Kay of Elton 9*s.* Chattels of the aforesaid Hugh the smith of Baucquell 3*s.* Chattels of the aforesaid John son of Simon son of Nalle of Tadington 5*s.* Chattels of the aforesaid Robert son of Simon of Assheford 65*s.* Chattels of William son of Alan de Cley of Teddeswell 5*s.* Chattels of William son of Richard at the mill of Hauersegge 4*s.* Chattels of the aforesaid Richard de Ryley son of Ralph le Streger of Hassop 23*s.* Chattels of the aforesaid Richard Cut of Hertingdon 10*s.* whereon the aforesaid sheriff shall answer since etc. And the others had no chattels.

[Richard de Ryley was given pardon of his outlawry for the death of Eustace (here described as "Eustace son of Reginald de Foulhowe") by letters patent of 28 February 1307, "he having been pardoned that death, 16 October, 29 Edward I [1301]" *Cal. Pat. Rolls 1301–7*, p. 501).]

[m. 3*d*] Still concerning the Peak Hundred. MAULAY

The jurors present that Agnes the wife of Robert de Byrleye on the day of St Bartholomew the Apostle [24 August] in the 33rd year etc. [1305] killed Rose her daughter in the vill of Haversegge and she was immediately captured and led to the prison of the lord the king at Nottingham. On that account the sheriff is instructed to cause the same to come here on the Friday next after the feast of the Translation of St Thomas the Martyr [7 July] in the 34th year etc. [1306]. On which day she herself came and having been asked how she wishes to clear herself of the aforesaid death she says she is not guilty thereof. And for this places herself upon the country. The jurors say upon their oath that the aforesaid Agnes on the day and in the year aforesaid lay in childbed in her house in the vill aforesaid, that within the third day after the birth for want of care and sustenance of her body she fell into a delirium and it seemed to her that a certain red dog entered the house where she lay and wanted to swallow the aforesaid Rose her daughter aged 1½ years who lay in a certain cradle before the bed of the said Agnes and Agnes herself raised a great clamour and took a certain knife and, meaning to have struck the aforesaid dog with the same knife as she thought, she struck the aforesaid Rose her daughter lying in the aforesaid cradle before her bed as has been said and gave her a certain wound in the head. So that she immediately died thereof; concerning which they say positively that the aforesaid Agnes killed the aforesaid Rose, her daughter, while she was in the aforesaid infirmity of delirium and out of her mind, and not by any felony or malice aforethought. On that account let her be sent back to prison to await the pardon of the lord the king.

[1306, 22 July, Beverley. Pardon to Agnes, wife of Robert de Birley, in Nottingham gaol for the death of Rose her daughter, as it appears by the record of Peter de Malo Lacu and his fellows, justices of oyer and terminer in the county of Derby, that she killed her in a fit of frenzy.[1]]

It is presented that Adam son of Geoffrey de Kynder and Hugh the shepherd of Worteley stole two oxen which belonged to William son of Simon de Kynder and one cow which belonged to Matilda de Lafford in the vill of Kynder on Wednesday next after the feast of St Michael [29 September] in the 32nd year etc. [1304]. And that Adam son of Peter del Mosse stole a cow which belonged to William Godknave in the vill of Boudon in the year aforesaid and that the aforesaid, Adam son of Geoffrey and the others, absconded because of the aforesaid thefts. And the sheriff was instructed to capture them if etc. And the sheriff testifies that they were not found. On that account let them be exacted and outlawed. They had no chattels.

It is presented that Henry Lumby of Derwent, Richard le Colier of the same and Adam his son are common thieves of divers thefts committed in this county for many years past and that they have committed many robberies on the moor of Basselowe from men crossing there and likewise that they are thieves of cattle stolen in this county. And that Thomas son of Mathew de Derwent is a common thief of all manner of thefts committed in this county within the time limited to the justices. And that Ivo son of Henry Wyldegos is a common thief of oxen and cows stolen in divers places in this county and that he stole an ox from Richard son of Hervy of Longdone Dale in the vill of Boudon in the year etc. And that the aforesaid Richard le Colier and Thomas son of Mathew and Ivo son of Henry Wyldegos, having been captured on account of this, are now come. And asked how they wish to clear themselves of the aforesaid felonies presented against them, they deny the robberies, thefts and all manner of felonies. And for good and ill place themselves upon the country. The jurors say upon their oath that the aforesaid Richard, Thomas and Ivo are guilty of the aforesaid felonies charged against them. On that account they etc. Chattels of the aforesaid Richard 3*s* 3*d*. Chattels of the aforesaid Ivo 35*s* 9*d* whereon Peter Pycot, the sheriff, shall answer since etc. The same Ivo had a cottage and one acre of land which are worth 4*s* a year and they shall be taken into the hand of the lord the king. And the sheriff shall be answerable to the lord the king in the next eyre etc. for the issues arising therefrom. And the aforesaid Thomas had no chattels. And the aforesaid Henry absconded because of the aforesaid felonies. And the sheriff was instructed to capture him if etc. And the sheriff testifies that he was not found. On that account let him be exacted and outlawed. He had no chattels.

[1] *Cal. Pat. Rolls 1301–7*, p. 458

It is presented that Robert del Hawe of Basselowe stole an ox from Elias de Boterhal in the vill of Basselowe in the 29th year etc. [1300–1] and that he received Robert de Bobenhill, a thief since hanged, knowing about his theft. And that the same Robert del Hawe is a common thief of thefts committed in this county. And that John Auker of Aistesley, Richard his brother, Roger de Merpil and Roger Maneris at the mill of Merpil were at the burglary and robbery committed at the house of Seuall de Midelcauel in the vill of Boudon in the 27th year etc. [1298–9]. And that they are common thieves of all manner of thefts committed in this county within the time limited to the justices. And that Richard Wyldesmyth of Hegham and Thomas his brother are common thieves and plunderers and have plundered many men crossing through the middle of Chattesworth moor of their goods within the said time. And the aforesaid Robert del Hawe and the others absconded because of the aforesaid felonies. And the sheriff was instructed to capture them if etc. And the sheriff testifies that they were not found. On that account let them be exacted and outlawed. They had no chattels.

It is presented that Robert Toggh of Hertingdon and William Grill of the same plundered Richard Knot of Bonteshall on Bracyington moor in the 34th year etc. [1305–6], namely, of one surcoat and other things to the value of ½ mark, and that they are common thieves of thefts committed in this county. And that John son of Robert son of Isabel of Cestreshire plundered John de Benteley on Foxelowe moor of goods to the value of ½ mark. And that he is a common thief of thefts committed in this county. On that account the sheriff was instructed to capture the aforesaid, Robert and the others, if etc. And the sheriff testifies that the aforesaid William and John were not found etc. On that account let them be exacted and outlawed. They had no chattels. And the aforesaid Robert was captured and is in the prison of the lord the king. Afterwards the aforesaid Robert Toggh came and, asked how he wishes to clear himself thereof, denies theft, robbery and common felony and for good and ill places himself upon the country. The jurors say on their oath that the aforesaid Robert did not plunder the aforesaid Richard, as he is charged with doing, nor is he guilty of any other theft or felony committed in the county within the time etc. or outside. On that account he is acquitted thereof.

[m. 4] Still the High Peak. MAULAY

It is presented that Richard le Stodhird is a thief of foals and bullocks stolen in divers places in the Peak within the time limited to the justices. On that account the sheriff was instructed to capture him if etc. Who being now captured comes and, asked how he wishes to clear himself thereof, denies all thefts and all felony and for good and ill places himself upon the country. The jurors say upon their oath that the aforesaid Richard is not at all guilty of the aforesaid thefts he is charged with or of any other theft or felony etc. On that account let him go acquitted thereof.

The jurors present that Richard Lippe son of William Wildegos of Feyrfeld and Robert Stickebuk stole a certain ox from Nicholas de Shirbrok on Bucstones moor and an ox and a calf from William Frost in the same vill of Bucstones in the 34th year etc. [1305–6] and that they are common thieves of thefts committed in this county within the time here limited to the justices. And that William son of Henry de Rountonstedes in the 31st year etc. [1302–3] stole a certain ox of John de la Boche in the forest of Croudecote and that he is a common thief and that the aforesaid Richard Lippe and the others absconded because of the aforesaid thefts. And the sheriff was instructed to capture them if etc. And the sheriff testifies that they were not found. On that count let them be exacted and outlawed. They had no chattels.

The jurors present that Adam son of Asser de Hokelowe is a thief of ewes stolen in this county. On that account the sheriff was instructed to capture him if etc. And the sheriff testifies that he was not found, nor had he anything etc. And because afterwards the jurors testify that only two ewes were stolen worth eleven pence, and that theft is so small that he would not lose life or limb if he were present, nothing about exacting is to be done against him for the aforesaid happening at present.

The jurors present that Richard Anvers of Glossop abducted the wife of Adam del Mosse against the peace etc. Afterwards the same jurors say that the aforesaid woman went from her house in the vill of Boudon and met the aforesaid Richard in the vill of Eclesmor and went of her own free will with the aforesaid Richard into the county of Cheshire. On that account nothing [must be done] about it at present.

The jurors present that Robert Batty on the Tuesday next after the feast of the Finding of the Holy Cross [3 May] in the 26th year etc. [1298] killed William his brother with a certain staff in the vill of Tyngewysel in the county of Cheshire. And because this happened in the county of Cheshire, the matter must therefore wait for the next eyre of the justices. And his chattels are likewise valued by the jurors at 14*s*. And the township of Glossop ought to be made responsible for it[1] in the aforesaid eyre.

It was presented that Richard son of Robert Ballgi the elder is the receiver of Philip his brother who killed William de Chelaston together with the others, as is presented elsewhere in the pleas of this wappentake.[2] On that account the sheriff was instructed to capture the aforesaid Richard if etc. And the sheriff testifies that he was not found, nor had he anything etc. And because the aforesaid Philip, of whose reception the said Richard is indicted, is not yet convicted, for that reason the matter of the same Richard must wait until the aforesaid Philip his brother is convicted . . .

[m. 13] PEAK

Richard Daniel Sworn.
Richard, son of William Folejaumb Sworn.
William de Hopton Sworn.
Henry de Graton Sworn.
Richard Folejaumb de Bucheles Sworn.
John Bortum de Edensovere.
John Folejaumb de Berde Sworn.
John del Smaleleys Sworn.

[1] *inde onerari*
[2] page 616 above. It will be observed from *Cal. Pat. Rolls 1301–7*, p. 28, that Philip had been pardoned in 1302, by reason of service in Scotland, for his share in the murder.

Alexander de Northleies Sworn.
Ricardus de Bokstones Sworn.
Philip de Stralee Sworn.
Henry de Hamelton Sworn.
Jordan de Steuresdal Sworn. . .

134. Notes classifying parliamentary business, 1318

(*Rot. Parl. Anglie hactenus inediti MCCLXXIX–MCCCLXXIII*, ed. H. G. Richardson and G. O. Sayles (Camden, 3rd ser., vol. 51 (1935)), pp. 70–80)

The following petitions for and against . . . delivered . . . except those which are marked "Concerning debts" – in D . . . Ashby.

Before the great council
[Specially] the petitions of
*the men of the community of the vill of Scarborough
*Gilbert Ackil
*Arnold de Cames
the clerks of the king's chancery
lords of liberties and burgesses and citizens about maintaining their liberties
two petitions on behalf of the clergy of the kingdom concerning prohibition
another petition about the extortions of the Roman court
the petition of John de Enderly
*John de Fre . . .
Christian who was the wife of Alexander de Bonkile
*Alice Love of co. Devon
Peter de Burgate
Robert de Umfraville, earl of Angus
Robert de Talliolu
the men formerly burgesses of Berwick
Hugh de Audley and Margaret his wife
*the community of Surrey about a way short . . .
Fulk son of Warin
*John of Weston'
a petition about ordaining who should wear furs
a petition against the marshal for[?] shoeing horses unduly
the petition of John de Mowbray
a petition about ordering greater certainty as to the keeping of the mints of London and Canterbury
a petition about corrodies granted by the king in various religious houses and abbeys which ought not to be burdened etc.

* Entries so marked are struck through.

Before the king[1]
[The petitions of] . . . de Burgh
. . .
. . .
the prior of Dover concerning . . .
Joan de Leylton
Walter de Gosewic
the men of Carlisle about provisioning
the prior of Malton
another petition of Hugh de Audley
Philip of Montgomery
John Cosyn
Agnes Burdon
John Dirland
John of Chester
Philip son of Richard de Ros
Ralph de Dreyton
Joan who was the wife of John de Chaumbre
Nicholas Kiriel
Robert le Taillour
Henry le Taillour
Beatrice of Ryle
Cassandra who was the wife of Wadin de Rosse
Luke de Wardon
Ankenny de Martmall
Richard de Reddyngs
the canons of Carlisle
John of Penrith
Agnes who was the wife of John Walton
John of Warthill
John Baudewyn
John son of Henry of Chester
William de Beneley
Roger le Flechcher
Peter Chichester
Thomas de Bekering
William de Hoveden
Gilbert de Birton
William of Weston
Robert de Blakeborn
Richard de Kirkbrigge
John Veys de Briseit

[1] *Coram Rege*. Not the king's bench, the law-court, but a special, quite unrelated tribunal (see *Rot. Parl. hactenus inediti*, p. xi, and p. 623, n. 2 below).

John of Shrewsbury
William Dacre
Alexander of Stanford
William de Horkesly
David de Beton
Richard of Denton
William Sauvage
Robert de Esslyngton
the bishop of Carlisle
Margaret who was the wife of Adam Banastre
John of Preston
William Sauvage and John Hardi
Edward Balliol
Dougal MacDowell
Dougal Mcdioll[1]

Wales
Madoc Glodeich
*Griffin de la Pole *Wales*
Madoc ap Griffith
Griffin Lloyd

Petitions before the king himself continued[2]
Two petitions of Gerard Salvayn – *It is reserved for Adam*
the petition of Thomas son and heir of Guy de Beauchamp
the petition of John Knokyn – *It is reserved for Adam*
*the petition of John of Brittany, earl of Richmond
John of Brittany[3]
*a petition of the clerks of the chancery
the petition of Henry Redmane
the petitions of the people of Northamptonshire
*Christine de Hauville – *because it is expedited*
those who stayed in Ber[wick] castle
John de Stirilisle
John Oggol
. . . ton

expedited

Also petitions concerning debts sought from the king, viz,
Manettus Fraunceys
Pierre de Bazas
John Cosyn, Arnald de Luk' and their partners of Gascony

[1] substituted for the preceding Dougal MacDowell
[2] cf. p. 622, n. 1 above
[3] written after deletion of preceding entry

Arnald de Luk'
Manettus Sausene, merchant of Gascony
all the vintners of Gascony
Richard Cosyn
*William Kelpyn
*the merchants of England about lending on sacks of wool
Warin Ballard
*William le Latimer
Ivo de Aldborough
Nicholas of Kingston
the abbot and convent of Cockersand
Richard Bret of Ireland
Gilbert Makaskil
the petition of Mary Heron
*the petition of Thomas de Heton
the petition of Ingelbright de Ferst and his partners, merchants of Almain

Petitions not fully expedited because of difficulties of some sort, viz,
The petitions of Richard of Ludgershall and Adam de Eglesfeld with a certain process etc. – *before the king*
*three petitions concerning the clerk of the market of the household
a petition of the community of the county of Nottingham asking for a perambulation to be made
a petition concerning merchants of Almain over a certain charter of the king
the petition of the archbishop of York about having a port at Hull
the petition of Robert Hastang, keeper of the vill of Hull
a petition of the county of Devon concerning a remedy over the levying of green wax
a petition of religious of the archbishopric of York
a petition of the archbishop, dean and chapter of York about having cornage
*two petitions of the clergy of England about prohibitions delivered in judgment
the petition of Henry de la Pomeray
the petition of Constance who was the wife of Henry de Mortimer
the petition of Thomas, earl of Norfolk
*the petition of Hugh de Audley and Margaret his wife
a petition of the merchants of England about half a mark the sack
William Kelpin
William le Latimer
*Thomas de Heton
Robert of Clitheroe
the abbots of Rievaulx and Byland
the prior of Nostell
Robert de Grimeby
Nicholas Pecche
John Vays and Katherine his wife

the advice of the people about some ordinance against provis[ors] etc.
a petition of the merchants of Almain written to the earl of Lancaster
the bishop of Ely

Petitions expedited[1]
Petitions delivered to Robert of Ashby
The petitions of the brethren of Burton Lazars
a petition on behalf of the citizens of London
the petition of Scolastica who was the wife of Godfrey of Meaux
the petition of Edmund de Passelawe
the petition of William de Furneys
the petition of Thomas of Warthill
a petition of the men of Derby
a petition of the men of the vill of Hedon
the petition of Nicholas Dauue
a petition on behalf of the men of Brampton
the petition of Edmund Everard
the petition of John de Cliff
the petition of Alexander de Montfort

a petition of the men of Cornwall
the petition of Gilbert de Ellesfeld
the petition of the prior of Kirkham
the petition of Walter of Bedwin
the petition of Cecilia de Beauchamp
the petition of Roger of Appleby
the petition of Robert de Mohaut
the petition of the bishop of Carlisle
} *are delivered to H. of Edwinstow*

two petitions of the men of Huntingdon
the petition of Thomas Danvers
a petition of the community of Devon
the petition of Matthew de Crouthorne
another petition of Devon
also a petition of Devon
} *Welford*

two petitions of Carmarthen – *are delivered to W. de Cliff*

the petition of Milo de Sanford
the petition of the abbot of Tupholm
} *Tynton*

the petition of William of Barton – *before the king*
the petition of mr John Bush – *through Cosyngton – Burgh*
a petition of the citizens of London – *Norton*
the petition of Stephen Guychard – *Burgh*

[1] The precise allocation to individual auditors of the petitions in this section is uncertain. But it is not a matter of major importance: all are petitions expedited.

a petition of Tamworth – *Cliff*
a petition of the executors of W. of Maidstone – *Cliff*
the record and petition of J. of Clavering – *to the same John*

the petition of the abbot of St Dogmael in Wales
the petition of the abbot of Leicester
} *Tynton*

the petition of the men of the garrison of Berwick
the petition of the men of Cambridge
} *Bamborough*

Also are delivered to Geoffrey of Welford
The petition of Henry of Stanton
the petition of the heir of Daubeny

a petition of the citizens of Canterbury – *is delivered to J. of Norton*

Edwinstow
The petition of the prior of Bridlington
the petition of John Osiom
the petition of Thomas de Goldesburgh

Airmyn
Petitions concerning Flemings
the petition of Robert Valoines, precentor of the church of York

a petition of the burgesses of Cambridge – *Norton*

a petition concerning the cocket of London
a petition about improving the vill of York
a petition about Windsor gaol
the petition of Walter Bedwin
the petition of Peter de Chenedon
a petition of the brethren of St Thomas of Acre
the petition of William Maghtild'
the petition of Richard of Houghton
the petition of Richard Arblaster
} *Burgh*

the petition of Matilda Berelem'
the petition of William of Ryle
the petition of John of Foxley
the petition of Alice of Lincoln
a petition of the canons of Beverley
the petition of John of Droxford
*the petition of John Osiom
the petition of J. de Ricardyn
} *to Richard of Nassington*

the petition of Arnald de Luk'[1]
the petition of the abbot of Peterborough – *Ashby*
a petition of the burgesses of Northampton – *Welford*
a petition of Yarmouth – *Botetourt*
two petitions of the abbot of Meaux – *are delivered to the same abbot*
a petition of Kepyer – *Herlaston*
the petition of John de Snayth }
the petition of William Percrik' } *Ashby*
a petition of the men of Wainfleet – *Tynton*
the petition of Edmund de Donyngton – *Bamborough*
the petition of the prioress of Marrick – *Herlaston*

Ashby
Simon de Wakfeld
Roger le Taillour
Marion of Newark
Andrew Harcla
Andrew Harcla
Adelard of Winchelsea
the men of Oxfordshire and Berkshire
the men of Pontefract
John Clareles
Philip of Kyme
Alina Lovel
Alina Lovel
William, prebendary of Corringham
Robert of Guisborough }
William of Sheppey } *W. Barton*
Nicholas de Boleville – *Tynton*
the community of Leicestershire
Beatrice of Ryle
Benet Athelard of Winchelsea
John de Osmundthorpe
Hugh of Houghton
the prior of Ellerton
John de Gysborn
William of Ryle
the tenants of the bishop of St David's
Nicholas le Latimer
the burgesses of the vill of Nottingham
the canons of Carlisle
Nicholas de Blokeville

[1] It is not clear to whom this petition is assigned.

for poor beneficed clerks
Edmund of Woodstock
John de Wroghale
Ralph of Boarstall
William de Bathel
John of Ferriby, clerk
merchants of the company of Spini
Richard of Houghton
the men of Cumberland
the countess of Lincoln – *Tynton*
the abbot of Thornton
William of Sheppey
the community of clergy at one time or another pluralist
Richard de Podmore
William de Stokhithe
William of Ryle
John Veys
John son of Roger de Doen
John de Cokeshale
the prioress of Brodholm
the prior of the hospital of St John
a petition against Robert of Kendal
Margery de Treverbyn
Nicholas of Linwood
Luke de Colevile
Philip de Rosse
about weighing lead on the tron
Henry of Buckton
the burgesses of Kingston
the community of the East Riding of Yorkshire
Margery who was the wife of John Cnokes
Ralph de Harlewod
Thomas of Weyland
John de Ridel
the master and brethren of the hospital of St Leonard, York
Ralph son of Iva Todde
Robert son of Angeis Daneby
Henry de Shiracos
Adam de Hoperton
Prior of Wirksop
John son of William of Hazleridge
Robert, parson of Saxmundham
the burgesses of Appleby
Robert de Hokesham

persona Lombard'
Owen of Montgomery
on behalf of the vill of Bulwell
John de Weston
John de Gore
Gilbert Makaskil
Robert of Clifton
Gilbert of Stapleton
concerning the Dover crossing
the men of Bamborough
the men of Carlisle
the men of Newcastle-upon-Tyne about the account of the eng[ineer]

Petitions expedited continued
the petition of Thomas de Heton
the petition of William of Felton
the petition of David of Langton
Thomas of Corbridge – *to the chancellor himself*
John of Cromwell
Philip de Laghton
Griffin de la Pole
the petitions of the men of Newcastle-upon-Tyne
also about changing suits in plea of debt
Philip of Montgomery
the community of Galtres Forest
Thomas de Condroi
Robert of Well
Henry son of Hugh
Robert de Hornclif'
on the ground that clerks of the chancery and exchequer are not to be attorned
John of Brittany, earl of Richmond
the executors of the will of William de Ros etc.
Griffin son of William de la Pole
Gilbert de Glenkarney
the citizens of Carlisle
Eleanor, abbess of Barking

Peter of Ashridge – *Burgh*

135. A parliamentary election, 1320

(*South Lancashire in the Reign of Edward II*, ed. G. H. Tupling (Manchester, for the Chetham Soc., 1949), p. 119)

... And that when a certain writ of the king had come to the same William[1] for the election of two knights to go to the king's parliament, which knights ought to have been elected by the whole community of the county, the same William elected Gilbert de Haydok and Thomas de Thornton without the consent of the community; and when they returned from the parliament they brought a writ for levying their expenses, by which the aforesaid Richard and William de Wynwyk the bailiffs were ordered to levy twenty pounds for the expenses of the aforesaid knights; whereas the community of that county could have had by their own election two sufficient men to go to the parliament for ten marks or ten pounds. And moreover the same bailiffs levied as much for their own use as they did for the use of the aforesaid knights. And they say that Henry de Malton, while he was sheriff, elected William de Slene and William de Walton to go to the parliament, without the consent etc. in the same manner.

[1] William le Gentil. He succeeded Henry de Malton (who is accused of similar misconduct of the election for the York parliament of 1319) in 1320. The earl of Lancaster was hereditary sheriff and both were in fact his deputies.

Part IV

THE CHURCH IN ENGLAND

INTRODUCTION

"ENGLISH history is more involved in general history in the thirteenth than it is even in the twelfth century" (Powicke). This is even more evident in religion than it is in other aspects of thirteenth-century English life. It is evident alike ecclesiastically and spiritually. The best general account is J. R. H. Moorman's *Church Life in England in the Thirteenth Century*. Its method, however, is descriptive and it should be supplemented by C. R. Cheney's *From Becket to Langton: English Church Government 1170–1213*, which emphasises change and sees it at work in England as much before as after the canons of the Fourth Lateran Council of 1215.

Because of this, Cheney is also essential reading as a corrective to Marion Gibbs and Jane Lang, *Bishops and Reform 1215–1272*, which analyses those canons and traces their application in England down to 1272. The canons themselves are given below (No. 136) in a complete English translation. There is, as yet, no good critical edition of the Latin text, though one is in preparation. The most serviceable and convenient one meanwhile (and the one used for No. 136) is that in *Conciliorum Oecumenicorum Decreta*, ed. J. Alberigo and others, *editio altera* (Rome, Herder, 1962), pp. 206–47. For further study of the impact of the Fourth Lateran Council on this country, after Gibbs and Lang as an introduction, the firm foundation is now, of course, *Councils and Synods . . . II (1205–1313)*, edited by Powicke and Cheney.

As great an influence as Pope Innocent and the Lateran Council was the *Rule* (and even more the spirit) of Francis of Assisi, a man who (we are told by one who heard him) "had not the manner of a preacher" and who certainly shunned power. The spirit is reflected in the chronicle of Brother Thomas, of which only the beginning is given here (No. 138 below) but which can be read in full in translations of an earlier and less authoritative edition of the Latin, Father Cuthbert's (1909) or E. Gurney Salter's (1926) given in the bibliography below. The Franciscan mission was not the only one, or even the first, to these islands in the thirteenth century (that of St Dominic's "preachers" preceded it by three years, and strongly rivalled it), but it is the best known, thanks to a tradition of fine scholarship established by A. G. Little and a British Society of Franciscan Studies (see E. L. C. Mullins, *Texts and Calendars* (R. Hist. Soc., 1958), pp. 115–18) and still alive in work such as that of Decima L. Douie on Archbishop Pecham. Here only illustrations can be given of the popular welcome the friars received, the attitudes of other religious to them, and some of the practical questions which arose from their coming.

Another influence from outside was what I have called "The University Movement". This, though associated with, indeed largely caused by, a renaissance, the "Recovery of Aristotle" it has been termed, resulting in not only a great advance in the method of intellectual inquiry but also a vast accession of knowledge, was essentially a concentration of teachers and students and subjects in convenient centres within a common ("university") organisation, instead of in cathedral or monastic or severely professional schools: essentially a different vehicle for higher education. The

Church was necessarily involved and did not wish to be otherwise, lest it completely lose control. What we have chosen to illustrate, however, is not this or the university *per se* (for university organisation, life and studies are matters covered by works in the bibliography), but how, to raise the standard of its priesthood, the Church found the means for scholarships for its best recruits to send them to university (No. 143). The monastic orders were slower to take the opportunity (or should one say to see the advantage in their case?). The *moine universitaire*, the monk who was also a university man, was not common: but, as Mr Pantin discovered (*Chapters of the English Black Monks*, III, p. ix), the Benedictines in England encouraged this new type of monk. The three pieces in No. 144 below span fourteen years of the career of one such.

The foundation alike of the government and the spiritual well-being of the Church was the bishop in his diocese. It had been so in the earliest days to which we can trace the office, the early years of the second century, long before the territorial diocese and the parochial system, and it was still so in the thirteenth. Archbishops could not regiment him. Between king and pope his position could be uncomfortable, but either of them could, and would, ensure that he was not completely subordinate to the other. It is not possible in the space to do more than indicate by a miscellany of texts at the same time the extent of his authority and the range of his problems, the complexity of his situations and the frailty of human nature which it was his pastorate to care for, but a task which, of necessity, he had in almost all cases to delegate. One can only recall that the quality of the episcopate of thirteenth-century England was high; that more leadership and example for the church in England (it could be maintained) emanated in the earlier part of that century from the diocese of Salisbury than from either of the archbishoprics.

SELECT BIBLIOGRAPHY

A brief bibliography for all periods of church history is Owen Chadwick's *The History of the Church: a Select Bibliography*, Historical Association "Helps" series pamphlet No. 66 (1962). Excellently selected, but necessarily general.

For the period and aspects more specialised bibliographies will be found in Kathleen Edwards's *The English Secular Cathedrals* (1967 edn); David Knowles's *The Monastic Order in England*, and *Religious Orders in England*, I; Hinnebusch, *Early English Friars Preachers*; Lunt, *Financial Relations of the Papacy with England to 1327*; Moorman's *Church Life in England in the Thirteenth Century*; Powicke's *Thirteenth Century 1216–1307*; *passim* in *Councils and Synods*, II (1205–1313), ed. Powicke and Cheney (Oxford, 1964); for Scotland, Wales and Ireland, the appropriate chapters and bibliographical sections of Powicke's *Thirteenth Century* (above), supplemented by such authors as, for Ireland, A. J. Otway-Ruthven, "Thirty years' work in Irish history", *Irish Historical Studies*, xv, No. 60 (September 1967), pp. 359–65, and *History of Medieval Ireland*, pp. 409–22, particularly the opening paragraph (p. 409) on projected bibliographies; as well as, of course, the periodicals, *Journal of Ecclesiastical History*, *English Historical Review*, and the other national historical journals of the British Isles, *History*, *Speculum*, for very recent publications. The Historical Association's *Annual Bulletin of Historical Literature*, though not confined to this country or this period, is extremely useful.

WORKS OF REFERENCE

Birch, W. de G., *History of Scottish Seals*, II (ecclesiastic and monastic seals) (Stirling, 1907)
Caulfield, Richard, *Sigilla ecclesiae Hibernicae illustrata* (Dublin, 1853[–6])
Cheney, C. R., *Handbook of Dates for Students of English History* (1945)
Davis, G. R. C., *Medieval Cartularies of Great Britain: a Short Catalogue* (1958)
Easson, D. E., Knowles, M. D., and Hadcock, R. N., *Medieval Religious Houses: Scotland* (1957)
Emden, A. B., *A Biographical Register of the University of Cambridge to 1500* (Cambridge, 1963)

Emden, A. B., *A Biographical Register of the University of Oxford to 1500*, 3 vols (Oxford, 1957–9)
Gwynn, A., and Hadcock, R. N., *Medieval Religious Houses: Ireland* (1970)
Hadcock, R. N., *The Map of Monastic Ireland* (Ordnance Survey, Dublin, 1959)
Harvey, J., and Oswald, A., *English Medieval Architects: a Biographical Dictionary to 1500* (1954)
Hope, W. H. St J., in *Proceedings of the Society of Antiquaries*, 2nd ser., xi (1885–7), pp. 271–306, and xv (1893–5), pp. 26–35, on the seals of English bishops and archdeacons
[Jenkinson, Hilary], *Guide to Seals in the Public Record Office* (H.M.S.O., 1954). More than a guide to the contents of the P.R.O.: a mine of information, bibliographical as well as technical
Ker, N. R., *Medieval Libraries of Great Britain: a List of Surviving Books*, 2nd edn (1964)
Knowles, M. D., and Hadcock, R. N., *Medieval Religious Houses: England and Wales*, 2nd rev. enl. edn (1971)
Le Neve, J., *Fasti Ecclesiae Anglicanae*, ed. T. Duffus Hardy, 3 vols (Oxford, 1854). Now being revised*: see* below
——, *Fasti Ecclesiae Anglicanae 1066–1300*, in progress (1968–), I, *St Paul's, London*, comp. D. E. Greenway (1968)
——, *Fasti Ecclesiae Anglicanae 1300–1541*, comp. J. M. Horn, B. Jones and H. P. F. King, 12 vols (1962–7)
Map of Monastic Britain: South Sheet (Ordnance Survey, Chessington, 1954)
Pedrick, Gale, *Monastic Seals of the Thirteenth Century* (1902)
Perceval, C. S., in *Proc. Soc. Antiquaries*, 2nd ser., v (1870–3), pp. 238–50, on Peculiars and their seals
Russell, J. C., *Dictionary of Writers of Thirteenth-Century England* (*Bull. Inst. Hist. Research*, Suppl., 1936)
Watt, D. E. R., *Fasti Ecclesiae Scoticanae Medii Aevi* (St Andrews, 1959)

FRIARS

Bryce, W. Moir, *The Black Friars of Edinburgh* (Edin., 1911)
——, *The Scottish Grey Friars*, 2 vols (Edin., 1909)
Clapham, A. W., "The architectural remains of the mendicant orders in Wales", *Archaeol. J.*, lxxxiv (1927), pp. 88–104
Cuthbert, Father, *Life of St Francis of Assisi* (1927)
——, *The Romanticism of St. Francis and other studies* (1924), pp. 190–235, on Adam Marsh, an English Franciscan of the thirteenth century
Emery, R. W., "The friars of the Sack", *Speculum*, xviii (1943), pp. 323–34
Fitzmaurice, E. B., and Little, A. G., *Materials for the History of the Franciscan Province of Ireland* (Manchester, 1920)
Galbraith, G. R., *The Constitution of the Dominican Order 1216–1360* (Manchester, 1925)
Goldthorp, L. M., "Franciscans and Dominicans in Yorkshire", *Yorkshire Archaeological Journal*, xxxiii (1935), pp. 365–428
Hinnebusch W. A., *The Early English Friars Preachers* (Rome, 1951)
Kingsford, C. L., *The Grey Friars of London* (1888)
Knowles, M. David, *The Religious Orders in England*, I (Cambridge, 1948), Pt. 2, "The friars 1216–1340"
Little, A. G., *A Guide to Franciscan Studies* (1920)
——, "A Record of the English Dominicans, 1314", *E.H.R.*, v (1890), pp. 107–12, and vi (1891), pp. 752–3
——, *Franciscan Papers, Lists and Documents* (Manchester, 1943)
——, *Studies in English Franciscan History* (Manchester, 1917)
——, "The administrative divisions of the mendicant orders in England", *E.H.R.*, xxxiii (1918), pp. 496–7, and xxxiv (1919), pp. 205–9
——, "The Franciscan friary at Romney", *Archaeol. Cantiana*, l (1938), pp. 151–2
—— (ed.), *Tractatus de adventu fratrum minorum in Angliam* (*fratris Thomae vulgo dicti de Eccleston*), new edn (Manchester, 1951)
——, "The friars of the Sack", *E.H.R.*, ix (1894), pp. 121–7
——, and Douie, Decima L., "Three sermons of Friar Jordan of Saxony, the successor of St. Dominic, preached in England, A.D. 1229", *E.H.R.*, liv (1939), pp. 1–19
Moorman, J. R. H., *Sources for the Life of St Francis* (Manchester, 1940)
Poland, E. B., *The Friars in Sussex* (1928)
Sabatier, P., *Life of St Francis of Assisi*, trans. Louis S. Houghton (1920)
Salter, E. Gurney, *The Coming of the Friars Minor to England and Germany* (1926). Translations of Thomas of Eccleston and Jordan of Giano
Steer, F. W., *The Grey Friars in Chichester*, Chichester Papers, No. 2 (Chichester, 1955)
Thorndike, L., "The true Roger Bacon", *American Hist. Review*, xxi (1916), pp. 237–57 and 468–80

UNIVERSITIES

Barbour, Ruth, "A manuscript of ps.-Dionysius Areopagita copied for Robert Grosseteste", *Bodleian Lib. Rec.*, vi, No. 2 (February 1958), pp. 401–16
Callus, D. A., "Introduction of Aristotelian learning to Oxford", *Proc. Brit. Acad.*, xxix (1943), pp. 229–81

——, "The date of Grosseteste's translations and commentaries on pseudo-Dionysius . . .", *Rech. de théologie ancienne et méd.*, xiv (1947), pp. 186–210

Callus, D. (ed.), *Robert Grosseteste, Scholar and Bishop: Essays in Commem. of the Seventh Centenary of his Death* (Oxford, 1955)

Cobban, Alan B., "Edward II, Pope John XXII and the university of Cambridge", *Bull. John Rylands Lib.*, xlvii (1964), pp. 49–78

Crombie, A. C., *Robert Grosseteste and the Origins of Experimental Science 1100–1700* (Oxford, 1953)

Emden, A. B., *An Oxford Hall in the Middle Ages* (Oxford, 1927)

Hackett, M. B., *The Original Statutes of Cambridge University: the Text and its History* (Cambridge, 1970)

Harris, C. R. S., *Duns Scotus*, 2 vols (Oxford, 1927)

Hill, Rosalind M. T., "Oliver Sutton, bishop of Lincoln, and the university of Oxford", *Trans. Royal Hist. Soc.*, 4th ser., xxxi (1949), pp. 1–16

Hunt, R. W., "Manuscripts containing the indexing symbols of Robert Grosseteste", *Bodleian Lib. Rec.*, iv, No. 5 (September 1953), pp. 241–55

Little, A. G., "Chronological notes on the life of Duns Scotus", *E.H.R.*, xlvii (1932), pp. 568–82

——, "Cistercian students at Oxford in the thirteenth century", *E.H.R.*, viii (1893), pp. 83–5

——, *The Grey Friars in Oxford* (Oxford, 1892)

——, "Theological schools in medieval England", *E.H.R.*, lv (1940), pp. 624–30

——, and Pelster, F., *Oxford Theology and Theologians* c. *1282–1302* (1934)

Moorman, J. R. H., *The Grey Friars in Cambridge* (Cambridge, 1951)

Rait, R. S., *Life in the Medieval University* (Cambridge, 1918)

Rashdall, Hastings, *Universities of Europe in the Middle Ages*, ed. F. M. Powicke and A. B. Emden, 3 vols (Oxford, 1936)

Sharp, D. E., *Franciscan Philosophy at Oxford in the Thirteenth Century* (Oxford, 1930)

Smalley, B., "Robert Bacon and the early Dominican school at Oxford", *Trans. Royal Hist. Soc.*, 4th ser., xxx (1948), pp. 1–19

Stevenson, F. S., *Robert Grosseteste* (1899)

Thomson, S. Harrison, *The Writings of Robert Grosseteste* (Cambridge, 1940)

Wieruszowski, Helene, *The Medieval University, Masters, Students, Learning, Readings* (New York, London, 1966). An anthology

GENERAL BOOKS AND ARTICLES

Adams, Norma, "The judicial conflict over tithes", *E.H.R.*, lii (1937), pp. 1–22

Arnold-Forster, *Studies in Church Dedications*, 3 vols (1899)

Barlow, F., *Durham Annals and Documents of the Thirteenth Century* (Surtees Soc., 1940)

Barraclough, G., *Papal Provisions* (1935)

——, "The making of a bishop in the Middle Ages: the part of the pope in law and fact", *Catholic Hist. Review*, xix (1933), pp. 275–319

Bilson, J., "The architecture of the Cistercians", *Archaeol. J.*, lxvi (1909), pp. 185–280

Bishop, E., "Fasting and abstinence of the Black Monks in England before the Reformation", *Downside Review*, xliii (1925), pp. 184–237

——, *Liturgica Historica* (Oxford, 1918), esp. pp. 238–59, "On the origins of the feast of the Conception of the Blessed Virgin Mary"; and 276–300, "Holy Week rites of Sarum, Hereford and Rouen"

——, T. A. M., "Monastic demesnes and the statute of Mortmain", *E.H.R.*, xlix (1934), pp. 303–6

Bond, Francis, *Dedications and Patron Saints of English Churches* (1914)

Brentano, R., *York Metropolitan Jurisdiction and Papal Judges Delegate 1279–96* (Berkeley, California, 1959)

Brooke, C. N. L., "Gregorian reform in action: clerical marriage in England 1050–1200", *Cambridge Hist. J.*, xii (1956), pp. 1–21

——, "Married men among the English higher clergy 1066–1200", ibid. pp. 187–8

——, "The deans of St Paul's *c.* 1090–1499", *Bull. Inst. Hist. Research*, xxix (1956), pp. 231–43

Butler, H. E., *The Autobiography of Giraldus Cambrensis* (1937)

Caplan, H., "The four senses of scriptural interpretation and the medieval theory of preaching", *Speculum*, iv (1929), pp. 282–90

Chambers, E. K., *The Medieval Stage*, 2 vols (Oxford, 1903)

Cheney, C. R., "Church-building in the Middle Ages", *Bull. John Rylands Lib*, xxxiv (1951–2), pp. 20–36

——, *Episcopal Visitation of Monasteries in the Thirteenth Century* (Manchester, 1931)

——, *From Becket to Langton: English Church Government 1170–1213* (Manchester, 1956)

——, *Hubert Walter* (1967)

——, "Legislation of the medieval English church", *E.H.R.*, l (1935), pp. 193–224, 385–417

——, *Notaries Public in England* (1972)

——, "The alleged deposition of King John ", pp. 100–16 of *Studies in Medieval History presented to F.M. Powicke*, ed. R. W. Hunt, W. A. Pantin and R. W. Southern (Oxford, 1948)

——, "The earliest English diocesan statutes", *E.H.R.*, lxxv (1960), pp. 1–29

——, "The papal legate and English monasteries in 1206", *E.H.R.*, xlvi (1931), pp. 443–52; cf. lxxvi (1961), pp. 654–8

——, "The punishment of felonious clerks", *E.H.R.*, li (1936), pp. 215–36
——, "The so-called statutes of archbishops John Pecham and Robert Winchelsey", *J. Ecclesiast. Hist.*, xii (1961) pp. 14–34
——, *The Study of the Medieval Papal Chancery* (Glasgow, 1966)
——, and Cheney, Mary G., *The Letters of Pope Innocent III (1198–1216) concerning England and Wales: a calendar with an appendix of texts* (Oxford, 1967)
Chettle, H. F., "The friars of the Holy Cross in England", *History*, xxxiv (1949), pp. 204–20
——, "The order of the Holy Cross in Ireland", in Watt, Morrall and Martin (eds), *Medieval Studies pres. to Aubrey Gwynn, S.J.* (Dublin, 1961)
Chew, H. M., *The English Ecclesiastical Tenants-in-Chief and Knight-Service* (Oxford, 1932)
Churchill, Irene J., *Canterbury Administration*, 2 vols (1933)
Cole, R. E. G., "Some papal provisions in the cathedral church of Lincoln 1300–20", *Assoc. Archit. Socs' Reports*, xxxiv (1918), pp. 219–58
Colledge, E., *The Medieval Mystics of England* (1961). An anthology, with bibliography
Colvin, H. M., *The White Canons in England* (Oxford, 1951)
Corish, P. J. (ed.), *A History of Irish Catholicism*, II (Dublin, 1968)
Councils and Synods with other documents relating to the English Church, II (1205–1313), ed. F. M. Powicke and C. R. Cheney, 2 vols (Oxford, 1964)
Cowan, I. B., "The development of the parochial system in medieval Scotland", *Scott. Hist. Review*, vol. 40, pp. 43–55
Craig, H., *English Religious Drama of the Middle Ages* (1955)
Darwin, F. D. S., *The English Mediaeval Recluse* (S.P.C.K., n.d.)
Deeley, Ann, "Papal provision and royal rights of patronage in the early fourteenth century", *E.H.R.*, xliii (1928), pp. 497 ff.
Deighton, H. S., "Clerical taxation by consent 1279–1301", *E.H.R.*, lxviii (1953), pp. 161–92
Dickinson, J. C., *Monastic Life in Medieval England* (1961)
Douie, Decima, "Archbishop Pecham's sermons and collations", *Studies in Med. Hist. pres. to F. M. Powicke*, ed. Hunt, Pantin and Southern (Oxford, 1948), pp. 269–82
——, Decima L., *Archbishop Pecham* (Oxford, 1952)
Dowden, J., *The Bishops of Scotland* (Glasgow, 1912)
——, *The Medieval Church in Scotland: its Constitution, Organisation and Law* (Glasgow, 1910)
Drew, C., *Early Parochial Organisation in England: the Origins of the Office of Churchwarden* (York, 1954)
Edwards, Kathleen, "Bishops and learning in the reign of Edward II", *Church Quarterly Review*, cxxxviii (1944), pp. 57–86
——, *The English Secular Cathedrals in the Middle Ages*, 2nd edn (Manchester, 1967)
——, "The political importance of the English bishops during the reign of Edward II", *E.H.R.*, lix (1944), pp. 311–47
——, "The social origins and provenance of the English bishops during the reign of Edward II", *Trans. Royal Hist. Soc.*, 5th ser., ix (1959), pp. 51–79
Emanuel, H. D., "Notaries public and their marks recorded in the archives of the dean and chapter of Hereford", *Nat. Lib. Wales J.*, viii (1953), pp. 147–63
Flahiff, G. B., "The use of prohibitions by clerics against ecclesiastical courts in England", *Mediaeval Studies* (Toronto), iii (1941), pp. 101–16
——, "The writ of prohibition to court christian in the thirteenth century", ibid., vi (1944), pp. 261–313, and vii (1945), pp. 229–90
Fowler, R. C., "Secular aid for excommunication", *Trans. Royal Hist. Soc.*, 3rd ser., viii (1914), pp. 113–17
Fraser, C. M., *A History of Antony Bek* (Oxford, 1957)
Gabel, L. C., *Benefit of Clergy in England in the later Middle Ages*, Smith Coll. Studies in History,XIV (1928–9)
Gibbs, M., and Lang, J., *Bishops and Reform 1215–72* (Oxford, 1934)
Graham, R., *English Ecclesiastical Studies* (1929)
——, "Sidelights on the rectors and parishioners of Reculver from the Register of Archbishop Winchelsey", *Archaeol. Cantiana*, lvii (1944), pp. 1–12
Graves, E. B., "*Circumspecte agatis*", *E.H.R.*, xliii (1928), pp. 1–20
Gray, J. W., "The *ius praesentandi* in England from the constitutions of Clarendon to Bracton", *E.H.R.*, lxvii (1952), pp. 481–509
Greenway, W., "Archbishop Pecham, Thomas Bek and St Davids", *J. Ecclesiast. Hist.*, xi (1960), pp. 152–63
Hand, G. J., "The rivalry of the cathedral chapters in medieval Dublin", *J. Royal Soc. Antiqu. Ireland*, xcii, Pt II (1962) pp. 193–206
Hill, Rosalind, "Bishop Sutton and his archives", *J. Ecclesiast. Hist.* (April 1951), ii, pp. 43–53
——, *Ecclesiastical Letter-Books of the Thirteenth Century* (privately printed, n.p., n.d.)
——, *Oliver Sutton, Dean of Lincoln, later Bishop of Lincoln (1280–99)* Lincoln Minster Pamphlets, No. 4 (Lincoln, 1950)
——, "Public penance: some problems of a thirteenth-century bishop", *History*, xxxvi (1951), pp. 213–26
——, "Theory and practice of excommunication in medieval England", *History*, xlii (1957), pp. 1–11
Hunt, R. W., "English learning in the late twelfth century", *Trans. Royal Hist. Soc.*, 4th ser., xix (1936), pp. 19–42

Kemp, E., "The origins of the Canterbury convocation", *J. Ecclesiast. Hist.*, iii (1952), pp. 132–43
Ker, N., and Pantin, W. A., *Oxford Formularies*, II (Oxford Hist. Soc., 1942). For letters of a Scottish master of arts at Paris and Oxford, *c.* 1250 (pp. 472–91)
Knowles, D., "The diet of Black Monks", *Downside Review*, lii (1934), pp. 275–90
——, M. D., *The Monastic Order in England*, 2nd edn (Cambridge, 1963)
——, *The Religious Orders in England*, I (Cambridge, 1948)
Lawrence, C. H., *St Edmund of Abingdon: a Study in Hagiography and History* (Oxford, 1960)
Levett, A. E., *Studies in Manorial History* (Oxford, 1938)
Lunt, W. E., *Financial Relations of the Papacy with England to 1327* (Cambridge, Mass., 1939)
——, *Papal Revenues in the Middle Ages*, 2 vols (New York, 1934)
——, "Papal taxation in England in the reign of Edward I", *E.H.R.*, xxx (1915), pp. 398–417
——, "The consent of the English lower clergy to taxation 1166–1216", *Facts and Factors in Economic History, articles by former students of E. F. Gay* (Cambridge, Mass., 1933), pp. 62–89
——, "The consent of the English lower clergy to taxation during the reign of Henry III", *Persecution and Liberty: Essays in honour of G. L. Burr* (New York, 1931)
——, *The Valuation of Norwich* (Oxford, 1926)
——, "William Testa and the parliament of Carlisle", *E.H.R.*, xli (1926), pp. 332–57
McRoberts, D., "The medieval Scottish liturgy illustrated by surviving documents", *Trans. Scott. Ecclesiol. Soc.*, xv (i) (1957), pp. 24–40
Maitland, F. W., *Roman Canon Law in the Church of England* (1898)
Major, Kathleen, "The finances of the dean and chapter of Lincoln from the twelfth to the fourteenth centuries", *J. Ecclesiast. Hist.*, v (1954), pp. 149–67
Mâle, Emile, *Religious Art in France: Thirteenth Century* (1913) (also in paperback, *The Gothic Image* (Fontana, 1961))
Mate, Mavis, "The indebtedness of Canterbury Cathedral Priory 1215–95", *Econ. Hist. Rev.*, 2nd ser., xxvi (1973), pp. 183–97
Moorman, J. R. H., *Church Life in England in the Thirteenth Century* (Cambridge, 1955)
——, "The medieval parsonage and its occupants", *Bull. John Rylands Lib.*, xxviii (1944–5), pp. 137–54
Owen, Dorothy M., *Church and Society in Medieval Lincolnshire* (Lincoln, 1971)
Owst, G. R., *Literature and Pulpit in Medieval England*, 2nd edn (Cambridge, 1961)
——, *Preaching in Medieval England* (Cambridge, 1926)
Pantin, W. A., *Chapters of the English Black Monks 1215–1540*, Royal Hist. Soc., Camden, 3rd ser., vols 45, 47 and 54 (1931–7)
——, "English monastic letter-books", *Historical Essays in honour of J. Tait* (Manchester, 1933), pp. 201–22
Poole, A. L., "Outlawry as a punishment of criminous clerks", *Historical Essays in honour of J. Tait* (Manchester, 1933), pp. 239–46
Power, Eileen, *Medieval English Nunneries* (Cambridge, 1922)
Powicke, F. M., *Stephen Langton* (Oxford, 1928)
——, *The Thirteenth Century 1216–1307* (Oxford, 1953)
Richardson, H. G., "The parish clergy of the thirteenth and fourteenth centuries", *Trans. Royal Hist. Soc.*, 3rd ser., vi (1912), pp. 89–128
Robinson, J. Armitage, "Convocation of Canterbury: its early history", *Church Quarterly Review*, lxxxi (1915) pp. 81–137
Rock D., *The Church of our Fathers as seen in St Osmund's Rite for the Cathedral of Salisbury*, ed. G. W. Hart and W. H. Frere, 4 vols (1903–4)
Salter, H. E., *Chapters of the Augustinian Canons* (Cant. and York Soc. and Oxford Hist. Soc., 1921–2)
Smalley, B., *The Study of the Bible in the Middle Ages*, 2nd edn (Oxford, 1952)
Smith, A. L., *Church and State in the Middle Ages* (Oxford, 1913)
——, R. A. L., *Canterbury Cathedral Priory: a study in monastic administration* (Cambridge, 1943)
——, *Collected Papers* (1947)
Snape, R. H., *English Monastic Finances in the later Middle Ages* (Cambridge, 1926)
Sommer-Seckendorff, E. M. F., *Studies in the Life of Robert Kilwardby, O.P.* (Rome, 1937)
Stone, E., "Profit-and-loss accountancy at Norwich Cathedral Priory", *Trans. Royal Hist. Soc.*, 5th ser., xii (1962), pp. 25–48
Stutz, Ulrich, "The proprietary church as an element of medieval Germanic ecclesiastical law", in G. Barraclough, *Mediaeval Germany 911–1250*, II (Oxford, 1938), pp. 35–70. Stutz's famous essay translated
Sutcliffe, D., "The financial condition of the see of Canterbury 1279–92", *Speculum*, x (1935), pp. 53–68
Sweet, Jennifer, "Some thirteenth-century sermons and their authors", *J. Ecclesiast. Hist.*, iv (1953), pp. 27–36
Thompson, A. Hamilton, "Cathedral builders of the Middle Ages", *History*, x (1925–6), pp. 139–50
——, "Diocesan organisation in the Middle Ages", *Proc. Brit. Acad.*, xxix (1943), pp. 153–94
——, *English monasteries* (Cambridge, 1913)
——, "Master Elias of Dereham and the King's Works", *Archaeol. J.*, xcviii (1941), pp. 1–35
——, *Parish History and Records* (1919). Indispensable for the writing of parochial history
——, *Rotuli Ricardi Gravesend 1258–79*, ed. Davis, Foster and Thompson (Cant. & York Soc. and Lincoln Rec. Soc., 1925). An important introduction
——, *The Cathedral Churches of England* (1925)

——, *The English Clergy and their Organisation in the later Middle Ages* (Oxford, 1947). Useful for this period also
——, *The Ground Plan of the English Parish Church* (Cambridge, 1911)
——, *The Historical Growth of the English Parish Church* (Cambridge, 1911)
——, M., *The Carthusian Order in England* (1930)
Tristam, E. W., *English Medieval Wall Painting in the Thirteenth Century*, 2 vols (1960)
Vaughan, R., *Matthew Paris* (Cambridge, 1958)
Watt, J. A., "The papacy and episcopal appointments in thirteenth-century Ireland", *Proc. Irish Catholic Hist. Com.* (1959), pp. 1–9
——, Morrall, J. B., and Martin, F. X., *Medieval Studies pres. to Aubrey Gwynn, S.J.* (Dublin, 1961)
Weske, D. B., *Convocation of the Clergy* (1937)
Whitwell, R. J., "The English monasteries and the wool trade", *Vierteljahrschrift für sozial- und Wirtschaftsgeschichte*, II (i) (1904), pp. 1–34
Williams, G., *The Welsh Church from the Conquest to the Reformation* (Cardiff, 1962)
Williamson, D. M., "Some aspects of the legation of Cardinal Otto in England 1237–41", *E.H.R.*, lxiv (1949), pp. 145–73
——, "The legate Otto in Scotland and Ireland 1237–40", *Scottish Hist. Review*, xxviii (1949), pp. 12–30
Wood, Susan, *English Monasteries and their patrons in the thirteenth century* (1955)
Woodcock, B. L., *Medieval Ecclesiastical Courts in the Diocese of Canterbury* (1952)
Wroot, H. E., "Yorkshire abbeys and the wool trade", *Thoresby Soc. Miscellany* (1935), pp. 1–21
Young, K., *The Drama of the Mediaeval Church*, 2 vols (Oxford, 1933)

SURVIVING EPISCOPAL REGISTERS OF THE PERIOD

(cf. App. III below for the bishops of the period)

C. & Y. Canterbury and York Society
R.S. "Rolls" series (Chronicles and Memorials . . .)
S.R.S. Somerset Record Society
S.S. Surtees Society

BATH AND WELLS

1264–6 Walter Giffard. (Fragment, preserved attached to his York archiepiscopal register) *Registers of W. G. . . . and of . . .*, ed. T. Scott Holmes (S.R.S., 1899). Abstract

1309–29 John Droxford. *Calendar of the Register of J. de D.*, ed. [Edmund] Hobhouse (S.R.S., 1887)

CANTERBURY

1279–92 John Pecham. *Registrum Epistolarum*, ed. C. T. Martin, 3 vols (R.S., 1882–6), a selection, supplemented by *Registrum Johannis Pecham* (in progress) (C. & Y., 1908–)

1293–1313 Robert Winchelsey. *Registrum*, ed. Rose Graham, 2 vols (C. & Y., 1952–6)

(Registers before Pecham's are said to have been removed by Kilwardby, Pecham's predecessor, when he was transferred to Rome and are now lost. The *acta* of Stephen Langton (1206–28) have been assembled from various sources: *Acta Stephani Langton . . .*, ed. Kathleen Major (C. & Y., 1950))

CARLISLE. 1292–1324 John of Halton. *The Register of J. de H.*, ed. W. N. Thompson, 2 vols (C. & Y., 1913)

CHESTER. *See* COVENTRY AND LICHFIELD

CHICHESTER. None

(The *acta* of the bishops from 1075 to 1207 have however, been assembled: *The Acta of the Bishops of Chichester, 1075–1207*, ed. H. M. R. E. Mayr-Harting (C. & Y., 1965))

COVENTRY AND LICHFIELD

1296–1321 Walter Langton. Register unpublished. An abstract of contents, also unpublished, is in the William Salt Library, Stafford

1321–58 Roger Northburgh. Register unpublished. In the *Coll. Hist. Staffs.*, I, 241–88 (William Salt Soc., 1880), by E. Hobhouse, "The Register of Roger de Norbury, 1322–58: an Abstract of Contents, and Remarks".

DURHAM

1311–16 Richard Kellaw. *Registrum Palatinum Dunelmense: the Register of R. de K. . . . 1314–16*, ed. T. Duffus Hardy, 4 vols (R.S., 1873–8)

(Miscellaneous documents emanating from or received by the chancery of Anthony Bek (1283–1311) have been assembled from various sources: *Records of Antony Bek, bishop and patriarch, 1283–1311*, ed. C. M. Fraser (S.S., 1953))

ELY. None

EXETER

1258–80 Walter Bronescombe. *Registers of W. B. ... and Peter Quivil ... with some records of the episcopate of Bishop Thomas de Bytton*, ed. F. C. Hingeston-Randolph (London and Exeter, 1889)

1280–91 Peter Quinel or Quivel. *do.*

1291–1307 Thomas Bitton. *do.*

1308–26 Walter Stapledon. *Register of W. de S.*, ed. F. C. Hingeston-Randolph (London and Exeter, 1892).
1326–7 James Berkeley. *See* below

1327–69 John Grandisson. *Register of J. de G. ..., with some account of the episcopate of James de Berekley*, ed, F. C. Hingeston-Randolph, 3 vols (London and Exeter, 1894–9)

HEREFORD

1275–82 Thomas Cantilupe. *Registrum*, ed. R. G. Griffiths and W. W. Capes (C. & Y., 1907, and by Cantilupe Society, 1906, jointly)

1282–1317 Richard Swinfield. *Registrum*, ed. W. W. Capes (C. & Y., 1909, and Cantilupe Soc., 1909, jointly)

1317–27 Adam Orleton. *Registrum*, ed. A. T. Banister (C. & Y., 1908, and Cantilupe Soc., 1907, jointly)

1327–44 Thomas Charlton. *Registrum*, ed., W. W. Capes (C. & Y., 1913, and Cantilupe Soc., 1912, jointly)

LICHFIELD. *See* COVENTRY AND LICHFIELD

LINCOLN

1209–35 Hugh of Wells. *Rotuli*, ed. W. P. Phillimore and F. N. Davis, 3 vols (C. & Y. and Lincoln Rec. Soc., 1907–9)

1235–53 Robert Grosseteste. *Rotuli*, ed. F. N. Davis (C. & Y. and Lincoln Rec. Soc., 1913)

1253–8 Henry Lexington. The only surviving roll of Lexington is edited with Grosseteste's rolls in *Rotuli*, above

1258–79 Richard Gravesend. *Rotuli*, ed. F. N. Davis, C. W. Foster and A. Hamilton Thompson (C. & Y. and Lincoln Rec. Soc., 1925)

1280–99 Oliver Sutton. *The Rolls and Register of Bishop Oliver Sutton*, ed. Rosalind M. T. Hill (Lincoln Rec. Soc., vols 1–6, 1948–69, in progress)

1300–20 John Dalderby. Register unpublished

1320–40 Henry Burghersh. *do.*

LONDON

1304–13 Ralph Baldock. *Registrum Radulphi Baldock, Gilberti Segrave, Ricardi Newport et Stephani Gravesend ... 1304–38*, ed. R. C. Fowler (C. & Y., 1911)

1313–16 Gilbert Segrave. *do.*

1317–18 Richard Newport. *do.*

1318–38 Stephen Gravesend. *do.*

NORWICH. Registers complete from 1299. None published.

ROCHESTER

1317–52 Hamo Hethe. *Registrum*, ed. Charles Johnson, 2 vols (C. & Y., 1948; also issued by Kent Archaeol. Soc.)

SALISBURY

1297–1315 Simon of Ghent. *Registrum*, ed. C. T. Flower and M. C. B. Dawes, 2 vols (C. & Y., 1934)

1315–30 Roger Martival. *The Registers of R. de M.*, ed. K. Edwards, C. R. Elrington and S. Reynolds, 4 vols (C. & Y., vols 1–3, 1959–65; in progress)

WINCHESTER

1282–1304 John of Pontoise. *Registrum J. de Pontissara*, ed. C. Deedes, 2 vols (C. & Y., 1915–24; also issued by Surrey Rec. Soc., 1913–24)

1305–16 Henry Woodlock. *Registrum*, ed. A.W. Goodman, 2 vols (C. & Y., 1940–1)

1316–19 John Sandale. *The Registers of John de Sandale and Rigaud de Asserio, bishops . . . 1316–23*, ed F. J. Baigent (Hants. Rec. Soc., 1897)

1319–23 Rigaud of Assier. *do.*

1323–33 John Stratford. Register unpublished

WORCESTER

1268–1302 Godfrey Giffard. *Episcopal registers, dioc. of Worcester. Register of Bishop Godfrey Giffard . . .*, ed. J. W. Willis Bund, 2 vols (Worcs. Hist. Soc., 1902). Calendar

1302–7 William Gainsborough. *The Register of W. de G.*, ed. J. W. Willis Bund and R. A. Wilson (Worcs. Hist. Soc., 1907–29). Calendar

1307–13 Walter Reynolds. *The Register of W. R.*, ed. R. A. Wilson (Worcs. Hist. Soc. and Dugdale Soc., 1929). Abstract.

1313–17 Walter Maidstone. Register unpublished

1317–27 Thomas Cobham. *The Register of T. de C.*, ed. E. H. Pearce (Worcs. Hist. Soc., 1930). Part transcript, part abstract

YORK

1215–55 Walter de Gray. *The Register or Rolls of Walter Gray*, ed. [James Raine, jun.] (S.S., 1872)

1266–79 Walter Giffard. *Register of Walter Giffard*, ed. [W. Brown] (S.S., 1904)

1279–85 William Wickwane. *Register of William Wickwane*, ed. [W. Brown] (S. S., 1907)

1285–96 John le Romeyn. *Registers of J. le R. . . . and of H. of Newark . . .*, ed. [W. Brown], 2 vols, (S.S., 1913–17)

1296–9 Henry Newark. *do.*

1299–1304 Thomas Corbridge. *Register of Thomas of Corbridge*, ed. [W. Brown and A. Hamilton Thompson], 2 vols (S.S., 1925–8)

1304–15 William Greenfield. *Register of William Greenfield*, ed. [W. Brown and A. Hamilton Thompson], 5 vols (S.S., 1931–40)

1316–40 William Melton. Register unpublished

WELSH DIOCESES (Bangor, Llandaff, St Asaph, St David's). None

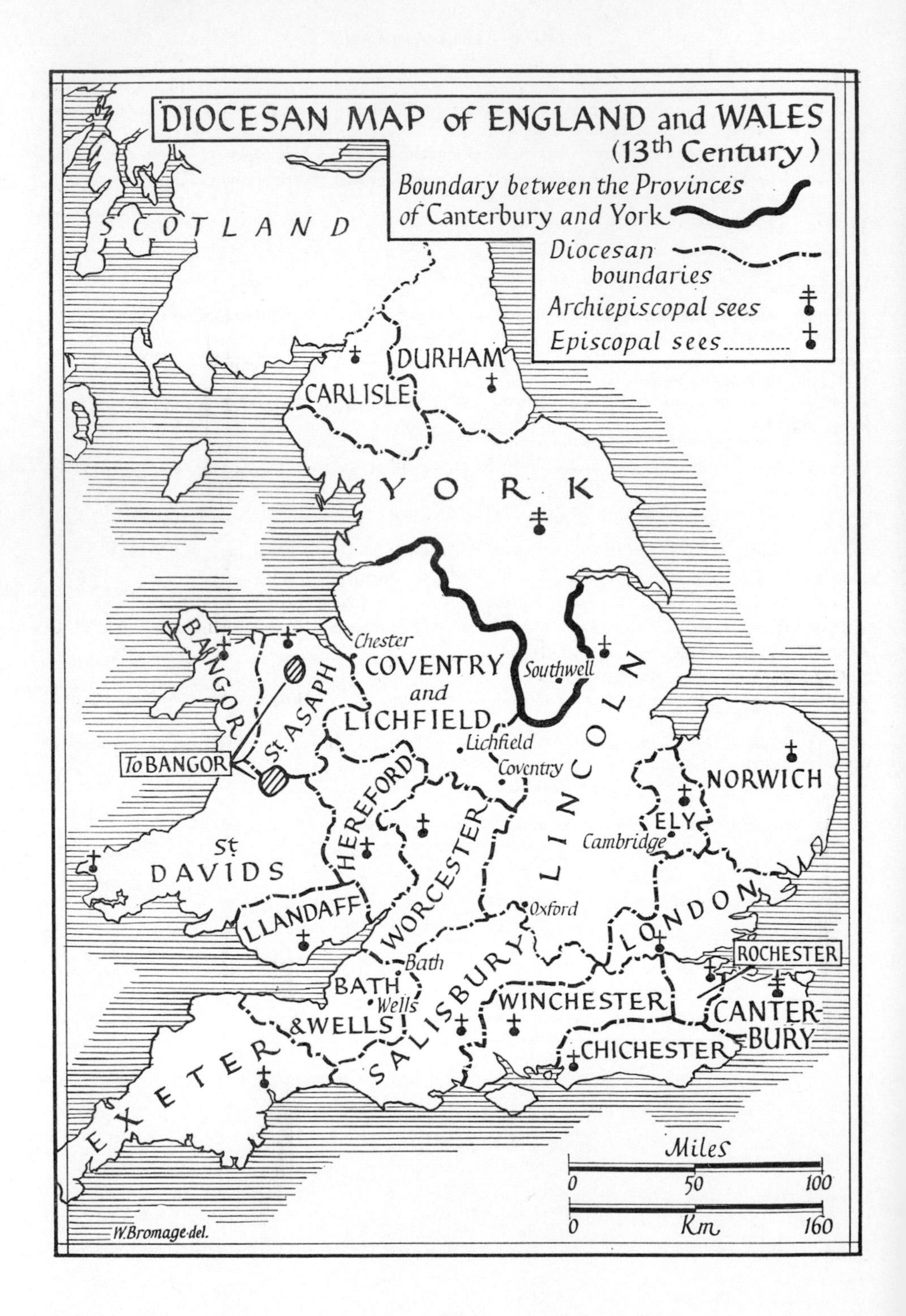
DIOCESAN MAP of ENGLAND and WALES
(13th Century)
Boundary between the Provinces of Canterbury and York
Diocesan boundaries
Archiepiscopal sees
Episcopal sees
SCOTLAND
DURHAM
CARLISLE
YORK
BANGOR
St ASAPH
To BANGOR
Chester
COVENTRY and LICHFIELD
Southwell
Lichfield
Coventry
LINCOLN
NORWICH
ELY
Cambridge
HEREFORD
WORCESTER
St DAVIDS
LLANDAFF
Oxford
LONDON
ROCHESTER
Bath
BATH &WELLS
Wells
SALISBURY
WINCHESTER
CANTERBURY
CHICHESTER
EXETER
Miles
0
50
100
0
Km
160
W.Bromage del.

A. THE WESTERN CHURCH

136. Canons of the Fourth Lateran Council, 1215

(*Conciliorum Oecumenicorum Decreta*, ed. J. Alberigo (and others), *editio altera* (Rome, Herder, 1962), pp. 206–47. In translating I have been helped on many points by the French rendering in Raymonde Foreville, *Latran I, II, III et Latran IV* (vol. 6 in the series *Histoire des Conciles Oecuméniques*, ed. G. Dumeige) (Paris, 1965), pp. 342–86)

1. We[1] firmly believe and simply confess, that there is one only true God, eternal, without measure, omnipotent, unchangeable, incomprehensible and ineffable, the Father, and the Son, and the Holy Spirit: three persons indeed, but one simple essence, substance or nature altogether; the Father of none, the Son of the Father alone, and the Holy Spirit of both alike, without beginning, always and without end; the Father begetting, the Son being born, and the Holy Spirit proceeding; consubstantial, and co-equal, co-omnipotent, and co-eternal; one principle of all things; the creator of all things visible and invisible, spiritual and corporal, who by His omnipotent virtue at once from the beginning of time established out of nothing both forms of creation, spiritual and corporal, that is the angelic and the mundane, and afterwards the human creature, composed as it were of spirit and body in common. For the devil and other demons were created by God naturally good, but they became evil by their own doing. Man, however, sinned by the suggestion of the devil.

This Holy Trinity, undivided as regards common essence, and distinct in respect of proper qualities of person, in accordance with the perfectly ordered plan of the ages, gave the teaching of salvation to the human race first by means of Moses and the holy prophets and others His servants. Finally the only-begotten Son of God, Jesus Christ, incarnate of the whole Trinity in common, being conceived of Mary ever Virgin by the cooperation of the Holy Spirit, made very man, compounded of a reasonable soul and human flesh, one person in two natures, shewed the way of life in all its clearness. He, while as regards His divinity He is immortal and incapable of suffering, nevertheless, as regards His humanity, was made capable of suffering and mortal. He also, having suffered for the salvation of the human race upon the wood of the cross and died, descended to hell, rose again from the dead, and ascended into heaven; but descended in spirit and rose again in flesh, and ascended in both alike to come at the end of the world to judge the quick and the dead, and to render to every man according to his works, both to the reprobate and to the elect, who all shall rise again with their own bodies which they now wear, that they may receive according to their works, whether they be good or bad, these perpetual punishment with the devil, and those everlasting glory with Christ.

There is moreover one universal church of the faithful, outside which no man at all is saved, in which the same Jesus Christ is both the priest and the sacrifice, whose body and blood are truly contained in the sacrament of the altar under the species of bread and wine, the bread being transubstantiated into the body and the wine into

[1] In canon 1, I have for the most part followed the rendering of A. Hamilton Thompson, *Cambr. Med. Hist.*, VI, pp. 634–5.

the blood by the divine power, in order that, to accomplish the mystery of unity, we ourselves may receive of His that which He received of ours. This sacrament no one can perform but a priest, who has been duly ordained, according to the keys of the church, which Jesus Christ Himself granted to the apostles and their successors.

But the sacrament of baptism, which is consecrated in water by invoking the indivisible Trinity, that is the Father, and the Son, and the Holy Spirit, is profitable to the salvation of children and adults alike when duly conferred in proper church fashion by anyone, whosoever he be. And if anyone, after receiving baptism, has fallen into sin, he can always be redeemed by true penitence. Not only virgins and the continent, but married people too, find favour with God by right faith and good works and deserve to attain to eternal blessedness.

2. We condemn therefore and reject the little book or treatise which the abbot Joachim has put out against mr Peter Lombard on the unity or essence of the Trinity, calling him a heretic and madman because he said in his *Sentences*, "There is a supreme reality[1] which is Father, Son and Holy Ghost and it does not beget, neither is it begotten, nor does it proceed," from which he asserts that Peter Lombard[2] makes God not so much a Trinity as a quaternity, that is to say three persons and the common essence, a sort of fourth, declaring plainly that there is no reality which is Father, Son and Holy Ghost, neither is it essence, substance or nature, although he concedes that Father, Son and Holy Ghost are one essence, one substance and one nature. He professes, however, that such a unity is not true and proper, but, as it were, a collective and analogous unity in the way many men are called one people and many believers one church, according to "The multitude of them that believed were of one heart and one soul", and "He that is joined unto the Lord is one spirit" with him; also "He that planteth and he that watereth are one", and all of us "are one body in Christ": again, in the book of Kings, "My people and thy people are one." But to establish this opinion he adduces above all what Christ says in the gospel about believers: "I wish, Father, that they may be one in us, even as we are one, that they may be made perfect in one."[3] For (so he says) Christians are not one, i.e. a single reality common to all: they are one in this way, i.e. one church because of the unity of the catholic faith and finally one kingdom because of the indissoluble union of charity. Thus one reads in the canonical Epistle of John, "For there are three that bear record in heaven, the Father, the Word and the Holy Ghost, and these three are one," and immediately the author adds, "And there are three that bear witness in earth, the spirit, the water, and the blood, and these three are one", according to certain manuscripts.[4]

But we, with the approbation of the holy and universal council, believe and confess with Peter [Lombard] that there is one single supreme reality, incomprehensible indeed and ineffable, who truly is Father, Son and Holy Ghost, the three persons together and each of them separately, and therefore in God there is a Trinity only, not a quaternity, because each of the three persons is that reality, that is to say essence, substance or divine nature, which alone is the principle of all things, apart from which

[1] *res*
[2] *ille*
[3] cf. John xvii. 21 ff.
[4] I Epist. John v. 7–8.

another cannot be found, and that reality does not beget, neither is it begotten, nor does it proceed, but it is the Father who begets, the Son who is begotten, and the Holy Ghost which proceeds, so there are distinctions of person and unity of nature. Although therefore one person is the Father, another is the Son, another the Holy Ghost, there is not another, but that which is the Father is the Son and the Holy Ghost, altogether the same, so, according to the orthodox and catholic faith, they are believed to be consubstantial. For the Father by begetting everlastingly the Son gave him his substance, as he himself testifies, "What the Father gave me is greater than all," and it cannot be said that he gave part of his substance to him and kept part for himself, as the substance of the Father is indivisible inasmuch as it is utterly simple; but neither can it be said that the Father transferred his substance to the Son in begetting him, as if he so gave it to the Son that he did not keep it himself, otherwise he would have ceased to be substance. It is clear therefore that in being born the Son received the substance of the Father without any diminution of it, and so the Father and the Son have the same substance and thus the Father and the Son and the Holy Ghost proceeding from both are the same reality. When therefore Truth prays to the Father for those believing in him, saying, "I wish that they may be one in us, as we also are one," this word "one" is taken to mean in the case of believers the union of charity in grace, in the case of divine persons the unity of identity in nature, as Truth says elsewhere, "Be ye perfect even as your heavenly Father is perfect," as if it were to say more plainly, "Be ye perfect" with the perfection of grace "as your heavenly Father is perfect" with the perfection of nature – each, that is, after his fashion, for between the Creator and a creature there can be remarked no similarity so great that a greater dissimilarity cannot be seen between them.

If therefore anyone ventures to defend or approve the opinion or teaching of the said Joachim on this matter, he is to be refuted by all as a heretic. By this however we do not wish to do anything at all to the detriment of the monastery of Fiore, of which Joachim was the founder, because there the foundation is according to rule and the observance is in a healthy state; particularly as this same Joachim ordered all his writings to be sent to us for approval or correction at the judgment of the apostolic see and composed a letter, signed by his own hand, in which he firmly confesses that he holds the faith held by the Roman church, the mother and teacher, by the divine plan, of all believers. We reject and condemn also the utterly perverse opinion of the impious Aymer whose mind the father of lies has blinded to such an extent that his teaching must be reckoned not so much heretical as insane.

3. We excommunicate and anathematise every heresy setting itself up against this holy, orthodox, catholic faith which we have expounded above, and condemn all heretics whatever names they go under: they have various faces indeed, but tails tied one to another, for they have vanity in common. Those condemned as heretics shall be handed over to the secular authorities present or to their bailiffs for punishment by the penalty deserved, clerks first being degraded from their orders. The goods of these condemned are, if they are laymen, to be confiscated, if clerks, assigned to the churches from which they drew their stipend. Those found no more than suspect of

heresy shall, unless they prove their innocence by a suitable purgation having regard to the reasons for suspicion and the character of the person, be struck by the sword of anathema, and until adequate satisfaction has been made they shall be avoided by everybody, so that if they continue under excommunication for a year they shall be condemned as heretics forthwith. Secular authorities, whatever functions they discharge, shall be instructed, exhorted and, if necessary, compelled by ecclesiastical censure, as they wish to be reputed Christian and treated as such, to take for the defence of the faith public oath that they will concern themselves and do their utmost in good faith to expel from lands under their jurisdiction all heretics pointed out by the church: accordingly from now on whenever anyone is raised to a position of authority spiritual or temporal he shall be bound to confirm this chapter on oath. If however a temporal lord, required and instructed by the church, neglects to purge his land of this heretical filth he shall be bound by the metropolitan and the other bishops of the same province with the bond of excommunication, and if he disdains to render satisfaction within the year it shall be reported to the supreme pontiff in order that he may forthwith declare his vassals absolved from their fealty to him, and make the land available for occupation by catholics, who when they have evicted the heretics are to have possession of it without opposition and keep it in the purity of the faith – saving the right of the principal lord, provided that in this matter he opposes no obstacle and puts no impediment in the way. The same rule is to be no less observed for those who do not have principal lords. Catholics who having taken the cross undertake to expel heretics shall enjoy the indulgence and be protected by the holy privilege allowed to those going to the help of the Holy Land. We decree that adherents of, besides receivers, defenders and helpers of heretics are liable to excommunication and firmly ordain that if any such, after being marked with excommunication refuses to render satisfaction within the year he shall forthwith be *ipso facto* branded with infamy, not to be admitted to public office or advisory functions or the electing of anyone to such, and his testimony shall not be acceptable; he shall also be *intestabilis*, i.e. he shall not have the right to make a will and he may not enter upon the succession to an inheritance; no one moreover shall be forced to answer to him about any matter whatever, but he shall answer to others. If he chances to be a judge, his sentence shall have no force, nor shall any causes be brought to his court; if he is an advocate his pleading shall not be listened to at all; if a notary, documents drawn up by him shall have no weight whatever, but be condemned with their condemned author; other cases we order to be treated similarly. If however he is a clerk he shall be deprived of every office and benefice, so that the heavier punishment may be employed against him whose fault is the greater. If any refuse to avoid heretics[1] after they have been pointed out by the church they shall be struck by the sentence of excommunication until proper satisfaction has been made. Clerks shall not, of course, administer the church's sacraments to such pestilent folk or presume to give them Christian burial or accept their alms or offerings; otherwise they shall be deprived of their office and never be restored to it without a special indult of the apostolic see. Similarly with regulars of whatever sort, and on them this too shall be inflicted – that

[1] *tales*

their privileges are not to be respected in the diocese in which they have presumed to commit such excesses. Because some "under a form of godliness denying (as the Apostle says) the power thereof" claim for themselves the authority to preach when the same Apostle says, "How shall they preach except they be sent?", all who are prohibited or not yet sent but presume to usurp publicly or privately the office of preaching without having received the authority of the apostolic see or the catholic bishop of the place shall be bound by the bond of excommunication, and unless they repent very promptly shall be punished by another appropriate penalty. We add moreover that every archbishop or bishop shall personally or through his archdeacon or other suitable and upright persons visit twice or at least once a year any parish of his in which there are said to be heretics and there compel three or more men of good reputation, or even if it seems expedient the whole neighbourhood, to swear that if anyone knows of heretics there or of any who hold secret conventicles or any whose life and habits differ from the normal way of living of Christians he will make it his business to point them out to the bishop. He, the bishop, shall summon the accused to his presence and if they do not clear themselves[1] of the accusation, or if after clearance they relapse into their former errors of faith, they shall be punished in accordance with canon law. If any of them, however, refuse with damnable obstinacy to be bound by oath and will not swear, they shall be from that very fact reckoned as heretics. We will, command and strictly order, on the strength of their obedience, bishops to see carefully to the effective execution of these things all over their dioceses, if they wish to escape canonical punishment; for if any bishop is negligent or slack over clearing the ferment of heresy from his diocese when it shows itself by unmistakable signs he shall be deposed from his office of bishop and in his place another suitable person substituted who has the will and the power to overthrow heresy.

4. Although we should like to cherish and honour the Greeks, who in our time are returning to the obedience of the apostolic see, by maintaining as much as we can under the Lord their customs and rites, we neither want to nor should we defer to them in things which breed danger to souls and detract from the decorum of the church. For after the Greek church withdrew with certain associates and supporters from the obedience of the apostolic see the Greeks began to loathe the Latins so much that, among other wicked things they did out of contempt for them, they would not, when Latin priests had celebrated on their altars, themselves sacrifice on them before they had washed them, as if by this they had been defiled. Also, those baptised by Latins these Greeks had the temerity to rebaptise and there are some still, we are told, who do not fear to do it. Wishing therefore to do away with such a scandal in the church of God, we on the advice of the holy council strictly command them not to venture to do such things in future and to conform like obedient sons to the holy Roman church, their mother, so that there may be "one fold and one shepherd". If anyone does venture to do such a thing he shall be struck with the sword of excommunication and deprived of every ecclesiastical office and benefice.

[1] by compurgation or ordeal

5. Renewing the ancient privileges of the patriarchal sees, we decree with the approbation of the holy universal council that, after the Roman church, which by the divine plan, has as mother and ruler of all Christians the primacy of ordinary power over all other churches, the church of Constantinople shall have the first place, that of Alexandria the second, that of Antioch the third, that of Jerusalem the fourth, each of them keeping its own authority – so that after their pontiffs have received the pallium, which is the distinguishing mark of the plenitude of the pontifical office, from the Roman pontiff and taken the oath of fealty and obedience to him, they may lawfully confer the pallium on their own suffragans and receive from them for themselves the canonical profession and for the Roman church the promise of obedience. They shall have the standard of the divine cross carried before them everywhere save in Rome or wherever the pope (or his legate) is present wearing the insignia of apostolic dignity. In all provinces under their jurisdiction appeal, when necessary, shall be made to them, except for appeals lodged with the apostolic see, to which all must humbly defer.

6. As is known to have been ordained of old by the holy fathers, metropolitans should not fail to hold provincial councils every year with their suffragans to consider diligently and in the fear of God the correction of excesses and the reform of morals, especially in the clergy, reciting the canonical rules (particularly those laid down by the present general council) to secure their observance, inflicting on transgressors the punishment due. In order that this may be the more effectively achieved, they are to set up in each diocese suitable persons, discreet that is and honest, who throughout the year shall carefully find out simply and summarily without any jurisdiction what things deserve correction or reform and faithfully report those things to the metropolitan and suffragans and others at the ensuing council, that they after careful deliberation may proceed against these things and others suitably and decently. What they decree, they shall cause to be observed, making it known in diocesan synods, which shall be held annually in each diocese. Whoever neglects to act upon this salutary statute is to be suspended from his benefices and his office until he is released by the decision of his superior.

7. By an irrevocable decree we ordain that persons in authority over churches shall prudently and diligently give their minds to correcting the excesses and reforming the morals of those, especially the clergy, subject to them, lest the blood of these be required at their hands. So that they can perform the task of correcting and reforming freely, we decree that no custom or appeal can impede the execution of their [sentences], unless they have exceeded the rules to be observed in such things. Let, however, the excesses of canons of a cathedral church which by custom have been corrected by the chapter be corrected by it, in churches which have had such a custom until now, at the instance and on the orders of the bishop within a sufficient time-limit, which the bishop shall fix. If this is not done, then the bishop, mindful of God and putting a stop to all opposition, shall not delay to correct them by ecclesiastical censure as the care of souls requires, and not omit to correct their other

excesses too as the charge of souls requires, due order nevertheless being observed in all things. For the rest, if canons stop celebrating divine service without manifest and reasonable cause, particularly in contempt of the bishop, the bishop may celebrate in the cathedral church notwithstanding if he wishes, and on complaint from him the metropolitan as our delegate for this may, when he has established the truth of the matter, chastise them with ecclesiastical censure in such fashion that for fear of the punishment they shall not venture such action in future. Let those in authority over churches carefully see to it therefore that they do not turn this salutary decree into a way of getting money or other exaction, but operate it zealously and faithfully if they wish to avoid canonical punishment, since the apostolic see will, with divine authority, watch over these things most particularly.

8. "By what right and in what way a prelate ought to proceed to enquire into and punish the excesses of subordinates is clearly shown from the testimony assembled in the New and Old Testament, from which the subsequent canon law sanctions derive," as we said distinctly some time ago and now with the approbation of the holy council confirm. For one reads in the gospel that the bailiff who was "denounced to his lord for having wasted his goods" heard from him, "What is this I hear of thee? Give an account of thy bailiwick for now thou canst no more be bailiff." And in Genesis God says, "I will go down now, and see whether they have done altogether according to the cry of it which is come unto me." From which authorities it is clearly proved that not only when a subordinate but even a prelate commits some excess and through complaint and rumour it reaches the ears of his superior, not from the ill-disposed and slanderous but from prudent and honest people, not just once but often (which complaint implies and rumour is manifest proof of), he, the superior, ought in the presence of senior people of the church to enquire into the truth and if the case demands it canonical distress shall smite the fault of the offender – not as if he were accuser and judge but with rumour informing and complaint denouncing, as one carrying out the duty of his office. While this is to be done in the case of subordinates, it must still more carefully be done in the case of prelates, who are set "as a mark for the arrow". And because they cannot please everybody since they are bound *ex officio* not only to reprove but also to blame, nay even at times to suspend, sometimes to bind, they frequently incur the hatred of many people and are liable to ambushes. For this reason the holy fathers wisely decreed that accusation of prelates is not to be allowed easily, for fear that if the columns are shaken the building may fall, unless there is careful provision for shutting the door against not only false but also malicious accusation. They wished so to provide for prelates not to be accused unjustly that they would take care all the same not to offend out of arrogance and they found a suitable preventative for either evil, viz, that a criminal accusation, which entails the *diminutio capitis*, i.e. degradation, shall in no wise be allowed unless it is preceded by the *inscriptio legitima*.[1] But when anyone is so notorious for his excesses that complaint now cannot be ignored any longer without scandal or without danger allowed to continue, action is to be taken without the slightest hesitation to enquire into and

[1] The accuser is named and he will be liable to a penalty if his accusation is not sustained.

punish his excesses, not out of hate but out of charity; with the condition that if it is a matter of a grave excess, though not one involving his degradation, he shall be deprived of all office, in accordance with the gospel sentence that the bailiff is to be removed from his bailiwick who cannot give a proper account of it. He ought therefore to be present about whom enquiry is to be made, unless out of contumacy he absents himself, and the points to be enquired into should be set out before him so that he can be in a position to defend himself, and not only the depositions of the witnesses but also their names, in order that he may know what has been said and who said it, are to be revealed to him, also legitimate exceptions and replications are to be allowed, lest through the suppression of names the audacious may prefer false charges or through the barring of exceptions, bear false witness. A prelate ought to be all the more zealous to correct the excesses of his subordinates, the more to blame he would be for leaving their offences unpunished. Against them, notorious cases aside, although three procedures are possible, viz, by accusation, denunciation and inquest, let careful precautions nevertheless be taken in all cases lest for the sake of a slight gain grave loss may be incurred: just as the *legitima inscriptio* ought to precede the accusation,[1] so a kindly warning ought to come before denunciation and entry of complaint before inquest, always with the rule applied that the method of pronouncing sentence shall be according to the mode of trial. This order, however, need not in our view be observed in all respects as regards regulars, who can at need be more easily and freely removed from their offices.

9. Since in many parts peoples of different languages with various rites and usages within the common faith are mixed together in the same city and diocese, we strictly command the bishops of cities or dioceses of this sort to appoint suitable men to celebrate divine service for them in the various rites and languages, administer the ecclesiastical sacraments to them and instruct them by word and by example alike. We utterly forbid one and the same city or diocese to have more than one bishop, like a body with more than one head as if it were a monster, yet if for the reasons aforesaid necessity requires it, the bishop of the place may after careful deliberation set up a catholic bishop appropriate for those nations as vicar for himself in the aforesaid matters, who will in all respects be under and obedient to him – as to which, if anyone behaves otherwise he shall know he is smitten by the sword of excommunication, and if he does not then recover his senses he is to be deposed from all ecclesiastical office, the help of the secular arm being invoked if necessary to curb such presumption.

10. Among the other things pertaining to the saving of Christian souls the bread of the gospel is recognised as the most necessary of all, for as the body is nourished by material food so is the soul by spiritual, because "Man does not live by bread alone, but by every word that proceedeth out of the mouth of God." Hence, since it often happens that bishops because of their manifold occupations or bodily ailments or enemy attacks or other reasons – not to mention lack of learning, in them a most grievous fault, not to be tolerated in future – are unable themselves to do all the

[1] see above

preaching of the gospel to the people that is needed, especially in large and scattered dioceses, we by a general constitution decree that bishops are to choose men effective in action and speech, suitable for executing the office of sacred preaching to advantage, to visit zealously the peoples committed to them in their place when they themselves cannot and edify them by word and example, and they are to furnish these men, when they need them, with what is appropriate and necessary lest for lack of the things necessary they be forced to abandon an undertaking. We order, in consequence, suitable men to be appointed as well in cathedral as in other conventual churches for the bishops to have as coadjutors and cooperators not only in preaching but also in hearing confessions and enjoining penances and everything else pertaining to the saving of souls. If any one neglects to carry this out, he shall be subject to rigorous punishment.

11. As because of their poverty some have neither the opportunity to study nor chance of advancement, the Lateran council[1] provided by a pious decree that "in each cathedral church some competent benefice should be given to a master, whose duty it should be to instruct for nothing the clerks of that church and other poor scholars, thus at once relieving the need of the teacher and opening up the path of knowledge to those who are learning". Since, however, this decree is very little observed in many churches, we confirm it, adding that not only in every cathedral church but also in others, whose resources are adequate, a suitable master, elected by the chapter or the greater and sounder part of the chapter, shall be established by the prelate. He is to instruct for nothing the clerks of those churches and of others in grammar and in other branches of study as far as possible. The metropolitan church shall maintain nonetheless a theologian to teach holy writ to priests and others and above all instruct them in those things which are recognised as having to do with the cure of souls. To each of the masters there is to be assigned by the chapter the income of a single prebend, and just as much by the metropolitan for the theologian, without his being made on that account a canon, though he shall get the revenues of one as long as he remains prepared to teach. If the metropolitan church finds the two a burden, let it provide for the theologian in the way stated, but for the grammarian get adequate provision made in another church of the city or diocese.

12. In each kingdom or province let there be held every three years, saving the right of diocesan bishops, a general chapter of abbots and of priors without an abbot of their own who have not been accustomed to hold one. They should all attend, if there is no canonical impediment, at one of the monasteries which is suitable for the purpose, with this limitation – that none of them shall bring with him more than six mounts and eight persons. Let them call in as a favour at the start of this innovation two neighbouring Cistercian abbots to furnish appropriate counsel and assistance, as they have long been accustomed to holding such chapters and are very knowledgable. They, with no opposition, shall coopt two they think would be a help from their own order, and these four shall preside over the general chapter, in such a way that

[1] Third Lateran Council, 1179

from this no one of them assumes leadership: so, if need be, they can, after careful deliberation be changed. This kind of chapter shall last several consecutive days, as is Cistercian practice, and in it there is to be careful consideration of the reform of the order and the observance of the rule, and what is decided with the approval of those four is to be inviolably observed by all, without any excuse, opposition or appeal. It shall be settled as well where the chapter is to be held next time. Those attending are to lead a common life and divide between them, proportionately, the common expenses. If they cannot all be put up in the same house, let them stay many together at least in several houses. In the same chapter too let there be appointed discreet religious who will make it their business to visit, in the way prescribed for them and on our behalf, every abbey of monks and of nuns of the kingdom or province to correct and reform what in their view needs correction and reform. If they consider that the superior of the place should be removed outright from the running of it, they shall denounce him to his bishop, that he may remove him, and if he does not do it, the visitors shall refer the matter to the consideration of the papal see. This same thing we will and command canons regular to observe according to their order. If any difficulty arises out of this innovation which cannot be resolved by the said visitors, let it be referred without fuss to the judgment of the papal see, the rest of what after careful discussion they have agreed upon being observed without being called in question again. On the other hand, diocesan bishops shall make it their business so to reform the monasteries under their jurisdiction that when the said visitors come they find more in them worthy of commendation than of correction; and shall be most careful lest the said monasteries are oppressed by them with undue burdens, for, just as we wish the rights of superiors to be upheld, we do not wish to support wrongs done to inferiors. Furthermore, we strictly command both diocesan bishops and those who preside at chapters to restrain by ecclesiastical censure, with no appeal from it, advocates, patrons, vidames, rectors and consuls, magnates and knights, or any others, from presuming to commit offences against monasteries in respect of their persons or their things, and should they have committed such an offence they shall without fail force them to give satisfaction, so that monasteries may serve Almighty God freely and quietly.

13. For fear too great a diversity of religious orders should lead to grave confusion in the church of God, we firmly forbid anyone in future to invent a new religious order: whoever wishes to become a religious must adopt one of the approved orders. Similarly, anyone wishing to found a new religious house must accept the rule and constitutions of one of the approved religious orders. We forbid also anyone to presume to have a place as a monk in more than one monastery, and one abbot to preside over more than one monastery.

14. That the morals and conduct of clerks may be improved, let all strive to live continently and chastely, especially those established in holy orders; let them seek to avoid completely the sin of lust – particularly that on account of which the anger of God comes from heaven upon the sons of disobedience – in order that they may be

able to minister in the sight of Almighty God with a pure heart and clean body. Lest too easy a pardon afford an incentive to sin, we decree that they who are caught giving way to the sin of incontinence shall in proportion to the degree of their sin be punished according to the rules of canon law, which we wish to be most effectively and rigorously observed in order that those whom the fear of God does not hold back from evil temporal punishment at least may restrain from sin. If anyone, therefore, suspended because of this, presumes to celebrate divine service he shall not only be deprived of ecclesiastical benefices but also for this twofold transgression be forever deposed from office. Prelates who venture to support such in their wickednesses, especially for money or other temporal advantage, shall be subject to like punishment. Those who, in the manner of their country, have not renounced the marriage bond shall if they fall into sin be punished more severely, since they can avail themselves of lawful matrimony.

15. All clerks shall carefully abstain from gluttony and drunkenness, by which means they may temper the wine to themselves and themselves to the wine; and let no one be urged to drink, as drunkenness both causes the loss of one's senses and rouses the temptation to lust. Accordingly we decree that that abuse is to be utterly abolished whereby in certain parts drinkers bind each other to drink measure for measure and he in their judgment is most praised who has made most people drunk and drained the deepest cups. If anyone shows himself to blame in these things, unless he makes suitable satisfaction when warned by his superior he is to be suspended from his benefice or office. Hunting and bird-catching we forbid for all clerks, hence let them not presume to have either hunting dogs or falcons.

16. Clerks are not to practice secular callings or business, especially if they are dishonourable, not to watch mimes, entertainers and actors and not to frequent taverns at all, unless compelled of necessity to do so on a journey. They are not to play at dice or the little dice[1] or be present at such games. They are to have a suitable crown and tonsure and apply themselves to the divine services and other good pursuits. They are to wear outer garments that are closed, not noticeable by being too short or too long; they are not to indulge in red or green cloths, long sleeves or shoes with embroidery or with curved toes, bridles, saddles, pectorals and spurs that are gilded or have other unnecessary ornamentation. Priests and those in minor dignities are not to wear cloaks with sleeves at divine service inside the church, and not even elsewhere, unless a justifiable fear requires a change of dress. They are not to wear buckles or belts ornamented with gold or silver, or even rings except those whose dignity it befits to have them. All bishops are to wear outer garments of linen in public and in church unless they are monks, when they should wear the monastic habit: they are not to wear their cloaks loose in public, but fastened on either side either behind the neck or at the chest.

17. We grieve to relate that not only certain lesser clerks but also some prelates spend nearly half the night in unnecessary feasting and forbidden conversation, not to

[1] *taxillos* (another kind of dice)

mention other things, and leaving for sleep what is left of the night, they are barely roused at the dawn chorus of the birds and doze away the whole morning. There are also others who celebrate mass barely four times a year or, what is worse, do not bother to attend it, and if they are present while it is being celebrated, they flee the silence of the choir and pay attention to the conversation of the laity outside and, while they are listening to things being said that they are not required to, their ears are not intent on the service. These things and the like we utterly forbid therefore on pain of suspension and strictly command them on the strength of their obedience to celebrate the divine service, day and night alike, as far as God allows them, with zeal and devotion.

18. No clerk may decree or pronounce a sentence of death; nor may he carry out a punishment which involves blood or be there when it is carried out. If anyone presumes to inflict injury on churches or ecclesiastical persons by transgressing this decree he shall be restrained by ecclesiastical censure. Nor shall any clerk write or dictate letters requiring a punishment which involves blood: in the courts of princes let this responsibility be given to laymen, not clerks. Also let no clerk be put in command of mercenaries, crossbowmen or suchlike men of blood; and no subdeacon, deacon, or priest is to practise the art of surgery, which involves burning and cutting; and none is to bestow any blessing or consecration on a purgation by ordeal of boiling water or of cold water or of the red-hot iron, saving nevertheless previously promulgated prohibitions concerning single combats or duels.

19. We do not wish it to be left uncorrected that certain clerks store their own furniture, and that of others, in churches, so that they look more like lay houses than houses of God, regardless of the fact that God would not suffer a vessel to be carried through the temple. There are others too who not only let churches fall into neglect, but also leave the sacred vessels and the liturgical vestments and the altar-cloths too and the very communion-cloths so dirty that at times they horrify some people. Now because the zeal of God's house has eaten us up, we firmly prohibit such furniture to be allowed into churches unless on account of enemy attacks or sudden fire or other emergencies they have to be taken in; yet so that when the emergency is over things are taken back to where they were. We command too that oratories, vessels, communion-cloths and the aforementioned vestments be kept clean and fresh. For it seems too absurd to neglect an uncleanness in sacred things which would be disgraceful even in profane.

20. We order the chrism and the eucharist in all churches to be kept locked away in a safe place so that no audacious hand can reach them to do anything horrible or impious. If he who is responsible for keeping them is careless and leaves them about he shall be suspended from office for three months, and if through his carelessness anything unspeakable happens to them he shall be subject to a greater punishment.

21. Every Christian of either sex after reaching the years of discretion shall confess all his sins at least once a year privately to his own priest and try as hard as he can to

perform the penance imposed on him; and receive with reverence the sacrament of the eucharist at least at Easter, unless for some reasonable cause, on the advice of his own priest, he thinks he should temporarily refrain from taking it. Otherwise he shall be barred from entering a church in his lifetime and at death shall not have Christian burial. This salutary decree shall be published frequently in churches, so that no one can find the veil of an excuse in the blindness of ignorance. Should, however, anyone for good reasons wish to confess his sins to another priest, let him first ask for and get the permission of his own priest, otherwise the other will not be able to absolve him or bind him. As for the priest, he should be discerning and prudent so that like a practised doctor he can pour wine and oil on the wounds of the injured, diligently enquiring into the circumstances both of the sinner and of the sin, from which to choose intelligently what sort of advice he ought to give him and what sort of remedy to apply, various means availing to heal the sick. Let him take the utmost care not to betray the sinner in some measure by word or sign or any other way whatever, but if he needs sage advice, let him seek it cautiously without mentioning the person: he who presumes to reveal a sin disclosed in the confessional we decree is to be not only deposed from his priestly office but also shut up to do penance for life in a monastery of strict observance.

22. As physical illness is sometimes the result of sin – the Lord said to a sick man whom he had cured, "Go and sin no more, lest worse befall you" – we by the present decree ordain and strictly command doctors, when it happens that they are called to the sick, to warn and exhort them before anything else to call in doctors of souls, so that after his spiritual health has been seen to, the sick man may respond better to the bodily medicine – for when the cause ceases, the effect ceases. This among other things has occasioned this decree: that some on a sickbed, when advised by doctors to arrange for the good of their souls, fall into a state of despair, whereby they incur more easily the danger of death. If any doctor shall transgress this our decree, after it has been published by the local prelates, he shall be barred from entering a church until he has performed the appropriate penance for this sort of transgression. Furthermore, as the soul is much more precious than the body, we forbid on pain of eternal anathema any doctor to prescribe anything for a sick man for his bodily health which might endanger his soul.

23. Lest for lack of a shepherd a rapacious wolf attack the Lord's flock and a bereaved church suffer grave injury to its good and wishing in this matter to counteract the danger to souls and provide protection for churches, we decree that a cathedral or monastic church may not be without a prelate for more than three months, and if, there being no lawful impediment, an election is not made within that time, those who should have elected shall be for that occasion deprived of the power to elect and it shall devolve upon him who is recognised as the immediate superior. He on whom the power has devolved shall, ever mindful of the Lord, not delay more than three months in supplying, with the counsel of his chapter and of other discreet men, the bereaved church canonically with a suitable person from that

church or from another church if one is not to be found in that, if he wishes to escape canonical penalty.

24. Owing to the various forms of election which some try to invent, both many impediments are produced and great dangers threaten bereaved churches. Because of this we decree that when an election is to be made, with all present who ought, want to and conveniently can be there, there shall be chosen three worthy of trust from the college who shall carefully find out in confidence one by one everybody's vote, and having written them down, shall quickly make known the result of the voting,[1] and no appeal shall be allowed to obstruct it, so that after scrutiny he shall be elected on whom the whole or the greater or sounder part of the chapter agree. Or else the power of electing shall be committed to some suitable men, who acting for everybody shall provide the bereaved church with a pastor. Otherwise no election made shall be valid, unless perchance it was made by all unanimously as if by divine inspiration and without flaw. Those who attempt to elect contrary to the aforesaid forms shall be deprived of the power of electing on that occasion. What we absolutely forbid is that anyone should appoint a proxy in the business of election unless he is away from the place where he ought to receive the summons and, detained by a lawful impediment, cannot come – as to which, if need be, he shall take an oath – and then if he wishes he may commission someone from the electoral college in his stead. We condemn also clandestine elections and decree that as soon as an election has taken place it be solemnly published.

25. Whoever consents to election of himself by misuse of secular power contrary to canonical freedom shall both be deprived of the advantage of having been elected and be rendered ineligible; nor can he without a dispensation be elected to any dignity. Those who presume to take part in this sort of election, which we declare *ipso jure* invalidated, shall be suspended completely from their offices and benefices for three years and during that time deprived of the power to elect.

26. There is nothing more harmful to the church of God than the elevation of unworthy prelates to the government of souls. Wishing therefore to apply the necessary medicine for this malady, we ordain by an irrevocable decree that when anyone is raised to the government of souls he who has the right to confirm him shall diligently examine both the election procedure and the character of the person elected, so that if everything is in order he may give him his confirmation, because if it were incautiously given in advance and everything was not in order, not only would the one unworthily promoted have to be rejected but also the one who promoted unworthily would have to be punished. The latter, we decree, is to suffer this punishment: if it is clearly a matter of negligence on his part, especially if he has confirmed the election of a man of insufficient learning or disgraceful life or uncanonical age, not only shall he be deprived of the power of confirming the first one to follow that man, but also (lest by any chance he escapes punishment) be debarred from receiving the

[1] *publicent in communi* (i.e. totals, not the individual votes)

fruits of his own benefice until he can justly obtain a pardon; if convicted of having intentionally transgressed in the matter, let him suffer a heavier penalty. Bishops too shall endeavour to promote to holy orders and ecclesiastical dignities such as are able to discharge worthily the office committed to them, if they themselves wish to escape canonical penalty. For the rest, those who are immediately under the Roman pontiff shall, to get confirmation of their office, appear personally before him if it can conveniently be done or send suitable persons, by means of whom careful inquiry into election procedure and into those who are elected can be made, so that in the end, on the strength of his informed judgment, they may attain the full authority of their office, when nothing in the canon law stands in their way – provided meanwhile that those who are in very distant posts, that is outside Italy, may by dispensation, if they were elected peaceably, where it meets the church's needs or is to its advantage administer in things spiritual and temporal, but shall alienate nothing whatever belonging to the church. They may be given the customary consecration or benediction.

27. As the governing of souls is the art of arts, we strictly command bishops carefully to prepare those who are to be promoted to the priesthood and instruct them, either personally or through other suitable men, in the divine services and the sacraments of the church, in order that they may know how to celebrate them properly: since if they presume in future to ordain the ignorant and unskilled (which could indeed be easily detected) we decree that both those who ordain and those who are ordained are to be subject to punishment. For it is better, particularly in the ordaining of priests, to have a few good than many bad ministers, because if the blind leads the blind both will fall into the ditch.

28. Certain people persistently demand leave to resign and having got it omit to do so. But in demanding such resignation they would seem to have in mind either the good of the churches over which they preside or their own well-being, neither of which things do we wish to be impeded by the advice of those seeking their own or even by any fickleness of purpose: we therefore decree that they are to be compelled to resign.

29. With great foresight it was prohibited in the Lateran council[1] for anyone to receive divers ecclesiastical dignities and several parish churches contrary to the ordinances of canon law on pain both of the receiver losing what he has thus received and of the one bestowing being deprived of the power to bestow. But as, owing to the presumption and greed of some, the said statute has borne no fruit, or very little, we, wishing to counter with a surer and stronger remedy,[2] ordain by the present decree that whoever receives a benefice with cure of souls attached, if he already has such a benefice shall automatically be deprived of that and if perchance he tries to keep it let him be deprived of the other one also. Also he who has the giving of the first benefice shall freely bestow it, after the receiving of the second, on a person on whom he

[3] Third Lateran Council, 1179

[2] *evidentius et expressius occurrere cupientes*

considers it can worthily be bestowed, but if he delays more than three months over bestowing it not only shall the bestowal of it devolve upon another in accordance with the statute of the Lateran council but also he shall be forced to assign for the use of the church of the benefice in question as much from his own income as is established was obtained from it while it was vacant. The very same we decree is to be done with regard to minor dignities, adding that no one shall presume to have several dignities or minor dignities in one and the same church even if they do not have cure of souls. As to men of birth and lettered persons, who should be honoured by greater benefices, they when reason demands it can be dispensed by the apostolic see.

30. It is very serious and improper that certain heads of churches, when they could promote suitable men to ecclesiastical benefices, fear not to adopt unworthy people recommended neither by upright living nor by learning, following the inclination of their heart, not the judgment of their reason. How much churches lose by this every man of right mind knows. Wishing therefore to cure this malady, we order them to pass over the unworthy and choose suitable people, who have both the desire and the ability to serve God and churches well, and let careful enquiry be made about this each year in provincial council, so that he who is found guilty after a first and a second correction shall be suspended by that council from conferring benefices, and a prudent and honest person appointed in that same council to take the place of the one suspended in conferring benefices; and the very same is to be done with regard to chapters who offend in these things. An offence by a metropolitan shall however be left by the council to be reported to the judgment of a superior. So that this salutary provision shall have its full effect, a sentence of suspension of this kind shall definitely not be lifted without the authority of the Roman pontiff or of the appropriate patriarch – that in this too the four patriarchal sees may be specially honoured.

31. To abolish a very bad corruption indeed which has been on the increase in many churches, we firmly prohibit sons of canons, particularly as they are bastards, being made canons in secular churches where their fathers are established; and if in spite of this it is attempted, we decree it not valid. And they who, as has been said, venture to make canons of such shall be suspended from their benefices.

32. A vicious custom that ought to be uprooted has established itself in some parts, namely that patrons of parish churches, and certain other persons, claim the incomes from them wholly for themselves, leaving the priests deputed to serve them so small a portion that they cannot fittingly live on it. We have learnt for certain that in some regions parish priests get for their support only a quarter of a quarter, that is a sixteenth, of the tithes. Whence it is that in these regions scarcely any parish priest can be found who has even a modicum of education. As the ox ought not to be muzzled when it treadeth out the corn, and he who serves the altar ought to live from the altar, we decree therefore, any custom of a bishop or patron or anyone else notwithstanding, that a sufficient portion shall be assigned to the priests. He who has a parish church shall serve it not by a vicar but personally in the due form which the care of

that church requires, unless perchance the parish church is annexed to a prebend or a dignity. In which case we allow that he who has such a prebend or dignity should, as he must serve in a greater church, make it his business to have in the parish church a suitable, canonically instituted perpetual[1] vicar, who, as has been said, shall have a fitting portion from the revenues of that church: otherwise, he shall know that by the authority of this decree he is deprived of that church and it is to be given freely to someone else who is willing and able to do as we have said. What we utterly forbid is that anyone should presume deceitfully to confer from the revenues of a church which has to maintain its own priest a pension on another as it were as a benefice.[2]

33. Procurations due, by reason of visitation, to bishops, archdeacons or anyone else, also to legates or nuncios of the apostolic see, should by no means, without manifest and necessary cause, be exacted save when they actually incur the expense of visitation, and then they shall observe the moderation in transport and retinue decreed in the Lateran council.[3] We add this modification as regards legates and nuncios of the apostolic see, that when they must necessarily stay in some place, so that this place may not be excessively burdened because of them they may receive moderate procurations from other churches or persons who have not yet been burdened with their procurations, on condition that the number of procurations shall not exceed the number of days they stayed in that place, and when any person has not sufficient means on his own, two or more may be combined into one. Rather, those performing the office of visitation shall not seek their own but the things which are Jesus Christ's, by devoting themselves to preaching, exhortation, correction and reformation, that they may bring back the fruit which does not perish. He who presumes to contravene this shall both restore what he has received and pay the same amount as compensation to the church he has thus burdened.

34. Many prelates, to meet the cost of a procuration or some service to a legate or some other person, extort more from their subordinates than they pay out, and trying to gain from their loss, seek booty rather than an aid from those under them. This we forbid to be done in future. And if perchance anyone ventures to do it let him both restore what has been thus extorted and be forced to distribute an equivalent amount to the poor. A superior with whom a complaint has been lodged about this shall, if he is negligent in executing this decree, suffer canonical punishment.

35. In order that due honour be paid to judges and thought taken for litigants in the matter of trouble and expense, we decree that when anybody sues an adversary before the competent judge, he shall not before judgment has been given appeal to a superior judge without reasonable cause, but proceed with his suit before that one and it shall not be open to him to obstruct by saying that he has sent a messenger to a superior judge or even procured letters from him before they were remitted to the

[1] i.e. with security of tenure, not removable
[2] For what could be involved in this last sentence, see Cheney, *From Becket to Langton* (Manchester, 1956), pp. 122–31.
[3] Third Lateran Council, 1179

judge delegate. When, however, in his view he has reasonable cause for appealing, and has stated before that same judge the grounds of the appeal and these are such that if they were proved they would be reckoned legitimate, the superior judge shall take cognisance of the appeal. If he finds it not reasonable he shall send the appellant back to the inferior judge and sentence him to bear the costs of the other party; otherwise he shall proceed with the case, saving the constitutions about referring major causes to the apostolic see.

36. As when the cause ceases the effect ceases, we decree that if a judge ordinary or a judge delegate has pronounced a comminatory or interlocutory sentence on anything, an order for the execution of which would prejudice one of the parties and on good advice refrains from putting it into effect, he shall proceed freely with the hearing of the case, notwithstanding any appeal made against such comminatory or interlocutory sentence (provided his action is not open to question on any other legal ground), in order that the action may not be held up for frivolous reasons.

37. Some abusing the grace of the holy see try to sue out writs from it to distant judges so that the one sued, tired of the trouble and expense of the action, shall have to give in to or come to terms with the bringer of the action. But since a way should not be opened by a court of justice for wrongs which observance of the law forbids, we decree that nobody can be dragged by papal writ to a court more than two days journey outside his diocese, unless it was procured with the assent of both parties and it expressly mentions this constitution. There are others too, who, turning to a new kind of trade, to revive complaints that are dormant or to introduce new questions invent causes, for which they sue out writs from the apostolic see without authority from their superiors and offer them for sale, either to the party sued that he may not be vexed by an outlay of trouble and expense because of them, or to the bringer of the action that he through them may tire out the adversary with undue vexations. But since lawsuits should be shortened rather than prolonged, we by this general edict decree that if anybody on any question presumes in future to sue out papal writs without special mandate from his superior, both the writs shall be invalid and he himself punished as a maker of false documents, unless he happens to be one of those from whom a mandate rightly ought not to be required.

38. Against a false assertion of an unjust judge an innocent litigator is never at any time able to prove the truth by a denial, as the act of denying is not in the nature of things at all a direct proof. So, lest the false should prejudice the truth or iniquity prevail over equity, we decree that in both ordinary and extraordinary judicial proceedings the judge shall always employ either a public official,[1] if he can get one, or two suitable men to draw up faithfully all judicial acts (that is to say, citations, adjournments, objections and exceptions, petitions and answers, interrogations, confessions, depositions of witnesses, productions of documents, interlocutions, appeals, renunciations, final decisions and the rest of the things that call for proper drafting)

[1] *publica persona* (i.e. a notary)

specifying places, times and persons; and everything thus written is to be given to the parties on condition that the originals are kept by the writers, so that if dispute arises over the handling of the case by the judge the truth can be established from them. With the application of this measure such deference will be paid to upright and experienced judges that justice will not be impaired for the innocent by imprudent and wicked judges. A judge who neglects to observe this decree shall, if any difficulty results from his neglect, be punished by a superior judge with the punishment he deserves, nor shall there be a presumption in favour of his procedure save to the extent that it accords with the legal documents.

39. It often happens that a man unjustly deprived of something loses in effect the right to it, because of the difficulty of proof when the one who deprived him of it has transferred it to a third party, there being no remedy at law for the deprived by means of an action for restitution against the possessor, the advantage of possession having changed hands. Wherefore, notwithstanding the strict civil law, we decree that if anyone in future knowingly receives such a thing (taking over as it were, too, the fault of the depredator because there is not much difference, particularly as regards peril to the soul, between unjustly withholding and seizing the property of another), as a help against this sort of possessor the deprived is to have the benefit of restitution.

40. It sometimes happens that a plaintiff who, on account of the contumacy of the opposing party, has the possession of a thing adjudged to him to look after, is not able to get it into his possession within a year because of force or fraud over it, or having got it loses it, and thus, since in the opinion of many he does not qualify as the true possessor at the end of the year, the defendant profits by his wickedness. Therefore so that a contumacious party shall not be in a better position than one who obeys a citation, we decree in the name of canonical equity that in the case aforesaid the plaintiff shall when a year has elapsed be accepted as the true possessor. Furthermore, we prohibit generally submission of spiritual matters to the arbitration of a layman, because it is not fitting for a layman to arbitrate in such things.

41. As "Whatsoever is not of faith is sin", we define by synodal decree that no prescription, canonical or civil, is valid without good faith, since generally any statute or custom is to be discounted which cannot be observed without committing mortal sin. So that it behoves one who claims a prescriptive right to have had no knowledge at any stage that the thing was someone else's.

42. Just as it is our will that laymen should not usurp the rights of clerks, so it ought to be our will that clerks should not lay claim to the rights of laymen. For which reason we forbid every clerk in future on the pretext of ecclesiastical freedom to extend his jurisdiction to the detriment of secular justice: let him be content with the written laws and the customs up to now approved, in order that by a right distribution "the things which are Caesar's" may be rendered unto Caesar and "the things that are God's" rendered unto God.

43. Some laymen try to encroach too far upon divine right when they force churchmen who hold nothing temporal from them to take oaths of fealty to them. Because, according to the apostle, a servant "to his own master standeth or falleth",[1] we prohibit by the authority of holy council such clerks to be compelled to take an oath of this sort to secular persons.

44. Laymen, however devout, have no power to dispose of church property: their lot is to obey, not to be in command. We deplore it, then, when in some of them charity grows so cold that the freedom of the church, which not only the holy fathers but secular rulers too have buttressed by many privileges, they do not fear to attack by their decrees, or rather their devices: by not only alienating fiefs and other ecclesiastical possessions and usurping jurisdictions but also illegally appropriating mortuaries as well as other things connected with spiritual property. It being our wish to ensure the immunity of churches from these things and to provide against such great injuries, we pronounce, with the approval of holy council, such decrees and the claiming of fiefs or other ecclesiastical goods appropriated under a decree of a lay power without the lawful assent of the ecclesiastical authorities, not valid, as it could be termed not a decree but a deprivation or molestation.[2] Those who expropriate the church are to be curbed by its censures.

45. In certain provinces, patrons or vidames and advocates of churches display so much arrogance that they not only create difficulties and snares when vacant churches have to be provided with suitable pastors but also presume to dispose of church possessions and other church goods as they like, and, dreadful to relate, fear does not deter them from murdering prelates. Since therefore what has been devised as a protection ought not to be turned into a roundabout way of oppression, we expressly forbid patrons or advocates or vidames in future to appropriate the aforesaid things to a greater extent than they are entitled to by law; and if contrary to this they do presume,[3] they are to be curbed with the utmost severity of the canon law. Equally, with the approbation of the sacred council we decree that if patrons or advocates or feudatories or vidames or others with benefices venture with unspeakable daring either in person or through others to kill or maim the rector of any church or other clerk of that church they shall surrender completely, patrons the right of patronage, advocates their patronage,[4] feudatories the fief, vidames the dignity of vidame,[5] the beneficed their benefice. And lest the punishment be less well remembered than the offence, not only shall nothing from the aforesaid things pass to their heirs, but also their posterity to the fourth generation shall by no means be admitted into a college of clerks or attain a position of any authority in houses of regulars, save when out of compassion they are given dispensation.

[1] Romans xiv. 4
[2] *non constitutio sed destitutio vel destructio*
[3] *praesumpserint* (presume, in the now archaic sense of take without right)
[4] *advocatiam*
[5] *vicedominatum*

46. With regard to consuls and rulers of cities and others who endeavour to oppress churches and churchmen by tallages or levies or other exactions, the Lateran council,[1] wishing to preserve ecclesiastical immunity, strictly forbade such presumption on pain of anathema, ordering offenders and their abettors to be subject to excommunication until they give suitable satisfaction. If, however, when for instance the bishop and his clergy together foresee a necessity or advantage so great that without any coercion, for the common good or the common need when the resources of laymen do not suffice, they consider churches should give subsidies, the aforesaid laymen shall humbly and devoutly receive them and give thanks. But as some are imprudent, let the Roman pontiff, whose business it is to see to the common good, be consulted beforehand. We decree further that, since as things now stand the malice of certain people towards the church of God has not abated, decrees and sentences promulgated by those excommunicated on this score or at their command shall be deemed null and void and never at any time to be valid. Besides, as fraud and guile ought not to protect anyone, let no one be duped by foolish error into resisting anathema during his time of authority as if after it he would not be compelled to give due satisfaction; for we decree that both he who has refused to give satisfaction and his successor (if he has not satisfied within a month) are to remain bound by ecclesiastical censure until suitable satisfaction is given, since he who succeeds to an office succeeds to its responsibilities.

47. With the approbation of the holy council we forbid anybody to venture to promulgate sentence of excommunication on anyone save after sufficient warning in the presence of suitable persons, who can if necessary testify to this warning. If anybody does contravene this, even if the sentence of excommunication is just, he shall know that entry to a church is forbidden him for a month and he shall nonetheless be punished with another penalty if that seems expedient. Let him also be careful not to proceed to the excommunication of anyone without manifest and reasonable cause. If perchance he does so proceed and, on being humbly requested, does not take the trouble to revoke the process without imposing punishment, the injured party may put in a complaint of unjust excommunication to a superior judge. This superior, if he can do it without danger from the delay, shall send him back to the one who excommunicated him with orders for him to be absolved by some suitably appointed date, otherwise he, the superior, will, either personally or through another as shall be expedient, on receiving sufficient security give him absolution. Whenever a case of unjust excommunication is made out against an excommunicator, he shall be condemned to pay the excommunicated compensation for damages, and be nonetheless punished in another way at the will of the superior judge if the nature of the offence calls for it – for it is not a light offence to inflict so great a punishment on someone innocent – unless it can be shown that he acted in error, particularly if he is of praiseworthy reputation. If, however, against the sentence of excommunication nothing reasonable is proved by the complainant, it is he who for the trouble caused by an unjustified complaint shall be condemned to be punished by having to pay

[1] Third Lateran Council, 1179

compensation or in another way at the discretion of the superior judge, unless in his case it can be shown that there is the excuse of error, and moreover he shall be compelled upon security to give satisfaction for that for which he was justly excommunicated or be subjected once more to the initial sentence until fully adequate satisfaction without remission has been given. Should, however, the judge of first instance acknowledge his error and be prepared to revoke the sentence but he for whose benefit it was passed appeals, for fear it may be revoked without satisfaction being exacted, appeal shall not be admitted in this regard unless the error is such that there can properly be doubt about it; in this case the judge, giving sufficient security that he will stand trial before the judge appealed to or one delegated by him, shall absolve the excommunicate and thus not be subject at all to the prescribed punishment – every precaution being taken that he does not with the wicked purpose of harming somebody pretend to have erred, if he wishes to escape strict canonical punishment.

48. As there is a special provision forbidding anybody to venture to promulgate sentence of excommunication on anyone save after sufficient warning[1] and as we wish to provide against the possibility of the one warned being able, by means of a fraudulent objection or appeal, to avoid examination by the giver of the warning, we decree that if he alleges he considers the judge suspect he shall, before this same judge, bring an action of just suspicion, and he himself in agreement with his adversary (or, if he happens not to have an adversary, with the judge) shall choose the arbiters or if it happens that they cannot reach agreement they shall choose without evil intent he one and the other another to take cognisance of the action of suspicion. If they, the arbiters, cannot reach an agreed decision they shall call in a third, so that what two of them decree shall have binding force.[2] They are to know also that this they are bound, in accordance with the command strictly enjoined by us in virtue of obedience under the testimony of the divine judgment, faithfully to give effect to. If the action of suspicion is not legally established before them within a sufficient time the judge shall exercise his jurisdiction. If on the other hand it is legally established, with the assent of the objector the judge objected to shall commit the matter to a suitable person or transmit it to a superior judge that he may conduct it as it should be conducted. Furthermore, if a person warned is resorting to appeal and his transgression is manifest from the evidence or by his confession or in some other lawful way – as the remedy of appeal has not been established to defend iniquity but to protect innocence – such an appeal is not to be allowed. If his transgression is in any doubt, the appellant, in order that he may not by the subterfuge of a frivolous appeal, impede the action of the judge, shall set out before him the verifiable grounds of the appeal, such that if they were verified would have to be considered legitimate. Then if he has an adversary, by a date to be fixed by the same judge according to the distance between places, the circumstances, and the nature of the business, he shall proceed with the appeal, and if he does not trouble to proceed with it, forthwith the judge himself shall proceed, notwithstanding the appeal. If no adversary appears, the judge

[1] The reference is, of course, to the preceding canon, No. 47.
[2] *robur obtineat firmitatis*

shall proceed *ex officio* and once the grounds of the appeal have been verified before the superior judge, the superior shall exercise his office as judge. But if the appellant fails to get the grounds of his appeal verified he shall be sent back to him from whom it has been established he appealed maliciously. We do not however wish the above two constitutions to apply to regulars, who have their own special observances.

49. Under the threat of divine judgment we absolutely forbid anyone out of cupidity to dare to bind someone with the bond of excommunication or to absolve anyone so bound, especially in those regions where by custom when an excommunicate is absolved he is punished by a money penalty; and we decree that when it is established that a sentence of excommunication was unjust he who imposed it shall be compelled by ecclesiastical censure to restore the money thus extorted, and, unless he demonstrably acted in error, he shall pay his victim as much again and if perchance he cannot pay he shall be punished in another way.

50. It should not be judged reprehensible if men's decrees are varied at some time or other in accordance with changing circumstances, especially when urgent necessity or evident advantage requires it, since God himself, of the things he decreed in the Old Testament, has changed some in the New. Since therefore the prohibitions about contracting marriage in the second or third degree of affinity and about uniting the offspring of a second marriage to the kindred of the first husband frequently lead to difficulty and sometimes endanger souls, we, inasmuch as when the prohibition ceases the effect ceases, revoke with the approval of the holy council decrees published on this subject and by the present constitution decree that contracting parties connected in these ways may in future be freely united. Also the prohibition of marriage shall not in future exceed the fourth degree of consanguinity and affinity, since in grades beyond that such prohibition cannot now be generally complied with without grave harm. The number four agrees well with bodily marriage – of which the apostle says, "The husband hath not power of his own body, but the wife, neither has the wife power of her own body, but the husband"[1] – because there are four humours in the body, which is composed of the four elements. As the prohibition of marriage is now restricted to the fourth degree it is our will that it should be unqualified,[2] notwithstanding decrees published before on this subject whether by others or by us, so that if any presume to be united contrary to this prohibition they shall not be protected by length of time, since lapse of time does not diminish a sin but increases it, and the graver offences are, the longer they keep the unfortunate soul in bondage.

51. As the prohibition of marriage in the three remotest degrees is repealed, we wish it to be strictly observed in the others. Hence, following in the steps of our predecessors, we absolutely prohibit clandestine marriages, forbidding also any priest to presume to be present at such. For which reason we extend the particular custom of certain countries to countries generally, decreeing that when marriages are to be contracted they shall be published in the churches by the priests, a suitable period

[1] I Cor. vii. 4 [2] *eam ita esse volumus perpetuam*

being fixed beforehand within which whoever wants and is able to may adduce a lawful impediment. Those priests shall nevertheless find out whether any impediment exists. When it seems probable that there is an impediment to contracting a union, the contract shall be expressly forbidden, until it is clear from documents produced what ought to be done about it. If any presume to enter into such clandestine marriages or forbidden marriages in a prohibited degree even in ignorance, the issue begotten of such union shall be reckoned truly illegitimate with no help to be had from the ignorance of the parents, since they by contracting such unions could be regarded as not devoid of knowledge or at least as affecting ignorance. Likewise the offspring shall be reckoned illegitimate if both parents, knowing of a lawful impediment, presume to contract marriage in the presence of the church, contrary to every prohibition. Certainly a parish priest who does not trouble to forbid such unions or any regular also, whatever his order, who ventures to be present at them, shall be suspended from office for three years, and more severely punished if the nature of the offence demands it. And for those too who presume to be united in such fashion, even in a permitted degree, an adequate penance shall be enjoined. If however any one, to impede a legitimate union, alleges out of wickedness an impediment, he shall not escape ecclesiastical punishment.

52. Although, contrary to normal practice, it was at one time of a certain necessity decided that in reckoning degrees of consanguinity and affinity hearsay evidence should be valid seeing that owing to the short life of man witnesses cannot testify from personal knowledge[1] in a reckoning as far as the seventh degree, nevertheless, because from numerous instances and definite proofs we have learnt that many dangers for lawful unions have arisen from this, we decree that in this matter witnesses from hearsay are not to be admitted in future (since the prohibition does not now go beyond the fourth degree) unless there exist persons of weight who are trustworthy and who testified before the cause was begun to things they learnt from their elders: not merely from one of them, since he alone if he were alive would not suffice, but from at least two, and they not of bad repute and suspect, but trustworthy and quite unexceptionable, since it would seem rather absurd to admit those whose actions would be rejected; nor if one got from a number what he testifies to, or if a number with bad reputations got what they testify to from men with good, should he be admitted as if he were more than one, or they as if they were suitable witnesses, since, according to normal legal practice, the assertion of a single witness is not sufficient even if he were resplendent with authority, and legal actions are forbidden to those of bad repute. Such witnesses shall declare on oath that in bearing witness in the cause they do not act from hate or fear or love or for advantage; shall indicate persons by their exact names or by gesture or by sufficient description; shall distinguish by clear reckoning every degree of relationship on either side; and, finally, shall include in their oath the statement that what they depose in evidence they got from their forefathers and they believe it to be correct. Still, they shall not be sufficient unless they declare on oath that to their knowledge the persons belonging to at least one of the

[1] *de visu*

aforesaid degrees regard each other as blood-relations. For it is preferable to allow some unions that are contrary to the laws of man than to contravene the law of God by parting those lawfully joined.

53. In some regions there are mingled certain peoples who in accordance with their rites by custom do not pay tithes, although they are counted as Christians. To these people some landed lords assign their lands to be cultivated in order, by cheating churches of the tithes, to get greater revenues from them. Wishing therefore to provide for the immunity of churches from these things, we ordain that, when lords make over their lands for cultivation to such persons in such a way, they shall pay the tithes to the churches without objection and in full, themselves, and if necessary be compelled to do so by ecclesiastical censure. Those tithes are of necessity payable inasmuch as they are due by divine law and[1] accepted local custom.

54. It is not in man's power for the seed to answer to the hopes of the sower, since in the words of the apostle, "Neither is he that planteth anything, neither he that watereth, but God that giveth the increase," he who from the dead seed bringeth forth much fruit, and some from excess of greed endeavour to cheat over the tithes, deducting from the crops and first-fruits the rents and dues, which meanwhile are got by untithed. But since as a sign of universal dominion, and by a certain special title as it were, the Lord has reserved tithes to himself, we, wishing to prevent both injury to churches and danger to souls, decree that in virtue of this general dominion payment of tithes is to precede payment of dues and rents, or at least those who receive untithed rents and dues shall, seeing that a thing carries with it its burden, be forced by ecclesiastical censure to tithe them for the churches to whom by right they are due.

55. Lately abbots of the Cistercian order assembled in general chapter wisely decreed at our instance that brothers of that order shall not in future buy property from which tithes are due to churches, unless it might be for founding new monasteries. And if such property is conferred on them by the pious devotion of the faithful or bought for founding new monasteries, they shall assign them for cultivation to others by whom the tithes shall be paid to churches, lest because of their privileges churches be permanently deprived. We accordingly decree that on lands assigned to others and on future acquisitions, even if they cultivate them with their own hands or at their own expense, they shall pay tithes to the churches to which because of the lands they were previously paid, unless they think fit to compound with those churches. Considering this sort of statute as acceptable and right, we will that it be extended to other regulars who enjoy like privileges and we command prelates of churches to be readier and prompter in affording them full justice with regard to those who wrong them and to be at pains to maintain their privileges more carefully and completely.

[1] *vel*

56. Many regulars, we understand, and sometimes secular clerks, in letting houses or granting fiefs add, to the prejudice of parish churches, a covenant that the tenants and vassals should pay them the tithes and choose burial in their ground.[1] Since it springs from avarice, we utterly disapprove of such a pact and decree that whatever is received because of such a pact shall be surrendered to the parish church.

57. In order that charters which the Roman church has granted to certain religious may remain intact, we have come to the conclusion that certain things in them should be clarified, lest through being not well understood they lead to abuse, on which account they could justly be revoked, for he deserves to lose his charter who abuses power granted to him.

The apostolic see has rightly given an indult to certain regulars that Christian burial shall not be denied to those who have become members of their fraternity if perchance the churches they belong to are under interdict and they happen to die, unless they are excommunicate or interdicted by name, and they may carry away members of their fraternity whom heads of churches will not permit to be buried in their churches to their own churches for burial, unless they were excommunicate or interdicted by name. But by members of their fraternity we understand this: either those who while still in this world have offered themselves to their order and changed their secular habit, or those who in their lifetime have given them their property, keeping for as long as they live the usufruct of it. They only are to be buried in the churches of these regulars or in churches not under interdict belonging to others which they have elected to be buried in, for if it were understood of anybody acquiring membership of their fraternity by paying them twopence or threepence a year ecclesiastical discipline would be at the same time loosened and cheapened, though even they may get a certain remission allowed them by the apostolic see.

Another indult has been given to such regulars: that if any of their brothers sent by them to receive dues or fraternity-money come to any city, castle or place which happens to be under an interdict, churches shall be opened once a year at their "joyous advent"[2] for divine services to be celebrated there, the excommunicate being excluded. This we wish to be understood thus – that in the same city or castle or place one church only shall be opened to the brothers of that order as has been said once a year. Because although it is said in the plural "churches shall be opened at their joyous advent", this on a rational explanation refers not to churches of one place but churches of the said places as a whole: for if in this way they visited all the churches of one place the sentence of interdict would incur too much contempt.

They who venture to usurp anything for themselves contrary to the above-written explanations shall undergo severe punishment.

58. The indult which has been given to some religious we extend to bishops in respect of their episcopal office, granting that when a country is under a general interdict they can sometimes – the excommunicate and persons interdicted being excluded – behind closed doors, in a lowered voice, and without the ringing of bells

[1] *apud eosdem* [2] *jucundo adventu*

celebrate divine service, unless this has been expressly forbidden them. We grant this, however, to those who have not in any way occasioned the interdict, lest they introduce any guile or fraud and turn the gain into a wicked loss.

59. What to certain religious is forbidden by the apostolic see we will and command to be extended to all: that no religious may without the leave of his abbot and the majority of his chapter be surety for anyone or accept a loan from another for a sum bigger than that decided on by the common opinion. Otherwise the community shall not be held at all responsible for these things, unless perchance the matter has manifestly redounded to the advantage of the house. And he who presumes to contravene this statute shall be subject to the severest discipline.

60. From complaints we get from bishops in various parts of the world, we have become aware of grave and great excesses committed by certain abbots, who not content with the frontiers of their own authority reach out to those of the episcopal dignity, taking cognisance of matrimonial causes, enjoining public penances, granting even letters of indulgence and like presumptions, from which it sometimes happens that for many episcopal authority is cheapened. Wishing therefore to provide in these things for both the dignity of bishops and the well-being of abbots, we by the present decree strictly forbid any of the abbots to presume to reach for such things, if he wishes to avoid danger for himself, unless perchance any of them by special concession or other legitimate cause is able to defend himself in respect of such things.

61. For any regulars to presume to receive churches or tithes from lay hands without the consent of the bishops or to admit to any divine services those under excommunication or those interdicted by name is known to have been prohibited in the Lateran council.[1] We now prohibit it more strongly and will see that offenders are punished by penalties which are adequate. We confirm, nevertheless, that in churches which do not fully belong to them they shall, in accordance with the statutes of that council, present priests who are to be instituted to the bishops for examination by them[2] about the care of people: to themselves they are to afford evidence of sufficient sense in things temporal. They shall not dare to remove them once they are instituted without first consulting the bishops; indeed we add that they shall try to present those who are either noted for their way of life or recommended on verifiable grounds by the bishops.

62. Because some put up saints' relics for sale and display them indiscriminately the Christian religion is very often disparaged. So, in order that it may not be disparaged in future, we ordain by the present decree that ancient relics from now on are not to be shown outside the reliquary or put up for sale. As for newly-discovered relics, let no one venture to venerate them publicly without their having first been approved

[1] Third Lateran Council, 1179, canon 9
[2] *ut illis . . . respondeant*

by the authority of the Roman pontiff. Neither should prelates in future allow those who come to their churches in order to venerate to be deceived by vain fictions or false documents, as has commonly happened in many places for the getting of alms. We forbid, too, questors of alms, some of whom deceive one another, advancing in their preaching a number of errors, to be recognised unless they show genuine letters from the pope or the diocesan bishop. Even then they shall be allowed to put forward to the people nothing beyond what is contained in those letters. We have indeed thought it well to give a copy of the form of letter which the apostolic see generally grants to such persons, in order that diocesan bishops may model their own letters on it. It is this:

> Since, as the apostle says, "we shall all stand before the judgment seat of Christ" to receive as we have "done in the body, whether it be good or bad", it behoves us to prepare for the day of the last judgment by works of mercy and for the sake of eternity to sow on earth what, God giving us it back multiplied, we should collect in heaven – keeping a firm hope and confidence, since "He that soweth sparingly shall reap also sparingly, and he that soweth in blessings, of blessings also shall reap" for life eternal. To support the brethren and the indigent who flock into such and such hospital its own resources do not suffice. We therefore admonish and exhort you all in the Lord and for the remission of your sins enjoin you from the goods God has conferred upon you to bestow pious alms and to give them grateful charitable assistance so that through your help their need may be cared for and you, by these and other good things which, God inspiring you, you have done, can attain eternal happiness.

Let those who are sent in quest of alms be modest and discreet, they are not to put up in taverns or other unsuitable places or incur unnecessary or excessive expense, being careful above all not to bear the garb of false religion. Moreover, because of indiscriminate and excessive indulgences, which certain heads of churches are not afraid to grant, the keys of the church are brought into contempt and at the same time penitential satisfaction loses force: we accordingly decree that when a church is dedicated the indulgence shall be for not more than a year, whether it is dedicated by one bishop or by more than one, and then for the anniversary of the dedication the remission granted shall not exceed forty days of the penance imposed. We order the letters of indulgence which are granted for various reasons at different times to fix this number of days also, since the Roman pontiff himself, who possesses the plenitude of power, generally observes this moderation in such things.

63. As we have learnt for certain, shameful and wicked exactions and extortions are levied in many places and by many persons, sellers of doves in the temple as it were, for the consecration of bishops, the blessing of abbots and the ordaining of clerks, and it is fixed how much is to be paid for this or that and how much for another or yet another, and, verging on the utterly damnable, there are some who strive to defend such base and crooked conduct on the grounds of old-established custom. Wishing to abolish so great an abuse, we thoroughly reject a custom such as this, which should rather be termed a corruption, and firmly decree that no one shall

presume to exact or extort anything under any pretext whatever for conferring things or for things conferred; otherwise both he who receives and he who gives so absolutely condemned a payment as this shall be condemned with Gehazi and Simon.[1]

64. The stain of simony has discoloured many nuns to such an extent that they admit scarcely any as sisters without payment – wishing to cover this vice with the pretext of poverty. We absolutely forbid this to happen in future and ordain that whoever commits such wickedness in future, both she who admits and she who is admitted, whether she is just a nun or in authority, shall be expelled from her convent without hope of reinstatement and thrust into a house of stricter observance to do perpetual penance. As to those who were admitted in such fashion before this conciliar decree we have thought fit to provide that they be removed from the convents they entered wrongly and placed in other houses of the same order. But if perchance there are too many of them to be conveniently placed elsewhere they are, by dispensation, so as not to roam about and perhaps imperil their souls in the world, to be admitted afresh to the same convent, with a change of superior and of the inferior officers of the houses. This, we decree, is to be observed with regard to monks and other regulars also. Yet, that they may not be able to excuse themselves on grounds of simplicity or ignorance, we command diocesan bishops to have this published all over their dioceses each year.

65. We have heard that certain bishops on the death of rectors of churches put these churches under an interdict and do not allow anyone to be instituted to them until they themselves have had a certain sum of money paid to them. Further, when a knight or a clerk enters a house of religion or chooses burial with religious, although he may have left nothing to the house, they cunningly make difficulties until their hand touches something in the way of a present. Therefore, since one should abstain not only from evil but also, according to the apostle,[2] "from all appearance of evil", we absolutely forbid exactions of this sort: and any transgressor shall restore double what was exacted, this to be faithfully used for the benefit of places prejudiced by the exactions.

66. It comes frequently to the ears of the pope that certain clerks exact and extort payment for funeral rites for the dead, the blessing of those being married, and the like, and if it happens that their greed is not satisfied they deceitfully set up false impediments. In retaliation some laymen, from a ferment of heretical wickedness, try to break with what is for holy church a laudable custom introduced by the pious devotion of the faithful, on the pretext of canonical scruples. For which reason we alike forbid the wicked exactions to be made in these matters and order the pious customs to be kept, ordaining that the sacraments of the church are to be given freely, but also that those who maliciously try to alter a laudable custom are, when the truth is known, to be restrained by the bishop of the place.

[1] cf. II Kings v. 20–7, and Acts viii. 9–24
[2] I Thessalonians v. 22

67. The more Christianity is restrained from exacting interest that much more strongly does the dishonesty of the Jews in these matters grow, so that in a short time they exhaust the means of Christians. Wanting therefore in this business to see that Christians are not savagely oppressed by Jews, we ordain by conciliar decree that if in future on any pretext whatever Jews extort oppressive and excessive interest from Christians they shall be allowed no contact with Christians until they have made suitable amends for the excessive burden. Christians too, if need be, shall be compelled by ecclesiastical censure without appeal to abstain from dealings with them. We enjoin upon rulers not to be hostile to Christians on this account, but, rather, zealous in restraining Jews from such great oppression. And by the same penalty Jews shall, we decree, be compelled to compensate churches for tithes and offerings due to them which they used to receive from Christians for houses and other possessions before these went by whatever title to the Jews, so that churches may be preserved from loss.

68. In some provinces a difference of dress distinguishes Jews or Saracens from Christians, but in certain others such confusion has developed that they are indistinguishable. Whence it sometimes happens that by mistake Christians unite with Jewish or Saracen women and Jews or Saracens with Christian. Therefore, in order that so reprehensible and outrageous a mixing cannot for the future spread under cover of the excuse of an error of this kind, we decree that such people of either sex in every Christian province and at all times shall be distinguished from other people by the character of their dress in public, seeing that in addition one finds that this was enjoined upon them by Moses himself. On the days of Lamentation and on Passion Sunday they shall not appear in public at all, because some of them on such days, so we have heard, do not blush to parade in their most elegant clothes and are not afraid to ridicule the Christians, who exhibit a memorial of the most holy Passion and display signs of grief. What we most strictly forbid is for them to venture to burst out at all in derision of the Redeemer. And as we ought not to ignore the insulting of Him who atoned for our sins, we order secular rulers to inflict condign punishment upon those who so venture, to restrain them from daring at all to blaspheme Him who was crucified for us.

69. It would be too absurd for a blasphemer of Christ to be in a position of authority over Christians and what the council of Toledo[1] providently laid down on this we, because of the boldness of transgressors, here[2] renew, forbidding Jews to be appointed to public office, since with such authority they are very hostile to Christians. Whoever commits such office to them shall by the provincial council – which we order to be held annually – be first admonished then curbed by an appropriate sanction. The officer so appointed[3] shall be denied communion with Christians in business and in other things as long as whatever he has got from Christians by reason of his office thus acquired is not converted in accordance with the stipulations of the diocesan

[1] A.D. 589 [2] *in hoc capitulo*
[3] *huiusmodi*

bishop to the use of poor Christians, and the office he disrespectfully assumed he shall surrender out of shame. We extend this same thing to pagans.

70. Some, we have learnt, who have come voluntarily to the water of holy baptism do not wholly cast off the old man to put on completely the new, when, keeping parts of their old rite, they upset by such mixing the decorum of the Christian religion. But since it is written Woe unto the man who goes into a land two ways and A garment ought not to be put on woven of linen and wool together, we decree that such persons shall be completely stopped by heads of churches from observing their old rite, in order that those who freely offered themselves to the Christian religion may by a salutary coercion be kept to its observance, for it is a lesser evil not to know the way of the Lord than to go back on it after knowing it.

71. It being our ardent aspiration to liberate the Holy Land from infidel hands, we decree, on the advice of men of experience who are fully aware of the circumstances of time and place and with the approbation of the holy council, that crusaders are to make ready so that all who have arranged to go by sea shall assemble in the kingdom of Sicily on the calends of June after next,[1] some as necessary and fitting at Brindisi, the others at Messina and places neighbouring it on either side, where we too have arranged to be in person at that time, God willing, in order that by our counsel and aid the Christian army may be in good order for setting out with divine and apostolic benediction. By the same date also they should take care to be ready who have decided to go by land. These shall forewarn us meanwhile, in order that we may grant them a suitable legate *a latere* for counsel and aid. Priests and other clerks, subordinates and prelates as well, who may be in the Christian army shall devote themselves to prayer and exhortation, teaching the troops[2] by word and example alike to have always before their eyes the fear and love of God and to say or do nothing which might offend the divine majesty. And if ever they fall into sin they shall through true penitence soon rise again, humble of mind[3] and body and observing moderation in way of life and of dress, avoiding all discord and rivalry, having put completely aside all bitterness and envy, so that thus armed with spiritual and material weapons they shall fight the enemies of the faith more safely, relying not on their own power but on that of God. To these clerks we grant that they may receive the fruits of their benefices in full for three years as if they were resident in the churches and, if necessary, have power to put them in pawn for that length of time. To prevent this holy purpose being hindered or delayed, we strictly enjoin on all heads of churches each in his own jurisdiction diligently to warn and induce those who have given up the cross to resume it, and them and others who have taken the cross and those who will still take it to fulfil their vows to God, and if necessary compel them to do so without further demur by sentences of excommunication against their persons and of interdict on their lands – those only being excepted who find themselves faced with an obstacle of such a sort that their vow may, in accordance with regulations laid down by the apostolic see, rightly be commuted or postponed. Furthermore, to

[1] i.e. on 1 June 1217 [2] *eos* [3] *cordis*

prevent anything connected with this matter of Jesus Christ being left undone, we will and command that patriarchs, archbishops, bishops, abbots and others who have cure of souls shall make it their business to preach the cross to those in their charge, earnestly entreating in the name of the Father, the Son and the Holy Ghost, one only true and eternal God, kings, dukes, princes, margraves, counts, barons and other magnates, also the communities of cities, vills and towns, that those who do not go in person to the help of the Holy Land should contribute, according to their means, the appropriate number of fighting men with their necessary expenses for three years, for the remission of their sins as is explained in encyclicals and for greater assurance will also be explained below. We wish not only those who furnish their own ships but also those who are zealous enough to build ships for this purpose to participate in this remission. To those who refuse, if there chance to be any so ungrateful to the Lord our God, we firmly declare in the name of the apostle they are to know they will be answerable to us before the awful judge at the latter day of strict judgment for this and let them ask themselves beforehand with what conscience, with what composure they can confess before the only-begotten Son of God Jesus Christ, to whom "the Father gave all things into his hands", if in this matter which is as it were peculiarly his they refuse to serve Him who was crucified for sinners, by whose beneficence they are sustained, nay more, by whose blood they are redeemed. Lest, however, we appear to put on men's shoulders heavy and unbearable burdens which we are unwilling to move a finger for, like those who say "by all means" but do not do, behold we from what we have been able to save over and above necessary and moderate expenses do grant and give to this work thirty thousand pounds, besides the ship which we are providing for the crusaders of Rome and neighbouring districts, and will nonetheless appropriate to this same purpose three thousand marks of silver which we have left over from the alms of certain faithful, the rest having been faithfully distributed for the needs and benefit of the said Land by the hands of Albert, patriarch of Jerusalem, of blessed memory, and the masters of the Temple and the Hospital. But desiring to have other heads of churches and all clerks participate and share in both the merit and the reward, we, with the general approbation of the council, have decreed that all clerks, subordinate as well as prelates, shall give a twentieth part of their ecclesiastical revenues for three years in aid of the Holy Land by means of those appointed for the purpose by apostolic provision, the only exceptions being that certain religious are rightly to be exempted from this taxation, likewise those who have taken or will take the cross and are to go in person. As for us and our brethren the cardinals of the holy Roman church, we shall pay a full tenth. And let them all know that they are obliged to observe this faithfully on pain of excommunication: so that those who knowingly commit fraud in this matter shall incur sentence of excommunication. Because those who continue in the service of the ruler of heaven ought certainly in justice to enjoy special privilege and as the date of departure is somewhat more than a year ahead, crusaders shall be exempt from levies, tallages and other burdens, and we take their persons and goods under the protection of St Peter and ourselves once the cross has been taken, ordaining that they are to be safeguarded by the archbishops, bishops and all prelates of the church, deputies to be specially appointed *ad hoc* for their protection so that until there is certain knowledge of their death or of their return their goods may remain intact and undisturbed. If anyone contravenes this he shall be curbed by ecclesiastical censure. If any of those setting out are bound by oath to pay interest, we command their creditors to be compelled by the same punishment to release them from the oath they have taken and to desist from exacting interest. But if any of the creditors does force them to pay interest we order him to be compelled by similar punishment to restore it. Jews we order to be compelled by the secular power to remit interest and until they do so all intercourse shall be refused them by Christians on pain of excommunication. For the benefit of those who are unable at present to pay off their debts to Jews, secular rulers shall so provide for them that from the start of their journey until there is certain knowledge of their death or return they shall not be liable to the inconvenience of interest, the Jews being compelled, after deduction of necessary expenses, to reckon the revenue they have received meanwhile from property held as security towards reduction of the debt: such a benefit does not seem to do much harm in that it defers payment in a way which does not devour the debt. Heads of churches who are negligent in doing justice to crusaders and their families are to know that they will be severely punished. Furthermore, because corsairs and pirates greatly hinder help to the Holy Land by capturing and plundering those going to or returning from it, we bind with the chain of excommunication those who help and support them. We forbid under threat of anathema anyone to be knowingly party to any contract of sale or purchase with them. We enjoin rulers of cities and their territories to restrain and constrain them from this iniquity: otherwise, because to be unwilling to overthrow wrongdoers is none other than to encourage them and he is not without a touch of secret complicity who does not oppose a manifest crime, it is our wish and command that ecclesiastical discipline be used against their persons and lands by heads of churches. Furthermore, we excommunicate and anathematise those false and impious Christians who affronting Christ himself and Christian people carry arms and iron and timber for galleys to the Saracens. Those too who sell them galleys or ships and those who pilot Saracen pirate ships or give them any advice or help with machines or anything else to the detriment of the Holy Land we decree are to be punished by being deprived of their possessions and are to be the slaves of those who capture them; and we order such a sentence to be renewed on Sundays and feast-days in every maritime city and the bosom of the church not to be opened for them unless they send in aid of the Holy Land the whole of what they have received of such damnable wealth and the same amount of their own so that they get a punishment proportionate to their offence. But if, perchance, they cannot pay, those guilty of such things shall be punished otherwise in order that through their punishment the audacity to attempt like things may be crushed in others.[1] In addition we prohibit and on pain of anathema forbid all Christians for four years to send or take their ships across to the lands of Saracens in eastern parts, in order that by this a greater supply of shipping may be got ready for those wanting to cross to the help of the Holy Land and the said Saracens deprived of the not inconsiderable help they

[1] *aliis interdicatur*

have been used to getting from it. Although tournaments have been forbidden on pain of a certain penalty in various councils in a general way, we, because the business of a crusade is greatly impeded by them at the present time, strictly forbid them to be held for three years. Because it is of the utmost necessity for the accomplishment of this business that rulers of Christian peoples should keep peace with each other, we ordain on the advice of the holy universal council that a general peace shall be kept throughout Christendom for at least four years, so that heads of churches may bring those at variance to conclude a peace or observe firmly and inviolably a truce. Those who refuse to agree shall be most strictly compelled to do so by excommunication of their persons and an interdict on their lands, unless their wrongdoing is so great that they ought not to have the enjoyment of such peace; but if perchance they make light of the church's censure they can, not without cause, dread the invocation by ecclesiastical authority of the secular arm against them as disturbers of the business of Him who was crucified. We therefore trusting in the mercy of Almighty God and the authority of the blessed apostles Peter and Paul, by that power of binding and unbinding which God has given us, though unworthy, grant to all who in person and at their own expense go on this journey full pardon of their sins about which they are profusely contrite in heart and have spoken in confession and at the retribution of the just we promise the further benefit of eternal salvation. To those who do not go there in person but send entirely at their own expense according to their means and status men suitably equipped,[1] and similarly to those who although at others' expense, go in person, we grant full pardon of their sins. We will and grant that all those shall participate too in this remission in proportion to the nature of their help and the intensity of their piety who contribute suitably from their goods to the support of the Holy Land or give useful advice and assistance. Likewise, the universal synod gives its full support and blessing to all starting out on this common enterprise that it may contribute worthily to their salvation.

137. The Rule of St Francis, 1223

(*Sbaralea*, *Bullarium Franciscanum* (Rome, 1759, etc.), I, pp. 15–19. Translation by H. Bettenson, *Documents of the Christian Church* (Oxford University Press, 1946), pp. 179–84)

This is not the original, but the final form approved by papal bull (the *Regula Bullata*), of the Rule of St Francis. In it the inspirer of the greatest religious movement of the thirteenth century, under pressure from his own followers and from ecclesiastical authority above him, compromised with his real wishes as expressed in his Primitive Rule (1210) and in his Testament (1226). He accepted finally, but still reluctantly, the need with growing numbers for organisation and authority, a toning down of the requirement of absolute poverty, and restriction of preaching and of missions. It was after this that he went into retirement.

Italics have been used here to draw attention to the main ways in which this Rule differed from the Primitive Rule, so far as the latter can now be reconstructed.

1. This is the Rule and way of life of the brothers minor; to observe the holy gospel of our Lord Jesus Christ, living in obedience, without personal possessions, and in chastity. Brother Francis promises obedience and reverence to our lord pope Honorius,

[1] *idoneos*

and to his canonical successors, and to the Roman Church. *And the other brothers shall be bound to obey brother Francis and his successors.*

2. If any wish to adopt this way of life, and shall come to our brothers, *they shall send them to their provincial ministers; to whom alone, and to no others, permission is given to receive brothers.* And the ministers shall carefully examine them in the catholic faith and the sacraments of the church. And if they believe all these, and will confess them faithfully and observe them steadfastly to the end; and if they have no wives, or if they have them and the wives have already entered a convent, or if with permission of the diocesan bishop they shall have given them permission to do so – they themselves having already taken a vow of continence, and their wives being of such age that no suspicion can arise in connection with them: the ministers shall tell them, in the words of the holy gospel, to go and sell all that they have and carefully give it to the poor. But if they shall not be able to do this, their good will is enough. And the brothers and their ministers shall be careful not to concern themselves about their temporal goods; so that they may freely do with those goods exactly as God inspires them. But if advice is required, the ministers shall be allowed to send them to some God-fearing men by whose counsel they shall dispense their goods to the poor. After that they shall be given the *garments of probation*: namely two gowns without cowls and a belt, and hose and a cape down to the belt: unless to these same ministers something else may at some time seem to be preferable in the sight of God. And, when the year of probation is over, they shall be received into obedience; promising always to observe this way of life and Rule. And, according to the mandate of the lord pope, they shall never be allowed to break these bonds. For according to the holy gospel, no one putting his hand to the plough and looking back is fit for the kingdom of God. And those who have now promised obedience shall have one gown with a cowl, and another, if they wish it, without a cowl. And those who really need them may wear shoes. And all the brothers shall wear humble garments, and may repair them with sack cloth and other remnants, with God's blessing. And I warn and exhort them lest they despise or judge men whom they shall see clad in soft garments and in colours, enjoying delicate food and drink; but each one shall rather judge and despise himself.

3. The clerical brothers shall perform the divine service according to the order of the holy Roman church; excepting the psalter, of which they may have extracts. But the lay brothers shall say twenty-four paternosters at matins, five at lauds, seven each at prime, terce, sext and none, twelve at vespers, seven at the completorium; and they shall pray for the dead. And they shall fast from the feast of All Saints to the Nativity of the Lord; but as to the holy season of Lent, which begins after the Epiphany of the Lord and continues forty days, a season the Lord consecrated by his holy fast – those who fast during this time shall be blessed of the Lord, and those who do not wish to fast shall not be bound to do so; but otherwise they shall fast until the Resurrection of the Lord. At other times the brothers shall not be bound to fast save on the sixth day [Friday]; but when there is a compelling reason the brothers shall not be bound to observe a physical fast. But I advise, warn and exhort my brothers in the Lord Jesus Christ, that, when they go into the world, they shall not quarrel, nor contend with words, nor judge others. But let them be gentle, peaceable, modest,

merciful and humble, with honourable conversation towards all, as is fitting. They ought not to ride, save when necessity or infirmity clearly compels them so to do. Into whatsoever house they enter let them first say, "Peace be to this house." And according to the holy gospel it is lawful for them to partake of all dishes placed before them.

4. I strictly command all the brothers never to receive coin or money either directly or through an intermediary. The ministers and guardians alone shall make provision, through spiritual friends, for the needs of the infirm and for other brothers who need clothing, according to the locality, season or cold climate, at their discretion; always providing that (as has been said) they do not receive coin or money.

5. Those brothers, to whom God has given the ability to work, shall work faithfully and devotedly and in such a way that, avoiding idleness, the enemy of the soul, they do not quench the spirit of holy prayer and devotion, to which other and temporal activities should be subordinate. As the wages of their labour they may receive corporal necessities for themselves and their brothers but not coin nor money, and this with humility, as is fitting for servants of God, and followers of holy poverty.

6. The brothers shall possess nothing, neither a house, nor a place, nor anything. But, as pilgrims and strangers in this world, serving God in poverty and humility, they shall confidently seek alms, and not be ashamed, for the Lord made Himself poor in this world for us. This is the highest degree of that sublime poverty, which has made you, my dearly beloved brethren, heirs and kings of the kingdom of Heaven; which has made you poor in goods but exalted in virtues. Let this be "your portion", which leads you to "the land of the living" [Ps. cxlii. 5]. If you cleave wholly to this, beloved, you will wish to have for ever in Heaven nothing save the name of our Lord Jesus Christ. Wherever the brethren are, and shall meet together, they shall shew themselves as members of one family; each shall with confidence unfold his needs to his brother. A mother loves and cherishes her son in the flesh; how much more eagerly should a man love and cherish his brother in the spirit? And if any of them fall sick the other brothers are bound to minister to him as they themselves would wish to be ministered to.

7. But if any of the brethren shall commit mortal sin at the prompting of the adversary: in the case of those sins concerning which it has been laid down that recourse must be had to the provincial ministers, the aforesaid brethren must have recourse to them without delay. Those ministers, if they are priests, shall with mercy enjoin penance: if they are not priests they shall cause it to be enjoined through others, who are priests of the order, as it seems to them most expedient in the sight of God. They must beware lest they become angry and disturbed on account of the sin of any brother; for anger and indignation hinder love in ourselves and others.

8. *All the brothers shall be bound always to have one of the brothers of the order as minister general and servant of the whole brotherhood, and shall be strictly bound to obey him.* On his death the election of a successor shall be made by the provincial ministers and guardians in the chapter at Pentecost, at which the provincial ministers shall always be bound to assemble, wherever the minister general provides; and this once in three years or at a greater or less interval, according as is ordered by the aforesaid minister.

And if at any time it shall be clear to the whole body of provincial ministers and guardians that the said minister does not suffice for the service and common advantage of the brethren, it shall be the duty of the said brethren who have the right of election to elect another as their guardian, in the name of God. But after the chapter held at Pentecost the ministers and guardians may (if they so wish and it seem expedient) call together their brethren, in their several districts, to a chapter, once in that same year.

9. The brothers shall *not preach in the diocese of any bishop who has forbidden them* to do so. And *none of the brothers shall dare to preach at all to the people unless he has been examined and approved by the minister general of this brotherhood and the privilege of preaching has been granted him.* I also exhort these same brothers that in all their preaching their language shall be pure and careful, to the advantage and edification of the people; preaching to them of vices and virtues, punishment and glory; and let their discourse be brief; for the words which the Lord spoke upon earth were brief.

10. The brothers who are the ministers and servants of the other brothers shall visit and admonish their brothers and humbly and lovingly correct them; not teaching them anything which is against their conscience and our Rule. But the brothers who are subjected to them shall remember that, before God, they have discarded their own wills. Wherefore I strictly charge them that they obey their ministers in all things which they have promised God to observe, and which are not contrary to their conscience and to our Rule. And wherever there are brothers who are conscious of their inability to observe the Rule in the spirit, they may and should have recourse to their ministers. But the ministers shall receive them lovingly and kindly, and shall exercise such familiarity towards them, that they may speak and act towards them as masters to their servants; for so it ought to be, that the ministers should be the servants of all the brothers. I warn and exhort, moreover, in Christ Jesus the Lord, that the brothers be on their guard against all pride, vainglory, envy, avarice, care and worldly anxiety, detraction and murmuring. And they shall not be concerned to teach those who are ignorant of letters, but shall take care that they desire to have the spirit of God and its holy workings; that they pray always to God with a pure heart; that they have humility, patience, in persecution and infirmity; and that they love those who persecute, revile and attack us. For the Lord saith: "Love your enemies, and pray for those that persecute you and speak evil against you; Blessed are they that suffer persecution for righteousness' sake, for of such is the kingdom of Heaven; He that is steadfast unto the end shall be saved."

11. I strictly charge all the brethren not to hold conversation with women so as to arouse suspicion, nor to take counsel with them. And, with the exception of those to whom special permission has been given by the apostolic chair, let them not enter nunneries. Neither may they become fellow god-parents with men or women, lest from this cause a scandal may arise among the brethren or concerning brethren.

12. Whoever of the brothers by divine inspiration may wish to go among the Saracens and other infidels, shall seek permission to do so from their provincial ministers. But to none shall the ministers give permission to go, save to those whom they shall see to be fit for the mission.

Furthermore, I charge the ministers on their obedience that they demand from the lord pope *one of the cardinals of the holy Roman church, who shall be the governor, corrector and protector* of the fraternity, so that, always submissive and lying at the feet of that same holy church, steadfast in the catholic faith, we may observe poverty and humility, and the holy gospel of our Lord Jesus Christ, as we have firmly promised.

B. THE COMING OF THE FRIARS

138. A passage from the chronicle of Brother Thomas "of Eccleston", *On the coming of the friars minor to England*

(*De Adventu fratrum minorum in Angliam*, ed. A. G. Little (Manchester, 1951))

Here beginneth the treatise concerning the coming of the friars minor to England, and their dispersion and multiplication therein.

Here beginneth the prologue

To his most beloved father, brother Simon of Ashby, in the sweetness of our Lord and Saviour Jesus Christ, Thomas, his brother, wisheth the consolation of the Holy Spirit.

Forasmuch as the just man ought to judge his own life by the examples of many, since examples are often better incentives than the precepts of reason, and in order that you may have examples from among your own people wherewith to strengthen your most dearly loved sons; in order, moreover, that those same sons – who, for the sake of following our order and condition, have yielded up so many and so great advantages, yea, and their own selves with them – should, when they read or hear the marvels of other orders, possess matter no less edifying in their own and give thanks unfailing to Him who called them, sweet Jesus: behold, most beloved father in sweet Jesus, I set before you the collections it is my joy to have acquired in twenty-six years from my dearest teachers and fellow-pupils. In honour, therefore, of Him in whom God the Father is well pleased, Jesus Christ our most sweet God and Lord, I send you this little work.

Of the first coming of the friars minor to England

In A.D. 1224, in the time of the lord pope Honorius, in the same year, that is, in which he confirmed the Rule of the blessed Francis, the eighth year of the reign of the lord king Henry, son of John, on the Tuesday after the feast of the Nativity of the Blessed Virgin, which in that year fell on a Sunday,[1] the friars minor first arrived in England at Dover, being four clerks and five laymen.

The clerks were these: first, brother Agnellus of Pisa, in orders a deacon, in age about thirty, who at the last chapter general had been designated by the blessed

[1] i.e. Tuesday, 10 September 1224

Francis as minister provincial for England: he had been custodian at Paris and had borne himself so discreetly as to win the highest favour among the brethren and lay folk alike by reason of his renowned holiness.

The second was brother Richard of Ingworth, an Englishman by birth, a priest and preacher, and an older man. He was the first of the order to preach to people north of the Alps. In course of time, under brother John Parenti of happy memory, he was sent to Ireland to be minister provincial; he had been brother Agnellus's vicar in England while Agnellus himself went to the chapter general in which the translation was effected of the remains of St Francis and had set a notable example of exceeding holiness. When he had fulfilled a ministry faithful and well-pleasing to God, he was absolved in chapter general by brother Albert of happy memory from all office among the brethren, and fired by zeal for the faith, set out for Syria and there, making a good death, fell on sleep.

The third was brother Richard of Devon, also an Englishman by birth, in orders an acolyte, in age a youth; he left us many examples of long-suffering and obedience. For after he had travelled through divers Provinces under obedience, he lived though frequently worn out by quartan fevers for eleven whole years at the place[1] at Romney.

The fourth was brother William of Ashby, still a novice wearing the hood of a probationer, likewise English by birth, young in years and in standing. He for a long time endured various offices in praiseworthy fashion, the spirit of Jesus Christ aiding him, and he showed us examples of humility and poverty, love and gentleness, obedience and patience and every perfection. For when brother Gregory, minister in France, enquired of him if he willed to go to England, he replied that he did not know. And when the minister marvelled at this reply, brother William at length said the reason he did not know what he willed was that his will was not his own but the minister's. Wherefore he willed whatsoever the minister willed him to will. Brother William of Nottingham testified of him that he was perfect in obedience, for when he offered him the choice of the place where he would live, he said that that place best pleased him which it pleased the brother to appoint for him.

> [And[2] because he was specially gifted with charm and a most prepossessing gentleness, he called forth the goodwill of many layfolk towards the order. Moreover, he brought into the way of salvation many meet persons of divers positions, ages and ranks, and in many ways he gave convincing proof that sweet Jesus knew how to do marvellous things and by locusts to vanquish giants.[3]]

> [He at a time of fleshly temptation mutilated himself in his zeal for chastity. After which he sought the pope, who, though severely reproving him, granted him a dispensation so that he might celebrate the divine offices. This same William after many years died peacefully in London.]

Now the laymen were these: first, brother Henry of Treviso, a Lombard by birth, who by reason of his saintliness and notable sagacity was afterward made guardian at London. When he had fulfilled the course of his labour in England, the number of

[1] the name given to small Franciscan houses

[2] This and other passages indented in square brackets are marginalia not incorporated in the text, but contemporary with it.

[3] cf. Num. xiii. 33

the brethren having already increased, he returned to his own country.[1] The second was brother Lawrence of Beauvais, who at first worked at his trade as the Rule decreed[2] and afterwards he returned to the blessed Francis and earned the privilege of seeing him often and being consoled by converse with him. Finally the holy father most generously bestowed on him his own tunic and sent him back to England gladdened by his most sweet blessing. This Lawrence, after many toils and, as I think, through the merits of that same father, reached the haven of rest, London, where now, sick beyond recovery, he awaits the end of his long and exhausting labours.[3] The third was brother William of Florence, who after the brethren had been received returned speedily to France. The fourth was brother Melioratus. The fifth was brother James from the other side of the Alps, still a novice in a probationer's hood.

These nine were out of charity conveyed across to England and courteously provided for in their need by the monks of Fécamp.[4] When they reached Canterbury, they stayed for two days at the priory of the Holy Trinity,[5] then without delay four of them set off to London, namely brother Richard of Ingworth, brother Richard of Devon, brother Henry and brother Melioratus. The other five went to the priests' hospital, where they remained until they had found themselves somewhere to live.[6] In fact a small room was soon afterwards granted them underneath the schoolhouse,[7] where they sat all day as if they were enclosed. But when the scholars returned home in the evening they went into the schoolhouse in which they had sat and there made themselves a fire and sat beside it. And sometimes they set on the fire a little pot containing dregs of beer when it was time to drink at the evening collation, and they put a dish in the pot and drank in turn, and one by one they spake some word of edification. And one who was their associate in this unfeigned simplicity and holy poverty, and merited to be a partaker thereof, bore witness that their drink was sometimes so thick that when it[8] had to be heated they put water in and so drank it joyfully . . .

Of the first separation of the brethren

Now the four brethren already named, when they reached London, betook them to the Friars Preachers,[9] and were by them graciously received. They remained with them for fifteen days, eating and drinking what was set before them quite as if they were members of the house. After this they hired a house for themselves in Cornhill and made cells for themselves in it stuffing grasses into gaps in the cells.[10] And they remained in that simple state until the following summer, with no chapel, for they had not yet

[1] A different view of the man and of his end is given in one of the contemporary marginalia (p. 683, below).
[2] No. 137 (Reg. Bullata 1223), cap. 5, but most explicitly in the Regula Prima, cap. 7.
[3] *diutinae fatigationis*
[4] a Benedictine abbey in Normandy with priories in England
[5] i.e. Christ Church Cathedral
[6] *sibi providissent de loco*
[7] the grammar school at Canterbury, which was under the control of the prior and monks of Christ Church Cathedral
[8] I have here preferred the readings of manuscript P (*De Adventu fratrum minorum in Angliam*, ed. A. G. Little, op. cit. p. 7).
[9] who had entered England and settled in London three years earlier, in 1221
[10] *consuentes herbas in cellarum interstitia*

been granted the privilege of setting up altars and celebrating the divine offices in their own places.[1]

And without delay, before the feast of All Saints[2] and even before brother Agnellus came to London, brother Richard of Ingworth and brother Richard of Devon set out for Oxford and there were similarly received in the friendliest manner by the Friars Preachers; they ate in their refectory and slept in their dormitory like members of their house for eight days. After that they hired a house for themselves in the parish of St Ebbe's, and there remained without a chapel until the following summer. There sweet Jesus sowed a grain of mustard-seed that afterward became greater than all herbs.[3] From there brother Richard of Ingworth and brother Richard of Devon set out for Northampton and were taken in at the Hospital. Afterward they hired a house for themselves in the parish of St Giles, where the first guardian was brother Peter the Spaniard, he who wore an iron corselet next to his skin and gave many other examples of perfection.

The first guardian at Oxford was brother William of Ashby, until then a novice; howbeit, the habit of his profession was granted him. The first guardian at Cambridge was brother Thomas of Spain, the first at Lincoln was brother Henry Misericorde, a layman:

[under whom brother John of Yarmouth was then a member of the house, a man of great holiness, who afterward died at Nottingham and is buried among the canons of Shelford[4]]

[Sir John Travers first received the brethren in Cornhill and hired them a house,[5] and a certain Lombard, a layman, Henry by name, was made guardian. He then for the first time learnt to read, by night, in the church of St Peter, Cornhill. Afterward he was made vicar of the English province while brother Agnellus was going to the chapter general. In the vicariate he had, however, as coadjutor brother Richard of Ingworth. But he did not support such a high state of happiness unto the end, rather growing luxurious in these honours and estranged from his true self, and he apostatised from the order in pitiable fashion.[6]]

[It is worthy of record that in the second year of the administration of brother Peter, the fifth minister in England, in the thirty-second year, to wit, from the coming of the brethren to England, the brethren living in England in forty-nine places were numbered at twelve hundred and forty-two.]

1 Friars Minor did not get this privilege before 3 December 1224 (*De Adventu*, ed. Little, p. 9, n. c).
2 1 November
3 cf. Matt. xiii. 32
4 a priory of Augustinian canons, co. Notts.
5 see above. Travers was a sheriff of the city at the time.
6 A different view of Brother Henry is given in the text, at pp. 681–2 above.

139. Franciscans at Scarborough, *c.* 1239–43

(*Roberti Grosseteste Epistolae*, ed. Luard (Rolls series, 1861), No. CIX, (with some amendment) as trans. in *Mon. Franciscana*, ed. Brewer (Rolls series, 1858), pp. 642–3)

Eccleston does not mention the opposition friars met from older religious orders, Cistercians, Benedictines, Augustinian canons, at Scarborough, Bury St Edmunds, Dunstable. The troubles at Scarborough occasioned the following letter of Robert Grosseteste (written about 1243).

To the venerable men, very dear in Christ, the abbot by God's grace of Cîteaux and the convent of that place, Robert by the same grace bishop of Lincoln greeting and sincere increase of grace in the Lord.[1] I have received a letter apostolic, to the effect that, on the authority therein contained, I should have the buildings of the Minorites of Scarborough demolished, if they be of such a nature, as is described in the aforesaid letter. I have accordingly summoned the friars, and on their appearing by proxy legally constituted before my official acting on my behalf, during two days' litigation it was objected on their part against the said letter that there was a flaw in its construction, and they exhibited a privilege to the effect that Friars Minor cannot be summoned before a tribunal[2] by letters apostolic unless express mention is made of the said indulgence and of their order. After much altercation on these and other points, on the third day the friars appeared by their proctor before me sitting in my own person, and one of their order said as follows:

That although, notwithstanding their profession, they thought they might innocently defend themselves in this regard by contending that they were supporting their own rights before me not for temporal matters but for the salvation of souls, arising from their inhabiting the said place, and that for the salvation of souls it was permissible not to observe, nay even to contravene ordinary law and right. [The spokesman cited in support of this Matth. xii. 3–4, I Maccab. ii. 40–1, and Acts xxv. 11], yet because, as the same friar asserted, they professed the gospel and its precept is [here the spokesman cited Matth. v. 39–41 and xvii. 26, II Timothy ii. 24, and I Corinthians vi. 7], they wish to withdraw completely from the suit and from the place about which dispute had arisen, lest [Grosseteste went on] they offer the slightest offence to you whom they regard as their most holy fathers and abundant benefactors. Furthermore, the same friar prostrating himself at the feet of your proctor and your other brethren then present before us, humbly requested pardon for his order inasmuch as for two days of the suit the foresaid friars, guided by the spirit of evil counsel, had as it were, in defending themselves, offended your charity. The proctor of the said Scarborough friars also approved what had been said and expressly renounced the aforementioned exception and privilege and all other defences open to them in this regard. But I, with your proctor and other discreet men then present who were members of your order, considering, nay rather taking it as certain, that if the said friars were to leave Scarborough immediately, as according to the assertion of their proctor they professed themselves with all humility prepared to do forthwith, it would not redound to the credit of your order, but rather greatly soil the dazzling whiteness of its reputation and put a distinct stain on its glory, as your discretion without any telling from me may

[1] To the abbot of Cîteaux because Scarborough was an alien cell, dependent on Cîteaux itself.
[2] *conveniri*

readily understand, have, with the counsel and consent of your said proctor and brethren, caused the Scarborough Friars Minor to stay there until I had reported the foregoing to you and have received a definite reply from you by letters patent of your will about their staying in that place or withdrawing from it. May your grace always fare well in the Lord.

140. Matthew Paris on the friars

(*Chron. Maj.*, IV, pp. 279–80, trans. J. A. Giles, I (1852), pp. 474–6)

[s.a. 1243]

And that the world might not appear to be devoid of increasing troubles on every side, a controversy arose between the Minorite brothers and Preachers, to the astonishment of many, because they seemed to have chosen perfection's path, viz, that of poverty and patience. On one side the Preachers declaring that they were instituted first, and on that account more worthy; that they were also more decent in their apparel, and had deservedly obtained their name and office from their preaching, and that they were more truly distinguished by the apostolic dignity: on the other side, the Minorites gave answer, that they had embraced, for God, a way of living more rigorous and humble, and so the more worthy, because more holy; and that the brothers could and certainly ought to pass over from the order of Preachers to their order, as from an inferior community to one more rigorous and superior. The Preachers contradicted them to their face, saying, that though the Minorites went barefoot, coarsely clad, and girded with a rope, the privilege of eating flesh or a more delicate article of diet was not denied them even in public, a thing which is forbidden to the community of Preachers, wherefore it could not be allowed that the Preachers could enter the order of Minorites, as one more rigorous and more worthy, but quite the contrary. Therefore, between these, even as between the Templars and Hospitallers, in the Holy Land, through the enemy to the human race sowing the seeds of dissension, a great and scandalous strife arose; and inasmuch as it was between learned men and scholars, it was more dangerous to the catholic church, and a sign of a great judgment impending at its threshold. And what is terrible, and a sad presage, for three or four hundred years, or more, the monastic order did not hasten to destruction so quickly as their order, of whom, now, the brothers, twenty-four years having scarcely elapsed, had first built, in England, dwellings which rivalled regal palaces in height. These are they who daily expose to view their inestimable treasures, in enlarging their sumptuous edifices, and erecting lofty walls, thereby impudently transgressing the limits of their original poverty, and violating the basis of their religion, according to the prophecy of the German Hildegarde. When noblemen and rich men are at the point of death, whom they know to be possessed of great riches, they, in their love of gain, diligently urge them, to the injury and loss of the ordinary pastors, and extort confessions and hidden wills, lauding themselves and their own order only, and placing themselves before all others. So no faithful man now believes he can be saved, except he is directed by the counsels of the Preachers and Minorites. Desirous of obtaining privileges in the courts of kings and potentates, they act the parts of councillors, chamberlains, treasurers, groomsmen, and mediators for marriages; they are the executors of the papal extortions; in their sermons, they either are flatterers, or most cutting reprovers, revealers of confessions, or impudent accusers. Despising, also, the authentic orders which were instituted by the holy fathers, namely, by St Benedict and St Augustine, and also the followers of them (as the thing clearly appears in the case of the church of Scarborough, when the Minorites shamefully retreated), they set their own community before the rest. They look upon the Cistercian monks as clownish, harmless, half-bred, or rather ill-bred, priests; and the monks of the Black order as proud epicures.

[Matthew Paris's account of the troubles at Bury St Edmunds and Dunstable, under the years 1258 and 1259, may be read in No. 4 above, where the entries for those years are given in full.]

141. The *Annals of Dunstable* on the friars

(*Ann. Monastici*, III, pp. 133–4, 213, 261, 278, 289–90, 336–7)

1233

... The same year Walter, a canon of Dunstable who had taken the vows, and John, one who had not, went out without permission by a broken window and leapt over the wall of the monastery and took the habit of the Friars Minor at Oxford. And the prior of Dunstable had them denounced in Oxford and elsewhere as excommunicate. As a result Walter with three friars of the Minorite order came back to the chapter of Dunstable and humbly begged to be absolved. And he swore that he would, saving his order, obey the commands of the prior in all things. And so he was absolved, on the prior's orders, by three canons with corporal discipline; and afterwards by word of mouth by the whole convent. Finally he was ordered, first to restore the quires and the habit he had gone off with, and think things over for a year, then if the order of the Minorites is harder than ours to remain there, but if not, to return to our order, where he could reckon on finding a welcome. John was found in London and after being found was by the prior similarly absolved: he, though, with his brother Nicholas set out for home, taking Henry Archer with him. In this year Richard Falco went over to the same order.

1259

... The same year the Friars Preachers by very great industry and deceit entered the vill of Dunstable against our will, and through[1] the lord king and the queen and certain magnates got our permission to stay there.

[1] This is confirmed by the royal records:

1259, 9 April, Westminster (*C.P.R. 1258–66*, p. 20).

To the prior and convent of Dunstable. Whereas the king lately directed his prayers to them for the Friars Preachers, whom the king holds in special devotion as men of the gospel and ministers of the Most High King, that they would permit the said friars without impeachment or any difficulty on their part, to acquire in the town of Dunstable, according to the custom of the said order, a competent area to dwell in, build houses, and there and in the adjoining country procure the fruit of souls. . . .

1259, 27 October, Westminster (*C.P.R. 1258–66*, p. 47).

To the prior and convent of Dunstable. Whereas at the king's petition they have kindly received the Friars Preachers . . . to dwell in the town of Dunstable, the king thanks them, and begs them to continue their kindness by giving the friars their counsel and aid in all their affairs and necessities, which he will regard as done to himself; the king, moreover . . . undertakes that if anything be attempted by any of the said friars against the form made between the prior and canons and the friars, it shall be fully amended. . . .

1274

... The same year Nicholas of Aldbury, who from the order of Friars Preachers had come to us and was a fellow-canon of ours for nine years, went back to that order.

1277

... Then the prior ate with the Friars Preachers in the vill for the first time.

1282

... A certain woman of St Giles, Dunstable, died and was buried among the Friars Preachers. Her corpse was first brought to our church; we celebrated the mass, and got the offering and eight candles; from which the sacrist gave the friars two candles, the nuns two, and kept all the rest.

Brother Philip of Marston of the order of Minorites died on our premises [*septa*]; and because he was a particular friend of ours and a lecturer in his order, he was buried in our cloister most becomingly.

1287

[The canons prevent the Dominicans from enlarging their site in Dunstable. This entry is given in No. 171 below, among illustrations of monastic business.]

C. THE UNIVERSITY MOVEMENT

142. Devorguilla's charter to Balliol College, Oxford, 1282

(*Source Book of Scottish History*, ed. Dickinson, Donaldson and Milne, I, pp. 190–3)

Dervorgulla of Galloway, lady of Balliol, to our beloved brother in Christ, Hugh of Hertilpoll and master William of Menyl: greeting in the lord everlasting. Desiring with maternal affection to provide for the profit of our sons and scholars sojourning at Oxford, we will, enjoin and command that all things noted below be by them inviolably observed. In honour then of our Lord Jesus Christ, and of His glorious mother Mary, as well as of all saints: First, we will and ordain that our scholars, all and several, be bound on Lord's days, and on the principal feasts, to attend divine office, and also the sermons or preachings on the same feasts and days, unless it happen that any of them be hindered by urgent necessity, or for evident utility. But on other days they shall diligently attend the schools, and apply themselves to study, according to the statutes of the university of Oxford, and according to the order set forth below. We ordain, further, that our scholars be bound to obey our procurators in all things which, by our ordinance, grant and commission, are known to belong to their rule and benefit. Further, we will that our scholars from among themselves elect a principal, whom all the others shall humbly obey in those matters which touch the office of principal, according to the statutes and customs amongst them used and approved.

Moreover, the foresaid principal, after he has been lawfully elected, shall be presented to our procurators; and he shall not exercise anything of his office until by them under our authority he has been instituted in the foresaid office. Further, we ordain that our scholars procure three masses to be solemnly celebrated every year, for the soul of our beloved husband lord J. of Balliol, and for the souls of our forefathers, and of all the faithful departed, as well as for our weal and safety; so that the first mass be celebrated in the first week of the Advent of our Lord, and the second in the week of Septuagesima Sunday, and the third in the first week after the octave of Easter, and the said masses shall be those of the Holy Ghost or the blessed Virgin, or for the dead, according to the order of the procurators. Also, every day, as well at dinner as at supper, they shall ask a blessing before they eat, and after their meal shall say grace, and they shall specially pray for the soul of our beloved husband above named, and for the souls of all our forefathers, as well as of our children deceased; for the safety also of us, and of our children and other friends living as also for our procurators, according to the form anciently used. And that better provision be made for the support of the poor, for whose profit we purpose to labour, we will that the richer in the society of our scholars study to live so temperately that the poorer be in no wise burdened on account of heavy expenses. And if it happen that the whole community of our scholars shall, in their common expenses in any week, exceed the portion provided for them by us, we will and strictly enjoin that, for the payment of those expenses in excess, nothing at all shall be received beyond one penny a week from those who, according to the discretion and decree of our procurators, are judged unable or too poor to make full payment of those expenses, if an equal portion were to be paid by all the members. We will, however, that the foresaid rules shall not be extended to the long vacation, which lasts from the translation of St Thomas the Martyr to the feast of St Luke, nor yet to those weeks in which occur the feasts of the Nativity of our Lord, of the Circumcision, of the Epiphany, of Easter and Pentecost, nor in other cases in which our procurators shall have determined that it be omitted. We will also that our procurators make diligent inquiry concerning the foresaid inability of our scholars, and that the scholars themselves go to our procurators with all confidence to make known their poverty. And if it happen that any one or more of our scholars, contrary to this decree, murmur, or, on occasion of this order, provoke the poorer by any word or sign, we will that our scholars be bound, under the oath taken to us, to reveal to our procurators, the names of those so murmuring or provoking. And the procurators, having taken sufficient proof on this matter by the authority of these presents, shall, without delay, expel such person or persons, without hope of returning. We ordain, moreover, that our scholars shall speak Latin in common, and that those who habitually do otherwise be rebuked by the principal; and if any one, after being twice or thrice rebuked, do not amend, he shall be separated from the common table to eat by himself, and shall be served last of all. And if he remain incorrigible for a week, he shall be expelled by our procurators. We will also that, in each alternate week, among our scholars in their house, a sophism shall be disputed and determined; and this shall be done in turn, and so that the sophisters oppose and reply, and those who have determined in the schools determine. But if any sophister shall be so advanced that he can deservedly in a short time determine in the schools, he shall then be told by the principal that he should first determine at home among his fellows. At the end of each disputation, the principal shall fix the day of the following one, and shall conduct the disputation, and shall restrain babblers, and shall assign a sophism for the next disputation, and appoint opponent, respondent and determiner, that they may be the better able to prepare themselves. In like manner shall it be done each alternate week concerning the question. We command also our scholars, and firmly enjoin them, to keep with special care the *Portitorium* which we have granted to them for the soul of our beloved husband, and that they shall not allow it to be pledged on any pretence, or alienated by any title whatsoever. Let our scholars also have one poor scholar, appointed by our procurators, to whom they shall be bound daily to give the leavings of their table, unless our procurators shall have ordained that it be omitted. Moreover, that all and each of the foresaid rules be inviolably observed by our scholars in the time of whatsoever procurators, we have ratified the present writing with the security of our seal. Given at Botel, on the octaves of the Assumption of the glorious Virgin Mary, in the year of grace one thousand two hundred and eighty-two.

143. Institutions to rectories, with licence to study and dispensation meanwhile, Winchester diocese, 1299

(*Registrum Johannis de Pontissara*, ed. C. Deedes, I (Cant. & York Soc., 1915), p. 91)

Institution of Peter de Colleshulle to the church of Stratfieldsaye – Be it remembered that on 20 December A.D. 1299 at Cheriton the lord bishop admitted Peter de Coleshulle, clerk of the church of Stratfieldsaye on the presentation of Thomas Say, the patron of that church.

Institution of Richard de Maundevile to the church of Weyhill – Be it remembered also that on the same day and at the same place Richard de Mandevile was admitted to the vacant church of Weyhill on the presentation of the prior of Wilmington and he had licence to study in this form.

The letter of Richard de Mandevile that he can study for seven years – John [etc.] to the beloved son Richard de Maundevile, clerk, rector of the church of Weyhill in our diocese greeting [etc.]. Wishing to help in your education and do a special favour to one eager to bear fruit in the church of God, we out of compassion grant by the authority of these presents dispensation that for seven years from the time of your institution to the aforesaid church you can persevere in the study of letters. Provided that within a year of the time of your institution you have yourself ordained as subdeacon and after the aforesaid seven years have yourself promoted to the orders of deacon and priest on pain of the canon of Gregory X of blessed memory, viz, the canon promulgated in the general council of Lyons. Given at Cheriton, 20 December in the year of the Lord as above.

A like letter was made for Peter de Colleshulle, rector of the church of Stratfieldsaye.

144. Ranulph de Calthrop

(a)

(J. M. Wilson, *The Worcester Liber Albus* (1920), p. 47)

[1304] Brother W.,[1] by Divine permission humble minister of the church of Worcester, to his beloved sons in Christ, the prior and convent of the same church, salvation, grace, and blessing.

Being desirous that, through the study and teaching of sacred literature, both the honour of God and the advance of our church should be augmented, we earnestly require and request your prompt attention, as you are bound to have the same desire as ourselves, that you will not permit our beloved in Christ, brother Ranulph de Catthrop, who, as we have learned, has up to this time made praiseworthy progress both in learned studies[2] and in uprightness of character, to be hindered in any way in so fruitful an occupation, but rather that by sending him to a place of study, you should procure, as far as in you lies, that what he has well begun should be even better completed.

Pray do not oppose our request; and be assured that what we now seek only by words we are prepared when the opportunity comes to support by deeds.

May you ever be strong in the Lord. Given at Alvechurch, 20 August 1304.

(b)

(ibid. p. 120)

[*c.* 1312] To the man of excellent discretion, the lord chancellor of the university of Oxford, brother John the humble prior of the cathedral church of Worcester wishes the joy of safety here and hereafter[3] in Him from whom all wisdom forever flows.

Since we well understand that, on grounds both of law and of reason, no one can be excused from the burdens attached to a position from which he desires to obtain advantage and honour, we grant special permission to our beloved fellow-monk and brother, Ranulph de Catthrop, to observe the statutes and customs of the university aforesaid, so far as they affect a religious who is a scholar; and for that purpose we permit him to take any lawful oath on his approaching inception, saving the regular institutes of our order. To you and to all who have honoured us and our order by promoting the said inception we give our heartiest possible thanks.

(c)

(*Chapters of the English Black Monks*, ed. W. A. Pantin (Camden, 3rd series, 1931-7), I, No. 101 (p. 182))

Ranulph had been lent as lecturer to Ramsey abbey. His prior recalls him to Worcester to lecture in his own house.

[December 1318] Greeting in Christ. Although we wrote to you lately to come to us without delay to occupy among us by general agreement the office of lecturer because of the absence of brother Richard de B[romwyk] who at the command of the presi-

[1] William Gainsborough, bp of Worcester 1302–7
[2] *in scientiali studio*
[3] *salutis gaudium utriusque*

dents of the order now has the office of visitor, you, disdaining such letter of ours if it reached you, or at least pretending to overlook it, have up to now put off directing your steps to us. We write again strictly commanding you in the name of holy obedience by the tenor of these presents to come to our monastery without delay and with no hope of going back; and to preclude in future your putting off the journey any longer or concocting vain excuses we are sending you a mount.[1] Farewell.

D. THE BISHOP AND HIS DIOCESE

145. Statutes of a diocesan synod, 1262–5

(*Reg. Pontissara*, ed. C. Deedes (Cant. & York Soc., 1915), pp. 218–39, as abstracted on pp. 207–18. The Latin original is now best consulted in the edited text in *Councils and Synods II*, ed. Powicke and Cheney (Oxford, 1964), pp. 700–23)

The bishop being appointed, though unworthy, as a keeper in the vineyard of the Lord of Hosts, is anxious to discharge his office watchfully, thwarting foxes, rooting up weeds, so that the vines may be fruitful and answer their Lord's expectations. He therefore exhorts that what this holy synod has decreed for the adornment of the church of God, the reformation of manners, and the general advantage, may be faithfully observed, saving in all points the councils of Oxford and London, and the salutary institutions of the holy fathers. Their appointments are to be held as God's appointments.

On the sacraments, and first on baptism

This being the door of all sacraments, without which none can reach the kingdom of Heaven, priests who have the cure of souls should often explain to their parishioners in the vulgar tongue the formula of baptism, that if inevitable necessity should arise, the priest's substitute should know the right form. In this case the priest should make diligent inquiry, so that if he should find anything omitted or not observed, he may himself use the full form. A child privately baptised on convalescence must be carried to the church for the supply of what was omitted. The vessel in which the child was baptised should be reserved for the use of the church or burnt, and the water poured into the fire or into the church font. The priest should instruct his parishioners that any lay persons, even the parents though unmarried, may baptise infants in case of urgent necessity. Water should be at hand when a woman is in labour lest it should be needed for this purpose.

Parents should be warned not to refuse, like soothsayers, to have their children baptised on the vigils of Easter and Whit-Sunday,[2] days specially appointed by the holy fathers for receiving the laver of salvation.

[1] The abbot of Ramsey, who evidently did not want to let Ranulph go, had said he hoped to have Ranulph back some day (hence the "with no hope of going back" earlier) and had said they could not provide him with a mount. An ill-natured correspondence between the two Benedictine houses is summarised in Wilson's *The Worcester Liber Albus*, pp. 179–81.

[2] See Bingham, *Antiquities*, Bk xi, sect. 7, and for the service *Ordo Romanus I* in Mabillon's *Museum Italicum*, ii, 24–9.

Also that no one on the ground of doubt may lack baptism, which is certainly necessary to salvation, children exposed, whether with or without salt,[1] and others of whose baptism there may be reasonable doubt, should be conditionally baptised.

On confirmation

Because our adversary the Devil, desiring to have partners in his ruin, makes his heavier attacks against the baptised, the church as a careful mother has thought good to add the sacrament of confirmation, that, strength being received hereby, every Christian may more bravely resist his foe. The parish priests therefore should frequently warn and lead their people to have their children confirmed as quickly as possible, so that, if within three years from their birth, provided there has been a bishop at hand,[2] children have not been confirmed, their parents should be compelled to fast for a day on bread and water. As confirmation should not be repeated, parents should instruct their children who have been confirmed as to the fact, and the priests should warn parents that by such iteration they incur irregularity, and parents who are guilty should be visited with heavy penance. The priests should warn lay persons that, a spiritual affinity being set up by sponsorship, such persons as are thus connected are forbidden to intermarry.

On the sacrament of the altar

Human strength being insufficient for the spiritual conflict, Christ gave His disciples the power of making a viaticum, that is, His Body, to increase their spiritual strength and console them for His departure. We therefore beseech all presbyters to practise diligent self-examination before they approach so great a mystery, and if they have committed mortal sin to receive penance from a priest. Masses are to be celebrated only on consecrated altars or complete super-altars, and in the celebration at least two lights shall be burning in the church – one of them of wax.

In imitation of the devotion and faith of our predecessors to all parishioners truly penitent and confessed who help to supply the torches burning in the canon of the mass we relax ten days of penance enjoined them.

The local presbyters should frequently urge the laity to bow reverently at the elevation of the Lord's Body, and to adore with great devotion.

When the Host is carried to a sick man, the priests vested in surplice and stole are to bear it in a clean box before their breast, with light and bell going before, and the faithful should be warned to adore.

The parishioners, when they hear the aforesaid bell, should follow it to the sick man's house and thence conduct it to the church. To those who do so, ten days' indulgence is granted for each occasion.

That the Eucharist may not be a cause of loathing to communicants it should be kept in a clean and dry place, and not reserved more than a week after consecration.

[1] For continental, but almost contemporary evidence to explain this, cf. G. G. Coulton, *Life in the Middle Ages* (Cambridge, 1930), I, No. 54.

[2] cf. No. 148 below

On penance

Such is human misery and frailty that man falls not only daily but almost continually. But Christ, lest He should lose man whom He redeemed, has provided after shipwreck a second plank, namely the sacrament of penance. Every priest therefore should warn his parishioners that each at least thrice in the year, if it may be, or at any rate once in Lent, and that as soon after the beginning as possible, so that he may not lack the suffrages of the church, should make full confession of his sins to his own priest, or with his licence, which for just cause should not be refused, to another.

We wish the laity to be expressly told that a foreign priest without the aforesaid licence is unable to loose or bind another man's parishioner.

One who has confessed to an alien priest in the manner aforesaid should make this clear to his parish priest, otherwise let him be held as unconfessed.

And, because what heals the eye is no remedy for the heel, let priests be discreet and wary so that like skilful physicians they may apply according to the nature of the wounds the wine or oil of health. Let them listen to their penitents in a gentle spirit and not look at anyone's face unless to estimate their contrition. Let the priests beware of enjoining any penance to husbands or their wives which might cause a mutual suspicion of serious crime.

When the sick of whose recovery there is doubt are commended to God's mercy, no fixed and precise penance should be enjoined, but it should rather be signified to them what is due, that, if they pass, the debt of eternal punishment may be commuted into that of purgatory. If they should recover they can discharge the penance alive.

Women expecting their confinement should confess for fear of being unfit afterwards in case of a difficult delivery. Priests are forbidden to enjoin on their penitents masses to be performed by themselves or other lucrative penances. Transgressors must fast that year every Friday in Lent on bread and water, and anyone convicted hereof shall be expelled from our diocese without hope of restitution.

No one subject to us shall prevent the Dominicans and Franciscans as they pass through the parishes, whether in Lent or at other times, from hearing the confessions of the faithful and enjoining penances, they having first obtained leave from their own priest, and the oblations accustomed and due to the parish church being paid. And since the preaching and holy conversation of the friars are known to bear no little fruit, we direct that when they pass through our diocese they shall be received everywhere with hospitality and respect.

On extreme unction

The mystery of extreme unction, serving as it does both for the relief of the body and the health of the soul, should be venerated among the other sacraments.

We enjoin therefore that parish priests should not venture to pass the night away from their parish without reasonable cause and then leaving another suitable priest in their place. Should anyone through the priest's absence, negligence, or other fault die without the last rites, the fault being proved, the priest himself shall be *ipso facto* suspended till he has expiated his fault by a condign penance. One who has been accustomed to do this shall incur perpetual suspension.

We have heard that some ignorant persons have such a dread of this sacrament that they are unwilling to receive it even at the last; we direct the parish priests to announce publicly that this sacrament can be repeated when needful, so that those who have been anointed, if they recover, are not bound to give up the usual duties of life.

On matrimony

We know that the sacrament of matrimony was ordained to check the concupiscence which we have contracted from the infected stock of our first parents: its virtue in the church of God is easily shown by the fact that only those lawfully begotten are admitted to ecclesiastical dignities and civil successions, and unless with canonical dispensation those otherwise born are rejected.

To avoid therefore the perils and perplexities which often happen from the irregularities of contracting parties, following canonical rule, we prohibit the contracting of matrimony unless after a threefold notice at proper intervals in the parishes where they reside. Priests who without such notice take part in a matrimonial contract or solemnise a marriage shall be canonically punished.

Also, because in cases of intoxication consent cannot be called lawful, we forbid a man and woman to pledge their troth mutually in taverns by any words, or unless fasting, and in the presence of trustworthy persons who can bear witness if asked.

Moreover, because some men, heedless of their own salvation, do not fear to contract with different women in different provinces, we strictly forbid that any unknown person should be allowed to enter into such contract in our diocese unless he first prove his banns by the letters of a bishop, his official, or an archdeacon, giving clear evidence that he can contract lawfully and without impediment.

We also prohibit, under a money-penalty, abjurations to be made by prostitutes, but let such delinquents contract mutually under this form: "I accept thee from this time as mine, if hereafter I should know thee carnally: and I thee as mine, if I allow myself to be known by thee." Lest afterwards doubts should be raised, we order that all should be clearly written down.

On ordination

We direct that the sacrament of orders, whereby those called into the Lord's heritage receive an increase of virtues and gifts of graces, be venerated with all reverence, and especially by those who have already received, or who desire, or are bound to receive them in the future.

We enjoin therefore, and very earnestly beseech you in Jesus Christ, that whoever approaches so great a sacrament, and especially holy orders, should take them with all purity and only after confession and penance.

We will and order that all who are beneficed in our diocese should apply for the orders which the cure of their benefices requires at our successive ordinations.

On churches and other holy places, and their ornaments

If the Israelites serving the shadow of the Law required places dedicated to worship the Lord, much more are Christians, to whom the kindness and love of the Saviour have appeared, bound with all their powers to procure the consecration of churches in which the Son of God is sacrificed. We then, being eager to carry out what is your business, order the rectors of unconsecrated churches to take pains to prepare them, so that we can dedicate them whenever it happens that we have leisure, yet so that we may have notice a week beforehand. We will that dedication-anniversaries be solemnly observed by the parishioners of the churches themselves and of adjacent undedicated chapels. And we will that the day and year of consecration, with the name of the consecrator and the endowment and indulgence then granted, be distinctly noted in the kalendar and other books of the church. Also, in order that the churches which are houses of prayer may not be made a den of thieves, we strictly forbid the holding of public markets in churches or churchyards; nor for this purpose let tents be pitched in the same, nor secular pleas be held, nor let buildings be constructed there, unless, which God forbid, war should break out. Any built must be pulled down before Easter.

We direct also that churchyards be properly enclosed with a ditch, hedge, or wall, by those whose customary duty it is, so that hereby unclean animals be kept out, and in them on the festivals of saints and at other times let not wrestling take place, nor dances or other showy sports be held: nor in them let any animals be fed.

Because of members of religious orders in our diocese some hold churches to their own uses, others certain portions of particular tithes, others receive and keep annual pensions from churches, lest prejudice should arise to such churches, the rectors of which are frequently slack and remiss in the prosecution of their own right, we sequestrate into our own hands all such churches, tithes, and pensions, until we are satisfied as to the right of the receivers.

We will, moreover, that in all churches which are commonly taxed up to fifty marks or more there shall be a deacon and subdeacon continually serving, and at least one solemn vestment with tunic and dalmatic.

Further, wishing to anticipate future perils which we hear have often arisen, we order that the rectors of churches who have chapels immediately subject to them, and receive all or some emoluments from them, if the said chapels are distant from the churches two miles or over, cause burial-grounds to be prepared, if this is not yet done, near the chapels, so that when we may happen to pass by such places, we may be able to consecrate them for the burial of the parishioners of those chapels, without prejudice to the rights of the mother churches, for whose indemnity we will then make provision, with careful and effectual regard for the rectors themselves.

Let no one, moreover, under any pretext give or receive to farm the churches of our diocese or lands belonging to them. Anyone whom we have allowed to do this is forbidden to serve in another man's church as stipendiary.

We direct also that churches and chapels be decked according to ability with proper ornaments, and that both they and their furniture be entrusted to good and safe custody, yet not of lay persons, unless this be clearly necessary. Moreover, no lay persons or married clergy may touch consecrated vessels or otherwise serve in church in the place of the clergy.

Moreover, we forbid under pain of anathema that fraudulently at our visitation or that of the archdeacons, when they have heard of our arrival, any rector, vicar, or priest whatsoever presume to receive or to lend to another as a loan any vestments or ornaments from the church, that so those who receive them may, for the deception of the Visitors, as we find has been done elsewhere, fraudulently assert that they are their own.

On the life and good conduct of the clergy[1]

Since the life of clerics ought to be a pattern and instruction to the laity, we direct that the clergy show themselves sober and respectable in habit and gesture, not wearing clothes of green or red silk nor using gilt trappings. Let them have a sufficient tonsure of hair and crown,[2] nor let any clerics frequent taverns or play at dice, or presume to take part in public shows.

We direct also that clergy, rejecting all sinful lust, whereby ecclesiastical propriety is grievously blackened, live continently, and do not keep concubines either in their houses or in other places. We have determined to compel them to this by suspending them from office, withdrawing the fruits of their benefices, and finally by deprivation if they remain obstinate.

We have decreed that their public concubines shall be suspended from entering the church which they disgrace. And if, being thrice warned, they fail to correct themselves, let them be excommunicated and their excommunication publicly announced. We inhibit also, under pain of anathema, that anyone should knowingly presume to entertain or otherwise receive them. And to show more fully our detestation of this vice, however willing we are that the last wills of departing clergy should be free, so far as concerns legacies to their housekeepers we decree that such shall be void. We will that such legacies, if there be any, shall be claimed by our Officials for the use of the poor. We order further that no clergy, beneficed or in holy orders, build or buy houses or possessions for the use of their concubines or sons, nay more, that they do not presume to apply any money for them. Let those convicted of this be condemned in the amount spent on such gifts.

Also since, according to the apostle, we must abstain not only from evil but from all appearance of evil, we forbid clergy to visit frequently nunneries or to have familiar conversation with nuns, or to have any women in their houses of whom any sinister rumour may reasonably arise.

Moreover, we inhibit clergy or religious from presuming to enter into business, especially for the purpose of trade, and from borrowing money or anything else with a consideration for passage of time or lending at interest. And since we are unwilling that the mouth of the ox treading out the corn should be muzzled,[3] we decree that, apart from the question of good and well-deserving presbyters, no parish priest should

[1] cp. Canons of the Fourth Lateran Council, 1215 (No. 136 above), esp. canons 14–18
[2] See note 53 in Rock, *Church of our Fathers*, i, 145, on the two forms of tonsure.
[3] cf. Canons of the Fourth Lateran Council, 1215 (loc. cit.), canon 32

have less than five marks a year for stipend. Since we believe that priests themselves take at least partial care of this, we give orders that, rejecting all appearance of disgraceful gain, none presume to say divers offices in one mass, or to celebrate more masses than one except on Christmas and Easter day, and when a funeral is arranged from his own parish and in his own church, and this in churches wherein on account of their poverty there is only one chaplain. Parish priests, moreover, are not to receive annual or triennial payments, by which the parish church may be deprived of obsequies due. Further, to avoid confusion, we inhibit deacons from hearing confessions or dispensing other sacraments restricted to priests alone, except in cases of necessity, in which even lay persons are permitted.

To avoid the return of the clergy to secular matters which they have abandoned, we inhibit clerks beneficed or in holy orders from being sheriffs or justiciaries or from taking up any such administration or temporal bailiwick, by which they are bound to render accounts to lay persons, especially to such as by secular influence may actually grasp at the goods of clergy. They are also forbidden to take in hand any case of bloodshed or to write or dictate letters on it, or to have anything to do with it. If any hold such bailiwicks at present, as they wish to escape a heavy penalty, they must resign them within a month.

Also under pain of excommunication we strictly forbid any clerk to draw another clerk into a case before a secular court on a spiritual matter or any action personal to himself or to any of his friends; nor let any parishioner, clerical or lay, maliciously presume to call any other cleric or layman of our diocese against whom he has no just complaint before an extraordinary judge outside our bishopric, so as to harass him with labours and expenses, or to take money from him to give over his vexatious conduct.

We also forbid all clergy to build on lay ground with the goods of the church, and to deposit their tithes outside the sanctuary of the church, and if they have no ground in the property of the church, we direct that ground be bought within a year for this purpose.

Let decent dwellings be provided for parish priests in the church's free land, lest for want of such they be compelled to lodge with lay persons not without scandal and peril.

We will also and by the present holy synod decree that rectors, vicars, and all others beneficed in our diocese, who from the nature of their charge are bound to residence, before Christmas repair to their benefices, prepared to reside henceforth continually therein, saving, however, special conditions made beforehand. Otherwise we shall proceed against them according to canonical sanctions which declare such benefices of those who decline to reside vacant. Except, however, some persons who for some reason have been dispensed by the apostolic see or ourselves; and those also who hold canonically more than one benefice in our own or another bishop's diocese, concerning whose residence we have thought good to appoint that, the number and amount of their rents being reckoned according to more or less, they arrange to reside, now in one, then in another. But to those who think themselves in this regard sufficiently protected by dispensations, but have not yet exhibited them before us in due form, so that we could judge whether they are sufficiently protected, we peremptorily require that they should show them to us before Christmas, otherwise we shall proceed against them thenceforth according to the tenor of the council published hereon.

Moreover, by the sanction of the synod, we direct that concerning the fruits of non-residents (which term should be understood as well of monks holding parish churches to their own uses, as of seculars), by the ordinance of ourself or our Official, some portion, not less then the tenth of the tithes, should be applied to the uses of the needy. Those monks, however, being excepted who hold parish churches within the enclosure of their monastery or adjoining the same in their monastery.

We also forbid any priest, except rectors or vicars who are bound to personal service of their own churches, to undertake the charge of a parish in the first year of his ordination.

In churches which are near the schools of the city of Winchester or of the castles of our diocese holy water is to be carried only by the scholars. Let rectors, vicars, and parish priests also take care that the boys of their parishes know the Lord's Prayer, the Creed, and the Hail Mary, and can sign themselves properly with the sign of the Cross. From the adult laity also, when they come in confession, let very careful inquiry be made whether they know these, that if perchance they are ignorant, as is very commonly the case, they may be instructed therein by the priests. Let parents also be induced, after their boys have learnt to read the Psalter, to keep up their knowledge, lest after they have learnt more difficult things, they may be compelled to go back to this study, or as being found ignorant of this they may be always reckoned unfit for divine service.

We further decree that a rector dying after Maundy Thursday shall receive fully the autumn fruits, then let him bear all the charges contingent to the church up to the next Maundy Thursday. But if the church should be one whose whole, greater, or mean revenue consists in oblations, which are payable in full to his successor immediately after his institution, let the successor meet all such charges, or a part of them in proportion to his receipts.

But if rectors should die before the feast aforesaid, we will that an allowance be made in full to their executors by their successors for the expenses incurred in the cultivation of church-lands, the same privilege being given concerning those who hold churches to farm with our licence, but die before the end of their term. Agreements which deceased rectors have made with their chaplains should bind their successors till the end of the year, unless there be lawful cause to the contrary.

On tithes and oblations

That there may be no default in the payment of tithes which the Lord has reserved to Himself as a token of His universal dominion, which ought to be paid fully on all things, we order that tithes be paid on all handicrafts, businesses, honey, windmills, watermills, fulling mills, and on all other things which are subject to annual renewal. But specially let tithe of hay be paid in full whether meadows be mowed once or twice in the year.

We order, moreover, that before corn is tithed at harvest-tide no sheaf should ever be delivered to anyone for the service of the reapers or in any other wise, so as to cheat the tithe.

We decree, moreover, that tithes be fully paid on pannage, unless a rector or vicar holds his pigs quit from pannage on account of the church not of the fee; and on herbage sold, unless it be sold to parishioners from whom the parish church may have tithes on the issues of animals, let tithes be paid in full.

But with regard to a certain custom which has grown up among some laity of our diocese, rather to be called an abuse, namely, that such lay persons decline to pay their tithes fully unless the rectors provide them with a banquet first, we order that apart from any banquet and gift such withholders of tithes be compelled by ecclesiastical censure to make full payment.

Since by driving flocks to different pastures contentions sometimes arise between rectors on tithes, we, wishing to make peace, decide that to the churches of those parishes in which sheep are fed and folded from their shearing-time till Easter, even if afterwards they are removed and shorn elsewhere, the tithe of wool shall be fully paid, and of cheese, lambs and milk at the same time, and that this may be done without any cheating, we appoint that before sheep are taken from their pastures or are even separated, care shall be fully taken for the payment of this tithe to rectors. But, if within the aforesaid time sheep are fed on different farms, let each parish receive their tithe in proportion of time, a space of less than a month not being reckoned in such proportions.

Since no one ought to lay violent hands on what can be demanded judicially, we excommunicate, by the authority of the said father and the present synod, all those with their abettors who dare to seize by force of arms the tithes of their neighbours or even their own, not hitherto in their possession, saving nevertheless the legal penalty published against such encroachers. All those who, against the rights and liberty of the church, intrude or procure admission into ecclesiastical benefices we strike with the same sentence.

We excommunicate, moreover, all those who shall rashly violate our sequestrations on ecclesiastical goods and revenues.

We decree also that by all parishioners who have passed their eighteenth year, provided they have movables, or are employed outside their parents' houses at fixed wages, at the four festivals, namely, Christmas, Easter, the festival [of a holy place], and the dedication of the church, due and accustomed oblations be paid.

We are willing also to give indulgence to rectors and vicars to excommunicate or suspend by themselves, after canonical monition thrice given, the withholders of tithes, oblations, and other rights of their churches, the possession of which is well known to have hitherto belonged to the rectors and vicars, but in other cases this must not be attempted.

Moreover, we will that the Paschal wax candle[1] already removed from the candlestick after the feast of Holy Trinity be left in the church for burning, or that private candles may be made of it, yet so that by reason hereof the accustomed lights of the church may not be diminished.

[1] See Rock, *Church of our Fathers*, iv, 283–5

On Wills

That the last wills of those departing may proceed duly, we enjoin that executors immediately after the deceased's death make a faithful and full inventory of all his movable goods and send a copy of it to us or our Official, before they make any administration of the goods, so that, in rendering to us an account of the goods aforesaid to which they acknowledge themselves bound, the proceeding may be safer. For, if they show themselves negligent or liable to suspicion in this or other matters, when the account of their receipts and expenses has been sent in they may be removed, and others appointed by ourself or the Official, if it seem expedient.

We do not wish that any executors should meddle with the goods of the deceased, except so far as to make an inventory, until the wills have been proved before us or our official or others appointed by us, and they should be careful to render an account when they are required.

Also under pain of excommunication we forbid such executors to buy personally or through others or mutually to exchange or under any title to acquire any of the goods of the deceased, unless in the presence of trustworthy persons and at a reasonable price, except what was left to them in the will.

And let no legacy be delivered, unless after sufficient caution for making needful restitution, if there be ground for suspecting forgery.

We forbid the religious of any profession to undertake executors' duties in our bishopric without our special licence.

Moreover, to confute the wickedness of forgers, all those who after the death of anyone have attempted to make or sign any will in his name, or, beside the testator's will, to add, withdraw, or to commit any such fraud in the will itself, with the approval of the sacred synod we excommunicate and publicly proclaim excommunicated, and those who may happen to be convicted of such crime we decree to be repulsed as forgers from any lawful action.

We prohibit under anathema anyone from hindering or disturbing the will of any person of whatsoever condition against the custom of the kingdom.

Concerning the principal legacy, which is otherwise called a mortuary, that contention may be removed and a uniform solution may obtain in our diocese, we have decided on this course, that, if a male testate or intestate or a widow should die, for their tithes wilfully or ignorantly detained or imperfectly paid, the second best possession, which in the partition of goods in the portion of the deceased we wish to be reckoned, be assigned to the mother church or chapel according to the custom of the place, unless perchance the person dying be so poor that such possession having been given up, nothing of value would remain to the heir or children. If this should happen, we will that when there is canonical proof of such poverty, nothing should be exacted from the dead man's goods except what he specially designed to leave to the church. But anything under the title of second best goods and legacy due to the church, in the case of a married woman, citizen, burgess, tradesman, or others who die not holding lands, we think should be left to the custom of the places. We wish, however, all such persons to be diligently advised and urged that of the goods belonging to the deceased some reasonable portion should be left to the church under the title of mortuary. And, because many people falsely allege that what is found second best among the goods of the deceased is their own, we direct that, if proof be given, such persons shall be excommunicate, decreeing, however, that persons should not be heard in favour of the church unless they have first given clear proof of their title.

Since the wishes of the dying in these days scarcely receive due effect, as well on account of the negligence of executors, as on account of fictitious creditors who maliciously demand from the executors what the deceased did not owe them, then also on account of debtors, who reckoning on the impossibility of proof refuse to pay what they are bound, we, desiring to apply such remedy as we can, by the authority of God and the holy synod excommunicate all who maliciously demand anything from executors in a trial, if they carry it on to a definitive sentence, and also those who knowing themselves bound to the deceased, allow themselves to be sued by executors, that in failure of due proof they may be freed from payment by judicial sentence.

On archdeacons, officials, deans, and their apparitors

As greater causes by their nature require greater judges, we inhibit archdeacons, their officials, or deans from presuming to handle matrimonial or civil causes which tend to deposition or deprivation of a benefice, whether the action is criminal or civil, or those which belong in any other way to our jurisdiction. Let them not claim or receive procurations from churches in our collation and exempt, or in any way take upon themselves to visit them.

And, moreover, let them not venture without our special licence to increase old procurations, or to accept those increased, or to impose new procurations on poor churches from which on account of their poverty none was payable in our predecessors' times, or to extort any so imposed.

Let not the archdeacons visit several churches on one day, and let not them nor their men dare on any pretext to claim gifts from those whom they visit.

Also, we enjoin that archdeacons do not presume to demand or receive procurations from churches which they do not visit personally, or when they visit that they do not exceed the amount of profits laid down by the Lateran council, but behave in their household and among all others quietly according to the tenor of the new constitution.

Moreover, we strictly forbid rectors and vicars of churches in our gift, in which the archdeacon has no place, either themselves, their chaplains, or parishioners to follow suit at the archdeacons' chapters or answer before them against the ancient custom of the church of Winchester.

But, allowing the correction of lesser offences and cognisance in lesser causes to the same rectors or vicars in their parishes according to ancient custom, we strictly forbid them to concern themselves with matrimonial or other greater causes, or with the correction of greater offences, or even that they handle the lesser through unlearned and unskilled chaplains or farmers.

We enjoin that priests unknown and of foreign ordination whom we will have examined by ourself or our Official be not admitted to celebrate without our special mandate.

Moreover, to the archdeacons themselves, their officials, and others having ordinary jurisdiction, we enjoin and command that, in assigning fines and amercements on their dependents, they show themselves so moderate that the receiver may not be considered greedy nor the giver too much burdened, so that for the future no clamour or complaint may din in our ears.

Nevertheless, we forbid the same under pain of canonical distraint to extort any money from our clerical or lay dependents by malicious evasions of our statutes or precepts.

Moreover, we firmly inhibit any archdeacon, official, dean, or apparitor from summoning anyone to a chapter unless he be first accused by good and weighty persons.

In fixing a period of expiation for persons thus accused, let them not exceed a term of five years for a light charge or ten or twelve for a greater and detestable crime.

Moreover, greatly desiring to study the quiet of our subjects, we enjoin that the general chapters of archdeacons be held in the middle of each deanery and not unless at intervals of four weeks. At which let rectors, vicars, parish priests, private persons, but not all be compelled to attend; only those who are nearest, and others who may have their own or their parishioners' business to see to there. And then we enjoin that they should be set free as soon as possible, lest they linger on outside their own parishes to the peril of souls.

And let none be vexatiously dragged from one deanery to another, or to distant spots.

But chaplains of parish churches engaged about the burials of their parishioners or other lawful business, provided they may be reasonably excused by their clerks or other messengers if they fail to come to any chapters, we will not have adjudged contumacious on this account.

Let no archdeacon's clerk except the official venture to publish sentences of excommunication or suspension against any dependent of the archdeacon, or in any way to practise jurisdiction unless a commission by letter has been given him by the archdeacon or his official for a lawful reason.

And as it is right that both we and our Official should often receive information by the assertions of the rural deans and apparitors about citations and other things, we appoint that for the future as well deans as apparitors be chosen by us or our Official, the archdeacons or their officials in common, and likewise be removed in common by the same persons. But there should be in each deanery only a single apparitor without a horse, except in the more scattered deaneries in which we allow their apparitors to be mounted, since they could not on foot accomplish with due speed all that we, our Official, or the archdeacons and their officials shall enjoin on them.

Let them not entrust citations to parochial chaplains outside their own parishes, lest meanwhile the cure of souls be left in danger.

Also, since it is a grievous sin to hinder the blessing of peace, we decree that provided the cause is one which can be duly terminated by a composition, the litigants can retire from a suit whenever they wish without penalty, and let no amercement be exacted from them on this account, unless there be clear proof of excessive injury and evil-doing on one side or the other.

Further, since the remedy of an appeal has been set on foot for the defence of innocence, we enjoin that archdeacons, their officials, and deans, when appeals have been lodged for our audience, accept them reverently, giving no trouble to the appellants or to their own people on this account, nor threatening them at all so as to make them withdraw their opposition. But when we or our Official can be easily approached, let a convenient term be fixed for such appellants, within which they can appear to prosecute their appeal.

Since every man ought to bear his own burden, we forbid the archdeacons, their officials, or the deans on account of the crimes of rectors or vicars to suspend churches from divine services, but let them restrain and curb such delinquents by sentences of suspension or excommunication against their persons, or by the compulsion of sequestration and distraint of their goods, if necessary.

But concerning the goods of those who die intestate, which, according to the custom of the church of England are known to be at the bishop's disposal, we do not wish that without our special licence anyone should interfere with them.

And since many ignorant and illiterate persons to the peril of their own souls usurp the pastoral office, we enjoin both our Official and the archdeacons, by the sprinkling of the Blood of Jesus Christ, that personally they make frequent and anxious inquiry whether any rectors or vicars are greatly deficient in learning; and concerning sacerdotal and parochial matters let frequent trial be made whether they know the decalogue and the ten precepts of the Mosaic law, the seven sacraments moreover, and the seven deadly sins, and whether they have at least a simple understanding of the faith; and whether they know how to explain all these to the laity in the vulgar tongue, and to instruct the people committed to them thereon.

We decree, moreover, that if any layman has been convicted of a heinous crime, for which, by right, public punishment ought to be inflicted or a solemn penance, it should by no means be commuted for another, unless perhaps for greater fruit of penance, or if, considering the person of the offender, he who has jurisdiction in the case considers it better to dispense otherwise.

Clergy also convicted of, or confessing to, similar crimes, we will to be suspended, and that the suspension should not be relaxed without our knowledge; and we enjoin that such, both clergy and laity, should be sent to our penitentiars to receive condign penance for their sins, and that they should return to their own priest with the penitentiars' letters containing the penance enjoined them, that he may be able in due course to bear witness that the penance has been carried out.

But archdeacons, their officials, and deans who permit clergy thus suspended or repeatedly convicted of incontinence, on payment of money, to carry out their office, we will to be *ipso facto* suspended from the execution of their office.

Archdeacons also and their officials or deans who in regard of cupidity, by occasion of gain, commute corporal penances justly due into others, or enjoin corporal penances where they are not due, that for fear of them they may be able to extort money, if convicted of this, must from their own purse restore double, and, notwithstanding, submit to another heavy punishment.

Moreover, we inhibit the archdeacons (by reason of a custom by which from some time back they have extorted twelve pence yearly from the several churches of their archdeaconry, which, to conceal the vice of simony inherent in it, some call a present, others a pork-butcher's gift, others by a feigned name the archdeacon's pig) from daring to extort any money, or the rectors or vicars from paying the exaction, until the archdeacons themselves have clearly shown us their right to receive this payment, and the rectors and vicars have other instructions from us hereon.

On the veneration of saints and the celebration of their festivals in the year

As it is prohibited in a general council[1] so we also strictly forbid anyone to venerate publicly newly discovered relics, until they have been approved by the pope's authority.

But let not stones, logs, trees, or wells on account of some dream be venerated as holy, since we believe that from such things many perils have come to the souls of the faithful.

Moreover, we strictly forbid anyone to admit a begging preacher to collect the alms of the faithful without letters; but not even then should they allow him to preach without our special licence, nor any indulgences to be offered, unless such as can be clearly proved by the authentic books of a pope, or by our letter; and not according to schedules, which we know to have been often forged.

We direct, moreover, that the feasts of the blessed Swithun and Birinus our patrons, also the festivities of Saints Edmund of Canterbury and Richard of Chichester, together with other feasts the solemnisation of which the holy fathers our predecessors have sanctioned, be solemnly celebrated everywhere through our diocese.

On the sentence of excommunication to be pronounced thrice in the year

We direct that the sentences of excommunication which are contained in the council of Oxford for curbing the ill-doing of perverse men be published thrice a year through all the churches of our diocese under this form: By the authority of God the Father and of the blessed Mary and all the saints we excommunicate all those who maliciously presume to deprive churches, and especially the church of Winchester or others of the diocese of Winchester of their right, and strive to infringe or disturb their liberties.

Also we bind with the sentence of excommunication all those who injuriously presume to disturb the peace and tranquillity of the lord king and of the kingdom, or who unjustly strive to keep back the rights of the lord king.

We add also as bound by a like sentence all those who knowingly and deliberately offer false witness or procure that it should be offered, or who knowingly bring forward or suborn such witnesses in a matrimonial cause where the action is against a marriage, or also where the action is for someone's disinheritance.

We also excommunicate all those advocates who in matrimonial causes move

[1] No. 136 above, canon 62

exceptions or cause them to be moved, so that true marriages may not attain their due effect, or that the process of the cause may be suspended against justice.

Moreover, we excommunicate all those who for the sake of gain or hatred or favour or for whatever other reason maliciously allege a crime against anyone, when he has not been ill-spoken of among good and weighty men, that so at least he may be forced to clear his character or be otherwise annoyed.

Moreover, we bind with the sentence of excommunication all those who when a church is vacant maliciously move a question on the right of patronage, that so for that time at least they may defraud the true patron of his collation.

And so we excommunicate all those who for the sake of gain or hatred or otherwise refuse to obey the king's mandate published against excommunicate persons, despising the keys of the church.

But we will that for the future every year the synod be celebrated in this place on the fifth day before the feast of St Denys. And, that no rector, vicar, or priest shall be able to pretend or plead ignorance about the aforesaid synodal statutes, we direct that they be transcribed before Easter in all churches of our diocese under canonical penalty to be inflicted for contempt or neglect. But to those who obey and keep them be health and life perpetual in our Lord Jesus Christ. Amen.

146. Episcopal visitation of a diocese: Canterbury diocese, 1292–4

(*Archaeologia Cantiana*, vol. 32 (1917), 143–80. Passages which the editor left untranslated, but which in our day it seems no longer necessary to leave in the obscurity of a learned language (i.e. passages marked *–*), are here translated by H. Rothwell.

[*Roll IX*] [*Woodchurch*]

At a chapter held in the church of the blessed Nicholas of Romene by brother R. de Clyve, commissary of Canterbury during the vacancy of the see, on the Friday next before the feast of the Conversion of the blessed Paul, in the year of our Lord *mcc nonagesimo secundo* [$129\frac{2}{3}$], Roger the chaplain of Wodechurch is cited to make canonical obedience to the prior and chapter of Canterbury *sede vacante*. He doth not appear, but since there is good reason to believe that he hath a corpse awaiting burial he is excused. On the morrow he appeared at hagene [Ageney][1] in the hall of the said prior and chapter and asked to be allowed to make his obedience there and then because he certified that he had another corpse awaiting burial on that day, and in order that he might bury the aforesaid corpse, he was permitted to make his obedience in the accustomed manner.

Woodchurch. Robert le Ster is noted for adultery committed with a certain Carter.[2] He doth not appear. Wherefore we suspend him from entering the church.

Juliana de Hornyngbroke is noted for adultery with Ralph de Pysinghe. The woman cited, does not appear, therefore suspended.

*John the chaplain who was at Woodchurch in a former year is noted in connection

[1] one of the Christ Church manors, near New Romney
[2] *carectar'*

with Joan the wife of William le Hert. The woman cited, does not appear, therefore suspended, subsequently again cited does not appear, therefore excommunicated.*

The same John is accused concerning the widow of le Spyle. The woman was cited, etc. [as the last].

William son of William Lucas got Juliana Bructyn with child. The man appears and confesses and renounces his sin and is whipped three times round the church. It is afterwards granted that he should receive one discipline humbly in the procession because he appeared humbly, and the woman is excused because she lies in childbed.

[*Old Romney*]

A visitation held in the churches of St Laurence and St Martin in Old Romney on the day and year above named. They have nothing to say except concerning the ornaments of the said churches.

Sir William, the chaplain, has a certain Agnes, his sister as they say, in his house.

[Then follow a number of charges against parishioners for detaining money, goods, or stock (chiefly cows) belonging to the church.]

In the church of St Martin the chrismatory and *Corpus Domini* are without locks, there are no books,[1] the chalice requires repair, the font has no lock, the roof of the chancel and of the church are in bad condition. For the defects found in the chrismatory and pix sir William, the chaplain, is suspended from the celebration of divine service.

[*New Romney*]

Verso. Visitation in the church of St Nicholas, Romney. Visitation held . . . in the year of our Lord 1294.

Alice the wife of Godfrey Tyter is noted for adultery committed with Richard called Burnet.

All the clerks[2] are married.

In St Nicholas' church there is no censer, both font and chrismatory are without locks, the churchyard fence is out of repair and in the same condition as it was last year.

1292 *St Mary in the Marsh*

The rector doth not reside continually, he hath another benefice in the diocese of . . . [?] Wherefore he must shew his title to these churches, and appear before the lord [commissary] to answer for his non residence.

Robert Godman, John Godman, and William, chaplain of Hope, have failed to pay tithes within the bounds of the parish of St Mary. Robert and John appear and say that they have paid their dues as they were bound to do, and that they were not called to answer for the other man. William the chaplain, who was suspected of appropriating the tithes, could not be found.

*John Wolnoth got Celestria daughter of John Andreu with child, as is said. The

[1] *libri penitus deficiunt*

[2] *clerici beneficiarii*

woman is dead. John was not cited because he lives in Cant'. Simon the servant, brother of Honychilde, is accused of the same.* The man did not appear, therefore he was suspended and is cited to appear on the morrow at Romney.

Matilda daughter of Alan Godefrey keepeth back two pounds of wax due to the church of St Mary yearly from certain land which is called Pennesland, and hath done so for two years. She was not cited because she lives at Winchelsea.

Eastbridge[1]

The rector did not appear to receive the lord's visitation, nor has he ever been in residence there, nor was a chaplain found therein at the time of the visitation, and the parishioners ask that a fit priest may be provided for them. Wherefore it was decreed that the fruits of the benefice should be sequestrated until other order be taken. The rector doth not appear and therefore he is suspended from celebrating divine service. And an inhibition was issued that no one should presume to violate this sequestration on pain of excommunication, also the rector is cited to appear at Braburn on Thursday after the feast of All Saints to answer to the premisses and to the charge of breaking the aforesaid sequestration. On the day he did not appear, nor did any proctor appear in his name. The case standeth over.[2]

Edward, vicar of Westhethe, hath the said church to farm and hath held it a long time. He was suspended and deprived of his vicarage.

Broomhill[3]

The vicar doth not reside, nor hath he done so since he was instituted. The abbess and convent of Gynes hold the church for their own uses. Adjourned.

Roger, who is now chaplain there, hath taken the vicarage to farm, out of which he payeth yearly to the archdeacon one mark, and the king taketh[4] all the fruits of the same. The chaplain appeared and saith on oath that in the first year of the institution of the vicar, he agreed with the vicar to serve the church, and give to the vicar that year four marks, out of which he paid one mark to the vicar, and two marks to the archdeacon, *pro incontinentia vicarii*, and one mark remains to be paid for that year, which he is keeping in his own hands, and he confesseth that he is bound to pay four marks the following year, of which he has not yet paid anything but keepeth the money in his own hands. M^d^ The chaplain retired to the diocese of Chichester.

The church lacks a surplice and a rochet. Proctors appear and promise that they would find what was required before the feast of All Saints.

*John de Gateberghe wished to marry Petronilla Faron whose relative Petronilla de Cruce he had previously had knowledge of. The said John and Petronilla Faron appear and say on oath that they had not contracted matrimony with each other and the man confesses that earlier he knew Petronilla the relative but did not know that the two were related and the wife confesses that when she was known by John she was well

[1] Estbregge
[2] *Pendet*
[3] Promhulle. A limb of the Cinque Port of Romney situated on the sea coast near the boundary between Kent and Sussex. The town was washed away in the great storm of 1287, which also destroyed old Winchelsea. The church, however, survived the *débâcle*, and continued to exist until the end of the fifteenth century.
[4] *percipit*

aware that he had previously known her relative Petronilla; in respect of which they renounce their sins and suspect places and they shall be whipped five times through Wereham market-place and five times round the church where both are parishioners.*

Walter son of John is noted for fornication with Deonise Kembestere. Cited, they do not appear. Afterwards it is testified that they are vagrant, wherefore they are to be cited when they can be found.

Thomas son of Hamo is noted in connection with Mabel Levechild. Cited, the man does not appear, therefore suspended, and the woman is excused because she is pregnant. Afterwards it is testified that the woman is dead and the man at sea.[1]

[*Roll X*]
Concerning the vacancy of the vicarage of Promhelle. Friday next before Palm Sunday, 1292. In the church of St Nicholas de Romenal an inquiry was held by the commissary into the cause of the vacancy of the vicarage. The jurors were the rector of Middele, the vicars of Romenal, Lyde and Newecherche, and the parish chaplains of Ivecherche, Fayrefeld, Northne, Lyde, Romenal, All Saints Hope, and St Clement's Old Romenal, who said that the jurisdiction of the church of Canterbury during the vacancy of the see rested with prior and chapter of Christ Church.

Hope All Saints
The rector does not reside because he is at school[2] by licence of the lord [archbishop], and mr Nicholas, master of the schools of Canterbury, keepeth[3] the fruits of the same church and answereth for the same. Adjourned.

William chaplain of that place harboured long ago Joan a serving-maid . . . [?] Dobyn, whom it is said he got with child. It is pending.

The vicar of Romene doth wrong to the church of All Saints in that he taketh a moiety of the tithe of the milk of beasts which are milked in the parish of the same vicar. Adjourned. Afterwards, because no one prosecuted, the case is dismissed.

The lady of Crawethorne[4] doth not come to church as she ought and is bound to do, nor does she contribute either to the work of the church, to the paschal candle, or the blessed bread, because she hath a chapel, in which her chaplains use a bucket for a font. Adjourned till the lord's visit.

The missal is in bad condition,[5] and through the poverty of the parishioners it is not possible to get it repaired or renovated, because the men of Romene possess almost all the lands in the said parish. Adjourned until the lord shall come to Romene.

The heirs of Hamo le Bret of Romney keep back xii*d* of annual rent of the lands which have been from ancient time assigned to the work of the said church, and they should be cited at Romney in March.

Alice, widow of John le Wyse, keepeth back two cows of the said church which she had of her husband because she was the executrix of his will. She appears and saith that she hath paid and made satisfaction concerning the rent due to the church from the two cows, and her evidence is supported by her chaplain.

[1] *in mari*
[2] *stat in scolis*
[3] *custodit*
[4] Crawthorne
[5] *debilis*

The Master of the *Domus Dei* of Dover, the chief parishioner,[1] hath purchased many lands which are not of the ancient demesne of his manor, out of which he hath contributed nothing to the work of the said church, or to any of the defects therein. The case is adjourned until the lord shall come to Romene. The Master did not appear, wherefore he is suspended from the celebration of divine service, and it is decreed that he should be summoned to appear on the Thursday next after the feast of All Saints at Brabourn. The Master appeared on the morrow at Aldington and obtained reinstatement,[2] but he is to appear at Romney on the Tuesday next after the feast of All Saints. On which day he appeared, and saith that none of the said lands have been acquired recently, but that some part of the lands of his ancient demesne has been exchanged for other lands. Wherefore it is decreed that an inquest be held on Wednesday at Romney. On which day the rector's proctors appeared and the parishioners, and because they say that they know nothing against the said Master and brethren, and the evidence is in his favour, and no inquest has been held, the said Master and brethren are dismissed [here a wide space is left blank] until other order be taken. Also the vicar should receive annually two marks from the nuns to whom the church is impropriated. The nuns' proctors appear and confessed that they were in times past liable to pay a pension of four marks, and that the money was reserved[3] in their own hands. The names of their proctors are Michael Evebroke and another. Also the chaplain swore that he would collect with all fidelity the altar dues, and render a faithful account of the same to the lord archbishop of Canterbury or his ministers when called upon to do so. Afterwards the said chaplain went away[4] and he lives at la Rye, and it is said that Henry Thomas, a layman, holdeth the said vicarage to farm. Wherefore it was decreed that the said Thomas should be cited and the fruits sequestrated. Afterwards the sequestration was relaxed at Aldington.

Bilsington[5]

Jordan de Newentone, canon regular of Bilsington priory, is noted in connection with Joan Kynet who is said to have borne him issue. It is not known where the woman is living. The man appears and denies the deed and submits himself to an inquisition which shall take place on Thursday, and because the woman has not appeared for that reason suspended and she is to be cited for the said day. On which day a certain Susannah widow of Matthew Mabeli' was called and said on oath and under interrogation that the aforesaid Jordan asked her that the said Joan could be in her house declaring that she was a relative of his, which Joan did indeed stay in her house.

Thomas Quikenam, farmer of sir Nicholas de Sandwych, knight, doth not reckon when paying his tithes, the tenth sheaf which he giveth to the reapers. And though he is a great merchant he giveth no tithe of his merchandise. He was summoned and did not appear, wherefore he was suspended. Afterwards he appeared and was enjoined to purge his contumacy by visiting the precincts[6] of the blessed Edmund barefoot within three weeks. To the other articles recited he saith on oath and confesseth that in

[1] *capitalis parochianus*
[2] *status sui reformacionem obtinuit*
[3] *sequestrata*
[4] *recessit*
[5] Bilsyntone
[6] *limina*

autumn he has some of his corn reaped for money, and some for the tenth sheaf which he giveth to the reapers before everything, and of the corn which is reaped for money he giveth the tenth sheaf to God and the church, and of the corn which he causeth to be reaped for the tenth sheaf he giveth the tithe after he has given the tenth to the reapers, and as for his merchandise he giveth tithe of his profits[1] in divers places where he maketh profit. Wherefore he is enjoined to give the tithe sheaf of his corn before he giveth anything to the reapers, or to give to the reapers first and the ninth sheaf to the church, and of his profit on merchandise he should give the tithe to the church where he liveth and receiveth the sacraments and sacramentals,[2] unless he hath built warehouses in certain markets and hath stayed there for some time, and that he should deduct nothing from the said profits except what must necessarily be put aside for buying and selling in his business, also he shall make satisfaction to the vicar of Bilsington, where the said Thomas liveth, and the said Thomas was bound by his corporal oath to do all these things under pain of excommunication.

Also the same Thomas, a layman and a married man, holdeth to farm the church of Brenset and the church of Promhelle and the church of Beusfeld[3] in the deanery of Dover, whose fruits he purchased for three years, and there was wont to be distributed four seams of corn at Brensete to poor parishioners at the feast of the Annunciation which hath been withheld by him, as is alleged, and yet it is believed that it is reckoned in his account. He appears and saith on oath that he entereth the corn of the churches of Brensete and Promhelle in autumn in the name of the rectors and not in his own name, and that afterwards he buyeth the said corn from them, and now the king hath everything, and on this he submitted himself to an inquest. As for the church of Beusfeld he confesseth that he bought it [the profits]. The roof of the nave of the church and the churchyard are in bad repair. Thomas de Cobery is said to be the warden, wherefore he was summoned. He appeared and denied [the charge]. Wherefore six parishioners of the better sort are summoned . . . the parishioners appeared and alleged that the said defects were now made good, and they are enjoined under pain of one mark to the archbishop's almonry that they make good the churchyard fence. Adjourned by leave of the Visitor.[4]

Orgarswick[5]

The prior and convent of Christ Church, Canterbury, have a certain manor in the said parish, and do not pay the small tithes, nor the tithes of hay which were wont to be paid in time past. Held over because the rector saith that it is not expedient to proceed against them.

Brenzett[6]

Hamo Corbyl is cited for adultery with Basilea Forne, and although he has often been corrected yet he does not fear to repeat the offence . . . An inquest was held and the jurors found that they were guilty and incorrigible, and that the man behaved badly towards his wife, who appeared, and they were reconciled and agreed to live together

[1] *lucri* [2] *sacramentalia* [3] Whitfield
[4] *domini* [5] Orgareswyke [6] Brensete

under pain of seven floggings in the neighbouring markets. And the said Hamo and Basilea were condemned by the same inquest and abjured their sins, and the suspected places, and were flogged five times through Romney market, and five times through Hythe market, and six times round their parish churches.

William Wolnoth kept Mabel la Wyte long ago in fornication and they never received any penance from any ordinary. They appear and confess the fame and the fact, and renounce one another on the bench of the church and are whipped three times round the aforesaid church.

Blackmanstone

Mass was wont to be celebrated in the said church of Blackmanstone every day, but in the time of the present parish priest it is not always said.[1] The said chaplain of the place appeareth, and was enjoined to serve the said church regularly and in seemly fashion, as far as his strength allowed, under pain of severe penalty if he should be negligent in the future.

Henry Tuke, farmer of the mill of Nicholas Barrok, hath not paid the tenth seam of wheat for tithe of the mill, although he payeth to the lord of the mill ten seams yearly . . . he saith that he gives to the said Nicholas for the farm of the mill only eight seams a year. He must pay to the rector of Blackmanstone two bushells of wheat for the arrears of half a year under pain of excommunication.

[*Roll XIII*] *Burmarsh*[2]

[Two cases of incontinence of no interest.]

The clerk of the church is married, and he carrieth the blessed water. He appeareth, and took oath that for the future he will not minister about the altar.

The archdeacon of Canterbury, rector of the church of Lymene, usurps to himself the tithes of ten acres which are within the boundaries of the said parish of Burewaremershe. Adjourned by request.

The rector of Demecherche usurpeth to himself the tithes of certain land within the boundaries of the said parish. It standeth over because both parties consent to a summary inquiry.

The rector of Burewaremershe is not continually in residence, nevertheless he is a good man, and does what good he can in the parish. Let the fruits of the rectory be sequestrated.

His chancel is badly covered. He appeared, and promised *bona fide* that he would make good all the defects.

Dymchurch[3]

Elias the clerk harbours a certain Agatha in his house in fornication. The man appears and confesses and renounced his sin. The man whipped three times round the church. . . . The woman whipped three times round the church of Dymchurch.

The roof of the church is in bad order, nevertheless some say it is being repaired.

Brother John of Honychilde, a layman, is cited concerning the wife of William

[1] *continue* [2] Burewaremerse [3] Demecherche

Feyne. They both appear and deny on oath the report and the fact, and because not much is known against them they are ordered to purge themselves *una manu* as quickly as they can; afterwards both solemnly purged themselves.

Snave

The rector is not in priest's orders, nevertheless he was instituted in the time of the legate Ottobon of good memory. He is, however, a deacon. He doth not reside continually. Adjourned by the direction of the Visitor.

The roof of the church is in bad order; they lack a chalice and towel, it is alleged through the fault of the rector or priest. The case is adjourned, and the proceedings before the Visitor are on another roll.

Adam Cook of Horton, married, keeps in adultery Lymna daughter of John de la Bregge. They both appear and confess etc. . . . and whipped five times through Romney market-place and five times through Warehorne market-place, and each five times round the church.

The beneficiary of the place is married. There is there, however, a clerk sufficient to serve the church and about the altar. The beneficiary appears and swore that he will not minister about the altar in future.

*John parochial chaplain of the place kept long ago and still keeps Agnes Hungerhern of Romney. He appears and denies on oath the fame and the fact and submits himself to an inquisition of clerks and laymen. It is however decreed that it be done *by laymen trustworthy and not suspect as well as by clerks*. It is pending in another roll before the lord [commissary].*

[*Roll XII*] *Newchurch*

Sir John de Berthen, rector of the same, doth not reside, he doeth no good in the parish, and all the granges[1] of the rectory have been destroyed, so that the greater part of the fruits [of the benefice] are sometimes entrusted to a layman's keeping, and he letteth those fruits to farm. He did not appear at the visitation, either in person or by his proctor, wherefore the fruits are sequestrated . . . Afterwards the rector's proctor gave satisfaction for his contumacy, and the sequestration was relaxed, and he was enjoined to distribute every year to the poor people of the parish five quarters of corn, the charge concerning non-residence, and the repair of the defects standeth over.[2]

There is in the same church a vicar, who used to have a chaplain to help him on account of the size of the parish, but for a long time he hath not had one on account of the small value of his vicarage, wherefore proceedings are being taken to augment the same. The vicar appeareth, and saith that he did not have a chaplain there because of the poorness of the vicarage. Wherefore it was decreed that the rector should be cited instead, on Monday after the feast of St Luke the Evangelist . . . the vicar saith he hath in writing the ordination which the lord [archbishop] made for the vicarage, and that he will shew it on the morrow, on which day he exhibited it, and he is dismissed.

A copy of the inquest concerning the vicarage of the church of Newchurch:

[1] *gran ia* [2] *pendet*

Thomas, rector of Chartham, certifies to the archbishop [Pecham] that in accordance with his *mandamus* he has summoned an inquest of jurors to enquire into the condition of the vicarage of Newchurch, and that the jury . . . had made the following return: That at one time there was a resident rector there and no vicar; that the rector served the church well with the aid of two chaplains, one a deacon, and other sufficient clerks; that after the death of that rector divers rectors were collated to the church at divers times who kept no residence, let the church to farm, and served the church in a miserable way with the aid of a single chaplain. The parishioners, feeling themselves aggrieved, complained to the archbishop for the time being, and the same archbishop ordained a perpetual vicarage therein, endowing it with all oblations and offerings of the altar, all small tithes, and the tithe of hay, and he served the church honourably with a chaplain as colleague[1] in deacon's orders, and other sufficient ministers. And the rector, for the time being, paid all pensions due from the same church, and the rectory at that time was reputed to be worth forty marks, and the vicarage twenty marks. At length Boniface of good memory, archbishop of Canterbury, collated to the church one of his clerks, mr John Poroges, who, being an astute and litigious person, withdrew from the vicar the tithe of hay, and at first made the vicar pay the pensions due from the said church, viz, to the church of Bilsington ten shillings, and to the church of St Martin at Canterbury sixteen shillings and ninepence-halfpenny. The vicar, for the time being, went to law with him [the rector], and while the suit was pending he died, and from that time forward the succeeding vicars have not received the hay-tithe, and have been improperly burdened with the payment of the pensions. They say also that the present vicar does not receive a sufficient portion [of the benefice] to enable him to sustain the burdens laid upon his vicarage for hospitality, such as the reception of friars[2] and other guests known and unknown who may come along, because his share at the present time is worth only ten marks, and the rectory upwards of sixty marks, because the lands which used to be in grass, and on which animals were pastured, which were of much profit and convenience to the vicars, are now under the plough on account of the drying up of the marsh,[3] wherefore the rector receiveth all the tithes and the vicar scarcely any.[4] Moreover, the rectors sustain none of the burdens there, nor do they keep any hospitality, but carry off everything; nor had the vicar any house except one belonging to a layman[5] which is highly rented and burdened with services. Nevertheless the said vicar hath built a sufficient house for himself and his successors out of his own private fortune. They say also that mr Richard de Coplond, who was at one time rector there and did much good, considering the share of the vicar to be insufficient, gave him, in some years, five seams of corn, and in some years eight seams, towards the support of the burdens incumbent upon the vicarage. Nevertheless, after his time the share of the vicar decreased very considerably from the causes above written. Asked how the share of the vicar might be augmented with the least and more tolerable loss to the rector, they say if the vicar were to have the tithe of hay and five acres of land, which are of

[1] *socio* [2] *fratres*
[3] For the changes man and nature between them were effecting in Romney Marsh, at this time, see J. A Williamson, *The English Channel* (1959), pp. 107–8.
[4] *quasi nihil* [5] *nisi in laico feudo*

the fee of the church, and are held by the rector and are of little profit to him, and which after deducting the various rents and services are estimated at ten shillings annually, together with some reasonable share of the corn, his share, together with what he now possesses, would then amount to twenty marks. He will then be able to maintain hospitality and all the burdens of the vicarage in an honourable manner.[1]

[*Roll VII*] *Lyminge*[2]

[1293] The visitation of the church of Lyminge and of the chapels annexed to the mother church.

The abbot of St Radegund doth not pay the small tithes issuing out of the manor of Paddlesworth, and as he used to do in times past. The vicar of Lymmeng was wont to have the great tithes of the sheaves[3] of the manor of Paddlesworth and in like manner of Stanford, paying ten marks to the rector, whereas now he hath nothing of the aforesaid tithes; nevertheless they know not why the aforesaid tithes are withdrawn from him. The rector is not resident in person, and it appeareth that he holdeth several benefices with cure of souls in England. At Paddlesworth the *stipend* [?] of the priest is withdrawn by the vicar . . . and sometimes the said J., chaplain of the said vicar, celebrateth so early[4] that the parishioners lack[5] the canonical hours and mass.

Also the fruits of the church of Lymminge and of its chapels are spent in foreign parts.[6] Also at Stanford the granary is ruinous. Also at Paddlesworth the rector hath caused a certain house to be pulled down and hath not rebuilt it.

The vicar of Lymminge published the banns in the aforesaid church between Henry de Hempstede and Emma, daughter of Thomas de Bredenheye, and although he knew that they were related in the fourth and fifth degree, the vicar solemnised marriage between them.

Richard Brunig hath put away[7] Alice, daughter of Simon Bedell, because the mother of the said Richard received the said Alice from the sacred font.

The proctor of the rector hath sold the fruits at Paddlesworth to William, called Bastard, before they were reaped.

Sir William, chaplain at Stanford, hath bought the corn of Stanford for five years of the proctor of the said rector.

John de Leche is noted for adultery committed with Joan daughter of William called Barun and the same John has a wife in his district.

William son of William de Prato keeps a certain Godelena daughter of his godmother.

Vincent de Heydon, executor of the will of Robert Box, detaineth two shillings to his own use, which were left for making Stanford bridge, and likewise he detaineth twelve pence left for the maintenance of a certain road near Stanford.

Thomas Charles, son of Thomas Charles, executor of the same T., hath not carried out the last will of the said Thomas, because he retaineth sixpence left to the hospital of the blessed Thomas at Canterbury, and sixpence to the hospital of poor priests.

[1] see also below, p. 721
[2] Lymmynge
[3] *garbarum*
[4] *ita mane*
[5] *careant*
[6] *in partibus citra marinis*
[7] *desponsavit*

Sir William, chaplain of Stanford, keeps in his house Alice de Werchorne.

*[*On the back.*] John son of Edya is noted for adultery committed with Joan . . .*

The rector is not in priest's orders, nevertheless he saith he obtained institution before the council of Lyons.

The chaplain of Stanford keeps his concubine as is said before. This he adds that he has kept her for ten years and more.

Dom de Leche keepeth back all the tithe of the wind-mill, and hath retained for a year and a half three bushels of barley, ten shillings.

A missal is lacking in the chapel of Stanford, which the parishioners are bound to find.

The vicar keeps his own daughter in his house, in respect of whom the said John his fellow chaplain is noted, and she is suitable enough for manly embraces.

Things lacking in the chapel of Paddlesworth

A psalter and legendary are lacking; the Body of the Lord is kept in a very unseemly pix; the font has no lock or cover; the chrismatory has no lock. Wherefore the sir J., chaplain there, is suspended from celebrating divine service, and the parishioners should be warned to repair the defects before the feast of St Michael under penalty of twenty shillings.

[A membrane attached to the above contains a list of persons excommunicated or suspended during the vacancy of the see, as follows:] Dunstan, vicar of Sellenge, Simon, rector of Boninton, John, parish chaplain of Heryngsselle,[1] Adam, vicar of Eghethorne,[2] dean of Sandwich, mr John de Moningham, rector of the same, Richard called domine, chaplain of the church of Ridelingwealde,[3] excommunicated; mr Richard, rector of the church of Ripple, Stephen, rector of Waldweressare,[4] Stephen, Godfrey, Matthew and William, vicars respectively of Colrede, Tilmanstone, Norbourne, Wodnisburg, suspended; John, rector of Horton, dean of Elham, suspended, and after repeated contumacy excommunicated, Geoffrey, vicar of Chileham, dean of Bregge, Robert and Richard, vicars of Preston and Pelham et William de Stodmersse . . . [?] . . . [on the back] John Boxley, dean of Wesbere, excommunicated; Peter, vicar of the church of Menstre, suspended; John de Watton, vicar of the church of Kingston [blank], mr Matthew, rector of the church of the blessed Mary Magdalene in Canterbury, suspended; John, vicar of the church of Monketone, excommunicated.

[Roll XI] Brookland

The church is badly covered, the gutters[5] and timber are rotten. Wherefore the parishioners are summoned, and because it is said that they are liable, it was enjoined on the wardens that they should cause all the said defects to be repaired before the next visit of the lord [?commissary] to the marsh under pain of twenty shillings.

The rents assigned to the fabric and lights of the church are not paid nor can they be levied except by the rector, whose duty it is to levy such dues. Adjourned.

[1] ?Hinxhill
[2] Eythorne
[3] Ringwould
[4] Waldershare
[5] *stillicidia*

Fairfield[1]

Roger of Kenardintone, clerk of the church, is married, and he carrieth the blessed water, and it is believed that he married a widow. He appeared and swore that he would no longer serve about the altar.

The present chaplain pastureth lambs in the churchyard and alloweth a young woman[2] to minister to him at the altar. He appeared and swore that on three or four occasions he was served in the manner aforesaid, and he swore that in future he would do so no more, nor would he pasture lambs in the churchyard except in gathering time.[3]

Simon once a chaplain there now living at Romney is noted in connection with Nutekina daughter of Hugh ate Walle. The man appears and confesses that at one time he did sin with her, for which he was corrected during a vacancy of the see, and he denies repetition . . . as to which he submits himself to an inquisition, etc.[4]

[5]The visitation of brother R. de Clyve, commissary of Canterbury, *sede vacante*, made in the church of Feyrefeld on the Saturday next after the feast of the Holy Trinity in the year of our Lord 1294, by sir Simon, chaplain of the same, and Will' Comffrey, Stephen de Longhe, Simon Cleys, Richard le Wolfe and Lovekyn Breke-bot, parishioners of the said church.

A frontal for the high altar is lacking, because there is only a poor[6] carpet before[7] the same.

A cloth[8] is required for the lectern,[9] because the one that is there is very dirty[10] and in poor condition.

There is an antiphoner which is of no use or value, and a legend of no value.

They lack a psalter, manual, processional, ordinal, collectar and martyrology.

The church was never dedicated, and the altars in the chancel are of wood badly put together, also the walls of the chancel are in bad condition[11] because they are full of holes in the lower parts; moreover the churchyard is dedicated, but not the church, because it is of wood and daub.[12]

The oil has not been changed this year, the church font has no lock as it ought to have.

The rector does no good in the parish, and this year has sold all the fruits at the same time and all together[13] to a layman, and the chaplain has so meagre a portion that he cannot live or sustain himself in a decent manner there.

Simon the chaplain is noted in connection with a certain Natekina and they believe that it is true rather than false. The clerk of the church is married.[14]

Sellinge[15]

John de Wylminton causeth injury to the church by impeding, as far as he can, the

[1] Feyrefeld
[2] *juvenculam*
[3] *tempore collectionis*
[4] see below
[5] This is from another document [F 29], but it probably was once part of the roll.
[6] *debile*
[7] *coram*
[8] *tuella*
[9] *lectonarium* [*sic*]
[10] *vilissima*
[11] *debiles*
[12] *de ligno et plastura terre*
[13] *simul et in summa*
[14] see above
[15] Selynghe

vicar from cultivating an acre of land which from old time belongeth to his vicarage, and the said John very rarely cometh to church, and in other ways behaveth badly in keeping back [church dues]. Adjourned by request.

The same vicar hath no clerks to serve him, except laymen, who are literates[1] and married. They appear [*sic*], and it was found that he hath a sufficient clerk . . . nevertheless the vicar was enjoined for the future to cause himself to be served by fit and sufficient clerks under pain of suspension.

Nicholas Cryel knt, is noted for adultery with Matilda de Hanlee whom the said John often conducted to him at Westenhanger, because of which woman the aforesaid Nicholas ill-treats his wife. The man is cited in his manor but not personally found, for which he is reckoned contumacious and it is decreed that he be called concerning John as above. William de Morstoke and Thomas of the same pay in the name of tithe the eleventh sheaf of their fields, and although they have often been corrected, they do not reform. They were cited, but did not appear, therefore they were suspended for contumacy . . . The rector of Orgareswyke taketh the small tithes of seventeen acres of land called Soleslonde, which was wont to belong to the church of Sellynghe. Adjourned by request.

The rector of Demecherche taketh tithes of Honnyngstone, viz, on three acres which used to belong to the vicarage of Sellynge. The matter is being considered by the rector and the master of the Maison Dieu.

[The next entry is omitted as the parchment is mutilated and the writing can only be partly read.]

It is certified that the said church lacks . . . [obliterated] because the chaplain is insufficient . . . afterwards the said chaplain appears, and was found to be incompetent[2] and insufficient to hold the cure, wherefore it was decreed that the rector should be recalled to the cure, unless he can get leave from the lord.

Westenhanger[3]

The rector of *Westenhanger is noted in connection with a certain widow of Heytone. The man appears and denies expressly on oath the fame and the fact and because there is no very great presumption against him he shall purge himself five-handed on Friday, on which day the said rector purged himself most solemnly.*

The rector is non-resident, but is at school, by licence of the lord [archbishop] as is alleged, and he doth no good in the parish, but taketh the money and departeth, and letteth the church and altarage to farm. Afterwards the rector doth not appear, wherefore he is considered contumacious, and his penance is reserved until it can be inflicted by the lord. The fruits were sequestrated. The church roof is in bad order, nevertheless it is being repaired.

Richard chaplain of the same place is accused concerning a certain Alice Gangard of Snergate who lieth in child-bed. They are not cited because they are not found. The clerk of the church is married, and he ministers about the altar. The clerk was not cited because he went away with the priest.

[1] *litteratos* [2] *impotens*
[3] Ostringehangre

[*Roll XIV*] *Lympne*
Lymene the clerk hath a wife, and he hath married a widow. He appeared, and was inhibited under pain of excommunication from ministering about the altar and from reading the epistle.

The archdeacon of Canterbury is rector of the same [church]. He did not appear to receive visitation on the day appointed for him. Afterwards he did not appear, nor was he summoned.

Thomas de Marynes knt keeps in adultery a certain Eleanor de Elmestede daughter of John de Wadesole, and earlier he kept another, Agnes Soppestre by name, whom he still supports, and he ill-treats and has long ill-treated his wife. The knight appeared on Thursday before the lord [commissary] and confesses that he sinned with each and with the said Ellen and he renounced both and suspect places on pain of forty marks to be spent at the will of the lord archbishop of Canterbury if they are incurred and because it is not seemly for a knight to do public penance he is commanded on the orders of the lord [commissary] to pay or cause to be paid twenty marks to poor villeins[1] of the district, to which the said knight agreed.

[On the back.] And on the same day the said Agnes Soppestre appears and on oath confesses that she cohabited with the said knight for nine years or so and given birth twice for him and says that it is a year and more since the man last knew her and renounced the said knight and suspect places and she will be whipped five times through the market-place and five times round the church in a chemise as is customary and because the said Ellen is pregnant . . . herself[2] this time and it is decreed that the said knight and his wife are to appear before the lord [commissary] on the morrow of the next feast of St Luke the Evangelist and receive for the dissension that has arisen between them what is right and the same knight agreed that he could be forced both to the aforesaid penance if incurred and to payment of the said marks to be paid on that account as aforementioned as touched on above by any ecclesiastical censures whatsoever without any remedy in lay law.

Godard de la Ree, Walter Rok and some other parishioners withhold certain laudable and customary offerings hitherto in use. They appear and say they have never withheld [anything]. The vicar appeared and gave evidence, and the said parishioners swore that in future they would withhold nothing, whereupon the vicar signified that he was content. The vicar of Aldintone taketh small tithes to the value of one hundred shillings within the bounds of the said parish, by what right is unknown. Both the vicars appear, he of Lymene and he of Aldintone, and the vicar of Aldintone exhibited an ordination of his vicarage in which the said tithes are contained, and the evidence having been heard, both were enjoined for the future not to hinder one another under pain of excommunication from taking what was theirs by right and approved custom. Afterwards both vicars appear, and the vicar of Aldintone saith that the said vicar of Lymene again hindered him from taking his said tithe. [More evidence is inscribed on the back of the roll about this case, but it does not seem to have been settled definitely by the commissary.]

[1] *pauperibus hosp'*
[2] *sibi*

Dunstan who was chaplain there now living as is said at Brookland is noted in connection with Matilda daughter of Godard de Ree the wife of Richard Taylur. The woman is vagrant because she follows her husband. It is said, however, that she is now at the manor of Smeeth and it is said that the priest is living at Brookland. He appears and says that three years ago he sinned once with her and not more, for which he was corrected and he submitted himself to an inquisition, which says that the said chaplain sinned with the said woman three years ago and for this he was corrected and the woman likewise and they did penance and they[1] understand that they never afterwards relapsed. And so he is dismissed.

John Salkyn has a wife who is old, and he is not willing to support her. The man stays with sir[2] William de Brochelle in the parish of Saltwood and let him be cited for Friday. The woman appears and says that her husband treats her well and she does not complain of him.

West Hythe[3] a chapel of Lympne

Aylward vicar of West Hythe kept in his house long ago a certain woman by whom he had ever so many children and who died in his house as if she were his wife, and at length he took a certain Chima Tukkyld a woman whom he keeps openly and he enfeoffed her with a certain house and he often knows her in a hut and on banks[4] to the scandal of the whole [priestly] order. The said vicar confesses in the visitation that he has indeed a bad reputation where Chima Tuckyld is concerned, though he is blameless concerning her as he says. He appears and sworn to speak the truth confesses that at some time or other he had two children by the one who is dead and eight years have elapsed since he last knew her, and a year since she died in his house. He says also on oath that he has no connection with the surviving woman mentioned, and on this he submitted himself to an inquisition to be made on Friday, and the said survivor, Chima, appears, denies on oath the fact and says that the said chaplain never enfeoffed her with any house and submitted herself to inquisition . . . afterwards that Aylward was deprived and the woman renounced her sin and suspect places and whipped three times through Hythe market-place and three times round the church of West Hythe.

Roll X

[1292] Proceedings in the church of Christ, Canterbury, before us, brother Richard of Clyve, commissary of Canterbury, during the vacancy of the see, on the third law-day next after the feast of the Epiphany in the year of our Lord 1292.

Rolvenden

Concerning the vacancy of the vicarage of Rolvenden. Tuesday next before . . . [?] 1292. The commissary on arriving at the church of Essettisfforde[5] for the purpose of inquiring into the cause of the vacancy, found the gates of the church closed against him, and mr Robert of Derby standing in the churchyard, who insultingly denied

[1] i.e. the inquest
[2] *dominus*
[3] Westhethe
[4] *in fossis*
[5] Ashford

him entrance to the church, to the prejudice, loss, and scandal of the church of Christ in Canterbury. At length the inquiry was held in the churchyard by the vicars of Charing, Aldinton, the parish chaplains of Godmersham, Westwell, Egerton and Smethe.

Ivychurch[1]
Sir Hugh de Notyngham, rector of the church there, doth not reside, and he letteth to farm the fruits and the altarage. The rector doth not appear because he is in the king's service, but his clerk appeared as his proctor, and sufficient evidence was given to shew that the fruits [of the benefice] are not let to farm, but are sold after collection by the rector; the charge of non-residence standeth over. Also there used to be a vicar in the same church and now there is none. This is denied on the part of the rector, and it was certified by the parishioners that there was formerly a vicar there a long time ago, and that in the time of the [last] four successive rectors there had been no vicar. The case is adjourned at the Visitor's pleasure.

Robert de Prato, clerk of the same church, hath a wife, and he serveth the priest at the altar, nevertheless another carrieth the blessed water, who is said to be unqualified.[2] The said Robert appeareth and was inhibited under pain of excommunication from approaching the altar. The lesser clerk is allowed to minister.

Mr Hugh de Panebrok, formerly rector of the same church, is said to have done nothing for his parish in his lifetime, nevertheless his executors were enjoined after his death by brother R. de Clyve, the commissary, *sede vacante*, to give seven marks of the goods of the deceased in the parish, and it is unknown whether this has been done. Mr Thomas, rector of Adesham and ex'or of the said Hugh, appeared and answered that he was ready to give an account of his administration, and if it should appear that there was any liability upon him he would give satisfaction according as the ordinary should decide.[3] Adjourned.

Monday next after the feast of the blessed Lucy the Virgin in the year of our Lord abovesaid, in the church of Christ, Canterbury, in full consistory by mandate of the above lords we held an inquiry concerning the vacancy of the church of Ivecherche by mr Martin, rector of the church of Icham, mr Gwydone, rector of Swalclyve, sir Rich., rector of Aldintone, sir Will', rector of St George, Canterbury, sir Matt', rector of St Mary de Castro, sir Thos', vicar of Aldintone, sir John, vicar of la Bredene, Canterbury, and sir John, parish chaplain of Netherhardres.

Aldinton and Smeeth
The vicar quarreleth with his parishioners on Sundays and holidays, and knoweth not how to carry on a discussion without getting into a great rage. And the same vicar pastureth his horses in the churchyard, and he employeth temporary[4] chaplains. The vicar appeared and denieth the first article, and was enjoined under pain of deprivation that for the future he should no longer quarrel with his parishioners; concerning the

[1] Ivecherche [2] *insufficiens*
[3] An inventory of the goods of Hugh de Panebrok is printed in *Kent Records*, vol. 3 (1888), p. 146.
[4] *momentaneos*

animals, he was bidden to keep the church gate shut; concerning the temporary chaplains, the vicar was enjoined, on pain of deprivation, that for the future he should employ properly qualified chaplains and competent assistants.

[Seven cases of incontinency follow, but as they are of no special interest they are omitted.]

The ornaments of the church of Aldintone and of the chapel of Smethe are visited.

The light of the church of Aldintone is badly kept, and this is thought to be the fault of Robert de la . . . [?] Robert appeareth and saith that he is not the warden of the light, but he hath twelve pence to buy a sheep for the light, and he is enjoined to buy the sheep before the feast of Easter, or return the money to the warden of the light.

The churchyard is badly fenced . . . [the rest is illegible].

Newchurch

Proceedings in the church of Newcherche . . . Tuesday next before the feast of St Katherine, in the year abovesaid. A mandate had been issued to sir John, rector of Seymetone, dean of Lymene, to summon the clergy of his deanery to inquire into the vacancy of the church of Newcherche in the gift of the king of England.

The dean appeared, and asserted that he had been so much occupied in certain arduous business relating to the subsidy for the Holy Land that he had not been able to reduce his certificate to writing, but confessed that he had received the mandate with due reverence, and asked to be allowed to certify by word of mouth that he had duly cited the following persons: mr William, rector of Broclonde, sir Simon, rector of Bonyntone, sir Thomas, rector of Bilsington, sir Adam, rector of Orgareswyke, sir Richard, rector of Aldintone, mr Peter, vicar of Lyde, sir Thomas, vicar of Aldintone, sir William, rector of Brensete, sir Thomas, vicar of Newcherche, and the parish chaplains of Wyttrishesham, St Nicholas de Romene, Ivecherche, Lyde, Smethe, Mersham, Stone, Apeldre, Lymene, Rokyng, Blakmannestone, Henxele and Estbregg.

[*Assessments for taxation of pope Nicholas IV*, 1291

(*Taxatio ecclesiastica . . . Nicholai IV*, 1291 (Rec. Com., 1802), pp. 2–3)

	£	s	d
Woodchurch	20	0	0
Old Romney	18	13	4
New Romney	20	0	0
St Mary-in-the-Marsh	20	0	0
Eastbridge	6	13	4
Broomhill	10	13	4
Hope, All Saints	13	16	8
Bilsington	16	13	4
Orgarswick [entered only as part of a Christ Church, Canterbury manor]	–	–	–

		£	s	d
Brenzett		13	6	8
	vicarage	4	13	4
Blackmanstone		5	0	0
Burmarsh		9	6	8
Dymchurch		11	6	8
Snave		13	6	8
Newchurch		40	0	0
Lyminge, with [Paddlesworth] chapel		60	0	0
	vicarage	8	0	0
Brookland		13	6	8
Fairfield [entered only as part of a Christ Church, Canterbury manor]		–	–	–
Selling		20	0	0
	vicarage	6	13	4
Westenhanger[1]		4	13	4
Lympne, with [West Hythe] chapel		20	0	0
Rolvenden		33	6	8
	vicarage	6	13	4
Ivychurch		35	6	8
Aldington, with [Smeeth] chapel		30	0	0]

147. To a negligent archdeacon, 1301

(*Reg. Simonis de Gandavo* (Cant. & York Soc.), p. 66. Based on the translation in C. J. Offer, *The Bishop's Register* (London, 1929), pp. 155–6)

To the archdeacon of Salisbury because of the manifest defects in the chancel of the church of Urchfont discovered by his lordship. – Coming in person lately to the church of Urchfont to proclaim the word of God we found the chancel of that place unroofed so much that if then rain snow or hail had fallen even lightly there would have been no more convenient place in it to celebrate the solemnities of the mass than under the open sky; in which case it certainly behoves our solicitude to make clear the default of the rector of the place and we cannot commend your diligence. Furthermore, we have found that the aforesaid rector without our leave has not only left the aforesaid church, but, in addition, from the time when he obtained possession of it, as is set out above, he has always been absent and has not hitherto come near it, but without licence sending to other places the revenues and offerings belonging to the rectory of that church, and by means of an illegal contract he has granted and still grants it to a layman to farm yet by some fraudulent subtlety of language inserted in the said contract by a change not of substance but of wording, as by the substitution of the word farmer for layman, to the peril of his own safety and the no mean prejudice of the parishioners of the said church and the scandal of very many. Since therefore we cannot with averted eyes let them go without correction, we, by the tenor of these presents,

[1] Ostringehangre

commit the aforementioned things to your zealous attention and order you in our place and by our authority for the aforesaid and certain other legitimate causes to sequestrate the aforesaid fruits, revenues and offerings and have them kept in safe sequestration by the vicars of that or neighbouring places until you have other orders from us touching these things. Farewell. Given at Poterne, 11 December A.D. 1301, and in the fifth year of our consecration.

148. Confirmations [late 12th cent.]

(Trans., *Life of St Hugh of Lincoln*, ed. Douie and Farmer (1962), I, pp. 127–8)

A story told to illustrate the saintliness of St Hugh, bishop of Lincoln 1186–1200, but valuable also for the light it throws on confirmations, one of the duties of a bishop of which there is little formal record. Bishops' registers of this period are usually silent on the subject, probably because, whether performed well or ill or indeed at all, it was a humdrum, routine duty and one which did not, out of common prudence as with appointments and property matters, require record. Even record of bishops' injunctions for children to be brought for confirmation is rare. This, therefore, is precious evidence; above all, of how unceremonious and casual (in every sense) the administration of the sacrament could be, and no doubt sometimes had to be.

Frequently when he was travelling about, people flocked to him to ask him to confirm them, or brought their children to be confirmed. As soon as he reached a suitable place he dismounted, and did his part with earnest devotion in whatever diocese it was. Neither fatigue nor sickness, nor the heed for hastening on his journey, nor the roughness of the road, nor the bad weather could persuade him to administer the sacrament on horseback.

To my shame and sorrow, I afterwards saw a certain young bishop, of exceptional strength, when the spot and the weather were both admirable and he had no reason to be in a hurry, sprinkle children with the sacred chrism whilst on horseback. The children howled and were terror-stricken, and in actual danger amongst the fiery and kicking horses. The ruffianly retainers cuffed and struck these innocents, but the bishop took no notice of their danger and panic. Our Hugh used to behave in a very different way. Although already advanced in years, and subject to all the inconveniences which often afflict travellers, he used to dismount and gently summon the children and their godparents to him one after another. If by chance his lay attendants laid their hands on them, his anger was terrible and sometimes he even restrained them by blows. Having given the bystanders the blessing they hoped for, he prayed to God for any sick persons who were there, thus arousing their hope of recovering their health, and went on his way accompanied by the blessings of the crowd.

149. A rural dean's court, 1300

(*Worcestershire Hist. Soc. Collectanea* (1912), 69–80)

The earliest known record of proceedings in a ruridecanal court, a rare and possibly unique survival from the period covered by this volume. The deanery is that of Wych (now the two deaneries of Droitwich and Bromsgrove) in the diocese of Worcester. On ecclesiastical discipline of the laity, see Moorman, *Church Life in England in the Thirteenth Century* (Cambridge, 1955), pp. 207 ff; H. S. Bennett, *Life on the English Manor* (Cambridge, 1948), pp. 246–8; and, more localised, R. H. Hilton, *A Medieval Society: The West Midlands at the End of the Thirteenth Century* (1966), pp. 261 ff. A particular case is mentioned in *The Worcester Liber Albus*, ed. J. M. Wilson (1920), p. 263. On public penance and on the theory and practice of excommunication, see two articles by Rosalind Hill in *History*, vol. 36 (1951), pp. 213–26, and vol. 42 (1957), pp. 1–11, respectively. For the procedure in such cases, see B. L. Woodcock, *Medieval Ecclesiastical Courts in the Diocese of Canterbury* (Oxford University Press, 1952), esp. ch. 10; after which, F. S. Hockaday, "The Consistory Court of the Diocese of Gloucester", *Trans. Bristol and Gloucestershire Arch. Soc.*, vol. 46 (for 1924), pp. 195–287, and J. S. Purvis, *An Introduction to Ecclesiastical Records* (1953), ch. 3.

[Chapter held in the church] of Dodderhill on the Friday before the feast of the Ascension in the year 1300 [Friday, 13 May] and there will be another at Salwarp on the Wednesday after the feast of St Barnabas in the aforesaid year [Wednesday, 15 June 1300].

... of ... fornicated with ... and confesses and is whipped in the usual way. The woman did [penance]. The man is not subject to the jurisdiction [of this court].

Henry son of John fornicated with Lucy de (Wych) Coker. Each appears and confesses and renounces his sin and is whipped in the usual way. They are doing [penance]. They did [penance].

Roger le Gardiner fornicated for the seventh time with Lucy de la Lynde. Each appears and confesses and renounces his sin and is whipped in the usual way. Each withdrew.[1]

Henry le coupere of Birmingham fornicated repeatedly with Isabella daughter of Richard le potter. Each is suspended for contumacy. Each is excommunicated. Each is reconciled and is whipped once for contumacy and confesses and is whipped in the usual way. They did [penance].

John of Hodscote fornicated with Julia daughter of Thomas de Colemor. The man is not found. Purgation six-handed[2] is decreed for the woman. The woman withdrew for[3] four compurgators.

Roger de la Berne fornicated with Christine daughter of Roger clerk. Each is suspended for contumacy. Each is reconciled and confesses and is whipped in the usual way once for contumacy. The woman did [penance]. The man withdrew.

Peter de la Holyok fornicated with Isabella Ketel. The man appears and confesses and is whipped in the usual way. The woman is infirm.

(Hanbury)[4] Nicholas veredarius fornicated for the second time with Evette Pinyng. The woman appears and confesses and renounces her sin and is whipped in the usual way once through the market place. The man confesses and is whipped in the usual way. He did [penance]. The woman withdrew.

[1] *recessit*

[2] *vj manu:* i.e. with five compurgators or oath-helpers

[3] *recessit pro*

[4] in the margin in the MS. The name of the parish covers the case opposite which it appears and any following, if there is more than one case from that parish.

Richard Suel fornicated with Margery le Senegar. Purgation six-handed is decreed for the man. The man makes his purgation. The woman is not subject to the jurisdiction.

(Bromsgrove) John son of William le Foler fornicated with Matilda le Koubestere. Each is suspended for contumacy. Each is reconciled and confesses and is whipped in the usual way once for contumacy. They withdrew.[1]

Adam Blouerd fornicated with Alice le beggestere. Each is suspended for contumacy. Each is excommunicated. Each is excommunicated *cum communi*. They withdrew.

(Stoke Prior) Richard le coupere committed adultery with Lucy the daughter of Christopher. The woman is suspended. She is not cited. Purgation nine-handed is decreed for the man. The man makes his purgation. The woman is suspended for contumacy. The woman is reconciled. Purgation ten-handed is decreed for the woman . . . William whose surname she does not know and whom she renounces and is whipped in the usual way three times through the market place. The woman is doing [penance]. The woman did [penance].

(St Nicholas's) Richard the servant of John Elliot fornicated with Christine Louchard. Each appears and confesses and is whipped in the usual way. They withdrew.

Thomas Louchard ill-treats his wife and this with the rod. The man appears and confesses and is whipped in the usual way once through the market place. He withdrew.

Thomas Tenor of Criche fornicated with Julia Thorn of Hampton. They renounce [their sin] with each other and are whipped in the usual way. Each withdrew.

John Colines a married man committed adultery with Agnes Smal. The man is suspended for contumacy. The woman appears and confesses and renounces her sin and is whipped in the usual way twice through the market place. The man is reconciled and confesses and is whipped in the usual way twice through the market place. They did [penance].

(Elmbridge) Richard Green chaplain committed adultery with Christine Brudeneburi of Bromyard. Purgation nine-handed by compurgators of the same status is decreed for the man. The man withdrew for[2] four compurgators.

(King's Norton) John son of William John fornicated with Isabella daughter of Adam de Lega. Each appears and confesses and is whipped in the usual way. Each withdrew.

Richard the servant of Henry de Wrodenhal fornicated repeatedly with Isabella daughter of Sontasse. Purgation six-handed is decreed for each. The man is not cleared by compurgation. The woman makes her purgation.

(Upton) Thomas Colier fornicated with Julia Godmon. Each appears and confesses and is whipped in the usual way. The woman withdrew The man did [penance].

[1] *recesserun* [2] *recessit pro*

Chapter held in the church of Salwarp on the Wednesday after the feast of St Barnabas [Wednesday, 15 June] in the year 1300 and there will be another at Northfield on the Tuesday after the feast of St Peter[1] in the aforesaid year.

(King's Norton) William le yrmongarre fornicated for the third time with Agnes Elyot. Purgation seven-handed is decreed for the man. The woman is suspended for contumacy. The man fails in the purgation and renounces his sin and is whipped in the usual way twice through the market place. The woman confesses and is whipped in the usual way once through the market place. The man withdrew.

Henry de Lee fornicated with Agnes of Alvechurch. Purgation six-handed is decreed for the man. The woman is suspended for contumacy. The woman withdrew. The man is cited.

William Miller fornicated with Alice de la Schave. Each appears and confesses and is whipped in the usual way. Each withdrew.

Edith Ythefrithe, pregnant, says on oath by Richard de Boscho whom she renounces and is whipped in the usual way. The man confesses and is whipped in the usual way. The woman did [penance]. The man withdrew.

(Bromsgrove) William de Coleweyk fornicated with Julia, a weaver. Each appears and confesses and is whipped in the usual way. Each did [penance].

Roger Miller fornicated with Isabella Clerk and with Alice Clerk, sister of the said Isabella. The man confesses with regard to each and is whipped in the usual way once through the market place. Isabella confesses and is whipped in the usual way. Each withdrew.

Thomas de Brandel[2] fornicated with Agnes daughter of Gilbert the smith. The man confesses and is whipped in the usual way. The woman is suspended for contumacy. The woman is excommunicated. The man is doing [penance]. The woman is reconciled and confesses and is whipped in the usual way. Withdrew.

Geoffrey of Langley fornicated for the fifth time with Agnes daughter of Aldich. Purgation six-handed is decreed for each. They each make their purgation.

Walter of Morton fornicated with Alice le Carter. The man is cited. The woman appears and confesses and is whipped in the usual way. The woman withdrew. The man is not found.

Thomas Noppe fornicated with Isabella of Holywalle. Each confesses and is whipped in the usual way. Each *recessit*.

Henry de Frankel fornicated with Matilda Honderwode. The woman confesses and renounces her sin and is whipped in the usual way once through the market place. The man is suspended for contumacy. The woman did [penance]. The man is excommunicated *cum communi*.

(St Peter's) Robert Bost fornicated with Alice Folk and with Christine Cubbel. The

[1] Error for the feast of SS Peter and Paul. In 1300 the Tuesday after would be Tuesday, 5 July, which gives the usual three weeks' interval between chapters and also makes better sense (see below, p. 727, n. 2).
[2] cf. below, p. 727, Thomas son of Richard of Barndel, also under Bromsgrove

man confesses as regards Alice and is whipped in the usual way. The man clears himself six-handed. The woman did [penance].

Nicholas Gryke fornicated for the third time with Alice de Hal. The woman confesses and is whipped in the usual way through the market place. The man is excommunicated. The man is reconciled. The man confesses and is whipped in the usual way through Droitwich market place. The woman pregnant. The man withdrew. The woman did [penance].

William Bolwynch fornicated with Christine Gryke. Purgation six-handed is decreed for the man. For the woman purgation nine-handed. They each make their purgation.

(St Andrew's) Walter Peperwyt fornicated for the third time with Agnes of Malvern. It is pending before the bishop.

Robert le coupere fornicated for the third time with Julia Poddyg. They renounce each other and are whipped in the usual way twice through the market place. Each withdrew.

William servant of Mariti Babe fornicated with Isabella Tirel. The woman is suspended for her contumacy. The woman is excommunicated. The woman is reconciled and confesses and is whipped in the usual way. She did [penance]. The man is corrected at Salwarp.

(Salwarp) Thomas a drover fornicated with Joan Crabbe. Purgation six-handed is decreed for the woman. The woman fails in the purgation. She is cited *pena d[uplicata]*. The woman is suspended for contumacy. The woman is reconciled, confesses and renounces [her sin] and is whipped in the usual way.

(Bromsgrove) Thomas son of Richard de Barndel[1] fornicated with Agnes daughter of Gilbert the smith. The man confesses and is whipped in the usual way. The woman is suspended for contumacy. The woman is excommunicated. The woman is reconciled and confesses and is whipped in the usual way. Withdrew. The man did [penance].

Alice de Totenhulle fornicated with Peter le tiler Warr. The woman confesses and is whipped in the usual way. The woman did [penance]. The man is not found.

(Dodderhill) Henry de Sawageburi fornicated for the second time with Alice daughter of John. The man appears and confesses and is whipped in the usual way once through the market place. The woman confesses and is whipped in the usual way once through the market place. Each withdrew.

(Salwarp) William de Home fornicated with Petronilla Blountus. Each appears, confesses and is whipped in the usual way. They did [penance].

Chapter held in the church of Northfield on the Tuesday after the feast of St Peter[2]

[1] cf. above, p. 726, Thomas de Brandel

[2] The error is repeated (above, p. 726, n. 1). Tuesday, 2 August (the Tuesday after St Peter's Chains, 1300) would be inconsistent with Monday, 18 July for the next chapter, and that Tuesday, 5 July (the Tuesday after SS Peter and Paul, 1300) is intended is shown by the note "Things done (*Acta*)" at the end of the document.

in the year 1300 and there will be another in the church of St Andrew, Droitwich, on the Monday after the feast of St Kenelm in the aforesaid year [Monday, 18 July 1300].

(Dodderhill) Roger le pallefray, servant of the rector, fornicated with Julia Wyleket. Each confesses and is whipped in the usual way. Each did [penance].

(Salwarp) Richard Kakenache committed adultery with Alice of Hartlebury. The man confesses and is whipped in the usual way. The man is doing [penance]. The woman is not subject to the jurisdiction. The man did [penance].

(Hadsor) John son of John de Pendok fornicated with Matilda of Hadsor. The same fornicated for the second time with Agnes daughter of Richard Red of Wychbold. Purgation six-handed is decreed for Agnes. Matilda is suspended for contumacy. The woman is excommunicated. Agnes fails in the purgation and confesses and is whipped in the usual way once through the market place. Agnes withdrew. Purgation six-handed is decreed for the man. The man fails in the purgation and is whipped in the usual way and renounces [his sin] in the court of the bishop. Once through the market place.

(St Andrew's) John Schappe fornicated for the second time with Matilda de Brugg. Each is suspended for contumacy. Each is reconciled. Each is reconciled and confesses and is whipped in the usual way once through the market place. Each withdrew. The man is excommunicated.

(Cofton *alias* Coston, Hackett) William the servant of the rector of Northfield fornicated with Margery de Cimiterio. The woman confesses and is whipped in the usual way. The woman is pregnant. The man is suspended for contumacy. The man is reconciled and confesses and is whipped in the usual way. Withdrew. The woman withdrew.

(Bromsgrove) William Dipel fornicated for the second time with Christine Protfot. Each is suspended for contumacy. Each is reconciled and confesses and is whipped in the usual way once for contumacy and once through the market place. Each did [penance].

Geoffrey Sarr fornicated with Agnes Primel. The woman appears and confesses and is whipped in the usual way. The man is not subject to the jurisdiction. The woman did [penance].

(Beoley) Nicholas Pinyng fornicated with Lece daughter of Reginald Symeon. The man is cited *sub pena di*[*midia*?]. The woman confesses and is whipped in the usual way. Withdrew. The man did [penance].

(King's Norton) John son of Nicholas the clerk fornicated for the second time with Julia Redes. Each appears and confesses and is whipped in the usual way once through the market place. The woman pregnant. The man withdrew.

William of Ombersley, a shepherd, committed adultery with Alice de Nortgraue. The man appears and confesses and is whipped in the usual way twice through the market place. The woman at Worcester. Each did [penance].

Chapter held in the church of St Andrew, Droitwich, on the Monday after the feast of St Kenelm *Rex* [Monday, 18 July 1300] and there will be another when needed.

(Dodderhill) William Byestrete fornicated with Agnes Magge. Purgation six-handed is decreed for the woman. The man is not subject to the jurisdiction. The man at Leburi. The woman is cited *pena red[uplicata*?]. The woman fails in the purgation and confesses and renounces [her sin] and is whipped in the usual way. The woman withdrew.

(Hampton Lovett) Isolda the nurse of Hampton, pregnant, is suspended for contumacy. The woman is excommunicated. The woman at Rock.

(Cofton *alias* Coston, Hackett) William Balaunse of Thoneworth committed adultery with Margery Chirheye. The man is suspended for contumacy. The woman is cited. The man is reconciled. They renounce their sin with each other and are whipped in the usual way.

Things done in the church of Northfield on the Tuesday after the feast of the Apostles Peter and Paul in the year 1300.

[Then follows a brief note of a larger meeting of the clergy of the whole archdeaconry "at the said day and place" on other matters not the business of a ruridecanal chapter.]

150. Punishment for violation of sanctuary

(Trans. Douie and Farmer (eds), *Life of St Hugh of Lincoln* (1962), II, pp. 197–9)

The church afforded sanctuary to those who sought its protection and, as the following story of the action of St Hugh as bishop of Lincoln in one case shows, inflicted severe punishment on those who violated it.

Not only wrongdoers, of course, sought shelter – the background of No. 212 (c) below, for instance, is political rather than legal and in No. 110 (a) Fleta recognises that timid men seek the protection of the church who have committed no felony and he has shrewd advice to give them – but, as far as we can tell from the records, criminals avoiding arrest predominated. They were certainly a normal element and English law evolved regular procedures for dealing with them. The object was to get them as quickly as possible to emerge either to stand trial or to abjure the realm. The law is described by *Fleta* in No. 110 (a); No. 110 (b) shows it in operation; the best modern statement of the subject, based on the records of sanctuary and abjuration in the coroners' rolls, is now that of R. F. Hunnisett, *The Medieval Coroner* (Cambridge, 1961), ch. 3. cf. his *Bedfordshire Coroners' Rolls* (Bedfordshire Hist. Record Soc., XLI (1961). It would appear that most criminals chose abjuration rather than trial, but did not in fact leave the country.

After this when he had just passed through the county of Troyes, a man came to him who with groans implored his compassion. He confessed that he had been excommunicated by him, as he richly deserved, for which reason he was haunted by the dread of eternal damnation besides having had to endure almost continuous misfortune.

The cause of his excommunication was as follows. Whilst he was bailiff of certain vills belonging to the earl of Leicester, a thief had taken sanctuary in the church of the vill of Brackley of which he was reeve. The manor was in the Lincoln diocese. The lord of the manor was a great warrior, of noble blood, and related to the best families of the kingdom. Being high in the king's favour he and his men confidently usurped rights which were not legally theirs. His officials, contrary to the instructions of holy writ, "Be not just to excess", had exacted the full penalty from one who had sought the church's protection, whom they hanged, after luring him from Christ's sanctuary by a trick.

The bishop was at that time abroad, and learning of the outrage on his return, he promulgated a general excommunication of the perpetrators of the crime and their accomplices. The rest, being conscience-stricken about the sacrilege, humbly submitted to the discipline of the church, but he, shrinking from the shame of penance, left England and sought refuge with his lord in Normandy.

In fact, those who had caused the death of the victim, or had by treachery removed him from the precincts of the church, naked except for their breeches, had been compelled to dig up the already putrid corpse of the man, and placing it on a bier to carry it on their bare shoulders from the place of execution to the village, a distance of almost a mile. After taking the body and limbs which were now in a state of corruption round all the churches of the district, and being beaten outside each of them by all the priests of the chapter, they were finally compelled to bury it with their own hands, still naked as I have described, in the cemetery of the church from which they had removed the man when still living. After this they were ordered to go barefoot to Lincoln, and outside all the churches of that immense city bare their backs for the scourge and perform other similar penances which were particularly severe in winter time.

The man about whom I am speaking, although he had been one of them, refused to submit, and preferred to leave England rather than make the angels rejoice by a fitting show of penance. . . . Being unready to accept punishment in spite of his guilt, at a time when he could still have kept his position in society, from henceforth he was buffeted by the storms of adversity and sustained such losses and misfortunes, that he declared his life became a burden to him. . . . Now he submitted joyfully to a seven-year's penance, having previously scorned a shorter one.

151. Relics

(Text and trans., *Life of St Hugh of Lincoln*, ed. Douie and Farmer (1962), II, pp. 153–4 and 167–70)

Let us now continue his journey to Burgundy. . . . His willingness to embark on such a strenuous journey at the beginning of the summer heat was due to the inspiration of the Holy Spirit and not, as some scandalmongers aver, to the ties of blood and friendship.[1] This is clearly proved by his visits out of devotion to famous shrines and monasteries, including not only those on or near his route, but many a good distance from it.

It was near the time of harvest which he was wont every year to devote to contem-

[1] St Hugh was Burgundian by birth

plation, that whilst others worked hard to fill their outward storehouses with earthly corn, wine and oil, he could increase the abundance of his interior spiritual graces. He decided now to spend the whole time in religious exercises, and return, as was his custom, to the cultivation of the field of the Lord, that is his church, at seed-time.

First, therefore, at Meulan he came to the shrine of St Nicasius, where, having prayed with deep devotion and made an offering of gold, he acquired a large bone, which he removed with his own hands from the head. This acquisition caused him immense joy. Whilst on his way to Paris he turned aside to go to St Denys. Although his attempt to extract one of the teeth of St Nicasius whilst holding the holy head uncovered and keep it as a blessed relic was a failure, he did manage to put his fingers in the nostrils which had always breathed the good odour of Christ, and easily removed a delicate little bone which had separated the martyr's two eye-sockets. This he received with fitting devotion as a precious gift and pledge of God's favour, and with renewed hope that the Lord would lead him along the way of peace and salvation, with the assistance of this renowned bishop who had condescended to bestow on him a part of his very frame which had always until then remained between his most blessed eyes.

. . . Whilst I am on the subject of the relics of the saints it would not be amiss to give certain anecdotes which contribute to their glory and to the edification of the reader. The bishop had ordered to be made for him a ring of the finest gold set with precious stones, which had in the part which encircled the outside of his finger a kind of hollow jewel which he intended to use as a repository for relics. This receptacle was about the width of four fingers, and in it he had collected thirty relics of the saints.

Although he tried with deep devotion and earnestness to acquire these priceless treasures, he wanted most of all to obtain a portion of the body of that great confessor of Christ and patriarch and law-giver of monks, Benedict. This ardent desire caused him to dispatch a pleading letter to the venerable abbot and monks of the monastery of Fleury where the most holy corpse of the saintly father reposed. . . . The sequel was that the bearer of the letter returned at last, and brought to the man of desires the reward of his prayers and longings, namely one of the teeth of the saint and a large portion of the cloth in which his remains had been wrapped. He also brought a letter . . . in which the greetings and compliments of the venerable bishop were courteously returned, and sure proof was furnished as to the genuineness of the gifts which had been dispatched. Having received and read these, the man of God was filled with gladness, and immediately summoned his goldsmith who lived in his town of Banbury . . . to open and then close up again the bishop's sacramental ring (he gave it this name because he often used it at ordination and consecration ceremonies as an incentive to devotion). . . . He frequently kissed the tooth with deep devotion before having it placed in his ring.

When he was at the celebrated monastery of Fécamp, he extracted by biting two small fragments of the bone of the arm of the most blessed lover of Christ, Mary Magdalen. This bone had never been seen divested of its wrappings by the abbot or any of the monks who were present on that occasion, for it was sewn very tightly into three cloths, two of silk and one of ordinary linen.

They did not dare to accede even to the bishop's prayer to be allowed to see it.

He, however, taking a small knife from one of his notaries, hurriedly cut the thread and undid the wrappings. After reverently examining and kissing the much venerated bone, he tried unsuccessfully to break it, with his fingers, and then bit it first with his incisors and finally with his molars. By this means he broke off the two fragments, which he handed immediately to the writer, with the words, "Take charge of this for me with especial care."

When the abbot and monks saw what had happened, they were first overcome with horror, and then became exceedingly enraged. They cried out, "What terrible profanity! We thought that the bishop had asked to see this holy and venerable relic for reasons of devotion, and he has stuck his teeth into it and gnawed it as if he were a dog." He mollified their anger with soothing words. Part of his speech is worth recording. "If, a little while ago I handled the most sacred body of the Lord of all the saints with my fingers, in spite of my unworthiness, and when I partook of it, touched it with my lips and teeth, why should I not venture to treat in the same way the bones of the saints for my protection, and by this commemoration of them increase my reverence for them and without profanity acquire them when I have the opportunity?"

On another occasion, at Peterborough where the arm of the glorious king and martyr Oswald is displayed with the bones and skin, and flesh still bloody as if recently severed from a living body, he severed with a knife a protruding sinew which was pliable and flexible enough to be drawn out by whoever handled it. This he kept and preserved with great devotion. It and other holy relics which it would take too long to describe he placed in the ring I have mentioned so often. . . .

152. The lay Christian

(Trans. Douie and Farmer, *Life of St Hugh of Lincoln*, II, pp. 46–7)

To lay persons who praised this angelic way of life[1] and lamented the hindrances of life in the world, and whom he knew had neither the intention nor the capacity to follow a better way of life, he gave the following advice, "The kingdom of God is not confined only to monks, hermits and anchorites. When at the last, the Lord shall judge every individual, he will not hold it against him that he has not been a hermit or a monk, but will reject each of the damned because he had not been a real Christian. A Christian is expected to possess three virtues, and if, on the day of judgment he lacks any of them, the name of Christian will be useless to him. The name without the reality is in itself a condemnation, for falsehood is the more horrible in a professor of truth. That blessed name must really represent the virtues it implies, and all sincere Christians must have loving hearts, truthful tongues and chaste bodies."

The man of God often developed this further, by describing and defining the properties and differences of these virtues. He taught that even married people, who never rose above the natural obligations of their state, should not be considered to be devoid of the virtue of chastity but equally with virgins and celibates would be admitted to the glory of the heavenly kingdom.

[1] Seen in the practice of St Hugh himself, who was a Carthusian monk as well as bishop of Lincoln and lived as a monk of that strict order as strictly as his episcopal duty permitted.

153. The Church defied

(*Life of St Hugh of Lincoln*, ed. and trans. Douie and Farmer (1962), II, pp. 31–2)

The story of a girl excommunicated by St Hugh, bishop of Lincoln 1186–1200. Oxford was, of course, in his diocese. The date is immaterial.

A young girl at Oxford, the daughter of one of the burgesses, and already wedded to a certain youth of the same town, was inflamed by a stronger love for another youth, and deserting her husband, actually lived with him as his wife. Her husband accused her and proved the charge, and the bishop earnestly admonished her to return without delay to him. She, however, was dissuaded by her mother, who showed herself another Herodias in her wicked advice to her daughter, and declared defiantly that she would rather die than live with him. The man of God then took her husband by his right hand, and combining persuasion with threats said, "If you desire to be my daughter, obey me and give your husband the kiss of peace with God's blessing. If you do not, I shall not spare you and your evil counsellors." He also ordered her husband to give her the kiss of peace, which he would willingly have done, but the wretched girl impudently spat in his face, although he was near the altar and the bishop himself was present in the church with many important ecclesiastics and a great multitude of the faithful. Everyone was deeply shocked at such outrageous behaviour towards her husband. The bishop said very sternly, "As you have spurned my blessing and have desired my curse, my curse shall fall upon you," and immediately excommunicated her. She went home still stubborn and during the few days vouchsafed to her by the divine mercy to come to a better frame of mind, her heart became more hardened and not in the least repentant. Then being suddenly strangled by the devil, her illicit and temporary delights were exchanged for perpetual torments as she richly deserved.

154. Simon Luvel provides for his mother, 1199/1201

(*Cartulary of St Mary Clerkenwell*, ed. W. O. Hassall (Camden Series, LXXI (London, 1949), No. 138)

To all sons of holy mother church Simon Luvel of Eversden greeting.

Know ye that I have given, granted and by this my present charter confirmed to God and St Mary and the nuns of the church of St Mary of Clerkenwell in perpetual alms with my mother Matilda six acres arable of my land in Eversden: namely four acres in one field and two in the other field. Of the four acres two selions lie at Chichelidole in Litlendene two selions on Prestehol one selion near Bentli one selion in the same furlong near Wido Wiringi one selion beyond Wodeweie two selions at the door of Peter four selions at Grenedich one selion in the other field. Of the two acres there lie at Marscodeswell three selions on seven acres two selions in Grenedich two selions at Brunneweie one selion: free and quit of all worldly service and all worldly exaction due to me and my heirs for the love of God and for the health of my soul and the souls of my father and my predecessors and my heirs.

I the aforesaid Simon and my heirs will warrant and defend the aforesaid six arable acres to the aforesaid nuns against all men and women.

In return for this gift, grant, warranty and defence and confirmation of this my charter the aforesaid nuns of Clerkenwell will provide my mother Matilda with as much as she needs in food and clothing as long as she lives.

These being witness. William de Bancis and sons Eustace, William and Roger. Baldwin de St George.

155. An episcopal indulgence for contributing to repair the fabric of St Paul's, 1308

(*Registrum R. Baldock, G. Segrave, R. Newport, et S. Gravesend*, ed. R. C. Fowler (Cant. & York Soc., 1911), p. 74, trans. C. J. Offer, *The Bishop's Register* (1929), p. 209)

Ralph Baldock was bishop of London 1304–13.

Appointment for the old work of St Paul's.—Ralph, etc. We by these presents commit to you the care and custody of the old fabric of our church of London, and all the rents and revenues of whatever kind, temporal or spiritual, belonging to the same fabric or such as can be lawfully acquired in any way by your industry, to your discretion, for the remission of your sins and under due oath profferred by you before us and also under invocation of divine justice, firmly enjoining that you shall so prudently, diligently and faithfully cause the said rents to be collected and repairs to be carried out in the said ancient fabric according to your power at opportune times, that besides the reward of human praise you may be able to obtain the prize of eternal glory. Wherefore we, desiring to excite the devoted minds of the faithful for the assistance of the said old fabric by the enticing rewards of indulgences, by these presents concede to all our subjects and to others whose diocesans hold our indulgences valid, truly repenting and confessing their sins, who shall stretch out helping hands to the support and repair of the said ancient fabric according to their capacities, forty days' indulgence, ratifying moreover all other indulgences hitherto conceded for this purpose. We intimate these things severally to all whom it concerns. Given at Stepney, 27 July 1308.

156. A reformer overruled, 1236

(*Cal. Papal Letters*, I (1198–1304), ed. Bliss, p. 154)

One of the faults of the rector of Urchfont in No. 147 above was to have "farmed" his living, i.e. in return for a lump sum (which would be less than the return the "farmer" could expect over the years) to let or lease the proceeds of the benefice to someone else for a given period. Such "business" in the cure of souls was opposed by all reformers. cf. J. R. H. Moorman, *English Church Life in England in the Thirteenth Century* (Cambridge, 1955), pp. 33–4. The interest of this particular case is that the bishop of Lincoln overruled in this wholesale way by papal authority, no less, and obviously through royal influence at Rome, is the ardently reforming bishop, Robert Grosseteste.

1236, 27 April, Viterbo

Mandate to the bishop of Lincoln to allow Hugh de Patasulle, the king's clerk and treasurer, to let his benefices in the diocese of Lincoln, which, however, must be properly served.

157. Creation of a vicarage, 1304

(*Worcester Liber Albus*, trans. J. M. Wilson (1920), No. 403, pp. 79–83. The text has been preserved in this, a cathedral priory register, as well as officially in the bishop's register (probably because the prior of Worcester was normally keeper of the spiritualities of the diocese *sede vacante*), whereas the *Register of William de Geynesburgh, 1302–1307*, ed. J. W. Willis Bund (Worcs. Hist. Soc., 1907) is a calendar, not a full text.)

To all members of holy mother church to whose knowledge this writing may come, brother[1] William [Gainsborough], by divine permission bishop of Worcester, everlasting salvation in the Lord.

We make it known by these presents to all of you that recently we found that the church of Child's Wickham[2] in our diocese, which under the title of appropriation had been applied to the personal needs of the men of religion, the abbot and convent of Bordesley of the Cistercian order, by the lord Godfrey of good memory our predecessor, was destitute of the solace of a vicar; and that no sufficient provision for the support of a vicar had been arranged by our predecessor or by any one else, or was in any way existing. We being anxious to keep in view that the said parish should suffer no loss; and that the souls of the parishioners should be provided for; anxious also to obey canonical laws as we are bound to do; having first obtained the written and explicit submission of brother J. the abbot, and of the convent of the said place, sealed by their seal and now in our custody, do make order henceforth that a vicar shall be appointed in that church with whom will rest the cure of souls, and who should reside there continually; and for his support in the aforesaid church of Wykewane[3] we make order as follows:

We . . . after inquiry made in accordance with our mandate by trustworthy men, rectors, vicars, chaplains, and laity in sufficient numbers, men who were likely to have the fullest knowledge of the true value of all sources of income, sworn and straitly charged to report the true value of all the income of the said church, and of every particular of its income, such as it produces in ordinary years, do hereby order, decree, appoint, and will that the support or suitable sustentation for the perpetual vicar whose duty it is to serve the said church shall consist of the payments written below.

To wit, of a certain area in the township of Wykewane, in which is situated a certain house called the priest's house, with all the area adjacent to it; and of a certain garden defined on the western side of the rectory manse by hedges and ditches, as are now included, lying between the manse on one side and the pool of the water-mill on the other, to be satisfactorily built by the abbot and convent before St John the Baptist's day [24 June] next occurring; and of tithes, and other payments to the said church written below.

That is to say, of the tithe of wool, milk, calves, young pigs, geese, eggs, honey and bees, gardens, curtilages, land dug with spade, doves, mills of every kind, flax, hemp.

Also of all mortuary fees save only those which have to be paid in live animals.

[1] Gainsborough was a Franciscan friar
[2] co. Gloucester; dioc. Worcester, archd. Gloucester, deanery Campden
[3] Child's Wickham

Also[1] of offerings of all kinds at the altar, annuals, trentals, oblations for the dead and in general all small tithes and contributions to the altar by whatever name either now or at a later time they may be described.

Also of the tenth of meadow land hitherto paid in money.

Also of one quarter of wheat, and of one quarter of barley, pure and clean grain, to be received from the grange of the abbot and convent in the town of Wykewane every year in future on St Martin's day in the winter.

We also ordain and decree that the said abbot and convent and their successors for ever, shall pay to the vicar for the time being of the aforesaid church of Wykewane sixty shillings sterling, at the times named below, viz, on the feast of the Purification of the glorious Virgin, twenty shillings; on the feast of the Annunciation, twenty shillings; and on the feast of the Holy Trinity, twenty shillings.[2]

We further order and decree that the said abbot and convent shall repair, rebuild, or reroof the chancel, whenever it shall be necessary, and shall for the future provide sufficient books in the same.

We further order and decree that the vicar for the time being shall entertain in future the archdeacon of the place, and besides his procuration shall pay him annually half a mark sterling, on the feast of the Purification of the glorious Virgin; and that he shall be bound to find linen,[3] vestments, and other ornaments necessary for divine service in the chancel, and also to provide a competent clerk.

We also ordain that both the said abbot and convent and the said vicar and their successors shall always acknowledge extraordinary claims from time to time, and bear their share, to be divided as in future may be decided.

To this ruling we hereby add that the archdeacons of the place and their officials for the time being shall, notwithstanding any privilege whatever obtained or to be obtained by the said abbot and convent and their successors, possess the free power to correct, punish, and otherwise exercise archidiaconal powers, as they have been accustomed to exercise them in their own time and that of their predecessors over the transgressions and sins of the parishioners of the said church, and also of the ministers and servants of the said abbot and convent, if committed in the parish itself, and those of all others of whatever state and condition, who have been guilty in the parish or in the rectory manse.

That this our ruling may have its due result in every detail, and not be exposed to blame in the future, we ordain that we, and the archdeacon of the place, and our successors, and our officials, shall possess the power, without troublesome judicial proceedings, or any form of law, or any warning given, of compelling, when occasion requires, the said abbot and convent and their successors to observe all the foregoing, if in any respect, which may God forbid, they wish to infringe our ruling; and to satisfy in the matter of losses or any interests those who may be interested in this matter, by sentences of suspension, excommunication, and interdict, or any other

[1] I have slightly emended this and the next item in the light of Willis Bund's calendar (*Reg. Geynesburgh*, pp. l and lvii).

[2] i.e. on 2 February, 25 March, and (according to the year) a date in May or June

[3] lights, according to Willis Bund (*Reg. Geynesburgh*, p. 2)

ecclesiastical censure, and by the sequestration of all their property, wherever found, whether in the parish itself or elsewhere in the diocese.

We reserve for ourselves and our successors four marks sterling as procuration, from the income of the said abbot and convent in the said church, to be paid every year in future, to those who are appointed by us or our successors to visit the church, under penalties notified above.

We reserve also for ourselves and our cathedral church of Worcester the dignity in all matters due to the bishop and the cathedral, and that of the archdeacon for the time being.

Given at Alvechurch, the 3rd of the Ides of January, A.D. 1303, in the second year of our consecration [i.e. 11 January 1304].[1]

[On 20 February 1304 on the presentation of the abbot and convent of Bordesley – who had themselves been inducted as rector on 14 November 1303 (*Reg. Geynesburgh*, p. 2) – Thomas de Aldulvestre, priest, was instituted to the vicarage (op. cit. p. 129).

Thomas ran into trouble by appointing a clerk who was in minor orders and not a deacon (op. cit. p. 2). The bishop overcame this and settled another matter – that synodals were to be paid by the rector, the abbot and convent, not the vicar – in an addition to his ordinance of 11 January 1304 (op. cit. pp. 2–3).]

158. Creation of a vicarage in an appropriated church in Wales, 1284

(*Cal. Chancery Rolls (Various) 1277–1326*, pp. 286–7)

1284, 16 July, Carnarvon

To archbishops, etc. Notification that the king has granted to the abbot and convent of Aberconewey [Conway] – whose site he wills shall be transferred to Maynan [Maenan] by the assent of the abbot and convent and of their fellow abbots of the Cistercian order, by whom the king has caused the place to be visited – that they shall have and hold all the church of Aberconewey, which they previously had and held as a conventual church, henceforth as a parish church appropriated to them, with all rights of patronage and ownership, in frank almoin, with all rights, possessions and things pertaining to the said parish church both within the walls and without, with all tithes of all lands and of the sea on both sides of [the river] Coneway pertaining of old time to the said church of Aberconewey, on condition that they cause the said church to be served by two fit and honest English chaplains, one of whom shall be perpetual vicar in the same and shall be presented by the abbot and convent to the diocesan upon each voidance, and by a third honest Welsh chaplain by reason of the difference of language.[2] Witnesses: Robert, bishop of Bath and Wells, Henry de Lacy, earl of Lincoln, Richard de Burgo, earl of Ulster, Otto de Grandisono, Reginald de Grey, John de Monte Alto, Peter de Chaumpvent. Given by the king's hand at Karnarvan.

[1] He was consecrated on 28 October 1302 and the second year of his consecration would begin 28 October 1303.

[2] *propter idiomatis diversitatem*

159. A papal provision, 1295

(*Records of Antony Bek*, ed. C. M. Fraser (Surtees Soc., CLXII (1953)), No. 49)

This is offered as an example of papal provision and one need not here enter into the details. But it is not a simple case. Another party had in fact already been instituted to the living and at Rome, behind the attempt to provide, powerful Colonna influences had been at work. As his register shows, *Reg. Pontissara*, ed. C. Deedes (Cant. & York Soc.), 2 vols (1915, 1924), pp. 804–21 and 830–5, Pontissara found himself in a difficult position.

10 April 1295, Chester. *Mandate of Antony Bek, bp of Durham, as papal executor, to bp of Winchester to induct to rectory of Middleton (now Longparish), Hants.*

Mandate from bp as co-executor with [William de Louth] bp of Ely and Richard de Monte Nigro, provost of Rheims, of letters of pope Celestine V, delivered him on 10 April 1295 by Nicodemus de Faisolano, proctor of Bartholomew son of Francis de St Angelo. These letters, dated from Aquila, 2 September 1294, notify the provision by Celestine V of the same Bartholomew to the parish church of St Nicholas, Middleton, in dioc. Winchester, vacant by reason of death at the curia of mr Berard de Neapoli, papal notary, lately its rector, wherefore provision pertains to the pope. The executors, jointly or singly, are to induct Bartholomew or his proctor to corporal possession, notwithstanding that Bartholomew is also canon of Bayonne and Teano, and archd. and prebendary of Bayonne. Bp Bek instructs John [de Pontissara] bp of Winchester, to induct Bartholomew's proctor to church of Middleton within six days of request by proctor, under pain of suspension from entry of church and execution of episcopal office. Should the church have been occupied by admission of some presentee or otherwise, the wrongful detainer is to be removed within eight days. All parishioners are to pay their dues to Bartholomew alone, under pain of excommunication with reservation of absolution to the papal executors, whose rights to proceed are safeguarded. The present letters are to remain with Bartholomew's proctor, but the bp of Winchester is to certify his execution of mandate.

160. Procurations, 1281

(*Reg. W. Wickwayn*, ed. W. Brown (Surtees Soc., 1907), pp. 248–9, trans. J. R. H. Moorman, *Church Life in England in the Thirteenth Century* (Cambridge, 1955), p. 122)

To the venerable, etc. . . . his loyal sons the rectors, vicars and parish priests of the deanery of Holderness, greeting etc.

If the beginnings of the early church are called to mind it will be remembered that its members were one in faith, one in spirit, one in baptism, and that having pooled their resources they all promised to supply the wants of the poor and to regard the needs of all as their own. Moreover the robe of Christ is one and seamless, and the bride of Christ has never been divorced nor borne the reproach of being a stranger and a harlot. As the Bridegroom Himself bears witness in the Song of Songs, "My dove, my undefiled, is but one." And although there are many churches, yet are they compactly joined together in one body, so that if one member suffer all the members suffer with it, or if one church be desolate or oppressed all the others must needs share in her grief. For God Himself once spoke of the church: "I will make thee an eternal excellency, a joy of many generations. Thou shalt also suck the milk of the Gentiles and shalt suck the breast of kings." But today the church is not only without nourishment but is even abandoned and rejected, weighed down with new burdens and unwonted oppressions, and there is scarcely anyone to bring her solace in all her troubles.

For when long since, beyond the memory of living men, the archdeacon's official with the rural dean and his clerk, or sometimes with only one of them, used to visit us and our churches to hold their chapters, they came with three or four mounted retainers[1] at the most; but nowadays the official brings his companion and the rural dean his clerk, with your sequestrator in addition, and an apparitor – recently inflicted upon us by your official – and thus they descend upon us with a retinue of eight or nine for holding their chapter. In this way, not only the rectors and the vicars but also the parish priests are unduly burdened at a time when their livings have been greatly reduced by various disturbances in the realm in these latter days, while at the same time the number of poor people (to whom the goods of the church belong) is daily increasing. Thus are the clergy grieved by reason of this oppression as were the children of Israel under Pharaoh.

Wherefore we approach your grace in whose sympathy and help we have the deepest trust in Christ, beseeching you, father, of your paternal affection to restore us to that condition which previously we enjoyed.

Farewell.

(Since our own seals are not known to you we have had the authentic seal of the deanery of Holderness attached to this letter.)

161. The teaching of theology at Worcester Cathedral Priory, 1305

(*Worcester Liber Albus*, ed. J. M. Wilson), (1920), pp. 54–5)

As required by the Lateran Council of 1215 (c. 12) Benedictine houses had adopted the Cistercian practice of meeting in general chapters. That council had also (c. 11) reaffirmed the need of provision for theological teaching, which if not binding on cathedral as well as metropolitan churches, had in fact been accepted by many English cathedral chapters, including the Benedictine chapters at Worcester. Here the president of the English Benedictine general chapter, writing on the matter to the prior and convent, reveals the uneasiness of dual visitation, by general chapter and by the diocesan, and the Order's preference for the former.

You have been accustomed in your monastery to elect a prudent, fit and learned man, who is able to discharge the office of lector by reading holy scripture, and we believe that this has usually been done not only in your church by election, but in all cathedral churches, as expressly decreed by the constitutions of the holy fathers the Roman pontiffs, and we find the custom to be observed in the great majority of them.

But you in your monastery, as we have learned from the report of trustworthy persons, have now for two years abandoned a practice so sanctioned, to the prejudice of your church, the blackness of your reputation, and the loss of both seculars and regulars. Compensation for things that have been lost does not go far to supply the benefit of restoration, as is not surprising.

[1] *evectionibus*

We are desirous, to the utmost of our power, to obviate the malicious and evil reports which have for these reasons spread among people about you, and therefore advise and command you, each and all, to take pains to recall the custom, or rather the solemn and venerable ordinance, by electing some one to read holy writ and preach the divine Word, as in past times had been the continued custom, lest the diocesan be forced to apply his helping hand, and at his coming the secrets of our order should be revealed, to the exclusion of the visitors of our general chapter, which we would not wish.

162. A new cathedral at Salisbury

(a) *Laying the foundation stones of the new cathedral of Salisbury, 1220*

(*Vetus Registrum Sarisberiense alias dictum Registrum S. Osmundi Episcopi*, ed. W. H. R. Jones (Rolls series, 2 vols, 1883–4), II, pp. 12–13, trans. L. F. Salzman, *Building in England down to 1540* (Oxford, 1967), pp. 380–1. For his purpose, Mr Salzman slightly abridged the passage. I have supplied what he omitted.)

1220

On the day of St Vital the martyr, which was 28 April, was laid the foundation of the new church of Salisbury. The lord bishop had reckoned on the lord king being there on that day, and the lord legate and the lord [archbishop] of Canterbury, and many of the magnates of England, and on account of this had gone to great expense, especially to lay on a grand banquet for all who came. But on account of the talks held at that time with the Welsh at Shrewsbury the said bishop was disappointed of his hope. Since however he could not postpone the affair because a public announcement of it had been made throughout the diocese, he came to it with great devotion on the day appointed for it, accompanied though by few earls or barons, but by a great multitude of ordinary people coming from all directions. When divine service was over and the grace of the Holy Spirit had been invoked, the bishop went barefoot in procession with the clergy of the church to the place of the stone-laying[1] chanting the litany. When the litany was finished and a sermon had first been preached to the people, the bishop himself laid the first stone on behalf of pope Honorius, who had given leave for the removal of the church of Salisbury; the second he laid on behalf of Stephen, archbishop of Canterbury and cardinal of the holy Roman church, who was at that time engaged with the king on the Welsh border; the third he added to the fabric on his own behalf; the fourth stone William Longsword, earl of Salisbury, who was present, laid; the fifth Ela de Viteri, countess of Salisbury, wife of the said earl, a woman worthy of praise as being full of the fear of God. After this certain nobles, but only a few, each laid their own stones; then A. the dean, W. the precentor, H. the chancellor, A. the treasurer; and the archdeacons and canons of the church of Salisbury who were present; the multitude of people who were there acclaiming and weeping for joy and readily contributing according to the means God had given them their alms to this. In the course of time, when the nobles came back from Wales,

[1] *fundatio*

some of them came to this place and each laid their own stones, binding themselves to some definite contribution during the next seven years.

(b) *Collections in the diocese of Lincoln for the building of the new Salisbury cathedral, 1224*

(*Rotuli Hugonis de Welles, episcopi Lincolniensis 1219-1235* (Cant. & York Soc.), II (1907), pp.207-8)

"The new church was so far advanced by 1225 that on 28 September three altars were dedicated, and next day service was held, the archbishop [Stephen Langton] preaching." (Salzman, *Building in England down to 1540*, p. 381)

Hugh by the grace of God bishop of Lincoln to the beloved sons in Christ the archdeacon of Northampton and the official, deans, parsons, vicars and chaplains established throughout the archdeaconry of Northampton, greeting, grace and benediction. Know ye that we with the assent of William the dean and of our chapter of Lincoln have granted to the venerable brother R., the bishop of Salisbury, and his chapter that they may send preachers all over the archdeaconry of Northampton to get alms given them from the bounty and devotion of the faithful for the building-fund of the new church of Salisbury, and we command and strongly enjoin you to receive those preachers kindly when they come to you on account of this and help them both liberally and efficaciously. We, trusting in God's mercy, remit twenty days of the penance enjoined on them to all of our diocese (and of other dioceses where the diocesans approve) who having confessed and being truly repentant contribute their alms to the said building fund, and we grant that this collection and our period of remission shall start next St Luke the Evangelist's day [18 October] and last for a year. Given by the hand of John de Tantone, chaplain, at Banbury, on 2 October in the fifteenth year of our pontificate [2 October 1224].

163. Founding a monastery: Selborne (Augustinian canons), co. Hants., 1233

(*Charters of Selborne Priory*, ed. W. C. Macray (Hants. Record Soc., 1891), and ibid. 2nd ser. (1894))

[The bishop of Winchester buys land for the site.]

1233. Grant from James de Ochangre to Peter, bishop of Winchester, for the sum of 40 marks, of the croft called la Lyghe, which goes down by the brook descending from Cratewelle to the land which John de Achangre, the grantor's uncle, held on the west of the brook, and extends from the brook westward to the land called Thornwik; also a croft called Brodecrofte which the said John his uncle held, opposite Edithesgrove up to the croft called La Bechecrofte; also a croft which Gilebert de Wik formerly held, near Brodecrofte and near the grantor's wood. Also a croft which Ralph le Niweeman held. Also a croft called Cavelescroft extending from a corner of the croft called la Lyghe to a corner between the grantor's wood and the wood which Rob. de la Rode held, alongside of the wood of de la Rode to the land of Thomas Coterel. Also a croft which Adam le But formerly held, with two increments of land on S. and E. – in order to enlarge and make therein a religious house of the order of St Augustine.

Witn.: Richard parson of Gretham, Oliver parson of Stokes, Guy chaplain of Seleburne, John de Wyndleshore, Will. de Ho, James de Nortune, Nicholas of the Mills, Roger But, Gilbert Cunan, Gilbert de Burhunte, clerk, John de Achangre. [55]

[1233] Grant from James de Nortune to Peter, bishop of Winchester, for the sum of 35 marks "*ad me acquietandum versus Judeos*", of his water-course going down from his mill of Durtone to the wood of Will. Mauduit, with one croft called Edrichescrofte extending from the wood of the said W. Mauduit to the old ditch of Steppe, and 9 perches from the head of the said ditch, towards the E., and all the land called Stepe as it was enclosed by the old ditch up to the croft which formerly belonged to Philip of the Mills, and the said croft, and a moiety of the croft of Peter de Durtone, and a moiety of the meadow of the said Philip, with all the meadow, wood, and pasture between the said crofts and the water, to found a house of religion of the order of St Augustine, with liberty to enclose the land, and make ponds and mills, and to have a way for cars and carts up to the highway.
Witn.: mr Elyas de Derham, mr Will. de St Mary Church, mr Robert Basset, mr Humphrey de Milleirs, Robert de Clinchampe, Oliver the clerk, Roger Wacelin then sheriff of Suh.,[1] John de Venuz, Will. de Ho, John Windeshore, Will. de Bira, Gilebert the canon, Peter the forester, Gilebert de Popham, Laurence de Heiges, Hugh de Popham, Gilibert de Burhunte, clerk. [294]

[The bishop gets charter from king for the foundation, 4 May 1233. On 20 January 1234 he issued his own charter of foundation. After the necessary preparation:]

[1233] Grant from Ralph the abbot and the convent of Mount St Michael "*de periculo maris*" to Peter [de Rupibus], bishop of Winchester, of the advowson of the churches of Basinges, Basingestoke, and Seleburne with whatever benefit or pension they receive from them. [14]

1233. 9 July, 17 Hen. [III], at Wyndlesore. "Inspeximus" by Henry III, confirming the grant made by Ralph, the abbot, and the convent of Mount St Michael "*de periculo maris*" to Peter [de Rupibus], bishop of Winchester, of the advowson of the churches of Basinges, Basingestoke, and Seleburne, and of all benefit or pension from the same.
Witnesses: W[illiam de Fortibus] earl of Albemarle, Stephen de Sedgrave [*sic*] justiciary of England, Peter de Rivallis, Hugh Dispenser, Peter de Malo Lacu, Ralph son of Nicholas, Philip de Albyn', John son of Philip, Robert le Lov, Will. de Picheforde, John de Plesseto, Barthol. Peche. [18]

1233[-4]. 15 January "*xviii kal. Feb.*" At Wlvese.[2] Grant by P[eter] bishop of Winchester to the prior and convent of Seleburne of the advowsons of the churches of Basinges, Basingestoke and Selebourne, with all their free land, rents and pensions belonging to them; to hold in free alms for their own uses and those of their church.

[1] He was sheriff of Southampton from October 1232 to October 1234.
[2] Wolvesey

Witnesses: sir Walter, abbot of Hyde, sir Walter, prior of St Swthun, sir . . . [*sic*] prior of Motisfonte, Alan de Stoke, mr William de St Mary Church the bishop's official, Luke archdeacon of Surrey, Peter Russinol. [35]

[He appropriated, two days later, the churches of Selborne, Basing and Basingstoke to the new foundation, 22 January 1233–4.]

[As corporately rector of these churches, the priory was, of course responsible for the cure of souls in these parishes. At Selborne, for which there is information, it seems to have carried out its duty through a chaplain and not until 1254 to have endowed a vicarage for the purpose. The endowment does not appear to have been satisfactory and it had to be augmented in 1271–2. It was raised again after the Black Death:]

1271[–2]. 8 February "*in f. S. Edelflede virg.*", at Seleburne. Agreement [indented] before the official of the bishop of Winchester, between sir Roger de Lechelade, vicar of Seleburne, and the prior and conv. of Seleburne, for settling of a controversy respecting augmentation of the vicarage, viz, that the said vicar shall have the tithes of flax of the parish, which he had formerly demised to them amongst other tithes granted to them in payment of a pension of 100*s*, and shall be released from an annual payment of 7*s* to which he was bound by the agreement formerly made, and shall receive one quarter of corn yearly during his life; in return, the vicar covenants never again to raise any question respecting the poverty of the vicarage. [70]

1282. 17 December "*die Jov. pr. p. f. S. Lucie virg.*", in the chapel of the Holy Ghost at Basinggestoke. "Memorandum" that at an enquiry held by the official of the bishop of Winchester respecting a claim made by sir Richard, vicar of the church of Selebourne, to one quarter of wheat, one quarter of barley, one quarter of oats, and one quarter of beans, from the prior and convent of Selebourne, brother Richard de Portes, the proctor of the latter, produced an ordinance of W[ill. Raleigh] formerly bishop of Winchester, and other instruments, by which it appeared that the said allowance was granted to a former vicar, Richard le Bel, only for his own personal merits and not by reason of his vicarage; and the claimant therefore acknowledged that he had no right to it. [117]

[Continued exertion and the interest of local families (reflected in the witnesses as well as the parties to the documents) enlarged both the site and the estate of the priory:]

1233. 21 July "*die Jovis prox. post fest. S. Margarete virg.*", 17 Hen. *fil.* Joh. At Aultone. Grant from John de Venuz to the church of B. Mary of Seleburne, to Peter bp of Winchester, and to the prior and canons in that church, in free alms, of the whole moor where the Beme rises, up to the head of the fishpond, that they may make in it a fishpond as great, as wide, and as deep as they wish, and pools and mills at their will; and also his meadow called Sidenemed lying on either side of the water which comes down from Beme and all the course of the water so descending to the mill which Paulinus held of the grantor to farm, and the mill itself, and the meadow which is called Hundeshammed and which lies on either side of the water called Lachemere, which Gilbert Oyn formerly gave to William de Venuz; also the reversion of one

virgate of land in Achangre on the north of the water-course, which William de Venuz, the grantor's father, gave to Richard atte Dene in marriage-dowry with Lucy his wife, and which on the decease of the said Richard should, for want of issue, revert to the now grantor, and of which the boundaries begin at the stone bridge of Achangre towards the west, through the lands of James de Achangre up to the meadow of sir William de Mauduyt, stretching towards the east through the lands and wood of the said sir William towards Byneswerthe and up to Kyngesly and Oxeneye, and thence by the old bank which goes down to the aforesaid mill of Sydenemed and from thence the bank itself divides the said virgate from the land of James de Achangre up to the aforesaid stone bridge; also a quit-rent of a pair of gloves worth one penny from the aforesaid Richard for the said virgate, paying annually after the life of the said Richard for the said virgate ten shillings to the king through his bailiffs of Aultone.
Witn.: Roger Wasseline, sheriff of Suhamptone, John de Wyndesores, James de Nortone, William de Hoo, Thomas the Welshman,[1] James de Achangre, Laurence de Hegzes, Roger de Bradeschate, clerk, Mathew de Monasterio, Peter the forester. [160]

1234. 9 March, 18 Hen. [III], at Northampton "*per manum Radulfi Cycenstren. episc. cancell.*" Grant from the king to Peter, bishop of Winchester, of all the land and rent in the manor of Seleburne which mr Stephen de Lucy formerly held, for the enlargement of the priory and its buildings which the bishop has there founded by the king's grant, in the land which he bought of James de Ochangre, with all liberties [everywhere] and with sok and sak, thol and them, infangenethef and utfangenethef and hamsocne and blodwite, and the money paid for murder, and forstal and flemenestriche, and acquittance from all scot and geld, and all aids of kings and sheriffs and all their ministers, and from hidage and armies and scutage and tallage and shires and hundreds and pleas and quarrels and ward and wardpeny, and the works of castles and bridges and enclosures of parks, and carriage and sumage, and building and repairing of royal houses, and all other liberties and free customs.
Witn.: J[ohn], earl of Chester and Huntingdon, J[ohn de Laci], earl of Lincoln and constable of Chester, W[illiam de Fortibus], earl of Albemarle, S. de Segrave, justiciary of England, Philip de Albiniaco, Hugh Dispenser, Godfrey de Craucumbe, John son of Philip, Geoffrey Dispenser, Geoffrey de Cauz, Barthol. Peche, John de Plesset[is]. [304]

[1234] Grant from James de Akhangre to John the prior and the canons of Seleburne, in free alms, of all the moor where the Beme rises, and the land round the same moor to make a fishpond[2] as great, as deep, as wide, and as long, as they wish, and mills and pools at their will, and sufficient land all round the fishpond for dragging and drying their nets.
Witn.: Roger Wascel', then sheriff of Suhamptes[ire], John de Windeshore, James

[1] "Wallensis"
[2] *vivarium*

de Nortone, William de Ho, Thomas Wallensis, Laurence de Heyes, Roger de Bradesete, clerk, Mathew de Monasterio, Peter the forester. [136]

[1234] Release from Hunfrid de Gollega to sir John the prior and the convent of Seleburne, for the sum of 30 marks, of all his right in the whole tenement and in one messuage in the vill of Seleburne.
Witn.: Roger Wascelin, sheriff of Suthamtpteshire,[1] John de la Stane, John de Venuz, John de Windlesore, James de Nortune, Thomas de Giminge, William de Ho, Thomas de Venuz, Gilebert de Popham, Laurence de Heyes, Hugh de Popham, Gilebert Cunan, Roger de Bradesete, clerk. [82]

[1234] Release and quit-claim from Hunfrid de Gollege to the prior and canons of B. Mary of Seleburne, for the sum of 13 marks of all his right in one virgate of land in Seleburne, which his brother, Gilebert de Gollega, formerly held by his gift, of the king in villenage, according to the custom of the manor.
Witn.: Roger Wacelin, sheriff of Suhamshire, John de la Stone, John de Venuz, John de Wildesore, James de Northune, Thomas de Giminge, William de Ho, Thomas de Venuz, Gilebert de Popham, James de Achangre, Alan de Haueclige, Gilebert Cunan, Roger de Bradesete, clerk. [71]

[1234] Release and quit-claim from Richard de Suanemere to the church of B. Mary of Seleburne, and the prior and canons there, for the sum of 33 marks, of all his right in one virgate of land in Seleburne, as the right of their church, which Gilebert de Gollega, his uncle, formerly held in Seleburne, by the gift of the king, in villenage, according to the custom of the manor.
Witn.: Roger Waceline, sheriff of Suhamtesire, John de la Stone, John de Venuz, John de Wildesore, James de Northune, Thomas de Giminge, William de Ho, Thomas de Venuz, Gilebert de Popham, James de Achangre, Alan de Haveclige, Gilebert Cunan, Roger de Bradesete, clerk. [3]

1234. 6 December "*die Veneris, scilicet die S. Nich'i*", 19 Hen. *fil.* Joh.[2] Release from Ameria, wife of the late Adam Gurdon, with the consent of her sons, to the prior and canons of B. Mary of Selebourne of all her right in heybote and housbote and common in their wood at Selebourne, and in the common pasture of Durton, which wood and pasture they have by the king's gift, of which the pasture lies between the vills of Selebourne and Thornwyke, extending in length by the water which goes down from Selebourne to the priory on the one side, and near the lands of the prior and canons, of which one is called la Wrthe, and through the lands of Thomas de Bercham, near la Middelwrthe, up to Lytecoumbe, on the other side, namely on the north, and abutting on two crofts of the prior and canons, one called Thornwyke and the other Farncrofte, at the east end, and on the vill of Selebourne at the west end; saving to all her men of Selebourne common with all their own animals in the

[1] sheriff in 1233–4
[2] [*sic*] but St Nicholas's day, 6 December, fell on Wednesday in that year

said pasture as in times past; releasing also all her right in all the land which Thomas de Bercham held near the water of Durtone, which lies between the land called Thornwyk and the ditch of the prior and canons which goes down to the said water through the middle of the meadow which was Philip of the Mill's, and in all the land which Gibert de Gollegze formerly held in Selebourne, saving an annual rent of 4*s* 10*d*; and her heir, when he comes of age, shall make his own charter of release which he has sworn to do, "*tactis sacrosanctis*", or else, if any dispute be made, eighteen marks which have been given for this release, are to be repaid; she and her eldest son, Adam (who seals with her), binding all their lands in Selebourne and Tistede for guarantee of fulfilment.
Witn.: sir Stephen, prior of Motesfonte, mr Elyas de Derham, John de Venuz, Laur. de Hegzes, Matthew de Monasterio. [24]

[The seal, so to speak, was set by another royal charter of 10 April 1234 and by a papal bull of 1 September 1235 confirming the foundation.]

[Thereafter the priory managed its own affairs. As rector of Selborne, it had a canonical responsibility for the poor of the parish and almost immediately it acquired a small endowment specifically towards this expense:]

1235. 19 Hen. *fil.* Joh. In the chapter of the priory of Seleburne. Indenture by which Roger de Cherlecote grants to J. the prior and the convent of Seleburne in perpetual fee-farm a messuage with a croft in Hakangre Bynorthebroke, on condition that they distribute annually among the poorer persons of the parish of Seleburne, for the soul of himself, his wife Isabella, and his ancestors, six pairs of shoes, each of the value of 5½*d*.
Witn.: John de Venuz, James de Nortune, knts, Henry de la Charite, John de Borhunte, James de Achangre, Gilbert Conan. [171]

[Next year, 1236, it added to its properties. Hugh de Bromdean, who had already had to raise money on his estate to meet his debts, sold out most of it to Selborne priory for a joint annuity for himself and his wife and for Bartholomew his son and heir:]

1234. 22 June "*die Jovis pr. ante Nat. S. Jo. Bapt.*", 15 Hen. *fil.* Jo. "*a coron. apud Westminster*".[1] Grant [indented] from Hugh de Bromdene to Alan son of Warin for the sum of 40 marks "*ad aquietandum me versus merum Judeum de Cauntebrigge*", of 140 acres of land in Bromdene, of which 32½ extend to the quick-hedge of Hentone, 3 are below the grantor's garden before his gate, together with the garden next on E., saving free ingress and egress to his land with cart and horse; and the rest of the said 140 acres he is to make up to the said Alan from his demesne in Bromdene, viz, from the whole of Sendrie londe, the whole of White Helle, and the whole of Hokescrofte; he grants also all his meadow in the same village, and 24*s* of quit-rent, of which Roger Picot pays 2*s* and Hervic 2*s*, William son of Herbert 3*s*, Ralph son of Robert 3*s*, Osilla de Tistede 6*d*, Nich. de Belewe 18*d*, the heir of Will. de Cadamo[2] 2*s*, for all services, Peter de la Stane 4*s* and his service, Walter Sahirman 2*s* and his service, the land which was Hugh Joye's 2*s* and service, and the land which was

[1] i.e. from his second coronation in 1220
[2] i.e. of Caen

Alured's 2*s* and service. Also he grants all his wood in Bromdene and all the aforesaid for the term of 40 years, reserving to himself and his heirs husbote, heibote, and forbote; also he grants the patronage and gift of the church of Bromdene; reserving to himself and his heirs 6 oxen, 2 cows, 60 two-year old sheep, and 10 pigs free in the pasture.
Witnesses: sir John de Venuz, sir Thomas de Gemiges the coroner, John de la Bere, Thos de Bromdene, Nicholas de Belewe, Roger Picot, John le Fraunkelein, Will. son of Herbert. [24]

[*c.* 1235] Grant from Hugh de Bromdene to Alan son of Gwarin of all his land of Bromdene, together with the advowson of the church, viz, that land which the said Alan held to farm of him for 40 years for the sum of 40 marks which he paid for him to the Jews; paying an annual quit-rent of one mark. And for this grant the said Alan gives him yearly during his life 12 quarters of wheat, 4 quarters of barley, and six marks.
Witnesses: Nich. de Blakedune, John de Clatforde, Hugh de Ho, Roger de Puncharde, Roger Picot, Thos de Putte, H. de Brams. [9]

[1236] Grant from Hugh de Bromdene to the church, the prior and canons, of St Mary of Seleborne, in perpetual alms, of his chief messuage of Bromdene and 62 acres of land, and also all the remainder of his land in Bromdene which he had farmed to Alan son of Warin for the term of 40 years, together with the advowson of the church of Bromdene, and with his wood which lies between the wood called Winely and the wood of Wudecote, and with the whole meadow belonging to the same land, after the completion of the term of the said Alan; paying to him and his heirs an annual quit-rent of 4*s*, and saving the service due to the king for the fifth part of one knight's fee, which service the men of the tenement, both free and villeins, are to pay.
Witnesses: John de Venuz, Roger Wascelin sheriff of Suthamptes', John de Windleshore, Rich. de Cardeville, Thos de Gyminges, Will. de Ho, James de Nortone, Laur. de Heyes, Gilebert de Popham, James de Achangre, Giles Cunan, Thos de Bromdene, Robert le Butillir. [16]

1236. 9 June "*die lune pr. ante f. S. Barn. ap.*", 20 Hen. *fil.* Joh. Fine in the king's court at Gloucester before Will. of York Will. de L'Isle, Ralph of Norwich, Thurstan le Despenser and Ralph de Chandos, judges itinerant, between John, the prior of Seleburne, plaintiff, and Hugh de Bromdene, defendant, respecting one messuage and 60 acres of land in Bromdene, by which the said Hugh acknowledges all the said land (which he had given to farm to Alan son of Warin, for the term of 40 years) together with the advowson of the church, to be the right of the said prior and his church of Seleburne as that which they have by his gift, to hold in free alms, rendering annually a quit-rent of 4*s*; and for this acknowledgment the said prior grants to the said Hugh and Maud his wife 6 loads[1] of wheat and 3 of barley, and 4 marks, annually during

[1] *summas*

their lives, provided that on the death of either of them one moiety of the payment be discontinued; and also to Bartholomew de Bromdene, son and heir of the said Hugh, 6 quarters of wheat and 1 of barley and 2 marks annually for the term of his life. And this agreement was made in the presence of Alan son of Warin, Nich. de Blakedone, and John his brother, who released to the said prior, etc., all their right in the said land and in the said advowson, for the sum of £100. [11]

[Both Hugh and his wife Maud appear to have been still alive in the 1240s but in much reduced circumstances. In the same decade the priory rescued another member of the Bromdene family from Jewish creditors:]

[*c.* 1240–50] Grant from Hervic de Bromdene, with the consent of his wife Juliana, to the prior and canons of Seleburne, for the sum of 40 shillings "*ad terram nostram redimendam versus omnes Judeos*", in free alms, of one acre of land with a messuage situate thereupon, between the messuage of John le Frankelain and that of Sibona, and extending from the highway northwards, in Bromdene; releasing also all his pasture for 100 sheep and 4 oxen and all his pigs in the pasture and wood of the said prior and canons free of herbage and pannage, which he had in their manor of Bromdene, saving only pasture for 4 oxen.
Witnesses: Rob. de Ho, Will. de Dunstigele, Will. de Draitune, Henry de la Putte, James de Acangre, Matth. de Monasterio, Will. Baion, Rob. de la Rode, Roger Picot. [51]

[By the fourteenth century the family appears to have sunk to humble status (*V.C.H. Hants.*, III, 46–7).]

[In the following year again, 1237, in return for a right to present to a canonry in the priory, the priory added to its Selborne interests:]

1236[–7]. 12 January "*secundo idus Jan.*" Decree of arbitration by E[lias] de Derham, canon of Salisbury, in a suit brought by authority of the pope before the dean, chancellor, and succentor of Sarum, between J., the prior, and the convent of Seleburne, J. de Nortone, knt, and G. de Burhunte, clerk, about a moiety of all the tithes issuing from the demesne of the said J. de Nortone, and from the dowry of his mother Alice; viz, that the said G. de Burhunte shall receive the said tithes during his life, offering yearly for them, on Easter day, to the mother church of Seleburne, at the high altar, 2*s*; that on his resignation of them, or death, they shall wholly and entirely remain for ever to the said prior and convent; and that on Burhunte's death or resignation the said J. de Nortune and his heirs shall present a fit clerk, who shall be admitted into the convent as a canon, and so on from time to time; and if any dispute arise as to the fitness of the presentee, it shall be determined by the official of the bishop.
Witn.: sir John de Venoiz, knt, mr John de Dertef[ord], mr H., vicar of Hertele, John Terri, vicar of Hamelede, John de Caneford, chaplain Roger de Cherlecote, Hugh de Popham, Will. de Venoiz, sir J. de Windleshore, James de Ochangre, Mathew de Monasterio, Thomas de Chabb', Reginald de Wiche, clerks. [326]

[Similarly in 1261, in return for a right to present to another canonry in the priory, it added to its interests in West Tisted:]

1261. 3 January "*iij nonas Jan. pontif. nostri anno vij*", at the Lateran. Bull from pope Alexander IV addressed to the dean and chapter of Sumallinges, diocese of Chichester, directing them to protect the prior and convent of Seleburne in the possession of the church of Westistede, the revenues of which do not exceed 10 marks, and which the said prior and convent have acquired for appropriation, at the presentation of the patroness Joan, who was the wife of Rob. le Hout. [274]

1261. 28 February "*ij kal. Marcii*", in the great church of Winchester. Indenture tripartite of a decree of arbitration by Constantine de Mildehale, official of Boniface, archbishop of Canterbury, in the diocese of Winchester during the vacancy of the see, in a controversy between Ralph de Camays, knt, and the prior and convent of Seleborne, respecting the right of patronage of the church of Westtisted, claimed by the said Ralph in virtue of his lordship of the manor of Westtisted, and who has thereupon presented mr John de Brideport, clerk, to the said church. The decree assigns the patronage absolutely to the said prior and canons as having been given to them by Peter de Rupibus, bishop of Winchester; but inasmuch as the said church is endowed with goods issuing from the said manor, and in order that the said nobleman[1] may be duly honoured by the said prior and canons[2] ordains that he and his heirs shall always have the right of presenting one fit clerk to be admitted as a canon into the said convent, supplied by him with clothes and other necessaries at his admission, who shall there celebrate for the souls of the said nobleman and his ancestors and successors; and the said prior and convent shall pay to the said mr John de Brideport 100*s* annually until they promote him, or procure his promotion, to some better ecclesiastical benefice; and the said nobleman shall execute a deed of quit-claim and confirmation of the patronage to the said prior and convent. [234]

[1261] Release from Ralph de Cameys, knt, to the prior and canons of Seleburne, in free alms, of all his right in the advowson and patronage of the church of Westtystede.
Witn.: sir Hugh son of Adam, the grantor's steward, sir Henry de Brettone, sir Henry de Chylderle, his knights, sir Thomas de Gemynge, sir Robert de Poppham, sir Adam Gurdone, Will. Huse, Rich. de la Bere, John de Burhunte, Thomas Wallensis, James de Akhangre. [249]

1261. 18 August "*die Jovis pr. p. f. Assumpt. B.M.*", at Schulebrede. Release from Ralph de Cameys, knt, to the prior and canons of Seleburne of all his right in the land called Trendledecroft and Rykemannesdone, and in the advowson and right of patronage of the church of Westtystede, which they hold by the gift of the lady Joan la Hood; granting them also the right of having 100 sheep in his pasture in the same village; and confirming all the other lands and tenements which they have there of his fee.

[1] *nobilis* [2] *condigna honoris munificentia veneretur*

Witn.: sir Hugh son of Adam, the grantor's steward, sir Henry de Brettone, sir Henry de Chylderly, his knights, sir Thomas de Gymmingges, James de Achangre. [256]

[The muniments calendared by Macray show the priory continuing to be active in business, adding to and rounding off its interests in a variety of transactions with neighbours, great and small. For example, in 1250 it acquired a mill in return for "brotherhood and benefits" and sold a corrody to Roger de Cherlecote, whom we met in 1235 (see above) as the friend of the poor of Selborne parish; in 1270 or earlier it gave thought to its water supply.]

[*c.* 1250] Grant from Robert Gaugy, with the consent of his wife Muriel, to the prior and canons of Seleburne, in free alms, of all his mill of la Sydenemed, which he had of the said prior and canons, with the pasture of the said meadow after haymaking; and the said prior and canons grant to him and his wife the brotherhood and benefits of their house for ever.
Witn.: sir John de Venuz, sir Thomas Makerel, Will. Huse, James de Molendinis, John de Burhunte and Andrew his brother, Nich. Svele, Mathew de Monasterio, James de Ackangre, Will. de Arundel de la Wyke. [353]

1250. 3 February "*a die S. Hillarii in tres sept.*", 34 Hen. *fil.* Joh. Fine before the judges at Westminster (Roger de Thurkelby, John de Gatesdene, Gilbert de Prestone, John de Cobbeham, Alan de Wassand, and Will. de Wyltone), by which Roger de Cherlecote conveys to John, the prior of Seleburne, and his church, in free alms, one messuage, one mill, and thirty-five acres of land in Bradechete, 10*s* of rent in la Wyke from the whole tenement which Will. de Arundel held of the said Roger in la Wyke, and one messuage, one acre of land, and three acres of meadow, in Akhangre; and the said prior covenants that he and his church shall provide every week for the said Roger and Isabella his wife, during their life, eighteen canonical loaves, twenty-eight servants' loaves, fifteen flagons[1] of the drink of the convent, fourteen flagons of the second beer, and 12*d* for meat[2] and pottage: the allowance to be reduced by one-half on the death of either of them. [177]

[*c.* 1270, or earlier?] Grant from William de la Rode, with the consent of his wife Alice, to the prior and convent of Seleburne, for the sum of 6*s* 8*d*, of a piece of land one perch in width, from the head of the well of Chyldewelle, through the middle of the grantor's garden, as it is marked by boundaries, which land the said prior and convent are bound to enclose from the beech above the well to their grove; to be held by them for the purpose of making a head in the well, "*ad lavacrum suum sustinendum*"; and for this the said prior and convent are to inscribe the names of the said William, his father and mother and wife, in their martiloge, and once in the year to celebrate for them.
Witn.: sir Adam de Gurdun, sir Robert de Poppham, knts, Henry Wyard, Robert Gaugy, James de Achangre, John Marescall de Burhunte, Walter Drueys, Robert Marescall de la Wyke, Will. Coterel de la Rode. [366]

[1] *lagenas*
[2] *ferculis*

164. Names "in religion", 1206

(Trans. Cheney and Semple (eds), *Selected Letters of Pope Innocent III* (London, 1953), p. 83)

To Brother Augustine, regular canon of the church of St Mary of Norton.

Because before you professed the monastic life you had from baptism borne the name Henry, and because later your prior decreed that you should be called Augustine as having by your profession been changed into a new man, you have humbly supplicated our apostolacy to deign either to restore you the first name or to confirm the second, since you fear that after death you may derive no benefit from the prayers which your loving brethren will make for you under the second of the two names.

On this matter we have thought fit thus to answer your devotion: you can with confidence keep the name given you at the time of your profession, just as we also unhesitatingly keep the altered name which, by the will of God, was bestowed on us when we undertook the office of apostolic servitude.

Ferentino, 30 July, in the ninth year of our pontificate.

165. A code of monastic signs

(Trans. H. F. Berry, in *Journal of the Royal Society of Antiquaries of Ireland*, xxii (Dublin, 1892), pp. 107-25)

The following code was used at St Thomas's Abbey, Dublin, a house of Augustinian canons of the Congregation of St Victor, in the thirteenth century. On the subject of monastic silence, D. Knowles, *The Monastic Order in England* (1950), pp. 453-6.

Of signs of certain things

Of those that specially appertain to the divine office

For the general sign of a book, extend the hand, and move it as the leaf [of a book] is usually turned.

For the sign of a missal, having first made the general sign, add the sign of the Cross.

For the sign of the text of the gospel, in addition, make the sign of the Cross on the forehead.

For the sign of a lection, press the finger to the hand or breast, and when drawn along a little, make it fillip as one who, by means of his nails, might try to remove wax fallen from the candle of a reader upon the leaf [of a book].

For the sign of the responsory, place the thumb beneath the joint of the forefinger, and so make it fillip.

For the sign of the antiphon, or of a responsory versicle, place the thumb beneath the joint of the little finger, and so make it fillip.

For the sign of allelujah, raise the hand and the tops of the fingers bent; move as if to fly, on account of the angels, because it is called their song.

For the sign of sequence, raise the hand bent, and in moving it from the breast, invert it so that what was first upward may be downward.

For the sign of tract, draw the hand over the stomach from below, which signifies long, and place the hand against the mouth, which signifies singing.

For the sign of the book which is read at nocturns, having first made the general sign of a book and of a lection, in addition place the hand on the cheek.

For the sign of the antiphonary, having first made the sign of a book, in addition bend the thumb, on account of the curves of the notes – the "neumæ", which are so bent.

For the sign of the Rule, add that you grasp the hair hanging over the ear with two fingers.

For the sign of the hymnary, in addition, bring forward the thumb and the finger next it, their tips being joined, [by] which the present time [or] what is first is signified.

For the sign of the psalter, in addition place the hollowed hand on the head, on account of the similitude of a crown which a king usually wears.

Of those which appertain to food

For the sign of bread, make a circle with both thumbs and the two next fingers.

For the sign of bread which is made with water, in addition, place the inside of one hand upon the outside of the other, and move the upper hand round as in mixing or moistening.

For the sign of bread, which is commonly called "turta", in addition make a cross through the middle of the palm, because this bread is wont to be so divided.

For the sign of half a loaf, bend the thumb of one hand with the finger next it, as though you would make a half circle.

For the sign of beans, place beneath the first joint of the thumb the top of the next finger, and so cause the thumb to stand out.

For the sign of millet, make a circuit with the finger, because it is so stirred with a spoon in a pot.

For the sign of pottage cooked with herbs, draw one finger over another, as one does who cuts up herbs for cooking.

For the general sign of fish, imitate with the hand the motion of a fish's tail in the water.

For the sign of cuttle fish, divide all the fingers one from another, and so move them together.

For the sign of an eel, shut up each hand as one who holds and presses an eel slipping away.

For the sign of a lamprey, simulate with the finger on the cheek the hollows that a lamprey has under the eyes.

For the sign of salmon, in addition, making a circle with the thumb and forefinger, place them round the right eye.

For the sign of a pike, in addition stroke the surface of the nose with the hand, because this fish has a long snout.

For the sign of a trout, in addition draw the finger from brow to brow, which is the sign of a woman, because the trout is pronounced to be feminine.

For the sign of crispels, take hold of the locks of hair with the hand, as if wanting to make them curled.

For the sign of cheese, join both hands obliquely, as one who presses cheese.

For the sign of cheese cakes, having first made the sign of bread and of cheese, bend all the fingers of one hand, and so place the hollowed hand on the surface of the other.

For the sign of rusks, having first made the sign of bread, imitate with two fingers the twistings which are made in them.

For the sign of milk, press the little finger with the lips, because an infant sucks milk.

For the sign of honey, make the tongue appear for a little, and apply the fingers as though you wanted to lick them.

For the sign of wine, bend the finger, and so apply it to the lips.

For the sign of water, join together all the fingers, and move them obliquely.

For the sign of vinegar, rub the throat with the finger, because vinegar is felt in the throat.

For the sign of fruit, especially the pear or apple, inclose the thumb within the other fingers.

For the sign of cherries, in addition place a finger under the eye.

For the sign of a raw leek, extend the thumb and finger next to it joined together.

For the sign of garlic or radish, extend the finger across the mouth a little opened, on account of the savour which is perceived from them.

For the sign of mustard, place the thumb beneath the first joint of the little finger.

For the sign of a bowl, bend three fingers a little and hold them up.

For the sign of a dish, extend the hand more widely.

For the sign of "justa" (or due allowance of wine), incline the hollowed hand downwards.

For the sign of a glass beaker, having first made the sign of a bowl, in addition, place two fingers round the eye.

For the sign of the cloak, hold its edge with three fingers (that is), with the little finger and the two next.

For the sign of an upper tunic, hold its sleeve with the same fingers.

For the sign of the mantle or furs, hold the edge of them.

For the sign of the tunic, expand all the fingers of one hand, and contract them placed on the breast, as one does who gathers up wool.

For the sign of a shirt, hold the sleeve of it.

For the sign of drawers, in addition draw the hand on the thigh from below, as one who puts on drawers.

For the sign of stockings, hold one and add the sign of drawers.

For the sign of a coverlet, make the sign of a tunic, and in addition draw the hand on the arm from below, as one who covers himself with a coverlet.

For the sign of a bolster or pillow, lift the hand and the tops of the fingers bent, move as if to fly, afterwards place on the cheek as one is accustomed to do when sleeping.

For the sign of the girdle, bring round finger to finger, and from each side bring together the fingers of each hand as one who ties a girdle round him.

For the sign of metal, strike the fist roughly with the fist.

For the sign of a knife, draw the hand across the middle of the palm.

For the sign of the sheath of a knife, place the top of one hand in the other hand, as if putting a knife into a sheath.

For the sign of a needle, having first made the sign of metal, feign as though you held the needle in one hand and the thread in the other, and that you wanted to put the thread through the eye of the needle.

For the sign of the stylus, having first made the sign of metal, with the extended thumb and forefinger imitate one who writes.

For the sign of tablets, fold both hands together, and separate them as if opening tablets.

For the sign of a comb, draw three fingers through the hair, as one who combs it.

For the sign of an angel, make the same sign as for allelujah.

For the sign of an apostle, draw the right hand downwards from the right side to the left, and again from the left to the right, for the "pallium" which archbishops use; which is also the sign of a bishop.

For the sign of a martyr, place the right hand on the neck, as though you wanted to cut something.

For the sign of a confessor if he be a bishop, make the same sign as for an apostle; if an abbot, make the sign of the Rule, namely, by taking hold of the hair.

For the sign of a holy virgin, make the sign for a woman.

For the sign of a festival, first make the sign of a lection, and bring forward all the fingers of each hand.

For the sign of an abbot, grasp the hair hanging over the ear with two fingers.

For the sign of a monk, hold the hair with the hand.

For the sign of a cleric, bring the finger round the ear.

For the sign of a canon Regular, with the thumb and forefinger imitate one wishing to bind his breast with the lap of the shirt.

For the sign of the laity, hold the chin with the right hand.

For the sign of a prior, feign with the thumb and forefinger to sound the small bell.

For the sign of the greater [prior] in addition extend the hand which always signifies anything great.

For the sign of the sub-[prior], extend the little finger, which always signifies what is little.

For the sign of the sacrist, with the hand imitate a hand ringing a bell.

For the sign of the librarian and chantor, lift the inner surface of the hand, and move as if giving the sign to sing together.

For the sign of master of novices, draw the hand obliquely through the hair over the forehead, which is the sign of a novice, and place the finger next the thumb under the eye, which is the sign of seeing.

For the sign of the chamberlain, imitate the counting of money.

For the sign of the cellarer [imitate] one holding a key in his hand, and as if turning it when fixed in the lock.

For the sign of the gardener, bend the finger [and draw it to you] as one who draws a rake along the ground.

For the sign of the almoner, draw the hand from the right shoulder to the left side, as the strap of a wallet is usually carried by beggars.

For the sign of the infirmarer, place the hand against the breast, and add the sign of seeing.

For the sign of the refectioner, make the sign of refection.

For the sign of the keeper of the garners, with both hands joined, feign as though you wanted to pour corn into a vessel.

For the sign of an old man, draw the hand straight through the hair over the ear.

For the sign of a youth, move the little finger to the lips.

For the sign of a fellow-countryman or blood relation, hold the hand against the face, and place the middle finger on the nose, on account of the blood which sometimes flows from it.

For the sign of speaking, hold the hand against the mouth, and so move it.

For the sign of silence, place a finger upon the closed mouth.

For the sign of hearing, place a finger over the ear.

For the sign of not knowing, wipe the lips with the finger.

For the sign of kissing, place the first finger on the lips.

For the sign of robing, catching the robe with the thumb and next finger on the breast, draw it downwards.

For the sign of disrobing, draw it upwards.

For the sign of eating, with the thumb and forefinger imitate one eating.

For the sign of drinking, move the finger bent to the lips.

For the sign of assent, lift the hand moderately, and move it not inverted, but so that the outer surface may be upwards.

For the sign of negation, place the tip of the middle finger under the thumb, and so make it fillip.

For the sign of blood-letting, strike on the arm with the thumb and middle finger, as one who lets blood.

For the sign of seeing, place the finger next the thumb under the eye.

For the sign of washing the feet, turn the inner parts of both hands to one another, and so move the tips [of the fingers] of the upper hand a little.

For the sign of good, place the thumb on one cheek and the other fingers on the other, and make them gently sink on the chin.

For the sign of evil, having placed the fingers spread out on the face, imitate the claw of a bird drawing something to it in tearing it in pieces.

For the sign of anything which has already been done, hold the hand equally against the breast, so that the inner part of the hand may be turned up, and so move it upwards still more from the breast.

166. An unruly monk, 1317

(Translated in *Worcester Liber Albus*, ed. J. M. Wilson (1920), pp. 65–8; the Latin original has since been printed by W. A. Pantin, *Chapters of the English Black Monks*, Camden Series (London), I (1931), pp. 178–80)

The treatment seems to have worked. After four months the monk, Simon of Defford, was taken back by Worcester.

To the reverend father in the Lord, by the grace of God the lord abbot of St Peter's, Gloucester, brother John, the humble prior of the cathedral church of Worcester, and the chapter of the same place, greeting and sincere charity in the Lord.

In the halls of the house of God it becomes and behoves those who serve together in the dress of our holy religion to walk in harmony, and to preserve in all things the bond of peace. But in our community there is a certain brother who, by his violent language, has greatly disturbed the peace and the quiet intercourse of the brethren. We have borne with it for many days, carrying this burden on our weary shoulders, in the hope of some amendment to come, of which, however, we see no signs. Many circumstances therefore, indeed urgent necessity, and the fear that such rebellion and unreasonableness may, if unpunished, set to others a pernicious example, and give them audacity in disobedience, compel us to think of some remedy.

When, therefore, recently we were carefully considering how to correct the excesses of our brother, and restore quiet in our community, there came among other things to our recollection that laudable statute, which in our last general chapter, held at Northampton, was drawn up almost precisely for chastising this sort of disturber of peace.[1] The statute referred to was, therefore, read aloud in our chapter, and a public inquiry was then made at the meeting as to the intolerable behaviour of the said brother; and it was found by the larger and saner part of the chapter, indeed by the whole convent, that the brother we have indicated was a perturber of peace, disturbing our customary quiet. We, therefore, by common consent decreed that this state[2] of things must be put an end to.

We hoped that our brother could be forced to penitence and amendment in your monastery more effectively and in accordance with the rule than anywhere else; and, therefore, we sent our brother and fellow-monk, sir John de Harley, to you with our letters of credence; and he in our name, by word of mouth, pleaded with your fatherly heart that you would admit the said brother for a time to perform his penance in your monastery, for his amendment and our quiet, and also for the honour of our order. To this request, as we have learned from the tenor of your letters, you have courteously consented.

For this consent, in addition to the reward which you will receive in the sight of God for your conspicuous obedience in this matter to the presidents and prelates of our order and to their statutes, we also convey to you our thanks, to be expressed in manifold actions.

. . . After being entertained among you as a guest for one night in any way you think best, let him on the morrow have a bed assigned him in some part of your

[1] This does not seem to have survived, but see *Chapters of the English Black Monks*, ed. Pantin, I, p. 179, n. 2, and II (1933), p. 52.

[2] The text is uncertain (ibid. I, p. 179): it should probably read "decreed that he should be sent out at once".

common dormitory; and after that let him be admitted in the chapter house in presence of all. Let him then be conducted outside, and, while the chapter meeting goes on, let him have a fixed place assigned him in your cloisters apart from the novices; and meantime let the brethren be informed of the reason of his coming. Thenceforward let him take his place in the convent as a novice not professed, and be placed last but one among the younger priests on the left side of the choir. When he has been instructed by some guardian as to your mode of chanting and reading in the church, let him take his share, as you may arrange, in the work of divine service, along with the rest of the juniors. Then, if it should seem to you expedient, let him be placed in order for everything except masses; we do not intend to impose on him the celebration of the solemnity of the mass until he has established peace with his neighbours and himself. In other matters let him do whatever he is asked to do, but not interfere at all with anyone else's work. He should dine only in the refectory; and on no account let him drink wine. Let him sleep in the dormitory; not go outside the cloister; and nowhere, except in the presence of some guardian of the order, hold conversation with any one, whether a stranger or known to you. Let secret confabulations in[1] the same way be forbidden; it will not be expedient, in a place of silence and quiet, to hear his noisy lips and braggart tongue.

Be good enough, if you please, when you see the right moment, to let us know concerning any signs of penitence and improvement in him, as soon as they seem to be established, and how he behaves in obeying the rules laid down; and we will certainly arrange for his further treatment by lightening, or if need be increasing, his burden, as his conduct may require.

If during the time he is with you he should be ill, treat him in all respects as you would treat one of similar position in your own community. It only remains to say that as to his expenses for the whole time of his sojourn with you we will fully satisfy you whenever you wish, according to the terms of the statute referred to.

May the Most High for ever guard your kind paternity.

167. Testimonial for a candidate for admission to a monastery, 1323

(*Worcester Liber Albus*, ed. J. M. Wilson (1920), No. 1008 (pp. 207–8))

Brother John of Worcester, monk of Glastonbury, and precentor, to the most holy prior and convent of Worcester, greeting.

I thank you, my lord prior and reverend father, that it hath pleased you to send me your fatherly letter, and to make trial of my humble services and reverence.

In that letter you have signified to me that you would be glad to receive Robert de Weston as a monk, seeing that he is commended for his learning and his character, had you not heard, somewhat doubtfully, that he comes of servile stock.[2] It is this doubt that you wish should be cleared up by my answer, addressed to yourself and the convent jointly; and that the clerk should himself be sent with my letter of

[1] Here too the text is uncertain (ibid. p. 180): it should probably read "with him be forbidden your brethren".
[2] *de servili genere*

testimonial, should I, after diligent examination, think him worthy to be admitted among you.

Your most blessed meeting may know certainly that the father of the said clerk holds land under our abbot in Weston, and that it is free land, not serf.[1] This fact is attested and asserted by the joint evidence of the cellarer of our house, the bailiff of the place, and other trustworthy persons who know. He possesses a creditable knowledge of letters[2] and is commended by our mr Edmund, and the scholar-monks now in our house. By the process of learning he will know more of song than he knows at present; and by practice in singing he will be able to improve his voice. Moreover, the said master and scholars, in speaking of his behaviour in study, and our neighbours in speaking of his good character when living at home, agree about him. He himself, the bearer of this letter, is worthy, as I judge, on the evidence of such high testimony, to be associated with your college.

And now that he has been so recommended, I commend myself to you and to your prayers. I beg your holiness to be pleased to absolve, and to commend to God, the soul of brother John de la Heeth, a name written on my heart.

May God in His mercy vouchsafe to keep you all in safety.

[Robert was admitted on 11 November 1323.]

168. A legate's powers, 1263–4

(*Cal. Papal Letters*, I (1198–1304), pp. 396–400)

The circumstances of the appointment of Gui Foulquois, cardinal bishop of Sabina, as legate to England in 1263 were even more exceptional than those implied in the appointment of any legate, and in fact he never landed in England,[3] but the following record even in digest shows how extensive the powers of a legate could be.[4]

1263 Orvieto 22 Nov.	Exhortation and mandate to Guy bishop of Sabina, papal legate in England, to execute his office, and procure peace and tranquillity to the king and realm, in which dissension has arisen between the royal family and the barons and others, to the injury of royalty and danger of the kingdom; some prelates have been seized, despoiled and imprisoned, collation to benefices is made by those who have no right, and in many ways ecclesiastical liberty is infringed, and crimes and excesses are committed. The legate is ordered to apply such remedies as he shall see fit in England, Wales, and Ireland.
ditto	Monition and mandate to archbishops, bishops, abbots, and all prelates in England to receive Guy, bishop of Sabina, as papal legate, and obey to his advice and orders.
12 Dec.	To Henry III, stating that the chief object of sending the legate is that the king and his house may be restored to their former position, and the

[1] *liberam non nativam*
[2] *literaturam laudabilem*
[3] cf. *Councils and Synods II (1205–1313)*, ed. F. M. Powicke and C. R. Cheney (Oxford, 1964), pp. 693–4; more fully in Powicke, *King Henry III and the Lord Edward* (Oxford, 1947), chaps 10–11
[4] Powicke, *King Henry III and the Lord Edward*, p. 454

kingdom quieted. The pope desires the king to receive the legate favourably and follow his advice.

13 Dec. The like to the queen.

The like to the earls and barons of the realm.

[?]14 Dec The like to Edward, the king's eldest son.

[n.d.] The like to Simon de Montfort, earl of Leicester, who, according to the report of some persons, is the chief among the disturbers of the realm.

12 Dec. Notification to the king of France that he has received the ambassadors, and letters of him and his queen, and the next day determined to send the bishop of Sabina to England, Wales, and Ireland, and urging him to assist the legate, who was attached to him when in a lower office, in whatever way he can, so that the king and his house being restored, ecclesiastical liberty may be preserved and peace return to the kingdom.

15 Dec. The like to the queen of France.

22 Nov. Commission to Guy, bishop of Sabina, papal legate, investing him with full powers to act in the pope's name, even in matters not, perhaps, appertaining to his office of legate.

ditto Faculty to the same to punish archbishops, bishops, heads of religious houses, exempt or not, convents, chapters or colleges, and all ecclesiastical persons who do not obey him in regard to his mission by suspension, citation to Rome, and deprivation.

ditto Power granted to the same to summon to his presence princes, prelates, and others, to make such orders and injunctions, and to demand their aid, as may be necessary to the success of his mission, and to compel obedience by ecclesiastical censure, any papal indult to the contrary notwithstanding.

1 Dec. Faculty to the same to cite persons of his legation to appear before him, even though he be beyond the sea.

ditto Faculty to the same to relax oaths taken by the king, the queen, their sons, Edward and Edmund, and any persons ecclesiastical or lay, and especially the oath said to have been taken by the queen and her sons with regard to their return to the realm.

24 Nov. Faculty to the same to apply, by himself or deputy, such ecclesiastical censures against prelates, converts, nobles and all persons and bodies of the realm, as he shall see fit.

ditto Faculty to the same to relax sentences of suspension, excommunication, and interdict; to remit injuries done to the Roman church, and to admit those who have committed them to the favour of the holy see; to collect troops and march against those who oppose his mission, and to use ecclesiastical censures against them as he shall see fit.

22 Nov. Mandate to the same to warn and induce all prelates, and nobles, and other clergy or laymen to keep their oaths of fealty to the king, and to dissolve and abjure all conspiracies and confederations made by them, keeping none of their statutes, even though they, the king, queen, and their sons, have

sworn to do so; also to compel the said prelates by sentence of suspension, and laymen, by depriving them of their fiefs and other goods which they withhold from certain churches of the realm and others, and to use any other spiritual or temporal coercion. Prelates so suspended are to be summoned to appear before the pope to receive a further sentence.

27 Nov. Mandate to the same to preach a crusade against the prelates and nobles of the realm who rebel against the king or the legate, granting to those penitents who directly or indirectly assist such crusade the same pardon of sins that is granted by the general council to those who go to the help of the Holy Land, with faculty to commute vows, even those for Jerusalem, for this object.

22 Nov. Mandate to the same to warn and induce prelates, nobles, and all other clergy and laymen of the realm, under pain of suspension and deprivation, to give up to the king all his cities, fortresses, lands, towns, castles, goods, and rights, no appeal being allowed; and to deprive, as he shall see fit, the clerks, brothers, sons, and nephews of those who resist him, of their benefices and honours, any grants or conventions to the contrary notwithstanding, by which he is to declare, if expedient, that the king, queen, and their sons, are not bound.

27 Nov. Power to the same to compel, as above, the Teutons and others who have assisted the rebels in England, applying sentences of excommunication and interdict, notwithstanding any papal indult to the contrary.

ditto Mandate to the archbishop of Cologne and his suffragans to obey whatever may be enjoined them by the above legate in regard to his mission in England, in which they are to assist him; if not, the pope will confirm whatever sentences the legate may issue against them.

19 Dec. Power to Guy, bishop of Sabina, papal legate, to deprive those secular clerks who are disobedient to him in matters concerning his mission of all papal favours granted to them, compelling by ecclesiastical censure the executors of the papal letters not to carry out their provisions.

27 Nov. Power to the same to exercise ecclesiastical censure against any who in any way injure him or his household, unless they make amends; and against places where such injury is done, unless the lords of those places, being laymen, make amends.

13 Dec. Declaration, that the legate's special commissions are not to interfere with the general object of his mission, which he is to prosecute fully and freely.

30 Nov. Licence to the same if obliged to leave England to return as often as the circumstances of his mission may require it; and to exercise his office even when not in England.

ditto Licence to the same to exercise his office even if he be hindered from entering the realm.

1 Dec. Order to the same that, even after the discords in England have ceased, his office of legate, and his commission on other matters, shall endure until he is recalled by the pope.

ditto	Similar order in regard to his powers of granting dispensations in certain cases, and other ways of fulfilling his mission.
22 Nov.	Power to the same to deprive religious of any order of their indults and privileges, if they refuse to obey him.
27 Nov.	Faculty to the same to compel by ecclesiastical censures Friars Preachers, Friars Minors, and other religious to do whatever he thinks will assist his mission.
1264 19 March	Licence to the same to relax a hundred days of enjoined penance to those penitants who attend his preaching of the crusade against those who oppose him.
1263 13 Dec.	Faculty to the same to grant to those who preach the crusade against the rebels power to grant a relaxation of forty days of enjoined penance to penitents who come to hear them.
ditto	Licence to the same to grant a relaxation of a year and forty days of enjoined penance to those penitents who attend conferences, congregations, solemn feasts and masses, and translations of saints, held and celebrated within and without the limits of his legation.
22 Nov.	Licence to the same to relax a hundred days of enjoined penance to those who attend his preaching, and a year and forty days to those present when he consecrates altars, or churches, or blesses nuns.
13 Dec.	Licence to the same to grant a relaxation of forty days of enjoined penance to those penitents who assist in building churches.
22 Nov.	Faculty to the same to grant dispensations, as shall seem to him expedient in furthering his mission, to three clerks of his legation, being illegitimate, but not sons of an adulterous, incestuous, or religious parent, to minister in the orders which they have received and be promoted, even to a bishopric, provided they are of good conversation, and otherwise fitted for the office.
24 Nov.	Faculty to the same to grant dispensations by himself or others to clerks of illegitimate birth (as above) to be ordained and hold benefices, but not bishoprics, provided they reside and take such orders as their benefice or dignity requires.
26 Nov.	Faculty to the same to grant dispensations to religious of illegitimate birth (as above) to be ordained and promoted to dignities and administrations of their order.
ditto	Licence to the same to grant dispensations to religious persons of his legation, of any order, who have committed simony during his mission.
ditto	Faculty to the same to grant dispensations to prelates and ecclesiastical persons of his legation, who have incurred irregularity by excommunicating others verbally, contrary to the constitution of pope Innocent.
ditto	Faculty to the same to grant dispensations by himself or others and enjoin penance on ecclesiastics, regular or secular, on account of any irregularity which they have contracted during his legation, by receiving orders or

ministering, when excommunicate or under sentence of suspension or interdict.

ditto Faculty to the same to absolve those prelates and monks who have incurred sentence of excommunication by disobeying statutes made for their monasteries by pope Gregory, and to dispense with them on account of irregularity contracted by joining in divine offices while under such sentence, a penance being enjoined them.

22 Nov. Faculty to the same to absolve those who have been excommunicated by judges delegated by the pope, some of whom have died, and have not been succeeded, others are not accessible, and the jurisdiction of others has expired; satisfaction being first made by the persons concerned.

ditto Faculty to the same to grant dispensations to ten persons within the limits of his legation to hold a plurality of benefices, provided that the churches are properly served.

ditto Faculty to the same to grant licence to noble women, with a suitable company of women, to enter monasteries of any order, once a year during his legation, for purposes of devotion, provided that they do not spend the night therein.

ditto Faculty to the same to grant dispensations to four noble persons, related in the fourth degree of kindred or affinity, to intermarry.

24 Nov. Faculty to the same to make provision to five fit persons of benefices, prebends, or dignities, in cathedral or other churches of his legation; any papal indult or statute to the contrary notwithstanding.

22 Nov. Faculty to the same to cause his clerks, to whom provision has been made in cathedral or other churches, to be received as canons, and have prebends provided for them; any statute as to the number of canons or any papal indult to the contrary notwithstanding.

23 Nov. Faculty to the same, to confer, by himself or others, on fit persons the benefices, with or without cure of souls, dignities and parsonages, void by the death or resignation, during his absence from Rome, of clerks in his retinue or service as legate, any statute or indult to the contrary notwithstanding.

ditto Faculty to the same to appoint one person to a canonry of Narbonne, and another to one of Le Puy, and cause them to be provided with prebends.

24 Nov. Indult to the same that clerks in his service may receive the fruits of their benefices and dignities, except daily distributions, while non-resident, any custom or statute to the contrary notwithstanding.

ditto Mandate to the same to cause to be paid to his clerks, being non-resident (as above), the fruits of their benefices and dignities.

169. Pluralism: Archbishop Pecham to Pope Nicholas III, 1280

(*Registrum epistolarum Johannis Pecham*, ed. C. Trice Martin (Rolls series, 1882–5), I, pp. 137–8 (No. CXVI). The translation is that of R. K. Richardson, in *Archaeologia Aeliana*, 3rd series, IX (1913), p. 100, completed and in certain respects corrected.)

To the most holy father and lord N[icholas], by God's grace supreme pontiff of the sacred Roman and universal church, brother J[ohn] by divine permission priest of the church of Canterbury with filial reverence kisses for the blessed feet. The eye of your illustrious consideration, most holy father, is not unaware how, taught by your holy instruction, I would have proceeded to extirpate the unbridled audacity of some, nay rather of many, who neglecting to obtain apostolic dispensation occupy very many benefices with cure of souls. Which pestilence was the more incurable in that it had slowly spread into many and since a superior rarely or never censured this evil, the statutes of the council of Lyons on it being rejected, it was simply thought lawful. Nor was it easy to reduce suddenly to modest poverty men of high birth, affluent and accustomed to honours. While therefore with combined severity and mildness I was taking thought concerning the fulfillment of this your – nay rather the divine – desire, I was very greatly comforted by sir Anthony, called Bek, very trusty secretary of the king of England, who on 3 August, by sufficient proxy, submitted to my will his status in the province of Canterbury as to benefices with cure of souls. Of which, when I inquired the number, I found from his proxy that he had five only with cure of souls in the province of Canterbury. One, belonging to the patronage of a certain priory, I adjudged should be conferred on the spot. Three of the remaining, in lay patronage, and the fourth too, about which there is dispute between a clerical and lay patron, I have thus far left in his hands until I am instructed by your wisdom what to do, because I am publicly assured that your Clemency is disposed to grant grace of dispensation as well to him as to certain other royal clerks. Wherefore I beseech your Piety, whose memory often consoles my distress, that you will deign to relieve the suspense of my mind in this matter, resting assured that with a little help I shall achieve your Clemency's intention in this matter, God willing, which by trying to be severe I should not have achieved or would not achieve in future. This assurance I none the less give your lordship, that I have not received and will not in future receive into the grace of episcopal honour without papal dispensation anyone having a plurality of benefices with cure of souls unless this fault has been purged. The Lord preserve your holy sublimity for his holy church for a long time.

170. Furthering a cause at the papal court, 1281

(*Reg. Thome de Cantilupo*, ed. R. G. Griffiths and W. W. Capes (Canterbury & York Society, 1907), pp. 273–6. The translation in C. J. Offer, *The Bishop's Register* (London, 1929) has been useful in a number of points.)

To our proctors staying at the Roman court. To masters William Brun and John de Bitterley greeting. Although word has passed between us before and an account by letter followed afterwards upon the same matter, i.e. of "visiting" every one of the cardinals, we think after deliberation that the burden of debt and the poverty of the bishopric do not permit this; yet, because we understand, know indeed, that affairs in the curia are not advanced at all unless there are visits general and particular, we send you on that account for the expediting of our affairs by letters of merchants of Pistoia one hundred pounds sterling to be received in sterling or *gros* of Tours. Which sum of money, though it seems little, can nevertheless be useful if carefully distributed, which in the judgment of some can be done in this way: viz, that sir Hugh, the English cardinal, should have thirty marks, sir Gerard, cardinal, our auditor,[1] ten pounds, and his household five marks. Sir Matthew Ruffus, cardinal, ten marks, sir Jordan, cardinal, ten marks, the vice-chancellor, fifteen pounds, the auditor of objections,[2] ten marks, B. de Neapoli and another notary who is particularly outstanding and particularly intimate with the lord pope, twenty marks in equal portions; the chamberlain of the lord pope ten marks, the usher of the lord pope, forty shillings sterling.

To others it seems that five marks can be deducted from the sum set aside for the vice-chancellor, so that he has ten marks only; from the two notaries and the chamberlain of the pope they can subtract seven and a half marks so that each of them has as much as the other. And so of the hundred pounds there will remain 33½ marks.[3]

To others it seems that it would be a good thing to bear in mind the pope, with whom the archbishop (from whom appeal is being made) is on familiar terms, to the extent of forty or fifty marks, first taking out of the list as many people as would together receive that amount of money. But to us it seems that the middle way is more profitable and honourable, though if necessity compels it, let the pope be considered in some way which will please him on whom it is recognised all favour depends. This however which we write about the pope we have no mind for, unless for lack of its being done our cause against St Asaph and our other affairs were to be manifestly in danger. For which reason we should very much like you to present forty or fifty marks, or jewels to that amount, to the said lord rather by raising a new loan than that you should subtract any part of the aforementioned sum. For contracting which loan we are not sending you our signet because we do not believe that it is necessary for us to do this this time. The merchants of Pistoia, we believe, will, to oblige us, lend us on any sort of bond of ours that amount of money. But if it is not possible to provide for our needs through them or our other friends, then you may take out of the hundred pounds for the lord's use[4] as much as you consider expedient, distributing what is left of the said money amongst the others as shall seem expedient for advancing our cause and our other affairs. In the cause against St Asaph let us hold in the main to the rule of the defendant, whose instinct is to drag out the cause as long as possible. In the aforementioned cause, however, in which we have an acceptance lately drawn up in legal form of the appeal from [the decision of] the lord archbishop of Canterbury, we do not wish to hunt for shameful and doubtful subterfuges with which to sway the mind of the judge or such things

[1] i.e. the judge delegated to hear the bishop's cause
[2] *auditor contradictorum*
[3] The arithmetic is faulty, but could be corrected by assuming a copyist's error and reading fifteen marks (instead of pounds) for the vice-chancellor in the first scheme.
[4] *ad opus Domini* – taken in the context to be the lord pope

as might render us suspect in his eyes or by which danger might threaten us if we are sent back to the former judge: a thing which perhaps might be preferred by our adversary. We wish instead to avoid the manifold dangers while the cause is at the aforesaid court; so long as our expenses incurred in sending a modest mission to obtain a decision[1] are first refunded to us, or at least claimed with sufficient force, before he from whose decision we are appealing defers to our appeal; on account of that, as in this method of distribution, with which as we have stated above we are in more agreement, there are 33½ marks left over for distribution, we very much wish our lord the Spanish cardinal (to whom we are writing) to have ten marks and sir Benedict, cardinal, and sir James, cardinal, or William, the French cardinal, whichever of these at the time of distribution is friendlier with the lord pope and in the promotion of our affairs is able to exert more influence for us, to have ten marks, indeed eleven marks. What is left over after these we leave you to deal with jointly, for one or more other visits or for other necessary expenditure.

After the distribution, though, we should like our envoys to return to us with the utmost speed, with your letters recounting what has been done and the attitude of the recipients, along with other news worth mentioning.

Because we are (praised be the Most High) so restored spiritually and improved bodily that our body suffices these days for the labours, troubles and duties of our office, we propose to return home about the feast of St Michael if the Lord allows, especially because the lord king has now written twice to us about this since Easter. And if you send back one of our envoys or someone else to us to tell us the exact state of our cause we shall be able to send back to you our pleasure in writing before our return by him or another from Fontaine, where we shall then be. Indeed we do not want you to retain even one of our envoys for too long, since messengers sufficiently reliable and faithful return from the curia every day, by whom you will be able to tell us what you have to say and we thank you for having reported the state of affairs at the curia to us by such hitherto.

We are indeed sending you the contents of the letters in which we write as you ask, and in the light of them you will be able to speak more circumspectly with them. Mr Adam de Fileby, according to what we have heard, will arrive at the curia soon. In what frame of mind he is, though, towards us we do not know at all.[2] If in addition to the amounts distributed[3] and necessary expenses four marks can be paid to mr E. de Warefelde[4] as salary, then by all means let it be done; that too among other things you might tell us about. And because in addition to the ten marks which you have received from us and which you have expended on difficult business of ours, you have spent eight shillings sterling and three shillings and one penny of *gros* of Tours, as we understand from a certain schedule of yours sent to us, we very much want you to recompense yourselves from the money sent to you, if it can be done conveniently for us.

If you can distribute the said money to better advantage than is set out in any of the

[1] *ad impetrandum*
[2] Relations were strained, cf. *Reg. Cantilupe*, pp. 244, lxix, and index, *s.v.* "Fileby".
[3] *distribuciones*
[4] cf. *Reg. Cantilupe*, p. 281

ways mentioned, then in the name of the Lord do as will be most useful to us, provided there is agreement about what is done. Farewell. Given at Brynum on 16 June, A.D. 1281.

171. The affairs of Dunstable priory, 1272–95

(*Annales Monastici*, ed. Luard, III (Rolls series, 1866), pp. 253–60, 263–7, 274–5, 277–280, 282, 285–7, 289–91, 299–300, 302, 305–6, 313–15, 317, 321, 325, 336–8, 341–2, 354, 358, 364–5, 370–1, 374, 377, 387–91, 393, 395–6, 398, 402)

Extracts from the chronicle under these years relating to the priory's affairs and to the weather in these years.

1272

... The same year, on the feast of All Saints, we bound ourselves on behalf of Ralph Pirot to the merchants of Cahors for six score marks. And they had our wool from the Peak, namely at 8 marks the sack until the said money was paid to them. We had the said Ralph's income from Harlington and Wenerugge, and incurred a very great loss by so doing.

... In the same year and on the same day [St Edmund the Confessor's day, 16 November] died John the parson of Harlington, who held that church for twelve years, and we presented mr William de la Mare to it. Ralph Pirot opposed our presentation. You will find the process about this in the following year.

... The same year on the morrow of St Fremund's day we bound ourselves and our successors to pray every day in the mass *de Domina* in the convent specially for the soul of John de Crachele thus, "Have pity we beseech thee on the soul of thy servant John", etc. Also we promised that for the ten following years we would have celebrated by one of us each week three requiem masses for the soul of the said John and three masses *de Domina* namely *salutationem*. And we deputed our fellow canon, brother John de Waltre to perform this office, and he began on the morrow of St Dunstan's day and duly completed it. Also for the soul of the said John we admitted to our almshouse Simon, a blind clerk from Westone, who remained there a very long time at our expense [namely for ten years[1]].

Mr John of Houghton and Gerard of Ely, executors of the said John with full powers of administration, pardoned us more than 134 marks as is contained in their letter. The schedule too of our indebtedness for that amount and more they restored to us, protesting that satisfaction had been given them for the whole amount owed by us to the said John from the beginning of the world.

1273

... The same year we leased Lidlington church for 5 years at 18 marks a year; and in addition we gave to their proctors 5 marks for palfreys.

... The same year the roof of our church of Dunstable was renewed at the expense of the parishioners, namely from the altar at the transept to the west door on the north side. Henry Chadde met the greater part of the cost of it.

[1] inserted later

. . . The same year we built a windmill on Schykes Acre.

. . . In the same year many people died in our district, and especially parsons, vicars and clerks.

. . . And our total income at that time was £107 a year, according to the taxation of mr Constantine and G. of Taunton.

. . . In the same year and at the same time Ralph Pirot was imprisoned in London because a certain merchant had appealed him.

. . . The same year, in March, there was a very hard frost and it lasted a long time.

1274

. . . We granted by deed from the chapter to Wyvian de Chetendone that we would admit one canon in succession in his name forever; and he gave us 60 marks.

. . . The same day we granted the fruits of Lidlington church for that year to Martin Pecham for 20 marks; and when they were stored in the barn these fruits were damaged and wasted by a certain John [ ] and his men, so that the said Martin got nothing from them.

. . . In the same year, on 23 October, Simon, our sixth prior, died; and he was prior for 11 years and 9 months; and at that time the house was burdened with debt totalling [ ].

. . . The same year we acknowledged before the dean of Lincoln that we owed mr John of Houghton 20 marks for corn, goods and other things which we had obtained on credit from him when he was alive and afterwards from his executors. And we paid the said 20 marks to the dean and chapter of Lincoln in accordance with the said mr John's bequest . . .

1275

. . . In the same year we sold our wool from the Peak in advance for a period of five years, namely at 9 marks a sack. We received as earnest money 30 marks. From this we paid 20 marks to the chapter of Lincoln on behalf of mr John, for which see above, and 1 mark as penalty.

. . . The same year, within the octave of the Nativity of the Blessed Mary, an earthquake was felt all over England; but it lasted for a short time.

The same summer we spent 100 marks on buying corn.

. . . The same year we granted Richard, the son of John Duraunt, 1 mark from our chamber until provision should be made for him by means of an ecclesiastical benefice.

The same year we took 100*s* from the oblations of St Fremund and bought oats with it . . .

1276

. . . At the same time we granted John of Elstow a room in our house and he gave us at most 20 marks, with the hope however of a larger gift . . .

1277

We sold John Duraunt all the wool from the Dunstable area, namely at 6 pence the woolfell, to be had at this price until he had in full 158 marks, 3 shillings and 11 pence worth. From the said money we paid 100 marks 44 shillings and 11 pence for the crusading tenth, 23 marks to Martin the clerk for Lidlington, and to the said John 32 marks we owed him.

The same year the executors of Peter de Radenhore pardoned us seven-score marks, and we granted the deceased special mention which is entered in our book of obits.

. . . At the same time our parishioners at Tebworth had us summoned before the said archbishop at St Neot's. And John, called Poleyn, one of the parishioners, appeared and asked our proctor, extra-judicially as it were, that we should have divine service celebrated in Tebworth chapel three days a week as used to be done formerly; or at least that we should restore to the said parishioners the 36 acres of land with the appurtenances, which their forbears, as is said, had given to the mother church of Chalgrave for that purpose. And it was so agreed between the aforesaid John Poleyn and our proctor that, on their plaint and every ground of action with regard to the aforesaid being dropped, we would as an act of friendship do in respect of the aforesaid what justice indicated. And this was done from prudence, because the said archbishop favoured the other side in this case.

Bartholomew Young of Dunstable died, and he had bequeathed 40 shillings to the high altar. Also 10 marks, for the celebration of two anniversary masses in our church. Also he bequeathed 10 pounds for the pittances of the convent, to be taken in rent. These pounds too prior William lent for the use of the cellarer, so, that is, that the pittancer should get 20 shillings a year from the cellarer, until the aforesaid ten pounds was paid in full; of which in his time 10 shillings and no more was paid. In return for this gift, the convent granted that the aforesaid Bartholomew and his wife were to have on their anniversaries the service and corrody of two professed canons.

The same year our manor of Catesby was leased to William the parson's brother for the term of 20 years, namely from Michaelmas 1277; in return for 12 marks according to the terms of the cirograph made between us on this.

The same year on the feast of St Thomas the Apostle we granted our manor of Stoke on a lease, namely from Michaelmas 1278 for the term of 20 years, in return for 5 marks p.a., and we received 25 marks for the entry . . .

1278

. . . Edelina de Bradewin had a writ of covenant for arrears of her corrody; we made peace with her.

Robert Ferrares, of St Albans confirmed to us lands and tenements which were his father, Robert Cheltone's in the parish of Studham, or elsewhere; and we gave him half a mark.

. . . The same year we conveyed for the term of 13 years our tithes at Brassington and Atlow, in return for 200 marks received in advance. And we made three records of this.

The same year Roger, the bishop of Coventry, confirmed the church of Bradborne with all its chapels to us. And he procured for us the confirmation of the Coventry and Lichfield chapters for this. In return for these things we gave the almonry of the bishop the aforesaid 200 marks. It was formally declared however by the bishop and by us that the said payment was made on account of a certain long-standing sequestration, which the same bishop said he had made in the said church of Bradborne.

. . . That winter there was neither snow nor ice in our district.

1279

. . . The same year and month [May] there was terrible thunder; trees were uprooted in many places and borne elsewhere; men were carried away in the clouds; buildings collapsed; pools of water too were dried up, and crosses reduced to fragments.

. . . The same year brother John, the archbishop, visited the diocese of Coventry and Lichfield. He, finding us sufficiently protected by patrons' collations, bishops' appropriations and chapters' confirmations, as well as papal confirmations and ratifications in respect of the church of Bradborne with its chapels, pronounced that we had canonical entry therein, and confirmed it to us by archiepiscopal authority. The same year we gave 40*s* a year from our chamber to mr Walter of Wooton who was the proctor and promoter of the confirmation . . .

1280

. . . And because the house was at that time excessively burdened with debt it was unanimously conceded by the bishop, prior and convent of Lincoln that many deductions should be made by head and members; and they should hold good until they were revoked again by the community. And this was done.

Our friend John Duraunt for the sake of concord gave 5 marks on his own account to the said archdeacon [of Bedford] for the palfrey he was asking for, that the installation of the prior should [not][1] be hindered.

. . . The same year a hard frost began on St Vincent's day [22 January] and lasted for forty days, so that all cultivation of the soil was stopped . . .

1281

. . . In the same year and at the same time we granted our place at Gledley to William de Chaurugge for the term of his life for 1 mark p.a., reserving to ourselves the greater trees. And he gave us 15 marks in advance. The same year we received from him 25 marks for corrodies.

. . . The same year we sold to Thomas the son of John Duraunt 14 small white loaves, 7 coarse loaves and 7 cobs and 14 gallons of better ale every week for the rest of his life, for 40 marks.

. . . The same year there was heavy snow and very hard frost. London bridge was for the most part broken; Rochester bridge likewise. And in other places throughout England on account of the hardness of the frost.

Near Biddenham bridge the ice broke under a certain woman and she was stranded on a floe; and from there she was carried resting firmly on the water as far as Bedford bridge: nor could anyone come to her aid. At Bedford bridge the ice broke and the woman was not seen again.

[1] supplied, as *praepediretur* would seem to require a negative

1282

... We bought of Robert Ingolf a certain part of his wood at Buckleshore for 30*s*. And we bought another parcel nearby the year before from him.

... We bought 1 acre of land at Buckleshore from William fitzWilliam: and it belongs to our fief and is within our land.

... The same year, on the day of St Peter's Chair [22 February], we granted and gave William Atte Hoo and Alexandra his wife certain corrodies in bread, ale and other things which are contained in their charter. And we received from them on account of these things 45 marks ...

1283

... The same year on the feast of All Saints mr Walter de Ludeford, principal executor of mr Peter de Radenhore, pardoned us all the money owed by us to the said mr Peter in any way from the beginning of time.

In the same year and at the same time we sold John de Ludeforde a certain corrody for his lifetime for 25 marks.

... The same year we caused to be enrolled in the Fine roll of 11 Edw. I: It is granted to the prior of Dunstable that for the 100*s* he owes the king for the escape of John le Peyvur and the 46*s* 8*d* he owes the king for arrears of the fifteenth, and for 1 mark he owes the king for a writ, and for 20*s* he owes the king for a trespass, he may pay the king 60*s* p.a., one half at Michaelmas and the other half at Easter ...

... The same year on the day of SS Vedast and Amand, John Duraunt of Dunstable laid on a great feast in Dunstable for the aforesaid lord of Caddington and certain people of importance in the neighbourhood, among whom, contrary to the accepted practice of our monastery, was our prior. But he could be excused for doing this because he was greatly indebted to the said John and so dared not offend him.

... The same year, because of the heavy rain which was very nearly continuous in the summer, almost all the sheep grazing in folds in shut-in valleys caught such dampness and grew so fat inside that a general mortality of sheep ensued. So that in the Dunstable district we had barely 200 sheep at the end of the following March. Our sheep in the Chilterns and the Peak, however, stayed healthy and vigorous. A remedy for the scab, which for the previous seven years had afflicted all the sheep of England generally we learnt of, though late in the day. We made up a certain ointment from stale fat, quicksilver and verdigris; and with it we anointed wherever the scab showed itself and the itching soon ceased. But it availed nothing against the illness caused by the damp.

1284

... The same year we gave Henry de Weyville about 14 marks for the redemption of the rent of 14*s* 10*d* we owed him annually for lands in Houghton.

In the same year William and Richard, sons of John Duraunt of Dunstable, incepted in Arts at Oxford; which John, their father, celebrated by feasting a large company.

. . . The same year we bought from Benedict Sporon a certain croft of arable and certain headlands of meadow which he held of us in Wadlow.

. . . The same year Robert son of Alan granted us in pure almoign 1 virgate of land in Stokehammond which we held of his fee by the gift of John Hasting. And we gave the said Robert 2½ marks for this.

. . . In the same year we had in the Peak only 5 sacks and 20 stones of wool; of which at least 2 sacks were from tithe; at which we were astonished and displeased, more especially because we had there in that shearing the wool from all our own sheep, 1200 by the long hundred.

. . . The same year the winter was very mild, so that the older of us had not hitherto seen its like.

1285

. . . In the aforesaid eyre we granted sir William de Cateby, the clerk of sir Roger Loveday, justice, a pension of 1 mark a year to be drawn on our chamber, until a suitable ecclesiastical benefice should be provided for him by us. And especially because the same William was useful to us.

The same year, we received from Philip Knyth for corrodies 30 marks, which were spent on harvest-work . . .

1286

. . . The same year the abbot of Dale[1] compounded with us over tithes in the Peak which we were demanding from him; and an agreement was drawn up between us before ecclesiastical judges subdelegate . . .

1287

. . . The same year to forestall the machinations and evil deeds of the Preaching Friars in Dunstable we caused Thomas our doorkeeper to buy a messuage, once Robert Francis's, in Dunstable next to the ground of the said friars; and by the said Thomas we were enfeoffed with the said messuage, lest the said friars enlarged their bounds against our will. And the chirograph between the said Thomas and the seller of the messuage is in the court of the lord king. And as a result of that transaction we were heavily burdened with yearly corrodies and other things.

. . . Immediately after the feast of All Saints, that year, the said prior of Dunstable visited in person his place at Bradborne and found in the granges there much grain of every kind on account of the abundant harvest there was generally throughout England that year. And the number of sheep there at that time amounted in all to 800, by the long hundred. The said place was extremely burdened with debt, owing to the shortage of corn and other mischances which had happened in that place in past years. The little wood, however, to the north, which brother Henry of Newton, a canon, had planted there a little time before with ash trees and other trees of divers kinds, was high by this time and very delightful to look at.

The same year there was such an abundance of produce that long after the following

[1] Dale or Depedale, co. Derby

Easter a quarter of wheat was being sold for 20 pence, a quarter of oats and of beans for 12 pence.

In the winter of that year there was very serious flooding from the rains and the North Sea from the Humber to Yarmouth overflowed its usual limits and for a breadth of sometimes three leagues, sometimes four whatever it found it submerged. An enormous multitude of men, sheep and beasts of burthen died by drowning.

1288

... The same year the summer was too dry and warm, as it had not been for many years, and a very great mortality of men followed. The winter was very cold and frost-bound, and there was heavy snow.

... The same year the abundance of produce continued, and a quarter was sold for the same price as in the previous year ...

1289

.. In the same year we bound ourselves to keep John de Badelesdene, a clerk; and we received 20 marks from him.

... The same year, specially on account of the aforesaid plea, we granted 20*s* p.a. to Roger de Hechem, 20*s* to Henry Spigurnel also, to Walter of Aylesbury too 20*s*, so that they might give their attention to our affairs, as is contained in their bonds.

In the same year we granted Henry Spigurnel our manor of Stoke, saving to Robert and Walter, clerks, the term of years they had in it.[1] Subsequently the said clerks granted their term of years to the said Henry.

The same year the parishioners of Dunstable completed two pinnacles on the north front of the church, and they likewise repaired the completely ruined stone ceiling in the north porch. For all which John Duraunt senior gave half the cost. In that year his wife died and for her he provided expensive funeral ceremonies hitherto unheard of in Dunstable.

1290

... The same year Ralph of Hengham compounded for us all the debts we owed him and as we could not repay, to pay 24 marks each year.

... The same year Richard le Juvene, lord of Humbershoe, gave us his meadow adjoining ours in Flitt, in return for having quittance of toll for himself and his sub-tenants and their heirs at Humbershoe in our market at Dunstable, as is contained in our charter, the fair of St Peter's Chains [1 August] excepted.

1291

... In the same year there was a great drought in summer, a rainy autumn and in winter severe cold and an extreme shortage of hay and fodder, with unheard-of prices for each of them.

... The same year on the feast of Mary Magdalene the predial tithes in Bracentone and Atlow, which William of Hamilton had at farm for 200 marks for 13 years, fell in.

The same year died Thomas, our head doorkeeper, for whom we had two anni-

[1] see above, s.a. 1277

versaries celebrated by the canons. And in return for this burden we had his sheep at Bukeleshore, namely [ ] . . .

. . . In the same year we had at Bradborne only 2½ sacks of good wool, John de Maydeneburi being custodian at that time; on which account our merchants were very much aggrieved . . .

1292

. . . The same year John Duraunt senior bought in fee the rent [ ] de Weyvile in Houghton; namely 11 marks per annum . . .[1]

1293

. . . The same year the justices in eyre at York acted very severely and put a certain nobleman Simon le Constable by name, apprehended for many felonies to the penance[2] of the statute, because he refused the verdict of the neighbourhood. And he died in prison.[3]

. . . The same year, with the assent of Peter le Loring, lord of Chalgrave, a new hedge was made in Chalgrave field, which is called [ ], from which we have had great benefit in the way of tithe and also from the land . . .

1294

. . . The same year because of the aforesaid payment to the king and to further the affairs of our monastery we granted on a lease our tithes at Newbottle for five years, namely in return for 15 marks p.a., of which we received 45 marks in advance. We also sold for the same reasons William of Marston a corrody of one free servant, in return for which we received 24 marks. For the same reason we also sold Walter de Cobilingtone many corrodies for a year[4] and the great solar and the little stable by the almonry; and we received 60 marks from him. The nature of the corrodies is contained in his charter. Also for the same reason we provided at Michaelmas for certain economies to be made and adhered to until we thought fit to revoke them when the payments to the king stopped and the finances of our monastery were relieved. The consumption of small white loaves we reduced by the weight of 10*s*. We decided that one portion of conventual dishes of every kind should be set before two brothers. Of the other economies made at that time, as regards the number of dishes in the convent, as regards the almonry, the reception of guests, and the management of the household, you will find the particulars[5] entered in the old book of obits.

. . . Also, Laurence of Ludlow, a very well-known merchant, was drowned at sea. He it was who induced the merchants of England to grant the king 40*s* on each sack of wool, namely as well on wool lost at sea as wool saved. And because he sinned against wool-merchants he was drowned in a ship laden with wool; and a king's clerk and one very rich merchant perished with him. All the rest of those who were in that ship, however, by God's grace escaped; of whom Robert Frude of Dunstable was one.

[1] Apparently a further transaction in the lands in Houghton referred to above, s.a. 1284.
[2] *poenitentiam*
[3] On the difficult birth of trial by jury, cf. Stat. Westm. I (No. 47 above), c. 12, and No. 109 above.
[4] *conredia annua* [5] *formam*

The same year, because of the robberies and homicides committed at sea, as said above, the crossing of merchants was forbidden. Wines gave out; the kinds of spices sold by weight and other merchandise from abroad did not come as usual; wool too was so very cheap because there was scarcely anyone who wanted to buy it. And we ourselves in that year accepted 16 marks for 4 sacks of wool in the Peak.

In the same year with the king's permission certain English merchants, in charge of whom should have been the aforementioned Laurence of Ludlow and the lord king's clerk, crossed with their wool with a safe-conduct from the pirates and sold it. And the money they got the lord king borrowed from them for the use of the king of Aragon.

The same year in the month of July, by the order of certain confidential agents of the lord king a scrutiny was made of money and treasure deposited in monasteries, cathedral churches, and other smaller churches, everywhere in England where it was believed anything was deposited, and certain clerks were deputed specially for this job. These sealed up the treasure they found in each place and left it there until the advice of the treasurers of the lord king in London could be got about it. The church of St Paul's London was searched and, as is said, about £2,000 deposited there by the bishop of Chichester was discovered there and borrowed for the king's use. Dunstable priory too was searched by Nicholas the rector of Toddington and laymen he had associated with him. But searching all our strong rooms and receiving from the bailiffs the keys of all the outbuildings, they found nothing except £40 deposited in our church by Walter of Rudham, which, after sealing it up, they left, to be paid later to the said Walter on the authority of a writ from the lord king's exchequer. This action greatly displeased the English church because such sacrilege had been unheard of hitherto. But it is said that the lord king had been innocent in this regard.

. . . The same year there was throughout England generally a great dearth of corn; so that a quarter of wheat was sold in the Peak for 21*s*, and at Dunstable for 16*s* 8*d*; and for a bigger price elsewhere. Also a quarter of salt was sold for 16*s*. Also the harvest, on account of the unseasonableness of the weather, was late, together with the hay harvest, and people were in despair about the following year.

. . . In the same year we paid nothing at the Quindene of Easter to sir Ralph of Hengham of what was due to him by the arrangement to pay off by instalments the great debt we owed him; but he himself let us off for that turn . . .

1295

. . . The suit between us and the Hospitallers over Marston church and about the fine that was made.

The writ. "Edward, by God's grace king of England, etc., to the sheriff of Buckinghamshire, greeting. Order the prior of Dunstable to pay the prior of the Hospital of St John of Jerusalem in England duly and without delay the 210 marks which are in arrears to him of the annual rent of 4 marks which he says, he owes him. And if he does not[1] . . ."

[1] The arrangement made in the end was that the prior agreed to pay the 4 marks p.a. in future, and the prior of the Hospitallers to forgo all but 12 marks of the 210 marks arrears.

. . . The same year we granted Walter of the Peak victuals for life in the house of our almonry. And for us he waived claim to his wages for many years and many other debts we owed him; and when he dies he will give us a half of all his goods.

The same year we granted Luke Bodyn 9 white loaves and 7 gallons of cellarer's ale[1] each week for life; in return for which we received 20 marks, to help the affairs of the house.

. . . In the same year the great dearth of corn of the year before persisted and the assize of bread was outrageously infringed by almost all the bakers of Dunstable. And the prior, because of the outcry of the populace when this was found out, immediately had it remedied by his bailiffs, with the assent of the body of the burgesses, punishing the bakers most severely in accordance with the usual custom of the borough.

The same year we withheld the feasts which it was our custom to lay on for the burgesses at Christmas.

. . . Crossing the sea with wine and almost [all] other merchandise was utterly forbidden to all merchants except those of Brabant, who freely took away the English wool they had bought, because their duke had to wife the king of England's daughter.

. . . The same year brother J[ohn] the carpenter made a new mill of a new and hitherto unheard-of design, promising that it could be worked by only one horse. But when the mill was finished and ought to have ground, four strong horses could scarcely move it, and on this account it was removed and the old horse-mill brought into use again.

172. The Scottish church declared independent of the English church, 1192

(Translated in *A Source Book of Scottish History*, I, ed. Dickinson, Donaldson and Milne, pp. 54–5)

The Scottish church with a parochial organisation and bishops but without an archbishop or metropolitan, had been in danger of falling subject to the archbishop of York. But in, it is now believed, 1192 (rather than 1189) Pope Celestine III declared it a "special daughter" of the papacy, subject to no archbishop. His bull has survived only in copies in English chronicles (see A. O. Anderson, *Scottish Annals from English Chroniclers A.D. 500 to 1286*, London, 1908, pp. 299–300) but officially and verbally almost identically in the reissue of it by Honorius III in 1218, here given.

Honorius, bishop, servant of the servants of God, to his dearest son in Christ Alexander, illustrious king of Scots, and his successors forever. While all the faithful ought to find at the apostolic see patronage and favour, yet it is fitting that those should more especially be cherished by the defence of its protection whose faith and devotion have been tried in most things, that they may be so much the more incited to the fervour of love for it, and be subdued by the more devout affection of reverence for it, as they know that they have more surely attained a pledge of its benevolence and grace. For this reason, dearest son in Christ, considering the reverence and devotion towards the Roman church which we know you and your predecessors to have had from times long past, by the page of this present writing (following the example of Celestine and Innocent, our predecessors of happy memory, popes of Rome) we most strictly forbid that it be permitted to anyone except the pope or a legate sent from his side to publish a sentence of interdict or excommunication in the

[1] *cervisia cellariae*

kingdom of Scotland, because the Scottish church (in which these episcopal sees are known to exist – St Andrews, Dunblane, Glasgow, Dunkeld, Brechin, Aberdeen, Moray, Ross and Caithness) is subject to the apostolic see as a special daughter, with no intermediary; and if such a sentence be pronounced, we decree it invalid. We add, also, that it be not permitted to any henceforth who is not of the kingdom of Scotland to exercise the office of legate in it unless one whom the apostolic see has specially sent from its body for that purpose. We forbid, too, that disputes which may arise in the same kingdom about its possessions be carried to the judgment of arbiters placed outside the kingdom, unless on appeal to the Roman church. And if any writings come to light which have been obtained contrary to the decree of this liberty, or chance in future to be obtained, without mention made of this concession, let nothing result to the prejudice of you or your successors, or of your kingdom, concerning the grant of this privilege. Besides, the liberties and immunities granted by the Roman church to you and your kingdom and the churches in that kingdom, and hitherto observed, we have confirmed and decree that they remain unimpaired in time to come, saving the authority of the apostolic see. Let it be permitted to no man at all to infringe this writing of our grant, prohibition and confirmation, or venture rashly to transgress it. But if any presume to attempt this, let him know that he shall incur the wrath of almighty God and of the blessed apostles Peter and Paul . . . Given at the Lateran by the hand of Ranerius, vice-chancellor of the holy Roman church, xi Kal. Decembris, the 7th indiction, the year of the Lord's incarnation MCCXVIII, and the third year of the pontificate of Honorius III.

173. A bishop's will: Richard bishop of Chichester (died 1253)

(Text and trans. from *Sussex Archaeological Collections*, I (1848), pp. 164–92)

Few wills as early as this of Richard Wich have survived.

In the name of the Father, Son and Holy Ghost, Amen.

I, Richard the second,[1] by divine permission bishop of Chichester, ordain and make my testament in the underwritten manner.

In the first place, to the most high Trinity and to the blessed Mary I commend and bequeath my soul, and my body to be buried in the great church of Chichester in the nave of the same church, near the altar of the blessed Edmund the Confessor,[2] against the column.

Also to the fabric[3] of the same church 40 pounds.

Also to those who serve in the choir 5 pounds.

Also my relics to the church of Chichester.

Also to the Friars Minor of Chichester my glossed Psalter[4] and 20 shillings.

[1] The first of the name was Richard Poore, bishop 1215–17 before being translated to Salisbury and then in 1228 to Durham.

[2] St Edmund (Rich) of Abingdon, archbishop of Canterbury (d. 1240), Wich's master and friend, was already canonised.

[3] Much work was done on Chichester Cathedral in the thirteenth century.

[4] The new communities of Franciscans and Dominicans, learning apart, were of course ill-provided even with books for their devotions.

Also to the Friars Minor of Lewes a book of Gospels, namely, Luke and John, and 20 shillings.

Also to the Friars Minor of Winchelsea Mark and Matthew and 20 shillings.

Also to the Preaching Friars of Arundel the book of Sentences and 20 shillings.

Also to the Preaching Friars of Canterbury Hosea glossed and 20 shillings.

Also to the Friars Minor of the same city Isaiah glossed and 20 shillings.

Also to the Preachers of London the book of Job, Acts, the Canonical Epistles, the Apocalypse glossed, in one volume and 20 shillings.

Also to the Friars Minor of the same city the Epistles of Paul glossed and 20 shillings.

Also to the Preaching Friars of Winchester the Summary of mr William of Auxerre and 20 shillings.

Also to the Friars Minor of the same city the Twelve Prophets glossed and 20 shillings.

Also I bequeath in aid of the Holy Land 50 marks [£33 6*s* 8*d*], to be paid and delivered to Robert Chaundos, my brother,[1] in order that he may go there, if he is willing, for me, and to be paid to another, if the said Robert should be unwilling to go.

Also to the house of Wymondham[2] 30 marks [£20], the debt for which I am bound to them not being computed in the said 30 marks.

Also to the abbey of Lacock my great cup of maplewood.

Also to the abbey of Marham in Norfolk my other cup of maplewood.

Also to Friar Garin the books of Damascenus with some other gatherings.[3]

Also to Friar William of Colchester, Preacher, the book of Anselm *Cur Deus Homo*.

Also to Friar Humphrey, the recluse of Pagham, 40 shillings.

Also to the female recluse of Houghton half a mark [6*s* 8*d*].

Also to the female recluse of Stopham half a mark.

Also to the recluse of Hardham [Heringham] half a mark.

Also to the female recluse of the Blessed Mary of Westoute at Lewes 5 shillings.

Also to the brethren of the House of God at Dover 20 shillings for a pittance.

Also to the monks of St Martin of the same town one mark.

Also I bequeath to Hugh of the Chamber[4] 10 pounds.

Also to Robert of Crowhurst [Crocherst] 20 pounds.

Also to Willard, formerly my cook, 10 marks [£6 13*s* 4*d*].

Also to Walter de Wyke 10 marks.

Also to Adam, the butler, 10 marks.

Also to Richard, the Baker, 10 marks.

Also to Ralph, the marshal, 100 shillings.

Also to Alexander, the keeper of the palfreys, 6 marks [£4].

Also to Lawrence, the farrier, 100 shillings.

Also to Walter Gray 100 shillings.

Also to William, my messenger, 100 shillings.

[1] possibly his sister's husband, i.e. brother-in-law
[2] Wymondham Priory (Benedictine), Norfolk
[3] *quaternis*
[4] *de Camera*

Also to William of Kempsey 20 pounds.

Also to the boy Henry, nephew of sir Simon de Terryng, 40 shillings.

Also to the boys who have waited on me, not named above, let my executors requite their services, in proportion to their service and the quality of their persons, at their own discretion.

Also to sir Simon de Terryng I bequeath my best palfrey and the book On Virtues, that is to say Distinctions on the Psalter.

Also to the same the goblet which the lord Stephen de Langespee gave me.

Also to sir Walter de Campeden a cup and two bowls of silver.

Also to sir William de Selsey, chaplain, my Bible and my gatherings in a hairy cover.[1]

Also to mr Robert de Hastyng my Decretals.

Also to mr Philip the goblet with a base, which sir Hugh Bigod gave me, and 20 pounds and a rouncey with harness.[2]

Also to sir William de Bramber, chaplain, a silver goblet and the book On Vices.

Also to Henry, clerk of the chapel, 10 marks [£6 13*s* 4*d*].

Also to Richard, the bailiff of Cacham, 100 shillings.

Also to Nigel, the bailiff of Aldingborne, 100 shillings (all which from the words "To Hugh of the Chamber" I consider rather as debts than legacies).

I also will that my rings be delivered to those to whom I have assigned them as is indicated in the attached[3] schedule of rings.

Also to the lady the queen a ring with[4] Henry the clerk.

Also to the bishop of Norwich a seal in a ring with[4] Hugh and my serpent-tongues[5] which stood before me at table.

Also to the bishop of Arles[6] a silver flagon which the abbot of Battle gave me.

Also to sir John Mansel and to mr Hugh de St Edmund's[7] the cloth which the bishop of Arles[6] gave me.

Also my cross which the earl of Lincoln[8] gave me to Edmund de Lacy with[4] William de Kempsey.

Also for marrying a daughter of my sister 20 marks [£13 6*s* 8*d*].

I also will and dispose and adjure my executors, calling to witness the divine judgment, that after paying the debts for which I am bound by deed to the church of Chichester, to sir Wybert of Kent, to sir Nicholas of Dover and to the lady Clavemunda as contained in my letters patent made for them, and my other debts and the legacies to my household and domestics (which I regard as equivalent to debts and

[1] *quaternos meos sub coopertorio piloso*

[2] *cum Runcino ad harnesuim*

[3] I have conjectured that the doubtful reading "*apponi?*" may be an abbreviated participle.

[4] *cum:* I do not know the force of this. Possibilities are "at present in the keeping of" (the person named), "to be conveyed by" (the person), or literally (the service of the person named being part of the legacy), in that order of probability.

[5] This piece of jewellery would seem to have found its way later into the king's possession. cf. *Liber Quotidianus Contrarotulatoris Garderoba e* [*28 Edw.* I] (Soc. Antiq., London, 1787), p. 352, and W. H. Blaauw, in *Sussex Archaeol. Collections*, I (1 848), p. 185, n. 57.

[6] Blaouw (ibid. p. 185) gives reason to suppose that this should be Orleans, not Arles.

[7] Two of the executors named in the will.

[8] The earl himself was dead by this time and Wich is returning the cross as a legacy to the earl's son, Edmund de Lacy.

reckon as such), they shall execute all the matters aforesaid according to my disposition set out above.

I will also that to carry out the foregoing there be exacted from the lord king by my executors the fruits of the bishopric of Chichester which he for two years took unjustly and which of right belong to me, and payment of which I will also seek in the court of the Most High unless he has fully satisfied my executors.[1]

I will also that my executors for the execution of the foregoing shall if they see fit dispose of my horses not assigned earlier and my silver food dishes and goblets not assigned earlier, and if all these things do not suffice the executors shall reduce, augment and arrange – in proportion to the legacies previously assigned and the quality of the persons – as seems to them most expedient for my soul. And if after my disposition set out above there is anything of my goods left over, let it be applied by my executors to help poor religious of my bishopric, and to help hospitals, to repair bridges and roads, and to help widows, orphans and wards, as seems to them expedient.

I excommunicate and anathematise all those who maliciously impede my will, in order that, in the words of the Apostle, "they may be delivered over for the destruction of the flesh, so that their spirit may be saved in the day of judgment."[2]

I appoint and constitute as executors of this my testament the venerable men sir John Mansel, provost of Beverley, the lords the dean of Chichester, the precentor of Chichester, and mr Hugh of St Edmund's, canon of St [Paul's] London, sir Simon de Teryngg, Walter de Campeden, William de Selesey, earnestly entreating them for charity's sake to execute my above-written will diligently and faithfully. And if it can be done without offence, I earnestly require my venerable father and lord, the archbishop of Canterbury, as principal executor and conservator of my goods (and, having asked permission, I constitute him principal executor and conservator of my goods) to direct, defend and deign to uphold against the opposition of disputants my underwritten [*sic*] will.

In witness of which matter, I have directed my seal to be affixed to the present writing.

We, B[oniface] archbishop of Canterbury, primate of all England, on the petition of the executors have caused our seal to be affixed to the present instrument, etc., etc.

[1] See *Cal. Pat. Rolls 1272–81*, p. 148 (Chichester, 18 June 1276, on the occasion of the translation of the body of the now canonised Richard), "200*l* due from Henry III to the aforesaid bishop", as calendared, but the full text (which I have not seen) is more informative: "to exonerate the soul of my father". See Blaauw (op. cit.), p. 188, n. 67.

[2] cf. I Corinthians v. 5

Part V
LAND AND PEOPLE

INTRODUCTION

This volume has so far illustrated the period 1189–1327 from chronicles, the royal records and ecclesiastical sources. Much as these tell us of the world as well as the cloister and of ordinary men as well as those at the head of affairs in church or state, they naturally see them and speak of them for the most part either as subjects or as the objects of pastoral care. There are, moreover, areas of living to which they hardly penetrate. They need both a corrective and a supplement. Part V sets out to be neither, but is intended to point the way.

It could not do more even if space permitted. The chief need is for an "economic history" of the period, to set alongside the political and ecclesiastical. The materials exist (in relative plenty in this country in this field as in others) but they are insufficiently worked and the discipline of economic history, though past infancy, is not yet mature. The early certainties are now being questioned. Contrary to H. L. Gray (*The English Field System*, Cambridge, Mass., 1915) and the Orwins,[1] Mrs Thirsk rejects an early origin for the open-field system and sees it not as the foundation for twelfth- and thirteenth-century agricultural conditions but a development in response to them. A newer orthodoxy, an industrial revolution in the thirteenth century (Carus-Wilson), has been queried: "the possibility arises that it was during the expansion of the fourteenth rather than during the contraction of the thirteenth century that the fulling mill most deeply influenced the location of the textile industry" (E. Miller, *Econ. Hist. Rev.*, 2nd ser., xviii (1965), p. 82). The emphasis on manorial custom and villein services has been corrected, the importance of paid labour as well as labour services in the heyday of the manor and not merely in its decline being now fully recognised (Postan, *The Famulus*). The picture of the thirteenth century as an age of expansion – of increasing population, growing villages and new towns, of high farming and the winning of new land for cultivation from wood, waste and fen, of rising prices, capital investment and expanding markets, a time when "if at any time during the Middle Ages, the flow of economic activity was in full flood"[2] – has been refined by Postan[3] into one not so much of boom as of impending doom. The argument here is of "inordinate expansion"; of "over-population" when a predominantly agrarian society already cultivating marginal land faced declining yields with little compensating improvement in agricultural techniques and with no alternative to agriculture for most men; a "starving and over-populated countryside" by the late thirteenth century; an economy, that is, moving into reverse long before the Black Death. This interpretation has received powerful support from, among others, Dr J. Z. Titow,[4] the scholar best acquainted with the main evidence

[1] In this and subsequent cases where authors and publications are not precisely indicated, reference should be made to the Select Bibliography for full information.

[2] E. Miller, *Econ. Hist. Rev.*, 2nd ser., xxiv (1971), p. 2

[3] *IXe. Congrès International des Sciences Historiques*, I, *Rapports* (Paris, 1950), pp. 225–41 and, with particular reference to this country, in subsequent writings

[4] in the introduction to his *English Rural Society 1200–1350*

for the period, viz, the accounts of the estate of the bishops of Winchester. On the other hand, it has never lacked critics – notably W. C. Robinson; J. C. Russell, who totally rejects the idea of over-population and maintains that England was "a prosperous country in all but the worst years" before 1348,[1] but who is severely criticised himself for his statistical methods;[2] Barbara F. Harvey;[3] and D. G. Watts, who supports Miss Harvey by evidence from the Titchfield Abbey estate. Meanwhile Postan himself can feel that he has succeeded in the purpose he had in 1950 when he remembers (as we should remember) that all he did then was to put forward a "hypothesis" and all he claimed for it was that it was "tentative in the extreme" and "a mere guess which may well turn out to be untrue".[4] Such debate and such readiness to retract in this and other fields are what should be in economic history at this stage. It is a healthy adolescence.

What is, above all, emerging is a recognition of the need for local studies. Thus, a weakness in Titow's support of Postan's hypothesis of over-population is the extent to which it depends on the evidence of one estate. Dr Titow is, of course, well aware of the danger in arguing from the particular to the general[5] and equally well aware of the other danger of assuming that a trend (when we are satisfied that there is one) operates uniformly. He writes, "What must not be assumed" because we find that something was universal is that "its character, extent, and chronology, was necessarily the same everywhere; much more work on a comparative basis will have to be done".[6] In fact, Titow's own work on the records of the estate of the bishops of Winchester and P. D. A. Harvey's study of the Merton College manor of Cuxham in Oxfordshire are examples of just what is needed. One a study of a large estate of many manors, permitting even within itself close comparisons annually, year after year from 1208 onwards with scarcely a break, a near perfect foundation for wider comparison with other estates. The other, precision work on a single manor from 1240 to 1400 in complete awareness of work elsewhere, with special attention not to matters in which Cuxham is recognisably normal but to those on which Cuxham throws new light, so providing material for comparisons without itself attempting them and then drawing conclusions "for which the evidence of a single community is quite inadequate". Equally fine work is possible on other estates. None may have surviving records to match those of the estate of the bishops of Winchester either for early date or for long, almost unbroken series, but there is from the late thirteenth century onwards an increasing volume and increasing variety

[1] "The pre-plague population of England", *Journal of British Studies*, v (1966)

[2] e.g. a very fair review of his *British Medieval Population* by R. S. Smith in *Speculum*, xxiv (1949), pp. 450–2; Titow in the introduction (particularly pp. 64–90) referred to in n. 1 above; R. Lennard in "Agrarian history: some vistas and pitfalls", *Agricultural History Review*, xii (1964); a short notice (of the "Ancient" part) of *Late Ancient and Medieval Population* (Philadelphia, 1958) by A. H. M. Jones in *History*, xliv (1959), pp. 37–8

[3] Miss Harvey's article in the *Transactions* of the Royal Historical Society and Dr Titow's introduction referred to in n. 1 above between them provide a good statement of the case for and against the "Postan" interpretation. It will be noticed that Titow, writing later, has had the advantage of being able to "reply" to Miss Harvey.

[4] *IXe. Congrès . . . Rapports* (Paris, 1950), p. 236

[5] *English Rural Society*, introduction, p. 53

[6] ibid. p. 35

of record, manorial court rolls as well as accounts, surveys, extents, custumals and rentals[1] – sufficient in the aggregate and by geographical spread to give an overall picture which we can accept as approximating to reality because it is compounded of local and regional diversities instead of ignoring them. How actively such work is now being done can be seen in the Select Bibliography which follows.[2] Local history is now in the mainstream of academic study. It is no longer left to the amateur or the professionally unambitious.

The emphasis rightly remains on rural England and such recent work as that, for instance, of Raftis on court rolls, Ault on the village community, Hallam on South Lincolnshire, Dodwell on peasant holdings and inheritance practice, Postan on animal husbandry, Brooke and Postan on a peasant land market, is bringing us noticeably closer to realities. Comparable attention to the minority who lived not on the land or its proceeds but by trade and industry and chiefly in towns would no doubt have a comparable result and is much needed. James Tait's *The Medieval English Borough* (Manchester, 1936) probably reaches the limits of a purely legal and institutional approach – even to the borough, the most distinctive and best documented and therefore most knowable form of association of non-rural elements in society. For further advance economic and social studies are needed. Borough records survive in increasing quantities from as early as 1196. A stocktaking of them for the thirteenth century and consideration of what can be done with them in conjunction with other sources is G. H. Martin's paper to the Royal Historical Society in *Transactions* (1963). An outstanding example of what can be done appeared the same year, G. A. Williams, *Medieval London from Commune to Capital*, followed in 1965 by Carus-Wilson's study of the first half-century of the borough of Stratford-upon-Avon, one of "those smaller English boroughs, founded after the Norman Conquest, which are often regarded as being distinguished from villages merely by the different legal status of their inhabitants – a difference which seems sometimes to have neither purpose nor meaning". Much fine work has been done on other places too, notably Canterbury (Urry), Lincoln (Hill), Winchester (Furley and – forthcoming – publications of the Winchester Excavations Committee and Research Unit), Southampton (Ruddock and – in 1973 – Colin Platt, *Medieval Southampton: an English Trading Community*) and in addition to G. A. Williams's work on London that of Sylvia Thrupp should be mentioned. More studies of the smaller boroughs are needed: Beresford's *New Towns*, like his work with others on deserted villages, is for all its topographical insights and archaeological contributions essentially a survey and a gazetteer, all that can be done for many places, but not if from surviving records it is possible to study the community itself as well as the evidence of the ground. The even-more-elusive market town (*villa mercatoria, ville marchaunde*) needs attention.

[1] For the different purposes of these types of record, see the introduction (pp. 24–33) to Titow's *English Rural Society*, with examples (chiefly from the Winchester episcopal records) in the text. G. R. Elton's statement in *England 1200–1640*, "The sources of history" (1969), is marred by being divided, on a somewhat artificial distinction, between two chapters (pp. 128–34 and 138–53).

[2] A very recent case of precision work on a single manor, relevant to the work of Ault as well as Raftis as village and manor coterminous, is E. B. DeWindt, *Land and People in Holywell-cum-Needingworth* (Toronto, 1972). According to the reviewer in *Econ. Hist. Rev.*, 2nd ser., xxvi (1973), p. 525, conclusions questionable but material valuable.

The amount of manorial traffic and agricultural trade is now being realised. At this level urban and rural history shade off into each other.

It is easier to picture the traffic (Jusserand's classic, *English Wayfaring Life*, trans. L. Toulmin Smith) than the roads, particularly the by-roads, of which there must have been a network when "except in the most sparsely populated areas, there was scarcely a peasant in the land who was not within reach of a market where he could dispose each week of his surplus produce and buy what he needed, walking there and back the same day".[1] There is no contemporary map of sufficient scale. The nearest in date and size is the Bodleian map known as the "Gough" (reproduced in facsimile, Oxford, 1958), on which the map "England circa 1300" in this volume relies. Nor is there any question of Ordnance Survey precision. Reconstructions such as that of Rees for South Wales and the Border are necessarily approximations. This applies even to maps on an Ordnance Survey base, such as the Survey's own period maps (for which see the section in Harley and Phillips, *The Historian's Guide to O.S. Maps*). For reconstruction the two pillars are our knowledge of the Roman road system in this country and current Ordnance Survey maps, the problem being, of course, to bridge the gap. Knowledge of the Roman system has been both extended and refined in recent years (besides the O.S. period map of Roman Britain, see Codrington, Margary, *Viatores*, Dymond in the Select Bibliography). At this end, the O.S. maps. reaching back in the Old Series or "First Edition" of the One Inch to the Mile map (the first sheet of which was published in 1801) to the last years of the eighteenth century, are themselves a record of change. The last sheet of the First Edition One Inch was not published until 1873, but at the very least the gap to be bridged is reduced for us by a century and by anything up to a century and three quarters in the case of earlier sheets.[2] Then the bridge starts, with large-scale county maps, estate maps and surveys, tithe and enclosure awards and maps, and road-books (especially John Ogilby's survey of roads, *Britannia, Volume the First* . . . , London, 1675), taking us back to the sixteenth century.[3] An arch forward of such strength from the Roman end is not to be expected. It is demonstrable that some of the Roman roads of this country continued to be used after Roman times, but how many, which in particular, whether over their whole length or only for part of it, the amount of traffic they carried, each of them, and each of them for how long, for it is inconceivable, however slowly society might change, that traffic did not look for new routes, shrinking or ceasing altogether on some in the course of centuries, these are questions which history has not, and archaeology is unlikely to produce in sufficient quantities,

[1] Professor Carus-Wilson in A. L. Poole (ed.), *Medieval England*, I, p. 241, on the position reached by the early fourteenth century.

[2] The actual survey began in 1795, six years before publication began. For some later sheets the interval is much greater. For the historian, therefore, the date of survey of a particular sheet is more important than that of its publication. On the surveyors' drawings, their dating, and their value in themselves to him, see Harley and Phillips, op. cit. pp. 7 ff.

[3] For printed maps of this country, and particularly the bibliographies of Sir H. G. Fordham, Thomas Chubb and Harold Whitaker of them, see the Preface and Introduction to Whitaker's *Descriptive List of the Printed Maps of Northamptonshire A.D. 1576–1900* (Northampton, 1948); for a union list of large-scale country maps, see below under "Roger" in the Select Bibliography, "The Land" section; for tithe and enclosure awards and maps, W. E. Tate's *The Parish Chest* (3rd rev. edn, Cambridge, 1969) and his lists of such records in local record societies' publications.

the evidence to answer. The firmest foundation is I. D. Margary's field work. Its precision enables one to compare Roman routes with modern – where the evidence permits with early modern. They may be identical, but only proof of use in the interval between them will be proof of continuity and they are a millennium and more apart. When found the evidence will fall casually, it will as often as not be mentioned in connection with something else and quite incidentally, and it will not be found frequently enough to be complete proof. The best we can expect is not a bridge, but stepping stones not too far apart. Anything as massive as the Gough map in the shorter gap from the modern end and a generation at most from the present volume is sheer luck.

The centre of the Roman road system, as of modern roads and railways, was London. And as the Gough map shows, it was so in the Middle Ages. This was primarily for economic reasons. London was the commercial capital of the country before there was a political. It was the one city in England which bore comparison for size with continental centres. Through it more than any other England operated its foreign trade, its alien communities were more numerous, more goods, exports or imports, passed through its port. London is well represented in the Select Bibliography. Williams's *Medieval London* is focussed on this period. It sees the London of this period "whole", grounding "political narrative and constitutional analysis in social reality". Unwin's *Gilds and Companies* and Sylvia Thrupp's *Merchant Class*, studies of this economic and social foundation, are not diminished thereby. All three should be regarded as essential reading. Other reading on London, on minor ports and inland centres of trade, on production for home markets or for export, and other aspects of the economy will be found in the Select Bibliography. The main lines of the traffic by road are shown in Map 6; England's closest economic interests on the continent (in France and the Low Countries) in Map 7.

The highly technical matters of coinage and currency and credit, public, commercial, and private, may be approached historically via P. Spufford's Appendix to *Cambridge Economic History of Europe*, III (Cambridge, 1963), S. L. Lopez, "Back to gold", *Econ. Hist. Rev*., 2nd ser., ix (1956–7), pp. 219–40, A. M. Watson, "Back to gold – and silver", ibid. xx (1967), pp. 1–34, and Cipolla on currency depreciation, ibid. xv (1962–3), pp. 413–22. For bibliography, P. Grierson, *Coins and Medals* (Hist. Assoc., 1954) or its revision and amplification, *Bibliographie Numismatique* (Brussels, 1966). For England, C. Johnson (ed.), *The De Moneta of Nicholas Oresme and English Mint Documents* (1956), C. G. Crump and A. Hughes, "The English currency under Edward I", *Econ. Journal*, v (1895), C. G. Crump and C. Johnson, "Tables of bullion coined under Edward I, II, and III", *Numismatic Chronicle*, 4th ser., xiii (1913), pp. 200–45, M. Prestwich, *Econ. Hist. Rev*., 2nd ser., xxii (1969), pp. 406–16 on Edward I's monetary policies. This last article ranges widely, but turns on Edward's action in 1299 by the statute of Stepney against the amount of bad foreign money in circulation (Nos 82 above and 226 below). A contemporary unofficial view is that of the Guisborough chronicler.[1] The increasing reliance of medieval

[1] [s.a. 1299] "*A Change of the Coinage:* The same year during the Christmas celebrations the king prohibited all foreign money in his territory to be current any longer in return for sterling. For foreign merchants had

society by the thirteenth century upon written record reveals the important part already played by credit in its economy. For public credit (with special reference to North-Western Europe) the best approach (in English) is chapter VII of *The Cambridge Economic History of Europe*, III (Cambridge, 1963). For commercial credit, Postan on "Credit in medieval trade", two articles by R. D. Face on the mechanism of the Champagne fairs in *Econ. Hist. Rev.*, 2nd ser., x (1957–8) and xii (1959–60), J. W. Baldwin on theories of the just price, involving the awkward matter of interest, H. G. Richardson on the English Jewry, and Plucknett on Edward I's commercial legislation offer a variety of approaches to the subject. E. B. Fryde on the younger Despenser's business with Italian bankers may be mentioned as one illustration of private transactions, a reminder that a reward for the risks of being a king's banker was the amount of private customers' business it brought.

Another economic factor, more important then than now and even more unpredictable then than now, was the weather. References to it in chronicles are collected in *A Meteorological Chronology to A.D. 1450*, ed. C. E. Britton (H.M.S.O., 1937). Evidence of the weather on the estates of the bishops of Winchester between 1209 and 1350 collected from the account rolls is published by Titow (Sel. Bibl.). There is a remarkable correspondence between this evidence and that of tree growth: see D. J. Schove and A. W. G. Lowther, "Tree-rings and medieval archaeology", *Medieval Archaeology*, I (1957), pp. 85–7. For Matthew Paris's evidence on weather at – or heard of at – St Albans, see No. 188 below.

---

brought coins of very bad metal into England in very large numbers: pollards, crockards, scaldings, brabantines, eagles, lions dormant and various other names. They were all white money simulating silver and were artificially compounded of silver, copper and sulphur and there was not in four of them, or five, one pennyweight of silver. And by the king's command two of them were current in return for a sterling until Easter. It was a very bad time because of the base currency and many changes occurred in the price of things. The following Easter, however, the king prohibited these coins entirely, and held exchange in many places. Five or six of them were given in return for one sterling, and men did not settle accounts with them because of the trifling value of the coins. Yet before a year had passed, after men had learnt by experiment the art of refining metal with lead melted with it in a fire, two were worth one penny: as Cato said '*Quod vile est carum, quod carum vile putato*' [Dion. Catonis Distich., i. 29]. And many men became rich by exchange who had bought that money while it was cheap. The king subsequently had enquiry made about those who had exchanged without special permission and had thus been rewarded, and he fined them a large sum of money." (*The Chronicle of Walter of Guisborough*, ed. H. Rothwell (Camden Third Series, LXXXIX (1957), p. 333.)

SELECT BIBLIOGRAPHY

THE LAND

Avery, D., *The Irregular Common Fields of Edmonton*, Edmonton Hundred Hist. Soc. Occasional Papers, n.s. No. 9 (1965)
Baker, A. D. H., "Local history in early estate maps", *Amateur Historian*, v (1962)
Barrow, G. W. S., "Rural settlement in central and eastern Scotland: the medieval evidence", *Scottish Studies*, vi (1962)
Barton, N. J., *The Lost Rivers of London* (1962)
Beresford, M. W., and St Joseph, J. K. S., *Medieval England: an Aerial Survey* (Cambridge, 1958)
Britton, C. E. (ed.), *A Meteorological Chronology to 1450* (H.M.S.O., 1957)
Bull, G. B. G., "Elizabethan maps of the lower Lea valley", *Geographical Journal*, cxxiv (1958)
Codrington, T. C. E., *Roman Roads in Britain* (1918)
Crone, G. R., "Early mapping of the British Isles", *Scottish Geographical Magazine*, lxxviii (1962)
——, Campbell, E. M. J., and Skelton, R. A., "Early cartographic activity in Britain", *Geographical Journal*, cxxviii (1962)
Darby, H. C., "The draining of the English claylands", *Geographische Zeitschrift*, band 52
——, *The Medieval Fenland* (Cambridge, 1940)
——, *The Draining of the Fens*, 2nd edn (Cambridge, 1956)
Drew, J. H., "The Welsh road and the drovers", *Birmingham Arch. Soc. Trans. and Proc.*, lxxxii (1967)
Dymond, D. P., "Roman bridges on Dere Street co. Durham, with a general appendix on the evidence for bridges in Roman Britain", *Arch. J.*, cxviii (1963), pp. 136–64
Emmison, F. G., "Estate maps and surveys", *History*, xlviii (1963), pp. 34–7
Glasscock, R. E., "The distribution of landed wealth in East Anglia in the early fourteenth century", *Instit. Brit. Geographers Trans. and Papers*, No. 32 (1964)
Green, C., "Broadland fords and causeways", *Norfolk Archaeology*, xxxii (1961)
——, "East Anglian coastline levels since Roman times", *Antiquity*, xxxv (1961), pp. 21–8
——, "Excavations on a medieval site at Water Newton in the county of Huntingdon in 1958", *Proc. Cambs. Antiqu. Soc.*, lvi–lvii (1964), pp. 68–87
Hallam, H. E., *The New Lands of Elloe*, Univ. Leicester Occasional Papers, No. 6 (Leicester, 1954)
Handford, C. C., *Some Maps of Derbyshire 1577–1850*, Derbyshire Miscellany, Supplement xi (1971)
Harley, J. B., "Maps for the local historian: a guide to British sources; 4, Maps of communications", *Local Historian*, viii (2) (1968)
——, "The settlement geography of early medieval Warwickshire", *Instit. Brit. Geographers Trans. and Papers*, No. 34 (1964)
——, and Phillips, C. W., *The Historian's Guide to Ordnance Survey Maps*, Nat. Council of Soc. Service (1964), repr. from *Amateur Historian* (1962–3) with additional material inc. a special chapter on the O.S. maps of Scotland; for Ireland, *see* p. 6, n. 1
Harris, Alan, *The Rural Landscape of the East Riding of Yorkshire 1700–1850* (1962)
Hayes-McCoy, G. A. (ed,), *Ulster and other Irish maps c. 1600*, Irish MSS Commission (Dublin, 1964)
Helm, P. J. "The Somerset levels in the Middle Ages 1086–1539", *J. Brit. Arch. Assoc.*, 3rd ser., xii (1949)
Hodgson, R. I., "Medieval colonisation in northern Ryedale, Yorkshire", *Geographical Journal*, cxxxv (1969)
Jarrett, M. G., "The deserted villages of West Whelpington, Northumberland", *Arch. Aeliana.*, 4th ser., xl (1962)
Jones, G. R. J., "The pattern of settlement on the Welsh border", *Agric. Hist. Rev.*, viii (1960)
Kestner, F. J. T., "The old coastline of the Wash", *Geographical Journal*, cxxviii (1962)
Lambert, J., and others, *The Making of the Broads*, Royal Geogr. Research ser., No. 3 (1960)
Lee, C. E., "Early industry and transport in East Yorkshire", *Trans. Newcomen Soc.*, xxxii (1961)
Map of Great Britain c. 1360 known as the Gough Map, facs. and introd., for Bodleian Lib. and Royal Geogr. Soc. (Oxford, 1958)
Margary, I. D., *Roman Roads in Britain*, 2 vols (1955–7)
——, *Roman Ways in the Weald* (1948)
Mowat, J. L. G., *Sixteen Old Maps of Properties in Oxfordshire* (1888)
Neilson, N., *A Terrier of Fleet, Lincolnshire* (1920)
Owen, A. E. B., "A thirteenth-century agreement on water for livestock in the Lindsey Marsh", *Agric. Hist. Rev.*, xiii (1965)
Postgate, M. R., "The field systems of Breckland", *Agric. Hist. Rev.*, x (1962)
Rees, William, *An Historical Atlas of Wales*, 3rd edn (1967)
——, *South Wales and the Border in the Fourteenth Century* (Cardiff, 1933), historical map 2 m. to 1 inch, 4 sheets with handbook

Roberts, B. K., "Study of medieval colonisation in the Forest of Arden [Tanworth]", *Agric. Hist. Rev.*, xvi (1968)
Rodley, J., "Peak District roads prior to the turnpike era", *Derbyshire Arch. J.*, lxxxiii (1964), pp. 39–50
Roger, E. M., *The Large Scale County Maps of the British Isles 1596–1850: a union list*, Bodleian Library (Oxford, 1960)
Schove, D. J., and Lowther, A. W. G., "Tree-rings and medieval archaeology", *Medieval Archaeology*, i (1957), pp. 85–7
Sheppard, June A., *The Draining of the Hull Valley;* and *The Draining of the Marshlands of South Holderness and of the Vale of York;* East Yorkshire Local History Society ser., Nos 8 and 20 (York, 1958, 1966)
Simmonds, L. F., "Some remnants of the medieval landscape in S. Worcestershire", *Trans. Worcs. Arch. Soc.*, xxxvii (1961)
Spufford, M., "The street and ditchways in S.E. Cambridgeshire", *Proc. Cambs. Antiqu. Soc.*, lix (1966)
Steer, F. W., *A Catalogue of Sussex Estate and Tithe Award Maps* (Lewes and Chichester, 1962)
——, "A catalogue of Sussex maps", *Sussex Rec. Soc.*, lxvi (1968)
Tann, Jennifer, "Some problems of water power: a study of mill-siting in Gloucestershire", *Trans. Bristol and Glos. Arch. Soc.*, lxxxiv (1965)
Titow, J., "Evidence of weather in the account rolls of the bishopric of Winchester 1209–1350", *Econ. Hist. Rev.*, 2nd ser., xii (1959–60), pp. 360–407
Viatores, The (pseud.), *Roman Roads in the South-East Midlands* (1964)
Waites, B., "Aspects of thirteenth and fourteenth century arable farming on the Yorkshire Wolds", *Yorks. Arch. J.*, xlii (1968)
——, "Medieval iron working in N.E. Yorkshire", *Geography*, xlix (1964)
——, *Moorland and Vale-land Farming in N.E. Yorkshire: the monastic contribution in the thirteenth and fourteenth centuries*, Borthwick Papers, No. 32 (York, 1967)
Weatherill, J., "The eighteenth-century Rievaulx bridge and its medieval predecessor", *Yorks. Arch. J.*, xli (1963), pp. 71–80
Whittington, G., "The distribution of strip lynchets", *Instit. Brit. Geographers Trans. and Papers*, xxxi (1961)
Wightman, W. E., "Open field agriculture in the Peak District", *Derbyshire Arch. J.*, lxxxi (1961); cf. A. R. H. Baker, "Open fields in Derbyshire: some reservations about recent arguments", ibid. lxxxiii (1963); and J. P. Carr, "Open field agriculture in mid-Derbyshire", ibid. lxxxiii (1964)
——, W. R., "The pattern of vegetation in the Vale of Pickering *c.* 1300", *Instit. Brit. Geographers Trans.*, xlv (1968)
Willan, T. S., *The Early History of the Don Navigation* (Manchester, 1965)
Williams, M., *The Draining of the Somerset Levels* (Cambridge, 1970)
Williamson, J. A., "Geographical history of the Cinque Ports", *History*, xi (1926–7), pp. 97–115
——, *The English Channel* (1959)

PEOPLE

Altschul, M., *A Baronial Family in Medieval England: the Clares 1217–1314* (Baltimore, 1966)
Arkell, A., *Oxford Stone* (1947)
Asplin, P. W. A., *Medieval Ireland c. 1170–1495: a bibliography of secondary works*, Royal Irish Academy (Dublin, 1971)
Ault, W. O., "By-laws of gleaning and the problems of harvest", *Econ. Hist. Rev.*, 2nd ser., xiv (1961–2), pp. 210–17
——, *Open Field Husbandry and the Village Community: a study of agrarian by-laws in medieval England*, Trans. Amer. Philos. Soc., n.s., No. 55, Pt 7 (Phila, 1965); cf. same author, *Open Field Farming in Medieval England* (1972), for trans. docs; and rev. in *Econ. Hist. Rev.*, xxvi (1973), pp. 339–40
——, "Some early village by-laws", *E.H.R.*, xlv (1930), pp. 208–31
——, "The village church and the village community in medieval England", *Speculum*, xlv (1970)
——, "Village by-laws by common consent", *Speculum*, xxix (1954), pp. 378–94
Baker, A. R. H., "Evidence in the *Nonarum Inquisitiones* of contracting arable lands in England during the early fourteenth century", *Econ. Hist. Rev.*, xix (1966), pp. 518–32
——, "Howard Levi Gray and English field systems: an evaluation", *Agric. Hist.* xxxix (1965)
——, "Open fields and partible inheritance on a Kent manor", *Econ. Hist. Rev.*, 2nd ser., xvii (1964–5), pp. 1–23
——, "Some terminological problems in studies of British field systems", *Agric. Hist. Rev.*, xvii (1969)
——, Timothy, *Medieval London* (1970)
Baldwin, J. W., *The Medieval Theories of the Just Price: Romanists, Canonists and Theologians in the Twelfth and Thirteenth Centuries*, Trans. Amer. Philos. Soc., n.s., No. 49, Pt 4 (Phila, 1959)
Barraclough, K. C., "Early steelmaking in the Sheffield area", *Steel Times Ann. Rev.* (October 1968)
Bartlett, J. N., "The expansion and decline of York in the later Middle Ages", *Econ. Hist. Rev.*, 2nd ser., xii (1959–60), pp. 17–33
Bazeley, M. L., "The extent of the English forests in the thirteenth century", *Trans. Royal Hist. Soc.*, 4th ser., iv (1921)

Bennett, H. S., *Life on the English Manor* (Cambridge, 1948)
Beresford, M. W., *New Towns of the Middle Ages: town plantation in England, Wales and Gascony* (1967)
——, "Six new towns of the bishops of Winchester 1200–55", *Medieval Archaeology*, iii (1959), pp. 187–215
——, and Hurst, J. G., *Deserted Medieval Villages* (1971)
Birnbaum, E., "Starrs of Aaron of York in the dean and chapter muniments of Durham", *Trans. Jewish Hist. Soc.*, xix (1960)
Birrell, J., "Peasant craftsmen in the medieval forest", *Agric. Hist. Rev.*, xvii (1969)
Bishop, T. A. M., "Assarting and the growth of the open fields", *Econ. Hist. Rev.*, vi (1935–6), pp. 13–29
——, "Rotation of crops at Westerham 1297–1350", *Econ. Hist. Rev.*, ix (1938–9), pp. 38–44
——, "The distribution of manorial demesne in the Vale of Yorkshire", *E.H.R.*, xlix (1934), pp. 386–406
Bridbury, A. R., *England and the Salt Trade in the Later Middle Ages* (Oxford, 1955)
Brooke, C. N. L., and Postan, M. M., *Carte Nativorum*, Northants Rec. Soc. (1960)
Brooks, F. W., "A medieval brickyard at Hull", *J. Brit. Arch. Assoc.*, 3rd ser., iv (1939), pp. 151–74
Buckatzsch, E. J., "The geographical distribution of wealth in England 1086–1843: an experimental study of certain tax assessments", *Econ. Hist. Rev.*, 2nd ser., iii (1950–1), pp. 180–201; contradicted for 14th and 15th cents by R. S. Schofield, ibid. xviii (1965), pp. 483–510
Butlin, R. A., "Recent developments in studies of the terminology of agrarian landscapes", *Agric. Hist. Rev.*, xvii (1969)
——, "Some terms used in agrarian history: a glossary", *Agric. Hist. Rev.*, ix (1961)
Cam, Helen, "Pedigrees of villeins and freemen in the thirteenth century", *Genealogists' Magazine* (September 1933), repr., *Liberties and Communities in Medieval England* (Cambridge, 1944)
——, "The early burgesses of Cambridge in relation to the surrounding countryside", *Wirtschaft und Kultur; Festschrift zum 70 Geburtstag von Alfons Dopsch* (Vienna, 1938), repr., *Liberties and Communities in Medieval England* (Cambridge, 1944)
Carus-Wilson, E. M., "An industrial revolution in the thirteenth century", *Econ. Hist. Rev.*, xi (1941), repr., *Medieval Merchant Venturers* (1954), pp. 183–210
——, "Haberget: a medieval textile conundrum", *Medieval Archaeology*, xiii (1971)
——, "The effects of the acquisition and of the loss of Gascony on the English wine trade", *Econ. Hist. Rev.*, xiv (1944–5), pp. 32–50, repr., *Medieval Merchant Venturers* (1954), pp. 265–78
——, "The English cloth industry in the late twelfth and early thirteenth centuries", *Econ. Hist. Rev.*, xiv (1944), repr., *Medieval Merchant Venturers* (1954)
——, "The first half-century of the borough of Stratford-upon-Avon", *Econ. Hist. Rev.*, 2nd ser., xviii (1965), pp. 46–63
——, "The medieval trade of the ports of the Wash", *Medieval Archaeology*, vi–vii (1962–3), Boston and Lynn
——, "The woollen industry", in *Cambridge Econ. Hist. Europe*, ed. Postan, etc., II (Cambridge, 1952), ch. 6
——, and Coleman, Olive, *England's Export Trade 1275–1547* (Oxford, 1963)
Cazel, F. A., "The Fifteenth of 1225", *Bull. Inst. Hist. Research*, xxxiv (1961)
Cipolla, C. M., "Currency depreciation in medieval Europe", *Econ. Hist. Rev.*, 2nd ser., xv (1962–3), pp. 413–22
Clapham, J. H., "A thirteenth century market town", *Cambridge Hist. J.*, iv (1932–4)
Colby, C. W., "The growth of oligarchy in English towns", *E.H.R.*, v (1890)
Colvin, H. M. (ed.), *Building Accounts of King Henry III* (Oxford, 1971)
——, *The History of the King's Works* (1963)
Cowley, F. G., "The Cistercian economy in Glamorgan 1130–1349", *Morgannwg*, xi (1967)
Darby, H. C. (ed.), *An Historical Geography of England before 1800* (Cambridge, 1936)
Davenport, Frances G., *The Economic Development of a Norfolk Manor* [Forncett] *1086–1565* (1906, repr., 1967)
Davies, E., *A Gazeteer of Welsh Place Names* (Cardiff, 1957)
——, R. R., "The survival of the blood-feud in medieval Wales", *History*, liv (1969), pp. 338–57
Davis, H. W. C., "The commune of Bury St Edmunds 1264", *E.H.R.*, xxiv (1909), pp. 313–17
Denholm-Young, N., "Feudal society in the thirteenth century: the knights", *History*, xxix (1944), pp. 107–19
——, *Seignorial Administration in England* (Oxford, 1937)
——, "The merchants of Cahors", *Medievalia et Humanistica*, iv (1946)
——, "The tournament in the thirteenth century", in *Studies in Medieval Hist. pres. to F. M. Powicke*, ed. Hunt, Pantin and Southern (Oxford, 1948), pp. 240–68
DeWindt, E. B., *Land and People in Holywell-cum-Needingworth* (Toronto, 1972)
Dobson, R. B., "Admissions to the freedom of the city of York in the later Middle Ages", *Econ. Hist. Rev.*, 2nd ser., xxvi (1973), pp. 1–22
Dodwell, Barbara, "Holdings and inheritance in medieval East Anglia", *Econ. Hist. Rev.*, 2nd ser., xx (1967), pp. 53–66
——, "The free tenantry of the Hundred Rolls", *Econ. Hist. Rev.*, xiv (1944–5), pp. 163–71
Donkin, R., "Cattle on the estates of medieval Cistercian monasteries in England and Wales", *Econ. Hist. Rev.*, 2nd ser., xv (1962–3), pp. 31–53
——, "Cistercian sheep-farming and wool sales in the thirteenth century", *Agric. Hist. Rev.*, vi (1958)

Donkin, R., "Settlement and depopulation on Cistercian estates during the twelfth and thirteenth centuries, especially in Yorkshire", *Bull. Inst. Hist. Research*, xxxiii (1960)
——, "Site changes of Cistercian monasteries", *Geography*, xliv (1959)
——, "The Cistercian order and the settlement of northern England", *Geogr. Rev.*, lix (1969)
——, "The Cistercian order in medieval England: some conclusions", *Inst. Brit. Geographers*, No. 33 (1963)
Dunning, G. C., "A group of English and imported pottery from Lesnes Abbey, Kent and the trade in early Hispano-Moresque pottery in England", *Antiquaries Journal*, xli (1961)
——, "Medieval pottery kilns", *Archaeol. News Letter*, I, xi, No. 8 (1949)
——, "Polychrome jugs found in England and Scotland", *Archaeologia*, lxxxiii (1933), pp. 126–38
Ekwall, E., *Street Names of Medieval London* (Oxford, 1954)
——, *Studies on the Population of Medieval London* (Stockholm, 1956)
——, *Variation in Surnames in Medieval London* (Lund, 1945)
Elman, P., "Economic causes of the expulsion of the Jews in 1290", *Econ. Hist. Rev.*, vii (1936–7), pp. 145–54
Emery, F. V., "Moated settlements in England", *Geography*, xlvii (1962)
English Rural Life in the Middle Ages, Bodleian Picture Book No. 14 (Oxford, 1965)
Evans, Joan, *Magical Jewels of the Middle Ages and the Renaissance, particularly in England* (Oxford, 1922)
Faith, R. J., "Peasant families and inheritance customs in medieval England", *Agric. Hist. Rev.*, xiv (1966)
Farmer, D. L., "Some grain price movements in thirteenth-century England", *Econ. Hist. Rev.*, 2nd ser., x (1957–8), pp. 207–20
——, "Some livestock price movements in thirteenth-century England", *Econ. Hist. Rev.*, 2nd ser., xxii (1969), pp. 1–16
——, "Some price fluctuations in Angevin England", *Econ. Hist. Rev.*, 2nd ser., ix (1956–7), pp. 34–43
Flower, C. T., *Public Works in Medieval Law*, 2 vols (1923)
Fowler, G. H. "Some notes on the pronunciation of medieval Latin in England", *History*, xxii (1937–8), pp. 97–109
Fox, L., "The early history of Coventry", *History*, xxx (1945), pp. 21–37
Fraser, C. M., "Medieval trading restrictions in the north-east", *Arch. Aeliana*, 4th ser., xxi (1961)
——, "The north-east coal trade until 1421", *Trans. Archit. and Arch. Soc. Durham and Northumberland*, xi (1962)
Fryde, E. B., "The deposits of Hugh Despenser the younger with Italian bankers", *Econ. Hist. Rev.*, 2nd ser., iii (1950–1), pp. 344–62
Furley, J. S., *The City Government of Winchester from the Records of the Fourteenth and Fifteenth Centuries* (Oxford, 1923)
Fussell, G. E., "Ploughs and ploughing before 1800", *Agric. Hist.*, xl (1966)
Gill, C., *Studies in Midland History* (Oxford, 1930). On Coventry
Graves, C. V., "The economic activities of the Cistercians in medieval England 1128–1307", *Analecta Sancti Ordinis Cisterciensis* (1957)
Haberley, L., *Medieval Paving-tiles* (Oxford, 1937)
Hall, Hubert (ed.), *Pipe Roll of the Bishopric of Winchester 1208–9* (1903)
Hallam, H. E., "Further observations on the Spalding serf lists", *Econ. Hist. Rev.*, 2nd ser., xvi (1963–4), pp. 338–50
——, "Population density in medieval Fenland", *Econ. Hist. Rev.*, 2nd ser., xiv (1961–2), pp. 71–81
——, "Salt making in the Lincolnshire fenland during the Middle Ages", *Lincs. Archit. and Arch. Soc.*, n.s., vol. 8 (1959–60), pp. 85–112
——, *Settlement and Society: a study of the early agrarian history of S. Lincolnshire* (Cambridge, 1965)
——, "Some thirteenth-century censuses", *Econ. Hist. Rev.*, 2nd ser., x (1957–8), pp. 340–61. On serf lists of Spalding priory, 1268–9
——, "The agrarian economy of medieval Lincolnshire before the Black Death", *Hist. Studies Austral. and N.Z.*, xi (1964)
Hancock, P. D., *A Bibliography of Works relating to Scotland 1916–50*, 2 vols (Edinb., 1959–60)
Harley, J. B., "Population trends and agricultural developments from the Warwickshire Hundred Rolls of 1279", *Econ. Hist. Rev.*, 2nd ser., xi (1958–9), pp. 8–18
Harvey, Barbara F., "The population trend in England between 1300 and 1348", *Trans. Royal Hist. Soc.*, 5th ser., xvi (1966), pp. 23–42
——, J., *English Medieval Architects: a biographical dictionary down to 1550* (1954)
——, P. D. A., *A Medieval Oxfordshire Village: Cuxham 1240–1400* (1965)
Hewitt, H. J., *Medieval Cheshire* (Manchester, 1929)
Higgs, E. S., and White, J. P., "Autumn killing [of stock]", *Antiquity*, xxxvii (1963)
Hill, J. W. F., *Medieval Lincoln* (Cambridge, 1948)
Hilton, R. H., *A Medieval Society: the West Midlands at the end of the thirteenth century* (1966)
——, "A thirteenth-century poem on disputed villein services", *E. H. R.*, lvi (1941), pp. 90–5
——, "Peasant movements in England before 1381", *Econ. Hist. Rev.*, 2nd ser., ii (1949–50), pp. 117–36
——, *The Decline of Serfdom in Medieval England* (1969)
——, "The origins of Robin Hood", *Past and Present*, xiv (1958), pp. 30–44
Hodgett, G. A. J., *Agrarian England in the Later Middle Ages*, Hist. Assoc. Aids for Teachers, No. 13 (1966)
Holt, J. C., "The ballads of Robin Hood", *Past and Present*, xviii (1960), pp. 89–110
——, N. R. (ed,), *The Pipe Roll of the Bishopric of Winchester 1210–11* (Manchester, 1964)

Homans, G. C., *English Villagers of the Thirteenth Century* (Cambridge, Mass., 1941; Harper Torchbooks, 1970)
——, "The explanation of English regional differences", *Past and Present*, No. 42 (1969)
Honeybourne, Marjorie B., "The leper hospitals of the London area: with an appendix on some other medieval hospitals of Middlesex", *Trans. London and Middx Arch. Soc.*, xxi (1963)
Hoskins, W. G., *Devon* (1954)
——, *Fieldwork in Local History* (1967)
——, *Leicestershire* (1957)
——, *The Making of the English Landscape* (1957)
——, *The Midland Peasant* (1957)
Hunt, T. J., and Keil, I. J., "Two medieval gardens", *Proc. Som. Arch. and Nat. Hist. Soc.*, civ (1959–60)
Hurry, J. B., *The Woad Plant and its Dye* (1930)
Hyams, P. R., "The origins of a peasant land market in England", *Econ. Hist. Rev.*, 2nd ser., xxiii (1970), pp. 18–31
James, M. K., *Studies in the Medieval Wine Trade* (Oxford, 1971)
Jenkins, Rhys, "Iron making in the Forest of Dean", *Newcomen Soc. Trans.*, vi (1925–6)
Jenkinson, Hilary, "Medieval tallies, public and private", *Archaeologia*, lxxiv (1925)
Johnstone, Hilda, "Everyday life in some medieval records", *History*, xii (1927–8), pp. 1–12
——, "Poor relief in the royal households of thirteenth-century England", *Speculum*, iv (1929), pp. 149–67
Jones, G. P., "Trading in medieval Caernarvon", *Trans. Caerns. Hist. Soc.*, x (1950)
Keen, M., "Robin Hood, peasant or gentleman?", with J. C. Holt's reply, *Past and Present*, xix (1961), pp. 7–18
Kerridge, E., "Ridge and furrow and agrarian history", *Econ. Hist. Rev.*, 2nd ser., iv (1951–2)
King, E., "Large and small landowners in thirteenth-century England: the case of Peterborough Abbey", *Past and Present*, No. 47 (1970)
Knoop, D., and Jones, G. P., *The Medieval Mason*, 3rd edn (Manchester, 1967)
Kosminsky, E. A., *Studies in the Agrarian History of England in the Thirteenth Century*, ed. R. H. Hilton (Oxford, 1956)
Krause, J., "The medieval household: large or small?", *Econ. Hist. Rev.*, 2nd ser., ix (1956–7), pp. 420–32
Kuhlicke, F. W., and Emmison, F. H. (eds), *English Local History Handlist*, Hist. Assoc. (1969)
Lane, F. C., "Tonnages, medieval and modern", *Econ. Hist. Rev.*, 2nd ser., xvii (1964–5), pp. 213–33
Lennard, R., "Agrarian history: some vistas and pitfalls", *Agric. Hist. Rev.*, xii (1964)
——, "Early manorial juries", *E.H.R.*, lxxvii (1962)
——, "Manorial traffic and agricultural trade in medieval England", *J. Proc. Agric. Econ. Soc.*, v (1938)
——, "Statistics of sheep in medieval England", *Agric. Hist. Rev.*, vii (1959)
——, "The composition of demesne plough teams in twelfth-century England", *E.H.R.*, lxxv (1960)
——, "The long and short hundred in agrarian statistics", *Agric. Hist. Rev.*, viii (1960)
——, "What is a manorial extent?", *E.H.R.*, xliv (1929), pp. 256–63
Le Patourel, J., *Documents Relating to the Manor and Borough of Leeds 1066–1400*, Thoresby Soc. (Leeds, 1957)
Lewis, E. A., "The development of industry and commerce in Wales during the Middle Ages", *Trans. Royal Hist. Soc.*, n.s., xvii (1903), pp. 121–73
——, G. R., *The Stannaries, a study of the English tin mines* (Cambridge, Mass., 1908)
Lipman, V. D., *The Jews of Medieval Ipswich* (1967)
Lloyd, T. H., "Some costs of cloth manufacturing in thirteenth-century England", *Textile History*, i (1971)
Lysons, S., *The Environs of London*, 4 vols (1792–6)
Major, K., "The local historian and the Middle Ages", *Bull. Local Hist. E. Midland Region*, iv (1969)
Marsh, F. B., *English Rule in Gascony, with special reference to the Towns* (Ann Arbor, 1912)
Martin, G. H., "The English borough in the thirteenth century", *Trans. Royal Hist. Soc.*, 5th ser., No. 13 (1963), pp. 123–44
Marwick, W. H., "A bibliography of Scottish economic history 1951–62", and "1963–70", *Econ. Hist. Rev.*, 2nd ser., xvi (1963–4), pp. 147–8, and xxiv (1971), pp. 469–70. Slight
May, A. N., "An index of thirteenth-century peasant impoverishment: manor court fines", *Econ. Hist. Rev.*, 2nd ser., xxvi (1973), pp. 389–402
——, Teresa, "The estates of the Cobham family in the later thirteenth century", *Arch. Cantiana*, lxxxiv (1969)
Miller, E., "England in the twelfth and thirteenth centuries: an economic contrast", *Econ. Hist. Rev.*, 2nd ser., xxiv (1971), pp. 1–14. Criticism of this by C. G. Reed and T. L. Anderson, with Miller's reply, is in ibid. xxvi (1973), pp. 134–40
——, *The Abbey and Bishopric of Ely* (Cambridge, 1951)
——, "The citizens of York in the twelfth and thirteenth centuries" (Report of Anglo-American Conference of Historians, 1957), *Bull. Inst. Hist. Research*, xxxi (1958)
——, "The English economy in the thirteenth century", *Past and Present*, No. 28 (1964), pp. 21–40
——, "The fortunes of the English textile industry during the thirteenth century", *Econ. Hist. Rev.*, 2nd ser., xviii (1965), pp. 64–82
Moor, C., *Knights of Edward I*, 5 vols, Harleian Soc., Nos 80–4 (1929–32)
Moore, J. H., "The ox in the Middle Ages", *Agric. Hist.*, xxxv (1961)

O'Neill, H., "Monastic mining and metallurgy in the British Isles", *Metals and Materials* (June 1967)
Orwin, C. S. and C. S., *The Open Fields*, 3rd edn, with new introd. by Joan Thirsk (Oxford, 1967)
Oswald, A., "The excavation of a thirteenth-century wooden building at Wesley Castle, Birmingham 1960-1", *Medieval Archaeology*, vi–vii (1964)
Page, F. M., "Bidentes Hoylandie, a medieval sheep farm", *Econ. J. Hist. Suppl.* (1929)
Painter, S., "The family and the feudal system in twelfth-century England", *Speculum*, xxxv (1960)
Pantin, W. A., "The merchant houses and warehouses of King's Lynn", *Medieval Archaeology*, vi–vii (1962–3), pp. 173–81
Pegolotti, F. B., *La Practica della Mercatura*, ed. A. Evans (Med. Acad. of America, 1936)
Perry, R., "The Gloucestershire woollen industry 1100-1696", *Trans. Bristol and Glos. Arch. Soc.*, lxvi (1947)
Pirenne, H., *Economic and Social History of Medieval Europe*, trans. I. E. Clegg (1936)
Plucknett, T. F. T. *The Legislation of Edward I* (Oxford, 1949). Relates Edw. I's statutes to the social background
——, *The Mediaeval Bailiff*, Creighton Lecture, 1953 (1954)
Pocock, E. A., "The first fields in an Oxfordshire parish [Clanfield]", *Agric. Hist. Rev.*, xvi (1968)
Poole, A. L., *Obligations of Society in the XII and XIII Centuries* (Oxford, 1946)
—— (ed.), *Medieval England*, 2 vols (Oxford, 1958)
Postan, M. M., "Credit in medieval trade", *Econ. Hist. Rev.*, i (1928)
——, "Investment in medieval agriculture", *J. Econ. Hist.*, xxvii (1967)
——, "Italy and the economic development of England in the Middle Ages", *J. Econ. Hist.*, xi (1951)
——, "Partnerships in English medieval commerce", *Studi in Onore di Armando Sapori* (Milan, 1957)
——, "Some economic evidence of declining population in the later Middle Ages", *Econ. Hist. Rev.*, 2nd ser., ii (1950)
——, "The chronology of labour services", *Trans. Royal Hist. Soc.*, 4th ser., xx (1937)
——, *The Famulus: the estate labourer in the XIIth and XIIIth centuries*, Econ. Hist. Rev. Suppl., No. 2 (1954)
——, "Village livestock in the thirteenth century", *Econ. Hist. Rev.*, 2nd ser., xv (1962–3), pp. 219–49
——, and others, *The Cambridge Economic History of Europe* (Cambridge, 1941–63), I, *Agrarian Life of the Middle Ages* (1941, 2nd edn, 1966); II, *Trade and Industry in the Middle Ages* (1952); III, *Economic Organisation and Policies in the Middle Ages* (1963)
Power, E. E., "Peasant life and rural conditions", *Camb. Med. Hist.*, VII (1932)
——, "The position of women", in *The Legacy of the Middle Ages*, ed. C. Crump and E. Jacob (Oxford, 1926)
——, *The Wool Trade in English Medieval History* (Oxford, 1941)
Pritchard, V., *English Medieval Graffiiti* (Cambridge, 1967)
Rackham, B., *Medieval English Pottery* (1948)
Raftis, J. A., "Peasant mobility and freedom in medieval England", Canadian Hist. Assoc. Ann. Rep. (1965)
——, "Social structure in five East Midland villages: a study of possibilities in the use of court roll data", *Econ. Hist. Rev.*, 2nd ser., xviii (1965), pp. 83–100
——, *The Estates of Ramsey Abbey* (Toronto, 1957)
Rees, W., *South Wales and the March 1284–1415* (Oxford, 1924)
Reynolds, R. L., "Some English settlers in Genoa in the late twelfth century", *Econ. Hist. Rev.*, iv (1933)
Richardson, H. G., *The English Jewry under the Angevin Kings* (1960)
——, "The medieval plough team", *History*, xxvi (1942), pp. 287–96
Roberts, B. K., "Medieval fishponds", *Amateur Historian*, vii, No. 4 (1966)
Robinson, W. C., "Money, population and economic change in late medieval Europe", *Econ. Hist. Rev.*, 2nd ser., xii (1959–60), pp. 63–76; reply by M. M. Postan, ibid., pp. 77–82
Roden, D., "Demesne farming in the Chiltern hills", *Agric. Hist. Rev.*, xvii (1969)
——, "Fragmentation of farms and fields in the Chiltern hills: thirteenth century and later", *Medieval Studies*, xxxi (1969)
Roper, M. (ed.), *Feet of Fines for the County of York 1300–14*, Yorks. Arch. Soc. Rec. ser. (1965)
Roth, C., "The economic history of the Jews", *Econ. Hist. Rev.*, 2nd ser., xiv (1961–2), pp. 131–5
Rowe, Margery, and Jackson, A., *Exeter Freemen 1266–1967* (Exeter, 1973)
Ruddock, A. A., *Italian Merchants and Shipping in Southampton 1270–1600* (Southampton, 1951)
Rudkin, E. H., and Owen, D. M., "The medieval salt industry in the Lindsey marshland", *Lincs. Archit. and Arch. Soc.*, n.s., viii (1959–60)
Russell, J. C., *British Medieval Population* (Albuquerque, New Mexico, 1948)
——, "Demographic limitations of the Spalding serf lists", *Econ. Hist. Rev.*, 2nd ser., xv (1962–3), pp. 138–144. Replies to articles of H. E. Hallam
——, *Late Ancient and Medieval Population*, Trans. Amer. Philos. Soc., n.s., No. 48, Pt 3 (Philadelphia, 1958)
——, "Recent advances in medieval demography", *Speculum*, xl (1965)
Ryder, M., "Follicle remains in some British parchments", *Nature*, clxxxvii (1960)
——, "Sheep breeds in history", *Year Book of the Nat. Sheep Breeders' Assoc.* (1960)
Sabine, E. L., "Butchering in medieval London", *Speculum*, viii (1933), pp. 335–53
——, "City cleaning in medieval London", *Speculum*, xii (1937), pp. 19–43
——, "Latrines and cesspools of medieval London", *Speculum*, ix (1934), pp. 303–21

Salzman, L. F., *Building in England down to 1540*, repr. (Oxford, 1967)
——, *English Industries of the Middle Ages*, new edn (Oxford, 1923)
——, *English Trade in the Middle Ages* (Oxford, 1931)
——, "The Legal status of markets", *Cambridge Hist. J.*, ii (1926–8)
Scott, E. K., "Early cloth fulling and its machinery", *Trans. Newcomen Soc.*, xii (1933), pp. 31–52
Sheehan, M. M., "A list of thirteenth-century English wills", *Genealogists' Magazine*, xiii (1961)
Shelby, L. R., "The role of the master mason in medieval English building", *Speculum*, xxxix (1964)
Sherborne, J. W., *The Port of Bristol in the Middle Ages*, Bristol branch Hist. Assoc. (Bristol, 1965)
Siddle, D. J., "The rural economy of medieval Holderness", *Agric. Hist. Rev.*, xv (1967)
Singer, C., Holmyard, E. J., etc., *A History of Technology*, II (Mediterranean civilisation and the Middle Ages) (Oxford, 1957)
Smith, A. H., *English Place-name Elements*, English Place-name Soc., vols 25 and 26 (1956)
——, J. T., "Medieval roofs: a classification", *Arch. J.*, cxv (1958), pp. 111–49
Stenton, D. M., *English Society in the Early Middle Ages (1066–1307)*, Pelican History (1951)
——, F. M., *Norman London*, Hist. Assoc. (1934)
——, "The free peasantry of the northern Danelaw", *Bull. de la Soc. Royale de Lettres de Lund* (Lund and London, 1926), Introduction
Stephenson, Mill, *A List of Monumental Brasses in the British Isles* (1926)
Stone, E., "Profit and loss accountancy at Norwich Cathedral Priory", *Trans. Royal Hist. Soc.*, 5th ser., xii (1962), pp. 25–48
Straker, S. E., *Wealden Glass* (Hove, 1933)
Strutt, J., *Sports and Pastimes of the People of England*, ed. J. C. Cox (1903). Not yet superseded
Thirsk, Joan, "The common fields", *Past and Present*, No. 29 (1964), pp. 3–25
——, "The family", *Past and Present*, No. 27 (1964), pp. 116–22
——, "The origin of the common fields", *Past and Present*, No. 33 (1966), pp. 142–7. A reply to J. Z. Titow, ibid. No. 32 (1965), pp. 86–102
Thomas, A. H., *Calendar of Early Mayor's Court Rolls of the City of London 1298–1307* (Cambridge, 1924)
——, Colin, "Thirteenth-century farm economies in North Wales", *Agric. Hist. Rev.*, xvi (1968)
Thompson, A. Hamilton, "Medieval building documents and what we learn from them", *Som. Arch. Soc. Trans.*, lxvi
——, D. V., "Medieval parchment making", *The Library*, 4th ser., xvi (1935), pp. 113–17
——, *The Materials of Medieval Painting* (1936)
Thrupp, S. L., "Medieval gilds reconsidered", *J. Econ. Hist.*, ii (1942), pp. 164–73
——, *The Merchant Class of Medieval London 1300–1500* (Chicago, 1948; and Ann Arbor paperback, 1962)
——, "The problem of replacement rates in late medieval English population", *Econ. Hist. Rev.*, 2nd ser., xviii (1965), pp. 101–19
——, and Johnson, H. B., "The earliest Canterbury freemen's rolls 1298–1363", *Documents Illustrative of Medieval Kentish Society*, ed. F. R. H. Du Boulay, Kent Arch. Soc. (1964)
Titow, J. Z., *English Rural Society 1200–1350* (1969)
——, "Medieval England and the open field system", *Past and Present*, No. 32 (1965), pp. 86-102. cf. Joan Thirsk, ibid. No. 29 (1964), pp. 3–25
——, "Some differences between manors and their effect on the condition of the peasant in the thirteenth century", *Agric. Hist. Rev.*, x (1962)
——, "Some evidence of the thirteenth-century population increase", *Econ. Hist. Rev.*, 2nd ser., xiv (1961–2), pp. 218–24
——, *Winchester Yields: a study in medieval agricultural productivity* (Cambridge, 1972)
Tout, T. F., "The beginnings of a modern capital: London and Westminster in the fourteenth century", *Proc. Brit. Acad.*, xi, repr. in *Collected Papers*, III (Manchester, 1934)
Treharne, R. F., "The knights in the period of reform and rebellion 1258–67: a critical phase in the rise of a new class", *Bull. Instit. Hist. Research*, xxi (1946–8)
Ugawa, J., "The economic development of some Devon manors in the thirteenth century", *Trans. Devon Assoc.*, xciv (1962)
Ulyanov, Y. U. R., "The Stonor family estates in the eleventh to thirteenth centuries: on the problem of genesis of small estates in medieval England", *Srednie Veka*, No. 30 (1967)
——, "Watlington Manor, Oxfordshire 1086–1300", *Srednie Veka*, No. 29 (1966)
Unwin, G., *The Gilds and Companies of London*, rev. edn (1938)
Urry, William, *Canterbury under the Angevin Kings* (1967)
Van Houtte, J. A., "The rise and decline of the market of Bruges", *Econ. Hist. Rev.*, 2nd ser., xix (1966), pp. 29–47
Veale, Elspeth M., "The rabbit in England", *Agric. Hist. Rev.*, v (1957)
Victoria County History: Wiltshire, VI (1962), Old Sarum, Wilton, New Sarum
——: *Yorkshire* (1961), city of York
——: *Yorkshire East Riding*, I (1969), Kingston upon Hull
Watts, D. G., "Model for the early fourteenth century", *Econ. Hist. Rev.*, 2nd ser., xx (1967), pp. 543–7. Price movements on Titchfield Abbey estates
Webb, J. J., *The Guilds of Dublin* (Dublin, 1929)

Wightman, W. E., *The Lacy Family in England and Normandy 1066–1194* (Oxford, 1966). See *Econ. Hist. Rev.*, 2nd ser., xx (1967), pp. 385–6
Willard, J. F., "Inland transportation in England during the fourteenth century", *Speculum*, iii (1926)
Williams, D. H., *The Welsh Cistercians: aspects of their economic history* (Pontypool, 1969)
——, G. A., *Medieval London: from Commune to Capital* (1963)
Willis, D. (ed.), *The Estate Book of Henry de Bray of Harleston*, Camden ser. (1916)
Wilson, A. E., "Farming in Sussex in the Middle Ages", *Sussex Arch. Coll.*, xcvii (1959)
Wretts-Smith, M., "The organisation of farming at Croyland Abbey 1257–1321", *J. Econ. and Bus. Hist.*, iv (1931)
Wright, E. C., "Common law in the thirteenth-century royal forest", *Speculum*, iii (1928)
——, N. R., "Buildings of the old port of Boston, Lincs.", *J. Indust. Arch.*, II, No. 4 (1965)

MISCELLANEOUS

Ackerman, R. W., "The knighting ceremonies in the Middle English romances", *Speculum*, xix (1944), pp. 285–313
Andersson, A., *English Influence in Norwegian and Swedish Sculpture in Wood, 1220–70* (Stockholm, 1940)
Baring, F., "Domesday and some thirteenth-century surveys", *E.H.R.*, xii (1897), pp. 285–90
Barron, E. M., *The Scottish War of Independence* (2nd edn, Inverness, 1934)
Barrow, G. W. S., "The Scottish clergy in the war of independence", *Scott. Hist. Rev.*, xli, pp. 1–22
Bassett, Margery, "Newgate prison in the Middle Ages", *Speculum*, xviii (1943), pp. 233–46
Bateson, M., "A London municipal collection of the reign of King John", *E.H.R.*, xvii (1902), pp. 480–511, 707–30
Beddie, J. S., "The ancient classics in the medieval libraries", *Speculum*, v (1930), pp. 3–20
Beloe, E. M., "Freebridge Marshland Hundred and the making of Lynn", *Norfolk Archaeology*, xii (1895)
Beresford, M. W., "Maps and the medieval landscape", *Antiquity*, xxiv (1950), pp. 114–18
Bilson, J., "The architecture of the Cistercians", *Arch. J.*, lxvi (1909), pp. 185–280
Boase, T. S. R., *English Art 1100–1216* (Oxford, 1953)
Brett-James, N. G., "John de Drokensford, bishop of Bath and Wells", *Trans. London and Middx Arch. Soc.*, new ser., x (1951)
Brieger, P. H., *English Art 1216–1307* (Oxford, 1957)
Bullough, V. L., "Medical study at medieval Oxford", *Speculum*, xxxvi (1961)
Butler, L. H., "Archbishop Melton, his neighbours and his kinsmen", *J. Eccles. Hist.*, ii (1951)
Chamot, M., *English Mediaeval Enamels* (1930)
Chew, H. M., "Mortmain in medieval London", *E.H.R.*, lx (1945), pp. 1–15
——, "The office of escheator in the city of London during the Middle Ages", *E.H.R.*, lviii (1943), pp. 319–30
Christie, A. G. I., *English Mediaeval Embroidery* (Oxford, 1938)
Crawford, O. G. S., *Archaeology in the Field* (1953, rev. edn, 1960)
——, "Southampton", *Antiquity*, xvi (1942), pp. 36–50
Crosby, Ruth, "Oral delivery in the Middle Ages", *Speculum*, xi (1936), pp. 88–110
Curwen, E. C., *Air Photography and the Evolution of the Corn Field* (2nd edn, 1938)
Darby, H. C., *The Domesday Geography of England* (Cambridge, 1952 – in progress). Vols I to V on Eastern, Midland, Northern, South-East, and South-West England, respectively, have so far appeared.
Denholm-Young, N., *The Country Gentry in the Fourteenth Century* (Oxford, 1969)
Dilley, J. W., "German merchants in Scotland 1297–1327", *Scott. Hist. Rev.*, xxvii
Duncan, A. A. M., and Brown, A. L., "Argyll and the Isles in the earlier Middle Ages", *Proc. Soc. Antiqu. Scotland*, xc, pp. 192–220
Edwards, (Sir) J. G(oronwy), "The battle of Maes Madog and the Welsh campaign of 1294–5", *E.H.R.*, xxxix (1924), pp. 1–12
——, "Edward I's castle-building in Wales", Sir John Rhŷs Memorial Lecture for 1944, *Proc. Brit. Academy, 1946*, xxxii (1950), pp. 15–81
——, "The site of the battle of 'Meismeidoc', 1295", *E.H.R.*, xlvi (1931), pp. 262–5
Egbert, D. D., *The Tickhill Psalter and related manuscripts* (New York, 1940)
Ekwall, E., *Two Early London Subsidy Rolls* (Lund, 1951)
Evans, J., *English Art 1307–1461* (Oxford, 1949)
Field Archaeology (H.M.S.O., rev. edn, 1963)
Fraser, C. M., "Law and society in Northumberland and Durham, 1290–1350", *Arch. Aeliana*, xlvii (1969)
——, "The pattern of trade in the N.E. of England, 1265–1350", *Northern History*, iv (1969)
Haskins, G. L., "Three English documents relating to Franciscus Accursius", *Law Quart. Rev.*, liv (1938), pp. 87–94
Hoskins, W. G., *Provincial England* (1963)
——, and Stamp, Sir Dudley, *Common Lands of England and Wales* (1963)
James, M. R., "The bestiary", *History*, xvi (1931–2), pp. 1–11
——, *Suffolk and Norfolk* (1930)
Jervoise, E., *The Ancient Bridges of Mid and Eastern England* (1932)

——, *The Ancient Bridges of the South of England* (1930)
——, *The Ancient Bridges of the North of England* (1931)
Ker, W. P., "On the history of ballads", *Proc. Brit. Academy*, iv (1909–10), pp. 179–205
Knoop, D., and Jones, G. P., "The English medieval quarry", *Econ. Hist. Rev.*, ix (1938–9), pp. 17–37
Lane, R. H., "Waggons and their ancestors", *Antiquity*, ix (1935), pp. 140–1
Lapsley, G., "Buzones", *E.H.R.*, xlvii (1932), pp. 177–93, 545–67
Leadman, D. H., "The battle of Boroughbridge", *Yorks, Arch. J.*, vii (1882), pp. 330–60
Legge, M. Dominica, "La piere d'Escoce", *Scott. Hist. Rev.*, xxxviii, pp. 109–13
Lennard, R., "Early English fulling mills: additional examples", *Econ. Hist. Rev.*, 2nd ser., iii (1950–1), pp. 342–3
Lethaby, W. R., "Medieval paintings at Westminster", *Proc. Brit. Academy*, xiii (1927), pp. 123–51
Lewis, T., "An English serjeanty in a Welsh setting", *History*, xxxi (1946), pp. 85–99
Little, A. G., "Grammar schools at Oxford, 1231", *E.H.R.*, vi (1891), pp. 152–3
Lobel, M. D., *The Borough of Bury St Edmunds* (Oxford, 1935)
Loomis, R. S., and Cohen, G., "Were there theatres in the twelfth and thirteenth centuries?", *Speculum*, xx (1945), pp. 92–8
Lopez, R., "The English and the manufacture of writing materials in Genoa", *Econ. Hist. Rev.*, x (1939–40), pp. 132–7
Lucas, H. S., "The great European famine of 1315, 1316, and 1317", *Speculum*, v (1930), pp. 343–77
Mackenzie, B. A., *The Early London Dialect* (Oxford, 1928)
Madan, Falconer, "The localisation of manuscripts", *Essays in History presented to R. Lane Poole*, ed. H. W. C. Davis (Oxford, 1927), pp. 5–29
Maitland, F. W., "A conveyancer in the thirteenth century", *Law Quart. Rev.*, vii (1891), pp. 63–9
——, "History of a Cambridgeshire manor", *E.H.R.*, ix (1894), pp. 417–39
——, "The laws of Wales: the kindred and the bloodfeud", *Collected Papers*, 3 vols (Cambridge, 1911), I, pp. 202–29
——, *Township and Borough* (Cambridge, 1898)
Maps and Plans in the Public Record Office, c. 1410–1860 (H.M.S.O., 1967)
Massingberd, W. O., "A Lincolnshire manor without a demesne farm", *E.H.R.*, xix (1904), pp. 297–8
——, "The Lincolnshire sokemen", *E.H.R.*, xx (1905), pp. 699–703
Melville, A. M. M., "The pastoral custom and local wool trade of mediaeval Sussex, 1085–1485", *Bull. Inst. Hist. Research*, x (1932–3), pp. 38–40
Messent, C. J. W., *The Ruined Churches of Norfolk* (Norwich, 1931)
Murray, K. M. E., *The Constitutional History of the Cinque Ports* (Manchester, 1935)
——, "Faversham and the Cinque Ports", *Trans. Royal Hist. Soc.*, 4th ser., xviii (1935), pp. 53–84
Nichols, J. F., "An early fourteenth century petition from the tenants of Bocking to their manorial lord", *Econ. Hist. Rev.*, ii (1929–30), pp. 300–7
Nicholson, Jennifer, "A contribution to the study of French as taught in England, 1250–1450", *Bull. Inst. Hist. Research*, xv (1937–8), pp. 185–6
——, Ranald, "The Franco-Scottish and Franco-Norwegian treaties of 1295", *Scott. Hist. Rev.*, xxxviii, pp. 114–32
Nightingale, M., "Ploughing and field shape", *Antiquity*, xxvii (1953), pp. 20–6
Otway-Ruthven, J., "The request of the Irish for English law, 1277–80", *Irish Historical Studies*, vi (1948–9), pp. 261–70
Page, W., "The origins and forms of Hertfordshire towns and villages", *Archaeologia*, lxix (1917–18)
Payne, R. C., "Agrarian conditions in the Wiltshire estates of the duchy of Lancaster, the lords Hungerford and the bishopric of Winchester in the thirteenth, fourteenth and fifteenth centuries", *Bull. Inst. Hist. Research*, xviii (1940–1), pp. 116–18
Pegues, F., "Royal support of students in the thirteenth century", *Speculum*, xxxi (1956), pp. 454–62
Penson, Eva, "Charters to some western boroughs in 1256", *E.H.R.*, xxxv (1920), pp. 558–64
Pevsner, *The Leaves of Southwell* (1945)
Platt, Colin, *Medieval Southampton: an English trading community* (1973)
——, *The Monastic Grange in Medieval England* (1969)
Rabinowitz, L., "The medieval Jewish counterpart to the gild merchant", *Econ. Hist. Rev.*, viii (1937–8), pp. 180–5
Raistrick, A., *The Story of the Pennine Walls* (Clapham, Yorks., 1952)
Reynolds, R. L., "Some English settlers in Genoa in the late twelfth century", *Econ. Hist. Rev.*, iv (1932–4), pp. 317–23
Rickert, M., *Painting in Britain: the Middle Ages* (1954)
Roberts, E., "The boundary and woodlands of Shotover forest, *c.* 1298", *Oxoniensia*, xxviii (1963)
Roth, C., "Pledging a book in medieval England", *The Library* (Trans. Bibliographical Soc.), 5th ser., xix, pp. 196–200
Salter, H., "An Oxfordshire will of 1230–1", *E.H.R.*, xx (1905), p. 291
——, "The ford of Oxford", *Antiquity*, ii (1928), pp. 458–60
Sanford, E. M., "The study of ancient history in the Middle Ages", *J. Hist. Ideas*, v (1944), pp. 21–43
Savage, Sir William, *The Making of our Towns* (1952)

Sayles, G. O., "The dissolution of a gild at York in 1306", *E.H.R.*, lv (1940), pp. 83–98
Schramm, P. E., *A History of the English Coronation*, trans. L. G. Wickham Legg (1937)
Shilson, J. W., "Weighing wool in the Middle Ages", *Antiquity*, xviii (1944), pp. 72–7
Smirke, E., "Winchester in the thirteenth century", *Arch. J.*, ix (1859)
Smith, R. A. L., "Marsh embankment and sea defence in medieval Kent", *Econ. Hist. Rev.*, x (1939–40), pp. 29–37
Stamp, A. E., "Legal proofs of age", *E.H.R.*, xxix (1914), pp. 323–5
Stenton, F. M., "The changing feudalism of the Middle Ages", *History*, xix (1934–5), pp. 289–301
——, "The road system of medieval England", *Econ. Hist. Rev.*, vii (1936–7), pp. 1–21
Stephenson, C., *Borough and Town: a study of urban origins in England* (Cambridge, Mass., 1933)
Stone, L., *Sculpture in Britain: the Middle Ages* (1955)
Strayer, J. R., "The laicisation of French and English in the thirteenth century", *Speculum*, xv (1940), 76–86
Tait, J., "Knight-service in Cheshire", *E.H.R.*, lvii (1942), pp. 437–59
——, *The Medieval English Borough* (Manchester, 1936)
Taylor, A. J., "The date of Caernarvon castle", *Antiquity*, xxvi (1952), pp. 25–34
Usher, A. P., "The origins of banking: the primitive bank of deposit, 1200–1600", *Econ. Hist. Rev.*, iv (1932–4), pp. 399–428
Wagner, (Sir) A(nthony), *A Catalogue of English Medieval Rolls of Arms* (Soc. Antiqu., 1950)
——, *Heralds and Heraldry* (2nd edn, Oxford, 1956)
Wake, Joan, "Local sources of history", *Bull. Inst. Hist. Research*, i (1923–4), pp. 81–8
Walsh, J. J., *Medieval Medicine* (1920)
Whitwell, R. J., "The libraries of a civilian and a canonist and of a common lawyer, 1294", *Law Quart. Rev.*, xxi (1905), pp. 393–400
——, and Johnson, C., "The 'Newcastle' galley, 1294", *Arch. Aeliana*, 4th ser., ii (1926), pp. 142–96
Willard, J. F., "The use of carts in the fourteenth century", *History*, xvii (1932–3), pp. 246–50
Wilson, R. M., "English and French in England 1100–1300", *History*, xxviii (1943), pp. 37–60
Wood, A. C., *A History of Nottinghamshire* (Nottingham, 1947)
Woodforde, C., *English Stained and Painted Glass* (Oxford, 1954)

174. Keeping open the port of Hythe, 1230

(*Cal. Close Rolls 1227–31*, p. 321)

Hythe itself did not succumb before the fifteenth century, but this record of action already needed in the thirteenth reflects a problem of the Channel ports generally: their fight with Nature to keep their ports open. A prevailing south-west wind, the eastward drift of sand or gale-driven shingle across the entrances, this in turn, by reducing the scouring effect of the tides, hastening the choking of the port by river-silt as well. Or it might be, at another point on the changing coastline, a fight against erosion, a fight for very life as at Old Winchelsea. For a general statement, J. A. Williamson, *The English Channel* (1959), pp. 95–113; for the coastline the same writer's "The Geographical History of the Cinque Ports", *History*, xi (1926–7), pp. 97–115; for Winchelsea, Old and New, whose diverse fates provide a classic case, *The Collected Papers of Thomas Frederick Tout*, III (Manchester, 1934), pp. 81–4, and No. 175 below.

1230
Word was sent to the sheriff of Kent to go in person to the port of Hythe, which is blocked, it is said, by the accumulation of sand and soil, and have the port reopened and repaired by the men of the neighbouring townships who have been accustomed and ought to open and repair that port. Witness the king at Reading, 12 April.

175. Winchelsea, Old and New, *c.* 1287

At once an interesting case of town-planning (for which, see "Medieval Town Planning", *Collected Papers of Thomas Frederick Tout*, III (Manchester, 1934), pp. 59–92) and the classic example in this period of English history of vain struggle with natural forces. Old Winchelsea, powerful and prosperous[1] but fighting erosion, washed away in the exceptional storms of 1287. New Winchelsea, safe enough from erosion, but trapped in the end by the other danger of silt and left as we see it today, a port high and dry. cf. No. 174 above.

(a)

(*Cal. Pat. Rolls 1272–81*, p. 151)

1276, 3 July, Romney
Grant in fee simple to Matthew de Horne of Winchelsea, of a place 100 ft by 50 ft, lying between his house in Winchelsea and the king's port there, so that the said Matthew may make a quay upon the said place for the defence of his house against inundation of the sea, and build upon it.

(b)

(ibid. p. 414)

1280, 11 November, Westminster
Commission to Ralph de Sandwyco, king's steward, to extend and buy or obtain by exchange certain lands of John de Langherst and John [le] Bon which are suitable for the new town of Winchelsea, which is to be built upon a hill called Yhamme, the old town being for the most part submerged by the sea.

(c)

(*Cal. Pat. Rolls 1281–92*, p. 3)

1281, 27 November, Westminster
Appointment of Stephen de Penecestre, Iter[ius] de Engolisma, and Henry le Waleys

[1] Matthew Paris s.a. 1254, trans. J. A. Giles, vol. 3 (Bohn's Antiquarian Library, 1854), p. 80; L. F. Salzman, *English Trade in the Middle Ages* (Oxford, 1931), pp. 354–5, and the sources cited, p. 354, n. 2.

to assess certain plots of land[1] at Ihamme, and to let them to the barons and goodmen of Winchelse for building; saving to the immediate lords of the aforesaid plots a reasonable extent of every acre.

(d)

(ibid. pp. 81–2)

1283, 13 October, Acton Burnell

Appointment of Stephen de Penecestre, Henry le Waleys and Gregory de Rokesle to plan and assess the new town of Yhamme, which the king is ordering to be built there, for the barons of the town and port of Wynchelsea, which is already in great part submerged by inundations of the sea and in danger of total submersion; to plan and give directions for streets and lanes[2] necessary for the said new town, for places suitable for a market, and for two churches, one to St Thomas, and the other to St Giles, as there are in the aforesaid town of Wynchelsea, to assign and deliver to the said barons competent places according to the requirements of their state, and to provide and give directions concerning harbours and all other things necessary for the said town.

Grant to the same barons to be as free in the new town as in the old town of Winchelsea, and have the same free customs according to their charters.

(e)

(*Cal. Fine Rolls*, I, p. 249)

1288, 23 June, Westminster

Order to the sheriff of Sussex to deliver to the barons of the port of Winchelse the site and place of Ihamme with the marsh, except 10 acres of land there which the king retains, which site the king had of the grant of William de Grandisono and Isabel his wife and which he has granted to the barons owing to the damage sustained by the said town through the violence of the sea, and the peril daily threatening them there; to inhabit the same and make there the town of Winchelse and to hold of the king and his heirs, so that the barons be as free there as before at Winchelse and enjoy the same liberties which they have used by charters of the king's ancestors, kings of England, and by the king's confirmation, and so that the bailiffs answer as before for the farm of the town; and the king on his coming to England will satisfy any who claim right in the premises.

Order to the same to deliver to the same barons the said site without the said conditions.

The like to Salamon de Roffa and his fellows, justices in eyre in Sussex, by two like writs, one with conditions as above, and one without.

[1] *placias* [2] *vicis et venellis*

176. Improvement of the port of Bristol, 1240

(*Bristol Charters 1155–1373*, ed. N. D. Harding (Bristol, 1930), p. 18)

Henry by the grace of God king of England, lord of Ireland, duke of Normandy [and] of Aquitaine and count of Anjou to all goodmen dwelling in Redcliffe in the suburb of Bristol greeting. Whereas our beloved burgesses of Bristol for the common benefit of the whole town of Bristol as of your suburb have begun a certain trench in St Augustine's Marsh so that ships coming to our port of Bristol can enter and leave more freely and without impediment but will not be able to complete it without great expense, WE, since from the improvement of that port no small advantage should accrue not only to the burgesses themselves but also to you who share the same liberties which our aforesaid burgesses have in the aforesaid town and in scot and in lot are fellows with them, since also it could be very useful and profitable to you for work on the aforesaid trench to be favourably completed, COMMAND YOU, in so far as it concerns you along with our aforesaid burgesses with whom you are fellows in the aforesaid liberties, to contribute as effective assistance as they do, lest the aforesaid work, which we regard as our own, should suffer delay through fault of yours. Witness myself, at Windsor, on the 27th day of April in the 24th year of our reign.

177. The river Severn, 1308

(*Cal. Pat. Rolls 1307–13*, p. 87)

1308, 15 March, Westminster
Commission of oyer and terminer to William de Mortuo Mari and Roger de Bella Fago, on complaint by Ralph son of Cicely de Bello Loco who had freighted a vessel at Bewdley (apud Bellum locum) with brushwood, merchandise and goods for Bristol, that William Roculf' of Worcester, Richard le Mercer, Richard Adam, Henry Pertrich, Thomas de Braunteford, Henry Gorney, Adam de Pidele "tanur", William Colle of Worcester and others of the same town seized his ship in the river Severn, near Worcester, imprisoned him and carried away his goods.

178. The river Trent, 1229

(*Cal. Close Rolls 1227–31*, p. 276)

A gift of oaks
Order to Thomas de Birkin' to cause Richard de Sancto Johanne, chaplain of H. de Burgo etc., to have oaks in Sherwood Forest where they can be most suitably taken and nearest to the R. Trent for conveyance by water to the parts of Norfolk, as a gift from the king for housing himself there. Witness [the king at Grimeston', 19 December 1229].

179. London Bridge, 1281

(*Cal. Pat. Rolls, 1272–81*, p. 422)

1281, 8 January, Walsingham
Protection with clause *rogamus*, directed to all bailiffs, for the keepers of London Bridge, or their messengers, collecting alms throughout the realm for the repair of the bridge which has fallen into a ruinous state, to the great danger of the almost innumerable people dwelling thereon.

The like directed to all archbishops, bishops, and ministers of holy mother church.

180. Between London and Westminster, 1315

(*Cal. Pat. Rolls 1313–17*, p. 340)

1315, 8 August, Langley
Grant for three years to William de Leyre, Richard Abbot, William le Rous, and Thomas Seman of pavage to be taken at the place which is called "la Charryng", in aid of the repair of the pavement between the Bar of the New Temple, London, and the gate of the king's palace of Westminster, upon all wares for sale passing through that place.

181. Bridge at Doncaster to be of stone, 1247

(*Cal. Pat. Rolls 1232–47*, p. 498)

Grant to the good men of Donecastre that to build the bridge of their town of stone they may take a custom of 1*d* on every cart with merchandise crossing the said bridge from Easter, 31 Henry III, for three years.

182. The crossing of the river Don at Doncaster, 1311

(*Cal. Pat. Rolls 1307–13*, p. 410)

1311, 20 December, Westminster
Mandate to John de Donecastre, Walter de Harom and Thomas de Cresacre to collect the customs granted for three years on all goods and wares brought along the causey, or way, which leads from the greater bridge of the town of Doncaster to le Bordel towards the north, in aid of the repair of that causey.

By K. on the information of Adam de Osgodeby.

183. The Fen country

(a)

(*Cal. Pat. Rolls 1301–7*, p. 196)

1303, 17 October, Dundee

Commission of oyer and terminer to William Haward, William de Ormesby and Lambert de Thrykingham, on complaint by the abbot of Thorneye, touching the persons who [broke closes and warrens and pounds at several places in Huntingdonshire belonging to the abbot] and by night raised a dyke across the highway at Eye by Paston, co. Northampton, which leads from the town of Peterborough and the parts of Stamford to the abbey of Thorneye, which is surrounded by marshes and the fresh water gravitating there, and which the abbot and his predecessors have been wont to use for carrying corn from their manors and for bringing in purveyance for their maintenance. By p.s.

(b)

(*Select Cases in the Court of King's Bench under Edward I*, I, ed. G. O. Sayles (Selden Soc., vol. 55, 1936), No. 86)

[In the court of King's Bench, Michaelmas term, 1283]

Lincolnshire

Because, on account of the inundation of the sea and the marsh and the failure to repair the causey of Holland, the banks, the dikes, the gutters, the bridges and the sewers in the lands of divers persons in the districts of Holland, great danger and loss may occur from day to day as well to the king as to others having lands in the parts of Holland and also to those crossing through those districts, the lord king, wishing to apply a remedy to this and to guard and watch over the safety of his people, has sent word to John de Vaux and his fellows, justices in eyre in the county of Lincoln, to search their rolls and send him not only the inquisitions made by themselves concerning the repair of the aforesaid causey, banks etc., but also the inquisitions made by Martin of Littlebury and his fellows, Gilbert of Preston and his fellows, and other justices long ago in eyre in the county of Lincoln in the time of king Henry his father. [These were sent, but for technical reasons action could not be taken on them and the judges of the King's Bench considered it necessary for the matter to be handled with all those it concerned present.] And because it seemed to them that it would be a serious and difficult matter to cause a great crowd of people to come before the king wherever he might be in England and also it would be easier to deal with and settle that business in those parts, the lord king by the counsel of his justices ordered John Beck, Nicholas of Stapleton and Roger Loveday to enquire who are held to repair and maintain the banks, ditches and bridges and to distrain them for those repairs and maintenance. And they first enquired about the bridge of Peckbridge and about two bridges in Spalding . . .

184. An agreement on water for livestock, 1240

(Public Record Office, D. L. 36/2, No. 83, ed. and trans. A. E. B. Owen, *Agricultural History Review*, xiii (1965), pp. 46 and 43)

This is the agreement made between Hawise de Quincey countess of Lincoln and Philip de Kyme at Lincoln three weeks after Easter in the 24th year of the reign of king Henry son of king John [1240] concerning the dispute between them about a certain obstruction of a certain water caused by the said Philip in Thorpe to the damage of the port of the said Hawise in Wainfleet, viz, that since it was then clear that the land on each side of the said watercourse to the port of Wainfleet belongs to the said Philip, the lordship of that ditch where the water runs is to remain to the said Philip and his heirs in this manner, viz, that the course of the water to the port of Wainfleet ought to be open and without obstruction of any kind every year from Michaelmas to the following Easter, and from Easter day for the following three weeks the said Philip and his heirs every year may and ought by this agreement to stop up the course of the water so as to refresh the ditches of his manor of Croft and to water his cattle. And immediately the three weeks have ended the said Philip and his heirs shall completely remove the obstruction of the water so that for the next three weeks the said Hawise and her heirs may have the course of the water completely open to her port of Wainfleet. And thus every year between Easter and Michaelmas the course of the said water is to be obstructed for three weeks and is to be open for the following three weeks. And immediately after Michaelmas every year the said Philip and his heirs are to open the said watercourse and it shall remain open every year until the following Easter as is written above. This agreement was enrolled in the rolls of Robert de Lexington, Jollan de Nevill, Robert de la Haye and Warner Engayne, justices of the lord king then itinerant at Lincoln. In witness of which, the aforesaid Hawise and Philip have affixed to this writing done in the form of a chirograph their seals alternately. These being witnesses, Norman de Areci, William de Well, Guy Wak, William de Beningworthe, John Gubaud, John de Criteleston, Walter Beck, Henry Chamberlain, Thomas de Turribus, William de Bilsby, Ketelbern de Keles, Henry de Tointon and others.

185. Salt

Salt was, above all, a preservative. It was made on the coasts, but especially in Lincolnshire, by evaporating sea-water, and it was imported in increasing quantities from the shores of the Bay of Biscay, as well as produced from the brine springs of Cheshire and of Droitwich in Worcestershire by a process of boiling. For Droitwich in particular as a centre for production and distribution, see R. H. Hilton, *A Medieval Society: the West Midlands at the end of the Thirteenth Century* (1966), with map on p. 12 and n. 11 on p. 282 for further reading. "Vat" can have the meaning of a measure of brine as well as of the boiler itself. The lord of Salwarpe would have capital enough for an industrial investment: there was, it will be noticed, woodland in the manor itself which could provide him with some at least of the fuel needed for boilings.

(a)

(*Cal. Inquisitions post mortem*, III, p. 47)

[Part of estate of Robert Burnell (d. 1292)]

Nantwich (de Wyco Malbano). A third part of the barony, held of the king in chief by service of 3 knight's fees; and a moiety of a saltpit held of Robert de Brescy doing service of 1*d* yearly, and a saltpit held of Richard de Batington doing service of 10*s*.

(b)

(ibid. V, p. 410)

[Part of estate of Guy Beauchamp, E. of Warwick (d. 1315)]
Salewarpe. The manor [full extent given], including a park, a wood called Lenediwode, rents from free tenants of the fee of Brudly in Droitwich (Wych), a way toll at Coppecote, a salt-pit at Droitwich with a boilery of eight vats . . . rents from free tenants at Hosyntre, and the advowson of the church.

List of free tenants of the manor of Salewarpe and of Bruyly etc.

186. Prospecting for iron-ore in Chippenham forest, 1229

(*Close Rolls of Henry III, 1227–31* (1902), pp. 268–9)

The main source by far of iron was still the Forest of Dean. Even the Weald of Sussex and Kent, with better access to markets, was no rival as yet. Output elsewhere, considerable though it was, was scattered and served local requirements. To a king quite aware of his profits already from the Forest of Dean the prospect of further finds in another royal forest would be worth pursuing.

The best introduction to the subject of iron-working in medieval England is L. F. Salzman's chapter in his *English Industries of the Middle Ages* (Oxford, 1923), pp. 21–40.

About looking for ore. Because the king is given to understand that ore for making iron can be found in the king's forest of Chippenham, John de Monmouth is ordered to have that ore searched for in that forest, and if it happen to be found, then to have forges provided to go round[1] in that forest for making the iron.

187. Safety at sea, 1247

(*Cal. Pat. Rolls 1232–47*, p. 500)

Because it is a pious work to help Christians exposed to the dangers of the sea so that they may be brought into the haven out of the waves of the deep, it is commanded to J. son of Geoffrey, justiciary of Ireland, that, so long as the lands late of W. Marshal, earl of Pembroke, in Ireland, are in his custody, he shall let the wardens and chaplains of St Saviour's Rendenan,[2] who are building there a tower as a signal and warning to those at sea to avoid danger, have such maintenance in money and other liveries out of the issues of the said lands [as they have had], with the arrears due to them.

[1] *itinerare:* although this in the case of machinery can mean no more than the working of the machine, we know from other sources that such forges could be quite temporary erections (*fabricae errantes*). I have therefore retained Mr Salzman's interpretation (*English Industries of the Middle Ages*, p. 30), though something rather less aimless than "wander about" seems called for.

[2] co. Wexford

188. The weather, 1236–59

(*Chronica Majora*, ed. H. R. Luard, 7 vols (Rolls series, 1872–4), trans. J. A. Giles, *Matthew Paris's English History*, 3 vols (1852–4))

A feature of Matthew Paris's "Greater Chronicle" is its information on the weather experienced – or heard of – at St Albans. The following extracts contain his observations on each of the years 1236 to 1259. That as a Benedictine he begins the year at Christmas, a week early on our reckoning, needs only occasionally to be remembered and attention has been drawn to it in every case when this is so.

1236

. . . About the same time, for two months and more, namely, in January, February, and part of March, such deluges of rain fell as had never been seen before in the memory of any one. About the feast of St Scholastica [10 February], when the moon was new, the sea became so swollen by the river torrents which fell into it, that all the rivers, especially those which fell into the sea, rendered the fords impassable, overflowing their banks, hiding the bridges from sight, carrying away mills and dams, and overwhelming the cultivated lands, crops, meadows, and marshes. Amongst other unusual occurrences, the river Thames overflowed its usual bounds, and entered the grand palace at Westminster, where it spread and covered the whole area, so that small boats could float there, and people went to their apartments on horseback. The water also forcing its way into the cellars could with difficulty be drained off. The signs of this storm which preceded it, then gave proofs of their threats; for on the day of St Damasus [i.e. 11 December 1235], thunder was heard, and on the Friday next after the conception of St Mary [i.e. Friday, 14 December 1235], a spurious sun was seen by the side of the true sun. . . . In the summer of this year, after a winter beyond measure rainy, as has been mentioned, a constant drought, attended by an almost unendurable heat, succeeded, which lasted for four months and more. The marshes and lakes were dried up to their very bottoms; watermills stood uselessly still – the water being dried up; and the earth gaped with numerous fissures; the corn too in a great many places scarcely grew to the height of two feet. . . . Near about the same time too, namely on the Monday following that feast [Michaelmas], deluges of rain fell in the northern parts of England, to such a degree that the rivers and lakes, overflowing their usual bounds, caused great damage by destroying bridges, mills, and other property near the banks. . . . On the day after the feast of St Martin [11 November], and within the octaves of that feast, great inundations of the sea suddenly broke forth by night, and a fierce storm of wind arose, which caused inundations of the rivers, as well as of the sea, and in places, especially on the coast, drove the ships from their ports, tearing them from their anchors, drowned great numbers of people, destroyed flocks of sheep, and herds of cattle, tore up trees by the roots, overthrew houses, and ravaged the coast. The sea rose for two days and the intermediate night, a circumstance before unheard of, and did not ebb and flow in its usual way, being impeded (as was said) by the violence of the opposing winds. The dead bodies of those drowned were seen lying unburied in caves formed by the sea, near the coast, and at Wisbeach and the neighbouring villages, and along the sea-coast, an endless number of human beings perished: in one town, and that not a populous one, about a hundred bodies were consigned to the tomb in one day. In the night of Christmas eve, also, a very fierce storm of wind raged, attended by thunder and a deluge of rain, and shook towers and other buildings, and the confusion of the elements rendered the roads and seas impassable. And thus in that year about the equinoctial season, the storm twice repeated ravaged England with irreparable damage. The Lord indeed seemed, owing to the sins of the people, to have sent this flood as a scourge to the earth, and to fulfil the threat contained in the Gospel: "There shall be upon the earth distress of nations, with perplexity; the sea and the waves roaring". . . .

1237

. . . As 1 March was drawing near, namely on the feast of St Valentine [14 February], heavy storms of rain inundated the country, which, by destroying the banks of the rivers, rendered the fords and roads impassable for eight successive days. And in order that, from some cases, other similar ones may be imagined, the Thames in England, and the Seine in France, with their swollen floods, washed away cities, bridges, and mills, lakes springing up in formerly dry places, and spreading over a wide extent of country, so that for fifteen days, in consequence of the floods, it was scarcely possible to distinguish the roads on the banks. . . . Amongst others who came to that council,[1] was one master Walter Pruz, a clerk, who publicly declared that almost all the planets were then coming together under one sign of the zodiac, namely Capricorn, and would cause great commotion in the elements, and stir up heavy storms of wind; and foretold that a great destruction of animals, especially horned ones (which we call flocks or herds), would ensue, and added, as if in jest, "May it not be of horned men", that is, "of bishops". This prediction of his was not altogether void of truth, for on a sudden, St Paul's church, where they were all assembled, was suddenly shaken by such a storm of wind, that great fear seized on all, and especially the legate. On the night of St Cecilia's day [22 November] too, the moon being in its first quarter, extraordinary black clouds, of tower-like form, appeared in the western part of the heavens; thunder began to roar, lightning to dart forth, and the wind to rise, and throughout that whole night and the following day such a heavy storm of wind raged as was never remembered to have occurred before, and this storm continued for fifteen days more without interruption. Oaks were torn up by the roots and fell; houses, towers, and other buildings, were thrown down or shaken, so that the elements seemed to join in the perturbation of man. . . . During the whole of this year, the atmosphere was stormy and unsettled, injurious to men, and unhealthy; and never, in the memory of any one, had so many people suffered from the quartan ague. . . .

1238

. . . On 20 January in this year dreadful thunder was heard, which was accompanied by a strong wind and heavy clouds. . . . About the feast of St Matthew [21 September], a storm of wind raged with such destructive violence that, without mentioning other incalculable and irreparable damage, more than twenty ships were sunk at Portsmouth. . . . In the same year, the rivers impetuously burst forth in an unusual

[1] the Legatine Council of Cardinal Otto at St Paul's, London, November 1237

and unnatural manner over great numbers of fields and level places, formerly free from water and quite dry, and increased suddenly to rapid torrents, so that fishes swam about in them. The inclemency and sickliness of the atmosphere, too, generated various diseases; so that the inclemency of the atmosphere was like a plague on the earth, and the country people and husbandmen, as well as knights, and nobles, and prelates, also felt this scourge of God . . . part of this year was cloudy and rainy, until the spring had passed, whence all confidence in the crops failed; and during two or more of the summer months, the weather was beyond measure and unusually dry and hot; as autumn, however, approached, it became moist and rainy; by which the crops were wonderfully restored, fresh plants springing up in place of those that had withered; and there was a great abundance of corn. At the end of autumn, however, those who delayed their reaping were deprived of their crops; for such deluges of rain fell, that the straw as well as the grain rotted; and this unnatural autumn, which was considered generally to be a dry and cold season, generated various kinds of dangerous diseases; so that the temperament was with difficulty maintained, and no one remembered ever to have seen so many afflicted with the quartan fever. . . .

1239

. . . As spring drew nigh, about Easter, the storms of wind and heavy rains ceased, which for the four preceding months successively had continued to make mud on the ground, to extend the lakes and marshes, to choke the corn, and disturb the atmosphere. . . . On 3 June, in this year, there was an eclipse of the sun about the sixth hour of the day. . . . In the same year, on the eve of the feast of St James [25 July], about dusk, before the stars had appeared, was seen in a clear blue sky, a very large star like a torch, which rose from the south, and flying along, not upwards, darted through the air, making its way towards the north, not swiftly, but as a hawk usually flies; when it had reached the middle of the firmament, which is in our hemisphere, it vanished, leaving, however, smoke and sparks in the air. This star was either a comet or a dragon, greater to the eye than Lucifer, having the form of a mullet, very bright at the foremost part of it, but at the hind part smoky and sparkling. All who saw this wonderful sign were struck with wonder, and did not know what it portended, but one thing is certain, that after the crops had been almost all choked by the protracted rains, the season was at this very hour changed into one of a most remarkable fertility, and preserved the ripe crops, which were only waiting for the sickle, and allowed them to be gathered in. . . .

1240

. . . Near about this time a terrible sound was heard, as if a huge mountain had been thrown forth with great violence, and fallen in the middle of the sea; and this was heard in a great many places at a distance from each other, to the great terror of the multitudes who heard. . . . During this time, namely throughout the whole of February, a dim sort of star appeared in the evening in the western part of the sky, sending forth rays towards the east, which many unhesitatingly declared to be a comet. . . . On the day after the feast of SS Perpetua and Felicitas [7 March], a storm of wind, beyond measure strong and violent, disturbed the whole atmosphere; which, among other wonderful occurrences, carried a stone, which a strong man could scarcely lift, from the pinnacle of the church to a great distance from it. . . . The course of events in this year was unfavourable to the kingdom of England, adverse to the holy church, and injurious to the eastern as well as the western countries; for three successive months, namely in March and the two following months, the season was dry – rainy throughout the rest of the months, yet producing abundance of corn and fruit – but the rainy autumn in a great measure choked the abundant crops. In the Italian provinces, the inundations caused by the rain, which poured down from the mountains into the plains, at the end of this year, scarcely left a single bridge entire. . . .

1241

. . . About the same time, particularly on the day of our Lord's Circumcision [1 January], and for several successive days, a wind from the north, beyond measure violent, caused irreparable damage, both by land and sea, bringing destruction on buildings and forests, and threatening imminent danger to those sailing on the sea; so that the disturbed state of the elements seemed well suited to the state of the human race. . . . On 6 October in this year, which was the day of St Faith, the sun underwent an eclipse, from the third hour till the sixth; and the heavens seemed to be of the same form as the earth; and this was the second eclipse of the sun which had happened in three years – an event hitherto unheard of. . . . This year was on the whole tolerably abundant in crops of fruit and corn; but from the feast of the Annunciation of the blessed Virgin [25 March] till that of the apostles Simon and Jude [28 October], a continued drought and intolerable heat dried up deep lakes and extensive marshes, drained many rivers, parched up the warrens and suspended the working of mills; hence the pastures withered away, herbage died, and consequently the flocks and herds pined away with hunger and thirst. In the winter too, namely about the Advent of our Lord, ice and snow, attended by intolerably severe cold, covered the earth, and hardened it to such a degree, at the same time freezing the rivers, that such great numbers of birds died, that the like was never remembered to have occurred before.

1242

. . . On the feast of St Edmund[1] in the same year, distinct thunder attended by lightning, a sad presage of the approach of a lengthened tempest, alarmed the hearts and ears of mortals; nor was the warning false, for it was followed by continued unseasonable weather, and by an unpleasant and disturbed state of the air, which continued for several days. Such deluges of rain fell, that the river Thames, overflowing its usual bounds and its ancient banks, spread itself over the country towards Lambeth, for six miles, and took possession, far and wide, of the houses and fields in that part. Owing to the inundation of the water, people rode into the great hall at

[1] More likely to be 20 November than the 16th, but in either case (and from the context) the month of November 1242.

Westminster on horseback. . . . Thus this year passed away, having afforded an abundance of fruits and vegetables, notwithstanding it was arid and hot, and towards the end, generating epidemics and quartan agues.

1243

. . . And in the same year, namely on 26 July, the night was most serene, and the atmosphere very pure, so that the Milky Way appeared as plainly as it is accustomed to do on the most placid winter night, the moon being eight days old. And behold, stars were seen to fall from heaven, swiftly darting to and fro. But, contrary to what usually happens, not little sparks shooting after the manner of stars (which is stated as a natural phenomenon in Aristotle's book on Meteors), like lightning, produced by thunder; but, in one instant, thirty or forty were seen to shoot about or fall, so that two or three at once appeared to fly in one train. Thus, if they were real stars (which no wise man can think), there would not have been one left in the heavens. Let astrologers declare what this kind of thing may portend, which appeared strange and miraculous to all beholders. . . . This year, therefore, passed over, threatening danger and trouble to the church, plentiful enough in vegetables and fruits, bringing death and annoyance to many nobles in Christendom, reproachful and prejudicial to the kingdom and king of England, bringing battles and hostilities for the Italians, and mistrust for the Holy Land, and generating schism and scandal between the Templars and Hospitallers.

1244

. . . In the month of November of this year, as a sad presage of coming events, thunder was plainly heard and lightning seen, which lasted for fifteen successive days, and was followed by a disturbed state of the weather. . . . Thus ended this year, which was throughout abundantly productive in fruit and corn, so much so, indeed, that the price of a measure of corn fell to two shillings; its events were most inimical to the Holy Land; marked with disturbances in England; fraught with peril to the French kingdom; raised suspicion in the church, and turbulence among the Italians.

1245

. . . This year throughout was remarkable for an abundance of corn, increased by the greater fertility of the preceding year; so much so, that the price of a measure of corn fell to two shillings only; but, owing to the unseasonableness and inclemency of the atmosphere during the summer, the fruit trees did not produce any fruit. The events of it were productive of prosperity and increase to France; of trouble and loss to England; to the Holy Land, of enmity and danger; to the Irish, of labour and toil; to the Welsh, of blood and misfortune; to the Poitevins, of such treatment as children get from their stepmothers; and it made the whole empire and court of Rome tremble.

1246

. . . On the day and during the night of the feast of St Mark the Evangelist [25 April], the frost and snow covered and bound the earth with such intensity of cold, and so weakened the shooting branches of the trees, together with their foliage, that the leaves as well as the grass irreparably faded away. . . . In order that the elements might be conformable with the affairs of the world, about this time, namely on the day preceding the feast of St Margaret [20 July], there arose a dreadful storm, attended by thunder and lightning, and also by hail, the stones of which were angular and most hard, and larger than almonds, which destroyed birds, and even some animals, disturbed the whole country throughout, tearing up oaks, throwing down buildings, burning men, destroying flocks and herds, breaking down bridges with the rush of water; and all this continued for sixteen hours, which was a whole night and part of a day. . . . It is related by credible persons, that during this year the sea did not rise upon the seacoast in the usual way for the space of four or five days; a circumstance which those dwelling on the coast, and the sailors who traffic on the great waters, testified they had never seen before. . . .

1247

. . . On 13 February in this year, that is on St Valentine's day, at various places in England, especially at London, and there mostly on the banks of the Thames, an earthquake was felt, which shook buildings, and was very injurious and terrible in its effect; for, as was believed, such an occurrence was significative, inasmuch as it was unusual and unnatural in these western countries, since the solid mass of England is free from those underground caverns and deep cavities (in which, according to philosophers, an earthquake is generally produced), nor could any reason for it be discovered. It was therefore expected, according to the threats of the Gospel, that the end of the world was at hand, and that this movement of the earth indicated corresponding movements in the world, so that the elements might be agitated and disturbed by frequent motions. The sea too for a few days previous, ebbed and flowed but little, if at all, for a great distance along the coast, as has been before stated, for about three months this year, a circumstance which no one remembered to have ever seen before; nor had there been an earthquake in England since the year 1133, which was the third year before the death of king Henry the first. This earthquake was followed by a protracted inclemency of the atmosphere, and by an unseasonable and winterly roughness, disturbed, cold, and rainy, so that the husbandmen and gardeners complained that the spring by a backward movement was changed to winter, and entertained great fears that they would be deceived in their hopes of their crops, plants, fruit trees, and corn. This disturbed state of the weather lasted uninterruptedly with scarcely the intervention of a single calm day, till the feast of the Translation of St Benedict [11 July]. . . . In the dog-days, and when the sun was declining in the zodiac, especially in the month of September, a pestilence and mortality began to rage amongst men, which lasted for three months; and so virulent was it; that nine or ten corpses were buried in one day in the cemetery of one church, namely that of St Peter, in the town of St Albans. . . . This year throughout was very abundant in corn, but barren of fruit; was productive of injury to England, of tyranny to Wales; was hostile to the Holy Land, a turbulent despoiler of the church; a source of bloodshed to Italy, and warlike and hostile to the empire and the Roman court, and especially so to the kingdom of Germany; generated hatred in the hearts of prelates and several others against the pope, because he forcibly despoiled their patrons, and suspended them from the collation of benefices, a circumstance hitherto unheard of, and adverse to the king, because he tolerated such proceedings.

1248

. . . On the first[1] of June in this year, just after sunset, the moon underwent an almost total eclipse. . . . On 24 November in this year, the sea overflowed its bounds to a great distance, and caused irreparable injury to those dwelling near the coast; for when the moon, according to the computation of the calendar, was in its fourth quarter, the tide flowed with swollen waters without any visible ebb or decrease. This is believed to have occurred in consequence of the strong wind which blew from the sea, and yet the sea itself did not rise in such a way; even old persons were astonished at this new and unusual occurrence. . . . In the same year, on the day of our Lord's Advent, which was the fourth day before Christmas, an earthquake occurred in England, by which (as was told to the writer of this work by the bishop of Bath, in whose diocese it occurred) the walls of buildings were burst asunder, the stones were torn from their places, and gaps appeared in the ruined walls. The vaulted roof which had been placed on the top of the church of Wells by the great efforts of the builder, a mass of great size and weight, was hurled from its place, doing much damage, and fell on the church, making a dreadful noise in its fall from such a height, so as to strike great terror into all who heard it. During this earthquake a remarkable occurrence happened: the tops of chimneys, parapets, and pillars were thrown from their places, but the bases and foundations of them were not at all disturbed, although the reverse ought naturally to have happened. This earthquake was the third which had occurred within three years on this side the Alps: one in Savoy, and two in England; a circumstance unheard of since the beginning of the world, and therefore the more terrible. . . . This year passed, temperate and calm, filling the barns with abundance of corn, and making the presses flow with wine; so much so, that a measure of corn fell in price to two shillings, and a cask of choice wine was freely sold for two marks; the orchard fruit was very abundant in some places, but scanty in others; but the gourd-worms entirely destroyed everything green where the disease made its way into the shrubs. The events of the year proved hostile to the Holy Land, inimical to Italy, deadly to Germany, adverse to England, and destructive to France; and, to sum up much in a few words, consumptive of money in almost every country of Christendom; by many indications it gave tokens of the end of the world approaching, as we read, "Nation shall rise against nation, and there shall be earthquakes in places", and other similar prophecies. To the Roman court it was a source of disgrace, pestiferous, and injurious, and evidently threatening the divine anger. The temperature of winter was entirely changed to that of spring, so that neither snow nor frost covered the face of the earth for two days together; trees might be seen shooting in February, and the birds singing and sporting as if it were April.

[1] As the Latin text says "kalends", "feast" in Giles's translation (II, p. 266) is probably no more than a printer's error. But in any case "first" is wrong: the eclipse was on 7 June (*Chron. Majora*, ed. Luard, V, p. 20).

1249

. . . About the same time, a general tournament was appointed to be held at Northampton on Ash Wednesday [17 February]; but it was prevented by the king's prohibition and his threats, and by the inclemency of the season. The knights grieved much at this, and especially the novices, as they eagerly desired to enter upon the initiatory contest in knightly discipline; and William de Valence, the king's uterine brother, who was a novice, sent word to them, that, notwithstanding the king's prohibition and frivolous suspicions, they should not fail, if a fine season smiled on them, to hold the tournament; for that he would interpose himself as a security between the king his brother and them, to prevent his venting his rage on them; and this message gave to the said William a no slight claim to knighthood, and added much to his honour. However, on that day, Ash Wednesday, a heavy fall of snow took place, and continued for two days, to such a degree that it covered the face of the earth to the depth of a foot, broke down the heavily loaded branches of the trees, and then melting, caused the furrows in the fields, now dilated like caverns, to fill with the rivulets which ran down them; and thus the said tournament was ruined by a double disadvantage. . . . At the commencement of the month of June, such a deluge of rain fell in the parts about Abingdon, that willows and other trees, and the adjacent houses, and even sheep-cots and the sheep in them, salt-pits and a chapel built near that town, were carried away by the swelling of the rivers and torrents. The green corn, with its shooting ears then in blossom, was levelled to the ground; owing to which the bread appeared to be made of bran instead of wheat. . . .

1250

. . . About the same time, namely on the first day of the month of October, the moon being in its first quarter, there appeared a new moon, swollen and red in appearance, as a sign of coming tempests; according to the experimental writings of the philosopher and poet:

> When Cynthia yet is new, and ruddy tints
> O'erspread her face, it threatens gusts of wind,
> Unless excess of heat or cold prevent.
> Her face, if swollen, portendeth storms; but, pale
> And bright, she clears the face of heaven.

The sky then, in the first week of the increase of the moon, was covered with a thick mist, and began to be much disturbed by the violence of the winds, which tore away the branches and the leaves which were then dying away on the trees, and carried them to a great distance through the air. What was more destructive, the disturbed sea transgressed its usual bounds, the tide flowing twice without any ebb, and emitted such a frightful roaring sound, that, even in parts remote from it, it created amazement in those who heard it, even in old men; and no one in modern times remembered ever to have seen the like before. In the darkness of the night too the sea appeared to burn like a fire, and the billows seemed to crowd together, as though fighting with one another, in such fury, that the skill of sailors could not save their sinking ships, and large and firmly-built vessels were sunk and lost. Not to mention other cases, at the port of Hertbourne alone three noble ships were swallowed up by the raging billows, besides small ones and others of moderate size. At Winchelsea, a port on the eastern coast, besides the salt-houses, and the abodes of fishermen, the bridges, and mills which were destroyed, more than three hundred houses in that village, with some churches, were thrown down by the impetuous rise of the sea. Holland in England, and Holland on the continent also, as well as Flanders and other level countries adjoining the sea, sustained irreparable damage. The rivers falling into the sea were forced back and swelled to such a degree that they overflowed meadows, destroyed mills, bridges, and the houses adjacent to them, and, invading the fields, carried away the corn which had not been stored away in the barns; that the anger of God plainly appeared to mortals in the sea as well as on land, and the punishment of sinners appeared imminent, according to the prophecy of Habakkuk: "Art thou angered in the rivers, O Lord, or is thy indignation in the sea?" And what wonder is it? For from the Roman court, which ought to be the fountain of all justice, there emanated unmentionable enormities, one of which, although unfit to be described, we have thought proper to insert in this work. . . . In the same year, on the day of St Lucia [13 December], about the third hour of the day, an earthquake occurred at St Albans and the adjacent districts, which are called Chiltern, where from time immemorial no such an event had ever been seen or heard of; for the land there is solid and chalky, not hollow or watery, nor near the sea; wherefore such an occurrence was unusual and unnatural, and more to be wondered at. This earthquake, if it had been as destructive in its effects as it was unusual and wonderful, would have shaken all buildings to pieces: it came on with a trembling motion, and attended by a sound as if it were dreadful subterranean thunder. A remarkable circumstance took place during the earthquake, which was this: the pigeons, jackdaws, sparrows, and other birds which were perched on the houses, and on the branches of the trees, were seized with fright, as though a hawk were hovering over them, and suddenly expanding their wings, took to flight, as if they were mad, and flew backwards and forwards in confusion, exciting fear and dread in those who saw the occurrence; but, after the trembling motion of the earth and the rumbling noise had ceased, they returned to their usual nests, which had been disturbed by the earthquake. This earthquake, indeed, struck horror into the hearts of all, which I think to be more than amazement or fear, and it was believed to be indicative of future events. In this year, the land as well as the sea was affected by unusual and dreadful commotions, which, according to the threatening words of the gospel, "there shall be earthquakes in divers places", threateningly foretold that the end of the world was at hand. . . . It is believed to be not without its signification, that in this last year all the elements suffered unusual and irregular detriment; fire, because on the night of Christmas lately past it shone forth in a terrible way, contrary to the usual course of nature; the air, because, in the diocese of Norwich and the neighbouring districts far and wide, it was covered with mist and disturbed by unnatural and unseasonable thunder for a length of time, and obscured by thick clouds; nor had there for a long time been heard such dreadful thunder or such lightning seen even in summer; the sea, because it transgressed its usual bounds and devastated the places adjacent to it; and the land, because it quaked in England, and even at Chiltern, which is a chalky and solid country.

1251

. . . About this time, namely on the night of Christmas day,[1] in token, as was believed, of God's anger, dreadful thunder was heard, especially in the diocese of Norwich and its adjacent districts, and fearful flashes of lightning darted forth, which, together with an unseasonable commotion of the air, struck the greatest fear and alarm into the hearts of all who heard and saw it; and diviners said that this occurred as a mournful prognostic of the future. . . . In the course of this year about the fruit-season, there appeared, in the orchards chiefly, some remarkable birds, which had never before been seen in England, somewhat larger than larks, which ate the kernel of the fruit and nothing else, whereby the trees were fruitless, to the loss of many. The beaks of these birds were crossed, so that by these means they opened the fruit, as if with pincers or a knife; and that part of the fruit which they left was as it were infected with poison. . . . In the night of St Lambert's day [17 September], which was Sunday, the darkness was dreadful, and there was such an abundant fall of rain, that the cataracts of the sky seemed to open, and the clouds to pour themselves on the earth as if to destroy it. . . . In the summer of the same year, on St Dunstan's day [19 May] a thick cloud arose early in the morning, which darkened, as it seemed, the world, both north and south, and east and west, and thunder was heard as if at a great distance, preceded by lightning. About the first hour of the day, the thunder and lightnings approaching nearer, one clap more terrible than the rest, as though it would bear the heavens down on the earth, struck the hearts and ears of those who heard it dumb by its sudden crash. With that crash a thunderbolt fell on the bed room of the queen, where she was then staying with her sons and family, and threw the bed to the ground, crushing it to powder, and shook the whole house. In the adjacent forest of Windsor, it threw down or split asunder thirty-five oak trees. It moreover destroyed some mills with their appurtenances, and some sheep-cots with their shepherds, and bruised some husbandmen and travellers, and brought many injuries on mankind, such as we who write this account have not heard of or seen before. At St Albans, moreover, the lightning fell on a bath and set it on fire, and in other places it fell on the convent itself, but did not do much harm; but the traces of it appeared on the walls for many years afterwards. But what is wonderful and worthy of relation is, that on the same day, some brethren of the order of Preachers or Minorites were received for shelter and food at St Albans, as was the almost daily custom, and could not be restrained from going forth at the urgent entreaty of the monk, who, according to custom, received and provided for them, although the storm had not yet ceased; and after they had gone out of the town, they saw meeting them on the road, which is a public one and much trodden by men and carriages, a torch, with the appearance of a drawn sword, but waving about, which was followed by incessant thunder and a dreadful murmuring. Turning aside, they signed themselves with the cross, and began with fear and devotion to invoke the Holy Ghost, and

[1] i.e. Christmas 1250

to chant the *Veni Creator Spiritus*, and what follows; and the thunder and lightning were deadened and passed over, whilst they remained uninjured. About the same time of the year, namely at the time of the equinox, the sea overflowed its usual bounds, causing no small injury in the provinces of England lying near the coast, and the shore was covered for the space of six feet further than had ever been seen before. . . . This year throughout was productive of corn and fruit in sufficiency, even to abundance, though it was stormy, turbulent, and awful with lightning. It was a laborious and expensive year to the pope and the Roman court, and dangerous on account of their return to Italy; to France and England it was full of suspicion under a fluctuating peace; to the Romans, Italians, Germans, Sicilians, Apulians, and Calabrians, who were without a head and chief, an anxious one; a bloody year to Dacia; and to Scotland, whose king was a boy, wavering and threatening, as Lucan says in the case of Pompey the great:

> His youthful age may well suspicion raise,
> For to be firm, one must have length of days;

silent and exposed as he, the king of Scotland, was to the oscillations of fortune.

1252

. . . In this same year, in the octaves of the Epiphany [6 January], the east wind blew till it stirred up the south-west wind to blow also, and many suffered from the effects. The south-west wind blowing with a dreadful roaring and with fierce violence, drove back the waves from the shore, and unroofed or destroyed houses. It tore up large oaks by the roots, or split them asunder, and stripped them of their leaves; it tore the lead off the churches, sunk the largest and strongest ships on the deep, and did irreparable injury to many. But if the damage was great on land, it was evidently ten times greater by sea. Not to mention other injuries and losses, we think it worth while to mention some which we know of and were witnesses of. At Winchelsea, which was a port of great use to the English, and especially to the people of London, the waves of the sea, as if indignant and enraged at being driven back on the day before, covered the places adjoining the shores, took possession of mills and houses, and drowned and washed away a great many of the inhabitants; and that we may be more fully informed of other unexpected circumstances which happened elsewhere, it tore up by the roots three oaks in the cemetery of St Albans, which three men could not encircle with their arms, and tore off the leaves of others in its fury. On the festival of St Valentine [14 February] the king arrived at London. . . . About this same time, namely on the day after the festival of St Gregory [12 March], on the fourth day of the week, when the change of the moon was near at hand, it appeared four days before its first day of appearance was foretold, for the day next before the Sabbath was, in the true order of things, the first day of its appearance. For fifteen successive days afterwards the sun, moon, and stars appeared of a reddish colour, and a day-cloud, as it were, or smoke, seemed to fill the wide space of the world, the wind at the time blowing from the north or east. During the greatest part of March, and the whole of April and May of this same year, the earth was parched up by the burning heat of the sun, the wind continually blowing from the east, north, or north-east. In consequence of the increased causes of heat and drought, and the cessation of refreshing dews, apples and other fruits, which had already appeared and become as plentiful as nuts, fell withered and useless, scarcely any portion of them thriving, although the blossoms had promised a great abundance of fruit. The loss of the fruits remaining was increased, when they attained the size of acorns, by a sudden frost in the morning, attended with unnatural lightnings (which natural philosophers call blasting), which burnt up the ripening apples, acorns, beech-nuts, and all kinds of fruit and herbage, to such a degree, that scarcely a tenth part remained. However, on account of the primitive abundance of the crops, the orchards still abounded with apples and the fields with corn; and, indeed, if all the buds had remained, the trees would not have been able to support the fruit they had produced. The sun rising to solstitial height in the heavens, its immoderate and unendurable heat so burnt up the surface of the earth, that all the herbage was withered, and the meadows refused all kinds of food to the cattle. The heat, too, continued during the nights, and generated flies, fleas, and other injurious insects, so that all living beings grew weary of life. . . . During the months of April, May, June, and July of this year, an intolerable heat and drought prevailed, and continued for that time, without any fall of rain or dew to refresh the earth; in consequence of which, the blossoms on the trees, which had promised an abundance of fruit, faded away and fell; the fields were stripped of their herbage, the foliage of plants withered, and the pastures refused food to the famishing cattle. The earth became hardened and gaped asunder, and, for want of moisture, could afford no nourishment to the corn; flies flitted buzzing about, and the birds, with drooping wings and open beaks, suspended their joyful songs. The burning sweats caused by this temperature gave promise to human beings of chronic diseases and gasping fevers during the fall of the year. . . . During this year, after an intensely hot summer, as autumn approached, a plague-like mortality, such as had never before been seen in the memory of man, arose amongst the cattle in many parts of England, but especially in Norfolk, the Marsh, and the southern districts. A remarkable feature of this pestilence was, that the dogs and crows that fed on the bodies of the cattle which died of this disease were at once infected, became swollen, and died on the spot; hence, no human being dared to eat the flesh of cattle, lest it should belong to a beast that died of the disease. Another wonderful circumstance was noticed amongst the cattle, which was, that cows and full-grown bullocks sucked the teats of the older cows like young calves; and another remarkable occurrence was also noticed; namely, that at this time of the year, when nature usually produces pears and apples, the trees showed themselves in blossom, as they usually do in the month of April. This mortality amongst the cattle, and the late appearance of the blossoms, with the unnatural wantonness of the cattle, were originally caused by the heat and drought which we have mentioned before; for, what is astonishing, the grass, even in the meadows, was so rotten, hard, and dry, during the months of May, June, and July, that, on being rubbed in the hands, it crumbled into powder. The equinoctial season, however, gave an abundant supply of rain and moisture to the parched-up earth, which it sucked into its opened pores, and became lavish in the production of its benefits, giving forth fertile herbage, though unnatural and inferior to the usual crops. The hungry, famished cattle devoured this so eagerly, that they became suddenly puffed up with fat, and their flesh was rendered useless for food, and extraordinary humours were produced in them. Finally, they went mad, and frisked about in an unusual manner, until, becoming suddenly infected with the disease, they fell dead; and the contagion from them, owing to the virulence of the disease, infected others as well. A similar cause can also be assigned for the trees blossoming out of season. . . . The king, moreover, compelled the citizens of London willy nilly to close shop[1] in the city of London, and to attend the fair which he had instituted on the feast of St Edward[2] at Westminster, to the injury of the fair at Ely, and which continued for fifteen days. Notwithstanding the wintry inclemency of the weather, the dirt, rain, and the unfitness of the place, they were compelled to stand in tents, having been ordered by the king, who feared not the imprecations of all, to expose their wares for sale, even though they could not meet with purchasers. All, therefore, were overcome with fatigue, both those who had come to the fair and those who dwelt there; for during the whole time that the vast crowds from all parts of the kingdom were travelling thither, sojourning there and returning, it rained to such a degree that they were all soaked with rain, covered with mud, and wearied; on their journey, too, they found the fords scarcely passable, the bridges having given way, the roads unfit for travelling, the city dirty and destitute of provisions and other necessaries, and everything very dear; so that they were involved in inextricable difficulties. Moreover, there was such a numerous host of persons arriving and staying at London, that the citizens, even the oldest amongst them, declared that they had never before seen such a great multitude. During all this time, angry feelings were aroused, and hatred increased against the pope and the king, who favoured and abetted each other in their mutual tyranny; and all being in ill-humour, called them the disturbers of mankind, so that the saying of the apostle was fulfilled, "Unless a separation shall take place, the son of iniquity shall not be revealed." For even now a manifest schism was imminent, and an almost universal feeling of exasperation was awakened, if not in the body at least in the heart (which was a more serious evil), against the church of Rome, and the small spark of devotion remaining was extinguished. . . . Thus then passed this year, moderately productive of corn and fruit, severe, owing to the deadly disease amongst the cattle; and to sum up briefly the state of human affairs, it was one of trouble to the whole of mankind. Of this state of trouble, the cause, amongst the Orientals, was said to be the unfortunate capture of the French king. Thus we see, when a bone is thrown amongst a lot of snappish dogs, each one endeavours to seize it, and in their struggle one attacks the other; and thus striving to gnaw the bone, they gnaw each other; whilst the bone remains untouched. The empire was in a state of danger, like a vessel without a helmsman. The French kingdom, deprived of rulers, barons, arms, and money, never before lamented such a comfortless and desolate state. England, trampled underfoot by foreigners, bowing the neck to many masters, and deprived of the sincere affection of its king, and submitting to the most abject

[1] *fenestris claussis*
[2] Translation of St Edward (13 October)

conditions, pined away in despair and inconsolable; and, what was most grievous, the deadly hatred existing between the church and the people daily increased.

1253

. . . About this same time, a wonderful circumstance occurred, and which was much talked of, namely, that although in the spring and summer of this year there had been a great and prolonged drought, yet at the end of the summer, and in the autumn the rivers overflowed their banks and rose to a level with the tops of the hills, covering the neighbouring country. Again, at the end of autumn, and after Michaelmas, the floods caused by heavy rains having dispersed, there succeeded such a drought, and diminution and scarcity of water in the rivers and springs, that those who wanted to grind corn were obliged to carry it nearly a day's journey to be ground. A similar wonderful occurrence took place in the spring of this same year, contrary to the nature of the season, for at the time of the equinox, as the whole atmosphere is moderate in temperature, there is peace in the elements. . . . On the morrow after St Lucia's day [13 December] in this year, the clouds poured forth snow in abundance, and winterly thunder gave forth dreadful prognostications. . . . In this year, too, the sea and rivers several times overflowed their usual bounds, doing irreparable damage to the adjacent country. . . . This year throughout was abundant in corn and fruit; so much so, that the price of a measure of corn fell to thirty pence. But the benefit which accrued to the earth was obviated by the damage done by the sea overflowing its bounds, which by its sudden inundations overwhelmed men and cattle, and when it happened by night it drowned many the more. This was a year of destruction to the Holy Land; of bloodshed to Flanders and its neighbouring countries; of loss and disgrace to France; and of vexation and trouble to the pope and his adherents. To England it was pregnant with trouble, and gave a depressed tendency to its spiritual and temporal welfare.

1254

. . . About midnight of the day of our Lord's Circumcision [1 January], the moon being eight days old, and the firmament studded with stars, and the air completely calm, there appeared in the sky, wonderful to relate, the form of a large ship, well-shaped, and of remarkable design and colour. This apparition was seen by some monks of St Albans, staying at St Amphibalus to celebrate the festival, who were looking out to see by the stars if it was the hour for chanting matins, and they at once called together all their friends and followers who were in the house to see the wonderful apparition. The vessel appeared for a long time, as if it were painted, and really built with planks; but at length it began by degrees to dissolve and disappear, wherefore it was believed to have been a cloud, but a wonderful and extraordinary one. . . . On the same day [12 March] too, the severity of the frost gave way, which had lasted uninterrupted for nearly the whole winter, at least, ever since the night of the Circumcision, when there was seen the wonderful apparition of the ship in the sky, or a cloud very like a ship. The apparition was believed, at the time, to be a sign of coming tempestuous weather, and was, moreover, followed by such a deadly disease amongst sheep and wild beasts, that the sheepfolds were void of sheep, and the forests of wild beasts; indeed, in large flocks scarcely one half survived. . . . In this year a remarkable occurrence took place as regards the wind; which was, that it blew continually from the north-east or the north for three months and some days, and destroyed the fruit and flowers of spring; and about 1 July, the time of the solstice, a deluge of rain with most violent hailstorms burst forth, such as we had never seen before; and which lasted for an hour and more, tearing away the tiles and laths of the houses, and rending away the branches of the trees. . . . On the eve of the feast of the Assumption of the blessed Mary [15 August] in this year, about six o'clock, in the midst of an unusually heavy fall of rain, a single clap of thunder was heard, and a flash of lightning which accompanied it fell on the tower of St Peter's church, in St Albans, penetrated the upper part of it with a horrible crash, twisted the oaken material as though it were mere network, and, wonderful to relate, crushed it, so to speak, into small shreds. It left behind it an intolerable stench of smoke throughout the whole of the tower. . . . In this same year, at the autumnal season, when agriculturists usually reaped the reward of their toils, they found all the lands in the vicinity of the sea, though carefully cultivated, to be devoid of any kind of crop, and drenched with brine; for, as before stated, during the winter, the sea had taken possession of the shores and the lands adjacent to them; so that no corn was visible, nor even did the woods or orchards show their leaves, or blossoms, or fruit. We may imagine the losses of others from the case of one, the prior of Spalding, who could not boast of having gathered one single sheaf of wheat on all his land adjacent to the seacoast. The trees, also, of the forest, as well as fruit trees, were so dried up, that they were only fit for cutting down. Flanders, also, and all maritime countries, suffered the same loss; nor did any old man remember to have ever before seen the like. A remarkable fact was noticed during that unusual and extraordinary fluctuation, by sailors and fishermen whilst plying their avocations in many parts of the sea; for they discovered, both whilst lying at anchor and when on a voyage, that the sea left its usual bed or channel, and laid bare sands in the midst of the ocean, where the water was usually of a great depth; but this has been mentioned before. . . . On the day after the festival of SS Crispin and Crispian [25 October], the ears and hearts of all were disturbed by dreadful thunder, though in the winter, accompanied by a deluge of rain. In this same year, also, from Ascension day [21 May] till that of All Saints [1 November], scarcely two or three days passed undisturbed by some commotion of the elements. . . . This year throughout was abundantly productive in fruit and corn, so that the price of a measure of corn fell to two shillings; and in like proportion oats and all other kinds of corn and pulse fell in price, to the benefit of the poor plebeians. To the Italians, French, and Flemings, this year was one of war and hostility, and one of suspicion to England. From the middle of autumn to spring it was troubled by storms, to such a degree that at Bedford more than forty men and an immense number of cattle perished.

1255

. . . In this year, from St Valentine's day [14 February] for a month following, the wind blew violently, attended by deluges of rain both day and night, causing great commotion not only on land but also on the sea. During that same time the sea cast up in the districts belonging to the diocese of Norwich an immense sea monster, which was disturbed by the violent commotions of the waves and was killed, as was believed, by the blows and wounds it received. This monster was larger than a whale, but was not considered to be of the whale kind: its carcass enriched the whole adjacent country. . . . The weather at this time[1] was quite unseasonable, the north wind, which is a great enemy to the budding flowers and trees, blowing during nearly the whole spring. Throughout the whole month of April too, neither rain nor dew moistened, or afforded the least refreshment to the parched earth. For a long time the nobles had fasted day after day, uselessly beating the air, and many of them were seized with divers kinds of disease and sickness. The atmosphere dried up by the blasts of the north and equinoctial winds, assumed a citron-like colour, and generated much sickness. . . . In this same summer a drought prevailed, owing to the continuance of the equinoctial winds, which altogether stopped the dews of the morning and checked those of the evening, and continued from the middle of March to the first of June. One might see the grains of corn lying in the dust whole, and not decaying as usual, so as to shoot and give increase. At length, however, by the kindness of Him who rains on the just and the unjust, the earth with its half-dead roots and seeds was refreshed by a seasonable supply of rain and dew, so that by the grace of God, the drought was turned to a living freshness, and all places revived, giving promise of abundant fruits and crops. . . . And in order that the condition of the heavenly bodies might not differ from that of those below, the moon underwent an extraordinary and unusual total eclipse in the month of July, during the night following St Margaret's day [20 July]. The eclipse began two hours before midnight and lasted for nearly four hours. . . . This year, I say, though not in accordance with our deserts, was throughout so productive in corn and fruit, that a measure of wheat fell in price to two shillings, and the same quantity of oats to twelvepence. . . .

1256

. . . Whilst the festivities of Christmas[2] were still being kept up, on the sixth day after Christmas day, the third before the Calends of January, which was the eve of St Sylvester, the sun underwent a partial eclipse. At Toledo the eclipse was total; and on the third day following, which was the Circumcision [1 January 1256], the moon, according to the calendar, was one day old. . . . On the third day after,[3] an extraordinary storm, or succession of storms of wind and rain, accompanied by hail, thunder, and lightning, alarmed men's hearts, and caused irreparable damage. One might see the wheels of mills torn from their axles and carried by the violence of the wind to great distances, destroying in their course the neighbouring houses; and what the water did to the water-mills, the wind did not fail to do to the windmills. Piles of bridges, stacks of hay, the huts of fishermen with their nets and poles, and even children in their cradles, were suddenly carried away, so that the deluge of Deucalion[4]

[1] The reference is to the inclemency of the weather during the sitting of the April parliament at Westminster in 1255.
[2] i.e. Christmas 1255
[3] after 16 June
[4] the son of Prometheus, and the Noah of Greek mythology

seemed to be renewed. Not to mention other places, Bedford, which is watered by the Ouse, suffered incomputable damages, as it had done a few years before. Indeed, in one place, six houses immediately adjoining each other were carried away by the rapidity of the torrents, their inhabitants having much difficulty in saving themselves; and other places contiguous to that river were exposed to similar perils. . . . Thus then closed this year, which had been tolerably productive of fruit and corn. To the church and the prelates it brought the vilest slavery, and to the French, envy, in consequence of the promotion of earl Richard. It was a year of pillage for England; barren, and rather injurious than otherwise, to the Holy Land; it brought war on Wales, and disquiet and turbulence to Scotland. It was beyond measure stormy and rainy, so that, indeed, the times of Deucalion seemed to be renewed. From the day of the Assumption of the blessed Virgin [15 August] to the anniversary of her Purification [2 February], the rain ceased not to fall daily in deluges, which rendered the roads impassable and the fields barren. Hence at the end of autumn the corn was rotted in the ear.

1257

. . . On the Innocents' day[1] in this year such a quantity of rain fell that it covered the surface of the ground, and the times of Deucalion seemed to be renewed. The furrows looked like caves or rivers, and the rivers covered the meadows and all the neighbouring country, so that it presented the appearance of a sea. That from one case other similar ones may be understood, I may mention, that one river alone in the northern parts of England carried away seven large bridges of wood and stone; the mills too, and the neighbouring houses, were carried away by the violence of the torrent-swollen streams and destroyed. On the aforesaid day, too, a fierce whirlwind, accompanied by a violent hailstorm, disturbed the atmosphere and obscured the sky with darkness like that of night. The clouds collected together, and from them the lightning darted forth with fearful vividness, followed by claps of thunder. This thunder was clearly a bad omen, for it was mid-winter, and the cold was equal to that generally felt in February. This weather was followed by sickly unseasonable weather, which lasted about three months. . . . About this time, that is to say at the commencement of the autumn, the abbot and brethren of St Albans, considering that the crops of hay and corn were in imminent danger of being spoiled by the excessive falls of rain, came to a determination in their chapter, as was the usual custom in cases of such danger, that a fast should be proclaimed through their archdeacon, to be observed by the public as well as the convent; and also that the bier of St Alban should be carried in solemn procession to the church of St Mary-in-the-Fields, the conventual brethren and the people following with bare feet and uttering devout prayers. This was accordingly done, and on the same day, through the merits of the martyr, the destructive rain ceased. . . . This year throughout was barren and meagre; for whatever had been sown in winter, had budded in spring, and grown ripe in summer, was stifled and destroyed by the autumnal inundations. The scarcity of money, brought on by the spoliation practised by the king and the pope in England,

[1] i.e. 28 December 1256

brought on unusual poverty. The land lay uncultivated, and great numbers of people died from starvation. About Christmas,[1] the price of a measure of wheat rose to ten shillings. Apples were scarce, pears more so; figs, beech-nuts, cherries, plums – in short all fruits which are preserved in jars were completely spoiled. This pestiferous year, moreover, gave rise to mortal fevers, which raged to such an extent that, not to mention other cases, at [Bury] St Edmunds alone more than two thousand dead bodies were placed in the large cemetery during the summer, the largest portion of them during the dog-days. There were old men, who had formerly seen a measure of wheat sold for a mark, and even twenty shillings, without the people being starved to death. To add to the misery, Richard, king of Germany, had stripped the kingdom of England of many thousand marks, which he had ordered to be raised from his lands in England. The Holy Land languished in desolation and in fear of the Tartars; for the king of the latter had four million of fighting men in his train; and, as we have heard from learned and credible persons, they had already reduced half the world to subjection to them by their ferocity. Any one making a careful search and inquiry at St Albans may find there an account of their most filthy mode of life. This year, too, generated chronic complaints, which scarcely allowed free power of breathing to any one labouring under them. Not a single frosty or fine day occurred, nor was the surface of the lakes at all hardened by the frost, as was usual; neither did icicles hang from the ledges of houses; but uninterrupted heavy falls of rain and mist obscured the sky until the Purification of the blessed Virgin.[2]

1258

[References to the weather in 1258 will be found in No. 4 above, where the entry under that year in the Chronicle is given in full.]

1259

[References to the weather in 1259 will be found in No. 4 above, where the entry under that year in the Chronicle is given in full.]

189. Medieval courtesies

(*Worcester Liber Albus*, ed. J. M. Wilson (1920), Nos 30, 844 and 360)

(a) *Invitation to dine, 1301*

Godfrey, by divine permission bishop of Worcester, to his beloved son in Christ, brother John de Wyke, prior of Worcester, salvation with the grace and blessing of God.

On Sunday next after St Martin's feast day [11 November], come to us, as you love us, at Alvechurch at one o'clock to dine with us on good fat and fresh venison, and an equally fat crane, which chance to have been sent us, and which we do not like to eat without you. It will be a pleasure to us both. Farewell in the Lord.

[1] presumably Christmas 1257
[2] i.e. until 2 February 1258

(b) *Invitation for Christmas, 1318*
To his confidential friend, A. de H., Wulstan, prior of the cathedral church of Worcester, greeting.

We by this letter specially beg and urge you, as a friend in whom we have full confidence, that you will come to us at Worcester for Christmas, which is now close at hand; and that you will stay with us a few days, dining at our table in this festal season, and thus at once gratify and honour us.

Be assured that we cannot bear with equanimity the thought of your absence at that feast.

Please to assure us by the bearer that you will come.

[The invited guest is perhaps Adam of Horwyntone, a commissary of Adam Orlton, bishop of Hereford.]

(c) *Invitation to a funeral, 1306*
[Prior of Gloucester to the prior of Worcester] Since, by the command of our supreme Creator, our meek father and most dear shepherd has been released from this life, from which fate no mortal can escape, and his body is to be buried with the rites of the church in the aforesaid monastery, on Tuesday after the Sunday on which *Misericordia Domini* is sung, we therefore humbly pray that in your charity you will be so good as to be present at the said funeral. May the Most High keep you.

190. Salmon fishing, 1305

(*Cal. Pat. Rolls 1301–7*, p. 356)

1305, 23 April, Westminster
The like [commission of oyer and terminer] to Thomas de Metham and William de Huk', touching persons of Yorkshire who take salmon in the waters of Humber, Use, Trente, Dove, Ayre, Derwent, Wherf, Nidde, Yore, Swale and These and other waters where salmon are to be taken, between 8 September and Martinmas [11 November], and who take little salmon with nets and other engines between the middle of April and midsummer against the statute.[1]

191. A court in difficulty, 1277

(*Select Cases in the Court of King's Bench under Edward I*, I, ed. Sayles (Selden Soc.), p. 33)

Included because the Middle Ages are not usually credited with regard for the delicacies any more than the courtesies of life. In this case the husband, who was claiming tenancy by courtesy, was amerced for a false claim as a result of the court's difficulty.

Afterwards, on the morrow of the Purification of the blessed Mary, before the king and his council at Woodstock, although it was proved by the jurors that there was born of the aforesaid Margery a certain boy, who was called at the naming of the women "John", yet because a woman is not admitted to make any inquisition in the king's court, and it cannot be clear to the court whether he was born a living

[1] Stat. Westm. II, 1285 (No. 57 above), c. 47

ENGLAND
circa 1300
Main roads
Important cross-country roads
Highlands
Fenland
SCOTLAND
Berwick-on Tweed
Alnwick
Morpeth
Newcastle-on-Tyne
Chester-le-Street
Durham
Carlisle
Penrith
Appleby
Bowes
Darlington
Shap
Brough
Gilling
Northallerton
Kendal
Kirkby Lonsdale
Leeming
Topcliffe
Boro'bridge
Lancaster
Settle
Wetherby
YORK
Skipton
Castle-ford
Tadcaster
Brotherton
Hull
Preston
Bradford
Pontefract
Wakefield
ISLE OF AXHOLME
Wigan
Doncaster
Blyth
Warrington
Worksop
Tuxford
Lincoln
Chesterfield

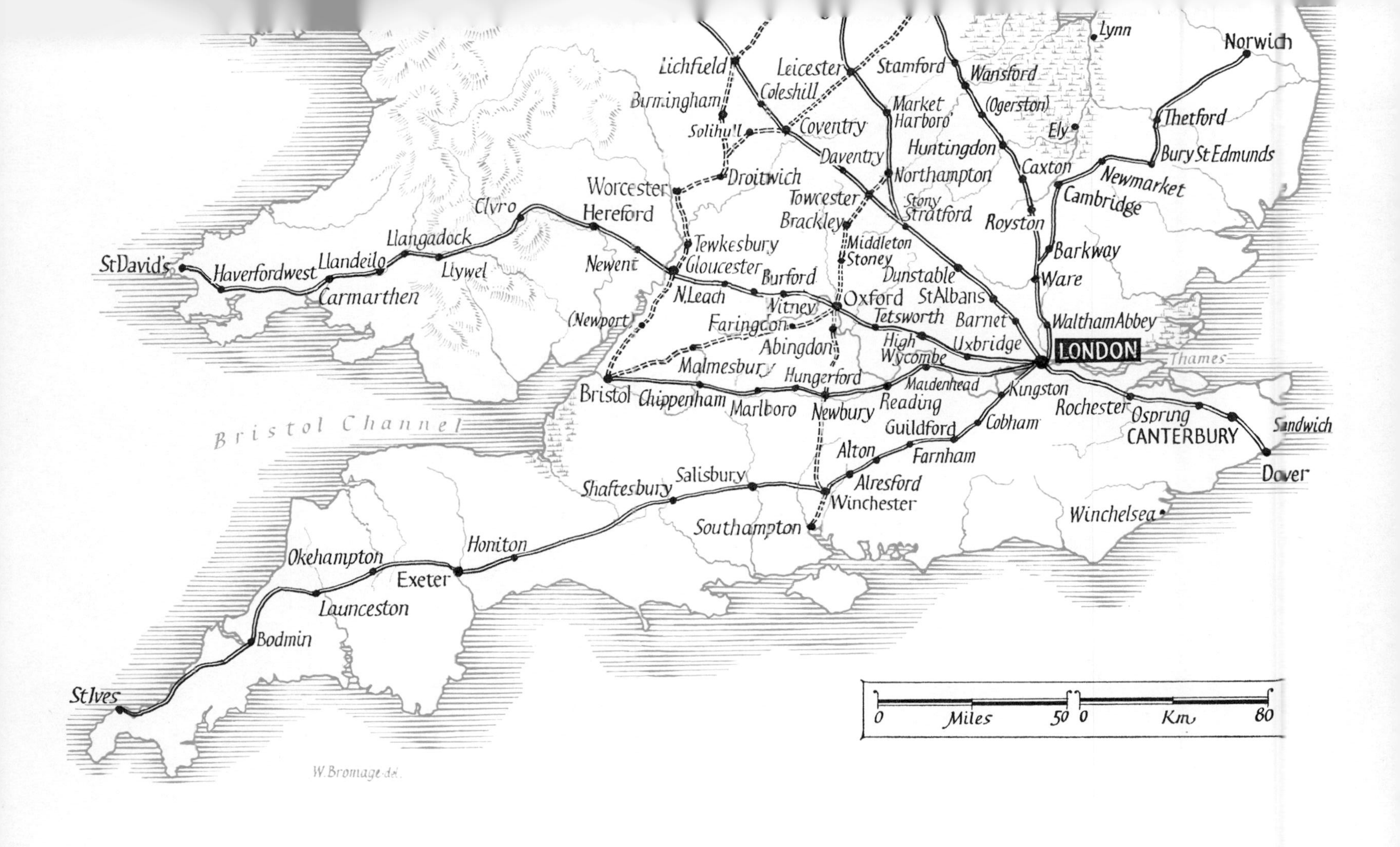

Lynn
Norwich
Lichfield
Leicester
Stamford
Wansford
Coleshill
Burmingham
Market
Harboro'
(Ogerston)
Ely
Thetford
Solihull
Coventry
Huntingdon
Bury St Edmunds
Daventry
Caxton
Droitwich
Northampton
Newmarket
Worcester
Towcester
Cambridge
Stony
Stratford
Royston
Clyro
Hereford
Brackley
Llangadock
Tewkesbury
Middleton
Stoney
Barkway
St David's
Llandeilo
Gloucester
Burford
Dunstable
Haverfordwest
Llywel
Newent
Ware
Carmarthen
N. Leach
Oxford
St Albans
Witney
Tetsworth
Barnet
(Newport)
Faringdon
Waltham Abbey
High
Wycombe
Uxbridge
Abingdon
LONDON
Thames
Malmesbury
Hungerford
Maidenhead
Bristol
Chippenham
Marlboro
Newbury
Reading
Kingston
Rochester
Ospring
CANTERBURY
Sandwich
Bristol Channel
Guildford
Cobham
Alton
Farnham
Dover
Salisbury
Alresford
Shaftesbury
Winchester
Winchelsea
Southampton
Honiton
Okehampton
Exeter
Launceston
Bodmin
St Ives
0
Miles
50
0
Km
80
W. Bromage del.

boy or not, and he had not been seen by males or heard by them to cry out and never by such was he seen alive, nor could he be seen because it is not permissible that males should be present at such intimate affairs, and similarly because it was proved by the jurors that never by any males was he heard to cry out, it does not seem to the court that the aforesaid John [the husband] ought to hold the inheritance of the aforesaid Margery by the law of England on account of the aforesaid boy.

192. Precautions on losing one's seal, 1267

(P.R.O., Curia Regis Roll, No. 180 (formerly 130), whence printed in *The Ancestor*, vol. 2 (1902), p. 120)

For similar precautions taken by a sheriff, *Select Cases in the Court of King's Bench under Edward I, II*, ed. G. O. Sayles (Selden Soc. No. 57), 1938, No. 18 (p. 30).

Memorandum that R.[1] earl of Gloucester and Hertford informed the justices here on Sunday next before the feast of St Peter in Cathedra [22 February] that in crossing a certain bridge he lately lost his seal, of which the impression was six small shields, together with his other equipment and he asked the justices to proclaim this publicly, and that for the future no credit may be given to that device, and that credit may be given to the device now sent to the same justices, in which the impression of one shield with the arms of the earl is contained: and the justices did this publicly.

193. Forgery

(*Cal. Papal Letters*, I, p. 194)

From the register of pope Gregory IX under date 5 March 1241.

Declaration to the convent of Canterbury that their good fame is not to suffer from the assertion of the late archbishop Edmund[2] that they had committed forgery in respect to certain privileges of Alexander III and St Thomas the Martyr. On enquiry made by Otho, cardinal of St Nicholas in Carcere,[3] it was found that three of them were guilty of having, in erroneous simplicity, rewritten a privilege of the said martyr, from which the seal had been torn, and affixed the said seal to the copy.

194. A lost ear

(a)

(*Cal. Pat. Rolls 1301–7*, p. 141)

1303, 20 May, Roxburgh. Notification, lest sinister suspicion arise hereafter, that the right ear of William son of John le Noble of Laghton was torn off in his minority by the bite of a pig. By K.

[1] An error for G.
[2] Edmund Rich was archbishop of Canterbury from 1233 to 16 November 1240
[3] The legation of Otto extended from July 1237 to January 1241.

(b)

(*Cal. Pat. Rolls 1258–66*, p. 64)

1259, 12 December, Westminster. Whereas Henry de Warwyk, bearer of these presents, lately before the king's justices at Westminster essoined Muriel de Bouley, his lady, who was impleaded there, and in awaiting the day of his essoin, had his right ear on suspicion of a trespass done before them cut off there by misrepresentation,[1] and whereas it appears on good testimony that he was not guilty of such trespass and no sign of such trespass was found on him or any proof thereof offered, the king notifies this—lest prejudice should arise to the said Henry hereafter—and commands that he be not molested on that account.

195. Proof of age

(*Cal. Inquisitions post mortem*, IV, No. 239)

Given as an example of the *method* of proving age for legal purposes. It is not suggested that the evidence adduced could be safely used by the historian for other purposes without corroboration. As in medieval tax assessments there was a strong tendency towards formalism, and in offices a strong tendency towards the use of formularies (cf. No. 215 below), so in this kind of record. If not already so in 1304, it very quickly became formal, and evidently untrustworthy when evidence in cases from different counties is identical even in wording: *E.H.R.*, xxii (1907), pp. 101–3 and 526–7; and ibid. xxix (1914), pp. 323–4. cf. C. T. Flower, *Introduction to the Curia Regis Rolls 1199–1230*, Selden Soc., vol. 62 (1944), p. 264.

John, son and heir of Richard Tempest

[York] Proof of age made at Skipton in Craven on Thursday after St Michael, 32 Edw. I [Thursday, 1 October 1304]

William de Marton, aged 60, says that the said John was born at Bracewell on the day of St Bartholomew 21 years ago, and was baptised in the baptistery of the church of St Michael there; and he recollects the day and year because on the day of the Exaltation of the Holy Cross following, a son Patrick was born to himself who was 21 at that feast last.

William de Cestrunt, aged 50, agrees, and recollects because Margery his own mother was married to one John de Ursewyck of Lonsdale on the day of St Martin next after the said John's birth, 21 years ago.

John de Kygheley, aged 60, agrees, and recollects because on the day of the Translation of St Cuthbert following the said birth, there was born to him a daughter Alice, who was 21 at that feast last.

Henry de Aula, aged 40, agrees, and recollects because one Cecily his stepmother was married to William de Aula his father on the day of the Decollation of St John the Baptist next after the said birth, twenty-one years ago.

Robert Buck, aged 41, agrees, and recollects because he was at school[2] at Clitheroe on the exhibition of sir Henry de Kygheley, and on the morrow of the Nativity of St John the Baptist next before the said birth he was so badly beaten there that he left the school, and from the day of that beating it was twenty-one years on the same morrow last past.

[1] *surreptionem*

[2] *in scolis*

Robert Forbraz, aged 50, agrees, and recollects because on the day of St Michael following the said birth he crossed to France, twenty-one years ago.

Elias de Stretton, aged 70, agrees, and recollects because Anabel his wife died at the feast of St Martin after the said John's birth twenty-one years ago.

Adam son of William de Brochton, aged 65, agrees, and recollects because he was a godfather of the said John and lifted him from the sacred font.

Robert son of Geoffrey de Bradeley, aged 80, agrees, and recollects because he impleaded one Adam Standefast by a writ of right in the court of Skipton, before John de Totenhow, constable of the castle, and recovered seisin of the tenement sought about the feast of St Martin next after the said John's birth, twenty-one years ago at the said feast next.

Richard de Bradeley, aged 60, agrees, and recollects because at Christmas next after the said John's birth, there was born to him a son Henry who will be 21 at that feast next if then living.

William de Brigham, aged 44, agrees, and recollects because at Whitsunday before the said birth he entered the service of sir William de Paterton, twenty-one years ago at that feast last.

Henry de Marton, aged 40, agrees and knows it because on the same day there was born to him a son William, who was 21 at the feast of St Bartholomew last.

196. Death by misadventure, 1267

(*Cal. Inquisitions Miscellaneous*, I, No. 2133)

On Wednesday before Ascension day 51 Henry III [25 May 1267] William de Stangate came down a road called Burleyesdam [in Sussex] with a cross-bow on his left shoulder and a poisoned[1] arrow, and he met Desiderata, late the wife of Robert le Champeneys, who was his child's godmother, and a particular friend. And she asked him in jest, whether he were one of the men who were going about the country with cross-bows, bows and other weapons, to apprehend robbers and evil-doers by the king's order; adding that she could overcome and take two or three like him. And putting out her arm she caught him by the neck and crooking her leg[2] behind his without his noticing it, she upset him and fell on him. And in falling she struck herself in the side with the arrow which he had under his belt, piercing to the heart, and died on the spot. *Verdict*. Death by misadventure. [*C. Inq. Misc.*, File 4 (32)]

[1] *toxicatam* [2] *tibiam*

197. A wedding brawl, 1268

(*Cal. Inquisitions Miscellaneous*, I, No. 359)

William Selisaule was in prison at York for killing Adam de Auwerne. On 18 September a writ was issued to John de Octon to enquire whether William killed Adam through mischance or malice. The inquisition returned the following answer.

A certain stranger being new-married was taking his wife and others who were with her to one end of the town of Byrun, when William Selisaule asked for a ball,[1] which it is the custom to give; and they having no ball gave him a pair of gloves for a pledge; afterwards other men of Byrun asked for a ball, and they said they would not give one, because they had already given a pledge for one, and the men of Byrun would not believe them, but still asked for the said ball; and so there arose a dispute, and the wedding party, being slightly drunk, assaulted the men of Byrun with axes and bows and arrows, and wounded very many; and the said William hearing the noise, and thinking it was for the ball for which he had a pledge, ran with a stick to appease the dispute; and when he had come near, one William son of Ralph de Rotil[?] drew an arrow at him and hit him in the breast, so that he thought he had got his death; as the said William son of Ralph, not yet content, was meaning to shoot at him again, he saw that he could only escape the arrow by hitting him back, so as to hinder his drawing; so he ran up to the said William son of Ralph to hit him on the arm, but by mischance, hit the said Adam [de Auwerne], who unwittingly came between them, so he died. Thus the said William Selisaule killed the said Adam by mischance, and not of malice prepense. [*C. Inq. Misc.*, File 15 (12)]

198. Christmas in Acton Scott, Shropshire, 1287

(*Cal. Inquisitions Miscellaneous*, I, No. 2306)

An inquisition in 1289 into the circumstances in which John de Quercubus killed Hugh de Weston at Christmas 1287.

John de Quercubus of Scottes Acton killed Hugh de Weston, chaplain, in self defence. On Christmas day 16 Edward I [1287] after sunset there were some men singing outside a tavern kept by Richard son of William de Skottesacton in that town. And Hugh came by the door immensely drunk, and quarrelled with the singers. Now John was standing by, singing, and Hugh hated him a little because he sang well, and desired the love of certain women who were standing by in a field and whom Hugh much affected. So Hugh took a naked sword in his hand and ran at John, striking him once, twice, thrice, on the head, and nearly cutting off two fingers of his left hand. And John went on his knees, and raised his hands asking God's peace and the king's, and then ran into a corner near the street under a stone wall. And Hugh ran after him and tried to kill him, so he drew his knife and wounded Hugh in the chest, killing him instantly. [*C. Inq. Misc.*, File 48 (45)]

[1] *pelota*

199. Villein status

The treatise on the laws and customs of the realm of England commonly called "Glanvill" was written at the very outset of the period with which we are concerned, probably between 1187 and 1189. These extracts from it, (a), deal with personal serfdom: villein tenure is referred to, but is not itself treated. The whole subject in its legal aspects is best approached via Pollock and Maitland, *History of English Law*, I, pp. 356–83 and 412–32. "Glanvill" itself is now best read in the edition (and translation) of G. D. G. Hall (1965).

The following case, (b), heard in the King's Bench in 1286, illustrates the working of the law. John son of Robert de Estgate, bringing an assize of *novel disseisin* against one William de Mortimer, has to overcome the fact that he had a villein grandmother.

(a)

(*Glanvill*, V, 3–6, ed. Hall, pp. 55–8)

. . . free status shall be proved as follows. He who claims to be free shall produce in court several near blood relatives descended from the same stock as himself, and if they are admitted or proved in court to be free, then the claimant himself will be freed from the yoke of servitude. If, however, their free status is denied or doubted, recourse must be had to the men of the neighbourhood by whose verdict it may be known whether they are free men or not, and judgment will be given according to this verdict. However, he who seeks to reduce the claimant to villein status may have produced others to prove the opposite, namely villeins of his who descend from one and the same stock as the man whom he claims as a villein; in such a case, if those produced by both parties are all admitted to be blood relatives, the men of the neighbourhood shall similarly be asked which of them are his nearest relatives, and judgment given accordingly. The same method is to be used if those produced by one party are admitted, and those produced by the other party are denied, to be blood relatives, or if there is doubt about it; all such doubt is resolved by the verdict of the neighbourhood.

When free status has been properly proved in court, then he whose free status is the subject of dispute shall be quit and free for ever from the claim of the man who alleged him to be a villein. But if he has failed in his proof, or if the other party has proved him to be his villein, then he and all his chattels shall be adjudged irrevocably to his lord.

This same form and order of pleading is to be used both when a man who has been enjoying freedom is reduced to villeinage and when a man of apparent villein status claims freedom on his own initiative . . .

The ways in which a person can be made free

A person of villein status can be made free in several ways. For example, his lord, wishing him to achieve freedom from the villeinage by which he is subject to him, may quit-claim him from himself and his heirs; or he may give or sell him to another with intent to free him. It should be noted, however, that no person of villein status can seek his freedom with his own money, for in such a case he could, according to the law and custom of the realm, be recalled to villeinage by his lord, because all the chattels of a villein are deemed to such an extent the property of his lord that he cannot redeem himself from villeinage with his own money as against his lord. If, however, a third party provides the money and buys the villein in order to free him, then he can maintain himself for ever in a state of freedom as against his lord who sold him . . . It should, however, be noted that anyone may make his villein free as against himself or his heirs, but not as against others. For if anyone formerly a villein, who has been freed in this way, is produced in court to make proof as a champion or to wage law, he can lawfully be excluded if his villein status is raised as an objection and proved, even if he has been made a knight since he was freed.

If any villein stays peaceably for a year and a day in a privileged town and is admitted as a citizen into their commune, that is to say, their gild, he is thereby freed from villeinage.

The ways in which people become villeins

Some persons are villeins from the moment of birth, for example a person born of a villein father and a villein mother, or one born of a free father and a villein mother; even to one born of a free mother and a villein father the same conclusion about civil condition applies. Therefore, if a free man marries a villein and lives on a villein tenement, so long as he is bound in this way by the villein tenure he loses, as a villein, all legal rights. If children are born of the villein of one lord and the villein mother of another they will be equally divided between the two lords.

(b)

(*Select Cases in the Court of King's Bench under Edward I*, III, ed. and trans. G. O. Sayles (Selden Soc., 1939), pp. 48–9)

Heard in King's Bench, Michaelmas Term 1296

. . . The jurors say on their oath that a certain Bartholomew Hauteyn, a free man, begot the aforesaid Robert de Estgate, father of the aforesaid John, with a certain female serf of Robert de Mortimer, father of the aforesaid William de Mortimer. And Robert de Estgate afterwards increased in goods and by his trading he improved himself so much that he acquired by charters some of the aforesaid tenements in the time of the aforesaid Robert de Mortimer and he held the same by the services contained in those charters, but because he frequently used to return and stay on the aforesaid Robert de Mortimer's land at Barnham because his mother lived there, the same Robert de Mortimer demanded from him a penny a year to be paid for chevage, and he paid that penny to the aforesaid Robert every year during all the time of that Robert de Mortimer. And after that Robert de Mortimer had died and the earl Warenne had seized the lands and tenements which the same Robert held because the aforesaid William was a minor in his wardship, he afterwards delivered the same to the same [William] for a fine which that William's friends had made to that earl for the wardship and marriage. The same William delivered the manor of Barnham to Henry de Mortimer, his uncle, to hold it for the term of that Henry's life. And they say that the aforesaid Robert de Estgate paid the aforesaid Henry during all his time the aforesaid penny every year for chevage. And after the aforesaid Henry's death the aforesaid manor reverted to the aforesaid William as the right heir. And they say that the aforesaid Robert de Estgate likewise acquired the remaining part of the aforesaid tenements, concerning which that assize etc., by charters . . . of the aforesaid Henry as well as, afterwards, of the aforesaid William, and he always held the same tenements according to the form of the aforesaid charters. And they say that thereupon a certain steward of the aforesaid William summoned all the tenants of the aforesaid manor on a certain day and held the court of that William, his lord, and enjoined upon all that, if they had acquired any lands by charters, they should give him their charters. Among them it happened that the aforesaid Robert de Estgate gave him his charters, and all these charters he afterwards returned to the aforesaid Robert for a fine of half a mark which he received from him for the use of the aforesaid William, his lord. And they say that the same Robert took as his wife a certain free woman in the same manor and with her he begot the aforesaid John, who has now brought this assize. And they say that the same Robert held all those tenements by the services in the charters etc. and he died seised thereof, and after his death the aforesaid William and the others removed the aforesaid John therefrom, and the aforesaid William afterwards held the same until now. Asked whether the aforesaid Robert during all his time did any servile services to the aforesaid Robert de Mortimer and Henry or William, they say that neither did they demand any servile services from him nor did he do them, only the services contained in his charters and one penny for chevage, as is abovesaid. Because it is manifest by this assize that the aforesaid Robert de Estgate, father of the aforesaid John, freely acquired the aforesaid tenements to be held by definite services etc., and he died seised of those tenements in his demesne as of fee, and he never did any servile services to the aforesaid William de Mortimer or his ancestors, and after the death of the aforesaid Robert, his son was seised of the aforesaid tenements until the aforesaid William de Mortimer and the others removed and disseised him thereof, therefore it is awarded that the aforesaid John should recover his seisin of the aforesaid tenements from the aforesaid William, and his damages, which are taxed by the jurors at twenty-four shillings. And the aforesaid William and the others in mercy . . .

200. A marriage-tangle, 1254

(*Cal. Inquisitions post mortem, Henry III* (1904), No. 303, pp. 79–80)

An inquisition post mortem on 31 March 1254 after the death of a Hampshire tenant-in-chief William de Cardevill' (Cardunvill) revealed a marriage-tangle and, in the opinion of the jury, a succession difficulty.

He solemnly espoused at the church door one Alice, and they lived together as husband and wife for sixteen years and had several children, of whom one named Richard, aged 4, lives. Afterwards came one Joan of whom long ago he had begotten a son named Richard, now aged 24, and claimed the said William as her husband in the court Christian by a promise[1] given to her, and intention having been proved it was so adjudged, and divorce from the said Alice solemnly pronounced, and so it has remained for a year and more. But as the said Joan was never solemnly espoused at the church door, the jury doubt whether her son or the son of the said Alice is the heir; if neither, then Robert de Cardunville, brother of the said William, is the heir.

[1] *fidem*

201. Provision for a mistress and her children (mid-13th cent.)

(*Sir Christopher Hatton's Book of Seals*, ed. L. C. Lloyd and D. M. Stenton (Oxford, 1950), No. 269)

Know those present and future that I Philip son of Roger Pantulf of Newbold have given and granted and by this my present charter confirmed to Denise of Warwick and the children begotten of me the said Philip and the said Denise for her service three half virgates of land with all their appurtenances in the district of Long Lawford, one virgate of which I had as a gift from Roger Pantulf my father with the men sitting on that land and all their issue and all their chattels namely the half virgate of land which Thomas de le Hul held, with the said Thomas and all his issue and all his chattels, and the half virgate of land which William son of Roger held, with the said William and all his issue and all his chattels, and the half virgate of land which I had as a gift from William Pantulf my brother, that namely which Roger Colling held, with the said Roger Colling and all his issue and all his chattels; To have and to hold of me and my heirs or my assigns to the said Denise and the children born of me the said Philip and the said Denise and their heirs freely quietly well and in peace and by inheritance forever, Rendering thence annually to me and my heirs and my assigns one pair of white gloves worth a halfpenny, or one halfpenny, at Easter for all secular services, suits of court, complaints, exactions, customs and demands. I Philip Pantulf however and my heirs and my assigns will warrant, acquit and defend the said three virgates[1] of land with all their appurtenances in meadows in pastures in ways and paths and all other places to the aforementioned Denise and the children begotten of me and the said Denise for the said service against all men and women forever. In order that this my gift and grant and the confirmation of my present charter may remain valid forever, I have confirmed this my present charter by the impression of my seal. These being witnesses, William de Wauere, lord of Church Lawford, Richard Cheynel of Lawford, John de Awers of Newbold, William Cosin of Newbold, Geoffrey son of Alexander of Lawford, John Rag of Lawford, Reginald Toft, Philip the cook of Lawford, Thomas Palle of Lawford and others.

202. A judicial separation, 1294

(*Cal. Pat. Rolls 1292–1301*, pp. 63–5 [French])

Edward I's rather shadowy cousin, Edmund earl of Cornwall, succeeded his father Richard, earl of Cornwall and king of the Romans, in 1272. He married in that year the earl of Gloucester's sister Margaret, who after twenty-two years here agrees to a separation: but the marriage had completely broken down long before this (cf. L. M. Midgley (ed.), *Ministers' Accounts of the Earldom of Cornwall 1296–1297*, p. xvi, n. 4).

To all those who shall see and hear this document Margaret, countess of Cornwall, greeting in God. Know that as there were wranglings and disputes between my lord sir Edmund, earl of Cornwall, my husband, of the one part and me, his wife, of the other part, because I demanded to be taken back to him and that he should receive me in his house and treat me also as his lawful wife, give me back my con-

[1] a slip, presumably, for half virgates

jugal rights and find and provide for me in all things as his wife, and my aforesaid lord persisted in rebutting me in these my demands in divers ways and by many exceptions, these wranglings and disputes have at last been brought to an end and terminated in the following manner. Namely, my lord has assigned to me 800 pounds worth of land and rent a year for the support of myself and my household in everything necessary to us. The lands he has assigned to me are these. Namely all his lands and tenements in Norfolk and Suffolk, which are estimated at 382 pounds 10 shillings and 8 pence worth of land a year; the manor of Kirton[1] in the county of Lincoln with the soke and its appurtenances, which is estimated at 368 pounds 15 shillings and 9 pence a year. And 40 pounds a year from the farms of Malmesbury and Winterslow in Wiltshire and from Queenhithe at London 8 pounds 13 shillings and 7 pence a year. And moreover I receive these lands and rents in such a way that I cannot alienate them or any part of them or grant or allow any possession of them to anyone, but shall retain these lands and rents in my hand for my support and shall not commit waste or exile therein, or destruction of villeins, but shall have *housbote* and *heybote* as is fitting.[2] And my lord who has granted me this retains nevertheless for himself the advowsons of priories and churches, the knight's fees and the escheats of the aforesaid lands and tenements. And if I should die before my lord the earl, the aforesaid lands and rents shall revert fully and freely to him and his heirs, saving to me full power of bequeathing the goods which I have received from these lands and rents and which are on the lands on the day of my death; the ownership and lordship of these lands remaining forever with my lord the earl. And should it happen that my lord dies before me, there shall be saved to me the claiming of my dower from the lands and tenements of my lord the earl only in accordance with the custom of England as long as I have less of the lands and rents of my lord the aforesaid earl than my dower should amount to, and this my lord the earl has granted that I may claim and have. And I have faithfully promised that nothing else ought to be or can be claimed by me or anyone else from the goods or chattels of my lord the earl either in his lifetime or after his death, but with these things in this form I will remain satisfied and content. And I, who wish to live chastely and serve and direct my thoughts to God alone, readily and of my own free will and with the assent of my lord the earl both swear on God's holy gospel and take a corporal oath before the honoured father sir Thomas by God's grace bishop of Rochester to stay chaste and continent as long as my lord the earl lives and will not claim conjugal rights from him, or to be in his house or to be taken back into his bed unless my lord pleases otherwise, nor will I from now on molest or vex him in any of these points. And if I do vex him in any of these points (which God preserve me from) in fact with a judgment or without a judgment[3] claiming anything else of him either personally or by someone else in my name, or molesting or vexing him in these aforesaid articles, or if I or anyone else in my name get absolution, either from the pope or other superior, from being bound to keep my aforesaid oath, or if I avail myself of any such absolution obtained by anyone else contrary to any of these points of my oath and this is evident, or if I am lawfully

[1] Kirton-in-Lindsey
[2] i.e. the right to take wood and/or thorns as necessary for repair of house or fences respectively
[3] *en jugement ou hors de jugement*

convicted before a competent judge of contravening any of the aforesaid points, I am willing from that time that the aforesaid lands and rents should revert freely to my lord the earl and that he himself can of his own authority take seisin of them and retain them for himself. And moreover my lord the earl has granted me that he will not wrongfully disturb me in the possession of the aforesaid lands and rents nor shall anyone for him either wholly or partly. And if he does and this is lawfully complained of and proved before our lord the king or other competent judge, my lord promises me to make restitution of damages and to pay the expenses I incur in suing for my rights, however long the aforesaid covenants retain their force and power. And I, who wish all these things set out above to remain firm and stable, renounce purely and absolutely in all these things above-written and in each article of them every kind of right and of action and everything which could be done at the discretion of the law or of a judge[1] which is or could be open to me against my lord the earl. And if any judge by any kind of discretion[2] does anything for me against my lord in any of the aforenamed articles, I promise that I shall not be willing to make use of this discretion[3] or receive or have any advantage from it. And I renounce every kind of benefit of *restitutio in integrum* and every other kind of benefit of law which could help me on any point aforenamed. And on top of this I wish all the proceedings between us over the aforesaid disputes and controversies before whatever person, whether judge ordinary or delegate, in England or at the court of Rome, and also the sentences of suspension and of excommunication imposed and ordained by whatever judge or auditor, to be null, void and forever henceforth treated as non-existent. And to the extent that they have in fact been stopped for a time, to that extent let them be in fact resumed and put an end to. And this I will take steps to achieve for my part and my lord will take steps to achieve as much for his part as regards proceedings against me. And I by the tenor of this document expressly renounce all my proceedings and all the rights which I could have by them against my lord. These things on each point I have promised of my own accord to keep and grant without any sort of distress or compulsion from anyone else. Nor will I ever contravene any of the points. In witness of which thing and for greater security of this business I have set my seal to this present document which stays with my lord the earl, and have got the honoured father sir Thomas, by God's grace bishop of Rochester, and sir Bogo de Clare, my brother, to set their seals to this same document. And the earl my lord has set his seal to the part which stays with me. Given at Rochester the thirteenth day of February, the year of the incarnation one thousand two hundred and ninety-three.[4] And the twenty-second year of the reign of king Edward.

[1] *chescun office de droit e de juyge*
[2] *par aukune manere de office*
[3] *cel office*
[4] Evidently the Christian year is being reckoned from the Annunciation (25 March), but as the regal year (22 Edward I = 20 November 1293 to 19 November 1294) shows, the date by our reckoning is 13 February 1294.

203. Popular canonisation

(*Cal. Inquisitions Miscellaneous*, II, No. 2103)

Earl Thomas of Lancaster was executed on 22 March 1322. Within weeks there were reports of miracles being worked at his tomb. For the background of the present document and the persistence of the cult, see J. R. Maddicott, *Thomas of Lancaster 1307–1322* (Oxford, 1970), pp. 329–30.

Commission to Henry le Scrop, John de Donecastr' and John de Denum. Barnard Castle, 9 September, 17 Edward II [1323]
The king formerly commanded Richard de Moseleye, his clerk, constable of Pontefract castle, to go in person to the place of execution of Thomas, late earl of Lancaster and prohibit a multitude of malefactors and apostates from praying and making oblations there in memory of the said earl not to God but rather to idols, in contempt of the king and contrary to his former command.

The said constable and his servants were assaulted at Pontefract, and two of them named Richard de Godeleye and Robert de la Hawe were killed.

The commissioners are to inquire into this and imprison such persons as should be indicted before them. By p.s.

204. Love-days

(a)

(*Select Cases of Proceedings without Writ*, ed. H. G. Richardson and G. O. Sayles (Selden Soc., vol. 60, 1941), pp. clxxx–clxxxi)

Be it known to all that on the day after the feast of St Thomas the Apostle[1] there came to Henry de Bohun, earl of Hereford, Richard abbot of Cirencester with his fellow-canons, mr Alexander[2] and Nicholas de la Mare, and Martin styled[3] prior of Gloucester,[4] with his fellow-canons, namely Walter the cellarer, the sub-prior Walter of Prestbury, William of St Oswald and William the Fleming, seeking on bended knees his grace and mercy in respect of the complaints he had against the prior of Llanthony. The aforesaid earl said to them, "I am not minded to listen to your petitions, for I have found this prior so unstable and faithless in word and deed that I am not willing and have not dared to believe him at all." The prior answered by his counsel, that is by the mouth of mr Alexander, "Lord, have pity on your own,[5] because you know, of a truth, that we have come to regain your peace and mercy. And prior Martin, here, has bound himself absolutely to do what Geoffrey fitz Peter, earl of Essex,[6] advises and you wish, concerning him personally and other complaints you have against them."[7] Earl Henry, replying to them, "What faith can I have in your word and his, when I have never found him, along with his fellow-canons,

[1] i.e. on 22 December: the year was 1204
[2] the famous scholar Alexander Neckham
[3] *dictus*
[4] The Augustinian priory of Llanthony Secunda was near Gloucester.
[5] *vestrorum*
[6] the justiciar
[7] *eos*: presumably his fellow-canons at Llanthony Secunda. The contrast would seem to be between him as prior and them, particularly in view of the earl's reply in the next sentence.

trusty in either word or deed?" The canons of Cirencester and of Llanthony,[1] answering him, "We tell you, of a truth, that the aforesaid prior Martin will stand firmly by an agreement and keep his word." Earl Henry answered, "I hear what you say. We are willing to go to the court of the lord king, and the lord justiciar will be there, and they will advise us, and I will give you a love-day about this if that should be their advice." And we went to the court and the advice of the lord justiciar came to this that I should give them a love-day, namely the Wednesday before Hilarytide.[2]

(b)

(*Selborne Charters*, ed. W. D. Macray (Hants. Rec. Soc., London and Winchester, 1891), p. 44)

1251, 24 February. Indenture of an agreement whereby sir James de Nortune, knt, gives to the prior and canons of Seleburne the width of fourteen feet of his lands to make a ditch between their meadow and his land, from the corner of Binlaund, and six feet of his meadow to make another ditch; and they mutually covenant that if their cattle trespass, they will, before going into their courts about it, call each other to the churchyard of Seleburne, and there state the damage, and have it satisfied according to the view of good men, Witness sir John de Venuz, sir William his son, sir John de la Stane, sir Thomas Makeril, knts, James de Accangre, John de Burrunte, James de Molendinis, William Band, Matthew de Monasterio.

205. A case for pardon, 1249

(*Crown Pleas of the Wiltshire Eyre, 1249*, ed. C. A. F. Meekings (Wilts. Archaeol. and Nat. Hist. Soc.: Records Branch, Devizes, 1961), p. 158 (No. 39))

[Wiltshire Eyre, 1249. Crown Pleas. Startley Hundred]

Robert the son of Henry Badding', in climbing up a hayrick in Segre meadow, fell from the rick so that he broke his neck. John son of Maud, William Skywe, Walter son of Alice and Robert Stormy were then present there. William Skywe, accused of the death of Robert, comes and denies the said death and for good [and ill he puts himself on the country]. The jurors say he is guilty of the said death, for they say that Robert fell from the rick on to William Skywe and William, startled by this, struck Robert twice on the head with his staff, so that he killed him. But they say that William did not do this in felony but rather out of witlessness because he is under age being twelve years old. So it is awarded that William be taken into custody and this case be told the king, etc. It is testified that Henry of Hertham the coroner received one mark to conceal this matter. Henry himself is present and cannot deny this, so he is in mercy.

[1] *Lantonensis ecclesie*
[2] i.e. on 12 January 1205

206. Further pardons for homicide

(*Cal. Pat. Rolls 1258–66*, p. 407; *Cal. Inquis. Miscell.*, 1, No. 2275 and *Cal. Close Rolls 1279–88*, p. 334; *Cal. Pat. Rolls 1292–1301*, p. 250)

For consideration of the whole question of clemency in such cases, Naomi D. Hurnard, *The King's Pardon for Homicide before A.D. 1307* (Oxford, 1969)

1265. Pardon, at the instance of Thomas de Ferrariis to William Pilche of Sankey, an idiot, for the death of Augustine le Fevere of Manchester, as it appears by testimony of Robert de Stockport, coroner in the county of Lancaster, and other trustworthy persons that the said William was passing along the high road by night when he was met by the said Augustine in the disguise of a terrible monster uttering groans and refusing to speak though adjured in God's name, on account of which the said William rushed upon him as a monster and killed him.
1285, June. James de Ardena, imprisoned at Norwich, killed Eve de Carleton in his madness,[1] and was mad both before and long after.
July. Order to deliver James de Ardena, imprisoned at Norwich . . . in bail to twelve men who shall mainpern to have him before the justices . . . if any one wish to speak against him, as the king learns by inquisition taken by the sheriff that James slew Eva in a fit of madness and not by felony or of malice aforethought.
1297. Pardon to John son of John Legat for the death of Robert de Turbervill, as it appears by the record of Hugh de Brunteston and John Neyrenuyt, justices appointed to deliver Oxford goal, that he is and from birth has been deaf and dumb, and therefore, according to law and the custom of the realm, cannot put himself upon the country.

207. Henry of Berwick and his nieces, 1285

(*Select Cases in the Court of King's Bench under Edward I*, I, ed. G. O. Sayles (Selden Soc., vol. 55, 1936), Nos 90 and 91 (pp. 134–7))

Gloucestershire. Henry of Berwick was attached to answer William Hirdeman and Christian his wife on a plea why he along with unknown men made an assault with force and arms upon the aforesaid Christian in Redcliff Street at Bristol and beat and ill-treated her and stole from her her goods and chattels that were found with her and took and abducted Cecily and Christian, daughters of that Christian in the charge of William and Christian. And with regard to this they complain that on the feast of St Thomas the Martyr in the ninth year of the present king's reign [29 December 1280] he did the aforesaid trespass to them, whereby they say that they are wronged and have suffered loss to the value of a hundred shillings, and thereof they produce suit etc.

And the aforesaid Henry comes and denies force and tort when etc. And concerning this he explicitly denies that ever on the aforesaid day and year did he beat and ill-treat the aforesaid Christian or abduct the aforesaid Cecily and Christian with force and arms from the custody of the aforesaid William and Christian, because he says that the same Christian had been excommunicated on account of her contumacy, wherefore the same Christian went away outside the town of Bristol so that the aforesaid children were wandering about in the aforesaid town of Bristol without protection. And when the mayor of the aforesaid town of Bristol had noticed the aforesaid

[1] *furia inventus*

children wandering about without protection, the same mayor, who has charge of orphans and all other things pertaining to the aforesaid town [on behalf of the] community of the town of Bristol, took the aforesaid Cecily, daughter of the aforesaid Christian, and [delivered her to Henry] as uncle of the aforesaid Cecily, on account of the danger besetting the aforesaid child wandering about in this way, because the aforesaid child is better looked after by reason of this affinity. And afterwards came the aforesaid Christian, sister of the aforesaid Cecily, of her own will to the house of that Henry, and Henry did not want to drive the aforesaid Christian away on account of the relationship. And that he did no other trespass and did not abduct the aforesaid children, he asks for enquiry to be made. And that he did do them the aforesaid trespass, she asks for enquiry to be made. Therefore the bailiffs are ordered to cause twelve to come on the morrow.

The jurors say on their oath that the aforesaid Henry is in nothing guilty. And therefore it is awarded that the aforesaid Henry go thereof without day. And the aforesaid William and Christian be in mercy for a false claim. It is pardoned because they are poor.

Gloucestershire. Henry of Berwick was attached to answer William Hirdeman and Christian his wife on a plea why he took and carried away their goods and chattels at Bristol. And with regard to this they complain that, when the aforesaid William and Christian had their honey in their cellar in Small Street on Tuesday after the feast of St Denis in the ninth year of the present king's reign [14 October 1281], to wit, nine tubs of honey, the price of each tub being seven marks, he took and carried them away as well as forty pence. They also complain of the aforesaid Henry that, whilst they had their houses in the same street of Small Street, the aforesaid Henry came there and took and carried off the keys of those houses and kept them for half a year, so that they lost the letting of the aforesaid houses, to wit, to the value of forty shillings. They also complain of the aforesaid Henry that when they had six sacks of wool at Southampton, the price of each sack being ten marks, the aforesaid Henry came there and unlawfully seized the said wool so that, when the aforesaid William and Christian should have carried the aforesaid wool to Flanders, they lost the sale of the aforesaid wool on account of that seizure, whereby they say that they are wronged and have suffered the loss of seven pounds, and thereof they produce suit etc.

And the aforesaid Henry comes and denies force and tort when etc. And as for taking away the honey, he says that a certain John Gilbert on his death made Henry his executor, and this John left a hundred and forty pounds to the aforesaid Cecily and Christian, his children, and handed the money over into the care of the aforesaid Christian his wife. And afterwards, by the award of the commonalty of the town aforesaid in the Guildhall, it was adjudged that the aforesaid goods and tenements should be delivered to the same Henry to be kept for the use of the aforesaid children, as is the custom of the town, and William and Christian through the aforesaid award and by their own will handed over the aforesaid honey in part payment of the aforesaid money. And that in no other way did he take and carry away the aforesaid honey, he asks for enquiry to be made.

And as for carrying off the keys, he says that the aforesaid keys belonged to the aforesaid cellar where the honey was lying. And the same William and Christian handed over the aforesaid keys to the same Henry of their own will and because of the award of the commonalty of the town aforesaid until the aforesaid honey could be sold. And that it is so, he asks for enquiry to be made.

And as for the seizure of the aforesaid wool in Hampshire, he says that he ought not to answer for it on their complaint, because he says that he is a free man and ought not to answer here of different trespasses done in different counties without a special writ of the chancery addressed to the sheriff of the place, because he says that if any free man were required to answer for different trespasses done in different counties without special writ and on the simple complaint of a plaintiff, then it would be necessary for the defendant to require security for costs from the plaintiff and this will be contrary to the law and custom of England, and on this he prays judgment etc.

The jurors say on their oath that the aforesaid Henry is not guilty of any trespass because whatever he had in the aforesaid tubs was by award of the whole commonalty of Bristol, as is the custom in the same town with regard to the chattels of orphans. And therefore it is awarded that the aforesaid Henry go thereof without day. And the aforesaid William and Christian his wife be in mercy for a false claim. And it is amerced at half a mark.

208. Feudalism and the family

(a)

(*Cal. Pat. Rolls 1247–58*, p. 631)

Traffic in wardships and marriages. In this case the widow has acquired the marriages.

1258, 29 May, Clarendon
Ratification, at the instance of [Simon de Montfort, earl of Leicester], to [John de Haya] of the sale by the abbot of Pipperwell to Ermetrude late the wife of Walter Leydet of the marriage of two daughters and heirs of the said Walter which the abbot recovered in the king's court as is said; and of the sale by the said Ermetruda of the said marriage to the said John to the use of two of his sons.

(b)

(*Cal. Close Rolls 1272–9*, p. 332)

The family and primogeniture.

1276. William de Warenna, son of John de Warenna, earl of Surrey, granted before William de Luton that the earl, when he dies, may dispose of all his lands in co. Norfolk, and that he [William] will esteem the disposition firm and stable until ten years after the earl's death, and that he will not contravene the assignment, but that he will protect the earl's executors and will warrant them until the end of the said term.

209. The *Dictum* of Kenilworth, 1266–1302

The *Dictum* of Kenilworth (No. 43 above) could cast a long shadow over an estate and its tenants. Its effect generally requires further investigation: the best account in print is that of F. M. Powicke in his *King Henry III and the Lord Edward* (1947), especially pp. 534–56.

(a)

(*Cal. Close Rolls 1279–88*, p. 88)

1281, 28 May, Westminster

To Richard de Holebrok, the king's steward. Order to cause Hugh le Despenser to have full and free administration of the lands of Hugh le Despenser, deceased, which were taken into the king's hands by reason of the death of Alina la Despenser, the ransom whereof the late king in the form of the *Dictum* of Kenilleworth gave to Philip Basset, who bequeathed it to Alina his daughter, who bequeathed it to Hugh le Despenser, her son and heir and executor of her will, and to cause Hugh to have everything received thence since Alina's death in order to make execution of her will.

(b)

(ibid. p. 319)

1285, 16 May, Westminster

To master Henry de Bray, escheator this side Trent. Whereas Peter de Chaluns has acknowledged before the king that William, son and heir of William de Birmingeham, who was slain in the battle of Evesham against the late king and the present king, has satisfied him both for the ransom of the lands that belonged to William in Dorton [Bucks.] and for a quarter of the lands that belonged to William in Hoggeston [Bucks.] that Isabella, late the wife of the said William, lately deceased, held for her maintenance between a third and a quarter, according to the form of the *Dictum* of Kenill[eworth], which ransom was given to Peter by Hamo Lestrange [Extraneus], to whom the late king granted the lands according to the *Dictum*; the king orders the escheator to restore to William the said lands, which he took into the king's hands by reason of Isabella's death, together with everything received from them since they were taken into the king's hands.

(c) *The Dictum and the manor of Frampton, Lincs.*

(*Cal. Close Rolls 1296–1302*, pp. 610–11)

1302, 28 October, Westminster

To the sheriff of Lincoln. Order to summon Roger de Huntingfield by two men of that county to be before the king in fifteen days from Martinmas to show cause why Geoffrey de Genevill ought not to have the manor of Francton, in accordance with the form of the *Dictum* of Kenilworth and with the agreement made between Geoffrey and William son of William de Huntingfield for the ransom of the dower of Joan, late the wife of William de Huntingfield [the father], when it should fall in, as the late king granted by his charter to Geoffrey all the lands that belonged to William son of William de Huntingfield, which were in the said king's hands as forfeited by reason of the enmity and rebellion of William during the time of the disturbance in England, to have with the dower of the said Joan when it should fall in, to be redeemed in accordance with the form of the *Dictum* and with the aforesaid agreement, as the said Roger, son and heir of William de Huntingfield, the younger, has now entered the manor upon Joan's death, and deforces it from Geoffrey contrary to the form of the *Dictum* and the agreement, and the king wills that Geoffrey shall not be wronged in this behalf, and Geoffrey has found him as security to prosecute his claim Richard de Walsingham, knight of co. Norfolk, and William son of Walter de Sharnefeld, of co. Hereford.

210. Contracts for military service, 1270–1

(a)

(Text and trans., H. G. Richardson and G. O. Sayles, *The Governance of Medieval England from the Conquest to Magna Carta* (Edinburgh, 1963), Appendix VI [French])

To all those who shall see or hear this writing Adam of Jesmond wishes salvation in our Lord. Know that I have agreed with my lord Edward, the eldest son of the king of England, to go with him to the Holy Land, accompanied by four knights, and to remain in his service for a whole year to commence at the coming voyage of September. And in return he has given me, to cover all expenses, six hundred marks in money and transport, that is to say the hire of a ship and water for as many persons and horses as are appropriate for knights. And should it happen that I am detained by sickness or any other accident, which God forbid, a knight in my place and my knights aforesaid will undertake his service fully for the year or else I will return to him so much money as shall be necessary to complete the period which is lacking from the year, and this shall be at my option. And if it should by chance happen that God's will shall be that my aforesaid lord, sir Edward, shall die, I shall be bound to him, whom my lord shall leave or send in his place, as to himself, according to the form above written. And in witness hereof I have caused my seal to be set to this writing.

Given at Westminster the twentieth day of July in the fifty-fourth year from the coronation of our lord king Henry, son of king John [20 July 1270].

(b)

(*Cal. Pat. Rolls 1266–72*, p. 515)

[Inspeximus and confirmation by the king] of letters patent dated at Westminster, 1 February, 55 Henry III [1 February 1271], made by the same Edmund [Henry III's other son] granting to Robert de Turbervill, his knight, to whom he gave 20*l* a year from the manor of Minsterworth by the hands of the farmer or bailiff thereof, because he is about to cross the sea with him, that he shall keep the said manor in his own hands, demise or let it at farm, for three years, with reversion of the said manor to the grantor charged with 20*l* a year as before.

211. Baronial legislation: county of Chester, 13 January 1260

(T. F. T. Plucknett, *Legislation of Edward I* (Oxford, 1949), pp. 108–9)

It is provided and adjudged by the whole county that no one shall enfeoff anyone in another's fee, nor shall anyone presume to enter another's fee in virtue of a feoffment, unless he first comes to an agreement with the immediate lord of that fee. And if anyone does enter in that way another's fee, against the will of the lord or perhaps without his knowledge, it shall be lawful for the lord of the fee to expel him from his seisin within forty days of learning of his entry into the fee; so that he who has been expelled in such fashion shall not be heard on the propriety of a writ of *novel disseisin*, or of other writs. Further, because deceitfully and to the disinheritance of the lords of many fees many demise their land to many people for a term and before the end of that term secretly enfeoff them and then assert that because they have been seised many days they ought not to be and cannot rightly be ejected, it is for that reason provided that when any enter another's fee in this way as termors[1] and the lord of that fee suspects they may be secretly enfeoffed, it shall be lawful for that lord to distrain by his chattels him who is holding the land until he comes to the county to declare whether he [holds] it for a term or by feoffment; and if by feoffment, be it done as is noted above. Witness [the case of] the abbot of Cumbermere, who on the strength of the aforesaid decision was compelled to acknowledge in full county that the toll he had from Richard de Willburgham in . . .[2] for the term of 10 years and he completely renounced the charters of the said Richard which he had for the said toll.

212. The village community

(a)

(Warren O. Ault, "Open-Field Husbanding and the Village Community", *Trans. of the American Philosophical Society*, n.s., vol. 55, Pt 7 (1965), pp. 56, 57, 60)

By-laws of the community of the vill of Newton Longville, Bucks.
1290 (Saturday, 1 July)
It is granted and ordained by the community of the vill that no one henceforth shall gather green crops in another's corn-field.

Also that no one shall gather beans, peas or vetches in the fields who holds land of the lord, except from the land which he himself has sown.

Also that everyone who wishes to gather beans, peas or suchlike shall gather them between sunrise and prime in le Hech' and this after the feast of the B.V. Mary.[3]

Also that no one [shall have or allow] his calves [to graze] among the corn in the fields before any other beasts.

Also that no one shall be allowed to glean who is able to earn food and a penny a day, or twopence a day without food, if he finds someone willing to hire him.

Also that no stranger be allowed to glean unless he who houses him is willing to answer for his actions.

[1] *per terminum*

[2] Roll torn.

[3] i.e. after 8 September, the Nativity of the BVM

Also that a pauper shall gather beans not inside, but at the head or alongside the selions. And if they do otherwise they are to surrender whatever they have gathered and not be allowed into the fields to gather beans again.

Also that no carting be done in the night time.

Also that everyone shall have his stiles and the lanes nearest him kept in good repair in order that no damage may be done to the lord or any of his tenants for lack of maintenance.

Also that no one shall cause his beasts to graze in any piece of cultivated land before [the crop] of at least one acre adjacent is wholly removed.

Also that no one shall cause his beasts to graze in le Heche before . . .

Also that no one shall cause his beasts to graze among the corn in the night time.

Also that no one carry away the peas . . . of anyone [or] any corn from the fields in the time [of autumn?] . . . especially before night.

And if anyone is found acting contrary . . . he shall give the lord *6d.* And if anyone is found offending against the foregoing at night he shall give the lord *12d.*

1291 (Tuesday, 19 June)
It is agreed by the lord and the community of the vill to observe all the statutes of autumn and ordinances of preceding years and to make presentments faithfully of those offending against the aforesaid statutes and ordinances there have been elected John Roberd Richard Carlyl John Gerard Henry Holden Geoffrey Haukyns Henry Roberd Henry le ferrour Walter H. . . . etc.

1295 (Thursday, 11 August)
All the tenants of the lord both free and customary agreed to observe all the statutes of autumn ordained at the court held on the Saturday after the feast of the apostles Peter and Paul in the eighteenth [year] of the reign of king Edward[1] and to well and faithfully observe these statutes and make presentments there have been elected Hugh Roberd John Hervey John Bouere Henry Simcan Ralph Robyns Henry Hakene and they took the oath.

1322 (Wednesday, 8 July)
All the customary tenants agree to the ordinances of autumn made the year before with this exception, that each one[2] can put his beasts to graze among his own corn in le Hecking growing from his own grain.

(b) *Village by-laws in the king's court, 1292*

(*Select Cases in the Court of King's Bench under Edward I*, II, ed. G. O. Sayles (Selden Soc., vol. 57, 1938), pp. 84–6)

[Court of King's Bench, Easter term 1292]
Nottinghamshire
Richard de Furneis of Carlton, Hugh Bussel, William del Hul, Lawrence of Lidgate,

[1] i.e. Saturday, 1 July 1290, above
[2] *cuiusquisque* is probably a corruption of *unusquisque*, and *crescentes*, of *crescentia*

William of Melton, Hugh de Coupere and Geoffrey of Warwick in mercy for several defaults.

The same Richard and the others were attached to answer Thomas of Evesham, parson of the church of Carlton in Lindrick, on this plea: wherefore did they with force and arms depasture with their beasts certain corn of that Thomas at Carlton in Lindrick and reap and carry away certain of that Thomas's corn growing there, and other outrages etc., to that Thomas's loss of twenty pounds and against the peace etc. And with respect to this he complains that on Sunday[1] the feast of St Mary Magdalene in the nineteenth year of the present king's reign they cut the rye in a certain field which is called Parson's Brake and depastured for a whole week with their beasts his oats growing there, wherefore he says that he is wronged and has suffered loss to the value of twenty pounds, and produces suit thereof etc.

And the aforesaid Richard and the others come and deny force and tort when etc. And Richard de Furneis says that he is the lord of the aforesaid vill of Carlton and that the aforesaid Thomas, the parson, sowed that Richard's soil while that Richard was unaware, and when he perceived this he sent his beasts into that pasture, as was lawful to him. And the aforesaid Hugh and all the others say that the place in which the aforesaid corn was sown is their common pasture and they along with the aforesaid Richard depastured that pasture with their beasts, and that they did him no other trespass they put themselves on the country etc.

And the aforesaid Thomas says that the land in which the aforesaid corn was sown is the soil and endowment of his aforesaid church and against the peace etc. they depastured it, thus sown with corn, at a time when they ought not to have had common there. And he asks for enquiry to be made into this by the country. And the aforesaid Richard and the others likewise. Therefore, a jury is to come before the king on the octave of Trinity, wherever etc.

Afterwards, on the octave of Michaelmas in the twentieth year of the present king's reign, came the parties and likewise the jurors, who say on their oath that the aforesaid land, of which there is question, does not belong to the aforesaid Richard nor to the aforesaid Thomas nor is it the severalty of the others, rather is it the common of the whole community of the aforesaid vill. And such of old was, and still is, the custom in the aforesaid vill that the lord of the vill and the parson and also each freeman of the aforesaid vill can come with his plough to the aforesaid place on the morrow of the Epiphany of the Lord after sunrise, and as many furrows as he shall be able to plough in one ploughing in any strip he can sow each year in the aforesaid place, if he wishes, without asking permission, provided, however, that he does not add manure, and, should he add manure, he cannot sow the manured land without permission of the community of the aforesaid vill, and if he shall sow the manured land without permission, they say that the community of the aforesaid vill can depasture with their beasts the sown and manured land at whatsoever time it wishes. And they say that the aforesaid Thomas manured five acres in the abovesaid year and sowed them with winter seed, everyone of the vill knowing this, and in the same year he sowed seven unmanured acres of the aforesaid place with lenten seed and hoed all

[1] 22 July 1291

the aforesaid land, and afterwards without any gainsaying he held it peacefully until the aforesaid feast of [St Mary] Magdalene when the aforesaid corn was almost ripe, and then came all those named in the writ and depastured with their beasts the aforesaid corn as well in unmanured as in manured lands. And they say that the crop of the manured land was worth fifteen shillings and the crop of the unmanured land ten shillings and sixpence. Asked whether the aforesaid Thomas asked for permission to sow the aforesaid manured land, they say that he did not. Asked how long the aforesaid Thomas sowed the aforesaid land, they say that it was from the time when he became rector of the aforesaid church, that is to say, for ten years. Asked whether his immediate predecessor sowed the aforesaid land, they say that he did, that is to say, for fifteen years. Asked about the damages that the same Thomas sustained by reason of the destruction of the aforesaid corn over and above the value of the same, they say that his damages amount to sixty shillings. And because it is found by the verdict of the jurors that the aforesaid Thomas's predecessor was in good and peaceful seisin of the aforesaid land for fifteen years and that the same Thomas found his church seised of the aforesaid land and continued the estate of his predecessor for ten years without disturbance by the community of the aforesaid vill, and because the aforesaid Richard and the others destroyed and depastured with their beasts the aforesaid corn at the time when it was ripe and ready for reaping, a deed which is obviously harmful and unsupportable by any bye-law, it is awarded that the aforesaid Thomas recover his loss for the corn destroyed, which is taxed by the jurors at twenty-five shillings and sixpence. And because it seems to the justices that damages of sixty shillings cannot arise from so small a matter, it is awarded that the aforesaid Thomas may recover his damages which he sustained, over and above the value of the aforesaid corn by reason of the destruction of the same, and these are taxed at the discretion of the justices at twenty shillings. And the aforesaid Richard and the others are to be taken.

Damages 45*s* 6*d*, 20*s* of which to the clerks.

(c) *The community of the vill of Peatling Magna, Leicestershire, 1265*

(*Select Cases of Procedure without writ under Henry III*, ed. H. G. Richardson and G. O. Sayles (Selden Soc., vol. 60, 1941), pp. 42–5)

Pleas before the king on the morrow[1] of Hilary
Leicestershire
Because the king has learned from the complaint of certain people that his beloved etc. Peter de Neville is wrongfully holding Geoffrey Bertram, Simon de Aune, William Barun, William son of Martin of Weston and Roger of Thorp, men of Peatling Magna, as hostages for the payment to him of a sum of money, by which Robert of Pillerton, Hugh his brother, Roger Musket, Thomas Musket, Thomas the reeve and Philip the clerk made fine with Peter on behalf of themselves and the commonalty of the township for a tort said to have been committed against him by the commonalty, therefore the king, wishing to be certified upon these matters and to show justice to Peter as well as the aforesaid men in this behalf, ordered the sheriff to have Robert,

[1] 14 January 1266

Hugh, Roger, Thomas, Thomas and Philip in court on this day to do and receive what is right in the aforegoing matters. For he has ordered Peter to have the aforesaid hostages then before him to receive and do what is right in these matters etc.

And Peter comes, bringing the hostages, and declares that he is willing to stand trial if anyone wishes to speak against him etc. And Robert of Pillerton, Hugh his brother, Roger Musket, Thomas Musket, Thomas the reeve and Philip the clerk come on behalf of themselves and the commonalty of the township and complain against Peter de Neville on this ground: that, whereas Eudes la Zuche had seized the village of Peatling on Friday[1] after St Peter's Chains, that is to say, after the battle of Evesham, Peter took the aforesaid Geoffrey, Simon, William, William and Roger as hostages for the township and wrongfully keeps them as hostages for a sum of money, by which the commonalty was said to have made fine with Peter but which they did not make with him: on the contrary, Peter, by the agency of his men, dragged the hostages out of church, by force and against their will and assent, and led them away and kept them in prison until now, when they have been released by the king. And thereby they say that they are wronged and have suffered loss to the value of forty pounds. And thereof etc.

And Peter came and brought the hostages, and he denies force and tort when etc., and freely acknowledges that Geoffrey, Simon and the others are in his custody as hostages for the fine of twenty marks which the aforesaid commonalty made with him for the trespass which the men of the township of Peatling did to him and his men as they were crossing through the village after the aforesaid battle. For they accused him and his men of treason and other heinous offences, saying that they were going against the welfare of the commonalty of the realm and against the barons, and they beat, wounded and maltreated his men. And he expressly states that it was on account of that trespass that Thomas the reeve and the others, together with the whole commonalty, delivered the aforesaid Geoffrey, Simon and the others to him as hostages until they should have paid him the aforesaid fine. And as to the truth of this, that he never took anything from them or accepted hostages against their will or did them any other damage, he puts himself on the country, as also do Robert of Pillerton and the others. Therefore the sheriff is ordered that etc. a fortnight after Easter wherever etc., twelve etc., by whom etc., and who neither etc., to make recognition etc. Because both etc. And it is granted by both sides etc. And each one mainprises the other that he will come at the day etc.

And the aforesaid Geoffrey Bertram, Simon and the others come and complain that on Wednesday[2] after St Lawrence's day in the forty-ninth year of the reign Thomas the reeve, as their bailiff, on behalf of himself and the whole commonalty of the township, against their will and assent, gave them to Peter as hostages for twenty marks, to be paid him on the following Sunday for a certain trespass said to have been done to Peter by that commonalty; and because they were given as hostages they lay in wretchedness in prison from that time until Hilary[3] in the fiftieth year of the reign, when the king of his grace had them released; and this happened because Thomas and

[1] 7 August 1265
[2] 12 August 1265
[3] 13 January 1266

the others and the aforesaid commonalty made default and the money was not paid. Wherefore they say that, inasmuch as they are free men and of free status, they are wronged and have suffered loss to the amount of a hundred marks. And thereof they produce suit etc. And Thomas and the others come and deny force and tort when etc. and expressly deny that Thomas ever gave them as hostages, either on behalf of himself or the aforesaid commonalty; on the contrary they say that Peter and his men dragged these hostages forcibly and unwillingly out of the church and churchyard, and that neither Thomas and the others nor the commonalty in any way meddled in the matter. And as to the truth of this, they put themselves on the country, as also do Geoffrey Simon and the others. And it is conceded that Geoffrey Bertram may sue for his fellows, because of their poverty.

Afterwards, on the morrow[1] of All Souls in the fifty-first year etc., the jurors, chosen with the consent of the parties, came before the king at Warwick and said on their oath that on Saturday after the battle of Evesham[2] a certain groom of Peter de Neville arrived, bringing a cart through Peatling village, and some foolish men of the village, seeking to arrest the cart and horses, wounded a carter in the arm above his hand. Therefore he went to his lord and laid a complaint against these men, and on the following Wednesday a great many of Peter's men came to the village and demanded that their lord should be given redress for that trespass or else they would set the village on fire, wherefore the men of the village ran in fear to the church. And at length the wife of Robert of Pillerton and some others of the village, for fear that it would be set on fire, made fine with Peter's men by twenty marks, to be paid him on the following Sunday, and the men demanded surety for due payment. And the woman and some men of the village who were with her said that their neighbours had fled to the church and dared not come out and would not at their instance, and, if these men had been outside the church, they would have made them find hostages for the money. So Peter's men entered the church and made the men who were in there come out against their will. And, when they were outside the churchyard, at the woman's request and on Thomas the reeve's authority, Geoffrey Bertram and the others, of their own free will and without any compulsion upon them at the time on the part of Peter's men, became hostages for the money until the following Sunday, and afterwards the whole of the township of Peatling sent them twenty-seven pence for their expenses. Wherefore the jurors say that the whole township signified to them its assent that they should be hostages for the money. And afterwards the men of the village let the hostages lie in prison until Hilary in the fiftieth year when the king had them released, nor would they acquit them of the debt. And because the jury found that, although all the men of the village had not been present when the hostages were given, yet they gave sufficient consent, in that they afterwards sent them money for their expenses, and Peter's men did not seize them except on the aforesaid reeve's authority, and also because the men of the village allowed them to lie so long in prison and would not acquit them for the fine they made with Peter's men for the trespass, it is awarded that Peter is to recover the aforesaid twenty marks for the fine

[1] 3 November 1266
[2] The battle took place on Tuesday, 4 August 1265

and the hostages their damages, which are taxed by the jurors at one mark each, and the whole township is to be amerced and especially Thomas the reeve. And because Peter's men made the aforesaid men come out of the church by force, let them be arrested etc. And the sheriff is ordered to have the aforesaid money levied from the lands etc. of the whole township and handed over both to Peter and to the hostages etc.

From the money to be recovered by Peter, one mark to the clerks.

213. Fire

(*Select Cases in the Court of King's Bench under Edward I*, I, ed. G. O. Sayles (Selden Soc., vol. 55, 1936), pp. 181–2)

[Court of King's Bench, Hilary term, 1290]
Devon
Herbert of Pinn and John his son in mercy for several defaults.

The same Herbert and John were attached to answer Walter de Brainton on the plea why they burnt the houses of that Walter at Holewey and his goods and chattels within them to the value of two hundred pounds, and other outrages etc., to the grievous loss of that Walter and against the peace etc. And with regard to this he complains that, whereas the aforesaid Herbert and John on Friday after the Assumption of the Blessed Mary in the sixteenth year of the present king's reign [20 August 1288] were being entertained at the house of that Walter in his manor of Kenn, by their foolishness and lack of care and through a badly guarded candle they burned the aforesaid houses, along with all his goods, that is to say, the corn in the barns and granaries, flesh-meat, fish, wool and linen cloths, silver spoons, gold rings, charters, deeds, household utensils and other goods, to the value of two hundred pounds, whereby he says that he is wronged and has suffered loss to the value of two hundred pounds, and thereof he produces suit etc.

And Herbert and John come by John Gerneis their attorney and say that they were being entertained in the houses of that Walter by his own good will, so that if any damage happened to the houses and other goods of that Walter through fire or other means, that was by accident and not by any lack of care or wickedness on their part. And concerning this they put themselves on the country etc. And Walter likewise. Therefore let a jury come three weeks after Easter wherever etc., unless the justices first etc.

Afterwards, three weeks after Easter in the twenty-first year of the present king's reign, the parties came and likewise the jurors, who say on their oath that the aforesaid Herbert and John his son together with a certain Thomas de la Weye, parson of the church of Upton, steward of that Herbert, put up on the aforesaid day and year in the manor of the aforesaid Walter de Brainton and whilst that Herbert was lying on his bed asleep in a certain grange of the aforesaid manor, the aforesaid Thomas did not allow the aforesaid John, son of that Herbert, to put out a certain candle which was fixed on a post of that grange, for which reason the aforesaid John went to bed whilst that candle was burning and immediately went off to sleep. And the aforesaid Thomas went away, and before he came back the aforesaid candle fell down and that grange was immediately set alight by it, and this at night, so that a certain part of the bed of the aforesaid Herbert was burned before he woke up, and also the whole manor aforesaid of that Walter, together with all his goods, was burnt by the aforesaid fire.[1]

214. Building by-laws: London, 1189

(*Liber de Antiquis Legibus seu chronica maiorum et vicecomitum Londoniarum*, ed. T. Stapleton (Camden Soc., 1846), pp. 206–11, in H. T. Riley's translation, *Chronicles of the Mayors and Sheriffs of London: the French Chronicle of London* (1863), pp. 179–87, with a number of modifications.)

The risk of fire was greater, of course, in towns. London took precautions quite early in a general building by-law.

In the year of our Lord 1189, in the first year, namely, of the reign of the illustrious king Richard, Henry Fitz-Aylewin (who was the first mayor of London) being then mayor, it was by the discreet men of the city provided and ordained, for the allaying of the contentions that at times arise between neighbours in the city touching boundaries made, or to be made, between their lands, and other things; to the end that, according to the provisions then made and ordained, such contentions might be allayed. And the said provision and ordinance is called the "assize."

To prosecute which assize, and carry the same into effect, twelve men of the city were elected in full Hustings; and were there sworn that they would attend faithfully to carry out the same and come at the summons of the mayor, unless by reasonable cause prevented. It is necessary, however, that the greater part of the twelve men aforesaid should be present with the mayor in carrying out the matter aforesaid.

It should be known that he who demands the assize must demand it in full Hustings; and the mayor shall assign him a day within the octave, for such assize by the twelve men aforesaid, or by the greater part of them, in manner already mentioned, to be determined.

But if the Hustings be not sitting, as at the time of Boston Fair or harvest-time or the time of the fair at Winchester, and anyone has need to ask for the said assize, the same shall be granted unto him gratuitously by the mayor, some of the citizens being present with the mayor, and be determined by the twelve jurors aforesaid in the manner already stated, or the greater part of them, and that always in the presence of the mayor.

The provision and ordinance aforesaid, which is called the "assize", is to the following effect: –

When it happens that two neighbours wish to build between them of stone, each of them ought to give one foot and a half of his land and so at their joint cost they shall build a stone-wall between them three feet in thickness and sixteen feet in height. And if they wish, they shall make a rain-gutter between them, at their joint cost, to take and carry away the water from their houses in such manner as they may deem most expedient. But if they do not wish to do so, either of them may make a gutter

[1] In the margin there is, in Latin, a note, "Damages, if any, 100*l*."

by himself to carry the water that falls from his house on to his own land unless he can carry it into the highway.

They may also, if they agree thereupon, raise the said wall as high as they please, at their joint cost. And if it happens that one wishes to raise such a wall, and the other not, it shall be fully lawful for him who so wishes it, to raise the part on his own foot and a half, as much as he may please, and to build upon his part without damage to the other, at his own cost; and he shall receive the falling water in manner already stated.

And if both wish to have arches[1] in the wall, such arches must be made on either side of the depth of one foot only: so that the thickness of the wall between such arches may be one foot. But if one wishes to have an arch, and the other not, then he who wishes to have the arch shall find free-stone and cause it to be cut, and the arch shall be set at their joint expense.

And if anyone wishes to build of stone, according to the assize, and his neighbour through poverty cannot, or perchance will not, then the latter ought to give unto him who desires to build by the assize, three feet of his own land; and the other shall make a wall upon that land at his own cost, three feet thick and sixteen feet in height; and he who gives the land shall have a whole half of the wall and put his framework[2] on it and build. And they shall make gutters to take and carry away the water falling from their houses in such manner as is before mentioned as to a wall built between neighbours at their joint expense. But it shall always be lawful for one desiring so to do, to raise his own part at his own cost, without damage to the other. And if they wish to have arches, they shall be made on each side, in manner already stated. But nevertheless, he who shall have found the land, shall find the freestone and shall have it cut; and the other at his own cost shall set the same.

But this assize is not granted unto anyone, so as to cause a doorway, entry or exit, or shop to be narrowed or restricted to the injury of a neighbour.

This assize is also granted unto him who demands it as to the land of his neighbour, even though such land shall have been built upon, provided the building done is not of stone.

If anyone shall have his own stone-wall upon his own land, of the height of sixteen feet, his neighbour ought to make a gutter below the eaves of the house that is situate upon such wall, and to receive in it the water falling from the said house and lead it on to his own land, unless he can carry it off into the highway; and he shall, notwithstanding, have no interest in the aforesaid wall, when he shall have built beside that wall. And in case he shall not have so built, he still ought always to receive the water falling from the house built on such wall on to his land and carry it off without damage to him whose wall it is.

Also, no one of those who have a common stone-wall built between them may, or ought to, pull down any portion of his part of such wall, or lessen its thickness, or make arches in it, without the assent and will of the other.

Also, concerning necessary chambers in the houses of citizens, it is so enacted and

[1] i.e. for making cupboards in the party-wall

[2] *panna*: pan or pane, a section or wall-frame (probably of timber) of a house

ordained that if the pit made in such chamber be lined with a stone-wall, the mouth of the said pit shall be distant two feet and a half from the land of the neighbour, even though they have a common stone-wall between them. But if it is not lined with a wall, it ought to be distant three feet and a half from his neighbour's land. And as to such pits, the assize is offered and granted to everyone who shall demand it, in reference as well to those of former construction as to new ones unless they were made before the provision and ordinance aforesaid, which was enacted in the first year of the reign of king Richard, as already mentioned; provided always that by view of such twelve men as are before-mentioned, or the greater part of them, it shall be determined whether such pits have been properly made or not.

Also, if anyone has windows looking out on his neighbour's land, although he may have been for a long time in possession of the view from such windows and even though his predecessors may have been in possession of the windows aforesaid, nevertheless, his neighbour may rightly block the view from such windows by building opposite them or by placing [something] there on his own land in such manner as may unto him seem the most expedient; unless the person who has such windows can show something in writing by reason of which his neighbour cannot block the view from those windows.

Also if anyone has corbels in his neighbour's wall, the whole of such wall belonging to his said neighbour, he may not remove the aforesaid corbels to put them in any other part of the said wall, except with the assent of him to whom such wall belongs; nor may he put more corbels in the wall aforesaid than he had before.

Be it known that if anyone builds close to the tenement of his neighbour and it appears unto such neighbour that such building is unjust and to the injury of his own tenement, he may rightly impede the building, pledge and surety being given to the sheriffs of the city that he will prosecute; and thereupon such building shall cease, until by the twelve men aforesaid, or the greater part of them, it shall be determined whether such building is unjust or not. And then it becomes necessary that he whose building is impeded shall demand the assize.

On the day appointed, the twelve men aforesaid being summoned, the mayor of the city, with the aforesaid men, ought to visit the tenements of those between whom the assize is demanded, and there by the view of the aforesaid twelve men, or the greater part of them, after hearing the case of the complainant and the answer of his adversary, settle the matter.

But either party may, on the day appointed, essoin himself, and they shall have day at the same place on that day fortnight.

If the party complaining shall make default, however, his adversary shall withdraw without day, and the sureties of the complainant shall be amerced by the sheriffs. But if it shall be the person against whom the complaint is made that makes such default, the assize shall nonetheless proceed and in accordance with the decision of the twelve men aforesaid, or the greater part of them; and what is decided by them ought to be intimated by the sheriffs to him who has made default, to the end that the award so made be carried into effect within the next forty days.

And it should be known that as often as such award shall not within forty days have been carried into effect and complaint shall have been made thereon unto the mayor of London, two men of the assize, or three, ought by order of the mayor to go to the place at once; and if they see that such is the case, then shall he against whom proceedings of assize were taken be amerced by a sheriff; and the sheriff is bound at that man's expense, to carry such judgment into effect.

Also, if anyone has a wall built between himself and his neighbour, completely covered on top by his wall-frame[1] and timber, his neighbour, although he may have in the aforesaid wall corbels or beams for the support of his solar, or even arches or aumbries – in whatsoever way he has them in such wall, whether by grant of him who has the wall covered, or of his predecessor, or even without their knowledge – may demand or have in the aforesaid wall, without the assent of him who owns the wall so covered, no more than he possesses; and he ought to receive the water falling from the house built on the wall, below the eaves of the said house, as before-mentioned in this book, and carry it off at his own cost.

Also if anyone has two parts of a wall and a neighbour has only a third part, the neighbour can all the same place his wall-frame[1] on his own part and build as freely as he who has the [other] two parts of that wall; and in the same way ought rain-gutters to be made between them as noted earlier in this book as regards those who have a wall wholly in common between them; provided however that such part is sixteen feet in height.

Also, it should be known that the assize aforesaid does not proceed unless it is testified that he against whom the assize is demanded has been summoned. And if this is testified, then on the appearance of him who demands the assize and of the twelve men of the assize, or the greater part of them, with the mayor of the city, the assize shall proceed, whether he who was summoned appears or not. He can, however, essoin himself at the aforesaid day and have day in a fortnight's time, as already stated.

Also, it should be known that if it is testified by the sheriffs that he against whom the assize is demanded was not in the city, then the assize shall stand over that day and the sheriffs shall tell those who are resident in the tenement concerning which the assize is demanded, that he whose tenement it is shall be warned to appear that day fortnight, and on that day whether he appears or not, unless he has essoined himself, the assize shall proceed.

Also, if it happens that because of some impediment the men of the assize do not appear on the land concerning which the assize is demanded, it will then be necessary for the assize to be demanded afresh, either in the Hustings or in the way in which it is usually done at the different times of year, as noted earlier in this book. But if they do appear on the land, with the parties to the dispute present, but the greater part of the twelve men are absent, then, although the assize will be stayed, they can adjourn that day's proceedings[2] until the morrow or to what day they will in the ensuing fortnight.

It should be remembered that of old the greater part of the city was built of wood and houses covered with straw and stubble and such like thack; so that when any

[1] *panna* (cf. p. 850, n. 2, above)
[2] *continuare diem illum*

house caught fire, the greater part of the city was burnt by the fire, as happened in the first year of king Stephen's reign (as noted in the chronicles written earlier in this book) when owing to a fire which broke out at London Bridge the church of St Paul was burnt, from which spot the fire spread, consuming houses and buildings, as far as the church of St Clement Danes. After that, many citizens, to avoid such danger as far as they could, built on their foundations a stone house roofed with thick tiles and [so] protected against the fierceness of the fire; from which circumstance it has often been the case that when a fire has broken out in the city and has destroyed many buildings, on reaching such a house it has been unable to harm anything and has stopped there and been extinguished, so that by that house many neighbours' houses have been completely saved from the fire.

For this reason was it in the aforesaid ordinance, which is called the assize, ordained and provided, in order that citizens might build willingly of stone, that every one who has a stone-wall on his own land sixteen feet high shall possess it as freely and deservedly as stated earlier in this book, namely, that his neighbour ought always to receive on his own land the water from the house built on that wall and carry it off at his own cost. And if he wishes to build close to the said wall, he ought to make his gutter below the eaves of the said house to take the water, so that the said house shall remain safe and capable of withstanding the fierceness of a fire when it comes, and so, through it, many neighbours' houses saved and kept intact from the violence of the flames.

If anyone wishes to build a wall wholly[1] on his own land and his neighbour demands the assize against him, he may choose either to join [with the neighbour] in building a common wall between them or to build the wall on his own land and have it as freely and deservedly as has been said. His neighbour can, however, if he wishes build another wall like it and of the same height close to the said wall: in which case a gutter or gutters shall be made between them in the same way that is stated earlier in reference to a wall that is shared.[2]

It should be remembered that as often as the men of the assize appear on the land concerning which the assize is demanded, with the parties to the dispute present, one of the men aforesaid ought always to ask him against whom the assize is demanded if he knows aught by reason of which the assize ought to be stayed. And if he says No, the assize shall proceed at once. But if he says he has a charter of him who is demanding the assize or of any ancestor of his and produces it, it shall immediately be allowed him. But if he says he will produce[3] the charter at a later stage on a given day,[4] then day shall be given him for that day fortnight; on which day he can essoin himself and have day at the end of another fortnight. On which day, if he produces the charter, it shall be allowed him; but if on that day he does not appear, or appears but does not produce the deed, the assize shall at once proceed without further delay.

It should be remembered that this assize proceeds in every way as stated earlier in this book, both as to pleading and defending, as well against persons under age as against those of full age; so that the aforesaid assize shall not be impeded by anyone's

[1] *murum totum*, i.e. with the whole breadth of three feet on his own land
[2] *de communi muro* [3] *habebit* [4] *ad diem et terminum*

tender age. But because such a person has not the discretion to know how to plead or defend himself in any plea, it is necessary that his guardian and he should be jointly summoned, so that his guardian may answer for him completely in all the ways in which he would have pleaded, if the cause had been his own; and then whatever is done on award shall remain firm and established without appeal[1] from him who is under age when he comes of age.

Also, if anyone wrongfully makes a pavement in the highway to the injury of the city and of his neighbour, such neighbour can rightfully prohibit it through the bailiffs of the city and, so shall it be stayed until it is discussed and determined by the men of the assize.

And it should be known that it does not pertain to the men of the assize to correct any occupation,[2] of which anyone has had peaceful possession for a year and a day.

215. Urban sanitation, 1298

(*Cal. Close Rolls 1296–1302*, p. 218)

The fact that much of this is common form (cf. Oxford three years later: *Cal. Close Rolls 1296–1302*, p. 484; and Ballard and Tait, *British Borough Charters 1216–1307* (1923), pp. 374–6) merely emphasises the general condition. Bootham, York, might otherwise be regarded as exceptional and its condition at this time due to the presence of the royal exchequer and the influx and traffic occasioned by war with the Scots.

1298, 20 August, Braid
To the bailiffs of the abbot of St Mary's, York, at Boutham. Whereas it is sufficiently evident that the pavement of the said town of Bouthum is so very greatly broken up that all and singular passing and going through that town sustain immoderate damages and grievances, and in addition the air is so corrupted and infected by the pigsties situate in the king's highways and in the lanes of that town and by the swine feeding and frequently wandering about in the streets and lanes and by dung and dunghills and many other foul things placed in the streets and lanes, that great repugnance overtakes the king's ministers staying in that town and also others there dwelling and passing through, the advantage of more wholesome air is impeded, the state of men is grievously injured, and other unbearable inconveniences and many other injuries are known to proceed from such corruption, to the nuisance of the king's ministers aforesaid and of others there dwelling and passing through, and to the peril of their lives, and to the manifest shame and reproach of the bailiffs and other the inhabitants of that town: the king, being unwilling longer to tolerate such great and unbearable defects there, orders the bailiffs to cause the pavement to be suitably repaired within their liberty before All Saints next, and to cause the pigsties aforesaid to be pulled down and removed without delay, and to cause the aforesaid streets and lanes to be cleansed from all dung and dunghills, and to cause them to be kept thus cleansed hereafter, and to cause proclamation to be made throughout their bailiwick forbidding any one, under pain of grievous forfeiture, to cause or permit their swine to feed or wander outside his house in the king's streets or the lanes aforesaid, so that

[1] *reclamatio* [2] i.e. of property

damage or danger shall not arise hereafter to anyone by the breaking of the pavement or the corruption aforesaid in the bailiff's default. They are also ordered to apply such remedy to ruinous houses within the liberty that extend to public streets through which there is frequent passage of men that any peril that might easily arise by such ruin shall be prevented. The king warns them that he will punish them as transgressors of his orders if they do not execute the premises in due manner.

216. Fairs

(a) *The four great fairs of England, 1240*

(*Cal. Pat. Rolls 1232–47*, pp. 238–9)

1240, 16 November, Westminster

Mandate to the bailiffs and good-men of Winchester to make known to all merchants coming to their city the provision of the king and council, that all the king's prises from merchants shall be paid at four terms of the year, to wit, the prises due in the fair of Northampton in the fair of St Ives, [the prises due in the latter] in the fair of Boston, the prises due in the latter in the fair of Winchester, and those due in the latter in the fair of Northampton.

(b) *Royal prises and purchases at fairs, 1242*

(ibid. p. 300)

1242, 14 July, Westminster

The king sends to the fair of Len[1] Henry of Wengham and Jordan de Eynho to make prises and purchases for the king of cloth by view and testimony of two good men of London and two others of Northampton, and it is commanded to all merchants coming to that fair to be intendant to them, knowing that the price at which the cloths taken by them are appraised will be paid at the next fair of Northampton.

217. Southampton and the bishop of Winchester's Fair of St Giles

(a)

(*Cal. Pat. Rolls 1247–58*, p. 109)

1251, 23 September, Windsor

Mandate to the sheriff of Southampton, upon information that the burgesses of Southampton and other merchants were wont to expose for sale all merchandise, whether from Ireland or from elsewhere, upon the hill of St Giles, Winchester, so long as the fair lasted there, of which fair P. and W. some time bishops of Winchester were in seisin (and the king afterwards in time of voidance) as also of amends received whenever by chance the merchants withdrew themselves; and that the said burgesses and merchants this year did not come with their goods as they used to do, but withdrew themselves, holding in their said town the tronage and pesage to the prejudice of the church of Winchester and of A. [bishop] elect of Winchester, and they would

[1] Lynn

not make amends; that inasmuch as the king has restored to the said elect the seisin which the said bishops and the king had, he shall let the said elect have the same and satisfy him for his said losses, saving the right of anyone who may wish to contend touching right after the said seisin.

By K.

(b)

(*Cal. Chart. Rolls, I (1226–57)*, p. 445)

1255, 24 April, Westminster

Inspeximus and confirmation of an agreement made at Merewell, the Sunday after the Annunciation, A.D. 1254, between A. elect of Winchester, on the one part, and the commonalty of the burgesses of the town of Southampton on the other, in settlement of a dispute between the said parties touching the sale, purchase and merchandise of vendible goods, and the tronage and pesage of them, all which during the fair of St Giles upon the Hill ought not to be carried on by anyone in the town of Southampton saving in the case of victuals; whereby the said burgesses and their commonalty have agreed and promised that in future no vendible goods or merchandise coming at any time[1] to the town of Southampton on account of the said fair or remaining in the said town for that reason shall be sold or bought in the town of Southampton by any merchant whether of that town or no, so long as the said fair continues, victuals being always excepted; and that no tronage or pesage shall be made of such things during the said fair, but that all merchants coming with vendible goods and merchandise for the said fair, or with merchandise remaining there for that reason, shall be distrained by their goods to come to the said fair; but if the merchant will swear that he did not come for that fair or on account of that fair, he may freely pass, return or remain without any compulsion to come to the said fair, provided that during its continuance he make no sale in the said fair [*sic*] save of victuals as aforesaid; saving herein the right of the king; in testimony whereof the burgesses have caused the seal of the commonalty of the town to be affixed to these letters.

218. Weights and measures, 13th-cent.

(*Statutes of the Realm*, I (Rec. Com., 1810), pp. 204–5)

By an ordinance of the whole realm of England the king's measure was devised, that is to say, that the English penny called the "sterling", round and without clipping, shall weigh 32 grains of wheat [that grew] in the middle of the ear. And an ounce ought to weigh 20 pennies. And 12 ounces make a London pound, and 8 lb. make a wine gallon, and 8 wine gallons make a London bushel, and 8 bushels make a London quarter. And 12½ lb. make a London stone. A sack of wool ought to weigh 28 stones. And in some parts 30 stones. And[2] they are the same according to the greater and the lesser pound.

[1] *termino*

[2] "And . . . pound": this is not found in the comparable texts (*Camd. Miscell.* XV, Hall and Nicholas, "Select Tracts . . .", pp. 9–10 and 11–12; or *Fleta*, II, ed. Richardson and Sayles, Seld. Soc., No. 72, pp. 119–20) and may be an interpolation.

Six score stones make a char[1] of lead, that is to say, the great char of London, but the char of the Peak is much less.

Furthermore, the char of lead consists of 30 fotmals, and each fotmal of 6 stones less 2 lb., and each stone of 12 lb., and each lb. has the weight of 25 shillings. The total number of lb. in the fotmal 70 lb. The total number of stones in the char is 8 score and 15 stones: this can be reckoned as 6 times 30, that is 9 score, but from every fotmal 2 lb. are to be subtracted in the above calculation, which makes 60 lb. or 5 stones to be subtracted, and so there are in the char 8 score and 15 stones, as was said.

According to certain others, however, the char consists of 12 weys and this is by tron weight; and then the total number of stones in the char is 8 score and 8; and this can be reckoned as 12 times 14, for weys alike of lead and wool, flax, tallow, and cheese weigh 14 stones. And 2 weys make one sack of wool, and 12 sacks constitute the last. The last of herring, however, consists of 10 thousands and each thousand consists of 10 hundreds and each hundred of 6 score. Also, the last of hides of 20 dickers, and each dicker consists of 10 hides. Also, the dicker of gloves of 10 pairs. The dicker of horseshoes, however, of 110[2] shoes. Also, a dozen of gloves, parchment, and tawed leather contains in its kind 12 skins or 12 pairs of gloves. Also, a hundredweight of wax, sugar, pepper, cumin, almonds, and wormwood, contains 13½ stones and each stone contains 8 lb. The total number of lb. in the hundredweight is 108 lb.; and the hundred consists of 5 score and each lb. of 25 shillings. And know that a lb. of pennies and spices and confections such as electuaries has the weight of 20 shillings; a pound of all other things, however, has the weight of 25 shillings. An ounce of an electuary, however, has the weight of 20 pennies and the lb. contains 12 ounces. In other things, though, the lb. contains 15 ounces. An ounce in either case has the weight of 20 pennies. The hundred of board, linen, canvas, and linen cloth, consists of 100 ells and each hundred consists of 6 score. The hundred of horseshoes, however, of 5 score. A sheaf of steel consists of 30 pieces. Also, a seam of glass consists of 20 stones and each stone of 5 lb., and so the seam consists of 5 score lb. Also, a dozen of iron of 6 pieces.[3] Also, a bind of eels consists of 10 sticks and each stick of 25 eels. A bind of skins consists of 30 timber. A timber[4] of rabbit-skins and of "gris"[5] consists of 40[6] skins. A chef of fustian consists of [13 ells. A chef of muslin consists of][7] 14 ells. The measure of garlic contains 15 bunches and each bunch contains 25 heads. Also, the hundred of mulvels and of dried fish consists of 8[8] score fish, and[9] in some and many places of 9 score and this of the dried fish called Aberdeen.

[1] a (cart)load [2] *sic*
[3] This item is not found in the comparable texts (see p. 856, n. 2 above) and may be an interpolation.
[4] *senellio*
[5] *gris* or *vair*, a kind of grey squirrel
[6] "x" (*Stat. Realm*, I, p. 205) is either corrupt in the manuscript (Liber Horn) or a misprint, for "xl"
[7] supplied from the comparable texts mentioned in p. 856, n. 2 above. Obviously an accidental omission here.
[8] "vj" (*Stat. Realm*, I, p. 205) emended from the comparable texts mentioned above.
[9] "and . . . Aberdeen": probably interpolated, given by none of the comparable texts.

219. Hull, 1230

(*Cal. Close Rolls 1227–31*, pp. 355–6 and 370)

Order to Saer de Sutton' and his fellows that notwithstanding the king's order to them to arrest shipping they shall allow the ship of Walter son of Randulf de Dunwich, laden with the wool of Hugh de Selby, mayor of York, which they had arrested at Hull, to go off freely and without impediment to the parts of Flanders. Witness S. de Sedgrave at Lincoln, 27 June 1230.

They are likewise written to about freeing the ship of Robert Blund', merchant of Douai, and its contents and allowing it to go where it wishes. Witness as above . . .

Order to Saer de Sutton' and his fellows, keepers of the ports and coast of Yorkshire, that notwithstanding etc. they shall allow the ship of William of Orford, laden with leather of Andrew Bukerel, citizen of London, which they arrested at Hull, to go with the aforesaid leather and other things in it freely and without impediment where it wishes. Witness as above.

They are likewise written to –

about allowing the ships of John Kyte, William le Masuer of Gravelines, arrested at Hull, to leave for home, given security that they are from the land of the count of Flanders.

about allowing the ship of Alelm Columbel, merchant of Abbeville of the land of the count of Ponthieu, arrested at Hull, to leave for home with its contents. Witness as above.

about allowing the ship of Nicholas de Damme, arrested at Hull, to leave for home, given security that it is from the land of the count of Flanders . . .

Order to the bailiffs of the port of Hull that notwithstanding etc. they shall allow the ship of William Curtore of Damme of the land of the count of Flanders, arrested in the port of Hull, which the same William captains, laden with wool and lead and other merchandise of the merchants of Beverley and of Ypres and of Damme, to leave for home freely and without impediment. Witness S. de Sedgrave, at York, 18 August 1230.

Order to the bailiffs of the port of Hull that notwithstanding etc. they shall allow the ship of Alein Columbel of Abbeville, laden with the goods and merchandise of the merchants of York and the merchants of Abbeville and arrested in the port of Hull, to go from there freely and without impediment to York. Witness S. de Sedgrave, at York, 25 August 1230.

220. Yarmouth and the Cinque Ports, 1277

(*Cal. Pat. Rolls 1272–81*, pp. 203–4 [French])

Not the beginning, and by no means the end of the wrangle between Yarmouth and the Cinque Ports. But a good illustration of the frictions and the situation generating them. The Ports had done most to make Yarmouth the centre for English fishing of the herring-grounds off the Norfolk and Lincolnshire coasts and build up its fair, and, well entrenched in the place as a result (as this document shows), they were not disposed to surrender control to Yarmouth itself. The situation had scarcely changed by 1305: cf. *Cal. Pat. Rolls 1301–7*, p. 329.

Award between the barons of the Ports and the men of Great Yarmouth. The said barons are to have their easement in strand and den which they claim at Yarmouth, without any appropriation of the soil and in the time of the fair without giving any manner of custom. The men of the town of Yarmouth are to clear the strand and den of old ships and timber[1] where people are to put in and dry their nets, except of such ships as are being made, and of the masts upon which the said drying is carried on; and not to raise more than five windmills upon the den more than they have formerly raised, and those mills to be raised to the least damage and nuisance of the den and of those who are to dry their nets there. The said barons to have and enjoy peaceably their rents, of which they are seised in the town of Yarmouth, and if any deforce them the provost and bailiffs of Yarmouth to aid them to levy such rent according to law and right, and if the said barons believe themselves to have right in other rents, of which they are deforced by the people of Yarmouth, they are to recover by writ or by the law and by custom used in the said town. With regard to the claim of the said barons to have at Yarmouth royal justice and the keeping of the king's peace in time of the fair lasting for 40 days, they are to have the keeping of the king's peace and to do royal justice together with the provost of Yarmouth, as follows, viz, during the fair they are to have four serjeants, of whom one shall carry the king's banner,[2] and another sound a horn to assemble the people and to be better heard, and two shall carry wands[3] for keeping the king's peace, and this office they shall do on horseback if they wish it. The bailiffs of the Ports, together with the provost of Yarmouth, to make attachments and plead pleas and determine plaints during the fair, according to law-merchant, and the amercements and profits of the people of the Ports to remain to the barons of the Ports at the time of the fair, and the profits and amercements of all others who are not of the Ports to remain to the king by the bailiffs of Yarmouth. The bailiffs of the barons of the Ports aforesaid, together with the provost of Yarmouth, to have the keeping of the prison of Yarmouth during the fair, and if any prisoner be taken for so grave a trespass that it cannot be determined by them in time of fair, by merchant law, nor the prisons delivered, such person to remain in the prison of Yarmouth until the coming of the justices. The said bailiffs of the barons of the Ports to receive the customary 2*d* a ship, called "fire penyes", to keep up fires in the usual places for the safety of the shore by night as long as they are willing to keep up the fires, and if they fail to keep up the said fires the provost of Yarmouth may receive the aforesaid pence and keep up the fires in form aforesaid. In discharge of the custom of 4*d* from each ship claimed by the said barons they shall receive 6*l* sterling from year to year by the hand of the provost of Yarmouth at their

[1] *merin* [2] *barrere* [3] *verges*

departure from the fair. With regard to the claim of the said barons to distrain for their debts by land and sea, their bailiffs are not to make any distraint without the provost of Yarmouth, except upon the people of the Ports, and it is to be reasonable according to the law-merchant so that the fair does not suffer thereby. No guard to be put henceforth on ships, merchants, and merchandise by the men of Yarmouth, whereby merchants are prevented from selling their goods freely. Neither the said barons nor the men of Yarmouth are to take anything from minstrels and women.[1] The said barons are not to take anything for window tax or stallage.

221. "Futures" in wool, 1276

(*Cal. Close Rolls 1272–9*, pp. 354–5)

Enrolment of deed of brother P. abbot of Fountains, of the Cistercian order, in the diocese of York, and the convent of the same, whereby they sell to Dunelinus Jonte and Bernard Thethaldi, buying and receiving for themselves and for Theclanus Thedaldi, brother of the said Bernard, and for other of their fellows, citizens and merchants of Florence, 62 sacks of wool of the crop[2] of the monastery without clack[3] and lock[4], cot[5] and breech-wool,[6] or black, grey, inferior fleece,[7] and without pelt-wool,[8] which wool the abbot and convent promise to deliver, prepared and weighed at their cost, by lawful stipulation at the terms following, to wit 17 sacks at the quinzaine of midsummer, 1277; 17 sacks at the same quinzaine in 1278; 14 sacks in 1279; 14 sacks at the said quinzaine in 1280, every year at Clifton to the said merchants or their attorney bearing this letter. For this wool the merchants have paid beforehand at London 697½ marks of good, new and lawful sterlings, 13*s* 4*d* sterling being counted for each mark, receipt of which the abbot and convent acknowledge, renouncing all exception that the money has not been counted or paid. If the wool be not delivered as agreed, the abbot and convent bind themselves to refund all the expenses, damages and interest incurred by the merchants through non-delivery, concerning which credence shall be given to their bare word without oath or other proof, which expenses, etc., the abbot and convent shall not count in the lot[9] of the wool, and they shall not retain the wool contrary to the will of the said merchants by pretext of the said expenses beyond the terms aforesaid. For the observance of the premises, the abbot and convent bind themselves, their church and successors and all their goods, ecclesiastical or secular, to the merchants and their fellows, which goods the abbot and convent acknowledge that they hold from the merchants in the name of a pledge[10] until the full observance of the premises. The abbot and convent renounce all aid of the canon and civil law, privilege of clergy, etc., letters, indulgences, and inhibitions from the pope or the king's court, the constitution of two days issued in the general council, appeals, etc., and especially the papal indulgence granted to the English[11] which provides that no Englishmen shall be drawn into pleas outside Eng-

[1] *femmes de vie*
[2] *collecta*
[3] *clack'*
[4] *lok'*
[5] *god*
[6] *card*
[7] *vilein tuysun*
[8] *pelliciis*
[9] *in sortem*
[10] *precari*
[11] *Anglice*

land by letters of the papal see, and they renounce generally all exceptions, rights and defences, personal and real, that might benefit them and their successors or injure the said merchants, and they will that they may freely be summoned[1] and drawn to judgment in all places by the merchants or their envoy concerning the premises. Dated at London, on Thursday before St Luke, 1276.

Memorandum, that the abbot came into chancery, and acknowledged the premises.

Afterwards Dunelinus came into chancery and put in his place Dietaiutus, merchant of Florence, to receive a moiety of the wool aforesaid.

222. Concealed interest

(a)

(*Cal. Pat. Rolls 1247–58*, p. 631)

1258, 29 May, Clarendon

Acknowledgement of the receipt at London from James Davanzati, Rukus Cambii and Gerard Ricobaldi, citizens and merchants of Florence, and Aldebrand Aldebrandini, citizen and merchant of Siena, for themselves and their societies, of a loan of 2,250 marks, 13*s* 4*d* to the mark, renouncing all exceptions; with promise to repay the same at the New Temple, London, on the quinzaine of next Michaelmas, and if not the king will make good all loss, interest and expenses thereby incurred by them. The king also places himself and his heirs under the coercion of the bishop of Florence and of John de Kancia, of the order of the Minors, papal nuncio in England, to compel payment. Upon payment, the present instrument, as also one of the abbot and convent of Westminster binding them to pay the said money to the said merchants, are to be surrendered.

This bond was made by John Maunsell and friar John de Kancia.

And be it known that the said 2,250[2] marks were borrowed to pay 2,000 marks wherein the king is bound to the pope for his yearly cess of 1,000 marks, for two years, and the remaining 250 marks the said merchants have for their profit.

Promise to the abbey and convent of Westminster to keep them harmless as to their bond to the said James Bavanzati [*sic*] and the others named above in the said sum.

(b)

(*Cal. Pat. Rolls 1258–66*, p. 257)

1263, 6 May, St Paul's, London

Notification that the king has ordered his clerk mr Henry de Gandavo, keeper of the wardrobe, to pledge, of the jewels which are in his keeping,

12 bowls, silver gilt, weighing 104*l* 6*s* 11*d*

19 cups, silver gilt, and chased, weighing 112*l* 3*s* 1*d*

[1] *conveniri*

[2] 2,000 (*Cal. Pat. Rolls 1247–58*, p. 631), but this is presumably an error for 2,250

62 cups, silver gilt and plain, weighing 246*l* 10*s* 3*d*
36 pairs of silver basins, weighing 167*l* 10*s* 7*d*
1 silver boat[1] weighing 7*l* 2*s* 6*d*
the total weight amounting to 637*l* 13*s* 4*d*.

He is to pledge them for 1,000 marks with some safe person by view of mr Nicholas, archdeacon of Ely, the treasurer, for purchases of cloths and other necessaries of the wardrobe made at the fair of St Ives by Luke de Luke, Reyner de Luk and their fellows, merchants of Lucca, by the hands of Richard de Ewell and Hugh de Turri, buyers of the wardrobe; on condition that if the said 1,000*l* [*sic*] be not repaid by Michaelmas at the latest, the money shall be levied without reclaim on the said jewels and paid in full to the said merchants.

223. A Jew tries to collect his debts, 1274

(*Cal. of Plea Rolls of the Exchequer of the Jews in the Public Record Office*, ed. J. M. Rigg (Edinburgh, 1910), II, pp. 130–1)

Robert Hue and seventeen others attached to answer Deudoné of Winchester touching a plea of trespass, to wit, that, the said Deudoné having come to Southampton with Henry de Stokesbroc, sheriff of the said town, to levy certain of his debts, the said Robert and the rest, with the assent and consent of all the community of the town of Southampton, on the Tuesday next after Easter octave in the present year, came at the third hour of the day with swords, axes, bows, arrows, and other arms, and caused ring the common bell of the said town against the said sheriff and him, Deudoné, and raised the hue and cry, and assaulted him, and threw him down from a horse on which he rode, and stripped him of his tabard and supertunic, value ½ mark, and robbed him of 6 marks of silver; and one of them, to wit, Roger, wounded him in the arm with a knife, and maltreated him, against the king's peace, to his damage, £200. Whereof he brings suit.

The said Robert and the rest make defence to the force, etc, and deny all of it word by word, and that they are in no wise guilty, put themselves upon the country, as does also the said Deudoné. Wherefore mandate to the sheriff, that he cause twelve, etc., of the venue of Southampton to come before etc., on Michaelmas quindene, to recognise, etc., and so many and such, etc. On which day the said Robert and the rest come, and the said Deudoné was essoined, and the sheriff sends the names of the jurors, and word that the mainpernors of some of them have them not; wherefore they are in mercy. Order, that he distrain by lands, etc., and have their bodies before, etc., on Martinmas quindene, to recognise, etc., and hear, etc. And Adam de Northampton, and others of the said inquest, who were present, have the same day. On which day the said Deudoné came, but none of the jurors; and likewise some of those who had put themselves on the said inquest made default of appearance, and others were essoined. And the sheriff sent word that he returned the writ to the bailiffs of the bishop of Winchester and the city of Winchester, who did nought in pursuance thereof. Wherefore mandate to the sheriff, that he omit not, etc., and distrain all the

[1] *nacellam*

jurors to recognise, etc., and those aforesaid who put themselves upon the inquest and made default of appearance, to appear, on the octave of St Hilary.

224. Prospecting for lead in Snowdonia, 1284

(*Cal. Chancery Rolls* (*Various*) *1277–1326*, pp. 288–9)

1284, 4 September, Rhuddlan

To all whom etc. Notification that the king has granted to Reginald de Lodelawe all his mine[1] of lead that can be found in the parts of Snaudon beyond the waters of Conewey, for three years from Michaelmas next, with the brushwood necessary for burning for this purpose and with all manner of easements in waters, fields and other places of those parts, on condition that[2] a seventh of the lead thence arising shall be the king's and that the king may take from the six parts remaining to Reginald as much as he shall need for his works in Wales, to wit each smaller cartload of lead for 28*s*, to be paid to him upon the receipt of the lead. The king prohibits any of his bailiffs or others from hindering Reginald in the premisses contrary to this grant.

225. Shipbuilding, 1294

(P.R.O. Accounts, etc. (Exch.), bundle 5, No. 20)

Information on medieval methods of shipbuilding is provided by a very detailed account for the building at Newcastle of one of twenty galleys ordered by the king after the outbreak of war with France in 1294. This is printed with a valuable introduction and a glossary of technical terms by R. J. Whitwell and C. Johnson, "The 'Newcastle' Galley, A.D. 1294", *in Archaeologia Aeliana*, II, 4th ser. (1926), pp. 142–96. This galley took forty weeks to build. The accounts for the first two weeks, spent in buying materials and laying the keel, are given below, as translated by C. Johnson (ibid.), pp. 148–50. The whole cost was £205 2*s* 4¾*d*. The entry allowing this in the Exchequer pipe roll for Northumberland in 1300–1 is also given below, again in C. Johnson's translation (ibid.), pp. 144–5. The marginal letters A–D etc. in the subsidiary account are, it will be seen, part of the accounting process.

Account of the king's galley built at Newcastle upon Tyne [Endorsed]

Cost laid out in building the galley of the town of Newcastle upon Tyne from Sunday, St Nicholas's eve, 23 Edward I [5 December 1294], to Sunday after St Alban's day, 24 Edward I [24 June 1296], as appears below, by Hugh de Karliolo, then chief bailiff of the said town and the other bailiffs thereof, and by the testimony of John de Burgo, Henry de Wermue, Andrew Skaket, and Henry Maryman, sworn men.

Writ

The king sent his writ to his bailiffs of Newcastle upon Tyne in these words:–

Edward by the grace of God, etc., to his bailiffs of Newcastle upon Tyne greeting. Whereas we have of our counsel provided that galleys be built for the defence of our realm and the safety of the sea; we do command you, and strictly charge you on the fealty in which you are bound to us, that on the sight of these presents you cause to

[1] i.e. ore

[2] These "royalties" may be compared with those required by the king from iron-working in the Forest of Dean in L. F. Salzman, *English Industries of the Middle Ages* (Oxford, 1923), p. 37.

be made at Newcastle upon Tyne one good galley of six score oars, so that it be ready and prepared in all things that pertain to such a galley about Christmas next [25 December 1294] at latest. And this by no means omit, as you love our honour and would avoid our undoing and keep yourselves harmless: and the cost which you shall have laid out on this, when we know it, we will cause to be allowed you in the farm of the aforesaid town. Moreover we will that you take the boards and timber fit for this purpose wherever they may be found, and whose soever they may be, within and without the aforesaid town, for making that galley. Witness W. bishop of Bath and Wells [William de Marchia] our treasurer, at Westminster, 16 November, in the twenty-second year of our reign.

Wherefore, according to the tenor of this writ, the aforesaid bailiffs caused to be chosen the best and wisest of the aforesaid town to provide and purchase boards, timber and other necessaries for the aforesaid galley by the oath of twelve lawful men, who, being sworn, present John de Burgo, Henry de Wermue, Andrew Skaket, and Henry Mariman, who swore before the aforesaid bailiffs to make such provision and purchases, and the same sworn men chose William de Wayneflete master builder of the aforesaid galley; which same William shall have by agreement every week so long as the aforesaid galley is a-building ii*s*; and at the end of the work of the same galley he shall have one gown worth xx*s*, and to this the same William was sworn, etc.

Wherefore the aforesaid bailiffs, receiving the aforesaid writ on Sunday, the eve of St Nicholas, in the aforesaid year [5 December 1294] provided and spent as appears below:

1st week

		£	*s*	*d*
D	They account in the pay of labourers clearing and making a place where the galley should be made, by contract	0	8	3½
A	They also account in 5 logs bought of Alan de Colpyl for the beams[1] of the galley on the morrow of St Nicholas [7 December 1294] by the sworn men	0	6	0
A	Also in 60 spars[2] bought of John Raynecoc for making stays[3] to support the galley	0	2	0
A	Also in 93 boards bought of William of Staver[en] on the Friday following [10 December]	1	2	6
B	Also the same day in 6 great barrels of pitch bought of the aforesaid William, by the same sworn men	2	2	0
	Sum	£4	0*s*	9½*d*
		Approved		

[1] *trabas* [2] *cheveronibus* [3] *excitus*

2nd week

		£	s	d
D	On Sunday before the feast of St Thomas the apostle [19 December 1294]. In the wages of mr William for the past week	0	2	0
D	Also in the wages of 4 carpenters for 6 days, and in the wages of 1 carpenter for 3 days, whereof to each 3*d* a day	0	6	9
D	Also in the wages of 2 men hammering[1] nails, viz, "clinkers", for 4 days, whereof to each 2½*d* a day	0	1	8
D	Also in the wages of 6 labourers for 2 days and 1 labourer for 1 day about the carrying of the boards, iron, timber, and other necessaries, whereof to each 1½*d* a day	0	1	7½
D	Also in the expenses of Henry Mariman aforesaid, sworn man, in going and returning from Hartlepool to buy boards there, for 4 days	0	1	8
A	Also in 1 lock bought for the gate of the garden in which the timber was put to be stored for the galley	0	0	1
A	Also in 120 st. of iron bought for necessaries of the galley of Robert de Byngfeld	1	5	0
D	Also in the wages of smiths for working 20 st. of the same into nails which are called "Semenayl", viz, 1½*d* a stone	0	2	6
A	Also in 110 boards bought of Henry de Qualynk' by the sworn men for the aforesaid galley	0	18	4
A	Also in 54 boards bought of Adam le Moyn, whereof each board of the length of 26 ft, price 8*d* a board	1	16	0
A	Also in 43 boards bought of Roger le Rus, price 3*d* a board	0	10	6
B	Also in 5 barrels of tar bought of the wife of Lemmem de Pampeden, price 3*s* 9*d* a barrel	0	18	9
A	Also in earthen pots bought for heating tar and blare	0	0	2
A	Also in ½ chaldron coals bought, with the carriage of them to the place of the galley	0	0	3½
A	Also in 100 boards of Moray bought of Andrew Skaket, price 3½*d* a board	1	9	2
A	Also in 20 boards bought of William de Dolfamby, price 2*d* a board	0	3	4
A	Also in 1 log bought of John de Burgo, 56 ft long for the keel of the galley	1	0	0
A	Also in 1 log bought of Elias of Dunwich for the keel of the same galley, 52 ft long	1	0	0
A	Also in 1 log bought of William le Despenser for "underloute"	0	2	2
A	Also in 1 log for "underloute" with 4 other logs for tholes[2] bought of Tunock' Skinner	0	9	6
A	In 2 logs for "scheldbemes" bought of John de Burgo	0	3	6

[1] *repercuscium*
[2] *scalmas*

A	In 2 logs for "scheldbemes" bought of Henry Sparu . . .	0	3	6
C	In 260 iron nails, viz, "spyking", with 5 iron bolts[1] made for joining the keel of the galley	0	2	11
B	In 2 st. "burre" bought of Thomas Palmer, and 4 st. "wilding" bought of Andrew Skaket's wife	0	1	8
	Sum	£11	1s	1d
		Approved		

(Pipe Roll, No. 147, r. 14d)

Account of the men of the town of Newcastle upon Tyne, Nicholas of Carlisle and Thomas de Frismareys, bailiffs, on their behalf, of the mises and expenses incurred by them in the building of one galley, one barge, one cock-boat[2] newly made for the safety of the realm in the twenty-second year, by the king's writ, by which the king orders them to have made one good galley of six score oars with all things pertaining thereto for the defence of the realm and the safety of the sea. And the king will cause the cost which they shall have laid out on it to be allowed them in the farm of their town. They account in:–

	£	s	d
Timber and boards bought from time to time for the aforesaid galley, barge, and cock-boat	50	8	4
[This is the sum of the items marked A in the "bill of parcels".]			
Nails and other ironwork bought for the same [marked C] . . .	22	16	7½
Pitch, tar, "windel",[3] oil, and other sundry dressings against the water[4] [marked B]	11	2	0
Wages of carpenters and other workmen [marked D]	66	4	1¾
Ropes and cables [marked F]	8	10	4
Oars [marked G]	1	9	0
Canvas and yarn[5] for sails and ropes, and iron, brass,[6] and wooden utensils [marked H]	8	11	4
Mast and yard for the barge, with scoops[7] [bailers] [marked K]	0	9	1
Mast and yard for the galley, anchors, a windlass, a mast for the cock-boat, and sails for the galley, barge, and cock-boat and other sundries [marked L]	35	11	6½
Total	£205	2s	4¾d

[1] *buzonis*
[2] *navicula*
[3] i.e. the straw of wild grass, or possibly waste wool or some other substitute for oakum
[4] *minutis unguentis contra aquam*
[5] *filo*
[6] *eneis*
[7] *scopis*

226. "Bad" money, 1299–1300

To deal with the large amount of "pollards" and "crockards" and other bad foreign money in circulation, the king and council ordained on 15 May 1299 the "statute of Stepney" (No. 82 above). On 28 May, to save those offending from ignorance of the new regulation, it was announced that the death penalty in it was not to operate before St John the Baptist's day (24 June). There were also administrative and interpretative difficulties – as well as, of course, evasions.

Strict enforcement of the statute proved impossible. The death penalty was still not being inflicted in August, even upon deliberate offenders,[1] and the traffic in currencies which is revealed by the second extract under (c) below and which had developed quite contrary to the statute had for the time being to be tolerated. At Christmas there was an attempt to control it at least by allowing foreign money to circulate at half its face value until the following Easter. At Easter it was prohibited entirely. By then the king and his advisers had other measures ready.

Easter 1300 fell on 10 April. On the 11th orders were given to inform authorities at the ports and in Wales, Ireland and the Channel Islands that the king "with the counsel of his leading subjects (*proceres*)" had prohibited pollards, crockards and such like and decreed that the only legal currency in future should be "sterlings of his own mint".[2] On 29 March among the affairs of the parliament of 1300, on the day after the climax of that parliament on 28 March when the king had confirmed the charters once again in the most binding manner known and in a solemn assembly of his leading subjects,[3] a recoinage, the second of the reign, bigger than the first even, had been decreed (No. 86 (a) above).

A contemporary and (on this) well-informed opinion is that of Walter of Guisborough's chronicle, s.a. 1299 (see Introduction to Part V above).

(a) *Administrative difficulties*

(*Cal. Close Rolls 1296–1302*, p. 264)

1299, 2 August, Westminster

To the bailiffs of Bristol. Whereas the king lately, because they arrested a certain sum of money belonging to Arnald the smith, a merchant of Gascony, who was passing through that town with the money, ordered them to certify him of the causes of the arrest, and they have signified to him that they understood that Arnald had come with that money from parts beyond sea to that town, for which reason they caused it to be examined, in accordance with the form of the king's late ordinance that no one should bring any false money into the realm from parts beyond sea, and to be arrested because 22*l* in pollards were found therein, but that they afterwards ascertained that Arnald had received the money at Haverford for his wines there sold, and that he crossed to Bristol with the money by water, in order to set out thence to London to make his advantage thereof, of which they were not aware at the time of the arrest of the money, as the king learns by the return of his writ sent to him in this matter: THE KING ORDERS THEM to cause the money to be released from arrest and restored to Arnald to make his advantage thereof, according to the form of the aforesaid ordinance.

(b) *Does not apply to bad money already in circulation*

(ibid. p. 267)

1299, 18 August, Chertsey

To John Wogan, justiciary of Ireland. Order to permit burgesses and merchants of

[1] This is implicit in the second extract under (c) below and explicit in (d). cf. the complete pardon of certain members of the society of the Friscobaldi on 3 August (*Cal. Pat. Rolls 1292–1301*, p. 430).

[2] *Cal. Close Rolls 1296–1302*, pp. 390–1

[3] For the attendance, *Studies in Medieval History presented to F. M. Powicke*, ed. Hunt, Pantin and Southern (Oxford, 1948), pp. 325–6, esp. 326, n. 4.

Bristol, of whom he shall be ascertained under the common seal or under the seal of the constable of the castle that they are coming to Ireland with the money called "pollard" and "crokard" for the purpose of trading there, to trade with the said money and make their advantage thereof until otherwise ordered, as it was not and is not the king's intention, although he lately ordained by his council that no one should bring such money into his realm or power, that such money should not be current both in his realm and in his land of Ireland until he should revoke it or should otherwise ordain.

(c) *Evasions*

(*Cal. Pat. Rolls 1292–1301*, pp. 432 and 435)

1299, 23 August, Guildford
Mandate to the sheriffs of London and the collectors of the custom on wools there to arrest all wool and other merchandise within their bailiwick, as the king is informed that goods are being sold or traded in divers places for crockards, pollards and other bad money contrary to the statute made by the king with the council of the prelates and magnates, and are being carried with all speed to the ports where a coket is so as to be laden and conveyed out of the realm before it can be known whether the sale has been contrary to the statute. The king also appoints Elias Russel, citizen of London, with the said sheriffs and collectors to enquire by jury of the city and to take evidence touching this matter: where there has been no fraud they are to restore the goods without delay, saving the custom; where there has been fraud, they are to take the goods by indentures between themselves and the persons from whom they receive the goods, and to have the said indentures at the exchequer on the morrow of Michaelmas next before the treasurer and barons, to certify the latter what they have done in the premisses. And they are to act circumspectly, so that none be unduly aggrieved nor any offender spared by grace or favour.

1299, 23 August, Guildford
Appointment of John de Cobeham and William de Carleton, with such others as they shall associate with themselves, on complaint that native and foreign merchants take out of the realm sterlings and vessels and jewels of silver and gold, and exchange them beyond seas for pollards, crockards, and other bad money which they bring back to England and re-exchange for fresh sterlings, to make inquisition in the city of London to discover all who have done this, and to inflict ransoms, fines and other things due from the offenders, and to levy these for the king.

(d)

(ibid. p. 473)

1299, 23 August, Guildford
Commission to John de Cobeham and William de Carleton, with such others as they shall associate with themselves for the purpose, to enquire, by jury of merchants and others of the city of London, touching the trespasses of the persons who were taken

into custody for bringing pollards, crockards and other false money into the realm, and who are detained in Newegate gaol; according to the ordinance made by the king and council, these persons should forfeit their lives and goods, but the king has remitted their lives to them and desires their present deliverance, wherefore the commissioners are to enquire more fully into the matter, to receive fines and ransoms, in lieu of forfeiture of life, from every one of them who is convicted, and afterwards to deliver the said prisoners from gaol.

227. Rioting in Bristol, 1313

(*Cal. Pat. Rolls 1313–17*, pp. 68–9)

The struggle lasted until 1316. A contemporary's view of it, emphasising its economic background, is given in No. 13 above.

10 November 1313, Westminster

Commission of oyer and terminer to William Inge, Henry Spigurnel, Robert son of Payn, Edmund de Malu Lacu, John de Foxle and John de Button. Although the king had lately committed to Bartholomew de Badelesmere the custody of his castle of Bristol and the town and barton of Bristol, to hold during his pleasure, for a certain farm to be rendered yearly at the exchequer, and frequently enjoined on the men of the town to answer to him as constable of the castle and keeper of the town and barton, or to his attorney in that behalf, in all matters which appertain to the custody of the castle, town and barton, William de Axe, then mayor of the town, and John le Taverner, Thomas de la Grave, John de Kerdyf, John Hasard, Richard Colpek, Robert de Holhurst, Robert Martin, William de Clyf, Richard de Wodehulle, Thomas Uppediche, Walter Fraunceys, clerk, Richard le White, "pesshoner", Thomas de Salop, Adam Wysman, John Fraunceys, the elder, Richard de Cheddre, John de Keynesham, Philip de Sweyneseye, John le Lang, "maryner", Roger Blanket, John Legat, Nicholas le Taillur, Philip le Spicer, Nicholas de Farleye, Gilbert de Derby, William Flemmynge, William Burgeys, Thomas Butiller and Richard Legat, with others of the town, ignoring the king's commands, refused to obey him or his attorney. Subsequently the king, having for divers causes taken the liberty of the town into his hands, and having committed it during his pleasure to the said Bartholomew de Badelesmere, who was to answer at the exchequer for the issues thereof, the same John le Taverner, William de Clyf, and Gilbert Pokerel, exercised the offices of mayor and bailiffs in the town, as if the liberty of the town had not been taken into the king's hands, and they with the other persons above named, by their own authority, usurped and converted to their own uses the profits accruing to the town, which Bartholomew de Badelesmere, as constable of the castle and keeper of the town and barton and of the liberty thereof by virtue of the king's commissions to him and to his attorney, ought to have received. They also forcibly impeded him and his attorney and the other ministers appointed by him for collecting, exercising and doing those things which appertain to such custody, in the collection and execution of the same, and beat, wounded, and imprisoned his deputies; and also in divers places in the town they made barricades and other impediments, not permitting victuals or other things to be borne or even carried from the town, or through it, to the castle for the strengthening and custody thereof. Furthermore they forcibly broke the king's mills by the castle and made frequent attacks, as against enemies, on the men who were in the castle for its custody, by shooting arrows and quarrels into the castle, and finally they erected and crenellated a wall of stone and lime in the street called "Wynchestrete" and made barricades in divers places opposite the castle, discharging arrows and quarrels through the battlements[1] against the castle. They also with armed force hindered Thomas de Berkele, John de Welyngton, mr Richard de Abyndon, and the same John de Button, sent by the king to Bristol to assess a tallage in that town for his use and to make divers inquisitions there, from doing those things which appertained to their office, and imprisoned them. Further they conspired together and entered into a confederacy among themselves to commit trespasses against the king, his constable and keeper, and the attorney of the latter. They assessed many tallages on the commonalty of the town by reason whereof they oppressed the people there, converted the greater part of the money accruing from such tallages to their own uses, and having no consideration of the caption of the liberty of the town into the king's hands, but rather treating with contempt his action in that matter, held an election among themselves of a mayor and bailiffs for the town, who cease not to execute such offices there in contempt of the king's mandates, to the manifest derogation of the king's right and to the impoverishment of the town and against the peace. The justices, of whom William Inge is to be one, are to enquire into these matters by oath of goodmen of the county of Gloucester.

By K.

228. Usages of the city of Winchester, late 13th cent.

(*The Ancient Usages of the City of Winchester*, ed. and trans. J. S. Furley (Oxford, 1927), from the Anglo-Norman of a late thirteenth-century MS. now in the possession of Winchester College [French])

The Usages, in this their earliest known form, give us the municipal practice and regulations of the city in the late thirteenth century and are remarkable apart from their economic interest for the definite picture they give of the mayoralty at that time. For the background, J. S. Furley, *City Government of Winchester from the Records* . . . (Oxford, 1923).

[1] These are the ancient usages of the city of Winchester. They were observed in the time of our ancestors; they are, and are intended to be, for the saving and sustaining of the franchise.

[2] It is to be known that there shall be in the city a mayor elected by common assent of the four-and-twenty jurats[2] and of the commons, principal sustainer of the franchise; which mayor is to be removable from year to year; he may receive no plaint, nor plead of himself any plaint, that touches the provosty[3] of the city.

[3] Furthermore there shall be in the city four-and-twenty jurats, elected from the most trustworthy and wise of the city to loyally aid and counsel the aforesaid mayor in saving and sustaining the franchise.

[1] *per kernella muri*

[2] jurats = jurati = under oath – in this case to be loyal to the king and the city

[3] the king's authority in the city, formerly exercised by his provost or reeve (*prepositura*)

[4] Which four-and-twenty shall come at the regular summons of the mayor, and if any be absent without reasonable cause he shall be amerced of one besant,[1] each time, for the profit of the city.
[5] Furthermore there shall be in the city two bailiffs, jurats, to keep the provosty loyally and to do right to all the commonalty, from which the mayor and the twenty-four shall elect four trusty men at the Burgh-mote of St Michael, and the commons elect from these four the two aforesaid.
[6] Furthermore there shall be four serjeants in the city, jurats, bearing staves, to execute the orders of the mayor and bailiffs aforesaid.
[7] Furthermore none of the aforesaid twenty-four shall maintain a party in the court of the city nor be a countor or advocate in a cause in prejudice of the franchise of the city.
[8] Furthermore there shall be in the city two coroners, jurats, on behalf of our lord the king or his justices to do their office as well in the soke[2] as in the city aforesaid.
[9] Furthermore the aforesaid bailiffs shall deliver up at the end of the year their rolls of pleadings and of terrage and put them in common keeping for cases that may arise therefrom.
[10] Furthermore no citizen shall cause burels or chaluns to be worked outside the walls of the city under pain of forfeiting the goods or their value.
[11] And be it known that every great loom whereon burels are worked owes to the farm of the city five shillings a year, unless it work but a single cloth.
[12] And be it known that no loom shall be free, whoever it be that keeps it, in his house or elsewhere, except one for the use of the mayor, and another for the hospital, and a third for the clerk of the town.
[13] And be it known that weavers who work burels shall take for the working of the cloth eighteen pence[3] from All Saints to the Annunciation of our Lady, two shillings till the following All Saints.
[14] And be it known that none shall cause burel to be worked if he be not of the franchise of the city, save every fuller one a year, and every weaver one, to pay the king's farm.
[15] For the smaller looms whereon chaluns are worked the usage is thus, that every double loom owes to the farm of the city twelve pence a year, a single loom six pence, unless they work no more than a single cloth a year.
[16] And be it known that none is free unless it pay so much.
[17] And that the cloths be of length and width according to the ancient assize of the mistery, under pain of forfeiting the cloths that shall be found different, or their value.
[18] And be it known that the chaluns of four ells long shall be two yards wide before the tapener[4]; the chaluns of three yards and a half in length shall have two yards, less a quarter, of width before the tapener; the chaluns of three yards and a quarter long shall be an ell and a half and a half quarter wide before the tapener; the chaluns of three ells in length shall be an ell and a half before the tapener.
[19] And be it known that no apprentice may be set to a tapener's loom to work, if

[1] two shillings
[2] the district under the authority of the bishop, on the east and south sides of the city
[3] i.e. per week
[4] weaver

he give not ten shillings to the king, unless he be son to him who sets him thereto or son of his sister; and that none of the mistery make agreement with the servant of another until St Andrew's day be past, on pain of paying half a mark to the king's use.

[20] And that none of the mistery of tapeners work by night, save from the feast of St Thomas the apostle until Christmas, on pain of amercement of six pence every time that he shall be convicted.

[21] And be it known that none of the mistery of burellers shall work at night save from St Nicholas's day until Christmas, under the same penalty.

[22] And that two trustworthy men of the mistery of tapeners be chosen and sworn, to keep all the ancient usages belonging to the mistery and to take pledges of all those that they shall find in default, which pledges they shall present to the bailiffs of the city at the next court, under pain of amercement to the king.

[23] And these two jurats shall keep the booth where yarn is sold, that no regrate be made before the hour of tierce, and if they find any regrater the goods which he shall have bought before the aforesaid hour, or their value, shall be forfeited to the farm of the city: and that no regrater have in the booth aforesaid hutch or place enclosed wherein he can conceal his regrate: and if the jurats find aught damped, or other fraud, they shall deliver it immediately to the bailiffs to pass sentence thereon as of that which is false.

[24] Furthermore no butcher or other man may have a stall in the High Street of Winchester without paying the due to the city.

[25] Furthermore no man may buy green hides or green skin in the city if he be not of the franchise on pain of forfeiting the goods to the farm of the city: and those who are of the franchise, whereby they have the right to buy them, shall not carry them green out of the franchise.

[26] Furthermore no fishmonger or poulterer shall buy fish or poultry to retail before tierce have rung.

[27] Furthermore no manner of victual that comes into the city for sale may be carried out of the city unsold without leave of a bailiff from the hour that it be once put for sale, under pain of forfeiting the goods.

[28] Furthermore no regrater may go outside the city to meet victual to buy it before it come into the city to raise the price of the victual, under pain of being forty days in the king's prison.

[29] The custom of fish is this, that no man may have a board save only the king; and every board owes to the king a farthing a day that there is fish thereon: and this can no man escape by any manner of franchise.

[30] Furthermore every cart that comes into the city with fish for sale, whatever fish it bring, of whatever franchise it be, owes to the king's rent one halfpenny, every time that it comes, for the board that stands before the seller.

[31] Furthermore every cart out of franchise owes to the king of custom two pence halfpenny, whatever fish it brings for sale: and every horse-load of fresh fish that comes into the city for sale and is out of franchise owes to the king three halfpence of custom, and of salted fish one halfpenny.

[32] Furthermore every cart out of franchise coming into the city with salmon owes to the king of custom four pence, unless it bring but a single salmon; and a horse-load, unless it bear but a single one, two pence; and on a man's back one penny.
[33] Furthermore every hundred of lampreys coming into the city owes five lampreys of custom to the bailiffs of the city for their own use, and no other custom.
[34] Furthermore every seller of herrings in lent by retail owes to the king six pence of custom, and to the bailiffs a pitcher of wine of whatsoever franchise he be.
[35] Furthermore the usage of the butchers is this, that every butcher out of franchise that holds a stall owes to the king, of custom, twenty-five pence a year.
[36] Furthermore all those out of franchise that buy beasts, sheep, or swine and sell again without slaughtering owe to the king five pence a year as custom of pens, and to the city clerk one penny for enrolling their name, unless he do it for not more than a single beast. And all dealers in beasts, sheep, or swine out of franchise that frequent the city, unless they do not come more than once a year, owe the same custom. And they shall place the beasts outside the west gate of Winchester, where are the pens, from Michaelmas to the feast of St Nicholas from daybreak till high tierce, and after tierce in Minster street, and there for the whole year save the time and hour aforesaid.
[37] Furthermore every baker of the city that makes bread for sale owes to the king for custom two shillings a year and to the clerk of the city one penny: and they shall make white, well-baked bread according to the selling price of wheat and the assize of the king's marshalcy, that is to say that if the farthing loaf is in default of aught beyond twelve penny weights the baker is in mercy, and for every default within the weight of three ounces according to the amount of the trespass; and when the farthing loaf is in default by aught beyond three ounces the baker shall bear the sentence of the city.
[38] Furthermore every woman out of franchise selling bread in the high street of Winchester owes to the king as custom two shillings a year, and to the clerk of the city one penny if she sell for the whole year; and if she sell for less, then according to the amount;[1] and in the blind streets six pence, or three pence, according to the length of time for which she is without trade: and be it known that none of them shall fetch bread [to sell] save where the baskets shall stand before the hour of noon on pain of amercement for the seller and the buyer: and that none of them fetch bread from any baker from whom she cannot have his warrant, and if she so do she herself warrant it: and that every baker have his known stamp on his bread which he cannot disown if it be found other than good.
[39] Furthermore all brewsters within the jurisdiction of the city that brew for sale shall make good ale according to the selling price of grain and to the assize delivered; and if they do otherwise they shall be in the king's mercy so often as the bailiffs shall be able to convict them.
[40] Furthermore no brewster out of franchise can brew within the jurisdiction of the city for sale if she do not satisfy the bailiffs according to the quantity that she brews.
[41] Furthermore no man out of franchise, of whatever mistery he be, may keep shop, sell, or buy within the jurisdiction of the city without satisfying the bailiffs of the city.

[1] the amount sold

[42] Furthermore every cart sold in the city to a man out of franchise owes to the king as custom one halfpenny.
[43] Of petty customs the usage is this, that a stone of wool coming separately into the city, that is out of franchise, owes to the king as custom a farthing, and two together a farthing, and three together a halfpenny, and four a halfpenny, and five a halfpenny, and six together three farthings, and eight a penny, that is to say from those that are out of franchise: and if there be nine stones together or severally, for one man at one time, the wool owes to the king two pence as pesage, of whatever franchise he be that brings it.
[44] For cheese, butter, grease, and tallow the usage is in all points in the same manner as is said before of the custom of wool: and be it known that for wool, cheese, butter, grease, and tallow, whereon the pesage belongs to the king, as much shall be taken for the half weight, by itself, as for the entire weight: and be it known that every kind of goods, whereon the pesage belongs to the king, that is brought for sale within the jurisdiction of the city, owes the pesage to the king, by whatever weight it be weighed, and of whatever franchise he be whose the goods are: and if there be any denizen or stranger who owes the pesage and conceals the fact over night, he is in the king's mercy according to the amount of the trespass.
[45] Furthermore when tallage is to be levied in the city by order of the king or for common needs of the city, six trustworthy men shall be elected by common assent and sworn, three from the twenty-four and three from the commons, to assess that tallage and to receive and lawfully expend it, and to render lawful account: and when mayor or bailiffs or other trustworthy men go out of the city for common profit, on common purse, they must on their return render lawful account to the aforesaid six without delay: and if any trustworthy man of the city lends his substance for the common need of the city it shall be borrowed by tally by the hand of these six jurats, and repaid by the same.
[46] Furthermore when it is intended to drink the gild merchant, inquiry shall be made by common assent among the misteries of the city to find such men as are of good report and suitable to admit to the gild merchant; and each of these shall have in chattels the value of four pounds or more, and those that shall be admitted shall be allotted into four houses as they were used to be at all times.

And when gild merchant shall have been drunk the four houses shall gather together to see what they shall have raised and what they shall be able to raise, and if there be fault it shall be amended by common consent.

And if the value of one house be greater than that of another it shall bear burdens according to its value.

And that the money which shall be raised from the four houses aforesaid shall be delivered to the aforesaid six trustworthy men elected and sworn by common assent to lawfully keep and lawfully expend and render lawful account to the trustworthy men of the city twice a year by tally or by deed.
[47] Furthermore if any of the twenty-four find any foreigner within the jurisdiction of the city that owes him debt, it is lawful for him to make the distress himself on his debtor until he can come to the bailiffs: and none of the franchise of the city need give

anything to the bailiffs of the city to take distress on his debtors, denizen or foreign, as long as he offer security and pledge against them that owe him the debt.
[48] Of the gates of Winchester, wherefrom the bailiffs of the city take custom of them that are out of franchise and owe custom, the usage is that every cart that brings wheat for sale owes one halfpenny as custom every time that it comes; a horse-load a farthing.
[49] Furthermore every cart that brings iron or steel two pence, a horse-load one penny.
[50] Furthermore every cart that brings new cart-saddles, drawing-bars large or small, traces of rope or leather, owes as custom two pence and a horse-load a penny.
[51] Furthermore every cart bringing millstone, four pence; and every cart that brings grindstone, two pence.
[52] Furthermore every cart that brings tin or lead for sale four pence, a horse-load two pence.
[53] Furthermore every cart that brings *korc*[1] for dyeing two pence, a horse-load one penny.
[54] Furthermore scythes and sickles coming in a cart owe as custom one penny, a horse-load one halfpenny.
[55] Furthermore every cart that brings tanned leather for sale owes two pence, a horse-load one penny.
[56] Furthermore madder coming in cart for sale two pence, a horse-load one penny.
[57] Furthermore every cart that brings woad for sale four pence, a horse-load one penny.
[58] Furthermore every countryman that brings into the city potash for use with woad owes to the king as custom six pence a year and one penny to the clerk for enrolling his name, unless he come not more than once in the year.
[59] Furthermore it is the usage of the dyers' mistery in the city that two trustworthy and lawful men be elected by common assent and sworn to assay the woad of foreign merchants that comes into the city for sale and lawfully execute the assize to buyer and seller.
[60] Furthermore every tanner that holds a stall in the High street of Winchester owes for the ground which he takes up two shillings a year, and to the clerk one penny as *tan-gable*: and every woman selling tallow or grease by retail owes at Easter eve one penny as *smer-gable*.
[61] Furthermore every shoemaker that makes new shoes of neat's leather owes to the same city two pence as *sco-gable*: and these usages are for them that are in franchise as well as for the rest.
[62] Furthermore there is in the aforesaid city a common and authentic seal wherewith are sealed the charters of feoffments of the city, which charters [before they are sealed] shall have been in the keeping of the aldermen, who shall have given seisin, for year and day without challenge from any one, of which sealing notice shall be cried through the city the third day before the sealing.

And the charters that shall be presented by the aldermen aforesaid, who will testify

[1] used for dyeing and producing a crimson dye

the seisin as good and the keeping of the charter as unchallenged, shall be sealed, and made safe by that seal for all time.

And be it known that every charter that is sealed with this seal owes seven pence for the sealing, for wax and everything.

And be it known that the aforesaid seal shall be kept under three keys, whereof two trustworthy men of the twenty-four jurats shall keep two, and one trustworthy man of the commons the third.

And this chest with the three keys shall be put in a larger chest shut with two locks, of which one trustworthy man of the twenty-four shall keep one key, and one of the commons the other.

[63] (1) The order of the pleas pleaded in the city is by usage this, that every man of the franchise of the city that is impleaded can have three regular summons before he makes appearance, if he wishes to have them, provided attachment does not lie, and for his household as many.

(2) And be it known that these three summons shall be made on three successive days, unless a festival interfere, or the court be not held from day to day, provided that the plaintiff present himself at every court to obtain the summons.

(3) And if a man is attached in a case where summons lies, the distress shall be released at the next court and he shall have his regular summons according to the usage of the city.

(4) And if he be not found in the city when the first summons is ordered to be made, none shall be made for him before he comes into the city, if it be not a summons for a plea of land by writ.

(5) And if a man not of the franchise be impleaded he shall have but one summons, over one night, provided he be found in the city.

(6) And if he be impleaded by writ on a plea of land he can have, if he so wishes, three successive summons, as those have who are in franchise.

(7) And if a man that is in franchise appear in court to the first or the second summons he is bound to answer, as much as to the third: and when he appears, without distraint, whoever he be, whether of franchise or no, and belongs to the city, he can have a town-day for answering, if he asks for it in due form: and by town-day a denizen, pleading against a denizen, has a week's adjournment and thus, either by essoin or by appearance, the whole case is pleaded from week to week until it be ended; and if foreigner implead denizen the denizen has only the third day after his appearance to answer the summons, either by town-day or any other adjournment.

(8) And when denizen impleads foreigner the foreigner has his adjournment from week to week without town-day; and in plea of land he is entitled to claim the view on appearance after essoin, provided that an exception do not preclude the view, and if the view does not affect right, and provided that common law be followed between plaintiff and defendant in a writ of right in prosecuting and defending, the essoin of sickness, trial by battle, and great assize not being admitted [as reasons for staying the action], in such manner that inquest taken by twelve true men on oath decide the right for all time.

(9) And be it known that writs pleaded in the city before justices or the bailiffs

of the city are these: writs of *novel disseisin*, and all forms of *justicies* (except annual rent), writs of dower, of *de rationabili parte*, and of pure right.

(10) And that plaintiff and defendant may make attorney in every kind of plea, whether there be writ or no writ, in presence of the opposite party.

(11) And that the essoin of *de ultra mare* be not allowed in any kind of plea if cast for one that is found in the city on summons; and if he be not found the essoin shall be cast on the first summons, or else not allowed at all; and thus he shall have forty days, and if he come to the city within forty days and the plaintiff wishes to sue, the defendant shall be summoned again on the aforesaid summons, and then if he so wish he can cast an essoin *de malo veniendi* and have a week's adjournment, provided that no other adjournment lie before he answer the summons, unless it be by forking of more parceners than one on a plea of land by writ.

(12) And to plea of debt the procedure after the answer in chief is as follows: that if the demandant bring tally or bond and demands payment in full, no day of account shall be granted by the court without assent of the plaintiff; but the defendant may allege by tally or by bond or by a countersuit that his payment has been made, provided that if he bring tally or bond he prove them according to their nature, and if he bring suit his adversary shall have his defence according to law of the land.

(13) Furthermore, after the death of every tenant in fee the bailiffs of the city shall take simple seisin of the tenements of which he dies seised in order to know for certain who is the nearest heir, and at the next court the aforesaid tenements shall be delivered to the nearest heir on appearance; provided that if any be alleged as nearer heir or parcener that be in the country, his friends may have a day appointed for causing him to come, according to the distance of the places; and if he be out of the country he shall have forty days; and if he come to his day he shall have the same standing as he would have had had he been present the day that his ancestor died; and if he do not come to his day and thinks that he has right, he shall have his claim according to law of the land.

(14) Furthermore, for year and day in usage in the city, be it known that whosoever has held land or tenements, by inheritance or purchase, whereof he has been seised by the bailiffs or by certain testimony of the neighbourhood for year and day without challenge from any, the demandant shall be barred for all time unless he were under age, or out of the country or in prison, or unless he be entitled to lawful partition, as of equally near kinship with the possessor, that is to say brother with sister, uncle with nephew, aunt with niece.

(15) Furthermore the usage of year and day aforesaid is that if there be any that takes rent from any tenement within the franchise of the aforesaid city and his rent be entirely in arrear one year or more, and he do not find aught to distrain and there be a building and people dwelling therein, he may take away the doors and windows by leave of the bailiffs of the city, and if he cannot thereby get possession of his tenement or find aught else there to distrain, then by award of the court, and on the view by the alderman of the street and of one serjeant, shall stake be placed, or lock where there is a door, and it be enrolled in the court and sued from one week to a second and to a third, and to forty days, for a complete year from the first day of the suit;

and if then no one come to make satisfaction the tenant shall lose without recovery whoever he be, of age or not, provided always that he shall be able to make satisfaction any day before judgment pass, which judgment shall not be delayed to the damage of the demandant; and like suit shall be made of void land where there is no crop; and no man shall lay hands upon the aforesaid lands or tenements so long as the king's sequestration is thereon.

229. Provisions for the government of the city of Lincoln, *c.* 1300

The original of the following document is now missing from the city muniments, but Samuel Lyon, town clerk of Lincoln, gave in his account of the city records in 1785 what appears to be a full translation of it. This is printed in J. W. F. Hill, *Medieval Lincoln* (Cambridge, 1948), App. VII, whence, by permission, I reproduce it. Lyon informs us that the original was in Latin.

We have no means of knowing to what extent these provisions, coming after a decade of civic discord (cf. ibid, p. 300), are new or whether they merely restate the practice, or theory, of before 1290.

These are provisions made together with the underwritten articles by the mayor and whole commonalty of the city of Lincoln for keeping the peace of our lord the king and for the perpetual observance of the liberties and improvements hereunder mentioned (that is to say)

That the commonalty shall by their common council elect a mayor from year to year of their own election; and that no mayor shall be elected unless he shall before be assessed to the public taxes, with other citizens of the said city; and that the mayor shall remain in his mayoralty so long as it pleases him and the commonalty; And that the same mayor shall be discharged of all taxes dues and talliages and of all other customs belonging to the city so long as he shall be mayor (saving the precept of our lord the king in all things); And also that it shall be lawful for such mayor to take his hansels[1] within the city and without, except of the citizens of Lincoln and their sons, and all those who pay scot and lot in the said city and who ought not to be anselled within the county of Lincoln;

And further it is provided that the commonalty with the advice of the mayor shall choose twelve fit and discreet men to be judges of the said city, but that those twelve men shall be assessed to the public taxes and dues, and to all royal customs with other citizens of the said city;

And it is further provided that the said citizens shall have bailiffs every year of their own election, and that those bailiffs shall faithfully discharge the fee farm rent of our lord the king at the end of the year; And if they do not do so the mayor and commonalty shall distrain such bailiffs by their lands and chattels until the fee farm rent of our lord the king be fully paid; And that if any damage happens to the city through default of paying the fee farm rent of our lord the king such damage shall be made good to the city out of the chattels of the said bailiffs; And those bailiffs ought to have two clerks and four sergeants who shall be presented before the mayor and commonalty at the feast of St Michael;

And that there shall be no weigher of goods unless he is elected by the common

[1] a customary present to the mayor out of a commodity brought by strangers into the city for sale

council and that the persons so elected shall take their corporal oath upon the holy Evangelists faithfully and firmly to fulfil all these things and to keep and observe the customs of the city;

And if it shall happen that the mayor or any bailiff shall be called into question unjustly for supporting the rights of the city the commonalty shall defend them within the city and without to the utmost of their power; And also shall faithfully restrain the mayor and bailiffs within their own liberties of the said city;

And it is further provided that four men worthy of trust shall be elected from amongst the citizens by a free election at the feast of St Michael to keep an account of outgoings talliages and arrears belonging to the city; and that they have one chest and four keys; And that they shall render up their account to the city at the end of the year;

Also it is provided for the keeping the peace of our lord the king that they who ought shall appoint two men out of each parish of the city worthy of trust to search their own parishes once a month; And that no person shall lodge a stranger more than one night unless he shall bring him forth to public view on the morrow if it shall be necessary; And if any person in any parish shall be suspected and he cannot find pledges he shall be sent out of town until he can find pledges; And if the said two men will not search their respective parishes as aforesaid, they shall remain in the mercy of the city, and the names of the aforesaid men shall be set down in writing, to be in the keeping of the mayor, and at the feast of St Michael there shall be other two such men appointed to succeed to the said office; And if a disturbance of the city and a tumult and clamour happens, and the mayor and bailiffs attend, all the commonalty ought to prosecute them to the keeping of the peace of our lord the king, and of the city;

And it is further provided that those who choose to defend themselves by the liberty of the city shall be assessed, together with the commonalty, to all taxes dues and royal customs belonging to the city; And if any person of the city shall oppose the mayor and commonalty concerning any matter of a public nature by them enacted, he shall be in the mercy of the city; And it shall be lawful for the mayor and citizens to distrain him for his amercement until he shall make them satisfaction according to the greatness of his offence; And if reasonable summonses have been issued by command of the mayor and commonalty, he who withdraws himself, and does not appear, shall be amerced to the amount of 2*s*, unless he can suggest some reasonable cause by way of excuse;

Also it is provided that no foreign merchant shall remain in the city more than forty days for selling his merchandises, unless he shall have licence of the mayor and commonalty; And it is further provided that no foreigner shall have the freedom of the city unless he shall receive it in the presence of the mayor and commonalty; Also it is provided that no foreign merchant of any kind of merchandise ought to be admitted to sell it within the city by retail; Also it is provided that if any broker of the city shall lead a foreign merchant out of town to buy wool, or any other thing, which is contrary to the liberty of the city, he shall remain in the mercy of the city; And if he shall a second time be convicted of the like offence, he shall lose his freedom, until he shall make satisfaction to the commonalty; And if any citizen shall deal with him, he shall be in the mercy of the city; And if any merchant citizen shall associate himself with a foreign merchant to make any kind of merchandises within the city he shall be in the mercy of the commonalty, and the property of the foreigner shall be seized, and be in the mercy of the city; Also it is provided that if any worker of wool, man or woman, shall go out of the city to work at their trade (except at markets) he or she shall be in the mercy of the city; and if again convicted of the same offence, no one shall employ them in their business;

Also it is forbid that anyone do go out of the gates of the city to buy anything that is coming towards it, and if anyone do so, he shall be in the mercy of the mayor and bailiffs of the city, and the thing bought shall be seized to the use of the city;

Also it is forbid that anyone shall exercise his right of common in the common pastures but in a reasonable degree as he ought; and that any hog shall be suffered to enter thereon to the injury of the pasture;

And it is provided that it shall be lawful for every citizen to distrain his foreign debtors found within the city for their known debts, without any denial of the bailiffs, except in the times when the judges shall be holding pleas in the city, and proceeding from thence into the county, and also except as to men coming to market with their merchandises;

Also so that no weaver or dyer shall dye the wool or cloths of foreigners, nor fuller full the same against the liberty of the city, and if he does so, and is thereof convicted, he shall be in the mercy of the city, and if he shall be again convicted, he shall forfeit his right of a citizen, until he shall submit and promise amendment, And if anyone shall knowingly hold communication with him, he shall be in the mercy of the city, and the wool or cloth shall remain in the mercy of the mayor bailiffs and commonalty of the city, And it shall be lawful for any citizen to seize such wool or cloth as aforesaid without cause until he can show it to the mayor and bailiffs; And it is provided that no merchant of the city shall buy cloth made out of the city to dye within the same; And if anyone shall be convicted of this offence, the cloth shall be in the mercy of the city, and the seller also; And further that neither the dyer, the weaver, nor the fuller, ought to dye any cloth for their own use; and if they shall be thereof convicted the cloths shall remain to the use of the commonalty; And it shall be lawful for any citizen without cause to seize any such cloths, wheresoever he shall find them, until he shall show them to the mayor and bailiffs; Also it is provided that if any citizen shall find his cloth injured thro' the default of the fuller, the fuller shall make good the damage to him whose cloth it shall be, by the view of lawful men; Also it is provided that the dyers and weavers shall be punished in like manner if their works are ill done;

And also that no regrator of flesh or fish shall buy any flesh or fish to sell which the church of Lincoln refused before it was offered to the mayor, and that it shall be lawful for any citizen to arrest the person and the thing so bought, and bring them before the mayor, if any one shall be found so to do;

And it is provided that no fisherman ought to fish in the free waters of the city, unless with nets provided and made by the consent of honest men of the commonalty of the said city, and if anyone shall do so, he shall be in the mercy of the said city, and if he shall again be convicted thereof, he shall be in the mercy of the city, and his nets shall be forfeited;

Also it is provided that if any citizen of Lincoln shall be arrested out of the town for any debt of another citizen of Lincoln, it shall be lawful for the mayor and commonalty to distrain him, by whom he is arrested, by his chattels, until the streets of our lord the king shall be made free to the citizens of Lincoln;

Also it is provided that if any seller of wool shall sell any false wool to a merchant, by reason of which sale complaints shall come to the mayor or commonalty, the seller of such wool shall remain in the mercy of the city, and the false wool shall be burnt in any place the mayor and commonalty please; and be it known that all false merchandise, as in cloths, shoes, tanned leather, and all other merchandises, found to be false, which ought to be subject to a like penalty, shall be punished by a like penalty as false wools.

230. Some thirteenth-century English places and their associations

(*English Historical Review*, xvi (1901), pp. 501–3; reprinted with identifications by J. C. Tingey in *The History Teacher's Miscellany*, V (No. 1) (Cambridge, January 1927), pp. 9–12. In translating the opportunity has been taken to revise. Identifications about which I still feel doubt are followed by the initials of those responsible: thus "[J. C. T.]" indicates J. C. Tingey as above; "[T. R.]", Thorold Rogers, *Six Centuries of Work and Wages* (1894), pp. 105–6). No. 91 in the list means that I offer "Pewter" as a translation of "Poyture" (J. C. T. had "Bridge" of Exeter) without being certain of it. [French])

Surely the product of an idle hour. The work of someone travelled enough to know a large number of places personally or by repute, probably a merchant because he so often associates a place with its products, and one (if the geographical distribution of the places he mentions is a guide) most at home in eastern England. Professor Carus-Wilson is almost certainly right in dating it "almost certainly mid-thirteenth century".

The Baronage of London
Regrating of York
Sanctuary of Canterbury
Relics of Westminster[1]
5 Prostitutes of Charing
The Pardon[2] of St Paul's
Sauce of Fleet[3]
Deer of Bury St Edmund's
School of Oxford
10 Scarlet of Lincoln
Hauberge[4] of Stamford
Blanket of Blyth
Burnet of Beverley
Russet of Colchester

[1] The abbey's relics would be on show at certain times of year and were one of the sights.
[2] a churchyard
[3] Presumably the London Fleet (river, street, prison?) but not necessarily, in view of the author's familiarity with E. Anglia and the Fens. Sauce, if gastronomic, could be a satirical reference to the filthy and odoriferous condition of the Fleet river (cf. Sabine in *Speculum*, vols 8, 9 and 12, esp. vol. 12 (1937), pp. 34–6, for its pollution by butchers and tanners; and *Cal. Pat. Rolls 1301–7*, p. 548).
[4] a cloth, like the rest of 10–14

15 Thieves of Grantham
Murderers of Royston[1]
Knives of Thaxted
Sleeves[2] of Durham
Shears of Huntingdon [J. C. T.]
20 Needles of Wilton
Razors of Leicester
Butchers of Winchester
Bachelery of Northampton
Eels of Cambridge
25 Iron of Gloucester
Plains of Salisbury
Cloister of Lichfield [T. R.]
The bath of Bath
The marvel of Stonehenge
30 Merchants of Lynn
Herring of Yarmouth
Plaice of Winchelsea
Merling of Rye
Dace of Kingston
35 Loches of Weybridge[3]
Barbels of St Ives
Salmon of Berwick
Ruffs of Bedford
The crossing of Chelmsford
40 Simnel of Wycombe[4]
Wastel of Hungerford
Treet of Newbury
Coverchief of Shaftesbury
Wimple of Lewes
45 Skins of Shrewsbury
The ferry of Tilbury
Archers of Wales
Robbers of Alton
[?] Empyrean of Meldon [J. C. T.]
50 Marble of Corfe
Plaster of Nower[5]

[1] A clue to date if an allusion to the incident mentioned in *Liber Memorandorum de Barnewelle*, ed. J. Willis Clark, p. 145.
[2] Maunches: in the context, possibly rivets
[3] L. F. Salzman, *Engl. Industries of the Middle Ages*, p. 262, suggests that "loches" may have been a kind of stockfish and "Weybridge", Weybourn co. Norfolk, about 5 miles from the fish fair of Blakeney.
[4] Simnel, white bread of the very finest flour; wastel, a second quality bread; treet, bread of the coarsest brown flour.
[5] Nore Down, Purbeck: one of the native sources of supply of gypsum for plaster of Paris. Even thus early not all plaster of Paris was imported from Montmartre and, as this shows, plaster of Nower was already famous in its own right (Salzman, *Building in England to 1540*, pp. 155–6).

Pottery of Henham[1]
Cattle of Nottingham
Linen cloth of Aylesham
55 Cord of Warwick
Cambric of Bridport
"Chalons" of Guildford[2]
Rymers of Worcester[3]
Fur of Chester
60 Shipping of Southampton
The warren of Walton
Quilts of Clare
Town of Bures [J. C. T.]
Jousters of Yardley
65 Tourneyers of Blyth
Tilters of Ipswich
Mills of Dunwich
Priory of Waltham[4]
Bread of St Albans
70 The harbour of Norwich
Mead of Hitchin
Bever of Banbury[5]
Ale of Ely
Cod of Grimsby
75 Covert of Sherwood
Chase of Englewood
Forest of Windsor
Horn of Carlisle
Saddlery of Ogerston[6]
80 Palfrey of Ripon
Colt of Rievaulx
Cheese of Jervaulx[7]
[?] Scurvy of Fountains [J. C. T.]
Soap of Coventry
85 Lodging of Dunstable[8]
Scoffers of Elstow [J. C. T.]

[1] Henham in Essex; Salzman, *English Industries*, p. 171, n. 3, prefers Hanley, Staffordshire
[2] on English "Chalons", see Salzman, op. cit. pp. 199–200
[3] Reamer, a specialised trade; for a Worcester connection, see Salzman, op. cit., p. 145
[4] *Praerie*: for Waltham, "priory" seems likelier than "prairie" (T. R.'s suggestion)
[5] a drink. cf. *Shorter Oxford Dictionary*
[6] Ogerston, now a decayed hamlet in Washingley, south of the R. Nene in Huntingdonshire; then, a stage between Huntingdon and Stamford on the medieval road to the north and shown as such on the Gough Map of *c.* 1360; cf. F. M. Stenton, "The Road System of Medieval England", *Econ. Hist. Review*, vol. 7 (1936). The ruins are marked in Lewis's *Topographical Dictionary: Atlas Volume* (1842).
[7] Today named after Wensley, higher up the dale.
[8] Dunstable was on the main road for the north-west and, via Leicester, for the north; and was (at a later date at least) noted for its accommodation for traders and travellers.

[?] of Dunmow [J. C. T.]
The leather [market] of Bristol [T. R.]
Girls of Hereford [J. C. T.]
90 Cord of Bridport
[?] Pewter of Exeter
Beggars of Chichester
The market of Pontefract
Tin of Cornwall [T. R.]
95 Hose of Tickhill [J. C. T.]
Gloves of Haverhill [T. R.]
Villeins of Tamworth[1]
Cingles of Doncaster[2]
Cake of Stamford
100 The manor of Woodstock
The hardihood of the Cinque Ports
The castle of Dover
The pride of Peterborough
The marsh of Ramsey
105 Tiles of Reading [J. C. T.]
Parish of Spalding[3]
Mules [or Mullet] of Dengie [J. C. T.]
The entrance to Thorney[4]

There's plenty of places
But too much to drink
And much more to say
But my wits are away[5]

[1] cf. J. Tait, *Medieval English Borough*, pp. 83–4. Tamworth's villein-burgesses were evidently a curiosity.
[2] For a purchase of this and other Doncaster horse-furniture, see Bain's *Calendar of Documents relating to Scotland*, II, p. 365.
[3] An exceptionally large parish (over 10,000 acres in 1842) and possibly mentioned for that reason.
[4] Not, as T. R. suggested, an allusion to the site of the palace of Westminster (which the position of this item in the list would in any case make unlikely) but to Thorney Abbey, which was almost an island in the Fens. The approach to it from Peterborough and the parts of Stamford was evidently a feature of the local landscape. See No. 183 (a), above.
[5] which gives the level, if not quite the letter of
Asetz iad des uiles
Mes trop iad des g'les
Emoud plus a dire
Mes sen ne put suffire
(*gille*: a measure, formerly a measure of wine)

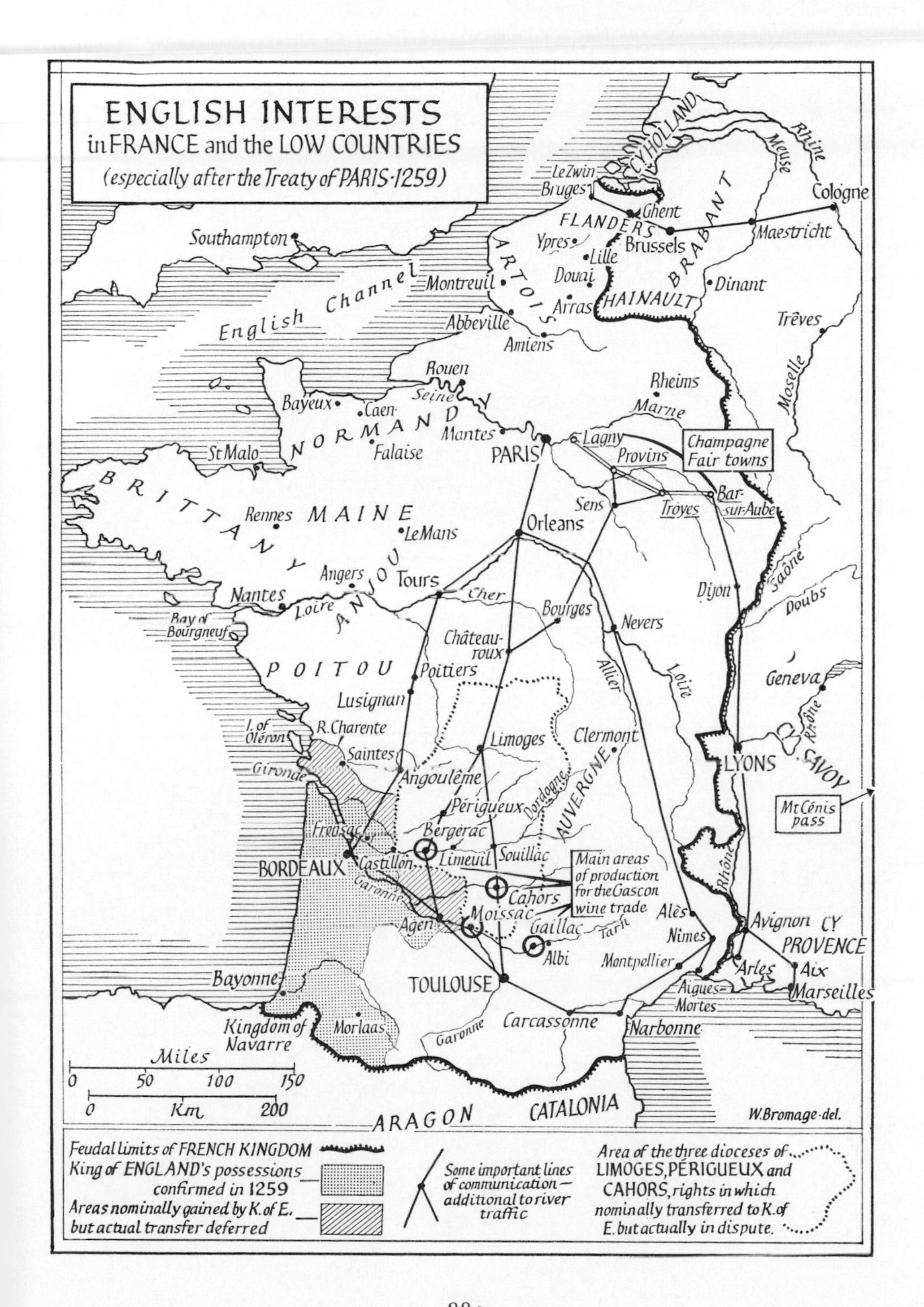
ENGLISH INTERESTS
in FRANCE and the LOW COUNTRIES
(especially after the Treaty of PARIS·1259)
Southampton
English Channel
Montreuil
Abbeville
Amiens
Le Zwin
Bruges
Ghent
FLANDERS
Ypres
Lille
Douai
Arras
ARTOIS
HAINAULT
Brussels
BRABANT
HOLLAND
Meuse
Rhine
Cologne
Maestricht
Dinant
Trêves
Moselle
Rouen
Seine
Bayeux
Caen
NORMANDY
Falaise
Mantes
PARIS
St Malo
BRITTANY
Rennes
MAINE
Le Mans
Rheims
Marne
Lagny
Provins
Champagne Fair towns
Sens
Troyes
Bar-sur-Aube
Orleans
Angers
ANJOU
Tours
Nantes
Loire
Cher
Bay of Bourgneuf
Bourges
Nevers
Dijon
Saône
Doubs
Château-roux
POITOU
Poitiers
Lusignan
I. of Oléron
R. Charente
Saintes
Gironde
Angoulême
Limoges
Clermont
Allier
Loire
AUVERGNE
Geneva
Rhône
LYONS
SAVOY
Mt Cénis pass
Périgueux
Dordogne
Bergerac
Fronsac
BORDEAUX
Castillon
Limeuil
Souillac
Main areas of production for the Gascon wine trade
Garonne
Cahors
Moissac
Agen
Gaillac
Tarn
Albi
Alès
Nimes
Avignon
PROVENCE
Arles
Aix
Marseilles
Montpellier
Aigues-Mortes
Bayonne
TOULOUSE
Carcassonne
Narbonne
Kingdom of Navarre
Morlaas
Garonne
Miles
0 50 100 150
0 Km 200
ARAGON
CATALONIA
W. Bromage · del.
Feudal limits of FRENCH KINGDOM
King of ENGLAND's possessions confirmed in 1259
Areas nominally gained by K. of E. but actual transfer deferred
Some important lines of communication — additional to river traffic
Area of the three dioceses of LIMOGES, PÉRIGUEUX and CAHORS, rights in which nominally transferred to K. of E. but actually in dispute.

Part VI

ILLUSTRATIONS OF THE THOUGHT OF THE PERIOD

INTRODUCTION

THE task of the student of any period of history so much earlier than our own that our present-day assumptions cannot be made or be our starting point is, in Frederick William Maitland's words, to "think the thoughts of our ancestors". This, though Maitland himself achieved it, is immensely difficult to do.

The nearest thing to it for the period covered by this volume is the writing of Sir Maurice Powicke. T. F. Tout recognised the value of Aquinas at least as a "source" for the historian, but chose a very different approach for his own contribution to understanding of the period. T. F. T. Plucknett followed Maitland's footsteps in the legal field, notably in his Ford Lectures on the *Legislation of Edward I*, a germinative work.

Such work shows the way. There is no facile synthesis of the thinking and the action of an age: much preliminary work has to be done, other specialists invoked, forbidding texts edited and interpreted, the thought of an age made plain, before the historian can make it his own. The amount of such preliminary work in English is so far not great, and little has been translated into English. The following selection of material with a direct bearing on English history illustrates at least the variety of material available. The bibliography directs attention to more such material.

SELECT BIBLIOGRAPHY OF WORKS ON THE THOUGHT OF THE PERIOD

To go direct to Aquinas is, of course, to begin work at the limits of thirteenth-century thought and understanding. To realise this and recognise those limits would be the historian's first lesson. His second would be to learn the nature of the task Aquinas had set himself as a churchman and a scholar, nothing less than to assimilate a new learning to the old faith. The learning was in fact Aristotle's, old but only recently recovered and new in its effect. His third lesson would be to realise that the process of assimilation did not begin with Aquinas; his fourth, that the debate did not end with him, his ideas by no means finding the acceptance they enjoy today.

As an introduction, R. L. Poole, *Illustrations of the History of Medieval Thought and Learning* (1920), a classic; on the migrations of Aristotle down to the twelfth century, P. H. Wicksteed, *Dante and Aquinas* (1913), chapter III; on his reception in the West in the eleventh and twelfth centuries, R. W. Southern, *The Making of the Middle Ages* (1953). The essential Aquinas can be read in English in A. C. Pegis, *The Basic Writings of Saint Thomas Aquinas* (2 vols, New York, 1945, with a short, but helpful introduction). For the *Summa Theologiae*, the Blackfriars edition, planned for 60 volumes and already well advanced in publication in London and New York, gives both the Latin text and a modern English translation and is on all counts up-to-date and authoritative. Quite the best approach to the thirteenth century and Aquinas's place in it among other scholars is now F. Van Steenberghen, *The Philosophical Movement in the Thirteenth Century* (1955) and the further reading there given. With D. E. Sharp, *Franciscan Philosophy at Oxford in the Thirteenth Century* (1930), this list would end worthily and, as it should, in this country.

Our extracts from Aquinas concern practical matters. A useful statement of scholastic positions on other practical matters is Bede Jarrett, *Social Theories of the Middle Ages 1200–1500* (1926). Brian Tierney's *Medieval Poor Law* (University of California, 1959) gives not only the canonical theory but the evidence for its application in England.

With "The Song of Lewes" (No. 232 below) we leave, not the society of educated men, but certainly disinterested scholarship. With true political songs we move into the (even then) socially indefinable between-world of the not-learned nor yet boorish but politically articulate. It is a world where Latin, the learned language, could pass but the vernaculars, native English or Anglo-Norman (English French), the latter especially, were ordinary currency: T. Wright, *The Political Songs of England from the Reign of John to that of Edward II* (Camden Soc., 1839), and I. S. T. Aspin, *Anglo-Norman Political Songs* (Oxford, 1953). It was a world which could also produce formal satire, as in "The Passion of the Judges" (No. 234 below). It produced also "The Mirror of Justices" (ed. W. J. Whittaker, with an introduction by F. W. Maitland, for the Selden Society as vol. 7 for 1893), whatever we make of it.

From this same literate world came No. 235, "How to hold a parliament". This, though we do not know the purpose behind it, was meant to be more than a squib. I have found it easier to attribute to Edward II's reign than to Richard II's, and, while it may have an Irish history as well as an English one, I see no reason to give it an Irish origin before production of proof thereof.

No. 236, select passages from *Britton*, a treatise on English common law (which was edited, with a translation, by F. M. Nichols in 1865 and whose place in our legal literature is indicated in T. F. T. Plucknett, *Early English Legal Literature*, Cambridge, 1958), is an example of a kind of practical, professional writing which, while not at all confined to England, is such a feature of this as compared with earlier, and even later, periods of English history. The first example (for us) would be Glanvill at the very outset ("written probably between 1187 and 1189"), edited and translated by G. D. G. Hall, *The treatise on the laws and customs of England commonly called Glanvill* (1965). The greatest would be Bracton on the laws, writing about the middle of the period. But for reasons explained by Plucknett (as above) he is not yet available as Glanvill is. The historian will use F. W. Maitland's *History of English Law* instead, and, of course, very much to his advantage. Thirteenth-century lawyers themselves preferred epitomes of Bracton. Of such epitomes, *Britton*, partly, no doubt, because it was the only one of them in Law-French instead of Law-Latin, was, it seems, the most successful.

A very different professional piece is No. 237, "The sea law of Oléron as preserved in the Oak Book of the port of Southampton", on which Sir Maurice Powicke, *The Thirteenth Century* (Oxford, 1953), p. 620, n. 3, and the further reading there given may be consulted. Other kinds of professional writing were of course, done; such as those lately re-edited by Dorothea Oschinsky, *Walter of Henley and other Treatises on Estate Management and Accounting* (Oxford, 1971), for a review of which and of the subject generally see a valuable article by P. D. A. Harvey, "Agricultural Treatises and Manorial Accounting in Medieval England", *Agricultural History Review*, vol. 20 (1972), Pt II, pp. 170–82.

With the last two items, Nos 238 and 239, we enter a different world again. No. 238 illustrates from the writings of two Englishmen (at least reputedly English in one case) the state of natural science at this period, a field in which another Englishman, Archbishop John Pecham of Canterbury, as well as, of course, Roger Bacon, not to mention Bishop Grosseteste of Lincoln earlier, was interested, and in which in the following century English Franciscans made even greater contributions. D. L. Douie, *Archbishop Pecham* (Oxford, 1952) and, for extracts from Pecham's own treatise on "The Sphere", Lynn Thorndike (ed. and trans.), *The "Sphere" of Sacrobosco and its Commentators* (copyright 1949 by the University of Chicago), App. I; A. C.

Crombie, *Robert Grosseteste and the Origins of Experimental Science, 1100–1700* (Oxford, 1953); and the further reading mentioned in the Historical Association's bibliography, *The Early History of Science* (Helps for Students of History, No. 52; 1950).

After this, No. 239, an extract from Roger Bacon, will be less of a surprise, especially if Mr Southern's whole article (*Trans. Royal Hist. Soc.*, 5th ser., vol. 22, 1972, pp. 159–80) is read along with it, but it points emphatically to the need to adjust oneself to think the thoughts of our ancestors.

231. Selections from the works of Thomas Aquinas

(a) *On law*

It is significant that Aquinas's theory of law, fundamental for his political theory, is stated as part of his theology: Summa Theologiae 1a2æ, Questions 90–108. Extracts from it on human law, the relation of this to the eternal law of God, the conditions of political obligation to such law, the admissibility of change in a law so based are here given – as translated in *Summa Theologiae*, vol. 28, *Law and Political Theory*, ed. Thomas Gilby (1966).

[Question 90] *The nature of Law*

. . . Law is a kind of direction or measure for human activity through which a person is led to do something or held back . . . Now direction and measure come to human acts from reason, from which, as we have shown, they start. It is the function of reason to plan for an end, and this purpose, as Aristotle notes, is the original source of what we do.

. . . Now the deeds we perform, these being the concern of the practical reason, all originate from our last end. We have shown that the last end of human living is happiness or well-being. Consequently law is engaged above all with the plan of things for human happiness. Again, since the subordination of part to whole is that of incomplete to rounded-off reality, and since a human individual man is part of the full life of the community, it must needs be that law properly speaking deals with this subordination to a common happiness . . . And since we speak of law most of all in terms of the common good, it follows that any other precept about more particular business will not have the nature of law except in so far as it enters into this plan for the common good.

. . . The chief and main concern of law properly so called is the plan for the common good. The planning is the business of the whole people or of their vicegerent. Therefore to make law is the office of the entire people or of the public personage who has care of them . . .

. . . to have binding force, which is an essential property of a law, it has to be applied to the people it is meant to direct. This application comes about when their attention is drawn to it by the fact of promulgation. Hence promulgation is required for a measure to possess the force of law.

To sum up . . . law is nought else than an ordinance of reason for the common good, made by the authority who has care of the community and promulgated.

[Question 91] *Varieties of Law*

. . . Granted that the world is ruled by divine Providence, and this we have shown in the First Part, it is evident that the whole community of the universe is governed by God's mind. Therefore the ruling idea of things which exists in God as the effective sovereign of them all has the nature of law. Then since God's mind does not conceive in time, but has an eternal concept, according to *Proverbs* viii. 23, it follows that this law should be called eternal.

. . . Since all things are regulated and measured by Eternal Law, as we have seen, it is evident that all somehow share in it, in that their tendencies to their own proper acts and ends are from its impression. Among them intelligent creatures are ranked under divine Providence the more nobly because they take part in Providence by their own providing for themselves and others. Thus they join in and make their own the Eternal Reason through which they have their natural aptitudes for their due activity and purpose. Now this sharing in the Eternal Law by intelligent creatures is what we call "natural law" . . . the light of natural reason by which we discern what is good and what evil, is nothing but the impression of divine light on us. Accordingly it is clear that natural law is nothing other than the sharing in the Eternal Law by intelligent creatures.

. . . just as from indemonstrable principles that are instinctively recognised the theoretic reason draws the conclusions of the various sciences not imparted by nature but discovered by reasoned effort, so also from natural law precepts as from common and indemonstrable principles the human reason comes down to making more specific arrangements. Now these particular arrangements human reason arrives at are called "human laws", provided they fulfil the essential conditions of law already indicated.

[Qu. 93] . . . the Eternal Law is nothing other than the exemplar of divine wisdom.

. . . all laws in so far as they share in right reason to that extent derive from the Eternal Law.

[Qu. 96] Human positive laws are either just or unjust. If they are just, they have binding force in the court of conscience from the Eternal Law from which they derive . . . Now laws are said to be just on three counts; from their end, when they are ordered to the common good, from their authority, when what is enacted does not exceed the lawgiver's power, and from their form, when for the good of the whole they place burdens in equitable proportions on subjects . . . Laws are unjust in two ways, as being against what is fair in human terms and against God's rights. They are contrary to human good on the three counts made above; from the end, when the ruler taxes his subjects rather for his own greed or vanity than the common benefit; from their author, when he enacts a law beyond the power committed to him; and from their form, when, although meant for the common good, laws are inequitably dispensed. These are outrages rather than laws . . . Such laws do not oblige in the court of conscience, unless perhaps to avoid scandal[1] or riot; on this account a man may be called to yield his rights . . . Laws can be unjust because they are contrary to God's rights; such are the laws of tyrants which promote idolatry or whatsoever is against divine law. To observe them is in no wise permissible . . .

. . . all who are subject to a governing authority are subject to the law it makes. There can be two reasons why a person is not subject, first because he owes no allegiance – thus those who belong to one state or kingdom are independent of the sovereign of another, being subject neither to his dominion nor his laws – and second, because he comes under a higher law; for instance one subject to a proconsul

[1] Not shocking behaviour, but the sin of causing moral harm to another.

ought to be ruled by his mandate, yet not in matters where he enjoys a dispensation from the emperor; the mandate of an inferior does not bind where a superior mandate directs. And so it happens that somebody who is simply subject to a body of law is not bound by one of its provisions because there he is ruled by a higher law . . .

As already stated, every law is ordained for the common well-being, and to that extent gets the force and quality of law; in so far as it falls short here it has no binding force . . . if a case crops up where its observance would be damaging to that common interest, then it is not to be observed . . . All the same notice this: if observing the letter of the law does not involve a sudden risk calling for instant decision and to be dealt with at once, it is not for anybody to construe the law and decide what is or what is not of service to the state. This is only for the governing authorities who, because of exceptional cases, have the power to grant dispensations from the laws. If, however, the danger is urgent, and admits of no delay, or time for recourse to higher authority, the very necessity carries a dispensation with it, for necessity knows no law.

[Qu. 97] In the statement that human law is a kind of dictate of reason directing human acts there are two clauses, and under both a cause for just change can arise . . . First, from the side of reason. To advance step by step from an undeveloped to a developed position seems natural to the human reason. We see this in the theoretic sciences, where the incomplete teachings of early thinkers have been followed by teachings more fully worked out by their successors. So also in practical questions; those who first attempted to draw up useful regulations for the human community were of themselves unable to take everything into consideration; they set up certain institutions which were lacking in many respects, yet which served for their successors to work on and make alterations, so that they might in fewer respects prove defective for the common benefit. Second, from the side of human beings whose acts it regulates. Law may be justly altered because of changed conditions of life, which make for differences in what is beneficial . . .

. . . human law is rightly altered so far as this will provide for the common benefit. Now a change in the law, looked at merely as a change, inflicts a kind of loss on the common well-being, because custom avails much for the observance of law, so much so that breaches of custom seem so much the graver on that account, though they be light matters otherwise. That is why when law is altered the restraining power of law is weakened in so far as custom is done away with. Hence a human law should never be altered, unless the gain to the common well-being on one head makes up for what has been lost on another. Such compensation comes either from some highly important and evident gain produced by the new statute; or from the urgent necessity for change, either because of the manifest wrong the old customary law contained or because its observance was highly harmful . . .

All law proceeds from the reason and will of the law-giver; divine and natural law from the intelligent will of God, human law from the will of man regulated by reason. Man's reason and will in matters of practice are manifested by what he says, and by what he does as well; each carries into execution what he has chosen because to him it seems good . . . words serve to alter a law as well as express its meaning. So also by repeated deeds, which set up a custom, a law can be changed and explained, and also a principle can be established which acquires the force of law, and this because what we inwardly mean and want is most effectively declared by what outwardly and repeatedly we do. When anything is done again and again it is assumed that it comes from the deliberate judgment of reason.

On these grounds custom has the force of law, and abolishes law, and is the interpreter of laws.

(b) *On government*

(*De Regimine Principum . . . et De Regimine Judaeorum . . . Politica Opuscula Duo*, ed. J. Mathis (Turin, 1924); *Summa Theologiae*, vol. 28, *Law and Political Theory*, ed. Thomas Gilby (1966), and vol. 29, *The Old Law*, ed. David Bourke (1969))

In his opuscule On Government (*De Regimine Principum*), written 1265–6, strongly influenced by Aristotle's Politics, which had only just become available in a Latin translation, Aquinas regards monarchy as the best form of government. The work retains its value as a thirteenth-century expression of the ideal of thirteenth-century kingship, noteworthy for the divine function accorded to the secular state, an awkward admission for the dispute between Philip IV of France and the papacy at the end of the century – "Aquinas opened", it has been observed, "a door which the Church tried in vain to close".

In the *Summa Theologiae*, 1a2æ, written, it would seem, some years later we have Aquinas's second thoughts, in which the best form of government is one which is a compound of monarchy, aristocracy and democracy, possible given the medieval social order and the medieval notion of monarchy as primarily elective. The two extracts from the *Summa Theologiae* on this point help to clarify each other and to reconcile it with the simpler reasoning of the *De Regimine Principum*.

[*De Regim. Principum* I. c. 1] Hence it is quite clear that it is the nature of a king to be one, to be in authority, and to be a shepherd seeking the common good and not his own advantage.

[I. c. 8] . . . a king in governing his people is an official of God.

[I. c. 8] . . . the reward of a king is honour and glory . . . what earthly, fleeting honour can equal this honour – that a man should be a citizen of God's and a member of his household,[1] reckoned among the sons of God and gaining the inheritance of the Heavenly Kingdom along with Christ?

[I. c. 9] . . . It remains to consider further what degree of heavenly bliss those will attain who fulfil their duty as kings in a fitting and praiseworthy manner . . . It is an outstanding virtue which enables a man to direct not only himself but others too; and the more so, the more people he rules . . . Thus greater virtue is required for ruling a household than for ruling oneself, and much greater for the rule of a city and kingdom. It is therefore surpassing virtue to fill well the office of king and it deserves a surpassing reward in heaven.

[I. c. 15] Because therefore the end of the life which we live well in the present is heavenly bliss, it is the duty of a king to promote the good life of the people in accordance with what contributes to the attaining of heavenly bliss, namely that he

[1] *civis et domesticus Dei*

should command what leads to heavenly bliss and, as far as possible, forbid what is contrary to it.

[I. c. 6] Because the rule of one is to be preferred as the best form of government, but can turn into tyranny, which is the worst form, the greatest pains must be taken to make such provision on the people's behalf concerning the king that they do not fall under a tyrant. First it is necessary that those to whom the appointment belongs should appoint as king a man of such sort that he is not likely to lapse into tyranny . . . Next, the constitution[1] should be so arranged that there be no opportunity of tyranny to the king thus appointed . . . Finally attention must be paid to the question, if the king should turn to tyranny, how he should be opposed.

If the tyranny is not excessive, it is better to tolerate it for a time, than by acting against a tyrant to be involved in many dangers which are worse than the tyranny itself . . .

If the tyranny is too great to be borne, it has seemed to some that it is for brave men to destroy the tyrant, risking death themselves for the sake of liberating the people . . . But this is not in accordance with apostolic teaching . . . against the ferocity of tyrants action is to be taken not by the private presumption of a few, but by public authority. In the first place, if it is the right of the people to provide for themselves with regard to their king, it cannot be wrong for that same people to destroy the king they have instituted, or to curb his power if he abuses his royal power tyrannically . . .

[*Summa Theolog.* 1a2æ Qu. 95] Thirdly, it is of the essence of law to be instituted by the governor of the political community . . . on this count law can be divided according to the type of the regime. One of these, according to Aristotle, is royal or kingly government, when the state is governed by one person, and corresponding to this you have princely ordinances; another is aristocracy, or the rule of the best or politically best, and corresponding to this you have the advice of learned counsel and senatorial resolutions; another is oligarchy, where a few rich or powerful men are in control, and from this you get praetorian law, also called honorary law; another is popular rule, called democracy, and from this come decrees of the commonalty. Another regime is tyranny, which is so thoroughly corrupt that it affords no law. There is another type of regime blended of the others, and this is the best, and provides law as Isidore understood it, namely that "which men of birth together with the common people have sanctioned".

[1a2æ Qu. 105] There are two things to be observed concerning the right ordering of rulers in a state or people. One is that all should take some share in government; this makes for peace among the people, and commends itself to all, and they uphold it, as Aristotle says. The other regards the kind of government, or how the rulers are instituted. There are various kinds of regimen, as he also points out, but the principal ones are royal or kingly government, in which one man rules as specially qualified,

[1] *regni gubernatio*

and aristocracy, that is the rule of the best, in which a few rule as specially qualified. Hence the best system in any state or kingdom is one in which one man, as specially qualified, rules over all, and under him are others governing as having special endowments, yet all have a share inasmuch as those are elected from all, and also are elected by all. This is the best form of constitution, a mixture of monarchy, in that one man is at the head, of aristocracy, in that many rule as specially qualified, and democracy, i.e. government by the people in that the rulers can be chosen from the people and by them.

(c) *On taxation*

(*De Regimine Principum . . . et De Regimine Judaeorum . . . Politica Opuscula Duo*, ed. J. Mathis (Turin, 1924))

Though from On the Government of Jews (*De Regimine Judaeorum*), this applies to Christian, i.e. ordinary, subjects.

Sixthly, you asked whether it is lawful for you to tax your Christian subjects: in regard to that you ought to bear in mind that earthly rulers are established by God not in order that they may seek their own private advantage, but to procure the common advantage of their people . . . Whence it is that landed revenues have been established for rulers in order that, living on them, they may refrain from despoiling their subjects . . . It sometimes happens, however, that rulers have not enough revenues of their own for the custody of the land and for the other reasonable purposes of a ruler: in which case it is just that subjects should provide what is necessary to secure their common good. And thus it is that in some countries by ancient custom lords impose taxes on their subjects, which, if they are not immoderate, can be exacted without sin . . . Similarly in the event of an emergency involving such expenditure for the common good or for maintaining the honourable estate of the ruler that neither the ruler's own resources nor the accustomed taxes combined suffice to meet it, for instance an enemy invasion or any similar emergency, then rulers may lawfully for the common good exact help from their subjects even beyond the accustomed exactions. To exact more than what is customary, however, simply from greed or because of inordinate and immoderate expenditure: that most certainly they may not lawfully do . . .

232. The Song of Lewes

(Trans. C. L. Kingsford (ed.), *The Song of Lewes* (Oxford, 1890), with certain revisions made by Sir Maurice Powicke, *Henry III and the Lord Edward*, pp. 471–2)

A Latin poem, written while Simon de Monfort was at the height of his power after the battle of Lewes by an enthusiastic supporter. It is obviously not a political song in the ordinary sense – language and content alike would bar any popular appeal – but an exposition for the benefit of educated men of the principles of opposition to Henry III in 1264. As a contemporary statement of the issues it is of the highest value. As a sustained "piece of forcible reasoning under the trammels of a metrical form" it is a literary feat.

His tongue is the pen of the writer who thus readily writes, laudably blessing thee, O right hand of God the Father, Lord of hosts, Who givest prosperity to Thine own, when Thou wilt, at Thy nod; in Thee may all now learn to trust, whom those, who are now brought to ruin, were desirous to ruin, whose head is captured, whose members are captive; the proud people are fallen, the faithful are glad. Now England breathes again hoping for liberty, to whom may God's grace grant prosperity! The English likened unto dogs were become vile, but now have they raised their head over their vanquished foes.

In the year of grace one thousand two hundred and sixty-four, on the Wednesday[1] also after the feast of Pancras, the populace of the English bore the shock of very grievous fight at the castle of Lewes; for to wrath yielded reason, life to the sword. On the day before the Ides of May they came together, they began the battle of terrible strife; in the county of Sussex was it done, and in the bishopric of Chichester. The sword waxed strong, many fell, truth prevailed, and the false fled. For the Lord of hosts withstood the perjured, and the shield of truth stood before the pure; the former the sword without and fear within has destroyed, the latter the favour of heaven has strengthened more fully. The feast of Victor and St Corona renders testimony on behalf of this contest; when the church honoured the said saints, victory crowned the true soldiers. The wisdom of God, that rules the whole world, has done marvellous things, and made a joyful war; has made the strong to flee, and the men of might to enclose themselves in a cloister, and also in safe places. Not by arms, but by the grace of Christianity, that is in a church, remained the sole refuge for the excommunicate; their horses abandoned, this plan occurred to the conquered. And to her, whom previously they had not feared to profane, whom they ought to have honoured in the place of a mother, to her although too little worthy, they flee, and fortify themselves with the embrace of the word of salvation. Those whom prosperity made to scorn their mother, wounds compelled to honour their mother. At Northampton[2] having prospered by treachery they despised the church; faithless sons they troubled the bowels of their holy mother with the sword, prospering they deserved not a prosperous war. Then did the mother bear her wrong patiently as though through indifference, but now she punishes abundantly this and the other offences which they afterwards added, for madmen they harmed many churches; and the monastery which is called Battle did the band of raging men, which is now disbanded, without mercy spoil of its goods, and in such wise prepared for themselves a battle.

[1] Wednesday, 14 May 1264
[2] Battle of Northampton, 5 April 1264

The Cistercian monks of Robertsbridge[1] would not have been secure from the fury of the sword, if they had not given five hundred marks to the prince, which Edward commanded to be taken, or they would have perished. For these and like deeds they deserved to yield and fall before their foes. May the Lord bless Simon de Montfort, his sons no less, and his company! Who nobly exposing themselves to death fought bravely, pitying the mournful lot of the English, who trampled on in a manner that can hardly be described, and well-nigh deprived of all liberties, nay of their life, languished under hard princes, even as the people of Israel under Pharaoh, groaning under a tyrannical devastation. But God beholding this suffering of the people, gives in the end of the age a new Mathathias, who, with his sons, zealous after the zeal of the law, yielded not to the wrong-doing nor to the fury of the king.

They call Simon a misleader and deceiver, but his deeds test him and prove him truthful. The treacherous fail in time of need; they who flee not death, are in the truth. But now says the envious man and plotter, whose evil eye is the disturber of peace: "If thou praisest the constancy, and the fidelity, which flees not the instancy of death, or punishment, those men shall equally be called constant, who go likewise to battle, fighting in their turn, likewise exposing themselves to hazard, and subjecting themselves to a hard epithet." But in our battle, wherewith we are now concerned, let us see of what kind is the difference of the case.

The earl had few men tried in arms; the party of the king was swollen great, having the trusty warriors and greater men of England gathered together, and those who were called the flower of the knighthood of the realm. Those who were furnished with arms from London would be the three hundred preferred to the many thousands; whence they were contemptible to those men, and detestable to the experienced. The earl's knights were for the most part striplings, novices in arms they knew too little of war. Now girt with his sword the tender youth stands at dawn in battle accustoming himself to arms; what wonder if a recruit so raw be fearful, and if the powerless lamb is wary of the wolf! Thus then are they inferior in knighthood who fight for England, and are also far fewer than the strong men, who were boasting enough of their own valour, so that they thought safely and without peril, as it were to swallow up all who rendered their aid to the earl. For also of those, whom the earl had led to the contest, from whom he had hoped for no small assistance, many presently withdrew themselves in terror, and as it were amazed betook themselves to flight; and of three parts the third deserted; the earl with his faithful few never yielded. We may compare the battle of Gideon with our own; in both of which we see the few of the faithful conquer the many in number that have not the faith, like Lucifer, trusting in themselves. "If I were to give victory to the many," says God, "the foolish would not give the glory to Me but to the foolish." So if God had given it to the strong to conquer, the common folk would have given the praise to such men and not unto God.

From this it can be gathered that the men of war feared not God, whence they did nothing which may prove their constancy or fidelity, but on the contrary their pride and cruelty; wishing to confound the party which they despised, rashly issuing forth

[1] Robertsbridge: about 5 miles from Battle on the R. Rother

they speedily perished. Exaltation of heart is the preparation of destruction, and lowliness deserves the divine grace to be given unto it; for he who trusts not in God, the pride of this man does God break down. We bring forward Aman and Mardocheus; we read that the one was proud, the other a true Jew. The gallows, which Aman had prepared for Mardocheus in the morning, the wretched man endures when hung thereon. The queen's banquet blinded Aman, the banquet which he regarded as a great privilege; but his vain hope is turned to confusion, when after the feast he is dragged to the hanging. Thus did sorrow seize on the last part of his joy, when it associated the end of the banquet with death. Very dissimilar is the fate of the Jew, whom the king honours highly, God so granting. Goliath is laid low by the hurling of a pebble; whom God pursues, for him does nothing avail. To the aforesaid divers reasons add that the foul bawds had gathered to themselves so many strumpets, even seven hundred, whom they ought to have known to be guileful disciples of Satan for deceiving souls, and firebrands for inflaming them, treacherous sharp knives for shearing the locks of Samson, and bringers of the stains of disgraceful conduct on the wretched who are not stout-hearted, nor confirmed by the grace of the divine gift, spiritual beings given to the lusts of the flesh, prepared with the brutish filthiness thereof they ought not to be worthy of victory, who were defiled with the foul debauchery of the flesh; they diminished their strength by the stews which they made, whence they were unworthy of knightly things. Let the knight be girded with his sword upon his thigh, let there be no loosening, let there be no vile acts; the body of the new-made knight is wont to be bathed, so that he may learn to be cleansed from forbidden deeds. They who had lately taken lawful wives, were not so fit for the Lord's war; the battle of Gideon is witness, much less are they, whom the furnace had injured with the fire of debauchery. Why therefore should God aid the adulterers, and not rather strengthen the clean children? Let them be cleansed who desire to conquer by fighting; they who subdue their faults are in the way of triumph; let them first conquer their vices, who desire to be with justice conquerors over sinners. If the just at times seems to be conquered by the impious, let him on the contrary be deemed the conqueror; for neither shall the just have been able to be conquered, nor the unjust to conquer so long as he shall be the enemy of justice.

Hear the equity of earl Simon! When the party of the king sought the sole penalty of his head and life, and would not admit the redemption of his head, but would have its severance; by whose confusion the most of the people would be confounded, and the greatest part of the realm would be put in peril; most grievous ruin would at once follow, which would not be repaired by the longest delay. Stephen,[1] by the divine grace, bishop of Chichester, sighing deeply for the boundless evils that were then already without fiction imminent, when the parties had been persuaded concerning the forming of peace, heard this answer from the earl: "Choose the best men, whose faith is lively, who have read the decretals, or have becomingly taught theology, and sacred philosophy, and who know how to rule the Christian faith; and whatever

[1] Stephen Berksted, bp of Chichester 1262–87, close enough to Simon at this time to be made with him and Gloucester one of the three electors after the battle of Lewes who were to choose the king's council of nine.

such men shall not fear through wholesome doctrine to counsel, or whatever they shall not fear to decide, what they shall say, that shall they find us ready to adopt; in such manner that we may not know the brand of perjury, but as sons of God may hold faith." Hence can they, who readily swear and hesitate little to reject what they swear, who quickly withdraw though they swear what is lawful, and render not wholly their promises to God, estimate with how great care they ought to preserve their oath, when they see a man flee neither torment nor death, for the sake of his oath, which was offered not rashly, but for the reforming of the state of the English nation which had fallen, which the treachery of an envious foe had violated. Behold! Simon obedient scorns the loss of property, subjecting himself to penalties, that he may not let go the truth, proclaiming openly to all men by deeds more than by words, that truth has no communication with falsehood. Woe to the wretched perjurers, who fear not God, denying Him for the hope of earthly reward, or fear of prison or of a light penalty; the new guide of the journey teaches us to bear whatever the world may have inflicted for the sake of truth, which is able to give perfect liberty. For the earl had formerly pledged his oath, that whatever the zeal of the wise had provided for the reformation of the royal honour, and the shunning of wandering error, in the parts of Oxford, that he would firmly preserve, and would not change the law of this decision; knowing that such canonical constitutions and such catholic ordinances for the peaceful preservation of the realm, on account of which he had previously sustained no slight persecution, were not to be scorned, and that, because he had sworn, they were to be stoutly maintained, unless the most perfect teachers of the faith should say, that those takers of an oath could be absolved, who had previously offered such an oath, and that what they had sworn was not to be attended to. Which, when the said bishop recited to the king, and the artificer of fraud was perhaps standing by, the voice of the throng of the arrogant is raised on high: "See! now is a knight subjected to the sayings of clerks. Knighthood put under clerks has become of little esteem." Thus was the wisdom of the earl despised; and Edward is said to have answered: "Peace is forbidden to them, unless they all bind themselves with halters on their necks, and bind themselves over to us for hanging or for drawing." What wonder if the earl's heart was then moved, since no penalty save that of the gallows was provided. He offered what he ought, but he was not heard; the king, forgetful of his safety, rejected moderation. But as the issue of the event on the morrow taught, the measure, which he then willed not, was not afterwards found. At even the devotion of the earl is derided, whose charge on the morrow will be felt to be victorious. This stone long refused by the enemy, was afterwards fitted to the two side-walls. The division of desolation of England was on our borders; but for a defence against division was present a corner-stone, the wholly singular religion of Simon. The faith and fidelity of Simon alone is become the security of the peace of all England; the rebels he humbles, he raises those lying in despair; the realm he reconciles, repressing the proud; and in what manner does he repress them? Certainly not by jesting, but the red juice he presses out by hard fighting; for truth compelled him to fight, or to abandon the truth, but he chose prudently to give his right hand to truth, and by the rough road that is joined unto probity, by the short and toilsome path unpleasant to the proud to obtain the reward which is given to the forceful, rather than to displease God by shrinking, and to advance the aims of the wicked by flight. For certain men had aimed to blot out the name of the English, whom they had already begun to hold in hatred; against whom God opposed a remedy, when He willed not the sudden ruin of them.

Hence may the English learn to call in foreigners, if they wish to be exiled by strangers; for they who wish to increase their own glory, and would wish their memory to stand for ever, are eager to associate many of their own nation with themselves, and soon to place them amongst the greatest; so the confusion of the natives increases, indignation increases, bitterness of heart increases, when the chief men of the realm feel that they are oppressed by those who make themselves equal to them, taking away what ought to have been theirs, growing by the things by which they were accustomed to grow. The king ought to honour with escheats and wardships his own men, who can aid him in divers ways, who, the stronger they are in might, are so much the surer in all chances. But if those, who brought nothing are endowed with his goods, if those, who were of no account, are made great, such men, when they have begun to grow, always climb on until they have supplanted the natural subjects; they are eager to turn away the heart of the prince from his own people, so that they may strip of glory those whom they wish to fall. And who would be able to bear such things patiently? Therefore let England learn prudently to take care that no such perplexity further befall her, that no such adversity touch the English. The earl was eager to obviate this evil, which had grown too strong, as it were a great sea, which could not be dried up by a small effort, but was to be crossed by the great assistance of God. Let foreigners come but quickly to withdraw, as though for the moment, but not to remain. One of the two hands helps the other, neither taking away the grace which more truly belongs to them both. Let each by keeping his own place aid and not injure, by so coming let the French be of service by doing good to the English, and by not misleading him through a sophistical countenance; and not the one by withdrawing the goods of the other; nay, rather by bearing his own burden. If it was his own advantage which had moved the earl he would have had no other zeal, nor would he have sought with his whole intent for the reformation of the realm, but a designing for lordship would seek its own advancement alone, and he would set before him the advancement of his own friends, would aim at the enrichment of his sons, and would neglect the safety of the community, and would veil the poison of falsehood with the cloak of duplicity; thus he would abandon the faith of Christianity, and would subject himself to the law of a terrible penalty, nor would he escape the weight of the storm. And who is able to believe that he would give himself to death, would be willing to ruin his friends, that he might thus exalt himself? Those who hunt after honour, and those who are always meditating how to escape death, cloak themselves cunningly; no men love the temporal life more, no men choose the station that is not of death more. Those who thirst for honours, dissimulate their aim; cautiously they make for themselves the name which they aim at; not so does the venerable Simon de Montfort, who, like unto Christ, gives himself to death for the many; Isaac dies not when he is ready to die, the ram is delivered to death, Isaac to honour. Neither fraud nor falsehood moved the earl, but the divine grace which knows who it may help. If you recall the hour and place of the conflict, you will be able to find that it promised him to be the conquered rather than the conqueror; but God provided that he should not succumb. Not by night does he steal down of a sudden in secret; nay, when the day has returned he fights in the open. Thus also was the place favourable to his enemies; so that hence it is clear to all that it is the gift of God, that victory yielded to him who does not trust in himself. Hence may the knighthood, which praises the exercise of the tournament, that it may thus be rendered ready for battle, learn how the party of the strong trained men was here crushed by the arms of the feeble and unpractised. In order that he may confound the strong places, God promotes the powerless, that he may strengthen the weak places, he lays low the powerful. So let no man now presume to trust in himself, but if he know how to place his hope in God, let him take up arms with constancy by doubting nothing, but by helping, since God is on behalf of justice. And thus it became God to help the earl, without Whom he could not overcome the enemy. Whose enemy shall I say? The earl's alone? Or shall I recognise the enemy of the English and of the whole realm? Perchance too of the church, therefore also of God? Because if this is so, what manner of grace would be fitting for him? He failed to deserve grace by trusting in himself, and by not fearing God did not deserve to be assisted. Therefore falls the boast of personal might. And evermore be blessed the Lord God of Vengeance, Who gives help to the destitute of strength, to the few against the many by crushing the foolish with the might of the faithful, Who sits afar in heaven on His throne; and by His own might treads upon the necks of the proud, subduing the great things beneath the feet of the less; He has subdued two kings and the heirs of kings, whom He has rendered captive as transgressors of the laws; and the pomp of the knighthood with its great following has He given unto shame; for the weapons, which the barons in their zeal for justice had taken up on behalf of the realm, they employed on the sons of pride, until victory was given from heaven with great glory which was not expected; for the bow of the mighty was then overcome, the assembly of the weak was made firm with strength. And we have said from heaven, lest any man glory; but unto Christ Whom we believe, let all the honour be given! For Christ at once commands, conquers, reigns; Christ delivers His own, to whom He has given faith. We pray God grant them, that the proud spirit of the conquerors kiss not their own hands, but that, what Paul advises, be observed by them: "He that rejoiceth, let him rejoice in the Lord." If any of our party be glad with vainglorying, may the Lord be indulgent, and not wrathful! And may He make our party cautious against the future; and that the doing may not fail, let them make themselves a wall! May the power of the Almighty complete what He has commenced, and may He restore the kingdom of the English nation! So that there may be glory to Himself, peace to His elect, conducted under His guidance until they are in their country. Read this, ye English, concerning Lewes's fight, under the protection whereof ye live defended. Because if victory had yielded to those who are now vanquished, the remembrance of the English would have been vanquished and become worthless.

Whereunto shall the noble Edward be compared? Perhaps he will be rightly called a leopard. If we divide the name it becomes lion and pard; lion, because we saw that he was not slow to attack the strongest places, fearing the onslaught of none, with the boldest valour making a raid amidst the castles, and wherever he does succeeding as it were at his wish, as though like Alexander he would speedily subdue the whole world, if Fortune's moving wheel would stand still for ever; wherein let the highest forthwith know that he will fall, and that he who reigns as lord will reign but a little time. And this has, it is clear, befallen the noble Edward, who, it is agreed, has fallen from his unstable position. A lion by pride and fierceness, he is by inconstancy and changeableness a pard, changing his word and promise, cloaking himself by pleasant speech. When he is in a strait he promises whatever you wish, but as soon as he has escaped he renounces his promise. Let Gloucester[1] be witness, where, when free from his difficulty, he at once revoked what he had sworn. The treachery or falsehood whereby he is advanced he calls prudence; the way whereby he arrives whither he will, crooked though it be, is regarded as straight; wrong gives him pleasure and is called right; whatever he likes he says is lawful, and he thinks that he is released from law, as though he were greater than the king. For every king is ruled by the laws which he makes; king Saul is rejected because he broke the laws; and David is related to have been punished as soon as he acted contrary to the law; hence, therefore, let him who makes laws, learn that he cannot rule who observes not the law; nor ought they, whose concern it is, to make this man king. O Edward! thou dost wish to become king without law; verily they would be wretched who were ruled by such a king! For what is more right than law, whereby all things are ruled? And what is more true than justice, whereby matters are decided? If thou desirest the kingdom, reverence the laws; the attacking of the law will give rough roads, rough and impassable roads, which will not lead thee through; if thou dost guard the laws, they shine as a lamp. Therefore avoid and abhor treachery, be zealous for truth, hate falsehood. Although treachery may flourish, it cannot bear fruit; this let the psalm teach thee: "My eyes," says God, "are on the faithful of the earth, whom verily I wish to sit with Me in the end of the world." See what now avails the treachery of Northampton, nor does the heat of deceit glow like a fire. If you wished to compare treachery to a fire, you would have been careful to feed such a fire with straw, which as soon as it has burnt up, ceases to blaze, and when it has scarcely begun comes to an end. So passeth away vanity that hath no roots; truth that is rooted undergoes no changes. Therefore desire only that which is lawful, and let not what the double-minded man shall say please thee. "A prince will think what is worthy of a prince"; therefore take upon thyself the law which shall render thee worthy of the rule over many; worthy of the office of prince, of the assistance of many, of a great company. And wherefore dost thou not love those whose king thou dost wish to be? Thou dost not choose to profit them, but only to be over them. He who seeks no one's glory but his own, through the pride of that man, whatever he rules perishes. So has all that which thou didst lately rule, perished; the glory which alone thou didst seek has passed away.

[1] Edward had saved himself at Gloucester in March 1264 by hoodwinking Simon's son, Henry de Montfort, with promises he afterwards repudiated.

See! we touch the root of the disturbance of the kingdom about which we are writing, and of the dissension of the parties who fought the said battle; to different objects did they turn their aim. The king with his party wished to be thus free, and urged that he ought to be so, and was of necessity, or that deprived of a king's right he would cease to be king, unless he should do whatever he might wish; that the magnates of the realm had not to heed, whom he set over his own counties, or on whom he conferred the wardenship of castles, or whom he would have to show justice to his people; and he would have as chancellor and treasurer of his realm anyone soever at his own will, and counsellors of whatever nation, and various ministers at his own discretion, without the barons of England interfering in the king's acts, as "the command of the prince has the force of law"; and that what he might command of his own will would bind each. For every earl also is thus his own master, giving aught of his own in what measure and to whom he will – castles, lands, and revenues, he entrusts to whom he will, and although he be a subject, the king permits it all. Wherein if he shall have done well, it is of profit to the doer, if not, he himself shall see to it; the king will not oppose him whilst injuring himself. Why is the prince made of worse condition, if the affairs of a baron, a knight, and a freeman are so managed? Wherefore they intrigue for the king to be made a servant, who wish to lessen his power, and to take away his dignity of prince; they wish to thrust down into wardship and subjection the royal power made captive through sedition, and to disinherit the king, that he may not have power to rule so fully as hitherto have done the kings who preceded him, who were in no wise subject to their own people, but managed their own affairs at their will, and conferred their own at their own pleasure. This is the king's pleading which seems true, and this allegation protects the right of the realm.

But now let my pen be turned to the opposite side. Let the proposal of the barons be subjoined to what has already been said; and when the parties have been heard let the statements be compared, and after comparison let them be closed by a definite termination, so that the truer part may be clear; the people are more prone to obey the more true. Therefore let the party of the barons now speak on its own behalf, and let it duly follow whither it is led by zeal. Which party in the first place openly makes protestation, that it devises naught against the royal honour, or seeks anything contrary to it; nay, is zealous to reform and magnify the kingly state; just as, if the kingdom were devastated by enemies, it would not then be reformed without the barons, to whom this would be proper and suitable; and he who should then falsify himself, him the law would punish as guilty of perjury, as a betrayer of the king. He who can contribute aught of aid to the king's honour, owes it to his lord when he is in peril, when the kingdom is deformed as it were in extremity.

The king's adversaries are enemies who make war, and counsellors who flatter the king, who by deceitful words mislead the prince, and with double tongues lead him into error; these are worse adversaries than the perverse, they make themselves out to be good, when they are misleaders, and they are procurers of their own honour; they deceive the unwary whom they render more careless through pleasant words, whence they are not guarded against but are looked on as speaking useful things.

These can deceive more than can the open, as they know how to feign themselves as not hostile. What, if such wretches and such liars should cleave to the side of the prince, full of all malice, fraud and falsehood, pricked with the stings of envy they would devise a deed of wickedness, through which they might bend to their own ostentation the rights of the realm; and should fashion some hard arguments, which would gradually confound the community, crush and impoverish the commonalty of the people, and subvert and infatuate the kingdom, so that no one might be able to obtain justice unless he were willing to foster the pride of such men by means of money amply bestowed? Who would endure so great a wrong to be imagined? And if such men by their aims were to alter the realm, so as to supplant right by unright; and after trampling on the natives were to call in strangers, and were to subdue the kingdom to foreigners; were not to regard the magnates and nobles of the land, and were to put mean men in the highest place, and were to cast down and humble the great, were to pervert order and turn it upside down; were to abandon the best, be urgent on the worst; would not those who should do thus, lay waste the kingdom? Although they might not be fighting with weapons of war from abroad, yet would they be contending with the devil's weapons, and pitifully violating the state of the realm, although their manner was different[1] they would do no less damage. Whether the king consenting through misguidance, or not perceiving such deceit, were to approve such measures destructive to the kingdom; or whether the king out of malice were to do harm, by preferring his own power to the laws, or by abusing his strength on account of his opportunity; or if thus or otherwise the kingdom be wasted, or the kingdom be made utterly destitute, then ought the magnates of the kingdom to take care, that the land be purged of all errors. And if to them belongs the purging of error, and to them belongs provision the governess of customs, how would it not be lawful for them to take foresight lest any evil happen which might be harmful; which, after it may have happened, they ought to remove, lest of a sudden it make the unweary to grieve. Thus that none of the aforesaid things may come about, which may impede the forming of peace or good customs; but that the zeal of the skilled may come in, which may be more expedient to the interest of the many; why should not improvement be admitted wherein no corruption is mingled? For the clemency of the king, and the majesty of the king ought to approve endeavours, which so temper baleful laws, that they be milder, and while less burdensome, be more welcome to God. For the oppression of the people pleases not God, nay rather does the compassion whereby the people may have leisure for God. Pharaoh, who thus afflicted the people of God, because he was scarcely able to hearken to the prophecy which Moses declared, was afterwards thus punished; he is compelled to let Israel go against his will, and he who trusted to catch him whom he had let go, was overwhelmed whilst he thinks to run through the deep. Solomon was unwilling to crush Israel, nor did he compel any of the race to be a slave; because he knew that it was God's people whom he ruled, and feared to injure the seal of God. The Father of Truth both praises mercy more than judgment, and peace more than punishment.

[1] literally, "differently"

Since it is agreed that all this is lawful for the barons, it remains to reply to the reasonings of the king. The king wishes, by the removal of his guardians, to be free, and wishes not to be subject to his inferiors, but to be over them, to command his subjects, and not to be commanded; nor does he wish to be humbled to those set in authority, for those, who are set in authority, are not set over the king, nay rather are men of distinction who support the right of the one; otherwise the king would not be without a rival[1] but they, whom the king was under, would reign equally. Yet this incongruity which seems so great, may, with God's assistance, be easily solved. For we believe that God, through Whom we thus dissolve this doubt, desires the truth. One alone is called, and is King in truth, through Whom the world is ruled by pure majesty. Who needs not assistance whereby He may be able to reign, nay nor counsel, Who cannot err. Therefore all-powerful and knowing He excels in infinite glory all, to whom He has granted to rule His people under Him and as it were to reign, who are able to fail and able to err, and who cannot stand by their own strength and overcome their enemies by their own valour, nor govern kingdoms by their own understanding, but go badly astray in the pathlessness of error; they need assistance that supports them, yea and counsel that keeps them right. The king says: "I agree to thy reasoning, but the election of these men falls under my choice; I will associate with me whom I will, by whose defence I will govern all things; and if my own men be insufficient, have not understanding, or be not powerful, or if they be evil-wishers, and be not faithful, but may perchance be treacherous, I wish thee to make clear, why I ought to be constrained to certain persons, and from whom I have power to get better assistance." The reasoning on which matter is quickly declared, if it be considered what the constraining of the king is. All constraint does not deprive of liberty, nor does all restriction take away power. Those that are princes wish for free power, those that are lords wish not for wretched slavery. To what purpose does free law wish kings to be bound? That they may not be able to be stained by an adulterine law. And this constraining is not of slavery, but is the enlarging of kingly virtue. So is the king's child preserved that he may not be hurt, yet he becomes not a slave when he is so constrained. Yea thus also are the angel spirits constrained, who are confirmed that they be not apostate. For that the Author of all is not able to err, that the Beginning of all is not able to sin, is not impotence but the highest power, the great glory of God and His great majesty. Thus he who is able to fall, if he be guarded that he fall not, is aided by such guardianship to live freely; neither is such sustenance of slavery, but is the protectress of virtue. Therefore let the king like everything that is good, but let him not dare evil; this is the gift of God. They who guard the king, that he sin not when tempted, are themselves the servants of the king, to whom let him be truly grateful, because they free him from being made a slave, because they do not surpass him, by whom he is led. But whoever is truly king is truly free, if he rule himself and his kingdom rightly; let him know that all things are lawful for him which are fitted for ruling the kingdom, but not for destroying it. It is one thing to rule, which is the duty of a king, another to destroy by resisting the law. Law is so called

[1] literally, "unique"

from binding,[1] which is so perfectly described as the law of liberty, as it is freely served.

Let every king understand that he is the servant of God; let him love that only which is pleasing to Him; and let him seek His glory in ruling, not his own pride by despising his equals. Let the king, who wishes the kingdom which is put under him to obey him, render his duty to God, otherwise let him truly know that obedience is not due to him, who denies the service by which it is held of God. Again, let him know that the people is not his own but God's, and let him be profitable to it as a help. And he who is for a short time set over the people, is soon closed in marble and laid beneath the earth. Let him make himself among them as one of them; let him regard David dancing with his handmaids; would that one like unto king David may succeed, a prudent man and humble, who may not wrong his own; verily one who would not hurt the people that was under him, but would spend on them the affection of love, and would seek the profit of his own salvation; him the commons would not allow to suffer loss. It is hard to love one who loves not himself, hard not to despise one who despises himself, hard not to resist one who forsakes himself; it is natural to applaud one who supports himself. It is the part of a prince not to crush, but to protect; it is the part of a prince not to oppress, but to earn by numerous benefits the favour of his own, even as Christ by His grace earned the love of all. If the prince has loved, he ought to be loved in return; if he has reigned rightly, he ought to be honoured; if the prince has erred, he ought to be called back, yea to be denied by those whom he has unjustly burdened, unless he is willing to be corrected; if he is willing to be improved, he ought at the same time to be raised up and assisted by them. Let a prince so rule that he does not need to rule without calling on his own subjects; ignorant princes, who confound their subjects, will find that the untamed will not let themselves be tamed. If the prince shall think that he alone has more of truth, and more of skill, and more knowledge than the commonalty, that he more abounds in grace and more in the gifts of God; if it be not presumption, nay be so in truth, then his own true instruction will shine through the hearts of his subjects with light, and will inform his own people with moderation.

We put forward Moses, David, Samuel; each of whom we know was a faithful prince. Who endured many things from their own subjects, yet did not for their deserts cast them off, nor set strangers over them, but ruled through those who were their own men. "I will set thee over a greater people and will slay this people," says God. "I would die rather than that this people should perish," let the kindly Moses, worthy of his office of prince, reply. And thus the wise prince will never reject his own men, but the foolish one will disturb the kingdom. Whence if the king be less wise than he ought, what service is he for ruling the kingdom? Shall he of his own proper understanding seek by whom he may be supported, by whom his own lack may be supplied? If he alone choose, he will be easily deceived, who has no knowledge who may be useful. Therefore let the community of the realm take counsel, and let that be decreed which is the opinion of the commonalty, to whom their own laws are most known; nor are all the men of the province such fools as not to know better

[1] *lex a ligando*

than others their own realm's customs, which those who are before bequeath to those who come after. Those, who are ruled by the laws, have more knowledge of them; those who apply them become more skilled in them. And because it is their own affair which is at stake, they will care more and will procure for themselves the means whereby peace is acquired. They can know little who are not experienced, they will profit the kingdom little except they are steadfast. From this it can be gathered that the kind of men who should be chosen for the service of the kingdom is the concern of the community; namely those who have the will and knowledge and power to be of profit, let such men be made counsellors and coadjutors of the king; men to whom the various customs of their country are known; who feel themselves injured if the kingdom is injured and who guard the kingdom lest the parts suffer with the whole; let them rejoice with it when it rejoices, if they be lovers of it. Let us put in our midst the noble judgment of king Solomon – she who shuddered not at the cruelty of the division of the child, because she grieved not with it, and had not motherly affection, showed, as the king witnessed, that she was not the mother; therefore let the prince choose such men as may grieve with the commonalty and have a motherly fear of the kingdom suffering hardship. But if there be one whom the ruin of many move not, if he alone obtain the pleas which he wishes, that man is not fitted for the rule of many, since he is wholly given to his own order alone. The man of common feeling is agreeable to the community, but the incompassionate man, whose heart is hardened, cares not if hard fortune comes upon the many; such walls alone are no defence against misfortunes.

If therefore the king has not the knowledge to choose by himself men who know how to counsel him, it is hence clear what ought then to be done; for it concerns the community that wretched men be not made guides of the royal dignity, but the best and chosen men, and the most approved who can be found. For since the governance of the realm is the safety or ruin of all, it matters much whose is the guardianship of the realm; just as it is on the sea, all things are confounded if fools are in command:[1] if any of the passengers placed in the ship, or if any of those belonging to it, misuse the rudder, it matters not if the ship be prosperously governed. Thus let care be given to those who ought to rule the realm, if anyone of the realm does not rule himself rightly, and goes in the wrong way, which perchance he has chosen. The affairs of the commonalty are best managed if the realm is directed by the way of truth; and moreover, if the subjects seek to waste their own, those set over them can refrain their folly and rashness, that the power of the realm be not weakened through the insolence or stupidity of the foolish, and courage against the realm be given to its enemies. For when any member of the body is injured, the body is made of less strength; thus, granted that it may even be lawful for men to misuse their own, although it be harmful to the realm, many will soon follow the injurious liberty and so multiply the disgrace of error, as to cause loss to the whole. Nor ought that properly to be named liberty which unwisely permits the foolish to have dominion; but let liberty be limited by the bounds of right, and when those limits are despised let it be deemed error. Otherwise thou wilt say that the madman is free, although everything pros-

[1] or (reading *naui* and *ignaui*), "or just as it is in a ship, if the slothful are in command"

perous be hateful to him. Therefore the king's pleading concerning his subjects carried whithersoever they will at their own pleasure, is through this sufficiently answered, sufficiently invalidated; while whoever is a subject is ruled by a greater, because we say that it is not lawful for any man to do whatever he wishes, but that each man has a lord to correct him in error; help him in well-doing, and raise him up whenever he falls. The commonalty comes first. We say also that law rules the royal dignity; for we believe that law is a light, without which we infer that the guide goes astray. Law, whereby is ruled the world and the kingdoms of the world, is described as fiery, because it contains a mystery of deep meaning; it shines, burns, glows; fire by shining prevents wandering, it avails against cold, purifies, and reduces to ashes, some hard things it softens, and cooks what was raw, takes away numbness, and does many other good things. Sacred law supplied like gifts to the king. This wisdom Solomon asked for; its friendship he sought for with all his might. If the king be without this law, he will go astray; if he hold it not, he will err shamefully. Its presence gives right reigning, and its absence the disturbance of the realm. That law speaks thus: "By me kings reign, by me is justice shown to those who make laws." That stable law shall no king alter, but through it shall he strengthen his changing self. If he conform to this law he shall stand, and if he disagree with it he will stagger. It is commonly said, "As the king wills, the law goes"; truth wills otherwise, for the law stands, the king falls. Truth and charity and the zeal of salvation are the integrity of law, the rule of virtue; truth is light, charity warmth, zeal burns; this variety of the law takes away all crime. Whatever the king determines, let it be consonant with these; for if he do otherwise the commons will be rendered sorrowful. The people will be confounded, if either the king's eye lacks truth, or if the prince's heart lacks charity, or does not always moderately fulfil its zeal with severity; these three being in support, let whatever pleases the king be done, but when they are in opposition, the king is resisting the law. But kicking against the pricks hurts not; thus does the instruction of Paul from heaven teach us. So there will be no disinheritance of the king if provision be made in accordance with just law. For dissimulation will not change the law, the firm reason of which will stand without end. Whence if anything useful has been long deferred, let it not be reprehended when it is late preferred. And let the king prefer nothing of his own to the common weal, as though the safety of all gave way to him who is but one;[1] for he is not set over them to live for himself, but so that this people which is put under him may be secure. Thou wilt know that the name of king is relative; thou wilt also understand that his name is protective; whence it was not lawful for him to live for himself alone, who ought by living to protect many; he who wishes to live for himself ought not to be in command, but to dwell apart and be as one alone. It is the glory of a prince to save very many; with trouble to himself to relieve many; let him not therefore allege his own profit, but his regard for his subjects by whom he is trusted; if he shall have saved the kingdom, he has done what is the duty of a king; whatever he shall have done otherwise, in that he has failed. From this is the true theory of a king sufficiently plain, that the position of king is unknown to one who is at leisure for his individual interest. For true charity is as it

[1] or (reading *quia*), "because the safety of all has been assigned to him alone"

were the contrary of self-interest, and an indissoluble bond to community; kindling like fire everything that is at hand, as happens in wood which gives increase to the fire, the passive to the active, and decrease when withdrawn in the contrary manner. If therefore the prince, so far as he may, is fervent with charity for the community, he will thus be anxious for it to be rightly ruled, and will never be glad if it suffer loss. Whence if the king loves the magnates of the kingdom, though he alone, like a great seer, knows what is needful for ruling the kingdom, what becomes him and what should be done, he will not hide what he has wisely decreed from those without whose aid he will be unable to bring to effect what he has decreed; therefore he will discuss with his own men those things which he will not think to do by himself. Why will he not communicate his plans to those from whom he will as a suppliant ask for aids? Whatever allures his people to kindliness, and makes them friends, and fosters unity, it becomes the king's prudence to declare to those who are able to increase his glory. The Lord showed all things to His disciples, distinguishing from servants those whom He made friends; and as though He were ignorant, He often asked of His followers what they thought, which He assuredly knew. Oh, if princes would but seek the honour of God, they would rule their realms rightly, and without error. If princes had knowledge of God, they would show their justice to all men. Knowing not the Lord, as it were blinded, they seek the praises of men, delighted with vain things. He who knows not how to rule himself, will rule many badly; if any one is willing to examine the psalms, he will read the same: how Joseph taught himself to teach princes, for which cause the king wished him to be preeminent; and how David in the innocence of his heart, and by understanding fed Israel. From all that has been said above, it will be clear that it is the duty of the magnates of the kingdom[1] to see what things are convenient for the governance of the kingdom,[2] and expedient for the preservation of peace; and that the king have natives at his side, whether as councillors or as the greater men of the realm, not strangers nor favourites who supplant others and the good customs. For such discord is the step-mother of peace, and brings in battles, devises treachery. For just as the envy of the devil brought in death, so does hate divide the court. The king shall keep the natives in their rank, and by this management shall rejoice in ruling. But if he have sought to degrade his own men, have overturned their rank, it is in vain that he will ask, why when so deranged they do not obey him; nay, they would be mad if they were to do so.

[1] or (reading *regem*), "it is the duty of the magnates to see to the king, what things", etc.
[2] or (reading *regis*), "of the king"

233. Select political songs of the period

(a) *The Order of Fair Ease*

(Anglo-Norman verse, trans. I. S. T. Aspin, *Anglo-Norman Political Songs* (Oxford, 1953), pp. 138–41)

Anonymous (though obviously English) work of the thirteenth or early fourteenth century, but not unprecedented – see David Knowles, *The Monastic Order in England* (Cambridge, 1950), p. 677.

Whoso will listen to me will hear and learn the tale of a new order, which is very attractive and fair. I will tell you how I heard of it from the brothers of my country. The order is so judiciously founded that it derives a feature from all orders; there is no order in this world of which there is not some feature in it. I want to tell you the name of the order, which no one could blame me for reading; whoso wishes to hear let him keep quiet; it is the order of fair ease.

I will tell you the whole story of the order, for in it is many a worthy man, and many a fair and good lady; to this order belong without shame squires, pages and men-at-arms. But bumpkins and louts are absolutely debarred from the order; may none ever be received into it, for they will disgrace it. When a rascal or a villein rises in station or authority, to where he can exercise control, there is no more moderation in them than in the wolf who devours lambs. I will have done with those fellows at this point and speak further about the order.

In this order of which I am telling you, it is laid down firstly, that those who shall belong to the order shall observe a rule of Sempringham, which will be very acceptable, such as the abbey of Sempringham has: brothers and sisters [shall be] together. It is an excellent order, it seems to me. But to this extent it will be altered, to be sure, that at Sempringham there must be between the brothers and sisters – which is unwelcome to many – moats and walls of great height. But in this order of fair ease there must be neither moat nor wall, nor any other hindrance which could prevent the brothers from coming to their sisters at will; and let them not be challenged. Neither will there be linen nor woollen between them, and if there is hair, it will not therefore be an obstacle. From thence it is likewise provided that those who shall have embraced the order must belong to the abbey, and this is our master's command, in order to be well fed and to their liking three times a day and more often. And if they do it because there is company, the order will not therefore lapse.

From Beverley they have taken a rule which will be well and strictly kept; in order to drink deeply at meals, and then afterwards until supper, and afterwards at collation, each must have a piece of candle as long as his forearm; and as long as a scrap of candle remains to be burned the brothers must sit and drink.

They have taken one rule from the hospitallers, who are right courtly knights and have becoming robes falling down to their feet, well-fitting shoes and leg coverings and fat, gently ambling palfreys. Such indeed must the brothers and sisters in our order have.

From the [regular] canons they have taken a rule which will be well established in the order; for the canons as a great privation eat meat in the refectory three days a week. So also must our sisters and our brothers eat meat in the refectory every day, except Friday only and Saturday likewise. And if it happens thus that on Saturday they have a guest, and there is not plenty of fish, they may have permission to take the provisions which are in the house; nor will the order be infringed.

They have derived a feature from the black monks, who drink readily indeed, and get drunk every day, for they do not know how else to live; but they do it for companionship and not in the least out of gluttony. Also it is ordained that each brother should be given drink from day to day most regularly, before and after meals. And if it should so happen that there come to see a brother some friend for whom they ought to bestir themselves in order to entertain the brothers, whoever knows how to play well of an evening – I tell you this of a truth – he shall sleep late in the morning, until the harmful vapour be gone from his head, because of the great danger to the eyesight.

From the secular canons, who willingly do service to ladies, our masters have derived a rule, and they wish this rule to be carefully kept and properly practised; because, mark well, it is the rule which is most essential to the order. In order to amuse the sisters, on pain of excommunication it is commanded very strictly that each brother must play the game of love with his sister before matins always, and after matins likewise. And if he plays it three times at his pleasure before leaving, the brother will not be censured, nor will the order be the worse.

Grey monks are a hardy race, and nevertheless our masters wish to burden our order by adopting one of their rules. And it is hardly genteel, for they go to matins without breeches; so must our brothers do also to be ready for their business. And when they say any prayer they must be on their knees, to carry out their work with greater devotion. And they ring one bell, no more, it is their rule and custom; but our brothers, in order to give double measure, must ring two bells.

In so far is our order divergent that our sisters must lie on their backs and pray facing upwards, they do it by great devoutness. Thus they take in patience this rule of the order of silence. Charterhouse is a good order and no mistake, there is no other which equals it; hence they desire to take some characteristic from this order for our purpose. Each is shut into his cell to be alone in quiet; so also must our brothers be. And each must have at his window some plants for solace, and the sister in his arms, and be shut up in privacy for fear of people dropping in.

If our order is to last, we must not at any price overlook the Friars Minor who serve God wholeheartedly. Thus we must adopt some characteristic of their order, to have the greater merit. Their order is based on poverty, by which they go the easy way to heaven quite freely; and I will tell you how they seek after poverty always. When they travel about the land they let the chief baron or knight put them up, or the principal person or priest, where they can take their ease. But by St Peter of Rome, they will not take shelter with a poor man! The richer the persons, the more readily will they ask lodging [from them]. Nor must our brothers go and seek hospitality in any place except where they know there is abundance. And there they must eat meat and whatever they have by charity, as the Minorites also do.

Since we have [taken] something from the Minorites, we shall have something from the Preachers. They do not walk bare foot like the others, but go preaching well shod. And if it happens sometimes that they have sore feet, they can, if they wish, ride freely all day long. But our brothers must behave in quite another manner, when they go about the country preaching. For they must always without exception ride far and near. And when they are not delivering a sermon they must be indoors. And always after meals they must by rights preach; for many a man is of such sort that his heart is harder than stone, but after he has had a few drinks, he will soon listen to the order, and hearts will be softened; they [the preachers] will be heard more readily, so that they [the hearers] will join the order when they have heard the sermon.

Our order is founded in this wise and our brothers have determined that each country should have an abbot, who has power to receive brothers and sisters and institute and keep orders in due form. And so that all the rules, which our masters have drawn up, should be kept, a provincial must go round the country and seek to find out who has obeyed the order. And the man who has infringed it will be chastised in private and reprimanded for his fault. And those who are found to have observed the order well, are to be promoted to high office for their humility, and made abbots or priors, to maintain the order in honour. Thus do the Augustinians do, who have so much occult knowledge, making full enquiry everywhere as to who are keeping the order loyally. And those who observe the order will be held in universal esteem.

Herewith finishes our order which is in harmony with all good orders; and it is the order of fair ease, which is very pleasing to many.

(b) *Song of the barons, or, Against Montfort's enemies (1263)*

(Aspin, op. cit. pp. 19–20)

But the good earl Warenne who owns so much wealth and property, and has been trained in warfare, he was conquering his foes in Norfolk, in that country, but now there is nothing for him to do.

Sir John Giffard is worthy of mention; he had few equals or rivals in that venture. And he was always at the fore, brave and skilful and bold and of high renown.

And sir John d'Ayvile, who never had any love for treason or deceit, was of the company. And sir Peter de Montfort was in sympathy with their pact, and he was very powerful.

And the good Roger Clifford behaved like a noble lord, and he was ever most just, he did not permit the humble nor yet the great to do any wrong, either behind his back or openly.

And sir Roger Leyburne who is always on the move, went on a round of conquests. He was at some pains to enrich himself, in order to make good the losses which the lord Edward had caused him previously.

Right worthy were the barons; but I know not how to enumerate them all, so great is their number. Therefore I go back to earl Simon, to give the interpretation of his name.

He is called of Montfort: he is in the world and he is strong, and great is his prowess; this is the truth and I concur: he loves right and hates wrong and he will get the upper hand.

Of a truth he is in the world, where the common folk of the land granted to him, acknowledge him; he is the earl of Leicester and he can be proud and rejoice in this renown.

The bishop of Hereford was well aware the earl was strong when he had experience of the matter. Before this he was very fierce, he thought to eat up all the English. But now he doesn't know what to do.

And the good shepherd of Norwich, who devours his sheep, knew much about this earl. In fact he lost a lot of his goods. Cursed be the man who left a mite to him, for he knew much about shame.

And as for sir John Langelé, his property was seized. Evil be to the man who is sorry for him! My lord Roger Clifford had all his belongings taken away; it was his will that nothing should remain.

Nor did they leave sir Matthew Besile a stick or a stone in town or on the land. All his property was embezzled and filched by a trick without trickery.

But sir John de Gray came to London, and I don't know what it was that provoked a quarrel between him and the Londoners, so that he lost bag and baggage. That was just his bad luck.

And sir William Latimer came to London on pleasure bent . . .

(c) *Lament for Simon de Montfort* (*c. 1267–8*)

(Aspin, op. cit. pp. 32–3)

I must sing, my heart wishes it, in a grievous strain; in tears was made the song of our gentle baronage, who for the sake of the peace so long deferred, let themselves be torn asunder, their bodies hacked and dismembered to save England.

Now he is slain, the flower of fame, who was so versed in warfare, Montfort the earl; the whole land bewailed his cruel death.

As I believe, on a Tuesday, they joined battle, all on horseback was the disaster, without any foot soldiers; they struck blows there to great harm with the burnished sword, so that lord Edward's party won the mastery.

Now he is slain, etc.

But by his death earl Montfort won the victory; like the martyr of Canterbury he ended his life. The good Thomas did not want holy church to be destroyed; the earl also fought and died without flinching.

Now he is slain, etc.

The fierce sir Hugh, the Despenser, most noble justiciar, now he is wrongly delivered up to death, in a most wicked manner, sir Henry – I tell the truth – son of the earl of Leicester, many others, as you will hear, through the earl of Gloucester.

Now he is slain, etc.

Whoever were prepared to die and maintain peace and justice, to them the holy martyr, who is ready to die and uphold the people of the land and accomplish his good desire, will insure the enjoyment of his pure conscience; for we are firmly minded to do it.

Now he is slain, etc.

Near his body, that great treasure, they found a hair shirt. The false knaves, they were so wicked, and those who killed him. It was worse that they had the good man dismembered, who knew so well all there was to know about fighting and keeping faith.

Now he is slain, etc.

Pray all of you, my gentle friends, to the Son of St Mary, that he lead the child, the mighty heir, in a godly life; I will not name the youth, I do not wish it to be mentioned; but for the love of the Saviour, pray for the clergy.

Now he is slain, etc.

I can find nothing that they did right, neither baron nor earl; the knights and squires are all brought low. Because of their loyalty and truthfulness which is all brought to naught, the flatterer will be able to reign, [and] the fool in virtue of his folly.

Now he is slain, etc.

Sir Simon, the just man, and his company joyfully go to Heaven above, to everlasting life. But may Jesus Christ, God who yielded himself to the Cross, take care of those who are put and kept in strict confinement.

Now he is slain, etc.

(d) *Song against the sheriffs (c. 1274–5)*

(From Brit. Mus., MS. Harl. 913, trans. in Helen M. Cam, *The Hundred and the Hundred Rolls* (1930), p. 106 [French])

Anonymous, but the translator describes the author as a contemporary and one who shared the outlook of the jurors of 1274–5, whose answers to the king's questions about the conduct of local government we have in the Hundred Rolls.

Who can tell truly
 How cruel sheriffs are?
Of their hardness to poor people
 No tale can go too far.
If a man cannot pay
 They drag him here and there,
They put him on assizes,
 The juror's oath to swear.
He dares not breathe a murmur,
 Or he has to pay again,
And the saltness of the sea
 Is less bitter than his pain.

When a sheriff comes
 To abbey or to hall

The best of meat, the best of drink,
Is brought at his call.
But all this store of dainties
Does the host no good
Unless a gift of jewels
Is dessert after food.
His grooms and his beadles
Must each have his share,
And his lady wife must have a gown
Of rainbow hues to wear.

Oh, the sheriff's clerks!
Needy folk at first,
Poor like others, suffering
From hunger and from thirst;
But when they get a bailiwick
How they grow and swell!
Their teeth grow long, their heads grow high,
Houses, lands, and rents they buy,
And pile up gold as well.
They scorn their poor neighbours,
They govern by new rules,
That is reckoned wisdom now
In our modern schools.

(e) *The treason of Thomas Turberville (1295–1325)*

(Aspin, op. cit. pp. 54–5)

Either within a few years of Turberville's exposure in 1295 or, more likely, a recollection of it in 1324–5 in the excitement of Charles IV's occupation of Gascony. I have not followed Miss Aspin in dating it more precisely.

My lords and ladies listen and you will hear about a great traitor who had plotted treason; Thomas Turberville was his name. He had promised Charles, and sworn by St Denis, that he would enable him to conquer all England by cunning and treachery. And Charles promised him large gifts, lands and goods of all kinds. The traitor asked Charles to equip without delay a big fleet of good ships, and a strong band of men, and said he would advise him in due time where he should make a sudden landing in England.

Without loss of time the traitor betook himself rapidly to England. He came to lord Edward, the king, and said that if he would act according to his [advice], he would conquer all the possessions which lord Charles had taken from him wrongly and by force. In the manner of the flatterer he betrayed both sides. Lord Edward did not grasp the trick which the traitor had planned thus. He received him with high honour, and at court he was a man of great authority. When he had spied out the whole situation and secret counsel of England, the traitor caused a letter to be written to lord Charles in secret, saying where his men should disembark in England and capture the country. This was made known to lord Edward, as God predestined, and the letter was shown to him, and the whole plot together. The king had the felon taken, Thomas the aforesaid traitor, who had caused the letter to be written. Through the city of London he had him drawn, wrapped in an ox hide; he was not otherwise accoutred, he had neither helmet nor hauberk. Round his sides were lots of cutting stones which made his blood flow. Afterwards the traitor was hanged and his soul was given over to Belzebub. There was no other way out; thus should a felon be treated. The unhappy man hangs on the gallows, bound with chains and irons; no one must bury him. As long as there is anything left of his body the trickster will hang there; such is the reward he gets for his pains.

Now truly Charles will long watch for him ere he come to ask of him the reward for his treason. Lord Edward did not give a leek for the great French fleet; he had the sea patrolled vigilantly from all sides by valorous men. The French failed to reach England and are disgraced. They remained at sea for a long space; the Ports slew many of them; they made a sudden assault on Dover and lost more than five hundred of their men there; never again did they achieve anything of advantage. Now they are all drowned I believe, or else gone back to their country and been hanged for their labours, because they did not take England; and Charles promised them this, if any of them came back.

Lord Charles,[1] noble knight, have done with your fighting, make peace with your cousin and consider the outcome. If you make war on England, you will never achieve success. Neither did your ancestors do so, who considered themselves such great champions: duke Louis, your relative, Eustace the monk likewise, and many other Frenchmen not named here. May the Lord God omnipotent grant you a good settlement. Amen.

(*f*) *Trailbaston* (*1305–7*)

(Aspin, op. cit. pp. 73–6)

The desire comes over me to rhyme and compose a story about an ordinance enacted in the land. It would have been better if the act had still to be carried out; if God does not prevent it, I believe war will flare up.

These are the articles of Trailbaston. Saving the king himself, may he have God's curse who first of all granted such a commission; for there is no sense of right in some of its points.

Sir, if I want to punish my boy with a cuff or two, to correct him, he will take out a summons against me and have me attached, and made to pay a big ransom before I get out of prison.

They take forty shillings for my ransom, and the sheriff comes for his reward for not putting me into a deep dungeon. Now judge, sirs, is this right?

Therefore I will keep within the woods, in the beautiful shade; there is no deceit there nor any bad law, in the forest of Belregard, where the jay flies and the nightingale always sings without ceasing.

[1] This may refer to Charles IV, but before this, for "Charles" read "Philip IV" in every case.

But the ill-favoured people on whom may God never have pity, out of their deceitful mouths they have indicted me for wicked thefts and other misdeeds, so that I do not dare to be received by my friends.

I have served my lord the king in peace and in war, in Flanders, Scotland, in Gascony his own land; but now I do not know how to make a living; I have spent all my time in vain to please such a man.

If these wicked jurors will not reform, so that I may go riding to my country, I will make their heads fly if I can get at them. I will not give a penny for all their threats.

Martyn and Knoville are pious men, and pray for the poor, that they may live in security. Spigurnel and Belflour are cruel men; if they were in my power there would be no help for them.

I will teach them the game of Trailbaston, and I will break their back and rump, their arms and their legs, it would be right; I will cut out their tongue and their mouth into the bargain.

Whoever first began these things will never be reformed all the days of his life. I tell you of a truth there is too much sin about it, because many a man will be a thief for fear of prison.

There are those who will become thieves who never were such, because, for fear of imprisonment, they dare not come into peace; one must have nourishment every day forthwith. Whoever began this business undertook a heavy burden.

Merchants and monks should indeed curse all those who have set up the Trailbaston; royal protection will not be worth a leek to them, unless they hand over their money without recompense.

You who are indicted, I advise you, come to me, to the green forest of Belregard, where there is no annoyance but only wild animals and beautiful shade; for the common law is too uncertain.

If you know your letters and are tonsured, you will be summoned before the justices. You may yet be brought back to prison, under the bishop's care until you have acquitted yourself.

. . . and suffer privation and very harsh penance, and in some cases you will never regain freedom.

Therefore it is better to stay with me in the woods, than to lie chained in the bishop's prison. The penance is too great and too hard to bear. Whoever can select the best is a fool not to choose.

Formerly I knew little [that was] worth while, now I am less wise; this is what the bad laws do to me by so great abuse, that I dare not come into peace among my kinsfolk. The rich are put to ransom, the poor dwindle away.

It would be a serious matter to pledge what cannot be discharged, that is to say a man's life which is so dear to him; and I have not the goods to be redeemed. But if I were in their power I would be delivered over to death.

I shall yet achieve pardon and hear people speak. Some who do not dare to come near me speak ill of me, and would willingly see me physically ill-treated; but God can save a man from a thousand devils.

Would that He who is the son of Mary should save me, for I was not guilty, I am indicted out of spite; may God curse whoever caused me to be in this place. The world is so fickle, he who trusts in it is a fool.

If I am a companion and have knowledge of archery, my neighbour will go about saying: "That man is of the band who go shooting in the wood and doing other foolish things. If he wants to live, he will live his life like a swine."

If I know the law better than they do, they will say: "That conspirator begins to be untrustworthy." And I will not come within ten leagues or two of home. May they be put to shame in all quarters.

I beg all good people that they should be good enough to pray for me that I may go riding to my country; I never killed a man, of my own free will to be sure, nor was I a wicked robber to do people harm.

This rhyme was made in the wood, beneath a laurel tree, there sing blackbird and nightingale and hovers the sparrow hawk; it was written on a parchment to keep it the more in remembrance, and thrown on the highroad that people should find it.

(g) *On the king's going back on his undertakings* (?*1306–7*)

(Aspin, op. cit. p. 64)

The occasion of this piece is uncertain. Version J, which appears to be the earlier, has the title, "On the Provision of Oxford"; on the other hand, its reference to "Merewell" (presumably Henry Woodlock of Marwell, bishop of Winchester 1305–16) suggests a much later date. Pope Clement V's bull of 29 December 1305, absolving Edward I from his constitutional concessions of 1297–1301, followed in 1306 by the king's forest ordinance, would be a sufficient occasion. Version A, another version, has no title and is so general that it offers no guidance. The interest of the piece remains, however: in the feeling expressed at such conduct on the king's part, whatever the immediate occasion.

VERSION J

On the Provision of Oxford

Rome can do and undo, she acts thus full often; that is neither good nor becoming; for this holy church is put to shame. Merewell, who agrees to such counsel is vicar of God. The man is not worth three eggs who does right and afterwards changes.

Our king of England, on the advice of his people, would set up a new law, and summoned a great parliament. All came there, the bishops and the barons likewise, and all who were there took an oath and held lighted tapers.

The provision is made of wax, I understand it and know it well, and it has been held too near the fire and has all melted away. I no longer know what to say, but all goes out of joint, court and law, hundred and shire, it all goes the way of the devil.

. . . .
. . . .
. . . .
. . . .[1]

[1] These lines of dots reflect the metre of a missing final quatrain.

234. The Passion of the Judges

(*State Trials of the Reign of Edward I, 1289–93*, ed. T. F. Tout and Hilda Johnstone (Camden series, 1906), pp. 93–9)

This "ribald travesty of biblical texts" (Powicke) is a satire on the many judges, including the chief justices of both benches, exposed when Edward I investigated complaints of misgovernment on his return from Gascony in 1289. The facts are given in Powicke, *The Thirteenth Century* (Oxford, 1953), pp. 361–6. The translation uses as much as possible of the English of the Authorised Version.

At that time a certain noble king went into a far country to receive for himself tribute, and he called his servants and delivered unto them his goods and gave them power to execute judgment. Each one according to his particular virtue prepared his throne for judgment and forgot the cry of the humble and took up a reproach against his neighbour. They sat with the rich in the secret places to murder the innocent and their right hand was full of bribes. And they said among themselves, "We will not have this man to reign over us": for in Proverbs it is written, "A reckless king ruineth his people and cities become populous through the prudence of their leading men." And because there is nothing hid that shall not be revealed, the king, when he heard of these sayings, entered into a ship, and passed over and came into his own country. But the children of Israel walked upon dry land next to the sea.

Some worshipped him with gifts: but some doubted. One of them, however, a certain Didimus, was not with them when their lord came, but saw the sea and fled and made as though he would have gone further, and he left his house and his wife, sons, brothers, fields, sheep and oxen and all the beasts of the field, and fled to the well of Babylon, and he was there in sheep's clothing[1] for fear of judgment by ordeal:[2] and all his wisdom was consumed and fear came on all that dwelt round about him and all these sayings were noised abroad throughout all the hill country of England. Then said the king to his men, "Have ye a watch on him: go your way, make it as sure as ye can, lest by chance the Romans come and take away both our place and nation: so the last error shall be worse than the first." So they went, sealing Babylon and setting a watch.

The king, going further on his way, said to his servants: "Go and walk through the land and survey it, and hearken unto the voices of my people which is in Egypt, for, because of the oppression of the poor, because of the sighing of the needy, now will I arise and render vengeance to mine enemies and will reward them that hate me." And they, diligently inquiring east and west and in the desert mountains, found some who were like as lions greedy of their prey[3] and as it were young lions lurking in secret places and whose garners were full affording all manner of store. And they which were sent were of the Pharisees. And they said to the king, "Behold, the whole world lieth in wickedness: wherefore do you not execute judgment and avenge our brethren?" To which the king replied, "The night will bring counsel."

And shortly afterwards the king, when he was come near to London, beheld the city and wept over it, saying, "If thou hadst known, even thou." And immediately

[1] for [Thomas called] Didimus, read Thomas de Weyland, the chief justice of Common Pleas, who took refuge in the house of the Franciscans at Babwell (*fons Babilonis*) and disguised himself as a Minorite

[2] *judiciorum*, a twist of John vii. 13 (*Judaeorum*)

[3] Ps. xvii. 12 (Auth. Version). Tout and Johnstone's printed text, p. 96 (*tanquam paratos ad predicta*), clearly should be emended to read *tanquam leones paratos ad predam*.

the people removed from their tents and bore the ark of the covenant of the Lord against him and said, "This is our King who hath delivered us from bondage to the Egyptians." But the king passing through the midst of them went his way and entering his paradise in search of the man whom he had created[1] he cried, "Adam, Adam, where art thou? Once before I should have lost thee, but thy money prayed for thee. Give an account of thy stewardship." Adam answered, "I cannot dig; to beg I am ashamed." And when he was accused of many things he answered not a word. At last came two ungrateful witnesses and said, "This fellow said, 'I am able to destroy your house in three days and never rebuild it.' He spoke and it was done, he commanded and it was destroyed." Then said the ruler unto him, "Hearest thou not how many things they witness against thee?" And he answered never a word, but went out and wept bitterly. Then the servants took him and threw him into prison. And the king said to his servants, "Go, gather up the fragments, that nothing be lost." Therefore they gathered them together and filled more than twelve baskets with money in the place of the tabernacle of his house and many other things which are not written in this book. When they therefore were come together, they asked their lord, saying, "Lord, wilt thou in due time restore anything to him?" And the king said, "It is not for you to know the treasure or money which he hath put in my power."

And after a little while there went out a decree from the said king that all the grievances of the land should be recorded. And all went to the city of London to give testimony. And there was a division among them. The people therefore that was there bare record that some servants of the king transgressed the tradition of the elders, loved the uppermost rooms at feasts and the chief seats in the synagogues and greetings in the markets, and to be called of men, Rabbi. And by them was hidden the gold and silver of the land. And the stores of the sanctuary were poured out in the top of every street. And when the king heard these words he groaned in the spirit and said, "Vengeance is mine: I will repay."

Also he made a great supper in London and bade many. And sent his servants at supper time to say to them that were bidden, "Come." And some began to make excuse. The first said, "I have bought pieces of ground for money untold and I must needs see them." And another said, "I have bought fifty yoke of oxen, and I go to prove them." And another said, "I have taken another man's wife and I go to prove her." So the servants came and shewed the lord king these things. Then said the king, "Go and compel them to come in into my presence. Tomorrow the iniquity of the earth will be destroyed. And I will see what their end shall be." Some said, "We perceive that we prevail nothing. Behold the world against us and our deeds. Let us go and offer unto him gifts, gold because he is a king, frankincense because he is a prelate, myrrh because he is immortal, and perhaps he will have mercy upon us." And when they had come to the king, he said, "Verily, I say unto you, that the hour cometh, and now is, that even in laughter your heart is sorrowful, but the people will rejoice. To me belongeth vengeance and I will repay in due time, for ye love wickedness and hate righteousness. Go into the village over against you and ye shall find others

[1] On Adam de Stratton, see N. Denholm-Young, *Seignorial Administration in England* (Oxford, 1937), pp. 77–84.

tied and many with them. There pray that ye enter not into temptation." And they said unto him, "Lord, thou hast the words of life; with whom shall we go?" Then the king said, "With the keeper of the city, that he may answer for you on the day of judgment." "O lord king, have mercy upon us." At which the king said, "I will not alter the thing that is gone out of my lips; once I have sworn in my wrath, ye have no part with me, for the king's strength loveth judgment." Whereupon they answered "Lord, thy will be done," and followed the keeper, and went back to Babylon another way, awaiting the coming of the lord of vengeance, the lord who will render to every man according to his deeds.

235. How to hold a parliament (1316–24)

(M. V. Clarke, *Medieval Representation and Consent* (1936), pp. 374–84)

Opinion on this important, but baffling because undated and anonymous treatise has fluctuated wildly. The issues are best stated by V. H. Galbraith in "The Modus Tenendi Parliamentum", *Journal of the Warburg and Courtauld Institutes*, xvi (1953), pp. 81–99, who gives reasons for assigning it, if not to 1321 or 1322, at least to "1316–24 or so" and to the authorship of "a working official – preferably a Chancery official – minutely informed regarding the rolls of parliament, who is also an ecclesiastic of sufficient education and broad outlook to express an unorthodox theory of the whole meaning of parliament in the later part of Edward II's reign", whom he would identify on incomplete but strong circumstantial evidence with a Yorkshireman, William Ayreminne, the best known Chancery official of the day. M. V. Clarke, *Medieval Representation and Consent* (1936) is an elaborate study of the treatise in both the English and the Irish traditions of the text in the light of thirteenth and fourteenth century parliamentary practice. The text given below is my translation of the provisional edition printed by Miss Clarke of the English tradition of the text. A definitive edition of both English and Irish, which could incidentally settle the question of priority (still disputed by Richardson and Sayles, *The Irish Parliament in the Middle Ages* (1952)), is greatly to be desired. See J. Taylor, "The Manuscripts of the 'Modus Tenendi Parliamentum' ", *E.H.R.*, lxxxiii (1968), pp. 673–88.

Here is described the way in which the parliament of the king of England and of his English was held in the time of king Edward the son of king Ethelred: which way was recited by the wiser men of the realm in front of William duke of Normandy, conqueror and king of England, on the conqueror's own orders, was approved by him, and was the customary way in his times and also in the times of his successors the kings of England.

Chapter 1 *The summoning of parliament*

The summoning of a parliament ought to precede the first day of parliament by forty days.

Chapter 2 *Concerning the clergy*

To parliament ought to be summoned and come archbishops, bishops, abbots, priors and other leading clergy who hold by earldom or barony by reason of such tenure, and no lower clergy unless their presence and attendance is required for reasons other than their tenures, as for example if they are of the king's council or their presence is considered necessary or useful to parliament, and the king is bound to provide them their keep and expenses in coming to and staying at the parliament; not that such lower clergy ought to be summoned to parliament, but the king used to send his writs to them at the same time asking them to be at his parliament.

Also, the king used to issue his summonses to archbishops bishops and other exempt persons, for example, abbots, priors, deans and other ecclesiastical persons who have jurisdiction by such separate exemptions and privileges, to cause to be elected for each deanery and archdeaconry of England by the deaneries and archdeaconries themselves two experienced and suitable proctors from their own archdeaconry to come and be present at parliament to answer, undertake, excuse themselves from and do[1] exactly what every one from those deaneries and archdeaconries would do, if every one of them was present in person.

And that such proctors come with their warrants in duplicate, sealed with the seals of their superiors, that they have been elected and sent to act as proctor: one of which letters shall be handed over to the clerks of parliament for enrolling and the other the proctors shall keep themselves. And so, with these two kinds of summons, the whole of the clergy ought to be summoned to the king's parliament.

Chapter 3 *Concerning the laity*

Also, ought to be summoned and come every one of the earls and barons, and their peers,[2] that is those who have lands and rents to the value of a whole earldom, viz, twenty fees of one knight, each fee reckoned at twenty librates,[3] making four hundred librates in all,[4] or to the value of one whole barony, that is, thirteen and one third fees of one knight, each fee reckoned at twenty librates, making in all four hundred marks;[5] and no lower laity ought to be summoned and come to parliament by reason of their tenure – they should be summoned and come only if their presence is useful or necessary to parliament on other grounds, and then in their case it should be done as has been said should be in the case of lower clergy, who by reason of their tenure are in no wise bound to come to parliament.

Chapter 4 *Concerning the barons of the ports*

Also, the king used to send his writs to the warden of the Cinque Ports to cause to be elected from each port by that port two suitable and experienced barons to come and be present at his parliament to answer, undertake, excuse themselves from and do exactly what their baronies would do, if every one from those baronies were there in person; and that such barons come with their warrants in duplicate, sealed with the common seals of their ports, that they have been duly elected and deputed for this purpose and sent on behalf of those baronies, of which [letters] one shall be handed over to the clerks of parliament and the other the barons shall keep themselves. And when such barons of the Ports, having obtained permission, were about to withdraw from parliament they then used to receive a writ under the great seal to the warden

1 *ad respondendum, subeundum allegandum et faciendum*

2 peers (*pares*), not, of course, in the modern sense, but in the non-technical sense of "equals" – here and everywhere else in this treatise, despite phrases such as "peers of parliament" (*pares parliamenti*) and "peers of the kingdom" (*pares regni*) in chapters 15 and 17, for example. Here in chapter 3 the equality is one of income. In *pares parliamenti* the equality is one of membership of a parliament, irrespective of grade or income. This is clear from chapter 15. *Pares regni* is defined in chapter 17 and clearly covers all grades, but in the context of chapter 19 is virtually synonymous with *pares parliamenti*.

3 i.e. lands and rents sufficient to produce an income of £20 a year

4 i.e. an income of £400 a year

5 i.e. an income of 400 marks (£266 13*s* 4*d*) a year

of the Cinque Ports for him to see that they got from their particular port their reasonable keep and expenses from the day they set out for parliament to the day they got home again, special mention being made in the writ of how long they had stayed at the parliament, of the day they arrived, the day they got permission to leave, and mention used sometimes to be made in the writ how much such barons ought to receive from their communities per day, some more no doubt and some less according to the abilities and standing of the persons concerned, but it was not usual for more than twenty shillings per day for the two barons to be paid out, taking into account how long they stayed, the work they did and their expenses, nor are such expenses usually repaid as a matter of course by the court for all persons so elected and sent instead of the communities, unless those persons have been esteemed and well-behaved in parliament.

Chapter 5 *Concerning the knights of the shires*

Also, the king used to send his writs to all the sheriffs of England for each to cause to be elected from his county by the county two suitable honourable and experienced knights to come to his parliament in the same way in which it has been said should be done in the case of the barons of the Ports, and in the same way for their warrants, but for the combined expenses of a shire's two knights it is not usual for more than one mark per day to be paid out.

Chapter 6 *Concerning the citizens*

In the same way word used to be sent to the mayor and sheriffs of London, the mayor and bailiffs or mayor and citizens of York and other cities for them to elect on behalf of the community of their city two suitable, honourable and experienced citizens to come and be present at parliament in the same way in which it has been said should be done in the case of the barons of the Cinque Ports and the knights of the shires; and the citizens used to be the peers of the knights of the shires on a level with them as to expenses while coming, staying and returning.

Chapter 7 *Concerning the burgesses*

Also, in the same way word used to be, and ought to be, sent to the bailiffs and good men of boroughs for them to elect from themselves and in place of themselves two suitable, honourable and experienced burgesses to come and be present at the king's parliament, in the same way in which it has been said should be done in the case of the citizens; but the two burgesses used not to receive more than ten shillings per day for their expenses and sometimes not more than half a mark, and this used to be assessed by the court according to the size and power of the borough and the standing of the persons sent.

Chapter 8 *The custom of parliament*

It having been shown first on what grounds, to whom, and how long in advance a summons of parliament ought to be issued and who ought to come by summons and who not, it must in the second place be said who they are who ought to come by reason of their offices and are bound to be present during the whole period of parliament without a summons. In which connection it is to be observed that the two principal clerks of parliament chosen by the king and his council and the other secondary clerks, of whom and whose offices there will be more particular mention later, and the chief crier of England with his under-criers and the chief doorkeeper of England, which two offices, that is the office of crier and that of doorkeeper, used to belong to one and the same person, these two officials are bound to be present on the first day.[1] The chancellor of England, the treasurer, the chamberlains and barons of the exchequer, the justices and all clerks and knights of the king, together with serjeants at the king's pleas, who are of the king's council are bound to be present on the second day, unless they have reasonable excuses for not being able to be present, and then they should send suitable excuses.

Chapter 9 *Concerning the opening of parliament*

The lord king shall sit in the middle of the greater bench and he is bound to be present first, sixth[2] day of parliament, and the chancellor, treasurer, barons of the exchequer and justices used to record non-attendances at parliament in the following order. On the first day the burgesses and citizens of all England shall be called, and if they do not come on that day a borough will be amerced at one hundred marks and a city at one hundred pounds. On the second day the knights of the shires of all England shall be called, and if they do not come on that day the county they are from shall be amerced at one hundred pounds. On the third day of parliament the barons of the Cinque Ports shall be called, and afterwards the barons and then the earls, and if the barons of the Cinque Ports do not come on that day[3] the barony they are from shall be amerced at one hundred marks: in the same way one who is himself a baron shall be amerced at one hundred marks and an earl at one hundred pounds, and the same for those who are equal to earls and barons, that is to say, who have lands and rents to the value of one earldom or of one barony, as said earlier in the section on summoning.[4] On the fourth day the proctors of the clergy shall be called and if they do not come their bishops shall be amerced at one hundred marks for each archdeaconry that has defaulted. On the fifth day the deans, priors, abbots, bishops and finally the archbishops shall be called and if they do not come each archbishop shall be amerced at one hundred pounds, a bishop holding a whole barony at one hundred marks, and the same for abbots, priors and others. On the first day proclamation should be made, first in the hall or the monastery or other public place where the parliament is being held, and afterwards publicly in the city or vill, that all those who wish to present petitions and plaints to parliament should deliver them not later than the fifth day following the first day of parliament.

[1] The obscurity of this sentence suggests interpolation!
[2] The printed text is obscure, possibly corrupt (*interesse primo, sexto die*).
[3] "*unde si*" treated as corruption of "*quo die si*"
[4] More precisely, No. 3 of the seven chapters into which modern editors have divided the section on summoning.

Chapter 10 *Concerning the sermon to parliament*

An archbishop or bishop or a prominent clerk of experience and eloquence, chosen by the archbishop in whose province the parliament is held, ought to preach on one of the first five days of parliament in full parliament and in the king's presence, and this when parliament has for the most part come together and assembled; and in his sermon suitably enjoin the whole parliament to make with him humble supplication and entreaty to God for the peace and tranquillity of king and kingdom, as will be more particularly mentioned in the following section concerning the pronouncement to parliament.

Chapter 11 *Concerning the pronouncement to parliament*

After the sermon the chancellor of England or the chief justice of England, the one that is who holds the pleas *coram rege*, or other justice, or clerk, of suitable standing and eloquence, chosen by the chancellor and chief justice, ought to declare the reasons for the parliament,[1] first generally but afterwards the particular reasons, standing while he does so; and in this connection be it known that everybody of the parliament, whoever he is, shall stand while speaking, the king excepted, so that everybody of the parliament may be able to hear him who speaks, and if he talks indistinctly or speaks in too low a voice let him say it over again and speak louder or let another speak for him.

Chapter 12 *Concerning the king's speech after the pronouncement*

The king after the pronouncement to parliament ought to ask the clergy and laity, naming all their grades, that is to say, archbishops, bishops, abbots, priors, archdeacons, proctors and others of the clergy, earls, barons, knights, citizens, burgesses and other laity, to apply themselves diligently, zealously and heartily to considering and reaching decisions upon the business of the parliament, as they understand and feel would be mainly and principally in accordance with God's will in the first place and after that be to his and their honour and advantage.

Chapter 13 *Concerning the absence of the king from parliament*

The king is absolutely bound to be present in person at parliament, unless he is prevented from coming by bodily illness and then he can keep to his chamber, provided that he does not lodge outside the manor, or the vill at all events, where the parliament is being held, and then he should send for twelve of the greater and better of those who have been summoned to the parliament, that is to say, two bishops, two earls, two barons, two knights of the shire, two citizens and two burgesses, to view his person and testify to his condition, and in their presence he should commission the archbishop of the province in which parliament is meeting,[2] the steward and his chief

[1] "*pronunciare causas Parliamenti*". This explains "pronouncement". The explanation is confirmed by *Mum and the Sothsegger*, a Middle English satire from the very end of the fourteenth century, as cited and translated in Helen M. Cam, *Liberties and Communities in Medieval England* (Cambridge, 1944), pp. 233 and 230 (note especially "And prononcid . . ." and ". . . cause of her comynge"). Another translation of the passage into modern English is given in the next volume in this series, *English Historical Documents*, IV, *1327–1485*, ed. A. R. Myers (1969), No. 266, p. 453.

[2] *archiepiscopo loci:* the happy rendering of Bagley and Rowley, *Documentary History of England 1066–1540* (Pelican, 1966), p. 179

justice jointly and severally to open and carry on parliament in his name, in the commission special mention being made there and then of the cause of his absence – which along with the clear testimony of their said twelve peers[1] ought to be enough to restrain the other nobles and magnates of parliament: the thing is that there used to be outcries and murmuring in parliament at the king's absence, because it is a harmful and dangerous thing for the whole community of parliament and kingdom when a king is absent from parliament, neither ought he to, nor can he absent himself, save in the one case aforesaid.

Chapter 14 *Concerning places and seating in parliament*

First, as was said before,[2] the king shall sit in the middle of the greater bench and on his right side shall sit the archbishop of Canterbury, the bishops of London and Winchester and after them in turn the other bishops, abbots and priors in rows, and on the king's left side shall sit the archbishop of York, the bishops of Durham and Carlisle and after them in turn the earls, barons and lords, there being always kept such a distribution of the aforesaid grades and their places that none shall sit except among his peers, and it is the responsibility of the steward of England to see to this unless the king wishes to assign someone else to it. At the right foot of the king shall sit the chancellor of England and the chief justice of England and his fellows, and their clerks who are of parliament; and at his left foot shall sit the treasurer, chamberlains and barons of the exchequer, the justices of the bench and their clerks who are of parliament.

Chapter 15 *Concerning the principal clerks of parliament*

Also, the two principal clerks of parliament shall sit amidst the justices and shall enrol all the pleas and business of parliament.

And be it understood that these two clerks are not subject to any of the justices – neither is any justice of England a justice in parliament, nor do they[3] in themselves have record in parliament except in so far as new power is assigned and given to them in parliament by the king and the peers of parliament, as when they are assigned with others attending parliament to hear and determine various petitions and plaints presented in parliament. On the contrary, these two clerks are immediately subject to the king and his parliament jointly unless perhaps one or two justices are assigned to them to examine and amend their enrolments. And when peers of parliament are assigned to hear and examine any petitions specially on their own and they are unanimously agreed in rendering their judgments on petitions of this kind they shall recite such petitions and the process[4] used in dealing with them and render judgment in full parliament, so that these two clerks as principals[5] may enrol all pleas and all judgments on the principal roll of parliament and deliver these same rolls to the treasurer before parliament is given leave to depart in order that the rolls may be in the treasury without fail before parliament does depart, saving to those two clerks

[1] Evidently "peers of parliament" in the sense of chapter 15, below. cf. the note to chapter 3, above.
[2] chapter 9, above
[3] i.e. the justices
[4] i.e. record of the proceedings
[5] *principaliter*

however a transcript thereof or a counter-roll if they want it. These two clerks, unless they hold other offices in the king's service and receive fees from him on which they can live suitably, shall receive from the king one mark a day divided equally between them for their expenses if they do not eat at the lord king's table, and if they do eat at his table they shall get besides their board half a mark a day divided equally between them for as long as parliament lasts.

Chapter 16 *Concerning the five clerks of parliament*

The lord king shall assign five skilled and approved clerks, of whom the first shall minister to and serve the bishops, the second the proctors of the clergy, the third the earls and barons, the fourth the knights of the shires, the fifth the citizens and burgesses, and each of them, unless he is in the service of the king and receives from him a fee or wages that he can live suitably on, shall receive from the king two shillings a day if he does not eat at the king's table, and if he does eat at his table he shall get twelve pence a day. And these clerks shall write down their[1] doubts and the answers they give to king and parliament [and] shall be present at their deliberations whenever they wish to have them there. And when they have nothing else to do they shall help the principal clerks with the enrolling.

Chapter 17 *Concerning difficult cases and judgments*

When contention, doubt or a difficult matter of peace or war arises in the kingdom or outside it, the question shall be referred in writing to and recited in full parliament and considered and argued there between the peers of parliament and, if it be necessary, be it enjoined on each grade of the peers by the king, or on behalf of the king if he is not present, that each grade go on its own, that the question be delivered to its clerk in writing and that in a place prescribed[2] they have it recited to them, in order that they may arrange and consider between themselves the best and justest possible way of proceeding in the matter as they, for the king and for themselves and for those they represent also, would wish to answer before God, and come back with their answers and observations in writing; and when all their answers, counsels and observations on either side[3] have been heard, let the matter be dealt with according to the better and sounder counsel and when at least the greater part of parliament are of one mind. But if through discord between the king and some magnates, or perhaps among the magnates themselves, the peace of the realm is rendered insecure, or the people or the country afflicted, so that it appears to the king and his council that it would be expedient for the matter to be considered and corrected through the deliberations of all the peers of his kingdom, or if the king and his kingdom are afflicted with war, or if a difficult case comes before the chancellor of England or a difficult judgment has to be given before the justices, and such like, and if perchance in such deliberations all or even the greater part are unable to agree, then the earl steward, the earl constable and the earl marshal, or two of them, shall from all the peers of the kingdom select twenty-five, that is to say two bishops and three proctors for the whole body of clergy, two

[1] *eorum* (i.e. of the particular grade they are assigned to)
[2] *in certo loco*
[3] *hinc inde*

earls and three barons, five knights of the shires, five citizens and five burgesses, which makes twenty-five, and these twenty-five can if they wish choose twelve of themselves and stand down in their favour, and these twelve six and stand down in their favour, and these six yet again three and stand down in their favour, but these three cannot stand down in favour of a smaller number without getting permission from the lord king, though, if the king agrees, the three can submit to two and of the two one can submit to the other, so that at length what he ordains will stand above the whole parliament; and by thus coming down from twenty-five persons to a single one, if a greater number is not able to agree and ordain, in the end a single person as has been said will ordain for all who cannot disagree with himself, saving to the lord king and his council that after ordinances of this sort have been put into writing they, if they know how to and wish to, may examine and amend them, provided that this is done there and then in full parliament and with the agreement of parliament, and not after parliament is over.

Chapter 18 *Concerning the order of dealing with the business of a parliament*
The business for which a parliament has been summoned ought to be dealt with according to the calendar of the parliament and in the order of the petitions presented and filed without regard for any persons whatsoever, instead let him who put in first go first. All the business of a parliament should be listed in the calendar of the parliament in this order: first, things to do with war if there is a war on, and other things touching the persons of the king, the queen and their children; second, matters concerning the kingdom generally – such as the making of laws for the defects of writs[1] original and judicial and writs of execution after judgment has been delivered, which are in the highest degree matters of general concern; third, individual matters should be listed and this in the order of the petitions as filed, as was said before.

Chapter 19 *Concerning the days and hours for parliament*
Parliament ought not to be held on Sundays but can be held on all other days, that day always excepted and three others, viz, All Saints, All Souls and the Nativity of St John the Baptist, and it ought to be begun each day at the hour of mid-prime, at which hour the king is bound to be present [at the] parliament, and all the peers of the kingdom.[2] Parliament ought to be held in a public place and not in a private or a secret place. On feast days parliament ought to be begun at the hour of prime[3] because of divine service.

Chapter 20 *Concerning the doorkeepers of parliament*
The principal doorkeeper of parliament shall stand inside the great door of the monastery, hall or other place where parliament is being held, and shall guard the door so that no one may enter parliament unless he owes suit and attendance at parliament or has been summoned on account of business he is prosecuting in parliament,

[1] emending, with V. H. Galbraith (*Journal of the Warburg and Courtauld Institutes*, xvi, p. 99), "*legum*" to "*brevium*"
[2] see above, chapter 3, n. 2
[3] i.e. half an hour earlier than usual, mid-prime being half way through the first hour of the day

and it is necessary for this doorkeeper to know the persons who ought to enter, so that no one is on any account refused admission whose presence in parliament is imperative. This doorkeeper can and, if it is necessary, ought to have several doorkeepers under him.

Chapter 21 *Concerning the crier of parliament*

The crier of parliament shall stand outside the door of the parliament and the doorkeeper shall tell him what to proclaim. The king used to direct his serjeants-at-arms to stand for a considerable distance[1] outside the door of the parliament to guard the door, so that none cause congestion or create disturbances around the doors by which parliament might be impeded on pain of arrest of their bodies, because by right the door of a parliament ought not to be closed but instead be guarded by the doorkeepers and the king's serjeants-at-arms.

Chapter 22 *Concerning standing while speaking in parliament*

All peers of parliament shall sit and none shall stand save when he is speaking, and he shall speak so that everyone in parliament is able to hear him; none shall enter parliament or go out of parliament except by the one door. And [if][2] anyone whatsoever is pleading any case which ought to be delivered by parliament, all who speak shall stand; the reason is for them to be heard by the peers, because all peers are judges and justices.

Chapter 23 *Concerning aids for the king*

The king used not to ask for an aid from his kingdom except when a war was imminent or for making his sons knights or marrying his daughters, and then aids of this sort ought to be asked for in full parliament, the request delivered to each grade of the peers of parliament in writing, and answered in writing. And be it known that for the granting of such aids all the peers of parliament ought to consent and it is to be understood that the two knights who come to parliament for the shire carry more weight[3] in parliament in granting and refusing than the greatest earl of England, and in like manner the proctors of the clergy of a diocese carry more weight[3] in parliament, if all are of the same mind, than the bishop himself. And so too[4] in all things which ought to be granted, refused or done by parliament: and this is clear from the fact that a king can hold a parliament with the community[5] of his kingdom without the bishops, earls and barons, provided they have been summoned to parliament even if no bishop, earl or baron comes in accordance with their summonses, for there was once a time when there was neither bishop, nor earl, nor baron, yet kings then held their parliaments. But it is otherwise the other way round. Supposing the communities,[6] clergy and laity, had been summoned to parliament (as of right they ought) but for certain reasons were not willing to come – for example if they alleged that the king was not ruling them as he should and were to state specifically in what points

[1] *per magnum spatium*
[2] conjectural, but the sense seems to require it
[3] *maiorem vocem habent*
[4] *et hoc* [5] *communitas* [6] *communitates*

he had misruled them – there would then be no parliament at all, even if all the archbishops, bishops, earls, barons and all their peers were present with the king. It is inescapable therefore that all things which ought to be affirmed or annulled, granted or refused, or done by parliament ought to be granted by the community[1] of parliament, which is made up of three grades or kinds [of people] of parliament, that is to say, the proctors of the clergy, the knights of the shires, citizens and burgesses, who represent the whole community[1] of England, and not of the magnates because each of them is at parliament for his own individual self and for no other person.

Chapter 24 *Concerning the dissolution of parliament*

Parliament ought not to be dissolved so long as any petition remains undiscussed, or, at least, the answer to it has not been decided, and if the king allows the contrary he is in breach of his oath.[2] Not a single one of all the peers of parliament can or should withdraw from parliament without getting permission for it from the king and from all his peers and this in full parliament; and[3] let a record of such permission be made in the roll of the parliament. And if any of the peers is taken ill during the parliament so that he is not able to attend the parliament, let him for three days send people to excuse him to parliament and on that day[4] if he has not come let there be sent to him two of his peers to view and attest such illness, and if there is ground for suspicion, the two peers shall be put to the oath that they will tell the truth of the matter, and if it is found that he had feigned himself sick let him be amerced as if he had defaulted, but if he had not feigned himself sick, he may then in their presence depute some sufficient person to attend parliament for him. And a healthy man cannot be excused if he is of sound mind.

Dissolution of parliament ought to be carried out so: in the first place it should be asked and proclaimed publicly in parliament and within the pale of parliament, if there is anyone who has presented a petition to parliament who has not yet had a reply; because if no one raises an objection it is to be supposed that everyone has his remedy,[5] or at least he has an answer as far as the law allows,[6] and then, and not before then, that is to say when no one objects who on that occasion tendered a petition, will[7] we "grant our parliament leave to depart".

Chapter 25 *Concerning transcripts of records and processes in parliament*

The clerks of parliament shall not refuse anyone a transcript of his process, but shall supply it to everyone who asks for it, and they may charge at the rate of ten lines a penny, unless perhaps poverty is proved on oath, in which case let them charge nothing. The rolls of parliament shall be ten inches wide. Parliament shall be held in whatever part of the kingdom the king pleases.

[1] *communitas* [2] *periurus*
[3] *et quod . . . fiat.* If, as is possible, "*quod*" is no more than an indication of quotation to follow, "let . . . roll of the parliament" should perhaps have been printed in inverted commas. The observant reader will notice that the first person (scarcely explicable except as a quotation) occurs at the end of this same chapter.
[4] i.e. the third day of non-appearance
[5] *cuilibet medetur*
[6] *quatenus potest de iure*
[7] *parliamentum nostrum licentiabimus*. The first person is noteworthy. cf. above, n. 3

Chapter 26 *Concerning the grades of peers of parliament*
The king is the head, beginning and end of parliament, hence he has no peer in his grade and so the first grade consists of the king alone. The second grade consists of the archbishops, bishops, abbots, priors[1] holding by barony. The third grade consists of the proctors of the clergy. The fourth grade consists of the earls, barons and other magnates and leading men with an income equivalent to that of[2] an earldom or barony as was stated earlier in the section on the laity.[3] The fifth grade consists of the knights of the shires; the sixth, of the citizens and burgesses. So parliament is made up of six grades. But it must be understood that even if any of the said five grades below the king is absent, provided they were all notified in advance by reasonable summonses of parliament,[4] it is nevertheless deemed to be a full one.

Here ends The Custom of Parliament.[5]

236. Select passages from *Britton*

(*Britton*, ed. and trans. F. M. Nichols, 2 vols (Oxford, 1865), I, pp. 1–24, 123–5, 125–34, 177–85, 194–212, 250–69, 293–309, 345–58; II, pp. 309–28 [French])

To judge by the number of surviving manuscripts, the most successful of a number of post-Bracton epitomes of English law of a practical kind composed in the second half of the thirteenth century. Unlike the others known to us, it is written in French, the working language of the courts. Its author is unknown, but it was a book for practitioners and he himself was probably one.

Book I

OF THE AUTHORITY OF JUSTICES AND OTHER OFFICERS, AND OF PERSONAL PLEAS, INCLUDING PLEAS OF THE CROWN

Prologus

Edward, by the grace of God, king of England, lord of Ireland, and duke of Aquitaine, to all his faithful people and subjects of England and Ireland, peace and grace of salvation.

Desiring peace among the people who by God's permission are under our protection, which peace cannot well be without law, we have caused such laws as have heretofore been used in our realm to be reduced into writing according to that which is here ordained. And we will and command, that throughout England and Ireland they be so used and observed in all points, saving to us the power of repealing extending restricting and amending them, whenever we shall see good, by the assent of our earls and barons and others of our council; saving also to all persons such customs as by prescription of time have been differently used, so far as such customs are not contrary to law.

[1] This list of clergy does not quite correspond to chapters 2 and 9 and it is possible that some such phrase as "and others" (*et aliis*) has dropped out here.
[2] *ternentibus ad valentiam*
[3] chapter 3, above
[4] "*Parliamenti*", but possibly a corruption of "*parliamentum*", in which case the translation would be "... summonses, parliament is ...".
[5] *Modus Parliamenti*

Chapter I

Of the Authority of Justices

1. First, with regard to ourselves and our court, we have ordained, that, inasmuch as we are not sufficient in our proper person to hear and determine all the complaints of our said people, we have distributed our charge in several portions, as is here ordained.

2. We will that our jurisdiction be superior to all jurisdictions in our realm; so that in all kinds of felonies trespasses and contracts, and in all manner of other actions personal or real, we have power to give, or cause to be given, such judgment as the case requires without any other process, whenever we have certain knowledge of the truth, as judge. And the steward of our household shall take our place within the verge of our household; and his office shall extend to the hearing and determining the presentments of the articles of our crown, when we shall see good.

3. Further, we will that justices itinerant be assigned to hear and determine the same articles in every county and franchise every seven years; and that our chief justices of Ireland and Chester have the like power.

4. With respect to the justices assigned to follow us and hold our place wheresoever we shall be in England, we will that they have cognisance of amending false judgments, and of determining appeals and other pleas of trespass committed against our peace, and that their jurisdiction and record shall extend so far as we shall authorise by our writs.

5. We will that the earl of Norfolk, by himself or another knight, be attendant upon us and upon our steward, to execute our commands and the attachments and executions of our judgments and those of our steward throughout the verge of our house, so long as he shall hold the office of marshal.

6. In our household let there be a coroner to execute the business of the crown throughout the verge and wheresoever we shall be or come within our realm; and let the same person or some other be assigned to assay all weights and measures in every our verge throughout our realm according to our standards; and these two duties he shall not fail to do by reason of any franchise, unless such franchise be granted in fee farm or in alms by us or our predecessors.

7. In every county let there be a sheriff who shall be attendant on our commands and those of our justices; and let him have record of pleas pleaded before him by our writs; and under the sheriffs let there be hundreders serjeants and beadles attendant on the sheriffs. And in every county let there be coroners chosen for keeping the pleas of our peace, as shall be authorised in the chapters concerning their office, and let them have record of things relating to their office.

8. Moreover our will is, that there be justices constantly remaining at Westminster, or at such other place as we shall be pleased to ordain, to determine common pleas according as we shall authorise them by our writs; and these justices shall have record of the proceedings held before them by virtue of our writs.

9. Also our will is, that at our exchequers at Westminster and elsewhere our treasurers and our barons there have jurisdiction and record of things which concern their

office, and to hear and determine all causes relating to our debts and seignories and things incident thereto, without which such matters could not be tried; and that they have cognisance of debts owing to our debtors, by means whereof we may the more speedily recover our own.

10. And we will, that justices be assigned in every county to have cognisance in such causes of petty assizes and other matters, as we shall assign them by our letters patent, of which causes we will that they have record. Let justices also be appointed to deliver the gaols in every county, once in every pleadable week, while they find anything to do; and let them likewise have record of the pleas brought before them and of their judgments.

11. And although we have granted to our justices to bear record of pleas pleaded before them, yet we will not that their record be any warrant to them in their own wrong, nor that they be permitted to erase their rolls or amend them or record contrary to the enrollment. And we will that the power of our justices be limited in this manner, that they go not beyond the articles of our writs, or of presentments of jurors, or of plaints before them made, save that they shall have the cognisance of vouchers to warranty, and of other incidental matters without which the original causes could not be determined. And we forbid, that any have power of amending any false judgment of our justices, except the justices who follow us in our court, who are authorised by us for that purpose, or ourselves, with our council; for this we specially reserve to our own jurisdiction.

12. We forbid all our coroners and justices, and all others to whom we have given authority of record, that any, except our steward and our justices of Ireland and of Chester, without our leave substitute another in his place, to do any act of which he himself ought to make record; and if anything be done before such substitutes, we will that it be of no force, though it should be of abjuration or outlawry.

13. We will also, that in counties and hundreds, and in every freeholder's court, the courts be held by the suitors; the like in cities boroughs and franchises, and in sheriffs' tourns and in view of frankpledge.

Chapter II

Of Coroners

1. And because our will is, that coroners shall in every county be the principal guardians of our peace, to bear record of the pleas of our crown, and of their views, and of abjurations and outlawries, we will that they be chosen according as is contained in our statute concerning their election; and when they shall be chosen, we will that in full county they take the oath before the sheriff, that they will lawfully and without demanding any reward make their inquests and enrollments, and do whatsoever belongs to the office of coroner.

2. Also, we will, when any felony or misadventure has happened, or if treasure be found under ground and wickedly concealed, and in case of rape of women, or of the breaking of our prison, or of a man wounded near to death, or of any other accident happening, that the coroner do speedily, as soon as he is informed of it, give notice to

the sheriff and the bailiff of the place, that at a certain day he cause to appear before him, at the place where the accident happened, the four adjacent townships and others if need be, whereby he may inquire of the truth of the casualty. And when he is come, let him swear the townships upon the Holy Evangelists, that they will speak the truth of such articles as he shall demand of them on our behalf. And in this case, and at the sheriffs' tourns, and at view of frankpledge, and in the office of escheators, and in our presence before our steward, and in the eyre of our justices, we will that people be sworn though our writ come not.

3. Afterwards, let the coroner with the jurors go and view the body, and the wounds and blows, or if any one hath been strangled or scalded or by other violence come to his end; and immediately after the view, let the body be buried. And if the coroner find the body buried before such view made, let him make an enrollment thereof; but let him nevertheless not fail to have the body disinterred, and view it openly, and have it viewed by the townships.

4. Those who are summoned, and come not to the coroner's inquest, shall be in our mercy at the coming of our justices at the next assizes in that county, if such defaults be entered in the roll of the coroner; so that neither our coroners, nor our escheators, nor any mere inquirers, have authority to amerce any one for any default.

5. When the coroner shall have a sufficient number by whom he may make his inquests, let him in the first place inquire, whether such person was killed by felony or misadventure; and if by felony, whether the felony was committed in or out of a house, or whether in a tavern, or at a wrestling-match or other meeting. Then let it be inquired, who were present at the fact, great and small, male and female; and who are guilty of the fact, and who of aid, or of force, or of commandment or consent, or of knowingly receiving such felons. And if the coroner on the first inquiry suspect concealment of the truth, or that there is need of further inquiry, and that by others, let inquiry be made again and again; but let him not for any contrariety in the verdicts alter or curtail his enrollment in any point. And further, he must inquire of the manner of the killing, and with what weapon, and of all the circumstances.

6. And let the sheriff forthwith cause all those who shall be indicted to be taken, if they be found. If they be not found, let the coroner inquire, who they are who have withdrawn themselves on that account; and let the sheriff forthwith seize their lands into our hand simply, without removing bailiffs or putting in any one on our behalf, until the parties are convicted by judgment or cleared of the felony. Next, let him seize all their chattels into our hand, and appraise them by good inquest, and that, whether they be the chattels of villeins, who have fled and are suspected, or of freemen, and cause the value to be enrolled in the coroner's roll, and the goods to be delivered to the townships to be answered for to us, in case the person indicted shall either refuse to submit himself to justice in our court, or be afterwards attainted as a felon. Afterwards let it be inquired, whether any of the persons indicted ever by virtue of our writ of menace found surety of our peace to the person killed; and let the names of the mainpernors be enrolled according as shall be found by the verdict.

7. If there be any one who would seek vengeance of the death by appeal of felony, let the male, of what age soever he be, be received before the female; and the next of

blood before one more remote. And if the plaintiff is willing to prosecute his appeal within the year and day, let him find in full county two sufficient pledges, distrainable to the sheriff of the county in whose bailiwick the felony was committed, that he will prosecute his appeal according to the law of the land, and thereupon let him be admitted thereto. Then let the coroner enter his appeal and the names of his pledges. Afterwards, let the bailiff of the place where the felony was committed be commanded to have the bodies of the appellees at the next county court to answer to the plaintiff.

8. And if he appeal several, some of the fact and some of the force or accessory facts, to every appeal let two pledges to prosecute be entered; and let the appeal be entered separately against each person. If the bailiff at the second county court testify that he could not find them, then let it be awarded that the principals appealed of the fact be solemnly demanded that they do come to our peace, to take their trial for the felony whereof they are appealed; and let them be so demanded from county court to county court until they appear or be outlawed. And if the plaintiff makes default at any county court, then let the exigent stand over till our coming into the county or the eyre of the justices; and if the plaintiff will resume his appeal, let him on finding other pledges to prosecute be received thereto, so as he pray it within the year and day.

9. But whether those who were appealed of consenting and of accessory facts withdraw themselves or appear, no exigent shall run against them, nor shall they be compelled to answer to the plaintiff before judgment be pronounced in the case of the principal. But if the principal be outlawed, then let exigents be immediately awarded against the accessories. And when any of them is outlawed, or hath withdrawn himself and is suspected, let the coroner inquire of whose tithing or whose mainpast such fugitive was, and make his enrollment according to the verdict; and let him inquire of the lands and chattels of every fugitive, and in what place he has had property elsewhere than in his bailiwick. And if they appear before the outlawry of the principal, let them be replevisable, and immediately after outlawry of the principal, let them come and answer to the plaintiff.

10. If the felony was committed out of a dwelling-house, then let the coroner inquire, who first found the body, and let him or them, if there be several, women as well as men, young as well as old, be taken and released by pledges, until our coming into the county or the eyre of the justices; and let the coroner cause their names and the names of the pledges to be imbreviated.

11. We forbid every coroner, upon pain of imprisonment and heavy ransom, to make his inquests of felonies accidents or other things belonging to his office, by procurement of friends, or to remove a juror on the challenge of any party, or to take anything by himself or other, or suffer anything to be taken by his clerk or any person belonging to him, for the executing of his office; or to erase, or alter, or practise any kind of fraud in his rolls, or suffer it to be done.

12. If he finds that any one has come to his death by accident, then let him inquire by what accident, whether he was drowned, or fell, or whether he was killed without felony prepensed of any other, or was a felon of himself; and if he was drowned, whether in the sea, or in an arm of the sea, in fresh water, or in a well, or ditch, and by what occasion he was drowned; also from what vessel he fell, and what things

were in such vessel, and to whose hands they came, and of what value they were, and who first found the body. If in a well, then let it be inquired, whose the well was. If by a fall, whether it was from a mill, or from a horse, or a house, or a tree. If from a mill, what things were then moving in the mill, who owned the mill, and the value of the things therein then moving; and likewise of houses, horses, trees, and carts.

13. If the person was killed, then let it be inquired, whether it was done by man or beast or any other thing; if by man, whether by the person himself, or by another; and if by another, whether the misadventure happened by chance, or from necessity to avoid death; if by a beast, whether by a dog, or other beast, and whether the beast was set on to do it, and encouraged to such mischief, or not, and by whom, and so of all the circumstances.

14. Of such as are drowned within our realm by falling from a vessel not at sea, our will is, that the vessel and whatsoever shall be found therein be appraised as a deodand and enrolled by the coroner, that is to say, whatsoever was moving; for if a man happens to fall from a ship under sail, nothing can be deemed the cause of his death, except the ship itself and the things moving in it; but the merchandise lying at the bottom of the ship, is not presumed to be the occasion of his death, and so in like cases. And of those drowned in fountains and wells, we will, as in the other cases, that the coroners admit to mainprise the first finders, and enroll their names and the names of their pledges; and of those who have come to their death by carts or mills, and in the like cases, let the coroner make his inquests and enrollments as above directed where persons are drowned.

15. Whenever the coroner takes his inquest on the body of a person feloniously killed, let him cause one or more of kin to the deceased on the side of the father or mother to appear before him in proof of Englishry according to the custom of the country, and enroll their names.

16. We will also that the coroners receive the confessions of felonies made by approvers in the presence of the sheriff, whom we intend to be his controller in every part of his office; and let them cause such confessions to be enrolled. And when any man has fled to church, we will that the coroner as soon as he has notice of it, command the bailiff of the place, that he cause the neighbours and the four nearest townships to appear before him at a certain day at the church where the fugitive shall be; and in their presence he shall receive the confession of the felony; and if the fugitive pray to abjure our realm, let the coroner immediately do what is incumbent on him. But if he does not pray abjuration, let him be delivered to the township to keep at their peril.

17. If the coroner be to take an inquest of rape, let him carefully inquire into all the circumstances of the force and of the felony, and make enrollment of the presumptive signs, such as stains of blood, and tearing of clothes. If of a wounding, let him inquire with what weapon, and of the length and depth of the wound. Let him likewise enter in his roll all judgments of death given in his bailiwick by any other than our justices; and in such cases, we will that their rolls be a record. And whereas it is declared above, that coroners ought to make enrollments of appeals of felonies of the death of a man, let them do the like in appeals of rape, robbery, larceny, and in appeals of every other kind of felony.

18. It also belongs to their office to inquire of ancient treasure found in the earth, of wreck of the sea, of sturgeons and whales, as soon as they shall have notice thereof; and to attach and let to mainprise those who have found or made away with them, and to enroll their names, and to secure such findings for our use. And we will that our sheriffs and bailiffs be attendant on our coroners, and execute their precepts.

Chapter III

Of Eyres of Justices

1. With respect to our coming, and the eyre of our justices, we will that general proclamation be solemnly made in the markets cities and boroughs throughout the county, as well within franchises as without, that all the freemen of the county, and four men and the provost of every vill, and all the mainpernors and those who have been let to mainprise throughout the county, appear at a certain day, which shall be forty days distant at least, before us, or such justices as shall be named in our precept to keep the eyre in the same county: and that all those who claim any franchise in the same county be the same day before us or the same justices, and that every one show distinctly in writing what franchises he claims; and that all those, who have any complaints to make against our ministers or bailiffs or those of others or any persons whatsoever, be there at the same day, to exhibit such complaints and find pledges to prosecute; and that the sheriff of the county have there all such writs as have been adjourned until the eyre, and all the assizes of *novel disseisin*, *mort d'ancester*, *darrein presentment*, *utrum*, and of dower, and all the prisoners and attachments. And meantime we will command our justices of the bench, that they adjourn all the pleas of the county and send them before us or such justices itinerant in that county, so that they be there at the day named.

2. And as to the coming of our justices, our will is, that as soon as they be come to the place appointed for holding the eyre, they produce the authority they have of us by our letters patent, and cause them to be read in the hearing of the people; and afterwards let him who is first named in the letters, show and declare to the people the occasions and advantages of their coming into that county; this done, let them receive the essoins of the common summons, which shall be immediately determined and adjourned. Then let the essoins of pleas of land be received; and let these be adjudged and the fourth day after adjourned.

3. Next let the letters whereby any persons whatever claim to hold franchises in that county be received, and let their claims be enrolled, and a transcript of the same enrollment be delivered to the sheriff; and as to all such franchises as are not claimed, let the sheriff be commanded to seize them into our hands by way of distress, and be answerable to us for the issues, until those who shall claim them have saved their defaults for not attending the summons; and let them then answer by what warrant they have held them.

4. Afterwards let the justices take the wands of the sheriff, and of the lords of the franchises, and of all the other inferior bailiffs, and then let the sheriff swear, that he will duly execute the lawful commands of our justices, and will well conceal the

secrets and counsels of their eyre, so help him God and the saints. And after this oath is taken, let the wand be delivered back to him. Then let the sheriff present all his officers and bailiffs, clerks and others, by whom the precepts of the justices and executions of their judgments are to be performed; and let them all take the same oath that the sheriff took, and their wands be delivered back to them.

5. And if there be any archbishop, bishop, abbot or prior, earl or baron, or other, that claims the franchise of return of our writs, let him take the same oath that the sheriff took; or let them take their wands in their hands, and present such bailiffs in their stead as will take the oath for them, and for whose acts they will be answerable as to that which to their office shall belong: and then let the wands be delivered by those lords to their bailiffs. Afterwards let proclamation be made, that all persons belonging to franchises, except the bailiffs, depart unto their own homes until further summons or until a certain day.

6. Next let the bailiffs of the sheriff swear, that they will truly present two or four of their bailiwick, or more or less, who are not appealed of any crime, nor are appellors, and such as shall best know and will inquire and discover secret acts concerning the breach of our peace. And when the names are given in, let those come and swear, that they will lawfully associate to themselves such others, by whom the truth may best appear. Afterwards, let them, together with those whom they have chosen for the most sufficient, swear, that they will lawful presentment make of such chapters as shall be delivered to them in writing, and that in this they will not fail for any love, hatred, fear, reward, or promise, and that they will conceal the secrets, so help them God, and the saints. And then let the chapters be read to them, and delivered to every dozen separately.

7. Afterwards, let proclamation be made, that none presume to amerce any man for making default in a court baron or hundred, who shall at that time be before us or our justices; and that no market be kept within ten miles, except in the town where our justices shall be, if the town is not able to find sufficient provision for such as shall abide there; and that, if any person be come who has no business on hand, he shall make his attorney, if he please, and depart home.

8. Afterwards, let the coroners, or their heirs, be commanded to deliver to the justices their rolls since the last eyre; and we will that the justices seal them under their seals, and forthwith without any examination deliver the rolls back to them, so that they be every day with their clerks before the justices, while they have occasion for them.

9. Afterwards, let the presentments upon the chapters delivered to the dozens be received in writing; and let the same be indented, so that the justices may have one part thereof and the other may remain with the presentors. The chapters which are to be delivered to them are not however of any certain number; for as crimes increase, so must the chapters and other remedies increase. Some of these chapters are concerning counterfeiters, murders, accidents, and other matters, as will appear from the following heads.

Chapter IV

Of the Chapters of the Eyre

In the first place, let the old articles presented in the last eyre in that county touching breaches of our peace, which then remained undetermined, be enquired of, heard, and determined. Of our mortal enemies abiding in our land presentment cannot properly be made, but accusation and appeal, as will appear in the chapter of appeals.

. . .

[Chapter XXVI]

2. Appeals of felony may also be brought for wounds, and for imprisonment of freemen, and for every other enormous trespass; but for avoiding the perilous risk of battle, it is better to proceed by our writs of trespass than by appeals; for if variance be found between the appeal as entered in the roll of the coroner and as set forth in the county court, or if there has been any omission, or any interruption of the county courts, or other error, the plaintiff shall be commanded to prison for not having performed what he bound himself to do, and shall make satisfaction to the defendant, and afterwards to us. But if the appeal be maintained, and the defendant have put himself for good or ill on the country, and the jury say that he is guilty, the same judgment shall be given against him, as would have been in case he had been vanquished in battle, to wit, wound for wound, imprisonment for imprisonment, and trespass for trespass. But in such cases our will is, that the execution of the judgment be so far mitigated, that the appellees be sent to prison, and there remain in irons till they have made satisfaction to the plaintiffs; and they shall afterwards be punished for breach of our peace.

3. The like judgment shall result where the proceeding is by our writ of trespass. But some trespasses deserve a greater punishment, as trespasses committed in time of peace against knights or other honourable persons by ribalds or other worthless people; in which case our pleasure is, that if a ribald be attainted at the suit of any knight of having feloniously struck him without any provocation from the knight, the ribald shall lose the hand wherewith he offended. We have said, in time of peace, because as to injuries done at tournaments and jousts, or such warlike feats, we will not interpose, unless the acts be done in our presence.

. . .

Chapter XXVII

Of Attachments, and other proceedings in actions of trespass: and of the conclusion of the Eyre

1. We have already treated of the manner of convicting offenders for breach of our peace by appeals and presentments; we must now show how the breach of our peace is to be convicted by way of trespass. In the first place, when any one has obtained our writ of trespass for a mayhem, imprisonment, or wound, or for anything stolen or robbed or in any other manner wrongfully carried away or detained, or for breaking parks, or for battery, or for other things committed against our peace, or against a bailiff for refusing to render account to his lord, let him begin by delivering his writ

to the sheriff; and afterwards let him find two pledges distrainable to the sheriff to prosecute his plaint. And let the sheriff cause the trespassers to be distrained by their cattle or by their chattels, and afterwards adjourn them to be in our court at the day prefixed according as shall be contained in our writs, to answer to the plaintiffs for the trespasses contained in the writs; so that every defendant may have notice of his adversary's case.

2. And if the writs are returnable in a franchise, and the bailiffs will not execute our precept unless the plaintiff will find them pledges distrainable to them, in such case the sheriff may make a return in our court, that he sent to the bailiffs of the person having the franchise of return of writs to do execution, but that they have nothing done; and we will immediately command the sheriff that he omit not by reason of the franchise to enter and do execution. And the plaintiff, if he will, may proceed against the bailiffs to recover his damages; for it would have been allowable for the plaintiffs to have found sureties to prosecute their plaints in our chancery without prejudice to any one; wherefore the surety found to the sheriff on every writ is sufficient.

3. If the defendants suffer distresses to be taken into the hands of the sheriffs, the sheriffs may return that they have distrained them by such cattle or by such chattels; and if the defendants do not thereupon come into court, then it must be distinguished whether the plaint is in our court, or elsewhere, as in the county, or in a court baron or other freeholder's court; and if in our court before us or before our justices, then we will that no default be adjudged in any plea until after the fourth day. If they do not come within the fourth day, and are not essoined, and the plaintiff offers himself and demands judgment for the default, the great distress shall be awarded, and the sheriff shall be charged to answer unto us for the issues of the first distress; and the justice shall adjourn the defendant to be in court on another day; at which day no essoin shall be allowed him, for we forbid the allowing of an essoin in any case after default, until such default be cleared in our court. And if upon this day the defendants make default, the issues shall be forfeited to us, and the sheriff shall be charged to answer unto us for the same, and these distresses shall be continued from day to day until they appear and answer.

4. If the plea be in any other court than ours, and the defendants have neither appeared nor caused themselves to be essoined, we will not that judgment be delayed until the fourth day; but immediately on the first day let it be awarded by the suitors, that such distresses be detained, and more be seized, and so from court to court. If the sheriff or the bailiff has not executed the precept, let him be in mercy.

5. The same process of distress is to be awarded in defaults after essoins in a writ of trespass committed against our peace; but in an attachment of felony no distress runs excepting against the body, if it can be found. And if in the above cases the sheriff return, that the trespassers have nothing in his bailiwick whereby they may be attached, it shall be awarded that he take their bodies; and if he return that the bodies are not found in his bailiwick, then let it be ordered by our writ of judgment, that they be demanded from county court to county court until they be outlawed, if they do not appear.

6. And when any person who has been distrained shall come into court, and cannot clear his default, let him be straightway adjudged in our mercy for his default; and if there be several defaults, let there be several amercements. And if any one be attached by pledges and make default, let the pledges be summoned to hear their judgment, for not having him in court for whom they were pledged. At which day if they do not appear, or cannot deny their being pledged they also shall be in our mercy; but if they will deny the plevin, the debate shall be between them and the sheriff.
7. When the defendants have appeared in court, and heard the plaintiffs count against them, and have defended themselves by proper words of defence, they may than aid themselves by exceptions general or special; and first, by exceptions to the judge; afterwards to the person of the plaintiff or to their own person, as shall be mentioned amongst exceptions in the writ of right; or they may except to the writ, as where a writ is sued out into any other county than where the fact is alleged to have been committed, or for a fault, error, or omission therein.
8. If there be no dilatory exception, let them answer to the action; to which they may say that they were previously acquitted of the same trespass, as against the same plaintiff; and if this be verified by record, let judgment be given accordingly. Or the defendants may say that the parties made accord of this trespass; and if the plaintiff deny it, let the truth be inquired by the country. And if the plaintiffs will not agree to the accord, let the defendants be awarded quit, and the plaintiffs in mercy.
9. With regard to receivers of trespassers, commanders, and accessories, there is not as yet any punishment ordained, except only against the principal trespassers. And if the plaintiff complains of a damage done to himself and to his men, or only on behalf of his men, the defendant may say that every man has a separate action; and in such cases we will that the plaintiffs recover nothing by their plaints beyond the damages which they can reasonably show they have sustained by the loss of the services of their men, who have been beaten or imprisoned, or so treated as to be incapable of service. And their action shall not be brought until after conviction of the trespass committed against the servants.
10. If the sheriff return that the defendant is a clerk, and refuses to submit to his jurisdiction, and that he has no lay fee in his bailiwick whereby he can be distrained, let his ordinary, as the archbishop or bishop, be commanded by our writ that he cause such a one his clerk to appear. And if he does not produce him at the day named in our writ, let the bishop be summoned to answer why he did not produce him at our precept. And if the bishop neglect our summons, let him be attached to come by distress; and if he does not come at the first distress, let the great distress, as above said, proceed against him until he shall come; and when he has appeared in court, if he cannot clear his default, let him be amerced.
11. There are however several actions of trespass which require greater expedition, as trespasses committed against us or our consort, or our children, or against foreign persons, as solemn ambassadors or alien friends, or against our officers, or against merchants, or against those who have taken the cross; in which cases no formality of attachment shall be required, but the bodies of the defendants shall be immediately attached, so that the sheriff shall have them to answer on the first day.

12. There are some actions also pleadable by like distresses as in trespass, where no outlawry ensues, and which are more dilatory by a day, and commence by summons; as a plea of debt, of covenant, in case of warranty of charter, waste, sale, destruction of houses or woods or other freehold, and pleas of *neifty*, and several others.

13. Whatever may be pleaded in the county court may also be pleaded in the eyre of the justices; as pleas *de vetito namio*, of debt, of *neifty*, of wards, and marriages; also presentments made in the sheriff's tourns and in views of frankpledge; and also pleas concerning false weights and measures, and many others, which are pleadable before our justices assigned to take assizes in the county, and writs pleadable before our justices of the bench at Westminster.

14. If any presentment upon the articles of our crown remain uncommenced or undetermined, then let the justices, unless they have a good and reasonable excuse, be punishable at our discretion. When the presentments on the articles of the eyre are determined, the pleas of land shall be immediately adjourned before them to another county; or if the eyre is not to be continued, they shall be adjourned into the bench, in the presence of the parties. The amercements are immediately to be assessed, and the estreats sent to our exchequer; the like as to fines and the chattels of felons and fugitives; and the names of the fugitives shall be enrolled in two rolls, whereof one shall remain with the coroners and the sheriff of the county under the seal of the justices thereto attached, and such persons are to be demanded by their names at the first county court after the eyre, to come and submit to justice in our court, and so from county court to county court, until they appear or be outlawed. The other roll, together with all the rolls of the eyre, shall be transmitted to our exchequer, and safely kept in our treasury.

15. If the suitors of the county be attainted of false judgment, or have made any other error in the usage of the law, the county shall be in our mercy. The hundreds also for the defaults of the suitors, and the townships for divers defaults; and the amercements shall be assessed according to our statutes of Westminster. And afterwards let the sheriff be commanded to aid the presentors by causing the neighbours to raise reasonable contributions towards their expenses.

. . .

Chapter XXX
Of the Sheriff's Tourns

1. There are some articles concerning our crown and the breach of our peace of which sheriffs may hold plea at other times than on the county days, and in a different place from that where the pleas of the county are held. These pleas are called the tourns of the sheriff, who ought to hold them twice in the year, within every hundred of his county. And that which before the sheriff is called the sheriff's tourn, is in the court of a freeman and in franchises, and in our hundreds, called view of frankpledge, where a more special inquiry is made concerning those who are not in any tithing, than is done in the sheriff's tourn.

2. At these tourns all the freemen of the hundred and other landholders being summoned, ought in general to appear, except clerks, persons in religion, and women.

At which day let the sheriff cause twelve of the most sage, lawful, and sufficient men out of the whole hundred to be chosen, and to swear they will present the truth of the articles hereinafter mentioned. Afterwards the rest shall be sworn by dozens, and by townships, that they will make lawful presentment to the first twelve jurors upon the articles wherewith they shall be charged by them. Next it shall be enjoined them, that if they find any offender, from whom there may be any danger of life or limb, the name of such offender be secretly presented. Afterwards the following articles shall be delivered to the twelve first jurors, who are to be charged upon their oaths that they will lawfully present the wrongs and offences which they shall find upon inquiry from the townships by means of these articles.

3. Of mortal enemies of the king or queen, or their children, and of those consenting to them; of counterfeiters of the king's seal and of his money; of homicides and murderers; of those who feloniously set fire to the houses or corn of others; of burglars, robbers and thieves; of breakers of the king's prison; of ravishers of women; of outlaws and abjurors of the realm who are returned; of sorcerers and sorceresses; of apostates and heretics; of traitors; of poisoners; of cut-purses; of usurers; of salesmen knowingly buying and selling stolen meat; of those who knowingly bleach skins of stolen beasts; and of menders of clothes knowingly buying stolen clothes and turning them into other shapes; of treasure hidden and found in the earth; of hue and cry wrongfully raised, or duly raised and not pursued; of waters stopped or narrowed or turned from their course; of roads stopped, narrowed, or turned; of boundaries removed or wrongfully altered; of walls, houses, gates, marlpits, ditches, or other nuisances raised or made in any common way to the annoyance of the same way and to the danger of passengers; of petty thieves, who shear or flay sheep or other cattle in the night to steal their skins; of those who take thefbote; and of those who have made a prison of their houses; or committed hamsoken, or breach of pound; and of offenders in parks or in vivaries; or takers of others' pigeons; of breach of the assize of bread and beer, and of those who buy and sell by weights and measures not according to the assize; of affrays, of brawlers, and of bloodshed; of watches not kept; of the king's highways not widened; of those who have detained approvers in any other prison than in our custody, or other felons elsewhere than in our prison above a day and night; of new franchises, customs, or instruments of correction, set up since the last tourn, in water or land; of waif, or wreck of sea found and retained; of bridges and highways broken, and who ought to repair them; of rights belonging to the king withheld, as wards, marriages, reliefs, demesnes, advowsons of churches, and all kinds of suits; and of those who claim royal franchises and powers of punishment; and of those of twelve years old and upwards in the hundred who have not come to the tourn.

4. All these articles shall also be inquired of at the view of frankpledge; and the following articles besides; whether all the headboroughs are come to the view, and whether they have their tithings complete; of those of twelve years old or upwards, excepts clerks, and knights and their children, and women, who are not in tithings, and of their receivers, and of whose mainpast they are; of vagrants through the country who are not of any one's mainpast, and are of suspicious character.

5. When the townships have given in their verdict to the first jurors, and they are certified of the truth, let the first jurors immediately go and deliver up their presentment to the sheriff, such as they will abide by without being questioned, and let them exhibit the presentments for felony privately, and the other presentments openly.
6. If any person indicted of felony be present, he shall be immediately apprehended and carried to our gaol, unless it be any thief or robber in possession of his theft "handhaving and backbearing", and the sakeber be present to make his suit, in which case let the evidence be examined, and judgment executed upon him, if the sakeber verifies the thing as his own, or as stolen or robbed out of his custody; and let the punishment be according to the quantity of the thing stolen as before is mentioned. As to such of the persons indicted as shall not be found present, let the presentment be sealed under the seals of the twelve presentors. And the sheriff shall cause them to be apprehended, and keep such as are not bailable safe in prison until the first gaol delivery, and bail those who are bailable until the same time.
7. What persons are bailable and what not, is mentioned in our statutes. Besides, those persons are not bailable, who are indicted or appealed of compassing our death, as is above said; nor those who are apprehended by the judgment of our justices, as persons convicted of open deceit committed in our court, nor those who are apprehended for re-disseisin, nor those who by judgment of our court are committed to prison for arrears of accounts, nor those who are taken for rape of women, or by statute merchant, nor those who are convicted of trespassing in parks and vivaries, or of impeding the execution of judgments of our court, nor those who have carried off religious women from their convent, nor those who have carried off infants whose marriages belong to others.
8. As to the presentments made of boundaries removed, ways and waters obstructed, and such other personal trespasses, let the trespassers, if they are present, immediately answer thereto; and if they will not, or if they are not present, then let the twelve presentors be commanded immediately to go and remedy such nuisances, if they have been done since the last tourn, by restoring matters to their lawful and usual state. And if such jurors have wrongfully aggrieved any persons in their absence by their presentment, in such case the persons aggrieved shall have an action to be reinstated, by plaint in the county court, or by our writ, if necessary, either against all the twelve presentors jointly, or against any of them severally. And if the plaintiffs cannot make good their plaints, then let the defendants recover their damage, and the plaintiffs be in mercy.
9. Afterwards let all those be amerced who shall be named as trespassers by the presentments, and those also of twelve years and upwards who have not appeared, except prelates, earls, barons, persons of religion, and women, and except also those who are not living or constantly resident in the hundreds, although they may have dwellings there. As to breach of assizes, let the proceedings be as mentioned in the next chapter. In views of frankpledge, let the headboroughs be amerced, who shall not have their tithings complete, there present, unless they are excusable by reason of the death of any one or more. Also let those be amerced who are twelve years old and upwards, and who ought to be in a tithing and have not been, and those also of

whose mainpast they are and have been; but if any person be elsewhere in a tithing, it is sufficient.

10. When any one is to be admitted into a tithing, first he shall find pledges to our bailiffs, that he will be amenable to justice in our court as often as there shall be occasion, and shall take the oath of fealty to us and to our heirs; and let him be delivered to his pledges, and let his name and the name of his pledges be enrolled.

11. Fealty shall be sworn in these words: Hear this you, N., bailiff, that I, P., from this day forward will be faithful and loyal to our lord E. king of England and his heirs, and will bear unto them faith and loyalty of life and limb, of body and chattels, and of earthly honour, and will neither know nor hear of their hurt or damage, but I will oppose it to the best of my power, so help me God and the saints.

. . .

Chapter XXXII
Of Villenage

1. We have above in part treated of the law of free persons; we must now treat of the condition of villeins. This condition was of ancient time changed from freedom to bondage by the constitution of nations, and not by the law of nature, as it stood at the time of the flood and earlier, when all things were common to every one, and all men were entirely free, and lived according to the law of nature. But from the increase of mankind and the appropriation of goods which before were common, battles arose in divers places in the world, and to avoid bloodshed and the perilous chances of battle, it was then ordained by the constitution of nations that men should not kill one another, but whenever one could take another in battle, that the person taken should for ever remain a bondman to him who took him, to do with him and all his issue that should proceed from him whatsoever he would, as with his beast or chattel, to give, to sell, and to kill. Afterwards it was ordained, on account of the cruelty of some lords, that no one should kill them, but that their lives and limbs, as well as those of free men, should be under the protection of kings and princes. Whence the law is this, that whosoever kills his villein, shall bear the same judgment as if he had killed a free man.

2. There is another kind of *neifs* who are not *neifs* by ancient birth, but are properly villeins, such as free men who have acknowledged themselves in our court to be villeins, or who have been in any manner convicted as villeins by plea under our writ of *neifty*. Beside those mentioned, there are no other kinds of villeins.

3. With respect to those who by reason of any tenement have made redemption of blood or done other villein services, although they and their ancestors have performed such services from one generation to another, if any one sprung from such a stock has fled from his lord, and is demanded by him as his villein, and such fugitive can prove his stock to be free by good inquest of the neighbourhood, and that the lord claiming him was not seised of him and his ancestors as his villeins by reason of their bodies, but by reason of the tenement which they held of him in villenage; in such case judgment shall be given against the lords. For justice will not allow that villenage, by any long

seisin of a servile tenement, shall make any freeman a bondman; nor, on the other hand, that long seisin of a free tenement shall change the condition of a villein into free estate. So that none can be a villein except by birth, or by recognisance. Nor can one be more a villein than another; for they are all of equal condition – whosoever is a bondman, is as absolutely a bondman as any other.

4. Nevertheless all who are begotten by villeins are not bondmen, for no one begotten by a bondman of a free woman out of matrimony is a bondman, although it happen that the issue be afterwards born within matrimony. Nor shall he be a bondman who was begotten on a bondwoman in matrimony, so as the father be free.

5. Where any one is by birth a bondman, he shall be merely the chattel of his lord to give and sell at his pleasure. But as bondmen are annexed to the freehold of the lord, they are not devisable by testament; and therefore holy church can take no cognisance of them in court Christian, although devised in a testament.

6. A villein may recover his freedom several ways, as if his lord enfeoff him of any tenement to him and his heirs, whether he receive his homage or not; for since it is the lord's pleasure that his bondman shall have heirs of his own other than the lord, and that his heirs shall succeed to his inheritance, it sufficiently appears that he intends his bondman to have the status of a freeman. A bondman also becomes free if he marries his lady, as well as a *neif* when her lord marries her; for otherwise so great inconvenience would ensue, that the heir should be villein to himself, and the land should escheat to the chief lord, who would hold the heir as his villein, when perhaps neither he nor any of his lineage were ever so. But if a villein espouses a free woman who has land in fee, their son born in matrimony is a villein, and his lord shall acquire the land of the mother either by his own entry or by means of his villein, heir to his mother, by assize of *mort d'ancester*, if she does not assign it over in her lifetime, and the son survives her, and she has no other issue which is free. Wherefore when any bondman or bondwoman once becomes free, or is enfranchised by the free bed of his lord or of any other, we ordain in favour of freedom and of matrimony that they and their issue shall for ever be held free, and the husbands be entitled to hold by the courtesy of England, and the wives to dower.

7. We will that villeins in all actions be answerable to every one, and every one to them, so that the exception of villenage shall only hold good between the lord and his villein, and that only when the lord has been in recent possession of him and of his suit, or at the least has been seised of him as his villein within a year and a day.

8. A bondman may be enfranchised also by the recognisance of his lord, as if his lord has acknowledged him to be free in a court of record. So also if he be waived by the lord, as where the lord has abandoned him. Likewise, by writing of his lord, as if his lord has for himself and his heirs quitclaimed to the bondman and his heirs all manner of right which he had or might have in the person of the *neif* by reason of the bondage of his blood. Villeins may also recover their freedom by the negligence of their lords, as if any lord suffer his villein to be fugitive for time of prescription limited in our writ of *mort d'ancester*; or to abide within our demesnes without challenge for a year and a day – a privilege which was heretofore granted to us by common allowance

for our profit and for the improvement of our towns. Likewise, if he permit his *neif* to be ordained clerk, or created a knight, at least until they be degraded from their orders; and so in the case of his *neif*, if he suffer her to be married to a freeman, she and all her issue shall for ever after be of free estate, as before is said.

9. Where any *neif* flies from his lord, his lord may pursue him as his chattel, to apprehend and bring him back into his fee wheresoever he shall find him within the year and day. But after that time they shall be deemed free as much as they please, until the lords can recover them by judgment of our court. It is not however necessary for every lord to keep his villein as a prisoner; but it is sufficient if the lords are in possession of their services, so as to take of some the services due from their tenements, and from others, who hold nothing in villenage, a penny a year for chevage and one day's work in harvest, or other service, small or great, according to their ability. So that the lord's right of action to recover his fugitive *neif* commences when the *neif* ceases to perform such services and to acknowledge him for his lord.

10. If the lord cannot find the fugitive in his fee, nor bring him to justice within the year and day, we will command the sheriff of the place in whose bailiwick the villein shall be residing, that he "justly and without delay cause such a one the plaintiff to have such a one his *neif* and fugitive with all his chattels and all his suit". In this plaint no summons lies, but the first process is distress, and the first distress is retained and others taken, if the plea be in the county court, until the defendant appears or is attached by pledges.

11. And because the fugitive may allege freedom, a matter which the sheriff has not jurisdiction to try, we have, in favour of freedom, granted to such fugitives that whenever they find themselves aggrieved by such proceedings of their lords, they shall have peace from such grievances until the eyre of our justices in that county, and that they shall have our writs for that purpose, whenever they wish to obtain them, upon finding pledges to the sheriffs to prove their freedom in the eyre aforesaid; and that in the meantime they shall have peace.

12. This writ of peace is called the writ *de libertate*, and in favour of freedom the pleadings are sooner dispatched than in a writ *de nativo*, unless the person who purchased the writ fail to appear, upon which he and his pledges shall be in mercy for his nonsuit. If, on the other hand, he prosecutes his suit, and the lord makes default, and the summons be in evidence, let it be awarded that he be free, and the lord in mercy, because he has wrongfully aggrieved him, and let the sheriff be commanded not to permit the lord to aggrieve him for the future. If the lord appears, it then lies on the bondman to prove his freedom, which he may do in divers ways, as appears by the several points, which have been stated in this chapter.

13. In a plea of *neifty* (as also in pleas of *replegiari facias*, *venire facias*, and the like) no essoin is to be allowed to the defendant until after appearance. And if the lord offers himself, and the fugitive makes default, let it be awarded on account of his default, that the fugitive and his pledges be in mercy, and that the plaintiff by the default of the fugitive do make proof of his *neifty* against the fugitive, so that the fugitive be never afterwards admitted in our court to prove his freedom, and that he be distrained by the grand distress until he appear.

14. If any lord has obtained a writ to remove the plaints by *pone* to a higher court, before any plaint upon the original writ is commenced in the county court, the *pone* shall thereby be abatable, on account of the false suggestion therein contained, which supposes a plaint to be in the county court, where in fact no summons was ever made. For before summons or attachment or appearance, a plaint is never in court. And this may be verified by the date of the *pone* and the day of the summons.

15. And when he is in court, let the plaintiff count against him by himself or his serjeant in this manner: "John who is here declareth this to you, that Peter who is there wrongfully fled from him, and herein wrongfully, that he is his villein who fled from his land within the term, etc., and of whom he was seised as of his villein until such a year when he fled from him." Forasmuch as the effect of this writ is to determine the possession as of a chattel, it is not proper to count in this plea by descent nor by resort, nor to touch at all upon the right, no mention being made thereof in the writ. For then there would be a variance between the writ and the declaration, and so the writ would be abatable. And besides, if one could so count, the defendant might then defend the right by battle, or by the great assize, which would be a great inconvenience to the lord. And because proof of *neifty* is made by suit, he must add thus, "and if he denies this, he denies it wrongfully, for the plaintiff hath thereof suit good and sufficient."

16. And immediately let the suit be examined, not only by taking their acknowledgements whether they are villeins to the plaintiff, but whether he against whom the plaint is prosecuted was ever upon the land of the plaintiff, and in what manner the plaintiff was seised of him. And if the suit be found to disagree, in so much is it bad and defective, and the plaint shall be lost.

17. But if the suit agrees, then let the defendant answer thus: "Peter who is here defends the wrong and force, and the flight from the land of John and the *neifty*, and will defend the same where and when he ought."

18. Afterwards he shall aid himself by exceptions to the judge, and then to the person of the plaintiff, and afterwards to his own person; and next by exception to the writ if there is any defect or error; and afterwards to the declaration, if there is any defect, omission, or variance in it; and lastly to the action.

19. Thus he may say that "he is a freeman, and Robert his father was free, and those of the suit were free, until they acknowledged themselves villeins; for in the reign of king Richard", or of some other king, "it came to pass that a certain knight begot one Theobald, great-grandfather of this same Peter, which Theobald married the *neif* of the ancestor of the same John, who held land of him in villenage, which Theobald as long as he lived performed the villein services to the tenement appertaining, and died in the same villenage; that from Theobald came Philip, from Philip William, from William Simon, from Simon Robert, from Robert Peter who is here, all of whom performed the services aforesaid by reason of the villein tenement, and not by reason of their persons, until the time of Robert, father of this same Peter." And if he can prove this by inquest, it shall be adjudged against the plaintiff.

20. The defendant may also aid himself by exceptions against the suit, for he may say that as to one of his kindred he is not admissible in evidence. For if there were three

of his male kindred, and five females, or more or less, and he can aver of one of the kinsmen that he was begotten out of matrimony of a free woman, and that the second kinsman who offers himself for suit was begotten in marriage by a freeman although his mother was a *neif*, notwithstanding he has no exception to make against the third kinsman of the suit, we will that if he demands judgment whether he ought to answer to the suit of a single man, it shall in such case be adjudged against the plaintiff; because the blood of a man cannot nor ought to be tried by means of women, neither is one male alone without more to be admitted as sufficient suit.

21. Or he may plead that he has done homage to his lord for a tenement; or that his lord has released him from all actions; or that he married his lady; or (if the defendant is a woman) that she was married to her lord or to another freeman. Or he may be aided by other peremptory exceptions, as above is mentioned.

22. If any one pleads that he is a clerk or knight, in such case judgment shall be given against the plaintiff, who must impute it to his own negligence. And if the clerk or the knight had not leave from the lord to take upon him such order, or those who ordained them to confer the same upon them, then the lord shall have his action to recover against those who ordained them to be knights or clerks such damages as he can reasonably assign. And if such knights or clerks refuse to perform honourable services becoming their station more readily and cheerfully to such natural lords than to others, or behave in any other manner unnaturally to them, in such cases we will that they be degraded; and if this cannot be done, that satisfaction be made to their lords out of their chattels; and if their chattels are not sufficient, let those who ordained them be answerable.

23. Or the defendant may say that the plaintiff is not entitled to an answer, inasmuch as this is an action limited within a certain term (as other actions are), and inasmuch as neither he nor any of his ancestors were ever within the term seised of him or any of his ancestors, as their villeins, he may demand judgment whether he is at this time bound to answer to him. And if this be proved, the plaintiff shall be convicted of false plaint. But to this, as in all other actions, he may reply that such plea ought not to avail the defendant, for that by continual claims he has been theretofore demanded and his ancestors likewise, by him and his ancestors by other like writs, but by the death of his ancestors or by the king's death those writs abated.

24. Or the defendant may plead that he has resided upon our demesne lands or elsewhere in any of our towns or cities for a year and a day without having been claimed by the plaintiff, and if he demands judgment whether in such case he ought to answer, and can verify this exception, the lord shall be forejudged of his action for his negligence. So also, where the defendant can prove by record of our court that the lord has knowingly suffered him to be upon juries and inquests in our court as a freeman. So, if he can verify by record that he has recovered frank tenement against him by judgment of our court, wherein the plaintiff did not allege any exception of villenage against him.

25. Or he may say that the plaintiff ought not to be answered until he has fully restored to him whatever goods of his he detains from him, or hath detained since he claimed free estate; which plea shall be allowable by reason of the words contained

in our writ, which says, "with all his chattels and all his suit", so that the plaintiff in his own writ supposes himself not to be seised of any of the chattels.

26. If judgment is given for the plaintiff, let it be awarded that the plaintiff recover him as his villein with all his suit and all his chattels and all his acquisitions, and that the villein have no heir other than the lord, and the villein shall remain in our mercy.

Here ends the book of personal pleas, and begins that of real pleas.

Book II

OF DISSEISINS AND THEIR REMEDIES

Chapter I

Of Suits concerning Land, pleadable by Attachment

Having gone through the form and manner of pleading personal pleas pleadable by attachments of the body or by distresses of movable goods, we must now treat of pleas concerning land, in which the process is by attachment of the very thing demanded. And first, of those pleas which more nearly concern the breach of our peace by fresh force, as when a person is wrongfully ejected or disturbed in the peaceable possession of his freehold, which act of violence is called disseisin, and fresh force. And in favour of complainants it is ordained that disseisins may be pleaded by petty assizes in the counties where the lands lie, in the absence as well as in the presence of the offenders.

2. There can be no disseisin except of a freehold. A freehold is a possession of soil or of services issuing out of the soil by a freeman holding in fee to him and his heirs, or at the least for term of life, whether the soil be charged with free or other services. Fee is a right vested in the person of the true heir, or of any other who hath acquired it by lawful title, whoever may be seised of the freehold. And this is the property, whereof one may have more and another less, as the heir of the disseisor has one kind of fee and of property, but the disseisee has a greater. But inasmuch as no one can be disseised unless he be first seised, we will therefore, before we proceed to pleas, show in what manner seisin may be acquired.

. . .

Chapter VIII

Of Charters

1. It has been said above in the chapter concerning debt that it is necessary for an obligation to be clothed in five different ways. The same clothing is also necessary for gifts and purchases. And as to that clothing by writing, which is called charter, it must be understood that there are several kinds of charters, as charters of kings and charters of private persons; and of the king's charters some are single, some common, some universal. Of simple charters, some are of pure feoffment and single, others of conditional feoffment; some are charters of confirmation, and some of quitclaim.

2. Single charters of pure feoffment without condition ought to remain with the purchasers and their heirs. Conditional charters ought to be indented in two or three

parts, so that one part sealed by the purchaser may remain with the donor, and another part sealed with the seal of the donor may remain with the purchaser and his heirs, and the third part be put into an impartial hand, so that no one may afterwards demand a right in anything by form of gift or by condition, but that our court may be certified of the form by the charter. For no action or exception avails unless it can be proved, and it is useless to pray the court that the adverse party may be compelled to produce a deed, because no one is obliged to arm his adversary.

3. As to royal charters, whether they are allowable, or false or doubtful, can be adjudged by none but ourselves. For it is the office of the author to determine and judge concerning them. Wherefore we will that such doubts and illegalities be referred to none but ourselves, and that all interpretations be made by us.

4. In single gifts it is sufficient to say thus: "Know all men present and to come that I, John, have given to Peter so much land with the appurtenances in such a town"; and it is proper to specify between what boundaries. And it is not necessary to say, "to Peter and his heirs", where Peter intends to purchase fee and frank tenement, but the heirs will be specified afterwards, thus: "To have and to hold to the same Peter and his heirs." Neither is it necessary to say, "grants and confirms", though it is usual to do so; nor is there occasion to say, "for homage", nor "for service", if it is not intended by the contract; for however homage or service are expressed in the charter, yet the chief lord of the fee shall not lose anything. Some persons however may do so in an exchange of seigniories, as in making a feoffment by custom of knight's service; and in such case it is proper to specify the homage in the feoffment. Appurtenances are named to include both corporeal things, such as hamlets appurtenant to chief manors, and common of pasture, turbary, fishery, or the like; and things incorporeal, as franchises, and servitudes of tenements. Then follows: "to have and to hold the aforesaid land with the appurtenances, to the same Peter and his heirs, doing therefore to the chief lords of the fee the services thereto belonging". And it should be understood, that it is a very necessary clause to specify the services by number, quality, and quantity, and to what persons they are due, so that neither the lords of the fee nor any other may demand more than right, without the feoffors being specially obliged to acquit and defend the purchasers. Then follows: "for all services, customs, and demands". And if the gift is made for term of life, or for term of years over, or in marriage, or in fee tail, or upon condition, the condition shall be specified in the charter indented, as above mentioned.

5. In absolute feoffments it is not proper to say, "to hold of the donor and of his heirs"; for whatever be said, it will not follow but that the purchaser will become tenant to the lord of the fee, in chief without mesne. And beyond this there is no occasion to say, "freely, quietly, well, and in peace". For these words belong rather to the form than to the substance of the business; but if such words are put in, they are harmless. With respect to tenements given in marriage, the form and issue supply the place of a charter; nevertheless a charter does no harm.

6. Sometimes a gift may be enlarged, sometimes restricted. It may be enlarged in this manner: "to have and to hold to the aforesaid Peter, his heirs, and assigns"; and sometimes further thus: "and to the heirs and assigns of his assigns". It may be restricted

as follows: "to hold until I pay him ten pounds", or "until I or my heirs pay him ten pounds", or "until I or my heirs or assigns pay Peter or his heirs or assigns". In another way thus: "to hold to him and his heirs without making alienation", or "without making alienation to such a one", or "except to such a one", or thus, "to hold during the life of Peter, and after his decease that the gift revert to Thomas and the heirs issuing from him, and if he has no such heirs, then return to Theobald, his heirs and assigns". And in all these cases we will that the intention of the donor be observed, so far forth as law and right will allow.

7. It must be understood that no feoffor is bound by the general clause of acquittance to acquit the fee from making contribution for the knighting of the lord's eldest son, or the marrying of his eldest daughter, nor from sheriff's aid, nor from common amercements or fines of the county or hundred, nor from suits due to the county or hundred court or elsewhere. Any one, however, may by a special clause bind himself to acquit his purchaser from all these services, and such obligations are enforced by writs of mesne.

8. Then there is the clause, "And I and my heirs will warrant the tenement with the appurtenances, and will acquit and defend the same to the aforesaid Peter, his heirs and assigns for ever." And this clause of warranty may be more full thus: "his heirs and assigns and the assigns of his assigns". And by reason of this clause it is useful in many cases for purchasers to take to themselves the charters of their feoffors, so that if the feoffors have nothing whereby they can warrant if need be, then the purchasers by virtue of the charters of their feoffors may vouch to warrant the feoffors of their feoffors, to which voucher they shall be admitted wheresoever it is found that the warranty of the first feoffors extends to warranty without mesne. Acquittance and defence are inserted to the intent that the person of whom the purchaser is to hold in chief may be obliged to acquit and defend him, in case any lord paramount or other should demand of him other services than the purchaser shall owe to the lord, of whom the purchaser holds in chief.

9. As to charters of confirmation and of quitclaim, let every one know that such charters made between persons out of seisin of any right are of no avail, where the parties to them are divested of the right of possession or the right of property. Therefore it is a good precaution for those who are having charters prepared, to take care that the date of the place and of the year be inserted.

10. Afterwards let some of the neighbours who are freemen be called as witnesses, in whose presence the charter should be read and sealed, and the names of the witnesses should be written in the charter. It would also be a good precaution to procure the seals of the witnesses to be affixed, together with the seal of the lord of the fee; or in the presence of the parties to have the charter enrolled in a court of record. And although the witnesses be not called, it is sufficient if the deed be afterwards recorded and acknowledged before them. If the feoffor has no seal of his own, a borrowed seal will be sufficient. There are many modes of purchase in which no charter is required; as by lawful judgment of our court; by surrender; by release and quitclaim; by default; by assignment of dower; by having issue by the law of England; and by several other ways.

11. But inasmuch as, although a charter is made, witnesses called, and the deed sealed in their presence, yet whatever has been done and said avails nothing unless livery of seisin be made by the donor to the purchaser, we must therefore say somewhat concerning induction into seisin, how seisin ought to be delivered, and how purchasers ought to receive it, of what things a man may be put into seisin immediately, and of what not until a certain time; and of what things induction into seisin is unnecessary.

Chapter IX

Of Seisins

1. Forasmuch as the mere grant and authorisation of the donor is not in general sufficient for purchasers, unless possession follows, with respect to possessions it must be understood, that possession is properly the seisin and holding of anything in fact and in intention, together with the property. There are some things however of which one cannot commonly retain possession or seisin; for of things incorporeal there can be no delivery; nor any proper seisin without a corporeal substance. But usage by long prescription supplies in time a legal title.

2. Livery and induction of seisin is a voluntary translation of a corporeal thing belonging to the person transferring it or to another, from the seisin of the true owner to the person of the purchaser, whether the owner transfers it in person, or by another on his behalf attorned and appointed by his letters patent. Such letters should be in duplicate, one to remain with the attorney, the other with the purchaser.

3. When any livery of seisin is to be made, the donor should first remove all his movable things which he has in the tenement, and his wife and children and all his family, so that there be nothing of his which he has not either removed or sold or let to farm, so that there may be no presumption that the donor intends to retain anything. For as long as he has any intention of retaining, no freehold ever accrues to the purchaser.

4. But if the donor vacates the tenement in fact and in intention, and delivers the seisin thereof to the purchaser, who receives it in fact and in intention, and so keeps it, a freehold, and fee (if the purchase be in fee) immediately accrue to the purchaser, by only setting his foot in the tenement, by virtue of the right, and of the union of wills which are joined, to wit, of the true owner in whose person both the right and the seisin were united, and of the purchaser who receives both the right and the seisin. Therefore, if any one ejected the purchaser from the land immediately after the gift, he should recover it by this assize as his freehold, although he had not taken any esplees, by virtue of the seisin. For neither user nor esplees are of the substance of the gift, but are equivalent to a declaration and evidence of seisin. And whereas the purchaser will thus have had the seisin in deed and in intention, so without both act and intention he can never so lose it, as not to be able to recover it.

5. But where any farmer has a term in the land, and is neither ejected nor attorns to the purchaser, if the donor dies during that term, his heir may recover the land by reason of the continuance of the seisin of the termor, who occupied it in the name of the donor. Wherefore no seisin can be legally delivered, except by judgment of our

court, unless while the seisin be vacant. The heir also shall recover seisin in case the seisin of the farmer has continued with that of the purchaser, inasmuch as the purchaser never had peaceable seisin in the lifetime of the donor. But if the farmer attorns to the purchaser, although he continues to hold his term, provided he has admitted that he holds of the purchaser, the gift is not thereby of less validity; for in such case the feoffment and term may well exist together in different persons.

6. Where there is nothing of the donor's in the tenement, and the tenement is a principal manor or mansion, there it is enough for the donor in the presence of some free neighbours as witnesses, and of some of the tenants, to deliver seisin to the purchaser by the hasp or ring of the door, or by shutting the gate; and thereby the purchaser becomes seised not only of the mansion, but of whatsoever was named in the charter and was properly the donor's, annexed to the mansion, as demesnes, rents, woods, meadows, pastures, and other frank tenements. But if a villein of the donor has made a free purchase, of which the donor has never been seised, the purchaser does not immediately become seised of such purchase. If seisin is to be made of a tenement where there is no house, then sufficient livery is made by a rod or by a glove in the presence of good witnesses.

7. It is to be understood, that the freehold never validly attaches to the purchaser until it is extinct in the donor, except by long and peaceable seisin. Nor can anything prevent the freehold from remaining in one of the two persons, and it may happen to remain in the person of the donor, although the donor may intend that the freehold and right should be transferred to the person of the purchaser, and although he may put the purchaser in seisin thereof – as by his family or chattels remaining in the tenement, which creates a presumption in favour of the heirs of the donor, that the donor retained the fee and freehold in intention, although he made it otherwise appear by colour of deed. And in such case if the purchaser be ejected by the heir of the donor, he shall not recover by this assize, by reason that the donor did not wholly divest himself in his lifetime, but the purchaser found the tenement full, and the donor always in seisin by his chattels and family; for by the continuance of the seisin it appears that the donor did not intend to part with the freehold. But if the chattels be stolen or otherwise lost upon the tenement, and the bailiffs and servants of the donor are ordered by him from that day forward not to remain there, unless to wait upon the purchaser as owner of the tenement, in such case there is no presumption that the donor meant to retain anything. So if it was not by the donor's consent or allowance that any of his family or of his chattels remained in the tenement in his name.

8. If a single person or a single beast abides on the part of the donor in the tenement given, the donor thereby retains the seisin as well as by several; as in the case of a feoffor who having given his common of pasture still causes the common to be fed by one beast; for by that one beast the donor retains all the common. So a lord may retain a rent by the hand of one tenant, where several tenants are jointly bound to pay the rent, and the lord has sold it and yet retains the rent, as above said, by means of one of the parceners. And because such presumptions are prejudicial, it is proper that in every regular livery of seisin the possession be absolutely vacant before the freehold can attach to the purchaser by the livery.

9. When a lawful livery of vacant seisin has been made with the solemnity of witnesses so that the donor is voluntarily ousted of the seisin and the purchaser put therein, the donor may not afterwards repent thereof. For if he should return immediately after his departure, and eject the purchaser, the ejected would recover by this assize.

10. If the donor perchance return after such seisin made to the purchaser and pray to be admitted into the tenement as a stranger, although the donor die in the tenement, yet by such abode and such seisin no right accrues to his heirs, unless they can prove that the donor conducted himself in the tenement as owner in the same way as he had before done, and not as bailiff or servant of the purchaser. But to remove all disputes, it is better for donors to make their abode elsewhere than in tenements of their own gift. And if any donor by the good nature of the purchaser is after the gift admitted into the tenement, and the purchaser perceives that the donor intends to eject or disturb him in his seisin, or to act as if in his own property, let him immediately proceed by this assize, or if he thinks it better, eject him without judgment. And if the assize pass in favour of the purchaser his estate is so far confirmed.

11. If the donor or the purchaser dies before livery of seisin, nothing accrues by the gift to the heirs of the purchaser, nor is anything lost to the heirs of the donor; and if the purchaser thrust himself in after the decease of the donor, the heir of the donor is not to be prevented from putting himself in; and if he be ejected or disturbed, he shall recover by this assize. And if by his own negligence he cannot avail himself of this assize, he shall recover by assize of *mort d'ancestor*, or by other writ according to the occasion.

12. If any person has made a purchase in another's name, and by virtue thereof keeps himself in seisin, and he in whose name the purchase is made disavows the deed and the purchase, and some stranger ejects the procurator, the ejected shall not recover by this assize, because he did not hold the seisin in his own name, neither shall he in whose name the purchase was made recover, since he never was in seisin either in deed or in intention. Therefore, as the freehold is not in the heirs of the purchaser, it still remains in the donor, and in such case the donor shall recover by this assize. Children however under age, and such as want discretion, cannot to their own detriment disavow a purchase; for, as a general rule, their estate may be rendered better but not worse.

13. If any donor appoints a servant or friend to put the purchaser in seisin, and livery of seisin is accordingly made to the purchaser in the lifetime of the feoffor, the feoffment shall be good. So likewise, if livery be made soon after the death of the feoffor, before the purchaser knows of his death. But if the heir of the feoffor after his death prohibits the seisin, before livery is made to the purchaser, the gift will be annulled, and the heir shall recover the tenements, because his ancestor died seised.

14. Advowsons of churches cannot be given or purchased simply without some corporeal thing annexed, as soil, rent, or other thing issuing out of the soil. And even if they should be so aliened, yet purchasers cannot be in full seisin of the advowsons until they have presented to the churches, and their presentees have been admitted and instituted by the bishop. For if the purchaser sell the advowson before he has been so seised by his clerk, and the buyer be impleaded by another, and thereupon

vouches his feoffor to warranty, the feoffor may plead that he is not bound to warranty by reason that he never was seised of the advowson, the church not having been void, but the seisin still remains in the first donor by reason that it never took effect in the person of another. And this reason would be allowable, inasmuch as no one can give that which he hath not – although the feoffor or the purchaser was fully seised of the manor with all the appurtenances.

15. It is to be understood, that in some cases an advowson may be included in appurtenances, and in some not. For if one give a manor with all the appurtenances without any reservation being specified in the gift, and the advowson of one or more churches is appendant thereto, in such a case the purchaser purchases the advowsons under the word appurtenances. But where the donor gives the manor entirely or by parcels, and in each gift the appurtenances are expressed, yet if the donor reserves to himself any parcel of the whole, entire with the appurtenances, in such case the advowson remains in this parcel, unless the advowson is specified in the alienation. So if the manor be aliened in parcels to divers persons, without anything being reserved to the donor, and each parcel be aliened with the appurtenances without specifying the advowson, the advowson shall belong to the last purchaser.

. . .

Chapter XIII

Of Remedies in Disseisin

1. The first remedy in disseisin is for the disseisee to gather friends and force, and without any delay after he may have knowledge of the disseisin to eject the disseisors. And if he can do no more, he should at least keep himself in possession with the disseisors, and make such use of his seisin as he can; in this way the disseisor will never gain a freehold without the consent of the true owner.

2. But if the disseisors have been for a long time in peaceable seisin in the presence of the disseisee, then it is not lawful for the disseisee to eject the disseisors without judgment. In such case inquiry may be made, where the disseisee was at the time of the disseisin; for if he was present, and knowingly suffered the disseisor to enjoy his peaceable seisin, the disseisee has no such right after a long space of time to eject the disseisor, but that the latter may recover his seisin by this assize, with his damages; for in such case it may reasonably be presumed that the disseisees were willing that the tenements should belong to the disseisors; inasmuch as they suffered their right to lie so long dormant.

3. But if the disseisee was in a distant country at the time when the disseisin was committed, then it is proper to consider and determine within what time his family might have reasonably given him intelligence of the disseisin, and in what time he might have returned to assemble his friends and eject the disseisors. And that such determination may not be arbitrary, we will that they be adjudged according to the periods allowed in essoins; so that if the disseisee be gone in a general passage to the land of Jerusalem, and after his return he eject the disseisor, or any other who may have been enfeoffed by the disseisor, it is lawful for him so to do, whether it be an

infant within age or any other whom he find therein, so as it be done within the fourth day from his return into the country, three days being allowed him to collect arms, friends and forces; and although the person so ejected brings this assize against the ejector, yet he shall not recover any freehold; for we will not that the absence of such persons be so prejudicial that they be in any way damaged thereby. If the disseisee went on a simple pilgrimage to the Holy Land, then let there be reckoned a year and a day, and one ebb and flow for delays at sea, and fifteen days for his journey to the land, and four days for assembling his force; and if he has within such time ejected whosoever was found in his tenement, the person ejected shall not recover the land by this assize, even though his ancestor died seised thereof. And if the pilgrimage of the disseisee was on this side of the Grecian sea, the reckoning shall be four months, one ebb and flow, fifteen days, and four days; if in England, fifteen days. And if the disseisee after that time eject the disseisors without judgment, inasmuch as they have been all that time or longer in peaceable seisin with the knowledge of the disseisees, the disseisors shall have recovery of their estate by this assize; for we will that all persons after the prescribed time of limitation proceed rather by judgment than force; and the first disseisees shall not be afterwards aided by this assize; for he who acts in opposition to the law has no right to claim aid of the law.

4. And as such disseisors have after a certain time and term a right of action to recover against the disseisees by this assize, so they have also before the time so limited a right of action to recover by this assize against all other disseisors having no right to eject them. For where neither of two persons has any right, the disseisee has a greater right than the disseisor. And although the original disseisor may thus recover by judgment of our court, yet the true owner shall not lose anything of the right when he shall choose to bring his plaint. So also, if during the time limited for ejectment he cannot recover his seisin without our aid, our writ shall be granted to him returnable at the eyre of our justices, or we will assign him justices to hear and determine the plaint according to the case.

5. Where a woman is disseised, and afterwards takes a husband, if they will afterwards proceed by this assize, the form of the writ shall be thus: "John and Peronel his wife have complained to us that Peter has wrongfully disseised the aforesaid Peronel." And if the husband desires to purchase a writ against his wife, then thus: "John and Peronel his wife have complained to us that Peronel of such a town has disseised the aforesaid Peronel"; so that the wife is plaintiff although she is disseisor; but the surname is altered before she is named as disseisor.

Chapter XIV

Of Views in Disseisin

1. If the person ejected cannot or ought not to eject his disseisor, or if the tenant hinders him from using his seisin together with him, he must then complain to us, and we will thereupon grant him our writ to the sheriff of the county in whose bailiwick the tenement is; which writ shall contain the names of the disseisors, of the

tenants, and of those who come with force and aid to help the disseisors, and the name of the plaintiff. But let every plaintiff beware of putting in his plaint any who were not wrongdoers, because for every one named in the writ who can acquit himself of the wrong the plaintiff shall be in mercy for his false plaint.

2. When any one has purchased our writs, and also letters from our justices to the sheriff to inform him of the day and place of their session; the original writ and the justices' letter shall be immediately taken to the sheriff; and the plaintiff shall keep our letters patent by him until the day of the plea, and then he shall deliver them up to the justices to be their warrant; for without either a general or special warrant they cannot determine anything.

3. In the next place it is the sheriff's duty to take pledges, two at least, distrainable to himself, that the plaintiff will prosecute his plaint, except where on account of his poverty we have permitted him to sue his plaint upon the pledge of his promise only; and then he shall find no other security to the sheriff. And if he goes without our aid, and is unable to recover his seisin, he may then obtain our writ, returnable at our eyre or that of our justices, or we will grant him justices to hear and determine the plaint according to the case. When pledges to prosecute are found to the sheriff, or to us in our chancery, whereof two pledges are sufficient though there are several plaintiffs in one writ, the plaintiffs are not to be required to find any other security, although the return is to be made in a franchise.

4. Security being thus taken if the writ require it, let two freeholders of the neighbourhood be immediately enjoined to summon the neighbours to be at a certain day and place before our justices to make recognisance upon their oaths, whether the plaintiff has been disseised, as he complains, of his freehold in such a certain place or not, and that in the meantime they view the tenements in this manner, whether the disseisin be made of land or of rent, of private property or of common; and if of common, whether common to everybody, or only to a certain number of people; also to how much in quantity the thing whereof the plaint is made amounts, so that they may be prepared with a certain answer when they shall be asked whether the plaintiff hath put too much or too little in his plaint. They ought also to see whether all the tenement is situate in the county and in the vill named in the writ or not. It is not the sheriff's or bailiff's office to give them the view, but the plaintiff's, who is bound to inform them within what boundaries and divisions the tenements named in the plaint lie.

5. If the plaint be made of corrodies or estovers, or of the delivery of corn yearly, or other provision or necessaries, or of bailiwicks or wardenships, or of the keepership of a park, or the ward of gates, or other kind of annual office, or of common of pasture, turbary, fishery, or other easements, then the jurors are required to make view of the tenement from whence the easements or estovers arise, or at least of those tenements where the annual necessaries are accustomed to be delivered or are assigned to be received.

6. And if the plaint be made of rent, then the jurors must view the soil from which the rent issues; and not only the soil, but the thing also for which the rent is paid; as in the following and like cases, where rent is granted by one neighbour to another

to have a right of driving cattle through any tenement, or where a rent issuing out of any tenement is partly or wholly released on condition of having an easement in another soil. For although the one party does not require the easement, yet he cannot refuse to pay the rent, or prevent the covenant from being binding in relation to him who is willing to keep it; and the contract shall never be dissolved but by common assent as it was at first made; and therefore, although the person who has granted a rent in fee or for term of life whereof the purchaser has been seised, does not wish to have the driftway or other easement in the soil of his neighbour, yet if he refuse to pay the rent according as it was covenanted between them, he to whom the rent is due may distrain for the arrears of the rent; and if he cannot find anything to distrain, or if he be hindered from distraining, he shall recover by this assize, if he can show that any soil is charged with the rent; and if not, it is sufficient to view the tenement for which the rent was given.

7. If the plaint is made of a nuisance, then let them view the nuisance, whether it be a wall, ditch, hedge, or market, or a pond raised or lowered, or otherwise injurious; and in such case it is not sufficient to view the nuisance only, but they must also view the tenement to which the annoyance is done. And in the preceding case also, if the disseisin be by a disturbance of an easement, such as having common in another's soil, or right of drift or way, or water at another's well, or other like easement, it is not sufficient to view the tenement subject to the easement, but the tenement to which the pasture belongs must likewise be viewed.

8. The parties, if they please, may be present at the view, and challenge the jurors; and if the parties agree upon jurors, the names of those upon whom they have agreed shall be imbreviated, to be presented to the justices at the day of plea.

9. Afterwards let the tenant and all the disseisors, or their bailiffs if they cannot themselves be found, be attached, and required to find pledges to be present at the day of the plea to hear the recognisance of the jurors upon the plaint, so that they may know of what offence they are to be accused.

Chapter XV

Of the Proceedings in Assizes

1. When the justices are come, they shall forthwith receive the essoins, and afterwards adjourn them. And if the plaintiff in this assize neither appears nor causes himself to be essoined, the writ shall be immediately taken out of the hands of the sheriff, and the names of the jurors presented; and the plaintiff shall be called. And if he makes default, let him and his pledges to prosecute be in mercy. Then let the tenant or his bailiff and the rest of the disseisors be demanded, and if they make default, or cause themselves to be essoined (since in this assize no essoin avails them), and it be proved by the sheriff that they were attached by pledges, then their pledges shall be in mercy, because they have not produced them in court according to their engagement. Afterwards let the jurors of the assize, according to the panel, be required to answer to their names; and let such as do not appear according as they have been summoned be in our mercy.

2. If the plaintiff appears, or causes himself to be essoined, and neither the tenant, nor his bailiff, nor his attorney, is present, the pledges as before mentioned shall be immediately amerced, and by way of punishment for the default of the parties it shall be awarded that they be not afterwards allowed to allege any reason for staying the assize, and that the assize be taken by their default.

3. And it should be known that in this and in no other assize every disseisor may answer either in person or by attorney, or by bailiff. Yet they have not all an equal power; for a bailiff cannot do all that his lord can. For a bailiff cannot acknowledge or grant that the disseisin was committed by his lord, so as to prevent the necessity of taking the recognisance, as the disseisor might himself do, if present. Moreover the bailiff cannot make any accord or partition, nor put the right of his lord into hotchpot, whereby the lord might lose any freehold without the recognisance of the assize. Yet the bailiff may, as well as his master, allege any objection, wherefore the assize ought not to pass, or for the purpose of barring the assize by dilatory or peremptory exceptions, as by an exception against the judge, or the plaintiff, or the jurors, or against the writ, and by all other exceptions and replications.

4. An attorney may do all that his lord can, except make accord, for as soon as the proceeding in court is ended, the power of the attorney ceases, and in making the accord another proceeding is begun, which was not before in court, when he was appointed attorney only in the proceeding then in court. This however must be understood of special, not of general attorneys. For a general attorney can do as much as his client from the commencement to the end of the suit.

5. When both the plaintiff and the defendants are in court, if the plaintiff declares that he will not further prosecute his writ, in whatever suit this may occur, he shall not afterwards resort to another like writ, but both he and his pledges to prosecute shall remain in our mercy. And if he withdraws himself from the action, he shall be barred of his action for ever; but if he has leave to seek a better writ, or if the writ be abated for error, or for other fault, and likewise if the plea be opened, and in the course of pleading the writ be found defective, although the plaintiff in such case say that he will not further prosecute that writ, yet he shall not thereby be barred from resorting to a better writ of the like kind, because no proceeding is as yet commenced upon the action, but the whole is to the writ, whereby the action remains entire. But if any one withdraw himself from his writ after the action is opened, he shall never resort to the like writ against the same persons for the same tenement, but the writ shall be liable to abate, if the fact be averred by exception. But if upon replication it can be averred that the tenant against whom the first writ was brought was not tenant of the tenement when the writ was abated, and that he obtained it by some means since that time by purchase, succession, or escheat, in such case the plaintiff may resort to another like writ, and the writ shall hold good, in respect of the right of action which commenced after the writ abated.

6. If any person attached declare in court that he has nothing in the tenement nor claims anything, without making any reservation, and such confession be recorded, he will be thereby for ever after foreclosed of every right which he may have had until that time in the tenement, if this exception be used against him.

7. If when the parties are come to trial the plaintiff has not our letters patent for trial of his suit, the justices have no power to hear or determine anything. And if the tenant enter nevertheless into his defence, and lose, he may still recover his former position, and whatsoever the justices shall do in such case shall be held entirely null and void. But if the plaintiff has the patent, let it be immediately read in audience, and if any doubt arises thereon, the tenant may have on that account a dilatory exception to ward off the assize. Afterwards let oyer be had of the writ close. And let it be immediately demanded of the plaintiff of what freehold he makes his plaint, and let the quality and quantity be imbreviated. Next let our justices examine how and by what title the plaintiff had a freehold therein; for in every demand it is not sufficient merely to demand, but the plaintiff must show by what right he demands; and this rule applies not only to things movable, but to things immovable, and not only to claims of possession, but to claims of right. And whoever will not make that appear, is not entitled to be answered.

. . .

Chapter XXI

Of the challenge of jurors, and of the trial of the assize

1. When the parties have pleaded to an assize or to a simple jury upon any exception, the day may be delayed many ways, as for default of jurors. Or if a sufficient number of jurors appear, yet some may be removable by the just challenge of the parties.

2. Sometimes the day is delayed on account of the season; for all seasons are not fit. For it is forbidden in the canon by holy church upon pain of excommunication, that from Septuagesima until the octaves of Easter, and from the beginning of Advent until the octaves of the Epiphany, and on Ember days, and on the days of the greater litanies, and on rogation days, and in the week of Pentecost, and in the time of harvest or vintage, which last from St Margaret's day until fifteen days after Michaelmas, and on solemn festivals of saints, no one shall be sworn upon the holy gospels, or hold any secular plea, or make any summons in the times aforesaid, so that all these seasons be set apart for prayer, and for appeasing of quarrels and reconciling those who are at variance, and for gathering the fruits of the earth which are to be the food of man. Nevertheless the bishops and prelates of holy church do sometimes grant dispensations, that assizes and juries be taken in such seasons for reasonable cause.

3. When the day cannot be put off on account of the season being improper, the jurors may be challenged, and sufficient and reasonable exceptions alleged why they ought not to be sworn or be in verdict against the party. For the same objections lie against jurors taking the oath as against a suspected witness giving his testimony, inasmuch as no one who has been once convicted of perjury ought to be sworn, for such are held to have forfeited their free law, so as not to be credited upon any oath which they take. Nor ought those to be sworn who have suffered judgment of life and limb, or punishment of pillory or tumbrel; nor those who want discretion; nor excommunicated persons; nor lepers removed from society; nor priests or clerks within holy orders; nor women; nor such as dwell away from the neighbourhood;

nor those who are above seventy years of age; nor allies in blood; nor such as can claim any right in the tenement; nor villeins; nor persons indicted or appealed of felony; nor those of the household of any of the parties; nor those who are liable to be distrained by either of the parties; nor their lords, or counsellors, or accountants.

4. When the parties have agreed upon the jury, then let the first juror, touching the holy gospels, swear after this manner. "Hear this, ye justices, that I will speak the truth of this assize" (if the assize is to be taken in manner of an assize and not as a jury) "of the tenement of which I have had the view by the king's precept"; or thus: "of the tenement whereout such rent is said to arise"; or thus: "of the pasture and of the tenement", or "of the common, whereof I have had the view". Thus the words of the oath must be varied according to the form of the writ and declaration; and if the plaint be made of nuisance, then it shall be said thus: "of the nuisance and of the tenement to which the nuisance is said to have been committed"; or thus: "of the wall, or pond, and of the tenement", without adding "whereof I have had the view". Then it continues thus: "and I will not fail for anything to speak the truth, so help me God and his saints". Then let the rest swear thus: "The same oath which such a one hath thus sworn, I for my part will keep, so help me God and the saints". Then let the gospels be kissed with all reverence as our faith and salvation. If several assizes are to be taken under one oath, then it shall be said: "of the assizes and of the tenements whereof I have had the view"; or thus: "of all assizes, and of those tenements whereout such rent is supposed to arise"; or thus: "of those tenements and of the common of pasture, or turbary, or other, and of the tenements to which it is said they ought to belong, whereof I have had the view"; or thus: "of this assize, and of the corrody, and of the tenement", and so of others. And in the other assizes of *mort d'ancester* and *darrein presentment* the oath shall be taken in the same manner.

5. When twelve are sworn, and their names enrolled, then let the writ be read to them by the clerk prothonotary, who shall address them in this manner: "You shall say by the oath you have taken whether such a one wrongfully and without judgment has disseised the plaintiff of his freehold in such a vill within the term, or not." The justice also shall straightway rehearse the substance of the plaint thus: "John, who is present here, complains of Peter that he has wrongfully and without judgment disseised him of his freehold in such a vill, whereof he puts in his view ten acres of land (or more or less), with the appurtenances"; and then let him mention the declaration of the plaintiff and the allegations of the defendant for the information of the jurors.

6. The jurors shall immediately withdraw by themselves to confer together; and then let them be so kept, that none of them speak with any other person except the jurors, nor any other person with them. And if any do so maliciously, and be found guilty thereof, let him be punished by imprisonment and fine, and let the jurors be amerced, if they have not themselves accused him. Moreover let the jurors be watched, that they do not give warning to any one, by motion of the eye or by other sign, against which of the parties they intend to pronounce their verdict; and whosoever shall do so, and be found guilty thereof, shall be amerciable or otherwise punishable according to the mischief which may arise.

7. If the jurors cannot agree, let others be added to the majority of the jury, if the

parties consent; and if not, let the judgment be against him who refuses to consent, so that if the plaintiff refuses, the seisin shall remain as before, and he be in mercy; and if the disseisor refuses, he shall be adjudged as undefended. If the jurors cannot pronounce the truth, nor return any verdict as to the fact, let the seisin remain in the tenant, and let the plaintiff be in mercy for not having proved the case made by his plaint. If the jury refuse to pronounce any verdict in the matter through favour to either of the parties, or for any other reason, then let them be shut up without meat or drink until they have given their verdict.

Chapter XXII

Of Judgments

1. When the jurors are all agreed, let them immediately go to the bar before the justices, and declare their verdict; and according to their verdict let judgment be given for one of the parties, unless any doubt or difficulty arise, which may make it necessary to examine the facts by the jurors or others, or to defer judgment until another day, so that the justices may in the mean time be advised and consult what is best to do therein. Where the justices however are doubtful about the verdict, and the jurors have not been sufficiently examined, or have been too hasty in their judgment on account of some word or sentence which might have a double intendment, in such case a certification may be taken by the same or other justices. But it is better and safer for the justices thoroughly to examine the reasons of the jurors so that they may give a good and sound judgment, and that no error may be found either in their office or in the proceedings.

2. When the jurors have declared their verdict upon the substance of the assize, or upon any exception, and such verdict is given against the plaintiff, then let it be awarded that the tenant and the others named in the writ go quit of that assize without day, and that the plaintiff take nothing by his writ, but be in our mercy for his false plaint. Nevertheless his pledges to prosecute shall not in such case be amerciable, inasmuch as the plaintiff has prosecuted his suit to the end.

3. When the assize is taken after the manner of an assize, regard must be had to the quantity and quality of the plaint, and how much the plaintiff has put in his view and set forth in his plaint; since the oath of the jurors does not extend to that which he has not put in his plaint. And if the justice awards to the plaintiff more than he has put in his plaint, or if the jurors give him seisin of more than he has put in his view, they commit a manifest disseisin on the tenant; as does the sheriff also, who puts in execution the command of the judge, because in such a case, or in any other where the justice's jurisdiction does not extend, no bailiff ought to obey him in executing his commands. The plaintiff is in a like position who receives such defective seisin. So likewise where the plaintiff encroaches upon the disseisor more than right under colour of judgment. And if the plaintiff puts too much in his view, he is amerciable for his excessive demand.

4. If the verdict be given for the plaintiff, it shall be forthwith inquired who were present at the disseisin, and the manner of the fact, whether the disseisin was committed

with banner displayed, or horses harnessed, or by other force of arms, and by what force, and by what arms. And it should be understood that there are divers sorts of arms and divers kinds of force. For all those are said to be armed who carry anything wherewith they may do hurt to people or overpower others, as well bows, arrows, knives, hatchets, and staves, as hauberks, lances, and swords. So there is armed force, and simple force without arms, as by multitude of people.

5. And because many a man, having no right, gains seisin by such force, upon which the tenant who has a right to retain and abide in possession leaves the tenement to avoid further mischief, and forasmuch as such ways of obtaining seisin are in part against our peace, we will that the justices inquire, who came in the force along with the principal disseisor, so that the disseisor and those of the force be punished by imprisonment and fine if they are convicted of a disseisin effected by force, and if by arms, then ransomed. And if any be convicted of a disseisin done under colour of right, and without breach of the peace, as by a simple disseisin done in the daytime, without force and arms, with a white wand in sign of peace; in such case let the disseisor be amerciable by their peers, and also make satisfaction to the plaintiff in damages. The penalty above mentioned, which is to be imposed upon disseisors who eject people from their freehold, whether by force or arms, or, as it should be done, after a peaceable manner, shall also be imposed upon disseisors who with force or arms, or simply without arms, keep a man out of his freehold when he expects to enter peaceably therein.

6. Sometimes it happens in this assize that the disseisors shelter themselves by us, and say that they neither have nor claim anything in the tenement, but whatsoever they did was done in our name, and that without us the assize cannot pass, nor the fact be brought in judgment without prejudice to us; in which cases we will not that under such pretext the assize shall stand over; but if the disseisin be clear and manifest, let it be adjudged for the plaintiff, and let the common law take its course against the tenant as against any other person; and if any doubt be perceived, let judgment be respited to another day, and let the proceedings in the meantime be laid before us, so that judgment may be ordained by our advice.

7. And because it often happens that the tenant has not committed any disseisin or wrong, but has possibly purchased the tenement by feoffment of the disseisor; in such case it is reasonable that the tenant should be able to vouch to warranty the disseisor, so that he who has done no wrong may not be punished for the trespass of another, without recovering to the value from his feoffor; and then let the same proceeding be observed as shall be mentioned concerning warranties in the assize of *mort d'ancester*. If two or more assizes are prosecuted by several persons against one, the last seisin shall be first tried, and so backwards to the first disseisin.

8. Afterwards let it be inquired of the jurors what damages the disseisors and the tenants have committed in houses, woods, gardens, warrens, vivaries, parks, rabbit-warrens, and elsewhere; and how much has or might have been by good husbandry received in the meantime of all kinds of issues of the tenement, and what profit in value the plaintiff might have had if he had not been disseised; and it shall be awarded accordingly that the plaintiff recover his full damages. And if the justices perceive that

the jurors are disposed to relieve the disseisor by assessing light damages, because on the other hand they have made him suffer by the loss of the tenement, let the lands be extended by the same jurors at their true value in the presence of the parties, if they will be there; and according to the yearly value let the damages be taxed by the justices, single or double, according to the ordinance of our statutes, and according as the assize shall have been falsely defended or not.

9. If the disseisors have taken away or detained from the plaintiff any vessel, robe, or chattel, it shall be in the election of the plaintiff either to sue for his chattels by appeal of robbery or trespass, or to have them taxed with the rest of his damages. The damages for wild animals taken in parks or chases, and for fish taken out of ponds, shall be assessed by the jurors; for in such cases the penalty of three years' imprisonment does not lie, nor in any case except where judgment of felony can be given, if the offender is in peril of life and limb. If houses have been burnt or other damage has happened in the meantime, although it was by an unforeseen accident, without any human malice, yet the disseisor is not thereby discharged from making satisfaction as well for the chattels of the disseisee as for the goods of others wrongfully detained by the disseisor.

. . .

Book VI

OF PROPRIETARY ACTIONS

Introduction

Of the Plea of Right

Having finished the form and manner of pleading the possessory right, we must now treat of the manner of pleading upon the right of property, which in the order of pleas is the last of all remedies; so that none can descend from a writ of right to a writ of a lower nature, although the reverse may be done.

Chapter I

Of Proximity of Heirs

1. This action alone by the manner of counting tries the proximity of heirs with respect to the succession to the inheritance. For inheritance is the succession of the heir to every right of which the ancestor died seised. And from inheritance is derived heir, who is the successor to every right which the ancestor had at the time of his death. And this right sometimes descends like a weighty body, and sometimes ascends. And although the possession does not always follow the mere right, yet in the end it will return to it, if the right heir proceeds in a proper manner. For to the right heir descends the mere right which his ancestor had when he died, whether the heir at the time of his ancestor's death be in the country or beyond sea, and whether he is in his mother's womb or already born.

2. All children however are not admissible to the inheritance, for some are natural and legitimate; and of those who are both legitimate and natural, some are sons and

heirs, others sons and not heirs; and some are heirs of their fathers, some of their mothers and some on both sides, and others are not heirs to either, although they are both legitimate and natural; and some begin by being heirs and afterwards perhaps cease to be so, and others not. And of natural and legitimate heirs, some are near and some again nearer, and some remote and others more remote. For all brothers on the father's side are near heirs of their father by reason of the share they have in the possession. This is undeniable, because if the younger brother keeps his elder brother out of his inheritance, and has taken the profits and peaceable seisin thereof, the eldest shall have no recovery in the right of possession, as before is mentioned, but he is driven to demand his inheritance by means of the writ of right, which writ alone tries who is nearest heir in blood. And according as it shall be found by counting of the proximity among brothers judgment shall be given. But in all cases that person is next heir at law to whom the mere right soonest descends.

Chapter II
Of Succession, and the Law of Inheritance

1. All those who first descend from the common stock from degree to degree in the direct line for ever are lawful and true heirs; and when default is found in the direct line, then those who are found to be nearest in the collateral degrees for ever are the right heirs; and lastly, when default is found in the transverse line descending, those who appear to be nearest in any transverse line ascending shall be admissible. But although the heirs so ascending for ever are lawful and right heirs, yet they are not all admissible at the same time to the succession, because the eldest, being nearest, excludes the youngest who is near, and he who is near excludes the remote, and the remote one more remote. And when all these fail, either by their blood becoming extinct, or by their right being forfeited by judgment of felony, the tenement must of necessity return to the lord of the fee, as to the source from which it first issued, for want of any other direction in which it can go; and in such case the homage received for the tenement is extinguished.

2. There are many things which constitute proximity, and confer an inheritance and right of succession, to wit, sex, age, line, a partible inheritance, plurality of female heirs, form of gift, and blood. Sex, because the male is to be received and the female rejected, so long as there is a male heir apparent of the father by the same mother; but the daughter begotten on the first wife is to be preferred in the succession to the marriage granted with her mother to the male begotten by the same father on the second wife.

3. Age is material; because he who is the first born is admissible before the younger son of the same father and mother, and the younger brother will remain nearest heir to the elder, or at least a near heir, according as the elder shall have issue or not. And if the elder brother dies without heir of his own in the lifetime of his father, the younger brother will take his place, and begin to be next heir to their common father, and the other younger ones will be near; and so of those more remote, without end.

4. If the elder brother dies in his father's lifetime, having begotten an heir, this issue remains under the authority of the grandfather, and shall be next heir to the grandfather by reason of the mere right descended to him by the death of his father, the grandfather's son, although the son did not live to attain any estate; and the uncle or aunt shall be only near heir, although he is one degree nearer than the grandson, who is next heir. Therefore if the uncle, or aunt, being out of seisin, demand the seisin of his father by assize of *mort d'ancester*, or by writ of right against the grandson, the exception of proximity shall bar him; and in like manner if he demand against a stranger. And if the uncle or aunt is in seisin, and keeps out the grandson, the grandson, being next heir, shall recover by means of the writ of right by pleading his descent. And what is here said of the younger brother, uncle to the near heir, may be taken as an example of the position of near heirs in all like cases.

5. Line is material; because the daughter found in the direct line descending is to be preferred before the male found in the transverse line.

6. Of a partible inheritance, the younger son, as before has been mentioned, shall have as great a share as the elder; and in this case the custom of the place shall be observed.

7. Plurality of female heirs affects the succession, as in case of sisters parceners, who, whether they are begotten of one or of several mothers, all present themselves in the place of one heir, and no one of them is to be preferred before another, neither can one be heir to the others; for that would imply a nearer proximity in one than in another, which there is not, since they are all equally nearest. And if one of them dies, the shares of the rest shall be thereby increased, but not by succession, but by a kind of right called that of accruer.

8. The form of gift is also material, as appears in the case of feoffments, whereby strangers are admissible to the succession in preference to the next heirs, who are excluded by the feoffors. For the wills of donors are to be observed as far as the law can permit; and although such strangers are not right heirs, yet they shall be in the place of heirs. And so shall all those stand in the place of heirs to whom lands or tenements fall by any manner of reversion or of escheat, whether it be by default of blood or by forfeiture.

9. Right of blood sometimes causes the female to exclude the male. For if A. begets by one wife a son and a daughter, and by another wife a son, the eldest son is next heir to the father and the mother, and if he dies without issue of his own, the sister is nearer heir to the deceased brother than the younger brother by the second or third wife. And so likewise the issue of the sister. But the first issue shall never demand any part of the inheritance of their step-mother until after the decease of her issue, and if she has no issue by their father, they can never demand any part of the inheritance of their step-mother; nor, although she has issue by their father, if her inheritance did not descend to their brothers or sisters, the children of their common father by their step-mother. But if the inheritance falls to their brothers or sisters, the children of the same father by a different mother, and the issue of their step-mother fails, an action immediately accrues to the first children, or to their issue, to demand the seisin of the last children or of their issue.

10. Of issue begotten upon the same mother by different fathers, the son by the first father and his issue are nearer, and are sooner to be admitted to every inheritance on the part of their mother, as well as on the part of their father, than the younger sons; and if they die seised and without issue, the sisters by the same father and mother are to be preferred to the brothers by the same mother and by different fathers. But if no male child of the first husband, or his issue, survive to attain the inheritance of his mother, then the males by the second husband are admissible to the inheritance of the mother before the females by the first husband; but if any male of the first husband has issue, male or female, this issue is to be admitted to the inheritance of the mother before the males by the second husband.

11. Sometimes also the younger sister excludes the elder brother, as where John begets by his first wife a son, and by his second wife a son and a daughter, and the younger son purchases lands or tenements, and dies without heir of his own body, the sister of the purchaser shall carry off the inheritance and exclude the elder brother, although the brother would be sooner admitted to the inheritance descending from the person of John the common father. And if John has issue two sons and two daughters by diverse mothers, the elder brother is nearest heir to John, and after him the younger, if the father survive the eldest son; but if one of these brothers makes a purchase, and dies without heirs of his own body, the sister of the same venter as the purchasor shall be the nearest heir, and shall exclude the brother and sister of the other venter, if not barred by homage.

12. If there are three or more brothers by the same father and mother, and the youngest of them all makes a purchase and dies without heir of his own body, the eldest brother shall be his next heir, and shall exclude the father and mother, although they are nearer in blood, because the brother is found to be the nearest in the same degree, which the father and the mother are not; and he shall also exclude the other brothers and sisters, although they are found in the same degree. And even if the intermediate or other brother be in seisin, yet the eldest shall obtain it by a writ of right. And if the eldest brother dies without heir of his own body, then it shall go to the next eldest brother, and so from brother to brother, until it comes to the sisters. And if neither brother nor sister nor any issue of them appear, then it shall go to the common father; or if the father be dead, and no other be found in any degree nearer on his side, to the common mother; and so of all the other degrees ascending. In what manner the degrees branch out will appear by the following tree of kindred.

Chapter III

Of Degrees of Kindred

1. There are various degrees of kindred, as will appear in the following figure. It must be observed, no one, whether male or female, found in any degree in the collateral line, either ascending or descending, is admissible to succeed, so long as any person is found alive in the direct line descending; but when no one is found there, then we are driven of necessity to seek the degrees in the collateral lines.

2. It is always proper to begin to count from the common stock last seised of both

THE LAW OF INHERITANCE

(The degrees of kindred reckoned in the direct line or through collateral lines)

father's side — *mother's side*

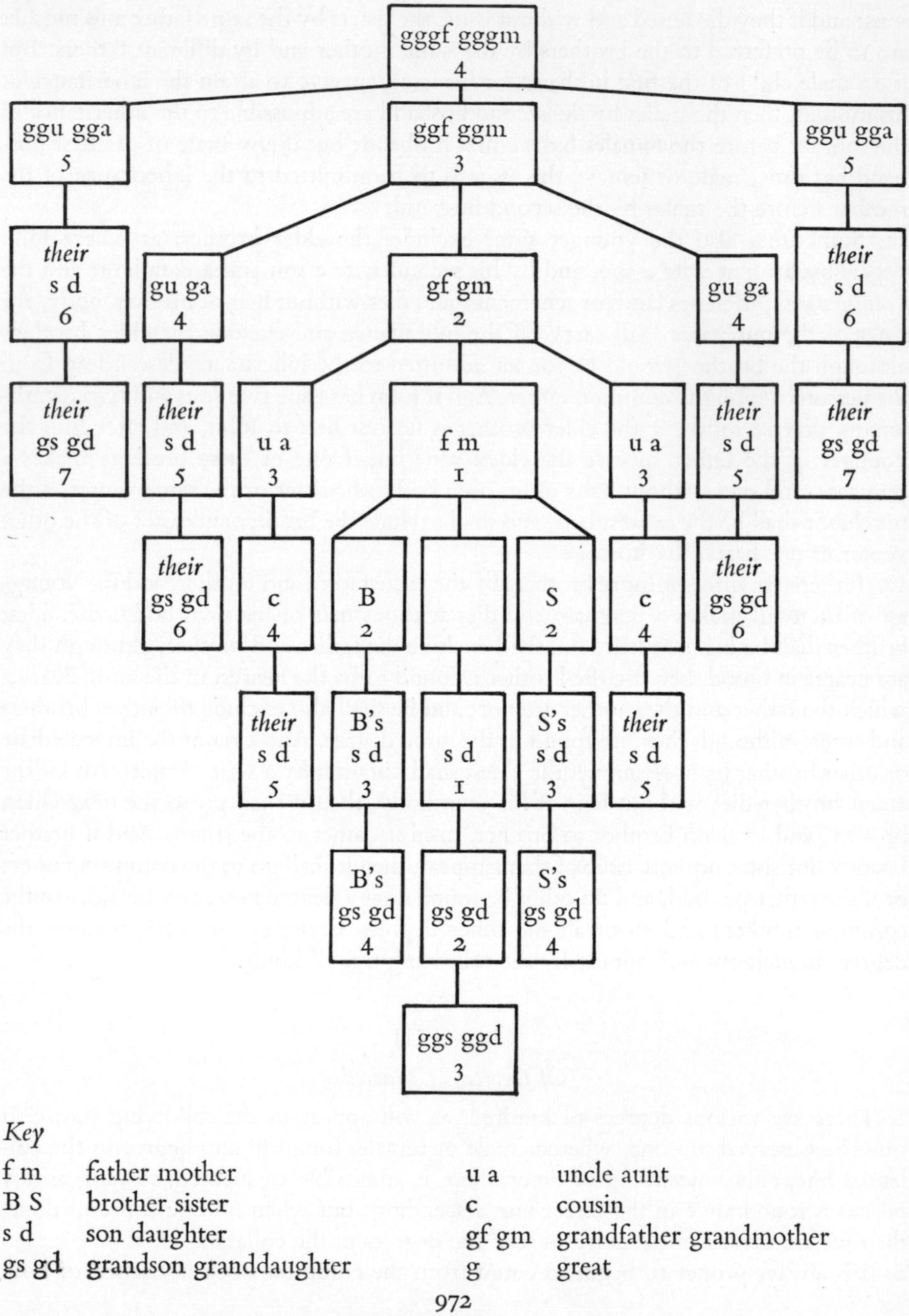

gggf gggm 4

ggu gga 5 | ggf ggm 3 | ggu gga 5

their s d 6 | gu ga 4 | gf gm 2 | gu ga 4 | *their* s d 6

their gs gd 7 | *their* s d 5 | u a 3 | f m 1 | u a 3 | *their* s d 5 | *their* gs gd 7

their gs gd 6 | c 4 | B 2 | [self] | S 2 | c 4 | *their* gs gd 6

their s d 5 | B's s d 3 | s d 1 | S's s d 3 | *their* s d 5

B's gs gd 4 | gs gd 2 | S's gs gd 4

ggs ggd 3

Key

f m	father mother	u a	uncle aunt
B S	brother sister	c	cousin
s d	son daughter	gf gm	grandfather grandmother
gs gd	grandson granddaughter	g	great

rights, and so descending in the direct line from degree to degree, without stepping over any, to the plaintiff, and not only through all the occupied degrees in the direct line, but sometimes through the vacant degrees; as in case where the eldest son, having issue, dies before his ancestor. Sometimes in counting by descent the vacant degrees are passed over, as, where the eldest sons die without heirs of their bodies in the lifetime of their ancestors; for if an eldest son dies without issue in the lifetime of his ancestor, it is never necessary to count through him, because he did not survive until any estate descended to him, but such degree is quite vacant; so also if he had an heir who died without issue; and in such case the next brother occupies his place by reason of the mere right, which attaches to him as the next of blood. And if there is not any brother, then the right of succession will attach to the sister or sisters; and if there is no sister, then it will resort to the next occupied degree on the side of that ancestor from whom the inheritance moves in some collateral line. And as soon as he becomes seised of both rights, he begins to make a direct line as to issue begotten by him, and to be a common stock with regard to the heirs derived from him. Yet if any one chooses to count through a person, or his children, who did not live until any estate descended to them by the death of the common ancestor, it does no harm; but in such case he ought not to say that the right of succession descended, but that from John ought the right to have descended to Peter, and from Peter to Thomas as his grandson and heir; but inasmuch as such son or grandson did not live until such right descended to him, because he died in the lifetime of the common ancestor, the right descended to the second brother or to the other next heir. And sometimes the count is divided into branches by reason of plurality of heirs, as in case of sisters parceners, where it is proper first to count through all the degrees of the issue of the first, and then of the second, and so of the rest.

3. For the assistance of learners, a figure may be made to show more plainly the degrees and the lines direct and collateral, whereby a person may be better acquainted with the law of successions. Let therefore a perpendicular line be drawn, and in the middle of it let a void space be left for the supposed plaintiff, and let his father or mother be placed above him as the first ancestor, and that will make the first degree. Above the father or mother let the grandfather or grandmother of the plaintiff be put as in the second degree, and above the grandfather the great-grandfather, or the great-grandmother, as in the third degree; and above the great-grandfather the great-great-grandfather, and so higher and higher by different degrees as far as the time limited in a writ of right will allow. And directly under the plaintiff let son or daughter be placed, which will make the first degree descending; and under him grandson or granddaughter, to make the second degree; and lower again the son or daughter of the grandson or granddaughter to make the third degree, and so descending from degree to degree *ad infinitum*.

4. If there be found no plaintiff in the direct line to whom the right of succession can descend, then of necessity it must descend to the collateral degrees, that is, to the nearest to the father or the mother, as, to the uncle or aunt, and so on, descending in that line from degree to degree so far as they continue, and then for default of degrees found in the first collateral line, it must resort to the grandfather in the direct line,

and afterwards for default there, resort to the brother or sister of the grandfather in the collateral line, and so from degree to degree so far as they shall be found full; and so of all the other higher degrees, so that the right of succession shall fall to those who shall be found in the direct line, if none can be found anywhere below him to whom the right may descend. And for default of him who would have made a degree in the direct line the right shall descend to one who shall be found in the collateral line, and for default of a degree in the collateral line the right shall resort again to the direct line at a higher degree, and if it find that degree full, it shall attach there; if not, it shall go on descending in the collateral line, and so of all the other degrees.

5. And if no degree be found where the right may rest – or even if any be found – the lord of the fee may seize his fee until he in whose person the mere right of succession rests shall come and demand it, and in the meantime the lord shall stand in the place of the heir.

6. How the degrees are placed in consanguinity, appears by the above figure, whereof the half might suffice, and then it would resemble a banner; but it is displayed on the one side to show the issue of male ancestors, and on the other to show the issue of female ancestors.

Chapter IV

Of the proceedings in a Plea of Right before the Court Baron and County Court, and of its removal into the Royal Court

1. Writs of right patent ought to be brought in the courts of the lords of whom the plaintiffs claim to hold; and therefore if they are brought or purchased in any other courts than those of the chief lords of the fees, such chief lords shall have their courts out of our court, as soon as they make demand thereof, and can prove the fees to be theirs; and the writs and proceedings shall fall to the ground, and the plaintiffs shall remain in our mercy.

2. The plaintiff, having purchased his writ, ought to carry and show it to him to whom the mandate is directed; and he forthwith, without demanding pledges to prosecute, is bound to appoint him a day at his first court, which ought to be within three weeks, upon the same fee; and the writ should be produced and read in full court, and entered on the roll, and the tenant summoned by award of the court.

3. If the plaintiff be longer delayed, and can prove the same, as hereafter mentioned, by plaint and proof, he may by reason of such wrong, and because his lord has failed to do him right, waive the court of his lord, and plead in the county court, whether the lord has the franchise of return of writs or not. And thus in some cases the plaint may be removed out of a court, and afterwards brought back into it again. And before proof made of default the plaint shall not be considered as in the county, but after that, and not before, a *pone* will lie to remove it before our justices.

4. There are many ways besides in which a cause is removable into the county court, as, where the lord refuses to intermeddle therein, or because he has no court, or because he has released his court by his letters patent; also for want of authority in the lord and his court, as where the tenant vouches a warrant out of his jurisdiction,

and whom he cannot compel to appear, or if the tenant cause himself to be essoined *de malo lecti* elsewhere than in the jurisdiction of his lord, or because he has not authority to send the four knights to judge of the sickness for which he is essoined, or if the tenant put himself upon the great assize, and for many other reasons. Sometimes also the plea is removable by the tenant, as where he does not hold anything of him to whom the writ is directed.

5. As to summonses and defaults and essoins in the courts of freemen, the practice ought to be according to the custom of the country; but in the demanding of view, vouching to warranty, counting by descents and resorts, defending, excepting, and joining in battle, let the same order of pleading be observed in the court of a freeman as is awarded in our court. . . .

237. The sea law of Oléron

(*The Oak Book of Southampton*, ed. P. Studer, II (Southampton, 1911), with translation)

1. This is the charter of Oleron of the judgments of the sea. First, a man is made master of a ship. The ship belongs to two or three. The ship departs from the country to which she belongs, and comes to Bordeaux, La Rochelle, or elsewhere, and is freighted to go to a strange country. The master may not sell the ship unless he has a mandate or procuration from the owners; but if he has need of provisions, he may well put some of the ship's apparel in pledge, upon consultation with the ship's company. And this is the judgment in this case.

2. A ship is in a haven, and stays to await her time, and the time comes for her departure, the master shall take counsel with the mariners, his companions, and say to them: "Sirs, you have this weather." There will be some who will say "the weather is not good", and some who will say, "the weather is fine and good". The master is bound to agree with the greater part of his companions. And if he does otherwise, he is bound to replace the ship and the goods, if they are lost, if he have wherewithal. And this is the judgment in this case.

3. If a ship is lost in any land or in any place whatever, the mariners are bound to save the most that they can; and if they assist, the master is bound, if he have not money, to pledge some of the goods which they have saved, and to convey them back to their country. And if they do not assist, he is not bound to furnish them with anything or to provide them with anything, on the contrary, they shall lose their wages, when the ship is lost. And the master has no power to sell the apparel of the ship, if he has not a mandate or procuration from the owners, but he ought to place them in safe deposit, until he knows the wish of the owners; and he ought to do this the most loyally that he can, and if he do otherwise, he is bound to make compensation, if he have wherewithal. And this is the judgment in this case.

4. A ship departs from Bordeaux or elsewhere; it happens sometimes that she is lost, and they save the most that they can of the wines and the other goods. The merchants and the master are in great dispute, and the merchants claim from the master to have their [goods]. They may well have them, paying their freight for such part of the

voyage as the ship has made, if it please the master. And if the master wishes, he may well repair his ship, if she is in a state to be speedily repaired; and if not, he may hire another ship to complete the voyage. And the master shall have his freight for as much of the cargo as has been saved in any manner. And this is the judgment in this case.

5. A ship departs from a port laden or empty, and arrives in another port; the mariners shall not go ashore without the leave of the master; for if the ship be lost or damaged by any accident, they are bound to make compensation, if they have wherewithal. But if the ship be in a place where she has been moored with four cables, they may well go ashore and return in time to their ship. And this is the judgment in this case.

6. Mariners hire themselves to their master, and there are some of them who go ashore without leave, and get drunk, and make quarrels, and some of them are hurt; the master is not bound to have them healed, or to provide them with anything; on the contrary, he may well put them ashore, and hire another in his place; and if the latter costs more than he did, the mariner ought to pay, if the master can find anything of his [i.e. any property of the mariner]. But if the master sends him [i.e. the mariner] on any service of the ship by his order, and he [the mariner] wounds himself and is hurt, he shall be cured and healed at the cost of the ship. And this is the judgment in this case.

7. It happens that sickness overtakes one of the ship's company, or two or three doing their service to the ship, and he cannot remain in the ship as long as he is ill, the master shall put him ashore, and seek a lodging for him, and furnish him with a cresset or a candle, and supply him with one of the ship's boys to tend him, or hire a woman to take care of him. He ought to provide him with such food as is used in the said ship, that is to say, with as much as he had when he was in health, and nothing more, unless it please the master. And if he [the sick man] wishes to have more delicate food, the master is not bound to find it, unless it be at his [i.e. the sick man's] own expense. The ship ought not to delay her voyage for him, on the contrary, she should proceed on it; and if he should recover, he ought to have his wages for the whole voyage; and if he should die, his wife or his near relatives ought to have them for him. And this is the judgment in this case.

8. A ship loads at Bordeaux, or elsewhere, and it happens that a storm overtakes her at sea, and that they cannot escape without casting over some of the goods on board, the master is bound to say to the merchants: "Sirs, we cannot escape without casting overboard some of these wines or goods." The merchants, if there are any, answer as they will, and agree readily to a jettison, the reasons of the master being, as it happens, most clear; and if they do not agree, the master ought not to refrain from casting over as much as he shall see fit, swearing himself and three of his companions upon the holy gospels, when they have arrived in safety on shore, that he did not do it, except in order to save the lives, and the ship, and the goods, and the wines. Those [goods] which are cast overboard, ought to be appraised at the market price of those which have arrived in safety, and shall be sold and shared pound by pound amongst the merchants; and the master ought to share [in the loss] reckoning his ship or his

freight at his choice, to reimburse the losses. Each mariner ought to have one tun free, and the rest [*lit.* the other] he ought to share in the jettison, according to what he may have on board, if he conduct himself as a man on the sea; and if he do not so conduct himself, he shall have nothing of the franchise; and the master shall be believed on his oath. And this is the judgment [in this case].

9. It happens that the master of a ship cuts his mast from stress of weather; he ought to call the merchants, and show them that it is expedient to cut the mast, to save the ship and the goods; [and sometimes it happens that cables are cut and anchors abandoned, to save the ship and the goods;] they ought to be reckoned pound by pound as jettison; and the merchants shall share and pay without any delay, before their goods are landed from the ship. And if the ship should be on hard ground, and the master tarry by reason of their disputes, and there be leakage, the master ought not to share [in the loss], but rather he ought to have his freight of these wines as of the other goods which are saved. And this is the judgment in this case.

10. A master of a ship comes in safety to her [port of] discharge; he ought to show the merchants the ropes with which he will hoist, and if he sees that there is something to repair, the master is bound to repair them, for if a tun is lost by fault of the hoisting tackle or ropes, the master is bound to make compensation, he and his mariners; and the master ought to share as much as he receives for the hoisting, and the hoisting [money] ought to be set to restore the damage in the first place, and the residue ought to be shared amongst them. But if the ropes break without their having shown them to the merchants, [they will be bound to make good all the damage. But if the merchants say that the ropes are fair and good, and they break, each ought to share the loss, that is to say, the merchants] to whom the wine belongs alone. And this is the judgment in this case.

11. A ship loads at Bordeaux, or elsewhere, and hires out her casks to stow the wines, and departs, and the master and mariners do not fasten as they ought [their bulkheads?] and bad weather overtakes them [on the sea] in such manner that the casks in the hold stave a tun or pipe; the ship arrives in safety, and the merchants say that the casks have destroyed their wines; the master says that it is not so; if the master can swear himself and [three of?] his companions, or four of those whom the merchants have chosen, that their [= the merchants'] wines were not destroyed by their [= the ship's] casks, even as the merchants surmise against them, they ought to be quit and set free, and if they are not willing to swear, they ought to make good to the merchants their damage, for they are bound to fasten well and surely their bulkheads[?] and their hatches, before they depart from the place where they have loaded. And this is the judgment in this case.

12. A master hires his mariners and he ought to keep them in peace, and be their judge, if there is any one who hurts another, because he [the master] puts bread and wine on the table[?]. He who shall give the lie to another ought to pay fourpence; and the master, if he gives the lie to any one, ought to pay eightpence; and if there is any one who gives the lie to the master, he ought to pay as much as the master. And if it be so that the master strikes one of his mariners, he [i.e. the mariner] ought to abide the first blow, whether it be of the fist or of the palm of the hand; and if he

[the master] strikes him more, he [the mariner] may defend himself. And if the mariner strikes the master first, he ought to lose a hundred shillings or his fist, at the choice of the mariners [i.e. mariner?]. And this is the judgment in this case.

13. A ship is freighted at Bordeaux or elsewhere, and comes to her [place of] loading, and a charter-party is made, towage and petty pilots are [a charge] upon the merchants. On the coast of Brittany all those whom they take after they have passed the Isle de Bas, [in Leon] are petty pilots, and those of Normandy and England [after they have passed Calais and those of Scotland] after they have passed Guernsey, and those of Flanders after they have passed Calais, and those of Scotland after they have passed Yarmouth. And this is the judgment in this case.

14. Contention arises on board of a ship between the master and the mariners. The master ought to take away the tablecloth before the mariners three times, before he orders them out [of the ship]. And if the mariner offers to make amends according to the award of the mariners who are at the table, and the master is so cruel that he will not do anything, and he puts him out, the mariner may go and follow the ship up to her [port of] discharge, and have as good wages as if he came on board the ship, making amends for his fault according to the award of the table [i.e. of the ship's company]. And if it should be that the master has not as good a mariner as he on board, and that he lose her [i.e. the ship] through any accident, the master is bound to make good the damage of the ship and of the merchandise which may be on board, if he have wherewithal. And this is the judgment in this case.

15. A ship is moored in a roadstead, and hastening on with the tide another ship [comes and strikes the ship] which is at rest. The ship is damaged by the blow which the other has given her, and wine of some [of the casks] is spilt; the damage ought to be appraised, and divided by halves between the two ships. And the wines which are in the two ships ought to share the damages between the merchants. The master of the ship which has struck the other is bound to swear, himself and his mariners, that they did not do it intentionally; and the reason why this judgment was so made, is that an old ship would willingly place herself in the way of a better ship, if she were to recover all her damages, in the hope of obtaining the other ship [by way of compensation]. But when she knows that she must share [the damage of both] by halves, she willingly places herself out of the way. And this is the judgment in this case.

16. A ship, or two, or more are in a haven where there is little water, and which dries; one of the ships is too near the other, the master of this ship ought to say to the other mariners, "Sirs, raise your anchor, for it is too near to us and might do damage," and [if] they will not raise it, the master and his men may proceed to raise it for them, and remove it to a distance from him. And if they [i.e. the crew of the other boat] hinder it from being raised, and the anchor does them damage, the others are bound to make compensation thoroughly. [And should there be any anchor without a buoy, which does damage, they are bound to make compensation thoroughly.] And if they are in a haven which dries, they are bound to put floats to the anchors which do not appear at high tide. And this is the judgment in this case.

17. The mariners of the coast of Brittany ought to have one kitchen [i.e. one cooked meal] a day, by reason that they have drink going and coming. And those of Nor-

mandy ought to have two a day, by reason that their master only supplies them with water in going. But when the ship arrives at the land where the wine grows, the mariners ought to have drink, and the master ought to find it for them. And this is the judgment in this case.

18. A ship arrives at her [place of] loading, at Bordeaux or elsewhere. The master is bound to say to his companions: "Sirs, will you freight your fares, or will you hire yourselves according to the freight of the ship?" They are bound to reply which they will do. And if they choose to hire themselves according to the freight of the ship, such freight as he [the master] shall have, they shall have. And if they wish to freight [their fares] for themselves, they ought to freight them in such manner that the ship shall not be delayed. And if it should happen that they find no freight, the master is not to blame. And the master ought to show them their fares and their hire, and each may place there the weight of his venture. And if they wish to place [there] a tun of water, they may well place it, and if jettison takes place, and their tun of water be cast over into the sea, it is to be reckoned for wine or other goods, pound by pound, so that the mariners may exert themselves reasonably on the sea [?] And if they freight their fares to merchants, [the same franchise as the mariners have, ought the merchants to have]. And this is the judgment in this case.

19. A ship arrives at [the place of] unloading. The mariners wish to have their wages. And there is someone who has neither cot nor chest in the ship, the master may well retain of his wages to take back the ship thither whence he brought it, if he [the mariner] do not give good security to perform the voyage. And this is the judgment in this case.

20. The master hires his mariners in the town whereof the ship is, and hires some of them for the venture, the others for money. Then they see that the ship cannot find any freight to come in those parts, and that it is necessary for them to go to a further distance. Those who go for a venture ought to follow the ship, but to those who are engaged for money the master is bound to increase their wages, view by view, and course by course, by reason that he had hired them [to go] to a certain place. And if they go a shorter distance than that for which the engagement was willingly made, he [the mariner] ought to have all his wages, but he ought to assist to bring the ship back to the place whence they brought it, if the master wish it, at the adventure of God. And this is the judgment [in this case].

21. It happens that a ship is at Bordeaux or elsewhere, of such kitchen as there shall be in the ship, two mariners may carry with them [ashore] one mess, at the time when they [the rations] are cut on board ship. And of such bread as there shall be in the ship, they ought to have according to what they can eat at one meal, and of drink, none ought to be given to those out of the ship. And they ought to return quickly to the ship, in order that the master lose not the service of the ship, for if the master lose it, and incurs damage, they shall be bound to make it good; or if one of the crew hurt himself from want of help, they are bound to contribute to his cure, and to make compensation to their companion, and to the master, and to their mess-men. And this is the judgment in this case.

22. A merchant freights a ship, and loads her, and sets her on her way, and the ship

enters a port, and remains there so long that money fails him; the master holds property, he may send to his own country to seek for money; but he ought not to lose time, for if he do so, he is bound to make compensation to the merchant for all the damage which he [the merchant] shall incur. But the master may take of the wines of the merchants and sell them to obtain provisions. And when the ship shall have arrived at her right discharge, the wines which the master shall have taken ought to be valued at the price at which the others shall be sold, neither at a higher nor at a lower price. And the master ought to have his freight of those wines, as he shall have of the others. And this is the judgment in this case.

23. A master freights his ship to a merchant, and willingly on either side it is devised between them, and a term is fixed for loading; when the merchant does not observe it, but detains the ship and the mariners for the space of fifteen days or more, the master sometimes loses his time and his expenses from the default of the merchant. The merchant is bound to make compensation to the master; and of the compensation that is made the mariners ought to have one fourth, and the master three fourths, for the reason that he provides the expenses. And this is the judgment in this case.

24. A young man is pilot of a ship, and he is hired to conduct her as far as the port where she ought to discharge. It happens that in this port there are closed parts where they place the ships to discharge, the master is bound to provide her berth, himself and his mariners, and to put floats [to the anchors?] which do not appear at high water, or [to see] that her berth is well buoyed, that the merchants may suffer no damage; for if they have damage the master is bound to make it good, unless he can give an explanation, and his explanation be not made void. And the pilot has well done his duty when he has brought the ship as far as her berth, for so far he ought to conduct her, and thenceforward the responsibility is with the master and his companions. And this is the judgment in this case.

25. Because great loss is often caused by pilots, for that he [the pilot] agrees to take a ship into a harbour, and steers her badly, whereby many a master and many a merchant are impoverished, it is our wish that if he [the pilot] undertake to steer a ship into any harbour to safety, and he steers her badly and the ship is lost through his not knowing the entrance into the precincts of the harbour, the statute ordains that he lose his right hand and his left eye, because he has treasonably led them. And this is the judgment in this case.

26. And on this matter, here is the commission of our lord the king of England. [A.D. 1285]

Edward, by the grace of God, king of England, lord of Ireland, and duke of Aquitaine, to all those whom these present letters shall reach, greeting. Whereas Gregory de Rokeslee and Henry Waleys, our citizens of London, and others, as well of the merchants of England . . .

27. *Wreck at Sea.* [A.D. 1275, Statute of Westminster, ch. IV.] It is agreed that if any man, dog, or cat escape quick out of the ship or out of the barge of the ship, that neither the ship, nor the barge, nor anything which was within them, be adjudged wreck: but the goods shall be saved and kept by view of the sheriff, the coroner, or the king's bailiff, [and be delivered] into the hands of those of the town where the goods

were found; so that if anyone come within a year and a day, and wish to sue for these goods, and be able to prove that those are they which belonged to his lord or which perished in his keeping, they shall be restored [to him] without delay; and if not, they shall remain to the king and be appraised by the sheriff, the coroner, and the bailiff, and shall be delivered to those of the town to answer before the justices of the wreck belonging to the king. And where wreck belongeth to another than to the king, he shall have it in like manner; and he that doth otherwise, and thereof be attainted, shall be awarded to prison, and shall remain [there] at the king's will, and shall render the damages ensuing; and if a bailiff do it, and it be disallowed by the lord, and the lord have appropriated to himself nothing of this, the bailiff shall answer, if he have whereof; and if not, the lord shall deliver the bailiff's body to the king.

238. The medieval universe

John de Sacrobosco, a master at Paris and, by tradition at least, an Englishman (his name has been variously translated as John of Holywood and John Halifax) wrote in the first half of the thirteenth century. His treatise on *The Sphere* became a university "set-book". Robert "the Englishman", his commentator, was a scholar of the next generation and, if his colophon is to be believed, lectured at Montpellier, or Paris, round about the year 1271. Both treatise and commentary are, apart from content, examples of thirteenth-century lecturing method.

(a) *Extracts from "The Sphere" of John de Sacrobosco*

(*The "Sphere" of Sacrobosco and its Commentators*, ed., with translations, by Lynn Thorndike (University of Chicago Press, 1949), pp. 118–23, 140–2.)

Proemium

The treatise on the sphere we divide into four chapters, telling, first, what a sphere is, what its centre is, what the axis of a sphere is, what the pole of the world is, how many spheres there are, and what the shape of the world is. In the second we give information concerning the circles of which this material sphere is composed and that supercelestial one, of which this is the image, is understood to be composed. In the third we talk about the rising and setting of the signs, and the diversity of days and nights which happens to those inhabiting diverse localities, and the division into climes. In the fourth the matter concerns the circles and motions of the planets, and the causes of eclipses.

Chapter 1

. . . The machine of the universe is divided into two, the ethereal and the elementary region. The elementary region, existing subject to continual alteration, is divided into four. For there is earth, placed, as it were, as the centre in the middle of all, about which is water, about water air, about air fire, which is pure and not turbid there and reaches to the sphere of the moon, as Aristotle says in his book of "Meteorology". For so God, the glorious and sublime, disposed. And these are called the "four elements" which are in turn by themselves altered, corrupted and regenerated. The elements are also simple bodies which cannot be subdivided into parts of diverse forms and from whose com-mixture are produced various species of generated things. Three of them, in turn, surround the earth on all sides spherically, except in so far as the dry land stays the sea's tide to protect the life of animate beings. All, too, are mobile except earth, which, as the centre of the world, by its weight in every direction equally avoiding the great motion of the extremes, as a round body occupies the middle of the sphere.

Around the elementary region revolves with continuous circular motion the ethereal, which is lucid and immune from all variation in its immutable essence. And it is called "Fifth Essence" by the philosophers. Of which there are nine spheres, as we have just said: namely, of the moon, Mercury, Venus, the sun, Mars, Jupiter, Saturn, the fixed stars, and the last, heaven. Each of these spheres encloses its inferior spherically.

And of these there are two movements. One is of the last heaven on the two extremities of its axis, the Arctic and Antarctic poles, from east through west to east again, which the equinoctial circle divides through the middle. Then there is another movement, oblique to this and in the opposite direction, of the inferior spheres on their axes, distant from the former by 23 degrees. But the first movement carries all the others with it in its rush about the earth once within a day and night, although they strive against it, as in the case of the eighth sphere one degree in a hundred years. This second movement is divided through the middle by the zodiac, under which each of the seven planets has its own sphere, in which it is borne by its own motion, contrary to the movement of the sky, and completes it in varying spaces of time – in the case of Saturn in thirty years, Jupiter in twelve years, Mars in two, the sun in three hundred and sixty-five days and six hours, Venus and Mercury about the same, the moon in twenty-seven days and eight hours.

That the sky revolves from east to west is signified by the fact that the stars, which rise in the east, mount gradually and successively until they reach mid-sky and are always at the same distance apart, and, thus maintaining their relative positions, they move towards their setting continuously and uniformly. Another indication is that the stars near the North Pole, which never set for us, move continuously and uniformly, describing their circles about the pole, and are always equally near or far from one another. Wherefore, from those two continuous movements of the stars, both those that set and those which do not, it is clear that the firmament is moved from east to west.

There are three reasons why the sky is round: likeness, convenience, and necessity. Likeness, because the sensible world is made in the likeness of the archetype, in which there is neither end nor beginning; wherefore, in likeness to it the sensible world has a round shape, in which beginning or end cannot be distinguished. Convenience, because of all isoperimetric bodies the sphere is the largest and of all shapes the round is most capacious. Since largest and round, therefore the most capacious. Wherefore, since the world is all-containing, this shape was useful and convenient for it, Necessity, because if the world were of other form than round – say, trilateral, quadrilateral, or many-sided – it would follow that some space would be vacant and some body without a place, both of which are false, as is clear in the case of angles projecting and revolved.

Also, as Alfraganus says, if the sky were flat, one part of it would be nearer to us than another, namely, that which is directly overhead. So when a star was there, it would be closer to us than when rising or setting. But those things which are closer to us seem larger. So the sun when in mid-sky should look larger than when rising or setting, whereas the opposite is the case; for the sun or another star looks bigger in the east or west than in mid-sky. But, since this is not really so, the reason for its seeming so is that in winter and the rainy season vapours rise between us and the sun or other star. And, since those vapours are diaphanous, they scatter our visual rays so that they do not apprehend the object in its true size, just as is the case with a penny dropped into a depth of limpid water, which appears larger than it actually is because of a like diffusion of rays.

That the earth, too, is round is shown thus. The signs and stars do not rise and set the same for all men everywhere but rise and set sooner for those in the east than for those in the west; and of this there is no other cause than the bulge of the earth. Moreover, celestial phenomena evidence that they rise sooner for orientals than for westerners. For one and the same eclipse of the moon which appears to us in the first hour of the night appears to orientals about the third hour of the night, which proves that they had night and sunset before we did, of which setting the bulge of the earth is the cause.

That the earth also has a bulge from north to south and *vice versa* is shown thus: To those living towards the north, certain stars are always visible, namely, those near the North Pole, while others which are near the South Pole are always concealed from them. If, then, anyone should proceed from the north southward, he might go so far that the stars which formerly were always visible to him now would tend towards their setting. And the farther south he went, the more they would be moved towards their setting. Again, that same man now could see stars which formerly had always been hidden from him. And the reverse would happen to anyone going from the south northwards. The cause of this is simply the bulge of the earth. Again, if the earth were flat from east to west, the stars would rise as soon for westerners as for orientals, which is false. Also, if the earth were flat from north to south and *vice versa*, the stars which were always visible to anyone would continue to be so wherever he went, which is false. But it seems flat to human sight because it is so extensive.

That the water has a bulge and is approximately round is shown thus: Let a signal be set up on the sea coast and a ship leave port and sail away so far that the eye of a person standing at the foot of the mast can no longer discern the signal. Yet if the ship is stopped, the eye of the same person, if he has climbed to the top of the mast, will see the signal clearly. Yet the eye of a person at the bottom of the mast ought to see the signal better than he who is at the top, as is shown by drawing straight lines from both to the signal. And there is no other explanation of this thing than the bulge of the water. For all other impediments are excluded, such as clouds and rising vapours.

Also, since water is a homogeneous body, the whole will act the same as its parts. But parts of water, as happens in the case of little drops and dew on herbs, naturally seek a round shape. Therefore, the whole, of which they are parts, will do so.

That the earth is in the middle of the firmament is shown thus. To persons on the earth's surface the stars appear of the same size whether they are in mid-sky or just rising or about to set, and this is because the earth is equally distant from them. For if the earth were nearer to the firmament in one direction than in another, a person at that point of the earth's surface which was nearer to the firmament would not see half of the heavens. But this is contrary to Ptolemy and all the philosophers, who say that, wherever man lives, six signs rise and six signs set, and half of the heavens is always visible and half hid from him.

That same consideration is a sign that the earth is as a centre and point with respect to the firmament, since, if the earth were of any size compared with the firmament, it would not be possible to see half the heavens. Also, suppose a plane passed through the centre of the earth, dividing it and the firmament into equal halves. An eye at the earth's centre would see half the sky, and one on the earth's surface would see the same half. From which it is inferred that the magnitude of the earth from surface to centre is inappreciable and, consequently, that the magnitude of the entire earth is inappreciable compared to the firmament. Also Alfraganus says that the least of the fixed stars which we can see is larger than the whole earth. But that star, compared with the firmament, is a mere point. Much more so is the earth, which is smaller than it.

That the earth is held immobile in the midst of all, although it is the heaviest, seems explicable thus. Every heavy thing tends towards the centre. Now the centre is a point in the middle of the firmament. Therefore, the earth, since it is heaviest, naturally tends towards that point. Also, whatever is moved from the middle towards the circumference ascends. Therefore, if the earth were moved from the middle towards the circumference, it would be ascending, which is impossible.

The total girth of the earth by the authority of the philosophers Ambrose, Theodosius, and Eratosthenes is defined as comprising 252,000 stades, which is allowing 700 stades for each of the 360 parts of the zodiac [*sic*]. For let one take an astrolabe on a clear starry night and, sighting the pole through both apertures in the indicator,[1] note the number of degrees where it is. Then let our measurer of the cosmos proceed directly north until on another clear night, observing the pole as before, the indicator stands a degree higher. After this let the extent of his travel be measured, and it will be found to be 700 stades. Then, allowing this many stades for each of 360 degrees the girth of the earth is found.

From these data the diameter of the earth can be found thus by the rule for the circle and diameter. Subtract the twenty-second part from the circuit of the whole earth, and a third of the remainder – that is, 80,181 stades and a half and third part of one stade – will be the diameter or thickness of the terrestrial ball.

. . .

Chapter 4

It should be noted that the sun has a single circle in which it is moved in the plane of the ecliptic, and it is eccentric. Any circle is called "eccentric" which, like that of

[1] The *mediclinium*, or "indicator", is described in the first part, fourth chapter, of Messahala's treatise on the astrolabe (English translation in R. G. Gunther, *Early Science at Oxford*, V (1929), pp. 142–4, "Of Making an Allidada which is called a Rule or Mediclinium").

the sun, dividing the earth into equal parts, does not have the same centre as the earth but one outside it. . . .

Moreover, there are two movements of the sun from west to east, one of which is its own in its eccentric, by which it is moved every day and night about 60 minutes. The other is the slower movement of the sphere itself on the poles of the axis of the circle of the signs, and it is equal to the movement of the sphere of the fixed stars, namely, 1 degree in a hundred years. From these two movements, then, is reckoned the sun's course in the circle of the signs from west to east, by which it cleaves the circle of the signs in 365 days and a fourth of one day, except for a small fraction which is imperceptible. . . .

Since the sun is larger than the earth, it is necessary that half the sphere of earth be always illuminated by the sun and that the shadow of the earth, extended into the air like a cone, diminish in circumference until it ends in the plane of the circle of the signs inseparable from the nadir of the sun. The nadir is a point in the firmament directly opposite to the sun. Hence, when the moon at full is in the head or tail of the dragon beneath the nadir of the sun, then the earth is interposed between sun and moon, and the cone of the earth's shadow falls on the body of the moon. Wherefore, since the moon has no light except from the sun, it actually is deprived of light and there is a general eclipse, if it is in the head or tail of the dragon directly but partial if it is almost within the bounds determined for eclipse. And it always happens at full moon or thereabouts. But, since in every opposition – that is, at full moon – the moon is not in the head or tail of the dragon or beneath the nadir of the sun, it is not necessary that the moon suffer eclipse at every full moon.

When the moon is in the head or tail of the dragon or nearly within the limits and in conjunction with the sun, then the body of the moon is interposed between our sight and the body of the sun. Hence it will obscure the brightness of the sun for us, and so the sun will suffer eclipse – not that it ceases to shine but that it fails us because of the interposition of the moon between our sight and the sun. From these it is clear that a solar eclipse should always occur at the time of conjunction or new moon. And it is to be noted that when there is an eclipse of the moon, it is visible everywhere on earth. But when there is an eclipse of the sun, that is by no means so. Nay, it may be visible in one clime and not in another, which happens because of the different point of view in different climes. Whence Virgil most aptly and concisely expresses the nature of either eclipse: "Varied defects of the moon, and of the sun travails."[1]

From the aforesaid it is also evident that, when the sun was eclipsed during the Passion and the same Passion occurred at full moon, that eclipse was not natural – nay, it was miraculous and contrary to nature, since a solar eclipse ought to occur at new moon or thereabouts. On which account Dionysius the Areopagite is reported to have said during the same Passion, "Either the God of nature suffers, or the mechanism of the universe is dissolved."

[1] *Georgics*, ii, 478

(b) *Extracts from the Commentary of Robertus Anglicus upon "The Sphere" of Sacrobosco*

(ibid. pp. 199–200, 203–15, 228–31, 236–7, 239–40, 243–6)

The commentary took fifteen lectures. Lectures 1–4 dealt with Sacrobosco's first chapter, 5–8 with his second, 9–13 with his third, and 14–15 with his fourth.

First lecture

One science is nobler or better than another for two reasons, either because it is about a nobler subject or because it proceeds by a more certain method. Among other sciences, therefore, astronomy deserves to be called the noblest, first, as being about a nobler subject, since it is concerning a celestial body ungenerable and incorruptible, which is the noblest body; second, as proceeding by a surer method, since demonstratively, for it proves the passions of the super-celestial bodies by most certain demonstrations, in which there is no error or ambiguity. And through knowledge of the passions or properties of those bodies the rational soul admires the marvellous work of the Creator, on which account man is strongly moved to come to knowledge of the Creator. And so Ptolemy says in the beginning of the "Almagest" that this science is, as it were, a road leading to God. As an introduction to which science this treatise was written, through which treatise a man is placed in the position of having in a compendium those things which are demonstrated more at length in the science of astronomy. Of this treatise the effective cause was the Englishman, mr John of Sacrobosco. The material cause is the heavens. The formal cause is as in other sciences. The final cause is its utility, which is clear through its exposition; for its usefulness is manifest in medical practice, because a physician cannot cure, if he does not know the cause of the disease, which cause cannot be understood if he is ignorant of the motion and disposition of the supercelestial bodies, which are the cause of every disposition of these inferiors. Therefore, if the superior cause is not known, the posterior cause is not known, especially since a primary cause influences its effect more than a secondary cause does, as is stated in the beginning of "On Causes". The usefulness of astronomy is also manifest in many other sciences.

The title is this: *Here begins the treatise on the sphere.* Moreover, it belongs under astronomy. It is divided into two parts, for in the first part, which is introductory, the author states his purpose and divides that treatise into four chapters. In the second, when he says, *A sphere therefore by Euclid . . .*, he pursues his purpose; and that second part is divided into four parts according as there are four chapters. Where they begin will become clear enough later. The first chapter is divided into three parts: in the first part he defines a sphere; in the second he divides the sphere when he says, *For the sphere is divided . . .*; in the third part he determines as to the form of the world when he says, *The machine of the universe. . . .* And the first of those parts has two parts; in the first part he gives one definition, in the second another when he says, *But by Theodosius a sphere. . . .* And that part where he divides is divided into two. In the first part he offers one division, in the second another when he says, *According to accident. . . .*

Those four sections with the first part, which is introductory, are the subject of this lecture. The meaning of all these parts is plain, after seeing what is notable. . . .[1]

[1] Most of the lecture is in fact explanatory, two points only being considered open to discussion.

Second lecture

The machine of the universe. This is the third part of this chapter in which he discusses the form of the world, and this part divides into two. In the first he divides the world into its integral parts. In the second part he determines the properties of the parts of the world, as there, *And of these there are two movements.* . . . The first is treated in this lecture and divides into four parts. In the first he divides the world into an elementary part and an ethereal, which are the parts of the world. In the second he proceeds with the elementary part of the world, dividing it into four parts, as here, *The elementary region, indeed.* . . . In the third he defines an element, as there, *The elements, moreover.* . . . In the fourth he discusses the other part of the world, namely, the ethereal, as there, *Around the elementary.* . . . The first part is plain. The text of the second part reads thus. *Indeed,* that is, surely. *Elementary region,* i.e. that part of the world which is called "elementary". *Pervious,* i.e. obedient. *To continual alteration,* i.e., is in continual transmutation, since ever from one element is generated another and *vice versa. Is divided into four,* namely, elements. The following text will be cleared up by the notabilia. The text of the fourth part reads thus. *Lucid ether,* i.e. that part of the world which contains the celestial orbs, which is lucid and full of light. *Existing about the elementary region,* this I repeat. *Immune,* i.e., lacking. *In its immutable essence,* i.e., by its substance, which is intransmutable. *Apart from all variation,* i.e. transmutation, this I repeat. *Proceeds,* i.e., is moved with a continuous motion. The text following is clear.

To complete this lecture one should note, first, the number of elements. Be it understood, then, that there cannot be a single element only, since all action is produced by contrariety. But where there is only one, there is no contrariety. So we must have two. If, then, there are supposed to be two extreme elements, such as fire and earth, it is necessary to assume two intermediates, since, if there is no intermediate, either there will be a vacuum between fire and earth, which is impossible in nature, or the fire will touch the earth and then, because of the agreement of fire with earth in dryness, the fire will burn the earth and ultimately convert it to its own nature. So there should be some middle element; but, if water is placed there, because of its agreement with earth in coldness and because of the heat of fire, in the end it will be converted either into earth or fire. So there must be some medium between water and fire which will share a property of either, and hence it is necessary to posit four elements. And so Plato says, "Between all cubic numbers may be placed two mean numbers which have the same ratios to the extremes." Hence between any two extreme elements it will be possible to place two mean elements, which form one proportion with the extremes. A cubic number is produced by multiplying any number by itself twice, whence the first cubic number is twice two twice, that is, 8, and the second is three times three times three, that is, 27, and between those two numbers may be placed two means which form one proportion with the extremes, such as 12 and 18. For all those numbers are in once and a half proportion because each larger one contains the small once and half of it. So it is with the elements for, as Boethius says, "All which have grown out of the primeval origin of things are formed in numerical ratio."

Second to be noted is the location of the elements. Every element is either very heavy or very light or relatively heavy or relatively light. If it is very heavy, it is at the centre of the world, as the earth is, because there is no point so remote from the place of light things as the centre. If it is very light, it is just below the last heaven, since that place is the highest there is under the sky. But if it is comparatively heavy, then it is above the earth, as water is. If it is comparatively light, it is below fire and above water, like air.

Third, note that all the elements surround the earth in all directions spherically except water, for which exception three reasons may be suggested. One, divine will to save animal life. Another, the dryness of earth absorbing parts of the water, as is stated in "On Generation and Corruption". Unless earth were mixed with water, it would crumble to dust. Third is the influence of the stars so that some conjunction above a part of the earth made it dry, a sign of which is that places which were once full of water are now dried out.

Note, fourth, that fire and air move circularly about the earth; and Alpetragi proves this because a comet in the air is moved with the motion of the firmament, wherefore the air bearing it is moved. By like reasoning it is certain of fire.

Fifth, it should also be noted that every element has two qualities, one essential, the other accidental, whence, in fire, heat is essential, dryness accidental; in air, humidity is essential, heat accidental; in water, cold is essential, humidity accidental; in earth, dryness is essential and cold accidental. In some elements the essential quality is more manifest than the accidental, as, in fire, heat is more manifest than dryness. In some the accidental quality is more manifest, as the humidity of water is more manifest than its coldness.

Also note that two qualities are active, hot and cold, and two passive, humid and dry. And two move from centre to circumference, hot and humid, but two in the opposite direction, cold and dry. Note, too, that those elements which have lots of form cannot lose their active qualities without their corruption, as the heat of fire, but those elements which have lots of matter can lose them without their corruption, as water loses coldness. Also note that an element is transmutable as far as its parts are concerned, but as a whole it is ungenerable and incorruptible. Also note that "simple" is used in two senses. In one it is contrasted with composition, and in this sense the elements are not simple. In another sense it is contrasted with mixture, and thus the elements are simple, since they are not mixtures.

Also, concerning the ethereal part of the world, it should be noted that the material of the supercelestial bodies is a pure lucid matter which is subject to no transmutation which might vary the substance of these bodies. And a star which is in an orb does not differ from the orb except in greater and less aggregation of light, and in greater and less density, wherefore a star is an aggregation of light in an orb with a greater density than the orb.

But the question might be raised whether there is a sphere of fire; and it appears not, since, if there were fire in its sphere, it would be either coal or flame or light. Not coal, because it is terrestrial matter. Not flame, because flame is aerial matter. Not light, because, if it were light, it would shine. But it does not shine, so no kind of fire is there. Also, since a celestial body is neither hot nor cold, it does not seem that a very hot body could be continuous with that body which is in no way hot; wherefore, there is no fire adjoining the sphere of the moon. Also, since air is nearer to the sky than earth is, and since there is greater heat on earth than in the air, it would seem that fire, since it is nearer to the sky than air is, would be colder than air. And if this is the case, there will not be fire there.

By way of solution I say that fire in its own sphere is light but it does not shine unless matter is supplied it from elsewhere, nor does it burn. Nor does it follow that, if there is light, it shines, since light is a condition and not an action, just as this does not follow: this is laughable, therefore it laughs.

To the second argument be it said that a celestial body is not hot itself and does not receive heat from anything next to it but is hot only effectively, so that by its motion it inflames bodies beneath it, yet it is not inflamed by those inflamed bodies.

To the third argument be it said that it does not follow that, if fire is nearer to the sky than air, it is colder, since heat is produced differently in fire and on earth, because in fire heat is caused by the motion of the sky, on earth by the reverberation of rays, as will be shown later.

Third lecture

The parts of the world have been discussed. Here the author intends to treat the properties of those parts; and this section is divided into seven parts. In the first he discusses the properties of the heavens; in the second the properties of the earth, and this with respect to figure; in the third the properties of water; in the fourth the properties of earth with respect to position; in the fifth the properties of earth as to size; in the sixth the properties of earth as to immobility; in the seventh the properties of earth as to measure. The second begins, *Moreover, that the earth is round. . . .* The third opens, *That the water. . . .* The fourth, *That the earth is in the middle. . . .* The fifth, *That same is a sign. . . .* The sixth, *That the earth in the middle of all. . . .* The seventh, *The total girth of the earth. . . .* The first three are covered in the present lecture.

The first part has three parts, for, first, he tells by what movements the sky is moved; second, he proves that it is moved, opening, *That the sky revolves . . .*; third, he determines the shape of the sky, opening, *That the sky is round. . . .* And that second section has four parts, for first he proves by one reason, second by another, third by another, fourth by another. The second here, *Convenience. . . .* The third here, *Necessity. . . .* The fourth here, *Also Alfraganus says. . . .* Then follows the second principal part, and it has two parts, since, first, it proves that the earth is round by one indication, then by another, opening, *That the earth also has a bulge. . . .* The third principal part likewise divides into two. In the first he proves that water is round by one indication, in the second by another when he says, *Also, since water is a homogeneous body. . . .*

The sense of the first part is this: The celestial spheres have two movements, one from east to west within a day and night once about the whole earth from point to point on the poles of the world. And by this movement all nine spheres are moved in uniform and continuous motion by the force of the first sphere and by some one mover, who is the Intelligence deputed to this, which is called the "world soul". The other movement is in eight celestial spheres only, from west to east by diverse movements on the poles of the zodiac. And it is twofold for certain, although it is not given in the text except as one. One is the movement from west to east of the eight spheres themselves; the other is the movement of the stars in the spheres. The first movement from west to east is uniform, one degree every hundred years. For thus are moved all eight spheres, according to the opinion of Ptolemy, by one Intelligence; but otherwise according to the opinion of Thebit, as will appear later. The other is the movement from west to east of stars in the spheres, which does not apply to the fixed stars, since they have no other movement than that of the sphere, but only to the seven planets. And by that movement the planets are moved against the movement of the spheres like a fly on a wheel. And in this way each planet has its own mover, namely, some Intelligence. And in this way Saturn completes its orbit in thirty years, Jupiter in twelve, and so with the others, as appears in the text.

The sense of the second part is clear after we have seen what the archetype world is; for it is a model of the world existent in the divine mind before the creation of the world after whose likeness the world was created. And, since that world was in the divine mind and that which is in God is one with God, as Augustine holds, therefore, as God had neither beginning nor end, so no more had that world. Moreover, a figure without beginning or end is circular, therefore, etc. And it is derived from *archi*, which is "chief", and *tipos*, which is "figure", as it were "chief of figures".

The sense of the third part is clear when we have understood the exposition of this word, "isoperimetric"; and it is derived from *idos*, which means "form", and *peri*, which is "about", and *metros*, "measure", as it were the greatest of all measurable circular forms. Which is evident, because if there were two equal lines and a square was made from one and a circle from the other, the circle will hold more than the square. The sense of the other parts is plain enough.

To complete this lecture be it noted, first, what moves the sky; second, why the sky is moved; and third, why it is moved by contrary movements. First, then, it should be noted that the mover of the sky is twofold, conjoined and separate. The First Cause is separate. Conjoined is some Intelligence deputed to move the sky, and it is twofold. For there is one which moves all the spheres from east to west, and it is the world soul; and there is a mover which moves by contrary movements, and those are several movers according to the plurality of movements from west to east, whence each planet has its own mover.

Second, it should be noted that there is a quadruple reason why the sky is moved continuously. The first is that it may be assimilated to its Creator; therefore, it is moved continuously in order that it may attain that which it seeks, and, because it never attains it completely, therefore it never ceases to be moved. The second reason is the continuation of heat in these inferiors; for natural heat, which is the principle of life, could not exist without the benefit of celestial heat. And since that heat is acquired by motion, therefore the sky is moved continuously. The third reason is the movement of these inferiors, since without the movement of the sky nothing could be moved here below. The fourth reason is the influence of the virtue of the stars on various parts of the earth. For if the heavens stood still, then a star existing in the sky would shed its influence only on one part of the earth; and then an effect which was in one part of the earth would not be in another part, which would be very inconvenient. Also it is moved by diverse movements, to this end that influence be exerted in different extensions of the earth, for in the case of movement from east to west influence is exerted on the stretch of earth from east to west, and by the contrary movement there is influence of the virtues of the stars on that extension of the earth which is from north to south. And so it is clear why the sky is moved by varied movements.

Also note that a star exerts influence in two ways, by motion and by ray. By motion it produces heat; by ray it produces heat and virtue. For it produces heat by the reflection of rays on the surface of a solid body, and it also produces virtue by the same ray. It is also to be noted that the planets and fixed stars have different influences, since the office of the fixed stars is to order inferior things so far as figure and the arrangement of parts is concerned, so that today there is no figure in these inferiors but that the same in likeness and virtue is found in the eighth sphere. For the Scorpion in the sky governs scorpions on earth, as Ptolemy has it. But the planets have dominion over the movement and virtue of these inferiors.

Also note that the properties of the seven planets are these: Saturn is of cold and dry nature; Jupiter of hot and moist nature; Mars of hot and dry nature which consumes by burning; but the sun is of a hot and dry nature, which heat is life-giving; Venus of cold and humid nature with aerial humidity; Mercury hot with the hot, cold with the cold, following the nature of the planet with which it is in conjunction; the moon of cold and humid nature with the humidity of water rather than that of air. But one wonders how those qualities can be in the heavens. But understand that those qualities can be in anything in three ways, either qualitatively and formally, or significatively, or effectively. Those qualities are in elementary bodies in the first way. They may be in supercelestial bodies in the second and third ways. For, as Averroes holds in the book, "*De substantia orbis*", just as not all that blackens is black, because, if this were so, it would go on *ad infinitum*, so not all that heats is hot, but one must suppose first that which heats and is not hot, like a celestial body which by its movement inflames and heats the bodies which are under it. Also it should be known that, of those planets, some are benevolent, some malevolent, and some indifferent. The malevolent are such as Saturn and Mars and are called "unfortunate". The benevolent are such as Jupiter, Venus, and the moon. The sun by conjunction is evil, by aspect good. Mercury is good with the good, evil with the evil.

Also it should be known that Saturn indicates a melancholy man, when it dominates in anyone's nativity, and is masculine and attests concerning melancholic humours and old age. Jupiter attests concerning a sanguine make-up and of ages designates youth towards its beginning and life and gladness, truth and religion and patience and every fine precept; and of figures a white man with ruddy face, as Messahala says, and is a masculine planet. Mars is masculine and of ages signifies the middle of youth and a choleric constitution and war and every occupation concerned with fire; and of human images a ruddy man with red hair and round face. The sun is masculine and signifies a wide rule and vital soul and light and splendour, and it rules the close of youth; and of human figures him who has a colour between yellow and black, that is, dark with redness, of short stature, curly-haired, bald, of beautiful body. Venus is feminine and is signifier of women and wives and youth as a whole. And of human types it indicates a white man tending towards blackness, with beautiful body and hair, having a round face, small jaw, and round eyes. Mercury is masculine and indicates love of concubines, and of occupations those who generate knowledge and philosophy and study and science and scriptures and youth; and of human figures not very white or black, having long fingers. The moon is feminine and indicates a phlegmatic constitution and boyhood and the beginning of growing; of occupations it controls legations and mandates; and of human figures a man with round face and beautiful appearance.

But now is asked whether, if the movement of the sky ceased, there could be motion in these inferiors. And it seems so because, if the sky stops, there is quiet, and if there is quiet, there is time, because all rest is in time. And if there is time, there is motion, since time is the measure of motion. Therefore, although the sky should not move, there would still be motion. Also supposing that, with the sky at rest, there is a millstone in the air, then I ask whether that stone will move or remain at rest. It does not remain at rest, I prove, because then a weight existing aloft with nothing to stop it would not fall downwards, which is impossible, since, if gravity moves a heavy body, as Aristotle and his commentator hold, and since this weight possesses gravity and the medium still exists through which motion occurs, it is evident that the weight is not prevented from falling. Suppose the sky is moving and begins to stop, then the last instant of its motion occurs. If it begins to move again, then you have the first instant of that motion. But between every two instants falls an intermediate period; therefore, there is some intermediate time in that instant in which the sky does not move. But there is no time without motion; therefore there will still be motion though the sky ceases to move.

Aristotle holds the contrary in the book of "Meteorology" and in several other places, that the movement of the sky is the cause of all motion.

To this question I say that, if the sky were not moved, nothing else could be moved, since the movement of the sky is the cause of every motion. And to the first argument be it said and to the second that to suppose that the sky does not move is to deprive the sky of its form, as Averroes holds in the book "*De substantia orbis*". So the impossible is assumed, and it is not surprising if the impossible follows. Yet to the first argument it may be said that rest is of two sorts. One is complete privation of any motion, and such is not in time; one is privation of a particular motion, and such is in time. To the second argument it should be said that, under the conditions named, the weight would be prevented from falling by the medium suddenly being condensed of necessity from the sky ceasing to move, so that the weight could not be moved further. To the third argument it should be said that those two instants are of different times and different continuums, and between different instants of different continuums middle time would not fall but only between instants of the same continuum, so the objection does not stand.

Fourth lecture

That the earth is in the middle of the firmament. In this part the author intends to treat of a certain property of the earth as to location, showing that the earth is in the middle of the firmament, first by one indication, second by another, when he says, *For if the earth were nearer.* . . . Then follows that part, *That same consideration* . . ., in which he treats of a property of the earth as to its size, showing that its quantity is insensible compared to the heavens, and this he shows in three ways. The second begins, *Also suppose a plane.* . . . The third way begins, *Also Alfraganus says.* . . . Then follows that part, *That the earth in the midst of all* . . . in which he proves a certain property of the earth as to immobility, showing that the earth is so situated in the midst of the firmament that it is not moved thence. And this he proves in two ways. The second opens, *Also, whatever is moved from the middle.* . . . Then follows that part, *The total girth of the earth* . . ., in which he instructs how to measure the earth; and that part has two parts. First, he teaches how to measure the circuit of the earth, opening, *From these data.* . . . And this is the sense of the text in general. The meaning of the whole lesson is plain except that of the two last parts.

The meaning of the next-to-the-last part is that if anyone wishes to measure the earth when he is in some city – Paris, for example – he should observe the altitude of the pole on a clear night through both sights which are on a quadrant or astrolabe, and he will find the altitude at Paris to be 48 degrees. Afterwards that same man should proceed straight north to some place until he shall have found the altitude of the pole greater than at Paris by 1 degree. Afterwards he shall measure the distance between Paris and that place, and he will find it 700 stades. Since, therefore, the circle of the earth and the circle of the sky are about the same centre – as is shown here in a figure – and, when two circles have the same centre, there are as many parts in the smaller as in the larger, although not equal, since 700 stades on earth corresponds to 1 degree in the sky, therefore as many degrees as there are in the sky, so many times 700 stades on earth. But there are 360 degrees in the sky, so there are 360 times 700 stades on earth. But 360 times 700 stades are 252,000 stades; wherefore in the circuit of the earth there are 252,000 stades. And understand that "cosmimeter" means "world measurer" and is derived from *cosmos*, which is "world", and *metros*, which is "measure". "Mediclinium" is the line or rule through the middle of the astrolabe where there are two perforated plates.

Towards understanding of the last part, note that you should first consider two rules, of which the former is that every circle contains its diameter three and one-seventh times and that, by this rule, if the measure of the diameter is known, the measure of the circumference is obtained. The second rule is that, having the measure of the circumference, I ought to take away one twenty-second part, and then a third of the remainder gives the length of the diameter. For instance, if the circumference contains 22 feet, I should take away 1 foot, which is a twenty-second part, and then take a third of 21 feet, which is 7; then the diameter will be 7 feet, and in this way is the operation performed in the text. Take the circumference of the earth, which is 252,000 stades. Then divide that number by 22, and the twenty-second part will appear in division, namely, 11,454; and there will remain 12 after dividing. Of those 12 you cannot take a twenty-second part in whole numbers. So you should use halves instead of wholes. Twelve are equivalent to 24 halves. A twenty-second part is one half, since two halves are thrown out, for they are not worth bothering about, since they are less than half of 22. So I determine that the twenty-second part of the said number will be 11,454 and one-half. Subtract that twenty-second part from the circumference of the earth, and there will remain the number 240,545 and one-half. Of that number you take a third part, dividing by 3, and after division there will be obtained the number 80,181; and there will remain 2½ stades after the division. Of the 2 stades you make four half-stades and plus one half, and there will be five halves. Of those five, remove 3 half-stades, and of those three take one half and it is a third. There remain two halves which equal 1 stade. Of that stade take a third and so you have got a third of the entire number, and you find that the diameter of the earth will contain 80,181 and one-half and one-third. This is the meaning of this part.

In this lecture further attention should be given to the properties of the planets. And it should be known that it was ordained by the virtue of the Creator in the first constitution of the world that the seven planets by their movements and their light move these inferior natures according to the order of their place in the succession of hours which augment the virtues of their operations. Therefore every planet in manifestation of its work dominates the first hour of the day that is named after the planet, as in the first hour of Monday the moon dominates, in the second Saturn, in the third Jupiter; and so, reckoning continuously by this computation, it happens that the third planet governs the last hour of Monday, that is, Jupiter. So, in the first hour of Tuesday, Mars rules; in the second the sun; in the third Venus; and so on, reckoning continuously in the manner aforesaid. And begin to compute unequal hours from sunrise according to the view of Alcabitius. Also it should be noted that the leadership of those planets in human conception is that the first month after the hour of conception is Saturn's, the second Jupiter's, the third Mars's, the fourth the sun's, the fifth of Venus, the sixth Mercury's, the seventh the moon's. The eighth again is Saturn's, and so he does not live who is born in the eighth month because he is born under the power of Saturn. Also note that the planets dispose the life of the child after birth in this fashion. The moon begins to dispose from the birth of the child through the years of nutrition, which are four. Then Mercury for four more, then Venus for eight, then the sun for nineteen, afterwards Mars for fifteen, Jupiter for twelve, then Saturn to the end of life.

Also it should be noted that the first hour of each day is masculine and similarly the first hour of the night. The second is feminine, the third masculine, the fourth feminine, and so reckoning continuously to the end.

Also it should be noted that Saturn has dominion over phlegmatic diseases, viscous and melancholy, congealed, and acute, such as leprosy, cancer, morphea, gout, and the like. And Jupiter has dominion over every disease of the blood which is not excessive beyond nature or from burned-up, convertible blood. Mars has dominion over hot fevers and frenzy from the blood and bloody pustules like impetigo and rubedo of the body, with roughness and foulness. The sun has dominion over hot and dry sicknesses. Venus has dominion over cold and humid sicknesses which happen about the genitals. Mercury has dominion over mental diseases, namely horrible thoughts, restlessness, doubts, and the like. The moon has dominion over gout and epilepsy and twisting of the face and junction of the members and whatever is in the guise of cold and damp.

Also about the moon it should be noted, further, that the first quarter of the moon is moist, the second is hot, the third is dry, the fourth is cold, according to Alcabitius. Also note that during the first quarter of the moon everything humid is augmented, in the second is diminished, in the third is increased, in the fourth is decreased. Moreover, it should be clearly understood that, while the moon increases, everything humid increases fantastically but not truly; for the moon works by a twofold ray, because it works by its own ray and when it so works it augments everything humid truly. This, however, is when it has less of the light of the sun after conjunction, not before conjunction because of its combustion by the sun's rays. And the more of the sun's rays it sends us, the more ebullition it makes in humidity and fantastic apparition; for it is a property of heat to cause ebullition and fantastic apparition. Moreover, physicians have in mind fantastic apparition of this sort when they say that when the moon waxes everything humid increases. And if anyone asks me how the moon by the light of the sun can produce ebullition in humidity when the sun by its light cannot do it, I think that the sunlight when it is received in the moon is somehow altered by the mediating virtue of the moon, according to the saying that every recipient changes what is received according to its own nature. Yet it is not entirely changed to the nature of the moon, but the moon as a mediating instrument suited to it works upon all humidity subject to it, just as effect is subject to cause.

Also it should be noted according to Ptolemy in the "*Centiloquium*" that the sun is the source of vital virtue, the moon of natural virtue, Saturn of retentive virtue, Jupiter of vegetative virtue, Mars of irascible, Venus concupiscible, Mercury discretive. Wherefore, Mars, Mercury, and Venus signify as to morals in the child's nativity. Also it should be noted that the moon and other planets have stronger dominion over inferior things when they are in their apogee than when they are in their perigee. The reason for this is that when a star is in its apogee it moves faster, and the faster it moves, the more strongly it influences these inferiors. And perhaps, if we are speaking of influence made by ray, the influence is then stronger when the star is in the lower part (of its orbit) because then the ray is shorter.[1]

. . .

Tenth lecture[2]

Astrological medicine. It should be noted here in continuing what was said before that, according to Messahala, the wise physician ought to watch in what part of the body

[1] Robert went on in lectures 5–8 to comment in similar scholastic fashion on Sacrobosco's second chapter.

[2] These extracts from lectures 10, 11 and 13 are interesting in their own right and are given although of Sacrobosco's third chapter, with which they deal, nothing is given.

the disease is and in what part of the sky the moon is, since, if the disease be in the head, throat, or breast, it should be cured while the moon is in Aries, Taurus, and Gemini. If the disease be in abdomen or groin, it should be cured while the moon is in Cancer, Leo, and Virgo. If the disease be in the stomach, heart, liver, or spleen, it is cured while the moon is in Capricorn, Aquarius, and Pisces. But if the ailment be in an inferior part, like the anus or lower, cure it while the moon is in Libra, Scorpio, or Sagittarius, and let the moon be joined with fortunate planets and waxing. And when the doctor wants to cure an eye complaint and cut with steel, let the moon be waxing and in lucky conjunction. If anyone wants to cure with cuppings, let the moon be waning and by no means joined with fortunate, and let Jupiter be above earth in the ascendant or the tenth or eleventh or ninth house and not in conjunction with Mars. And, if this cannot be done, take care that the moon be not in earthly signs or in conjunction with Mars. And in eye cures watch out that Mars is not in its own house, and not only of the eyes but also of the entire body, and do not operate while the moon is in a common or mobile sign. And if anyone wants to give evacuative medicine, do it while the moon is in aquatic signs in the ascendant. Wherefore Ptolemy says that aquatic signs are better in taking purgatives, and, of them, the better is Scorpio, the worse Cancer. And let the moon be fortunate, and beware of a conjunction with Saturn.

Eleventh lecture

. . . Yet for comprehension of the last part it may be noted that there are two kinds of hours in astronomy, equal and unequal. An equal hour is the twenty-fourth part of a natural day; wherefore, if an entire natural day were divided into 24 equal parts, then each of those parts would be called an "equal hour", and those hours are reckoned according to the rising of parts of the equinoctial, and an hour is nothing else than the time during which 15 degrees of the equinoctial rise. An unequal hour is the twelfth part of an artificial day, so if we understand that an artificial day is divided into 12 equal parts and the night into 12 others, then each of these is called an "unequal hour", and they are reckoned according to the rise of parts of the zodiac, and an hour is nothing else than the time in which 15 degrees of the zodiac rise. And those hours are called "unequal", not because the hours of the day are unequal to one another or the hours of the night to one another, but because the hours of the day are unequal to the hours of the night. And speaking of the first hours, it is said that the day has so many hours and the night so many. And we speak of the other hours, namely, the unequal, in the reckoning of hours by astronomical instruments and also by astronomical clocks. Nor is it possible for any clock to follow the judgment of astronomy with complete accuracy. Yet clockmakers are trying to make a wheel which will make one complete revolution for every one of the equinoctial circle, but they cannot quite perfect their work. But if they could, it would be a really accurate clock and worth more than astrolabe or other astronomical instrument for reckoning the hours, if one knew how to do this according to the method aforesaid.

The method of making such a clock would be this, that a man make a disc of uniform weight in every part so far as could possibly be done. Then a lead weight should be hung from the axis of that wheel and this weight should move that wheel so that it would complete one revolution from sunrise to sunrise, minus as much time as about 1 degree rises according to an approximately correct estimate. For from sunrise to sunrise the whole equinoctial rises and about 1 degree more, through which degree the sun moves against the motion of the firmament in the course of a natural day. Moreover, this could be done more accurately if an astrolabe were constructed with a network on which the entire equinoctial circle was divided up. Then the degree in which the sun was at rising would be noted, then the point of time or degree on the equinoctial which touched the horizon. And similarly on the day following would be noted the degree when the sun touched the horizon and likewise the degree of the equinoctial touching the horizon, and it would be about 1 degree more than the revolution of the entire equinoctial. Then let the time corresponding to 1 degree of the equinoctial be subtracted from the entire time from sunrise to sunrise; then have the said wheel complete its revolution in that time and let it be divided into 24 equal parts; then the situation of each part would show the hour in the sky.

If, too, anyone should wish to find when it is noon on any day that the sun is shining, let him make a circle on a plane surface, at whose centre let him erect a stick standing perpendicular to the surface of that circle, and let it be put on a high place where the sun touches it on the south, east, and west. Then at sunrise let the place be noted where the shadow of the upright touches the circumference of the circle. Do likewise when the sun is in the west, and then the arc intercepted between the two points of the first and second division should be divided into two equal parts, and from the point of division a diameter of the circle should be drawn through the centre. Then, whenever the shadow of the upright is on that diametral line, it will be true noon.

Moreover, the utility of that instrument is not slight, for by that circle is found most certainly the latitude of the region, which is the distance of the zenith from the equinoctial; and, since this distance corresponds to the altitude of the pole, consequently the altitude of the pole, too, is shown in every region. For with the sun in the first degree of Aries or in the first degree of Libra when its shadow falls on the diametral line of the circle, let the altitude of the sun be subtracted from 90 degrees, and the remainder will be the latitude of the region. This is the distance of the zenith from the equinoctial or the elevation of the pole without any error. But if a person wishes to take the altitude of the pole in any region in another way, let him at night sight some notable star which is near the pole in the Great or Little Bear and let him suspend an astrolabe or quadrant above the rod, sighting that star until it is at its highest point and then note the number of degrees of altitude of the star on the indicator. Then let him wait until the same star is at its greatest descent and in like manner take the number of degrees of the altitude of the star at that time. Then subtract the lesser number from the greater and divide the remainder into two equal halves and add one of those halves to the smaller number, and what you get will be the true altitude of the pole. But concerning the longitude of a region, how it is to be determined will be stated later.

. . .

Thirteenth lecture

. . . To develop this lecture, in the first place, it is to be seen how we ought to imagine the climes. Be it known, then, that if anyone was at the equator and had a quadrant or astrolabe and observed the pole, the pole would be at the bottom of his vision. And if the same person moves north in a straight line as far as where the pole is raised above the horizon by 12½ degrees and a quarter of one, than he will be at the beginning of the first clime, and this can be observed by the aforesaid quadrant or astrolabe. And if afterwards the same person proceeds farther until he sees the altitude of the pole at 27½ degrees and a quarter of one part, and so on continuously proceeding northwards, he can know at what place on earth the climes begin. And the last clime ends, as is said in the text and as Alfraganus states, where the altitude is 50½ degrees, and this is hardly across the English Channel, so that almost all England is outside a clime. And the reason for this is not because it is unfit to live in, as some will have it, but it is because it was not inhabited at the time of the division into climes.

Praise of England. This is a land which ministers whatever is suited to mortal use with unfailing fertility; for, fecund in every kind of metal, it has fields widely scattered; hills, too, in flourishing cultivation, on which varied crops spring in their season from the rich glebe. It has forests, too, full of all sorts of game, in whose dells and alternate pastures grass grows for the animals and flowers of varied colours distribute honey to the roving bees. It has verdant meadows, also, pleasantly situated at the foot of its hills, where clear springs, flowing with gentle murmur through clean streams, refresh those reclining on their fragrant banks.

Concerning which country a spirit spoke to the Greek Brutus who was the first settler in England and the spirit addressed him in this fashion:

> Brutus, beneath setting sun beyond Gallic kingdoms,
> There is an island in the ocean enclosed on all sides by the sea
> Which was once for a long time inhabited by giants.
> Now it is deserted, fit for your folk.
> This should be sought by you as a seat perennial;
> This will be another land for your children.
> Here from your offspring kings will be born,
> And the whole earth will be subject to them.

. . . And much is contributed to this conclusion by what I heard from a wise man in England who was of good and holy life, who asserted that he was present where an incantation was being performed, and the spirit told a man that he would bring him ripe figs at any time of year. Then the enchanter asked how that could be. And the spirit said, "There is a place on earth which is believed to be non-habitable by men where all year long are found ripe fruit in great variety which I will bring from that place to you." And next day, which was around Christmas, he brought him ripe figs, and it seems sure that that place is at the equator. . . .

. . .

Fifteenth lecture[1]

Since the sun is larger than the earth, etc. This is the second part of this chapter, in which the author treats of the causes of eclipses. . . .

But some things may be noted along the line of what is being said here. The first is about happenings in this generable and corruptible world which occur as a sequel to an eclipse. Be it known, then, according to what Alcabitius holds, that an eclipse of the moon when it is in the cold signs signifies severe cold in the time next following, unless a great conjunction from another direction impedes in whole or part. And in watery signs it signifies abundance of rain, especially if it is winter. If it is summer, the weather will be temperate, and so ever judge sanely according to the agreement of particular causes. In the other signs it happens similarly according to the natures of the signs, as I have said in speaking of them. Also be it known that if, at the time of the eclipse, fortunate stars are in conjunction or aspect with the moon, the conjunction will have a good effect. But if unfortunate stars are in conjunction or aspect with the moon, the eclipse will have an ill effect. And then one should especially beware of sowing seed, since no crop will grow thence, as I have learned by experience in certain parts of England, since someone sowed barley at the time of an eclipse in most fertile soil, yet the seed died as if none had been sown, and the people of the country believed that there had been an incantation, until I showed them that such a happening was natural. And a major truth in this matter is that the ascendant be observed in mid-eclipse and the lord of the ascendant noted, which, if fortunate and well placed, is a sure sign that the eclipse will have a good effect. But if it is unfortunate, many times manifold evils befall, such as famine, pestilential air, and the like.

Telling longitude from eclipses. Also be it known that from an eclipse a man can learn most certainly the longitude of a city; for it is known from the Toledan tables when an eclipse begins at Toledo. Also the distance of Toledo from the west is known, which is called its "longitude". Therefore, let the hour of the beginning of the eclipse where you are be observed and then see whether that hour is earlier or later than the hour at Toledo. If it is earlier, then your city is farther west than Toledo. Note, then, by how much it is earlier and subtract this from the longitude of the city of Toledo, and you will have the longitude of your city. But if the hour of the eclipse at Toledo is earlier, then your city will be more eastern; see by how much it is and add this to the longitude of the city of Toledo and you will have the longitude of your city. For example, according to the tables of Toledo the longitude of Toledo is 11 degrees, that is, two-thirds of an hour and one-sixtieth of an hour. And if an eclipse of the moon begins in the first hour of the night at Toledo, at Montpellier it will begin in the second hour of the night, since Toledo is farther west than Montpellier by 1 hour. And 1 hour is equivalent to 15 degrees. If, then, we should add 15 degrees to 11 degrees, we would have 26, and this is the longitude of Montpellier.

Illumination of the moon by the sun. Also, note should be taken of the cause of the diversity in reception of the moon's light from the sun. In connection with which, be

[1] The 14th lecture mainly supplemented Sacrobosco's chapter 4 on certain topics; lecture 15 supplements his treatment of eclipses.

it known that the moon has no light which can affect our vision except from the sun and that half of the moon which faces the sun is always lighted by the sun. Therefore, when the moon is in conjunction with the sun, then the half of the moon facing us is dark and the other half facing the sun is completely illuminated. And, since the moon is swifter in its movement then the sun, it passes the sun and some part of the half which was facing the sun begins to be turned towards us and to appear in the figure of a crescent. And the farther it recedes from the sun, so much larger a part begins to appear illuminated to us, until the moon is in opposition to the sun, and then the entire half of it which faces the sun appears to us completely illuminated, so that the moon seems to us full of light. And when the moon moves out of opposition, it follows the sun until it is in conjunction with it again, and then the half illuminated by the sun begins gradually to be hid from our sight until none of it is visible to us. And so every month that diversity in waxing and waning of the moon happens as it did before.

The man in the moon. There is another oddity in the moon whose truth I have not found discussed by any author fully as it should be, namely, that obscurity in the form of a man which appears in the moon, which, according to the stories of the rustics, is said to be a certain peasant who stole thorns and he, with a load of these on his back, was stellified in the moon and that darkness is his image. There is another opinion about that spot on the moon, that the moon, as a body half way between celestials and terrestrials, shares the nature of both. And as it shares the nature of celestials, clearness appears in it; and as it participates in the nature of terrestrial bodies, obscurity and darkness appear in it. Another more probable explanation is that the moon is like a polished, smooth and pure body, in which the forms of things facing it shine as in a pure mirror. Therefore, the parts of the earth which are covered by water appear in the moon clearly and the parts of the earth uncovered by water appear in the moon obscurely, and according to the shape of the site of these parts on earth appears the image in the moon. But against this opinion someone might raise this objection: when the form of anything is reflected in a mirror, the entire form of the same thing will appear in half of the mirror or a smaller portion of it. But it is evident that when there is a half-moon, the whole image does not appear in the moon but part of it, as is clear to sense. Therefore, the image in the moon is not made that way. To this it might be said that the objection is not valid because it makes a false supposition, namely, that a half-moon is really only half of the moon, which is false because it is always all there, although it is so called in its reception of light to our view. Wherefore, if the moon were always completely illuminated by the sun, that figure would always be seen, but, since it is not completely illuminated, not all the image is always visible. Another possible explanation – and I believe a better one – would be to assume that in the body of the moon there is greater rarity in some parts and greater density in others. Then those parts which are rarer receive more sunlight and more deeply, wherefore they appear brighter. The denser parts receive less and so appear darker, and such a figure appears corresponding to the location of that density. But should anyone raise an objection and say that I am wrong to posit rarity and density in the heavens, I answer that this is not impossible according to Averroes in the book, "*De substantia orbis*" who holds that rarity and density may be posited in the heavens just as here below, though perhaps equivocally or by more or less, as is there stated.

Completed is this compilation on the matter of the celestial sphere for the ampler introduction to the subject of scholars studying at Montpellier (or, Paris), which mr Robert of England composed and he finished it in A.D. 1271, while the sun was in the first degree of Taurus and Scorpio was in the ascendant.

239. Roger Bacon on prophecy as an intellectual enquiry, 1266–7

(*E.H.R.*, xii (1897), pp. 514–15. Translation by R. W. Southern in *Trans. Royal Hist. Soc.*, 5th ser., vol. 22 (1972), pp. 172–3)

If only the church would examine the prophecies of the Bible, the sayings of the saints, the sentences of sibyl and Merlin and other pagan prophets, and would add thereto astrological considerations and experimental knowledge, it would without doubt be able to provide usefully against the coming of Antichrist. For it is a great question whence he will arise and who he will be . . . and if the church would do all it can, I believe that God would give a fuller revelation, especially if a special prayer for this were ordained throughout the whole church. For not all prophecies are irrevocable . . . and many things are said in the prophets about the coming of Antichrist which will come to pass only through the negligence of Christians. They would be changed if Christians would strenuously enquire when he will come, and seek all the knowledge which he will use when he comes.

Appendices

I. CONTEMPORARY RULERS 1189–1327

	ENGLAND	SCOTLAND	FRANCE	FLANDERS	CASTILE	ARAGON	SICILY ("REGNO")	HOLY ROMAN EMPIRE	POPES	
1189	Richard I	William I (the lion)	Philip II (Augustus)	Philip of Alsace	Alfonso IX	Alfonso II	William II (Norman)	Frederick I (Hohenstaufen)	Clement III	1189
1190	"	"	"	"	"	"	Tancred of Lecce (Norman)	Henry VI	"	1190
1191	"	"	"	Baldwin of Hainault	"	,	"	"	Celestine III	1191
1192	"	"	"	"	"	"	"	"	"	1192
1193	"	"	"	"	"	"	"	"	"	1193
1194	"	"	"	Baldwin IX[1]	"	"	Henry VI (Hohenstaufen)	"	"	1194
1195	"	"	"	"	"	"	"	"	"	1195
1196	"	"	"	"	"	Peter II	"	"	"	1196
1197	"	"	"	"	"	"	"	"	"	1197
1198	"	"	"	"	"	"	Frederick II[2]	Philip of Swabia *v.* Otto (of Brunswick) IV (Philip) (Otto)	Innocent III	1198
1199	John	"	"	"	"	"	"	" "	"	1199
1200	"	"	"	"	"	"	"	" "	"	1200
1201	"	"	"	"	"	"	"	" "	"	1201
1202	"	"	"	"	"	"	"	" "	"	1202
1203	"	"	"	"	"	"	"	" "	"	1203
1204	"	"	"	"	"	"	"	" "	"	1204
1205	"	"	"	Joan	"	"	"	" "	"	1205
1206	"	"	"	"	"	"	"	" "	"	1206
1207	"	"	"	"	"	"	"	" "	"	1207
1208	"	"	"	"	"	"	"	" " (assassinated)	"	1208
1209	"	"	"	"	"	"	"	"	"	1209
1210	"	"	"	"	"	"	"	"	"	1210
1211	"	"	"	"	"	"	"	Frederick II	"	1211
1212	"	"	"	"	"	"	"	"	"	1212
1213	"	"	"	"	"	James I (the Conqueror)	"	"	"	1213

1214	,,	Alexander II	,,	,,	Henry I	,,	,,	,,	,,	1214
1215	,,	,,	,,	,,	,,	,,	,,	,,	,,	1215
1216	Henry III	,,	,,	,,	,,	,,	,,	,,	Honorius III	1216
1217	,,	,,	,,	,,	(St) Ferdinand III	,,	,,	,,	,,	1217
1218	,,	,,	,,	,,	,,	,,	,,	,,	,,	1218
1219	,,	,,	,,	,,	,,	,,	,,	,,	,,	1219
1220	,,	,,	,,	,,	,,	,,	,,	,,	,,	1220
1221	,,	,,	,,	,,	,,	,,	,,	,,	,,	1221
1222	,,	,,	,,	,,	,,	,,	,,	,,	,,	1222
1223	,,	,,	Louis VIII	,,	,,	,,	,,	,,	,,	1223
1224	,,	,,	,,	,,	,,	,,	,,	,,	,,	1224
1225	,,	,,	,,	,,	,,	,,	,,	,,	,,	1225
1226	,,	,,	(St) Louis IX	,,	,,	,,	,,	,,	,,	1226
1227	,,	,,	,,	,,	,,	,,	,,	,,	Gregory IX	1227
1228	,,	,,	,,	,,	,,	,,	,,	,,	,,	1228
1229	,,	,,	,,	,,	,,	,,	,,	,,	,,	1229
1230	,,	,,	,,	,,	,,	,,	,,	,,	,,	1230
1231	,,	,,	,,	,,	,,	,,	,,	,,	,,	1231
1232	,,	,,	,,	,,	,,	,,	,,	,,	,,	1232
1233	,,	,,	,,	,,	,,	,,	,,	,,	,,	1233
1234	,,	,,	,,	,,	,,	,,	,,	,,	,,	1234
1235	,,	,,	,,	,,	,,	,,	,,	,,	,,	1235
1236	,,	,,	,,	,,	,,	,,	,,	,,	,,	1236
1237	,,	,,	,,	,,	,,	,,	,,	,,	,,	1237
1238	,,	,,	,,	,,	,,	,,	,,	,,	,,	1238
1239	,,	,,	,,	,,	,,	,,	,,	,,	,,	1239
1240	,,	,,	,,	,,	,,	,,	,,	,,	,,	1240
1241	,,	,,	,,	,,	,,	,,	,,	,,	Celestine IV	1241
1242	,,	,,	,,	,,	,,	,,	,,	,,	*vacancy*	1242
1243	,,	,,	,,	,,	,,	,,	,,	,,	Innocent IV	1243
1244	,,	,,	,,	Margaret	,,	,,	,,	,,	,,	1244
1245	,,	,,	,,	,,	,,	,,	,,	,,	,,	1245
1246	,,	,,	,,	,,	,,	,,	,,	,,[3]	,,	1246
1247	,,	,,	,,	,,	,,	,,	,,	,,[3]	,,	1247

[1] Latin Emperor of Constantinople 1204–5

[2] Frederick's claims to succeed his father Henry VI in the Empire too were ignored by the Hohenstaufen themselves, who obtained the election of his uncle, Philip of Swabia. Otto of Brunswick was put up by their Saxon rivals. Frederick's eventual succession was secured by Pope Innocent III.

[3] After Frederick II had been declared deposed at the Council of Lyons (1245) Henry Raspe, landgrave of Thuringia, was raised against him as anti-king in 1246. He was followed in 1247 by William, count of Holland. His death in 1256, after that of Frederick II in 1250 and that of Conrad in 1254, should have left the way clear for an undisputed election, but led in fact to international rivalry, with the election of Richard of Cornwall of England, and of Alfonso IX of Castile, both in 1257.

CONTEMPORARY RULERS

	ENGLAND	SCOTLAND	FRANCE	FLANDERS	CASTILE	ARAGON	SICILY ("REGNO")	HOLY ROMAN EMPIRE	POPES	
1248	"	"	"	"	"	"	"	"	"	1248
1249	"	Alexander III	"	"	"	"	"	"	"	1249
1250	"	"	"	"	"	"	Conrad IV	Conrad IV	"	1250
1251	"	"	"	"	"	"	"	"	"	1251
1252	"	"	"	"	Alfonso X (the Wise)	"	"	"	"	1252
1253	"	"	"	"	"	"	"	"	"	1253
1254	"	"	"	"	"	"	Conradin	*The Great Interregnum*	Alexander IV	1254
1255	"	"	"	"	"	"	"	...	"	1255
1256	"	"	"	"	"	"	"	...	"	1256
1257	"	"	"	"	"	"	"	...[1]	"	1257
1258	"	"	"	"	"	"	Manfred	...	"	1258
1259	"	"	"	"	"	"	"	...	"	1259
1260	"	"	"	"	"	"	"	...	"	1260
1261	"	"	"	"	"	"	"	...	Urban IV	1261
1262	"	"	"	"	"	"	"	...	"	1262
1263	"	"	"	"	"	"	"	...	"	1263
1264	"	"	"	"	"	"	"	...	"	1264
1265	"	"	"	"	"	"	"	...	Clement IV	1265
1266	"	"	"	"	"	"	Charles I[2] (Angevin)	...	"	1266
1267	"	"	"	"	"	"	"	...	"	1267
1268	"	"	"	"	"	"	"	...	"	1268
1269	"	"	"	"	"	"	"	...	*vacancy*	1269
1270	"	"	Philip III	"	"	"	"	...	...	1270
1271	"	"	"	"	"	"	"	...	Gregory X	1271
1272	Edward I	"	"	"	"	"	"	...	"	1272
1273	"	"	"	"	"	"	"	Rudolf I (Hapsburg)	"	1273
1274	"	"	"	"	"	"	"	"	"	1274
1275	"	"	"	"	"	"	"	"	"	1275
1276	"	"	"	"	"	Peter III (the Great)	"	"	Innocent V Adrian V John XXI	1276

1277	,,	,,	,,	,,	,,	,,	,,		,,	Nicholas III	1277
1278	,,	,,	,,	,,	,,	,,	,,		,,	,,	1278
1279	,,	,,	,,	,,	,,	,,	,,		,,	,,	1279
1280	,,	,,	,,	Guy of Dampierre	,,	,,	,,		,,	,,	1280
1281	,,	,,	,,	,,	,,	,,	,,		,,	Martin IV	1281
							(*island* *Sicily*)	(*mainland* *Sicily:* *"Naples"*)			
1282	,,	,,	,,	,,	,,	,,	→ Peter III of Aragon	,,	,,	,,	1282
1283	,,	,,	,,	,,	,,	,,	,,	,,	,,	,,	1283
1284	,,	,,	,,	,,	Sancho IV	,,	,,	,,	,,	,,	1284
1285	,,	,,	Philip IV (the Fair)	,,	,,	Alfonso III	James [II]	Charles II	,,	Honorius IV	1285
1286	,,	Margaret (Maid of Norway)	,,	,,	,,	,,	,,	,,	,,	,,	1286
1287	,,	,,	,,	,,	,,	,,	,,	,,	,,	,,	1287
1288	,,	,,	,,	,,	,,	,,	,,	,,	,,	Nicholas IV	1288
1289	,,	,,	,,	,,	,,	,,	,,	,,	,,	,,	1289
1290	,,	*Interregnum*	,,	,,	,,	,,	,,	,,	,,	,,	1290
1291	,,	...	,,	,,	,,	James II ←	,,	,,	,,	,,	1291
1292	,,	John (Balliol)	,,	,,	,,	,,	,,	,,	Adolf of Nassau	,,	1292
1293	,,	,,	,,	,,	,,	,,	,,	,,	,,	*vacancy*	1293
1294	,,	,,	,,	,,	,,	,,	,,	,,	,,	Celestine V Boniface VIII	1294
1295	,,	,,	,,	,,	Ferdinand IV	,,	,,	,,	,,	,,	1295
1296	,,	*English occupation*	,,	,,	,,	,,	Frederick II	,,	,,	,,	1296
1297	,,	...	,,	,,	,,	,,	,,	,,	,,	,,	1297
1298	,,	...	,,	,,	,,	,,	,,	,,	Albert I (Hapsburg)	,,	1298
1299	,,	...	,,	,,	,,	,,	,,	,,	,,	,,	1299

[1] See n. 3 on previous page

[2] Mainland Sicily remained in Charles I's hands until his death in 1285. Island Sicily revolted from the mainland in 1282 (where the column divides), calling in the king of Aragon to rule them. Island Sicily was a breakaway, but the mainland remained Angevin for centuries.

CONTEMPORARY RULERS

	ENGLAND	SCOTLAND	FRANCE	FLANDERS	CASTILE	ARAGON	ARAGONESE SICILY	ANGEVIN NAPLES	HOLY ROMAN EMPIRE	POPES	
1300	,,	...	,,	,,	,,	,,	,,	,,	,,	,,	1300
1301	,,	...	,,	,,	,,	,,	,,	,,	,,	,,	1301
1302	,,	...	,,	,,	,,	,,	,,	,,	,,	,,	1302
1303	,,	...	,,	,,	,,	,,	,,	,,	,,	Benedict XI	1303
1304	,,	...	,,	,,	,,	,,	,,	,,	,,	,,	1304
1305	,,	...	,,	Robert III	,,	,,	,,	,,	,,	Clement V	1305
1306	,,	Robert (Bruce)	,,	,,	,,	,,	,,	,,	,,	,,	1306
1307	Edward II	,,	,,	,,	,,	,,	,,	,,	,,	,,	1307
1308	,,	,,	,,	,,	,,	,,	,,	,,	Henry VII (Luxemburg)	,,	1308
1309	,,	,,	,,	,,	,,	,,	,,	Robert	,,	,,	1309
1310	,,	,,	,,	,,	,,	,,	,,	,,	,,	,,	1310
1311	,,	,,	,,	,,	,,	,,	,,	,,	,,	,,	1311
1312	,,	,,	,,	,,	Alfonso XI	,,	,,	,,	,,	,,	1312
1313	,,	,,	,,	,,	,,	,,	,,	,,	,,	,,	1313
1314	,,	,,	Louis X	,,	,,	,,	,,	,,	Lewis IV (Bavaria)	,,	1314
1315	,,	,,	,,	,,	,,	,,	,,	,,	,,	*vacancy*	1315
1316	,,	,,	Philip V	,,	,,	,,	,,	,,	,,	John XXII	1316
1317	,,	,,	,,	,,	,,	,,	,,	,,	,,	,,	1317
1318	,,	,,	,,	,,	,,	,,	,,	,,	,,	,,	1318
1319	,,	,,	,,	,,	,,	,,	,,	,,	,,	,,	1319
1320	,,	,,	,,	,,	,,	,,	,,	,,	,,	,,	1320
1321	,,	,,	,,	,,	,,	,,	,,	,,	,,	,,	1321
1322	,,	,,	Charles IV	Louis de Nevers	,,	,,	,,	,,	,,	,,	1322
1323	,,	,,	,,	,,	,,	,,	,,	,,	,,	,,	1323
1324	,,	,,	,,	,,	,,	,,	,,	,,	,,	,,	1324
1325	,,	,,	,,	,,	,,	,,	,,	,,	,,	,,	1325
1326	,,	,,	,,	,,	,,	,,	,,	,,	,,	,,	1326
1327	Edward III	,,	,,	,,	,,	Alfonso IV	,,	,,	,,	,,	1327

II. SELECT PEDIGREES 1189–1327

A. FAMILIES OF THE KINGS OF ENGLAND

[Square brackets indicate that the person concerned had died before the beginning of the reign.]

FAMILY OF RICHARD I

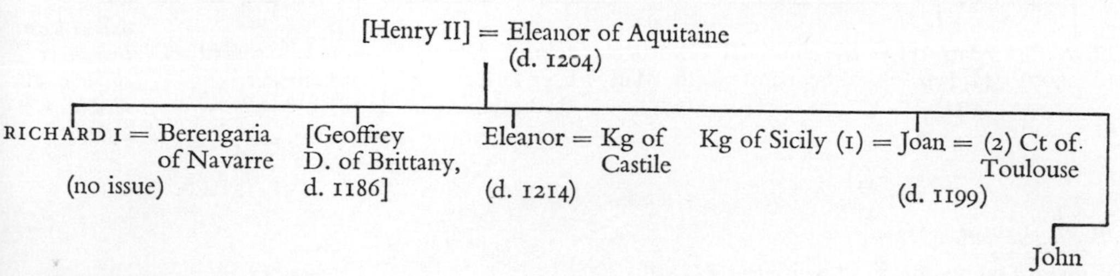

Illegitimate brothers of Richard

Geoffrey (archbp of York 1189–) d. 1212
William Longsword (E. of Salisbury 1198–) d. 1226

Illegitimate son

Philip (married a dau. of the lord of Cognac) d. after 1211

FAMILY OF JOHN

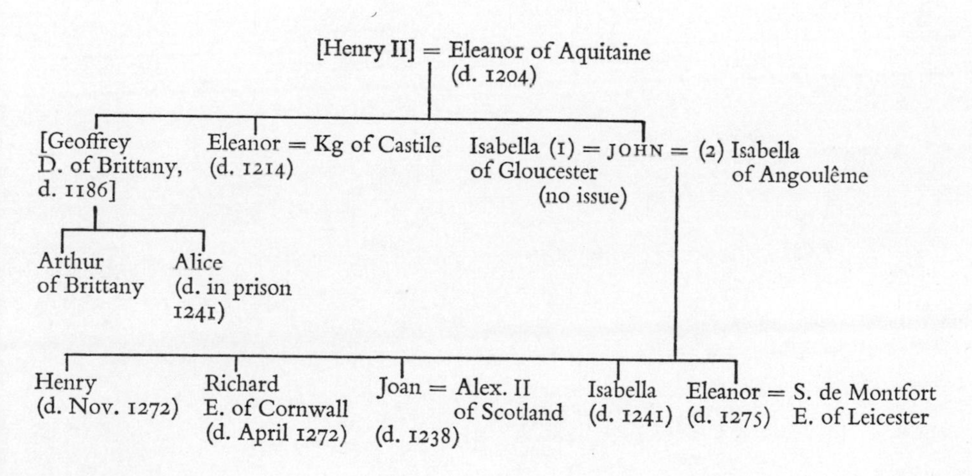

Illegitimate brothers of John

(as for Richard I)

Illegitimate children include

Joan (married Llywelyn ap Iorwerth, ruler of Gwynedd) d. 1237
Richard de Warenne, lord of Chilham (Kent), d. after May 1242

FAMILY OF HENRY III

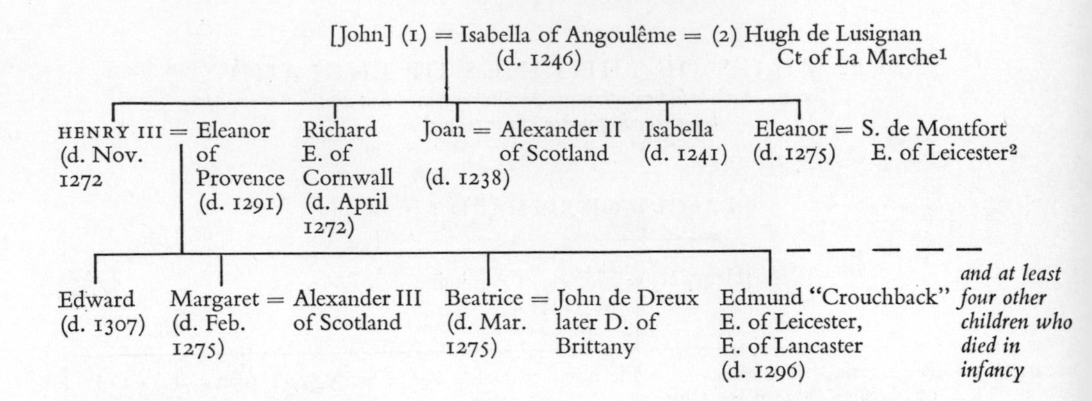

Illegitimate uncle of Henry

William Longsword, E. of Salisbury, d. 1226

[1] For Henry III's half-brothers, issue of this second marriage, see the Lusignan table.

[2] Eleanor's second marriage, at the age of twenty-three. She had been married, at nine, to William Marshal, the younger, E. of Pembroke, and widowed at sixteen when he died in 1231.

FAMILY OF EDWARD I

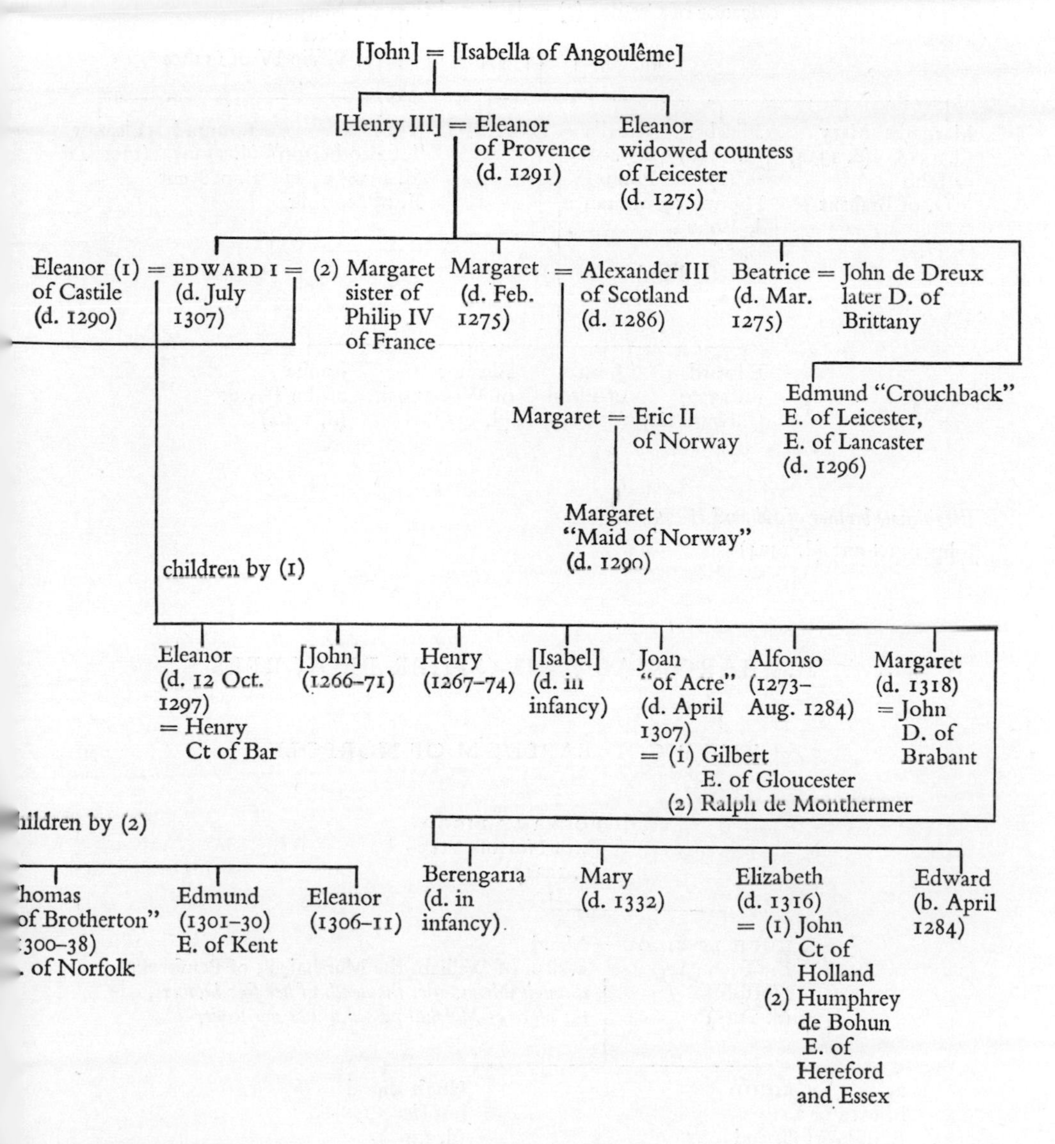

Illegitimate son of Edward I

John Botetourt (d. 1324)

FAMILY OF EDWARD II

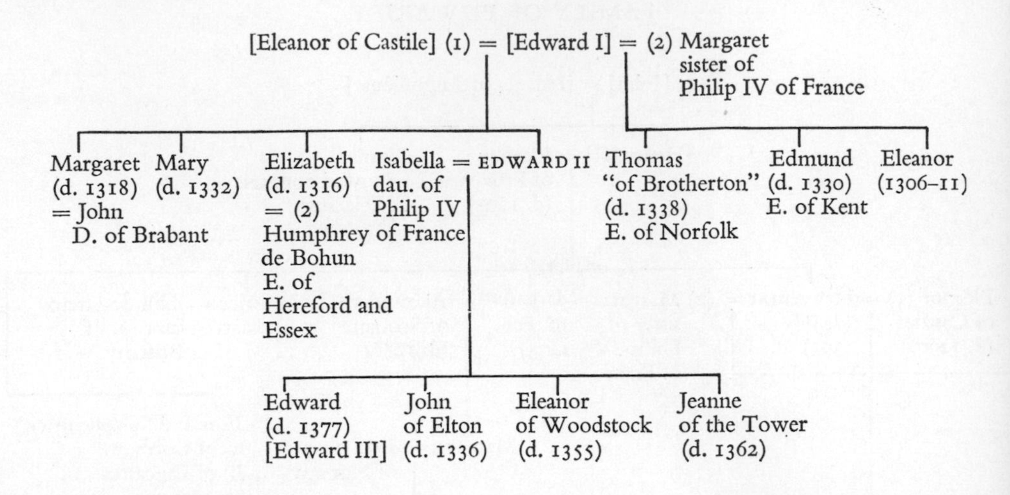

Illegitimate brother of Edward II
John Botetourt (d. 1324)

B. BARONIAL AND OTHER PEDIGREES

THE BIGOD EARLDOM OF NORFOLK

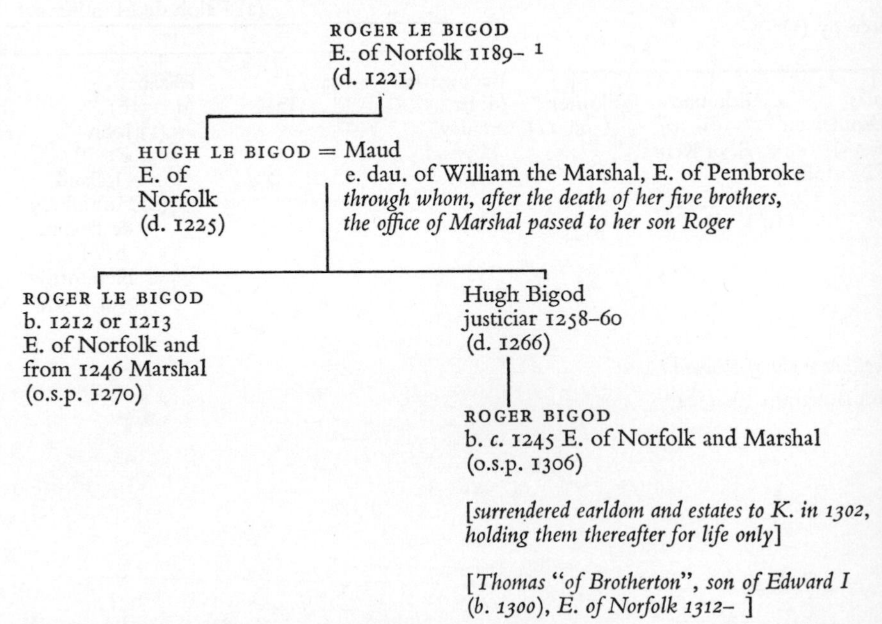

[1] His father, the first earl, had died in 1177, but Henry II would not allow him to inherit the earldom.

THE BOHUN EARLS OF HEREFORD AND ESSEX

Humphrey de Bohun
(d. *c.* 1187)

HENRY DE BOHUN = Maud de Mandeville
cr. E. of Hereford 1200 (d. 1220) | sister and heiress of William de M., E. of Essex (d. 1236)

HUMPHREY DE BOHUN
b. *c.* 1200
E. of Hereford; E. of Essex 1236–
(d. 1275)

Humphrey de Bohun the younger
[*Montfortian captured at Evesham and d. of wounds 1265*]

HUMPHREY DE BOHUN
b. *c.* 1249
E. of Hereford and Essex
Constable
(d. 1298)

HUMPHREY DE BOHUN = Elizabeth
E. of Hereford and Essex
Constable
(slain Boroughbridge 1322) | dau. of Edward I

JOHN DE BOHUN
E. of Hereford and Essex
(d. 1336)

THE DE CLARE EARLS OF GLOUCESTER

Roger of Clare (Clare, Suffolk)
E. of Hertford
(d. 1173)

RICHARD OF CLARE = Amice
E. of Hertford
(d. 1217) | dau. of E. of Gloucester

GILBERT OF CLARE = Isabel Marshal
E. of Gloucester and Hertford
(d. 1230) | dau. of William Marshal, E. of Pembroke

Margaret de Burgh (1) = RICHARD OF CLARE = (2) Maud de Lacy
Margaret de Burgh: dau. of Hubert de Burgh
Richard of Clare: majority 1243, E. of Gloucester and Hertford (d. 1262)
Maud de Lacy: dau. of John de Lacy, E. of Lincoln

Alice de Lusignan (1) = GILBERT OF CLARE = (2) in 1290 Joan of Acre
Alice de Lusignan: dau. of Ct of La Marche
Gilbert of Clare: b. 1243, E. of Gloucester and Hertford (d. 1295)
Joan of Acre: dau. of Edward I, b. 1272

GILBERT OF CLARE
E. of Gloucester and Hertford
(o.s.p. Bannockburn 1314)

Eleanor = (1) Hugh le Despenser the younger (hanged 1326)

Margaret = (1) Piers Gavaston (hanged 1312)

THIRTEENTH-CENTURY EARLS OF PEMBROKE

WILLIAM MARSHAL *rector regni*
married (1189) into the family of
the preceding earls of Pembroke
cr. E. of Pembroke 1199
(d. 1219)

WILLIAM MARSHAL	RICHARD MARSHAL	GILBERT MARSHAL	WALTER MARSHAL	Anselm
E. of Pembroke [*m. a sister of Henry III, Eleanor, who later m. Simon deMontfort*] (o.s.p. 1231)	E. of Pembroke (o.s.p. 1234)	E. of Pembroke (o.s.p. legit. 1241)	E. of Pembroke (o.s.p. 1245)	(o.s.p. 1245 never invested with earldom)

Joan = WILLIAM "OF VALENCE" (IN POITOU) OR "OF LUSIGNAN"
E. of Pembroke
(d. 1296)

[*niece of the foregoing brothers; lived into the fourteenth century and usu. styled "countess of Pembroke"; m., not later than 1247, Henry III's half-brother William of Valence*]

AYMER OF VALENCE
styled E. of Pembroke 6 Nov. 1307
(o.s.p. 1324)

THE FERRERS (DE FERRARIIS) FAMILY

WILLIAM DE FERRIÈRES
E. of Derby
(d. 1190)

WILLIAM DE FERRERS
E. of Derby
[*loyal to K. John*]
(d. 1247)

WILLIAM DE FERRERS
E. of Derby
(d. 1254)

ROBERT DE FERRERS
E. of Derby
[*sided with S. de Montfort. Picked out by name in Dictum of Kenilworth for specially severe redemption and by 1269 forced to surrender his earldom and lands – which were granted to the king's younger son Edmund "Crouchback", E. of Leicester (1265–) and E. of Lancaster (1267–)*]
(d. 1279)

John de Ferrers
[*like his father petitioned in vain for redress. Sided with Bohun and Bigod in 1297 and with them pardoned by name in pardons of 10 Oct. and 5 Nov. 1297 and in "De Tallagio non Concedendo". Sought justice from the pope until forbidden in 1301 to do so. Accuser of Walter Langton, the treasurer, in Carlisle parliament 1307*]
(d. 1312)

THE DESPENSERS

Hugh le Despenser
(d. 1238)

|

Hugh le Despenser
[*Montfortian slain at Evesham 1265*

|

Hugh le Despenser
b. 1261
[*cr. E. of Winchester 1322*]
(hanged 1326)

|

Hugh le Despenser the younger
(hanged 1326)

THE MORTIMERS (MORTEMER) OF WIGMORE

[a Domesday Book honour with lands in twelve counties, with *caput* at Wigmore]

Roger de Mortimer of Wigmore
[*on loss of Normandy in 1204 adhered to John and forfeited his Norman lands*]
(d. before 19 August 1214)

Children of Roger de Mortimer:

- Hugh de M. of Wigmore (o.s.p. 1227)
- Ralph de M. of Wigmore (d. 1246) = Gladys

Joan dau. of K. John = Llywelyn ap Iorworth ("the Great") (d. 1240)
→ Gladys

Ralph de M. of Wigmore = Gladys
→ Roger de M. of Wigmore (d. 1282) = Maud, e. dau. and co-h. of William de Braose lord of Brecon, Builth and Abergavenny who was executed in 1230

Roger de M. of Wigmore = Maud
→ Edmund de M. of Wigmore (d. 1304) = Margaret de Fiennes cousin of Q. Eleanor of Castile, the wife of Edward I

Edmund de M. of Wigmore = Margaret de Fiennes
→ Roger de M. of Wigmore
[*cooperated with Q. Isabella to dethrone Edward II*
E. of March 1328–]
(executed 1330)

THE MORTIMER LORDSHIP OF CHIRK

ROGER DE MORTIMER the younger
the third son of Roger de Mortimer of Wigmore (d. 1282) by Maud (d. 1301), eldest dau. and coheiress of William de Braose, lord of Brecon, Builth and Abergavenny (d. 1230)

In 1282 granted lands of Llywelyn ap Gruffudd, becoming lord of a new marcher lordship of Chirk

[*Important and powerful in Edward II's reign. With other marcher lords joined E. of Lancaster against the Despensers, but surrendered 1322 and prisoner in the Tower until death in 1326. All his possessions forfeited.*]

THE MORTIMERS OF RICHARD'S CASTLE

Robert de Mortimer of Essex

Robert de Mortimer (2) (d. in or before 1219) = in 1210 Margaret de Say, dau. and heiress of Hugh de Say, lord of barony of Burford (Salop) and Richard's Castle (Hereford), who d. 1197

Hugh de Mortimer
aged about 40 in 1259
[*royalist in 1264 and 1265 and rewarded for it afterwards*]
(d. 1274)

Robert de Mortimer
(d. 1287)

Hugh de Mortimer
minor in 1287
of age in 1295
(o.s.p. male 1304)

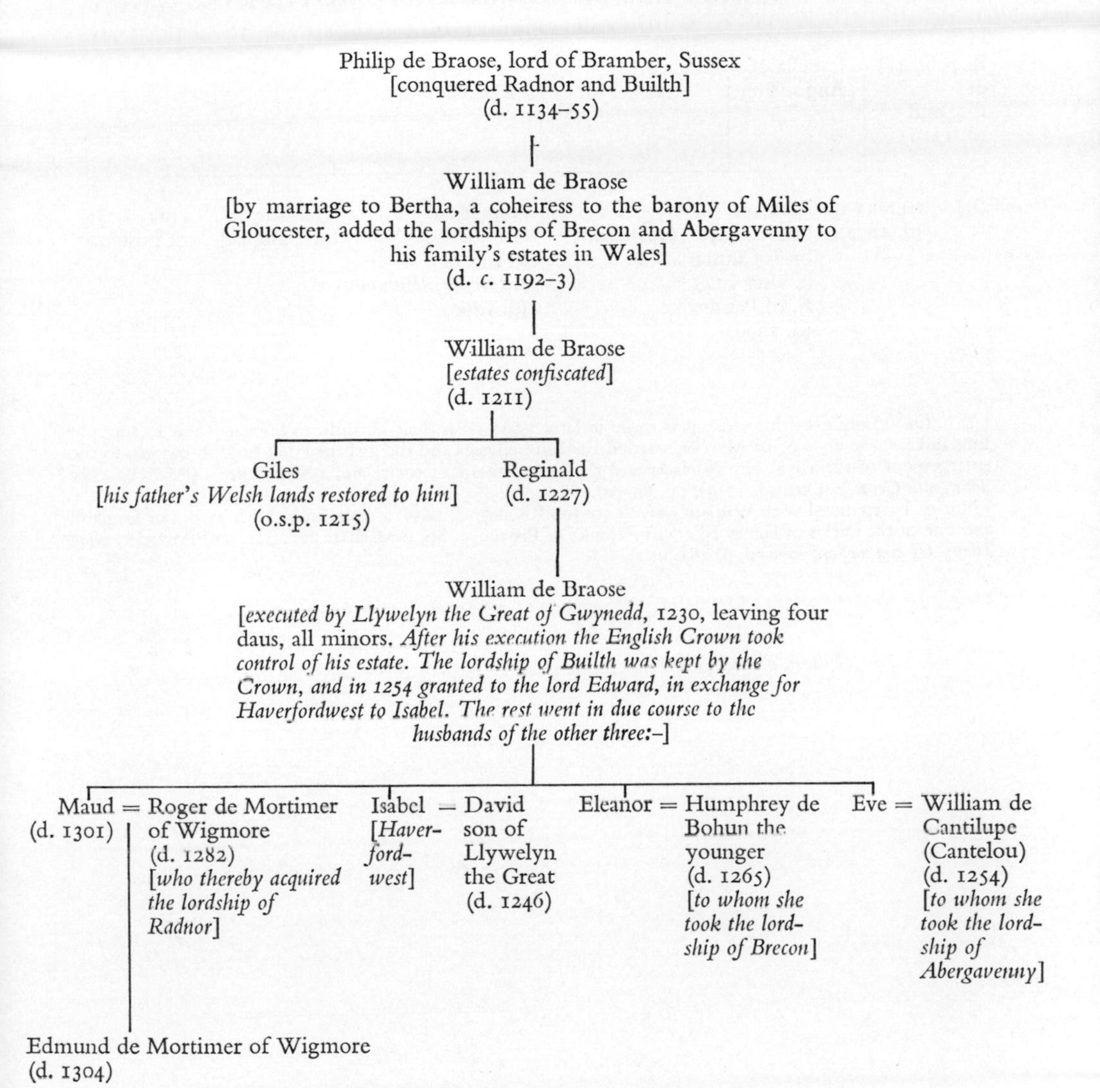
Philip de Braose, lord of Bramber, Sussex
[conquered Radnor and Builth]
(d. 1134–55)
William de Braose
[by marriage to Bertha, a coheiress to the barony of Miles of Gloucester, added the lordships of Brecon and Abergavenny to his family's estates in Wales]
(d. c. 1192–3)
William de Braose
[estates confiscated]
(d. 1211)
Giles
[his father's Welsh lands restored to him]
(o.s.p. 1215)
Reginald
(d. 1227)
William de Braose
[executed by Llywelyn the Great of Gwynedd, 1230, leaving four daus, all minors. After his execution the English Crown took control of his estate. The lordship of Builth was kept by the Crown, and in 1254 granted to the lord Edward, in exchange for Haverfordwest to Isabel. The rest went in due course to the husbands of the other three:–]
Maud = Roger de Mortimer of Wigmore
(d. 1301)
(d. 1282)
[who thereby acquired the lordship of Radnor]
Isabel = David son of Llywelyn the Great
[Haverford-west]
(d. 1246)
Eleanor = Humphrey de Bohun the younger
(d. 1265)
[to whom she took the lordship of Brecon]
Eve = William de Cantilupe (Cantelou)
(d. 1254)
[to whom she took the lordship of Abergavenny]
Edmund de Mortimer of Wigmore
(d. 1304)

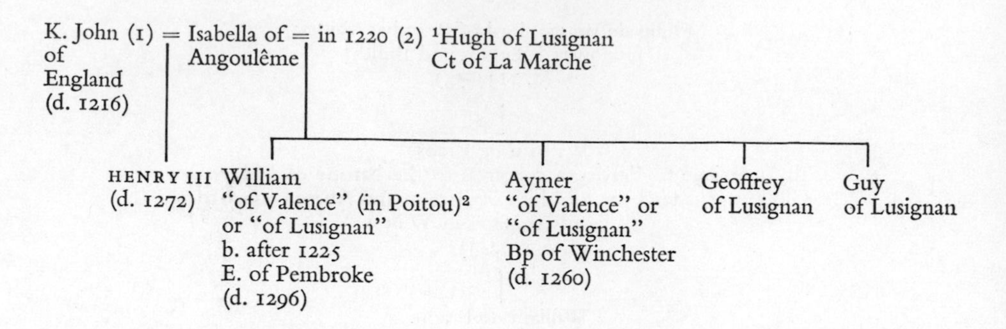

[1] "... the offspring of this virile pair came in later years with their kinsfolk to increase their fortunes in England ... the boys of La Marche married English heiresses and the girls married English barons, to the enlargement of the royal family circle and the bedevilment of social and political life" (Powicke, *The Thirteenth Century* (Oxford, 1953), pp. 89-90).

[2] Not to be confused with William of Valence (on Rhône), d. 1239, a churchman with livings in England and one of the uncles of Henry III's wife Eleanor of Provence. See next chart pedigree, and Powicke, *King Henry III and the lord Edward*, p. 264, n. 1.

ELEANOR OF PROVENCE'S SAVOYARD RELATIVES

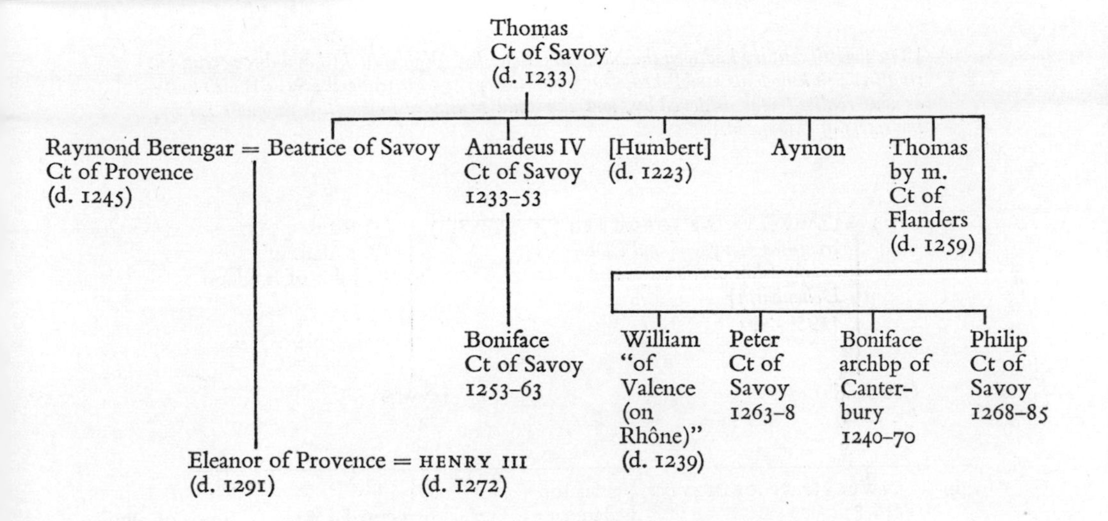

ELEANOR OF PROVENCE'S SISTERS

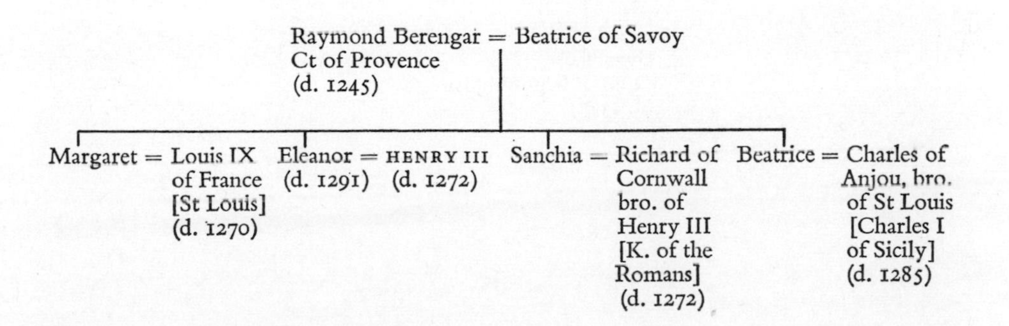

THE FAMILY OF SIMON DE MONTFORT

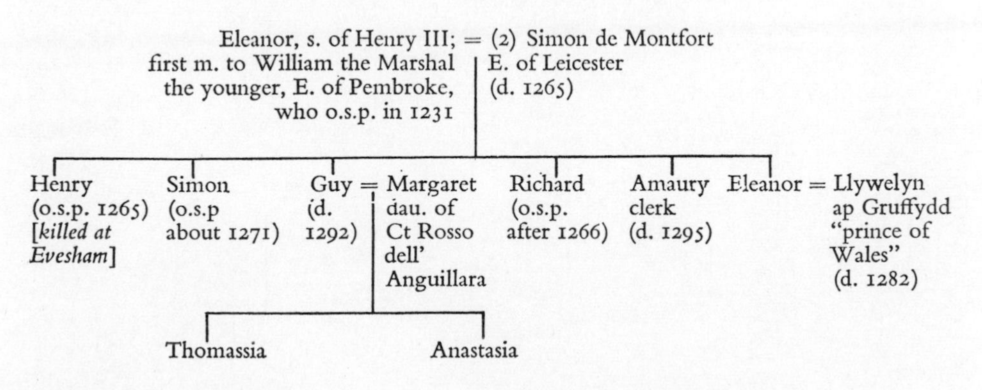

THE RULING FAMILY OF GWYNEDD

[*The twelfth century had seen the Norman conquest of Wales checked and three great, but rival, Welsh kingdoms established, Gwynedd, Powys and Deheubarth. Such Welsh unity as was realised was achieved by, and the final resistance to English conquest led by, the rulers of Gwynedd.*]

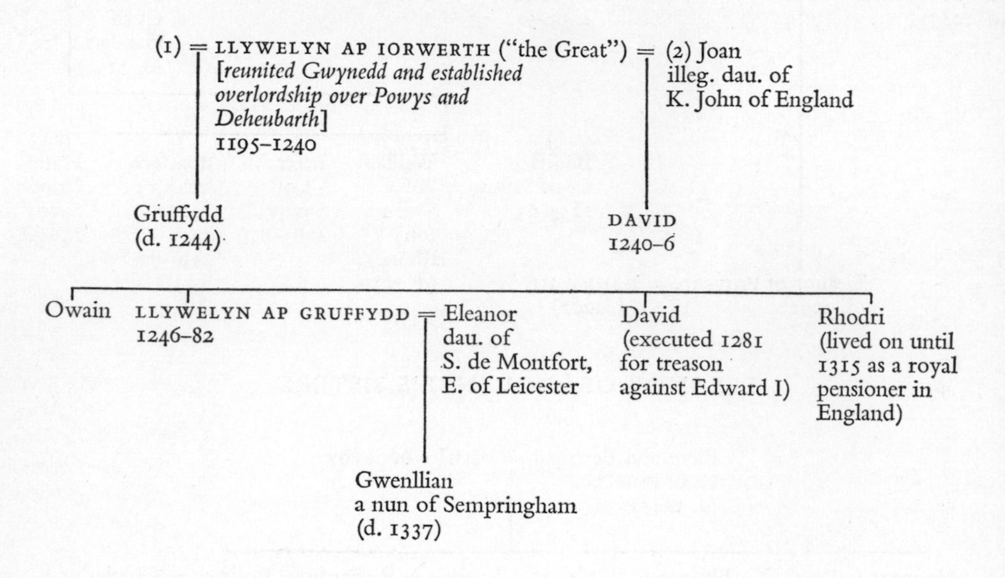

III. BISHOPS EXERCISING JURISDICTION IN ENGLAND 1189–1327

The dioceses are arranged alphabetically irrespective of province.

BATH AND WELLS

Bath

Reginald FitzJocelin 1173–91
(d. as elect of Canterbury)

Savaric FitzGeldewin 1191–1205

Bath and Glastonbury

Jocelin of Wells 1206–42

Bath and Wells

Roger of Salisbury 1244–7

William of Bitton I 1248–64

Walter Giffard 1264–6
trs. to York

William of Bitton II 1267–74

Robert Burnell 1275–92

William of March 1293–1302

Walter Haselshaw 1302–8

John Droxford 1309–29

CANTERBURY

Baldwin 1184–90

[Reginald FitzJocelin
el. Nov., d. Dec. 1191]

Hubert Walter 1193–1205

[Reginald
el. 1205, quashed 1206]

[John de Gray
postulated 1205, quashed 1206]

Stephen Langton 1206–28

[Walter of Evesham
el. 1228, quashed 1229]

Richard Grant (Wethershed) 1229–31

[Ralph Nevill
postulated 1231, quashed 1232]

[John of Sittingbourne
el. March, quashed June 1232]

[John Blund
el. 1232, quashed 1233]

Edmund Rich 1233–40
canonised 1246

Boniface of Savoy 1241–70

[Adam of Chillenden
el. 1270, quashed 1272]

Robert Kilwardby 1272–8
trs. to Porto on becoming cardinal

[Robert Burnell
postulated 1278, quashed 1279]

John Pecham 1279–92

Robert Winchelsey 1293–1313

[Thomas Cobham
el. May, quashed October 1313]

Walter Reynolds 1313–27

Simon Mepham 1327–33

CARLISLE

Bernard 1203–14

Hugh of Beaulieu 1218–23

Walter Mauclerc 1223–46
resigned

Silvester Everdon 1246–54

Thomas Vipont 1254–6

Robert de Chaury or Chause 1257–78

Ralph Ireton 1278–92

John of Halton 1292–1324

[William Ayermine
el. Jan., quashed Feb. 1325]

John Ross 1325–32

CHESTER

see COVENTRY AND LICHFIELD

CHICHESTER

Seffrid II 1180–1204

Simon FitzRobert 1204–7

[Nicholas de l'Aigle
el. 1209, quashed before 1214]

Richard Poore 1215–17
trs. to Salisbury

Ranulf of Wareham 1217–22

Ralph Nevill 1222–44

[Robert Passelewe
el. before 19 April, quashed June 1244]

Richard Wich 1244–53
canonised 1262
John Climping 1253–62
Stephen Bersted 1262–87
Gilbert of St Leofard 1288–1305
John Langton 1305–37

COVENTRY AND LICHFIELD

Note. The see was first at Lichfield, was transferred to Chester in 1075 and to Coventry in 1102. The continuing claim of Lichfield to be a see was recognised in 1228 in the new title "Coventry and Lichfield". Chester got no such recognition: "bishop of Chester" is found between 1189 and 1327, but only as an unofficial description of the bishops of Coventry or Coventry and Lichfield.

Coventry
Hugh de Nonant 1185–98
Geoffrey Muschamp 1198–1208
William Cornhill 1214–23
resigned
Alexander Stavensby 1224–38

Coventry and Lichfield
Hugh Pattishall 1239–41
Roger Weseham 1245–56
resigned
Roger Longespee (Meuland) 1257–95
Walter Langton 1296–1321
Roger Northburgh 1321–58

DURHAM

Hugh du Puiset 1153–95
Philip of Poitiers 1195–1208
Richard Marsh 1217–26
Richard Poore 1228–37
Nicholas Farnham 1241–9
resigned
Walter Kirkham 1249–60
Robert Stichill 1260–74
Robert of Holy Island 1274–83
Anthony Bek 1283–1311
Richard Kellaw 1311–16
Lewis de Beaumont 1317–33

ELY

Geoffrey Ridel 1173–89
William Longchamp 1189–97
Eustace 1197–1215
[Robert of York
el. 1215, quashed 1219]
John of Fountains 1220–5
Geoffrey de Burgo 1225–8
Hugh of Northwold 1229–54
William of Kilkenny 1254–6
Hugh Balsham 1256–86
John of Kirkby 1286–90
William of Louth 1290–8
Ralph Walpole 1299–1302
Robert Orford 1303–10
John Ketton 1310–16
John Hotham 1316–37

EXETER

John the Chanter 1186–91
Henry Marshal 1194–1206
Simon of Apulia 1214–23
William Briwere 1223–44
Richard Blund 1245–57
Walter Bronescombe 1258–80
Peter Quinel or Quivel 1280–91
Thomas Bitton 1291–1307
Walter Stapledon 1308–26
James Berkeley 1326–7
[John Godele
el. 1327, quashed 1327]
John Grandisson 1327–69

HEREFORD

William de Vere 1186–98
Giles de Braose 1200–15
Hugh de Mapenore 1216–19
Hugh Foliot 1219–34
Ralph Maidstone 1234–9
resigned
Peter D'Aigueblanche 1240–68
John Breton 1268–75
Thomas Cantilupe 1275–82
canonised 1320
Richard Swinfield 1282–1317
Adam Orleton 1317–27
trs. to Worcester
Thomas Charlton 1327–44

LICHFIELD

see COVENTRY AND LICHFIELD

LINCOLN

Hugh of Avalon 1186–1200
William of Blois 1203–6
Hugh of Wells 1209–35
Robert Grosseteste 1235–53
Henry Lexington 1253–8
Richard Gravesend 1258–79
Oliver Sutton 1280–99
John Dalderby 1300–20
[Anthony Bek
el. 1320, quashed 1320]
Henry Burghersh 1320–40

LONDON

Richard FitzNeal 1189–98
William of Sainte-Mère-Église 1198–1221
resigned
Eustace of Fauconberg 1221–8
Roger Niger 1228–41
Fulk Basset 1241–59
Henry of Wingham 1259–62
Henry of Sandwich 1262–73
John Chishull 1273–80
Richard Gravesend 1280–1303
Ralph Baldock 1304–13
Gilbert Segrave 1313–16
Richard Newport 1317–18
Stephen Gravesend 1318–38

NORWICH

John of Oxford 1175–1200
John de Gray 1200–14
Pandulf Masca 1215–26
Thomas Blundeville 1226–36
[Simon of Elmham
el. 1236, quashed 1239]
William Raleigh 1239–43
trs. to Winchester
Walter Suffield 1244–57
Simon Walton 1257–66
Roger Skerning 1266–78
William Middleton 1278–88
Ralph Walpole 1288–99
trs. to Ely

John Salmon 1299–1325
[Robert Baldock
el. July, resigned Sept. 1325]
William Ayermine 1325–36

ROCHESTER

Gilbert Glanvill 1185–1214
Benedict de Sausetun 1214–26
Henry Sandford 1226–35
Richard Wendene 1235–50
Lawrence of St Martin 1250–74
Walter of Merton 1274–7
John Bradfield 1277–83
Thomas Ingoldsthorpe 1283–91
Thomas Wouldham 1292–1317
Hamo Hethe 1317–52
resigned

SALISBURY

Hubert Walter 1189–93
trs. to Canterbury
Herbert Poore 1194–1217
Richard Poore 1217–28
trs. to Durham
Robert Bingham 1228–46
William of York 1246–56
Giles of Bridport 1256–62
Walter de la Wyle 1263–71
Robert Wickhampton 1271–84
Walter Scammel 1284–6
Henry Brandeston 1287–8
William de la Corner 1288–91
Nicholas Longespee 1291–7
Simon of Ghent 1297–1315
Roger Martival 1315–30

WINCHESTER

Godfrey de Lucy 1189–1204
Peter des Roches 1205–38
William Raleigh 1243–50
Aymer de Valence 1250–60
John Gervais 1262–8
Nicholas of Ely 1268–80
[Robert Burnell
el. 1280, quashed 1280]
[Richard de la More
el. 1280, resigned 1282]

John of Pontoise 1282–1304
Henry Woodlock 1305–16
John Sandale 1316–19
Rigaud of Assier 1319–23
John Stratford 1323–33
trs. to Canterbury

Walter Maidstone 1313–17
Thomas Cobham 1317–27
[Wulston Bransford
el. 1327, quashed 1327]
Adam Orleton 1327–33
trs. to Winchester

WORCESTER

William of Northall 1186–90
Robert FitzRalph 1190–3
Henry de Sully 1193–5
John of Coutances 1196–8
Mauger 1199–1212
Walter de Gray 1214–15
trs. to York
Sylvester 1216–18
William de Blois 1218–36
Walter Cantilupe 1236–66
Nicholas of Ely 1266–8
trs. to Winchester
Godfrey Giffard 1268–1302
[John St German
el. Mar., quashed Oct. 1302]
William Gainsborough 1302–7
Walter Reynolds 1307–13
trs. to Canterbury

YORK

Geoffrey 1189–1212
[Simon Langton
el. June, quashed Aug. 1215]
Walter de Gray 1215–55
Sewal de Bovill 1255–8
Godfrey Ludham 1258–65
[William Langton
el. March, quashed Nov. 1265]
[Bonaventura
provided 1265, resigned 1266]
Walter Giffard 1266–79
William Wickware 1279–85
John le Romeyn 1285–96
Henry Newark 1296–9
Thomas Corbridge 1299–1304
William Greenfield 1304–15
William Melton 1316–40

IV. EASTER TABLE 1189–1327

In the texts contained in this volume many events are dated by reference to Easter or by other feasts of the Church whose incidence is dependent upon that of Easter. In nearly every case when this has occurred the day of the month has been indicated. But in view of the language of many documents it may be convenient to list the date on which Easter fell in each year of this period; and it may also be noted for reference that:

Septuagesima falls *9 weeks before* Easter
Sexagesima falls *8 weeks before* Easter
Quinquagesima falls *7 weeks before* Easter
Quadragesima falls *6 weeks before* Easter
Ascension day falls *39 days after* Easter
Whitsunday falls *7 weeks after* Easter

DATES OF EASTER

Leap years are shown in bold type

9 April	1189	26 March	1217	16 April	1245	9 April	1273	2 April	1301
25 March	1190	15 April	1218	8 April	**1246**	1 April	1274	22 April	1302
14 April	1191	7 April	1219	31 March	1247	14 April	1275	7 April	1303
5 April	**1192**	29 March	**1220**	19 April	**1248**	5 April	**1276**	29 March	**1304**
28 March	1193	11 April	1221	4 April	1249	28 March	1277	18 April	1305
10 April	1194	3 April	1222	27 March	1250	17 April	1278	3 April	1306
2 April	1195	23 April	1223	16 April	1251	2 April	1279	26 March	1307
21 April	**1196**	14 April	**1224**	31 March	**1252**	21 April	**1280**	14 April	**1308**
6 April	1197	30 March	1225	20 April	1253	13 April	1281	30 March	1309
29 March	1198	19 April	1226	12 April	1254	29 March	1282	19 April	1310
18 April	1199	11 April	1227	28 March	1255	18 April	1283	11 April	1311
9 April	**1200**	26 March	**1228**	16 April	**1256**	9 April	**1284**	26 March	**1312**
25 March	1201	15 April	1229	8 April	1257	25 March	1285	15 April	1313
14 April	1202	7 April	1230	24 March	1258	14 April	1286	7 April	1314
6 April	1203	23 March	1231	13 April	1259	6 April	1287	23 March	1315
25 April	**1204**	11 April	**1232**	4 April	**1260**	28 March	**1288**	11 April	**1316**
10 April	1205	3 April	1233	24 April	1261	10 April	1289	3 April	1317
2 April	1206	23 April	1234	9 April	1262	2 April	1290	23 April	1318
22 April	1207	8 April	1235	1 April	1263	22 April	1291	8 April	1319
6 April	**1208**	30 March	**1236**	20 April	**1264**	6 April	**1292**	30 March	**1320**
29 March	1209	19 April	1237	5 April	1265	29 March	1293	19 April	1321
18 April	1210	4 April	1238	28 March	1266	18 April	1294	11 April	1322
3 April	1211	27 March	1239	17 April	1267	3 April	1295	27 March	1323
25 March	**1212**	15 April	**1240**	8 April	**1268**	25 March	**1296**	15 April	**1324**
14 April	1213	31 March	1241	24 March	1269	14 April	1297	7 April	1325
30 March	1214	20 April	1242	13 April	1270	6 April	1298	23 March	1326
19 April	1215	12 April	1243	5 April	1271	19 April	1299	12 April	1327
10 April	**1216**	3 April	**1244**	24 April	**1272**	10 April	**1300**		

INDEX TO TEXTS

The figures refer to the numbered documents. In a few cases when, for the sake of clarity, it has been found necessary to add a page reference, this has been placed within parentheses.